סידור וחומש קורן למחנה קיץ • נוסח אשכנז

The Koren Siddur and Ḥumash for Summer Camp
Nusaḥ Ashkenaz

קורן ירושלים

THE MAGERMAN EDITION

סידור וחומש קורן אני תפילה למחנה קיץ

THE KOREN ANI TEFILLA SIDDUR AND ḤUMASH FOR SUMMER CAMP

WITH TRANSLATION BY

Rabbi Lord Jonathan Sacks שליט״א

AND COMMENTARY BY

Rabbi Dr. Jay Goldmintz שליט״א

•

KOREN PUBLISHERS JERUSALEM

The Koren Ani Tefilla Siddur and Ḥumash for Summer Camp
First Hebrew/English Ashkenaz Edition, 2019
Combined American/Canadian Edition

Koren Publishers Jerusalem Ltd.
POB 4044, Jerusalem 91040, ISRAEL
POB 8531, New Milford, CT 06776, USA

www.korenpub.com

The English translation and commentary in this edition are based on the English translation and commentary first published in Great Britain in 2006 in the Authorised Daily Prayer Book of the United Hebrew Congregations of the Commonwealth: New Translation and Commentary by Chief Rabbi Jonathan Sacks (Fourth Edition, Compilation © United Synagogue) by Collins, a division of HarperCollins Publishers, London.

Printed in the PRC

Standard Size, Hardcover, ISBN 978 965 301 752 8
Compact Size, Soft cover, ISBN 978 965 301 753 5

CATA03

PREFACE

It is with great excitement that we present the Magerman Edition of the *Koren Ani Tefilla Siddur and Ḥumash for Summer Camp,* an engaging and thoughtful siddur for the inquiring student and thoughtful adult alike. This Siddur is part of the Magerman Series of appropriately designed siddurim for students from first to twelfth grade, and beyond. Each siddur has been created to inspire and develop connections to prayer and to God. These goals are achieved through encouraging personal reflection, spiritual and emotional connection, and cognitive learning.

Jewish summer camps provide a unique experience and opportunity for students to learn in an informal environment. Unlike schools, summer camps provide a way of "living Jewish" and not just learning about Judaism. The Siddur has been produced in response to the specific needs of summer camps: a single volume including prayers for weekdays and Shabbat, the fasts of Shiva Asar B'Tammuz and Tisha B'Av (including *Eikha* and a selection of *Kinot*), and all of the Torah readings and Haftarot of the summer months.

It is always a privilege to collaborate on a project with those who share our commitment and enthusiasm for bringing out the beauty of *Tefilla.* We are grateful to Debra and David Magerman for their critical support and encouragement, and for enabling the creation of this and all the volumes in the series. On behalf of the campers who will use this Siddur, we are forever in your debt.

We wish to thank Rabbi Sacks for his foreword and translation, and his ongoing support for this project. Special thanks go to Rabbi Dr. Jay Goldmintz who provided the vision for this Siddur, and its exceptional commentary. The small but highly professional team at Koren was led by Rabbi Dr. Daniel Rose, Director of Educational Projects, and included Rabbi David Fuchs and Rabbi Ḥanan Benayahu, who reviewed the

Tefillot; Esther Be'er who designed and typeset the text; Rachel Meghnagi, our Language Editor; and Tani Bayer, our Art Director.

It is our sincere hope and prayer that this Siddur will provide a platform for the educational and spiritual growth of present and upcoming generations of committed Jews, throughout the year.

Matthew Miller, Publisher
Jerusalem, 5775 (2015)

FOREWORD

Philosophers speculate about God. Scientists argue about God. Theologians theorize about God. We as Jews do something simpler and ultimately more profound. We talk to God. We bring Him our thanks and our hopes, our fears and our dreams. That conversation is what we call prayer, and Jews have engaged in it ever since the days of Abraham. The Siddur, the book you have in your hand, grew out of those conversations. Every time we pray we become part of the long dialogue between earth and heaven that has lasted now for almost four thousand years. Prayer was our ancestors' source of strength, and when we learn to pray it becomes ours also.

This new Siddur was designed for you and others like you, as you begin to wonder why we pray as we do, why in these words not those, how the various elements that make up a service relate to each other, and how these ancient texts relate to us in the present, in the immediacy of our lives. I hope you will enjoy this new Koren edition with its multiple commentaries and beautiful design. I wish it had existed when I was growing up, but in those days we tended to take prayer for granted. We prayed because Jews pray. Our parents did. So did our grandparents. So did countless generations before them. We didn't ask questions. We didn't read commentaries. We just prayed, often not really understanding what we were doing. I think that the new approach is better, because the more we understand what we say, the more deeply we enter into the act of prayer, and the more profoundly it changes us.

If I were to try to summarize briefly what prayer is, I would call it a journey in three stages. The first stage is *opening our eyes to wonder*. We are here, but we might not have been. The universe exists in almost infinite dimensions, as does the earth in all its sublime beauty. Scientists are just beginning to understand how finely tuned the universe had to be for stars, planets and life to emerge. Biologists, having mapped the human genome,

are just beginning to understand how complex the human body is. There is wonder here, and the opening sequences of prayer give expression to that wonder in the majestic poetry we call *Pesukei DeZimra*, "the verses of praise." In these poems, mostly taken from the last chapters of *Sefer Tehillim*, we move from creation to the Creator, from the universe to God, Architect of the universe. It is almost as if we were taking a rocket journey into space, seeing the earth in all its beauty while traveling beyond it.

The second stage, beginning with *Barekhu* and ending with *Kaddish Titkabal* after the *Amida*, is *approaching the presence of God*. This is a difficult idea and each of us has to find our own way of thinking about it. Imagine this, for example. You have been invited to meet the President (or King or Queen) of your country. It is a huge honor, and as the day approaches, you find yourself full of excitement. You prepare yourself. You dress in your best clothes. You rehearse exactly how you are going to conduct yourself and what you are going to say. The day comes. You enter the building. You are taken through many rooms and corridors until you finally find yourself face to face with the most powerful person in the country. You have to pinch yourself to make sure that this is really happening; it is not just a dream. Whatever is said and whatever is left unsaid, the memory of that encounter will stay with you for a lifetime.

That, multiplied a billion times over, is what it means to be in the presence of God. Only the fact that we do it several times a day, every day, takes away some of the wonder. Yet that is what is happening when, for example, we say the *Amida*. We are having a direct, personal encounter with the Creator of the universe. God, who has seven billion people to worry about, three million other life forms, and a hundred billion galaxies, *cares about us*, personally and individually. That may just be the most remarkable, empowering idea in the entire history of human thought. We matter. We count. God created us in love, and in love He listens to us as we declare our needs and ask for His help. In that moment we are rescued from insignificance and powerlessness. We are here because we are loved by God Himself. If we are fully open to it – and this may take years of practice and concentration – that encounter is life-changing.

Finally, from the second *Ashrei* to *Aleinu*, we come back down to earth, a little different than we were before we began the journey. We have seen the beauty of the created world. We have had a personal meeting with the

Creator Himself. And now we know there is work to do, because there is much in the world around us that is not as it should be. There is poverty, sickness, loneliness and injustice. People are cruel to one another. There is too much conflict and too little love. God wants us to bring a little of His light into other people's lives. He wants us to become "His partners in the work of creation." He has given us a sacred mission, to show by the way we live that God exists and that His existence makes a difference. Meeting God helps us become, in some small way, a little more like God, by doing acts of *tzedek umishpat, ḥesed veraḥamim*, righteousness and justice, kindness and compassion. We are small; God is great. But by opening ourselves to One so much greater than us, we become greater than we would have been if all we cared about was ourselves.

Those are the three phases of *Shaḥarit*, the Morning Prayer, and they correspond to the three ways in which we come to know God: through *creation* (the universe and its wonders), *revelation* (direct experience of the Divine Presence), and *redemption* (God's work in making the world more loving and just). *Minḥa* and *Ma'ariv*, the Afternoon and Evening prayers, have a somewhat different and more abridged structure.

Prayer matters. It changes the world because it changes us. It brings the Divine Presence into our lives and gives us strength we didn't know we had. It is to the soul (the mind, the self, our inner life) what exercise is to the body. Like exercise, it is important that we do it daily at set times, and like exercise, it makes us healthier (though in a different way) and more highly charged with positive energy. Prayer aligns us with the creative energies that run through the universe, the energies we call life and love, the supreme gifts of God.

So I hope you use this Siddur not just to pray but also to reflect on what we are doing when we pray. May God hear and answer all your prayers, and may we be worthy of the great challenge He has set us: of being His children, His ambassadors, His partners in creating a world worthy of His Presence. May He bless us, helping us to become a blessing to those whose lives we touch.

Rabbi Lord Jonathan Sacks
Ḥanukka 5775 (December 2014)

INTRODUCTION

There is an inherent tension that exists in our form of worship. On the one hand, we are encouraged to pour out our hearts to Hashem in a very personal way, to carry on a private dialogue with Him, to acknowledge His role in our own lives, to confide in Him, to ask for help and support – it is what the Rabbis called *avoda shebalev*, service of the heart – emotional, spontaneous, heartfelt.

On the other hand, for a variety of reasons, prayer has also become a ritual, a standardized fixed text with a myriad number of rules associated with it: what exactly one must say, when one should bow, when to stand or sit, when to speak and when not. At times, it can feel for some like it is entirely *avoda* – service, to be sure, but not a lot of heart.

But the truth is that, as the name indicates, *avoda shebalev* is supposed to be a combination of the two. The text is one that has developed over millennia. It contains unique contributions from almost every major Jewish community in Jewish history, as well as different elements of Jewish philosophy, history, language, law and custom. It is made up of prayers that we are all supposed to say both because of the importance of those contents and because prayer is not only an individual activity but a communal one as well. There is added power, effectiveness and holiness when a community prays together in a single voice. That's the "we're-all-together-on-the-same page" aspect. How, then, does one make one's prayer more personal?

Aside from adding one's own prayers, which one is indeed encouraged to do, one solution lies in the standardized text itself. Certainly, the words of the prayers are supposed to be understood literally but, at the same time, their meaning need not end there. Rather, the words can have almost whatever additional meaning we give them. This is because although the words themselves may not change, we do. Sometimes we are more tired, sometimes more awake, sometimes more in need, sometimes

more thankful. Each of us comes to *Tefilla* with different experiences and backgrounds, at different stages of our lives and our development, at different times of the day with different needs, moods and desires. The prayer does not change, but the pray-er does.

And so this commentary and guide has been designed to help you create your own meaning. The prayer book has a particular path that leads to a personal and communal encounter with Hashem – that is why it is called a siddur, from the Hebrew word *seder*, which means order or pattern, making sure that we all get to the same destination together as a community. Each one of the legs of the journey has its own function and style, its own theme and rhythm. But how we experience it along the way, what meaning we take from it or bring to it, is up to each and every one of us.

The commentary for this Siddur is thus divided into different sections, each designed to help connect to the text in a different way. Even so, some of the comments do not easily lend themselves to precise categorization, as the fixed and the fluid, the past and the present, the intellectual and the emotional can meld together as different sides of the same coin.

TRANSLATION

There is first and foremost the accessible and elegant translation of Rabbi Lord Jonathan Sacks, which has been included because gaining fluency in the meanings of words is but one prerequisite for more meaningful prayer.

BIUR TEFILLA – ביאור תפילה

The *Biur Tefilla* helps in gaining a thorough understanding of the text and context of the prayers. It examines the micro-understanding of a specific word or phrase in the text of the *Tefilla*, as well as presenting a wider understanding of the historical background of the *Tefilla*, and its place in the context of the overall structure of the service.

IYYUN TEFILLA – עיון תפילה

Iyyun Tefilla explores the deeper meaning behind the *tefillot*, taking a broader approach to the text. It presents a macro-understanding of the prayers, including philosophical and theological approaches to *Tefilla* in general and the text in particular.

HILKHOT TEFILLA – הלכות תפילה

This section ensures that one is aware of the ritual requirements surrounding the mitzva to pray. These comments are interspersed throughout the Siddur as well as concentrated in an appendix at the back which focuses on the laws of daily prayer and changes that need to be made during the course of the year.

ANI TEFILLA – אני תפילה

The expressed aim of the *Ani Tefilla* sections is to encourage connection to the *tefillot* in a direct and personal way. It is hoped this will be achieved through encouraging the reader to consider the prayers in an experiential way through inspiring and thought-provoking quotes and narratives, as well as through a process of personal creative thinking.

The name for this section derives from a statement made by King David in *Tehillim* 109:4 which says: וַאֲנִי תְפִלָּה. This could be translated as "I pray"; but it could also mean "I am prayer." At its best, prayer is an extension of the person who says it. It is shaped by who you are and what thoughts, emotions, memories, moods, feelings and expression you bring to it. The words of the Siddur, then, are not only to be taken literally, they are also signposts to help generate the range of thoughts and emotions and associations that reside within you on any given day. Think and feel beyond the words.

FREQUENTLY ASKED QUESTIONS

In addition, I have appended a section on frequently asked questions about *Tefilla* that I have heard from young people and adults over the years (although adults are unfortunately often much more shy about asking difficult questions). The answers to these questions are purposely brief. They should be considered introductions rather than comprehensive and complete. As Hillel said to the person who wanted to learn the entire Torah at once, "*Tzeh ulmad*, go and learn" (*Shabbat* 30a). For rest assured that during the last two thousand years, you are not the only one to have these questions, and others have no doubt come up with more if not better answers than I.

SOME SUGGESTIONS FOR ENHANCING ONE'S KAVANA

Despite our sincere attempts to make the words more meaningful, there can be times when the demands and distractions of everyday life can make it difficult to focus. One needs to find ways to recharge one's

וְשִׁנַּנְתָּם לְבָנֶיךָ

Dedicated to my wife,
Debra צביה אהובה
and our children,
Elijah Matthew מנחם מנדל
Zachary Noah יצחק אבנר
Sydney Rachel אלקה שיינה
Lexie Belle רחל לאה

In celebration
of our joint and individual journeys
toward a better understanding of Torah
and our relationship to Hashem.

David Magerman

CONTENTS

spiritual batteries. This section contains some practical suggestions from over the ages, for the challenge is not a new one. It faces everyone, even the most practiced and well-intentioned.

SHEMONEH ESREH

This particular prayer is the climax of any service and so it deserves special attention. Especially when one knows the prayer by heart or one is in a particular rush, the words can fly by without getting much consideration. In an attempt to get one to slow down, each blessing has been placed on its own page to encourage greater focus on the words, themes and meaning than one might otherwise apply. Recognizing, too, that one might want to approach this experience in different ways on different days, we have designed two different formats. In *Shaḥarit* and *Minḥa,* the text appears with a full commentary. In *Ma'ariv,* we have provided a traditional continuous format for someone who wishes to say the prayer with greater fluency. Each format can be used for any service although one must be careful to make the appropriate changes when necessary.

Acknowledgments

To the extent that this work is an outgrowth of my own personal development, I owe a long overdue word of thanks to Rabbi Dr. David Eliach, a master teacher and educator who first inspired me over thirty-five years ago to think and teach beyond the words of the Siddur. My thanks to some of my former students who provided suggestions, encouragement or feedback, especially when I first began thinking about this project. Among them: Gabi Agus, Sarah Emmerich, Eliza Ezrapour, Chloe Fein, Alison Goldberg, Esther Malka Issever, Sara Malamut, Sarah Marlowe, Deborah Pollack, Yossi Quint, Nina Rohr, Ethan Stein, Zach Weiner and Josh Wildes. My thanks go as well to Dr. Scott Goldberg for first involving me in this project and additionally to Dr. David Pelcovitz for his ongoing interest and support of my work. To Mrs. Rivka Kahan, Rabbi Dr. Barry Kislowicz, Rebbetzin Peshi Neuburger and Rabbi Dr. Gil Perl who each provided their own encouragement or support to see this project to its end.

Special thanks to Rabbi Dr. Daniel Rose, Director of Educational Projects at Koren who served as project coordinator and a welcome virtual *ḥavruta*; his influence, educational sensitivity and editorial contributions can be found in numerous places in this work. Thanks, as well, to Koren

◀ Rabbi

Rabbi David Fuchs for his meticulous care in reviewing portions of the commentary and making important suggestions for changes in both form and content, to Rachel Meghnagi for her careful editing of my text, and to Esther Be'er for the complicated task of typesetting and making all of the pieces come together. Particular heartfelt thanks to Matthew Miller, Publisher of Koren, whose gracious spirit made itself felt from the moment I met him informally years ago and only further intensified when we became reacquainted only months ago. We are all in his debt for his lasting contribution to the world of Jewish books.

The Weekday edition of this work was dedicated in part to the memory of my father David Goldmintz, David Mordechai ben Menachem Mendel, ז״ל, whose kind and gentle soul was manifest to all who knew him. His spontaneous tears at the Kotel once prompted a passerby to ask if he was a Holocaust survivor, not realizing that heartfelt prayer from the depths of one's being need not necessarily come from a place of crisis, but only from a place of sincerity, dependence and a desire for connection.

The Shabbat edition was dedicated to the memory of my father-in-law, Werner Rosenbaum, Aharon Meir ben Menachem, ז״ל, a gentleman and a scholar, a survivor of the Shoah who never saw himself as such, a man of profound humility who cast a giant shadow. His appreciation for the need to preserve one's minhag or family tradition, especially but not exclusively in prayer, was an inspiration to both those who did not have such a tradition and those who did not always appreciate what they had.

May the prayers that emanate from this Siddur, be a merit for them both and, in addition, for my mother and mother-in-law, עמו״ש. It seems appropriate to mention in this particular context the thanks I owe to my children, both old and new, who are not only the embodiment of the fact that prayers really can be answered, but who also stand as living testimony to the unique power that summer experiences can bring to the development of one's religious growth in general and in particular to one's relationship with HaKadosh Barukh Hu. With His help, may this Siddur help serve that function for you too, and may it strengthen your resolve to take that reinvigorated relationship into the months which follow, so that you may live not only a life filled with prayer but a prayerful life as well.

Rabbi Jay Goldmintz Ed.D.
Teaneck, NJ, 5775 (2015)

THE STRUCTURE OF SHAḤARIT*

Recall that the word Siddur means "arrangement" or "order." To the untrained eye, it may seem like just a random collection of verses and sentences but, in truth, there is an order that is designed to take one on a step-by-step journey toward a rendezvous with God. How all of the pieces fit together is a question to which you can provide your own answer. On this page and the next are the brief outlines of just two possibilities.

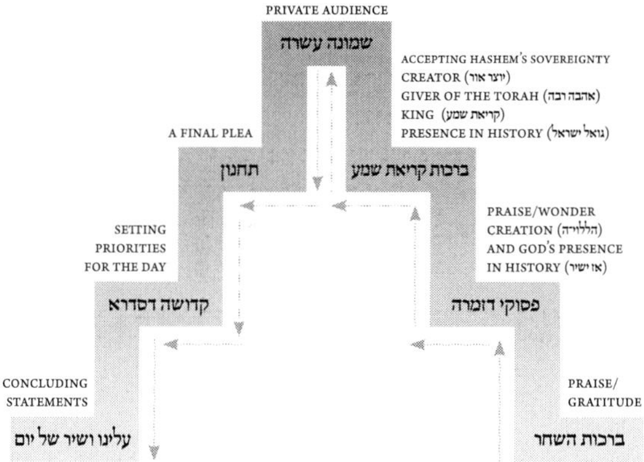

* Based on a diagram conceived by Rabbi Moshe Drelich.

THE STRUCTURE OF THE SHABBAT MORNING PRAYERS

SHAḤARIT

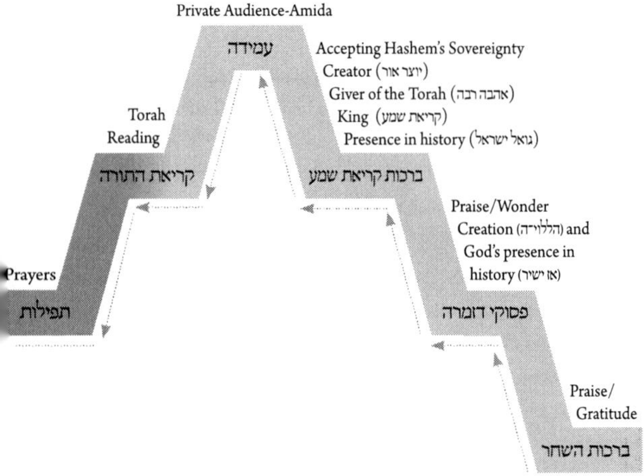

The name of the prayerbook, *siddur*, comes from the Hebrew word *seder* which means order or sequence. The implication is that despite what might seem to the uninitiated like a disconnected collection of liturgical compositions, is in fact an intricate arrangement designed to not only help direct one's thoughts and feelings but to help generate them as well. The diagram above gives an overview of that progression in the Shabbat morning service.

◂ In truth

MUSAF

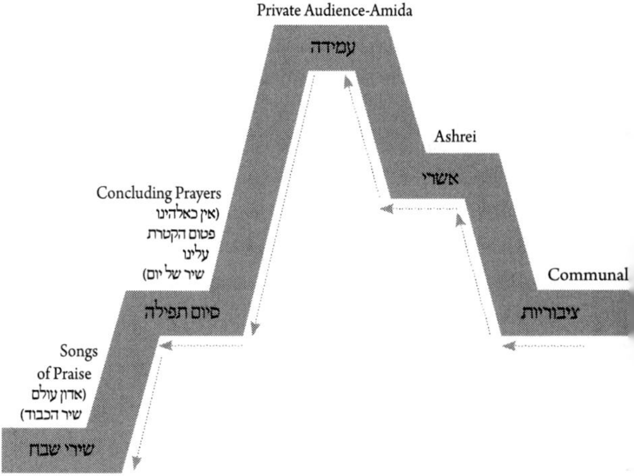

In truth, there are really two services that take place, the Shabbat morning *Shaḥarit* and the special additional service called *Musaf*. As we shall see, there were times when the two were separate but today they have generally been combined into one, thus accounting for the ups and downs of the overall theme of a rendezvous with the Divine.

Service of the heart

Rav Shimon Schwab (d. 1995) the leader of the German Jewish community in Washington Heights for close to 40 years, suggests that our "service of the heart" (עבודה שבלב) corresponds to the Service (עבודה) in the *Beit HaMikdash*. All of *Shaḥarit* can therefore be seen as a symbolic path toward a private meeting with God.

What follows is but a brief summary of his more detailed and poetic description.

1. The *Ezrat Nashim* – the place where everyone congregated before the doors opened. Corresponds to things said before *Shaḥarit* begins: אדון עולם, נטילת ידים, אשר יצר, אלקי נשמה.
2. The 15 steps leading up to the *Ezrat Yisrael*. Corresponds to the 15 ברכות השחר.
3. The *Ezrat Kohanim*, location of the *Mizbe'aḥ* (Altar). Corresponds to the *Korbanot* section.
4. Steps leading from the *Ezrat Kohanim* to the *Ulam*. The 12 steps plus the platform correspond to the 13 *midot* of Rabbi Yishmael.
5. The *Ulam* or antechamber. Corresponds to *Pesukei DeZimra*.
6. The *Heikhal* or Holy Place, location of the *Shulḥan* and *Menora*. Corresponds to the two blessings before *Shema*, one which focuses on the material world (יוצר אור) and the other on the spiritual (אהבה רבה).
7. The *Mizbe'aḥ HaKetoret* – the Incense Altar, corresponding to the *Shema*.

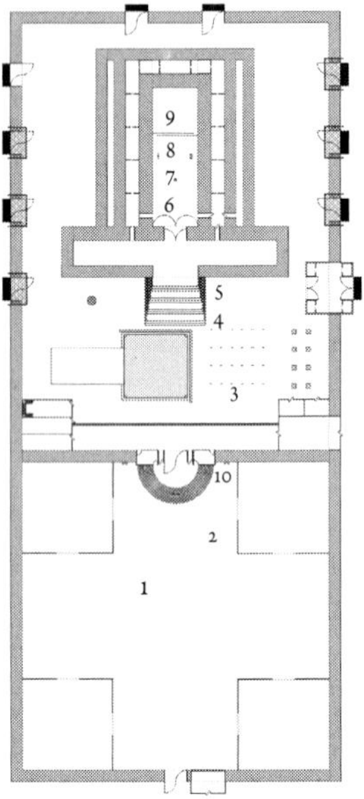

◂ 8. The *Parokhet*

8. The *Parokhet* – the curtain adjoining the *Kodesh HaKodashim*. Corresponds to the blessing of *geula* which must be attached to *Shemoneh Esreh*.
9. The *Kodesh HaKodashim* – the innermost sanctum where one is alone with God. Corresponds to *Shemoneh Esreh*.
10. At the conclusion of the *Shemoneh Esreh*, we take three steps back, past the *Heikhal*, the *Ulam*, to the *Azara*, where we stop for the Repetition of the *Shemoneh Esreh*.
11. From there we continue backwards, reciting the remainder of the service, finding ourselves back in the *Ezrat Nashim* where we first began our journey.

ימי חול

WEEKDAYS

Shaḥarit

The following order of prayers and blessings, which departs from that of most prayer books, is based on the consensus of recent halakhic authorities. See laws 40–47.

ON WAKING

On waking, our first thought should be that we are in the presence of God. Since we are forbidden to speak God's name until we have washed our hands, the following prayer is said, which, without mentioning God's name, acknowledges His presence and gives thanks for a new day and for the gift of life.

מוֹדֶה I thank You, living and eternal King,
for giving me back my soul in mercy.
Great is Your faithfulness.

Wash hands and say the following blessings.
Some have the custom to say "Wisdom begins" below at this point.

בָּרוּךְ Blessed are You, LORD our God, King of the Universe,
who has made us holy through His commandments,
and has commanded us about washing hands.[ABH]

Some say:

רֵאשִׁית חָכְמָה Wisdom begins in awe of the LORD; all who fulfill [His com- *Ps. 111*
mandments] gain good understanding; His praise is ever-lasting. The Torah *Deut. 33*
Moses commanded us is the heritage of the congregation of Jacob. Listen, my *Prov. 1*
son, to your father's instruction, and do not forsake your mother's teaching. May the Torah be my faith and Almighty God my help. Blessed be the name of His glorious kingdom for ever and all time.

---

to ourselves that our actions today must also contain an element of sanctity.

How will I use my hands today to serve a higher purpose?

HILKHOT TEFILLA • הלכות תפילה

The custom is to say these blessings after waking in the morning but, if one did not, then they may be recited before communal services begin.

שחרית

The following order of prayers and blessings, which departs from that of most prayer books, is based on the consensus of recent halakhic authorities. See laws 40–47.

השכמת הבוקר

On waking, our first thought should be that we are in the presence of God. Since we are forbidden to speak God's name until we have washed our hands, the following prayer is said, which, without mentioning God's name, acknowledges His presence and gives thanks for a new day and for the gift of life.

men מוֹדֶה/ women מוֹדָה/ אֲנִי לְפָנֶיךָ מֶלֶךְ חַי וְקַיָּם
שֶׁהֶחֱזַרְתָּ בִּי נִשְׁמָתִי בְּחֶמְלָה
רַבָּה אֱמוּנָתֶךָ.

Wash hands and say the following blessings.
Some have the custom to say רֵאשִׁית חָכְמָה *below at this point.*

בָּרוּךְ אַתָּה יהוה אֱלֹהֵינוּ מֶלֶךְ הָעוֹלָם
אֲשֶׁר קִדְּשָׁנוּ בְּמִצְוֹתָיו וְצִוָּנוּ עַל נְטִילַת יָדַיִם. אבה

Some say:

רֵאשִׁית חָכְמָה יִרְאַת יהוה, שֵׂכֶל טוֹב לְכָל־עֹשֵׂיהֶם, תְּהִלָּתוֹ עֹמֶדֶת לָעַד: תהלים קיא
תּוֹרָה צִוָּה־לָנוּ מֹשֶׁה, מוֹרָשָׁה קְהִלַּת יַעֲקֹב: שְׁמַע בְּנִי מוּסַר אָבִיךָ וְאַל־תִּטֹּשׁ דברים לג משלי א
תּוֹרַת אִמֶּךָ: תּוֹרָה תְּהֵא אֱמוּנָתִי, וְאֵל שַׁדַּי בְּעֶזְרָתִי. בָּרוּךְ שֵׁם כְּבוֹד מַלְכוּתוֹ
לְעוֹלָם וָעֶד.

BIUR TEFILLA • ביאור תפילה

עַל נְטִילַת יָדַיִם – *Washing hands.* We wash our hands with a vessel rather than directly from the faucet, for that is how the *kohanim* did it in the *Beit HaMikdash* (*Shemot* 30:17-21). We thereby signal

ANI TEFILLA • אני תפילה

עַל נְטִילַת יָדַיִם – *Washing hands.* Water is life giving. We wash our hands in the morning in order to remind ourselves that each day we are born anew. I am thankful to God to be able to start all over again (Rashba).

How would I like my today to be different from my yesterday?

בָּרוּךְ Blessed are You, Lord our God, King of the Universe,
who formed man[IA] in wisdom
and created in him many orifices and cavities.
It is revealed and known before the throne of Your glory
that were one of them to be ruptured or blocked,
it would be impossible to survive and stand before You.
Blessed are You, Lord,
Healer of all flesh who does wondrous deeds.

אֱלֹהַי My God,
the soul[IB] You placed within me is pure.
You created it, You formed it, You breathed it into me,
and You guard it while it is within me.
One day You will take it from me,
and restore it to me in the time to come.
As long as the soul is within me, I will thank You,
Lord my God and God of my ancestors,
Master of all works, Lord of all souls.
Blessed are You, Lord,
who restores souls to lifeless bodies.

ANI TEFILLA • אני תפילה

אֲשֶׁר יָצַר – *Who formed man.*
Close your eyes and think for a moment about the miracle of your own body.

IYUN TEFILLA • עיון תפילה

אֱלֹהַי נְשָׁמָה – *My God, the soul.* We cannot see love or time or yearning, yet we know they exist. So, too, we cannot see the soul, but we know that it is there within us.

BIUR TEFILLA • ביאור תפילה

אַתָּה בְרָאתָהּ, אַתָּה יְצַרְתָּהּ – *You created it, You formed it. Bara*, "create," usually means creation out of nothing. *Yatzar* means to form something new from that which already exists. The first means that God created my soul in its body, as in all humans; the second means that He made me different from anyone else. I have different ideas and a unique personality. Thus, God created my soul in its body and then gave the soul its individual endowments. We are all created by God, yet we are all different, and hence we need both words. (Rabbi Wohlgemuth)

בָּרוּךְ אַתָּה יהוה אֱלֹהֵינוּ מֶלֶךְ הָעוֹלָם
אֲשֶׁר יָצַר[עא] אֶת הָאָדָם בְּחָכְמָה
וּבָרָא בוֹ נְקָבִים נְקָבִים, חֲלוּלִים חֲלוּלִים.
גָּלוּי וְיָדוּעַ לִפְנֵי כִסֵּא כְבוֹדֶךָ
שֶׁאִם יִפָּתֵחַ אֶחָד מֵהֶם אוֹ יִסָּתֵם אֶחָד מֵהֶם
אִי אֶפְשַׁר לְהִתְקַיֵּם וְלַעֲמֹד לְפָנֶיךָ.
בָּרוּךְ אַתָּה יהוה, רוֹפֵא כָל בָּשָׂר וּמַפְלִיא לַעֲשׂוֹת.

אֱלֹהַי
נְשָׁמָה[עב] שֶׁנָּתַתָּ בִּי טְהוֹרָה הִיא.
אַתָּה בְרָאתָהּ, אַתָּה יְצַרְתָּהּ, אַתָּה נְפַחְתָּהּ בִּי
וְאַתָּה מְשַׁמְּרָהּ בְּקִרְבִּי, וְאַתָּה עָתִיד לִטְּלָהּ מִמֶּנִּי
וּלְהַחֲזִירָהּ בִּי לֶעָתִיד לָבוֹא.
כָּל זְמַן שֶׁהַנְּשָׁמָה בְקִרְבִּי, men מוֹדֶה/women מוֹדָה/ אֲנִי לְפָנֶיךָ
יהוה אֱלֹהַי וֵאלֹהֵי אֲבוֹתַי
רִבּוֹן כָּל הַמַּעֲשִׂים, אֲדוֹן כָּל הַנְּשָׁמוֹת.
בָּרוּךְ אַתָּה יהוה, הַמַּחֲזִיר נְשָׁמוֹת לִפְגָרִים מֵתִים.

IYUN TEFILLA • עיון תפילה

אֲשֶׁר יָצַר – *Who formed man.* Imagine what it would be like not to be able to go to the bathroom! Imagine the pain or discomfort, the inability to focus on anything else in one's life. And yet for all of its complexity and all of its importance, precisely because it is something that is so natural and so everyday and so private, we take it for granted. And precisely because we have a tendency to take it for granted, the Siddur tries to get us to focus upon it first thing in the morning. Blessings are opportunities to not take life for granted.

ANI TEFILLA • אני תפילה

אֲשֶׁר יָצַר – *Who formed man.*

I could prove God statistically. Take the human body alone – the chances that all the functions of an individual would just happen is a statistical monstrosity.

(Attributed to pollster George Gallup, *Readers Digest,* October 1943)

TZITZIT

The following blessing is said before putting on tzitzit. Neither it nor the subsequent prayer is said by those who wear a tallit. The blessing over the latter exempts the former. See laws 49–55.

בָּרוּךְ Blessed are You, LORD our God, King of the Universe,
who has made us holy through His commandments,
and has commanded us about the command of tasseled garments.

After putting on tzitzit, say:

יְהִי רָצוֹן May it be Your will, LORD my God and God of my ancestors,
that the commandment of the tasseled garment be considered before You
as if I had fulfilled it in all its specifics, details and intentions,
as well as the 613 commandments dependent on it, Amen, Selah.

BLESSINGS OVER THE TORAH

In Judaism, study is greater even than prayer. So, before beginning to pray, we engage in a miniature act of study, preceded by the appropriate blessings. The blessings are followed by brief selections from Scripture, Mishna and Gemara, the three foundational texts of Judaism.

בָּרוּךְ Blessed are You, LORD our God, King of the Universe,
who has made us holy through His commandments,
and has commanded us to engage in study
of the words of Torah.
Please, LORD our God, make the words of Your Torah
sweet in our mouths and in the mouths of Your people,
the house of Israel,
so that we, our descendants (and their descendants)
and the descendants of Your people, the house of Israel,
may all know Your name
and study Your Torah for its own sake.
Blessed are You, LORD, who teaches Torah to His people Israel.

---

who studied did so for the respect it would bring them or just for the intellectual challenge or for some other reward. As a result, Torah was devalued perhaps in their own eyes as well as in the eyes of others. In our own day, the equivalent might be studying Torah solely for grades or so that others might see us in a particular way. Saying *Birkhot HaTorah* first thing in the morning is thus a reminder that the things we are going to study today are a value in their own right.

לבישת ציצית

The following blessing is said before putting on a טלית קטן. Neither it nor יְהִי רָצוֹן is said by those who wear a טלית. The blessing over the latter exempts the former. See laws 49–55.

בָּרוּךְ אַתָּה יהוה אֱלֹהֵינוּ מֶלֶךְ הָעוֹלָם
אֲשֶׁר קִדְּשָׁנוּ בְּמִצְוֹתָיו וְצִוָּנוּ עַל מִצְוַת צִיצִת.

After putting on the טלית קטן, say:

יְהִי רָצוֹן מִלְּפָנֶיךָ, יהוה אֱלֹהַי וֵאלֹהֵי אֲבוֹתַי
שֶׁתְּהֵא חֲשׁוּבָה מִצְוַת צִיצִית לְפָנֶיךָ
כְּאִלּוּ קִיַּמְתִּיהָ בְּכָל פְּרָטֶיהָ וְדִקְדּוּקֶיהָ וְכַוָּנוֹתֶיהָ
וְתַרְיַ״ג מִצְוֹת הַתְּלוּיוֹת בָּהּ, אָמֵן סֶלָה.

ברכות התורה[ע]

In Judaism, study is greater even than prayer. So, before beginning to pray, we engage in a miniature act of study, preceded by the appropriate blessings. The blessings are followed by brief selections from תנ״ך, משנה and גמרא, the three foundational texts of Judaism.

בָּרוּךְ אַתָּה יהוה אֱלֹהֵינוּ מֶלֶךְ הָעוֹלָם
אֲשֶׁר קִדְּשָׁנוּ בְּמִצְוֹתָיו וְצִוָּנוּ לַעֲסֹק בְּדִבְרֵי תוֹרָה.
וְהַעֲרֶב נָא יהוה אֱלֹהֵינוּ אֶת דִּבְרֵי תוֹרָתְךָ
בְּפִינוּ וּבְפִי עַמְּךָ בֵּית יִשְׂרָאֵל
וְנִהְיֶה אֲנַחְנוּ וְצֶאֱצָאֵינוּ (וְצֶאֱצָאֵי צֶאֱצָאֵינוּ)
וְצֶאֱצָאֵי עַמְּךָ בֵּית יִשְׂרָאֵל
כֻּלָּנוּ יוֹדְעֵי שְׁמֶךָ וְלוֹמְדֵי תוֹרָתְךָ לִשְׁמָהּ.
בָּרוּךְ אַתָּה יהוה, הַמְלַמֵּד תּוֹרָה לְעַמּוֹ יִשְׂרָאֵל.

IYUN TEFILLA · עיון תפילה

ברכות התורה – *Blessings over the Torah.* Rabbi Yehuda (*Nedarim* 81a) claims that the *Beit HaMikdash* was destroyed because people did not recite the *Birkhot HaTorah* before they learned. Why such a huge consequence for such a seemingly small omission? Rabbeinu Yona suggests that it was because the lack of a recitation of the blessing means that Torah was not being studied as a religious value. Perhaps those

בָּרוּךְ Blessed are You, LORD our God, King of the Universe,
who has chosen us from all the peoples
and given us His Torah.
Blessed are You, LORD, Giver of the Torah.

יְבָרֶכְךָ May the LORD bless you[B] and protect you. *Num. 6*
May the LORD make His face shine on you
and be gracious to you.
May the LORD turn His face toward you
and grant you peace.

אֵלּוּ These are the things *Mishna Pe'ah 1:1*
for which there is no fixed measure:
the corner of the field, first-fruits,
appearances before the LORD
[on festivals, with offerings],
acts of kindness and the study of Torah.

אֵלּוּ These are the things *Shabbat 127a*
whose fruits we eat in this world
but whose full reward awaits us
in the World to Come:
honoring parents; acts of kindness;
arriving early at the house of study
morning and evening;
hospitality to strangers; visiting the sick;
helping the needy bride; attending to the dead;
devotion in prayer;
and bringing peace between people –
but the study of Torah is equal to them all.

---

ately after the recitation of the blessing. The next three paragraphs thus represent selections respectively from Torah, Mishna, and Gemara, thereby symbolically incorporating all of the Written Torah and the Oral Torah into our learning – for its own sake.

בָּרוּךְ אַתָּה יהוה אֱלֹהֵינוּ מֶלֶךְ הָעוֹלָם
אֲשֶׁר בָּחַר בָּנוּ מִכָּל הָעַמִּים
וְנָתַן לָנוּ אֶת תּוֹרָתוֹ.
בָּרוּךְ אַתָּה יהוה, נוֹתֵן הַתּוֹרָה.

יְבָרֶכְךָ יהוה וְיִשְׁמְרֶךָ: במדבר ו
יָאֵר יהוה פָּנָיו אֵלֶיךָ וִיחֻנֶּךָּ:
יִשָּׂא יהוה פָּנָיו אֵלֶיךָ וְיָשֵׂם לְךָ שָׁלוֹם:

אֵלּוּ דְבָרִים שֶׁאֵין לָהֶם שִׁעוּר משנה, פאה א:א
הַפֵּאָה וְהַבִּכּוּרִים וְהָרֵאָיוֹן
וּגְמִילוּת חֲסָדִים וְתַלְמוּד תּוֹרָה.

אֵלּוּ דְבָרִים שֶׁאָדָם אוֹכֵל פֵּרוֹתֵיהֶם בָּעוֹלָם הַזֶּה שבת קכז.
וְהַקֶּרֶן קַיֶּמֶת לוֹ לָעוֹלָם הַבָּא
וְאֵלּוּ הֵן
כִּבּוּד אָב וָאֵם, וּגְמִילוּת חֲסָדִים
וְהַשְׁכָּמַת בֵּית הַמִּדְרָשׁ שַׁחֲרִית וְעַרְבִית
וְהַכְנָסַת אוֹרְחִים, וּבִקּוּר חוֹלִים
וְהַכְנָסַת כַּלָּה, וּלְוָיַת הַמֵּת
וְעִיּוּן תְּפִלָּה
וַהֲבָאַת שָׁלוֹם בֵּין אָדָם לַחֲבֵרוֹ
וְתַלְמוּד תּוֹרָה כְּנֶגֶד כֻּלָּם.

BIUR TEFILLA • ביאור תפילה

יְבָרֶכְךָ יהוה – *May the Lord bless you.* We just recited blessings over Torah study. In order to ensure that the blessings not be in vain, the custom is to "learn" some Torah immedi-

TALLIT

Say the following meditation before putting on the tallit. Meditations before the fulfillment of mitzvot are to ensure that we do so with the requisite intention (kavana). This particularly applies to mitzvot whose purpose is to induce in us certain states of mind, as is the case with tallit and tefillin, both of which are external symbols of inward commitment to the life of observance of the mitzvot.

בָּרְכִי נַפְשִׁי Bless the LORD, my soul. LORD, my God, You are very great, *Ps. 104*
clothed in majesty and splendor, wrapped in a robe of light, spreading out the heavens like a tent.

Some say:

For the sake of the unification of the Holy One, blessed be He, and His Divine Presence, in reverence and love, to unify the name *Yod-Heh* with *Vav-Heh* in perfect unity in the name of all Israel.

I am about to wrap myself in this tasseled garment (tallit). So may my soul, my 248 limbs and 365 sinews be wrapped in the light of the tassel (*hatzitzit*) which amounts to 613 [commandments]. And just as I cover myself with a tasseled garment in this world, so may I be worthy of rabbinical dress and a fine garment in the World to Come in the Garden of Eden. Through the commandment of tassels may my life's-breath, spirit, soul and prayer be delivered from external impediments, and may the tallit spread its wings over them like an eagle stirring up its nest, hovering over its *Deut. 32*
young. May the commandment of the tasseled garment be considered before the Holy One, blessed be He, as if I had fulfilled it in all its specifics, details and intentions, as well as the 613 commandments dependent on it, Amen, Selah.

Before wrapping oneself in the tallit, say:

בָּרוּךְ Blessed are You, LORD our God, King of the Universe,
who has made us holy through His commandments,
and has commanded us to wrap ourselves
in the tasseled garment.

According to the Shela (R. Isaiah Horowitz), one should say these verses after wrapping oneself in the tallit:

מַה־יָּקָר How precious is Your loving-kindness, O God, *Ps. 36*
and the children of men find refuge under the shadow of Your wings.
They are filled with the rich plenty of Your House.
You give them drink from Your river of delights.
For with You is the fountain of life; in Your light, we see light.
Continue Your loving-kindness to those who know You,
and Your righteousness to the upright in heart.

עטיפת טלית

Say the following meditation before putting on the טלית*. Meditations before the fulfillment of* מצוות *are to ensure that we do so with the requisite intention (*כוונה*). This particularly applies to* מצוות *whose purpose is to induce in us certain states of mind, as is the case with* טלית *and* תפילין*, both of which are external symbols of inward commitment to the life of observance of the* מצוות*.*

בָּרְכִי נַפְשִׁי אֶת־יהוה, יהוה אֱלֹהַי גָּדַלְתָּ מְּאֹד, הוֹד וְהָדָר לָבָשְׁתָּ: תהלים קד
עֹטֶה־אוֹר כַּשַּׂלְמָה, נוֹטֶה שָׁמַיִם כַּיְרִיעָה:

Some say:

לְשֵׁם יִחוּד קֻדְשָׁא בְּרִיךְ הוּא וּשְׁכִינְתֵּהּ בִּדְחִילוּ וּרְחִימוּ, לְיַחֵד שֵׁם י״ה בו״ה בְּיִחוּדָא שְׁלִים בְּשֵׁם כָּל יִשְׂרָאֵל.

הֲרֵינִי מִתְעַטֵּף בַּצִּיצִית. כֵּן תִּתְעַטֵּף נִשְׁמָתִי וּרְמַ״ח אֵבָרַי וּשְׁסָ״ה גִידַי בְּאוֹר הַצִּיצִית הָעוֹלָה תַּרְיַ״ג. וּכְשֵׁם שֶׁאֲנִי מִתְכַּסֶּה בְּטַלִּית בָּעוֹלָם הַזֶּה, כָּךְ אֶזְכֶּה לַחֲלוּקָא דְרַבָּנָן וּלְטַלִּית נָאָה לָעוֹלָם הַבָּא בְּגַן עֵדֶן. וְעַל יְדֵי מִצְוַת צִיצִית תִּנָּצֵל נַפְשִׁי רוּחִי וְנִשְׁמָתִי וּתְפִלָּתִי מִן הַחִיצוֹנִים. וְהַטַּלִּית תִּפְרֹשׂ כְּנָפֶיהָ עֲלֵיהֶם וְתַצִּילֵם,
כְּנֶשֶׁר יָעִיר קִנּוֹ, עַל גּוֹזָלָיו יְרַחֵף: וּתְהֵא חֲשׁוּבָה מִצְוַת צִיצִית לִפְנֵי הַקָּדוֹשׁ בָּרוּךְ דברים לב
הוּא, כְּאִלּוּ קִיַּמְתִּיהָ בְּכָל פְּרָטֶיהָ וְדִקְדּוּקֶיהָ וְכַוָּנוֹתֶיהָ וְתַרְיַ״ג מִצְוֹת הַתְּלוּיוֹת בָּהּ, אָמֵן סֶלָה.

Before wrapping oneself in the טלית*, say:*

בָּרוּךְ אַתָּה יהוה אֱלֹהֵינוּ מֶלֶךְ הָעוֹלָם
אֲשֶׁר קִדְּשָׁנוּ בְּמִצְוֹתָיו וְצִוָּנוּ לְהִתְעַטֵּף בַּצִּיצִית.

According to the Shela (R. Isaiah Horowitz), one should say these verses after wrapping oneself in the טלית*:*

מַה־יָּקָר חַסְדְּךָ אֱלֹהִים, וּבְנֵי אָדָם בְּצֵל כְּנָפֶיךָ יֶחֱסָיוּן: תהלים לו
יִרְוְיֻן מִדֶּשֶׁן בֵּיתֶךָ, וְנַחַל עֲדָנֶיךָ תַשְׁקֵם:
כִּי־עִמְּךָ מְקוֹר חַיִּים, בְּאוֹרְךָ נִרְאֶה־אוֹר:
מְשֹׁךְ חַסְדְּךָ לְיֹדְעֶיךָ, וְצִדְקָתְךָ לְיִשְׁרֵי־לֵב:

TEFILLIN[H]

Some say the following meditation before putting on the tefillin.

For the sake of the unification of the Holy One, blessed be He, and His Divine Presence, in reverence and love, to unify the name *Yod-Heh* with *Vav-Heh* in perfect unity in the name of all Israel.

By putting on the tefillin I hereby intend to fulfill the commandment of my Creator who commanded us to wear tefillin, as it is written in His Torah: "Bind them as a sign on your hand, and they shall be an emblem on the center of your head." They contain these four sections of the Torah: one beginning with *Shema* [Deut. 6:4–9]; another with *Vehaya im shamo'a* [ibid. 11:13–21]; the third with *Kadesh Li* [Ex. 13:1–10]; and the fourth with *Vehaya ki yevi'akha* [ibid. 13:11–16]. These proclaim the uniqueness and unity of God, blessed be His name in the world. They also remind us of the miracles and wonders which He did for us when He brought us out of Egypt, and that He has the power and the dominion over the highest and the lowest to deal with them as He pleases. He commanded us to place one of the tefillin on the arm in memory of His "outstretched arm" (of redemption), setting it opposite the heart, to subject the desires and designs of our heart to His service, blessed be His name. The other is to be on the head, opposite the brain, so that my mind, whose seat is in the brain, together with my other senses and faculties, may be subjected to His service, blessed be His name. May the spiritual influence of the commandment of the tefillin be with me so that I may have a long life, a flow of holiness, and sacred thoughts, free from any suggestion of sin or iniquity. May the evil inclination neither incite nor entice us, but leave us to serve the LORD, as it is in our hearts to do.

Deut. 6

And may it be Your will, LORD our God and God of our ancestors, that the commandment of tefillin be considered before You as if I had fulfilled it in all its specifics, details and intentions, as well as the 613 commandments dependent on it, Amen, Selah.

---

an idea and to have that idea realized. Speaking between placement of the two is prohibited by halakha (*Oraḥ Ḥayyim* 25:9) because this interruption represents a disconnect between thought and action. Many Jews express identification with Judaism, but they do not act as Jews, reflecting this very difference. (Rabbi Soloveitchik)

הנחת תפילין[ה]

Some say the following meditation before putting on the תפילין.

לְשֵׁם יִחוּד קֻדְשָׁא בְּרִיךְ הוּא וּשְׁכִינְתֵּהּ בִּדְחִילוּ וּרְחִימוּ, לְיַחֵד שֵׁם י״ה בו״ה בְּיִחוּדָא שְׁלִים בְּשֵׁם כָּל יִשְׂרָאֵל.

הִנְנִי מְכַוֵּן בַּהֲנָחַת תְּפִלִּין לְקַיֵּם מִצְוַת בּוֹרְאִי, שֶׁצִּוָּנוּ לְהָנִיחַ
תְּפִלִּין, כַּכָּתוּב בְּתוֹרָתוֹ: וּקְשַׁרְתָּם לְאוֹת עַל־יָדֶךָ, וְהָיוּ לְטֹטָפֹת בֵּין דברים ו
עֵינֶיךָ: וְהֵן אַרְבַּע פָּרָשִׁיּוֹת אֵלּוּ, שְׁמַע, וְהָיָה אִם שָׁמֹעַ, קַדֶּשׁ לִי, וְהָיָה כִּי יְבִאֲךָ, שֶׁיֵּשׁ בָּהֶם יִחוּדוֹ וְאַחְדוּתוֹ יִתְבָּרַךְ שְׁמוֹ בָּעוֹלָם, וְשֶׁנִּזְכֹּר נִסִּים וְנִפְלָאוֹת שֶׁעָשָׂה עִמָּנוּ בְּהוֹצִיאוֹ אוֹתָנוּ מִמִּצְרַיִם, וַאֲשֶׁר לוֹ הַכֹּחַ וְהַמֶּמְשָׁלָה בָּעֶלְיוֹנִים וּבַתַּחְתּוֹנִים לַעֲשׂוֹת בָּהֶם כִּרְצוֹנוֹ. וְצִוָּנוּ לְהָנִיחַ עַל הַיָּד לְזִכְרוֹן זְרוֹעַ הַנְּטוּיָה, וְשֶׁהִיא נֶגֶד הַלֵּב, לְשַׁעְבֵּד בָּזֶה תַּאֲווֹת וּמַחְשְׁבוֹת לִבֵּנוּ לַעֲבוֹדָתוֹ יִתְבָּרַךְ שְׁמוֹ. וְעַל הָרֹאשׁ נֶגֶד הַמֹּחַ, שֶׁהַנְּשָׁמָה שֶׁבְּמֹחִי עִם שְׁאָר חוּשַׁי וְכֹחוֹתַי כֻּלָּם יִהְיוּ מְשֻׁעְבָּדִים לַעֲבוֹדָתוֹ, יִתְבָּרַךְ שְׁמוֹ. וּמִשֶּׁפַע מִצְוַת תְּפִלִּין יִתְמַשֵּׁךְ עָלַי לִהְיוֹת לִי חַיִּים אֲרוּכִים וְשֶׁפַע קֹדֶשׁ וּמַחֲשָׁבוֹת קְדוֹשׁוֹת בְּלִי הִרְהוּר חֵטְא וְעָוֹן כְּלָל, וְשֶׁלֹּא יְפַתֵּנוּ וְלֹא יִתְגָּרֶה בָּנוּ יֵצֶר הָרָע, וְיַנִּיחֵנוּ לַעֲבֹד אֶת יהוה כַּאֲשֶׁר עִם לְבָבֵנוּ.

וִיהִי רָצוֹן מִלְּפָנֶיךָ, יהוה אֱלֹהֵינוּ וֵאלֹהֵי אֲבוֹתֵינוּ, שֶׁתְּהֵא חֲשׁוּבָה מִצְוַת הֲנָחַת תְּפִלִּין לִפְנֵי הַקָּדוֹשׁ בָּרוּךְ הוּא, כְּאִלּוּ קִיַּמְתִּיהָ בְּכָל פְּרָטֶיהָ וְדִקְדּוּקֶיהָ וְכַוָּנוֹתֶיהָ וְתַרְיַ״ג מִצְוֹת הַתְּלוּיוֹת בָּהּ, אָמֵן סֶלָה.

HILKHOT TEFILLA • הלכות תפילה

הנחת תפילין – *Tefillin*. In Ashkenazic practice, the two tefillin each have their own blessing because each one represents something different. The one for the arm represents the world of action; the one for the head, the world of thought. The success of man is actualized through the merging of thought and action, through his ability to conceive

Stand and place the hand-tefillin on the biceps of the left arm (or right arm if you are left-handed), angled toward the heart, and before tightening the strap, say:

בָּרוּךְ Blessed are You, LORD our God, King of the Universe,
who has made us holy through His commandments,
and has commanded us to put on tefillin.

Wrap the strap of the hand-tefillin seven times around the arm.
Place the head-tefillin above the hairline, centered between the eyes, and say quietly:

בָּרוּךְ Blessed are You, LORD our God, King of the Universe,
who has made us holy through His commandments,
and has commanded us about the commandment of tefillin.

Adjust the head-tefillin and say:

בָּרוּךְ Blessed be the name of His glorious kingdom
for ever and all time.

Some say:

From Your wisdom, God most high, grant me [wisdom],
and from Your understanding, give me understanding.
May Your loving-kindness be greatly upon me,
and in Your might may my enemies and those who rise against me be subdued.
Pour Your goodly oil on the seven branches of the menora
so that Your good flows down upon Your creatures.
You open Your hand, and satisfy every living thing with favor. *Ps. 145*

Wind the strap of the hand-tefillin three times around the middle finger, saying:

וְאֵרַשְׂתִּיךְ I will betroth you to Me for ever; *Hos. 2*
I will betroth you to Me in righteousness and justice,
loving-kindness and compassion;
I will betroth you to Me in faithfulness;
and you shall know the LORD.

After putting on the tefillin, say the following:

וַיְדַבֵּר The LORD spoke to Moses, saying, "Consecrate to Me every *Ex. 13*
firstborn male. The first offspring of every womb among the Israelites,
whether man or beast, belongs to Me." Then Moses said to the people,

Stand and place the תפילין של יד on the biceps of the left arm (or right arm if you are left-handed), angled toward the heart, and before tightening the strap, say:

בָּרוּךְ אַתָּה יהוה אֱלֹהֵינוּ מֶלֶךְ הָעוֹלָם
אֲשֶׁר קִדְּשָׁנוּ בְּמִצְוֹתָיו
וְצִוָּנוּ לְהָנִיחַ תְּפִלִּין.

Wrap the strap of the תפילין של יד seven times around the arm.
Place the תפילין של ראש above the hairline, centered between the eyes, and say quietly:

בָּרוּךְ אַתָּה יהוה אֱלֹהֵינוּ מֶלֶךְ הָעוֹלָם
אֲשֶׁר קִדְּשָׁנוּ בְּמִצְוֹתָיו
וְצִוָּנוּ עַל מִצְוַת תְּפִלִּין.

Adjust the תפילין של ראש and say:

בָּרוּךְ שֵׁם כְּבוֹד מַלְכוּתוֹ לְעוֹלָם וָעֶד

Some say:

וּמֵחָכְמָתְךָ אֵל עֶלְיוֹן תַּאֲצִיל עָלַי, וּמִבִּינָתְךָ תְּבִינֵנִי
וּבְחַסְדְּךָ תַּגְדִּיל עָלַי, וּבִגְבוּרָתְךָ תַּצְמִית אוֹיְבַי וְקָמַי.
וְשֶׁמֶן הַטּוֹב תָּרִיק עַל שִׁבְעָה קְנֵי הַמְּנוֹרָה
לְהַשְׁפִּיעַ טוּבְךָ לִבְרִיּוֹתֶיךָ.
פּוֹתֵחַ אֶת־יָדֶךָ וּמַשְׂבִּיעַ לְכָל־חַי רָצוֹן: תהלים קמה

Wind the strap of the תפילין של יד three times around the middle finger, saying:

וְאֵרַשְׂתִּיךְ לִי לְעוֹלָם הושע ב
וְאֵרַשְׂתִּיךְ לִי בְּצֶדֶק וּבְמִשְׁפָּט וּבְחֶסֶד וּבְרַחֲמִים:
וְאֵרַשְׂתִּיךְ לִי בֶּאֱמוּנָה, וְיָדַעַתְּ אֶת־יהוה:

After putting on the תפילין, say the following:

וַיְדַבֵּר יהוה אֶל־מֹשֶׁה לֵּאמֹר: קַדֶּשׁ־לִי כָל־בְּכוֹר, פֶּטֶר כָּל־רֶחֶם שמות יג
בִּבְנֵי יִשְׂרָאֵל, בָּאָדָם וּבַבְּהֵמָה, לִי הוּא: וַיֹּאמֶר מֹשֶׁה אֶל־הָעָם,

"Remember this day on which you left Egypt, the slave-house, when the LORD brought you out of it with a mighty hand. No leaven shall be eaten. You are leaving on this day, in the month of Aviv. When the LORD brings you into the land of the Canaanites, Hittites, Amorites, Hivites and Jebusites, the land He swore to your ancestors to give you, a land flowing with milk and honey, you are to observe this service in this same month. For seven days you shall eat unleavened bread, and make the seventh day a festival to the LORD. Unleavened bread shall be eaten throughout the seven days. No leavened bread may be seen in your possession, and no leaven shall be seen anywhere within your borders. On that day you shall tell your son, 'This is because of what the LORD did for me when I left Egypt.' [These words] shall also be a sign on your hand, and a reminder above your forehead, so that the LORD's Torah may always be in your mouth, because with a mighty hand the LORD brought you out of Egypt. You shall therefore keep this statute at its appointed time from year to year."

וְהָיָה After the LORD has brought you into the land of the Canaanites, as He swore to you and your ancestors, and He has given it to you, you shall set apart for the LORD the first offspring of every womb. All the firstborn males of your cattle belong to the LORD. Every firstling donkey you shall redeem with a lamb. If you do not redeem it, you must break its neck. Every firstborn among your sons you must redeem. If, in time to come, your son asks you, "What does this mean?" you shall say to him, "With a mighty hand the LORD brought us out of Egypt, out of the slave-house. When Pharaoh stubbornly refused to let us leave, the LORD killed all the firstborn in the land of Egypt, both man and beast. That is why I sacrifice to the LORD the first male offspring of every womb, and redeem all the firstborn of my sons." [These words] shall be a sign on your hand and as an emblem above your forehead, that with a mighty hand the LORD brought us out of Egypt.

זָכוֹר אֶת־הַיּוֹם הַזֶּה, אֲשֶׁר יְצָאתֶם מִמִּצְרַיִם מִבֵּית עֲבָדִים, כִּי בְּחֹזֶק יָד הוֹצִיא יהוה אֶתְכֶם מִזֶּה, וְלֹא יֵאָכֵל חָמֵץ: הַיּוֹם אַתֶּם יֹצְאִים, בְּחֹדֶשׁ הָאָבִיב: וְהָיָה כִי־יְבִיאֲךָ יהוה אֶל־אֶרֶץ הַכְּנַעֲנִי וְהַחִתִּי וְהָאֱמֹרִי וְהַחִוִּי וְהַיְבוּסִי, אֲשֶׁר נִשְׁבַּע לַאֲבֹתֶיךָ לָתֶת לָךְ, אֶרֶץ זָבַת חָלָב וּדְבָשׁ, וְעָבַדְתָּ אֶת־הָעֲבֹדָה הַזֹּאת בַּחֹדֶשׁ הַזֶּה: שִׁבְעַת יָמִים תֹּאכַל מַצֹּת, וּבַיּוֹם הַשְּׁבִיעִי חַג לַיהוה: מַצּוֹת יֵאָכֵל אֵת שִׁבְעַת הַיָּמִים, וְלֹא־יֵרָאֶה לְךָ חָמֵץ וְלֹא־יֵרָאֶה לְךָ שְׂאֹר, בְּכָל־גְּבֻלֶךָ: וְהִגַּדְתָּ לְבִנְךָ בַּיּוֹם הַהוּא לֵאמֹר, בַּעֲבוּר זֶה עָשָׂה יהוה לִי בְּצֵאתִי מִמִּצְרָיִם: וְהָיָה לְךָ לְאוֹת עַל־יָדְךָ וּלְזִכָּרוֹן בֵּין עֵינֶיךָ, לְמַעַן תִּהְיֶה תּוֹרַת יהוה בְּפִיךָ, כִּי בְּיָד חֲזָקָה הוֹצִאֲךָ יהוה מִמִּצְרָיִם: וְשָׁמַרְתָּ אֶת־הַחֻקָּה הַזֹּאת לְמוֹעֲדָהּ, מִיָּמִים יָמִימָה:

וְהָיָה כִּי־יְבִאֲךָ יהוה אֶל־אֶרֶץ הַכְּנַעֲנִי כַּאֲשֶׁר נִשְׁבַּע לְךָ וְלַאֲבֹתֶיךָ, וּנְתָנָהּ לָךְ: וְהַעֲבַרְתָּ כָל־פֶּטֶר־רֶחֶם לַיהוה, וְכָל־פֶּטֶר שֶׁגֶר בְּהֵמָה אֲשֶׁר יִהְיֶה לְךָ הַזְּכָרִים, לַיהוה: וְכָל־פֶּטֶר חֲמֹר תִּפְדֶּה בְשֶׂה, וְאִם־לֹא תִפְדֶּה וַעֲרַפְתּוֹ, וְכֹל בְּכוֹר אָדָם בְּבָנֶיךָ תִּפְדֶּה: וְהָיָה כִּי־יִשְׁאָלְךָ בִנְךָ מָחָר, לֵאמֹר מַה־זֹּאת, וְאָמַרְתָּ אֵלָיו, בְּחֹזֶק יָד הוֹצִיאָנוּ יהוה מִמִּצְרַיִם מִבֵּית עֲבָדִים: וַיְהִי כִּי־הִקְשָׁה פַרְעֹה לְשַׁלְּחֵנוּ, וַיַּהֲרֹג יהוה כָּל־בְּכוֹר בְּאֶרֶץ מִצְרַיִם, מִבְּכֹר אָדָם וְעַד־בְּכוֹר בְּהֵמָה, עַל־כֵּן אֲנִי זֹבֵחַ לַיהוה כָּל־פֶּטֶר רֶחֶם הַזְּכָרִים, וְכָל־בְּכוֹר בָּנַי אֶפְדֶּה: וְהָיָה לְאוֹת עַל־יָדְכָה וּלְטוֹטָפֹת בֵּין עֵינֶיךָ, כִּי בְּחֹזֶק יָד הוֹצִיאָנוּ יהוה מִמִּצְרָיִם:

PREPARATION FOR PRAYER

On entering the synagogue:

HOW GOODLY *Num. 24*

are your tents, Jacob, your dwelling places, Israel.
As for me, *Ps. 5*
in Your great loving-kindness,
I will come into Your House.
I will bow down to Your holy Temple
in awe of You.
LORD, I love the habitation of Your House, *Ps. 26*
the place where Your glory dwells.

As for me,
I will bow in worship;

I will bend the knee
before the LORD my Maker.

As for me, *Ps. 69*
may my prayer come to You, LORD,

at a time of favor.
God, in Your great loving-kindness,
answer me with Your faithful salvation.

הכנה לתפילה

On entering the בית כנסת*:*

במדבר כד
מַה־טֹּבוּ אֹהָלֶיךָ יַעֲקֹב, מִשְׁכְּנֹתֶיךָ יִשְׂרָאֵל:
תהלים ה
וַאֲנִי בְּרֹב חַסְדְּךָ אָבוֹא בֵיתֶךָ
אֶשְׁתַּחֲוֶה אֶל־הֵיכַל־קָדְשְׁךָ
בְּיִרְאָתֶךָ:
תהלים כו
יהוה אָהַבְתִּי מְעוֹן בֵּיתֶךָ
וּמְקוֹם מִשְׁכַּן כְּבוֹדֶךָ:

וַאֲנִי אֶשְׁתַּחֲוֶה
וְאֶכְרָעָה
אֶבְרְכָה לִפְנֵי יהוה עֹשִׂי.

תהלים סט
וַאֲנִי תְפִלָּתִי־לְךָ יהוה
עֵת רָצוֹן
אֱלֹהִים בְּרָב־חַסְדֶּךָ
עֲנֵנִי בֶּאֱמֶת יִשְׁעֶךָ:

The following poems, on this page and the next, both from the Middle Ages, are summary statements of Jewish faith, orienting us to the spiritual contours of the world that we actualize in the mind by the act of prayer.

LORD OF THE UNIVERSE,
who reigned before the birth of any thing –

When by His will all things were made
then was His name proclaimed King.

And when all things shall cease to be
He alone will reign in awe.

He was, He is, and He shall be
glorious for evermore.

He is One, there is none else,
alone, unique, beyond compare;

Without beginning, without end,
His might, His rule are everywhere.

He is my God; my Redeemer lives.
He is the Rock on whom I rely –

My banner and my safe retreat,
my cup, my portion when I cry.

Into His hand my soul I place,
when I awake and when I sleep.

The LORD is with me, I shall not fear;
body and soul from harm will He keep.

The following poems, on this page and the next, both from the Middle Ages, are summary statements of Jewish faith, orienting us to the spiritual contours of the world that we actualize in the mind by the act of prayer.

אֲדוֹן עוֹלָם

אֲשֶׁר מָלַךְ בְּטֶֽרֶם כָּל־יְצִיר נִבְרָא.
לְעֵת נַעֲשָׂה בְחֶפְצוֹ כֹּל אֲזַי מֶֽלֶךְ שְׁמוֹ נִקְרָא.
וְאַחֲרֵי כִּכְלוֹת הַכֹּל לְבַדּוֹ יִמְלֹךְ נוֹרָא.
וְהוּא הָיָה וְהוּא הֹוֶה וְהוּא יִהְיֶה בְּתִפְאָרָה.
וְהוּא אֶחָד וְאֵין שֵׁנִי לְהַמְשִׁיל לוֹ לְהַחְבִּֽירָה.
בְּלִי רֵאשִׁית בְּלִי תַכְלִית וְלוֹ הָעֹז וְהַמִּשְׂרָה.
וְהוּא אֵלִי וְחַי גֹּאֲלִי וְצוּר חֶבְלִי בְּעֵת צָרָה.
וְהוּא נִסִּי וּמָנוֹס לִי מְנָת כּוֹסִי בְּיוֹם אֶקְרָא.
בְּיָדוֹ אַפְקִיד רוּחִי בְּעֵת אִישַׁן וְאָעִֽירָה.
וְעִם רוּחִי גְּוִיָּתִי יהוה לִי וְלֹא אִירָא.

GREAT

is the living God and praised.
He exists, and His existence is beyond time.

He is One, and there is no unity like His.
Unfathomable, His oneness is infinite.

He has neither bodily form nor substance;
His holiness is beyond compare.

He preceded all that was created.
He was first: there was no beginning to His beginning.

Behold He is Master of the Universe; and every creature
shows His greatness and majesty.

The rich flow of His prophecy He gave
to His treasured people in whom He gloried.

Never in Israel has there arisen another like Moses,
a prophet who beheld God's image.

God gave His people a Torah of truth
by the hand of His prophet, most faithful of His House.

God will not alter or change His law
for any other, for eternity.

He sees and knows our secret thoughts;
as soon as something is begun, He foresees its end.

He rewards people with loving-kindness according to their deeds;
He punishes the wicked according to his wickedness.

At the end of days He will send our Messiah
to redeem those who await His final salvation.

God will revive the dead in His great loving-kindness.
Blessed for evermore is His glorious name!

יִגְדַּל

אֱלֹהִים חַי וְיִשְׁתַּבַּח, נִמְצָא וְאֵין עֵת אֶל מְצִיאוּתוֹ.

אֶחָד וְאֵין יָחִיד כְּיִחוּדוֹ, נֶעְלָם וְגַם אֵין סוֹף לְאַחְדוּתוֹ.

אֵין לוֹ דְּמוּת הַגּוּף וְאֵינוֹ גוּף, לֹא נַעֲרֹךְ אֵלָיו קְדֻשָּׁתוֹ.

קַדְמוֹן לְכָל דָּבָר אֲשֶׁר נִבְרָא, רִאשׁוֹן וְאֵין רֵאשִׁית לְרֵאשִׁיתוֹ.

הִנּוֹ אֲדוֹן עוֹלָם, וְכָל נוֹצָר יוֹרֶה גְדֻלָּתוֹ וּמַלְכוּתוֹ.

שֶׁפַע נְבוּאָתוֹ נְתָנוֹ אֶל־אַנְשֵׁי סְגֻלָּתוֹ וְתִפְאַרְתּוֹ.

לֹא קָם בְּיִשְׂרָאֵל כְּמֹשֶׁה עוֹד נָבִיא וּמַבִּיט אֶת תְּמוּנָתוֹ.

תּוֹרַת אֱמֶת נָתַן לְעַמּוֹ אֵל עַל יַד נְבִיאוֹ נֶאֱמַן בֵּיתוֹ.

לֹא יַחֲלִיף הָאֵל וְלֹא יָמִיר דָּתוֹ לְעוֹלָמִים לְזוּלָתוֹ.

צוֹפֶה וְיוֹדֵעַ סְתָרֵינוּ, מַבִּיט לְסוֹף דָּבָר בְּקַדְמָתוֹ.

גּוֹמֵל לְאִישׁ חֶסֶד כְּמִפְעָלוֹ, נוֹתֵן לְרָשָׁע רָע כְּרִשְׁעָתוֹ.

יִשְׁלַח לְקֵץ יָמִין מְשִׁיחֵנוּ לִפְדּוֹת מְחַכֵּי קֵץ יְשׁוּעָתוֹ.

מֵתִים יְחַיֶּה אֵל בְּרֹב חַסְדּוֹ, בָּרוּךְ עֲדֵי עַד שֵׁם תְּהִלָּתוֹ.

MORNING BLESSINGS[IH]

The following blessings are said aloud by the Leader, but each individual should say them quietly as well. It is our custom to say them standing.

בָּרוּךְ Blessed are You, LORD our God,
King of the Universe,
who gives the heart understanding[B]
to distinguish day from night.

Blessed are You, LORD our God,
King of the Universe,
who has not made me a heathen.

Blessed are You, LORD our God,
King of the Universe,
who has not made me a slave.[A]

BIUR TEFILLA • ביאור תפילה

אֲשֶׁר נָתַן לַשֶּׂכְוִי בִינָה – *Who gives the heart understanding.* The word שֶׂכְוִי can mean rooster or it can mean the human heart. An animal with a brain the size of a pea, and the most intelligent species on the planet nevertheless share an intuitive sense of the world. There are different ways to "know" something to be true.

ANI TEFILLA • אני תפילה

שֶׁלֹּא עָשַׂנִי עָבֶד – *Who has not made me a slave.*

One day, and for days thereafter, in the Kovno Ghetto during the Nazi oppression, the ḥazan Rabbi Avraham Yosef was leading the prayers, and when he got to this blessing he cried aloud to God in a bitter voice:

"How can I recite this blessing to You when we are imprisoned this way? How can I, a slave, recite the blessing of a free man, when death hangs over me, when I have no bread to eat? How can I recite the blessing 'who did not make me a slave?' I would be making fun of God were I to say it! My mouth and my heart would not be in accord." Rabbi Ephraim Oshry responded that the blessing is a reference to the fact that a Canaanite slave is not permitted to do mitzvot; that is why one thanks God, for the opportunity to do more mitzvot than others may be obligated to do. The blessing is therefore not about physical slavery at all but about spirituality. As such, Heaven forbid that one should stop saying this blessing! Let us be reminded and let the enemy see that despite the fact that they work us like slaves, we are still free, free to do mitzvot, and free to serve our Creator. (*Responsa MiMa'amakim* III:6)

ברכות השחר[עה]

The following blessings are said aloud by the שליח ציבור, but each individual should say them quietly as well. It is our custom to say them standing.

בָּרוּךְ אַתָּה יהוה אֱלֹהֵינוּ מֶלֶךְ הָעוֹלָם
אֲשֶׁר נָתַן לַשֶּׂכְוִי בִינָה[ב]
לְהַבְחִין בֵּין יוֹם וּבֵין לָיְלָה.

בָּרוּךְ אַתָּה יהוה אֱלֹהֵינוּ מֶלֶךְ הָעוֹלָם
שֶׁלֹּא עָשַׂנִי גּוֹי.

בָּרוּךְ אַתָּה יהוה אֱלֹהֵינוּ מֶלֶךְ הָעוֹלָם
שֶׁלֹּא עָשַׂנִי עָבֶד.[א]

IYUN TEFILLA • עיון תפילה

ברכות השחר – *Morning Blessings.* The Gemara (*Berakhot* 60b) rules that one should recite a blessing of praise upon every act related to getting up in the morning. These *berakhot*, with some exceptions, are what constitute the 15 *Birkhot HaShaḥar* that appear here. Yet according to current practice, these blessings are unlike most other similar ones. For in general, we recite certain blessings of praise or thanks, *after* having experienced something, such as an act of nature (e.g., the blessing on hearing thunder) or eating (*Birkat HaMazon*) or the like. In the present case, however, we recite these blessings even if we have not experienced the occurrence ourselves. For example, if one were blind, one would still recite the blessing of **פּוֹקֵחַ עִוְרִים**, "Who opens the eyes of the blind"; if one was sick and stayed in one's pajamas all day, one would still recite **מַלְבִּישׁ עֲרֻמִּים**, "Who clothes the naked," etc. We thus begin our day with blessings for the many natural things in our lives that we and others derive benefit from. Imagine if you were unable to see, or couldn't straighten up in the morning, or didn't have clothes to wear; what would your life be like? Someone who reflects upon these things is able to start each day with a new appreciation for the things that we otherwise tend to take for granted. Each day is a new day, even if at first it may have felt the same as the day before. Each day represents a fresh slate, a new beginning.

HILKHOT TEFILLA • הלכות תפילה

ברכות השחר – *Morning Blessings.* Given the reasons for these *berakhot*, one should ideally recite them at home after one washes in the morning. Nevertheless, in many communities they are the first thing recited aloud by the *ḥazan*, to which the listeners should respond *Amen*. (*Shulḥan Arukh*, 46:1-2)

Blessed are You, LORD our God,
King of the Universe,
men: who has not made me a woman.
women: who has made me according to His will.

Blessed are You, LORD our God,
King of the Universe,
who gives sight to the blind.[A]

Blessed are You, LORD our God,
King of the Universe,
who clothes the naked.[I]

Blessed are You, LORD our God,
King of the Universe,
who sets captives free.[I]

Blessed are You, LORD our God,
King of the Universe,
who raises those bowed down.

Blessed are You, LORD our God,
King of the Universe,
who spreads the earth above the waters.

---

them with clothes since they were embarrassed by their nakedness. They had given in to their desires which then changed their perception of the world. Clothes remind us that we are not animals, that we can restrain ourselves with modesty. Another word for clothes is בֶּגֶד, the same root as the word "traitor." Clothes remind us not to betray our superiority over the animals.

מַתִּיר אֲסוּרִים – *Who sets captives free.* This blessing was said when one stretched for the first time in the morning. The ability to stretch one's limbs should never be taken for granted. At the same time, is there some habit to which you feel bound? If I could only stop being lazy, overeating, staying up so late, wasting my time... This blessing says that freedom from bad habits is possible.

בָּרוּךְ אַתָּה יהוה אֱלֹהֵינוּ מֶלֶךְ הָעוֹלָם
men שֶׁלֹּא עָשַׂנִי אִשָּׁה.
women שֶׁעָשַׂנִי כִּרְצוֹנוֹ.

בָּרוּךְ אַתָּה יהוה אֱלֹהֵינוּ מֶלֶךְ הָעוֹלָם
פּוֹקֵחַ עִוְרִים.[א]

בָּרוּךְ אַתָּה יהוה אֱלֹהֵינוּ מֶלֶךְ הָעוֹלָם
מַלְבִּישׁ עֲרֻמִּים.[ע]

בָּרוּךְ אַתָּה יהוה אֱלֹהֵינוּ מֶלֶךְ הָעוֹלָם
מַתִּיר אֲסוּרִים.[ע]

בָּרוּךְ אַתָּה יהוה אֱלֹהֵינוּ מֶלֶךְ הָעוֹלָם
זוֹקֵף כְּפוּפִים.

בָּרוּךְ אַתָּה יהוה אֱלֹהֵינוּ מֶלֶךְ הָעוֹלָם
רוֹקַע הָאָרֶץ עַל הַמָּיִם.

IYUN TEFILLA • עיון תפילה

מַלְבִּישׁ עֲרֻמִּים – *Who clothes the naked.* On one level, we must be thankful that unlike so many other people in the world, we have clothes to wear, often an amazing collection of clothes when others have but one outfit they wear all of the time. But as well, we can be reminded that in an act of *ḥesed*, after Adam and Ḥava sinned, Hashem provided

ANI TEFILLA • אני תפילה

פּוֹקֵחַ עִוְרִים – *Who gives sight to the blind.*

Try closing your eyes tight. Then open them. Then say this blessing.

Blessed are You, LORD our God,
King of the Universe,
who has provided me with all I need.[IA]

Blessed are You, LORD our God,
King of the Universe,
who makes firm the steps of man.[I]

Blessed are You, LORD our God,
King of the Universe,
who girds Israel with strength.[B]

Blessed are You, LORD our God,
King of the Universe,
who crowns Israel with glory.

Blessed are You, LORD our God,
King of the Universe,
who gives strength to the weary.

IYUN TEFILLA • עיון תפילה

הַמֵּכִין מִצְעֲדֵי גָבֶר – *Who makes firm the steps of man.* Hashem cares about each individual and what you can accomplish in this world. He therefore grants each person only a certain number of steps in life. Make each step you take count today (based on *Shomer Emunim, hashgaḥa pratit*). The ability to walk comes from Him; the direction you take is up to you.

BIUR TEFILLA • ביאור תפילה

אוֹזֵר יִשְׂרָאֵל בִּגְבוּרָה – *Who girds Israel with strength.* This blessing literally means "who girds Israel with heroism," which is different from the request for strength. "Heroic action means sacrificial action; if one does not sacrifice, he cannot be called a hero. A Jew may not be strong physically, but he can engage in heroic activity, and, indeed, has been engaging in heroic action for millennia... Jewish existence has been a heroic existence. Even today, our task is to defy everybody, which is a very difficult job and demands a great deal of heroism" (Rabbi J.B. Soloveitchik).

בָּרוּךְ אַתָּה יהוה אֱלֹהֵינוּ מֶלֶךְ הָעוֹלָם
שֶׁעָשָׂה לִּי כָּל צָרְכִּי.עא

בָּרוּךְ אַתָּה יהוה אֱלֹהֵינוּ מֶלֶךְ הָעוֹלָם
הַמֵּכִין מִצְעֲדֵי גָבֶר.ע

בָּרוּךְ אַתָּה יהוה אֱלֹהֵינוּ מֶלֶךְ הָעוֹלָם
אוֹזֵר יִשְׂרָאֵל בִּגְבוּרָה.ב

בָּרוּךְ אַתָּה יהוה אֱלֹהֵינוּ מֶלֶךְ הָעוֹלָם
עוֹטֵר יִשְׂרָאֵל בְּתִפְאָרָה.

בָּרוּךְ אַתָּה יהוה אֱלֹהֵינוּ מֶלֶךְ הָעוֹלָם
הַנּוֹתֵן לַיָּעֵף כֹּחַ.

IYUN TEFILLA • עיון תפילה

שֶׁעָשָׂה לִּי כָּל צָרְכִּי – *Who has provided me with all I need.* Almost all of the blessings are in the present tense yet this one is expressed in the past tense. Why not say "who gives me all I need"? Oftentimes sadness, hardship, and misfortune may appear to be filling up our lives but it truly is only later, further on down the road, that we can see that it all happened for a reason. Only then can we thank Hashem for what previously seemed to have been bad. A man could have found what seemed to be the perfect job: great pay, great location, and great facilities. He goes in for an interview, thinks he got the job, gets excited, and then finds out that he did not get the position. He is distraught, upset, and quite puzzled. Why would he want to thank God for all He does? Only after he gets his new job with better pay, a better location, and better facilities can he thank God for not granting him his originally desired position. Only then can he distinguish the forest from the trees. The Siddur helps give perspective to our lives. (Based on Rabbi A. Twerski)

ANI TEFILLA • אני תפילה

שֶׁעָשָׂה לִּי כָּל צָרְכִּי – *Who has provided me with all I need.*

In early life, Rabbi Yeḥiel Mikhel of Zlotchov lived in great poverty but he was always happy. Someone once asked him:

"Rabbi, how can you pray every day 'Who provided me with all I need' when you surely lack everything a man has need of!"

He replied: "My need is, most likely, to be poor, and that is what I have been supplied with."

בָּרוּךְ Blessed are You, Lord our God, King of the Universe,
who removes sleep from my eyes and slumber from my eyelids.
And may it be Your will, Lord our God
and God of our ancestors, to accustom us to Your Torah,[B]
and make us attached to Your commandments.
Lead us not into error, transgression, iniquity,[B] temptation or disgrace.
Do not let the evil instinct dominate us.
Keep us far from a bad man and a bad companion.[A]
Help us attach ourselves to the good instinct and to good deeds
and bend our instincts to be subservient to You.
Grant us, this day and every day, grace, loving-kindness
and compassion in Your eyes and in the eyes of all who see us,
and bestow loving-kindness upon us.
Blessed are You, Lord,
who bestows loving-kindness on His people Israel.[I]

יְהִי רָצוֹן May it be Your will, Lord my God and God of my ancestors, to save me today and every day, from the arrogant and from arrogance itself, from a bad man, a bad friend, a bad neighbor, a bad mishap, a destructive adversary, a harsh trial and a harsh opponent, whether or not he is a son of the covenant. *Berakhot 16b*

BIUR TEFILLA • ביאור תפילה

לֹא לִידֵי חֵטְא וְלֹא לִידֵי עֲבֵרָה וְעָוֹן – *Not into error, transgression, iniquity.* A חֵטְא is a sin which one commits by accident; an עֲבֵרָה is a transgression, a sin which one commits over and over again until it becomes habitual to the point that it seems totally permissible. An עָוֹן is a sin which is done on purpose, knowing that it is wrong. Each kind of sin stands on its own, yet it is also possible that each one eventually leads to the other. (Rabbi Schwab)

ANI TEFILLA • אני תפילה

וּמֵחָבֵר רָע – *A bad companion.*
What is a bad friend? If he or she is really a friend, then how could they be bad?

IYUN TEFILLA • עיון תפילה

גּוֹמֵל חֲסָדִים טוֹבִים לְעַמּוֹ יִשְׂרָאֵל – *Who bestows loving-kindness on His people Israel.* There is a rule that the theme at the end of a "long" blessing must relate to the theme at the opening of the blessing. What is the connection here? We began by acknowledging that Hashem relieves us of sleepiness. We conclude by acknowledging that our ability to begin a new day, refreshed and alert, even if we are tired, is an act of *ḥesed* by God (Rabbeinu Tam, *Berakhot* 46a). Each day is a new adventure to be embraced and appreciated.

בָּרוּךְ אַתָּה יהוה אֱלֹהֵינוּ מֶלֶךְ הָעוֹלָם
הַמַּעֲבִיר שֵׁנָה מֵעֵינַי וּתְנוּמָה מֵעַפְעַפָּי.
וִיהִי רָצוֹן מִלְּפָנֶיךָ יהוה אֱלֹהֵינוּ וֵאלֹהֵי אֲבוֹתֵינוּ
שֶׁתַּרְגִּילֵנוּ בְּתוֹרָתֶךָ,ב וְדַבְּקֵנוּ בְּמִצְוֹתֶיךָ
וְאַל תְּבִיאֵנוּ לֹא לִידֵי חֵטְא
וְלֹא לִידֵי עֲבֵרָה וְעָוֹןב
וְלֹא לִידֵי נִסָּיוֹן וְלֹא לִידֵי בִזָּיוֹן
וְאַל תַּשְׁלֶט בָּנוּ יֵצֶר הָרָע
וְהַרְחִיקֵנוּ מֵאָדָם רָע וּמֵחָבֵר רָעא
וְדַבְּקֵנוּ בְּיֵצֶר הַטּוֹב וּבְמַעֲשִׂים טוֹבִים
וְכֹף אֶת יִצְרֵנוּ לְהִשְׁתַּעְבֶּד לָךְ
וּתְנֵנוּ הַיּוֹם וּבְכָל יוֹם לְחֵן וּלְחֶסֶד וּלְרַחֲמִים
בְּעֵינֶיךָ, וּבְעֵינֵי כָל רוֹאֵינוּ
וְתִגְמְלֵנוּ חֲסָדִים טוֹבִים.
בָּרוּךְ אַתָּה יהוה, גּוֹמֵל חֲסָדִים טוֹבִים לְעַמּוֹ יִשְׂרָאֵל.ע

ברכות טז: יְהִי רָצוֹן מִלְּפָנֶיךָ יהוה אֱלֹהַי וֵאלֹהֵי אֲבוֹתַי, שֶׁתַּצִּילֵנִי הַיּוֹם וּבְכָל יוֹם מֵעַזֵּי פָנִים וּמֵעַזּוּת פָּנִים, מֵאָדָם רָע, וּמֵחָבֵר רָע, וּמִשָּׁכֵן רָע, וּמִפֶּגַע רָע, וּמִשָּׂטָן הַמַּשְׁחִית, מִדִּין קָשֶׁה, וּמִבַּעַל דִּין קָשֶׁה בֵּין שֶׁהוּא בֶן בְּרִית וּבֵין שֶׁאֵינוֹ בֶּן בְּרִית.

BIUR TEFILLA • ביאור תפילה

שֶׁתַּרְגִּילֵנוּ בְּתוֹרָתֶךָ – *To accustom us to Your Torah.* We ask that Hashem "accustom us to Torah" or "make Torah habitual for us." Perhaps it is a reference to the studying of Torah or perhaps it is about living our lives according to Torah values and commandments. Regardless, these things come about only when they become habits for us, things that we practice every day. "We are what we repeatedly do," said Aristotle. "Excellence, then, is not an act, but a habit."

THE BINDING OF ISAAC

On the basis of Jewish mystical tradition, some have the custom of saying daily the biblical passage recounting the Binding of Isaac, the supreme trial of faith in which Abraham demonstrated his love of God above all other loves. Some omit and continue with "A person should" on page 36.

Our God and God of our ancestors, remember us with a favorable memory, and recall us with a remembrance of salvation and compassion from the highest of high heavens. Remember, Lord our God, on our behalf, the love of the ancients, Abraham, Isaac and Yisrael Your servants; the covenant, the loving-kindness, and the oath You swore to Abraham our father on Mount Moriah, and the Binding, when he bound Isaac his son on the altar, as is written in Your Torah:

It happened after these things that God tested Abraham. He said to him, "Abraham!" "Here I am," he replied. He said, "Take your son, your only son, Isaac, whom you love, and go to the land of Moriah and offer him there as a burnt-offering on one of the mountains which I shall say to you." Early the next morning Abraham rose and saddled his donkey and took his two lads with him, and Isaac his son, and he cut wood for the burnt-offering, and he set out for the place of which God had told him. On the third day Abraham looked up and saw the place from afar. Abraham said to his lads, "Stay here with the donkey while I and the boy go on ahead. We will worship and we will return to you." Abraham took the wood for the burnt-offering and placed it on Isaac his son, and he took in his hand the fire and the knife, and the two of them went together. Isaac said to Abraham his father, "Father?" and he said "Here I am, my son." And he said, "Here are the fire and the wood, but where is the sheep for the burnt-offering?" Abraham said, "God will see to the sheep for the burnt-offering, my son." And the two of them went together. They came *Gen. 22*

פרשת העקדה

On the basis of Jewish mystical tradition, some have the custom of saying daily the biblical passage recounting the Binding of Isaac, the supreme trial of faith in which Abraham demonstrated his love of God above all other loves. Some omit and continue with לְעוֹלָם יְהֵא אָדָם *on page 37.*

אֱלֹהֵינוּ וֵאלֹהֵי אֲבוֹתֵינוּ, זָכְרֵנוּ בְּזִכְרוֹן טוֹב לְפָנֶיךָ, וּפָקְדֵנוּ בִּפְקֻדַּת יְשׁוּעָה וְרַחֲמִים מִשְּׁמֵי שְׁמֵי קֶדֶם, וּזְכָר לָנוּ יהוה אֱלֹהֵינוּ, אַהֲבַת הַקַּדְמוֹנִים אַבְרָהָם יִצְחָק וְיִשְׂרָאֵל עֲבָדֶיךָ, אֶת הַבְּרִית וְאֶת הַחֶסֶד וְאֶת הַשְּׁבוּעָה שֶׁנִּשְׁבַּעְתָּ לְאַבְרָהָם אָבִינוּ בְּהַר הַמּוֹרִיָּה, וְאֶת הָעֲקֵדָה שֶׁעָקַד אֶת יִצְחָק בְּנוֹ עַל גַּבֵּי הַמִּזְבֵּחַ, כַּכָּתוּב בְּתוֹרָתֶךָ:

וַיְהִי אַחַר הַדְּבָרִים הָאֵלֶּה, וְהָאֱלֹהִים נִסָּה אֶת־אַבְרָהָם, בראשית כב
וַיֹּאמֶר אֵלָיו אַבְרָהָם, וַיֹּאמֶר הִנֵּנִי: וַיֹּאמֶר קַח־נָא אֶת־בִּנְךָ
אֶת־יְחִידְךָ אֲשֶׁר־אָהַבְתָּ, אֶת־יִצְחָק, וְלֶךְ־לְךָ אֶל־אֶרֶץ
הַמֹּרִיָּה, וְהַעֲלֵהוּ שָׁם לְעֹלָה עַל אַחַד הֶהָרִים אֲשֶׁר אֹמַר
אֵלֶיךָ: וַיַּשְׁכֵּם אַבְרָהָם בַּבֹּקֶר, וַיַּחֲבֹשׁ אֶת־חֲמֹרוֹ, וַיִּקַּח אֶת־
שְׁנֵי נְעָרָיו אִתּוֹ וְאֵת יִצְחָק בְּנוֹ, וַיְבַקַּע עֲצֵי עֹלָה, וַיָּקָם וַיֵּלֶךְ
אֶל־הַמָּקוֹם אֲשֶׁר־אָמַר־לוֹ הָאֱלֹהִים: בַּיּוֹם הַשְּׁלִישִׁי וַיִּשָּׂא
אַבְרָהָם אֶת־עֵינָיו וַיַּרְא אֶת־הַמָּקוֹם מֵרָחֹק: וַיֹּאמֶר אַבְרָהָם
אֶל־נְעָרָיו, שְׁבוּ־לָכֶם פֹּה עִם־הַחֲמוֹר, וַאֲנִי וְהַנַּעַר נֵלְכָה עַד־
כֹּה, וְנִשְׁתַּחֲוֶה וְנָשׁוּבָה אֲלֵיכֶם: וַיִּקַּח אַבְרָהָם אֶת־עֲצֵי הָעֹלָה
וַיָּשֶׂם עַל־יִצְחָק בְּנוֹ, וַיִּקַּח בְּיָדוֹ אֶת־הָאֵשׁ וְאֶת־הַמַּאֲכֶלֶת,
וַיֵּלְכוּ שְׁנֵיהֶם יַחְדָּו: וַיֹּאמֶר יִצְחָק אֶל־אַבְרָהָם אָבִיו, וַיֹּאמֶר
אָבִי, וַיֹּאמֶר הִנֶּנִּי בְנִי, וַיֹּאמֶר, הִנֵּה הָאֵשׁ וְהָעֵצִים, וְאַיֵּה
הַשֶּׂה לְעֹלָה: וַיֹּאמֶר אַבְרָהָם, אֱלֹהִים יִרְאֶה־לּוֹ הַשֶּׂה לְעֹלָה,
בְּנִי, וַיֵּלְכוּ שְׁנֵיהֶם יַחְדָּו: וַיָּבֹאוּ אֶל־הַמָּקוֹם אֲשֶׁר אָמַר־לוֹ

to the place God had told him about, and Abraham built there an altar and arranged the wood and bound Isaac his son and laid him on the altar on top of the wood. He reached out his hand and took the knife to slay his son. Then an angel of the Lord called out to him from heaven, "Abraham! Abraham!" He said, "Here I am." He said, "Do not reach out your hand against the boy; do not do anything to him, for now I know that you fear God, because you have not held back your son, your only son, from Me." Abraham looked up and there he saw a ram caught in a thicket by its horns, and Abraham went and took the ram and offered it as a burnt-offering instead of his son. Abraham called that place "The Lord will see," as is said to this day, "On the mountain of the Lord He will be seen." The angel of the Lord called to Abraham a second time from heaven, and said, "By Myself I swear, declares the Lord, that because you have done this and have not held back your son, your only son, I will greatly bless you and greatly multiply your descendants, as the stars of heaven and the sand of the seashore, and your descendants shall take possession of the gates of their enemies. Through your descendants, all the nations of the earth will be blessed, because you have heeded My voice." Then Abraham returned to his lads, and they rose and went together to Beersheba, and Abraham stayed in Beersheba.

Master of the Universe, just as Abraham our father suppressed his compassion to do Your will wholeheartedly, so may Your compassion suppress Your anger from us and may Your compassion prevail over Your other attributes. Deal with us, Lord our God, with the attributes of loving-kindness and compassion, and in Your great goodness may Your anger be turned away from Your people, Your city, Your land and Your inheritance. Fulfill in us, Lord our God, the promise You made in Your Torah through the hand of Moses Your servant, as it is said: "I will remember My covenant with Jacob, *Lev. 26* and also My covenant with Isaac, and also My covenant with Abraham I will remember, and the land I will remember."

הָאֱלֹהִים, וַיִּבֶן שָׁם אַבְרָהָם אֶת־הַמִּזְבֵּחַ וַיַּעֲרֹךְ אֶת־הָעֵצִים, וַיַּעֲקֹד אֶת־יִצְחָק בְּנוֹ, וַיָּשֶׂם אֹתוֹ עַל־הַמִּזְבֵּחַ מִמַּעַל לָעֵצִים: וַיִּשְׁלַח אַבְרָהָם אֶת־יָדוֹ, וַיִּקַּח אֶת־הַמַּאֲכֶלֶת, לִשְׁחֹט אֶת־בְּנוֹ: וַיִּקְרָא אֵלָיו מַלְאַךְ יהוה מִן־הַשָּׁמַיִם, וַיֹּאמֶר אַבְרָהָם אַבְרָהָם, וַיֹּאמֶר הִנֵּנִי: וַיֹּאמֶר אַל־תִּשְׁלַח יָדְךָ אֶל־הַנַּעַר, וְאַל־תַּעַשׂ לוֹ מְאוּמָה, כִּי עַתָּה יָדַעְתִּי כִּי־יְרֵא אֱלֹהִים אַתָּה, וְלֹא חָשַׂכְתָּ אֶת־בִּנְךָ אֶת־יְחִידְךָ מִמֶּנִּי: וַיִּשָּׂא אַבְרָהָם אֶת־עֵינָיו, וַיַּרְא וְהִנֵּה־אַיִל, אַחַר נֶאֱחַז בַּסְּבַךְ בְּקַרְנָיו, וַיֵּלֶךְ אַבְרָהָם וַיִּקַּח אֶת־הָאַיִל, וַיַּעֲלֵהוּ לְעֹלָה תַּחַת בְּנוֹ: וַיִּקְרָא אַבְרָהָם שֵׁם־הַמָּקוֹם הַהוּא יהוה יִרְאֶה, אֲשֶׁר יֵאָמֵר הַיּוֹם בְּהַר יהוה יֵרָאֶה: וַיִּקְרָא מַלְאַךְ יהוה אֶל־אַבְרָהָם שֵׁנִית מִן־הַשָּׁמָיִם: וַיֹּאמֶר, בִּי נִשְׁבַּעְתִּי נְאֻם־יהוה, כִּי יַעַן אֲשֶׁר עָשִׂיתָ אֶת־הַדָּבָר הַזֶּה, וְלֹא חָשַׂכְתָּ אֶת־בִּנְךָ אֶת־יְחִידֶךָ: כִּי־בָרֵךְ אֲבָרֶכְךָ, וְהַרְבָּה אַרְבֶּה אֶת־זַרְעֲךָ כְּכוֹכְבֵי הַשָּׁמַיִם, וְכַחוֹל אֲשֶׁר עַל־שְׂפַת הַיָּם, וְיִרַשׁ זַרְעֲךָ אֵת שַׁעַר אֹיְבָיו: וְהִתְבָּרְכוּ בְזַרְעֲךָ כֹּל גּוֹיֵי הָאָרֶץ, עֵקֶב אֲשֶׁר שָׁמַעְתָּ בְּקֹלִי: וַיָּשָׁב אַבְרָהָם אֶל־נְעָרָיו, וַיָּקֻמוּ וַיֵּלְכוּ יַחְדָּו אֶל־בְּאֵר שָׁבַע, וַיֵּשֶׁב אַבְרָהָם בִּבְאֵר שָׁבַע:

רִבּוֹנוֹ שֶׁל עוֹלָם, כְּמוֹ שֶׁכָּבַשׁ אַבְרָהָם אָבִינוּ אֶת רַחֲמָיו לַעֲשׂוֹת רְצוֹנְךָ בְּלֵבָב שָׁלֵם, כֵּן יִכְבְּשׁוּ רַחֲמֶיךָ אֶת כַּעַסְךָ מֵעָלֵינוּ וְיִגֹּלוּ רַחֲמֶיךָ עַל מִדּוֹתֶיךָ. וְתִתְנַהֵג עִמָּנוּ יהוה אֱלֹהֵינוּ בְּמִדַּת הַחֶסֶד וּבְמִדַּת הָרַחֲמִים, וּבְטוּבְךָ הַגָּדוֹל יָשׁוּב חֲרוֹן אַפְּךָ מֵעַמְּךָ וּמֵעִירְךָ וּמֵאַרְצְךָ וּמִנַּחֲלָתֶךָ. וְקַיֶּם לָנוּ יהוה אֱלֹהֵינוּ אֶת הַדָּבָר שֶׁהִבְטַחְתָּנוּ בְּתוֹרָתֶךָ עַל יְדֵי מֹשֶׁה עַבְדֶּךָ, כָּאָמוּר: וְזָכַרְתִּי ויקרא כו
אֶת־בְּרִיתִי יַעֲקוֹב וְאַף אֶת־בְּרִיתִי יִצְחָק, וְאַף אֶת־בְּרִיתִי אַבְרָהָם אֶזְכֹּר, וְהָאָרֶץ אֶזְכֹּר:

ACCEPTING THE SOVEREIGNTY OF HEAVEN

לְעוֹלָם A person should always be God-fearing, privately and publicly, acknowledging the truth and speaking it in his heart. *Tanna DeVei Eliyahu, ch. 21*

He should rise early and say:

Master of all worlds,[I]
not because of our righteousness *Dan. 9*
do we lay our pleas before You,
but because of Your great compassion.

What are we?
What are our lives?
What is our loving-kindness?
What is our righteousness?
What is our salvation?
What is our strength?
What is our might?
What shall we say before You,
LORD our God and God of our ancestors?
Are not all the mighty like nothing before You,
the men of renown as if they had never been,
the wise as if they know nothing,
and the understanding as if they lack intelligence?
For their many works are in vain,
and the days of their lives like a fleeting breath before You.
The pre-eminence of man over the animals is nothing,[B] *Eccl. 3*
for all is but a fleeting breath.

BIUR TEFILLA • ביאור תפילה

וּמוֹתַר הָאָדָם מִן־הַבְּהֵמָה אָיִן – *The pre-eminence of man over the animals is nothing.*

The word אָיִן means "nothing." But there are those who suggest that the three letters can be read as an acronym for אָדָם יֵשׁ נְשָׁמָה – the preeminence of man over the animal is that man has a soul.

קבלת עול מלכות שמים

לְעוֹלָם יְהֵא אָדָם יְרֵא שָׁמַיִם בְּסֵתֶר וּבְגָלוּי תנא דבי אליהו, פרק כא
וּמוֹדֶה עַל הָאֱמֶת, וְדוֹבֵר אֱמֶת בִּלְבָבוֹ
וְיַשְׁכֵּם וְיֹאמַר
רִבּוֹן כָּל הָעוֹלָמִים[ע]
לֹא עַל־צִדְקוֹתֵינוּ אֲנַחְנוּ מַפִּילִים תַּחֲנוּנֵינוּ לְפָנֶיךָ דניאל ט
כִּי עַל־רַחֲמֶיךָ הָרַבִּים:

מָה אָנוּ, מֶה חַיֵּינוּ, מֶה חַסְדֵּנוּ, מַה צִּדְקוֹתֵינוּ
מַה יְּשׁוּעָתֵנוּ, מַה כֹּחֵנוּ, מַה גְּבוּרָתֵנוּ
מַה נֹּאמַר לְפָנֶיךָ, יהוה אֱלֹהֵינוּ וֵאלֹהֵי אֲבוֹתֵינוּ
הֲלֹא כָּל הַגִּבּוֹרִים כְּאַיִן לְפָנֶיךָ
וְאַנְשֵׁי הַשֵּׁם כְּלֹא הָיוּ
וַחֲכָמִים כִּבְלִי מַדָּע, וּנְבוֹנִים כִּבְלִי הַשְׂכֵּל
כִּי רֹב מַעֲשֵׂיהֶם תֹּהוּ, וִימֵי חַיֵּיהֶם הֶבֶל לְפָנֶיךָ
וּמוֹתַר הָאָדָם מִן־הַבְּהֵמָה אָיִן[ב] קהלת ג
כִּי הַכֹּל הָבֶל:

IYUN TEFILLA • עיון תפילה

רִבּוֹן כָּל הָעוֹלָמִים – *Master of all worlds.* The prayer is divided into two parts. In the first, we are reminded that we are but creatures with our weaknesses and faults; in the second, we are reminded that we are chosen by Hashem for greatness. According to Rabbi Bunim of Peshis-ḥa, everyone should have two pockets, each containing a slip of paper. On one should be written: "I am but dust and ashes," and on the other: "The world was created for me." Sometimes we must reach into one pocket; other times we must reach into the other. The secret of living comes from knowing when to reach into each.

אֲבָל Yet we are Your people, the children of Your covenant,
the children of Abraham, Your beloved,
to whom You made a promise on Mount Moriah;
the offspring of Isaac his only one who was bound on the altar;
the congregation of Jacob Your firstborn son
whom – because of the love with which You loved him
and the joy with which You rejoiced in him –
You called Yisrael and Yeshurun.

לְפִיכָךְ Therefore it is our duty
to thank You, and to praise, glorify, bless, sanctify
and give praise and thanks to Your name.
Happy are we, how good is our portion,
how lovely our fate, how beautiful our heritage.

▸ Happy are we who, early and late,
evening and morning,
say twice each day –

Listen, Israel: the LORD is our God, the LORD is One. *Deut. 6*

Quietly: Blessed be the name of His glorious kingdom for ever and all time.

Some congregations say the entire first paragraph of the Shema (below) at this point. If there is a concern that the Shema will not be recited within the prescribed time, then all three paragraphs should be said. See law 65.

Love the LORD your God with all your heart, with all your soul, and with all your might. These words which I command you today shall be on your heart. Teach them repeatedly to your children, speaking of them when you sit at home and when you travel on the way, when you lie down and when you rise. Bind them as a sign on your hand, and they shall be an emblem between your eyes. Write them on the doorposts of your house and gates.

אַתָּה הוּא It was You who existed
before the world was created,
it is You now that the world has been created.
It is You in this world
and You in the World to Come.

אֲבָל אֲנַחְנוּ עַמְּךָ בְּנֵי בְרִיתֶךָ
בְּנֵי אַבְרָהָם אֹהַבְךָ שֶׁנִּשְׁבַּעְתָּ לּוֹ בְּהַר הַמּוֹרִיָּה
זֶרַע יִצְחָק יְחִידוֹ שֶׁנֶּעֱקַד עַל גַּבֵּי הַמִּזְבֵּחַ
עֲדַת יַעֲקֹב בִּנְךָ בְּכוֹרֶךָ
שֶׁמֵּאַהֲבָתְךָ שֶׁאָהַבְתָּ אוֹתוֹ, וּמִשִּׂמְחָתְךָ שֶׁשָּׂמַחְתָּ בּוֹ
קָרָאתָ אֶת שְׁמוֹ יִשְׂרָאֵל וִישֻׁרוּן.

לְפִיכָךְ אֲנַחְנוּ חַיָּבִים לְהוֹדוֹת לְךָ וּלְשַׁבֵּחֲךָ וּלְפָאֶרְךָ
וּלְבָרֵךְ וּלְקַדֵּשׁ וְלָתֵת שֶׁבַח וְהוֹדָיָה לִשְׁמֶךָ.
אַשְׁרֵינוּ, מַה טּוֹב חֶלְקֵנוּ, וּמַה נָּעִים גּוֹרָלֵנוּ, וּמַה יָּפָה יְרֻשָּׁתֵנוּ.

◂ אַשְׁרֵינוּ, שֶׁאֲנַחְנוּ מַשְׁכִּימִים וּמַעֲרִיבִים עֶרֶב וָבֹקֶר
וְאוֹמְרִים פַּעֲמַיִם בְּכָל יוֹם

דברים ו **שְׁמַע יִשְׂרָאֵל, יהוה אֱלֹהֵינוּ, יהוה אֶחָד:**

Quietly בָּרוּךְ שֵׁם כְּבוֹד מַלְכוּתוֹ לְעוֹלָם וָעֶד.

Some congregations say the entire first paragraph of the שמע *(below) at this point. If there is a concern that the* שמע *will not be recited within the prescribed time, then all three paragraphs should be said. See law 65.*

וְאָהַבְתָּ אֵת יהוה אֱלֹהֶיךָ, בְּכָל־לְבָבְךָ, וּבְכָל־נַפְשְׁךָ, וּבְכָל־מְאֹדֶךָ: וְהָיוּ הַדְּבָרִים הָאֵלֶּה, אֲשֶׁר אָנֹכִי מְצַוְּךָ הַיּוֹם, עַל־לְבָבֶךָ: וְשִׁנַּנְתָּם לְבָנֶיךָ, וְדִבַּרְתָּ בָּם, בְּשִׁבְתְּךָ בְּבֵיתֶךָ, וּבְלֶכְתְּךָ בַדֶּרֶךְ, וּבְשָׁכְבְּךָ וּבְקוּמֶךָ: וּקְשַׁרְתָּם לְאוֹת עַל־יָדֶךָ וְהָיוּ לְטֹטָפֹת בֵּין עֵינֶיךָ: וּכְתַבְתָּם עַל־מְזֻזוֹת בֵּיתֶךָ וּבִשְׁעָרֶיךָ:

אַתָּה הוּא עַד שֶׁלֹּא נִבְרָא הָעוֹלָם
אַתָּה הוּא מִשֶּׁנִּבְרָא הָעוֹלָם.
אַתָּה הוּא בָּעוֹלָם הַזֶּה
וְאַתָּה הוּא לָעוֹלָם הַבָּא.

▸ Sanctify Your name
through those who sanctify Your name,
and sanctify Your name
throughout Your world.
By Your salvation may our pride be exalted;
raise high our pride.
Blessed are You, Lord,
who sanctifies His name among the multitudes.

אַתָּה הוּא You are the Lord our God
in heaven and on earth, and in the highest heaven of heavens.
Truly, You are the first and You are the last,
and besides You there is no god.
Gather those who hope in You
from the four quarters of the earth.
May all mankind recognize and know
that You alone are God
over all the kingdoms on earth.

You made the heavens and the earth,
the sea and all they contain.
Who among all the works of Your hands,
above and below,
can tell You what to do?

Heavenly Father, deal kindly with us
for the sake of Your great name
by which we are called,
and fulfill for us, Lord our God,
that which is written:
"At that time I will bring you home, *Zeph. 3*
and at that time I will gather you,
for I will give you renown
and praise among all the peoples of the earth
when I bring back your exiles before your eyes,
says the Lord."

◂ קַדֵּשׁ אֶת שִׁמְךָ עַל מַקְדִּישֵׁי שְׁמֶךָ
וְקַדֵּשׁ אֶת שִׁמְךָ בְּעוֹלָמֶךָ
וּבִישׁוּעָתְךָ תָּרוּם וְתַגְבִּיהַּ קַרְנֵנוּ.
בָּרוּךְ אַתָּה יהוה
הַמְקַדֵּשׁ אֶת שְׁמוֹ בָּרַבִּים.

אַתָּה הוּא יהוה אֱלֹהֵינוּ
בַּשָּׁמַיִם וּבָאָרֶץ וּבִשְׁמֵי הַשָּׁמַיִם הָעֶלְיוֹנִים.
אֱמֶת, אַתָּה הוּא רִאשׁוֹן, וְאַתָּה הוּא אַחֲרוֹן
וּמִבַּלְעָדֶיךָ אֵין אֱלֹהִים.
קַבֵּץ קֹוֶיךָ מֵאַרְבַּע כַּנְפוֹת הָאָרֶץ.
יַכִּירוּ וְיֵדְעוּ כָּל בָּאֵי עוֹלָם
כִּי אַתָּה הוּא הָאֱלֹהִים לְבַדְּךָ לְכֹל מַמְלְכוֹת הָאָרֶץ.

אַתָּה עָשִׂיתָ אֶת הַשָּׁמַיִם וְאֶת הָאָרֶץ
אֶת הַיָּם וְאֶת כָּל אֲשֶׁר בָּם
וּמִי בְּכָל מַעֲשֵׂי יָדֶיךָ בָּעֶלְיוֹנִים אוֹ בַתַּחְתּוֹנִים
שֶׁיֹּאמַר לְךָ מַה תַּעֲשֶׂה.

אָבִינוּ שֶׁבַּשָּׁמַיִם, עֲשֵׂה עִמָּנוּ חֶסֶד
בַּעֲבוּר שִׁמְךָ הַגָּדוֹל שֶׁנִּקְרָא עָלֵינוּ
וְקַיֶּם לָנוּ יהוה אֱלֹהֵינוּ
מַה שֶּׁכָּתוּב:
בָּעֵת הַהִיא אָבִיא אֶתְכֶם, וּבָעֵת קַבְּצִי אֶתְכֶם צפניה ג
כִּי־אֶתֵּן אֶתְכֶם לְשֵׁם וְלִתְהִלָּה בְּכֹל עַמֵּי הָאָרֶץ
בְּשׁוּבִי אֶת־שְׁבוּתֵיכֶם לְעֵינֵיכֶם
אָמַר יהוה:

OFFERINGS[B]

The sages held that, in the absence of the Temple, studying the laws of sacrifices is the equivalent of offering them. Hence the following texts. There are different customs as to how many passages are to be said, and one should follow the custom of one's congregation. The minimum requirement is to say the verses relating to The Daily Sacrifice on the next page.

THE BASIN

The LORD spoke to Moses, saying: Make a bronze basin, with its bronze stand for washing, and place it between the Tent of Meeting and the altar, and put water in it. From it, Aaron and his sons are to wash their hands and feet. When they enter the Tent of Meeting, they shall wash with water so that they will not die; likewise when they approach the altar to minister, presenting a fire-offering to the LORD. They must wash their hands and feet so that they will not die. This shall be an everlasting ordinance for Aaron and his descendants throughout their generations. *Ex. 30*

TAKING OF THE ASHES

The LORD spoke to Moses, saying: Instruct Aaron and his sons, saying, This is the law of the burnt-offering. The burnt-offering shall remain on the altar hearth throughout the night until morning, and the altar fire shall be kept burning on it. The priest shall then put on his linen garments, and linen breeches next to his body, and shall remove the ashes of the burnt-offering that the fire has consumed on the altar and place them beside the altar. Then he shall take off these clothes and put on others, and carry the ashes outside the camp to a clean place. The fire on the altar must be kept burning; it must not go out. Each morning the priest shall burn wood on it, and prepare on it the burnt-offering and burn the fat of the peace-offerings. A perpetual fire must be kept burning on the altar; it must not go out. *Lev. 6*

(אֵיזֶהוּ מְקוֹמָן), and Gemara (רַבִּי יִשְׁמָעֵאל אוֹמֵר) (Tosafot, *Kiddushin* 30a).

סדר הקרבנות – *Offerings.* The word *korban* shares the same root as the word *karov*, meaning closeness. The sacrifices are designed to bring one closer to God, as is their recitation. Nevertheless, with perhaps one exception, their inclusion in one's prayers is not generally considered obligatory, although it is still common for most of them to be recited.

סדר הקרבנות[ב]

חז״ל held that, in the absence of the Temple, studying the laws of sacrifices is the equivalent of offering them. Hence the following texts. There are different customs as to how many passages are to be said, and one should follow the custom of one's congregation. The minimum requirement is to say the verses relating to the קרבן תמיד on the next page.

פרשת הכיור

שמות ל וַיְדַבֵּר יהוה אֶל־מֹשֶׁה לֵּאמֹר: וְעָשִׂיתָ כִּיּוֹר נְחֹשֶׁת וְכַנּוֹ נְחֹשֶׁת לְרָחְצָה, וְנָתַתָּ אֹתוֹ בֵּין־אֹהֶל מוֹעֵד וּבֵין הַמִּזְבֵּחַ, וְנָתַתָּ שָׁמָּה מָיִם: וְרָחֲצוּ אַהֲרֹן וּבָנָיו מִמֶּנּוּ אֶת־יְדֵיהֶם וְאֶת־רַגְלֵיהֶם: בְּבֹאָם אֶל־אֹהֶל מוֹעֵד יִרְחֲצוּ־מַיִם, וְלֹא יָמֻתוּ, אוֹ בְגִשְׁתָּם אֶל־הַמִּזְבֵּחַ לְשָׁרֵת, לְהַקְטִיר אִשֶּׁה לַיהוה: וְרָחֲצוּ יְדֵיהֶם וְרַגְלֵיהֶם וְלֹא יָמֻתוּ, וְהָיְתָה לָהֶם חָק־עוֹלָם, לוֹ וּלְזַרְעוֹ לְדֹרֹתָם:

פרשת תרומת הדשן

ויקרא ו וַיְדַבֵּר יהוה אֶל־מֹשֶׁה לֵּאמֹר: צַו אֶת־אַהֲרֹן וְאֶת־בָּנָיו לֵאמֹר, זֹאת תּוֹרַת הָעֹלָה, הִוא הָעֹלָה עַל מוֹקְדָה עַל־הַמִּזְבֵּחַ כָּל־הַלַּיְלָה עַד־הַבֹּקֶר, וְאֵשׁ הַמִּזְבֵּחַ תּוּקַד בּוֹ: וְלָבַשׁ הַכֹּהֵן מִדּוֹ בַד, וּמִכְנְסֵי־בַד יִלְבַּשׁ עַל־בְּשָׂרוֹ, וְהֵרִים אֶת־הַדֶּשֶׁן אֲשֶׁר תֹּאכַל הָאֵשׁ אֶת־הָעֹלָה, עַל־הַמִּזְבֵּחַ, וְשָׂמוֹ אֵצֶל הַמִּזְבֵּחַ: וּפָשַׁט אֶת־בְּגָדָיו, וְלָבַשׁ בְּגָדִים אֲחֵרִים, וְהוֹצִיא אֶת־הַדֶּשֶׁן אֶל־מִחוּץ לַמַּחֲנֶה, אֶל־מָקוֹם טָהוֹר: וְהָאֵשׁ עַל־הַמִּזְבֵּחַ תּוּקַד־בּוֹ, לֹא תִכְבֶּה, וּבִעֵר עָלֶיהָ הַכֹּהֵן עֵצִים בַּבֹּקֶר בַּבֹּקֶר, וְעָרַךְ עָלֶיהָ הָעֹלָה, וְהִקְטִיר עָלֶיהָ חֶלְבֵי הַשְּׁלָמִים: אֵשׁ, תָּמִיד תּוּקַד עַל־הַמִּזְבֵּחַ, לֹא תִכְבֶּה:

BIUR TEFILLA • ביאור תפילה

סדר הקרבנות – *Offerings.* The Gemara (*Ta'anit* 27b; *Megilla* 31b) raises the question of how people will be able to atone if we can no longer bring sacrifices to the *Beit HaMikdash*. The answer is provided in the name of Hashem: "If they read [about the sacrifices] before Me, I will count it as if they offered them before Me, and I will forgive them for their sins."

Similarly elsewhere (*Menaḥot* 110a) *Ḥazal* tell us that in the absence of the *Beit HaMikdash*, the recitation of the *korbanot* will be tantamount to actually offering them. Hence it has become customary to read the descriptions of the different *korbanot* as they appear in *Torah Shebikhtav* and *Torah Shebe'al Peh*, the Written and Oral Law. There are selections from each of Torah (תָּמִיד), Mishna

May it be Your will, Lord our God and God of our ancestors, that You have compassion on us and pardon us all our sins, grant atonement for all our iniquities and forgive all our transgressions. May You rebuild the Temple swiftly in our days so that we may offer You the continual-offering that it may atone for us as You have prescribed for us in Your Torah through Moses Your servant, from the mouthpiece of Your glory, as it is said:

THE DAILY SACRIFICE

וַיְדַבֵּר The Lord said to Moses,[H] "Command the Israelites and tell them: 'Be careful to offer to Me at the appointed time My food-offering consumed by fire, as an aroma pleasing to Me.' Tell them: 'This is the fire-offering you shall offer to the Lord – two lambs a year old without blemish, as a regular burnt-offering each day. Prepare one lamb in the morning and the other toward evening, together with a meal-offering of a tenth of an ephah of fine flour mixed with a quarter of a hin of oil from pressed olives. This is the regular burnt-offering instituted at Mount Sinai as a pleasing aroma, a fire-offering made to the Lord. Its libation is to be a quarter of a hin [of wine] with each lamb, poured in the Sanctuary as a libation of strong drink to the Lord. Prepare the second lamb in the afternoon, along with the same meal-offering and libation as in the morning. This is a fire-offering, an aroma pleasing to the Lord.'" *Num. 28*

וְשָׁחַט He shall slaughter it at the north side of the altar before the Lord, and Aaron's sons the priests shall sprinkle its blood against the altar on all sides. *Lev. 1*

May it be Your will, Lord our God and God of our ancestors,
that this recitation be considered accepted and favored before You
as if we had offered the daily sacrifice at its appointed time and place,
according to its laws.

It is You, Lord our God, to whom our ancestors offered fragrant incense
when the Temple stood, as You commanded them through Moses Your prophet,
as is written in Your Torah:

---

day corresponds to three periods related to the sacrifice of the daily *Tamid* offering (*Berakhot* 26b). *Tamid* means consistency, a reflection of the daily service in the *Beit HaMikdash* and the daily service of the heart that we perform today.

יְהִי רָצוֹן מִלְּפָנֶיךָ יהוה אֱלֹהֵינוּ וֵאלֹהֵי אֲבוֹתֵינוּ, שֶׁתְּרַחֵם עָלֵינוּ, וְתִמְחֹל לָנוּ עַל כָּל חַטֹּאתֵינוּ וּתְכַפֵּר לָנוּ עַל כָּל עֲוֹנוֹתֵינוּ וְתִסְלַח לָנוּ עַל כָּל פְּשָׁעֵינוּ, וְתִבְנֶה בֵּית הַמִּקְדָּשׁ בִּמְהֵרָה בְיָמֵינוּ, וְנַקְרִיב לְפָנֶיךָ קָרְבַּן הַתָּמִיד שֶׁיְּכַפֵּר בַּעֲדֵנוּ, כְּמוֹ שֶׁכָּתַבְתָּ עָלֵינוּ בְּתוֹרָתֶךָ עַל יְדֵי מֹשֶׁה עַבְדֶּךָ מִפִּי כְבוֹדֶךָ, כָּאָמוּר

פרשת קרבן התמיד

וַיְדַבֵּר יהוה אֶל־מֹשֶׁה לֵּאמֹר: צַו אֶת־בְּנֵי יִשְׂרָאֵל וְאָמַרְתָּ אֲלֵהֶם, אֶת־קָרְבָּנִי לַחְמִי לְאִשַּׁי, רֵיחַ נִיחֹחִי, תִּשְׁמְרוּ לְהַקְרִיב לִי בְּמוֹעֲדוֹ: וְאָמַרְתָּ לָהֶם, זֶה הָאִשֶּׁה אֲשֶׁר תַּקְרִיבוּ לַיהוה, כְּבָשִׂים בְּנֵי־שָׁנָה תְמִימִם שְׁנַיִם לַיּוֹם, עֹלָה תָמִיד: אֶת־הַכֶּבֶשׂ אֶחָד תַּעֲשֶׂה בַבֹּקֶר, וְאֵת הַכֶּבֶשׂ הַשֵּׁנִי תַּעֲשֶׂה בֵּין הָעַרְבָּיִם: וַעֲשִׂירִית הָאֵיפָה סֹלֶת לְמִנְחָה, בְּלוּלָה בְּשֶׁמֶן כָּתִית רְבִיעִת הַהִין: עֹלַת תָּמִיד, הָעֲשֻׂיָה בְּהַר סִינַי, לְרֵיחַ נִיחֹחַ אִשֶּׁה לַיהוה: וְנִסְכּוֹ רְבִיעִת הַהִין לַכֶּבֶשׂ הָאֶחָד, בַּקֹּדֶשׁ הַסֵּךְ נֶסֶךְ שֵׁכָר לַיהוה: וְאֵת הַכֶּבֶשׂ הַשֵּׁנִי תַּעֲשֶׂה בֵּין הָעַרְבָּיִם, כְּמִנְחַת הַבֹּקֶר וּכְנִסְכּוֹ תַּעֲשֶׂה, אִשֵּׁה רֵיחַ נִיחֹחַ לַיהוה: במדבר כח

וְשָׁחַט אֹתוֹ עַל יֶרֶךְ הַמִּזְבֵּחַ צָפֹנָה לִפְנֵי יהוה, וְזָרְקוּ בְּנֵי אַהֲרֹן הַכֹּהֲנִים אֶת־דָּמוֹ עַל־הַמִּזְבֵּחַ, סָבִיב: ויקרא א

יְהִי רָצוֹן מִלְּפָנֶיךָ, יהוה אֱלֹהֵינוּ וֵאלֹהֵי אֲבוֹתֵינוּ
שֶׁתְּהֵא אֲמִירָה זוֹ חֲשׁוּבָה וּמְקֻבֶּלֶת וּמְרֻצָּה לְפָנֶיךָ
כְּאִלּוּ הִקְרַבְנוּ קָרְבַּן הַתָּמִיד בְּמוֹעֲדוֹ וּבִמְקוֹמוֹ וּכְהִלְכָתוֹ.

אַתָּה הוּא יהוה אֱלֹהֵינוּ שֶׁהִקְטִירוּ אֲבוֹתֵינוּ לְפָנֶיךָ אֶת קְטֹרֶת הַסַּמִּים בִּזְמַן שֶׁבֵּית הַמִּקְדָּשׁ הָיָה קַיָּם, כַּאֲשֶׁר צִוִּיתָ אוֹתָם עַל יְדֵי מֹשֶׁה נְבִיאֶךָ, כַּכָּתוּב בְּתוֹרָתֶךָ:

HILKHOT TEFILLA • הלכות תפילה

וַיְדַבֵּר יהוה אֶל־מֹשֶׁה – *The Lord said to Moses.* Of all of the sacrifices mentioned in this section, the one describing the *Korban Tamid* is the one considered most obligatory (Rema 48:1). It is of special significance because the timing of the three prayer services in the

THE INCENSE

> The Lord said to Moses: Take fragrant spices – balsam, onycha, galbanum and pure frankincense, all in equal amounts – and make a fragrant blend of incense, the work of a perfumer, well mixed, pure and holy. Grind it very finely and place it in front of the [Ark of] Testimony in the Tent of Meeting, where I will meet with you. It shall be most holy to you. *Ex. 30*

And it is said:

> Aaron shall burn fragrant incense on the altar every morning when he cleans the lamps. He shall burn incense again when he lights the lamps toward evening so that there will be incense before the Lord at all times, throughout your generations.

The rabbis taught: How was the incense prepared? It weighed 368 manehs, 365 corresponding to the number of days in a solar year, a maneh for each day, half to be offered in the morning and half in the afternoon, and three additional manehs from which the High Priest took two handfuls on Yom Kippur. These were put back into the mortar on the day before Yom Kippur and ground again very thoroughly so as to be extremely fine. The incense contained eleven kinds of spices: balsam, onycha, galbanum and frankincense, each weighing seventy manehs; myrrh, cassia, spikenard and saffron, each weighing sixteen manehs; twelve manehs of costus, three of aromatic bark; nine of cinnamon; nine kabs of Carsina lye; three seahs and three kabs of Cyprus wine. If Cyprus wine was not available, old white wine might be used. A quarter of a kab of Sodom salt, and a minute amount of a smoke-raising herb. Rabbi Nathan the Babylonian says: also a minute amount of Jordan amber. If one added honey to the mixture, he rendered it unfit for sacred use. If he omitted any one of its ingredients, he is guilty of a capital offence. *Keritot 6a*

Rabban Simeon ben Gamliel says: "Balsam" refers to the sap that drips from the balsam tree. The Carsina lye was used for bleaching the onycha to improve it. The Cyprus wine was used to soak the onycha in it to make it pungent. Though urine is suitable for this purpose, it is not brought into the Temple out of respect.

It was taught, Rabbi Nathan says: While it was being ground, another would say, "Grind well, well grind," because the [rhythmic] sound is good for spices. If it was mixed in half-quantities, it is fit for use, but we have not heard whether this applies to a third or a quarter. Rabbi Judah said: The general rule is that if it was made in the correct proportions, it is fit for use even if made in half-quantity, but if he omitted any one of its ingredients, he is guilty of a capital offence.

It was taught, Bar Kappara says: Once every sixty or seventy years, the accumulated surpluses amounted to half the yearly quantity. Bar Kappara also taught: If a minute quantity of honey had been mixed into the incense, no one could have resisted the scent. Why did they not put honey into it? Because the Torah says, "For you are not to burn any leaven or honey in a fire-offering made to the Lord." *JT Yoma 4:5* *Lev. 2*

פרשת הקטורת

שמות ל וַיֹּאמֶר יהוה אֶל־מֹשֶׁה, קַח־לְךָ סַמִּים נָטָף וּשְׁחֵלֶת וְחֶלְבְּנָה, סַמִּים וּלְבֹנָה זַכָּה, בַּד בְּבַד יִהְיֶה: וְעָשִׂיתָ אֹתָהּ קְטֹרֶת, רֹקַח מַעֲשֵׂה רוֹקֵחַ, מְמֻלָּח, טָהוֹר קֹדֶשׁ: וְשָׁחַקְתָּ מִמֶּנָּה הָדֵק, וְנָתַתָּה מִמֶּנָּה לִפְנֵי הָעֵדֻת בְּאֹהֶל מוֹעֵד אֲשֶׁר אִוָּעֵד לְךָ שָׁמָּה, קֹדֶשׁ קָדָשִׁים תִּהְיֶה לָכֶם:

וְנֶאֱמַר

וְהִקְטִיר עָלָיו אַהֲרֹן קְטֹרֶת סַמִּים, בַּבֹּקֶר בַּבֹּקֶר בְּהֵיטִיבוֹ אֶת־הַנֵּרֹת יַקְטִירֶנָּה: וּבְהַעֲלֹת אַהֲרֹן אֶת־הַנֵּרֹת בֵּין הָעַרְבַּיִם יַקְטִירֶנָּה, קְטֹרֶת תָּמִיד לִפְנֵי יהוה לְדֹרֹתֵיכֶם:

כריתות ו. תָּנוּ רַבָּנָן: פִּטּוּם הַקְּטֹרֶת כֵּיצַד, שְׁלֹשׁ מֵאוֹת וְשִׁשִּׁים וּשְׁמוֹנָה מָנִים הָיוּ בָהּ. שְׁלֹשׁ מֵאוֹת וְשִׁשִּׁים וַחֲמִשָּׁה כְּמִנְיַן יְמוֹת הַחַמָּה, מָנֶה לְכָל יוֹם, פְּרַס בְּשַׁחֲרִית וּפְרַס בֵּין הָעַרְבַּיִם, וּשְׁלֹשָׁה מָנִים יְתֵרִים שֶׁמֵּהֶם מַכְנִיס כֹּהֵן גָּדוֹל מְלֹא חָפְנָיו בְּיוֹם הַכִּפּוּרִים, וּמַחֲזִירָן לְמַכְתֶּשֶׁת בְּעֶרֶב יוֹם הַכִּפּוּרִים וְשׁוֹחֲקָן יָפֶה יָפֶה, כְּדֵי שֶׁתְּהֵא דַקָּה מִן הַדַּקָּה. וְאַחַד עָשָׂר סַמָּנִים הָיוּ בָהּ, וְאֵלּוּ הֵן: הַצֳּרִי, וְהַצִּפֹּרֶן, וְהַחֶלְבְּנָה, וְהַלְּבוֹנָה מִשְׁקַל שִׁבְעִים שִׁבְעִים מָנֶה, מֹר, וּקְצִיעָה, שִׁבֹּלֶת נֵרְדְּ, וְכַרְכֹּם מִשְׁקַל שִׁשָּׁה עָשָׂר שִׁשָּׁה עָשָׂר מָנֶה, הַקֹּשְׁטְ שְׁנֵים עָשָׂר, קִלּוּפָה שְׁלֹשָׁה, קִנָּמוֹן תִּשְׁעָה. בֹּרִית כַּרְשִׁינָה תִּשְׁעָה קַבִּין, יֵין קַפְרִיסִין סְאִין תְּלָת וְקַבִּין תְּלָתָא, וְאִם לֹא מָצָא יֵין קַפְרִיסִין, מֵבִיא חֲמַר חִוַּרְיָן עַתִּיק. מֶלַח סְדוֹמִית רֹבַע, מַעֲלֶה עָשָׁן כָּל שֶׁהוּא. רַבִּי נָתָן הַבַּבְלִי אוֹמֵר: אַף כִּפַּת הַיַּרְדֵּן כָּל שֶׁהוּא, וְאִם נָתַן בָּהּ דְּבַשׁ פְּסָלָהּ, וְאִם חִסַּר אֶחָד מִכָּל סַמָּנֶיהָ, חַיָּב מִיתָה.

רַבָּן שִׁמְעוֹן בֶּן גַּמְלִיאֵל אוֹמֵר: הַצֳּרִי אֵינוֹ אֶלָּא שְׂרָף הַנּוֹטֵף מֵעֲצֵי הַקְּטָף. בֹּרִית כַּרְשִׁינָה שֶׁשָּׁפִין בָּהּ אֶת הַצִּפֹּרֶן כְּדֵי שֶׁתְּהֵא נָאָה, יֵין קַפְרִיסִין שֶׁשּׁוֹרִין בּוֹ אֶת הַצִּפֹּרֶן כְּדֵי שֶׁתְּהֵא עַזָּה, וַהֲלֹא מֵי רַגְלַיִם יָפִין לָהּ, אֶלָּא שֶׁאֵין מַכְנִיסִין מֵי רַגְלַיִם בַּמִּקְדָּשׁ מִפְּנֵי הַכָּבוֹד.

תַּנְיָא, רַבִּי נָתָן אוֹמֵר: כְּשֶׁהוּא שׁוֹחֵק אוֹמֵר, הָדֵק הֵיטֵב הֵיטֵב הָדֵק, מִפְּנֵי שֶׁהַקּוֹל יָפֶה לַבְּשָׂמִים. פִּטְּמָהּ לַחֲצָאִין כְּשֵׁרָה, לִשְׁלִישׁ וְלִרְבִיעַ לֹא שָׁמַעְנוּ. אָמַר רַבִּי יְהוּדָה: זֶה הַכְּלָל, אִם כְּמִדָּתָהּ כְּשֵׁרָה לַחֲצָאִין, וְאִם חִסַּר אֶחָד מִכָּל סַמָּנֶיהָ חַיָּב מִיתָה.

ירושלמי תַּנְיָא, בַּר קַפָּרָא אוֹמֵר: אַחַת לְשִׁשִּׁים אוֹ לְשִׁבְעִים שָׁנָה הָיְתָה בָאָה שֶׁל שִׁירַיִם
יומא ד, הלכה ה לַחֲצָאִין. וְעוֹד תָּנֵי בַּר קַפָּרָא: אִלּוּ הָיָה נוֹתֵן בָּהּ קוֹרְטוֹב שֶׁל דְּבַשׁ אֵין אָדָם יָכוֹל
ויקרא ב לַעֲמֹד מִפְּנֵי רֵיחָהּ, וְלָמָּה אֵין מְעָרְבִין בָּהּ דְּבַשׁ, מִפְּנֵי שֶׁהַתּוֹרָה אָמְרָה: כִּי כָל־שְׂאֹר
וְכָל־דְּבַשׁ לֹא־תַקְטִירוּ מִמֶּנּוּ אִשֶּׁה לַיהוה:

The following three verses are each said three times:

The LORD of hosts is with us; the God of Jacob is our stronghold, Selah. *Ps. 46*
LORD of hosts, happy is the one who trusts in You. *Ps. 84*
LORD, save! May the King answer us on the day we call. *Ps. 20*

You are my hiding place; You will protect me from distress and surround me with *Ps. 32*
songs of salvation, Selah. Then the offering of Judah and Jerusalem will be pleasing *Mal. 3*
to the LORD as in the days of old and as in former years.

THE ORDER OF THE PRIESTLY FUNCTIONS

Abaye related the order of the daily priestly functions in the name of tradition and *Yoma 33a*
in accordance with Abba Shaul: The large pile [of wood] comes before the second pile for the incense; the second pile for the incense precedes the laying in order of the two logs of wood; the laying in order of the two logs of wood comes before the removing of ashes from the inner altar; the removing of ashes from the inner altar precedes the cleaning of the five lamps; the cleaning of the five lamps comes before the blood of the daily offering; the blood of the daily offering precedes the cleaning of the [other] two lamps; the cleaning of the two lamps comes before the incense-offering; the incense-offering precedes the burning of the limbs; the burning of the limbs comes before the meal-offering; the meal-offering precedes the pancakes; the pancakes come before the wine-libations; the wine-libations precede the additional offerings; the additional offerings come before the [frankincense] censers; the censers precede the daily afternoon offering; as
it is said, "On it he shall arrange burnt-offerings, and on it he shall burn the fat of *Lev. 6*
the peace-offerings" – "on it" [the daily offering] all the offerings were completed.

Please, by the power of Your great right hand, set the captive nation free.
Accept Your people's prayer. Strengthen us, purify us, You who are revered.
Please, mighty One, guard like the pupil of the eye those who seek Your unity.
Bless them, cleanse them, have compassion on them,
grant them Your righteousness always.
Mighty One, Holy One, in Your great goodness guide Your congregation.
Only One, exalted One, turn to Your people, who proclaim Your holiness.
Accept our plea and heed our cry, You who know all secret thoughts.
Blessed be the name of His glorious kingdom for ever and all time.

Master of the Universe, You have commanded us to offer the daily sacrifice at its appointed time with the priests at their service, the Levites on their platform, and the Israelites at their post. Now, because of our sins, the Temple is destroyed and the daily sacrifice discontinued, and we have no priest at his service, no Levite
on his platform, no Israelite at his post. But You said: "We will offer in place of *Hos. 14*
bullocks [the prayer of] our lips." Therefore may it be Your will, LORD our God and God of our ancestors, that the prayer of our lips be considered, accepted and favored before You as if we had offered the daily sacrifice at its appointed time and place, according to its laws.

The following three verses are each said three times:

יהוה צְבָאוֹת עִמָּנוּ, מִשְׂגָּב לָנוּ אֱלֹהֵי יַעֲקֹב סֶלָה: תהלים מו

יהוה צְבָאוֹת, אַשְׁרֵי אָדָם בֹּטֵחַ בָּךְ: תהלים פד

יהוה הוֹשִׁיעָה, הַמֶּלֶךְ יַעֲנֵנוּ בְיוֹם־קָרְאֵנוּ: תהלים כ

אַתָּה סֵתֶר לִי, מִצַּר תִּצְּרֵנִי, רָנֵּי פַלֵּט תְּסוֹבְבֵנִי סֶלָה: תהלים לב

וְעָרְבָה לַיהוה מִנְחַת יְהוּדָה וִירוּשָׁלָםִ כִּימֵי עוֹלָם וּכְשָׁנִים קַדְמֹנִיּוֹת: מלאכי ג

סדר המערכה

אַבַּיֵי הֲוָה מְסַדֵּר סֵדֶר הַמַּעֲרָכָה מִשְּׁמָא דִגְמָרָא, וְאַלִּבָּא דְאַבָּא שָׁאוּל: יומא לג.
מַעֲרָכָה גְדוֹלָה קוֹדֶמֶת לְמַעֲרָכָה שְׁנִיָּה שֶׁל קְטֹרֶת, וּמַעֲרָכָה שְׁנִיָּה שֶׁל
קְטֹרֶת קוֹדֶמֶת לְסִדּוּר שְׁנֵי גִזְרֵי עֵצִים, וְסִדּוּר שְׁנֵי גִזְרֵי עֵצִים קוֹדֵם לְדִשּׁוּן
מִזְבֵּחַ הַפְּנִימִי, וְדִשּׁוּן מִזְבֵּחַ הַפְּנִימִי קוֹדֵם לַהֲטָבַת חָמֵשׁ נֵרוֹת, וַהֲטָבַת
חָמֵשׁ נֵרוֹת קוֹדֶמֶת לְדַם הַתָּמִיד, וְדַם הַתָּמִיד קוֹדֵם לַהֲטָבַת שְׁתֵּי נֵרוֹת,
וַהֲטָבַת שְׁתֵּי נֵרוֹת קוֹדֶמֶת לִקְטֹרֶת, וּקְטֹרֶת קוֹדֶמֶת לְאֵבָרִים, וְאֵבָרִים
לְמִנְחָה, וּמִנְחָה לַחֲבִתִּין, וַחֲבִתִּין לִנְסָכִין, וּנְסָכִין לְמוּסָפִין, וּמוּסָפִין לְבָזִיכִין,
וּבָזִיכִין קוֹדְמִין לְתָמִיד שֶׁל בֵּין הָעַרְבַּיִם. שֶׁנֶּאֱמַר: וְעָרַךְ עָלֶיהָ הָעֹלָה, ויקרא ו
וְהִקְטִיר עָלֶיהָ חֶלְבֵי הַשְּׁלָמִים: עָלֶיהָ הַשְׁלֵם כָּל הַקָּרְבָּנוֹת כֻּלָּם.

אָנָּא, בְּכֹחַ גְּדֻלַּת יְמִינְךָ, תַּתִּיר צְרוּרָה.
קַבֵּל רִנַּת עַמְּךָ, שַׂגְּבֵנוּ, טַהֲרֵנוּ, נוֹרָא.
נָא גִבּוֹר, דּוֹרְשֵׁי יִחוּדְךָ כְּבָבַת שָׁמְרֵם.
בָּרְכֵם, טַהֲרֵם, רַחֲמֵם, צִדְקָתְךָ תָּמִיד גָּמְלֵם.
חֲסִין קָדוֹשׁ, בְּרֹב טוּבְךָ נַהֵל עֲדָתֶךָ.
יָחִיד גֵּאֶה, לְעַמְּךָ פְּנֵה, זוֹכְרֵי קְדֻשָּׁתֶךָ.
שַׁוְעָתֵנוּ קַבֵּל וּשְׁמַע צַעֲקָתֵנוּ, יוֹדֵעַ תַּעֲלוּמוֹת.
בָּרוּךְ שֵׁם כְּבוֹד מַלְכוּתוֹ לְעוֹלָם וָעֶד.

רִבּוֹן הָעוֹלָמִים, אַתָּה צִוִּיתָנוּ לְהַקְרִיב קָרְבַּן הַתָּמִיד בְּמוֹעֲדוֹ וְלִהְיוֹת כֹּהֲנִים
בַּעֲבוֹדָתָם וּלְוִיִּם בְּדוּכָנָם וְיִשְׂרָאֵל בְּמַעֲמָדָם, וְעַתָּה בַּעֲוֹנוֹתֵינוּ חָרַב בֵּית הַמִּקְדָּשׁ
וּבָטַל הַתָּמִיד וְאֵין לָנוּ לֹא כֹהֵן בַּעֲבוֹדָתוֹ וְלֹא לֵוִי בְּדוּכָנוֹ וְלֹא יִשְׂרָאֵל בְּמַעֲמָדוֹ,
וְאַתָּה אָמַרְתָּ: וּנְשַׁלְּמָה פָרִים שְׂפָתֵינוּ: לָכֵן יְהִי רָצוֹן מִלְּפָנֶיךָ יהוה אֱלֹהֵינוּ וֵאלֹהֵי הושע יד
אֲבוֹתֵינוּ, שֶׁיְּהֵא שִׂיחַ שִׂפְתוֹתֵינוּ חָשׁוּב וּמְקֻבָּל וּמְרֻצֶּה לְפָנֶיךָ, כְּאִלּוּ הִקְרַבְנוּ
קָרְבַּן הַתָּמִיד בְּמוֹעֲדוֹ וּבִמְקוֹמוֹ וּכְהִלְכָתוֹ.

On Shabbat:

וּבְיוֹם הַשַּׁבָּת On the Shabbat day, make an offering of two lambs a year old, without blemish, together with two-tenths of an ephah of fine flour mixed with oil as a meal-offering, and its appropriate libation. This is the burnt-offering for every Shabbat, in addition to the regular daily burnt-offering and its libation. *Num. 28*

On Rosh Hodesh:

וּבְרָאשֵׁי חָדְשֵׁיכֶם On your new moons, present as a burnt-offering to the LORD, two young bulls, one ram, and seven yearling lambs without blemish. There shall be a meal-offering of three-tenths of an ephah of fine flour mixed with oil for each bull, two-tenths of an ephah of fine flour mixed with oil for the ram, and one-tenth of an ephah of fine flour mixed with oil for each lamb. This is the burnt-offering – a fire-offering of pleasing aroma to the LORD. Their libations shall be: half a hin of wine for each bull, a third of a hin for the ram, and a quarter of a hin for each lamb. This is the monthly burnt-offering to be made at each new moon throughout the year. One male goat should be offered as a sin-offering to God, in addition to the regular daily burnt-offering and its libation. *Num. 28*

LAWS OF OFFERINGS, MISHNA ZEVAHIM

אֵיזֶהוּ מְקוֹמָן What is the location for sacrifices?[1] The holiest offerings were slaughtered on the north side. The bull and he-goat of Yom Kippur were slaughtered on the north side. Their blood was received in a sacred vessel on the north side, and had to be sprinkled between the poles [of the Ark], toward the veil [screening the Holy of Holies], and on the golden altar. [The omission of] one of these sprinklings invalidated [the atonement ceremony]. The leftover blood was to be poured onto the western base of the outer altar. If this was not done, however, the omission did not invalidate [the ceremony]. *Zevahim Ch. 5*

The bulls and he-goats that were completely burnt were slaughtered on the north side, their blood was received in a sacred vessel on the north side, and had to be sprinkled toward the veil and on the golden altar. [The omission of] one of these sprinklings invalidated [the ceremony]. The leftover blood was to be poured onto the western base of the outer altar. If this was not done, however, the omission did not invalidate [the ceremony]. All these offerings were burnt where the altar ashes were deposited.

The communal and individual sin-offerings – these are the communal sin-offerings: the he-goats offered on Rosh Hodesh and Festivals were slaughtered on the north side, their blood was received in a sacred vessel on the north side, and required four

בשבת: וּבְיוֹם הַשַּׁבָּת, שְׁנֵי־כְבָשִׂים בְּנֵי־שָׁנָה תְּמִימִם, וּשְׁנֵי עֶשְׂרֹנִים סֹלֶת מִנְחָה בְּלוּלָה בַשֶּׁמֶן, וְנִסְכּוֹ: עֹלַת שַׁבַּת בְּשַׁבַּתּוֹ, עַל־עֹלַת הַתָּמִיד וְנִסְכָּהּ: במדבר כח

בראש חודש: וּבְרָאשֵׁי חָדְשֵׁיכֶם תַּקְרִיבוּ עֹלָה לַיהוה, פָּרִים בְּנֵי־בָקָר שְׁנַיִם, וְאַיִל אֶחָד, כְּבָשִׂים בְּנֵי־שָׁנָה שִׁבְעָה, תְּמִימִם: וּשְׁלֹשָׁה עֶשְׂרֹנִים סֹלֶת מִנְחָה בְּלוּלָה בַשֶּׁמֶן לַפָּר הָאֶחָד, וּשְׁנֵי עֶשְׂרֹנִים סֹלֶת מִנְחָה בְּלוּלָה בַשֶּׁמֶן לָאַיִל הָאֶחָד: וְעִשָּׂרֹן עִשָּׂרוֹן סֹלֶת מִנְחָה בְּלוּלָה בַשֶּׁמֶן לַכֶּבֶשׂ הָאֶחָד, עֹלָה רֵיחַ נִיחֹחַ, אִשֶּׁה לַיהוה: וְנִסְכֵּיהֶם, חֲצִי הַהִין יִהְיֶה לַפָּר, וּשְׁלִישִׁת הַהִין לָאַיִל, וּרְבִיעִת הַהִין לַכֶּבֶשׂ, יָיִן, זֹאת עֹלַת חֹדֶשׁ בְּחָדְשׁוֹ לְחָדְשֵׁי הַשָּׁנָה: וּשְׂעִיר עִזִּים אֶחָד לְחַטָּאת לַיהוה, עַל־עֹלַת הַתָּמִיד יֵעָשֶׂה, וְנִסְכּוֹ: במדבר כח

דיני זבחים

זבחים פרק ה אֵיזֶהוּ מְקוֹמָן שֶׁל זְבָחִים.[ע] קָדְשֵׁי קָדָשִׁים שְׁחִיטָתָן בַּצָּפוֹן. פַּר וְשָׂעִיר שֶׁל יוֹם הַכִּפּוּרִים, שְׁחִיטָתָן בַּצָּפוֹן, וְקִבּוּל דָּמָן בִּכְלִי שָׁרֵת בַּצָּפוֹן, וְדָמָן טָעוּן הַזָּיָה עַל בֵּין הַבַּדִּים, וְעַל הַפָּרֹכֶת, וְעַל מִזְבַּח הַזָּהָב. מַתָּנָה אַחַת מֵהֶן מְעַכָּבֶת. שְׁיָרֵי הַדָּם הָיָה שׁוֹפֵךְ עַל יְסוֹד מַעֲרָבִי שֶׁל מִזְבֵּחַ הַחִיצוֹן, אִם לֹא נָתַן לֹא עִכֵּב.

פָּרִים הַנִּשְׂרָפִים וּשְׂעִירִים הַנִּשְׂרָפִים, שְׁחִיטָתָן בַּצָּפוֹן, וְקִבּוּל דָּמָן בִּכְלִי שָׁרֵת בַּצָּפוֹן, וְדָמָן טָעוּן הַזָּיָה עַל הַפָּרֹכֶת וְעַל מִזְבַּח הַזָּהָב. מַתָּנָה אַחַת מֵהֶן מְעַכָּבֶת. שְׁיָרֵי הַדָּם הָיָה שׁוֹפֵךְ עַל יְסוֹד מַעֲרָבִי שֶׁל מִזְבֵּחַ הַחִיצוֹן, אִם לֹא נָתַן לֹא עִכֵּב. אֵלּוּ וָאֵלּוּ נִשְׂרָפִין בְּבֵית הַדָּשֶׁן.

חַטֹּאת הַצִּבּוּר וְהַיָּחִיד. אֵלּוּ הֵן חַטֹּאת הַצִּבּוּר: שְׂעִירֵי רָאשֵׁי חֳדָשִׁים וְשֶׁל

IYUN TEFILLA • עיון תפילה

אֵיזֶהוּ מְקוֹמָן שֶׁל זְבָחִים – *What is the location for sacrifices.* This particular chapter of Mishna was chosen because in all of its *mishnayot* there is not a single disagreement reported among the sages, reflecting perhaps the accuracy of its transmission, and the fact that peace is a value with which to begin one's day.

sprinklings, one on each of the four corners of the altar. How was this done? The priest ascended the ramp and turned [right] onto the surrounding ledge. He came to the southeast corner, then went to the northeast, then to the northwest, then to the southwest. The leftover blood he poured onto the southern base. [The meat of these offerings], prepared in any manner, was eaten within the [courtyard] curtains, by males of the priest-hood, on that day and the following night, until midnight.

The burnt-offering was among the holiest of sacrifices. It was slaughtered on the north side, its blood was received in a sacred vessel on the north side, and required two sprinklings [at opposite corners of the altar], making four in all. The offering had to be flayed, dismembered and wholly consumed by fire.

The communal peace-offerings and the guilt-offerings – these are the guilt-offerings: the guilt-offering for robbery; the guilt-offering for profane use of a sacred object; the guilt-offering [for violating] a betrothed maidservant; the guilt-offering of a Nazirite [who had become defiled by a corpse]; the guilt-offering of a leper [at his cleansing]; and the guilt-offering in case of doubt. All these were slaughtered on the north side, their blood was received in a sacred vessel on the north side, and required two sprinklings [at opposite corners of the altar], making four in all. [The meat of these offerings], prepared in any manner, was eaten within the [courtyard] curtains, by males of the priesthood, on that day and the following night, until midnight.

The thanksgiving-offering and the ram of a Nazirite were offerings of lesser holiness. They could be slaughtered anywhere in the Temple court, and their blood required two sprinklings [at opposite corners of the altar], making four in all. The meat of these offerings, prepared in any manner, was eaten anywhere within the city [Jerusalem], by anyone during that day and the following night until midnight. This also applied to the portion of these sacrifices [given to the priests], except that the priests' portion was only to be eaten by the priests, their wives, children and servants.

Peace-offerings were [also] of lesser holiness. They could be slaughtered anywhere in the Temple court, and their blood required two sprinklings [at opposite corners of the altar], making four in all. The meat of these offerings, prepared in any manner, was eaten anywhere within the city [Jerusalem], by anyone, for two days and one night. This also applied to the portion of these sacrifices [given to the priests], except that the priests' portion was only to be eaten by the priests, their wives, children and servants.

The firstborn and tithe of cattle and the Pesaḥ lamb were sacrifices of lesser holiness. They could be slaughtered anywhere in the Temple court, and their blood required only one sprinkling, which had to be done at the base of the altar. They differed in their consumption: the firstborn was eaten only by priests, while the tithe could be eaten by anyone. Both could be eaten anywhere within the city, prepared in any manner, during two days and one night. The Pesaḥ lamb had to be eaten that night until midnight. It could only be eaten by those who had been numbered for it, and eaten only roasted.

מוֹעֲדוֹת. שְׁחִיטָתָן בַּצָּפוֹן, וְקִבּוּל דָּמָן בִּכְלִי שָׁרֵת בַּצָּפוֹן, וְדָמָן טָעוּן אַרְבַּע מַתָּנוֹת עַל אַרְבַּע קְרָנוֹת. כֵּיצַד, עָלָה בַכֶּבֶשׁ, וּפָנָה לַסּוֹבֵב, וּבָא לוֹ לְקֶרֶן דְּרוֹמִית מִזְרָחִית, מִזְרָחִית צְפוֹנִית, צְפוֹנִית מַעֲרָבִית, מַעֲרָבִית דְּרוֹמִית. שְׁיָרֵי הַדָּם הָיָה שׁוֹפֵךְ עַל יְסוֹד דְּרוֹמִי. וְנֶאֱכָלִין לִפְנִים מִן הַקְּלָעִים, לְזִכְרֵי כְהֻנָּה, בְּכָל מַאֲכָל, לְיוֹם וָלַיְלָה עַד חֲצוֹת.

הָעוֹלָה קֹדֶשׁ קָדָשִׁים. שְׁחִיטָתָהּ בַּצָּפוֹן, וְקִבּוּל דָּמָהּ בִּכְלִי שָׁרֵת בַּצָּפוֹן, וְדָמָהּ טָעוּן שְׁתֵּי מַתָּנוֹת שֶׁהֵן אַרְבַּע, וּטְעוּנָה הֶפְשֵׁט וְנִתּוּחַ, וְכָלִיל לָאִשִּׁים.

זִבְחֵי שַׁלְמֵי צִבּוּר וַאֲשָׁמוֹת. אֵלּוּ הֵן אֲשָׁמוֹת: אֲשַׁם גְּזֵלוֹת, אֲשַׁם מְעִילוֹת, אֲשַׁם שִׁפְחָה חֲרוּפָה, אֲשַׁם נָזִיר, אֲשַׁם מְצֹרָע, אָשָׁם תָּלוּי. שְׁחִיטָתָן בַּצָּפוֹן, וְקִבּוּל דָּמָן בִּכְלִי שָׁרֵת בַּצָּפוֹן, וְדָמָן טָעוּן שְׁתֵּי מַתָּנוֹת שֶׁהֵן אַרְבַּע. וְנֶאֱכָלִין לִפְנִים מִן הַקְּלָעִים, לְזִכְרֵי כְהֻנָּה, בְּכָל מַאֲכָל, לְיוֹם וָלַיְלָה עַד חֲצוֹת.

הַתּוֹדָה וְאֵיל נָזִיר קָדָשִׁים קַלִּים. שְׁחִיטָתָן בְּכָל מָקוֹם בָּעֲזָרָה, וְדָמָן טָעוּן שְׁתֵּי מַתָּנוֹת שֶׁהֵן אַרְבַּע, וְנֶאֱכָלִין בְּכָל הָעִיר, לְכָל אָדָם, בְּכָל מַאֲכָל, לְיוֹם וָלַיְלָה עַד חֲצוֹת. הַמּוּרָם מֵהֶם כַּיּוֹצֵא בָהֶם, אֶלָּא שֶׁהַמּוּרָם נֶאֱכָל לַכֹּהֲנִים, לִנְשֵׁיהֶם, וְלִבְנֵיהֶם וּלְעַבְדֵיהֶם.

שְׁלָמִים קָדָשִׁים קַלִּים. שְׁחִיטָתָן בְּכָל מָקוֹם בָּעֲזָרָה, וְדָמָן טָעוּן שְׁתֵּי מַתָּנוֹת שֶׁהֵן אַרְבַּע, וְנֶאֱכָלִין בְּכָל הָעִיר, לְכָל אָדָם, בְּכָל מַאֲכָל, לִשְׁנֵי יָמִים וְלַיְלָה אֶחָד. הַמּוּרָם מֵהֶם כַּיּוֹצֵא בָהֶם, אֶלָּא שֶׁהַמּוּרָם נֶאֱכָל לַכֹּהֲנִים, לִנְשֵׁיהֶם, וְלִבְנֵיהֶם וּלְעַבְדֵיהֶם.

הַבְּכוֹר וְהַמַּעֲשֵׂר וְהַפֶּסַח קָדָשִׁים קַלִּים. שְׁחִיטָתָן בְּכָל מָקוֹם בָּעֲזָרָה, וְדָמָן טָעוּן מַתָּנָה אֶחָת, וּבִלְבַד שֶׁיִּתֵּן כְּנֶגֶד הַיְסוֹד. שִׁנָּה בַאֲכִילָתָן, הַבְּכוֹר נֶאֱכָל לַכֹּהֲנִים וְהַמַּעֲשֵׂר לְכָל אָדָם, וְנֶאֱכָלִין בְּכָל הָעִיר, בְּכָל מַאֲכָל, לִשְׁנֵי יָמִים וְלַיְלָה אֶחָד. הַפֶּסַח אֵינוֹ נֶאֱכָל אֶלָּא בַלַּיְלָה, וְאֵינוֹ נֶאֱכָל אֶלָּא עַד חֲצוֹת, וְאֵינוֹ נֶאֱכָל אֶלָּא לִמְנוּיָיו, וְאֵינוֹ נֶאֱכָל אֶלָּא צָלִי.

THE INTERPRETIVE PRINCIPLES OF RABBI YISHMAEL

רַבִּי יִשְׁמָעֵאל Rabbi Yishmael says:
The Torah is expounded by thirteen principles:

1. An inference from a lenient law to a strict one, and vice versa.
2. An inference drawn from identical words in two passages.
3. A general principle derived from one text or two related texts.
4. A general law followed by specific examples
[where the law applies exclusively to those examples].
5. A specific example followed by a general law
[where the law applies to everything implied in the general statement].
6. A general law followed by specific examples
and concluding with a general law:
here you may infer only cases similar to the examples.
7. When a general statement requires clarification by a specific example,
or a specific example requires clarification by a general statement
[then rules 4 and 5 do not apply].
8. When a particular case, already included in the general statement,
is expressly mentioned to teach something new,
that special provision applies to all other cases
included in the general statement.
9. When a particular case, though included in the general statement,
is expressly mentioned with a provision similar to the general law,
such a case is singled out to lessen the severity of the law,
not to increase it.
10. When a particular case, though included in the general statement,
is explicitly mentioned with a provision differing from the general law,
it is singled out to lessen in some respects, and in others to increase,
the severity of the law.
11. When a particular case, though included in the general statement,
is explicitly mentioned with a new provision,
the terms of the general statement no longer apply to it,
unless Scripture indicates explicitly that they do apply.
12. A matter elucidated from its context, or from the following passage.
13. ▸ Also, when two passages [seem to] contradict each other,
[they are to be elucidated by] a third passage that reconciles them.

May it be Your will, Lord our God and God of our ancestors, that the Temple be speedily rebuilt in our days, and grant us our share in Your Torah. And may we serve You there in reverence, as in the days of old and as in former years.

ברייתא דרבי ישמעאל

רַבִּי יִשְׁמָעֵאל אוֹמֵר: בִּשְׁלֹשׁ עֶשְׂרֵה מִדּוֹת הַתּוֹרָה נִדְרֶשֶׁת

א מִקַּל וָחְמֶר

ב וּמִגְּזֵרָה שָׁוָה

ג מִבִּנְיַן אָב מִכָּתוּב אֶחָד, וּמִבִּנְיַן אָב מִשְּׁנֵי כְתוּבִים

ד מִכְּלָל וּפְרָט

ה מִפְּרָט וּכְלָל

ו כְּלָל וּפְרָט וּכְלָל, אִי אַתָּה דָן אֶלָּא כְּעֵין הַפְּרָט

ז מִכְּלָל שֶׁהוּא צָרִיךְ לִפְרָט, וּמִפְּרָט שֶׁהוּא צָרִיךְ לִכְלָל

ח כָּל דָּבָר שֶׁהָיָה בִּכְלָל, וְיָצָא מִן הַכְּלָל לְלַמֵּד
לֹא לְלַמֵּד עַל עַצְמוֹ יָצָא
אֶלָּא לְלַמֵּד עַל הַכְּלָל כֻּלּוֹ יָצָא

ט כָּל דָּבָר שֶׁהָיָה בִּכְלָל, וְיָצָא לִטְעֹן טְעַן אֶחָד שֶׁהוּא כְעִנְיָנוֹ
יָצָא לְהָקֵל וְלֹא לְהַחֲמִיר

י כָּל דָּבָר שֶׁהָיָה בִּכְלָל, וְיָצָא לִטְעֹן טְעַן אַחֵר שֶׁלֹּא כְעִנְיָנוֹ
יָצָא לְהָקֵל וּלְהַחֲמִיר

יא כָּל דָּבָר שֶׁהָיָה בִּכְלָל, וְיָצָא לִדּוֹן בַּדָּבָר הֶחָדָשׁ
אִי אַתָּה יָכוֹל לְהַחֲזִירוֹ לִכְלָלוֹ
עַד שֶׁיַּחֲזִירֶנּוּ הַכָּתוּב לִכְלָלוֹ בְּפֵרוּשׁ

יב דָּבָר הַלָּמֵד מֵעִנְיָנוֹ, וְדָבָר הַלָּמֵד מִסּוֹפוֹ

יג וְכֵן שְׁנֵי כְתוּבִים הַמַּכְחִישִׁים זֶה אֶת זֶה
עַד שֶׁיָּבוֹא הַכָּתוּב הַשְּׁלִישִׁי וְיַכְרִיעַ בֵּינֵיהֶם.

יְהִי רָצוֹן מִלְּפָנֶיךָ, יהוה אֱלֹהֵינוּ וֵאלֹהֵי אֲבוֹתֵינוּ, שֶׁיִּבָּנֶה בֵּית הַמִּקְדָּשׁ בִּמְהֵרָה בְיָמֵינוּ, וְתֵן חֶלְקֵנוּ בְּתוֹרָתֶךָ, וְשָׁם נַעֲבָדְךָ בְּיִרְאָה כִּימֵי עוֹלָם וּכְשָׁנִים קַדְמוֹנִיּוֹת.

In Ashkenazi communities many have the custom to stand for Kaddish because of the holiness associated with the sanctification of Hashem's name in the prayer in general and in the central response by the congregation in particular. (In Sephardic communities the custom is to sit, while others have the custom to remain standing if they are already doing so.)

THE RABBIS' KADDISH[B]

The following prayer, said by mourners, requires the presence of a minyan. A transliteration can be found on page 1140.

Mourner: יִתְגַּדַּל Magnified and sanctified
may His great name be,
in the world He created by His will.
May He establish His kingdom in your lifetime
and in your days,
and in the lifetime of all the house of Israel,
swiftly and soon –
and say: Amen.

All: May His great name[A] be blessed for ever and all time.

Mourner: Blessed and praised, glorified and exalted,
raised and honored, uplifted and lauded
be the name of the Holy One,
blessed be He,

---

of the congregation whereas this version of the prayer is said by an individual.

Kaddish DeRabbanan (Rabbis') includes a prayer for scholars and is recited at the conclusion of a section of public learning of Rabbinic literature – Halakha, Aggada, Gemara.

Its ancient origins are attested to by the unusual language which is a combination of Hebrew and a form of Aramaic used millennia ago. So important was the prayer considered, so especially inspiring is the one line at its center, that it is one of those that can only be said with a minyan (a *davar shebikedusha* – דָּבָר שֶׁבִּקְדֻשָּׁה).

ANI TEFILLA • אני תפילה

יְהֵא שְׁמֵהּ רַבָּא - *May His great name.*

Whoever says "yeheh shemeh raba..." with all his strength, the Heavenly Court rips up any negative decree against him. (*Shabbat* 119b)

In Ashkenazi communities many have the custom to stand for קדיש because of the holiness associated with the sanctification of Hashem's name in the prayer in general and in the central response by the congregation in particular. (In Sephardic communities the custom is to sit, while others have the custom to remain standing if they are already doing so.)

קדיש דרבנן[ב]

The following prayer, said by mourners, requires the presence of a מנין.
A transliteration can be found on page 1140.

אבל: יִתְגַּדַּל וְיִתְקַדַּשׁ שְׁמֵהּ רַבָּא (קהל: אָמֵן)
בְּעָלְמָא דִּי בְרָא כִרְעוּתֵהּ
וְיַמְלִיךְ מַלְכוּתֵהּ
בְּחַיֵּיכוֹן וּבְיוֹמֵיכוֹן וּבְחַיֵּי דְכָל בֵּית יִשְׂרָאֵל
בַּעֲגָלָא וּבִזְמַן קָרִיב
וְאִמְרוּ אָמֵן. (קהל: אָמֵן)

קהל ואבל: יְהֵא שְׁמֵהּ רַבָּא[א] מְבָרַךְ לְעָלַם וּלְעָלְמֵי עָלְמַיָּא.

אבל: יִתְבָּרַךְ וְיִשְׁתַּבַּח וְיִתְפָּאַר וְיִתְרוֹמַם וְיִתְנַשֵּׂא
וְיִתְהַדָּר וְיִתְעַלֶּה וְיִתְהַלָּל
שְׁמֵהּ דְּקֻדְשָׁא בְּרִיךְ הוּא (קהל: בְּרִיךְ הוּא)

INTRODUCTION TO KADDISH

There are four variations of this prayer in the siddur.

The shorter one, called *Ḥatzi* (Half) *Kaddish*, serves to separate between sections of the service; it acts as a transition. Despite its name, this is the oldest and original version.

Kaddish Titkabal or *Shalem* (Full) has three extra lines at the end, added during the times of the Geonim, which speak of the acceptance of our prayers. It is usually recited to mark a conclusion of a service defined here as one involving *Seliḥot* or the *Shemoneh Esreh* (even if some other prayers like *Taḥanun* or *Uva LeTziyon* were subsequently attached to the end of the *Shemoneh Esreh*).

Kaddish Yatom (of the Orphan) is recited on behalf of someone who has passed away. The text is similar to *Kaddish Shalem* except that it is missing the primary line of *Titkabal,* which asks for the acceptance of our prayers, since that is reserved for a Ḥazan on behalf

beyond any blessing,
song, praise and consolation
uttered in the world –
and say: Amen.

To Israel,
to the teachers,
their disciples
and their disciples' disciples,
and to all who engage in the study of Torah,
in this (*in Israel add:* holy) place or elsewhere,
may there come to them and you great peace,
grace, kindness and compassion,
long life, ample sustenance and deliverance,
from their Father in Heaven –
and say: Amen.

May there be
great peace from heaven,
and (good) life
for us and all Israel –
and say: Amen.

Bow, take three steps back, as if taking leave of the Divine Presence, then bow, first left, then right, then center, while saying:

May He who makes peace in His high places,
in His compassion make peace
for us and all Israel –
and say: Amen.

On Shabbat, continue Shaḥarit on page 516.

לְעֵלָּא מִן כָּל בִּרְכָתָא
וְשִׁירָתָא, תֻּשְׁבְּחָתָא וְנֶחֱמָתָא
דַּאֲמִירָן בְּעָלְמָא
וְאִמְרוּ אָמֵן. (קהל: אָמֵן)

עַל יִשְׂרָאֵל וְעַל רַבָּנָן
וְעַל תַּלְמִידֵיהוֹן וְעַל כָּל תַּלְמִידֵי תַלְמִידֵיהוֹן
וְעַל כָּל מָאן דְּעָסְקִין בְּאוֹרַיְתָא
דִּי בְּאַתְרָא (בארץ ישראל: קַדִּישָׁא) הָדֵין, וְדִי בְּכָל אֲתַר וַאֲתַר
יְהֵא לְהוֹן וּלְכוֹן שְׁלָמָא רַבָּא
חִנָּא וְחִסְדָּא, וְרַחֲמֵי, וְחַיֵּי אֲרִיכֵי, וּמְזוֹנֵי רְוִיחֵי
וּפֻרְקָנָא מִן קֳדָם אֲבוּהוֹן דִּי בִשְׁמַיָּא
וְאִמְרוּ אָמֵן. (קהל: אָמֵן)

יְהֵא שְׁלָמָא רַבָּא מִן שְׁמַיָּא
וְחַיִּים (טוֹבִים) עָלֵינוּ וְעַל כָּל יִשְׂרָאֵל
וְאִמְרוּ אָמֵן. (קהל: אָמֵן)

Bow, take three steps back, as if taking leave of the Divine Presence, then bow, first left, then right, then center, while saying:

עֹשֶׂה שָׁלוֹם בִּמְרוֹמָיו
הוּא יַעֲשֶׂה בְרַחֲמָיו שָׁלוֹם
עָלֵינוּ וְעַל כָּל יִשְׂרָאֵל
וְאִמְרוּ אָמֵן. (קהל: אָמֵן)

On שבת, continue שחרית on page 517.

A PSALM BEFORE VERSES OF PRAISE

מִזְמוֹר שִׁיר A psalm of David. *Ps. 30*
A song for the dedication of the House.[B]
I will exalt You, LORD, for You have lifted me up,
and not let my enemies rejoice over me.
LORD, my God, I cried to You for help and You healed me.
LORD, You lifted my soul from the grave;
You spared me from going down to the pit.
Sing to the LORD, you His devoted ones,
and give thanks to His holy name.
For His anger is for a moment, but His favor for a lifetime.
At night there may be weeping, but in the morning there is joy.
When I felt secure, I said, "I shall never be shaken."
LORD, when You favored me,
You made me stand firm as a mountain,
but when You hid Your face, I was terrified.
To You, LORD, I called; I pleaded with my LORD:
"What gain would there be if I died and went down to the grave?
Can dust thank You? Can it declare Your truth?
Hear, LORD, and be gracious to me; LORD, be my help."
▸ You have turned my sorrow into dancing.
You have removed my sackcloth and clothed me with joy,
so that my soul may sing to You and not be silent.
LORD my God, for ever will I thank You.

---

as an adequate substitute. We dedicate ourselves since we cannot yet dedicate the *Beit HaMikdash*. On the other hand, perhaps it has nothing to do with what precedes. Instead, we sometimes come to prayer too upset or not in the mood to pray and therefore not open to the messages of *Pesukei DeZimra* that the world is a beautiful place protected by God. King David reminds us that he, too, went through sadness and despair yet awoke to the possibility of happiness and a sense of security because of his awareness of God's presence in his life. (Based on Rabbi E. Munk)

מזמור לפני פסוקי דזמרה

מִזְמוֹר שִׁיר־חֲנֻכַּת הַבַּיִת לְדָוִד: תהלים ל
אֲרוֹמִמְךָ יהוה כִּי דִלִּיתָנִי, וְלֹא־שִׂמַּחְתָּ אֹיְבַי לִי:
יהוה אֱלֹהָי, שִׁוַּעְתִּי אֵלֶיךָ וַתִּרְפָּאֵנִי:
יהוה, הֶעֱלִיתָ מִן־שְׁאוֹל נַפְשִׁי, חִיִּיתַנִי מִיָּרְדִי־בוֹר:
זַמְּרוּ לַיהוה חֲסִידָיו, וְהוֹדוּ לְזֵכֶר קָדְשׁוֹ:
כִּי רֶגַע בְּאַפּוֹ, חַיִּים בִּרְצוֹנוֹ, בָּעֶרֶב יָלִין בֶּכִי וְלַבֹּקֶר רִנָּה:
וַאֲנִי אָמַרְתִּי בְשַׁלְוִי, בַּל־אֶמּוֹט לְעוֹלָם:
יהוה, בִּרְצוֹנְךָ הֶעֱמַדְתָּה לְהַרְרִי עֹז
הִסְתַּרְתָּ פָנֶיךָ הָיִיתִי נִבְהָל:
אֵלֶיךָ יהוה אֶקְרָא, וְאֶל־אֲדֹנָי אֶתְחַנָּן:
מַה־בֶּצַע בְּדָמִי, בְּרִדְתִּי אֶל שָׁחַת
הֲיוֹדְךָ עָפָר, הֲיַגִּיד אֲמִתֶּךָ:
שְׁמַע־יהוה וְחָנֵּנִי, יהוה הֱיֵה־עֹזֵר לִי:
◂ הָפַכְתָּ מִסְפְּדִי לְמָחוֹל לִי, פִּתַּחְתָּ שַׂקִּי, וַתְּאַזְּרֵנִי שִׂמְחָה:
לְמַעַן יְזַמֶּרְךָ כָבוֹד וְלֹא יִדֹּם, יהוה אֱלֹהַי, לְעוֹלָם אוֹדֶךָּ:

BIUR TEFILLA • ביאור תפילה

מִזְמוֹר שִׁיר־חֲנֻכַּת הַבַּיִת לְדָוִד – *A psalm of David. A song for the dedication of the House.* The inclusion of chapter 30 of *Tehillim* is a relatively late addition to the Ashkenazi siddur, first appearing around the seventeenth century. But on the surface the prayer may be said to serve as a transition between the two parts of the service. On the one hand, one tradition has it that it was sung at the time of the inauguration of the First *Beit HaMikdash*. Having just completed a long recitation of the various sacrifices, we conclude with this reminder and hope that the prayers which we are about to offer serve

MOURNER'S KADDISH

The following prayer, said by mourners, requires the presence of a minyan.
A transliteration can be found on page 1141.

Mourner: יִתְגַּדַּל Magnified and sanctified
may His great name be,
in the world He created by His will.
May He establish His kingdom
in your lifetime and in your days,
and in the lifetime of all the house of Israel,
swiftly and soon –
and say: Amen.

All: May His great name be blessed
for ever and all time.

Mourner: Blessed and praised,
glorified and exalted,
raised and honored,
uplifted and lauded
be the name of the Holy One,
blessed be He,
beyond any blessing,
song, praise and consolation
uttered in the world –
and say: Amen.

May there be great peace from heaven,
and life for us and all Israel –
and say: Amen.

Bow, take three steps back, as if taking leave of the Divine Presence,
then bow, first left, then right, then center, while saying:
May He who makes peace in His high places,
make peace for us and all Israel –
and say: Amen.

קדיש יתום

The following prayer, said by mourners, requires the presence of a מנין*.*
A transliteration can be found on page 1141.

אבל: יִתְגַּדַּל וְיִתְקַדַּשׁ שְׁמֵהּ רַבָּא (קהל: אָמֵן)
בְּעָלְמָא דִּי בְרָא כִרְעוּתֵהּ
וְיַמְלִיךְ מַלְכוּתֵהּ
בְּחַיֵּיכוֹן וּבְיוֹמֵיכוֹן וּבְחַיֵּי דְכָל בֵּית יִשְׂרָאֵל
בַּעֲגָלָא וּבִזְמַן קָרִיב
וְאִמְרוּ אָמֵן. (קהל: אָמֵן)

קהל ואבל: יְהֵא שְׁמֵהּ רַבָּא מְבָרַךְ לְעָלַם וּלְעָלְמֵי עָלְמַיָּא.

אבל: יִתְבָּרַךְ וְיִשְׁתַּבַּח וְיִתְפָּאַר
וְיִתְרוֹמַם וְיִתְנַשֵּׂא וְיִתְהַדָּר וְיִתְעַלֶּה וְיִתְהַלָּל
שְׁמֵהּ דְּקֻדְשָׁא בְּרִיךְ הוּא (קהל: בְּרִיךְ הוּא)
לְעֵלָּא מִן כָּל בִּרְכָתָא
וְשִׁירָתָא, תֻּשְׁבְּחָתָא וְנֶחֱמָתָא
דַּאֲמִירָן בְּעָלְמָא
וְאִמְרוּ אָמֵן. (קהל: אָמֵן)

יְהֵא שְׁלָמָא רַבָּא מִן שְׁמַיָּא
וְחַיִּים, עָלֵינוּ וְעַל כָּל יִשְׂרָאֵל
וְאִמְרוּ אָמֵן. (קהל: אָמֵן)

Bow, take three steps back, as if taking leave of the Divine Presence, then bow, first left, then right, then center, while saying:

עֹשֶׂה שָׁלוֹם בִּמְרוֹמָיו
הוּא יַעֲשֶׂה שָׁלוֹם עָלֵינוּ וְעַל כָּל יִשְׂרָאֵל
וְאִמְרוּ אָמֵן. (קהל: אָמֵן)

PESUKEI DEZIMRA

The introductory blessing to the Pesukei DeZimra (Verses of Praise) is said standing. There is a custom to hold the two front tzitziot of the tallit until the end of the blessing at "songs of praise" (on page 68) whereupon they are kissed and released. From the beginning of this prayer to the end of the Amida, conversation is forbidden.

Some say:

I hereby prepare my mouth to thank, praise and laud my Creator,
for the sake of the unification of the Holy One,
blessed be He, and His Divine Presence,
through that which is hidden and concealed, in the name of all Israel.

---

is to cut away the thoughts and feelings that get in the way of our ability to grow spiritually. Reciting these verses is designed to prepare our souls for the encounter that we are hopefully to have with Hashem during the *Shemoneh Esreh*. We first need to nurture our soul, to give it fresh air to breathe and the space to be able to come to the fore, before the demands of our day send it back into the recesses of our being. *Pesukei DeZimra* is an opportunity to get back in touch with the core of who we are and before whom we stand.

The goal here, then, is to get into the mood, to get focused. As such, it is all about quality not quantity. Go slow. Skip parts if necessary in order to maintain your own slower pace (see the guide on what to do when you are pressed for time, in the Halakha section, law 70). Our sages tell us that we should utter each word as if it were a valuable coin being counted. Make the words count.

HILKHOT TEFILLA · הלכות תפילה

בָּרוּךְ שֶׁאָמַר – *Blessed is He who spoke.* The following is the opening blessing of *Pesukei DeZimra*. It is generally recited while standing. If you are running out of time, you should minimally say this prayer before moving on to *Ashrei*.

If one understands the purpose of the different parts of *Pesukei DeZimra* as being a single unit of praise that is designed to prepare us psychologically and spiritually for *Shemoneh Esreh*, then one can appreciate the fact that Halakha deems it important that its recitation not be interrupted by unnecessary speech. Its identity as a single unit is indicated by the opening blessing we are about to recite and the similar concluding blessing at the end of *Yishtabaḥ*, thereby making *Pesukei DeZimra* one long blessing of praise. This is also the reason why during its recitation one may respond *Amen* on hearing someone else's blessing, since *Amen*, too, is considered a song of praise, something that cannot be said of extraneous conversation.

פסוקי דזמרה

The introductory blessing to the פסוקי דזמרה *is said standing. There is a custom to hold the two front* ציציות *of the* טלית *until the end of the blessing at* בַּתִּשְׁבָּחוֹת *(on page 69) whereupon they are kissed and released. From the beginning of this prayer to the end of the* עמידה*, conversation is forbidden.*

Some say:

הֲרֵינִי מְזַמֵּן אֶת פִּי לְהוֹדוֹת וּלְהַלֵּל וּלְשַׁבֵּחַ אֶת בּוֹרְאִי
לְשֵׁם יִחוּד קֻדְשָׁא בְּרִיךְ הוּא וּשְׁכִינְתֵּהּ
עַל יְדֵי הַהוּא טָמִיר וְנֶעְלָם בְּשֵׁם כָּל יִשְׂרָאֵל.

AN INTRODUCTION TO THE INTRODUCTION – PESUKEI DEZIMRA

Praying isn't always easy – especially in the morning; especially when you have been up late the night before. The Rabbis understood that even in the best of times, prayer required psyching yourself, getting into the mood or the zone that is familiar to athletes before they play or performers before they go on stage. That's what *Pesukei DeZimra* is: the prelude to *tefilla*. It is a kind of prayer before one prays.

The Rabbis mandated, based upon a request that Moshe made to God, that before one asks anything of God, one should first praise Him.

When I was younger, I cynically thought that this was like trying to bribe God, to butter Him up before I got what I wanted. Yet it gnawed at me: if God is so great, does He really need my praise?! It wasn't until later that I realized that in fact God doesn't need our praise; we do. If we're going to ask God for something, don't we need to first acknowledge the good that we already have from Him? Don't we need to acknowledge what He is capable of doing for us? Don't we need to first remind ourselves of the beauty of creation, the wonder of the cosmos, the miracle of life, the marvel of God's presence in our history? Only when we know before whom we are standing, when we can admit what His power is relative to our own, can we dare to ask. That's what these seemingly random verses of song, *Pesukei DeZimra*, are supposed to accomplish.

That is why the *Menorat HaMaor* once suggested that the word used here for "song" is related to another Hebrew word, a homonym – **זָמַר** – meaning "to prune." When one wants a plant to grow to be healthy and strong, one often needs to prune it, to cut back the limbs or foliage that prevent it from getting the full measure of air and light required for continued sustenance. So, too, in *Pesukei DeZimra* our goal

BLESSED IS HE WHO SPOKE[BI]

and the world came into being, blessed is He.
Blessed is He who creates the universe.
Blessed is He who speaks and acts.
Blessed is He who decrees and fulfills.
Blessed is He who shows compassion to the earth.
Blessed is He who shows compassion to all creatures.
Blessed is He who gives a good reward
to those who fear Him.
Blessed is He who lives for ever and exists to eternity.
Blessed is He who redeems and saves.
Blessed is His name.

---

praying. But note that it's not just about the fact that He created the world, but the *way* in which He created it: simply by uttering His desire to do so. Recall the phrase at the beginning of *Bereshit*, "And God *said*, 'Let there be...' And there was..." Hashem simply willed the world into existence through speech.

But it doesn't end there. The second line, בָּרוּךְ עוֹשֶׂה בְרֵאשִׁית, refers not to the world in general but specifically to the rest of creation. In fact, over and over again in the following verses in *Bereshit* (according to *Ḥazal* ten times in total), God spoke and the different parts of creation came into being. But what is especially noteworthy is the difference between the verb tense here and in the previous line. Do you see it? The verb here is in the present tense whereas the previous line is in the past tense. Perhaps that's because the initial creation of the world happened only once, but if you look around you, you can see the world being re-created every day: the dawn of a new day, the birth of a baby, the changing of the seasons – all point to ongoing creation. That's why בָּרוּךְ עוֹשֶׂה בְרֵאשִׁית is written in the present tense, because if I would just open my eyes (sleepy as they may be this time of morning) I would realize how amazing the world is.

IYUN TEFILLA • עיון תפילה

בָּרוּךְ שֶׁאָמַר – *Blessed is He who spoke.* There has been much written about this prayer, the meaning of each one of the phrases, the philosophical content of each, and the like. Suffice it to say that what we have here is a series of statements that go to the essence of our beliefs about God and the way He runs the universe. In fact, if you look at all of the rest of the statements in this introductory paragraph, you will see that each can

This **IYUN TEFILLA** *continues on page 69.*

בָּרוּךְ שֶׁאָמַר בע

וְהָיָה הָעוֹלָם, בָּרוּךְ הוּא.
בָּרוּךְ עוֹשֶׂה בְרֵאשִׁית
בָּרוּךְ אוֹמֵר וְעוֹשֶׂה
בָּרוּךְ גּוֹזֵר וּמְקַיֵּם
בָּרוּךְ מְרַחֵם עַל הָאָרֶץ
בָּרוּךְ מְרַחֵם עַל הַבְּרִיּוֹת
בָּרוּךְ מְשַׁלֵּם שָׂכָר טוֹב לִירֵאָיו
בָּרוּךְ חַי לָעַד וְקַיָּם לָנֶצַח
בָּרוּךְ פּוֹדֶה וּמַצִּיל
בָּרוּךְ שְׁמוֹ

BIUR TEFILLA • ביאור תפילה

בָּרוּךְ שֶׁאָמַר – *Blessed is He who spoke.*
The first section of the *tefilla*, which you can easily tell consists of a number of repetitions of the word בָּרוּךְ (ten of them if you don't include בָּרוּךְ הוּא, which is part of Hashem's name and not a blessing) followed by some descriptions of what Hashem can do and does.

In the very first one, for example, בָּרוּךְ שֶׁאָמַר וְהָיָה הָעוֹלָם בָּרוּךְ הוּא, we declare that Hashem created the world. Sounds like an appropriate way to start off *tefilla*, no? After all, if we are about to pray, it makes sense for us to remind ourselves to whom we are

בָּרוּךְ שֶׁאָמַר – *Blessed is He who spoke.*
The origin of this prayer is shrouded in mystery. One source claims that a note fell down from heaven upon which this prayer was written. In fact, it may date as far back as the *Tanna'im* but the legend attests to the mystical content of the prayer as well. So holy was this prayer considered, so important was it deemed to be as an introduction to *Pesukei DeZimra*, that there are reports of some communities in medieval Germany that used to spend one full hour reciting it. (And you thought *tefilla* today takes a long time!)

Blessed are You, LORD our God, King of the Universe,
God, compassionate Father, extolled by the mouth of His people,
praised and glorified by the tongue of His devoted ones
and those who serve Him.
With the songs of Your servant David[B]
we will praise You, O LORD our God.
With praises and psalms
we will magnify and praise You, glorify You,
Speak Your name and proclaim Your kingship,
our King, our God, ▸ the only One, Giver of life to the worlds,
the King whose great name is praised
and glorified to all eternity.
Blessed are You, LORD,
the King extolled with songs of praise.[B]

ANI TEFILLA · אני תפילה

But just a few days before my arrest, I received [a book of Psalms from my wife, which the authorities confiscated from me] ... It took me three years to fight, to force authorities to give me this book... It was difficult for me to read, with my [limited] knowledge of Hebrew, this ancient language where you cannot even understand where is the end of the sentence. It was difficult to understand, but when you are reading day after day, you understand a word here, a word there, a phrase here, a phrase there, you compare, and some moment you start understanding. I remember the first psalm which I suddenly understood, the phrase which I understood was [Hebrew], "And when I go through the valley of death, I'll fear no evil, because You are with me." It was such a powerful feeling, as if King David himself, together with my wife, together with my friends, came to prison to save me from this, and to support me. Suddenly all these connections of thousands of years are restored, and you feel exactly as King David, 3000 years ago, wrote this. This was sending me a message to be strong... That was a very powerful feeling, and it gave me a lot of strength. I felt all the time that if this book of psalms was with me, nothing would happen. I fought each time they took it from me: I was on hunger strikes, I spent hundreds of days on hunger strikes and in punishment cells, in order not to permit them to take it from me. Even when I was released, and I still didn't know that I was released, but I was brought to the airplane from the prison, and they took all the clothes, and gave me different ones, and I suddenly understood that maybe some big changes are happening, but my book of psalms was not with me. I was so scared to be without it that I lay in the snow and refused to enter the airplane until they brought it back to me. And that's the only piece of property with which I came to freedom from Soviet prison. (Natan Sharansky)

בָּרוּךְ אַתָּה יהוה אֱלֹהֵינוּ מֶלֶךְ הָעוֹלָם
הָאֵל הָאָב הָרַחֲמָן הַמְהֻלָּל בְּפִי עַמּוֹ
מְשֻׁבָּח וּמְפֹאָר בִּלְשׁוֹן חֲסִידָיו וַעֲבָדָיו
וּבְשִׁירֵי דָוִד עַבְדֶּךָ נְהַלֶּלְךָ יהוה אֱלֹהֵינוּ.
בִּשְׁבָחוֹת וּבִזְמִירוֹת, נְגַדֶּלְךָ וּנְשַׁבֵּחֲךָ וּנְפָאֶרְךָ
וְנַזְכִּיר שִׁמְךָ וְנַמְלִיכְךָ מַלְכֵּנוּ אֱלֹהֵינוּ, › יָחִיד חֵי הָעוֹלָמִים
מֶלֶךְ, מְשֻׁבָּח וּמְפֹאָר עֲדֵי עַד שְׁמוֹ הַגָּדוֹל
בָּרוּךְ אַתָּה יהוה, מֶלֶךְ מְהֻלָּל בַּתִּשְׁבָּחוֹת.

BIUR TEFILLA • ביאור תפילה

בָּרוּךְ שֶׁאָמַר – *Blessed is He who spoke.*
The prayer really consists of two parts. The second part is, in effect, a *berakha* that we recite before saying *Pesukei DeZimra*. You can find that section because it begins and ends with the traditional formula of ...בָּרוּךְ אַתָּה. In it, we declare that we are about to praise Hashem using the psalms of King David which mostly speak about the beauty of creation that we too often take for granted. In fact, from here until *Yishtabaḥ*, the concluding blessing of *Pesukei DeZimra*, we recite 13 paragraphs of praise, the same number of times that the word בָּרוּךְ appears in this introductory prayer.

be interpreted to reflect a different important belief that we hold dear. In effect, the siddur is directing us at this very beginning of prayer to recall and reflect upon before whom we stand.

This is heady stuff: to think about God, to feel His presence, to reflect upon His name, His attributes, what He has done, what He continues to do, how He treats us every day... It's amazing that it only took those people in medieval Germany an hour to say this whole thing with *kavana*. How long does it take you?

BIUR TEFILLA • ביאור תפילה

מֶלֶךְ מְהֻלָּל בַּתִּשְׁבָּחוֹת – *The King extolled with songs of praise.* This blessing sets the tone for *Pesukei DeZimra*, namely, praising Hashem. As we mentioned above, Hashem doesn't need our praises. *We* need them.

וּבְשִׁירֵי דָוִד עַבְדֶּךָ – *With the songs of Your servant David.* This is a reference to King David and the songs referred to are the psalms that we know as the book of *Tehillim* which he authored. This opening blessing thus says that we will praise God specifically using David's *Tehillim* and it therefore alludes to the core of *Pesukei DeZimra*, namely, the last six chapters of the book of *Tehillim* which we will begin to say a little later on, starting with the prayer *Ashrei*.

הוֹדוּ לַיהוה Thank the LORD,[B] call on His name, make His acts known among the peoples. Sing to Him, make music to Him, tell of all His wonders. Glory in His holy name; let the hearts of those who seek the LORD rejoice. Search out the LORD and His strength; seek His presence at all times. Remember the wonders He has done, His miracles, and the judgments He pronounced. Descendants of Yisrael His servant, sons of Jacob His chosen ones: He is the LORD our God. His judgments are throughout the earth. Remember His covenant for ever, the word He commanded for a thousand generations. He made it with Abraham, vowed it to Isaac, and confirmed it to Jacob as a statute and to Israel as an everlasting covenant, saying, "To you I will give the land of Canaan as your allotted heritage." You were then small in number, few, strangers there, wandering from nation to nation, from one kingdom to another, but He let no man oppress them, and for their sake He rebuked kings: "Do not touch My anointed ones, and do My prophets no harm." Sing to the LORD, all the earth; proclaim His salvation daily. Declare His glory among the nations, His marvels among all the peoples. For great is the LORD and greatly to be praised; He is awesome beyond all heavenly powers. ▸ For all the gods of the peoples are mere idols; it was the LORD who made the heavens. *1 Chr. 16*

Before Him are majesty and splendor; there is strength and beauty in His holy place. Render to the LORD, families of the peoples, render to the LORD honor and might. Render to the LORD the glory due to His name; bring an offering and come before Him; bow

---

the *Beit HaMikdash* was built by King Solomon. At that point, different sacrifices and songs were instituted.

This historical information explains the difference between Ashkenazic and Sephardic practice regarding this prayer. Sephardim associate it with the sacrifices and therefore recite it before the prayer of *Barukh She'amar* which marks the beginning of *Pesukei DeZimra*. Ashkenazim, however, associate it with the *Tehillim* composed and recited by David since, once the *Beit HaMikdash* was built, this prayer was no longer said with the sacrifices and thus stands on its own as a song of David (*Beit Yosef* 50, Tur 51).

דברי הימים א, טז

הוֹדוּ לַיהוה קִרְאוּ בִשְׁמוֹ, הוֹדִיעוּ בָעַמִּים עֲלִילֹתָיו: שִׁירוּ לוֹ,
זַמְּרוּ־לוֹ, שִׂיחוּ בְּכָל־נִפְלְאוֹתָיו: הִתְהַלְלוּ בְּשֵׁם קָדְשׁוֹ, יִשְׂמַח לֵב
מְבַקְשֵׁי יהוה: דִּרְשׁוּ יהוה וְעֻזּוֹ, בַּקְּשׁוּ פָנָיו תָּמִיד: זִכְרוּ נִפְלְאֹתָיו
אֲשֶׁר עָשָׂה, מֹפְתָיו וּמִשְׁפְּטֵי־פִיהוּ: זֶרַע יִשְׂרָאֵל עַבְדּוֹ, בְּנֵי יַעֲקֹב
בְּחִירָיו: הוּא יהוה אֱלֹהֵינוּ בְּכָל־הָאָרֶץ מִשְׁפָּטָיו: זִכְרוּ לְעוֹלָם
בְּרִיתוֹ, דָּבָר צִוָּה לְאֶלֶף דּוֹר: אֲשֶׁר כָּרַת אֶת־אַבְרָהָם, וּשְׁבוּעָתוֹ
לְיִצְחָק: וַיַּעֲמִידֶהָ לְיַעֲקֹב לְחֹק, לְיִשְׂרָאֵל בְּרִית עוֹלָם: לֵאמֹר,
לְךָ אֶתֵּן אֶרֶץ־כְּנָעַן, חֶבֶל נַחֲלַתְכֶם: בִּהְיוֹתְכֶם מְתֵי מִסְפָּר,
כִּמְעַט וְגָרִים בָּהּ: וַיִּתְהַלְּכוּ מִגּוֹי אֶל־גּוֹי, וּמִמַּמְלָכָה אֶל־עַם
אַחֵר: לֹא־הִנִּיחַ לְאִישׁ לְעָשְׁקָם, וַיּוֹכַח עֲלֵיהֶם מְלָכִים: אַל־
תִּגְּעוּ בִּמְשִׁיחָי, וּבִנְבִיאַי אַל־תָּרֵעוּ: שִׁירוּ לַיהוה כָּל־הָאָרֶץ,
בַּשְּׂרוּ מִיּוֹם־אֶל־יוֹם יְשׁוּעָתוֹ: סַפְּרוּ בַגּוֹיִם אֶת־כְּבוֹדוֹ, בְּכָל־
הָעַמִּים נִפְלְאֹתָיו: כִּי גָדוֹל יהוה וּמְהֻלָּל מְאֹד, וְנוֹרָא הוּא
עַל־כָּל־אֱלֹהִים: ‹ כִּי כָּל־אֱלֹהֵי הָעַמִּים אֱלִילִים, וַיהוה שָׁמַיִם
עָשָׂה:

הוֹד וְהָדָר לְפָנָיו, עֹז וְחֶדְוָה בִּמְקֹמוֹ: הָבוּ לַיהוה מִשְׁפְּחוֹת
עַמִּים, הָבוּ לַיהוה כָּבוֹד וָעֹז: הָבוּ לַיהוה כְּבוֹד שְׁמוֹ, שְׂאוּ
מִנְחָה וּבֹאוּ לְפָנָיו, הִשְׁתַּחֲווּ לַיהוה בְּהַדְרַת־קֹדֶשׁ: חִילוּ מִלְּפָנָיו

BIUR TEFILLA • ביאור תפילה

הודו לַיהוה – *Thank the Lord.* The first set of verses was recited by David and actually come from *Divrei HaYamim* I 16:8–36. Once the Ark had been returned by the Pelishtim, David built a special enclosure in Yerushalayim to protect it there. A special *Tamid* sacrifice in its honor was instituted, once in the morning and once in the evening, each with its own song sung by a choir of *Levi'im*. And thus it was for 43 years until

down to the LORD in the splendor of holiness. Tremble before Him, all the earth; the world stands firm, it will not be shaken. Let the heavens rejoice and the earth be glad; let them declare among the nations, "The LORD is King." Let the sea roar, and all that is in it; let the fields be jubilant, and all they contain. Then the trees of the forest will sing for joy before the LORD, for He is coming to judge the earth. Thank the LORD for He is good; His loving-kindness is for ever. Say: "Save us, God of our salvation; gather us and rescue us from the nations, to acknowledge Your holy name and glory in Your praise. Blessed is the LORD, God of Israel, from this world to eternity." And let all the people say "Amen" and "Praise the LORD."

▸ Exalt the LORD our God and bow before His footstool: He is *Ps. 99*
holy. Exalt the LORD our God and bow at His holy mountain; for holy is the LORD our God.

He is compassionate. He forgives iniquity and does not destroy. *Ps. 78*
Repeatedly He suppresses His anger, not rousing His full wrath.
You, LORD: do not withhold Your compassion from me. May Your *Ps. 40*
loving-kindness and truth always guard me. Remember, LORD, *Ps. 25*
Your acts of compassion and love, for they have existed for ever.
Ascribe power to God, whose majesty is over Israel and whose *Ps. 68*
might is in the skies. You are awesome, God, in Your holy places.
It is the God of Israel who gives might and strength to the people,
may God be blessed. God of retribution, LORD, God of retribu- *Ps. 94*
tion, appear. Arise, Judge of the earth, to repay the arrogant their
just deserts. Salvation belongs to the LORD; may Your blessing *Ps. 3*
rest upon Your people, Selah! ▸ The LORD of hosts is with us, the *Ps. 46*
God of Jacob is our stronghold, Selah! LORD of hosts, happy is *Ps. 84*
the one who trusts in You. LORD, save! May the King answer us *Ps. 20*
on the day we call.

Save Your people and bless Your heritage; tend them and carry *Ps. 28*
them for ever. Our soul longs for the LORD; He is our Help and *Ps. 33*
Shield. For in Him our hearts rejoice, for in His holy name we

כָּל־הָאָרֶץ, אַף־תִּכּוֹן תֵּבֵל בַּל־תִּמּוֹט: יִשְׂמְחוּ הַשָּׁמַיִם וְתָגֵל
הָאָרֶץ, וְיֹאמְרוּ בַגּוֹיִם יהוה מָלָךְ: יִרְעַם הַיָּם וּמְלוֹאוֹ, יַעֲלֹץ
הַשָּׂדֶה וְכָל־אֲשֶׁר־בּוֹ: אָז יְרַנְּנוּ עֲצֵי הַיָּעַר, מִלִּפְנֵי יהוה, כִּי־בָא
לִשְׁפּוֹט אֶת־הָאָרֶץ: הוֹדוּ לַיהוה כִּי טוֹב, כִּי לְעוֹלָם חַסְדּוֹ:
וְאִמְרוּ, הוֹשִׁיעֵנוּ אֱלֹהֵי יִשְׁעֵנוּ, וְקַבְּצֵנוּ וְהַצִּילֵנוּ מִן־הַגּוֹיִם,
לְהֹדוֹת לְשֵׁם קָדְשֶׁךָ, לְהִשְׁתַּבֵּחַ בִּתְהִלָּתֶךָ: בָּרוּךְ יהוה אֱלֹהֵי
יִשְׂרָאֵל מִן־הָעוֹלָם וְעַד־הָעֹלָם, וַיֹּאמְרוּ כָל־הָעָם אָמֵן, וְהַלֵּל
לַיהוה:

‹ רוֹמְמוּ יהוה אֱלֹהֵינוּ וְהִשְׁתַּחֲווּ לַהֲדֹם רַגְלָיו, קָדוֹשׁ הוּא: תהלים צט
רוֹמְמוּ יהוה אֱלֹהֵינוּ וְהִשְׁתַּחֲווּ לְהַר קָדְשׁוֹ, כִּי־קָדוֹשׁ יהוה
אֱלֹהֵינוּ:

וְהוּא רַחוּם, יְכַפֵּר עָוֹן וְלֹא־יַשְׁחִית, וְהִרְבָּה לְהָשִׁיב אַפּוֹ, תהלים עח
וְלֹא־יָעִיר כָּל־חֲמָתוֹ: אַתָּה יהוה לֹא־תִכְלָא רַחֲמֶיךָ מִמֶּנִּי, חַסְדְּךָ תהלים מ
וַאֲמִתְּךָ תָּמִיד יִצְּרוּנִי: זְכֹר־רַחֲמֶיךָ יהוה וַחֲסָדֶיךָ, כִּי מֵעוֹלָם תהלים כה
הֵמָּה: תְּנוּ עֹז לֵאלֹהִים, עַל־יִשְׂרָאֵל גַּאֲוָתוֹ, וְעֻזּוֹ בַּשְּׁחָקִים: תהלים סח
נוֹרָא אֱלֹהִים מִמִּקְדָּשֶׁיךָ, אֵל יִשְׂרָאֵל הוּא נֹתֵן עֹז וְתַעֲצֻמוֹת
לָעָם, בָּרוּךְ אֱלֹהִים: אֵל־נְקָמוֹת יהוה, אֵל נְקָמוֹת הוֹפִיעַ: תהלים צד
הִנָּשֵׂא שֹׁפֵט הָאָרֶץ, הָשֵׁב גְּמוּל עַל־גֵּאִים: לַיהוה הַיְשׁוּעָה, תהלים ג
עַל־עַמְּךָ בִרְכָתֶךָ סֶּלָה: ‹ יהוה צְבָאוֹת עִמָּנוּ, מִשְׂגָּב לָנוּ אֱלֹהֵי תהלים מו
יַעֲקֹב סֶלָה: יהוה צְבָאוֹת, אַשְׁרֵי אָדָם בֹּטֵחַ בָּךְ: יהוה הוֹשִׁיעָה, תהלים פד תהלים כ
הַמֶּלֶךְ יַעֲנֵנוּ בְיוֹם־קָרְאֵנוּ:

הוֹשִׁיעָה אֶת־עַמֶּךָ, וּבָרֵךְ אֶת־נַחֲלָתֶךָ, וּרְעֵם וְנַשְּׂאֵם עַד־ תהלים כח
הָעוֹלָם: נַפְשֵׁנוּ חִכְּתָה לַיהוה, עֶזְרֵנוּ וּמָגִנֵּנוּ הוּא: כִּי־בוֹ יִשְׂמַח תהלים לג

have trusted. May Your loving-kindness, LORD, be upon us, as we
have put our hope in You. Show us, LORD, Your loving-kindness Ps. 85
and grant us Your salvation. Arise, help us and redeem us for the Ps. 44
sake of Your love. I am the LORD your God who brought you Ps. 81
up from the land of Egypt: open your mouth wide and I will fill
it. Happy is the people for whom this is so; happy is the people Ps. 144
whose God is the LORD. ▸ As for me, I trust in Your loving-kind- Ps. 13
ness; my heart rejoices in Your salvation. I will sing to the LORD
for He has been good to me.

The following psalm recalls the thanksgiving-offering in Temple times.
ITo emphasize its sacrificial nature, the custom is to say it standing.

מִזְמוֹר A psalm of thanksgiving.[IA] Shout joyously to the LORD, Ps. 100
all the earth. Serve the LORD with joy. Come before Him with jubilation. Know that the LORD is God. He made us and we are His. We are His people and the flock He tends. Enter His gates with thanksgiving, His courts with praise. Thank Him and bless His name. ▸ For the LORD is good, His loving-kindness is everlasting, and His faithfulness is for every generation.

ANI TEFILLA • אני תפילה

מִזְמוֹר לְתוֹדָה – *A psalm of thanksgiving.* We go through a myriad of potential disasters every day. We are surrounded by germs; we cross the street in busy traffic; our car brakes are supposed to stop our vehicle when we press them but they could just as easily not do so; accidents happen around us all of the time and we walk away unscathed. Think about your morning thus far, about your trip to get here, about the things that could have gone wrong, but didn't. We go about our lives as if nothing could have happened…or will happen. We take such things for granted. This prayer is part of the antidote to that lack of awareness. What might have gone wrong? What didn't go wrong? **What do I have to be thankful for? Now say this prayer of thanks.**

לִבֵּנוּ, כִּי בְשֵׁם קׇדְשׁוֹ בָטָחְנוּ: יְהִי־חַסְדְּךָ יהוה עָלֵינוּ, כַּאֲשֶׁר
יִחַלְנוּ לָךְ: הַרְאֵנוּ יהוה חַסְדֶּךָ, וְיֶשְׁעֲךָ תִּתֶּן־לָנוּ: קוּמָה עֶזְרָתָה תהלים פה תהלים מד
לָּנוּ, וּפְדֵנוּ לְמַעַן חַסְדֶּךָ: אָנֹכִי יהוה אֱלֹהֶיךָ הַמַּעַלְךָ מֵאֶרֶץ תהלים פא
מִצְרָיִם, הַרְחֶב־פִּיךָ וַאֲמַלְאֵהוּ: אַשְׁרֵי הָעָם שֶׁכָּכָה לּוֹ, אַשְׁרֵי תהלים קמד
הָעָם שֶׁיהוה אֱלֹהָיו: ◂ וַאֲנִי בְּחַסְדְּךָ בָטַחְתִּי, יָגֵל לִבִּי בִּישׁוּעָתֶךָ, תהלים יג
אָשִׁירָה לַיהוה, כִּי גָמַל עָלָי:

The following psalm recalls the קרבן תודה *in Temple times.*
To emphasize its sacrificial nature, the custom is to say it standing.

מִזְמוֹר לְתוֹדָה,[עא] הָרִיעוּ לַיהוה כׇּל־הָאָרֶץ: עִבְדוּ אֶת־ תהלים ק
יהוה בְּשִׂמְחָה, בֹּאוּ לְפָנָיו בִּרְנָנָה: דְּעוּ כִּי־יהוה הוּא
אֱלֹהִים, הוּא עָשָׂנוּ וְלוֹ אֲנַחְנוּ, עַמּוֹ וְצֹאן מַרְעִיתוֹ: בֹּאוּ
שְׁעָרָיו בְּתוֹדָה, חֲצֵרֹתָיו בִּתְהִלָּה, הוֹדוּ לוֹ, בָּרְכוּ שְׁמוֹ:
◂ כִּי־טוֹב יהוה, לְעוֹלָם חַסְדּוֹ, וְעַד־דֹּר וָדֹר אֱמוּנָתוֹ:

IYUN TEFILLA • עיון תפילה

מִזְמוֹר לְתוֹדָה – *A psalm of thanksgiving.* Rashi believes that the saying of this prayer is directly related to the sacrifice known as the *Korban Toda* which was brought in the *Beit HaMikdash*. The circumstances for bringing this sacrifice are fairly well known: "Four kinds of people are supposed to bring this kind of sacrifice: someone who survives an ocean voyage, a journey through the desert, an illness, or a period of time in prison" (*Berakhot* 54b).

Imagine if you had been in such a situation. Did you turn to God and say "If You just get me through this, I promise I'll…" And when the moment of danger passed, were you filled with elation and just wanted to scream in thanks? Or did you forget to give thanks altogether? The Torah commanded that on such occasions we go to the *Beit HaMikdash* to give thanks to Hashem, for, no matter what the circumstances of our delivery, we believe that behind it all Hashem is there pulling the strings.

יְהִי כְבוֹד May the LORD's glory[IAB] be for ever; may the LORD rejoice *Ps. 104*
in His works. May the LORD's name be blessed, now and for ever. *Ps. 113*
From the rising of the sun to its setting, may the LORD's name be
praised. The LORD is high above all nations; His glory is above the
heavens. LORD, Your name is for ever. Your renown, LORD, is for all *Ps. 135*
generations. The LORD has established His throne in heaven; His *Ps. 103*
kingdom rules all. Let the heavens rejoice and the earth be glad. Let *1 Chr. 16*
them say among the nations, "The LORD is King." The LORD is King,
the LORD was King, the LORD will be King for ever and all time. The *Ps. 10*
LORD is King for ever and all time; nations will perish from His land.
The LORD foils the plans of nations; He frustrates the intentions of *Ps. 33*
peoples. Many are the intentions in a person's mind, but the LORD's *Prov. 19*
plan prevails. The LORD's plan shall stand for ever, His mind's intent *Ps. 33*
for all generations. For He spoke and it was; He commanded and
it stood firm. For the LORD has chosen Zion; He desired it for His *Ps. 132*
dwelling. For the LORD has chosen Jacob as His own, Israel as His *Ps. 135*
special treasure. For the LORD will not abandon His people; nor will *Ps. 94*
He forsake His heritage. ▸ He is compassionate. He forgives iniquity *Ps. 78*
and does not destroy. Repeatedly He suppresses His anger, not rous-
ing His full wrath. LORD, save! May the King answer us on the day *Ps. 20*
we call.

INTRODUCTION TO THE LAST SIX PSALMS

What follows next is the "core" of *Pesukei DeZimra*, the oldest and most significant parts of this section of *tefilla*. Rabbi J.B. Soloveitchik suggested that it derives from the practice reported in the Gemara (*Berakhot* 30b), wherein the pious men of old would wait for an hour before praying *Shemoneh Esreh* in order to properly collect and direct their thoughts. They recited psalms of praise in keeping with the directive of Rav Simlai (*Berakhot* 32a) that one must first praise Hashem and only afterwards ask for one's needs.

This next section we are about to say comprises a discrete unit since, rather than being seemingly random verses, it consists of the last six psalms of the book of *Tehillim* (chapters 145–150), as if to say that with their recitation, it is as if we recited the entire book of praises. Even so, these psalms share a common theme; they are a kind of *Hallel* in which Hashem reveals Himself not through miracles but through the forces of nature that surround us daily. Nourishment of one's faith lies in the everyday, not in supernatural wonders. As Rabbi Soloveitchik once noted, is there truly any greater miracle than the sun rising in the morning?

יְהִי כְבוֹד[עאב] יהוה לְעוֹלָם, יִשְׂמַח יהוה בְּמַעֲשָׂיו: יְהִי שֵׁם יהוה תהלים קד תהלים קיג
מְבֹרָךְ, מֵעַתָּה וְעַד־עוֹלָם: מִמִּזְרַח־שֶׁמֶשׁ עַד־מְבוֹאוֹ, מְהֻלָּל
שֵׁם יהוה: רָם עַל־כָּל־גּוֹיִם יהוה, עַל הַשָּׁמַיִם כְּבוֹדוֹ: יהוה שִׁמְךָ תהלים קלה
לְעוֹלָם, יהוה זִכְרְךָ לְדֹר־וָדֹר: יהוה בַּשָּׁמַיִם הֵכִין כִּסְאוֹ, וּמַלְכוּתוֹ תהלים קג
בַּכֹּל מָשָׁלָה: יִשְׂמְחוּ הַשָּׁמַיִם וְתָגֵל הָאָרֶץ, וְיֹאמְרוּ בַגּוֹיִם יהוה דברי הימים א׳ טז
מָלָךְ: יהוה מֶלֶךְ, יהוה מָלָךְ, יהוה יִמְלֹךְ לְעוֹלָם וָעֶד. יהוה מֶלֶךְ תהלים י
עוֹלָם וָעֶד, אָבְדוּ גוֹיִם מֵאַרְצוֹ: יהוה הֵפִיר עֲצַת־גּוֹיִם, הֵנִיא תהלים לג
מַחְשְׁבוֹת עַמִּים: רַבּוֹת מַחֲשָׁבוֹת בְּלֶב־אִישׁ, וַעֲצַת יהוה הִיא משלי יט
תָקוּם: עֲצַת יהוה לְעוֹלָם תַּעֲמֹד, מַחְשְׁבוֹת לִבּוֹ לְדֹר וָדֹר: כִּי הוּא תהלים לג
אָמַר וַיֶּהִי, הוּא־צִוָּה וַיַּעֲמֹד: כִּי־בָחַר יהוה בְּצִיּוֹן, אִוָּהּ לְמוֹשָׁב לוֹ: תהלים קלב
כִּי־יַעֲקֹב בָּחַר לוֹ יָהּ, יִשְׂרָאֵל לִסְגֻלָּתוֹ: כִּי לֹא־יִטֹּשׁ יהוה עַמּוֹ, תהלים קלה תהלים צד
וְנַחֲלָתוֹ לֹא יַעֲזֹב: ◂ וְהוּא רַחוּם, יְכַפֵּר עָוֹן וְלֹא־יַשְׁחִית, וְהִרְבָּה תהלים עח
לְהָשִׁיב אַפּוֹ, וְלֹא־יָעִיר כָּל־חֲמָתוֹ: יהוה הוֹשִׁיעָה, הַמֶּלֶךְ יַעֲנֵנוּ תהלים כ
בְיוֹם־קָרְאֵנוּ:

IYUN TEFILLA • עיון תפילה

יְהִי כְבוֹד – *May the Lord's glory.* "May Hashem's glory be forever; may Hashem rejoice in His works." Hashem's "glory" parallels "His works" and is thus a reference to creation. The Gemara says that when an angel uttered this verse at the time of creation, all of the plants began to emerge (*Ḥullin* 60a). The phrase thus introduces the theme of God's presence in nature that will be at the center of *Pesukei DeZimra*.

BIUR TEFILLA • ביאור תפילה

יְהִי כְבוֹד – *May the Lord's glory.*
Numbers: There is a tradition that in this prayer there are 21 references to Hashem's name, paralleling the 21 verses in the prayer of *Ashrei* which follows (*Tehilla* 145). Can you find the 21? (Hint: most are explicit; one is hidden in the initials of the first four words of one of the verses.)

ANI TEFILLA • אני תפילה

יְהִי כְבוֹד – *May the Lord's glory.*
The Gemara (*Berakhot* 10a) notes that "there is no artist like God."

Where can I see Hashem's artistry this morning?

The line beginning with "You open Your hand" should be said with special concentration, representing as it does the key idea of this Psalm, and of Pesukei DeZimra as a whole, that God is the creator and sustainer of all. Some have the custom to touch the hand-tefillin at °, and the head-tefillin at °°.

אַשְׁרֵי Happy are those who dwell in Your House;[AB] *Ps. 84*
they shall continue to praise You, Selah!
Happy are the people for whom this is so; *Ps. 144*
happy are the people whose God is the LORD.

A song of praise by David. *Ps. 145*
א I will elevate You, my God, the King,
and bless Your name for ever and all time.
ב Every day I will bless You,
and praise Your name for ever and all time.
ג Great is the LORD and greatly to be praised;
His greatness is unfathomable.
ד One generation will praise Your works to the next,[A]
and tell of Your mighty deeds.

ANI TEFILLA • אני תפילה

דּוֹר לְדוֹר יְשַׁבַּח מַעֲשֶׂיךָ – *One generation will praise Your works to the next.* Every generation passes its firsthand experience along to the next generation. We are who we are thanks to the traditions passed along to us by our parents, grandparents and previous generations (Radak). **What has the previous generation contributed to my development and growth as a person and as a Jew?**

דּוֹר לְדוֹר יְשַׁבַּח מַעֲשֶׂיךָ – *One generation will praise Your works to the next.* Every generation is capable of uncovering scientific knowledge that was unavailable to its predecessors, so that in each generation it is possible to gain an even better and more accurate understanding and appreciation of God's world (Malbim). **What inventions or discoveries have previous generations enabled me to benefit from?**

ANI TEFILLA • אני תפילה

Imagine a king who asks his servant to go up to the attic. If the servant doesn't jump up from the ground to the attic in a single leap, the king won't be angry. He expects that the servant will need to go up a ladder, one rung at a time. That, then, is what Hashem demands of us; to raise ourselves, in steps, one rung at a time. (Rabbi Hayyim of Volozhin)

The line beginning with פּוֹתֵחַ אֶת יָדֶךָ *should be said with special concentration, representing as it does the key idea of this psalm, and of* פסוקי דזמרה *as a whole, that God is the creator and sustainer of all. Some have the custom to touch the* תפילין של יד *at °, and the* תפילין של ראש *at °°.*

אַשְׁרֵי יוֹשְׁבֵי בֵיתֶךָ, עוֹד יְהַלְלוּךָ סֶּלָה: תהלים פד
אַשְׁרֵי הָעָם שֶׁכָּכָה לּוֹ, אַשְׁרֵי הָעָם שֶׁיהוה אֱלֹהָיו: תהלים קמד

תְּהִלָּה לְדָוִד תהלים קמה
אֲרוֹמִמְךָ אֱלוֹהַי הַמֶּלֶךְ, וַאֲבָרְכָה שִׁמְךָ לְעוֹלָם וָעֶד:
בְּכָל־יוֹם אֲבָרְכֶךָּ, וַאֲהַלְלָה שִׁמְךָ לְעוֹלָם וָעֶד:
גָּדוֹל יהוה וּמְהֻלָּל מְאֹד, וְלִגְדֻלָּתוֹ אֵין חֵקֶר:
דּוֹר לְדוֹר יְשַׁבַּח מַעֲשֶׂיךָ, וּגְבוּרֹתֶיךָ יַגִּידוּ:

ANI TEFILLA • אני תפילה

אַשְׁרֵי יוֹשְׁבֵי בֵיתֶךָ – *Happy are those who dwell in Your House.* Happy are those who take time out every morning to get back in touch with You and with themselves. Research shows that people who pray regularly are healthier, have greater coping skills and resilience than those who don't. In short, they can indeed be happier.

BIUR TEFILLA • ביאור תפילה

אַשְׁרֵי יוֹשְׁבֵי בֵיתֶךָ – *Happy are those who dwell in Your House.* This verse is from *Tehilla* 84:5 and the next one is from *Tehilla* 144:15. They were added as a prelude to *Tehilla* 145 but the combination is known as *Ashrei*. Rabbi Soloveitchik once suggested that they were added because, viewed in context, they are a declaration of a longing to be in God's presence, just as Jews felt it during the times of the *Beit HaMikdash*. The language is therefore similar to the very first verse of *Tehillim* which also begins with the word אַשְׁרֵי. But *Ḥazal* added a verse at the end of this prayer that is not part of the original psalm and thereby makes the last word הַלְלוּיָהּ. Stylistically it is thus similar to the end of the book of *Tehillim* (and all of the ones we are about to say) which also ends with הַלְלוּיָהּ. This psalm thus reflects the entire book of *Tehillim* both in substance (the acrostic representing the entire *Alef-Beit*) and in form.

ה On the glorious splendor of Your majesty I will meditate,
and on the acts of Your wonders.
ו They shall talk of the power of Your awesome deeds,
and I will tell of Your greatness.
ז They shall recite the record of Your great goodness,
and sing with joy of Your righteousness.
ח The LORD is generous and compassionate,
slow to anger and great in loving-kindness.
ט The LORD is good to all,[I]
and His compassion extends to all His works.
י All Your works shall thank You,[IA] LORD,
and Your devoted ones shall bless You.
כ They shall talk of the glory of Your kingship,
and speak of Your might.
ל To make known to mankind His mighty deeds
and the glorious majesty of His kingship.
מ Your kingdom is an everlasting kingdom,
and Your reign is for all generations.
ס The LORD supports all who fall,[I]
and raises all who are bowed down.
ע All raise their eyes to You in hope,
and You give them their food in due season.

יוֹדוּךָ יהוה כָּל מַעֲשֶׂיךָ – *All Your works shall thank You.* The moon and stars, the sea creatures, the deserts, the mountains and valleys, the vegetation and trees and animals and insects and birds; a song to God emanates from all of them. (*Tehillot Hashem*)

ANI TEFILLA • אני תפילה

יוֹדוּךָ יהוה כָּל מַעֲשֶׂיךָ – *All Your works shall thank You.*

Imagine yourself in a place where you have heard nature sing.

IYUN TEFILLA • עיון תפילה

סוֹמֵךְ יהוה לְכָל הַנֹּפְלִים – *The LORD supports all who fall.* Even people who sin – Hashem supports them so that they do not fall even further (Maharsha). Remember that self improvement is always possible.

הֲדַר כְּבוֹד הוֹדֶךָ, וְדִבְרֵי נִפְלְאֹתֶיךָ אָשִֽׂיחָה:
וֶעֱזוּז נוֹרְאֹתֶיךָ יֹאמֵרוּ, וּגְדוּלָּתְךָ אֲסַפְּרֶנָּה:
זֵכֶר רַב־טוּבְךָ יַבִּיעוּ, וְצִדְקָתְךָ יְרַנֵּנוּ:[ע]
חַנּוּן וְרַחוּם יהוה, אֶרֶךְ אַפַּיִם וּגְדָל־חָסֶד:
טוֹב־יהוה לַכֹּל,[ע] וְרַחֲמָיו עַל־כָּל־מַעֲשָׂיו:
יוֹדוּךָ יהוה כָּל־מַעֲשֶׂיךָ,[עא] וַחֲסִידֶיךָ יְבָרְכוּכָה:
כְּבוֹד מַלְכוּתְךָ יֹאמֵרוּ, וּגְבוּרָתְךָ יְדַבֵּרוּ:
לְהוֹדִיעַ לִבְנֵי הָאָדָם גְּבוּרֹתָיו, וּכְבוֹד הֲדַר מַלְכוּתוֹ:
מַלְכוּתְךָ מַלְכוּת כָּל־עֹלָמִים, וּמֶמְשַׁלְתְּךָ בְּכָל־דּוֹר וָדֹר:
סוֹמֵךְ יהוה לְכָל־הַנֹּפְלִים,[ע] וְזוֹקֵף לְכָל־הַכְּפוּפִים:
עֵינֵי־כֹל אֵלֶיךָ יְשַׂבֵּרוּ, וְאַתָּה נוֹתֵן־לָהֶם אֶת־אָכְלָם בְּעִתּוֹ:

IYUN TEFILLA • עיון תפילה

וְצִדְקָתְךָ יְרַנֵּנוּ – *And sing with joy of Your righteousness. Tzedaka* may be understood as righteousness or charity. I sing with joy to Hashem, because when I think about it, everything good that I have in my life is really just a result of His charity and *ḥesed*. (Malbim)

טוֹב־יהוה לַכֹּל – *The Lord is good to all.*

"God is good to all, and His compassion extends to all His works." Therefore, so too should we be careful to preserve animal life unless it is to protect ourselves or for some other worthwhile purpose. (Radak)

"God is good to all, and His compassion extends to all His works." Therefore, so too should we act this way toward people who are not of our faith, to visit their sick and bury their dead and to support their poor. (Rambam)

Even when seemingly bad things happen, one must believe that ultimately there is some good that will result, for "God is good... to all His works." (*Me'am Loez*)

"God's mercy is in all of His creations." He has implanted His mercy in each of us so that we too can act toward others with compassion. (*Bereshit Raba* 33:3)

פ °You open Your hand,[HA] °°and satisfy every living thing with favor.
צ The LORD is righteous in all His ways,[I] and kind in all He does.[I]
ק The LORD is close to all who call on Him,[I]
to all who call on Him in truth.
ר He fulfills the will of those who fear Him;
He hears their cry and saves them.
ש The LORD guards all who love Him,
but all the wicked He will destroy.
ת ▸ My mouth shall speak the praise of the LORD,
and all creatures shall bless His holy name for ever and all time.
We will bless the LORD now and for ever. Halleluya! *Ps. 115*

---

sensitive to the people around me, I realized that there were a lot of people who were starving in the world and it made me wonder whether in fact God really was satisfying all of the needs of every living thing. I continued to say the verse, but I had my nagging doubts.

It was only later that I came to believe that perhaps God provides all of the resources necessary for all of the world's needs, but it is man's fault that those resources are not shared fairly. And so, whenever I recited the verse, I asked myself what I was doing to ensure that people in need were being helped. After all, if I want God to provide for my needs, shouldn't I be doing my share to provide for others? Perhaps my role was to be an agent for God's generosity to those around me. And every time I praised God, I also challenged myself to be a better person.

And then, while I became more sensitive to the needs of others, I became more aware of how much I already have in my own life, how many of my needs are already satisfied, how much I take for granted and how I am so fortunate and in many ways so very, very rich.

And then I realized that maybe Mr. Deutsch was right after all.

IYUN TEFILLA • עיון תפילה

צַדִּיק יהוה בְּכָל־דְּרָכָיו – *The LORD is righteous in all His ways.* And should one wonder why some people have some things while others do not, know that Hashem gives each according to his unique needs, just as a doctor does not give the same medicine to each person. (Ibn Ezra)

וְחָסִיד בְּכָל־מַעֲשָׂיו – *And kind in all He does.* If a person is punished, one can look at it as a lack of kindness; alternatively, it is possible that he is getting less of a punishment than he really deserves. (*Me'am Loez*)

קָרוֹב יהוה לְכָל־קֹרְאָיו – *The LORD is close to all who call on Him.* To all those who call out to Him in sincerity." God is close to everyone who calls out to Him; but only those who are sincere walk away realizing that He is close. (Rabbi S.R. Hirsch)

°פּוֹתֵחַ אֶת־יָדֶךָ, °° וּמַשְׂבִּיעַ לְכָל־חַי רָצוֹן:
צַדִּיק יהוה בְּכָל־דְּרָכָיו, וְחָסִיד בְּכָל־מַעֲשָׂיו:
קָרוֹב יהוה לְכָל־קֹרְאָיו, לְכֹל אֲשֶׁר יִקְרָאֻהוּ בֶאֱמֶת:
רְצוֹן־יְרֵאָיו יַעֲשֶׂה, וְאֶת־שַׁוְעָתָם יִשְׁמַע, וְיוֹשִׁיעֵם:
שׁוֹמֵר יהוה אֶת־כָּל־אֹהֲבָיו, וְאֵת כָּל־הָרְשָׁעִים יַשְׁמִיד:
· תְּהִלַּת יהוה יְדַבֶּר פִּי, וִיבָרֵךְ כָּל־בָּשָׂר שֵׁם קָדְשׁוֹ לְעוֹלָם וָעֶד:
וַאֲנַחְנוּ נְבָרֵךְ יָהּ מֵעַתָּה וְעַד־עוֹלָם, הַלְלוּיָהּ: תהלים קטו

ANI TEFILLA • אני תפילה

פּוֹתֵחַ אֶת־יָדֶךָ – *You open Your hand.*
Anyone who says this verse in the context of this prayer is guaranteed a place in the World to Come. (*Berakhot* 4b)

HILKHOT TEFILLA • הלכות תפילה

פּוֹתֵחַ אֶת־יָדֶךָ – *You open Your hand.*
So critical is this verse that the *Shulḥan Arukh* says (51:7) that if one did not recite it with proper *kavana*, then one must go back and repeat it again, apparently because it contains the essence of *Pesukei DeZimra*. Why do you think this is so?

ANI TEFILLA • אני תפילה

פּוֹתֵחַ אֶת־יָדֶךָ – *You open Your hand.*
When I was in elementary school, my teacher Mr. Deutsch told us that if we just said the phrase from Ashrei, **פּוֹתֵחַ אֶת־יָדֶךָ וּמַשְׂבִּיעַ לְכָל־חַי רָצוֹן**, *"You open Your hand, and satisfy every living thing with favor," then we would grow up to be very rich. As a young child, I understood it almost as a magic formula: acknowledge God's ability to make you rich, tell Him so as if you really mean it, and you will get rich. No doubt, this interpretation is one of the things that kept me saying that phrase with any amount of kavana any time I prayed, even as I mumbled the rest of the words of the prayer.*

As I grew older, I realized two things: the first was that prayer didn't really work that way. It is not a magic incantation that you recite and then, poof, you get what you want, even if you pray really, really hard. And so I thought that Mr. Deutsch had really just led me on. But secondly, I came to learn that this prayer appears not in a section related to requests, bakashot, but that it was in a section of the siddur that is related to shevaḥ, giving praise to Hashem. In other words, I wasn't necessarily supposed to be asking for anything at all at this point in the service but rather was supposed to be praising God for giving all people the food that they need. And so I thought of the corn fields and wheat fields that make this country so rich and so prosperous and praised God for that.

As I grew yet older and became more

הַלְלוּיָהּ Halleluya! Praise the LORD, my soul.[I] I will praise the LORD all my life;[IA] I will sing to my God as long as I live. Put not your trust in princes,[I] or in mortal man who cannot save. His breath expires,[I] he returns to the earth; on that day his plans come to an end. Happy is he whose help is the God of Jacob,[I] whose hope is in the LORD his God who made heaven and earth, the sea and all they contain; He who keeps faith for ever. He secures justice for the oppressed.[I] He gives food to the hungry.[I] The LORD sets captives free. The LORD gives sight to the blind.[IA] The LORD raises those bowed down. The LORD loves the righteous. The LORD protects the stranger. He gives courage to the orphan and widow. He thwarts the way of the wicked. ▸ The LORD shall reign for ever. He is your God, Zion, for all generations. Halleluya! *Ps. 146*

---

day his plans come to an end." Man is finite. God is eternal. Whose values and plans will last longer?

אַשְׁרֵי שֶׁאֵל יַעֲקֹב בְּעֶזְרוֹ – *Happy is he whose help is the God of Jacob.* He is called the God of Yaakov here because Yaakov (see *Bereshit* 34:10) represents the survival of the Jewish people long after the other nations of the world have disappeared (Sforno). God has continued to watch over us. History proves it.

עֹשֶׂה מִשְׁפָּט לַעֲשׁוּקִים – *He secures justice for the oppressed.* Someone who sets out to harm another, very often inadvertently ends up helping him. The brothers of Yosef thought they were oppressing him when, in fact, their plot against him played right into God's plan. (Rabbi Yosef Albo)

נֹתֵן לֶחֶם לָרְעֵבִים – *He gives food to the hungry.* There is hunger that comes from not eating, and there is the hunger of the soul that comes from being out of touch. God can satisfy both.

יהוה פֹּקֵחַ עִוְרִים – *The LORD gives sight to the blind.* There are those whose eyesight is 20/20, yet they can still be described as being blind. Belief in God can open one's eyes.

ANI TEFILLA • אני תפילה

When I went to the moon, I was as pragmatic a test pilot, engineer, and scientist as any of my colleagues... But there was another aspect to my experience during Apollo 14, and it contradicted the "pragmatic engineer" attitude. It began with the breathtaking experience of seeing planet Earth floating in the vastness of space...the presence of divinity became almost

This **ANI TEFILLA** *continues on page 87.*

הַלְלוּיָהּ, הַלְלִי נַפְשִׁי אֶת־יהוה: אֲהַלְלָה יהוה בְּחַיָּי, אֲזַמְּרָה תהלים קמו
לֵאלֹהַי בְּעוֹדִי: אַל־תִּבְטְחוּ בִנְדִיבִים, בְּבֶן־אָדָם שֶׁאֵין לוֹ תְשׁוּעָה:
תֵּצֵא רוּחוֹ, יָשֻׁב לְאַדְמָתוֹ, בַּיּוֹם הַהוּא אָבְדוּ עֶשְׁתֹּנֹתָיו: אַשְׁרֵי
שֶׁאֵל יַעֲקֹב בְּעֶזְרוֹ, שִׂבְרוֹ עַל־יהוה אֱלֹהָיו: עֹשֶׂה שָׁמַיִם וָאָרֶץ,
אֶת־הַיָּם וְאֶת־כָּל־אֲשֶׁר־בָּם, הַשֹּׁמֵר אֱמֶת לְעוֹלָם: עֹשֶׂה מִשְׁפָּט
לָעֲשׁוּקִים, נֹתֵן לֶחֶם לָרְעֵבִים, יהוה מַתִּיר אֲסוּרִים: יהוה פֹּקֵחַ
עִוְרִים, יהוה זֹקֵף כְּפוּפִים, יהוה אֹהֵב צַדִּיקִים: יהוה שֹׁמֵר אֶת־
גֵּרִים, יָתוֹם וְאַלְמָנָה יְעוֹדֵד, וְדֶרֶךְ רְשָׁעִים יְעַוֵּת: ‹ יִמְלֹךְ יהוה
לְעוֹלָם, אֱלֹהַיִךְ צִיּוֹן לְדֹר וָדֹר, הַלְלוּיָהּ:

IYUN TEFILLA · עיון תפילה

הַלְלִי נַפְשִׁי אֶת־יהוה – *Praise the Lord, my soul.* Besides the human soul, there is no other creation that is able to recognize God's presence in the world. (Rabbi S.R. Hirsch)

אֲהַלְלָה יהוה בְּחַיָּי – *I will praise the Lord all my life.* "I will praise Hashem while I live; I will sing praises to my God while I have my being."

The verse can also be read: "I will praise Hashem for the fact that I am alive and I will sing praises for the fact that He also watches over me" (Malbim).

No matter what else is going on in my life, I have much to be thankful for.

ANI TEFILLA · אני תפילה

אֲהַלְלָה יהוה בְּחַיָּי – *I will praise the Lord all my life.*

Compare these interpretations:

I will praise Hashem as long as I am alive. (Meiri)

I will praise Hashem while I still have my health. (Roke'aḥ)

I will praise Hashem with the way I live my life.

Which of these speaks most to you today?

IYUN TEFILLA · עיון תפילה

אַל־תִּבְטְחוּ בִנְדִיבִים – *Put not your trust in princes.* King David, himself a monarch and a wealthy man, warns us that only God is worthy of our trust; people who are wealthier than us may seem to "have it all," but money and prestige can disappear quickly. Faith in God is the only way to maintain one's true self-worth.

תֵּצֵא רוּחוֹ – *His breath expires.* "His breath expires, he returns to the earth; on that

הַלְלוּיָהּ Halleluya! How good it is to sing songs to our God; how pleasant and fitting to praise Him. The LORD rebuilds Jerusalem. He gathers the scattered exiles of Israel. He heals the brokenhearted[I] and binds up their wounds. He counts the number of the stars,[AI] calling each by name. Great is our LORD and mighty in power; His understanding has no limit.[I] The LORD gives courage to the humble, but casts the wicked to the ground. Sing to the LORD in thanks; make music to our God on the harp.[I] He covers the sky with clouds. He provides the earth with rain and makes grass grow on the hills.[A] He gives food to the cattle and to the ravens when they cry. He does not take delight in the strength of horses nor pleasure in the fleetness of man.[I] The LORD takes pleasure in those who fear Him, who put their hope in His loving care. Praise the LORD, Jerusalem;[I] sing to your God, Zion, for He has strengthened the bars of your gates and blessed your children in your midst. He has brought peace to your borders, and satisfied you with the finest wheat. He sends His *Ps. 147*

לִתְבוּנָתוֹ אֵין מִסְפָּר – *His understanding has no limit.* The full capacity of one's understanding cannot be measured by standardized tests such as SATs or IQs. And what is true of man is all the more true of God. (Based on Rabbi S.R. Hirsch)

זַמְּרוּ לֵאלֹהֵינוּ בְכִנּוֹר – *Make music to our God on the harp.* Song and music are both instruments for praising Hashem. They both can express emotions of thanks when words might otherwise fail. Sing.

ANI TEFILLA • אני תפילה

הַמַּצְמִיחַ הָרִים חָצִיר – *Makes grass grow on the hills.*

Have you ever seen lush foliage, green pastures, mountains covered with clouds and vegetation? Imagine yourself there now.

IYUN TEFILLA • עיון תפילה

לֹא־בְשׁוֹקֵי הָאִישׁ יִרְצֶה – *Nor pleasure in the fleetness of man.* The true value of a person is not in his physical prowess, but in how much he fears God. Even if he has athletic talents, he needs to acknowledge that those come from Hashem.

שַׁבְּחִי יְרוּשָׁלַםִ אֶת־יהוה – *Praise the LORD, Jerusalem.* "Sing to your God, Zion, for He has strengthened the bars of your gates and blessed your children in your midst." Since 1948, the Jewish people have had sovereignty over Jerusalem.

הַלְלוּיָהּ, כִּי־טוֹב זַמְּרָה אֱלֹהֵינוּ, כִּי־נָעִים נָאוָה תְהִלָּה: בּוֹנֵה תהלים קמז
יְרוּשָׁלַםִ יהוה, נִדְחֵי יִשְׂרָאֵל יְכַנֵּס: הָרוֹפֵא לִשְׁבְוּרֵי לֵב,ע וּמְחַבֵּשׁ
לְעַצְּבוֹתָם: מוֹנֶה מִסְפָּר לַכּוֹכָבִים,אע לְכֻלָּם שֵׁמוֹת יִקְרָא: גָּדוֹל
אֲדוֹנֵינוּ וְרַב־כֹּחַ, לִתְבוּנָתוֹ אֵין מִסְפָּר:ע מְעוֹדֵד עֲנָוִים יהוה,
מַשְׁפִּיל רְשָׁעִים עֲדֵי־אָרֶץ: עֱנוּ לַיהוה בְּתוֹדָה, זַמְּרוּ לֵאלֹהֵינוּ
בְכִנּוֹר:ע הַמְכַסֶּה שָׁמַיִם בְּעָבִים, הַמֵּכִין לָאָרֶץ מָטָר, הַמַּצְמִיחַ
הָרִים חָצִיר:א נוֹתֵן לִבְהֵמָה לַחְמָהּ, לִבְנֵי עֹרֵב אֲשֶׁר יִקְרָאוּ: לֹא
בִגְבוּרַת הַסּוּס יֶחְפָּץ, לֹא־בְשׁוֹקֵי הָאִישׁ יִרְצֶה:ע רוֹצֶה יהוה
אֶת־יְרֵאָיו, אֶת־הַמְיַחֲלִים לְחַסְדּוֹ: שַׁבְּחִי יְרוּשָׁלַםִ אֶת־יהוה,ע
הַלְלִי אֱלֹהַיִךְ צִיּוֹן: כִּי־חִזַּק בְּרִיחֵי שְׁעָרָיִךְ, בֵּרַךְ בָּנַיִךְ בְּקִרְבֵּךְ:
הַשָּׂם־גְּבוּלֵךְ שָׁלוֹם, חֵלֶב חִטִּים יַשְׂבִּיעֵךְ: הַשֹּׁלֵחַ אִמְרָתוֹ אָרֶץ,

---

palpable, and I knew that life in the universe was not just an accident based on random processes... It was knowledge gained through private subjective awareness, but it was – and still is – every bit as real as the objective data upon which, say, the navigational program or the communications system was based. (Captain Edgar D. Mitchell)

IYUN TEFILLA • עיון תפילה

הָרוֹפֵא לִשְׁבְוּרֵי לֵב – *He heals the brokenhearted.* Sometimes when other people cannot understand you, Hashem is the only One who can.

ANI TEFILLA • אני תפילה

מוֹנֶה מִסְפָּר לַכּוֹכָבִים – *He counts the number of the stars.*

Imagine yourself in a place where you have seen a star-filled sky. Close your eyes. Count them.

IYUN TEFILLA • עיון תפילה

מוֹנֶה מִסְפָּר לַכּוֹכָבִים – *He counts the number of the stars.* Hashem counts each one of His creations because He cares about them. (Rashi)

Every person has a star in the heavens which corresponds to him and shines according to the actions of that person. (*Midrash Shoḥer Tov 148:1*)

Hashem knows the name of every one of His creations – including me.

commandment to earth; swiftly runs His word. He spreads snow like fleece,[A] sprinkles frost like ashes, scatters hail like crumbs. Who can stand His cold? He sends His word and melts them; He makes the wind blow and the waters flow. ▸ He has declared His words to Jacob, His statutes and laws to Israel. He has done this for no other nation; such laws they do not know. Halleluya![A]

הַלְלוּיָהּ Halleluya! Praise the Lord from the heavens,[BI] praise Him in the heights. Praise Him, all His angels; praise Him, all His hosts. Praise Him, sun and moon; praise Him, all shining stars. Praise Him, highest heavens and the waters above the heavens. Let them praise the name of the Lord, for He commanded and they were created. He established them for ever and all time, issuing a decree *Ps. 148*

ANI TEFILLA • אני תפילה

Think about the complexity of creation as you know it from biology or any of the other physical sciences. Close your eyes and imagine being in a place where you were once overwhelmed by the beauty, symmetry and complexity of nature.

IYUN TEFILLA • עיון תפילה

הַלְלוּיָהּ, הַלְלוּ אֶת־יהוה מִן־הַשָּׁמַיִם – *Halleluya! Praise the Lord from the heavens.* This psalm describes the entire universe in dynamic terms. Borrowing heavily from the terminology and images used in *Bereshit*, the psalm in both content and structure reflects one who is overcome by the realization of the varied yet unified nature of the world around us. The first section begins "Praise Hashem from the heavens"; the second section begins "Praise Hashem from the earth"; the concluding section begins "His majesty is above [both] the earth and the heavens."

ANI TEFILLA • אני תפילה

At a meeting of Alcoholics Anonymous (AA), a man related that he had been sober for seven years.

"I walked out on my first contact with AA. They were talking about having a Higher Power, and I was an avowed atheist. When I could not get sober, I returned and said that I want to join the program, but I don't want any of the God talk, and they said 'Okay.' They told me I had to get a sponsor, which I did, and my

This **ANI TEFILLA** *continues on page 91.*

עַד־מְהֵרָה יָרוּץ דְּבָרוֹ: הַנֹּתֵן שֶׁלֶג כַּצָּמֶר,[א] כְּפוֹר כָּאֵפֶר יְפַזֵּר:
מַשְׁלִיךְ קַרְחוֹ כְפִתִּים, לִפְנֵי קָרָתוֹ מִי יַעֲמֹד: יִשְׁלַח דְּבָרוֹ וְיַמְסֵם,
יַשֵּׁב רוּחוֹ יִזְּלוּ־מָיִם: ‹ מַגִּיד דְּבָרָו לְיַעֲקֹב, חֻקָּיו וּמִשְׁפָּטָיו
לְיִשְׂרָאֵל: לֹא עָשָׂה כֵן לְכָל־גּוֹי, וּמִשְׁפָּטִים בַּל־יְדָעוּם, הַלְלוּיָהּ:[א]

תהלים קמח הַלְלוּיָהּ, הַלְלוּ אֶת־יהוה מִן־הַשָּׁמַיִם,[בע] הַלְלוּהוּ בַּמְּרוֹמִים:
הַלְלוּהוּ כָל־מַלְאָכָיו, הַלְלוּהוּ כָּל־צְבָאָו: הַלְלוּהוּ שֶׁמֶשׁ וְיָרֵחַ,
הַלְלוּהוּ כָּל־כּוֹכְבֵי אוֹר: הַלְלוּהוּ שְׁמֵי הַשָּׁמָיִם, וְהַמַּיִם אֲשֶׁר מֵעַל
הַשָּׁמָיִם: יְהַלְלוּ אֶת־שֵׁם יהוה, כִּי הוּא צִוָּה וְנִבְרָאוּ: וַיַּעֲמִידֵם
לָעַד לְעוֹלָם, חָק־נָתַן וְלֹא יַעֲבוֹר: הַלְלוּ אֶת־יהוה מִן־הָאָרֶץ,

---

ANI TEFILLA • אני תפילה

הַנֹּתֵן שֶׁלֶג כַּצָּמֶר – *He spreads snow like fleece.* The next three verses speak of Hashem's control over precipitation and the weather, which can have both positive and negative effects on man. The religious personality sees God's hand in the cycle of nature; "when the snow melts...the waters flow," and the cycle of life continues.

Look outside. What is the weather like today? Don't take it for granted.

BIUR TEFILLA • ביאור תפילה

הַלְלוּיָהּ, הַלְלוּ אֶת־יהוה מִן־הַשָּׁמַיִם – *Halleluya! Praise the Lord from the heavens.* The diversity of creation is highlighted by the listing of creations. In the first section (verses 1–6) they are listed according to their stature, moving mostly from "higher" to "lower." In the second section, the reverse is true: the creations are listed from the bottom of the sea up to the sky and back down again but according to their stature not their place. Especially toward the end, one sees movement from the inanimate (mountains) to the animate (animals) to mankind. Indeed, even within each category there is an attempt to convey a sense of all of its members by the use of opposites (fire and hail etc.). The all-encompassing nature of the description in both sections is emphasized by the recurring use of the word כָּל. It is as if the reader is immersed in all of the parts of creation. Man, reflecting upon the world around him, is overwhelmed by its diversity and complexity. At the same time, however, man is called upon to recognize the thread which ties together all of these diverse elements: namely, the One who created them all.

that will never change. Praise the LORD from the earth: sea monsters and all the deep seas; fire and hail, snow and mist, storm winds that obey His word; mountains and all hills, fruit trees and all cedars; wild animals and all cattle, creeping things and winged birds; kings of the earth and all nations, princes and all judges on earth; youths and maidens, old and young. ▸ Let them praise the name of the LORD,[A] for His name alone is sublime; His majesty is above earth and heaven. He has raised the pride of His people, for the glory of all His devoted ones, the children of Israel, the people close to Him. Halleluya!

הַלְלוּיָהּ Halleluya! Sing to the LORD a new song,[I] His praise in the assembly of the devoted. Let Israel rejoice in its Maker; let the children of Zion exult in their King. Let them praise His name with dancing; sing praises to Him with timbrel and harp. For the LORD delights in His people; He adorns the humble with salvation. Let the devoted revel in glory; let them sing for joy on their beds. Let high praises of God be in their throats, and a two-edged sword in their hand: to impose retribution on the nations, punishment on the peoples, ▸ binding their kings with chains, their nobles with iron fetters, carrying out the judgment written against them. This is the glory of all His devoted ones. Halleluya! *Ps. 149*

ANI TEFILLA • אני תפילה

One night I dreamed I was walking on the beach with God. I saw many scenes from my life flash across the sky. In each scene I noticed footprints in the sand. Sometimes there were two sets of footprints and sometimes there was only one.

This bothered me because I noticed that during the low periods in my life, when I was suffering from anguish, sorrow or defeat, I could see only one set of footprints, so I said to God, "You promised me that if I followed You, You would walk with me always. But I have noticed that during the most trying periods of my life there has been only one set of footprints in the sand. Why, when I have needed You most, have You not been there for me?"

God replied, "The years when you have seen only one set of footprints, my child, is when I carried you." (Author unknown)

תַּנִּינִים וְכׇל־תְּהֹמוֹת: אֵשׁ וּבָרָד שֶׁלֶג וְקִיטוֹר, רוּחַ סְעָרָה עֹשָׂה דְבָרוֹ: הֶהָרִים וְכׇל־גְּבָעוֹת, עֵץ פְּרִי וְכׇל־אֲרָזִים: הַחַיָּה וְכׇל־בְּהֵמָה, רֶמֶשׂ וְצִפּוֹר כָּנָף: מַלְכֵי־אֶרֶץ וְכׇל־לְאֻמִּים, שָׂרִים וְכׇל־שֹׁפְטֵי אָרֶץ: בַּחוּרִים וְגַם־בְּתוּלוֹת, זְקֵנִים עִם־נְעָרִים: ‹ יְהַלְלוּ אֶת־שֵׁם יהוה,[א] כִּי־נִשְׂגָּב שְׁמוֹ לְבַדּוֹ, הוֹדוֹ עַל־אֶרֶץ וְשָׁמָיִם: וַיָּרֶם קֶרֶן לְעַמּוֹ, תְּהִלָּה לְכׇל־חֲסִידָיו, לִבְנֵי יִשְׂרָאֵל עַם קְרֹבוֹ, הַלְלוּיָהּ:

הַלְלוּיָהּ, שִׁירוּ לַיהוה שִׁיר חָדָשׁ,[ע] תְּהִלָּתוֹ בִּקְהַל חֲסִידִים: תהלים קמט
יִשְׂמַח יִשְׂרָאֵל בְּעֹשָׂיו, בְּנֵי־צִיּוֹן יָגִילוּ בְמַלְכָּם: יְהַלְלוּ שְׁמוֹ בְמָחוֹל, בְּתֹף וְכִנּוֹר יְזַמְּרוּ־לוֹ: כִּי־רוֹצֶה יהוה בְּעַמּוֹ, יְפָאֵר עֲנָוִים בִּישׁוּעָה: יַעְלְזוּ חֲסִידִים בְּכָבוֹד, יְרַנְּנוּ עַל־מִשְׁכְּבוֹתָם: רוֹמְמוֹת אֵל בִּגְרוֹנָם, וְחֶרֶב פִּיפִיּוֹת בְּיָדָם: לַעֲשׂוֹת נְקָמָה בַּגּוֹיִם, תּוֹכֵחוֹת בַּלְאֻמִּים: ‹ לֶאְסֹר מַלְכֵיהֶם בְּזִקִּים, וְנִכְבְּדֵיהֶם בְּכַבְלֵי בַרְזֶל: לַעֲשׂוֹת בָּהֶם מִשְׁפָּט כָּתוּב, הָדָר הוּא לְכׇל־חֲסִידָיו, הַלְלוּיָהּ:

IYUN TEFILLA · עיון תפילה

הַלְלוּיָהּ, שִׁירוּ לַיהוה שִׁיר חָדָשׁ – *Halleluya! Sing to the* Lord *a new song.* Each of us is called upon to create our own personal praise of Hashem's presence in our lives. Each day we should create our own new song. Alternatively, each day we are different than we were the day before and so our song is a new one, unlike the one we sang yesterday, not because the words are different but because we are.

What's your song today?

sponsor told me I had to pray every day. I said: 'Hold it! I was assured that I would not be bothered about God.' My sponsor said, 'Look here, do you want to get sober or stay drunk? If you want to get sober, you're going to pray every day.'

"Well, I prayed every day, but I didn't pray to God because I didn't believe in God. But when I prayed, that reminded me that I was not God."

The first step in recovery from addiction and in the effort to achieve a relationship with God, is humility, the realization that we are not God. Only then can we have emuna. Until then, our prayers may only help us realize that we are not God. (Rabbi A.J. Twerski)

Ps. 150

הַלְלוּיָהּ Halleluya! Praise God in His holy place;
praise Him in the heavens of His power.
Praise Him for His mighty deeds;
praise Him for His surpassing greatness.
Praise Him with blasts of the shofar;
praise Him with the harp and lyre.
Praise Him with timbrel and dance;
praise Him with strings and flute.
Praise Him with clashing cymbals;
praise Him with resounding cymbals.
▸ Let all that breathes praise the LORD. Halleluya!
Let all that breathes praise the LORD. Halleluya![B]

IYUN TEFILLA • עיון תפילה

כֹּל הַנְּשָׁמָה תְּהַלֵּל יָהּ – *Let all that breathes praise the* LORD. Words, music and song are all but modes of expression for that which lies at our core – the human soul. It is like "an inner drive that breaks out like a flame inside a volcano, but cannot do so in the form of words or logical sentences" (Rabbi J.B. Soloveitchik). Alternatively, the word for soul is related to the word for breath (נשימה) – wherever we are, we should look for God's presence in our lives and celebrate with every breath we take.

BIUR TEFILLA • ביאור תפילה

כֹּל הַנְּשָׁמָה תְּהַלֵּל יָהּ – *Let all that breathes praise the* LORD. The repetition of the final sentence is a traditional way of conveying the fact that this represents the conclusion of a section; here it marks the end of the last chapter of *Tehillim*, the core of *Pesukei DeZimra* (*Tur* 51, *Sefer Pardes*).

ANI TEFILLA • אני תפילה

We can only pray the way prayer is supposed to be when we recognize that in fact the soul is always praying.

Without stop, the soul soars and yearns for its Beloved. It is at the time of outward prayer [as we are doing now], that the perpetual prayer of the soul reveals itself in the realm of action.

This is prayer's pleasure and joy, its glory and beauty. It is like a rose, opening its elegant petals toward the dew, facing the rays of the sun as they shine over it with the sun's light. (Rabbi A.I. Kook)

My soul is always praying. Now is the time to hear its voice.

תהלים קנ

הַלְלוּיָהּ, הַלְלוּ־אֵל בְּקָדְשׁוֹ
הַלְלוּהוּ בִּרְקִיעַ עֻזּוֹ:
הַלְלוּהוּ בִגְבוּרֹתָיו
הַלְלוּהוּ כְּרֹב גֻּדְלוֹ:
הַלְלוּהוּ בְּתֵקַע שׁוֹפָר
הַלְלוּהוּ בְּנֵבֶל וְכִנּוֹר:
הַלְלוּהוּ בְתֹף וּמָחוֹל
הַלְלוּהוּ בְּמִנִּים וְעֻגָב:
הַלְלוּהוּ בְצִלְצְלֵי־שָׁמַע
הַלְלוּהוּ בְּצִלְצְלֵי תְרוּעָה:
› כֹּל הַנְּשָׁמָה תְּהַלֵּל יָהּ, הַלְלוּיָהּ:
כֹּל הַנְּשָׁמָה תְּהַלֵּל יָהּ, הַלְלוּיָהּ:

IYUN TEFILLA • עיון תפילה

הַלְלוּ־אֵל בְּקָדְשׁוֹ – *Halleluya! Praise God in His holy place. praise Him in the heavens.* His holy place is the *Beit HaMikdash* and represents God's revelation to man in the moral sphere. The heavens represent His revelation to man in the world of nature (Rabbi S.R. Hirsch). The study of Torah represents man's education about what God wants in the moral sphere; the study of the sciences represents man's education about God's presence in the physical sphere.

Science can be a religious quest.

הַלְלוּהוּ כְּרֹב גֻּדְלוֹ – *Praise Him for His surpassing greatness.* One might think one should continue to praise with words. However, sometimes words are inadequate to express how beautiful, complex, and overwhelming the beauty of the world and its creations can be. Did you ever witness something so amazing that it was indescribable? And so, when words fail, sometimes only music and song can best express what our heart is feeling. What follows, then, is reference to a variety of ancient musical instruments whose sounds are sometimes better equipped to express the praise we feel.

בָּרוּךְ Blessed be the LORD for ever.[B] Amen and Amen. *Ps. 89*
Blessed from Zion be the LORD who dwells in Jerusalem. Halleluya! *Ps. 135*
Blessed be the LORD, God of Israel, who alone does wonders. *Ps. 72*
▸ Blessed be His glorious name for ever,
and may all the earth be filled with His glory.
Amen and Amen.[B]

Stand until after "Bless the LORD" on page 106.

וַיְבָרֶךְ David blessed the LORD[A] in front of the entire assembly. *1 Chr. 29*
David said, "Blessed are You, LORD, God of our father Yisrael, for ever and ever. Yours, LORD, are the greatness and the power, the glory, majesty and splendor, for everything in heaven and earth is Yours. Yours, LORD, is the kingdom; You are exalted as Head over all. Both riches and honor are in Your gift and You reign over all things. In Your hand are strength and might. It is in Your power to make great and give strength to all. Therefore, our God, we thank You and praise Your glorious name." You alone are the LORD.[B] *Neh. 9*

---

at this point to set aside money to donate to *tzedaka* (*Magen Avraham* 51). In so doing, we state our awareness that the money that we have, no matter the amount, is a gift from God. My giving some of it to others is an acknowledgment that He also gives to me. The prevalent custom is to stand for these verses, perhaps because the practice of some was to stand when doing a mitzva like giving *tzedaka*, or because people once stood in honor of others who came to collect it.

ANI TEFILLA • אני תפילה

וַיְבָרֶךְ דָּוִיד אֶת יהוה – *David blessed the LORD.*

Rabbi Elazar would give a coin to a poor person and only then would he begin to pray (Bava Batra 10a).

If you haven't set aside some money for *tzedaka*, do so now. To ask for help one should be prepared to give help.

BIUR TEFILLA • ביאור תפילה

אַתָּה־הוּא יהוה לְבַדֶּךָ – *You alone are the LORD.* What follows in the next prayers is a brief history of our relationship with Hashem from Creation until the splitting of the Sea at the time of the exodus. This represents a shift from focusing primarily on Hashem's presence in nature to Hashem's presence in history. The bridge between the two is Avraham who, according to one tradition, discovered Hashem in nature and then went on to find His place in human affairs.

בָּרוּךְ יהוה לְעוֹלָם,[ב] אָמֵן וְאָמֵן: תהלים פט
בָּרוּךְ יהוה מִצִּיּוֹן, שֹׁכֵן יְרוּשָׁלָםִ, הַלְלוּיָהּ: תהלים קלה
בָּרוּךְ יהוה אֱלֹהִים אֱלֹהֵי יִשְׂרָאֵל, עֹשֵׂה נִפְלָאוֹת לְבַדּוֹ: תהלים עב
◂ וּבָרוּךְ שֵׁם כְּבוֹדוֹ לְעוֹלָם, וְיִמָּלֵא כְבוֹדוֹ אֶת־כׇּל־הָאָרֶץ
אָמֵן וְאָמֵן:[ב]

Stand until after בָּרְכוּ *on page 107.*

וַיְבָרֶךְ דָּוִיד אֶת־יהוה[א] לְעֵינֵי כׇּל־הַקָּהָל, וַיֹּאמֶר דָּוִיד, בָּרוּךְ דברי הימים א, כט
אַתָּה יהוה, אֱלֹהֵי יִשְׂרָאֵל אָבִינוּ, מֵעוֹלָם וְעַד־עוֹלָם: לְךָ יהוה
הַגְּדֻלָּה וְהַגְּבוּרָה וְהַתִּפְאֶרֶת וְהַנֵּצַח וְהַהוֹד, כִּי־כֹל בַּשָּׁמַיִם
וּבָאָרֶץ, לְךָ יהוה הַמַּמְלָכָה וְהַמִּתְנַשֵּׂא לְכֹל לְרֹאשׁ: וְהָעֹשֶׁר
וְהַכָּבוֹד מִלְּפָנֶיךָ, וְאַתָּה מוֹשֵׁל בַּכֹּל, וּבְיָדְךָ כֹּחַ וּגְבוּרָה, וּבְיָדְךָ
לְגַדֵּל וּלְחַזֵּק לַכֹּל: וְעַתָּה אֱלֹהֵינוּ מוֹדִים אֲנַחְנוּ לָךְ, וּמְהַלְלִים
לְשֵׁם תִּפְאַרְתֶּךָ: אַתָּה־הוּא יהוה לְבַדֶּךָ,[ב] אַתְּ עָשִׂיתָ נחמיה ט

BIUR TEFILLA • ביאור תפילה

בָּרוּךְ יהוה לְעוֹלָם – *Blessed be the* Lord *for ever.* The prayers which follow add other dimensions to the *Pesukei DeZimra*. As they are not directly a part of the core *Tehillim* we just concluded, the Maharam would recite the following series of verses, reminiscent of the language of a closing blessing, in order to separate the two sections. (Abudarham)

אָמֵן וְאָמֵן – *Amen and Amen.* The word *amen* can have two meanings:

(a) a declaration – I agree with everything that was just said;
(b) a prayer – I pray that everything that was just said will come true. (*Tzeluta DeAvraham*)

HILKHOT TEFILLA • הלכות תפילה

וַיְבָרֶךְ דָּוִיד אֶת יהוה – *David blessed the* Lord. These verses of thanks were recited by King David toward the end of his life when he had amassed the wealth necessary to build the *Beit HaMikdash* that would be constructed by his son. As a result, there is a custom

You made the heavens, even the highest heavens, and all their hosts, the earth and all that is on it, the seas and all they contain. You give life to them all, and the hosts of heaven worship You. ▸ You are the LORD God who chose Abram[A] and brought him out of Ur of the Chaldees, changing his name to Abraham. You found his heart faithful toward You, ◂ and You made a covenant with him to give to his descendants the land of the Canaanites, Hittites, Amorites, Perizzites, Jebusites and Girgashites. You fulfilled Your promise for You are righteous. You saw the suffering of our ancestors in Egypt. You heard their cry at the Sea of Reeds. You sent signs and wonders against Pharaoh, all his servants and all the people of his land, because You knew how arrogantly the Egyptians treated them. You created for Yourself renown that remains to this day. ▸ You divided the sea before them, so that they passed through the sea on dry land, but You cast their pursuers into the depths, like a stone into mighty waters.

וַיּוֹשַׁע That day the LORD saved Israel from the hands of the Egyptians, and Israel saw the Egyptians lying dead on the seashore. ▸ When Israel saw the great power[I] the LORD had displayed against the Egyptians, the people feared the LORD, and believed in the LORD and in His servant, Moses. *Ex. 14*

---

be your seed," so shall be the history of your people, your children. Your great destiny is just as enigmatic and mysterious and incomprehensible as the great story of the heavens. Why try to rationalize it? ... The story of your people is the story of the heavens; no one will ever be able to understand it. (Rabbi J.B. Soloveitchik)

IYUN TEFILLA • עיון תפילה

וַיַּרְא יִשְׂרָאֵל אֶת־הַיָּד הַגְּדֹלָה – *When Israel saw the great power.* But were there not times subsequently when *Benei Yisrael* did not believe in Hashem?! What happened to their faith? Rather, faith is not something that is binary, an either/or proposition. Instead, faith is akin to an analog signal that varies with different intensities and strengths at different points in one's life. (Rabbi. S. Aviner)

Indeed, it can be argued that a faith that relies upon supernatural miracles is inferior. The stronger faith is the one that sees the miracles in the everyday.

What miracles surround your life this morning?

אֶת־הַשָּׁמַיִם, שְׁמֵי הַשָּׁמַיִם וְכָל־צְבָאָם, הָאָרֶץ וְכָל־אֲשֶׁר עָלֶיהָ,
הַיַּמִּים וְכָל־אֲשֶׁר בָּהֶם, וְאַתָּה מְחַיֶּה אֶת־כֻּלָּם, וּצְבָא הַשָּׁמַיִם לְךָ
מִשְׁתַּחֲוִים: ◂ אַתָּה הוּא יהוה הָאֱלֹהִים אֲשֶׁר בָּחַרְתָּ בְּאַבְרָם,[א]
וְהוֹצֵאתוֹ מֵאוּר כַּשְׂדִּים, וְשַׂמְתָּ שְּׁמוֹ אַבְרָהָם: וּמָצָאתָ אֶת־
לְבָבוֹ נֶאֱמָן לְפָנֶיךָ, ◂ וְכָרוֹת עִמּוֹ הַבְּרִית לָתֵת אֶת־אֶרֶץ הַכְּנַעֲנִי
הַחִתִּי הָאֱמֹרִי וְהַפְּרִזִּי וְהַיְבוּסִי וְהַגִּרְגָּשִׁי, לָתֵת לְזַרְעוֹ, וַתָּקֶם
אֶת־דְּבָרֶיךָ, כִּי צַדִּיק אָתָּה: וַתֵּרֶא אֶת־עֳנִי אֲבֹתֵינוּ בְּמִצְרָיִם,
וְאֶת־זַעֲקָתָם שָׁמַעְתָּ עַל־יַם־סוּף: וַתִּתֵּן אֹתֹת וּמֹפְתִים בְּפַרְעֹה
וּבְכָל־עֲבָדָיו וּבְכָל־עַם אַרְצוֹ, כִּי יָדַעְתָּ כִּי הֵזִידוּ עֲלֵיהֶם, וַתַּעַשׂ־
לְךָ שֵׁם כְּהַיּוֹם הַזֶּה: ◂ וְהַיָּם בָּקַעְתָּ לִפְנֵיהֶם, וַיַּעַבְרוּ בְתוֹךְ־הַיָּם
בַּיַּבָּשָׁה, וְאֶת־רֹדְפֵיהֶם הִשְׁלַכְתָּ בִמְצוֹלֹת כְּמוֹ־אֶבֶן, בְּמַיִם עַזִּים:

שמות יד וַיּוֹשַׁע יהוה בַּיּוֹם הַהוּא אֶת־יִשְׂרָאֵל מִיַּד מִצְרָיִם, וַיַּרְא יִשְׂרָאֵל
אֶת־מִצְרַיִם מֵת עַל־שְׂפַת הַיָּם: ◂ וַיַּרְא יִשְׂרָאֵל אֶת־הַיָּד הַגְּדֹלָה[ע]
אֲשֶׁר עָשָׂה יהוה בְּמִצְרַיִם, וַיִּירְאוּ הָעָם אֶת־יהוה, וַיַּאֲמִינוּ
בַּיהוה וּבְמֹשֶׁה עַבְדּוֹ:

ANI TEFILLA • אני תפילה

When Avraham was a lad, when he was a shepherd and remained in the field at night, he couldn't sleep because he was restless. He could not understand the cosmos; the grandeur of the cosmic drama puzzled him. Chaldea [Ur Kasdim] was the land where astronomy was born. They were the first ones to describe the skies, draw maps of the heavens. Avraham counted the stars; he discovered God with the stars. When a sensitive and refined person lifts his eyes and watches the stars and the heavenly drama, he begins to think of the enormous distances and is confronted by the Ein Sof, by infinity, by endlessness itself. The sensitive soul will sense the complete worthlessness of man in comparison with infinity and will finally find God in the infinite spaces separating galaxies and stars…

God tells Avraham not merely to count the stars, but to try to comprehend them. Can you enumerate the stars, Avraham? Can you explain the cosmic drama, the flying nebulae on the outskirts of the universe? … "So shall

אָז יָשִׁיר־מֹשֶׁה Then Moses and the Israelites sang[HA] this song to the LORD, saying: *Ex. 15*
I will sing to the LORD, for He has triumphed gloriously;
horse and rider He has hurled into the sea.
The LORD is my strength and song; He has become my salvation.
This is my God, and I will beautify Him,
my father's God, and I will exalt Him.
The LORD is a Master of war; LORD is His name.
Pharaoh's chariots and army He cast into the sea;
the best of his officers drowned in the Sea of Reeds.
The deep waters covered them;
they went down to the depths like a stone.
Your right hand, LORD, is majestic in power.
Your right hand, LORD, shatters the enemy.
In the greatness of Your majesty, You overthrew those who rose against You.
You sent out Your fury; it consumed them like stubble.
By the blast of Your nostrils the waters piled up.
The surging waters stood straight like a wall;
the deeps congealed in the heart of the sea.
The enemy said, "I will pursue. I will overtake. I will divide the spoil.
My desire shall have its fill of them.
I will draw my sword. My hand will destroy them."
You blew with Your wind; the sea covered them.
They sank in the mighty waters like lead.
Who is like You, LORD, among the mighty?
Who is like You – majestic in holiness, awesome in glory, working wonders?

---

all lifted up the hems of their clothes to keep them from getting wet, for it actually seemed to them that they had gone down into the Sea which had split before them. Such is the power of imagination during tefilla.

אָז יָשִׁיר־מֹשֶׁה וּבְנֵי יִשְׂרָאֵל^הא^ אֶת־הַשִּׁירָה הַזֹּאת לַיהוה, וַיֹּאמְרוּ שמות טו
לֵאמֹר, אָשִׁירָה לַיהוה כִּי־גָאֹה גָּאָה, סוּס
וְרֹכְבוֹ רָמָה בַיָּם: עָזִּי וְזִמְרָת יָהּ וַיְהִי־לִי
לִישׁוּעָה, זֶה אֵלִי וְאַנְוֵהוּ, אֱלֹהֵי
אָבִי וַאֲרֹמְמֶנְהוּ: יהוה אִישׁ מִלְחָמָה, יהוה
שְׁמוֹ: מַרְכְּבֹת פַּרְעֹה וְחֵילוֹ יָרָה בַיָּם, וּמִבְחַר
שָׁלִשָׁיו טֻבְּעוּ בְיַם־סוּף: תְּהֹמֹת יְכַסְיֻמוּ, יָרְדוּ בִמְצוֹלֹת כְּמוֹ־
אָבֶן: יְמִינְךָ יהוה נֶאְדָּרִי בַּכֹּחַ, יְמִינְךָ
יהוה תִּרְעַץ אוֹיֵב: וּבְרֹב גְּאוֹנְךָ תַּהֲרֹס
קָמֶיךָ, תְּשַׁלַּח חֲרֹנְךָ יֹאכְלֵמוֹ כַּקַּשׁ: וּבְרוּחַ
אַפֶּיךָ נֶעֶרְמוּ מַיִם, נִצְּבוּ כְמוֹ־נֵד
נֹזְלִים, קָפְאוּ תְהֹמֹת בְּלֶב־יָם: אָמַר
אוֹיֵב אֶרְדֹּף, אַשִּׂיג, אֲחַלֵּק שָׁלָל, תִּמְלָאֵמוֹ
נַפְשִׁי, אָרִיק חַרְבִּי תּוֹרִישֵׁמוֹ יָדִי: נָשַׁפְתָּ
בְרוּחֲךָ כִּסָּמוֹ יָם, צָלֲלוּ כַּעוֹפֶרֶת בְּמַיִם
אַדִּירִים: מִי־כָמֹכָה בָּאֵלִם יהוה, מִי
כָּמֹכָה נֶאְדָּר בַּקֹּדֶשׁ, נוֹרָא תְהִלֹּת עֹשֵׂה

ANI TEFILLA • אני תפילה

Then Moses and the Israelites sang. Once, Rabbi Shmelke of Nikolsburg said the Song at the Sea as Ḥazan with such power that when the congregation recited with him the verses about the crossing of the Reed Sea, they

HILKHOT TEFILLA • הלכות תפילה

אָז יָשִׁיר־מֹשֶׁה וּבְנֵי יִשְׂרָאֵל – *Then Moses and the Israelites sang.* One should say the Song at the Sea with great joy, and imagine that at that very moment he crossed through it and was liberated. And if one does so, then all of his sins will be forgiven (*Mishna Berura* 51:17). In other words, this is not just about reciting or retelling the event; it is about reliving it.

You stretched out Your right hand,
the earth swallowed them.
In Your loving-kindness, You led the people You redeemed.
In Your strength, You guided them to Your holy abode.
Nations heard and trembled;
terror gripped Philistia's inhabitants.
The chiefs of Edom were dismayed,
Moab's leaders were seized with trembling,
the people of Canaan melted away.
Fear and dread fell upon them.
By the power of Your arm, they were still as stone –
until Your people crossed, LORD,
until the people You acquired crossed over.
You will bring them and plant them
on the mountain of Your heritage –
the place, LORD, You made for Your dwelling,
the Sanctuary, LORD, Your hands established.
The LORD will reign for ever and all time.

The LORD will reign for ever and all time.
The LORD's kingship is established for ever and to all eternity.

When Pharaoh's horses, chariots and riders went into the sea,
the LORD brought the waters of the sea back over them,
but the Israelites walked on dry land through the sea.

▸ For kingship is the LORD's *Ps. 22*
and He rules over the nations.
Saviors shall go up to Mount Zion *Ob. 1*
to judge Mount Esau,
and the LORD's shall be the kingdom.

Then the LORD shall be King over all the earth; *Zech. 14*
on that day the LORD shall be One and His name One,

(as it is written in Your Torah, saying:
Listen, Israel: the LORD is our God, the LORD is One.) *Deut. 6*

פֶּֽלֶא: נָטִ֙יתָ֙ יְמִ֣ינְךָ֔ תִּבְלָעֵ֖מוֹ אָֽרֶץ: נָחִ֥יתָ
בְחַסְדְּךָ֖ עַם־ז֣וּ גָּאָ֑לְתָּ, נֵהַ֥לְתָּ בְעָזְּךָ֖ אֶל־נְוֵ֥ה
קָדְשֶֽׁךָ: שָֽׁמְע֥וּ עַמִּ֖ים יִרְגָּז֑וּן, חִ֣יל
אָחַ֔ז יֹשְׁבֵ֖י פְּלָֽשֶׁת: אָ֤ז נִבְהֲלוּ֙ אַלּוּפֵ֣י
אֱד֔וֹם, אֵילֵ֣י מוֹאָ֔ב יֹֽאחֲזֵ֖מוֹ רָ֑עַד, נָמֹ֕גוּ
כֹּ֖ל יֹשְׁבֵ֥י כְנָֽעַן: תִּפֹּ֨ל עֲלֵיהֶ֤ם אֵימָ֙תָה֙
וָפַ֔חַד, בִּגְדֹ֥ל זְרוֹעֲךָ֖ יִדְּמ֣וּ כָּאָ֑בֶן, עַד־
יַעֲבֹ֤ר עַמְּךָ֙ יהוה, עַד־יַעֲבֹ֖ר עַם־ז֥וּ
קָנִֽיתָ: תְּבִאֵ֗מוֹ וְתִטָּעֵ֙מוֹ֙ בְּהַ֣ר נַחֲלָֽתְךָ֔, מָכ֧וֹן
לְשִׁבְתְּךָ֛ פָּעַ֖לְתָּ יהוה, מִקְּדָ֕שׁ אֲדֹנָ֖י כּוֹנְנ֥וּ
יָדֶֽיךָ: יהוה ׀ יִמְלֹ֖ךְ לְעֹלָ֥ם וָעֶֽד:

יהוה יִמְלֹךְ לְעֹלָם וָעֶד.
יהוה מַלְכוּתֵהּ קָאֵם לְעָלַם וּלְעָלְמֵי עָלְמַיָּא.

כִּ֣י
בָא֩ ס֨וּס פַּרְעֹ֜ה בְּרִכְבּ֤וֹ וּבְפָרָשָׁיו֙ בַּיָּ֔ם, וַיָּ֧שֶׁב יהוה עֲלֵהֶ֖ם אֶת־מֵ֣י
הַיָּ֑ם, וּבְנֵ֧י יִשְׂרָאֵ֛ל הָלְכ֥וּ בַיַּבָּשָׁ֖ה בְּת֥וֹךְ הַיָּֽם:

› כִּי לַיהוה הַמְּלוּכָה וּמשֵׁל בַּגּוֹיִם: תהלים כב
וְעָלוּ מוֹשִׁעִים בְּהַר צִיּוֹן לִשְׁפֹּט אֶת־הַר עֵשָׂו עובדיה א
וְהָיְתָה לַיהוה הַמְּלוּכָה:
וְהָיָה יהוה לְמֶלֶךְ עַל־כָּל־הָאָרֶץ זכריה יד
בַּיּוֹם הַהוּא יִהְיֶה יהוה אֶחָד וּשְׁמוֹ אֶחָד:

(וּבְתוֹרָתְךָ כָּתוּב לֵאמֹר, שְׁמַע יִשְׂרָאֵל, יהוה אֱלֹהֵינוּ יהוה אֶחָד:) דברים ו

יִשְׁתַּבַּח May Your name be praised[BH]
for ever, our King,
the great and holy God,
King in heaven and on earth.
For to You,
LORD our God and God of our ancestors,
it is right to offer song and praise,
hymn and psalm,
strength and dominion,
eternity, greatness and power,
song of praise and glory,
holiness and kingship,
▸ blessings and thanks,
from now and for ever.
Blessed are You, LORD,
God and King,
exalted in praises,
God of thanksgivings,
Master of wonders,
who delights in hymns of song,
King, God, Giver of life to the worlds.[B]

HILKHOT TEFILLA • הלכות תפילה

יִשְׁתַּבַּח שִׁמְךָ – *May Your name be praised.* As we have noted, *Pesukei DeZimra* is a single unit bounded by the blessing *Barukh She'amar* at the beginning and the blessing *Yishtabaḥ* at the end. As such, no interruptions are generally permitted. What about between *Yishtabaḥ* and *Barekhu*? If the first unit (*Pesukei DeZimra*) is complete, and the next unit (*Birkhot Keriat Shema*) has not yet begun, should any talking be permitted? There are those authorities who say it is not (Rif on *Berakhot* 23a; Rosh 5, 5; *Kol Bo, siman* 4). Their reasoning is because if *Pesukei DeZimra* is really intended as the praise one should say before one prays, then isn't it contradictory to interrupt that process? After all, traveling on a straight path it makes no sense to take a detour,

This **HILKHOT TEFILLA** *continues on page 105.*

יִשְׁתַּבַּח

שִׁמְךָ[בה] לָעַד, מַלְכֵּנוּ
הָאֵל הַמֶּלֶךְ הַגָּדוֹל וְהַקָּדוֹשׁ בַּשָּׁמַיִם וּבָאָרֶץ
כִּי לְךָ נָאֶה, יהוה אֱלֹהֵינוּ וֵאלֹהֵי אֲבוֹתֵינוּ
שִׁיר וּשְׁבָחָה, הַלֵּל וְזִמְרָה
עֹז וּמֶמְשָׁלָה
נֶצַח, גְּדֻלָּה וּגְבוּרָה
תְּהִלָּה וְתִפְאֶרֶת, קְדֻשָּׁה וּמַלְכוּת
‹ בְּרָכוֹת וְהוֹדָאוֹת, מֵעַתָּה וְעַד עוֹלָם.
בָּרוּךְ אַתָּה יהוה
אֵל מֶלֶךְ גָּדוֹל בַּתִּשְׁבָּחוֹת
אֵל הַהוֹדָאוֹת
אֲדוֹן הַנִּפְלָאוֹת
הַבּוֹחֵר בְּשִׁירֵי זִמְרָה
מֶלֶךְ, אֵל, חֵי הָעוֹלָמִים.[ב]

BIUR TEFILLA • ביאור תפילה

יִשְׁתַּבַּח שִׁמְךָ – *May Your name be praised.* It is said that the 15 nouns here correspond to the 15 steps leading from one part of the *Beit HaMikdash* to another. As we conclude this part of the service, we get one step closer to our personal encounter with Hashem in the *Shemoneh Esreh.*

מֶלֶךְ, אֵל, חֵי הָעוֹלָמִים – *King, God, Giver of life to the worlds.* At the beginning of *Pesukei DeZimra* we said that we would praise Hashem and make His name great in our eyes via the recitation of *Tehillim*: בִּשְׁבָחוֹת...נְגַדֶּלְךָ. We conclude here by saying that, thanks to our focusing on the *Tehillim* that we just said, we are now more aware of how great You are: מֶלֶךְ גָּדוֹל בַּתִּשְׁבָּחוֹת.

HALF KADDISH

Leader: יִתְגַּדַּל Magnified and sanctified
may His great name be,
in the world He created by His will.
May He establish His kingdom
in your lifetime
and in your days,
and in the lifetime
of all the house of Israel,
swiftly and soon –
and say: Amen.

All: May His great name[A] be blessed
for ever and all time.

Leader: Blessed and praised,
glorified and exalted,
raised and honored,
uplifted and lauded
be the name of the Holy One,
blessed be He,
beyond any blessing, song,
praise and consolation
uttered in the world –
and say: Amen.

ANI TEFILLA • אני תפילה

יְהֵא שְׁמֵהּ רַבָּא – *May His great name.* Whoever says *yeheh shemeh raba*... with all his strength, the Heavenly Court rips up any negative decree against him (*Shabbat* 119b). "With all his strength" – with his complete concentration (Rashi).

חצי קדיש

ש״ץ: יִתְגַּדַּל וְיִתְקַדַּשׁ שְׁמֵהּ רַבָּא (קהל: אָמֵן)
בְּעָלְמָא דִּי בְרָא כִרְעוּתֵהּ
וְיַמְלִיךְ מַלְכוּתֵהּ
בְּחַיֵּיכוֹן וּבְיוֹמֵיכוֹן
וּבְחַיֵּי דְכָל בֵּית יִשְׂרָאֵל
בַּעֲגָלָא וּבִזְמַן קָרִיב,
וְאִמְרוּ אָמֵן. (קהל: אָמֵן)

קהל וש״ץ: יְהֵא שְׁמֵהּ רַבָּא[א] מְבָרַךְ לְעָלַם וּלְעָלְמֵי עָלְמַיָּא.

ש״ץ: יִתְבָּרַךְ וְיִשְׁתַּבַּח וְיִתְפָּאַר וְיִתְרוֹמַם וְיִתְנַשֵּׂא
וְיִתְהַדָּר וְיִתְעַלֶּה וְיִתְהַלָּל
שְׁמֵהּ דְּקֻדְשָׁא בְּרִיךְ הוּא (קהל: בְּרִיךְ הוּא)
לְעֵלָּא מִן כָּל בִּרְכָתָא
וְשִׁירָתָא, תֻּשְׁבְּחָתָא וְנֶחֱמָתָא
דַּאֲמִירָן בְּעָלְמָא
וְאִמְרוּ אָמֵן. (קהל: אָמֵן)

---

especially one that will get in the way of reaching one's destination with the right frame of mind. Why work so hard getting into the mood, only to get sidetracked and have to start over? Nevertheless, one sees that interrupting at this point, between units, is probably different from interrupting in the middle of a unit itself, and so some communities have the practice to allow certain interruptions (such as the recitation of *Shir HaMa'alot*) that are still related to the act of prayer or some other community related need (See Rema and *Mishna Berura* 54:3).

BLESSINGS OF THE SHEMA

The following blessing and response are said only in the presence of a minyan. They represent a formal summons to the congregation to engage in an act of collective prayer. The custom of bowing at this point is based on I Chronicles 29:20, "David said to the whole assembly, 'Now bless the LORD your God.' All the assembly blessed the LORD God of their fathers and bowed their heads low to the LORD and the King."

The Leader says the following, bowing at "Bless," standing straight at "the LORD." The congregation, followed by the Leader, responds, bowing at "Bless," standing straight at "the LORD."

Leader: **BLESS**
the LORD, the blessed One.

Congregation: Bless the LORD, the blessed One,
for ever and all time.

Leader: Bless the LORD, the blessed One,
for ever and all time.

---

a powerful experience. We aspire to that same experience in communal prayer. If I'm not in the mood, or am having a difficult time focusing, the presence of other people helps me to get into the right frame of mind. I allow myself to be drawn in to their devotion or excitement or participation.

And so the *Ḥazan* here issues an invitation to the entire congregation to join him in the recitation of the *berakhot* of *Keriat Shema* which are about to follow. In effect, he says, "Please join me so that I am not saying this alone, but rather we can all say this together as a community. Join with me, and have the intention to sanctify God's name, to fulfill the commandment regarding the recitation of the *Shema*. Join me, so that I can help you and you can help me. We're on the verge of entering the palace of the *Shemoneh Esreh*; let's go together." Implied here as well is the thought that if for some reason you are having a particularly difficult time focusing today, then listen to me, answer *Amen* to the blessings of the *Shema* and to the *Shema* itself. We thus transform our prayer from being not only a private affair but a communal one as well.

קריאת שמע וברכותיה

The following blessing and response are said only in the presence of a מנין.
They represent a formal summons to the קהל *to engage in an act of collective prayer.*
The custom of bowing at this point is based on דברי הימים א׳ כט, כ*, "David said to the whole assembly, 'Now bless the Lord your God.' All the assembly blessed the Lord God of their fathers and bowed their heads low to the Lord and the King."*
The שליח ציבור *says the following, bowing at* בָּרְכוּ*, standing straight at* ה׳*. The* קהל*, followed by the* שליח ציבור*, responds, bowing at* בָּרוּךְ*, standing straight at* ה׳*.*

ש״ץ: **בָּרְכוּ**
אֶת יהוה הַמְבֹרָךְ.

קהל: בָּרוּךְ יהוה הַמְבֹרָךְ לְעוֹלָם וָעֶד.

ש״ץ: בָּרוּךְ יהוה הַמְבֹרָךְ לְעוֹלָם וָעֶד.

INTRODUCTION TO BAREKHU

Commentary on Blessings of Keriat Shema can be found on page 581.

Until this point, although we have been praying with a *minyan*, the truth is that our prayer has been relatively individualistic. The service until now has been a warm-up exercise, a way for us to begin to get into the right frame of mind for the prayers which are to come, especially the *Shemoneh Esreh*. At this point, then, we move one step closer to our encounter with Hashem by formally joining together with the rest of the *tzibbur* or congregation.

One benefit of joining with others is that I am sometimes able to get "into it" much better, when everyone around me is doing the same thing, than when I am alone. Have you ever been to a sporting event or a concert and looked around at the thousands of people surrounding you, all experiencing the same emotions as you at that moment? That can be such

The custom is to sit from this point until the Amida, since the predominant emotion of this section of the prayers is love rather than awe. Conversation is forbidden until after the Amida.

בָּרוּךְ Blessed are You, LORD our God, King of the Universe,
who forms light and creates darkness,[B] makes peace and creates all.[B] *Is. 45*

הַמֵּאִיר In compassion He gives light to the earth and its inhabitants,[I]
and in His goodness continually renews the work of creation,[A]
day after day.[I]
How numerous are Your works, LORD;[A] *Ps. 104*
You made them all in wisdom;
the earth is full of Your creations.

---

of the planet is dependent upon His *raḥamim* (mercy).

מְחַדֵּשׁ בְּכָל יוֹם – *Renews the work of creation, day after day.* Creation was not a one-time event. It happens anew every day; one need only open one's eyes to the miracle of it all. The sun comes up, the flowers reappear, babies are born. Creation is dynamic and ongoing; life is beautiful.

If at the beginning of the blessing there was a refutation of there being more than one God, here the siddur refutes the idea advanced by the Greek philosopher Aristotle that God created the world and walked away. Instead, Hashem's presence is always felt, if one only looks for it.

Where have I seen it thus far today? Where can I see it?

ANI TEFILLA • אני תפילה

תָּמִיד מַעֲשֵׂה בְרֵאשִׁית – *Renews the work of creation.*

Rav Schwab relates that when he flew overseas in the early days of aviation, they flew close to the ocean and he recited the blessing "Oseh Ma'aseh Bereshit" that one is obligated to say when one sees an unusual aspect of nature. The first time he flew on a jet, though, he was above the clouds for the first time in his life and was even more amazed when he said these words of prayer. He went back to Rav Breuer and told him that he never had such kavana. Rav Breuer said that he has the same kavana when he looks at a flower.

מָה־רַבּוּ מַעֲשֶׂיךָ יהוה – *How numerous are Your works, LORD.*

People ask me every day if I get bored of delivering children, or if the deliveries become routine. I can say quite assuredly that the opposite is true: the more I see and the more I know, the more I am aware how miraculous it is each and every time. In fact, I probably am more in awe of the birth than the parents are. I tell patients every day that there are billions of ways the reproductive process can go wrong. The fact that it ever goes right is a miracle. (Dr. Nathan S. Fox, MD)

The custom is to sit from this point until the עמידה, since the predominant emotion of this section of the prayers is love rather than awe. Conversation is forbidden until after the עמידה.

בָּרוּךְ אַתָּה יהוה אֱלֹהֵינוּ מֶלֶךְ הָעוֹלָם
ישעיה מה יוֹצֵר אוֹר וּבוֹרֵא חֹשֶׁךְ, עֹשֶׂה שָׁלוֹם וּבוֹרֵא אֶת הַכֹּל.

הַמֵּאִיר לָאָרֶץ וְלַדָּרִים עָלֶיהָ בְּרַחֲמִים
וּבְטוּבוֹ מְחַדֵּשׁ בְּכָל יוֹם תָּמִיד מַעֲשֵׂה בְרֵאשִׁית.
תהלים קד מָה־רַבּוּ מַעֲשֶׂיךָ יהוה, כֻּלָּם בְּחָכְמָה עָשִׂיתָ
מָלְאָה הָאָרֶץ קִנְיָנֶךָ:

BIUR TEFILLA • ביאור תפילה

יוֹצֵר אוֹר וּבוֹרֵא חֹשֶׁךְ – *Who forms light and creates darkness.* Continuing the theme of *Pesukei DeZimra*, the theme of this first blessing before the *Shema* is "Hashem as Creator." From the beginning, we acknowledge that He is the One solely responsible for the world as we know it in all of its perfect harmony. At the same time, the blessing slides a step further into the theme of a similar relationship that Hashem has with the heavenly world, where He is also acknowledged as Creator. There is thus a balance between the lower world and the upper, which means that the whole universe is in harmony. The blessing thereby serves as an important prelude to our recitation of the *Shema* where we are called upon to declare His Oneness.

וּבוֹרֵא אֶת הַכֹּל – *And creates all.* There are those who say that the phrasing of this blessing was chosen specifically to deny the claim of those believers in ancient religions who thought there was a god of light and a god of darkness, one who reigned when good things happened and one who reigned when bad things happened. Interestingly, the phrasing is taken from a verse in *Yishayahu* but was actually changed here. The original says that God "makes peace and creates evil," whereas here the Rabbis changed the ending to say "makes peace and creates everything" (*Yishayahu* 45:7). The lesson is clear as we approach the *Shema* – there is only one God.

IYUN TEFILLA • עיון תפילה

הַמֵּאִיר לָאָרֶץ וְלַדָּרִים עָלֶיהָ בְּרַחֲמִים – *In compassion He gives light to the earth and its inhabitants.* If the sun were closer to the Earth, we would be like Venus – the oceans would boil away. If it were further away, we would be like Mars – the oceans would be frozen. We would no longer be in what astronomers call a Goldilocks Zone, a place that is situated in just the right location relative to its star. The continued existence

He is the King exalted alone since the beginning of time –
praised, glorified and elevated since the world began.
Eternal God,
in Your great compassion, have compassion on us,
LORD of our strength, Rock of our refuge,
Shield of our salvation, You are our stronghold.
The blessed God,[B] great in knowledge,[A]
prepared and made the rays of the sun.
He who is good formed glory for His name,
surrounding His power with radiant stars.[I]
The leaders of His hosts, the holy ones, exalt the Almighty,[I]
constantly proclaiming God's glory and holiness.[A]

---

to God: "I don't know the prayers. All I know is the letters of the Alef-Beit. Please take the letters and turn them into the right words to reflect what I feel in my heart." The Ba'al Shem Tov said that the boy's prayer not only broke through the gates of heaven, but enabled everyone else's prayers to enter as well.

IYUN TEFILLA • עיון תפילה

מְאוֹרוֹת נָתַן סְבִיבוֹת עֻזּוֹ – *Surrounding His power with radiant stars.* God is hidden behind His creations. On the one hand, one might think this means that He cannot be found. On the other hand, one can also say that if you want to know God, look carefully at all of His creations. As the Rambam (*Yesodei HaTorah* 2:2) says:

> What is the path [a person should take to attain] love and fear of Him? When a person contemplates His wondrous and great deeds and creations and appreciates His infinite wisdom that surpasses all comparison, he will immediately love, praise, and glorify [Him], yearning with tremendous desire to know [God's] great name, as David stated: "My soul thirsts for Hashem, for the living God" [Psalms 42:3].

Seen in this light, the siddur may be understood to mean that astronomy, biology, anatomy and the like can all be used as vehicles for getting to know God better.

When you read about these subjects, do you see them as aspects of human knowledge or as a way to come to a better knowledge of God?

פִּנּוֹת צְבָאָיו קְדוֹשִׁים, רוֹמְמֵי שַׁדַּי – *The leaders of His hosts, the holy ones, exalt the Almighty.* Only the angels can recognize God's attribute of שַׁדַּי. The meaning of this name is found in *Ḥagiga* 12a: "During the Creation of the universe, it was constantly expanding until God demanded that it stop." When we look through telescopes we think the universe is ever expanding, but no earthly creature knows where it stops. For us, it remains a mystery. Look at photos of outer space. You can feel the mystery (Rabbi S. Schwab).

The **ANI TEFILLA** *is on page 113.*

הַמֶּלֶךְ הַמְרוֹמָם לְבַדּוֹ מֵאָז
הַמְשֻׁבָּח וְהַמְפֹאָר וְהַמִּתְנַשֵּׂא מִימוֹת עוֹלָם.
אֱלֹהֵי עוֹלָם
בְּרַחֲמֶיךָ הָרַבִּים רַחֵם עָלֵינוּ
אֲדוֹן עֻזֵּנוּ, צוּר מִשְׂגַּבֵּנוּ
מָגֵן יִשְׁעֵנוּ, מִשְׂגָּב בַּעֲדֵנוּ.
אֵל בָּרוּךְ[ב] גְּדוֹל דֵּעָה[א]
הֵכִין וּפָעַל זָהֳרֵי חַמָּה
טוֹב יָצַר כָּבוֹד לִשְׁמוֹ
מְאוֹרוֹת נָתַן סְבִיבוֹת עֻזּוֹ[ע]
פִּנּוֹת צְבָאָיו קְדוֹשִׁים, רוֹמְמֵי שַׁדַּי[ע]
תָּמִיד מְסַפְּרִים כְּבוֹד אֵל וּקְדֻשָּׁתוֹ.[א]

BIUR TEFILLA • ביאור תפילה

אֵל בָּרוּךְ – *The blessed God.* This is the first instance thus far in the siddur where a prayer is written out as an alphabetical acrostic incorporating all 22 letters of the Hebrew alphabet. It is one of a number of prayers that are constructed this way, including this prayer's parallel "sister" prayer said on Shabbat morning – אֵל אָדוֹן.

Why are certain prayers constructed this way? There is no one correct answer. One possibility comes from the experience that some of us have had of being in a place that was of such overwhelming beauty, a place that filled us with such awe, that we could not adequately describe it. There is a word here for every letter of the alphabet, but these are just representatives for every word in the entire language that we could possibly use to describe the feelings that we have at this moment. It's not only about what the words mean but about how they help us feel.

Alternatively, the blessing grapples with the old question of why did God bring the world into being? The letters of the *Alef-Beit* symbolize the written word of the Torah, the demands of which bring purpose and meaning to our world (Rabbi I. Wohlgemuth).

ANI TEFILLA • אני תפילה

אֵל בָּרוּךְ גְּדוֹל דֵּעָה – *The blessed God, great in knowledge.*

A young illiterate boy came to shul and wanted to pray but had never been taught how to read. And so he simply recited the Alef-Beit over and over again. He then said

Be blessed, LORD our God, for the magnificence of Your handiwork
and for the radiant lights You have made.
May they glorify You, Selah!

תִּתְבָּרַךְ May You be blessed,
our Rock, King and Redeemer, Creator of holy beings.[1]
May Your name be praised for ever,
our King, Creator of the ministering angels,
all of whom stand in the universe's heights,
proclaiming together, in awe, aloud,
the words of the living God, the eternal King.
They are all beloved, all pure, all mighty,
and all perform in awe and reverence the will of their Maker.
▸ All open their mouths in holiness and purity, with song and psalm,
and bless, praise, glorify,
revere, sanctify and declare the sovereignty[A] of – ◂
The name of the great, mighty and awesome God and King,
holy is He.

IYUN TEFILLA · עיון תפילה

בּוֹרֵא קְדוֹשִׁים – *Creator of holy beings.* What goes on in our world of ongoing creation takes place in the upper worlds as well. While focusing on the skies above us, the blessing now shifts from the physical world to the spiritual world, from the sun and the moon and the stars to the angels, the Seraphim and Ophanim. Our knowledge of these angels comes from the prophetic visions of Yishayahu and Yeḥezkel, and therefore our understanding is limited. But the blessing assures us that there is such a world, one which in many ways parallels our own. Alternatively, in Hebrew, the word "angel" and the word for "emissary" are the same, in which case we could say that aspects of nature are themselves the angels/emissaries of Hashem. Thus, the sun and moon and stars are "angels," that is, emissaries and servants of God, who obey His will and sing His praises, as it were, just by the way they function.

When was the last time you listened to their song? Listen to it now if you can.

ANI TEFILLA · אני תפילה

וּמְבָרְכִים וּמְשַׁבְּחִים וּמְפָאֲרִים וּמַעֲרִיצִים וּמַקְדִּישִׁים וּמַמְלִיכִים – *And bless, praise, glorify, revere, sanctify and declare the sovereignty.* There are six verbs here listed in rapid succession. It has been suggested that these reflect the six wings that Yishayahu saw on each one of the angels in his vision.

Close your eyes. What does it sound like?

תִּתְבָּרַךְ יהוה אֱלֹהֵינוּ
עַל שֶׁבַח מַעֲשֵׂה יָדֶיךָ.
וְעַל מְאוֹרֵי אוֹר שֶׁעָשִׂיתָ
יְפָאֲרוּךָ סֶּלָה.

תִּתְבָּרַךְ
צוּרֵנוּ מַלְכֵּנוּ וְגוֹאֲלֵנוּ, בּוֹרֵא קְדוֹשִׁים[ע]
יִשְׁתַּבַּח שִׁמְךָ לָעַד
מַלְכֵּנוּ, יוֹצֵר מְשָׁרְתִים
וַאֲשֶׁר מְשָׁרְתָיו כֻּלָּם עוֹמְדִים בְּרוּם עוֹלָם
וּמַשְׁמִיעִים בְּיִרְאָה יַחַד בְּקוֹל
דִּבְרֵי אֱלֹהִים חַיִּים וּמֶלֶךְ עוֹלָם.
כֻּלָּם אֲהוּבִים, כֻּלָּם בְּרוּרִים, כֻּלָּם גִּבּוֹרִים
וְכֻלָּם עוֹשִׂים בְּאֵימָה וּבְיִרְאָה רְצוֹן קוֹנָם
◂ וְכֻלָּם פּוֹתְחִים אֶת פִּיהֶם בִּקְדֻשָּׁה וּבְטָהֳרָה
בְּשִׁירָה וּבְזִמְרָה
וּמְבָרְכִים וּמְשַׁבְּחִים וּמְפָאֲרִים
וּמַעֲרִיצִים וּמַקְדִּישִׁים וּמַמְלִיכִים[א] ◂
אֶת שֵׁם הָאֵל הַמֶּלֶךְ הַגָּדוֹל, הַגִּבּוֹר וְהַנּוֹרָא
קָדוֹשׁ הוּא.

ANI TEFILLA • אני תפילה

תָּמִיד מְסַפְּרִים כְּבוֹד אֵל וּקְדֻשָּׁתוֹ – *Constantly proclaiming God's glory and holiness.* If life seems humdrum and boring sometimes, it is because of our perception. The world is in constant motion. Nature is constantly in flux. Beauty and the miraculous surround us all of the time. As Keats wrote "The poetry of the earth is never dead." The siddur reminds us to open our eyes.

▸ All accept on themselves, one from another,
the yoke of the kingdom of heaven,
granting permission to one another
to sanctify the One who formed them, in serene spirit,
pure speech and sweet melody.
All, as one, proclaim His holiness,
saying in awe:

All say aloud: Holy, holy, holy[H] is the LORD of hosts; *Is. 6*
the whole world is filled with His glory.

▸ Then the Ophanim and the Holy Ḥayyot, with a roar of noise,
raise themselves toward the Seraphim and,
facing them, give praise, saying:

All say aloud: Blessed is the LORD's glory from His place. *Ezek. 3*

HILKHOT TEFILLA · הלכות תפילה

קָדוֹשׁ, קָדוֹשׁ, קָדוֹשׁ – *Holy, holy, holy.* This section of the prayer is known in halakhic literature as the "sitting *Kedusha*" (קְדֻשָּׁה דִישִׁיבָה) as opposed to the "standing *Kedusha*" (קְדֻשָּׁה דַעֲמִידָה) which is found in *Shemoneh Esreh*. What distinguishes the two is that in this one we do not actually sanctify God's name, otherwise we would not be able to sit down when reciting it, nor would we be able to say it without a *minyan* as normally required in a דָּבָר שֶׁבִּקְדֻשָּׁה (a prayer of such sanctity that it requires a *minyan*); rather, we merely describe the way that the angels praise Him and sanctify His name. The description is one step removed from our own experience.

IYUN TEFILLA · עיון תפילה

קָדוֹשׁ, קָדוֹשׁ, קָדוֹשׁ... בָּרוּךְ כְּבוֹד – *Holy, holy, holy… Blessed is the LORD's glory.* The two primary lines of the *Kedusha* contain a contradiction of sorts. On the one hand, God is distant, unfathomable, beyond anything we can understand or relate to – קָדוֹשׁ, קָדוֹשׁ, קָדוֹשׁ. The distance between infinity and mortality is too huge for us to cross. On the other hand, it says that God is nearby – בָּרוּךְ כְּבוֹד יהוה מִמְּקוֹמוֹ. He is located in a particular place, able to be perceived and praised. His presence thus fills the entire universe and yet He can be found in one place. He is *Kadosh* in a way that we cannot fathom; on the other hand, the whole world is filled with His glory. How can He be far and yet be here? Yet this is precisely the relationship we have with Him. Like a parent who is far away; we can feel very close despite the distance. And we can send messages and thereby maintain our relationship even though

This **IYUN TEFILLA** *continues on page 117.*

‹ וְכֻלָּם מְקַבְּלִים עֲלֵיהֶם עֹל מַלְכוּת שָׁמַיִם זֶה מִזֶּה[ב]
וְנוֹתְנִים רְשׁוּת זֶה לָזֶה[ע]
לְהַקְדִּישׁ לְיוֹצְרָם בְּנַחַת רוּחַ
בְּשָׂפָה בְרוּרָה וּבִנְעִימָה
קְדֻשָּׁה כֻּלָּם כְּאֶחָד
עוֹנִים וְאוֹמְרִים בְּיִרְאָה

ישעיה ו *All say aloud* קָדוֹשׁ, קָדוֹשׁ, קָדוֹשׁ[ה] יהוה צְבָאוֹת
מְלֹא כָל־הָאָרֶץ כְּבוֹדוֹ:

‹ וְהָאוֹפַנִּים וְחַיּוֹת הַקֹּדֶשׁ בְּרַעַשׁ גָּדוֹל מִתְנַשְּׂאִים לְעֻמַּת שְׂרָפִים
לְעֻמָּתָם מְשַׁבְּחִים וְאוֹמְרִים

יחזקאל ג *All say aloud* בָּרוּךְ כְּבוֹד־יהוה מִמְּקוֹמוֹ:[ע]

BIUR TEFILLA • ביאור תפילה

וְכֻלָּם מְקַבְּלִים עֲלֵיהֶם עֹל מַלְכוּת שָׁמַיִם זֶה מִזֶּה – *All accept on themselves, one from another, the yoke of the kingdom of heaven.* Just as there is a unity and balance in the physical world, so too is there unity in the spiritual world. Here the emissaries gather together, as it were, to take upon themselves the yoke of heaven, קַבָּלַת עֹל מַלְכוּת שָׁמַיִם, just as we are about to do in the first paragraph of the *Shema*. And they do so as a prelude to sanctifying God's name in the *Kedusha*, just as we will do in the *Shemoneh Esreh*. In our collective praise, the upper and lower worlds, the physical and the spiritual, will be united.

IYUN TEFILLA • עיון תפילה

וְנוֹתְנִים רְשׁוּת זֶה לָזֶה – *Granting permission to one another.* "They give permission to one another." In the spiritual world there is no place for selfishness. At first, they defer to one another, "You go first." "No, it's really ok, you go first." But in the end, they join together as one, כְּאֶחָד, in keeping with the theme of the *Shema* that we are about to say. The Midrash says that herein lies a challenge to all of us – to get rid of our selfishness in all aspects of life, both physical and spiritual.

ANI TEFILLA • אני תפילה

From the angels one learns that spirituality can be found in acknowledging the holiness of the other person. For in the other person I recognize that all of us are created in the image of Hashem. As one anonymous person wrote:

"I searched for God but could not find Thee. I searched for myself but could not find me. I searched for the other and there I found all three."

לָאֵל To the blessed[B] God they offer melodies.
To the King, living and eternal God,
they say psalms and proclaim praises.
For it is He alone
who does mighty deeds
and creates new things,
who is Master of battles,
and sows righteousness,
who makes salvation grow
and creates cures,
who is revered in praises,
LORD of wonders,
who in His goodness,
continually renews the work of creation,
day after day,
as it is said:
"[Praise] Him who made the great lights, *Ps. 136*
for His love endures for ever."
▸ May You make a new light shine over Zion,[B]
and may we all soon be worthy of its light.
Blessed are You, LORD,
who forms the radiant lights.

BIUR TEFILLA · ביאור תפילה

אוֹר חָדָשׁ עַל צִיּוֹן תָּאִיר – *May You make a new light shine over Zion.* It is not clear what this "new light" is. In *Bereshit* it says that God created light before He created the luminaries. According to *Ḥazal*, this therefore refers not to the light that we know but to one that was subsequently hidden from man for some future time. Here we pray for its restoration. Others suggest that it is a metaphoric light, the light of redemption or the restoration of the entire Jewish people to the Land.

ANI TEFILLA · אני תפילה

It is told that Rabbi Menachem Mendel Morgenstern, known as the Kotzker Rebbe, once asked a group of scholars "Where does God live?" They laughed and replied, "Doesn't it say that the whole world is filled with His glory!" But the Kotzker Rebbe then responded to his own question:

"God lives wherever man decides to let Him in."

לְאֵל בָּרוּךְ נְעִימוֹת יִתֵּנוּ, לְמֶלֶךְ אֵל חַי וְקַיָּם
זְמִירוֹת יֹאמֵרוּ וְתִשְׁבָּחוֹת יַשְׁמִיעוּ
כִּי הוּא לְבַדּוֹ
פּוֹעֵל גְּבוּרוֹת, עוֹשֶׂה חֲדָשׁוֹת
בַּעַל מִלְחָמוֹת, זוֹרֵעַ צְדָקוֹת
מַצְמִיחַ יְשׁוּעוֹת, בּוֹרֵא רְפוּאוֹת
נוֹרָא תְהִלּוֹת, אֲדוֹן הַנִּפְלָאוֹת
הַמְחַדֵּשׁ בְּטוּבוֹ בְּכָל יוֹם תָּמִיד מַעֲשֵׂה בְרֵאשִׁית
כָּאָמוּר
לְעֹשֵׂה אוֹרִים גְּדֹלִים, כִּי לְעוֹלָם חַסְדּוֹ: תהלים קלו
‹ אוֹר חָדָשׁ עַל צִיּוֹן תָּאִיר וְנִזְכֶּה כֻלָּנוּ מְהֵרָה לְאוֹרוֹ.
בָּרוּךְ אַתָּה יהוה, יוֹצֵר הַמְּאוֹרוֹת.

---

sometimes the gap which separates seems huge.

Alternatively, there are times when belief is very difficult, when God cannot be seen. Yet at other times, belief is easy and natural, times when God feels close. Sometimes we feel one way, sometimes we feel the other. Both are natural.

BIUR TEFILLA · ביאור תפילה

לְאֵל בָּרוּךְ – *To the blessed.* As the blessing draws to a close, we return to the original theme. The angels sing about the wonderful things that God continues to do for the entire universe, including us, through His involvement in the ongoing creation of the world.

Each of the expressions can be understood to reflect some aspect of His role in nature or in human affairs. For example:

פּוֹעֵל גְּבוּרוֹת, *He does mighty deeds* – He is the force behind hurricanes and man's ability to conquer space.

עוֹשֶׂה חֲדָשׁוֹת, *He creates new things* – from the cotton gin to the microchip.

בַּעַל מִלְחָמוֹת, *He is Master of battles* – the force behind successful human military strategy, victory and defeat.

אֲדוֹן הַנִּפְלָאוֹת, *He is Lord of wonders* – from the Seven Wonders of the World to the birth of a baby.

Look around you right now. Where can His hand be seen?

אַהֲבָה You have loved us with great love,[B] Lord our God,
and with surpassing compassion
have You had compassion on us.[I]
Our Father, our King,
for the sake of our ancestors who trusted in You,
and to whom You taught the laws of life,
be gracious also to us and teach us.
Our Father, compassionate Father,
ever compassionate,
have compassion on us.
Instill in our hearts
the desire to understand[B] and discern,
to listen, learn and teach,
to observe, perform and fulfill
all the teachings of Your Torah in love.

IYUN TEFILLA • עיון תפילה

חֶמְלָה גְדוֹלָה וִיתֵרָה חָמַלְתָּ עָלֵינוּ – *And with surpassing compassion have You had compassion on us.* The only person in the Torah who is described as having the kind of compassion meant by חֶמְלָה was the daughter of Pharaoh (*Shemot* 2:6), who had pity on the baby she found. Hashem, You have had that kind of compassion for us.

BIUR TEFILLA • ביאור תפילה

לְהָבִין – *understanding* the difficult theoretical issues of Torah study.

וּלְהַשְׂכִּיל – *understanding* in order to be able to carry out in practice what we learn in theory.

לִשְׁמֹעַ – *listening* to the Rabbis as the qualified interpreters of Torah tradition.

לִלְמֹד – we have to review our *learning* until it becomes part of our Torah knowledge.

וּלְלַמֵּד – *teaching/sharing our knowledge* with others.

לִשְׁמֹר – *guarding/reviewing* our knowledge lest we forget it.

וְלַעֲשׂוֹת – *performing/carrying out* the commandments.

וּלְקַיֵּם – *fulfilling* the commandments in a meaningful way. (Rabbi I. Wohlgemuth)

אַהֲבָה רַבָּה[ב] אֲהַבְתָּנוּ, יהוה אֱלֹהֵינוּ
חֶמְלָה גְדוֹלָה וִיתֵרָה חָמַלְתָּ עָלֵינוּ.[ע]
אָבִינוּ מַלְכֵּנוּ
בַּעֲבוּר אֲבוֹתֵינוּ שֶׁבָּטְחוּ בְךָ
וַתְּלַמְּדֵם חֻקֵּי חַיִּים
כֵּן תְּחָנֵּנוּ וּתְלַמְּדֵנוּ.
אָבִינוּ, הָאָב הָרַחֲמָן, הַמְרַחֵם
רַחֵם עָלֵינוּ
וְתֵן בְּלִבֵּנוּ לְהָבִין[ב] וּלְהַשְׂכִּיל
לִשְׁמֹעַ, לִלְמֹד וּלְלַמֵּד
לִשְׁמֹר וְלַעֲשׂוֹת, וּלְקַיֵּם[ב]
אֶת כָּל דִּבְרֵי תַלְמוּד תּוֹרָתֶךָ בְּאַהֲבָה.

BIUR TEFILLA • ביאור תפילה

אַהֲבָה רַבָּה – *Great love.* The first blessing, *Yotzer Or*, focused on Hashem's role as Creator. Its theme was quite universalistic. This second blessing, however, is more particularistic, moving us one step closer to focusing on our special relationship with Hashem. That unique relationship is exemplified by the Torah, which was given to us as a gift. Just as a groom presents his bride with a ring under the *ḥuppa*, so, too, Hashem gave us the Torah at Sinai. This relationship also carries with it certain responsibilities, including the requirement to declare our belief in Him as the One God, which we will do shortly in the *Shema*.

אַהֲבָה רַבָּה – *Great love.* רַבָּה in this context could mean not only "great" but also "constantly increasing" (Rabbi S. Schwab). His love is manifest in the fact that He helped expand the understanding of Torah over time. Torah has been at the center of Jewish intellectual history and Jewish identity for millennia. In each generation, scholars and lay people alike have expanded and enhanced our appreciation of its depth, beauty, and relevance to contemporary life. And the older we get, the more mature is our ability to understand and to appreciate what a gift it is. Appreciate Torah as our families did in previous generations.

Enlighten our eyes in Your Torah[B]
and let our hearts cling to Your commandments.[B]
Unite our hearts to love and revere Your name,[B]
so that we may never be ashamed.
And because we have trusted
in Your holy, great and revered name,
may we be glad and rejoice in Your salvation.

At this point, gather the four tzitziot of the tallit, holding them in the left hand.

Bring us back in peace from the four quarters of the earth
and lead us upright to our land.
▸ For You are a God who performs acts of salvation,
and You chose us from all peoples and tongues,
bringing us close to Your great name for ever in truth,
that we may thank You
and proclaim Your oneness in love.
Blessed are You, Lord,
who chooses His people Israel in love.

INTRODUCTION TO KERIAT SHEMA

In the first blessing, *Yotzer Or*, we focused on God as Creator; in the second it was the God of Israel. In the first, God is distant; in the second He is close. In the first, our relationship is marked by awe and wonder, or יִרְאָה; in the second it is marked by love, אַהֲבָה. Having experienced both emotions, we are now ready to speak about the Unity of God. (Rabbi M. Angel)

Contrary to popular belief, the *Shema* is not a prayer, as is commonly understood, as much as it is a declaration. That's why it is not called תְּפִלַּת שְׁמַע but rather קְרִיאַת שְׁמַע, for it is similar to reading a proclamation. Think of it a little like a national anthem. We sing it as much for ourselves as for anyone else. Rabbi Yitzḥak Arama in *Akedat Yitzḥak* (58:1) explains that it is a description of the roots of faith upon which prayer and belief are built. If in much of the rest of prayer man talks to God, here God talks to man. "Listen Israel" to what He has to say.

The first paragraph is about קַבָּלַת עֹל מַלְכוּת שָׁמַיִם – accepting God as the ultimate ruler in one's life.

The second paragraph is about קַבָּלַת עֹל מִצְוֹת – accepting the responsibility of doing mitzvot.

The first paragraph focuses on love.

The second paragraph focuses on awe and the concept of reward and punishment.

The first paragraph is in the singular.

The second paragraph is in the plural.

The path to accepting God in one's life is through love not fear.

This **INTRODUCTION** *continues on page 123.*

וְהָאֵר עֵינֵינוּ בְּתוֹרָתֶךָ, וְדַבֵּק לִבֵּנוּ בְּמִצְוֹתֶיךָ
וְיַחֵד לְבָבֵנוּ לְאַהֲבָה וּלְיִרְאָה אֶת שְׁמֶךָ
וְלֹא נֵבוֹשׁ לְעוֹלָם וָעֶד.
כִּי בְשֵׁם קָדְשְׁךָ הַגָּדוֹל וְהַנּוֹרָא בָּטָחְנוּ
נָגִילָה וְנִשְׂמְחָה בִּישׁוּעָתֶךָ.

At this point, gather the four ציציות *of the* טלית*, holding them in the left hand.*

וַהֲבִיאֵנוּ לְשָׁלוֹם מֵאַרְבַּע כַּנְפוֹת הָאָרֶץ
וְתוֹלִיכֵנוּ קוֹמְמִיּוּת לְאַרְצֵנוּ.
› כִּי אֵל פּוֹעֵל יְשׁוּעוֹת אָתָּה
וּבָנוּ בָחַרְתָּ מִכָּל עַם וְלָשׁוֹן
וְקֵרַבְתָּנוּ לְשִׁמְךָ הַגָּדוֹל סֶלָה, בֶּאֱמֶת
לְהוֹדוֹת לְךָ וּלְיַחֶדְךָ בְּאַהֲבָה.
בָּרוּךְ אַתָּה יהוה, הַבּוֹחֵר בְּעַמּוֹ יִשְׂרָאֵל בְּאַהֲבָה.

BIUR TEFILLA • ביאור תפילה

וְהָאֵר עֵינֵינוּ בְּתוֹרָתֶךָ – *Enlighten our eyes in Your Torah.*
We declare our willingness to learn the Torah for which you chose us. The two blessings of *Keriat Shema* are thus connected: the first blessing spoke of the lights of creation which help our physical lives. Here we speak about the enlightenment of Torah, a key to our spiritual lives.

וְדַבֵּק לִבֵּנוּ בְּמִצְוֹתֶיךָ – *And let our hearts cling to Your commandments.* We not only want to learn Torah but to actualize it in our lives through the mitzvot.

וְיַחֵד לְבָבֵנוּ לְאַהֲבָה וּלְיִרְאָה אֶת שְׁמֶךָ – *Unite our hearts to love and revere Your name.* And through Torah and mitzvot we wish to unify our hearts in both love and awe. Chosenness, Torah, mitzvot, love, awe, unity, the Land – these are all themes that we will further describe in the *Shema*.

IYUN TEFILLA • עיון תפילה

The Maggid of Mezeritch said that the *Shema* is not a command to love God, nor is it a way to manipulate yourself into thinking you do. Rather it is a call for mindfulness. Be mindful. Hashem is our God. If you get that, says the Maggid, then *ve'ahavta* will be an inevitable result.

The Shema must be said with intense concentration. In the first paragraph one should accept, with love, the sovereignty of God; in the second, the mitzvot as the will of God. The end of the third paragraph constitutes fulfillment of the mitzva to remember, morning and evening, the exodus from Egypt. See laws 71–80.

When not praying with a minyan, say:

God, faithful King!

The following verse should be said aloud, while covering the eyes with the right hand:

Listen, Israel: the LORD is our God, the LORD is One.

Deut. 6

Quietly: Blessed be the name of His glorious kingdom for ever and all time.

BIUR TEFILLA • ביאור תפילה

שְׁמַע יִשְׂרָאֵל – *Listen, Israel.*
"Know" (Rabbi Sa'adia Gaon)
"Believe and accept" (*Hovot HaLevavot, ot* 5)
"Hear and understand" (Abudarham, *ot* 17)
"Listen, Israel" (Rabbi J. Sacks)
Which one do you need to emphasize most today?

IYUN TEFILLA • עיון תפילה

The covering of one's eyes during the recitation of the sentence beginning *Shema Yisrael* is to indicate our exclusion of every possible argument for not accepting *HaKadosh Barukh Hu* – and there are thousands of them. (Rabbi S. Schwab)

ANI TEFILLA • אני תפילה

שְׁמַע יִשְׂרָאֵל – *Listen, Israel.*
Rabbi Eliezer Silver, a leader of American Orthodox Jewry in the twentieth century, was president of the Va'ad Hatzala or the Rescue Committee for Jews who survived the Shoah. In that capacity he traveled in post-war Europe looking for Jewish children who had ended up in non-Jewish orphanages, most often sponsored by the Church. In one such case he came to an orphanage in Alsace Lorraine asking if there were Jewish children there. He was told that there were none or that they could not be identified as such; their origins were unknown and they themselves had forgotten where they were from. Rabbi Silver insisted that he nevertheless be permitted to see the children and he was finally allowed to do so for a few moments before their bedtime. He walked into a room filled with beds of children preparing to go to sleep. He called out "Shema Yisrael Hashem Elokeinu Hashem Ehad" and immediately a young child cried out "Mommy!" Soon other voices joined in as children began to come forward crying out for their mothers. "These children are mine," he said to the priest. "I will take them now."

The שמע must be said with intense concentration. In the first paragraph one should accept, with love, the sovereignty of God; in the second, the מצוות as the will of God. The end of the third paragraph constitutes fulfillment of the מצווה to remember, morning and evening, the exodus from Egypt. See laws 71–80.

When not praying with a מנין, say:

אֵל מֶלֶךְ נֶאֱמָן

The following verse should be said aloud, while covering the eyes[ע] with the right hand:

שְׁמַע יִשְׂרָאֵל, יְהוָה אֱלֹהֵינוּ, יְהוָה ׀ אֶחָד׃ דברים ו

Quietly בָּרוּךְ שֵׁם כְּבוֹד מַלְכוּתוֹ לְעוֹלָם וָעֶד.

The path to accepting the mitzvot is through reward and punishment.

WHY THESE DIFFERENCES?

Love of God is a matter for the individual who strives to attain it through self-perfection, whilst the acceptance of the yoke of the mitzvot and their fulfillment is only conceivable in human society. Robinson Crusoe living on his desert island isolated from human society could indeed have implemented "you should love Hashem your God," but he could not have fulfilled "if you [plural] listen to my commandments" which, for the most part, relate to the life of man amidst society and his bonds with his family, friends, the state, and the human race. (Nechama Leibowitz)

The third paragraph contains the mitzva to recall the exodus from Egypt, another basic tenet of Jewish life, without which the Jewish people would have disappeared from the stage of history. It also contains a reference to *tzitzit*, as well as a reminder that our eyes and our hearts can sometimes mislead us.

In sum, it has been suggested that *Birkhot HaShaḥar* are about Hashem's providence over our individual lives, *Pesukei DeZimra* are about Hashem's mastery over the world, and *Keriat Shema* is about our relationship with the God of Israel. The first paragraph of the *Shema* focuses on Hashem as King – similar to the theme of the first blessing of *Birkhot Keriat Shema;* the second paragraph of the *Shema* speaks of Hashem's unique relationship with the Jewish people – similar to the theme of the second blessing of *Birkhot Keriat Shema*. The third paragraph speaks to Hashem's involvement in history, just like the third blessing of *Birkhot Keriat Shema*.

Step by step we move closer to our personal encounter with Hashem in the *Shemoneh Esreh* where all of these themes, and more, will come together. We are almost there.

Touch the hand-tefillin at ° and the head-tefillin at °°.

וְאָהַבְתָּ Love[I] the LORD your God with all your heart, with all your soul, and with all your might.[I] These words which I command you today shall be on your heart. Teach them repeatedly to your children, speaking of them when you sit at home and when you travel on the way, when you lie down and when you rise. °Bind them as a sign on your hand, and °°they shall be an emblem between your eyes. Write them on the doorposts of your house and gates. *Deut. 6*

Touch the hand-tefillin at ° and the head-tefillin at °°.

וְהָיָה If you indeed heed My commandments with which I charge you today, to love the LORD your God and worship Him with all your heart[B] and with all your soul, I will give rain in your land in its season, the early and late rain; and you shall gather in your grain, wine and oil. I will give grass in your field for your cattle, and you shall eat and be satisfied. Be careful lest your heart be tempted and you go astray and worship other gods, bowing down to them. Then the LORD's anger will flare against you and He will close the heavens so that there will be no rain. The land will not yield its crops, and you will perish swiftly from the good land that the LORD is giving you. Therefore, set these, My words, on your heart and soul. °Bind them as a sign on your hand, °°and they shall be an emblem between your eyes. Teach them to your children, speaking of them *Deut. 11*

---

phrase as, "You shall love Hashem your God with all of your *very-muchness*." This would refer to the extra talents or abilities which *HaKadosh Barukh Hu* has given a person, מְאֹד, more than that which he has given to other people. Examples would be utilizing one's great intelligence or musical or artistic ability, or building skills, to demonstrate his love for *HaKadosh Barukh Hu*. (Rabbi S. Schwab)

Which part of my מְאֹד can I better use today to enhance my spirituality?

IYUN TEFILLA • עיון תפילה

וּלְעָבְדוֹ, בְּכָל לְבַבְכֶם – *And worship Him with all your heart.*

What is service of the heart? *Tefilla*. (*Ta'anit* 2a)

Touch the תפילין של יד *at* ° *and the* תפילין של ראש *at* °°.

דברים ו וְאָהַבְתָּ[ע] אֵת יהוה אֱלֹהֶיךָ, בְּכָל־לְבָבְךָ וּבְכָל־נַפְשְׁךָ וּבְכָל־
מְאֹדֶךָ:[ע] וְהָיוּ הַדְּבָרִים הָאֵלֶּה, אֲשֶׁר אָנֹכִי מְצַוְּךָ הַיּוֹם, עַל־
לְבָבֶךָ: וְשִׁנַּנְתָּם לְבָנֶיךָ וְדִבַּרְתָּ בָּם, בְּשִׁבְתְּךָ בְּבֵיתֶךָ וּבְלֶכְתְּךָ
בַדֶּרֶךְ, וּבְשָׁכְבְּךָ וּבְקוּמֶךָ: °וּקְשַׁרְתָּם לְאוֹת עַל־יָדֶךָ °°וְהָיוּ
לְטֹטָפֹת בֵּין עֵינֶיךָ: וּכְתַבְתָּם עַל־מְזֻזוֹת בֵּיתֶךָ וּבִשְׁעָרֶיךָ:

Touch the תפילין של יד *at* ° *and the* תפילין של ראש *at* °°.

דברים יא וְהָיָה אִם־שָׁמֹעַ תִּשְׁמְעוּ אֶל־מִצְוֹתַי אֲשֶׁר אָנֹכִי מְצַוֶּה אֶתְכֶם
הַיּוֹם, לְאַהֲבָה אֶת־יהוה אֱלֹהֵיכֶם וּלְעָבְדוֹ, בְּכָל־לְבַבְכֶם[ב] וּבְכָל־
נַפְשְׁכֶם: וְנָתַתִּי מְטַר־אַרְצְכֶם בְּעִתּוֹ, יוֹרֶה וּמַלְקוֹשׁ, וְאָסַפְתָּ
דְגָנֶךָ וְתִירֹשְׁךָ וְיִצְהָרֶךָ: וְנָתַתִּי עֵשֶׂב בְּשָׂדְךָ לִבְהֶמְתֶּךָ, וְאָכַלְתָּ
וְשָׂבָעְתָּ: הִשָּׁמְרוּ לָכֶם פֶּן־יִפְתֶּה לְבַבְכֶם, וְסַרְתֶּם וַעֲבַדְתֶּם
אֱלֹהִים אֲחֵרִים וְהִשְׁתַּחֲוִיתֶם לָהֶם: וְחָרָה אַף־יהוה בָּכֶם, וְעָצַר
אֶת־הַשָּׁמַיִם וְלֹא־יִהְיֶה מָטָר, וְהָאֲדָמָה לֹא תִתֵּן אֶת־יְבוּלָהּ,
וַאֲבַדְתֶּם מְהֵרָה מֵעַל הָאָרֶץ הַטֹּבָה אֲשֶׁר יהוה נֹתֵן לָכֶם:
וְשַׂמְתֶּם אֶת־דְּבָרַי אֵלֶּה עַל־לְבַבְכֶם וְעַל־נַפְשְׁכֶם, °וּקְשַׁרְתֶּם
אֹתָם לְאוֹת עַל־יֶדְכֶם, °°וְהָיוּ לְטוֹטָפֹת בֵּין עֵינֵיכֶם: וְלִמַּדְתֶּם

IYUN TEFILLA · עיון תפילה

וְאָהַבְתָּ – *Love.* How does one come to love God? By studying His Torah and by studying nature, for through His creations, one comes to better understand and know the Creator.

And you should love Hashem. The Kotzker rebbe once called over one of his followers whom he heard reciting the Shma. Tell me the truth, he said, when you said v'ahavta, is it really Hashem you love or yourself? When someone says "I love fish" it's not really the fish he loves, but himself! So too here, do you love Hashem or do you love yourself? (*Sneh Bo'er BeKotzk p. 110*)

מְאֹדֶךָ – *Your might.* The phrase literally means "very much." I would translate the

when you sit at home and when you travel on the way, when you lie down and when you rise. Write them on the doorposts of your house and gates, so that you and your children may live long in the land that the LORD swore to your ancestors to give them, for as long as the heavens are above the earth.

Hold the tzitziot in the right hand also (some transfer to the right hand), kissing them at °.

וַיֹּאמֶר The LORD spoke to Moses, saying: Speak to the Israelites and tell them to make °tassels on the corners of their garments for all generations. They shall attach to the °tassel at each corner a thread of blue. This shall be your °tassel, and you shall see it and remember all of the LORD's commandments and keep them, not straying after your heart and after your eyes,[A] following your own sinful desires. Thus you will be reminded to keep all My commandments, and be holy to your God. I am the LORD your God, who brought you out of the land of Egypt[I] to be your God. I am the LORD your God. *Num. 15*

°True[B] –

The Leader repeats:

▸ The LORD your God is true –

BIUR TEFILLA • ביאור תפילה

אֱמֶת – *True.* We now begin the third and final *berakha* before the *Shemoneh Esreh*, called *Birkat Geula*, referring to our being freed from Egypt. The last paragraph of the *Shema* served as an introduction to this theme in its declaration that God took us out of Egypt in order to be His people. The blessing here conveys the point that it wasn't just that He gave us our freedom at that one point in history, but, like a parent, He continued to watch over us and protect us. This relationship is highlighted by the subsequent threat at *Yam Suf* and the destruction of our enemies in light of overwhelming odds, a phenomenon that has repeated itself numerous times throughout our history. Here we therefore emphasize not the God of Creation (*Yotzer or*), or the God of Sinai (*Ahava raba*), but the God of history who remains a powerful force in our personal and collective lives.

אֹתָם אֶת־בְּנֵיכֶם לְדַבֵּר בָּם, בְּשִׁבְתְּךָ בְּבֵיתֶךָ וּבְלֶכְתְּךָ בַדֶּרֶךְ,
וּבְשָׁכְבְּךָ וּבְקוּמֶךָ: וּכְתַבְתָּם עַל־מְזוּזוֹת בֵּיתֶךָ וּבִשְׁעָרֶיךָ: לְמַעַן
יִרְבּוּ יְמֵיכֶם וִימֵי בְנֵיכֶם עַל הָאֲדָמָה אֲשֶׁר נִשְׁבַּע יהוה לַאֲבֹתֵיכֶם
לָתֵת לָהֶם, כִּימֵי הַשָּׁמַיִם עַל־הָאָרֶץ:

Hold the ציציות *tin the right hand also (some transfer to the right hand), kissing them at °.*

וַיֹּאמֶר יהוה אֶל־מֹשֶׁה לֵּאמֹר: דַּבֵּר אֶל־בְּנֵי יִשְׂרָאֵל וְאָמַרְתָּ במדבר טו
אֲלֵהֶם, וְעָשׂוּ לָהֶם °צִיצִת עַל־כַּנְפֵי בִגְדֵיהֶם לְדֹרֹתָם, וְנָתְנוּ °עַל־
צִיצִת הַכָּנָף פְּתִיל תְּכֵלֶת: וְהָיָה לָכֶם °לְצִיצִת, וּרְאִיתֶם אֹתוֹ
וּזְכַרְתֶּם אֶת־כָּל־מִצְוֹת יהוה וַעֲשִׂיתֶם אֹתָם, וְלֹא תָתֻרוּ אַחֲרֵי
לְבַבְכֶם[א] וְאַחֲרֵי עֵינֵיכֶם, אֲשֶׁר־אַתֶּם זֹנִים אַחֲרֵיהֶם: לְמַעַן תִּזְכְּרוּ
וַעֲשִׂיתֶם אֶת־כָּל־מִצְוֹתָי, וִהְיִיתֶם קְדֹשִׁים לֵאלֹהֵיכֶם: אֲנִי יהוה
אֱלֹהֵיכֶם, אֲשֶׁר הוֹצֵאתִי אֶתְכֶם מֵאֶרֶץ מִצְרַיִם,[ע] לִהְיוֹת לָכֶם
לֵאלֹהִים, אֲנִי יהוה אֱלֹהֵיכֶם:

°אֱמֶת[ב]

The שליח ציבור *repeats:*

› יהוה אֱלֹהֵיכֶם אֱמֶת

ANI TEFILLA • אני תפילה

וְלֹא תָתוּרוּ אַחֲרֵי לְבַבְכֶם – *Not straying after your heart and after your eyes.* "You should not wander after your hearts and your eyes."

Do your eyes follow your heart or do you let your heart follow your eyes?

IYUN TEFILLA • עיון תפילה

אֲנִי יהוה אֱלֹהֵיכֶם, אֲשֶׁר הוֹצֵאתִי אֶתְכֶם מֵאֶרֶץ מִצְרַיִם – *I am the Lord your God, who brought you out of the land of Egypt.* In an age when might triumphed over right, the Torah records one of the great turning points in the human story, when the Creator of heaven and earth intervened in defense of the powerless. (Rabbi J. Sacks)

וְיַצִּיב And firm, established and enduring, right, faithful,
beloved, cherished, delightful, pleasant,
awesome, mighty, perfect, accepted,
good and beautiful[I]
is this faith[B] for us for ever.
True is the eternal God, our King,
Rock of Jacob, Shield of our salvation.
He exists and His name exists
through all generations.
His throne is established,
His kingship and faithfulness endure for ever.

At °, kiss the tzitziot and release them.

His words live and persist,
faithful and desirable
°for ever and all time.
▸ So they were for our ancestors, so they are for us,
and so they will be for our children
and all our generations
and for all future generations
of the seed of Israel, Your servants. ◂

---

are about to have a private audience with Him. Imagine yourself 15 steps away.

Alternatively, it has been suggested that including the word אֱמֶת there are 16 adjectives corresponding to the 16 verses from *Shema* to the end of the second paragraph. We declare each one of those verses to be true (*Etz Yosef*).

BIUR TEFILLA • ביאור תפילה

הַדָּבָר הַזֶּה – *Is this faith.* There are numerous adjectives added here, all of which describe "הַדָּבָר הַזֶּה." What is "this thing?" Most likely it is a reference to the final theme we mentioned in the *Shema*, namely, we hereby reaffirm our belief in the fact that "I am Hashem your God who took you out of Egypt." It is thus a reference to our belief in the historical truth of the exodus (*Tosafot, Berakhot* 12a). Alternatively, there are those who say it is a reference to our belief in Hashem, that it was He who took us out (*Emek Berakha*).

וְיַצִּיב, וְנָכוֹן וְקַיָּם, וְיָשָׁר וְנֶאֱמָן
וְאָהוּב וְחָבִיב, וְנֶחְמָד וְנָעִים
וְנוֹרָא וְאַדִּיר, וּמְתֻקָּן וּמְקֻבָּל
וְטוֹב וְיָפֶה[ע]
הַדָּבָר הַזֶּה[ב] עָלֵינוּ לְעוֹלָם וָעֶד.
אֱמֶת אֱלֹהֵי עוֹלָם מַלְכֵּנוּ
צוּר יַעֲקֹב מָגֵן יִשְׁעֵנוּ
לְדוֹר וָדוֹר הוּא קַיָּם וּשְׁמוֹ קַיָּם
וְכִסְאוֹ נָכוֹן
וּמַלְכוּתוֹ וֶאֱמוּנָתוֹ לָעַד קַיָּמֶת.

At °, kiss the ציציות *and release them.*

וּדְבָרָיו חָיִים וְקַיָּמִים, נֶאֱמָנִים וְנֶחֱמָדִים
°לָעַד וּלְעוֹלְמֵי עוֹלָמִים
◂ עַל אֲבוֹתֵינוּ וְעָלֵינוּ
עַל בָּנֵינוּ וְעַל דּוֹרוֹתֵינוּ
וְעַל כָּל דּוֹרוֹת זֶרַע יִשְׂרָאֵל עֲבָדֶיךָ. ◂

IYUN TEFILLA · עיון תפילה

There are 15 adjectives here connected with one another by the conjunction "and," thus indicating that they are intended to form a single unit. This 15 is reminiscent of the 15 chapters of *Tehillim* composed by King David which begin with the phrase **שִׁיר הַמַּעֲלוֹת** (song of *ascents*), which in turn are reminiscent of the 15 steps in the *Beit HaMikdash* leading from the outer courtyard to the inner courtyard, as well as the 15 **מַעֲלוֹת טוֹבוֹת** (rising levels of favors) which Hashem did for us during and after the exodus mentioned in *Dayeinu* in the Haggada (Abudarham). These allusions remind us that we are moving ever closer to the encounter with Hashem in the *Shemoneh Esreh*.

Imagine yourself at the bottom of a long staircase or at the end of a long hallway leading up to the office of the King. You

For the early and the later generations
this faith has proved good and enduring for ever –
True and faithful, an irrevocable law.

True You are the LORD: our God and God of our ancestors,
▸ our King and King of our ancestors,
our Redeemer and Redeemer of our ancestors,
our Maker,
Rock of our salvation,
our Deliverer and Rescuer:
this has ever been Your name.
There is no God but You.

עֶזְרַת You have always been the help of our ancestors,
Shield and Savior of their children after them
in every generation.
Your dwelling is in the heights of the universe,
and Your judgments and righteousness
reach to the ends of the earth.
Happy is the one who obeys Your commandments
and takes to heart Your teaching and Your word.
True You are the Master of Your people
and a mighty King who pleads their cause.
True You are the first and You are the last.
Besides You, we have no king,
redeemer or savior.

---

knew them all to be true because they saw "Truth" when God revealed Himself to them. We approach faith based upon their experiences which they handed down to us. But we can also have our own absolute faith that the Torah is true, for it has proven itself as the foundation of the laws of civilization, from one generation to the next, and it will never disappear.

עַל הָרִאשׁוֹנִים וְעַל הָאַחֲרוֹנִים [ע]
דָּבָר טוֹב וְקַיָּם לְעוֹלָם וָעֶד
אֱמֶת וֶאֱמוּנָה, חֹק וְלֹא יַעֲבֹר.
אֱמֶת שָׁאַתָּה הוּא יהוה אֱלֹהֵינוּ וֵאלֹהֵי אֲבוֹתֵינוּ
› מַלְכֵּנוּ מֶלֶךְ אֲבוֹתֵינוּ
גּוֹאֲלֵנוּ גּוֹאֵל אֲבוֹתֵינוּ
יוֹצְרֵנוּ צוּר יְשׁוּעָתֵנוּ
פּוֹדֵנוּ וּמַצִּילֵנוּ מֵעוֹלָם שְׁמֶךָ
אֵין אֱלֹהִים זוּלָתֶךָ.

עֶזְרַת אֲבוֹתֵינוּ אַתָּה הוּא מֵעוֹלָם
מָגֵן וּמוֹשִׁיעַ לִבְנֵיהֶם אַחֲרֵיהֶם בְּכָל דּוֹר וָדוֹר.
בְּרוּם עוֹלָם מוֹשָׁבֶךָ
וּמִשְׁפָּטֶיךָ וְצִדְקָתְךָ עַד אַפְסֵי אָרֶץ.
אַשְׁרֵי אִישׁ שֶׁיִּשְׁמַע לְמִצְוֹתֶיךָ
וְתוֹרָתְךָ וּדְבָרְךָ יָשִׂים עַל לִבּוֹ.
אֱמֶת אַתָּה הוּא אָדוֹן לְעַמֶּךָ
וּמֶלֶךְ גִּבּוֹר לָרִיב רִיבָם.
אֱמֶת אַתָּה הוּא רִאשׁוֹן וְאַתָּה הוּא אַחֲרוֹן
וּמִבַּלְעָדֶיךָ אֵין לָנוּ מֶלֶךְ גּוֹאֵל וּמוֹשִׁיעַ.

IYUN TEFILLA • עיון תפילה

עַל הָרִאשׁוֹנִים וְעַל הָאַחֲרוֹנִים – *For the early and the later generations.* There are some mitzvot in the Torah that make sense to us, and others that do not. Our ancestors

From Egypt You redeemed us,[B] LORD our God,
and from the slave-house You delivered us.
All their firstborn You killed,
but Your firstborn You redeemed.
You split the Sea of Reeds
and drowned the arrogant.
You brought Your beloved ones across.
The water covered their foes; *Ps. 106*
not one of them was left.

For this, the beloved ones praised and exalted God,
the cherished ones sang psalms, songs and praises,
blessings and thanksgivings to the King,
the living and enduring God.
High and exalted, great and awesome,
He humbles the haughty and raises the lowly,
freeing captives and redeeming those in need,
helping the poor
and answering His people when they cry out to Him.

Stand in preparation for the Amida. Take three steps back before beginning the Amida.

▸ Praises to God Most High,
the Blessed One who is blessed.
Moses and the children of Israel
recited to You a song with great joy,
and they all exclaimed:
"Who is like You, LORD, among the mighty? *Ex. 15*
Who is like You, majestic in holiness,
awesome in praises, doing wonders?"

---

erful was that experience that they burst into song and praise of Hashem, just as we are about to do in the first three blessings of the *Shemoneh Esreh*. We thus fulfill the Rabbis' insistence that we precede our prayer by recalling that we were freed from Egypt and saved as a people (סוֹמֵךְ גְּאֻלָּה לִתְפִלָּה).

מִמִּצְרַיִם גְּאַלְתָּנוּ, יהוה אֱלֹהֵינוּ
וּמִבֵּית עֲבָדִים פְּדִיתָנוּ
כָּל בְּכוֹרֵיהֶם הָרָגְתָּ, וּבְכוֹרְךָ גָּאָלְתָּ
וְיַם סוּף בָּקַעְתָּ
וְזֵדִים טִבַּעְתָּ
וִידִידִים הֶעֱבַרְתָּ
וַיְכַסּוּ־מַיִם צָרֵיהֶם, אֶחָד מֵהֶם לֹא נוֹתָר: תהלים קו

עַל זֹאת שִׁבְּחוּ אֲהוּבִים, וְרוֹמְמוּ אֵל
וְנָתְנוּ יְדִידִים זְמִירוֹת, שִׁירוֹת וְתִשְׁבָּחוֹת
בְּרָכוֹת וְהוֹדָאוֹת לְמֶלֶךְ אֵל חַי וְקַיָּם
רָם וְנִשָּׂא, גָּדוֹל וְנוֹרָא
מַשְׁפִּיל גֵּאִים וּמַגְבִּיהַּ שְׁפָלִים
מוֹצִיא אֲסִירִים, וּפוֹדֶה עֲנָוִים וְעוֹזֵר דַּלִּים
וְעוֹנֶה לְעַמּוֹ בְּעֵת שַׁוְּעָם אֵלָיו.

Stand in preparation for the עמידה. Take three steps back before beginning the עמידה.

◂ תְּהִלּוֹת לְאֵל עֶלְיוֹן, בָּרוּךְ הוּא וּמְבֹרָךְ
מֹשֶׁה וּבְנֵי יִשְׂרָאֵל
לְךָ עָנוּ שִׁירָה בְּשִׂמְחָה רַבָּה
וְאָמְרוּ כֻלָּם
מִי־כָמֹכָה בָּאֵלִם, יהוה שמות טו
מִי כָּמֹכָה נֶאְדָּר בַּקֹּדֶשׁ, נוֹרָא תְהִלֹּת, עֹשֵׂה פֶלֶא:

BIUR TEFILLA • ביאור תפילה

מִמִּצְרַיִם גְּאַלְתָּנוּ – *From Egypt You redeemed us.* The Torah says that when Israel saw the splitting of the *Yam Suf*, they "believed in God and in Moshe His servant." So pow-

▸ With a new song, the redeemed people praised
Your name at the seashore.
Together they all gave thanks, proclaimed Your kingship,
and declared:
"The LORD shall reign for ever and ever." *Ex. 15*

Congregants should end the following blessing together with the Leader so as to be able to move directly from the words "redeemed Israel" to the Amida, without the interruption of saying Amen.

▸ צוּר יִשְׂרָאֵל Rock of Israel! Arise to the help of Israel.
Deliver, as You promised, Judah and Israel.
Our Redeemer, the LORD of hosts is His name, *Is. 47*
the Holy One of Israel.
Blessed are You, LORD, who redeemed Israel.

INTRODUCTION TO THE AMIDA: THE STRUCTURE OF THE SHEMONEH ESREH

There are nineteen blessings that comprise the *Shemoneh Esreh*. They are known by the following names:

1. אבות – Patriarchs
2. גבורות – Divine Might
3. קדושת שם – Holiness
4. דעת – Knowledge
5. תשובה – Repentance
6. סליחה – Forgiveness
7. גאולה – Redemption
8. רפואה – Healing
9. ברכת השנים – Prosperity
10. קיבוץ גלויות – Ingathering of Exiles
11. משפט – Justice
12. ברכת המינים – Against Informers
13. על הצדיקים – The Righteous
14. בניין ירושלים – Rebuilding Jerusalem
15. מלכות בית דוד – Kingdom of David
16. שומע תפלה – Response to Prayer
17. עבודה – Temple Service
18. מודים – Thanksgiving
19. שלום – Peace

Numerous attempts have been made to define the overall structure of the prayer. The most traditional division is the following: the first three blessings consist of praise/שֶׁבַח; the middle thirteen blessings constitute requests/בַּקָּשׁוֹת and the final three blessings are thanks/הוֹדָאָה.

This is the way that Rabbi Ḥanina (*Berakhot* 34a) characterized this structure: "The first blessings are like a servant who organizes his praise before his master; the middle blessings are like a servant who requests his allotment from his master; and the last blessings are like a servant who received his allotment from his master and takes his leave."

As we have mentioned before, one begins with describing Hashem's relation-

This **INTRODUCTION** *continues on page 137.*

◂ שִׁירָה חֲדָשָׁה שִׁבְּחוּ גְאוּלִים
לְשִׁמְךָ עַל שְׂפַת הַיָּם
יַחַד כֻּלָּם הוֹדוּ וְהִמְלִיכוּ
וְאָמְרוּ
יהוה יִמְלֹךְ לְעֹלָם וָעֶד: שמות טו

The קהל *should end the following blessing together with the* שליח ציבור *so as to be able to move directly from the words* גָּאַל יִשְׂרָאֵל *to the* עמידה*, without the interruption of saying* אמן.

◂ צוּר יִשְׂרָאֵל, קוּמָה בְּעֶזְרַת יִשְׂרָאֵל
וּפְדֵה כִנְאֻמֶךָ יְהוּדָה וְיִשְׂרָאֵל.
גֹּאֲלֵנוּ יהוה צְבָאוֹת שְׁמוֹ, קְדוֹשׁ יִשְׂרָאֵל: ישעיה מז
בָּרוּךְ אַתָּה יהוה, גָּאַל יִשְׂרָאֵל.

ANI TEFILLA • אני תפילה

Rabbi Yose ben Elyakim testified in the name of the holy community of Jerusalem:

If one joins the blessing of Geula to the Tefilla [Shemoneh Esreh], he will not meet with any mishap for the whole of the day. (Berakhot 9b)

IYUN TEFILLA • עיון תפילה

We know these events took place because they have been passed along to us by our parents and their parents going back to the moment when it all happened. We are living only a short period of time after the Holocaust, though there are people who deny it ever took place. It is all the more understandable that there are those who would deny the exodus and the splitting of the Sea. Yet, says Rabbi Yehuda HaLevi, our tradition has been unbroken and our historical experience ever since has proven over and over again that God has been an ongoing presence in our history, even if He is sometimes hard to see.

ANI TEFILLA • אני תפילה

At this point we transport ourselves in time, seeing ourselves as having been there at the moment of liberation. Imagine the joy, the gratitude, the sense of awe and wonder, the sense of intimacy with Hashem and with one another.

Close your eyes and imagine actually coming into contact with the Presence of the Divine. Now begin the *Shemoneh Esreh.*

THE AMIDA

The Amida until "in former years" on page 186, is said standing with feet together. The Amida is said silently, following the precedent of Hannah when she prayed for a child (1 Sam. 1:13). If there is a minyan, it is repeated aloud by the Leader. Take three steps forward, as if formally entering the place of the Divine Presence. At the points indicated by ˅, bend the knees at the first word, bow at the second, and stand straight before saying God's name.

O LORD, open my lips,[BA] so that my mouth may declare Your praise. *Ps. 51*

---

someone, before going back to finish the text of the blessing itself. So, too, if one wanted to ask for prosperity in **ברכת השנים**. The same is true for all of the other blessings as well, as long as one does not forgo the text of the blessing and as long as one keeps within the theme of that blessing (*Shulḥan Arukh* 119:1). Any request that doesn't seem to fit into the theme of an existing blessing may be included in **שומע תפלה**. In short, there is a tremendous amount of room for personal expression.

We conclude with three blessings whose primary theme is thanks, like a servant who departs from his master, grateful for the audience, relieved that he has had the opportunity to express his innermost thoughts, confident that his prayers have been heard and hopeful that they will be answered.

For more on the *Amida* go to page 606.

BIUR TEFILLA • ביאור תפילה

אֲדֹנָי, שְׂפָתַי תִּפְתָּח – *O LORD, open my lips.* This is actually a verse from *Tehillim*, (51) recited by King David in the wake of his sin with Batsheva. Knowing that Hashem does not want sacrifices or ritual offerings empty of heartfelt emotion or a change in one's behavior, he asks that Hashem help him to open his mouth in sincere prayer.

Other approaches to this verse include:

Forgive me, Hashem, so that my prayer will be acceptable. (Rashi)

Help me, Hashem, so that I may pray with kavana so that my prayers will be accepted. In effect, this is a prayer for proper prayer. (Rabbeinu Yona)

Help me, Hashem, to feel dependent enough upon You to want to pray out of a true sense of need.

Help me, Hashem, to feel other people's sense of sorrow and pain, without my having to actually suffer these, so that I may pray to You out of a true sense of need. (Rabbi Tzaddok of Lublin)

ANI TEFILLA • אני תפילה

אֲדֹנָי, שְׂפָתַי תִּפְתָּח – *O LORD, open my lips.* *A rabbi was seen coming late to shul on a regular basis, despite the fact that he was also regularly seen up and about from the time*

This **ANI TEFILLA** *continues on page 139.*

עמידה

The עמידה *until* קַדְמֹנִיּוֹת *on page 187, is said standing with feet together. The* עמידה *is said silently, following the precedent of Hannah when she prayed for a child* (שמואל א׳ א, יג). *If there is a* מנין, *it is repeated aloud by the* שליח ציבור. *Take three steps forward, as if formally entering the place of the Divine Presence. At the points indicated by* ▾, *bend the knees at the first word, bow at the second, and stand straight before saying God's name.*

תהלים נא

אֲדֹנָי, שְׂפָתַי תִּפְתָּח,בא וּפִי יַגִּיד תְּהִלָּתֶךָ:

ship with us and His power over the world, not because Hashem needs our praise, but because before one can ask for something, one needs to first acknowledge His ability to grant such requests. I need to first remind myself of who Hashem is, what role He plays in the world, and only then can I truly stand before Him as a servant before his master.

The requests speak to a central feature of prayer. Yet to see prayer as only this is to do an injustice to the concept of *tefilla*, which can be very different than prayer. Many Jewish philosophers have suggested that *tefilla* is less for God than it is for man. It is a way for me to understand myself, to clarify my values and priorities, to get me to change. Rabbi S.R. Hirsch famously suggested that this is why the word *tefilla* is derived from the root פלל which refers to judging or clarifying a matter. The Hebrew reflexive verb לְהִתְפַּלֵּל would thus mean "to judge oneself" or "to clarify things for oneself," and denotes "to step out of active life in order to attempt to gain a true judgment about oneself, that is, about one's ego, about one's relationship to God and the world, and of God and the world to oneself" (Hirsch, *Ḥorev*). The middle blessings are therefore not only opportunities to ask things of Hashem but also opportunities for asking things of ourselves.

There have been many attempts to understand the internal structure of the middle blessings. Are the various blessings related? Are they listed in a particular way? There are those who suggest that the first set of six refer to individual needs and the second set to communal ones, with the last blessing (**שומע תפילה**) being a summative one. Some have seen the blessings to be sequential (e.g., one needs health before one asks for material prosperity) and that perhaps there is even a symmetrical and causal relationship among them (e.g., blessing 4 must precede blessing 5, but it also is linked to blessing 10; 6 precedes 7 but is linked to 11 etc.) (cited in Abudarham). An additional explanation has a further internal division in which blessings 4–6 refer to spiritual needs, and 7–9 refer to physical needs, while 10–12 refer to national rebuilding, and 13–15 are components of their realization.

Regardless, there is a tradition that each of the blessings can also be understood as a category within which one can subsume one's related needs. So, for example, one can break from the text of the blessing of **רְפָאֵנוּ**, ideally toward the end (*Mishna Berura* 119:3), to insert one's own personal plea for

PATRIARCHS[IA]

▾בָּרוּךְ▾ Blessed are You, LORD our God and God of our fathers,[BA]
God of Abraham, God of Isaac and God of Jacob;[B]
the great, mighty and awesome God, God Most High,
who bestows acts of loving-kindness and creates all,
who remembers the loving-kindness of the fathers
and will bring a Redeemer to their children's children
for the sake of His name, in love.
King, Helper, Savior, Shield:[A]
▾Blessed are You,
LORD, Shield of Abraham.

BIUR TEFILLA • ביאור תפילה

אֱלֹהֵינוּ וֵאלֹהֵי אֲבוֹתֵינוּ – *Our God and God of our fathers.* The blessing says "our God and God of our fathers." Why does it say both? Isn't it the same God?!

The Ba'al Shem Tov answered that our knowledge of God comes from two sources: (1) our parents and the way they raised us, and (2) the knowledge of God we acquire on our own by ourselves as we mature.

ANI TEFILLA • אני תפילה

וֵאלֹהֵי אֲבוֹתֵינוּ – *God of our fathers.*

How did your parents or family convey to you a sense of Jewish tradition? Have this in mind when you say וֵאלֹהֵי אֲבוֹתֵינוּ.

How have you tried to make your knowledge of God your own? Have this in mind when you say אֱלֹהֵינוּ.

אֱלֹהֵינוּ וֵאלֹהֵי אֲבוֹתֵינוּ – *Our God and God of our fathers.*

Did you ever have difficulty relating to the existence of God? Some people find strength in recalling that Hashem has had a historical relationship with the Jewish people going all the way back to the Avot, that is, with our Fathers and with our fathers.

What event or phenomenon in Jewish history gives you reason to believe?

מֶלֶךְ עוֹזֵר וּמוֹשִׁיעַ וּמָגֵן – *King, Helper, Savior, Shield.*

How has Hashem been a King, Helper, Savior and Shield for the Jewish people in the past? Today?

How has Hashem been that in your family's life?

How has Hashem been that in your own life? What do I have to be grateful for?

אבות[עא]

בָּרוּךְ אַתָּה יהוה, אֱלֹהֵינוּ וֵאלֹהֵי אֲבוֹתֵינוּ[בא]
אֱלֹהֵי אַבְרָהָם, אֱלֹהֵי יִצְחָק, וֵאלֹהֵי יַעֲקֹב[ב]
הָאֵל הַגָּדוֹל הַגִּבּוֹר וְהַנּוֹרָא, אֵל עֶלְיוֹן
גּוֹמֵל חֲסָדִים טוֹבִים, וְקוֹנֵה הַכֹּל
וְזוֹכֵר חַסְדֵי אָבוֹת
וּמֵבִיא גוֹאֵל לִבְנֵי בְנֵיהֶם לְמַעַן שְׁמוֹ בְּאַהֲבָה.
מֶלֶךְ עוֹזֵר וּמוֹשִׁיעַ וּמָגֵן.[א]
בָּרוּךְ אַתָּה יהוה, מָגֵן אַבְרָהָם.

---

of sunrise early in the morning. When asked what he was doing during all of that time, he responded: "I pray that I may be able to pray." **Pray for a moment before you pray.**

IYUN TEFILLA • עיון תפילה

אבות – *PATRIARCHS.* The *Shulḥan Arukh* says about this blessing that one should have *kavana* in one's heart for the meaning of the words that one says with one's mouth. Also one should imagine that the *Shekhina* is standing right in front of your eyes and you should therefore remove all foreign thoughts which might distract you. You should think that you are standing before a human king or president, in which case you would be very careful about what you say and you would make sure that it was expressed well and with proper intention. All the more so if you are standing in front of the King of kings, *HaKadosh Barukh Hu*, the One who knows all of man's thoughts…

ANI TEFILLA • אני תפילה

אבות – *PATRIARCHS.*
If you could meet the President of the United States, how would you act? What would you say? **You are standing in front of the President of the world.**

What do you want to say?

אבות – *PATRIARCHS.* The *Sefat Emet*, a Rebbe of the Ger Hasidim, wrote that there is a spark of the *Avot* that resides in each and every one of us. That is why the *Shemoneh Esreh* begins with referring to them, for it is through them that we can more easily come to cleave to Hashem. **Which sparks of the *Avot* can you recognize in yourself?**

DIVINE MIGHT

אַתָּה גִּבּוֹר You are eternally mighty,[A] LORD.
You give life to the dead[B] and have great power to save.

In Israel: He causes the dew to fall.

He sustains the living with loving-kindness,
and with great compassion revives the dead.
He supports the fallen, heals the sick, sets captives free,
and keeps His faith with those who sleep in the dust.
Who is like You, Master of might,
and who can compare to You,
O King who brings death and gives life,[A]
and makes salvation grow?
Faithful are You to revive the dead.
Blessed are You, LORD,
who revives the dead.

When saying the Amida silently, continue with "You are holy" on page 144.

---

of Hashem's power over the physical world than that. Even so, many have suggested alternative possibilities for the meaning of the phrase "gives life to the dead."

Which interpretation appeals to you the most today?

(1) He supports and cures those who were at death's door whom doctors said could not be cured. Hashem thus revives the dead in this way. (Abudarham)
(2) By virtue of the fact that He provides good to those who are still alive, this provides life/satisfaction to those who are dead. (Tiferet Shlomo)
(3) Hashem grants life to those who are downcast or enveloped by sadness, who may feel like they are dead.
(4) Hashem sends rain on a regular basis which revives life on earth.
(5) Hashem enables us to awake every morning when we are otherwise like dead people.

Rabbi Avraham Weinberg, a leader of the Hasidim of Slonim, noted that the phrase סוֹמֵךְ נוֹפְלִים – "who raises those who fall," is written in the present tense and not in the past tense. From here one learns that no matter how many times you may have stumbled or fallen, Hashem is still there every day, in the present, to support you and make sure that you can get up again. Every day brings with it new hope for a fresh beginning.

גבורות

אַתָּה גִּבּוֹר לְעוֹלָם,[א] אֲדֹנָי
מְחַיֵּה מֵתִים[ב] אַתָּה, רַב לְהוֹשִׁיעַ

בארץ ישראל בקיץ: מוֹרִיד הַטָּל

מְכַלְכֵּל חַיִּים בְּחֶסֶד, מְחַיֵּה מֵתִים בְּרַחֲמִים רַבִּים
סוֹמֵךְ נוֹפְלִים, וְרוֹפֵא חוֹלִים, וּמַתִּיר אֲסוּרִים
וּמְקַיֵּם אֱמוּנָתוֹ לִישֵׁנֵי עָפָר.
מִי כָמוֹךָ, בַּעַל גְּבוּרוֹת, וּמִי דּוֹמֶה לָּךְ
מֶלֶךְ, מֵמִית וּמְחַיֶּה[א] וּמַצְמִיחַ יְשׁוּעָה.
וְנֶאֱמָן אַתָּה לְהַחֲיוֹת מֵתִים.
בָּרוּךְ אַתָּה יהוה, מְחַיֵּה הַמֵּתִים.

When saying the עמידה *silently, continue with* אַתָּה קָדוֹשׁ *on page 145.*

ANI TEFILLA • אני תפילה

אַתָּה גִּבּוֹר לְעוֹלָם – *You are eternally mighty*. Have you ever been in a place in nature where you felt the presence of God? Have you ever witnessed a natural phenomenon when you felt like there was a force or Presence that was beyond you?

Close your eyes. Imagine yourself there now.

מְכַלְכֵּל חַיִּים בְּחֶסֶד – *He sustains the living with loving-kindness*. The Ḥafetz Ḥayyim once wrote that the fulfillment of our prayers is dependent upon our actions. If we do acts of *Ḥesed* for other people, then it is much more likely that Hashem will do acts of *Ḥesed* for us (*Ahavat Ḥesed* II:6). For how can we ask Him to do something for us that we ourselves are not prepared to do for others?

What *Ḥesed* did you do for someone yesterday?

Whom can you reach out to today?

BIUR TEFILLA • ביאור תפילה

מְחַיֵּה מֵתִים – *Who revives the dead*. The *berakha* mentions the cardinal Jewish belief in the revival of the dead no less than five times, for there can be no greater example

KEDUSHA[BI]

During the Leader's Repetition, the following is said standing with feet together, rising on the toes at the words indicated by ▴.

Cong. then Leader: נְקַדֵּשׁ We will sanctify Your name on earth,
as they sanctify it in the highest heavens,
as is written by Your prophet,
"And they [the angels] call to one another saying: *Is. 6*

Cong. then Leader: ▴Holy, ▴holy, ▴holy[A] is the LORD of hosts
the whole world is filled with His glory."
Those facing them say "Blessed – "

Cong. then Leader: ▴"Blessed is the LORD's glory from His place." *Ezek. 3*
And in Your holy Writings it is written thus:

Cong. then Leader: ▴"The LORD shall reign for ever. He is your God, Zion, *Ps. 146*
from generation to generation, Halleluya!"

Leader: From generation to generation we will declare Your greatness,
and we will proclaim Your holiness for evermore.
Your praise, our God, shall not leave our mouth forever,
for You, God, are a great and holy King.
Blessed are You, LORD, the holy God.

The Leader continues with "You grace humanity" on page 146.

ANI TEFILLA • אני תפילה

קָדוֹשׁ, קָדוֹשׁ קָדוֹשׁ – *Holy, holy, holy.* Rudolph Otto was a famous German scholar of religion. In 1911, he traveled to Morocco and visited a small synagogue on Shabbat. He wrote:

> *I have heard the* Sanctus, sanctus, sanctus *of the cardinals in Saint Peter's, the* Swiat, swiat, swiat *in the cathedral in the Kremlin, and the* Hagios, hagios, hagios *of the patriarch in Jerusalem. In whatever language these words are spoken, the most sublime words that human lips have ever uttered, they always seize one in the deepest ground of the soul, arousing and stirring with a mighty shudder the mystery of the other-worldly that sleeps therein. That happens here more than anywhere else, here in this deserted place, where they resound in the language in which Isaiah first heard them and on the lips of this people whose heritage they initially were.* (*Rudolph Otto,* Autobiographical and Social Essays, *ed. Gregory D. Alles [The Hague: Mouton, 1996], 81*)

קדושה[בע]

During חזרת הש״ץ, *the following is said standing with feet together, rising on the toes at the words indicated by ˄.*

then קהל ש״ץ: נְקַדֵּשׁ אֶת שִׁמְךָ בָּעוֹלָם
כְּשֵׁם שֶׁמַּקְדִּישִׁים אוֹתוֹ בִּשְׁמֵי מָרוֹם
כַּכָּתוּב עַל יַד נְבִיאֶךָ, וְקָרָא זֶה אֶל־זֶה וְאָמַר — ישעיה ו

then קהל ש״ץ: ˄קָדוֹשׁ, ˄קָדוֹשׁ, ˄קָדוֹשׁ,[א] יהוה צְבָאוֹת
מְלֹא כָל־הָאָרֶץ כְּבוֹדוֹ:
לְעֻמָּתָם בָּרוּךְ יֹאמֵרוּ

then קהל ש״ץ: ˄בָּרוּךְ כְּבוֹד־יהוה מִמְּקוֹמוֹ: — יחזקאל ג
וּבְדִבְרֵי קָדְשְׁךָ כָּתוּב לֵאמֹר

then קהל ש״ץ: ˄יִמְלֹךְ יהוה לְעוֹלָם, אֱלֹהַיִךְ צִיּוֹן לְדֹר וָדֹר, הַלְלוּיָהּ: — תהלים קמו

ש״ץ: לְדוֹר וָדוֹר נַגִּיד גָּדְלֶךָ
וּלְנֵצַח נְצָחִים קְדֻשָּׁתְךָ נַקְדִּישׁ
וְשִׁבְחֲךָ אֱלֹהֵינוּ מִפִּינוּ לֹא יָמוּשׁ לְעוֹלָם וָעֶד
כִּי אֵל מֶלֶךְ גָּדוֹל וְקָדוֹשׁ אָתָּה.
בָּרוּךְ אַתָּה יהוה, הָאֵל הַקָּדוֹשׁ.

The שליח ציבור *continues with* אַתָּה חוֹנֵן *on page 147.*

קדושה – *KEDUSHA*. An Introduction to *HAZARAT HASHATZ* can be found on page 611.

IYUN TEFILLA · עיון תפילה

קדושה – *KEDUSHA*. In the *Kedusha* we move beyond the priestly prayer-as-sacrifice and the prophetic prayer-as-dialogue, to prayer as a mystic experience. So holy is it that in Israel in ancient times it was said only on Shabbat and festivals [*Sanhedrin* 37b; *Massekhet Soferim* 20:3]. The *Zohar* interprets Jacob's vision of a ladder stretching from earth to heaven, with angels ascending and descending (Gen. 28:12) as a metaphor for prayer, and this, too, is part of the meaning of *Kedusha*. We have climbed the ladder from earth to heaven. As the Leader repeats the prayer on behalf of the entire community, we reach the summit of religious experience. (Rabbi J. Sacks)

HOLINESS

אַתָּה קָדוֹשׁ You are holy[BIA] and Your name is holy,
and holy ones praise You daily, Selah![B]
Blessed are You, LORD,
the holy God.

---

placed within you a spark of My own *kedusha*, the *Tzelem Elokim*, which is the ability of the human being to overpower and separate himself from his *yetzer hara*. Just as *HaKadosh Barukh Hu* is *kadosh* above and not bound by His nature, He has imbued the human being with a similar power of *kedusha*: that of being able to transcend his own urges and inclinations, and separate himself from them.

What inclination can I try to overcome just once today?

The Ramban says that we can become holy by living a life of balance. **How can you balance your life a little today?**

אַתָּה קָדוֹשׁ – *You are holy.* The Alsheikh HaKadosh asks: Just because God is holy, why should that mean that I should be holy? After all, I am not like Him! The answer is that Hashem gave us the ability to be holy by living a life that separates us, enriches us, and makes us special. By living our lives this way, we acknowledge His being holy, to ourselves and to others.

ANI TEFILLA • אני תפילה

אַתָּה קָדוֹשׁ – *You are holy.*

What one act can I do today that will reflect my living a life of *kedusha*?

In my interactions with a non-Jew today, how can I be a representative of a life lived apart?

In my interactions with others today, how can I reflect the *kedusha* of Hashem?

BIUR TEFILLA • ביאור תפילה

וּקְדוֹשִׁים בְּכָל יוֹם יְהַלְלוּךָ סֶּלָה – *And holy ones praise You daily, Selah.* Who are the "holy ones?" Two possibilities: (a) the angels, (b) we Jews. **Which interpretation appeals to you most today?**

Alternatively, perhaps both are possible. We Jews are meant to strive to be like angels. **Close your eyes. Imagine yourself to be an angel.**

קדושת השם

אַתָּה קָדוֹשׁ[בעא] **וְשִׁמְךָ קָדוֹשׁ**
וּקְדוֹשִׁים בְּכָל יוֹם יְהַלְלוּךָ סֶּלָה.[ב]
בָּרוּךְ אַתָּה יהוה, הָאֵל הַקָּדוֹשׁ.

BIUR TEFILLA • ביאור תפילה

אַתָּה קָדוֹשׁ – *You are holy.* What does the word **קָדוֹשׁ** really mean? At its core, the word is derived from the Hebrew word for "separation." The Hebrew word for betrothal, "קִדּוּשִׁין," for example, suggests that, once engaged, the woman is off limits or *separated* from any other man who may want to marry her. Similarly, **קִדּוּשׁ** which we say on Friday night is designed to establish that we are acknowledging that Shabbat is a day *separate* from all others. Finally, there is the *parasha* in the Torah of **קְדֹשִׁים תִּהְיוּ** – the commandment that the Jewish people be *separate* from all other nations.

Based on this, the meaning of the present blessing becomes clear: we declare Hashem as being *Kadosh* – totally separate, not only from man but from all life as we know it. Here we acknowledge that He is indescribable, seemingly distant, and beyond anything we can imagine. After having praised Hashem in history (the first blessing – *Avot*) and in nature (the second blessing – *Gevurot*), we here admit that those descriptions are limited and that, in the end, He is beyond our understanding.

This is the meaning of the declaration at the beginning of the blessing which states simply "You are *Kadosh*." There is simply no better way to describe how indescribable You really are.

IYUN TEFILLA • עיון תפילה

אַתָּה קָדוֹשׁ – *You are holy.*
Parashat Kedoshim begins: **קְדֹשִׁים תִּהְיוּ כִּי קָדוֹשׁ אֲנִי יהוה** – we need to be holy because Hashem is holy. Rabbi Shimon Schwab wrote that here Hashem asks that we separate ourselves from our *yetzer hara* (inclination to act badly) because Hashem is **קָדוֹשׁ**, that is, you can be *kadosh because* I have

KNOWLEDGE[IA]

אַתָּה חוֹנֵן You grace humanity with knowledge[BA]
and teach mortals understanding.[B]
Grace us with the knowledge, understanding
and discernment that come from You.
Blessed are You, LORD,
who graciously grants knowledge.

---

infer and make deductions based upon the knowledge one has acquired. In this blessing we ask for both, for as the Mishna in *Avot* (3:21) says, "If there is no בִּינָה, there can be no דַּעַת; and if there is no דַּעַת, then there can be no בִּינָה."

What does it mean to have one without the other?

What added knowledge would I like to pray for today?

What added understanding would I like to pray for today?

דַּעַת – *Knowledge.* On Saturday night during *Ma'ariv*, a special blessing is inserted here which serves as a kind of verbal *Havdala*. The Gemara (Yerushalmi, *Berakhot* 5:2) explains that this *Havdala* was inserted into this particular blessing because "if there is no understanding, one can make no distinctions [*havdala*]."

What distinctions can I make in my life today between the holy and the secular?

What aspect of my life today can I make holy?

אַתָּה חוֹנֵן לְאָדָם דַּעַת – *You grace humanity with knowledge.* This is the only one of the middle *berakhot* of the *Shemoneh Esreh* that begins with a declarative statement of praise, namely, "You grace humanity with knowledge..." All of the other *berakhot* simply begin with a request. What makes this particular request so important that it requires us to begin by declaring that Hashem gives us the very thing that we are asking for? Consider one possibility: without intellect, prayer would be impossible.

ANI TEFILLA • אני תפילה

אַתָּה חוֹנֵן לְאָדָם דַּעַת – *You grace humanity with knowledge.* If one has trouble remembering what one has learned, one should spend some extra time on the blessing of אַתָּה חוֹנֵן. (Rashi, *Avoda Zara* 8a)

דעת[עא]

אַתָּה חוֹנֵן לְאָדָם דַּעַת[בא]
וּמְלַמֵּד לֶאֱנוֹשׁ בִּינָה.[ב]
חָנֵּנוּ מֵאִתְּךָ דֵּעָה בִּינָה וְהַשְׂכֵּל.
בָּרוּךְ אַתָּה יהוה, חוֹנֵן הַדָּעַת.

IYUN TEFILLA • עיון תפילה

דעת – *KNOWLEDGE.* Unlike any other creation on earth, man is created in the image of God. What is the image of God? According to some, it refers to man's intelligence, his ability to think. Hence the opening of the blessing declares that Hashem gave intelligence to Adam/Man. It was an act of grace (חֵן) not just to Adam but to all of humanity (אֱנוֹשׁ).

ANI TEFILLA • אני תפילה

דעת – *KNOWLEDGE.*

Why did God give man intelligence? For what purpose?

How has mankind used human intelligence for positive purposes?

How has mankind used human intelligence for negative purposes?

How can I use my intelligence today?

There are those who say that these words refer not just to the physical realm but to the spiritual realm as well.

What spiritual knowledge would I like to pray for today?

What spiritual understanding would I like to pray for today?

BIUR TEFILLA • ביאור תפילה

דַּעַת... בִּינָה – *Knowledge... understanding.* What is the difference between knowledge (דַּעַת) and understanding (בִּינָה)? One possibility is that knowledge refers to basic information; understanding refers to the ability to manipulate that information, to

REPENTANCE

הֲשִׁיבֵנוּ Bring us back,[IA] our Father,[I]
to Your Torah.
Draw us near, our King,
to Your service.
Lead us back to You in perfect repentance.[B]
Blessed are You, LORD, who desires repentance.

---

roots, my legacy." So too when a Jew becomes preoccupied with frivolous things, if after some time he decides to return, he is not embarrassed to do so for he says, "I am returning to my inheritance, my roots." That is why we say אָבִינוּ – for we are like a son returning to his inheritance which he received from his Father.

ANI TEFILLA • אני תפילה

הֲשִׁיבֵנוּ – *Bring us back.*

Which part of my spiritual inheritance have I been ignoring?

What will be my attitude to Torah study today?

How can I live more of a Torah life today?

BIUR TEFILLA • ביאור תפילה

וְהַחֲזִירֵנוּ בִּתְשׁוּבָה שְׁלֵמָה לְפָנֶיךָ – *Lead us back to You in perfect repentance.* לְפָנֶיךָ – this word literally means "in front of You." One must always believe that Hashem is there in front of you. Sforno says that people do not repent because they think that it is futile, because they feel that Hashem is not always there. In truth, says Sforno, bad things sometimes happen not because of the absence of Hashem, but because people do not recognize His presence.

Close your eyes and imagine that you are actually standing in His presence.

What can I do today to be more conscious of His presence?

ANI TEFILLA • אני תפילה

A young boy is found crying by his grandfather. "Why are you crying?" asks the old man. "Grandfather," the child responds, "I was playing hide-and-seek with my friends, and I was hiding but no one came to find me!"

Tears welled up in the old man's eyes, and he said, "My child, that is what Hashem says, 'I am hiding, and people don't try to find Me.'"

תשובה

הֲשִׁיבֵנוּ עא **אָבִינוּ** ע **לְתוֹרָתֶךָ**
וְקָרְבֵנוּ מַלְכֵּנוּ לַעֲבוֹדָתֶךָ
וְהַחֲזִירֵנוּ בִּתְשׁוּבָה שְׁלֵמָה לְפָנֶיךָ. ב
בָּרוּךְ אַתָּה יהוה, הָרוֹצֶה בִּתְשׁוּבָה.

IYUN TEFILLA • עיון תפילה

הֲשִׁיבֵנוּ – *Bring us back.* Asking for the ability to "return" to a destination implies that we want to go back to a place where we have been before. What is that place?

Rav Simlai (*Nidda* 30b) suggests that when a child is in the womb the knowledge of the entire Torah is implanted within him. Just before birth, however, an angel comes and taps him on the mouth (hence that small indentation in the middle of our upper lip) and the child is thereby made to forget everything. According to some, this is the meaning of the request to "return us," that is, return us to the state of knowing the entire Torah.

Alternatively, I know who I am or have the potential to be when I am at my best, both as a person and as a Jew. I just haven't been able to actualize that as often or as fully as I would like. Today I would like to move one step closer. Help me.

ANI TEFILLA • אני תפילה

הֲשִׁיבֵנוּ – *Bring us back.* The Ba'al HaTanya, the founder of Lubavitch, said that you should imagine two people standing back to back. They can't be much closer together than that, but neither could they be further away from one another. One needs to stand face to face. *Teshuva* means "to return." People tend to think that God is very far away. It's not true – He's right behind you. All you need to do to return is to turn around.

What can I do to "turn around" today?

IYUN TEFILLA • עיון תפילה

הֲשִׁיבֵנוּ אָבִינוּ – *Bring us back, our Father.* We pray that we should be dear to You like a son is to a father. There is a midrash (*Shemot Raba* 33:7) which states that this may be compared to the son of a king, a prince, who was taken captive overseas as a young child until he became steeped in the ways of the foreigners. If after many years he would seek to return to his father, he would not be ashamed to do so, for he would say, "I am returning to my inheritance, my

FORGIVENESS[A]

Strike the left side of the chest at °.

סְלַח לָנוּ Forgive us, our Father,[I]
for we have °sinned.
Pardon us, our King,[A]
for we have °transgressed;[BA]
for You pardon and forgive.
Blessed are You, LORD,
the gracious One who repeatedly forgives.

Is there a difference in the reaction of your father versus your friend?

Did your parent ever forgive you for something you did even if you didn't necessarily deserve it?

Imagine that you break someone's computer. You need to ask forgiveness. But you also need to pay back the damage. Imagine that he pardons you and tells you to forget about the payment. Here we ask God for both. The first is about asking for forgiveness because we have hurt our relationship with our Father. But we also ask for pardon from the consequences; that's our relationship with Him as King (Rabbi D. Aaron).

The word חֵטְא in Tanakh is also used as a term in archery for missing the target. As such, a sin is not a catastrophe but a reason to redouble one's efforts to focus and correct one's aim.

How will I do that today?

סְלִיחָה – *Forgiveness.*

What does it feel like to be insulted or to be wronged? When was the last time it happened to you? Do you recall how you felt when someone did something to you intentionally? Unintentionally? How do you think God feels?

When was the last time you had the chance to do a mitzva and you passed it up?

What amends can I make today?

סְלִיחָה – *Forgiveness.* If a friend were to forgive you and then you did it again, he wouldn't be so quick to forgive you again, and certainly not after the third or fourth time. Not so Hashem. Every time you sin, forgiveness is possible. (Ba'al HaTanya)

The Hebrew word for past is *kedem*. The word for progress is *lehitkadem*. In Judaism, progress doesn't always mean going on to something new but rather returning to oneself, to one's past.

When we lose sight of our own godliness, we lose contact with our true selves. This requires a return. (Rabbi D. Aaron)

Prayer changes the world because it changes us. (Rabbi J. Sacks)

סליחה[א]

Strike the left side of the chest at °.

סְלַח לָנוּ אָבִינוּ[ע] כִּי °חָטָאנוּ
מְחַל לָנוּ מַלְכֵּנוּ[א] כִּי °פָשָׁעְנוּ[בא]
כִּי מוֹחֵל וְסוֹלֵחַ אָתָּה.
בָּרוּךְ אַתָּה יהוה, חַנּוּן הַמַּרְבֶּה לִסְלֹחַ.

IYUN TEFILLA • עיון תפילה

סְלַח לָנוּ אָבִינוּ – *Forgive us, our Father.* Only this blessing and the one that precedes it emphasize Hashem as "Father. "Why? The Tur (*OḤ* 115) explains that we remind Hashem that it is a father's obligation to teach rather than simply punish his child. So, too, we ask Hashem here to have mercy, to be kind to us, just as a father would be forgiving of a child, and to teach us how to return to Him.

BIUR TEFILLA • ביאור תפילה

כִּי חָטָאנוּ... כִּי פָשָׁעְנוּ – *For we have sinned...for we have transgressed.*

Two types of sins are described here:
A **חֵטְא** is a sin that is committed inadvertently.
A **פֶּשַׁע** is a sin which is committed intentionally.

Note the parallels:
סְלַח לָנוּ אָבִינוּ כִּי חָטָאנוּ → **סְלַח** = total forgiveness
חֵטְא = unintentional sin
מְחַל לָנוּ מַלְכֵּנוּ כִּי פָשָׁעְנוּ → **מְחַל** = partial forgiveness
פֶּשַׁע = intentional sin

Why does one phrase address Hashem as Father and the other as King?

Which kind of sin does the entire blessing end with? Why?

ANI TEFILLA • אני תפילה

כִּי חָטָאנוּ... כִּי פָשָׁעְנוּ – *For we have sinned...for we have transgressed.*

What חֵטְא might you have committed in the last 24 hours?

What פֶּשַׁע might you have committed in the last 24 hours?

אָבִינוּ... מַלְכֵּנוּ – *Our Father... Our King.* Imagine that you sin against a friend and ask forgiveness and he grants it to you. Imagine the same when you ask forgiveness from your father.

REDEMPTION[BA]

רְאֵה Look on our affliction,[IA] plead our cause,[I]
and redeem us soon for Your name's sake,

them and did not look away. He came closer to them than He otherwise might, had they not prayed at that moment.

What do you want Hashem to "see" in your life?

Are there people in your life who would want you to really "see" them?

When was the last time that you "saw" someone's pain?

BIUR TEFILLA • ביאור תפילה

רְאֵה בְעָנְיֵנוּ – *Look on our affliction.* The root of the word עָנְיֵנוּ is the same one that the Torah uses for the five "afflictions" of Yom Kippur. They are things that we are deprived of, things that make us feel uncomfortable.

What things make you uncomfortable, that you wish were not a part of your life?

ANI TEFILLA • אני תפילה

רְאֵה בְעָנְיֵנוּ – *Look on our affliction.* Rabbi Elimelekh Szapira of Grodzisk explained that we ask that Hashem not only see our afflictions but that He sees "*into* our afflictions" (as indicated here by the letter ב). This is because we know that in our heart of hearts, in the essence of our being, we want to be closer to Hashem and to do the right thing. But externally we are not always able to be that way, to live our daily lives that way. And so we ask Hashem here to see what is really going on beneath the surface, at the core of our being. Please, see into my heart and how much I am bothered by the lack of consistency in my life. Help me help myself.

IYUN TEFILLA • עיון תפילה

וְרִיבָה רִיבֵנוּ – *Plead our cause.* Why should we be asking Hashem to fight our battles? There are some Hasidic masters who maintain that the battle we seek help with is the battle with our own *yetzer hara* (evil inclination). This is the bad side of us that gets in our way, that we give in to sometimes when we know we shouldn't. Here we ask Hashem's help to overcome it.

What battles have you been fighting with your own *yetzer hara*? Ask Hashem for help.

גאולה[כא]

רְאֵה בְעָנְיֵנוּ,[עב] וְרִיבָה רִיבֵנוּ[א]
וּגְאָלֵנוּ מְהֵרָה לְמַעַן שְׁמֶךָ

BIUR TEFILLA • ביאור תפילה

גאולה – *REDEMPTION.* The Hebrew word for "redemption" – **גאולה** – often refers to that time in the future predicted by the prophets when the Jewish people will be whole again in its own Land. The problem is that this theme is already touched upon in later blessings of *Shemoneh Esreh*. Here, then, it must mean something else, especially since this section of *Shemoneh Esreh* focuses more on individual concerns. What does it mean?

Redemption can mean to set someone loose from bondage, to free them from the limitations that prevent them from reaching self-fulfillment. The blessing could therefore refer to the suffering of those individuals who are actually in prison or being persecuted in some way or, alternatively, it could refer to personal suffering or other misfortunes, or other factors which you find limiting in your life.

ANI TEFILLA • אני תפילה

גאולה – *REDEMPTION.* Are there individual Jews you know of who are in jail or being persecuted for their Jewishness?

Think about them when you say this *tefilla*. What are the afflictions, misfortunes, absences in your own life that you think would make you more whole?

IYUN TEFILLA • עיון תפילה

רְאֵה בְעָנְיֵנוּ – *Look on our affliction.* Why do we ask God to "see" our afflictions; after all, doesn't He see everything?

Compare this to the story we cite in the Haggada, when *Benei Yisrael* were suffering under the yoke of the Egyptians and finally called out to Hashem for help. Note what the verse says (*Shemot* 2:24–25), "And God heard their mourning, and God recalled His covenant with Avraham, Yitzḥak and Yaakov; and God *saw* the children of Israel, and God *knew*."

What was it that Hashem saw? Rashi explains that He paid close attention to

for You are a powerful Redeemer.[B]
Blessed are You, LORD, the Redeemer of Israel.[B]

On Fast Days the Leader adds:

עֲנֵנוּ Answer us, LORD, answer us[I] on our Fast Day, for we are in great distress. Look not at our wickedness. Do not hide Your face from us and do not ignore our plea. Be near to our cry; please let Your loving-kindness comfort us. Even before we call to You, answer us, as is said, "Before they call, I will answer. While they are still speaking, I will hear." For You, LORD, are the One who answers in time of distress, redeems and rescues in all times of trouble and anguish. Blessed are You, LORD, who answers in time of distress. *Is. 65*

fast and so one adds it during *Minḥa*. The *Ḥazan* nevertheless recites it here because he is praying on behalf of the congregation and we assume that there will always be at least ten people who are fasting. (Rabbi I. Wohlgemuth)

IYUN TEFILLA • עיון תפילה

עֲנֵנוּ יהוה עֲנֵנוּ – *Answer us, LORD, answer us.* There are days when the Jewish people fast because of calamities that befell us, in order to arouse our hearts and to open our eyes to the need to repent. This is designed to help us focus on our own misdeeds and those of our ancestors which were similar to ours, to the point that we were all affected by those calamities; the purpose of this memorializing is therefore in order for us to change our ways. The primary goal then is not the fasting itself; rather, fasting is but a preparation for our changing something within ourselves. Therefore, those people who fast but spend their time doing frivolous things not in keeping with the spirit of the day, have grabbed onto what is secondary and have abandoned that which is essential (based on *Ḥayyei Adam* 2:133).

ANI TEFILLA • אני תפילה

What can I try to improve about myself today?

כִּי גּוֹאֵל חָזָק אָתָּה. ב

בָּרוּךְ אַתָּה יהוה, גּוֹאֵל יִשְׂרָאֵל. ב

On Fast Days the שליח ציבור *adds:*

עֲנֵנוּ יהוה עֲנֵנוּ הע בְּיוֹם צוֹם תַּעֲנִיתֵנוּ, כִּי בְצָרָה גְדוֹלָה אֲנָחְנוּ. אַל תֵּפֶן אֶל רִשְׁעֵנוּ, וְאַל תַּסְתֵּר פָּנֶיךָ מִמֶּנּוּ, וְאַל תִּתְעַלַּם מִתְּחִנָּתֵנוּ. הֱיֵה נָא קָרוֹב לְשַׁוְעָתֵנוּ, יְהִי נָא חַסְדְּךָ לְנַחֲמֵנוּ, טֶרֶם נִקְרָא אֵלֶיךָ עֲנֵנוּ, כַּדָּבָר שֶׁנֶּאֱמַר:
ישעיה סה וְהָיָה טֶרֶם יִקְרָאוּ וַאֲנִי אֶעֱנֶה, עוֹד הֵם מְדַבְּרִים וַאֲנִי אֶשְׁמָע: כִּי אַתָּה יהוה הָעוֹנֶה בְּעֵת צָרָה, פּוֹדֶה וּמַצִּיל בְּכָל עֵת צָרָה וְצוּקָה. בָּרוּךְ אַתָּה יהוה, הָעוֹנֶה בְּעֵת צָרָה.

BIUR TEFILLA • ביאור תפילה

כִּי גּוֹאֵל חָזָק אָתָּה – *For You are a powerful Redeemer.* You can operate above nature, You can turn the tide, just as You did in Egypt when You redeemed *Benei Yisrael*. So too, I acknowledge that You can change what now seems to be the natural course of nature, and redeem me.

בָּרוּךְ... גּוֹאֵל יִשְׂרָאֵל – *Blessed... the Redeemer of Israel.* Note that in the blessing before the *Shemoneh Esreh*, the conclusion was **גָּאַל יִשְׂרָאֵל** in the past tense, whereas here it says **גּוֹאֵל יִשְׂרָאֵל** in the present tense. Why? The blessing before the *Shemoneh Esreh* refers to the redemption that took place in the past, in Egypt, whereas here we reaffirm Hashem's redemption of us each and every day.

How can I look at the coming day as a redeeming experience?

HILKHOT TEFILLA • הלכות תפילה

עֲנֵנוּ יהוה עֲנֵנוּ – *Answer us, Lord, answer us.* If there is a *minyan* of people fasting, then the *Ḥazan* recites this in the Repetition. It is recited in this particular blessing because of the theme of Hashem helping us, redeeming us (**גְּאָלֵנוּ**), in our moment of need (**צָרָה**).

Although the *tefilla* was originally said three times during the day, the concern was that if someone said it in the morning and had to break his fast later in the day, then he would have said this blessing in vain. Once one fasts until later in the day, however, the likelihood is that he will complete the

HEALING

רְפָאֵנוּ Heal us, LORD, and we shall be healed.
Save us and we shall be saved,
for You are our praise.
Bring complete recovery for all our ailments,

The following prayer for a sick person may be said here:
May it be Your will, O LORD my God and God of my ancestors, that You speedily send a complete recovery from heaven, a healing of both soul and body, to the patient (*name*), son/daughter of (*mother's name*) among the other afflicted of Israel.

---

for You, God, King, are a faithful and compassionate Healer.
Blessed are You, LORD, Healer of the sick of His people Israel.

---

friend) who was obviously in physical pain? Who was obviously in emotional pain?

What ability do I have to help relieve someone of their pain or discomfort today? What is holding me back?

רְפָאֵנוּ יהוה וְנֵרָפֵא – *Heal us, LORD, and we shall be healed.*

Do I suffer from a spiritual illness?

What doesn't feel right?

If you were to speak to Hashem about the fact that you don't feel well spiritually, what would you ask for? Try it now.

Assuming my prayer would be answered, what responsibility might that then confer upon me?

ANI TEFILLA • אני תפילה

Praying on behalf of another person is a fulfillment of the commandment of *ve'ahavta lere'akha kamokha* וְאָהַבְתָּ לְרֵעֲךָ כָּמוֹךָ – and you should love your neighbor as yourself. (*Yesod VeShoresh HaAvoda* 5:4)

Rabbi Isaac the son of Rabbi Judah said: Let one always pray for mercy not to fall sick; for if he falls sick he is asked to show by what merit he should be healed. (*Shabbat* 32a)

One cannot always know what is going on inside one's own body. We know today that one's immune system is constantly at work, even when it is under siege yet the symptoms may not be felt for days or weeks or months or even years. One must therefore always pray not only for others, but for oneself, for a person who experiences a miracle is not always aware that he is living that miracle.

רפואה

רְפָאֵנוּ יהוה וְנֵרָפֵא[כא]
הוֹשִׁיעֵנוּ וְנִוָּשֵׁעָה, כִּי תְהִלָּתֵנוּ אָתָּה
וְהַעֲלֵה רְפוּאָה שְׁלֵמָה לְכָל מַכּוֹתֵינוּ

The following prayer for a sick person may be said here:

יְהִי רָצוֹן מִלְּפָנֶיךָ יהוה אֱלֹהַי וֵאלֹהֵי אֲבוֹתַי, שֶׁתִּשְׁלַח מְהֵרָה רְפוּאָה שְׁלֵמָה מִן הַשָּׁמַיִם רְפוּאַת הַנֶּפֶשׁ וּרְפוּאַת הַגּוּף לַחוֹלֶה/לַחוֹלָה *name of patient* בֶּן/בַּת *mother's name* בְּתוֹךְ שְׁאָר חוֹלֵי יִשְׂרָאֵל.

כִּי אֵל מֶלֶךְ רוֹפֵא נֶאֱמָן וְרַחֲמָן אָתָּה.
בָּרוּךְ אַתָּה יהוה, רוֹפֵא חוֹלֵי עַמּוֹ יִשְׂרָאֵל.

BIUR TEFILLA • ביאור תפילה

רְפָאֵנוּ יהוה וְנֵרָפֵא – *Heal us, Lord, and we shall be healed.* Perhaps the prayer is not speaking only about physical illness, but psychological illness or spiritual illness as well. The Etz Yosef suggests that whereas in physical illness we simply ask Hashem for a cure and we are passive agents, when it comes to spiritual illness, the cure does not come on its own. Hashem will respond to our prayer for restoring our spiritual health, but after that it is up to us. The soul cannot be cured unless we ourselves take an active part, a willing part, a purposeful part in changing the way we feel or think or act. But starting out can be difficult – we therefore ask Hashem to first help us get going, to do His part – **רְפָאֵנוּ** – and we promise that we will then do our part – **וְנֵרָפֵא**.

ANI TEFILLA • אני תפילה

רְפָאֵנוּ יהוה וְנֵרָפֵא – *Heal us, Lord, and we shall be healed.*

A doctor was once thanked by a patient for saving her life. "Don't thank me," said the doctor, "I'm only His messenger."

What role does man play in the relief of human suffering?

What call to action might this blessing represent? What might it be demanding not of God but of me?

When was the last time you did ***bikur ḥolim***?

When was the last time I reached out to help an acquaintance (not a close

PROSPERITY[AB]

בָּרֵךְ Bless this year for us,[A]
Lord our God,
and all its types of produce for good.[B]
Grant blessing on the face of the earth,
and from its goodness satisfy us,[IB]
blessing our year
as the best of years.
Blessed are You, Lord,
who blesses the years.

BIUR TEFILLA • ביאור תפילה

וְשַׂבְּעֵנוּ מִטּוּבֶךָ\מִטּוּבָהּ – *And from its/Your goodness satisfy us.* There are two different versions of this blessing in various siddurim.

This Siddur has וְשַׂבְּעֵנוּ מִטּוּבָהּ which means "satisfy us from its [=the Land's] goodness."

Other siddurim have the phrase וְשַׂבְּעֵנוּ מִטּוּבֶךָ which means "satisfy us from Your goodness."

What do you think is the basis behind the two different versions?

ANI TEFILLA • אני תפילה

The Hasidic leader, Rabbi Simḥa Bunim of Peshischa, was once asked: How was the serpent cursed by being told that he would have to eat the dust of the earth all the days of his life? What type of punishment is this? After all, dust is plentiful and therefore the serpent will never lack sustenance! To this, Rabbi Simḥa Bunim replied: The very fact that the serpent is always provided for and there is no need whatsoever for it to have to turn to Hashem, this is a punishment! Man, on the other hand, whom Hashem loves and wants to benefit by having contact with him, does not always have everything he needs. The necessities of life will lead him to pray and thereby enable him to derive a relationship with God.

ברכת השנים[אב]

בָּרֵךְ עָלֵינוּ[א] יהוה אֱלֹהֵינוּ אֶת הַשָּׁנָה הַזֹּאת
וְאֶת כָּל מִינֵי תְבוּאָתָהּ, לְטוֹבָה[ב]
וְתֵן בְּרָכָה עַל פְּנֵי הָאֲדָמָה
וְשַׂבְּעֵנוּ מִטּוּבָהּ[עב]
וּבָרֵךְ שְׁנָתֵנוּ כַּשָּׁנִים הַטּוֹבוֹת.
בָּרוּךְ אַתָּה יהוה, מְבָרֵךְ הַשָּׁנִים.

BIUR TEFILLA • ביאור תפילה

לְטוֹבָה – *For good.* Isn't a blessing always something good? Why add this word?

Sometimes the material things we acquire are not necessarily "good" for us.

Can you think of things you have asked for in the past that ultimately were not really in your best interests? We therefore ask that whatever we do acquire has only positive and not negative influences.

IYUN TEFILLA • עיון תפילה

וְשַׂבְּעֵנוּ מִטּוּבָהּ – *And from its goodness satisfy us.* A verse in *Kohelet* 5:9 says: אֹהֵב כֶּסֶף לֹא יִשְׂבַּע כֶּסֶף – "The person who loves money will never get enough money." There is a midrash (*Kohelet Raba* 1:32) which says that this is because a person leaves this world having fulfilled only half of his desires – if he has 100, then he wants 200; if he has 200, then he wants 400. In other words, we are insatiable – we always want more than we have.

Based on this, what do you think is the meaning of the word in the blessing: וְשַׂבְּעֵנוּ – "and satisfy/satiate us"? One answer: I should distinguish between what I want versus what I really need.

A person should consider that he has what he needs and he needs what he already has.

INGATHERING OF EXILES

תְּקַע Sound the great shofar[B] for our freedom,
raise high the banner to gather our exiles,[B]
and gather us together from the four quarters of the earth.[A]
Blessed are You, LORD,
who gathers the dispersed of His people Israel.[A]

What kind of "shofar" do you think would rally the Jewish people around a return to Israel today?

What could I do to bring the ingathering to Israel to reality?

מְקַבֵּץ נִדְחֵי עַמּוֹ יִשְׂרָאֵל – *Who gathers the dispersed of His people Israel.* Rabbi Shimon Schwab notes that we are separated from one another not only geographically but ideologically as well. All Jews do not necessarily believe the same thing; not all Jews practice Judaism in the same way. Even within the Orthodox community there can be disagreement about practices and views of the world. And so here we ask that all Jews come together to see the commonalities which unite us, so that we may no longer be exiled from ourselves as a people.

In a similar vein, Rabbi Soloveitchik used to note that in the gas chambers there was no distinction made between religious Jews and secular ones, between the learned and the unlearned. All Jews share a common fate.

What can I do today to focus on what I have in common with the Jews around me, rather than on what makes us different?

IYUN TEFILLA • עיון תפילה

מְקַבֵּץ נִדְחֵי עַמּוֹ יִשְׂרָאֵל – *Who gathers the dispersed of His people Israel.* Rabbi Menaḥem Naḥum Twersky of Chernobyl, a student of the Ba'al Shem Tov, once suggested that there are two kinds of *galut* (exile). There is the general exile of the Jewish people among the nations of the world, but there is also a private exile, wherein each person feels like he is alone, with his own private trials and tribulations.

How do you wish your life could "come together" for you?

ANI TEFILLA • אני תפילה

A reporter for ABC News once asked Rabbi David Aaron why Jews were drawn to the Land of Israel. He responded: "I don't know. Why are salmon drawn upstream?"

קבוץ גלויות

תְּקַע בְּשׁוֹפָר גָּדוֹל[ב] לְחֵרוּתֵנוּ
וְשָׂא נֵס לְקַבֵּץ גָּלֻיּוֹתֵינוּ[ב]
וְקַבְּצֵנוּ יַחַד מֵאַרְבַּע כַּנְפוֹת הָאָרֶץ.[א]
בָּרוּךְ אַתָּה יהוה, מְקַבֵּץ נִדְחֵי עַמּוֹ יִשְׂרָאֵל.[ע]

BIUR TEFILLA • ביאור תפילה

תְּקַע בְּשׁוֹפָר גָּדוֹל – *Sound the great shofar.* The phrase is based upon a verse in *Yishayahu* (27:13) which says than on that day in the future a big shofar will be blown and all of the lost Jews will come to the Land of Israel. We pray that now is the time of "our freedom" and ask Hashem that He blow the great shofar.

וְשָׂא נֵס לְקַבֵּץ גָּלֻיּוֹתֵינוּ – *Raise high the banner to gather our exiles.* The word *nes* can mean "banner" or it can mean "miracle."

The State of Israel's population has doubled a number of times since 1948. Since independence, more than three million people have immigrated there "from the four corners of the earth." For the first time in millennia, there are more Jews living in Israel than in any other country in the world. Jerusalem is the leading center of absorption. The miracle of the "ingathering of exiles" has been taking place before our very eyes.

ANI TEFILLA • אני תפילה

וְקַבְּצֵנוּ יַחַד מֵאַרְבַּע כַּנְפוֹת הָאָרֶץ – *And gather us together from the four quarters of the earth.* There are still pockets of "lost" Jews in the world who want to live in Israel, but who are prevented from doing so because of the lack of political freedom or economic freedom. Pray for them.

There are millions of Jews who are "lost" not geographically or physically, but spiritually; Jews who do not know they are Jewish, or do not appreciate their Jewishness. Pray for them to actively rejoin the Jewish people.

Can you think of times in Jewish history when Jews had the opportunity to live in Israel but gave up the opportunity?

What does the State of Israel mean to you?

What prayers do you have for the State as the national homeland of the Jewish people?

For the first time in millennia, the Jewish people has its own sovereign state, with its own Jewish holidays and Jewish flavor. Yet there are still millions of Jews who live outside of the homeland.

JUSTICE[B]

הָשִׁיבָה Restore our judges as at first,
and our counselors as at the beginning,
and remove from us sorrow and sighing.[B]
May You alone, LORD, reign over us
with loving-kindness and compassion,[A] and vindicate us in justice.
Blessed are You, LORD,
the King who loves righteousness and justice.[BA]

According to the Malbim, מִשְׁפָּט refers to the strict letter of the law; in other words, whatever the rule and its consequence, someone should be judged and held accountable. צְדָקָה on the other hand, refers to the extenuating circumstances that may have been present; that even though the law requires one thing, the special considerations of time or place or the individual requires that the rules be bent. Here we ask Hashem to balance both the letter of the law and its spirit, צְדָקָה וּמִשְׁפָּט.

ANI TEFILLA • אני תפילה

בְּחֶסֶד וּבְרַחֲמִים – *Loving-kindness and compassion.* What would it mean for me to judge someone בְּחֶסֶד וּבְרַחֲמִים today?

Whom have I treated unjustly in the last 24 hours?

Whom have I misjudged in the last 24 hours?

בְּחֶסֶד וּבְרַחֲמִים – *Loving-kindness and compassion.* There is no hope for a society, even a religious one, that corrupts social justice.

How can I volunteer to help increase social justice in the world?

(Be informed, write a postcard, raise consciousness, attend a rally, donate to a cause, stand up when I see someone being treated inappropriately even by a friend or colleague…)

צְדָקָה וּמִשְׁפָּט – *Righteousness and justice.*

Were you ever judged unfairly because someone was strictly following the letter of the rules?

Whom can I judge with a little more צְדָקָה today?

BIUR TEFILLA • ביאור תפילה

בָּרוּךְ אַתָּה יהוה מֶלֶךְ אוֹהֵב צְדָקָה וּמִשְׁפָּט – *Blessed are You, LORD, the King who loves righteousness and justice.* The conclusion suggests not only that Hashem loves צְדָקָה וּמִשְׁפָּט but also that He loves *the people who do* צְדָקָה וּמִשְׁפָּט.

ANI TEFILLA • אני תפילה

The Sefat Emet (Shofetim 5647) suggested that every person needs to assume the attributes of a judge, the ability to understand truth as it is found in Torah and Talmud, and through that to be able to rule over himself.

השבת המשפט[ב]

הָשִׁיבָה שׁוֹפְטֵינוּ כְּבָרִאשׁוֹנָה וְיוֹעֲצֵינוּ כְּבַתְּחִלָּה
וְהָסֵר מִמֶּנּוּ יָגוֹן וַאֲנָחָה[ב]
וּמְלֹךְ עָלֵינוּ אַתָּה יהוה לְבַדְּךָ בְּחֶסֶד וּבְרַחֲמִים[א]
וְצַדְּקֵנוּ בַּמִּשְׁפָּט.
בָּרוּךְ אַתָּה יהוה
מֶלֶךְ אוֹהֵב צְדָקָה וּמִשְׁפָּט.[בא]

BIUR TEFILLA • ביאור תפילה

השבת המשפט – *JUSTICE.* Why does this blessing follow the previous one about the ingathering of the exiles?

In the previous one, we essentially ask for the revival of the Jewish State. But here we say that having a State is not enough; it must be one that is founded on the principles of Hashem's justice and compassion.

Imagine living in a society that was even more just and compassionate than it is now.

In what ways would it look different? Pray for it.

ANI TEFILLA • אני תפילה

הָשִׁיבָה שׁוֹפְטֵינוּ – *Restore our judges.* "Our people need leaders," said Rabbi S.R. Hirsch, "men who will champion the truth..."

Pray for the success of such leaders.

הָשִׁיבָה שׁוֹפְטֵינוּ – *Restore our judges.* Rebbe Yose ben Elisha said: If you see a generation upon whom befall many tragedies, go and check the judges of Israel. For every calamity that comes to the world only happens because of the actions of the judges of Israel... They are evil, but they trust in God. (*Shabbat* 139a)

BIUR TEFILLA • ביאור תפילה

יָגוֹן וַאֲנָחָה – *Sorrow and sighing.* What's the difference between יָגוֹן and אֲנָחָה?

The son of the Gaon of Vilna suggested that אֲנָחָה refers to the kind of pain and suffering that is inflicted upon one by an enemy or outside force; יָגוֹן refers to the sadness that one can sometimes experience from within.

Think of someone you know of who is in pain. Pray for them.

Can I think of anyone whose "sorrow and sighing" I might be able to help relieve today, even a little?

צְדָקָה וּמִשְׁפָּט – *Righteousness and justice.* What's the difference between them?

AGAINST INFORMERS

וְלַמַּלְשִׁינִים For the slanderers let there be no hope,
and may all wickedness perish in an instant.
May all Your people's enemies swiftly be cut down.
May You swiftly uproot, crush, cast down
and humble the arrogant swiftly in our days.
Blessed are You, LORD,
who destroys enemies and humbles the arrogant.

BIUR TEFILLA • ביאור תפילה

ברכת המינים – *AGAINST INFORMERS.* The Gemara (*Sanhedrin* 11a) says that when the time came to compose this prayer, the Rabbis all turned to a man by the name of Shmuel HaKatan (lit. Shmuel the Small). Why was he called "the small" if he was great enough to be acknowledged by all of the Rabbis? The answer may lie precisely in his being considered "small," not in physical size, but in reference to his humility. Only a humble person may have the correct frame of mind to distinguish between the sin and the sinner. This is borne out by the fact that in *Pirkei Avot* (4:19) it says that "Shmuel HaKatan used to say: Do not rejoice at the downfall of your enemies." Perhaps only a humble person could appropriately compose a prayer that asks that Hashem "humble the arrogant."

Do I know any arrogant people?

How can I increase my own humility today?

ANI TEFILLA • אני תפילה

The story is told that the Gaon of Vilna was riding in a wagon and the wagon driver allowed the horse to veer off to the side and ride through the garden of a non-Jew. The non-Jew came running over to the wagon and started hitting the Gaon. The Gaon later said that it was on the tip of his tongue to say "It's not my fault, it's the fault of the wagon driver; why are you hitting me?!" But he did not do so because he thought he would be guilty of being a מַלְשִׁין *– one who informs on other Jews – for after all, it was an accident, and even if it wasn't, at most the wagon driver should have to pay damages instead of getting hit. And so the Gaon took the beating without saying anything.* (Ḥafetz Ḥayyim, *Shem Olam, Ḥelek beit*)

The Ba'al Shem Tov said that true humility takes place inside a person. A king once went on a short trip but instructed his coach and horseman to go ahead of him while he walked behind them. When asked to explain, he said that he was trying to display his humility to his people. A wise man told him: "Humility is not something one advertises to other people. Rather, the true test is to sit inside the coach and still be humble."

ברכת המינים[בעא]

וְלַמַּלְשִׁינִים אַל תְּהִי תִקְוָה, וְכָל הָרִשְׁעָה כְּרֶגַע תֹּאבֵד
וְכָל אוֹיְבֵי עַמְּךָ מְהֵרָה יִכָּרֵתוּ
וְהַזֵּדִים מְהֵרָה תְעַקֵּר וּתְשַׁבֵּר וּתְמַגֵּר וְתַכְנִיעַ בִּמְהֵרָה בְיָמֵינוּ.
בָּרוּךְ אַתָּה יהוה, שׁוֹבֵר אוֹיְבִים וּמַכְנִיעַ זֵדִים.

BIUR TEFILLA • ביאור תפילה

ברכת המינים – *AGAINST INFORMERS.* Although *Shemoneh Esreh* means 18, the truth is that there are 19 blessings in total. According to many, this particular blessing is the nineteenth, and was added at a later date. Historically, this blessing was created to address those who worked against the Jewish community in Roman times. Since then, the blessing continued to be said against any enemy who would undermine Judaism and the Jewish people.

ברכת המינים – *AGAINST INFORMERS.* There are variants of this text which also include a prayer against **מִינִים** and **מְשֻׁמָּדִים**, disbelievers and apostates who would work with authorities against the Jewish religion. As such, this blessing is not just about physical threats to the Jewish people, but spiritual threats as well.

What forces around you could be interpreted as trying to undermine Judaism today? Have them in mind.

ANI TEFILLA • אני תפילה

ברכת המינים – *AGAINST INFORMERS.* The Gemara (*Berakhot* 10a) relates that Rabbi Meir was once being harassed by a man in his community, and he was therefore praying for God to destroy this person who was harassing him. Beruria, Rabbi Meir's wife, renowned for her Torah knowledge, corrected him, pointing out, "The verse in *Tehillim* [104:35] says: '**יִתַּמּוּ חַטָּאִים מִן הָאָרֶץ** – Let *sins* be wiped out from the earth.' It doesn't say, 'Let *sinners* be wiped out.'" We do not seek vengeance or violence; we seek an end to the existence of "**רִשְׁעָה**" – wickedness. Hence the blessing does not say "may all the wicked perish" but, rather, "may all wickedness perish."

What can I do today to help eradicate the sin that comes through slandering other people?

IYUN TEFILLA • עיון תפילה

ברכת המינים – *AGAINST INFORMERS.* The *Ya'arot Devash* (*Ḥelek* 1, *derush* 1) says that with the recitation of this blessing one fulfils the mitzva to remember Amalek. The eradication of the Jewish people was a goal of Amalek. Have them in mind, for as Rabbi Soloveitchik has said, Amalek is not necessarily a people, but an ideology that still exists in modern times.

What enemies can I think of who are trying to undermine the Jewish people in the present? Have them in mind.

THE RIGHTEOUS

עַל הַצַּדִּיקִים To the righteous,[BA] the pious,
the elders of Your people the house of Israel,
the remnant of their scholars,
the righteous converts, and to us,
may Your compassion be aroused, LORD our God.
Grant a good reward[A] to all who sincerely trust in Your name.
Set our lot with them,[A]
so that we may never be ashamed,[B] for in You we trust.
Blessed are You, LORD,
who is the support and trust of the righteous.

עַל הַצַּדִּיקִים – *To the Righteous.* There are people in your life who are older and wiser just because they have lived life and experienced things.

Who are these people in your life? What do you wish you could learn from them?

עַל הַצַּדִּיקִים – *To the Righteous.* The simple but true fact of life is that you become like those with whom you closely associate – for the good and the bad (see Rashi on *Bemidbar* 3:29, 38).

שָׂכָר טוֹב – *Grant a good reward.* Note that in the blessing we ask for "a good reward."

Did you ever get a "bad reward" – something that you wanted badly but turned out to be not so great after all?

How does one tell the difference between a good reward and a bad one?

What kind of good reward would you like to pray for today?

וְשִׂים חֶלְקֵנוּ עִמָּהֶם – *Set our lot with them.* We ask that "You set our lot with them" – that we be associated with the categories of people who are working on themselves spiritually.

Do I associate with those kinds of people?

Do people look at me that way?

What one thing can I do today to change?

BIUR TEFILLA • ביאור תפילה

וּלְעוֹלָם לֹא נֵבוֹשׁ – *So that we may never be ashamed.* Some say that this refers to the World to Come when we stand before Hashem and we get to see all of our actions, good and bad, laid out before us for all to see.

What can I do today to avoid adding something to my profile that will ultimately make me embarrassed?

על הצדיקים

עַל הַצַּדִּיקִים^[כא] וְעַל הַחֲסִידִים, וְעַל זִקְנֵי עַמְּךָ בֵּית יִשְׂרָאֵל
וְעַל פְּלֵיטַת סוֹפְרֵיהֶם, וְעַל גֵּרֵי הַצֶּדֶק, וְעָלֵינוּ
יֶהֱמוּ רַחֲמֶיךָ יהוה אֱלֹהֵינוּ
וְתֵן שָׂכָר טוֹב^[א] לְכָל הַבּוֹטְחִים בְּשִׁמְךָ בֶּאֱמֶת
וְשִׂים חֶלְקֵנוּ עִמָּהֶם,^[א] וּלְעוֹלָם לֹא נֵבוֹשׁ^[ב] כִּי בְךָ בָּטָחְנוּ.
בָּרוּךְ אַתָּה יהוה, מִשְׁעָן וּמִבְטָח לַצַּדִּיקִים.

BIUR TEFILLA • ביאור תפילה

עַל הַצַּדִּיקִים – *To the Righteous.* After having prayed for the physical restoration of the State, and for the establishment of a system of justice, we now turn to the prayer for spiritual leadership and redemption in which each of us has a part to play. For sovereignty in our own state to work we not only need a justice system but also strong spiritual leadership, and it is to this that we now turn our attention. Look at the list of categories of people who are described at the beginning of the *tefilla*. There are those who say that the list appears in descending order.

הַצַּדִּיקִים – the truly righteous who do everything possible that a servant of Hashem can do.

הַחֲסִידִים – the pious, those who go beyond the letter of the law and do more than is required.

זִקְנֵי יִשְׂרָאֵל – the elders, not only in age but in wisdom born of life experience.

סוֹפְרֵיהֶם – the people who spend their lives teaching Torah to others.

גֵּרֵי הַצֶּדֶק – the converts who join Judaism because they truly believe in Torah.

וְעָלֵינוּ – and on us, the everyday, ordinary Jew, who, while not the same as the other people on the list, nevertheless has an important contribution to make.

עַל הַצַּדִּיקִים – *To the Righteous.* Earlier, we said the blessing for our physical sustenance. Here, says Rabbi S.R. Hirsch, we ask for the spiritual sustenance of the nation. **How could I contribute to the spiritual well-being of the community today?**

ANI TEFILLA • אני תפילה

עַל הַצַּדִּיקִים – *To the Righteous.*

Can you think of a different person for each one of these categories for whom you could pray today?

Do you know any converts? Why do you think they get special mention here?

What do you think your spiritual contribution could be to the community?

Ask Hashem for help.

REBUILDING JERUSALEM[B]

וְלִירוּשָׁלַיִם To Jerusalem, Your city,[A]
may You return in compassion,[B]
and may You dwell in it[A] as You promised.
May You rebuild it rapidly in our days[B]
as an everlasting structure,
and install within it soon the throne of David.
Blessed are You, LORD, who builds Jerusalem.

Think of a beautiful place you have seen or heard of in Jerusalem. Imagine yourself there now.

וְלִירוּשָׁלַיִם עִירְךָ – *To Jerusalem, Your city.* Rabbi Yehoshua ben Levi said, "*HaKadosh Barukh Hu* said to Israel: You caused the destruction of My House and the exile of My children. Inquire of the welfare of Yerushalayim and I will grant you peace." (*Derekh Eretz Zuta, Perek HaShalom*)

Pray for the peace of Yerushalayim.

BIUR TEFILLA • ביאור תפילה

בְּרַחֲמִים תָּשׁוּב – *May You return in compassion.* Wherever the Jews went into exile, the *Shekhina* went with them (*Megilla* 29a). In this *berakha* we ask Hashem to return the *Shekhina* to Yerushalayim.

בְּיָמֵינוּ – *In our days.* Rabbi Naftali of Ropshitz explained that the phrase "in our days" may also be translated "with our days." In other words, may the *Beit HaMikdash* be rebuilt with the way we spend our days, that is, every mitzva we do, how we spend each and every day has the potential to contribute to the rebuilding of Jerusalem and the *Beit HaMikdash*. It has also been pointed out that this is the reason that the blessing ends in the present tense: every day we can contribute to its rebuilding.

What can I do today to help move one step closer to the rebuilding of Yerushalayim?

ANI TEFILLA • אני תפילה

וְתִשְׁכֹּן בְּתוֹכָהּ – *And may You dwell in it.* Rav Aḥa said, "The *Shekhina* never departs from the Western Wall of the *Beit HaMikdash*." (*Tanḥuma Shemot*)

"In Tel Aviv I feel like a 16-year-old Israeli. In Jerusalem I feel like a 3000-year-old Jew." (A sixteen-year-old boy from Yerushalayim)

בניין ירושלים[ב]

וְלִירוּשָׁלַיִם עִירְךָ[א] בְּרַחֲמִים תָּשׁוּב[ב]
וְתִשְׁכֹּן בְּתוֹכָהּ[א] כַּאֲשֶׁר דִּבַּרְתָּ
וּבְנֵה אוֹתָהּ בְּקָרוֹב בְּיָמֵינוּ[ב] בִּנְיַן עוֹלָם
וְכִסֵּא דָוִד מְהֵרָה לְתוֹכָהּ תָּכִין.
בָּרוּךְ אַתָּה יהוה, בּוֹנֵה יְרוּשָׁלָיִם.

BIUR TEFILLA • ביאור תפילה

בניין ירושלים – *REBUILDING JERUSALEM.* For thousands of years the Jewish people has mourned the destruction of Jerusalem. Every single day, in our prayers, when we say *Birkat HaMazon*, at weddings, and on holy days, we have always declared our connection to Yerushalayim. "Let my tongue cling to the roof of my mouth if I do not remember you, if I do not consider Jerusalem my highest joy" (*Tehillim* 137).

There are actually three interrelated requests in this blessing:

(a) The return to Jerusalem and the *Beit HaMikdash* being rebuilt.
(b) The dwelling of the *Shekhina* there.
(c) That the monarchy be reestablished there.

The desire is expressed not just for the rebuilding of the *Beit HaMikdash* itself but for the residence of the *Shekhina* there. Hence the fact that we have Yerushalayim in our hands today is not a sufficient fulfillment of the request in the blessing.

ANI TEFILLA • אני תפילה

וְלִירוּשָׁלַיִם עִירְךָ – *To Jerusalem, Your city.* The first part of the name Yerushalayim is traditionally understood to come from the Hebrew word **יראה**, "will be seen" – meaning Hashem will be seen there.

Have you ever been to Yerushalayim? Have you ever felt something special there? Try to recapture those feelings.

Imagine that you are standing at the *Kotel*. You can feel the warm rays of the sun on your neck. You reach out to touch the stones of the wall. They are cool and smooth.

Close your eyes. What do you want to say?

וְלִירוּשָׁלַיִם עִירְךָ – *To Jerusalem, Your city.* The Rabbis said (*Kiddushin* 49b) that there are ten measures of beauty that descended to this world. Nine of them belong to Yerushalayim and one went to the rest of the world. Whoever has not seen Yerushalayim in her glory has never seen a beautiful city in his life.

KINGDOM OF DAVID[BI]

אֶת צֶמַח May the offshoot of Your servant David soon flower,[B]
and may his pride be raised high by Your salvation,
for we wait for Your salvation all day.[ABI]
Blessed are You, LORD, who makes the glory of salvation flourish.

---

progress. Salvation is not about achieving perfection; it's about being on the road of progress. The road to the Mashiaḥ is not only about the goal of getting there; it's about the process, and the progress we make to get there. (Rabbi E. Bick)

What can I do today to make progress toward a more perfect world?

BIUR TEFILLA • ביאור תפילה

כִּי לִישׁוּעָתְךָ קִוִּינוּ כָּל הַיּוֹם – *For we wait for Your salvation all day.* In all of the other blessings, we ask Hashem for something because He is the One who is capable of effecting it (i.e., "because You are a Redeemer," "because You are a faithful and merciful Healer.") In this blessing, however, we explain our request for redemption not because He is a Redeemer but because "we wait for Your salvation all day." The promise lies within each of us.

IYUN TEFILLA • עיון תפילה

כִּי לִישׁוּעָתְךָ קִוִּינוּ כָּל הַיּוֹם – *For we wait for Your salvation all day.* The mitzva here may well lie not only in belief in the Mashiaḥ, but in the *anticipation* of his coming. Like a soldier standing lookout in a tower awaiting relief, he is ever vigilant, ever hopeful, even when he cannot see anything on the horizon. (Rabbi A.I. Kook)

מלכות בית דוד – *KINGDOM OF DAVID.* There are those who suggest that in ancient Israel this blessing about the Mashiaḥ and the previous blessing about the restoration of the *Beit HaMikdash* were merged into one since they share the same theme. The Jews of Babylonia split it into two. Rabbi Soloveitchik suggested that it was because they feared that when they went into exile they would be pressured by other religious beliefs who believed that the Messiah had already come. This blessing, then, is also a plea for keeping our identity even in the Diaspora.

ANI TEFILLA • אני תפילה

Trees only bear fruit after the seedling has been cultivated and nourished. So, too, in relationships, meaningfulness comes about only after a period of growth. Friendship has to be cultivated in order to be meaningful and lasting. Love needs to be nourished in order for it to flourish and not stagnate. Knowledge cannot come about through impatience. So, too, with tefilla.

מלכות בית דוד[בע]

אֶת צֶמַח דָּוִד עַבְדְּךָ מְהֵרָה תַצְמִיחַ,[ב]
וְקַרְנוֹ תָּרוּם בִּישׁוּעָתֶךָ
כִּי לִישׁוּעָתְךָ קִוִּינוּ כָּל הַיּוֹם.[אבע]
בָּרוּךְ אַתָּה יהוה, מַצְמִיחַ קֶרֶן יְשׁוּעָה.

BIUR TEFILLA • ביאור תפילה

אֶת צֶמַח דָּוִד עַבְדְּךָ מְהֵרָה תַצְמִיחַ – *May the offshoot of Your servant David soon flower.* Why do we use the imagery of "flowering" and "flourishing" like plants?

There are two possible answers:

First, the process of growth is such that a seed is planted in the ground, rots, and from its decay grows anew something greater than what was planted. The world we live in is simply a preparation for a greater world yet to come.

Second, a plant doesn't grow all at once but in increments. So too, will Israel's redemption come in increments, slowly, step by step, measured in years and not in minutes.

מלכות בית דוד – *KINGDOM OF DAVID.* This blessing is essentially a prayer for the coming of Mashiaḥ. King David, the paradigm of a leader who combined the political and the religious, was promised that the monarchy would always belong to his family. Here we pray for the restoration of that period of time when the world in which we live is balanced by leadership that combines a knowledge of politics with the morality and spiritual values of religiosity.

How have today's political leaders succeeded politically but failed morally?

ANI TEFILLA • אני תפילה

כִּי לִישׁוּעָתְךָ קִוִּינוּ כָּל הַיּוֹם – *For we wait for Your salvation all day.*

How can I see the coming of Mashiaḥ as being more possible today than 100 years ago?

What can I do today to bring Mashiaḥ closer?

כִּי לִישׁוּעָתְךָ קִוִּינוּ כָּל הַיּוֹם – *For we wait for Your salvation all day.* Rava said: When one comes to the next world for judgment, one will be asked, "Were you honest in business, did you establish set times for learning Torah? Did you have a family? Did you anticipate the redemption?" This is your chance: anticipate. (*Shabbat* 31a)

כִּי לִישׁוּעָתְךָ קִוִּינוּ כָּל הַיּוֹם – *For we wait for Your salvation all day.* There is a student who always earns marks in the 90s. There is another student who always gets in the 70s. On the next test, the first student gets a mark of 95 but the second student gets a mark in the 80s. In absolute terms, the first student is the better student. But in relative terms, the second student has made more

RESPONSE TO PRAYER

שְׁמַע קוֹלֵנוּ Listen to our voice,[BIA] LORD our God.
Spare us and have compassion on us,
and in compassion and favor accept our prayer,
for You, God, listen to prayers and pleas.[BA]
Do not turn us away, O our King,
empty-handed from Your presence,[B]
for You listen with compassion to the prayer of Your people Israel.
Blessed are You, LORD, who listens to prayer.

---

plural, as opposed to the previous reference to תְּפִלָּתֵנוּ, meaning "our prayer" in the singular. This is because the prayers mentioned here refer not only to the prayers of the individual, and not only to the prayers of the other Jews in your *minyan*, and not only to the prayers of all Jews, but to the prayers of all mankind as well. (Rabbi S. Schwab)

What prayer might you have in common with the rest of humanity?

What prayer can I offer for the entire human race today?

BIUR TEFILLA • ביאור תפילה

כִּי אֵל שׁוֹמֵעַ תְּפִלּוֹת וְתַחֲנוּנִים אָתָּה – *For You, God, listen to prayers and pleas.* Listen to the prayer of all Israel, lest my own individual prayer is found lacking in some way. May my prayer be considered as part of theirs.

וּמִלְּפָנֶיךָ מַלְכֵּנוּ רֵיקָם אַל תְּשִׁיבֵנוּ – *Do not turn us away, O our King, empty-handed from Your presence.* This could mean, "Please give us at least something we asked for," or it could mean, "Let our prayers not be empty of content. Let us leave You with at least a meaningful prayer to our credit" (Rabbi S.R. Hirsch). Make this prayer meaningful.

ANI TEFILLA • אני תפילה

I thought I knew something about prayer, but I found out otherwise. I was at the Kotel saying Tehillim and thinking that I was really praying. I saw a blind man being led down to the Kotel. He ran his fingers over the stones, feeling thousands of years of history. Then he kissed the Wall, and began talking to God. He spoke very rapidly, and I could not understand anything he said. Abruptly he stopped, paused momentarily, then said, "Ok, I told you about that yesterday," and resumed his communication. I realized that he was really communicating with God, and knew that He listened. I resumed saying Tehillim, but with a much different kavana. (Rabbi A.J. Twerski)

The **ANI TEFILLA** *on* שומע תפילה *continues on page 175.*

שומע תפילה

שְׁמַע קוֹלֵנוּ[בעא] יהוה אֱלֹהֵינוּ
חוּס וְרַחֵם עָלֵינוּ, וְקַבֵּל בְּרַחֲמִים וּבְרָצוֹן אֶת תְּפִלָּתֵנוּ
כִּי אֵל שׁוֹמֵעַ תְּפִלּוֹת וְתַחֲנוּנִים אָתָּה[בא]
וּמִלְּפָנֶיךָ מַלְכֵּנוּ רֵיקָם אַל תְּשִׁיבֵנוּ[ב]
כִּי אַתָּה שׁוֹמֵעַ תְּפִלַּת עַמְּךָ יִשְׂרָאֵל בְּרַחֲמִים.
בָּרוּךְ אַתָּה יהוה, שׁוֹמֵעַ תְּפִלָּה.

BIUR TEFILLA • ביאור תפילה

שְׁמַע קוֹלֵנוּ – *Listen to our voice.* Listen, even if we ourselves have not understood all of the messages of the words we have just said in the previous blessings. (*Etz Yosef*)

"Listen to our voice" – even if we could not muster all of the correct *kavana* for the words because it is so hard to focus and so many other thoughts interfere. (*Siaḥ Yitzḥak*)

IYUN TEFILLA • עיון תפילה

שְׁמַע קוֹלֵנוּ – *Listen to our voice.* "Prayer…is a dialogue not a monologue. A dialogue exists when one person addresses another, even if the other is temporarily silent…. In praying, we do not seek a response to a particular request as much as we desire a fellowship with God" (Rabbi J.B. Soloveitchik). Hashem is like a friend on the other end of the phone who doesn't always speak. But there is comfort in knowing that He is always listening whenever we want to speak to Him. Hashem is always a **שׁוֹמֵעַ תְּפִלָּה**.

ANI TEFILLA • אני תפילה

שְׁמַע קוֹלֵנוּ – *Listen to our voice.* We ask Hashem to "listen to the sound of our voices." When the Jews suffered all of those years of slavery in Egypt, what was it that finally caused God to remember His covenant and to set the exodus in motion? The answer: "And the children of Israel sighed by reason of the bondage, and they cried, and their cry came up to God by reason of the bondage" (*Shemot* 2:23). God heard their voices, their pain, their sighing. Not their words. Sometimes, if we have the right *kavana,* just using the right voice can be enough.

Don't just read the words; use your voice.

כִּי אֵל שׁוֹמֵעַ תְּפִלּוֹת – *For You, God, listen to prayers.* Here the word **תְּפִלּוֹת** is in the

TEMPLE SERVICE[B]

רְצֵה Find favor,[B] LORD our God,
in Your people Israel and their prayer.[B]
Restore the service to Your most holy House,
and accept in love[B] and favor
the fire-offerings[B] of Israel and their prayer.
May the service of Your people Israel
always find favor with You.

The עֲבוֹדָה could be a reference to the specific *Avoda* of Yom Kippur performed by the *Kohen Gadol* in the Holy of Holies. (דְּבִיר בֵּיתֶךָ refers to the place where the word [דִּבּוּר] of God is heard.)

The עֲבוֹדָה could be a reference to the prayers which were offered then and which we offer now, the עֲבוֹדָה שֶׁבַּלֵּב, the service of the heart.

Which interpretation speaks to you today?

וְאִשֵּׁי – *The fire-offerings.* This could refer to the fire-offerings in the *Beit HaMikdash*. We ask that the Temple service be restored. Prayers there are different than our prayers here. How?

וְאִשֵּׁי could refer to the martyrs of Israel (from the word אִישׁ) who sacrificed their lives for Your name. Accept their sacrifice and their prayers. (*Tosafot Menahḥot* 110a)

וְאִשֵּׁי could refer to the fire that was always lit on the Altar. So, too, in the heart of every Jew there is a hidden flame that seeks to cleave to Hashem that is never extinguished.

Which interpretation speaks to you today?

בְּאַהֲבָה – *In love.* "Love" could describe the prayers – we ask that the prayers we offer out of love should be accepted.

"Love" could describe the acceptance – we ask that the prayers we offer should be accepted with love.

ANI TEFILLA • אני תפילה

If you saw somebody pulling a boat to the shore and were mistaken about mechanics and motion, you might think that he was pulling the shore to the boat. That's what prayer is like. You think that you're pulling God to you, but in fact, if you pray well, you pull yourself to God. (Attributed to Yehuda Aryeh MiModena)

עבודה

רְצֵה יהוה אֱלֹהֵינוּ בְּעַמְּךָ יִשְׂרָאֵל וּבִתְפִלָּתָם
וְהָשֵׁב אֶת הָעֲבוֹדָה לִדְבִיר בֵּיתֶךָ
וְאִשֵּׁי יִשְׂרָאֵל וּתְפִלָּתָם בְּאַהֲבָה תְקַבֵּל בְּרָצוֹן
וּתְהִי לְרָצוֹן תָּמִיד עֲבוֹדַת יִשְׂרָאֵל עַמֶּךָ.

ANI TEFILLA • אני תפילה

As a friend of mine once explained to me, people are unhappy because they want what they cannot have, and they don't want what they already have. We can alleviate this cycle of negativity in two ways. First, we must learn to want what we already have and be grateful to God. If we don't, we will not be ready to receive anything more. Next, we need to learn to desire what God wants to give us. When our will is aligned with God's will, and we sincerely ask for what God has wanted to give us all along, then His blessings flow freely into our lives. (Rabbi D. Aaron)

BIUR TEFILLA • ביאור תפילה

עבודה – *TEMPLE SERVICE.* This is the first of the final three blessings of the *Shemoneh Esreh*, the *birkhot hodaya*, blessings of thanks. What they all have in common, despite elements of additional requests, is the acknowledgment of and gratitude to Hashem for the personal and communal relationship we have with Him.

רְצֵה – *Find favor.* Here we ask that our prayers be found acceptable in terms of their content. Here we ask that our prayers be found acceptable in terms of their sincerity.

וּבִתְפִלָּתָם – *And their prayer.* We first ask Hashem to find favor in "Your people," and only afterwards in "their prayers." This is to teach us that if we make a sincere effort to make our own lives worthy, to become better people and better Jews, only then can we hope that our prayers will be found worthy. (Rabbi S.R. Hirsch)

How have your prayers until this point moved you to become a better person today?

How can I make myself a better person and a better Jew today?

הָעֲבוֹדָה – *The service.* The **עֲבוֹדָה** could be a reference to general worship in the *Beit HaMikdash* (**דְבִיר בֵּיתֶךָ**).

On Rosh Ḥodesh, say:

אֱלֹהֵינוּ Our God and God of our ancestors, may there rise, come, reach, appear, be favored, heard, regarded and remembered[I] before You, our recollection and remembrance, as well as the remembrance of our ancestors, and of the Messiah son of David Your servant, and of Jerusalem Your holy city, and of all Your people the house of Israel – for deliverance and well-being, grace, loving-kindness and compassion, life and peace, on this day of Rosh Ḥodesh. On it remember us, LORD our God, for good; recollect us for blessing, and deliver us for life. In accord with Your promise of salvation and compassion, spare us and be gracious to us; have compassion on us and deliver us, for our eyes are turned to You because You, God, are a gracious and compassionate King.

וְתֶחֱזֶינָה And may our eyes witness[B]
Your return to Zion in compassion.
Blessed are You, LORD,
who restores His Presence to Zion.[B]

ANI TEFILLA • אני תפילה

Make a picture in your mind when you are praying that you are really standing in Israel and in the Holy Temple and that you are actually seeing everything with your own eyes.... And when you imagine this is so, that you are standing in Israel, you will achieve great clarity in your prayer. (Rabbi Elimelech of Lizhensk)

IYUN TEFILLA • עיון תפילה

וְיִפָּקֵד וְיִזָּכֵר – *Regarded and remembered.* Why is there so much discussion here about remembering; after all, does Hashem really forget anything? Rather, just as there are distractions which cause us to be unable to recall things we really know, so too there are things about our actions which act as barriers to Hashem's "remembering" the good things that we do. For example, each person is born with his own unique potential which he must realize on his own. We ask that Hashem remember (וְיִפָּקֵד) the potential that we have and that he recall (וְיִזָּכֵר) the good deeds we have done to try to realize that potential. Rosh Ḥodesh and the holy days are times for introspection, for that, too, is a form of service of the heart.

On ראש חודש, *say:*

אֱלֹהֵינוּ וֵאלֹהֵי אֲבוֹתֵינוּ, יַעֲלֶה וְיָבוֹא וְיַגִּיעַ, וְיֵרָאֶה וְיֵרָצֶה וְיִשָּׁמַע, וְיִפָּקֵד וְיִזָּכֵר[ע] זִכְרוֹנֵנוּ וּפִקְדוֹנֵנוּ וְזִכְרוֹן אֲבוֹתֵינוּ, וְזִכְרוֹן מָשִׁיחַ בֶּן דָּוִד עַבְדֶּךָ, וְזִכְרוֹן יְרוּשָׁלַיִם עִיר קָדְשֶׁךָ, וְזִכְרוֹן כָּל עַמְּךָ בֵּית יִשְׂרָאֵל, לְפָנֶיךָ, לִפְלֵיטָה לְטוֹבָה, לְחֵן וּלְחֶסֶד וּלְרַחֲמִים, לְחַיִּים וּלְשָׁלוֹם בְּיוֹם רֹאשׁ הַחֹדֶשׁ הַזֶּה. זָכְרֵנוּ יהוה אֱלֹהֵינוּ בּוֹ לְטוֹבָה, וּפָקְדֵנוּ בוֹ לִבְרָכָה, וְהוֹשִׁיעֵנוּ בוֹ לְחַיִּים. וּבִדְבַר יְשׁוּעָה וְרַחֲמִים, חוּס וְחָנֵּנוּ וְרַחֵם עָלֵינוּ וְהוֹשִׁיעֵנוּ, כִּי אֵלֶיךָ עֵינֵינוּ, כִּי אֵל מֶלֶךְ חַנּוּן וְרַחוּם אָתָּה.

וְתֶחֱזֶינָה עֵינֵינוּ[ב] בְּשׁוּבְךָ לְצִיּוֹן בְּרַחֲמִים.
בָּרוּךְ אַתָּה יהוה
הַמַּחֲזִיר שְׁכִינָתוֹ לְצִיּוֹן.[ב]

BIUR TEFILLA • ביאור תפילה

וְתֶחֱזֶינָה עֵינֵינוּ – *And may our eyes witness.* An alternative translation is "and may You enable us to see." The existence of the State of Israel can be seen as a sign that You are a presence in history and that the State is the beginning of Your return to Zion. May You enable our eyes to see Israel not only as a political entity, but as the miracle that it really is.

IYUN TEFILLA • עיון תפילה

הַמַּחֲזִיר שְׁכִינָתוֹ לְצִיּוֹן – *Who restores His Presence to Zion.* I thank You Hashem because I know that You will return Your Presence to Jerusalem. I only pray that it be sooner rather than later.

While this *berakha* is found in the final section of the *Amida*, the section of "Thanks," it sounds like a request for the restoration of the Temple service, which more appropriately belongs in the middle section, and it can be argued these themes are already found there. However, if we approach this as a statement of faith rather than a request, that we have total faith that this will happen, and we merely desire it in a speedy fashion, then it certainly belongs here.

THANKSGIVING

Bow at the first nine words.

מוֹדִים We give thanks to You,[BA]
for You are the LORD our God
and God of our ancestors
for ever and all time.
You are the Rock of our lives,
Shield of our salvation
from generation to generation.
We will thank You and
declare Your praise for our lives,[B]
which are entrusted into Your hand;
for our souls,[B]
which are placed in Your charge;
for Your miracles[B]
which are with us every day;
and for Your wonders[B] and favors[B]
at all times, evening,
morning and midday.
You are good –
for Your compassion never fails.
You are compassionate –
for Your loving-
kindnesses never cease.
We have always
placed our hope in You.

During the Leader's Repetition, the congregation says quietly:

מוֹדִים We give thanks[B] to You,
for You are the LORD
our God
and God of our ancestors,
God of all flesh,
who formed us
and formed the universe.
Blessings and thanks are due
to Your great and holy name
for giving us life
and sustaining us.
May You continue
to give us life and sustain us;
and may You gather
our exiles
to Your holy courts,
to keep Your decrees,
do Your will and serve You
with a perfect heart,
for it is for us
to give You thanks.
Blessed be God
to whom
thanksgiving is due.

---

granted. I know that there is more to me as a person than my physical body.

וְעַל נִסֶּיךָ – *For Your miracles.* We thank You for the everyday miracles in our lives of which we are not aware, for example, a virus I did not catch, a moment when my life was imperiled on my way here today but I walked by, totally unaware.

וְעַל נִפְלְאוֹתֶיךָ – *And for Your wonders.* We thank You for the everyday wonders to which we may be oblivious. I will not take for granted the vibrant life which surrounds me.

וְטוֹבוֹתֶיךָ – *And favors.* We thank You even for the things which seem bad, because ultimately we know that You want good to emerge from them.

ANI TEFILLA *on* מודים *is on page 181.* **BIUR TEFILLA** *on* מודים דרבנן *is on page 180.*

הודאה

Bow at the first five words.

יְמוֹדִים אֲנַחְנוּ לָךְ[בא]
שָׁאַתָּה הוּא יהוה אֱלֹהֵינוּ
וֵאלֹהֵי אֲבוֹתֵינוּ לְעוֹלָם וָעֶד.
צוּר חַיֵּינוּ, מָגֵן יִשְׁעֵנוּ
אַתָּה הוּא לְדוֹר וָדוֹר.
נוֹדֶה לְּךָ וּנְסַפֵּר תְּהִלָּתֶךָ
עַל חַיֵּינוּ[ב] הַמְּסוּרִים בְּיָדֶךָ
וְעַל נִשְׁמוֹתֵינוּ[ב] הַפְּקוּדוֹת לָךְ
וְעַל נִסֶּיךָ[ב] שֶׁבְּכָל יוֹם עִמָּנוּ
וְעַל נִפְלְאוֹתֶיךָ[ב] וְטוֹבוֹתֶיךָ[ב]
שֶׁבְּכָל עֵת
עֶרֶב וָבֹקֶר וְצָהֳרָיִם.
הַטּוֹב, כִּי לֹא כָלוּ רַחֲמֶיךָ
וְהַמְרַחֵם, כִּי לֹא תַמּוּ חֲסָדֶיךָ
מֵעוֹלָם קִוִּינוּ לָךְ.

During חזרת הש״ץ, *the* קהל *says quietly:*

יְמוֹדִים[ב] אֲנַחְנוּ לָךְ
שָׁאַתָּה הוּא יהוה אֱלֹהֵינוּ
וֵאלֹהֵי אֲבוֹתֵינוּ
אֱלֹהֵי כָל בָּשָׂר
יוֹצְרֵנוּ, יוֹצֵר בְּרֵאשִׁית.
בְּרָכוֹת וְהוֹדָאוֹת
לְשִׁמְךָ הַגָּדוֹל וְהַקָּדוֹשׁ
עַל שֶׁהֶחֱיִיתָנוּ וְקִיַּמְתָּנוּ.
כֵּן תְּחַיֵּנוּ וּתְקַיְּמֵנוּ
וְתֶאֱסֹף גָּלֻיּוֹתֵינוּ
לְחַצְרוֹת קָדְשֶׁךָ
לִשְׁמֹר חֻקֶּיךָ
וְלַעֲשׂוֹת רְצוֹנֶךָ וּלְעָבְדְּךָ
בְּלֵבָב שָׁלֵם
עַל שֶׁאֲנַחְנוּ מוֹדִים לָךְ.
בָּרוּךְ אֵל הַהוֹדָאוֹת.

BIUR TEFILLA · ביאור תפילה

מוֹדִים אֲנַחְנוּ לָךְ – *We give thanks to You.* The word מוֹדִים can mean "thank" in which case the sense is that we thank You for all of the good that there is in our lives.

The word can mean "acknowledge" in which case the sense is that we acknowledge that You are our God and the God of our ancestors. We acknowledge that God exists based upon all of the good things we have in our lives.

Do I want to thank God today or to acknowledge His existence?

עַל חַיֵּינוּ – *For our lives.* We thank You for our physical life. I will not take my physical health for granted. There are so many people who are worse off than me.

וְעַל נִשְׁמוֹתֵינוּ – *For our souls.* We thank You for our souls which animate our bodies.

I will not take my spiritual life for

וְעַל כֻּלָּם For all these things may Your name be blessed and exalted, our King, continually, for ever and all time.
Let all that lives thank You, Selah! and praise Your name in truth, God, our Savior and Help, Selah!
▾Blessed are You, LORD, whose name is "the Good" and to whom thanks are due.

The following is said by the Leader during the Repetition of the Amida, except in a house of mourning and on Tisha B'Av. In Israel, if Kohanim bless the congregation, *turn to page 1008.*

Our God and God of our fathers, bless us with the threefold blessing in the Torah, written by the hand of Moses Your servant and pronounced by Aaron and his sons the priests, Your holy people, as it is said:[B]

May the LORD bless you and protect you. *Num. 6*
Cong: May it be Your will.
May the LORD make His face shine on you and be gracious to you.
Cong: May it be Your will.
May the LORD turn His face toward you, and grant you peace.
Cong: May it be Your will.

BIUR TEFILLA • ביאור תפילה

מודים דרבנן – *THE RABBIS' MODIM.* The Gemara (*Sota* 40a) asks what the congregation is supposed to recite when the *Hazan* reaches this point. Yet why ask? After all, in no other blessing during the *Hazan*'s repetition of the *Shemoneh Esreh* is there a different blessing that we ourselves say; the *Hazan* is our emissary for all of those other blessings. Why might it be different here? One answer was offered by Abudarham: because when it comes to saying "thank you" one cannot appoint a messenger. Each of us must offer thanks in our own personal way.

BIUR TEFILLA • ביאור תפילה

ברכת כהנים – *BIRKAT KOHANIM.* In the times of the *Beit HaMikdash*, after the sacrifices were offered, the *kohanim* would fulfill the positive commandment of blessing the people (*Bemidbar* 6:22–26.; *Vayikra* 9:22). Ultimately, however, it is understood that the blessing comes from Hashem, whose love for Israel is manifest in the blessings that we receive in our daily lives all around us. Note that each phrase has two verbs with Hashem at the center, and each phrase has 3, 5 and 7 words respectively, symbolizing the incremental growth inherent in each blessing (*berakha*), like a spring of water (*bereikha*) which bubbles up and gives life.

וְעַל כֻּלָּם יִתְבָּרַךְ וְיִתְרוֹמַם שִׁמְךָ מַלְכֵּנוּ תָּמִיד לְעוֹלָם וָעֶד.
וְכֹל הַחַיִּים יוֹדְוּךָ סֶּלָה, וִיהַלְלוּ אֶת שִׁמְךָ בֶּאֱמֶת
הָאֵל יְשׁוּעָתֵנוּ וְעֶזְרָתֵנוּ סֶלָה.
ׂבָּרוּךְ אַתָּה יהוה, הַטּוֹב שִׁמְךָ וּלְךָ נָאֶה לְהוֹדוֹת.

The following is said by the שליח ציבור *during* חזרת הש״ץ, *except in a house of mourning and on* תשעה באב. *In* ארץ ישראל *if* כהנים *say* ברכת כהנים *turn to page 1009.*

אֱלֹהֵינוּ וֵאלֹהֵי אֲבוֹתֵינוּ, בָּרְכֵנוּ בַּבְּרָכָה הַמְשֻׁלֶּשֶׁת בַּתּוֹרָה, הַכְּתוּבָה עַל
יְדֵי מֹשֶׁה עַבְדֶּךָ, הָאֲמוּרָה מִפִּי אַהֲרֹן וּבָנָיו כֹּהֲנִים עַם קְדוֹשֶׁיךָ, כָּאָמוּר:
יְבָרֶכְךָ יהוה וְיִשְׁמְרֶךָ: קהל: כֵּן יְהִי רָצוֹן במדבר ו
יָאֵר יהוה פָּנָיו אֵלֶיךָ וִיחֻנֶּךָּ: קהל: כֵּן יְהִי רָצוֹן
יִשָּׂא יהוה פָּנָיו אֵלֶיךָ וְיָשֵׂם לְךָ שָׁלוֹם: קהל: כֵּן יְהִי רָצוֹן

ANI TEFILLA • אני תפילה

מוֹדִים אֲנַחְנוּ לָךְ – *We give thanks to You.* In short, one can thank God here for anything and everything: the people in our lives who care about us, our family, our relatives, our friends and acquaintances, the material comforts we have, the air we breathe. Sometimes we do not appreciate things enough until they are gone. Don't wait. Be thankful.

What is on your list today?

ANI TEFILLA • אני תפילה

The story is told of two angels who were assigned the task of going around the world to collect people's prayers. Each one set out with a bag, determined to beat the other one out. At the end of the prescribed time, one angel returned with a bag that was bulging, he was bent over from the burden of his load. The other angel, however, clearly did not have the same success. His bag was half empty, or, at best, half full, and as he turned his bag over to empty it, it became clear that he had returned with a paltry sum of prayers. What accounted for the difference?

It turns out that they were collecting different prayers. The first angel was collecting only those prayers which contained requests, people's expressions of the things they wanted or thought they wanted or thought they needed. The other angel, however, the one with the emptier bag, only collected prayers of thanks. The point of the story is clear. We simply do not thank as much as we could, as much as we should.

PEACE

שִׂים שָׁלוֹם Grant peace,[ABI] goodness and blessing,
grace, loving-kindness and compassion[B]
to us and all Israel Your people.
Bless us, our Father, all as one, with the light of Your face,
for by the light of Your face[B] You have given us, LORD our God,
the Torah of life and love of kindness,
righteousness, blessing, compassion, life and peace.
May it be good in Your eyes to bless Your people Israel
at every time, in every hour, with Your peace.
Blessed are You, LORD, who blesses His people Israel with peace.[A]

---

angry so that peace and holiness can reign.

שִׂים שָׁלוֹם – *Grant peace. Shalom* comes about when everyone knows his or her place in the world, where there is no struggle because there is acceptance of others.

Can you think of someone whom you might have a hard time accepting?

What small change can you try to make today in your relationship?

שִׂים שָׁלוֹם – *Grant peace.* When one says this blessing, one should have in mind the mitzva of וְאָהַבְתָּ לְרֵעֲךָ כָּמוֹךָ – love your neighbor as yourself (*Ya'arot Devash*).

Whom can I have in mind for this mitzva today?

BIUR TEFILLA • ביאור תפילה

חֵן וָחֶסֶד וְרַחֲמִים – *Grace, loving-kindness and compassion.*

Hen, grace, is when the receiver finds favor in the eyes of the giver.

Hesed comes from the generosity of the giver, whether the recipient deserves it or not.

Rahamim, mercy, is granted when it is not deserved.

Which ones are most relevant for me today?

בְּאוֹר פָּנֶיךָ – *With the light of Your face.* "Bless us with the light of Your face" – this could be a request to God to stop hiding from us. The Ba'al HaTanya wrote that we are asking Him to enlighten us with belief in Him so that we can live with the clear understanding that everything comes from Him, and that He should reveal Himself to us in our daily lives. Peace can come from that knowledge.

How can I try harder to see the presence of God somewhere in my life today?

ANI TEFILLA • אני תפילה

הַמְבָרֵךְ אֶת עַמּוֹ יִשְׂרָאֵל בַּשָּׁלוֹם – *Who blesses His people Israel with peace.* One of God's names is "Peace" (*Shabbat* 10b). That is one meaning of the greeting *Shalom Aleikhem* – May peace be upon you. May Hashem's name be upon you. Without peace, there is nothing.

ברכת שלום

שִׂים שָׁלוֹם אבע טוֹבָה וּבְרָכָה
חֵן וָחֶסֶד וְרַחֲמִים ב עָלֵינוּ וְעַל כָּל יִשְׂרָאֵל עַמֶּךָ.
בָּרְכֵנוּ אָבִינוּ כֻּלָּנוּ כְּאֶחָד בְּאוֹר פָּנֶיךָ
כִּי בְאוֹר פָּנֶיךָ ג נָתַתָּ לָּנוּ יהוה אֱלֹהֵינוּ
תּוֹרַת חַיִּים וְאַהֲבַת חֶסֶד
וּצְדָקָה וּבְרָכָה וְרַחֲמִים וְחַיִּים וְשָׁלוֹם.
וְטוֹב בְּעֵינֶיךָ לְבָרֵךְ אֶת עַמְּךָ יִשְׂרָאֵל
בְּכָל עֵת וּבְכָל שָׁעָה בִּשְׁלוֹמֶךָ.
בָּרוּךְ אַתָּה יהוה, הַמְבָרֵךְ אֶת עַמּוֹ יִשְׂרָאֵל בַּשָּׁלוֹם. א

ANI TEFILLA • אני תפילה

שִׂים שָׁלוֹם – *Grant peace.* One vision of peace is surely that all Jews live together harmoniously. Although no one person can unify the world, every person is still obligated to feel united and connected to *Klal Yisrael*. (*Rinat Ḥayyim*)

To whom in my world could I feel more connected than I do?

שִׂים שָׁלוֹם – *Grant peace.* With whom am I angry?

I resolve to let my anger go so that I can feel more complete, so that the other person can feel more complete, so that the world can be more complete.

There can be no inner peace and no peace with others in a place where there is jealousy.

I resolve not to be jealous of others today.

There can be no inner peace or peace with others where there is unhealthy competitiveness.

I resolve not to be competitive today in an unhealthy way.

BIUR TEFILLA • ביאור תפילה

שִׂים שָׁלוֹם – *Grant peace. Shalom* is related to the word *shalem*, meaning "whole" or "complete." There cannot be peace unless people feel complete within themselves; until they are at peace with their physical selves, their ethical selves, their emotional selves. We ask Hashem to help us become more complete people today so that we may be at peace with ourselves and with others.

What can I do today to make myself into a more complete person physically? Ethically? Emotionally? Religiously?

IYUN TEFILLA • עיון תפילה

שִׂים שָׁלוֹם – *Grant peace.* Where there is anger, there cannot be peace. In a place where there is holiness, anger cannot exist. Therefore we ask Hashem to help us not be

The following verse concludes the Leader's Repetition of the Amida. Some also say it here as part of the silent Amida.

May the words of my mouth[IH] and the meditation of my heart find favor before You, LORD, my Rock and Redeemer. *Ps. 19*

אֱלֹהַי My God, *Berakhot 17a*
guard[BI] my tongue from evil
and my lips from deceitful speech.

IYUN TEFILLA • עיון תפילה

יִהְיוּ לְרָצוֹן אִמְרֵי־פִי – *May the words of my mouth.* The verse comes from the nineteenth chapter of *Tehillim*. Just as King David uttered this verse after reciting 18 psalms, so, too, do we express the same sentiment after reciting the prayer known as the Eighteen Blessings (*Berakhot* 9b).

BIUR TEFILLA • ביאור תפילה

אֱלֹהַי, נְצֹר – *My God, guard.* The major theme of this concluding prayer is the request that we be protected against the sin of **לָשׁוֹן הָרַע**, evil speech. Think about what negative effects **לָשׁוֹן הָרַע** has upon us, our relationships, and our daily lives. Think about it enough, suffer from it once, try not speaking it for any length of time, and you'll begin to understand why we need God's help.

IYUN TEFILLA • עיון תפילה

אֱלֹהַי, נְצֹר – *My God, guard.* The Ḥafetz Ḥayyim once said:

To be sure, in this prayer we ask Hashem for His help. We ask Him to help us not speak **לָשׁוֹן הָרַע** and not speak lies. But do we do our part? Do we expend energy to "protect our tongue from speaking evil and our lips from uttering deceit?"

Do we do our part?

And if we do not do our part, then how can we possibly ask Him for His help? For we have learned that there is a law (*Devarim* 22:4) that if you see someone's donkey fallen under too heavy a load, you must help the owner pick it up. And the verse says **הָקֵם תָּקִים עִמּוֹ** – you shall surely lift it *with him*. From here the Gemara in *Bava Metzia* 32b says it must happen "with him," meaning with the owner of the donkey; for the owner might sit by the wayside and say "Okay, since you are obligated to lift up your fellow man's donkey, you lift it up while I sit back and watch." Hence the Gemara says "you must lift it *with him*," meaning, the owner of the donkey must participate.

So, too, in our case, said the Ḥafetz Ḥayyim, if we ask Hashem to help unload us from this sin, then Hashem may say, "Help Me by doing your share, otherwise I am under no obligation to help you."

The following verse concludes the חזרת הש״ץ.
Some also say it here as part of the silent עמידה.

יִהְיוּ לְרָצוֹן אִמְרֵי־פִי וְהֶגְיוֹן לִבִּי לְפָנֶיךָ, יהוה צוּרִי וְגֹאֲלִי: תהלים יט

אֱלֹהַי ברכות יז.
נְצֹר לְשׁוֹנִי מֵרָע וּשְׂפָתַי מִדַּבֵּר מִרְמָה

HILKHOT TEFILLA • הלכות תפילה

יִהְיוּ לְרָצוֹן אִמְרֵי־פִי – *May the words of my mouth.* The Gemara *Berakhot* 9b says that one should conclude one's *Shemoneh Esreh* with this verse from *Tehillim* 19 just as one began one's prayer with the words, "Hashem, open my lips so that my mouth may declare Your praise." Now at the conclusion, we therefore say this parallel request: "May the words of my mouth and the meditation of my heart find favor..." We thus begin and end the prayer with a very personal request (unlike all of the other blessings, these words are in the singular and not the plural) that our prayers be heard, both those uttered aloud and those expressed in the inner recesses of our soul.

The question is whether this verse is part and parcel of the *Shemoneh Esreh* itself or, given that it is not really a blessing and given that it is in the singular and not the plural, whether it is part of a private supplication. The practical difference would be if, for example, you had not yet said the verse but had already concluded *Sim Shalom* and, in the meantime the rest of the congregation had reached *Kedusha*; would you respond or would you have to remain silent because you haven't really finished *Shemoneh Esreh* yet?

At the same time, there developed a practice to add even more supplications after the *Tefilla* was over as will be explained in the *Taḥanun* prayer found below. One such supplication, *Elokai Netzor* which appears next, was authored by one of the last of the Amoraim, Mar the son of Ravina (fifth century CE), and it was ultimately incorporated into the fixed text. Note that toward the end he includes this concluding verse of **יִהְיוּ לְרָצוֹן**. As such, where exactly does *Shemoneh Esreh* end – after *Sim Shalom*? after the recitation of the verse **יִהְיוּ לְרָצוֹן** the first time? after the recitation of *Elokai Netzor*?

The *Shulḥan Arukh* (122:1) rules that one should not utter any interruption until one has said **יִהְיוּ לְרָצוֹן**. The Rema disagrees, clearly believing that one's *Shemoneh Esreh* already formally concluded after *Sim Shalom*. The *Mishna Berura* suggests that one should say the verse **יִהְיוּ לְרָצוֹן** twice, once here and once in *Elokai Netzor* in order to remove oneself from doubt.

To those who curse me, let my soul be silent;[BA]
may my soul be to all like the dust.
Open my heart to Your Torah
and let my soul pursue Your commandments.
As for all who plan evil against me,
swiftly thwart their counsel and frustrate their plans.
Act for the sake of Your name; act for the sake of Your right hand;
act for the sake of Your holiness; act for the sake of Your Torah.
That Your beloved ones may be delivered,[B] *Ps. 60*
save with Your right hand and answer me.
May the words of my mouth and the meditation of my heart *Ps. 19*
find favor before You, LORD, my Rock and Redeemer.

Bow, take three steps back, then bow, first left, then right, then center, while saying:

May He who makes peace in His high places,
make peace for us and all Israel – and say: Amen.

יְהִי רָצוֹן May it be Your will, LORD our God and God of our ancestors,
that the Temple be rebuilt speedily in our days,
and grant us a share in Your Torah.
And there we will serve You with reverence,
as in the days of old and as in former years.
Then the offering of Judah and Jerusalem will be pleasing to the LORD *Mal. 3*
as in the days of old and as in former years.

When praying with a minyan, the Amida is repeated aloud by the Leader.

On days when Tahanun is said (see page 194), start Taḥanun on page 202.
On Mondays and Thursdays start Taḥanun on page 194.

On fast days (except Tisha B'Av) most congregations say Seliḥot
on page 870 before Avinu Malkenu on page 188.

On Rosh Ḥodesh say Hallel on page 842.

On other days when Taḥanun is not said (see page 194),
the Leader says Half Kaddish on page 208.

---

word יֵחָלְצוּן comes not from the word "to free," but rather from the word "to rest" (just as we say on Shabbat רְצֵה וְהַחֲלִיצֵנוּ in ברכת המזון). If so, then in this prayer I am asking that Hashem allow me to achieve mental rest, a release from pressure, tension, and worry.

וְלִמְקַלְלַי נַפְשִׁי תִדֹּם,[בא] וְנַפְשִׁי כֶּעָפָר לַכֹּל תִּהְיֶה.
פְּתַח לִבִּי בְּתוֹרָתֶךָ, וּבְמִצְוֹתֶיךָ תִּרְדֹּף נַפְשִׁי.
וְכָל הַחוֹשְׁבִים עָלַי רָעָה, מְהֵרָה הָפֵר עֲצָתָם וְקַלְקֵל מַחֲשַׁבְתָּם.
עֲשֵׂה לְמַעַן שְׁמֶךָ, עֲשֵׂה לְמַעַן יְמִינֶךָ
עֲשֵׂה לְמַעַן קְדֻשָּׁתֶךָ, עֲשֵׂה לְמַעַן תּוֹרָתֶךָ.
לְמַעַן יֵחָלְצוּן יְדִידֶיךָ,[ב] הוֹשִׁיעָה יְמִינְךָ וַעֲנֵנִי: תהלים ס
יִהְיוּ לְרָצוֹן אִמְרֵי־פִי וְהֶגְיוֹן לִבִּי לְפָנֶיךָ, יהוה צוּרִי וְגֹאֲלִי: תהלים יט

Bow, take three steps back, then bow, first left, then right, then center, while saying:

עֹשֶׂה שָׁלוֹם בִּמְרוֹמָיו
הוּא יַעֲשֶׂה שָׁלוֹם עָלֵינוּ וְעַל כָּל יִשְׂרָאֵל, וְאִמְרוּ אָמֵן.

יְהִי רָצוֹן מִלְּפָנֶיךָ יהוה אֱלֹהֵינוּ וֵאלֹהֵי אֲבוֹתֵינוּ
שֶׁיִּבָּנֶה בֵּית הַמִּקְדָּשׁ בִּמְהֵרָה בְיָמֵינוּ, וְתֵן חֶלְקֵנוּ בְּתוֹרָתֶךָ
וְשָׁם נַעֲבָדְךָ בְּיִרְאָה כִּימֵי עוֹלָם וּכְשָׁנִים קַדְמוֹנִיּוֹת.
וְעָרְבָה לַיהוה מִנְחַת יְהוּדָה וִירוּשָׁלָֽם כִּימֵי עוֹלָם וּכְשָׁנִים קַדְמֹנִיּוֹת: מלאכי ג

When praying with a מנין, *the* עמידה *is repeated aloud by the* שליח ציבור.

On days when תחנון *is said (see page 195), start* תחנון *on page 203.*
On Mondays and Thursdays start תחנון *on page 195.*

On fast days (except תשעה באב*) most congregations say* סליחות *on page 871 before* אבינו מלכנו *on page 189.*

On ראש חודש, *say* הלל *on page 843.*

On other days when תחנון *is not said (see page 195), the* שליח ציבור *says* חצי קדיש *on page 209.*

BIUR TEFILLA • ביאור תפילה

וְלִמְקַלְלַי נַפְשִׁי תִדֹּם – *To those who curse me, let my soul be silent.* Perhaps this is a reference to being on the receiving end of לָשׁוֹן הָרָע; if I am ever put in that position where people speak about me or against me, I hope I have the strength not to answer them in kind; otherwise, I will be no different than they are, and my prayer will now be meaningless.

לְמַעַן יֵחָלְצוּן יְדִידֶיךָ – *That Your beloved ones may be delivered.* The Meiri suggests that the

AVINU MALKENU[BA]

On fast days (except Tisha B'Av) most congregations say Seliḥot on page 870 before Avinu Malkenu.

The Ark is opened.

אָבִינוּ מַלְכֵּנוּ Our Father, our King, we have sinned before You.

Our Father, our King, we have no king but You.

Our Father, our King, deal kindly with us for the sake of Your name.

Our Father our King, bless us with a good year.

Our Father, our King, nullify all harsh decrees against us.

Our Father, our King, nullify the plans of those who hate us.

Our Father, our King, thwart the counsel of our enemies.

Our Father, our King, rid us of every oppressor and adversary.

Our Father, our King, close the mouths of our adversaries and accusers.

Our Father, our King, eradicate pestilence, sword, famine, captivity and destruction, iniquity and eradication from the people of Your covenant.

Our Father, our King, withhold the plague from Your heritage.

---

nation to not observe mitzvot that made no sense to him. In short, he had faith, a faith born of his own struggles. A lesson to all of us as we are about ask for Hashem's help.

ANI TEFILLA · אני תפילה

אָבִינוּ מַלְכֵּנוּ – *Our Father, our King.*
The story is told about a young prince whose father, the king, was also his teacher. Whenever the boy misbehaved, the king would be very hard on him. One day the father found the boy at home in tears and asked him why he was crying so intensely. The prince responded: "My teacher is too hard on me." His father replied, "I will speak to your teacher." Sometimes Hashem can relate to us as a king meting out punishment that we deserve; but we ask that he also relate to us to the extent possible with the compassion of a father, and so we say, "My Father, my King."

אבינו מלכנו [בא]

On fast days (except תשעה באב*) most congregations say* סליחות *on page 871 before* אבינו מלכנו.

The ארון קודש *is opened.*

אָבִינוּ מַלְכֵּנוּ, חָטָאנוּ לְפָנֶיךָ.

אָבִינוּ מַלְכֵּנוּ, אֵין לָנוּ מֶלֶךְ אֶלָּא אָתָּה.

אָבִינוּ מַלְכֵּנוּ, עֲשֵׂה עִמָּנוּ לְמַעַן שְׁמֶךָ.

אָבִינוּ מַלְכֵּנוּ, בָּרֵךְ עָלֵינוּ שָׁנָה טוֹבָה.

אָבִינוּ מַלְכֵּנוּ, בַּטֵּל מֵעָלֵינוּ כָּל גְּזֵרוֹת קָשׁוֹת.

אָבִינוּ מַלְכֵּנוּ, בַּטֵּל מַחְשְׁבוֹת שׂוֹנְאֵינוּ.

אָבִינוּ מַלְכֵּנוּ, הָפֵר עֲצַת אוֹיְבֵינוּ.

אָבִינוּ מַלְכֵּנוּ, כַּלֵּה כָּל צַר וּמַשְׂטִין מֵעָלֵינוּ.

אָבִינוּ מַלְכֵּנוּ, סְתֹם פִּיּוֹת מַשְׂטִינֵנוּ וּמְקַטְרְגֵינוּ.

אָבִינוּ מַלְכֵּנוּ, כַּלֵּה דֶּבֶר וְחֶרֶב וְרָעָב וּשְׁבִי וּמַשְׁחִית וְעָוֹן וּשְׁמַד מִבְּנֵי בְרִיתֶךָ.

אָבִינוּ מַלְכֵּנוּ, מְנַע מַגֵּפָה מִנַּחֲלָתֶךָ.

BIUR TEFILLA • ביאור תפילה

אָבִינוּ מַלְכֵּנוּ – *Our Father, our King.* This very ancient prayer is recited on days related to repentance, particularly on fast days and the days between Rosh HaShana and Yom Kippur. The Gemara (*Ta'anit* 25b) relates that there was a horrible drought and the prayers for relief were not answered until Rabbi Akiva got up and recited the introductory formula for this prayer, whereupon it began to rain. And what made his prayer more effective than those of others? One possibility offered is that it was because, as a *ba'al teshuva*, he had to forge his own relationship with Hashem, rather than rely first upon a religious upbringing. Another possibility is that he overcame his own initial incli-

Our Father, our King, forgive and pardon all our iniquities.

Our Father, our King, wipe away and remove our transgressions and sins from Your sight.

Our Father, our King, erase in Your abundant mercy all records of our sins.

The following nine sentences are said responsively, first by the Leader, then by the congregation:

Our Father, our King, bring us back to You in perfect repentance.

Our Father, our King, send a complete healing to the sick of Your people.

Our Father, our King, tear up the evil decree against us.

Our Father, our King, remember us with a memory of favorable deeds before You.

Our Father, our King, remember us for a good life.

Our Father, our King, remember us for redemption and salvation.

Our Father, our King, remember us for livelihood and sustenance.

Our Father, our King, remember us for merit.

Our Father, our King, remember us for pardon and forgiveness.

End of responsive reading.

Our Father, our King, let salvation soon flourish for us.

Our Father, our King, raise the honor of Your people Israel.

Our Father, our King, raise the honor of Your anointed.

Our Father, our King, fill our hands with Your blessings.

Our Father, our King, fill our storehouses with abundance.

Our Father, our King, hear our voice, pity and be compassionate to us.

Our Father, our King, accept, with compassion and favor, our prayer.

Our Father, our King, open the gates of heaven to our prayer.

Our Father, our King, remember that we are dust.

אָבִינוּ מַלְכֵּנוּ, סְלַח וּמְחַל לְכָל עֲוֹנוֹתֵינוּ.
אָבִינוּ מַלְכֵּנוּ, מְחֵה וְהַעֲבֵר פְּשָׁעֵינוּ וְחַטֹּאתֵינוּ מִנֶּגֶד עֵינֶיךָ.
אָבִינוּ מַלְכֵּנוּ, מְחֹק בְּרַחֲמֶיךָ הָרַבִּים כָּל שִׁטְרֵי חוֹבוֹתֵינוּ.

The following nine sentences are said responsively, first by the שליח ציבור*, then by the* קהל*:*

אָבִינוּ מַלְכֵּנוּ, הַחֲזִירֵנוּ בִּתְשׁוּבָה שְׁלֵמָה לְפָנֶיךָ.
אָבִינוּ מַלְכֵּנוּ, שְׁלַח רְפוּאָה שְׁלֵמָה לְחוֹלֵי עַמֶּךָ.
אָבִינוּ מַלְכֵּנוּ, קְרַע רֹעַ גְּזַר דִּינֵנוּ.
אָבִינוּ מַלְכֵּנוּ, זָכְרֵנוּ בְּזִכְרוֹן טוֹב לְפָנֶיךָ.
אָבִינוּ מַלְכֵּנוּ, זָכְרֵנוּ לְחַיִּים טוֹבִים.
אָבִינוּ מַלְכֵּנוּ, זָכְרֵנוּ לִגְאֻלָּה וִישׁוּעָה.
אָבִינוּ מַלְכֵּנוּ, זָכְרֵנוּ לְפַרְנָסָה וְכַלְכָּלָה.
אָבִינוּ מַלְכֵּנוּ, זָכְרֵנוּ לִזְכֻיּוֹת.
אָבִינוּ מַלְכֵּנוּ, זָכְרֵנוּ לִסְלִיחָה וּמְחִילָה.

End of responsive reading.

אָבִינוּ מַלְכֵּנוּ, הַצְמַח לָנוּ יְשׁוּעָה בְּקָרוֹב.
אָבִינוּ מַלְכֵּנוּ, הָרֵם קֶרֶן יִשְׂרָאֵל עַמֶּךָ.
אָבִינוּ מַלְכֵּנוּ, הָרֵם קֶרֶן מְשִׁיחֶךָ.
אָבִינוּ מַלְכֵּנוּ, מַלֵּא יָדֵינוּ מִבִּרְכוֹתֶיךָ.
אָבִינוּ מַלְכֵּנוּ, מַלֵּא אֲסָמֵינוּ שָׂבָע.
אָבִינוּ מַלְכֵּנוּ, שְׁמַע קוֹלֵנוּ, חוּס וְרַחֵם עָלֵינוּ.
אָבִינוּ מַלְכֵּנוּ, קַבֵּל בְּרַחֲמִים וּבְרָצוֹן אֶת תְּפִלָּתֵנוּ.
אָבִינוּ מַלְכֵּנוּ, פְּתַח שַׁעֲרֵי שָׁמַיִם לִתְפִלָּתֵנוּ.
אָבִינוּ מַלְכֵּנוּ, זְכֹר כִּי עָפָר אֲנָחְנוּ.

Our Father, our King, please do not turn us away from You empty-handed.

Our Father, our King, may this moment be a moment of compassion and a time of favor before You.

Our Father, our King, have pity on us, our children and our infants.

Our Father, our King, act for the sake of those who were killed for Your holy name.[A]

Our Father, our King, act for the sake of those who were slaughtered for proclaiming Your Unity.

Our Father, our King, act for the sake of those who went through fire and water to sanctify Your name.

Our Father, our King, avenge before our eyes the spilt blood of Your servants.

Our Father, our King, act for Your sake, if not for ours.

Our Father, our King, act for Your sake, and save us.

Our Father, our King, act for the sake of Your abundant compassion.

Our Father, our King, act for the sake of Your great, mighty and awesome name by which we are called.

▸ Our Father, our King, be gracious to us and answer us, though we have no worthy deeds; act with us in charity and loving-kindness and save us.

The Ark is closed.

---

up in front of a river. One soldier with a machine gun started shooting from the right side of the line and moved his gun toward the left until he killed all of the men. When the shooting began, all of the men started reciting the *Shema* together. The people on the right were killed as they said "*Hashem Elokeinu*"; they did not manage to finish the verse. Those people were הֲרוּגִים עַל שֵׁם קָדְשֶׁךָ (they died saying God's name). The people further left managed to stay alive for long enough to say "*Hashem eḥad*;" they died עַל יִחוּדֶךָ (for Your Unity). Rav Itzikel could not stop crying after hearing this.

אָבִינוּ מַלְכֵּנוּ, נָא אַל תְּשִׁיבֵנוּ רֵיקָם מִלְּפָנֶיךָ.
אָבִינוּ מַלְכֵּנוּ, תְּהֵא הַשָּׁעָה הַזֹּאת שְׁעַת רַחֲמִים
וְעֵת רָצוֹן מִלְּפָנֶיךָ.
אָבִינוּ מַלְכֵּנוּ, חֲמֹל עָלֵינוּ וְעַל עוֹלָלֵינוּ וְטַפֵּנוּ.
אָבִינוּ מַלְכֵּנוּ, עֲשֵׂה לְמַעַן הֲרוּגִים עַל שֵׁם קָדְשֶׁךָ.[א]
אָבִינוּ מַלְכֵּנוּ, עֲשֵׂה לְמַעַן טְבוּחִים עַל יִחוּדֶךָ.
אָבִינוּ מַלְכֵּנוּ, עֲשֵׂה לְמַעַן בָּאֵי בָאֵשׁ וּבַמַּיִם עַל קִדּוּשׁ שְׁמֶךָ.
אָבִינוּ מַלְכֵּנוּ, נְקֹם לְעֵינֵינוּ נִקְמַת דַּם עֲבָדֶיךָ הַשָּׁפוּךְ.
אָבִינוּ מַלְכֵּנוּ, עֲשֵׂה לְמַעַנְךָ אִם לֹא לְמַעֲנֵנוּ.
אָבִינוּ מַלְכֵּנוּ, עֲשֵׂה לְמַעַנְךָ וְהוֹשִׁיעֵנוּ.
אָבִינוּ מַלְכֵּנוּ, עֲשֵׂה לְמַעַן רַחֲמֶיךָ הָרַבִּים.
אָבִינוּ מַלְכֵּנוּ, עֲשֵׂה לְמַעַן שִׁמְךָ הַגָּדוֹל הַגִּבּוֹר וְהַנּוֹרָא
שֶׁנִּקְרָא עָלֵינוּ.
◂ אָבִינוּ מַלְכֵּנוּ, חָנֵּנוּ וַעֲנֵנוּ, כִּי אֵין בָּנוּ מַעֲשִׂים
עֲשֵׂה עִמָּנוּ צְדָקָה וָחֶסֶד וְהוֹשִׁיעֵנוּ.

The ארון קודש *is closed.*

ANI TEFILLA • אני תפילה

עֲשֵׂה לְמַעַן הֲרוּגִים עַל שֵׁם קָדְשֶׁךָ – *Act for the sake of those who were killed for Your holy name.*

The story is told that a Holocaust survivor asked Rav Itzikel from Antwerp the following question: We say in *Avinu Malkenu* "הֲרוּגִים עַל שֵׁם קָדְשֶׁךָ, those who were killed for Your holy name," and then "טְבוּחִים עַל יִחוּדֶךָ, slaughtered for proclaiming Your Unity." Why do we say two distinct phrases, שֵׁם קָדְשֶׁךָ and יִחוּדֶךָ? The Holocaust survivor answered his own question by explaining that when the Nazis marched into a town, they assembled 100 men and lined them

TAḤANUN

On Mondays and Thursdays, when Taḥanun is said, begin with "He is compassionate" below. On other days when Taḥanun is said, begin with "David said" on page 202.

Taḥanun is not said on: Rosh Ḥodesh, Tisha B'Av and Tu B'Av.

Taḥanun is also not said: on the morning of a Brit Mila, either where the brit will take place or where the father, Sandek or Mohel are present; if a groom is present (and some say a bride) on the day of his wedding or during the week of Sheva Berakhot; in a house of mourning.

The following until "David said" on page 202 is said standing.

וְהוּא רַחוּם He is compassionate. He forgives iniquity and does not destroy. *Ps. 78*
Repeatedly He suppresses His anger, not rousing His full wrath. Lord, do not withhold Your compassion from us. May Your loving-kindness and
truth always protect us. Save us, Lord our God, and gather us from among *Ps. 106*
the nations, that we may give thanks to Your holy name and glory in Your
praise. If You, Lord, should keep account of sins, O Lord, who could *Ps. 130*
stand? But with You is forgiveness, that You may be revered. Do not deal with us according to our sins; do not repay us according to our iniquities.
Though our iniquities testify against us, Lord, act for Your name's sake. *Jer. 14*
Remember, Lord, Your compassion and loving-kindness, for they are *Ps. 25*
everlasting. May the Lord answer us when we are in distress; may the *Ps. 20*
name of Jacob's God protect us. Lord, save! May the King answer us when we call. Our Father, our King, be gracious to us and answer us, though we have no worthy deeds; act charitably with us for Your name's sake. Lord our God, hear the sound of our pleas. Remember for us the covenant of our ancestors, and save us for Your name's sake.

---

regularly, both as individuals and as a nation, and that we are in need of God's help.

וְהוּא רַחוּם is one of those prayers of profound beauty, and the depth of individual and national longing that the prayer expresses is sometimes lost with a recitation that is too quick and cursory.

While the source of the prayer is not known for certain, there are a number of differing traditions. One of the most famous, and the one that may be closest to the historical truth, can be found in the siddur of the Roke'aḥ (Rabbi Elazar of Worms, one of the Torah giants of his generation), although the story itself was already known in the times of the Geonim, centuries before.

> *Vespasian drove three groups of distinguished Jerusalemites into exile. He placed each group in a separate ship without any navigator, and they traveled as far as Europe: one group arriving at Lyon, another at Arles and the third at Bordeaux. This last group was cordially received by the local duke. He allotted them fields and vineyards and they lived there*

This **INTRODUCTION** *continues on page 197.*

סדר תחנון

On Mondays and Thursdays, when תחנון *is said, begin with* וְהוּא רַחוּם *below.*
On other days when תחנון *is said, begin with* וַיֹּאמֶר דָּוִד *on page 203.*

תחנון *is not said on:* ראש חודש, תשעה באב, *and* ט״ו באב.

תחנון *is also not said: on the morning of a* ברית מילה, *either where the* ברית *will take place or where the father,* סנדק *or* מוהל *are present; if a* חתן *is present (and some say a* כלה*) on the day of his wedding or during the week of* שבע ברכות*; in a house of mourning.*

The following until וַיֹּאמֶר דָּוִד *on page 203 is said standing.*

וְהוּא רַחוּם, יְכַפֵּר עָוֺן וְלֹא־יַשְׁחִית, וְהִרְבָּה לְהָשִׁיב אַפּוֹ וְלֹא־יָעִיר תהלים עח
כָּל־חֲמָתוֹ: אַתָּה יהוה לֹא־תִכְלָא רַחֲמֶיךָ מִמֶּנּוּ, חַסְדְּךָ וַאֲמִתְּךָ תָּמִיד
יִצְּרוּנוּ. הוֹשִׁיעֵנוּ יהוה אֱלֹהֵינוּ וְקַבְּצֵנוּ מִן־הַגּוֹיִם, לְהוֹדוֹת לְשֵׁם קָדְשֶׁךָ, תהלים קו
לְהִשְׁתַּבֵּחַ בִּתְהִלָּתֶךָ: אִם־עֲוֺנוֹת תִּשְׁמָר־יָהּ, אֲדֹנָי מִי יַעֲמֹד: כִּי־עִמְּךָ תהלים קל
הַסְּלִיחָה לְמַעַן תִּוָּרֵא: לֹא כַחֲטָאֵינוּ תַּעֲשֶׂה לָּנוּ, וְלֹא כַעֲוֺנוֹתֵינוּ תִּגְמֹל
עָלֵינוּ. אִם־עֲוֺנֵינוּ עָנוּ בָנוּ, יהוה עֲשֵׂה לְמַעַן שְׁמֶךָ: זְכֹר־רַחֲמֶיךָ יהוה ירמיה יד / תהלים כה
וַחֲסָדֶיךָ, כִּי מֵעוֹלָם הֵמָּה: יַעֲנֵנוּ יהוה בְּיוֹם צָרָה, יְשַׂגֶּבְךָ שֵׁם אֱלֹהֵי
יַעֲקֹב. יהוה הוֹשִׁיעָה, הַמֶּלֶךְ יַעֲנֵנוּ בְיוֹם־קָרְאֵנוּ: אָבִינוּ מַלְכֵּנוּ, חָנֵּנוּ תהלים כ
וַעֲנֵנוּ, כִּי אֵין בָּנוּ מַעֲשִׂים, צְדָקָה עֲשֵׂה עִמָּנוּ לְמַעַן שְׁמֶךָ. אֲדוֹנֵינוּ
אֱלֹהֵינוּ, שְׁמַע קוֹל תַּחֲנוּנֵינוּ, וּזְכָר לָנוּ אֶת בְּרִית אֲבוֹתֵינוּ וְהוֹשִׁיעֵנוּ
לְמַעַן שְׁמֶךָ.

INTRODUCTION TO THE "LONG TAḤANUN" OF MONDAYS AND THURSDAYS

Mondays and Thursdays have long been known as fortuitous days in Jewish life, marked especially as days that are worthy of prayers being answered. The most famous Thursday-Monday combination took place when Moshe Rabbeinu went up Mount Sinai a second time to get the commandments after *Benei Yisrael* erred the first time; according to tradition, Moshe went up the mountain on a Thursday and came back down with the second Tablets on a Monday (Tur, 134). Ever since, Mondays and Thursdays have been known as יְמֵי רָצוֹן, days that are particularly favorable for getting a positive response from Hashem, especially in response to requests for forgiveness and atonement. So advantageous were these days for repentance that another tradition is to fast every Monday and Thursday, as if each were a mini Yom Kippur!

As a result, Mondays and Thursdays became days for adding lots of prayers that focus on our recognition that we sin all too

וְעַתָּה And now, My LORD, our God, who took Your people out of the land of Egypt with a mighty hand, creating for Yourself renown to this day: we have sinned and acted wrongly. LORD, in keeping with all Your righteousness, please turn Your wrath and anger away from Jerusalem, Your holy mountain. Because of our sins and the iniquities of our ancestors, Jerusalem and Your people have become the scorn of all those around us. And now, our God, heed Your servant's prayer and pleas, and let Your face shine on Your desolate Sanctuary, for Your sake, O LORD. Incline Your ear, my God, and hear. Open Your eyes and see our desolation and that of the city called by Your name. Not because of our righteousness do we lay our pleas before You, but because of Your great compassion. LORD, hear! LORD, forgive! LORD, listen and act! Do not delay – for Your sake, my God, because Your city and Your people are called by Your name. *Dan. 9*

אָבִינוּ Our Father, compassionate Father, show us a sign for good, and gather our scattered ones from the four quarters of the earth. Let all the nations recognize and know that You are the LORD our God. And now, *Is. 64* LORD, You are our Father. We are the clay and You are our Potter; we are all the work of Your hand. Save us for the sake of Your name, our Rock, our King and our Redeemer. Pity Your people, LORD. Let not Your heri- *Joel 2* tage become an object of scorn, a byword among nations. Why should they say among the peoples, "Where is their God?" We know we have sinned and that there is no one to stand up for us. Let Your great name stand up for us in time of trouble. We know we have no merits of our own: therefore deal with us charitably for Your name's sake. As a father has compassion on his children, so, LORD, have compassion on us, and save us for the sake of Your name. Have mercy on Your people; have compassion for Your heritage; take pity in Your great compassion. Be gracious to us and answer us, for righteousness is Yours, LORD. Always You do wondrous things.

All of these prayers are culled from as many as 58 biblical sources, although in fewer than half are the verses quoted verbatim. The rest are merely modeled, in respect of their language, on biblical sentences. The expressions, "our Father, our King," "Merciful and gracious," "Save us for Your name's sake," "Look down..." (*Habet, habita*) especially, keep being repeated. There are 13 words in the sentence *Vehu Raḥum,* corresponding, perhaps, to the 13 *Middot*: *Hashem Hashem Kel Raḥum* etc.

וְעַתָּה אֲדֹנָי אֱלֹהֵינוּ, אֲשֶׁר הוֹצֵאתָ אֶת־עַמְּךָ מֵאֶרֶץ מִצְרַיִם בְּיָד חֲזָקָה דניאל ט
וַתַּעַשׂ־לְךָ שֵׁם כַּיּוֹם הַזֶּה, חָטָאנוּ רָשָׁעְנוּ: אֲדֹנָי, כְּכָל־צִדְקֹתֶךָ יָשָׁב־
נָא אַפְּךָ וַחֲמָתְךָ, מֵעִירְךָ יְרוּשָׁלַםִ הַר־קָדְשֶׁךָ, כִּי בַחֲטָאֵינוּ וּבַעֲוֹנוֹת
אֲבֹתֵינוּ, יְרוּשָׁלַםִ וְעַמְּךָ לְחֶרְפָּה לְכָל־סְבִיבֹתֵינוּ: וְעַתָּה שְׁמַע אֱלֹהֵינוּ
אֶל־תְּפִלַּת עַבְדְּךָ וְאֶל־תַּחֲנוּנָיו, וְהָאֵר פָּנֶיךָ עַל־מִקְדָּשְׁךָ הַשָּׁמֵם, לְמַעַן
אֲדֹנָי: הַטֵּה אֱלֹהַי אָזְנְךָ וּשְׁמָע, פְּקַח עֵינֶיךָ וּרְאֵה שֹׁמְמֹתֵינוּ וְהָעִיר
אֲשֶׁר־נִקְרָא שִׁמְךָ עָלֶיהָ, כִּי לֹא עַל־צִדְקֹתֵינוּ אֲנַחְנוּ מַפִּילִים תַּחֲנוּנֵינוּ
לְפָנֶיךָ, כִּי עַל־רַחֲמֶיךָ הָרַבִּים: אֲדֹנָי שְׁמָעָה, אֲדֹנָי סְלָחָה, אֲדֹנָי הַקְשִׁיבָה
וַעֲשֵׂה אַל־תְּאַחַר, לְמַעַנְךָ אֱלֹהַי, כִּי־שִׁמְךָ נִקְרָא עַל־עִירְךָ וְעַל־עַמֶּךָ:

אָבִינוּ הָאָב הָרַחֲמָן, הַרְאֵנוּ אוֹת לְטוֹבָה וְקַבֵּץ נְפוּצוֹתֵינוּ מֵאַרְבַּע
כַּנְפוֹת הָאָרֶץ. יַכִּירוּ וְיֵדְעוּ כָּל הַגּוֹיִם כִּי אַתָּה יהוה אֱלֹהֵינוּ. וְעַתָּה ישעיה סד
יהוה אָבִינוּ אָתָּה, אֲנַחְנוּ הַחֹמֶר וְאַתָּה יֹצְרֵנוּ וּמַעֲשֵׂה יָדְךָ כֻּלָּנוּ:
הוֹשִׁיעֵנוּ לְמַעַן שְׁמֶךָ, צוּרֵנוּ מַלְכֵּנוּ וְגוֹאֲלֵנוּ. חוּסָה יהוה עַל־עַמֶּךָ, יואל ב
וְאַל־תִּתֵּן נַחֲלָתְךָ לְחֶרְפָּה לִמְשָׁל־בָּם גּוֹיִם, לָמָּה יֹאמְרוּ בָעַמִּים אַיֵּה
אֱלֹהֵיהֶם: יָדַעְנוּ כִּי חָטָאנוּ וְאֵין מִי יַעֲמֹד בַּעֲדֵנוּ, שִׁמְךָ הַגָּדוֹל יַעֲמָד
לָנוּ בְּעֵת צָרָה. יָדַעְנוּ כִּי אֵין בָּנוּ מַעֲשִׂים, צְדָקָה עֲשֵׂה עִמָּנוּ לְמַעַן
שְׁמֶךָ. כְּרַחֵם אָב עַל בָּנִים כֵּן תְּרַחֵם יהוה עָלֵינוּ, וְהוֹשִׁיעֵנוּ לְמַעַן
שְׁמֶךָ. חֲמֹל עַל עַמֶּךָ, רַחֵם עַל נַחֲלָתֶךָ, חוּסָה נָּא כְּרֹב רַחֲמֶיךָ, חָנֵּנוּ
וַעֲנֵנוּ. כִּי לְךָ יהוה הַצְּדָקָה, עֹשֵׂה נִפְלָאוֹת בְּכָל עֵת.

---

peacefully for a long time, until that duke died and a new king arose over them. He imposed new restrictions upon them and they suffered very much. Among them were two brothers, Joseph and Benjamin, and their cousin, Samuel. They cried out to God in their distress, fasted, donned sackcloth on their flesh, and the three together composed the Vehu Raḥum prayer. Joseph is designated as the composer of the first part, Vehu Raḥum, to the end of the paragraph Habet Na, which also ends with the words Vehu Raḥum. The second part, from Ana Melekh to the end of the paragraph Raḥum, the last words of which are Raḥum Ata, was composed by Samuel. The third part, from Ein Kamokha to the end of the paragraph beginning with Hapote'aḥ, was composed by Benjamin.

הַבֵּט נָא Please look, please swiftly have compassion for Your people for Your name's sake. In Your great compassion, LORD our God, have pity and compassion, and rescue the flock You tend. Let us not be ruled by wrath, for our eyes are turned toward You. Save us for Your name's sake. Have compassion on us for the sake of Your covenant. Look and answer us in time of trouble, for Yours, LORD, is the power to save. Our hope is in You, God of forgiveness. Please forgive, good and forgiving God, for You are a gracious, compassionate God and King.

אָנָּא מֶלֶךְ Please, gracious and compassionate King, remember and call to mind the Covenant between the Pieces [with Abraham] and let the binding of his only son [Isaac] appear before You for Israel's sake. Our Father, our King, be gracious to us and answer us, for we are called by Your great name. You who work miracles at all times, deal with us according to Your loving-kindness. Gracious and compassionate One, look and answer us in time of trouble, for salvation is Yours, LORD. Our Father, our King, our Refuge, do not act with us according to our evil deeds. Remember, LORD, Your tender mercies and Your love. Save us in Your great goodness, and have mercy on us, for we have no other god but You, our Rock. Do not abandon us, LORD our God, do not be distant from us, for we are worn out by the sword and captivity, pestilence and plague, and by every trouble and sorrow. Rescue us, for in You lies our hope. Put us not to shame, LORD our God. Let Your face shine upon us. Remember for us the covenant of our ancestors and save us for Your name's sake. See our troubles and heed the voice of our prayer, for You heed the prayer of every mouth.

אֵל רַחוּם וְחַנּוּן O Compassionate and gracious God, have compassion on us and on all Your works, for there is none like You, LORD our God. Please, we beg You, forgive our sins, our Father, our King, our Rock, our Redeemer, living and eternal God, mighty in strength, loving and good to all Your works, for You are the LORD our God. O God, slow to anger and full of compassion, act with us according to Your great compassion and save us for Your name's sake. Hear our prayer, our King, and save us from our enemies' hands. Heed our prayer, our King, and save us from all distress and sorrow. You are our Father, our King. We are called by Your name. Do not desert us. Do not abandon us, our Father. Do not cast us away, our Creator. Do not forget us, our Maker – for You are a gracious and compassionate God and King.

הַבֶּט נָא, רַחֵם נָא עַל עַמְּךָ מְהֵרָה לְמַעַן שְׁמֶךָ בְּרַחֲמֶיךָ הָרַבִּים יהוה אֱלֹהֵינוּ. חוּס וְרַחֵם וְהוֹשִׁיעָה צֹאן מַרְעִיתֶךָ, וְאַל יִמְשָׁל בָּנוּ קֶצֶף, כִּי לְךָ עֵינֵינוּ תְלוּיוֹת. הוֹשִׁיעֵנוּ לְמַעַן שְׁמֶךָ. רַחֵם עָלֵינוּ לְמַעַן בְּרִיתֶךָ. הַבִּיטָה וַעֲנֵנוּ בְּעֵת צָרָה, כִּי לְךָ יהוה הַיְשׁוּעָה. בְּךָ תוֹחַלְתֵּנוּ אֱלוֹהַּ סְלִיחוֹת, אָנָּא סְלַח נָא אֵל טוֹב וְסַלָּח, כִּי אֵל מֶלֶךְ חַנּוּן וְרַחוּם אָתָּה.

אָנָּא מֶלֶךְ חַנּוּן וְרַחוּם, זְכֹר וְהַבֵּט לִבְרִית בֵּין הַבְּתָרִים, וְתֵרָאֶה לְפָנֶיךָ עֲקֵדַת יָחִיד לְמַעַן יִשְׂרָאֵל. אָבִינוּ מַלְכֵּנוּ, חָנֵּנוּ וַעֲנֵנוּ, כִּי שִׁמְךָ הַגָּדוֹל נִקְרָא עָלֵינוּ. עֹשֵׂה נִפְלָאוֹת בְּכָל עֵת, עֲשֵׂה עִמָּנוּ כְּחַסְדֶּךָ. חַנּוּן וְרַחוּם, הַבִּיטָה וַעֲנֵנוּ בְּעֵת צָרָה, כִּי לְךָ יהוה הַיְשׁוּעָה. אָבִינוּ מַלְכֵּנוּ מַחֲסֵנוּ, אַל תַּעַשׂ עִמָּנוּ כְּרֹעַ מַעֲלָלֵינוּ. זְכֹר רַחֲמֶיךָ יהוה וַחֲסָדֶיךָ, וּכְרֹב טוּבְךָ הוֹשִׁיעֵנוּ, וַחֲמָל נָא עָלֵינוּ, כִּי אֵין לָנוּ אֱלוֹהַּ אַחֵר מִבַּלְעָדֶיךָ צוּרֵנוּ. אַל תַּעַזְבֵנוּ יהוה אֱלֹהֵינוּ אַל תִּרְחַק מִמֶּנּוּ. כִּי נַפְשֵׁנוּ קְצָרָה, מֵחֶרֶב וּמִשְּׁבִי וּמִדֶּבֶר וּמִמַּגֵּפָה. וּמִכָּל צָרָה וְיָגוֹן הַצִּילֵנוּ, כִּי לְךָ קִוִּינוּ. וְאַל תַּכְלִימֵנוּ יהוה אֱלֹהֵינוּ, וְהָאֵר פָּנֶיךָ בָּנוּ, וּזְכָר לָנוּ אֶת בְּרִית אֲבוֹתֵינוּ וְהוֹשִׁיעֵנוּ לְמַעַן שְׁמֶךָ. רְאֵה בְצָרוֹתֵינוּ, וּשְׁמַע קוֹל תְּפִלָּתֵנוּ, כִּי אַתָּה שׁוֹמֵעַ תְּפִלַּת כָּל פֶּה.

אֵל רַחוּם וְחַנּוּן, רַחֵם עָלֵינוּ וְעַל כָּל מַעֲשֶׂיךָ, כִּי אֵין כָּמְוֹךָ יהוה אֱלֹהֵינוּ. אָנָּא שָׂא נָא פְשָׁעֵינוּ, אָבִינוּ מַלְכֵּנוּ צוּרֵנוּ וְגוֹאֲלֵנוּ, אֵל חַי וְקַיָּם הַחֲסִין בַּכֹּחַ, חָסִיד וָטוֹב עַל כָּל מַעֲשֶׂיךָ, כִּי אַתָּה הוּא יהוה אֱלֹהֵינוּ. אֵל אֶרֶךְ אַפַּיִם וּמָלֵא רַחֲמִים, עֲשֵׂה עִמָּנוּ כְּרֹב רַחֲמֶיךָ, וְהוֹשִׁיעֵנוּ לְמַעַן שְׁמֶךָ. שְׁמַע מַלְכֵּנוּ תְּפִלָּתֵנוּ, וּמִיַּד אוֹיְבֵינוּ הַצִּילֵנוּ. שְׁמַע מַלְכֵּנוּ תְּפִלָּתֵנוּ, וּמִכָּל צָרָה וְיָגוֹן הַצִּילֵנוּ. אָבִינוּ מַלְכֵּנוּ אָתָּה, וְשִׁמְךָ עָלֵינוּ נִקְרָא. אַל תַּנִּחֵנוּ, אַל תַּעַזְבֵנוּ אָבִינוּ וְאַל תִּטְּשֵׁנוּ בּוֹרְאֵנוּ וְאַל תִּשְׁכָּחֵנוּ יוֹצְרֵנוּ, כִּי אֵל מֶלֶךְ חַנּוּן וְרַחוּם אָתָּה.

אֵין כָּמְוֹךָ There is none like You in grace and compassion, LORD our God. There is none like You, God, slow to anger and abounding in loving-kindness and truth. Save us in Your great compassion; rescue us from storm and turmoil. Remember Your servants Abraham, Isaac and Jacob; do not attend to our stubbornness, wickedness and sinfulness. Turn from Your fierce anger, and relent *Ex. 32* from the evil meant for Your people. Remove from us the scourge of death, for You are compassionate. This is Your way, to show unearned loving-kindness to every generation. Have pity on Your people, LORD, and save us from Your wrath. Remove from us the scourge of plague and the harsh decree, for You are the Guardian of Israel. You are right, my LORD, and we are shamefaced. How can we complain? What can we say? What can we plead? How can we justify ourselves? Let us search our ways and examine them and return to You, for Your right hand is outstretched to receive those who return. Please, *Ps. 118* LORD, please save. Please, LORD, please send success. Please, LORD, answer us when we call. For You, LORD, we wait. For You, LORD, we hope. For You, LORD, we long. Do not be silent while we suffer, for the nations are saying, "Their hope is lost." To You alone every knee must bend, and those who hold themselves high bow down.

הַפּוֹתֵחַ יָד You who hold out an open hand of repentance to receive transgressors and sinners – our soul is overwhelmed by our great sorrow. Do not forget us for ever. Arise and save us, for we seek refuge in You. Our Father, our King, though we lack righteousness and good deeds, remember for us the covenant of our fathers, and our testimonies daily that "The LORD is One." Look on our affliction, for many are our sufferings and heartaches. Have pity on us, LORD, in the land of our captivity. Do not pour out Your wrath on us, for we are Your people, the children of Your covenant. God, see how low our glory has sunk among the nations. They abhor us as if we were impure. How long will Your strength be captive, and Your glory in the hand of the foe? Arouse Your strength and zeal against Your enemies. Let them be shamed and deprived of power. Let not our hardships seem small to You. Swiftly may Your compassion reach us in the day of our distress. If not for our sake, act for Yours, so that the memory of our survivors be not destroyed. Be gracious to the nation who, in constant love, proclaim twice daily the unity of Your name, saying, "Listen, *Deut. 6* Israel, the LORD is our God, the LORD is One."

According to the Tur, Rabbi Yaakov ben Asher, that's the meaning of *Nefilat Apayim* or "falling down on one's face" immediately after the *Shemoneh Esreh*. You've just finished asking for everything, you've just finished saying everything there was to say, but somehow words have failed you and now there's nothing left to do but throw

This **INTRODUCTION** *continues on page 203.*

אֵין כָּמְוֹךָ חַנּוּן וְרַחוּם יהוה אֱלֹהֵינוּ, אֵין כָּמְוֹךָ אֵל אֶרֶךְ אַפַּיִם וְרַב חֶסֶד
וֶאֱמֶת. הוֹשִׁיעֵנוּ בְּרַחֲמֶיךָ הָרַבִּים, מֵרַעַשׁ וּמֵרֹגֶז הַצִּילֵנוּ. זְכֹר לַעֲבָדֶיךָ
לְאַבְרָהָם לְיִצְחָק וּלְיַעֲקֹב, אַל תֵּפֶן אֶל קָשְׁיֵנוּ וְאֶל רִשְׁעֵנוּ וְאֶל חַטָּאתֵנוּ.
שׁוּב מֵחֲרוֹן אַפֶּךָ, וְהִנָּחֵם עַל־הָרָעָה לְעַמֶּךָ: וְהָסֵר מִמֶּנּוּ מַכַּת הַמָּוֶת כִּי שמות לב
רַחוּם אָתָּה, כִּי כֵן דַּרְכֶּךָ, עוֹשֶׂה חֶסֶד חִנָּם בְּכָל דּוֹר וָדוֹר. חוּסָה יהוה עַל
עַמֶּךָ וְהַצִּילֵנוּ מִזַּעְמֶךָ, וְהָסֵר מִמֶּנּוּ מַכַּת הַמַּגֵּפָה וּגְזֵרָה קָשָׁה, כִּי אַתָּה
שׁוֹמֵר יִשְׂרָאֵל. לְךָ אֲדֹנָי הַצְּדָקָה וְלָנוּ בֹּשֶׁת הַפָּנִים: מַה נִּתְאוֹנֵן, מַה נֹּאמַר, דניאל ט
מַה נְּדַבֵּר וּמַה נִּצְטַדָּק. נַחְפְּשָׂה דְרָכֵינוּ וְנַחְקֹרָה וְנָשׁוּבָה אֵלֶיךָ, כִּי יְמִינְךָ
פְשׁוּטָה לְקַבֵּל שָׁבִים. אָנָּא יהוה הוֹשִׁיעָה נָּא, אָנָּא יהוה הַצְלִיחָה נָא: תהלים קיח
אָנָּא יהוה עֲנֵנוּ בְּיוֹם קָרְאֵנוּ. לְךָ יהוה חִכִּינוּ, לְךָ יהוה קִוִּינוּ, לְךָ יהוה
נְיַחֵל. אַל תֶּחֱשֶׁה וּתְעַנֵּנוּ, כִּי נָאֲמוּ גוֹיִם, אָבְדָה תִקְוָתָם. כָּל בֶּרֶךְ וְכָל
קוֹמָה, לְךָ לְבַד תִּשְׁתַּחֲוֶה.

הַפּוֹתֵחַ יָד בִּתְשׁוּבָה לְקַבֵּל פּוֹשְׁעִים וְחַטָּאִים, נִבְהֲלָה נַפְשֵׁנוּ מֵרֹב עִצְּבוֹנֵנוּ.
אַל תִּשְׁכָּחֵנוּ נֶצַח, קוּמָה וְהוֹשִׁיעֵנוּ כִּי חָסִינוּ בָךְ. אָבִינוּ מַלְכֵּנוּ, אִם אֵין
בָּנוּ צְדָקָה וּמַעֲשִׂים טוֹבִים, זְכָר לָנוּ אֶת בְּרִית אֲבוֹתֵינוּ וְעֵדוֹתֵינוּ בְּכָל
יוֹם יהוה אֶחָד. הַבִּיטָה בְעָנְיֵנוּ, כִּי רַבּוּ מַכְאוֹבֵינוּ וְצָרוֹת לְבָבֵנוּ. חוּסָה
יהוה עָלֵינוּ בְּאֶרֶץ שִׁבְיֵנוּ, וְאַל תִּשְׁפֹּךְ חֲרוֹנְךָ עָלֵינוּ, כִּי אֲנַחְנוּ עַמְּךָ בְּנֵי
בְרִיתֶךָ. אֵל, הַבִּיטָה, דַּל כְּבוֹדֵנוּ בַּגּוֹיִם וְשִׁקְּצוּנוּ כְּטֻמְאַת הַנִּדָּה. עַד מָתַי
עֻזְּךָ בַּשְּׁבִי, וְתִפְאַרְתְּךָ בְּיַד צָר. עוֹרְרָה גְבוּרָתְךָ וְקִנְאָתְךָ עַל אוֹיְבֶיךָ. הֵם
יֵבֹשׁוּ וְיֵחַתּוּ מִגְּבוּרָתָם. וְאַל יִמְעֲטוּ לְפָנֶיךָ תְּלָאוֹתֵינוּ, מַהֵר יְקַדְּמוּנוּ רַחֲמֶיךָ
בְּיוֹם צָרָתֵנוּ. וְאִם לֹא לְמַעֲנֵנוּ, לְמַעַנְךָ פְעַל, וְאַל תַּשְׁחִית זֵכֶר שְׁאֵרִיתֵנוּ,
וְחֹן אֹם הַמְיַחֲדִים שִׁמְךָ פַּעֲמַיִם בְּכָל יוֹם תָּמִיד בְּאַהֲבָה, וְאוֹמְרִים, שְׁמַע דברים ו
יִשְׂרָאֵל, יהוה אֱלֹהֵינוּ, יהוה אֶחָד:

INTRODUCTION TO TAHANUN – תחנון: נפילת אפיים

Did you ever try to say something important, but couldn't get the words out just right?

Did you ever try to say something, but couldn't say it with enough feeling or passion?

Did you ever have an emotion so deep (love, frustration, anger) that you couldn't even speak, but needed to physically act out by giving someone a hug or throwing yourself onto your bed?

LOWERING THE HEAD

On Sundays, Tuesdays, Wednesdays and Fridays, begin Taḥanun here. The following, until "We do not know" on page 208, is said sitting. When praying in a place where there is a Torah scroll, one should lean forward, resting one's head on the left arm (unless you are wearing tefillin on the left arm, in which case rest on the right arm out of respect for the tefillin), until in "sudden shame."

וַיֹּאמֶר דָּוִד David said[H] to Gad, "I am in great distress. *II Sam. 24*
Let us fall into God's hand, for His mercy is great;
but do not let me fall into the hand of man."

Compassionate and gracious One, I have sinned before You.
LORD, full of compassion, have compassion on me and accept my pleas.

LORD, do not rebuke me in Your anger or chastise me in Your wrath. Be gracious to me,[B] LORD, for I am weak. Heal me, LORD,[B] for my bones are in agony.[B] My soul is in anguish, and You, O LORD – how long? Turn, LORD, set my soul free; save me for the sake of Your love. For no one remembers You when he is dead. Who can praise You from the grave? I am weary with my sighing.[I] Every night I drench my bed, I soak my couch with my tears. My eye grows dim from grief, worn out because of all my foes. Leave me, all you evildoers, for the LORD has heard the sound of my weeping.[A] The LORD has heard[I] my pleas. The LORD will accept my prayer. All my enemies will be shamed and utterly dismayed. They will turn back in sudden shame. *Ps. 6*

Sit upright.

The Tefilla continues on page 206.

---

of Moshe's life and leadership, you can just imagine how heartfelt, how desperate, how pleading was that prayer. That's *Taḥanun*.

There's a verse in *Mishlei* (18:23) which says: תַּחֲנוּנִים יְדַבֶּר רָשׁ וְעָשִׁיר יַעֲנֶה עַזּוֹת – "The poor person speaks entreatingly (*taḥanunim*)…" Did you ever see a homeless person on the street asking for some money for a cup of coffee? Did you ever encounter a poor person at the *Kotel* asking for *tzedaka*, and you were truly moved by the sense of need the person seemed to convey? Did you ever have someone stand outside your door asking for a small amount and you felt so badly for them because of the way they spoke to you or appeared to you that you felt like you just had to give them something? How did these needy people present themselves? How did they speak? How did they act?

Imagine yourself the poor person. Now say *Taḥanun*.

HILKHOT TEFILLA • הלכות תפילה

וַיֹּאמֶר דָּוִד – *David said. Ḥazal* learn that there is a prohibition from the Torah to fully prostrate oneself on a stone floor. This is learned from the verse: "You shall not make idols for yourselves, neither shall you raise up an engraved image or a pillar, neither

This **HILKHOT TEFILLA** *continues on page 205. The commentary on Psalm 6 is on page 204.*

נפילת אפיים

On Sundays, Tuesdays, Wednesdays and Fridays, begin תחנון *here. The following, until* וַאֲנַחְנוּ לֹא נֵדַע *on page 209, is said sitting. When praying in a place where there is a* ספר תורה*, one should lean forward, resting one's head on the left arm (unless you are wearing* תפילין *on the left arm, in which case rest on the right arm out of respect for the tefillin), until in* יֵבֹשׁוּ רָגַע.

וַיֹּאמֶר דָּוִד ה אֶל־גָּד, צַר־לִי מְאֹד שמואל ב, כד
נִפְּלָה־נָּא בְיַד־יהוה, כִּי רַבִּים רַחֲמָו, וּבְיַד־אָדָם אַל־אֶפֹּלָה:

רַחוּם וְחַנּוּן, חָטָאתִי לְפָנֶיךָ.
יהוה מָלֵא רַחֲמִים, רַחֵם עָלַי וְקַבֵּל תַּחֲנוּנָי.

תהלים ו יהוה, אַל־בְּאַפְּךָ תוֹכִיחֵנִי, וְאַל־בַּחֲמָתְךָ תְיַסְּרֵנִי: חָנֵּנִי יהוה, ב כִּי אֻמְלַל אָנִי,
רְפָאֵנִי יהוה, ב כִּי נִבְהֲלוּ עֲצָמָי: ב וְנַפְשִׁי נִבְהֲלָה מְאֹד, וְאַתָּ יהוה, עַד־מָתָי:
שׁוּבָה יהוה, חַלְּצָה נַפְשִׁי, הוֹשִׁיעֵנִי לְמַעַן חַסְדֶּךָ: כִּי אֵין בַּמָּוֶת זִכְרֶךָ, בִּשְׁאוֹל
מִי יוֹדֶה־לָּךְ: יָגַעְתִּי בְּאַנְחָתִי, ע אַשְׂחֶה בְכָל־לַיְלָה מִטָּתִי, בְּדִמְעָתִי עַרְשִׂי
אַמְסֶה: עָשְׁשָׁה מִכַּעַס עֵינִי, עָתְקָה בְּכָל־צוֹרְרָי: סוּרוּ מִמֶּנִּי כָּל־פֹּעֲלֵי אָוֶן,
כִּי שָׁמַע יהוה קוֹל בִּכְיִי: א שָׁמַע יהוה ע תְּחִנָּתִי, יהוה תְּפִלָּתִי יִקָּח: יֵבֹשׁוּ
וְיִבָּהֲלוּ מְאֹד כָּל־אֹיְבָי, יָשֻׁבוּ יֵבֹשׁוּ רָגַע:

Sit upright.

The תפילה *continues on page 207.*

your body down and prostrate yourself before the Creator of the Universe who knows and understands all.

Apparently prayer isn't just something you do with your heart alone. You can do it with your body too. In fact, what we do with our bodies can have an effect on our hearts. (Why stand for the national anthem?) At other times, our heart comes first – you feel so strongly about something that you just have to physically display your emotion, for example, jump for joy, stand at attention, throw yourself on your bed.

That seems to be what the Tur is saying: during *tefilla* we resort to different physical displays of emotion, and if we don't feel that emotion, the physical action is supposed to help us to feel it – to get us in the mood. Throughout *Keriat Shema* and its *berakhot*, we remain seated. Then, in the *Shemoneh Esreh*, standing upright is the appropriate posture – that, after all, is why it is called the *Amida*. There is but one physical pose left to express ourselves, namely falling to the ground and throwing ourselves, as it were, at Hashem's mercy. That's *Taḥanun*.

Interestingly, much about this prayer is learned from Moshe Rabbeinu. In particular, note that in *Parashat VaEt-ḥanan*, Moshe pleads with Hashem to permit him to enter the Promised Land. If you recall the story

BIUR TEFILLA • ביאור תפילה

חָנֵּנִי יהוה – *Be gracious to me, Lord.* Note the word חָנֵּנִי (find favor, or חֵן) is related to the word תַּחֲנוּן. Find another related word later in this psalm.

רְפָאֵנִי יהוה – *Heal me, Lord.* There are those who say that the word רְפָאֵנִי asks for a cure from a physical illness. Others say it refers to spiritual illness.

Which do you think is more in keeping with the rest of the psalm?

כִּי נִבְהֲלוּ עֲצָמָי – *For my bones are in agony.* Note that the translation which appears here translates the word נִבְהֲלוּ differently in this verse and the next verse.

Why? Would you have done the same?

IYUN TEFILLA • עיון תפילה

יָגַעְתִּי בְּאַנְחָתִי – *I am weary with my sighing.* This verse refers specifically to crying in one's bed at night.

Why does it use this analogy? Did you ever cry at night? What for? Did you ever cry to God at night? What for?

Radak suggests that this expression is used because, (a) one is so worried and in pain that one cries oneself to sleep every night; (b) it is harder to bear things at night than it is during the day; (c) at night everyone else is asleep and one can cry in the privacy of one's room without anyone else seeing or hearing.

Which, if any, of these means the most to you today?

ANI TEFILLA • אני תפילה

קוֹל בִּכְיִי – *The sound of my weeping.*

To what may this be compared? To a wealthy man who bought his son very expensive clothes. The young man walked outside in the clothes in order to show off in front of his friends, and he jumped into a muddy puddle and dirtied his clothes. The boy said: Better that I should go personally and tell my father that I ruined my clothes, than he should hear about it from others. And so it happened. When he came to his father and admitted his wrongdoing, his father forgave him. That is the same thing that the poet said to his enemies: סוּרוּ מִמֶּנִּי כָּל־פֹּעֲלֵי אָוֶן, כִּי שָׁמַע יהוה קוֹל בִּכְיִי. (Me'am Loez)

Explain the parable: (a) Who is the king? (b) Who is the son? (c) What does the muddy puddle represent? (d) What do the expensive clothes represent? (e) What is the cause of the crying in the psalm?

IYUN TEFILLA • עיון תפילה

שָׁמַע יהוה – *The Lord has heard.* Verse 10 from this chapter of *Tehillim* (beginning with the words שָׁמַע יהוה) is very positive in outlook. It may well be that verse 10 corresponds to, and is a response to, verse 3 (beginning with the words חָנֵּנִי יהוה – look in the Hebrew.

Can you spot the recurring root? How is it a response?

shall you place any figured stone in your land, to bow down to it; for I am Hashem your God" (*Vayikra* 26:1). The Gemara (*Megilla* 22b) concludes from this that one may not fully prostrate oneself on a stone floor other than that of the *Beit HaMikdash*: "אֲבָל אַתָּה מִשְׁתַּחֲוֶה עַל אֲבָנִים שֶׁל בֵּית הַמִּקְדָּשׁ אִי אַתָּה מִשְׁתַּחֲוֶה בְּאַרְצְכֶם"

Needless to say, the Gemara and subsequent authorities don't leave it at that. For example, what constitutes prostrating oneself? (Answer: כְּרִיעָה refers to bowing; קִדָּה refers to bowing down on the floor and covering one's face; הִשְׁתַּחֲוָיָה is considered getting down on the floor and extending one's hands and legs.) Which one is forbidden? And where? And on what kind of floor? And why? Is it forbidden because it is a pagan practice? Or is it forbidden because you may not do a *Beit HaMikdash*-like act outside of the *Beit HaMikdash*?

The bottom line is that except for Yom Kippur and Rosh HaShana, we never bow down on the floor. But then how is one supposed to do *Taḥanun*, given that its very definition is to "fall on one's face"?! The custom therefore developed instead to compromise by bowing one's head down on one's arm, usually tilted to the side, and covering one's face with something. It's a kind of symbolic "falling on one's face," or נְפִילַת אַפַּיִם.

Now just as your face is hidden when you lie face-down on the floor, so, too, ideally, should one's face be covered during *Taḥanun*. But here, too, we compromise by making sure that there is still some kind of separation between our head and the surface. That's one reason why many people make sure to wear long sleeves when they pray, because there are authorities which suggest that if you try to cover a body part (your face) with a body part (your bare arm) that's not really the kind of external separator that is required. (Similarly, there are those who say that men shouldn't use their hand on their head instead of a *kippa* in order to make a blessing.) So next time you see someone struggling to pull their short sleeve down further to cover their arm, know that it's not their arm they are worried about, but their נְפִילַת אַפַּיִם.

One generally leans on one's left side, for that is the way of "free men and kings" (Rabbi Hai Gaon), as we do during the Pesaḥ Seder, although the Ashkenazi *minhag* is for men to lean on the right side when tefillin are on their left, so as not to "embarrass" the tefillin (Rema 131:1). Still, there are some who lean on the left hand regardless (the Vilna Gaon, Rabbi J.B. Soloveitchik).

There is a widespread custom not to "fall down" unless there is a *sefer Torah* present, since we learn the "falling down" from King David, who did so in the presence of a *sefer Torah*. Others suggest that having printed *sefarim* in the vicinity would also suffice. Interestingly, if you are in Jerusalem (perhaps only the Old City), then you are always considered to be in front of *Aron Hashem*, and so no *sefer Torah* is necessary.

Because of the somber mood of the prayer that focuses on our frailties, *Taḥanun* is not recited on festive days or days of great gladness, thus leading to frequent disputes in *shul*s as to what days would qualify. For example, Hasidim often don't say it on the day of the *yahrtzeit* of a great *tzaddik* (considered a festive rather than a sad day from a kabbalistic perspective), although there are those who disagree with this practice.

On Mondays and Thursdays, say the following.
On other days, continue with "Guardian of Israel" below.

LORD, God of Israel, turn away from Your fierce anger,
and relent from the evil against Your people.

Look down from heaven and see how we have become an object of scorn and derision among the nations. We are regarded as sheep led to the slaughter, to be killed, destroyed, beaten and humiliated. Yet, despite all this, we have not forgotten Your name. Please do not forget us.

LORD, God of Israel, turn away from Your fierce anger,
and relent from the evil against Your people.

Strangers say, "You have no hope or expectation." Be gracious to the nation whose hope is in Your name. O Pure One, bring our deliverance close. We are exhausted. We are given no rest. May Your compassion suppress Your anger against us. Please turn away from Your fierce anger, and have compassion on the people You chose as Your own.

LORD, God of Israel, turn away from Your fierce anger,
and relent from the evil against Your people.

Have pity on us, LORD, in Your compassion, and do not hand us over to cruel oppressors. Why should the nations say, "Where is their God now?" For Your own sake, deal kindly with us, and do not delay. Please turn away from Your fierce anger, and have compassion on the people You chose as Your own.

LORD, God of Israel, turn away from Your fierce anger,
and relent from the evil against Your people.

Heed our voice and be gracious. Do not abandon us into the hand of our enemies to blot out our name. Remember what You promised our fathers: "I will make your descendants as many as the stars of heaven" – yet now we are only a few left from many. Yet, despite all this, we have not forgotten Your name. Please do not forget us.

LORD, God of Israel, turn away from Your fierce anger,
and relent from the evil against Your people.

Help us, God of our salvation, for the sake of the glory of Your name. Save us and pardon our sins for Your name's sake. *Ps. 79*

LORD, God of Israel, turn away from Your fierce anger,
and relent from the evil against Your people.

On all days continue here:

שׁוֹמֵר יִשְׂרָאֵל Guardian of Israel, guard the remnant of Israel,
and let not Israel perish, who declare, "Listen, Israel."

Guardian of a unique nation, guard the remnant of a unique people,
and let not that unique nation perish, who proclaim the unity
of Your name [saying], "The LORD is our God, the LORD is One."

On Mondays and Thursdays, say the following.
On other days, continue with שׁוֹמֵר יִשְׂרָאֵל *below.*

יהוה אֱלֹהֵי יִשְׂרָאֵל, שׁוּב מֵחֲרוֹן אַפֶּךָ וְהִנָּחֵם עַל הָרָעָה לְעַמֶּךָ.

הַבֵּט מִשָּׁמַיִם וּרְאֵה כִּי הָיִינוּ לַעַג וָקֶלֶס בַּגּוֹיִם, נֶחְשַׁבְנוּ כַּצֹּאן לַטֶּבַח יוּבָל, לַהֲרֹג וּלְאַבֵּד וּלְמַכָּה וּלְחֶרְפָּה. וּבְכָל זֹאת שִׁמְךָ לֹא שָׁכָחְנוּ, נָא אַל תִּשְׁכָּחֵנוּ.

יהוה אֱלֹהֵי יִשְׂרָאֵל, שׁוּב מֵחֲרוֹן אַפֶּךָ וְהִנָּחֵם עַל הָרָעָה לְעַמֶּךָ.

זָרִים אוֹמְרִים אֵין תּוֹחֶלֶת וְתִקְוָה, חֹן אֹם לְשִׁמְךָ מְקַוֶּה, טָהוֹר יְשׁוּעָתֵנוּ קָרְבָה, יָגַעְנוּ וְלֹא הוּנַח לָנוּ, רַחֲמֶיךָ יִכְבְּשׁוּ אֶת כַּעַסְךָ מֵעָלֵינוּ. אָנָּא שׁוּב מֵחֲרוֹנְךָ וְרַחֵם סְגֻלָּה אֲשֶׁר בָּחָרְתָּ.

יהוה אֱלֹהֵי יִשְׂרָאֵל, שׁוּב מֵחֲרוֹן אַפֶּךָ וְהִנָּחֵם עַל הָרָעָה לְעַמֶּךָ.

חוּסָה יהוה עָלֵינוּ בְּרַחֲמֶיךָ, וְאַל תִּתְּנֵנוּ בִּידֵי אַכְזָרִים. לָמָּה יֹאמְרוּ הַגּוֹיִם אַיֵּה נָא אֱלֹהֵיהֶם, לְמַעַנְךָ עֲשֵׂה עִמָּנוּ חֶסֶד וְאַל תְּאַחַר. אָנָּא שׁוּב מֵחֲרוֹנְךָ וְרַחֵם סְגֻלָּה אֲשֶׁר בָּחָרְתָּ.

יהוה אֱלֹהֵי יִשְׂרָאֵל, שׁוּב מֵחֲרוֹן אַפֶּךָ וְהִנָּחֵם עַל הָרָעָה לְעַמֶּךָ.

קוֹלֵנוּ תִשְׁמַע וְתָחֹן, וְאַל תִּטְּשֵׁנוּ בְּיַד אֹיְבֵינוּ לִמְחוֹת אֶת שְׁמֵנוּ. זְכֹר אֲשֶׁר נִשְׁבַּעְתָּ לַאֲבוֹתֵינוּ כְּכוֹכְבֵי הַשָּׁמַיִם אַרְבֶּה אֶת זַרְעֲכֶם, וְעַתָּה נִשְׁאַרְנוּ מְעַט מֵהַרְבֵּה. וּבְכָל זֹאת שִׁמְךָ לֹא שָׁכָחְנוּ, נָא אַל תִּשְׁכָּחֵנוּ.

יהוה אֱלֹהֵי יִשְׂרָאֵל, שׁוּב מֵחֲרוֹן אַפֶּךָ וְהִנָּחֵם עַל הָרָעָה לְעַמֶּךָ.

עָזְרֵנוּ אֱלֹהֵי יִשְׁעֵנוּ עַל־דְּבַר כְּבוֹד־שְׁמֶךָ, וְהַצִּילֵנוּ וְכַפֵּר עַל־חַטֹּאתֵינוּ לְמַעַן שְׁמֶךָ׃ תהלים עט

יהוה אֱלֹהֵי יִשְׂרָאֵל, שׁוּב מֵחֲרוֹן אַפֶּךָ וְהִנָּחֵם עַל הָרָעָה לְעַמֶּךָ.

On all days continue here:

שׁוֹמֵר יִשְׂרָאֵל, שְׁמֹר שְׁאֵרִית יִשְׂרָאֵל, וְאַל יֹאבַד יִשְׂרָאֵל הָאוֹמְרִים שְׁמַע יִשְׂרָאֵל.

שׁוֹמֵר גּוֹי אֶחָד, שְׁמֹר שְׁאֵרִית עַם אֶחָד, וְאַל יֹאבַד גּוֹי אֶחָד הַמְיַחֲדִים שִׁמְךָ, יהוה אֱלֹהֵינוּ יהוה אֶחָד.

Guardian of a holy nation, guard the remnant of that holy people,
and let not the holy nation perish, who three times repeat
the threefold declaration of holiness to the Holy One.

You who are conciliated by calls for compassion and placated by pleas,
be conciliated and placated toward an afflicted generation,
for there is no other help.

Our Father, our King, be gracious to us and answer us, though we have no
worthy deeds; act with us in charity and loving-kindness and save us.

Stand at ▴.

וַאֲנַחְנוּ We do not know ▴what to do, but our eyes are turned to You. Remem- *II Chr. 12*
ber, LORD, Your compassion and loving-kindness, for they are everlasting. *Ps. 25*
May Your loving-kindness, LORD, be with us, for we have put our hope in *Ps. 33*
You. Do not hold against us the sins of those who came before us. May Your *Ps. 79*
mercies meet us swiftly, for we have been brought very low. Be gracious to us, *Ps. 123*
LORD, be gracious to us, for we are sated with contempt. In wrath, remember *Hab. 3*
mercy. He knows our nature; He remembers that we are dust. ▸ Help us, God *Ps. 103*
of our salvation, for the sake of the glory of Your name. Save us and grant *Ps. 79*
atonement for our sins for Your name's sake.

HALF KADDISH

Leader: יִתְגַּדַּל Magnified and sanctified may His great name be,
in the world He created by His will.
May He establish His kingdom in your lifetime and in your days,
and in the lifetime of all the house of Israel,
swiftly and soon – and say: Amen.

All: May His great name[A] be blessed for ever and all time.

Leader: Blessed and praised, glorified and exalted,
raised and honored, uplifted and lauded
be the name of the Holy One, blessed be He,
beyond any blessing, song, praise and consolation
uttered in the world – and say: Amen.

ANI TEFILLA · אני תפילה

יְהֵא שְׁמֵהּ רַבָּא – *May His great name.* Whoever says *yeheh shemeh raba*... with all his strength, the Heavenly Court rips up any negative decree against him (*Shabbat* 119b). "With all his strength" – with all of one's heart and soul (*Mishna Berura* 56:1).

שׁוֹמֵר גּוֹי קָדוֹשׁ, שְׁמֹר שְׁאֵרִית עַם קָדוֹשׁ, וְאַל יֹאבַד גּוֹי קָדוֹשׁ
הַמְשַׁלְּשִׁים בְּשָׁלֹשׁ קְדֻשּׁוֹת לְקָדוֹשׁ.

מִתְרַצֶּה בְּרַחֲמִים וּמִתְפַּיֵּס בְּתַחֲנוּנִים, הִתְרַצֵּה וְהִתְפַּיֵּס לְדוֹר עָנִי
כִּי אֵין עוֹזֵר.

אָבִינוּ מַלְכֵּנוּ, חָנֵּנוּ וַעֲנֵנוּ, כִּי אֵין בָּנוּ מַעֲשִׂים
עֲשֵׂה עִמָּנוּ צְדָקָה וָחֶסֶד וְהוֹשִׁיעֵנוּ.

Stand at ▸.

דברי הימים ב׳ יב, תהלים כה — וַאֲנַחְנוּ לֹא נֵדַע ׳מַה־נַּעֲשֶׂה, כִּי עָלֶיךָ עֵינֵינוּ: זְכֹר־רַחֲמֶיךָ יהוה וַחֲסָדֶיךָ,
תהלים לג, תהלים עט — כִּי מֵעוֹלָם הֵמָּה: יְהִי־חַסְדְּךָ יהוה עָלֵינוּ, כַּאֲשֶׁר יִחַלְנוּ לָךְ: אַל־תִּזְכָּר־לָנוּ
תהלים קכג — עֲוֹנֹת רִאשֹׁנִים, מַהֵר יְקַדְּמוּנוּ רַחֲמֶיךָ, כִּי דַלּוֹנוּ מְאֹד: חָנֵּנוּ יהוה חָנֵּנוּ,
חבקוק ג, תהלים קג — כִּי־רַב שָׂבַעְנוּ בוּז: בְּרֹגֶז רַחֵם תִּזְכּוֹר: כִּי־הוּא יָדַע יִצְרֵנוּ, זָכוּר כִּי־עָפָר
תהלים עט — אֲנָחְנוּ: ▸ עָזְרֵנוּ אֱלֹהֵי יִשְׁעֵנוּ עַל־דְּבַר כְּבוֹד־שְׁמֶךָ, וְהַצִּילֵנוּ וְכַפֵּר עַל־
חַטֹּאתֵינוּ לְמַעַן שְׁמֶךָ:

חצי קדיש

ש״ץ: יִתְגַּדַּל וְיִתְקַדַּשׁ שְׁמֵהּ רַבָּא (קהל: אָמֵן)
בְּעָלְמָא דִּי בְרָא כִרְעוּתֵהּ
וְיַמְלִיךְ מַלְכוּתֵהּ
בְּחַיֵּיכוֹן וּבְיוֹמֵיכוֹן וּבְחַיֵּי דְכָל בֵּית יִשְׂרָאֵל
בַּעֲגָלָא וּבִזְמַן קָרִיב, וְאִמְרוּ אָמֵן. (קהל: אָמֵן)

קהל וש״ץ: יְהֵא שְׁמֵהּ רַבָּא[א] מְבָרַךְ לְעָלַם וּלְעָלְמֵי עָלְמַיָּא.

ש״ץ: יִתְבָּרַךְ וְיִשְׁתַּבַּח וְיִתְפָּאַר וְיִתְרוֹמַם וְיִתְנַשֵּׂא
וְיִתְהַדָּר וְיִתְעַלֶּה וְיִתְהַלָּל
שְׁמֵהּ דְּקֻדְשָׁא בְּרִיךְ הוּא (קהל: בְּרִיךְ הוּא)
לְעֵלָּא מִן כָּל בִּרְכָתָא
וְשִׁירָתָא, תֻּשְׁבְּחָתָא וְנֶחֱמָתָא
דַּאֲמִירָן בְּעָלְמָא, וְאִמְרוּ אָמֵן. (קהל: אָמֵן)

REMOVING THE TORAH FROM THE ARK

On Mondays and Thursdays, Rosh Ḥodesh and Fast Days, the Torah is read when a minyan is present. On all other days, continue with "Happy are those" on page 224.

Before taking the Torah out of the Ark, on Mondays and Thursdays, stand while reciting "God, slow to anger." It is not said on Rosh Ḥodesh, Tisha B'Av or in a house of mourning.

Most people say both paragraphs; some say only the first.

God, slow to anger, abounding
in loving-kindness and truth,
do not rebuke us in Your anger.
Have pity on Your people, LORD,
and save us from all evil.
We have sinned against You, LORD.
Please forgive in accordance with
Your great compassion, God.

God, slow to anger, full of compassion,
do not hide Your face from us.
Have pity on the remnant of Israel
Your people, LORD,
and deliver us from all evil.
We have sinned against You, LORD.
Please forgive in accordance with
Your great compassion, God.

The Ark is opened and the congregation stands. All say:

וַיְהִי בִּנְסֹעַ Whenever the Ark set out, Moses would say, *Num. 10*
"Arise, LORD, and may Your enemies be scattered.
May those who hate You flee before You."
For the Torah shall come forth from Zion, *Is. 2*
and the word of the LORD from Jerusalem.
Blessed is He who in His holiness
gave the Torah to His people Israel.

---

and not the learning, of Torah). The mere act of reading or hearing it sanctifies the listener. In doing so, I attach myself to my people, my tradition, my God. I am a part of something bigger than myself and I am uplifted.

אֵל אֶרֶךְ אַפַּיִם – *God, slow to anger.* Many suggest that this *Keriat HaTorah* represents a kind of reenactment of the giving of the Torah at Sinai. If so, then perhaps this introductory passage of supplication to Hashem can be reminiscent of the days in which *Benei Yisrael* prepared for receiving the Torah, days no doubt filled with a sense of excitement and anticipation. Recall how very young children often approach the open *Aron Kodesh* for the first time, in awe and wonder at the beauty and the pageantry. There is no reason to lose that feeling. There is no reason to lose that feeling just because we are older.

הוצאת ספר תורה[ע]

On Mondays and Thursdays, ראש חודש *and Fast Days, the* תורה *is read when a* מנין *is present. On all other days, continue with* אשרי *on page 225.*

Before taking the תורה *out of the* ארון קודש*, on Mondays and Thursdays, stand while reciting* אֵל אֶרֶךְ אַפַּיִם*. It is not said on:* ראש חודש*,* תשעה באב *or in a house of mourning.*

Most people say both paragraphs, some say only the first.

אֵל אֶרֶךְ אַפַּיִם[ע] וְרַב חֶסֶד וֶאֱמֶת
אַל בְּאַפְּךָ תוֹכִיחֵנוּ.
חוּסָה יהוה עַל עַמֶּךָ
וְהוֹשִׁיעֵנוּ מִכָּל רָע.
חָטָאנוּ לְךָ אָדוֹן
סְלַח נָא כְּרֹב רַחֲמֶיךָ אֵל.

אֵל אֶרֶךְ אַפַּיִם וּמָלֵא רַחֲמִים
אַל תַּסְתֵּר פָּנֶיךָ מִמֶּנּוּ.
חוּסָה יהוה עַל שְׁאֵרִית יִשְׂרָאֵל עַמֶּךָ
וְהַצִּילֵנוּ מִכָּל רָע.
חָטָאנוּ לְךָ אָדוֹן
סְלַח נָא כְּרֹב רַחֲמֶיךָ אֵל.

The ארון קודש *is opened and the* קהל *stands. All say:*

וַיְהִי בִּנְסֹעַ הָאָרֹן וַיֹּאמֶר מֹשֶׁה במדבר י
קוּמָה יהוה וְיָפֻצוּ אֹיְבֶיךָ וְיָנֻסוּ מְשַׂנְאֶיךָ מִפָּנֶיךָ:
כִּי מִצִּיּוֹן תֵּצֵא תוֹרָה וּדְבַר־יהוה מִירוּשָׁלָםִ: ישעיה ב
בָּרוּךְ שֶׁנָּתַן תּוֹרָה לְעַמּוֹ יִשְׂרָאֵל בִּקְדֻשָּׁתוֹ.

IYUN TEFILLA • עיון תפילה

קריאת התורה – *PUBLIC READING OF THE TORAH.* Education in Jewish life has always been democratic. It is not only for the elite but for every person, rich or poor. Amazingly, universal schooling has been a part of Jewish life for close to 2000 years. So it should come as no surprise that from the very outset Moshe instituted that the Torah be read publicly three times a week (*Bava Kama* 82a), not just to keep the content of Torah alive, for that would happen in schools and private study regardless, but, rather, to remind us as a community that Torah is our life, as water is to a thirsty person, as water is to fish. We cannot live without it. According to Rabbi Soloveitchik, that is why there is not necessarily a need to even understand this public Torah reading or to learn from it (perhaps that is why it is simply called *Keriat HaTorah*: the reading,

Blessed is the name[B] of the Master of the Universe. Blessed is Your crown and Your place. May Your favor always be with Your people Israel. Show Your people the salvation of Your right hand in Your Temple. Grant us the gift of Your good light, and accept our prayers in mercy. May it be Your will to prolong our life in goodness. May I be counted among the righteous, so that You will have compassion on me and protect me and all that is mine and all that is Your people Israel's. You feed all; You sustain all; You rule over all; You rule over kings, for sovereignty is Yours. I am a servant of the Holy One, blessed be He, before whom and before whose glorious Torah I bow at all times. Not in man do I trust, nor on any angel do I rely, but on the God of heaven who is the God of truth, whose Torah is truth, whose prophets speak truth, and who abounds in acts of love and truth. ▸ In Him I trust, and to His holy and glorious name I offer praises. May it be Your will to open my heart to the Torah, and to fulfill the wishes of my heart and of the hearts of all Your people Israel for good, for life, and for peace. *Zohar, Vayak-hel*

The Leader takes the Torah scroll in his right arm, bows toward the Ark and says:

Magnify the LORD[B] with me, and let us exalt His name together. *Ps. 34*

The Ark is closed. The Leader carries the Torah scroll to the bima and the congregation says:

לְךָ Yours, LORD, are the greatness and the power, the glory and the majesty and splendor, for everything in heaven and earth is Yours. Yours, LORD, is the kingdom; You are exalted as Head over all. *1 Chr. 29*

רוֹמְמוּ Exalt the LORD our God and bow to His footstool; He is holy. Exalt the LORD our God, and bow at His holy mountain, for holy is the LORD our God. *Ps. 99*

אַב הָרַחֲמִים May the Father of compassion have compassion on the people borne by Him. May He remember the covenant with the mighty [patriarchs], and deliver us from evil times. May He reproach the evil instinct in the people carried by Him, and graciously grant that we be an everlasting remnant. May He fulfill in good measure our requests for salvation and compassion.

גַּדְּלוּ לַיהוה – *Magnify the LORD.* This call to the congregation by the *Ḥazan* urges us to be uplifted by the presence and revelation of the Torah. Symbolically, there is a custom for him to physically raise the Torah up accordingly. The phrase has six words which, according to one opinion, symbolize the series of six steps that the bearers of the Ark took when David led the amazing celebration of the repossession of the Ark (*Shmuel* II 6:13). Others point to the fact that the phrase has 26 letters, the *gematria* or numerical equivalent of the name of Hashem. All of these traditions simply try to convey the joy, pride and awe that it is possible to feel at this moment, if only we would allow ourselves not to take it for granted. Give in to the moment.

זוהר ויקהל
בְּרִיךְ שְׁמֵהּ דְּמָרֵא עָלְמָא, בְּרִיךְ כִּתְרָךְ וְאַתְרָךְ. יְהֵא רְעוּתָךְ עִם עַמָּךְ יִשְׂרָאֵל לְעָלַם, וּפֻרְקַן יְמִינָךְ אַחֲזֵי לְעַמָּךְ בְּבֵית מַקְדְּשָׁךְ, וּלְאַמְטוּיֵי לָנָא מִטּוּב נְהוֹרָךְ, וּלְקַבֵּל צְלוֹתַנָא בְּרַחֲמִין. יְהֵא רַעֲוָא קֳדָמָךְ דְּתוֹרִיךְ לַן חַיִּין בְּטִיבוּ, וְלֶהֱוֵי אֲנָא פְקִידָא בְּגוֹ צַדִּיקַיָּא, לְמִרְחַם עֲלַי וּלְמִנְטַר יָתִי וְיַת כָּל דִּי לִי וְדִי לְעַמָּךְ יִשְׂרָאֵל. אַנְתְּ הוּא זָן לְכֹלָּא וּמְפַרְנֵס לְכֹלָּא, אַנְתְּ הוּא שַׁלִּיט עַל כֹּלָּא, אַנְתְּ הוּא דְשַׁלִּיט עַל מַלְכַיָּא, וּמַלְכוּתָא דִּילָךְ הִיא. אֲנָא עַבְדָּא דְקֻדְשָׁא בְּרִיךְ הוּא, דְּסָגֵדְנָא קַמֵּהּ וּמִקַּמֵּי דִּיקַר אוֹרַיְתֵהּ בְּכָל עִדָּן וְעִדָּן. לָא עַל אֱנָשׁ רָחִיצְנָא וְלָא עַל בַּר אֱלָהִין סָמִיכְנָא, אֶלָּא בֶּאֱלָהָא דִשְׁמַיָּא, דְּהוּא אֱלָהָא קְשׁוֹט, וְאוֹרַיְתֵהּ קְשׁוֹט, וּנְבִיאוֹהִי קְשׁוֹט, וּמַסְגֵּא לְמֶעְבַּד טַבְוָן וּקְשׁוֹט. ‹ בֵּהּ אֲנָא רָחִיץ, וְלִשְׁמֵהּ קַדִּישָׁא יַקִּירָא אֲנָא אֵמַר תֻּשְׁבְּחָן. יְהֵא רַעֲוָא קֳדָמָךְ דְּתִפְתַּח לִבַּאי בְּאוֹרַיְתָא, וְתַשְׁלִים מִשְׁאֲלִין דְּלִבַּאי וְלִבָּא דְכָל עַמָּךְ יִשְׂרָאֵל לְטָב וּלְחַיִּין וְלִשְׁלָם.

The שליח ציבור *takes the* ספר תורה *in his right arm, bows toward the* ארון קודש *and says:*

תהלים לד
גַּדְּלוּ לַיהוה אִתִּי וּנְרוֹמְמָה שְׁמוֹ יַחְדָּו:

The ארון קודש *is closed. The* שליח ציבור *carries the* ספר תורה *to the* בימה *and the* קהל *says:*

דברי הימים א, כט
לְךָ יהוה הַגְּדֻלָּה וְהַגְּבוּרָה וְהַתִּפְאֶרֶת וְהַנֵּצַח וְהַהוֹד, כִּי־כֹל בַּשָּׁמַיִם וּבָאָרֶץ, לְךָ יהוה הַמַּמְלָכָה וְהַמִּתְנַשֵּׂא לְכֹל לְרֹאשׁ:

תהלים צט
רוֹמְמוּ יהוה אֱלֹהֵינוּ וְהִשְׁתַּחֲווּ לַהֲדֹם רַגְלָיו, קָדוֹשׁ הוּא: רוֹמְמוּ יהוה אֱלֹהֵינוּ וְהִשְׁתַּחֲווּ לְהַר קָדְשׁוֹ, כִּי־קָדוֹשׁ יהוה אֱלֹהֵינוּ:

אַב הָרַחֲמִים הוּא יְרַחֵם עַם עֲמוּסִים, וְיִזְכֹּר בְּרִית אֵיתָנִים, וְיַצִּיל נַפְשׁוֹתֵינוּ מִן הַשָּׁעוֹת הָרָעוֹת, וְיִגְעַר בְּיֵצֶר הָרָע מִן הַנְּשׂוּאִים, וְיָחֹן אוֹתָנוּ לִפְלֵיטַת עוֹלָמִים, וִימַלֵּא מִשְׁאֲלוֹתֵינוּ בְּמִדָּה טוֹבָה יְשׁוּעָה וְרַחֲמִים.

BIUR TEFILLA · ביאור תפילה

בְּרִיךְ שְׁמֵהּ – *Blessed is the name.* Added to the service by kabbalists about four centuries ago or more, this prayer is really a quote from the *Zohar* which says that "when the congregation takes the Torah from the Ark to read from it, the Gates of Mercy are opened in heaven and love is awakened on high; therefore this prayer should be spoken." Thus this prayer makes use, as it were, of a favorable circumstance to pray for the fulfillment of our hearts' deepest desires. (Rabbi E. Munk)

The Torah scroll is placed on the bima and the Gabbai calls a Kohen to the Torah.

May His kingship over us be soon revealed and made manifest. May He be gracious to our surviving remnant, the remnant of His people the house of Israel in grace, loving-kindness, compassion and favor, and let us say: Amen. Let us all render greatness to our God and give honor to the Torah. *Let the Kohen come forward. Arise (*name* son of *father's name*), the Kohen.

**If no Kohen is present, a Levi or Yisrael is called up as follows:*

/As there is no Kohen, arise (*name* son of *father's name*) in place of a Kohen./

Blessed is He who, in His holiness, gave the Torah to His people Israel.

Congregation followed by the Gabbai:

You who cling to the LORD your God are all alive today. *Deut. 4*

The appropriate Torah portions are to be found from page 1014.

The Reader shows the oleh the section to be read.
The oleh touches the scroll at that place with the tzitzit of his tallit,
which he then kisses. Holding the handles of the scroll, he says:

Oleh: Bless[B] the LORD, the blessed One.

Cong: Bless the LORD, the blessed One, for ever and all time.

Oleh: Bless the LORD, the blessed One, for ever and all time.

Blessed are You, LORD our God, King of the Universe,
who has chosen us from all peoples
and has given us His Torah.
Blessed are You, LORD, Giver of the Torah.

After the reading, the oleh says:

Oleh: Blessed are You, LORD our God, King of the Universe,
who has given us the Torah of truth,
planting everlasting life in our midst.
Blessed are You, LORD, Giver of the Torah.

---

long reading in which all were involved (*Megilla* 4a). Today, each individual recites two blessings. The first refers to "His [God's] Torah" while the second seems to suggest that the Torah is now a part of us. Perhaps that is the goal of this reading; namely, that we should walk away feeling like it is part of us.

For a guide to getting an aliya see Shaḥarit for Shabbat, page 639.

The ספר תורה is placed on the שולחן and the גבאי calls a כהן to the תורה.

וְתִגָּלֶה וְתֵרָאֶה מַלְכוּתוֹ עָלֵינוּ בִּזְמַן קָרוֹב, וְיָחֹן פְּלֵיטָתֵנוּ וּפְלֵיטַת עַמּוֹ בֵּית יִשְׂרָאֵל לְחֵן וּלְחֶסֶד וּלְרַחֲמִים וּלְרָצוֹן וְנֹאמַר אָמֵן. הַכֹּל הָבוּ גֹדֶל לֵאלֹהֵינוּ וּתְנוּ כָבוֹד לַתּוֹרָה.

*כֹּהֵן קְרַב, יַעֲמֹד (פלוני בֶּן פלוני) הַכֹּהֵן.

**If no כהן is present, a לוי or ישראל is called up as follows:*

/אֵין כָּאן כֹּהֵן, יַעֲמֹד (פלוני בֶּן פלוני) בִּמְקוֹם כֹּהֵן./

בָּרוּךְ שֶׁנָּתַן תּוֹרָה לְעַמּוֹ יִשְׂרָאֵל בִּקְדֻשָּׁתוֹ.

קהל followed by the גבאי:

דברים ד וְאַתֶּם הַדְּבֵקִים בַּיהוה אֱלֹהֵיכֶם חַיִּים כֻּלְּכֶם הַיּוֹם:

The appropriate תורה portions are to be found from page 1014.

The קורא shows the עולה the section to be read.
The עולה touches the ספר תורה at that place with the ציצית of his טלית,
which he then kisses. Holding the handles of the ספר תורה, he says:

עולה: בָּרְכוּ[ב] אֶת יהוה הַמְבֹרָךְ.

קהל: בָּרוּךְ יהוה הַמְבֹרָךְ לְעוֹלָם וָעֶד.

עולה: בָּרוּךְ יהוה הַמְבֹרָךְ לְעוֹלָם וָעֶד.
בָּרוּךְ אַתָּה יהוה, אֱלֹהֵינוּ מֶלֶךְ הָעוֹלָם
אֲשֶׁר בָּחַר בָּנוּ מִכָּל הָעַמִּים וְנָתַן לָנוּ אֶת תּוֹרָתוֹ.
בָּרוּךְ אַתָּה יהוה, נוֹתֵן הַתּוֹרָה.

After the קריאת התורה, the עולה says:

עולה: בָּרוּךְ אַתָּה יהוה אֱלֹהֵינוּ מֶלֶךְ הָעוֹלָם
אֲשֶׁר נָתַן לָנוּ תּוֹרַת אֱמֶת וְחַיֵּי עוֹלָם נָטַע בְּתוֹכֵנוּ.
בָּרוּךְ אַתָּה יהוה, נוֹתֵן הַתּוֹרָה.

BIUR TEFILLA · ביאור תפילה

בָּרְכוּ – *Bless.* Here the person getting the *aliya* invites us all to join in with him. Indeed, there was a time when there was only one blessing cited before the first *aliya* and a second blessing recited only at the end of all of the *aliyot* as if it were one

One who has survived a situation of danger says:

Blessed are You, LORD our God, King of the Universe,
who bestows good on the unworthy, who has bestowed on me much good.

The congregation responds:

Amen. May He who bestowed much good on you
continue to bestow on you much good, Selah.

Special blessings and memorial prayers may be said at this point (below and next page).

FOR A SICK MAN

May He who blessed our fathers, Abraham, Isaac and Jacob, Moses and Aaron, David and Solomon, bless and heal one who is ill, (*sick person's name*, son of *mother's name*), on whose behalf (*name of the one making the offering*) is making a contribution to charity. As a reward for this, may the Holy One, blessed be He, be filled with compassion for him, to restore his health, cure him, strengthen and revive him, sending him a swift and full recovery from heaven to all his 248 organs and 365 sinews, amongst the other sick ones in Israel, a healing of the spirit and a healing of the body, now, swiftly and soon, and let us say: Amen.

FOR A SICK WOMAN

May He who blessed our fathers, Abraham, Isaac and Jacob, Moses and Aaron, David and Solomon, bless and heal one who is ill, (*sick person's name*, daughter of *mother's name*), on whose behalf (*name of the one making the offering*) is making a contribution to charity. As a reward for this, may the Holy One, blessed be He, be filled with compassion for her, to restore her health, cure her, strengthen and revive her, sending her a swift and full recovery from heaven to all her organs and sinews, amongst the other sick ones in Israel, a healing of the spirit and a healing of the body, now, swiftly and soon, and let us say: Amen.

For a male close relative:

אֵל מָלֵא רַחֲמִים God, full of mercy, who dwells on high, grant fitting rest on the wings of the Divine Presence, in the heights of the holy and the pure who shine like the radiance of heaven, to the soul of (*name* son of *father's name*) who has gone to his eternal home, and to this I pledge (without formal vow) to give charity in his memory, may his resting place be in the Garden of Eden. Therefore, Master of compassion, shelter him in the shadow of Your wings forever and bind his soul in the bond of everlasting life. The LORD is his heritage; may he rest in peace, and let us say: Amen.

One who has survived a situation of danger says:

בָּרוּךְ אַתָּה יהוה אֱלֹהֵינוּ מֶלֶךְ הָעוֹלָם
הַגּוֹמֵל לְחַיָּבִים טוֹבוֹת, שֶׁגְּמָלַנִי כָּל טוֹב.

The קהל *responds:*

אָמֵן. מִי שֶׁגְּמָלְךָ כָּל טוֹב הוּא, יִגְמָלְךָ כָּל טוֹב, סֶלָה.

Special מי שברך *and memorial prayers may be said at this point (below and next page).*

מי שברך לחולֶה

מִי שֶׁבֵּרַךְ אֲבוֹתֵינוּ אַבְרָהָם יִצְחָק וְיַעֲקֹב, מֹשֶׁה וְאַהֲרֹן דָּוִד וּשְׁלֹמֹה הוּא יְבָרֵךְ וִירַפֵּא אֶת הַחוֹלֶה (פלוני בֶּן פלונית) בַּעֲבוּר שֶׁ(פלוני בֶּן פלוני) נוֹדֵר צְדָקָה בַּעֲבוּרוֹ. בִּשְׂכַר זֶה הַקָּדוֹשׁ בָּרוּךְ הוּא יִמָּלֵא רַחֲמִים עָלָיו לְהַחֲלִימוֹ וּלְרַפְּאתוֹ וּלְהַחֲזִיקוֹ וּלְהַחֲיוֹתוֹ וְיִשְׁלַח לוֹ מְהֵרָה רְפוּאָה שְׁלֵמָה מִן הַשָּׁמַיִם לִרְמַ״ח אֵבָרָיו וּשְׁסָ״ה גִּידָיו בְּתוֹךְ שְׁאָר חוֹלֵי יִשְׂרָאֵל, רְפוּאַת הַנֶּפֶשׁ וּרְפוּאַת הַגּוּף, הַשְׁתָּא בַּעֲגָלָא וּבִזְמַן קָרִיב, וְנֹאמַר אָמֵן.

מי שברך לחולָה

מִי שֶׁבֵּרַךְ אֲבוֹתֵינוּ אַבְרָהָם יִצְחָק וְיַעֲקֹב, מֹשֶׁה וְאַהֲרֹן דָּוִד וּשְׁלֹמֹה הוּא יְבָרֵךְ וִירַפֵּא אֶת הַחוֹלָה (פלונית בַּת פלונית) בַּעֲבוּר שֶׁ(פלוני בֶּן פלוני) נוֹדֵר צְדָקָה בַּעֲבוּרָהּ. בִּשְׂכַר זֶה הַקָּדוֹשׁ בָּרוּךְ הוּא יִמָּלֵא רַחֲמִים עָלֶיהָ לְהַחֲלִימָהּ וּלְרַפְּאתָהּ וּלְהַחֲזִיקָהּ וּלְהַחֲיוֹתָהּ וְיִשְׁלַח לָהּ מְהֵרָה רְפוּאָה שְׁלֵמָה מִן הַשָּׁמַיִם לְכָל אֵבָרֶיהָ וּלְכָל גִּידֶיהָ בְּתוֹךְ שְׁאָר חוֹלֵי יִשְׂרָאֵל, רְפוּאַת הַנֶּפֶשׁ וּרְפוּאַת הַגּוּף, הַשְׁתָּא בַּעֲגָלָא וּבִזְמַן קָרִיב, וְנֹאמַר אָמֵן.

For a male close relative:

אֵל מָלֵא רַחֲמִים, שׁוֹכֵן בַּמְּרוֹמִים, הַמְצֵא מְנוּחָה נְכוֹנָה עַל כַּנְפֵי הַשְּׁכִינָה, בְּמַעֲלוֹת קְדוֹשִׁים וּטְהוֹרִים, כְּזֹהַר הָרָקִיעַ מַזְהִירִים, לְנִשְׁמַת (פלוני בֶּן פלוני) שֶׁהָלַךְ לְעוֹלָמוֹ, בַּעֲבוּר שֶׁבְּלִי נֶדֶר אֶתֵּן צְדָקָה בְּעַד הַזְכָּרַת נִשְׁמָתוֹ, בְּגַן עֵדֶן תְּהֵא מְנוּחָתוֹ. לָכֵן, בַּעַל הָרַחֲמִים יַסְתִּירֵהוּ בְּסֵתֶר כְּנָפָיו לְעוֹלָמִים, וְיִצְרֹר בִּצְרוֹר הַחַיִּים אֶת נִשְׁמָתוֹ, יהוה הוּא נַחֲלָתוֹ, וְיָנְוּחַ בְּשָׁלוֹם עַל מִשְׁכָּבוֹ, וְנֹאמַר אָמֵן.

For a female close relative:

אֵל מָלֵא רַחֲמִים God, full of mercy, who dwells on high, grant fitting rest on the wings of the Divine Presence, in the heights of the holy and the pure who shine like the radiance of heaven, to the soul of (*name* daughter of *father's name*) who has gone to her eternal home, and to this I pledge (without formal vow) to give charity in her memory, may her resting place be in the Garden of Eden. Therefore, Master of compassion, shelter her in the shadow of Your wings forever and bind her soul in the bond of everlasting life. The LORD is her heritage; may she rest in peace, and let us say: Amen.

HALF KADDISH

After the Reading of the Torah, the Reader says Half Kaddish:

Reader: יִתְגַּדַּל Magnified and sanctified may His great name be,
in the world He created by His will.
May He establish His kingdom in your lifetime and in your days,
and in the lifetime of all the house of Israel,
swiftly and soon – and say: Amen.

All: May His great name[A] be blessed for ever and all time.

Reader: Blessed and praised, glorified and exalted,
raised and honored, uplifted and lauded
be the name of the Holy One, blessed be He,
beyond any blessing, song, praise and consolation
uttered in the world – and say: Amen.

The Torah scroll is lifted and the congregation says:

וְזֹאת הַתּוֹרָה This is the Torah *Deut. 4*
that Moses placed before the children of Israel,
at the LORD's commandment, by the hand of Moses. *Num. 9*

Some add: It is a tree of life to those who grasp it, *Prov. 3*
and those who uphold it are happy.
Its ways are ways of pleasantness, and all its paths are peace.
Long life is at its right hand; at its left, riches and honor.
It pleased the LORD for the sake of [Israel's] righteousness, *Is. 42*
to make the Torah great and glorious.

ANI TEFILLA · אני תפילה

יְהֵא שְׁמֵהּ רַבָּא – *May His great name.* Whoever says *yeheh shemeh raba...* with all his strength, the Heavenly Court rips up any negative decree against him (*Shabbat* 119b). "With all his strength" – in a loud voice (Tosafot).

For a female close relative:

אֵל מָלֵא רַחֲמִים, שׁוֹכֵן בַּמְּרוֹמִים, הַמְצֵא מְנוּחָה נְכוֹנָה עַל כַּנְפֵי הַשְּׁכִינָה, בְּמַעֲלוֹת קְדוֹשִׁים וּטְהוֹרִים, כְּזְהַר הָרָקִיעַ מַזְהִירִים, לְנִשְׁמַת (פלונית בַּת פלוני) שֶׁהָלְכָה לְעוֹלָמָהּ, בַּעֲבוּר שֶׁבְּלִי נֶדֶר אֶתֵּן צְדָקָה בְּעַד הַזְכָּרַת נִשְׁמָתָהּ, בְּגַן עֵדֶן תְּהֵא מְנוּחָתָהּ. לָכֵן, בַּעַל הָרַחֲמִים יַסְתִּירֶהָ בְּסֵתֶר כְּנָפָיו לְעוֹלָמִים, וְיִצְרֹר בִּצְרוֹר הַחַיִּים אֶת נִשְׁמָתָהּ, יהוה הוּא נַחֲלָתָהּ, וְתָנְוּחַ בְּשָׁלוֹם עַל מִשְׁכָּבָהּ, וְנֹאמַר אָמֵן.

חצי קדיש

After the קריאת התורה*, the* קורא *says* חצי קדיש:

קורא: יִתְגַּדַּל וְיִתְקַדַּשׁ שְׁמֵהּ רַבָּא (קהל: אָמֵן)
בְּעָלְמָא דִּי בְרָא כִרְעוּתֵהּ
וְיַמְלִיךְ מַלְכוּתֵהּ
בְּחַיֵּיכוֹן וּבְיוֹמֵיכוֹן וּבְחַיֵּי דְכָל בֵּית יִשְׂרָאֵל
בַּעֲגָלָא וּבִזְמַן קָרִיב, וְאִמְרוּ אָמֵן. (קהל: אָמֵן)

קורא וקהל: יְהֵא שְׁמֵהּ רַבָּא מְבָרַךְ לְעָלַם וּלְעָלְמֵי עָלְמַיָּא.

קורא: יִתְבָּרַךְ וְיִשְׁתַּבַּח וְיִתְפָּאַר וְיִתְרוֹמַם וְיִתְנַשֵּׂא
וְיִתְהַדָּר וְיִתְעַלֶּה וְיִתְהַלָּל
שְׁמֵהּ דְּקֻדְשָׁא בְּרִיךְ הוּא (קהל: בְּרִיךְ הוּא)
לְעֵלָּא מִן כָּל בִּרְכָתָא וְשִׁירָתָא, תֻּשְׁבְּחָתָא וְנֶחֱמָתָא
דַּאֲמִירָן בְּעָלְמָא, וְאִמְרוּ אָמֵן. (קהל: אָמֵן)

The ספר תורה *is lifted and the* קהל *says:*

וְזֹאת הַתּוֹרָה אֲשֶׁר־שָׂם מֹשֶׁה לִפְנֵי בְּנֵי יִשְׂרָאֵל: דברים ד
עַל־פִּי יהוה בְּיַד־מֹשֶׁה: במדבר ט

Some add עֵץ־חַיִּים הִיא לַמַּחֲזִיקִים בָּהּ וְתֹמְכֶיהָ מְאֻשָּׁר: משלי ג
דְּרָכֶיהָ דַרְכֵי־נֹעַם וְכָל־נְתִיבוֹתֶיהָ שָׁלוֹם:
אֹרֶךְ יָמִים בִּימִינָהּ, בִּשְׂמֹאולָהּ עֹשֶׁר וְכָבוֹד:
יהוה חָפֵץ לְמַעַן צִדְקוֹ יַגְדִּיל תּוֹרָה וְיַאְדִּיר: ישעיה מב

On those Mondays and Thursdays when Taḥanun is said, the Leader says the following while the Torah scroll is being bound:

יְהִי רָצוֹן May it be the will of our Father in heaven
to establish (the Temple), home of our life,
and to restore His Presence to our midst,
swiftly in our days –
and let us say: Amen.

יְהִי רָצוֹן May it be the will of our Father in heaven
to have compassion on us and our remnant,
and to keep destruction and plague away from us
and from all His people the house of Israel –
and let us say: Amen.

יְהִי רָצוֹן May it be the will of our Father in heaven
to preserve among us the sages of Israel:
them, their wives, their sons and daughters,
their disciples and their disciples' disciples,
in all their dwelling places –
and let us say: Amen.

יְהִי רָצוֹן May it be the will of our Father in heaven
that we may hear and be given good tidings
of salvation and consolation,
and that our dispersed be gathered
from the four quarters of the earth –
and let us say: Amen.

All:

אַחֵינוּ As for our brothers of the whole house of Israel
who are in distress or captivity, on sea or land,
may the All-Present have compassion on them
and lead them from distress to relief,
from darkness to light,
and from oppression to freedom,
now, swiftly and soon –
and let us say: Amen.

On those Mondays and Thursdays when תחנון *is said,*
the שליח ציבור *says the following while the* ספר תורה *is being bound:*

יְהִי רָצוֹן מִלִּפְנֵי אָבִינוּ שֶׁבַּשָּׁמַיִם
לְכוֹנֵן אֶת בֵּית חַיֵּינוּ
וּלְהָשִׁיב אֶת שְׁכִינָתוֹ בְּתוֹכֵנוּ
בִּמְהֵרָה בְיָמֵינוּ, וְנֹאמַר אָמֵן.

יְהִי רָצוֹן מִלִּפְנֵי אָבִינוּ שֶׁבַּשָּׁמַיִם
לְרַחֵם עָלֵינוּ וְעַל פְּלֵיטָתֵנוּ
וְלִמְנֹעַ מַשְׁחִית וּמַגֵּפָה מֵעָלֵינוּ
וּמֵעַל כָּל עַמּוֹ בֵּית יִשְׂרָאֵל, וְנֹאמַר אָמֵן.

יְהִי רָצוֹן מִלִּפְנֵי אָבִינוּ שֶׁבַּשָּׁמַיִם
לְקַיֵּם בָּנוּ חַכְמֵי יִשְׂרָאֵל
הֵם וּנְשֵׁיהֶם וּבְנֵיהֶם וּבְנוֹתֵיהֶם
וְתַלְמִידֵיהֶם וְתַלְמִידֵי תַלְמִידֵיהֶם
בְּכָל מְקוֹמוֹת מוֹשְׁבוֹתֵיהֶם, וְנֹאמַר אָמֵן.

יְהִי רָצוֹן מִלִּפְנֵי אָבִינוּ שֶׁבַּשָּׁמַיִם
שֶׁנִּשְׁמַע וְנִתְבַּשֵּׂר בְּשׂוֹרוֹת טוֹבוֹת, יְשׁוּעוֹת וְנֶחָמוֹת
וִיקַבֵּץ נִדָּחֵינוּ מֵאַרְבַּע כַּנְפוֹת הָאָרֶץ, וְנֹאמַר אָמֵן.

All:

אַחֵינוּ כָּל בֵּית יִשְׂרָאֵל
הַנְּתוּנִים בְּצָרָה וּבַשִּׁבְיָה
הָעוֹמְדִים בֵּין בַּיָּם וּבֵין בַּיַּבָּשָׁה
הַמָּקוֹם יְרַחֵם עֲלֵיהֶם וְיוֹצִיאֵם מִצָּרָה לִרְוָחָה
וּמֵאֲפֵלָה לְאוֹרָה, וּמִשִּׁעְבּוּד לִגְאֻלָּה
הַשְׁתָּא בַּעֲגָלָא וּבִזְמַן קָרִיב, וְנֹאמַר אָמֵן.

RETURNING THE TORAH TO THE ARK

The Ark is opened. The Leader takes the Torah scroll and says:

יְהַלְלוּ Let them praise the name of the LORD, Ps. 148
for His name alone is sublime.

The congregation responds:

הוֹדוֹ His majesty is above earth and heaven.
He has raised the horn of His people,
for the glory of all His devoted ones,
the children of Israel, the people close to Him.
Halleluya!

As the Torah scroll is returned to the Ark, say:

לְדָוִד מִזְמוֹר A psalm of David. The earth is the LORD's and all it contains, Ps. 24
the world and all who live in it. For He founded it on the seas and established it on the streams. Who may climb the mountain of the LORD? Who may stand in His holy place? He who has clean hands and a pure heart, who has not taken My name in vain, or sworn deceitfully. He shall receive blessing from the LORD, and just reward from God, his salvation. This is a generation of those who seek Him, the descendants of Jacob who seek Your presence, Selah! Lift up your heads, O gates; be uplifted, eternal doors, so that the King of glory may enter. Who is the King of glory? It is the LORD, strong and mighty, the LORD mighty in battle. Lift up your heads, O gates; lift them up, eternal doors, so that the King of glory may enter. Who is He, the King of glory? The LORD of hosts, He is the King of glory, Selah!

As the Torah scroll is placed into the Ark, say:

וּבְנֻחֹה יֹאמַר When the Ark came to rest, Moses would say: "Return, O Num. 10
LORD, to the myriad thousands of Israel." Advance, LORD, to Your resting Ps. 132
place, You and Your mighty Ark. Your priests are clothed in righteousness, and Your devoted ones sing in joy. For the sake of Your servant
David, do not reject Your anointed one. For I give you good instruction; Prov. 4
do not forsake My Torah. It is a tree of life to those who grasp it, and Prov. 3
those who uphold it are happy. Its ways are ways of pleasantness, and all
its paths are peace. ▸ Turn us back, O LORD, to You, and we will return. Lam. 5
Renew our days as of old.

The Ark is closed.

הכנסת ספר תורה

The ארון קודש *is opened. The* שליח ציבור *takes the* ספר תורה *and says:*

יְהַלְלוּ אֶת־שֵׁם יהוה, כִּי נִשְׂגָּב־שְׁמוֹ, לְבַדּוֹ תהלים קמח

The קהל *responds:*

הוֹדוֹ עַל־אֶרֶץ וְשָׁמָיִם:
וַיָּרֶם קֶרֶן לְעַמּוֹ
תְּהִלָּה לְכָל־חֲסִידָיו
לִבְנֵי יִשְׂרָאֵל עַם קְרֹבוֹ, הַלְלוּיָהּ:

As the ספר תורה *is returned to the* ארון קודש*, say:*

לְדָוִד מִזְמוֹר, לַיהוה הָאָרֶץ וּמְלוֹאָהּ, תֵּבֵל וְיֹשְׁבֵי בָהּ: כִּי־הוּא עַל־ תהלים כד
יַמִּים יְסָדָהּ, וְעַל־נְהָרוֹת יְכוֹנְנֶהָ: מִי־יַעֲלֶה בְהַר־יהוה, וּמִי־יָקוּם
בִּמְקוֹם קָדְשׁוֹ: נְקִי כַפַּיִם וּבַר־לֵבָב, אֲשֶׁר לֹא־נָשָׂא לַשָּׁוְא נַפְשִׁי
וְלֹא נִשְׁבַּע לְמִרְמָה: יִשָּׂא בְרָכָה מֵאֵת יהוה, וּצְדָקָה מֵאֱלֹהֵי יִשְׁעוֹ:
זֶה דּוֹר דֹּרְשָׁו, מְבַקְשֵׁי פָנֶיךָ, יַעֲקֹב, סֶלָה: שְׂאוּ שְׁעָרִים רָאשֵׁיכֶם,
וְהִנָּשְׂאוּ פִּתְחֵי עוֹלָם, וְיָבוֹא מֶלֶךְ הַכָּבוֹד: מִי זֶה מֶלֶךְ הַכָּבוֹד, יהוה
עִזּוּז וְגִבּוֹר, יהוה גִּבּוֹר מִלְחָמָה: שְׂאוּ שְׁעָרִים רָאשֵׁיכֶם, וּשְׂאוּ
פִּתְחֵי עוֹלָם, וְיָבֹא מֶלֶךְ הַכָּבוֹד: מִי הוּא זֶה מֶלֶךְ הַכָּבוֹד, יהוה
צְבָאוֹת הוּא מֶלֶךְ הַכָּבוֹד, סֶלָה:

As the ספר תורה *is placed into the* ארון קודש*, say:*

וּבְנֻחֹה יֹאמַר, שׁוּבָה יהוה רִבְבוֹת אַלְפֵי יִשְׂרָאֵל: קוּמָה יהוה במדבר י תהלים קלב
לִמְנוּחָתֶךָ, אַתָּה וַאֲרוֹן עֻזֶּךָ: כֹּהֲנֶיךָ יִלְבְּשׁוּ־צֶדֶק, וַחֲסִידֶיךָ יְרַנֵּנוּ:
בַּעֲבוּר דָּוִד עַבְדֶּךָ אַל־תָּשֵׁב פְּנֵי מְשִׁיחֶךָ: כִּי לֶקַח טוֹב נָתַתִּי משלי ד
לָכֶם, תּוֹרָתִי אַל־תַּעֲזֹבוּ: עֵץ־חַיִּים הִיא לַמַּחֲזִיקִים בָּהּ, וְתֹמְכֶיהָ משלי ג
מְאֻשָּׁר: דְּרָכֶיהָ דַרְכֵי־נֹעַם וְכָל־נְתִיבֹתֶיהָ שָׁלוֹם: › הֲשִׁיבֵנוּ יהוה איכה ה
אֵלֶיךָ וְנָשׁוּבָ, חַדֵּשׁ יָמֵינוּ כְּקֶדֶם:

The ארון קודש *is closed.*

CONCLUSION OF THE SERVICE

Some have the custom to touch the hand-tefillin at °, and the head-tefillin at °°.

אַשְׁרֵי Happy[B] are those who dwell in Your House; Ps. 84
they shall continue to praise You, Selah!
Happy are the people for whom this is so; Ps. 144
happy are the people whose God is the LORD.

The prayer thus ensures that one begins one's day with Torah learning before venturing out of *shul*.

A second theory, presented in the name of Rashi, suggests that there was a time when the government would not permit Jews to say the *Kedusha* in the *Shemoneh Esreh* because the Jews rejected the understanding of the threefold repetition of *kadosh* as a reference to different manifestations of God. They therefore sent spies into the *shul* at that time to make sure it was not recited. By the end of the service, however, the spies had left and so the congregants slipped in this *Kedusha* in order to be able to sanctify God's name before starting one's day (*Sefer HaPardes*). *Kedusha* follows a specific order, or *seder*, and therefore it is known as *Kedusha deSidra*.

Finally, there is another theory which suggests that there were people who came late to *shul* (can you believe that?!) and thus missed saying the *Kedusha* in the *Shemoneh Esreh*. These people were generally the more unlearned and therefore the *Kedusha* was translated into the vernacular so that they would understand it. Indeed, the entire prayer may be a kind of summary of the *Shemoneh Esreh* (God's name is mentioned 18 times) (Abudarham). Its insertion at this point in the service ensures that before we embark on our day, we come together as a community to sanctify God's name.

There are a few parts to this very ancient prayer. The first part speaks about the coming of the Redeemer, a fitting hope to have before one walks away from *tefilla* to begin one's day, especially after the allusion that we just made in Psalm 20 to the fact that life can have its sad or tragic moments.

Another section refers to Torah study. Before leaving *shul* to begin our day we restate the importance of learning as a core value, reflecting our millennia-old commitment to Torah as that which has kept us alive as a people. Indeed, Rabbi Meir Simḥa of Dvinsk suggested that this is the difference between this *Kedusha* and the other ones we have recited. In *Pesukei DeZimra* we described the *Kedusha* that the angels say on high; in the repetition of the *Shemoneh Esreh* we said the *Kedusha* as if we were angels ourselves; here, we create *Kedusha* through our Torah study, a sound that not even the angels can make (*Meshekh Ḥokhma Vayikra* 19).

But the sum total of the prayer seems to point toward putting one's faith in God and His Torah. In a world in which people are often asking "Why was I created?" or "What is the purpose of life?" Judaism's response

The continuation of this **INTRODUCTION** *and* **BIUR TEFILLA** *on* אַשְׁרֵי *are on page 227.*

סיום התפילה

Some have the custom to touch the תפילין של יד *at* °*, and the* תפילין של ראש *at* °°*.*

אַשְׁרֵי יוֹשְׁבֵי בֵיתֶךָ, עוֹד יְהַלְלוּךָ סֶּלָה: תהלים פד
אַשְׁרֵי הָעָם שֶׁכָּכָה לּוֹ, אַשְׁרֵי הָעָם שֶׁיהוה אֱלֹהָיו: תהלים קמד

INTRODUCTION TO KEDUSHA DESIDRA: קדושה דסדרא

The service begins to draw to a close. *Shemoneh Esreh* is over, *Kaddish* has been recited to complete the previous section, and we now move toward the final segment. The entire section is called by the prayer which concludes it, known as *Kedusha deSidra*, literally "the *Kedusha* of the order," the most important part of which is, as one would imagine, the *Kedusha* that is recited with its Aramaic translation. The section actually consists of three parts. The first is *Ashrei*, repeated here for a second time in *Shaḥarit*, in keeping with the Talmud's statement that "whoever says *Ashrei* three times a day is guaranteed a place in the World to Come" (*Berakhot* 4b). The third recitation will take place at *Minḥa*. Indeed, just as in *Minḥa* we have *Ashrei* followed by the *Kedusha* of *Shemoneh Esreh*, so too, here, we have *Ashrei* followed by the *Kedusha deSidra*. *Ashrei* describes a perfect world, an ideal state in which all of the world is in harmony; a fitting way to view the beginning of one's day.

The second component of this section is Psalm 20. This particular psalm also exudes confidence and optimism that all of our prayers will be answered (יְמַלֵּא יהוה כָּל מִשְׁאֲלוֹתֶיךָ). Indeed, it has been suggested that this twentieth psalm is the culmination of the previous 19 in *Sefer Tehillim*, and thus serves as a fitting summary here for a different 19, namely, the 19 blessings of the *Shemoneh Esreh* that we just recited. Because of its suggestion that God will even answer us on a *yom tzara*, a day of distress, it is omitted on holidays which cannot be characterized in such a negative way. Conversely, it is also omitted in the house of a mourner because we do not want to add to the distress which is already felt.

The final prayer in the section is the prayer from which the section derives its name: *Kedusha deSidra*. While the Gemara itself mentions this *tefilla* ("The world subsists on the *Kedusha deSidra*" – *Sota* 49a), it is not clear why it was instituted. The oldest explanation is that of Rabbi Natronai Gaon, who said that in Talmudic times before leaving *shul* they learned Torah together, which included the recitation of verses and their translation into the vernacular, which was Aramaic. Unfortunately, time constraints eventually dictated that this learning be curtailed and all that remains are some representative parts of Tanakh, specifically the sections that we know as *Kedusha*. A block of time dedicated to learning is known as a *seder*, hence this section became known as *Kedusha deSidra*, or the *Kedusha* which follows a *seder* of learning (*Teshuvot HaGeonim*).

A song of praise by David. *Ps. 145*

א I will elevate You, my God, the King,
and bless Your name for ever and all time.
ב Every day I will bless You,
and praise Your name for ever and all time.
ג Great is the LORD and greatly to be praised;
His greatness is unfathomable.
ד One generation will praise Your works to the next,
and tell of Your mighty deeds.
ה On the glorious splendor of Your majesty I will meditate,
and on the acts of Your wonders.
ו They shall talk of the power of Your awesome deeds,
and I will tell of Your greatness.
ז They shall recite the record of Your great goodness,
and sing with joy of Your righteousness.
ח The LORD is generous and compassionate,
slow to anger and great in loving-kindness.
ט The LORD is good to all,
and His compassion extends to all His works.
י All Your works shall thank You, LORD,
and Your devoted ones shall bless You.
כ They shall talk of the glory of Your kingship,
and speak of Your might.
ל To make known to mankind His mighty deeds
and the glorious majesty of His kingship.
מ Your kingdom is an everlasting kingdom,
and Your reign is for all generations.
ס The LORD supports all who fall,
and raises all who are bowed down.

---

out our day. Numerous studies have correlations that indicate that people who pray are better able to cope with the challenges that each day brings. Belief brings relief.

תהלים קמה

תְּהִלָּה לְדָוִד

אֲרוֹמִמְךָ אֱלוֹהַי הַמֶּלֶךְ, וַאֲבָרְכָה שִׁמְךָ לְעוֹלָם וָעֶד:
בְּכָל־יוֹם אֲבָרְכֶךָּ, וַאֲהַלְלָה שִׁמְךָ לְעוֹלָם וָעֶד:
גָּדוֹל יהוה וּמְהֻלָּל מְאֹד, וְלִגְדֻלָּתוֹ אֵין חֵקֶר:
דּוֹר לְדוֹר יְשַׁבַּח מַעֲשֶׂיךָ, וּגְבוּרֹתֶיךָ יַגִּידוּ:
הֲדַר כְּבוֹד הוֹדֶךָ, וְדִבְרֵי נִפְלְאֹתֶיךָ אָשִׂיחָה:
וֶעֱזוּז נוֹרְאֹתֶיךָ יֹאמֵרוּ, וּגְדוּלָּתְךָ אֲסַפְּרֶנָּה:
זֵכֶר רַב־טוּבְךָ יַבִּיעוּ, וְצִדְקָתְךָ יְרַנֵּנוּ:
חַנּוּן וְרַחוּם יהוה, אֶרֶךְ אַפַּיִם וּגְדָל־חָסֶד:
טוֹב־יהוה לַכֹּל, וְרַחֲמָיו עַל־כָּל־מַעֲשָׂיו:
יוֹדוּךָ יהוה כָּל־מַעֲשֶׂיךָ, וַחֲסִידֶיךָ יְבָרְכוּכָה:
כְּבוֹד מַלְכוּתְךָ יֹאמֵרוּ, וּגְבוּרָתְךָ יְדַבֵּרוּ:
לְהוֹדִיעַ לִבְנֵי הָאָדָם גְּבוּרֹתָיו, וּכְבוֹד הֲדַר מַלְכוּתוֹ:
מַלְכוּתְךָ מַלְכוּת כָּל־עֹלָמִים, וּמֶמְשַׁלְתְּךָ בְּכָל־דּוֹר וָדֹר:
סוֹמֵךְ יהוה לְכָל־הַנֹּפְלִים, וְזוֹקֵף לְכָל־הַכְּפוּפִים:

---

is that each of us is unique and was created for a specific purpose, even if we are not yet aware of what that purpose is. We have an identity that binds us to thousands of years of tradition and commitment, and faith which assures us that a bright future lies ahead. Life, especially a life in which one has pride for one's identity, is full of beauty and meaning, even as some individual days can seem overbearing and difficult. The person who puts his or her faith in God knows that such setbacks are temporary and can be overcome. Thus fortified, one can begin a new day.

BIUR TEFILLA · ביאור תפילה

אַשְׁרֵי – *Happy*. There are no requests here. The prayer speaks only of Hashem's watching out for the world, and so we now remind ourselves that He will continue to do so through-

ע All raise their eyes to You in hope,
and You give them their food in due season.
פ °You open Your hand,
°°and satisfy every living thing with favor.
צ The LORD is righteous in all His ways,
and kind in all He does.
ק The LORD is close to all who call on Him,
to all who call on Him in truth.
ר He fulfills the will of those who fear Him;
He hears their cry and saves them.
ש The LORD guards all who love Him,
but all the wicked He will destroy.
ת ▸ My mouth shall speak the praise of the LORD,
and all creatures shall bless His holy name
for ever and all time.
We will bless the LORD now and for ever. Halleluya! *Ps. 115*

Omit on Rosh Hodesh and Tisha B'Av, or in a house of mourning.

לַמְנַצֵּחַ For the conductor of music. A psalm of David.[B] May the LORD answer you when you are in distress; may the name of Jacob's God protect you. May He send you help from the Sanctuary and support from Zion. May He remember all your meal-offerings and accept your burnt-offerings, Selah! May He give you your heart's desire and make all your plans succeed. We will shout for joy at Your salvation and lift a banner in the name of our God. May the LORD grant all your requests. Now I know that the LORD saves His anointed; He answers him from His holy heaven with the saving power of His right hand. Some trust in chariots, others in horses, but we call on the name of the LORD our God.[I] They were brought to their knees and fell, but we rose up and stood firm. ▸ LORD, save! May the King answer us on the day we call. *Ps. 20*

battlefield of war and of life lies elsewhere. Our greatest enemy is our own lack of faith and optimism that things will work out; our greatest source of strength lies above.

עֵינֵי־כֹל אֵלֶיךָ יְשַׂבֵּרוּ, וְאַתָּה נוֹתֵן־לָהֶם אֶת־אָכְלָם בְּעִתּוֹ:
°פּוֹתֵחַ אֶת־יָדֶךָ, °°וּמַשְׂבִּיעַ לְכָל־חַי רָצוֹן:
צַדִּיק יהוה בְּכָל־דְּרָכָיו, וְחָסִיד בְּכָל־מַעֲשָׂיו:
קָרוֹב יהוה לְכָל־קֹרְאָיו, לְכֹל אֲשֶׁר יִקְרָאֻהוּ בֶאֱמֶת:
רְצוֹן־יְרֵאָיו יַעֲשֶׂה, וְאֶת־שַׁוְעָתָם יִשְׁמַע, וְיוֹשִׁיעֵם:
שׁוֹמֵר יהוה אֶת־כָּל־אֹהֲבָיו, וְאֵת כָּל־הָרְשָׁעִים יַשְׁמִיד:
› תְּהִלַּת יהוה יְדַבֶּר פִּי, וִיבָרֵךְ כָּל־בָּשָׂר שֵׁם קָדְשׁוֹ לְעוֹלָם וָעֶד:
וַאֲנַחְנוּ נְבָרֵךְ יָהּ מֵעַתָּה וְעַד־עוֹלָם, הַלְלוּיָהּ: תהלים קטו

Omit on ראש חודש *and* תשעה באב*, or in a house of mourning.*

לַמְנַצֵּחַ מִזְמוֹר לְדָוִד: ב יַעַנְךָ יהוה בְּיוֹם צָרָה, יְשַׂגֶּבְךָ שֵׁם אֱלֹהֵי תהלים כ
יַעֲקֹב: יִשְׁלַח־עֶזְרְךָ מִקֹּדֶשׁ, וּמִצִּיּוֹן יִסְעָדֶךָּ: יִזְכֹּר כָּל־מִנְחֹתֶךָ,
וְעוֹלָתְךָ יְדַשְּׁנֶה סֶלָה: יִתֶּן־לְךָ כִלְבָבֶךָ וְכָל־עֲצָתְךָ יְמַלֵּא: נְרַנְּנָה
בִּישׁוּעָתֶךָ, וּבְשֵׁם־אֱלֹהֵינוּ נִדְגֹּל, יְמַלֵּא יהוה כָּל־מִשְׁאֲלוֹתֶיךָ:
עַתָּה יָדַעְתִּי כִּי הוֹשִׁיעַ יהוה מְשִׁיחוֹ, יַעֲנֵהוּ מִשְּׁמֵי קָדְשׁוֹ,
בִּגְבוּרוֹת יֵשַׁע יְמִינוֹ: אֵלֶּה בָרֶכֶב וְאֵלֶּה בַסּוּסִים, וַאֲנַחְנוּ בְּשֵׁם־
יהוה אֱלֹהֵינוּ נַזְכִּיר: ע הֵמָּה כָּרְעוּ וְנָפָלוּ, וַאֲנַחְנוּ קַמְנוּ וַנִּתְעוֹדָד:
› יהוה הוֹשִׁיעָה, הַמֶּלֶךְ יַעֲנֵנוּ בְיוֹם־קָרְאֵנוּ:

BIUR TEFILLA • ביאור תפילה

לַמְנַצֵּחַ מִזְמוֹר לְדָוִד – *For the conductor of music. A psalm of David.* The psalm reassures a king (David) that as he goes out to do battle, Hashem will be with him. We too are encouraged to believe the same thing as we are about to begin our day.

IYUN TEFILLA • עיון תפילה

וַאֲנַחְנוּ בְּשֵׁם־יהוה אֱלֹהֵינוּ נַזְכִּיר – *But we call on the name of the Lord our God.* Nations have too often believed that their success lies in the development of the ultimate weapon, from horses and chariots to a nuclear arsenal. Yet we Jews are reminded that no such device is reliable. The ultimate answer on the

In a house of mourning and on Tisha B'Av omit the verse beginning "As for Me" and continue with "You are the Holy One."

וּבָא לְצִיּוֹן גּוֹאֵל "A redeemer will come to Zion, *Is. 59*
to those in Jacob who repent of their sins," declares the LORD.
"As for Me, this is My covenant with them," says the LORD.
"My spirit, that is on you,
and My words I have placed in your mouth
will not depart from your mouth,
or from the mouth of your children,
or from the mouth of their descendants from this time on
and for ever," says the LORD.

▸ You are the Holy One, enthroned on the praises of Israel. *Ps. 22*
And (the angels) call to one another, saying, "Holy, holy, holy *Is. 6*
is the LORD of hosts; the whole world is filled with His glory."
And they receive permission from one another, saying: *Targum Yonatan Is. 6*
"Holy in the highest heavens, home of His Presence; holy on earth,
the work of His strength; holy for ever and all time is the LORD of hosts;
the whole earth is full of His radiant glory."

▸ Then a wind lifted me up and I heard behind me *Ezek. 3*
the sound of a great noise, saying,
"Blessed is the LORD's glory from His place."
Then a wind lifted me up and I heard behind me *Targum Yonatan Ezek. 3*
the sound of a great tempest of those who uttered praise, saying,
"Blessed is the LORD's glory from the place of the home of His Presence."

The LORD shall reign for ever and all time. *Ex. 15*
The LORD's kingdom is established for ever and all time. *Targum Onkelos Ex. 15*

יהוה LORD, God of Abraham, Isaac and Yisrael, our ancestors, may You *1 Chr. 29*
keep this for ever so that it forms the thoughts in Your people's heart,
and directs their heart toward You. He is compassionate. He forgives *Ps. 78*
iniquity and does not destroy. Repeatedly He suppresses His anger,
not rousing His full wrath. For You, my LORD, are good and forgiving, *Ps. 86*
abundantly kind to all who call on You. Your righteousness is eternally *Ps. 119*

---

residence of the Divine. The second "holy" refers to God's holiness on earth, the residence of His creation. The third "holy" refers to God's holiness in time, forever and ever.

In a house of mourning and on תשעה באב *omit the verse beginning* וַאֲנִי זֹאת בְּרִיתִי *and continue with* וְאַתָּה קָדוֹשׁ.

וּבָא לְצִיּוֹן גּוֹאֵל, וּלְשָׁבֵי פֶשַׁע בְּיַעֲקֹב, נְאֻם יהוה: ישעיה נט
וַאֲנִי זֹאת בְּרִיתִי אוֹתָם, אָמַר יהוה
רוּחִי אֲשֶׁר עָלֶיךָ וּדְבָרַי אֲשֶׁר־שַׂמְתִּי בְּפִיךָ
לֹא־יָמוּשׁוּ מִפִּיךָ וּמִפִּי זַרְעֲךָ וּמִפִּי זֶרַע זַרְעֲךָ
אָמַר יהוה, מֵעַתָּה וְעַד־עוֹלָם:

▸ וְאַתָּה קָדוֹשׁ יוֹשֵׁב תְּהִלּוֹת יִשְׂרָאֵל: וְקָרָא זֶה אֶל־זֶה וְאָמַר תהלים כב / ישעיה ו
קָדוֹשׁ, קָדוֹשׁ, קָדוֹשׁ, יהוה צְבָאוֹת, מְלֹא כָל־הָאָרֶץ כְּבוֹדוֹ:
וּמְקַבְּלִין דֵּין מִן דֵּין וְאָמְרִין, קַדִּישׁ בִּשְׁמֵי מְרוֹמָא עִלָּאָה בֵּית שְׁכִינְתֵהּ תרגום יונתן ישעיה ו
קַדִּישׁ עַל אַרְעָא עוֹבַד גְּבוּרְתֵּהּ, קַדִּישׁ לְעָלַם וּלְעָלְמֵי עָלְמַיָּא
יהוה צְבָאוֹת, מַלְיָא כָל אַרְעָא זִיו יְקָרֵהּ.

▸ וַתִּשָּׂאֵנִי רוּחַ, וָאֶשְׁמַע אַחֲרַי קוֹל רַעַשׁ גָּדוֹל יחזקאל ג
בָּרוּךְ כְּבוֹד־יהוה מִמְּקוֹמוֹ:
וּנְטָלַתְנִי רוּחָא, וּשְׁמָעִית בַּתְרַי קָל זִיעַ סַגִּיא, דִּמְשַׁבְּחִין וְאָמְרִין תרגום יונתן יחזקאל ג
בְּרִיךְ יְקָרָא דַיהוה מֵאֲתַר בֵּית שְׁכִינְתֵהּ.

יהוה יִמְלֹךְ לְעֹלָם וָעֶד: שמות טו
יהוה מַלְכוּתֵהּ קָאֵם לְעָלַם וּלְעָלְמֵי עָלְמַיָּא. תרגום אונקלוס שמות טו

יהוה אֱלֹהֵי אַבְרָהָם יִצְחָק וְיִשְׂרָאֵל אֲבֹתֵינוּ, שָׁמְרָה־זֹּאת לְעוֹלָם דברי הימים א׳ כט
לְיֵצֶר מַחְשְׁבוֹת לְבַב עַמֶּךָ, וְהָכֵן לְבָבָם אֵלֶיךָ: וְהוּא רַחוּם יְכַפֵּר תהלים עח
עָוֹן וְלֹא־יַשְׁחִית, וְהִרְבָּה לְהָשִׁיב אַפּוֹ, וְלֹא־יָעִיר כָּל־חֲמָתוֹ:
כִּי־אַתָּה אֲדֹנָי טוֹב וְסַלָּח, וְרַב־חֶסֶד לְכָל־קֹרְאֶיךָ: צִדְקָתְךָ תהלים קיט

IYUN TEFILLA • עיון תפילה

קָדוֹשׁ, קָדוֹשׁ, קָדוֹשׁ – *Holy, holy, holy.* Why does the verse from *Yishayahu* repeat the word *kadosh* three times? The first "holy" refers to God's holiness in heaven above, the

righteous, and Your Torah is truth. Grant truth to Jacob, loving-kindness Mic. 7
to Abraham, as You promised our ancestors in ancient times. Blessed Ps. 68
is my LORD for day after day He burdens us [with His blessings];[i] God
is our salvation, Selah! The LORD of hosts is with us; the God of Jacob Ps. 46
is our refuge, Selah! LORD of hosts, happy is the one who trusts in You. Ps. 84
LORD, save![A] May the King answer us on the day we call. Ps. 20

בָּרוּךְ Blessed is He, our God, who created us for His glory, separating us from those who go astray; who gave us the Torah of truth, planting within us eternal life. May He open our heart to His Torah, imbuing our heart with the love and awe of Him, that we may do His will and serve Him with a perfect heart, so that we neither toil in vain nor give birth to confusion.

יְהִי רָצוֹן May it be Your will, O LORD our God and God of our ancestors,
that we keep Your laws in this world, and thus be worthy to live, see and
inherit goodness and blessing in the Messianic Age and in the life of the
World to Come. So that my soul may sing to You and not be silent. LORD, Ps. 30
my God, for ever I will thank You. Blessed is the man who trusts in the Jer. 17
LORD, whose trust is in the LORD alone. Trust in the LORD for evermore, Is. 26
for God, the LORD, is an everlasting Rock. ▸ Those who know Your name Ps. 9
trust in You, for You, LORD, do not forsake those who seek You. The LORD Is. 42
desired, for the sake of Israel's merit, to make the Torah great and glorious.

On Rosh Ḥodesh, the Leader says Half Kaddish, page 218.
The service then continues on page 854.

On other days, the Leader continues with Full Kaddish on the next page.

ANI TEFILLA • אני תפילה

A pauper once encountered a wealthy man on the street and begged him for some money. The rich man said that he hadn't enough with him but if the pauper were to come to his home that evening, he would give him even more than he asked for. The wealthy man waited all night but the pauper did not come. The next day, the rich man was accosted by the same pauper who once again pleaded with him for money. Again the wealthy man told him to come to his home and again the poor man did not show up. The next day, the pauper found the potential benefactor once more, but this time the wealthy man yelled at him that he was a liar and a charlatan.

Every day we ask Hashem in our prayers for the ability to understand and learn and live Torah. And He is willing to help us with that and more. He asks only one thing: we need to show up and be willing to do so earnestly and honestly. (Ḥafetz Ḥayyim)

מיכה ז צֶדֶק לְעוֹלָם וְתוֹרָתְךָ אֱמֶת: תִּתֵּן אֱמֶת לְיַעֲקֹב, חֶסֶד לְאַבְרָהָם,
תהלים סח אֲשֶׁר־נִשְׁבַּעְתָּ לַאֲבֹתֵינוּ מִימֵי קֶדֶם: בָּרוּךְ אֲדֹנָי יוֹם יוֹם יַעֲמָס־
תהלים מו לָנוּ,ע הָאֵל יְשׁוּעָתֵנוּ סֶלָה: יהוה צְבָאוֹת עִמָּנוּ, מִשְׂגָּב לָנוּ אֱלֹהֵי
תהלים פד יַעֲקֹב סֶלָה: יהוה צְבָאוֹת, אַשְׁרֵי אָדָם בֹּטֵחַ בָּךְ: יהוה הוֹשִׁיעָה,א
תהלים כ הַמֶּלֶךְ יַעֲנֵנוּ בְיוֹם־קָרְאֵנוּ:

בָּרוּךְ הוּא אֱלֹהֵינוּ שֶׁבְּרָאָנוּ לִכְבוֹדוֹ, וְהִבְדִּילָנוּ מִן הַתּוֹעִים, וְנָתַן לָנוּ תּוֹרַת אֱמֶת, וְחַיֵּי עוֹלָם נָטַע בְּתוֹכֵנוּ. הוּא יִפְתַּח לִבֵּנוּ בְּתוֹרָתוֹ, וְיָשֵׂם בְּלִבֵּנוּ אַהֲבָתוֹ וְיִרְאָתוֹ וְלַעֲשׂוֹת רְצוֹנוֹ וּלְעָבְדוֹ בְּלֵבָב שָׁלֵם, לְמַעַן לֹא נִיגַע לָרִיק וְלֹא נֵלֵד לַבֶּהָלָה.

יְהִי רָצוֹן מִלְּפָנֶיךָ יהוה אֱלֹהֵינוּ וֵאלֹהֵי אֲבוֹתֵינוּ, שֶׁנִּשְׁמֹר חֻקֶּיךָ
בָּעוֹלָם הַזֶּה, וְנִזְכֶּה וְנִחְיֶה וְנִרְאֶה וְנִירַשׁ טוֹבָה וּבְרָכָה, לִשְׁנֵי
תהלים ל יְמוֹת הַמָּשִׁיחַ וּלְחַיֵּי הָעוֹלָם הַבָּא. לְמַעַן יְזַמֶּרְךָ כָבוֹד וְלֹא יִדֹּם,
ירמיה יז יהוה אֱלֹהַי, לְעוֹלָם אוֹדֶךָּ: בָּרוּךְ הַגֶּבֶר אֲשֶׁר יִבְטַח בַּיהוה, וְהָיָה
ישעיה כו יהוה מִבְטַחוֹ: בִּטְחוּ בַיהוה עֲדֵי־עַד, כִּי בְּיָהּ יהוה צוּר עוֹלָמִים:
תהלים ט ◂ וְיִבְטְחוּ בְךָ יוֹדְעֵי שְׁמֶךָ, כִּי לֹא־עָזַבְתָּ דֹרְשֶׁיךָ, יהוה: יהוה חָפֵץ
ישעיה מב לְמַעַן צִדְקוֹ, יַגְדִּיל תּוֹרָה וְיַאְדִּיר:

On ראש חודש*, the* שליח ציבור *says* חצי קדיש*, page 219.*
The service then continues on page 855.

On other days the שליח ציבור *continues with* קדיש שלם *on the next page.*

ANI TEFILLA • אני תפילה

יהוה הוֹשִׁיעָה – *Lord, save.* The verse says: Don't worry, Hashem will save us, take care of us, He loves us and will answer us on the day we call out to Him. He listens to us, He is connected to us (Rabbi S. Aviner). It has always been so. I have reason to be optimistic.

IYUN TEFILLA • עיון תפילה

יַעֲמָס־לָנוּ – *He burdens us* [*with His blessings*]. Yet how many of us focus on the things we don't have instead? Think of all of the good things in your life that others do not have. They would look at us and say that we are burdened with blessings. We need to recognize it too. What do I have that many others do not?

FULL KADDISH

Leader: יִתְגַּדַּל Magnified and sanctified may His great name be,
in the world He created by His will.
May He establish His kingdom in your lifetime
and in your days, and in the lifetime
of all the house of Israel, swiftly and soon –
and say: Amen.

All: May His great name[A] be blessed for ever and all time.

Leader: Blessed and praised, glorified and exalted,
raised and honored, uplifted and lauded be
the name of the Holy One, blessed be He,
beyond any blessing,
song, praise and consolation uttered in the world –
and say: Amen.

On Tisha B'Av, omit the next verse and continue with "May there be great peace."

May the prayers and pleas of all Israel
be accepted by their Father in heaven –
and say: Amen.

May there be great peace from heaven,
and life for us and all Israel –
and say: Amen.

Bow, take three steps back, as if taking leave of the Divine Presence, then bow, first left, then right, then center, while saying:

May He who makes peace in His high places,
make peace for us and all Israel –
and say: Amen.

ANI TEFILLA · אני תפילה

יְהֵא שְׁמֵהּ רַבָּא – *May His great name.* Whoever says *yeheh shemeh raba...* with all his strength, the Heavenly Court rips up any negative decree against him (*Shabbat* 119b). "With all his strength" – one should enunciate the words clearly (Maharal).

קדיש שלם

ש״ץ: יִתְגַּדַּל וְיִתְקַדַּשׁ שְׁמֵהּ רַבָּא (קהל: אָמֵן)
בְּעָלְמָא דִּי בְרָא כִרְעוּתֵהּ
וְיַמְלִיךְ מַלְכוּתֵהּ
בְּחַיֵּיכוֹן וּבְיוֹמֵיכוֹן וּבְחַיֵּי דְכָל בֵּית יִשְׂרָאֵל
בַּעֲגָלָא וּבִזְמַן קָרִיב, וְאִמְרוּ אָמֵן. (קהל: אָמֵן)

קהל וש״ץ: יְהֵא שְׁמֵהּ רַבָּא[א] מְבָרַךְ לְעָלַם וּלְעָלְמֵי עָלְמַיָּא.

ש״ץ: יִתְבָּרַךְ וְיִשְׁתַּבַּח וְיִתְפָּאַר
וְיִתְרוֹמַם וְיִתְנַשֵּׂא וְיִתְהַדָּר וְיִתְעַלֶּה וְיִתְהַלָּל
שְׁמֵהּ דְּקֻדְשָׁא בְּרִיךְ הוּא (קהל: בְּרִיךְ הוּא)
לְעֵלָּא מִן כָּל בִּרְכָתָא
וְשִׁירָתָא, תֻּשְׁבְּחָתָא וְנֶחֱמָתָא
דַּאֲמִירָן בְּעָלְמָא, וְאִמְרוּ אָמֵן. (קהל: אָמֵן)

On תשעה באב*, omit the next verse and continue with* יְהֵא שְׁלָמָא.

תִּתְקַבַּל צְלוֹתְהוֹן וּבָעוּתְהוֹן דְּכָל יִשְׂרָאֵל
קֳדָם אֲבוּהוֹן דִּי בִשְׁמַיָּא, וְאִמְרוּ אָמֵן. (קהל: אָמֵן)

יְהֵא שְׁלָמָא רַבָּא מִן שְׁמַיָּא
וְחַיִּים, עָלֵינוּ וְעַל כָּל יִשְׂרָאֵל, וְאִמְרוּ אָמֵן. (קהל: אָמֵן)

Bow, take three steps back, as if taking leave of the Divine Presence, then bow, first left, then right, then center, while saying:

עֹשֶׂה שָׁלוֹם בִּמְרוֹמָיו
הוּא יַעֲשֶׂה שָׁלוֹם עָלֵינוּ וְעַל כָּל יִשְׂרָאֵל
וְאִמְרוּ אָמֵן. (קהל: אָמֵן)

Stand while saying Aleinu. Bow at ▾.

עָלֵינוּ It is our duty[B] to praise the Master of all,
and ascribe greatness to the Author of creation,
who has not made us like the nations of the lands
nor placed us like the families of the earth;
who has not made our portion like theirs,
nor our destiny like all their multitudes.
(For they worship vanity and emptiness,
and pray to a god who cannot save.)
▾But we bow in worship
and thank the Supreme King of kings,
the Holy One, blessed be He,
who extends the heavens and establishes the earth,
whose throne of glory is in the heavens above,
and whose power's Presence is in the highest of heights.
He is our God; there is no other.
Truly He is our King, there is none else,
as it is written in His Torah:
"You shall know and take to heart this day *Deut. 4*
that the LORD is God, in heaven above and on earth below.
There is no other."

---

misguided. The second paragraph, however, lays out our dream for the future, a time when all of the people of the world will accept God's sovereignty and adopt the basic standards of morality and justice exemplified in the seven laws of Noaḥ (Rabbi S.R. Hirsch). How will this happen? When we ourselves become the most religious, moral, and just people that we can be. Unlike other nations, who want to accomplish their mission via military conquest, we hope to spread our message by leading exemplary lives. In short, the more particular we are in how we live our lives, the more universal is our message. As we get ready to leave *shul* for the "outside" world, we remind ourselves that our goal is not simply to pray, but to live a prayerful life.

Stand while saying עָלֵינוּ*. Bow at* ׳.

עָלֵינוּ לְשַׁבֵּחַ לַאֲדוֹן הַכֹּל, לָתֵת גְּדֻלָּה לְיוֹצֵר בְּרֵאשִׁית
שֶׁלֹּא עָשָׂנוּ כְּגוֹיֵי הָאֲרָצוֹת, וְלֹא שָׂמָנוּ כְּמִשְׁפְּחוֹת הָאֲדָמָה
שֶׁלֹּא שָׂם חֶלְקֵנוּ כָּהֶם וְגוֹרָלֵנוּ כְּכָל הֲמוֹנָם.
(שֶׁהֵם מִשְׁתַּחֲוִים לְהֶבֶל וָרִיק וּמִתְפַּלְלִים אֶל אֵל לֹא יוֹשִׁיעַ.)
׳וַאֲנַחְנוּ כּוֹרְעִים וּמִשְׁתַּחֲוִים וּמוֹדִים
לִפְנֵי מֶלֶךְ מַלְכֵי הַמְּלָכִים, הַקָּדוֹשׁ בָּרוּךְ הוּא
שֶׁהוּא נוֹטֶה שָׁמַיִם וְיוֹסֵד אָרֶץ
וּמוֹשַׁב יְקָרוֹ בַּשָּׁמַיִם מִמַּעַל
וּשְׁכִינַת עֻזּוֹ בְּגָבְהֵי מְרוֹמִים.
הוּא אֱלֹהֵינוּ, אֵין עוֹד.
אֱמֶת מַלְכֵּנוּ, אֶפֶס זוּלָתוֹ
כַּכָּתוּב בְּתוֹרָתוֹ
וְיָדַעְתָּ הַיּוֹם וַהֲשֵׁבֹתָ אֶל־לְבָבֶךָ דברים ד
כִּי יהוה הוּא הָאֱלֹהִים בַּשָּׁמַיִם מִמַּעַל וְעַל־הָאָרֶץ מִתָּחַת
אֵין עוֹד:

BIUR TEFILLA • ביאור תפילה

עָלֵינוּ – *It is our duty.* The appearance of this prayer as the conclusion of the service is a relatively late development of the past 500 years, even though the prayer itself is at least three times that age. It is comprised of two paragraphs which in effect lay out two themes, one particularistic and the other universalistic. In the first, we declare that we are the Chosen People. We believe in one God who alone is the Creator of heaven and earth and He chose us above all other nations whose beliefs are simply untrue or

Therefore, we place our hope in You, LORD our God,
that we may soon see the glory of Your power,
when You will remove abominations from the earth,
and idols will be utterly destroyed,
when the world will be perfected
under the sovereignty of the Almighty,
when all humanity will call on Your name,
to turn all the earth's wicked toward You.
All the world's inhabitants will realize and know
that to You every knee must bow and every tongue swear loyalty.
Before You, LORD our God, they will kneel and bow down
and give honor to Your glorious name.
They will all accept the yoke of Your kingdom,
and You will reign over them soon and for ever.
For the kingdom is Yours,
and to all eternity You will reign in glory,
as it is written in Your Torah:
"The LORD will reign for ever and ever." *Ex. 15*
▸ And it is said:
"Then the LORD shall be King over all the earth; *Zech. 14*
on that day the LORD shall be One and His name One."

Some add:

Have no fear of sudden terror or of the ruin when it overtakes the wicked. *Prov. 3*
Devise your strategy, but it will be thwarted; propose your plan, *Is. 8*
but it will not stand, for God is with us.
When you grow old, I will still be the same. *Is. 46*
When your hair turns gray, I will still carry you.
I made you, I will bear you, I will carry you, and I will rescue you.

---

too, are a nation with a mission. But unlike others who would influence the world through the use of military force, we seek to influence the world through the force of who we are as people. We seek to be role models of morality and ethics, religiosity and spirituality. We will improve the world by improving ourselves. As I change myself, I can change the world. What one thing can I do today to live up to this mission?

עַל כֵּן נְקַוֶּה לְּךָ יהוה אֱלֹהֵינוּ, לִרְאוֹת מְהֵרָה בְּתִפְאֶרֶת עֻזֶּךָ
לְהַעֲבִיר גִּלּוּלִים מִן הָאָרֶץ, וְהָאֱלִילִים כָּרוֹת יִכָּרֵתוּן
לְתַקֵּן עוֹלָם בְּמַלְכוּת שַׁדַּי.
וְכָל בְּנֵי בָשָׂר יִקְרְאוּ בִשְׁמֶךָ לְהַפְנוֹת אֵלֶיךָ כָּל רִשְׁעֵי אָרֶץ.
יַכִּירוּ וְיֵדְעוּ כָּל יוֹשְׁבֵי תֵבֵל
כִּי לְךָ תִּכְרַע כָּל בֶּרֶךְ, תִּשָּׁבַע כָּל לָשׁוֹן.
לְפָנֶיךָ יהוה אֱלֹהֵינוּ יִכְרְעוּ וְיִפֹּלוּ, וְלִכְבוֹד שִׁמְךָ יְקָר יִתֵּנוּ
וִיקַבְּלוּ כֻלָּם אֶת עֹל מַלְכוּתֶךָ
וְתִמְלֹךְ עֲלֵיהֶם מְהֵרָה לְעוֹלָם וָעֶד.
כִּי הַמַּלְכוּת שֶׁלְּךָ הִיא וּלְעוֹלְמֵי עַד תִּמְלֹךְ בְּכָבוֹד
כַּכָּתוּב בְּתוֹרָתֶךָ, יהוה יִמְלֹךְ לְעֹלָם וָעֶד: שמות טו
◂ וְנֶאֱמַר, וְהָיָה יהוה לְמֶלֶךְ עַל־כָּל־הָאָרֶץ זכריה יד
בַּיּוֹם הַהוּא יִהְיֶה יהוה אֶחָד וּשְׁמוֹ אֶחָד:

Some add:

אַל־תִּירָא מִפַּחַד פִּתְאֹם וּמִשֹּׁאַת רְשָׁעִים כִּי תָבֹא: משלי ג
עֻצוּ עֵצָה וְתֻפָר, דַּבְּרוּ דָבָר וְלֹא יָקוּם, כִּי עִמָּנוּ אֵל: ישעיה ח
וְעַד־זִקְנָה אֲנִי הוּא, וְעַד־שֵׂיבָה אֲנִי אֶסְבֹּל ישעיה מו
אֲנִי עָשִׂיתִי וַאֲנִי אֶשָּׂא וַאֲנִי אֶסְבֹּל וַאֲמַלֵּט:

ANI TEFILLA • אני תפילה

Every nation needs a reason to exist and many find in that reason a sense of mission that they want to bring to the rest of the world. America wanted to "make the world safe for democracy" and Britain once claimed that its influence was so vast that "the sun never set on the British Empire." The Soviet Union once wanted to unite all of the world's workers under the banner of Communism, and in most recent years there have been terror groups who sought to impose their views on other nations. We,

MOURNER'S KADDISH

The following prayer, said by mourners, requires the presence of a minyan. A transliteration can be found on page 1141.

Mourner: יִתְגַּדַּל Magnified and sanctified
may His great name be,
in the world He created by His will.
May He establish His kingdom
in your lifetime and in your days,
and in the lifetime of all the house of Israel,
swiftly and soon –
and say: Amen.

All: May His great name be blessed
for ever and all time.

Mourner: Blessed and praised,
glorified and exalted,
raised and honored,
uplifted and lauded
be the name of the Holy One,
blessed be He,
beyond any blessing, song,
praise and consolation
uttered in the world –
and say: Amen.

May there be great peace from heaven,
and life for us and all Israel –
and say: Amen.

Bow, take three steps back, as if taking leave of the Divine Presence, then bow, first left, then right, then center, while saying:

May He who makes peace in His high places,
make peace for us and all Israel –
and say: Amen.

קדיש יתום

The following prayer, said by mourners, requires the presence of a מנין*.*
A transliteration can be found on page 1141.

אבל: יִתְגַּדַּל וְיִתְקַדַּשׁ שְׁמֵהּ רַבָּא (קהל: אָמֵן)
בְּעָלְמָא דִּי בְרָא כִרְעוּתֵהּ
וְיַמְלִיךְ מַלְכוּתֵהּ
בְּחַיֵּיכוֹן וּבְיוֹמֵיכוֹן וּבְחַיֵּי דְכָל בֵּית יִשְׂרָאֵל
בַּעֲגָלָא וּבִזְמַן קָרִיב
וְאִמְרוּ אָמֵן. (קהל: אָמֵן)

קהל ואבל: יְהֵא שְׁמֵהּ רַבָּא מְבָרַךְ לְעָלַם וּלְעָלְמֵי עָלְמַיָּא.

אבל: יִתְבָּרַךְ וְיִשְׁתַּבַּח וְיִתְפָּאַר
וְיִתְרוֹמַם וְיִתְנַשֵּׂא וְיִתְהַדָּר וְיִתְעַלֶּה וְיִתְהַלָּל
שְׁמֵהּ דְּקֻדְשָׁא בְּרִיךְ הוּא (קהל: בְּרִיךְ הוּא)
לְעֵלָּא מִן כָּל בִּרְכָתָא
וְשִׁירָתָא, תֻּשְׁבְּחָתָא וְנֶחֱמָתָא
דַּאֲמִירָן בְּעָלְמָא
וְאִמְרוּ אָמֵן. (קהל: אָמֵן)

יְהֵא שְׁלָמָא רַבָּא מִן שְׁמַיָּא
וְחַיִּים, עָלֵינוּ וְעַל כָּל יִשְׂרָאֵל
וְאִמְרוּ אָמֵן. (קהל: אָמֵן)

Bow, take three steps back, as if taking leave of the Divine Presence, then bow, first left, then right, then center, while saying:

עֹשֶׂה שָׁלוֹם בִּמְרוֹמָיו
הוּא יַעֲשֶׂה שָׁלוֹם עָלֵינוּ וְעַל כָּל יִשְׂרָאֵל
וְאִמְרוּ אָמֵן. (קהל: אָמֵן)

THE DAILY PSALM

One of the following psalms is said on the appropriate day of the week as indicated. After the psalm, the Mourner's Kaddish on page 240 is said.

After the Daily Psalm, on Rosh Hodesh, add Barekhi Nafshi, page 250 (in Israel, some only say Barekhi Nafshi). From the second day of Rosh Hodesh Elul through Shemini Atzeret (in Israel, through Hoshana Raba), add Psalm 27 on page 254. In a house of mourning the service concludes on page 256.

Sunday: Today is the first day of the week,[B]
on which the Levites used to say this psalm in the Temple:

לְדָוִד מִזְמוֹר A psalm of David. The earth is the LORD's and all it contains,[1] *Ps. 24* the world and all who live in it. For He founded it on the seas and established it on the streams. Who may climb the mountain of the LORD? Who may stand in His holy place? He who has clean hands and a pure heart, who has not taken My name in vain or sworn deceitfully. He shall receive a blessing from the LORD, and just reward from the God of his salvation. This is a generation of those who seek Him, the descendants of Jacob

---

and consequently the other days do not have their own names, but only numbers. Our week is, in effect, all about getting to Shabbat. As such, we refer to them as "the first day of the week/Shabbat," "the second day of the week/Shabbat," etc. On each day we are thereby reminded that Shabbat rest and re-creation are just around the corner. Hang in there!

BIUR TEFILLA • ביאור תפילה

הַיּוֹם יוֹם רִאשׁוֹן בְּשַׁבָּת – *Today is the first day of the week.* Hashem is the Creator, not in the remote heavens but on earth. Especially when we might enter into the beginning of the week wanting to conquer the world, it behooves us to recall that the world is not of our making. And how does one acknowledge this? By being a person who has "clean hands and a pure heart." What a great challenge for the week ahead!

IYUN TEFILLA • עיון תפילה

לַיהוה הָאָרֶץ וּמְלוֹאָהּ – *The earth is the LORD's and all it contains.* The Gemara (*Berakhot* 35a) asks, "But is there not a contradiction to this from another verse which says (*Tehillim* 115:16) 'And Hashem gave the land to man.' Does the land belong to God or to man?" To which the Gemara answers: "The earth belongs to God. But when man makes a blessing on food before he eats it, then the earth belongs to man." Blessings are how we get permission for, and take ownership of, what does not belong to us.

שיר של יום

One of the following psalms is said on the appropriate day of the week as indicated. After the psalm, קדיש יתום *on page 241 is said.*

After שיר של יום*, on* ראש חודש*, add* בָּרְכִי נַפְשִׁי*, page 251 (in* ארץ ישראל*, some only say* בָּרְכִי נַפְשִׁי*). From the second day of* ראש חודש אלול *through* שמיני עצרת *(in* ארץ ישראל*, through* הושענא רבה*), add* לְדָוִד, יהוה אוֹרִי *on page 255. In a house of mourning the service concludes on page 257.*

Sunday הַיּוֹם יוֹם רִאשׁוֹן בְּשַׁבָּת,[ב] שֶׁבּוֹ הָיוּ הַלְוִיִּם אוֹמְרִים בְּבֵית הַמִּקְדָּשׁ:

תהלים כד לְדָוִד מִזְמוֹר, לַיהוה הָאָרֶץ וּמְלוֹאָהּ,[ע] תֵּבֵל וְיֹשְׁבֵי בָהּ: כִּי־הוּא עַל־
יַמִּים יְסָדָהּ, וְעַל־נְהָרוֹת יְכוֹנְנֶהָ: מִי־יַעֲלֶה בְהַר־יהוה, וּמִי־יָקוּם
בִּמְקוֹם קָדְשׁוֹ: נְקִי כַפַּיִם וּבַר־לֵבָב, אֲשֶׁר לֹא־נָשָׂא לַשָּׁוְא נַפְשִׁי,
וְלֹא נִשְׁבַּע לְמִרְמָה: יִשָּׂא בְרָכָה מֵאֵת יהוה, וּצְדָקָה מֵאֱלֹהֵי יִשְׁעוֹ:
זֶה דּוֹר דֹּרְשָׁו, מְבַקְשֵׁי פָנֶיךָ יַעֲקֹב סֶלָה: שְׂאוּ שְׁעָרִים רָאשֵׁיכֶם,

---

INTRODUCTION: שיר של יום – THE DAILY PSALM

In the times of the *Beit HaMikdash*, during the offering of the daily *Korban Tamid*, the *Levi'im* were charged with providing musical accompaniment, singing a different chapter of *Tehillim* each day (Mishna *Tamid* 7:3–4). Why these particular chapters were chosen is really not so clear. The Gemara (*Rosh HaShana* 31a) suggests that each daily chapter reflects a different theme of each corresponding day of creation. Later sources have suggested that there is a cumulative theme that connects them all, while still others have focused on the independent message of each. We have followed the latter by suggesting a lesson that one can take away as one greets the new day. Nevertheless, examine them carefully and create your own meaning.

What they all certainly have in common is the introduction, which calls upon us to identify the days not by their secular name (many of which are pagan in origin, e.g., Sunday is the day of the sun; Monday, the day of the moon...) but rather by their relationship to Shabbat. The Ramban (on *Shemot* 20:8) notes that this is in fulfillment of the Torah's commandment to "remember the Sabbath day" constantly, even throughout the week. If a person were to be lost in the desert and lose track of time, he is supposed to begin counting the days and observe the seventh as Shabbat, for all revolves around that day. Indeed, it has been suggested that the first three days of the week draw a certain holiness from the previous Shabbat, while the last three days are drawn to the holiness of the next (*Ḥayyei Adam* II:1).

Given how central a role Shabbat plays in our personal and religious lives, all of the other days of the week revolve around it,

who seek Your presence, Selah! Lift up your heads, O gates; be uplifted, eternal doors, so that the King of glory may enter. Who is the King of glory? It is the LORD, strong and mighty, the LORD mighty in battle. Lift up your heads, O gates; lift them up, eternal doors, that the King of glory may enter. ▸ Who is He, the King of glory? The LORD of hosts, He is the King of glory, Selah!

Mourner's Kaddish (page 240)

Monday: Today is the second day of the week,[B]
on which the Levites used to say this psalm in the Temple:

שִׁיר מִזְמוֹר A song. A psalm of the sons of Koraḥ. Great is the LORD and *Ps. 48*
greatly to be praised in the city of God, on His holy mountain – beautiful in its heights, joy of all the earth, Mount Zion on its northern side, city of the great King. In its citadels God is known as a stronghold. See how the kings joined forces, advancing together. They saw, they were astounded, they panicked, they fled. There fear seized them, like the pains of a woman giving birth, like ships of Tarshish wrecked by an eastern wind. What we had heard, now we have seen, in the city of the LORD of hosts, in the city of our God. May God preserve it for ever, Selah! In the midst of Your Temple, God, we meditate on Your love. As is Your name, God, so is Your praise: it reaches to the ends of the earth. Your right hand is filled with righteousness. Let Mount Zion rejoice, let the towns of Judah be glad, because of Your judgments. Walk around Zion and encircle it.[A] Count its towers, note its strong walls, view its citadels, so that you may tell a future generation ▸ that this is God, our God, for ever and ever. He will guide us for evermore.

Mourner's Kaddish (page 240)

A score of conquerors have held it as their choicest prize; and more than a dozen times has it been utterly destroyed. The Babylonians burnt it, and deported its population; the Romans slew a million of its inhabitants, razed it to the ground, passed the ploughshare over it, and strewed its furrows with salt; Hadrian banished its very name from the lips of men, changed it to Aelia Capitolina, and prohibited any Jew from entering its precincts on pain of death. Persians and Arabs, Barbarians and Crusaders and Turks took it and retook it, ravaged it and burnt it; and yet, marvelous to relate, it ever rises from its ashes to renewed life and glory. It is the Eternal City of the Eternal People. (Rabbi J.H. Hertz)

וְהִנָּשְׂאוּ פִּתְחֵי עוֹלָם, וְיָבוֹא מֶלֶךְ הַכָּבוֹד: מִי זֶה מֶלֶךְ הַכָּבוֹד, יהוה עִזּוּז וְגִבּוֹר, יהוה גִּבּוֹר מִלְחָמָה: שְׂאוּ שְׁעָרִים רָאשֵׁיכֶם, וּשְׂאוּ פִּתְחֵי עוֹלָם, וְיָבֹא מֶלֶךְ הַכָּבוֹד: › מִי הוּא זֶה מֶלֶךְ הַכָּבוֹד, יהוה צְבָאוֹת הוּא מֶלֶךְ הַכָּבוֹד סֶלָה:

קדיש יתום (*page 241*)

Monday הַיּוֹם יוֹם שֵׁנִי בְּשַׁבָּת,[ב] שֶׁבּוֹ הָיוּ הַלְוִיִּם אוֹמְרִים בְּבֵית הַמִּקְדָּשׁ:

שִׁיר מִזְמוֹר לִבְנֵי־קֹרַח: גָּדוֹל יהוה וּמְהֻלָּל מְאֹד, בְּעִיר אֱלֹהֵינוּ, הַר־ תהלים מח
קָדְשׁוֹ: יְפֵה נוֹף מְשׂוֹשׂ כָּל־הָאָרֶץ, הַר־צִיּוֹן יַרְכְּתֵי צָפוֹן, קִרְיַת מֶלֶךְ רָב: אֱלֹהִים בְּאַרְמְנוֹתֶיהָ נוֹדַע לְמִשְׂגָּב: כִּי־הִנֵּה הַמְּלָכִים נוֹעֲדוּ, עָבְרוּ יַחְדָּו: הֵמָּה רָאוּ כֵּן תָּמָהוּ, נִבְהֲלוּ נֶחְפָּזוּ: רְעָדָה אֲחָזָתַם שָׁם, חִיל כַּיּוֹלֵדָה: בְּרוּחַ קָדִים תְּשַׁבֵּר אֳנִיּוֹת תַּרְשִׁישׁ: כַּאֲשֶׁר שָׁמַעְנוּ כֵּן רָאִינוּ, בְּעִיר־יהוה צְבָאוֹת, בְּעִיר אֱלֹהֵינוּ, אֱלֹהִים יְכוֹנְנֶהָ עַד־עוֹלָם סֶלָה: דִּמִּינוּ אֱלֹהִים חַסְדֶּךָ, בְּקֶרֶב הֵיכָלֶךָ: כְּשִׁמְךָ אֱלֹהִים כֵּן תְּהִלָּתְךָ עַל־קַצְוֵי־אֶרֶץ, צֶדֶק מָלְאָה יְמִינֶךָ: יִשְׂמַח הַר־צִיּוֹן, תָּגֵלְנָה בְּנוֹת יְהוּדָה, לְמַעַן מִשְׁפָּטֶיךָ: סֹבּוּ צִיּוֹן וְהַקִּיפוּהָ,[א] סִפְרוּ מִגְדָּלֶיהָ: שִׁיתוּ לִבְּכֶם לְחֵילָה, פַּסְּגוּ אַרְמְנוֹתֶיהָ, לְמַעַן תְּסַפְּרוּ לְדוֹר אַחֲרוֹן: › כִּי זֶה אֱלֹהִים אֱלֹהֵינוּ עוֹלָם וָעֶד, הוּא יְנַהֲגֵנוּ עַל־מוּת:

קדיש יתום (*page 241*)

BIUR TEFILLA • ביאור תפילה

הַיּוֹם יוֹם שֵׁנִי בְּשַׁבָּת – *Today is the second day of the week.* If yesterday we declared Hashem as our Master, today we declare Israel and Jerusalem as our place.

ANI TEFILLA • אני תפילה

סֹבּוּ צִיּוֹן וְהַקִּיפוּהָ – *Walk around Zion and encircle it.*

Do I see Israel as a destination or as my destiny?

Tuesday: Today is the third day of the week,
on which the Levites used to say this psalm in the Temple:

מִזְמוֹר לְאָסָף A psalm of Asaph. God stands in the divine assembly. Among the *Ps. 82*
judges He delivers judgment. How long will you judge unjustly, showing favor to the wicked? Selah. Do justice to the weak and the orphaned. Vindicate the poor and destitute. Rescue the weak and needy. Save them from the hand of the wicked. They do not know nor do they understand. They walk about in darkness while all the earth's foundations shake. I once said, "You are like gods, all of you are sons of the Most High." But you shall die like mere men, you will fall like any prince. ▸ Arise, O LORD, judge the earth, for all the nations are Your possession.

Mourner's Kaddish (page 240)

Wednesday: Today is the fourth day of the week,
on which the Levites used to say this psalm in the Temple:

אֵל־נְקָמוֹת God of retribution, LORD, God of retribution, appear! Rise up, *Ps. 94*
Judge of the earth. Repay to the arrogant what they deserve. How long shall the wicked, LORD, how long shall the wicked triumph? They pour out insolent words. All the evildoers are full of boasting. They crush Your people, LORD, and oppress Your inheritance. They kill the widow and the stranger. They murder the orphaned. They say, "The LORD does not see. The God of Jacob pays no heed." Take heed, you most brutish people. You fools, when will you grow wise? Will He who implants the ear not hear? Will He who formed the eye not see? Will He who disciplines nations – He who teaches man knowledge – not punish? The LORD knows that the thoughts of man

---

IYUN TEFILLA • עיון תפילה

הַיּוֹם יוֹם רְבִיעִי בְּשַׁבָּת – *Today is the fourth day of the week.* For all of the justice that we try to pursue in this world, the reality is that evil still exists; in trying to become like gods, men can become beasts. And we may sometimes wonder why it is that the wicked seem to succeed and flourish as often as they do. All one can do is have faith that Hashem has a plan and rest assured that the evil and corrupt will be eradicated. For my part, I will continue to believe in and stand up for what is right, as I begin a day that may be marked by individuals or nations who seek my downfall. It is my faith that will carry me through. That may be why two verses from the next psalm in *Tehillim* were added to this one, for they indicate two related notions. The first is that no matter what the challenge, one must always be optimistic about the future; faith allows one to always see the bright side. Hold on to that! In addition, these two verses are also the first two verses of the *Kabbalat Shabbat* service on Friday night, as if to say: "Shabbat is coming! Hold on to that!"

Tuesday הַיּוֹם יוֹם שְׁלִישִׁי בְּשַׁבָּת, שֶׁבּוֹ הָיוּ הַלְוִיִּם אוֹמְרִים בְּבֵית הַמִּקְדָּשׁ:

תהלים פב מִזְמוֹר לְאָסָף, אֱלֹהִים נִצָּב בַּעֲדַת־אֵל, בְּקֶרֶב אֱלֹהִים יִשְׁפֹּט: עַד־מָתַי תִּשְׁפְּטוּ־עָוֶל, וּפְנֵי רְשָׁעִים תִּשְׂאוּ־סֶלָה: שִׁפְטוּ־דַל וְיָתוֹם, עָנִי וָרָשׁ הַצְדִּיקוּ: פַּלְּטוּ־דַל וְאֶבְיוֹן, מִיַּד רְשָׁעִים הַצִּילוּ: לֹא יָדְעוּ וְלֹא יָבִינוּ, בַּחֲשֵׁכָה יִתְהַלָּכוּ, יִמּוֹטוּ כָּל־מוֹסְדֵי אָרֶץ: אֲנִי־אָמַרְתִּי אֱלֹהִים אַתֶּם, וּבְנֵי עֶלְיוֹן כֻּלְּכֶם: אָכֵן כְּאָדָם תְּמוּתוּן, וּכְאַחַד הַשָּׂרִים תִּפֹּלוּ: › קוּמָה אֱלֹהִים שָׁפְטָה הָאָרֶץ, כִּי־אַתָּה תִנְחַל בְּכָל־הַגּוֹיִם:

קדיש יתום (*page 241*)

Wednesday הַיּוֹם יוֹם רְבִיעִי בְּשַׁבָּת, שֶׁבּוֹ הָיוּ הַלְוִיִּם אוֹמְרִים בְּבֵית הַמִּקְדָּשׁ:

תהלים צד אֵל־נְקָמוֹת יהוה, אֵל נְקָמוֹת הוֹפִיעַ: הִנָּשֵׂא שֹׁפֵט הָאָרֶץ, הָשֵׁב גְּמוּל עַל־גֵּאִים: עַד־מָתַי רְשָׁעִים, יהוה, עַד־מָתַי רְשָׁעִים יַעֲלֹזוּ: יַבִּיעוּ יְדַבְּרוּ עָתָק, יִתְאַמְּרוּ כָּל־פֹּעֲלֵי אָוֶן: עַמְּךָ יהוה יְדַכְּאוּ, וְנַחֲלָתְךָ יְעַנּוּ: אַלְמָנָה וְגֵר יַהֲרֹגוּ, וִיתוֹמִים יְרַצֵּחוּ: וַיֹּאמְרוּ לֹא יִרְאֶה־יָּהּ, וְלֹא־יָבִין אֱלֹהֵי יַעֲקֹב: בִּינוּ בֹּעֲרִים בָּעָם, וּכְסִילִים מָתַי תַּשְׂכִּילוּ: הֲנֹטַע אֹזֶן הֲלֹא יִשְׁמָע, אִם־יֹצֵר עַיִן הֲלֹא יַבִּיט: הֲיֹסֵר גּוֹיִם הֲלֹא יוֹכִיחַ, הַמְלַמֵּד אָדָם דָּעַת: יהוה יֹדֵעַ מַחְשְׁבוֹת אָדָם, כִּי־הֵמָּה הָבֶל: אַשְׁרֵי הַגֶּבֶר אֲשֶׁר־תְּיַסְּרֶנּוּ יָּהּ, וּמִתּוֹרָתְךָ תְלַמְּדֶנּוּ: לְהַשְׁקִיט לוֹ מִימֵי רָע, עַד יִכָּרֶה

IYUN TEFILLA • עיון תפילה

הַיּוֹם יוֹם שְׁלִישִׁי בְּשַׁבָּת – *Today is the third day of the week.* The place spoken of yesterday can only be realized when it is built upon principles of fairness and justice for all. Today we declare our understanding that a just society is one that must be founded upon religious principles, for as long as laws are dependent solely on people, they are subject to change according to human whim and self-interest. The laws of God, however, cannot ever be changed.

What can I do on this day of the week to be more conscious of the need to judge fairly?

בְּקֶרֶב אֱלֹהִים יִשְׁפֹּט – *Among the judges He delivers judgment.* A judge should always remember that when he sits in judgment of other people, he does not sit alone. God sits there with him, among the judges, listening and watching (*Midrash Shoḥer Tov*). Good advice for the rest of us as well. If I should judge someone today or be judgmental, I must remember Who is looking over my shoulder.

are a mere fleeting breath. Happy is the man whom You discipline, LORD, the one You instruct in Your Torah, giving him tranquility in days of trouble, until a pit is dug for the wicked. For the LORD will not forsake His people, nor abandon His heritage. Judgment shall again accord with justice, and all the upright in heart will follow it. Who will rise up for me against the wicked? Who will stand up for me against wrongdoers? Had the LORD not been my help, I would soon have dwelt in death's silence. When I thought my foot was slipping, Your loving-kindness, LORD, gave me support. When I was filled with anxiety, Your consolations soothed my soul. Can a corrupt throne be allied with You? Can injustice be framed into law? They join forces against the life of the righteous, and condemn the innocent to death. But the LORD is my stronghold, my God is the Rock of my refuge. He will bring back on them their wickedness, and destroy them for their evil deeds. The LORD our God will destroy them.

▸ Come, let us sing for joy to the LORD; let us shout aloud to the Rock of our salvation. Let us greet Him with thanksgiving, shout aloud to Him with songs of praise. For the LORD is the great God, the King great above all powers. *Ps. 95*

Mourner's Kaddish (page 240)

Thursday: Today is the fifth day of the week,[B]
on which the Levites used to say this psalm in the Temple:

לַמְנַצֵּחַ For the conductor of music. On the Gittit. By Asaph. Sing for joy to God, our strength. Shout aloud to the God of Jacob. Raise a song, beat the drum, play the sweet harp and lyre. Sound the shofar on the new moon, on our feast day when the moon is hidden. For it is a statute for Israel, an ordinance of the God of Jacob. He established it as a testimony for Joseph when He went forth against the land of Egypt, where I heard a language that I did not know. I relieved his shoulder of the burden. His hands were freed from the builder's basket. In distress you called and I rescued you. I answered you from the secret place of thunder; I tested you at the waters of Meribah, Selah! Hear, My people, and I will warn you. Israel, if you would only listen to Me! Let there be no strange god among you.[B] Do not bow down to an alien god. I am the LORD your God who brought you out of the land of Egypt. Open *Ps. 81*

---

our part of the covenant? The week is not over. There is still time.

לֹא־יִהְיֶה בְךָ אֵל זָר – *Let there be no strange god among you.* This phrase can also be read "Let there be no strange god *within* you. "What strange god exists in the human body? The answer – the evil inclination (*Shabbat* 105b).

Alternatively, the Kotzker Rebbe used to paraphrase the verse as "Let God not be a stranger in you."

לָרָשָׁע שָׁחַת: כִּי לֹא־יִטֹּשׁ יהוה עַמּוֹ, וְנַחֲלָתוֹ לֹא יַעֲזֹב: כִּי־עַד־צֶדֶק יָשׁוּב מִשְׁפָּט, וְאַחֲרָיו כָּל־יִשְׁרֵי־לֵב: מִי־יָקוּם לִי עִם־מְרֵעִים, מִי־יִתְיַצֵּב לִי עִם־פֹּעֲלֵי אָוֶן: לוּלֵי יהוה עֶזְרָתָה לִּי, כִּמְעַט שָׁכְנָה דוּמָה נַפְשִׁי: אִם־אָמַרְתִּי מָטָה רַגְלִי, חַסְדְּךָ יהוה יִסְעָדֵנִי: בְּרֹב שַׂרְעַפַּי בְּקִרְבִּי, תַּנְחוּמֶיךָ יְשַׁעַשְׁעוּ נַפְשִׁי: הַיְחָבְרְךָ כִּסֵּא הַוּוֹת, יֹצֵר עָמָל עֲלֵי־חֹק: יָגוֹדּוּ עַל־נֶפֶשׁ צַדִּיק, וְדָם נָקִי יַרְשִׁיעוּ: וַיְהִי יהוה לִי לְמִשְׂגָּב, וֵאלֹהַי לְצוּר מַחְסִי: וַיָּשֶׁב עֲלֵיהֶם אֶת־אוֹנָם, וּבְרָעָתָם יַצְמִיתֵם, יַצְמִיתֵם יהוה אֱלֹהֵינוּ:

תהלים צה
› לְכוּ נְרַנְּנָה לַיהוה, נָרִיעָה לְצוּר יִשְׁעֵנוּ: נְקַדְּמָה פָנָיו בְּתוֹדָה, בִּזְמִרוֹת נָרִיעַ לוֹ: כִּי אֵל גָּדוֹל יהוה, וּמֶלֶךְ גָּדוֹל עַל־כָּל־אֱלֹהִים:

קדיש יתום (*page 241*)

Thursday הַיּוֹם יוֹם חֲמִישִׁי בְּשַׁבָּת, שֶׁבּוֹ הָיוּ הַלְוִיִּם אוֹמְרִים בְּבֵית הַמִּקְדָּשׁ:

תהלים פא
לַמְנַצֵּחַ עַל־הַגִּתִּית לְאָסָף: הַרְנִינוּ לֵאלֹהִים עוּזֵּנוּ, הָרִיעוּ לֵאלֹהֵי יַעֲקֹב: שְׂאוּ־זִמְרָה וּתְנוּ־תֹף, כִּנּוֹר נָעִים עִם־נָבֶל: תִּקְעוּ בַחֹדֶשׁ שׁוֹפָר, בַּכֵּסֶה לְיוֹם חַגֵּנוּ: כִּי חֹק לְיִשְׂרָאֵל הוּא, מִשְׁפָּט לֵאלֹהֵי יַעֲקֹב: עֵדוּת בִּיהוֹסֵף שָׂמוֹ, בְּצֵאתוֹ עַל־אֶרֶץ מִצְרָיִם, שְׂפַת לֹא־יָדַעְתִּי אֶשְׁמָע: הֲסִירוֹתִי מִסֵּבֶל שִׁכְמוֹ, כַּפָּיו מִדּוּד תַּעֲבֹרְנָה: בַּצָּרָה קָרָאתָ וָאֲחַלְּצֶךָּ, אֶעֶנְךָ בְּסֵתֶר רַעַם, אֶבְחָנְךָ עַל־מֵי מְרִיבָה סֶלָה: שְׁמַע עַמִּי וְאָעִידָה בָּךְ, יִשְׂרָאֵל אִם־תִּשְׁמַע־לִי: לֹא־יִהְיֶה בְךָ אֵל זָר, וְלֹא תִשְׁתַּחֲוֶה לְאֵל נֵכָר: אָנֹכִי יהוה אֱלֹהֶיךָ, הַמַּעַלְךָ מֵאֶרֶץ מִצְרָיִם, הַרְחֶב־פִּיךָ

BIUR TEFILLA • ביאור תפילה

הַיּוֹם יוֹם חֲמִישִׁי בְּשַׁבָּת – *Today is the fifth day of the week.* As the week begins to draw to a close, and we move closer to Shabbat, there may be reason to celebrate. The psalm begins with a joyous call to sing to God, and to prepare for a revelation comparable to Rosh HaShana, when He answered the prayers of the matriarchs and others (*Rosh HaShana* 8a; 11a). At the same time, in the second section, we are reminded not to rest upon our laurels. Are we ready to hear what He wants from us? Have we been living up to

your mouth wide and I will fill it. But My people would not listen to Me. Israel would have none of Me. So I left them to their stubborn hearts, letting them follow their own devices. If only My people would listen to Me, if Israel would walk in My ways, I would soon subdue their enemies, and turn My hand against their foes. Those who hate the LORD would cower before Him and their doom would last for ever. ▸ He would feed Israel with the finest wheat – with honey from the rock I would satisfy you.

Mourner's Kaddish (page 240)

Friday: Today is the sixth day of the week,[I]
on which the Levites used to say this psalm in the Temple:

יהוה מָלָךְ The LORD reigns. He is robed in majesty. The LORD is robed, girded with strength. The world is firmly established; it cannot be moved. Your throne stands firm as of old; You are eternal. Rivers lift up, LORD, rivers lift up their voice, rivers lift up their crashing waves. Mightier than the noise of many waters, than the mighty waves of the sea is the LORD on high. ▸ Your testimonies are very sure;[B] holiness adorns Your House, LORD, for evermore. *Ps. 93*

Mourner's Kaddish (page 240)

On Rosh Hodesh, the following psalm is said:

בָּרְכִי נַפְשִׁי Bless the LORD, my soul.[B] LORD, my God, You are very great, clothed in majesty and splendor, wrapped in a robe of light. You have spread out the heavens like a tent. He has laid the beams of His lofts in the waters. He makes the clouds His chariot, riding on the wings of the wind. He makes *Ps. 104*

ANI TEFILLA • אני תפילה

What can I do to prepare for Shabbat today, to make it more meaningful? What can I do beforehand to enhance the spirit of Shabbat tonight?

BIUR TEFILLA • ביאור תפילה

בָּרְכִי נַפְשִׁי – *Bless the LORD, my soul.* This psalm is a kind of *shir shel yom* for Rosh Hodesh, ostensibly because of its reference in verse 19 to "He made the moon to mark the seasons" (*Tur* 423). The chapter is an exquisite celebration of the beauty of nature and an acknowledgment of its Source. Yet if He is present in nature, He certainly abides in man, which in turn implies that no sinner is beyond redemption (Rabbi Soloveitchik). As the chapter concludes, and as Beruria, the wife of Rabbi Meir explained, it does not say "let sinners vanish from the earth" but, rather, "let sins vanish from the earth." Just as the moon renews itself each month, so, too, can we.

וַאֲמַלְאֵהוּ: וְלֹא־שָׁמַע עַמִּי לְקוֹלִי, וְיִשְׂרָאֵל לֹא־אָבָה לִי: וָאֲשַׁלְּחֵהוּ בִּשְׁרִירוּת לִבָּם, יֵלְכוּ בְּמוֹעֲצוֹתֵיהֶם: לוּ עַמִּי שֹׁמֵעַ לִי, יִשְׂרָאֵל בִּדְרָכַי יְהַלֵּכוּ: כִּמְעַט אוֹיְבֵיהֶם אַכְנִיעַ, וְעַל־צָרֵיהֶם אָשִׁיב יָדִי: מְשַׂנְאֵי יהוה יְכַחֲשׁוּ־לוֹ, וִיהִי עִתָּם לְעוֹלָם: ◂ וַיַּאֲכִילֵהוּ מֵחֵלֶב חִטָּה, וּמִצּוּר, דְּבַשׁ אַשְׂבִּיעֶךָ:

קדיש יתום (page 241)

Friday הַיּוֹם יוֹם שִׁשִּׁי בְּשַׁבָּת, שֶׁבּוֹ הָיוּ הַלְוִיִּם אוֹמְרִים בְּבֵית הַמִּקְדָּשׁ

תהלים צג יהוה מָלָךְ, גֵּאוּת לָבֵשׁ, לָבֵשׁ יהוה עֹז הִתְאַזָּר, אַף־תִּכּוֹן תֵּבֵל בַּל־תִּמּוֹט: נָכוֹן כִּסְאֲךָ מֵאָז, מֵעוֹלָם אָתָּה: נָשְׂאוּ נְהָרוֹת יהוה, נָשְׂאוּ נְהָרוֹת קוֹלָם, יִשְׂאוּ נְהָרוֹת דָּכְיָם: מִקֹּלוֹת מַיִם רַבִּים, אַדִּירִים מִשְׁבְּרֵי־יָם, אַדִּיר בַּמָּרוֹם יהוה: ◂ עֵדֹתֶיךָ נֶאֶמְנוּ מְאֹד, לְבֵיתְךָ נַאֲוָה־קֹדֶשׁ, יהוה לְאֹרֶךְ יָמִים:

קדיש יתום (page 241)

On ראש חודש*, the following psalm is said:*

תהלים קד בָּרְכִי נַפְשִׁי אֶת־יהוה, יהוה אֱלֹהַי גָּדַלְתָּ מְּאֹד, הוֹד וְהָדָר לָבָשְׁתָּ: עֹטֶה־אוֹר כַּשַּׂלְמָה, נוֹטֶה שָׁמַיִם כַּיְרִיעָה: הַמְקָרֶה בַמַּיִם עֲלִיּוֹתָיו, הַשָּׂם־עָבִים רְכוּבוֹ, הַמְהַלֵּךְ עַל־כַּנְפֵי־רוּחַ: עֹשֶׂה מַלְאָכָיו רוּחוֹת,

---

IYUN TEFILLA • עיון תפילה

הַיּוֹם יוֹם שִׁשִּׁי בְּשַׁבָּת – *Today is the sixth day of the week.* Today is the remaining day of Creation before Shabbat. Interestingly, although it is the day when, according to tradition, man himself was created, nowhere in this psalm does man appear. Rather, man takes his position as a part of creation to acknowledge the Creator. Shabbat is coming. We will soon be enveloped by that island in time. To appreciate it fully we cannot simply fall into it. We transition into its holiness even now, while the last day of the week is just beginning. The more we prepare, the more we will appreciate her presence.

BIUR TEFILLA • ביאור תפילה

עֵדֹתֶיךָ נֶאֶמְנוּ מְאֹד – *Your testimonies are very sure.* What is this a reference to? The predictions of Your prophets? Your commandments which testify to Your presence in history? The crashing waves of the oceans that testify to Your very existence?

the winds His messengers, flames of fire His ministers. He has fixed the earth on its foundations so that it will never be shaken. You covered it with the deep like a cloak; the waters stood above the mountains. At Your rebuke they fled; at the sound of Your thunder they rushed away, flowing over the hills, pouring down into the valleys to the place You appointed for them. You fixed a boundary they were not to pass, so that they would never cover the earth again. He makes springs flow in the valleys; they make their way between the hills, giving drink to all the beasts of the field; the wild donkeys quench their thirst. The birds of the sky dwell beside them, singing among the foliage. He waters the mountains from His lofts: the earth is sated with the fruit of Your work. He makes grass grow for the cattle, and plants for the use of man, that he may produce bread from the earth, wine to cheer the heart of man, oil to make the face shine, and bread to sustain man's heart. The trees of the LORD drink their fill, the cedars of Lebanon which He planted. There, birds build their nests; the stork makes its home in the cypresses. High hills are for the wild goats; crags are shelter for the badgers. He made the moon to mark the seasons, and makes the sun know when to set. You bring darkness and it is night; then all the beasts of the forests stir. The young lions roar for prey, seeking their food from God. When the sun rises, they slink away and seek rest in their lairs. Man goes out to his work and his labor until evening. How numerous are Your works, LORD; You made them all in wisdom; the earth is full of Your creations. There is the vast, immeasurable sea with its countless swarming creatures, living things great and small. There ships sail. There is Leviathan You formed to sport there. All of them look to You in hope, to give them their food when it is due. What You give them, they gather up. When You open Your hand, they are sated with good. When You hide Your face, they are dismayed. When You take away their breath, they die and return to dust. When You send back Your breath, they are created, giving new life to the earth. May the glory of the LORD be for ever; may the LORD rejoice in His works. When He looks at the earth, it trembles. When He touches the mountains, they pour forth smoke. I will sing to the LORD as long as I live; I will sing psalms to my God all my life. ▸ May my meditation be pleasing to Him; I shall rejoice in the LORD. May sinners vanish from the earth, and the wicked be no more. Bless the LORD, my soul. Halleluya!

Mourner's Kaddish (page 240)

---

of their own special blessings, rather than being subsumed under a broader more general blessing. Each has its own unique qualities.

מְשָׁרְתָיו אֵשׁ לֹהֵט: יָסַד־אֶרֶץ עַל־מְכוֹנֶיהָ, בַּל־תִּמּוֹט עוֹלָם וָעֶד: תְּהוֹם
כַּלְּבוּשׁ כִּסִּיתוֹ, עַל־הָרִים יַעַמְדוּ־מָיִם: מִן־גַּעֲרָתְךָ יְנוּסוּן, מִן־קוֹל רַעַמְךָ
יֵחָפֵזוּן: יַעֲלוּ הָרִים, יֵרְדוּ בְקָעוֹת, אֶל־מְקוֹם זֶה יָסַדְתָּ לָהֶם: גְּבוּל־שַׂמְתָּ
בַּל־יַעֲבֹרוּן, בַּל־יְשׁוּבוּן לְכַסּוֹת הָאָרֶץ: הַמְשַׁלֵּחַ מַעְיָנִים בַּנְּחָלִים, בֵּין
הָרִים יְהַלֵּכוּן: יַשְׁקוּ כָּל־חַיְתוֹ שָׂדָי, יִשְׁבְּרוּ פְרָאִים צְמָאָם: עֲלֵיהֶם עוֹף־
הַשָּׁמַיִם יִשְׁכּוֹן, מִבֵּין עֳפָאיִם יִתְּנוּ־קוֹל: מַשְׁקֶה הָרִים מֵעֲלִיּוֹתָיו,
מִפְּרִי מַעֲשֶׂיךָ תִּשְׂבַּע הָאָרֶץ: מַצְמִיחַ חָצִיר לַבְּהֵמָה,[ע] וְעֵשֶׂב לַעֲבֹדַת
הָאָדָם, לְהוֹצִיא לֶחֶם מִן־הָאָרֶץ: וְיַיִן יְשַׂמַּח לְבַב־אֱנוֹשׁ, לְהַצְהִיל פָּנִים
מִשָּׁמֶן, וְלֶחֶם לְבַב־אֱנוֹשׁ יִסְעָד: יִשְׂבְּעוּ עֲצֵי יהוה, אַרְזֵי לְבָנוֹן אֲשֶׁר
נָטָע: אֲשֶׁר־שָׁם צִפֳּרִים יְקַנֵּנוּ, חֲסִידָה בְּרוֹשִׁים בֵּיתָהּ: הָרִים הַגְּבֹהִים
לַיְּעֵלִים, סְלָעִים מַחְסֶה לַשְׁפַנִּים: עָשָׂה יָרֵחַ לְמוֹעֲדִים, שֶׁמֶשׁ יָדַע
מְבוֹאוֹ: תָּשֶׁת־חֹשֶׁךְ וִיהִי לָיְלָה, בּוֹ־תִרְמֹשׂ כָּל־חַיְתוֹ־יָעַר: הַכְּפִירִים
שֹׁאֲגִים לַטָּרֶף, וּלְבַקֵּשׁ מֵאֵל אָכְלָם: תִּזְרַח הַשֶּׁמֶשׁ יֵאָסֵפוּן, וְאֶל־
מְעוֹנֹתָם יִרְבָּצוּן: יֵצֵא אָדָם לְפָעֳלוֹ, וְלַעֲבֹדָתוֹ עֲדֵי־עָרֶב: מָה־רַבּוּ
מַעֲשֶׂיךָ יהוה, כֻּלָּם בְּחָכְמָה עָשִׂיתָ, מָלְאָה הָאָרֶץ קִנְיָנֶךָ: זֶה הַיָּם גָּדוֹל
וּרְחַב יָדָיִם, שָׁם־רֶמֶשׂ וְאֵין מִסְפָּר, חַיּוֹת קְטַנּוֹת עִם־גְּדֹלוֹת: שָׁם אֳנִיּוֹת
יְהַלֵּכוּן, לִוְיָתָן זֶה־יָצַרְתָּ לְשַׂחֶק־בּוֹ: כֻּלָּם אֵלֶיךָ יְשַׂבֵּרוּן, לָתֵת אָכְלָם
בְּעִתּוֹ: תִּתֵּן לָהֶם יִלְקֹטוּן, תִּפְתַּח יָדְךָ יִשְׂבְּעוּן טוֹב: תַּסְתִּיר פָּנֶיךָ
יִבָּהֵלוּן, תֹּסֵף רוּחָם יִגְוָעוּן, וְאֶל־עֲפָרָם יְשׁוּבוּן: תְּשַׁלַּח רוּחֲךָ יִבָּרֵאוּן,
וּתְחַדֵּשׁ פְּנֵי אֲדָמָה: יְהִי כְבוֹד יהוה לְעוֹלָם, יִשְׂמַח יהוה בְּמַעֲשָׂיו:
הַמַּבִּיט לָאָרֶץ וַתִּרְעָד, יִגַּע בֶּהָרִים וְיֶעֱשָׁנוּ: אָשִׁירָה לַיהוה בְּחַיָּי,
אֲזַמְּרָה לֵאלֹהַי בְּעוֹדִי: ‹ יֶעֱרַב עָלָיו שִׂיחִי, אָנֹכִי אֶשְׂמַח בַּיהוה: יִתַּמּוּ
חַטָּאִים מִן־הָאָרֶץ, וּרְשָׁעִים עוֹד אֵינָם, בָּרְכִי נַפְשִׁי אֶת־יהוה, הַלְלוּיָהּ:

קדיש יתום (*page 241*)

IYUN TEFILLA · עיון תפילה

מַצְמִיחַ חָצִיר לַבְּהֵמָה – *He makes grass grow for the cattle.* The Gemara (*Berakhot* 35b) uses these two verses as prooftexts for the fact that wine and bread are each deserving

During the month of Elul (except Erev Rosh HaShana), the shofar is sounded (some sound the shofar after the psalm below). From the second day of Rosh Hodesh Elul through Shemini Atzeret (in Israel through Hoshana Raba), the following psalm is said:

לְדָוִד By David. The LORD is my light[B] and my salvation – whom then shall I fear? The LORD is the stronghold of my life – of whom shall I be afraid? When evil men close in on me to devour my flesh, it is they, my enemies and foes, who stumble and fall. Should an army besiege me, my heart would not fear. Should war break out against me, still I would be confident. One thing I ask of the LORD, only this do I seek: to live in the House of the LORD all the days of my life, to gaze on the beauty of the LORD and worship in His Temple.[I] For He will keep me safe in His pavilion on the day of trouble. He will hide me under the cover of His tent. He will set me high upon a rock. Now my head is high above my enemies who surround me. I will sacrifice in His tent with shouts of joy. I will sing and chant praises to the LORD. LORD, hear my voice when I call. Be gracious to me and answer me. On Your behalf my heart says, "Seek My face." Your face, LORD, will I seek. Do not hide Your face from me. Do not turn Your servant away in anger. You have been my help. Do not reject or forsake me, God, my Savior. Were my father and my mother to forsake me,[I] the LORD would take me in. Teach me Your way, LORD, and lead me on a level path, because of my oppressors. Do not abandon me to the will of my foes, for false witnesses have risen against me, breathing violence. ▸ Were it not for my faith that I shall see the LORD's goodness in the land of the living. Hope in the LORD. Be strong and of good courage, and hope in the LORD! *Ps. 27*

Mourner's Kaddish (page 240)

---

suggested that when we are visitors we notice everything for the first time, and we fall in love with the experience. As time goes on, however, and things become routine, the specialness is lost to us and we take things for granted. So it can sometimes be with our passion for Jewish life. When we were young, everything seemed exciting, but as time wore on our enthusiasm waned. And so we pray to live in the house of Hashem as permanent residents, but that our mindset and disposition always be that of the enthusiastic guest, experiencing all of Jewish life as if for the first time. What can I do to regain some of the passion I once had?

כִּי־אָבִי וְאִמִּי עֲזָבוּנִי – *Were my father and my mother to forsake me.* There are times when one can feel that, despite the presence of parents, friends or spouse, one is still very much alone. Faith enables one to overcome that loneliness, for Hashem is always there and knows you better than you know yourself.

During the month of אלול *(except* ערב ראש השנה*), the* שופר *is sounded (some sound the* שופר *after the psalm below). From the second day of* ראש חודש אלול *through* שמיני עצרת *(in* ארץ ישראל *through* הושענא רבה*), the following psalm is said:*

תהלים כז

לְדָוִד, יהוה אוֹרִי וְיִשְׁעִי, מִמִּי אִירָא, יהוה מָעוֹז־חַיַּי, מִמִּי אֶפְחָד:
בִּקְרֹב עָלַי מְרֵעִים לֶאֱכֹל אֶת־בְּשָׂרִי, צָרַי וְאֹיְבַי לִי, הֵמָּה כָשְׁלוּ וְנָפָלוּ:
אִם־תַּחֲנֶה עָלַי מַחֲנֶה, לֹא־יִירָא לִבִּי, אִם־תָּקוּם עָלַי מִלְחָמָה, בְּזֹאת
אֲנִי בוֹטֵחַ: אַחַת שָׁאַלְתִּי מֵאֵת־יהוה, אוֹתָהּ אֲבַקֵּשׁ, שִׁבְתִּי בְּבֵית־יהוה
כָּל־יְמֵי חַיַּי, לַחֲזוֹת בְּנֹעַם־יהוה, וּלְבַקֵּר בְּהֵיכָלוֹ: כִּי יִצְפְּנֵנִי בְּסֻכֹּה
בְּיוֹם רָעָה, יַסְתִּרֵנִי בְּסֵתֶר אָהֳלוֹ, בְּצוּר יְרוֹמְמֵנִי: וְעַתָּה יָרוּם רֹאשִׁי
עַל אֹיְבַי סְבִיבוֹתַי, וְאֶזְבְּחָה בְאָהֳלוֹ זִבְחֵי תְרוּעָה, אָשִׁירָה וַאֲזַמְּרָה
לַיהוה: שְׁמַע־יהוה קוֹלִי אֶקְרָא, וְחָנֵּנִי וַעֲנֵנִי: לְךָ אָמַר לִבִּי בַּקְּשׁוּ פָנָי,
אֶת־פָּנֶיךָ יהוה אֲבַקֵּשׁ: אַל־תַּסְתֵּר פָּנֶיךָ מִמֶּנִּי, אַל תַּט־בְּאַף עַבְדֶּךָ,
עֶזְרָתִי הָיִיתָ, אַל־תִּטְּשֵׁנִי וְאַל־תַּעַזְבֵנִי, אֱלֹהֵי יִשְׁעִי: כִּי־אָבִי וְאִמִּי
עֲזָבוּנִי, וַיהוה יַאַסְפֵנִי: הוֹרֵנִי יהוה דַּרְכֶּךָ, וּנְחֵנִי בְּאֹרַח מִישׁוֹר, לְמַעַן
שׁוֹרְרָי: אַל־תִּתְּנֵנִי בְּנֶפֶשׁ צָרָי, כִּי קָמוּ־בִי עֵדֵי־שֶׁקֶר, וִיפֵחַ חָמָס: לוּלֵא
הֶאֱמַנְתִּי לִרְאוֹת בְּטוּב־יהוה בְּאֶרֶץ חַיִּים: קַוֵּה אֶל־יהוה, חֲזַק וְיַאֲמֵץ
לִבֶּךָ, וְקַוֵּה אֶל־יהוה:

קדיש יתום (page 241)

BIUR TEFILLA · ביאור תפילה

לְדָוִד יהוה אוֹרִי – By David. The Lord is my light. Included in the siddur only a few hundred years ago, this *tefilla* is added as a kind of daily *shir shel yom* from Rosh Ḥodesh Elul until Shemini Atzeret. The psalm has numerous references that are appropriate during this time of year. Find the ones that speak to you the most as you prepare for these Days of Awe.

IYUN TEFILLA · עיון תפילה

וּלְבַקֵּר בְּהֵיכָלוֹ – *And worship in His Temple.* The word *levaker* could be interpreted to mean "to visit," in which case there would be a contradiction: the one thing I ask is to *live* in Your house, yet I also want to visit it. What's the point? Rabbi Soloveitchik once

After the regular service, the following psalm is read in a house of mourning during the shiva week. On those days on which Taḥanun is not said, Psalm 16 (below) is substituted.

לַמְנַצֵּחַ For the conductor of music. Of the sons of Koraḥ. A sacred song. Hear this, all you peoples. Listen, all inhabitants of the world, low and high, rich and poor alike. My mouth will speak words of wisdom; the utterance of my heart will give understanding. I listen with care to a parable; I expound my mystery to the music of the harp. Why should I fear when evil days come, when the wickedness of my foes surrounds me, trusting in their wealth, boasting of their great riches? No man can redeem his brother or pay God the price of his release, for the ransom of a life is costly; no payment is ever enough that would let him live for ever, never seeing the grave. For all can see that wise men die, that the foolish and senseless all perish and leave their wealth to others. They think their houses will remain for ever, their dwellings for all generations; they give their names to their estates. But man, despite his splendor, does not endure; he is like the beasts that perish. Such is the fate of the foolish and their followers who approve their words, Selah. Like sheep they are destined for the grave: death will be their shepherd. The upright will rule over them in the morning. Their forms will decay in the grave, far from their mansions. But God will redeem my life from the grave; He will surely take me to Himself, Selah. Do not be overawed when a man grows rich, when the glory of his house increases, for he will take nothing with him when he dies; his wealth will not descend with him. Though while he lived he counted himself blessed – men always praise you when you prosper – he will join the generation of his ancestors who will never again see the light. A man who, despite his splendor, lacks understanding, is like the beasts that perish. *Ps. 49*

Mourner's Kaddish (page 240)

On those days on which Taḥanun is not said, substitute:

מִכְתָּם לְדָוִד A musical composition of David. Protect me, God, for in You I have found refuge. I have said to the LORD: You are my LORD: from You alone comes the good I enjoy. All my delight is in the holy ones, the mighty in the land. Those who run after other gods multiply their sorrows. I shall never offer them libations of blood, nor will their names pass my lips. The LORD is my allotted portion and my cup: You direct my fate. The lines have fallen for me in pleasant places; I am well content with my inheritance. I will bless the LORD who has guided me; at night my innermost being admonishes me. I have set the LORD before me at all times. He is at my right hand: I shall not be shaken. Therefore my heart is glad, my spirit rejoices, and my body rests secure. For You will not abandon me to the grave, nor let Your faithful one see the pit. You will teach me the path of life. In Your presence is fullness of joy; at Your right hand, bliss for evermore. *Ps. 16*

Mourner's Kaddish (page 240)

After the regular service, the following psalm is read in a house of mourning during the שבעה *week. On those days on which* תחנון *is not said,* תהלים טז *(below) is substituted.*

תהלים מט לַמְנַצֵּחַ לִבְנֵי־קֹרַח מִזְמוֹר: שִׁמְעוּ־זֹאת כׇּל־הָעַמִּים, הַאֲזִינוּ כׇּל־יֹשְׁבֵי
חָלֶד: גַּם־בְּנֵי אָדָם, גַּם־בְּנֵי־אִישׁ, יַחַד עָשִׁיר וְאֶבְיוֹן: פִּי יְדַבֵּר חׇכְמוֹת,
וְהָגוּת לִבִּי תְבוּנוֹת: אַטֶּה לְמָשָׁל אׇזְנִי, אֶפְתַּח בְּכִנּוֹר חִידָתִי: לָמָּה
אִירָא בִּימֵי רָע, עֲוֺן עֲקֵבַי יְסֻבֵּנִי: הַבֹּטְחִים עַל־חֵילָם, וּבְרֹב עׇשְׁרָם
יִתְהַלָּלוּ: אָח לֹא־פָדֹה יִפְדֶּה אִישׁ, לֹא־יִתֵּן לֵאלֹהִים כׇּפְרוֹ: וְיֵקַר פִּדְיוֹן
נַפְשָׁם, וְחָדַל לְעוֹלָם: וִיחִי־עוֹד לָנֶצַח, לֹא יִרְאֶה הַשָּׁחַת: כִּי יִרְאֶה
חֲכָמִים יָמוּתוּ, יַחַד כְּסִיל וָבַעַר יֹאבֵדוּ, וְעָזְבוּ לַאֲחֵרִים חֵילָם: קִרְבָּם
בָּתֵּימוֹ לְעוֹלָם, מִשְׁכְּנֹתָם לְדֹר וָדֹר, קָרְאוּ בִשְׁמוֹתָם עֲלֵי אֲדָמוֹת: וְאָדָם
בִּיקָר בַּל־יָלִין, נִמְשַׁל כַּבְּהֵמוֹת נִדְמוּ: זֶה דַרְכָּם, כֵּסֶל לָמוֹ, וְאַחֲרֵיהֶם
בְּפִיהֶם יִרְצוּ סֶלָה: כַּצֹּאן לִשְׁאוֹל שַׁתּוּ, מָוֶת יִרְעֵם, וַיִּרְדּוּ בָם יְשָׁרִים
לַבֹּקֶר, וְצוּרָם לְבַלּוֹת שְׁאוֹל מִזְּבֻל לוֹ: אַךְ־אֱלֹהִים יִפְדֶּה נַפְשִׁי מִיַּד
שְׁאוֹל, כִּי יִקָּחֵנִי סֶלָה: אַל־תִּירָא כִּי־יַעֲשִׁר אִישׁ, כִּי־יִרְבֶּה כְּבוֹד בֵּיתוֹ:
כִּי לֹא בְמוֹתוֹ יִקַּח הַכֹּל, לֹא־יֵרֵד אַחֲרָיו כְּבוֹדוֹ: כִּי־נַפְשׁוֹ בְּחַיָּיו יְבָרֵךְ,
וְיוֹדֻךָ כִּי־תֵיטִיב לָךְ: תָּבוֹא עַד־דּוֹר אֲבוֹתָיו, עַד־נֵצַח לֹא יִרְאוּ־אוֹר:
אָדָם בִּיקָר וְלֹא יָבִין, נִמְשַׁל כַּבְּהֵמוֹת נִדְמוּ:

קדיש יתום (*page 241*)

On those days on which תחנון *is not said, substitute:*

תהלים טז מִכְתָּם לְדָוִד, שָׁמְרֵנִי אֵל כִּי־חָסִיתִי בָךְ: אָמַרְתְּ לַיהוה, אֲדֹנָי אָתָּה,
טוֹבָתִי בַּל־עָלֶיךָ: לִקְדוֹשִׁים אֲשֶׁר־בָּאָרֶץ הֵמָּה, וְאַדִּירֵי כׇּל־חֶפְצִי־
בָם: יִרְבּוּ עַצְּבוֹתָם אַחֵר מָהָרוּ, בַּל־אַסִּיךְ נִסְכֵּיהֶם מִדָּם, וּבַל־אֶשָּׂא
אֶת־שְׁמוֹתָם עַל־שְׂפָתָי: יהוה, מְנָת־חֶלְקִי וְכוֹסִי, אַתָּה תּוֹמִיךְ גּוֹרָלִי:
חֲבָלִים נָפְלוּ־לִי בַּנְּעִמִים, אַף־נַחֲלָת שָׁפְרָה עָלָי: אֲבָרֵךְ אֶת־יהוה
אֲשֶׁר יְעָצָנִי, אַף־לֵילוֹת יִסְּרוּנִי כִלְיוֹתָי: שִׁוִּיתִי יהוה לְנֶגְדִּי תָמִיד, כִּי
מִימִינִי בַּל־אֶמּוֹט: לָכֵן שָׂמַח לִבִּי וַיָּגֶל כְּבוֹדִי, אַף־בְּשָׂרִי יִשְׁכֹּן לָבֶטַח:
כִּי לֹא־תַעֲזֹב נַפְשִׁי לִשְׁאוֹל, לֹא־תִתֵּן חֲסִידְךָ לִרְאוֹת שָׁחַת: תּוֹדִיעֵנִי
אֹרַח חַיִּים, שֹׂבַע שְׂמָחוֹת אֶת־פָּנֶיךָ, נְעִמוֹת בִּימִינְךָ נֶצַח:

קדיש יתום (*page 241*)

Minḥa for Weekdays

אַשְׁרֵי Happy[B] are those who dwell in Your House; Ps. 84
they shall continue to praise You, Selah!
Happy are the people for whom this is so; Ps. 144
happy are the people whose God is the LORD.

A song of praise by David. Ps. 145
א I will exalt You,[I] my God, the King,
and bless Your name for ever and all time.
ב Every day I will bless You,
and praise Your name for ever and all time.
ג Great is the LORD and greatly to be praised;
His greatness is unfathomable.

BIUR TEFILLA • ביאור תפילה

אַשְׁרֵי – *Happy.* In some ways, *Ashrei* here serves the same function as all of *Pesukei DeZimra* did in *Shaḥarit.* It is a prelude to *Tefilla* (the *Shemoneh Esreh*), a way for us to get into the right mindset before our afternoon rendezvous with *HaKadosh Barukh Hu.*

What is that mindset? The Gemara (*Berakhot* 31a) explains that one should not pray out of a sense of frivolity, or sadness, or while carrying on trivial conversation, but rather with a sense of joy. Rashi explains that reminding us of the joy in our lives is exactly the purpose of *Ashrei* – "Hashem protects those who love Him," "Hashem will fulfill the desires of those who are in awe of Him." We are reminded that we are not alone, that we have much to be thankful for. Once we acknowledge that, we are ready to say the *Shemoneh Esreh.*

What do I have to be thankful for this afternoon? Let *Ashrei* point the way.

IYUN TEFILLA • עיון תפילה

אֲרוֹמִמְךָ – *I will exalt You.* One of the reasons that the Rabbis decreed that this psalm should be said three times a day was because it is written as an acrostic, wherein each line begins with another letter of the *Alef-Beit.* It is as if one is saying, "Any praise I give You is incomplete. Therefore let each letter of the alphabet represent all of the praises that begin with that letter, of which I will offer just one line as an example." In a certain sense, then, the alphabetic listing of words is designed to convey the impression that all words fall short. It's not only about the meaning of the words but the feeling of the *Alef-Beit.*

מנחה לחול

אַשְׁרֵי[ב] יוֹשְׁבֵי בֵיתֶךָ, עוֹד יְהַלְלוּךָ סֶּלָה: תהלים פד
אַשְׁרֵי הָעָם שֶׁכָּכָה לּוֹ, אַשְׁרֵי הָעָם שֶׁיהוה אֱלֹהָיו: תהלים קמד

תְּהִלָּה לְדָוִד תהלים קמה
אֲרוֹמִמְךָ[ע] אֱלוֹהַי הַמֶּלֶךְ, וַאֲבָרְכָה שִׁמְךָ לְעוֹלָם וָעֶד:
בְּכָל־יוֹם אֲבָרְכֶךָּ, וַאֲהַלְלָה שִׁמְךָ לְעוֹלָם וָעֶד:
גָּדוֹל יהוה וּמְהֻלָּל מְאֹד, וְלִגְדֻלָּתוֹ אֵין חֵקֶר:

INTRODUCTION TO MINḤA

The word *minḥa* can mean an offering or a gift. Already in the twelfth century, Avraham ben Yitzḥak of Narbonne wrote in his work *HaEshkol* that people are so busy all day long at their jobs that they forget to say this important prayer service altogether. And yet, *Ḥazal* said (*Berakhot* 6a) that one should be especially careful about making sure to pray *Minḥa*, for that was the time when the prophet Eliyahu called out to Hashem "Answer me! Answer me!" and his prayers were answered (*Melakhim* I 18:36–38). Apparently, then, *Minḥa* is a time when one's prayers could be particularly effective. Why should this be so? One answer lies in the words of *HaEshkol* cited above. Precisely because *Minḥa* occurs during the most inconvenient time of the day, it is the easiest to ignore. In the morning one gets up refreshed, ready to begin one's day; prayer is natural. So, too, in the evening, the end of the day brings its own mood of reflection. But in the middle of the day, we are so preoccupied with our work and routine that stopping is difficult, if not an outright intrusion (Rabbi Yehoshua ben Alexander HaKohen Falk, *Perisha*). But perhaps that's exactly the point. For that is the time of the day when we would benefit the most from stopping to take stock, to center ourselves Jewishly, to ask ourselves if our day is going the way it should, the way it could, to gain perspective on what's really important in our lives and not what might be filling our time or our minds. Viewed in this light, *Minḥa* is not an intrusion, rather, it is, as its name implies, a gift. If only we would take the time to see it that way. Take the time now.

ד One generation will praise Your works to the next,
and tell of Your mighty deeds.
ה On the glorious splendor of Your majesty I will meditate,
and on the acts of Your wonders.
ו They shall talk of the power of Your awesome deeds,
and I will tell of Your greatness.
ז They shall recite the record of Your great goodness,
and sing with joy of Your righteousness.
ח The LORD is generous and compassionate,
slow to anger and great in loving-kindness.
ט The LORD is good to all,
and His compassion extends to all His works.
י All Your works shall thank You, LORD,
and Your devoted ones shall bless You.
כ They shall talk of the glory of Your kingship,
and speak of Your might.
ל To make known to mankind His mighty deeds
and the glorious majesty of His kingship.
מ Your kingdom is an everlasting kingdom,
and Your reign is for all generations.
ס The LORD supports all who fall,
and raises all who are bowed down.
ע All raise their eyes to You in hope,
and You give them their food in due season.
פ You open Your hand,
and satisfy every living thing with favor.
צ The LORD is righteous in all His ways,
and kind in all He does.
ק The LORD is close to all who call on Him,
to all who call on Him in truth.
ר He fulfills the will of those who fear Him;
He hears their cry and saves them.
ש The LORD guards all who love Him,
but all the wicked He will destroy.
ת ▸ My mouth shall speak the praise of the LORD,
and all creatures shall bless His holy name for ever and all time.

We will bless the LORD now and for ever. Halleluya! *Ps. 115*

דּוֹר לְדוֹר יְשַׁבַּח מַעֲשֶׂיךָ, וּגְבוּרֹתֶיךָ יַגִּידוּ:
הֲדַר כְּבוֹד הוֹדֶךָ, וְדִבְרֵי נִפְלְאֹתֶיךָ אָשִׂיחָה:
וֶעֱזוּז נוֹרְאֹתֶיךָ יֹאמֵרוּ, וּגְדוּלָּתְךָ אֲסַפְּרֶנָּה:
זֵכֶר רַב־טוּבְךָ יַבִּיעוּ, וְצִדְקָתְךָ יְרַנֵּנוּ:
חַנּוּן וְרַחוּם יהוה, אֶרֶךְ אַפַּיִם וּגְדָל־חָסֶד:
טוֹב־יהוה לַכֹּל, וְרַחֲמָיו עַל־כָּל־מַעֲשָׂיו:
יוֹדוּךָ יהוה כָּל־מַעֲשֶׂיךָ, וַחֲסִידֶיךָ יְבָרְכוּכָה:
כְּבוֹד מַלְכוּתְךָ יֹאמֵרוּ, וּגְבוּרָתְךָ יְדַבֵּרוּ:
לְהוֹדִיעַ לִבְנֵי הָאָדָם גְּבוּרֹתָיו, וּכְבוֹד הֲדַר מַלְכוּתוֹ:
מַלְכוּתְךָ מַלְכוּת כָּל־עֹלָמִים, וּמֶמְשַׁלְתְּךָ בְּכָל־דּוֹר וָדֹר:
סוֹמֵךְ יהוה לְכָל־הַנֹּפְלִים, וְזוֹקֵף לְכָל־הַכְּפוּפִים:
עֵינֵי־כֹל אֵלֶיךָ יְשַׂבֵּרוּ, וְאַתָּה נוֹתֵן־לָהֶם אֶת־אָכְלָם בְּעִתּוֹ:
פּוֹתֵחַ אֶת־יָדֶךָ, וּמַשְׂבִּיעַ לְכָל־חַי רָצוֹן:
צַדִּיק יהוה בְּכָל־דְּרָכָיו, וְחָסִיד בְּכָל־מַעֲשָׂיו:
קָרוֹב יהוה לְכָל־קֹרְאָיו, לְכֹל אֲשֶׁר יִקְרָאֻהוּ בֶאֱמֶת:
רְצוֹן־יְרֵאָיו יַעֲשֶׂה, וְאֶת־שַׁוְעָתָם יִשְׁמַע, וְיוֹשִׁיעֵם:
שׁוֹמֵר יהוה אֶת־כָּל־אֹהֲבָיו, וְאֵת כָּל־הָרְשָׁעִים יַשְׁמִיד:
◂ תְּהִלַּת יהוה יְדַבֶּר פִּי, וִיבָרֵךְ כָּל־בָּשָׂר שֵׁם קָדְשׁוֹ לְעוֹלָם וָעֶד:
וַאֲנַחְנוּ נְבָרֵךְ יָהּ מֵעַתָּה וְעַד־עוֹלָם, הַלְלוּיָהּ: תהלים קטו

ANI TEFILLA · אני תפילה

"Imagine a man," said the Ba'al Shem Tov, "whose business hounds him through many streets and across the marketplace the entire day. He almost forgets that there is a Maker of the world. Only when Minḥa comes along does he remember: 'I must pray.' And then, from the bottom of his heart, he heaves a sigh of regret that he has spent his day on vain and idle matters, and he runs into a side street and stands there and prays. God holds him dear, very dear, and his prayer pierces the firmament."

HALF KADDISH

Leader: יִתְגַּדַּל Magnified and sanctified may His great name be,
in the world He created by His will.
May He establish His kingdom
in your lifetime and in your days,
and in the lifetime of all the house of Israel,
swiftly and soon – and say: Amen.

All: May His great name[A] be blessed for ever and all time.

Leader: Blessed and praised, glorified and exalted,
raised and honored, uplifted and lauded
be the name of the Holy One, blessed be He,
beyond any blessing,
song, praise and consolation
uttered in the world – and say: Amen.

On fast days, go to Removing the Torah from the Ark on page 210.
The Torah reading and Haftara for fast days are on pages 1095–1096.
After the Torah is returned to the Ark, the Leader says Half Kaddish.

Shaḥarit we gave a number of suggestions for the kinds of ways to expand your *kavana* for each one of the blessings. Here, we provide you with an alternative strategy, namely, to write down your own personal thoughts, associations, requests, hopes and dreams. Fill in the blank spaces, either figuratively or literally. Use an erasable pencil or post a temporary note so that you can make changes over time to reflect the fact that you yourself change over time. Such additions, however, should not act as a distraction (see Rema 90:23). Alternatively, just leave the spaces blank and fill them in with your mind.

The Ben Ish Ḥai (*Ḥayyei Sara* 17) reports that there were those who wrote the word *tefillin* on every page of their siddur so that they would not lose sight of the fact that they were wearing them, and could thereby recall their holiness.

Rabbi Meir Margoliot (Ostrog; d. 1790) and his brother were devoted students of the Ba'al Shem Tov. He said to them: "You are very beloved to me. Ask me for anything and I will do it for you." They responded: "Do what you think is best." He said: "I have a handwritten siddur that I use every day. Write your names and the name of your mother next to any blessing in the *Shemoneh Esreh* and I will have you in mind." They wrote their names next to the blessing of שׁוֹמֵעַ תְּפִלָּה (*Emunat Tzaddikim* pp. 7–8).

חצי קדיש

ש״ץ: יִתְגַּדַּל וְיִתְקַדַּשׁ שְׁמֵהּ רַבָּא (קהל: אָמֵן)
בְּעָלְמָא דִּי בְרָא כִרְעוּתֵהּ
וְיַמְלִיךְ מַלְכוּתֵהּ
בְּחַיֵּיכוֹן וּבְיוֹמֵיכוֹן וּבְחַיֵּי דְכָל בֵּית יִשְׂרָאֵל
בַּעֲגָלָא וּבִזְמַן קָרִיב, וְאִמְרוּ אָמֵן. (קהל: אָמֵן)

קהל וש״ץ: יְהֵא שְׁמֵהּ רַבָּא[א] מְבָרַךְ לְעָלַם וּלְעָלְמֵי עָלְמַיָּא.

ש״ץ: יִתְבָּרַךְ וְיִשְׁתַּבַּח וְיִתְפָּאַר וְיִתְרוֹמַם וְיִתְנַשֵּׂא
וְיִתְהַדָּר וְיִתְעַלֶּה וְיִתְהַלָּל
שְׁמֵהּ דְּקֻדְשָׁא בְּרִיךְ הוּא (קהל: בְּרִיךְ הוּא)
לְעֵלָּא מִן כָּל בִּרְכָתָא
וְשִׁירָתָא, תֻּשְׁבְּחָתָא וְנֶחֱמָתָא
דַּאֲמִירָן בְּעָלְמָא, וְאִמְרוּ אָמֵן. (קהל: אָמֵן)

On fast days, go to הוצאת ספר תורה *on page 211.*
The תורה *reading and* הפטרה *for fast days are on pages 1095–1096.*
After the תורה *is returned to the* ארון קודש, *the* שליח ציבור *says* חצי קדיש.

ANI TEFILLA • אני תפילה

יְהֵא שְׁמֵהּ רַבָּא – *May His great name.* Whoever says *yeheh shemeh raba*... with all his strength, the Heavenly Court rips up any negative decree against him (*Shabbat* 119b). "With all his strength" – with all of your physical strength. (Ritva)

INTRODUCTION TO THE MINḤA AMIDA

Tefilla is supposed to be a time of reflection about personal as well as communal issues. The standardized text of the siddur provides guidelines for what to be thinking about, but that still leaves room for lots of personal input (see our Introduction to this Siddur). In

THE AMIDA

The Amida, until "in former years" on page 282, is said silently, standing with feet together. If there is a minyan, the Amida is repeated aloud by the Leader. Take three steps forward and at the points indicated by ▾, bend the knees at the first word, bow at the second, and stand straight before saying God's name.

When I proclaim the LORD's name, give glory to our God. *Deut. 32*
O LORD, open my lips,[A] so that my mouth may declare Your praise. *Ps. 51*

PATRIARCHS

▾בָּרוּךְ▾ Blessed are You, LORD our God and God of our fathers,
God of Abraham, God of Isaac and God of Jacob;
the great, mighty and awesome God, God Most High,
who bestows acts of loving-kindness and creates all,
who remembers the loving-kindness of the fathers
and will bring a Redeemer to their children's children
for the sake of His name, in love.
King, Helper, Savior, Shield:
▾Blessed are You, LORD,
Shield of Abraham.

DIVINE MIGHT

אַתָּה גִּבּוֹר You are eternally mighty, LORD.
You give life to the dead and have great power to save.

In Israel: He causes the dew to fall.

He sustains the living with loving-kindness,
and with great compassion revives the dead.
He supports the fallen, heals the sick,
sets captives free,
and keeps His faith with those who sleep in the dust.

---

seconds in an hour and about 500 words in *Shemoneh Esreh*, that would be mean one word every seven seconds (Rabbi A. Kaplan). That may not be realistic for you right now, but the lesson is clear – slow down!

עמידה

The עמידה*, until* קַדְמֹנִיּוֹת *on page 283, is said silently, standing with feet together. If there is a* מנין*, the* עמידה *is repeated aloud by the* שליח ציבור*. Take three steps forward and at the points indicated by* ׳*, bend the knees at the first word, bow at the second, and stand straight before saying God's name.*

כִּי שֵׁם יהוה אֶקְרָא, הָבוּ גֹדֶל לֵאלֹהֵינוּ: דברים לב

אֲדֹנָי, שְׂפָתַי תִּפְתָּח,א וּפִי יַגִּיד תְּהִלָּתֶךָ: תהלים נא

אבות

׳בָּרוּךְ אַתָּה יהוה, אֱלֹהֵינוּ וֵאלֹהֵי אֲבוֹתֵינוּ
אֱלֹהֵי אַבְרָהָם, אֱלֹהֵי יִצְחָק, וֵאלֹהֵי יַעֲקֹב
הָאֵל הַגָּדוֹל הַגִּבּוֹר וְהַנּוֹרָא, אֵל עֶלְיוֹן
גּוֹמֵל חֲסָדִים טוֹבִים, וְקוֹנֵה הַכֹּל, וְזוֹכֵר חַסְדֵי אָבוֹת
וּמֵבִיא גוֹאֵל לִבְנֵי בְנֵיהֶם לְמַעַן שְׁמוֹ בְּאַהֲבָה.
מֶלֶךְ עוֹזֵר וּמוֹשִׁיעַ וּמָגֵן.
׳בָּרוּךְ אַתָּה יהוה, מָגֵן אַבְרָהָם.

גבורות

אַתָּה גִּבּוֹר לְעוֹלָם, אֲדֹנָי
מְחַיֵּה מֵתִים אַתָּה, רַב לְהוֹשִׁיעַ
בארץ ישראל: מוֹרִיד הַטָּל
מְכַלְכֵּל חַיִּים בְּחֶסֶד, מְחַיֵּה מֵתִים בְּרַחֲמִים רַבִּים
סוֹמֵךְ נוֹפְלִים, וְרוֹפֵא חוֹלִים, וּמַתִּיר אֲסוּרִים
וּמְקַיֵּם אֱמוּנָתוֹ לִישֵׁנֵי עָפָר.

ANI TEFILLA · אני תפילה

אֲדֹנָי, שְׂפָתַי תִּפְתָּח – *O Lord, open my lips.* The Gemara (*Berakhot* 32b) says that the *Ḥasidim Rishonim* would spend an hour on the *Shemoneh Esreh*. If there are 3600

Who is like You, Master of might,
and who can compare to You,
O King who brings death and gives life,
and makes salvation grow?
Faithful are You to revive the dead.
Blessed are You, LORD,
who revives the dead.

When saying the Amida silently, continue with "You are holy" on the next page.

KEDUSHA

During the Leader's Repetition, the following is said standing with feet together, rising on the toes at the words indicated by ˄.

Cong. then Leader: נְקַדֵּשׁ We will sanctify Your name on earth,
as they sanctify it in the highest heavens,
as is written by Your prophet,
"And they [the angels] call to one another saying: *Is. 6*

Cong. then Leader: ˄Holy, ˄holy, ˄holy is the LORD of hosts
the whole world is filled with His glory."
Those facing them say "Blessed – "

Cong. then Leader: ˄"Blessed is the LORD's glory from His place." *Ezek. 3*
And in Your holy Writings it is written thus:

Cong. then Leader: ˄"The LORD shall reign for ever. He is your God, Zion, *Ps. 146*
from generation to generation, Halleluya!"

Leader: From generation to generation
we will declare Your greatness,
and we will proclaim Your holiness for evermore.
Your praise, our God, shall not leave our mouth forever,
for You, God, are a great and holy King.
Blessed are You, LORD,
the holy God.

The Leader continues with "You grace humanity" on the next page.

מִי כָמְוֹךָ, בַּעַל גְּבוּרוֹת
וּמִי דּוֹמֶה לָּךְ
מֶלֶךְ, מֵמִית וּמְחַיֶּה וּמַצְמִיחַ יְשׁוּעָה.
וְנֶאֱמָן אַתָּה לְהַחֲיוֹת מֵתִים.
בָּרוּךְ אַתָּה יהוה, מְחַיֵּה הַמֵּתִים.

When saying the עמידה *silently, continue with* אַתָּה קָדוֹשׁ *on the next page.*

קדושה

During the חזרת הש״ץ*, the following is said standing with feet together, rising on the toes at the words indicated by* ˄.

then קהל ש״ץ: נְקַדֵּשׁ אֶת שִׁמְךָ בָּעוֹלָם, כְּשֵׁם שֶׁמַּקְדִּישִׁים אוֹתוֹ בִּשְׁמֵי מָרוֹם
כַּכָּתוּב עַל יַד נְבִיאֶךָ:
וְקָרָא זֶה אֶל־זֶה וְאָמַר ישעיה ו

then קהל ש״ץ: ˄קָדוֹשׁ, ˄קָדוֹשׁ, ˄קָדוֹשׁ, יהוה צְבָאוֹת, מְלֹא כָל־הָאָרֶץ כְּבוֹדוֹ:
לְעֻמָּתָם בָּרוּךְ יֹאמֵרוּ

then קהל ש״ץ: ˄בָּרוּךְ כְּבוֹד־יהוה מִמְּקוֹמוֹ: יחזקאל ג
וּבְדִבְרֵי קָדְשְׁךָ כָּתוּב לֵאמֹר

then קהל ש״ץ: ˄יִמְלֹךְ יהוה לְעוֹלָם, אֱלֹהַיִךְ צִיּוֹן לְדֹר וָדֹר, הַלְלוּיָהּ: תהלים קמו

ש״ץ: לְדוֹר וָדוֹר נַגִּיד גָּדְלֶךָ, וּלְנֵצַח נְצָחִים קְדֻשָּׁתְךָ נַקְדִּישׁ
וְשִׁבְחֲךָ אֱלֹהֵינוּ מִפִּינוּ לֹא יָמוּשׁ לְעוֹלָם וָעֶד
כִּי אֵל מֶלֶךְ גָּדוֹל וְקָדוֹשׁ אָתָּה.
בָּרוּךְ אַתָּה יהוה, הָאֵל הַקָּדוֹשׁ.

The שליח ציבור *continues with* אַתָּה חוֹנֵן *on the next page.*

HOLINESS

אַתָּה קָדוֹשׁ You are holy and Your name is holy,
and holy ones praise You daily, Selah!
Blessed are You, LORD,
the holy God.

KNOWLEDGE

אַתָּה חוֹנֵן You grace humanity with knowledge
and teach mortals understanding.
Grace us with the knowledge, understanding
and discernment that come from You.
Blessed are You, LORD,
who graciously grants knowledge.

REPENTANCE

הֲשִׁיבֵנוּ Bring us back, our Father, to Your Torah.
Draw us near, our King, to Your service.
Lead us back to You in perfect repentance.
Blessed are You, LORD,
who desires repentance.

FORGIVENESS

Strike the left side of the chest at °.

סְלַח לָנוּ Forgive us, our Father, for we have °sinned.
Pardon us, our King, for we have °transgressed;
for You pardon and forgive.
Blessed are You, LORD,
the gracious One who repeatedly forgives.

REDEMPTION

רְאֵה Look on our affliction, plead our cause,
and redeem us soon for Your name's sake,
for You are a powerful Redeemer.
Blessed are You, LORD,
the Redeemer of Israel.

קדושת השם

אַתָּה קָדוֹשׁ וְשִׁמְךָ קָדוֹשׁ
וּקְדוֹשִׁים בְּכָל יוֹם יְהַלְלוּךָ סֶּלָה.
בָּרוּךְ אַתָּה יהוה, הָאֵל הַקָּדוֹשׁ.

דעת

אַתָּה חוֹנֵן לְאָדָם דַּעַת, וּמְלַמֵּד לֶאֱנוֹשׁ בִּינָה.
חָנֵּנוּ מֵאִתְּךָ דֵּעָה בִּינָה וְהַשְׂכֵּל.
בָּרוּךְ אַתָּה יהוה, חוֹנֵן הַדָּעַת.

תשובה

הֲשִׁיבֵנוּ אָבִינוּ לְתוֹרָתֶךָ
וְקָרְבֵנוּ מַלְכֵּנוּ לַעֲבוֹדָתֶךָ
וְהַחֲזִירֵנוּ בִּתְשׁוּבָה שְׁלֵמָה לְפָנֶיךָ.
בָּרוּךְ אַתָּה יהוה, הָרוֹצֶה בִּתְשׁוּבָה.

סליחה

Strike the left side of the chest at °.

סְלַח לָנוּ אָבִינוּ כִּי °חָטָאנוּ
מְחַל לָנוּ מַלְכֵּנוּ כִּי °פָשָׁעְנוּ
כִּי מוֹחֵל וְסוֹלֵחַ אָתָּה.
בָּרוּךְ אַתָּה יהוה, חַנּוּן הַמַּרְבֶּה לִסְלֹחַ.

גאולה

רְאֵה בְעָנְיֵנוּ, וְרִיבָה רִיבֵנוּ
וּגְאָלֵנוּ מְהֵרָה לְמַעַן שְׁמֶךָ
כִּי גּוֹאֵל חָזָק אָתָּה.
בָּרוּךְ אַתָּה יהוה, גּוֹאֵל יִשְׂרָאֵל.

On fast days the Leader adds:

עֲנֵנוּ Answer us, LORD, answer us on our Fast Day, for we are in great distress. Look not at our wickedness. Do not hide Your face from us and do not ignore our plea. Be near to our cry; please let Your loving-kindness comfort us. Even before we call to You, answer us, as it is said, "Before they call, I will answer. While they are still speaking, I will hear." For You, LORD, are the One who answers in time of distress, redeems and rescues in all times of trouble and anguish. Blessed are You, LORD, who answers in time of distress. *Is. 65*

HEALING

רְפָאֵנוּ Heal us, LORD, and we shall be healed.
Save us and we shall be saved,
for You are our praise.
Bring complete recovery for all our ailments,

The following prayer for a sick person may be said here:

May it be Your will, O LORD my God and God of my ancestors, that You speedily send a complete recovery from heaven, a healing of both soul and body, to the patient (*name*), son/daughter of (*mother's name*) among the other afflicted of Israel.

for You, God, King, are a faithful and compassionate Healer.
Blessed are You, LORD,
Healer of the sick of His people Israel.

PROSPERITY

בָּרֵךְ Bless this year for us, LORD our God,
and all its types of produce for good.
Grant blessing on the face of the earth,
and from its goodness satisfy us,
blessing our year as the best of years.
Blessed are You, LORD,
who blesses the years.

On fast days the שליח ציבור *adds:*

עֲנֵנוּ יהוה עֲנֵנוּ בְּיוֹם צוֹם תַּעֲנִיתֵנוּ, כִּי בְצָרָה גְדוֹלָה אֲנָחְנוּ. אַל תֵּפֶן אֶל רִשְׁעֵנוּ, וְאַל תַּסְתֵּר פָּנֶיךָ מִמֶּנּוּ, וְאַל תִּתְעַלַּם מִתְּחִנָּתֵנוּ. הֱיֵה נָא קָרוֹב לְשַׁוְעָתֵנוּ, יְהִי נָא חַסְדְּךָ לְנַחֲמֵנוּ, טֶרֶם נִקְרָא אֵלֶיךָ עֲנֵנוּ, כַּדָּבָר שֶׁנֶּאֱמַר:
ישעיה סה וְהָיָה טֶרֶם יִקְרָאוּ וַאֲנִי אֶעֱנֶה, עוֹד הֵם מְדַבְּרִים וַאֲנִי אֶשְׁמָע: כִּי אַתָּה יהוה הָעוֹנֶה בְּעֵת צָרָה, פּוֹדֶה וּמַצִּיל בְּכָל עֵת צָרָה וְצוּקָה. בָּרוּךְ אַתָּה יהוה, הָעוֹנֶה בְּעֵת צָרָה.

רפואה

רְפָאֵנוּ יהוה וְנֵרָפֵא
הוֹשִׁיעֵנוּ וְנִוָּשֵׁעָה, כִּי תְהִלָּתֵנוּ אָתָּה
וְהַעֲלֵה רְפוּאָה שְׁלֵמָה לְכָל מַכּוֹתֵינוּ

The following prayer for a sick person may be said here:

יְהִי רָצוֹן מִלְּפָנֶיךָ יהוה אֱלֹהַי וֵאלֹהֵי אֲבוֹתַי, שֶׁתִּשְׁלַח מְהֵרָה רְפוּאָה שְׁלֵמָה מִן הַשָּׁמַיִם רְפוּאַת הַנֶּפֶשׁ וּרְפוּאַת הַגּוּף לַחוֹלֶה/לַחוֹלָה *name of patient* בֶּן/בַּת *mother's name* בְּתוֹךְ שְׁאָר חוֹלֵי יִשְׂרָאֵל.

כִּי אֵל מֶלֶךְ רוֹפֵא נֶאֱמָן וְרַחֲמָן אָתָּה.
בָּרוּךְ אַתָּה יהוה, רוֹפֵא חוֹלֵי עַמּוֹ יִשְׂרָאֵל.

ברכת השנים

בָּרֵךְ עָלֵינוּ יהוה אֱלֹהֵינוּ אֶת הַשָּׁנָה הַזֹּאת
וְאֶת כָּל מִינֵי תְבוּאָתָהּ, לְטוֹבָה
וְתֵן בְּרָכָה עַל פְּנֵי הָאֲדָמָה, וְשַׂבְּעֵנוּ מִטּוּבָהּ
וּבָרֵךְ שְׁנָתֵנוּ כַּשָּׁנִים הַטּוֹבוֹת.
בָּרוּךְ אַתָּה יהוה, מְבָרֵךְ הַשָּׁנִים.

INGATHERING OF EXILES

תְּקַע Sound the great shofar for our freedom,
raise high the banner to gather our exiles,
and gather us together from the four quarters of the earth.
Blessed are You, Lord,
who gathers the dispersed of His people Israel.

JUSTICE

הָשִׁיבָה Restore our judges as at first,
and our counselors as at the beginning,
and remove from us sorrow and sighing.
May You alone, Lord,
reign over us with loving-kindness and compassion,
and vindicate us in justice.
Blessed are You, Lord,
the King who loves righteousness and justice.

AGAINST INFORMERS

וְלַמַּלְשִׁינִים For the slanderers let there be no hope,
and may all wickedness perish in an instant.
May all Your people's enemies swiftly be cut down.
May You swiftly uproot, crush, cast down
and humble the arrogant swiftly in our days.
Blessed are You, Lord,
who destroys enemies and humbles the arrogant.

THE RIGHTEOUS

עַל הַצַּדִּיקִים To the righteous, the pious,
the elders of Your people the house of Israel,
the remnant of their scholars,
the righteous converts, and to us,
may Your compassion be aroused, Lord our God.

קבוץ גלויות

תְּקַע בְּשׁוֹפָר גָּדוֹל לְחֵרוּתֵנוּ
וְשָׂא נֵס לְקַבֵּץ גָּלֻיּוֹתֵינוּ
וְקַבְּצֵנוּ יַחַד מֵאַרְבַּע כַּנְפוֹת הָאָרֶץ.
בָּרוּךְ אַתָּה יהוה, מְקַבֵּץ נִדְחֵי עַמּוֹ יִשְׂרָאֵל.

השבת המשפט

הָשִׁיבָה שׁוֹפְטֵינוּ כְּבָרִאשׁוֹנָה וְיוֹעֲצֵינוּ כְּבַתְּחִלָּה
וְהָסֵר מִמֶּנּוּ יָגוֹן וַאֲנָחָה
וּמְלֹךְ עָלֵינוּ אַתָּה יהוה לְבַדְּךָ בְּחֶסֶד וּבְרַחֲמִים
וְצַדְּקֵנוּ בַּמִּשְׁפָּט.
בָּרוּךְ אַתָּה יהוה
מֶלֶךְ אוֹהֵב צְדָקָה וּמִשְׁפָּט.

ברכת המינים

וְלַמַּלְשִׁינִים אַל תְּהִי תִקְוָה, וְכָל הָרִשְׁעָה כְּרֶגַע תֹּאבֵד
וְכָל אוֹיְבֵי עַמְּךָ מְהֵרָה יִכָּרֵתוּ
וְהַזֵּדִים מְהֵרָה תְעַקֵּר וּתְשַׁבֵּר וּתְמַגֵּר וְתַכְנִיעַ בִּמְהֵרָה בְיָמֵינוּ.
בָּרוּךְ אַתָּה יהוה, שׁוֹבֵר אוֹיְבִים וּמַכְנִיעַ זֵדִים.

על הצדיקים

עַל הַצַּדִּיקִים וְעַל הַחֲסִידִים
וְעַל זִקְנֵי עַמְּךָ בֵּית יִשְׂרָאֵל
וְעַל פְּלֵיטַת סוֹפְרֵיהֶם
וְעַל גֵּרֵי הַצֶּדֶק, וְעָלֵינוּ
יֶהֱמוּ רַחֲמֶיךָ יהוה אֱלֹהֵינוּ

Grant a good reward
to all who sincerely trust in Your name.
Set our lot with them,
so that we may never be ashamed, for in You we trust.
Blessed are You, Lord,
who is the support and trust of the righteous.

REBUILDING JERUSALEM

וְלִירוּשָׁלַיִם To Jerusalem, Your city, may You return in compassion,
and may You dwell in it as You promised.
May You rebuild it rapidly in our days as an everlasting structure,
and install within it soon the throne of David.
*Blessed are You, Lord,
who builds Jerusalem.

**On Tisha B'Av all conclude as follows:*

נַחֵם Console, O Lord our God, the mourners of Zion and the mourners of Jerusalem, and the city that is in sorrow, laid waste, scorned and desolate; that grieves for the loss of its children, that is laid waste of its dwellings, robbed of its glory, desolate without inhabitants. She sits with her head covered like a barren childless woman. Legions have devoured her; idolaters have taken possession of her; they have put Your people Israel to the sword and deliberately killed the devoted followers of the Most High. Therefore Zion weeps bitterly, and Jerusalem raises her voice. My heart, my heart grieves for those they killed; I am in anguish, I am in anguish for those they killed. For You, O Lord, consumed it with fire, and with fire You will rebuild it in the future, as is said, "And I Myself will be a wall of fire around it, says the *Zech. 2*
Lord, and I will be its glory within." Blessed are You, Lord, who consoles Zion and rebuilds Jerusalem.

Continue with "May the offshoot" below.

KINGDOM OF DAVID

אֶת צֶמַח May the offshoot of Your servant David soon flower,
and may his pride be raised high by Your salvation,
for we wait for Your salvation all day.
Blessed are You, Lord,
who makes the glory of salvation flourish.

וְתֵן שָׂכָר טוֹב לְכָל הַבּוֹטְחִים בְּשִׁמְךָ בֶּאֱמֶת
וְשִׂים חֶלְקֵנוּ עִמָּהֶם
וּלְעוֹלָם לֹא נֵבוֹשׁ כִּי בְךָ בָּטָחְנוּ.
בָּרוּךְ אַתָּה יהוה, מִשְׁעָן וּמִבְטָח לַצַּדִּיקִים.

בניין ירושלים
וְלִירוּשָׁלַיִם עִירְךָ בְּרַחֲמִים תָּשׁוּב
וְתִשְׁכֹּן בְּתוֹכָהּ כַּאֲשֶׁר דִּבַּרְתָּ
וּבְנֵה אוֹתָהּ בְּקָרוֹב בְּיָמֵינוּ בִּנְיַן עוֹלָם
וְכִסֵּא דָוִד מְהֵרָה לְתוֹכָהּ תָּכִין.
*בָּרוּךְ אַתָּה יהוה, בּוֹנֵה יְרוּשָׁלָיִם.

**On תשעה באב, all conclude as follows:*

נַחֵם יהוה אֱלֹהֵינוּ אֶת אֲבֵלֵי צִיּוֹן וְאֶת אֲבֵלֵי יְרוּשָׁלָיִם, וְאֶת הָעִיר הָאֲבֵלָה וְהֶחֳרֵבָה וְהַבְּזוּיָה וְהַשּׁוֹמֵמָה. הָאֲבֵלָה מִבְּלִי בָנֶיהָ, וְהֶחֳרֵבָה מִמְּעוֹנוֹתֶיהָ, וְהַבְּזוּיָה מִכְּבוֹדָהּ, וְהַשּׁוֹמֵמָה מֵאֵין יוֹשֵׁב. וְהִיא יוֹשֶׁבֶת וְרֹאשָׁהּ חָפוּי, כְּאִשָּׁה עֲקָרָה שֶׁלֹּא יָלָדָה. וַיְבַלְּעוּהָ לִגְיוֹנוֹת, וַיִּירָשׁוּהָ עוֹבְדֵי פְסִילִים, וַיָּטִילוּ אֶת עַמְּךָ יִשְׂרָאֵל לֶחָרֶב, וַיַּהַרְגוּ בְזָדוֹן חֲסִידֵי עֶלְיוֹן. עַל כֵּן צִיּוֹן בְּמַר תִּבְכֶּה, וִירוּשָׁלַיִם תִּתֵּן קוֹלָהּ. לִבִּי לִבִּי עַל חַלְלֵיהֶם, מֵעַי מֵעַי עַל חַלְלֵיהֶם, כִּי אַתָּה יהוה בָּאֵשׁ הִצַּתָּהּ, וּבָאֵשׁ אַתָּה עָתִיד לִבְנוֹתָהּ. כָּאָמוּר: וַאֲנִי אֶהְיֶה־לָּהּ, זכריה ב
נְאֻם־יהוה, חוֹמַת אֵשׁ סָבִיב, וּלְכָבוֹד אֶהְיֶה בְתוֹכָהּ: בָּרוּךְ אַתָּה יהוה, מְנַחֵם צִיּוֹן וּבוֹנֵה יְרוּשָׁלָיִם.

Continue with אֶת צֶמַח below.

משיח בן דוד
אֶת צֶמַח דָּוִד עַבְדְּךָ מְהֵרָה תַצְמִיחַ
וְקַרְנוֹ תָּרוּם בִּישׁוּעָתֶךָ
כִּי לִישׁוּעָתְךָ קִוִּינוּ כָּל הַיּוֹם.
בָּרוּךְ אַתָּה יהוה, מַצְמִיחַ קֶרֶן יְשׁוּעָה.

RESPONSE TO PRAYER

שְׁמַע קוֹלֵנוּ Listen to our voice, LORD our God.
Spare us and have compassion on us,
and in compassion and favor accept our prayer,
for You, God, listen to prayers and pleas.
Do not turn us away, O our King,
empty-handed from Your presence,*
for You listen with compassion
to the prayer of Your people Israel.
Blessed are You, LORD,
who listens to prayer.

**At this point on fast days, the congregation adds "Answer us".*

עֲנֵנוּ Answer us, LORD, answer us on our Fast Day, for we are in great distress. Look not at our wickedness. Do not hide Your face from us and do not ignore our plea. Be near to our cry; please let Your loving-kindness comfort us. Even before we call to You, answer us, as is said, "Before they call, I will answer. While they are still speaking, I will hear." For You, LORD, are the One who answers in time of distress, redeems and rescues in all times of trouble and anguish. *Continue with "for You listen" above.*

TEMPLE SERVICE

רְצֵה Find favor, LORD our God,
in Your people Israel and their prayer.
Restore the service to Your most holy House,
and accept in love and favor
the fire-offerings of Israel and their prayer.
May the service of Your people Israel always find favor with You.

On Rosh Ḥodesh, say:

אֱלֹהֵינוּ Our God and God of our ancestors, may there rise, come, reach, appear, be favored, heard, regarded and remembered before You, our recollection and remembrance, as well as the remembrance of our ancestors, and of the Messiah son of David Your servant, and of Jerusalem Your holy city, and of all Your people the house of Israel – for deliverance and

שומע תפלה

שְׁמַע קוֹלֵנוּ יהוה אֱלֹהֵינוּ
חוּס וְרַחֵם עָלֵינוּ
וְקַבֵּל בְּרַחֲמִים וּבְרָצוֹן אֶת תְּפִלָּתֵנוּ
כִּי אֵל שׁוֹמֵעַ תְּפִלּוֹת וְתַחֲנוּנִים אָתָּה
וּמִלְּפָנֶיךָ מַלְכֵּנוּ רֵיקָם אַל תְּשִׁיבֵנוּ*
כִּי אַתָּה שׁוֹמֵעַ תְּפִלַּת עַמְּךָ יִשְׂרָאֵל בְּרַחֲמִים.
בָּרוּךְ אַתָּה יהוה, שׁוֹמֵעַ תְּפִלָּה.

**At this point on fast days, the* קהל *adds* עֲנֵנוּ.

עֲנֵנוּ יהוה עֲנֵנוּ בְּיוֹם צוֹם תַּעֲנִיתֵנוּ, כִּי בְצָרָה גְדוֹלָה אֲנָחְנוּ. אַל תֵּפֶן אֶל רִשְׁעֵנוּ, וְאַל תַּסְתֵּר פָּנֶיךָ מִמֶּנּוּ, וְאַל תִּתְעַלַּם מִתְּחִנָּתֵנוּ. הֱיֵה נָא קָרוֹב לְשַׁוְעָתֵנוּ, יְהִי נָא חַסְדְּךָ לְנַחֲמֵנוּ, טֶרֶם נִקְרָא אֵלֶיךָ עֲנֵנוּ, כַּדָּבָר שֶׁנֶּאֱמַר: וְהָיָה טֶרֶם יִקְרָאוּ וַאֲנִי אֶעֱנֶה, עוֹד הֵם מְדַבְּרִים וַאֲנִי אֶשְׁמָע: כִּי אַתָּה יהוה הָעוֹנֶה בְּעֵת צָרָה, פּוֹדֶה וּמַצִּיל בְּכָל עֵת צָרָה וְצוּקָה.

Continue with כִּי אַתָּה שׁוֹמֵעַ *above.*

עבודה

רְצֵה יהוה אֱלֹהֵינוּ בְּעַמְּךָ יִשְׂרָאֵל וּבִתְפִלָּתָם
וְהָשֵׁב אֶת הָעֲבוֹדָה לִדְבִיר בֵּיתֶךָ
וְאִשֵּׁי יִשְׂרָאֵל וּתְפִלָּתָם בְּאַהֲבָה תְקַבֵּל בְּרָצוֹן
וּתְהִי לְרָצוֹן תָּמִיד עֲבוֹדַת יִשְׂרָאֵל עַמֶּךָ.

On ראש חודש*, say:*

אֱלֹהֵינוּ וֵאלֹהֵי אֲבוֹתֵינוּ, יַעֲלֶה וְיָבוֹא וְיַגִּיעַ, וְיֵרָאֶה וְיֵרָצֶה וְיִשָּׁמַע, וְיִפָּקֵד וְיִזָּכֵר זִכְרוֹנֵנוּ וּפִקְדוֹנֵנוּ וְזִכְרוֹן אֲבוֹתֵינוּ, וְזִכְרוֹן מָשִׁיחַ בֶּן דָּוִד עַבְדֶּךָ, וְזִכְרוֹן יְרוּשָׁלַיִם עִיר קָדְשֶׁךָ, וְזִכְרוֹן כָּל עַמְּךָ בֵּית יִשְׂרָאֵל, לְפָנֶיךָ, לִפְלֵיטָה לְטוֹבָה, לְחֵן וּלְחֶסֶד וּלְרַחֲמִים,

well-being, grace, loving-kindness and compassion, life and peace, on this day of Rosh Ḥodesh. On it remember us, LORD our God, for good; recollect us for blessing, and deliver us for life. In accord with Your promise of salvation and compassion, spare us and be gracious to us; have compassion on us and deliver us, for our eyes are turned to You because You, God, are a gracious and compassionate King.

וְתֶחֱזֶינָה And may our eyes witness
Your return to Zion in compassion.
Blessed are You, LORD, who restores His Presence to Zion.

THANKSGIVING

Bow at the first nine words.

מוֹדִים We give thanks to You,
for You are the LORD our God
and God of our ancestors
for ever and all time.
You are the Rock of our lives,
Shield of our salvation
from generation to generation.
We will thank You and
declare Your praise for our lives,
which are entrusted into Your hand;
for our souls,
which are placed in Your charge;
for Your miracles
which are with us every day;
and for Your wonders and favors
at all times,
evening, morning and midday.
You are good –
for Your compassion never fails.
You are compassionate –
for Your loving-kindnesses never cease.
We have always placed our hope in You.

During the Leader's Repetition, the congregation says quietly:
מוֹדִים We give thanks
to You, for You are
the LORD our God
and God of our ancestors,
God of all flesh,
who formed us
and formed the universe.
Blessings and thanks
are due to Your great
and holy name for giving us
life and sustaining us.
May You continue
to give us life
and sustain us;
and may You gather our
exiles to Your holy courts,
to keep Your decrees,
do Your will and serve You
with a perfect heart,
for it is for us
to give You thanks.
Blessed be God to whom
thanksgiving is due.

וְעַל כֻּלָּם For all these things may Your name be blessed and exalted, our King, continually, for ever and all time.

לְחַיִּים וּלְשָׁלוֹם בְּיוֹם רֹאשׁ הַחֹדֶשׁ הַזֶּה. זָכְרֵנוּ יהוה אֱלֹהֵינוּ בּוֹ לְטוֹבָה, וּפָקְדֵנוּ בוֹ לִבְרָכָה, וְהוֹשִׁיעֵנוּ בוֹ לְחַיִּים. וּבִדְבַר יְשׁוּעָה וְרַחֲמִים, חוּס וְחָנֵּנוּ וְרַחֵם עָלֵינוּ וְהוֹשִׁיעֵנוּ, כִּי אֵלֶיךָ עֵינֵינוּ, כִּי אֵל מֶלֶךְ חַנּוּן וְרַחוּם אָתָּה.

וְתֶחֱזֶינָה עֵינֵינוּ בְּשׁוּבְךָ לְצִיּוֹן בְּרַחֲמִים.
בָּרוּךְ אַתָּה יהוה, הַמַּחֲזִיר שְׁכִינָתוֹ לְצִיּוֹן.

הודאה

Bow at the first five words.

מוֹדִים אֲנַחְנוּ לָךְ
שָׁאַתָּה הוּא יהוה אֱלֹהֵינוּ
וֵאלֹהֵי אֲבוֹתֵינוּ לְעוֹלָם וָעֶד.
צוּר חַיֵּינוּ, מָגֵן יִשְׁעֵנוּ
אַתָּה הוּא לְדוֹר וָדוֹר.
נוֹדֶה לְּךָ וּנְסַפֵּר תְּהִלָּתֶךָ
עַל חַיֵּינוּ הַמְּסוּרִים בְּיָדֶךָ
וְעַל נִשְׁמוֹתֵינוּ הַפְּקוּדוֹת לָךְ
וְעַל נִסֶּיךָ שֶׁבְּכָל יוֹם עִמָּנוּ
וְעַל נִפְלְאוֹתֶיךָ וְטוֹבוֹתֶיךָ
שֶׁבְּכָל עֵת
עֶרֶב וָבֹקֶר וְצָהֳרָיִם.
הַטּוֹב, כִּי לֹא כָלוּ רַחֲמֶיךָ
וְהַמְרַחֵם, כִּי לֹא תַמּוּ חֲסָדֶיךָ
מֵעוֹלָם קִוִּינוּ לָךְ.

During the חזרת הש״ץ*, the* קהל *says quietly:*

מוֹדִים אֲנַחְנוּ לָךְ
שָׁאַתָּה הוּא יהוה אֱלֹהֵינוּ
וֵאלֹהֵי אֲבוֹתֵינוּ
אֱלֹהֵי כָל בָּשָׂר
יוֹצְרֵנוּ, יוֹצֵר בְּרֵאשִׁית.
בְּרָכוֹת וְהוֹדָאוֹת
לְשִׁמְךָ הַגָּדוֹל וְהַקָּדוֹשׁ
עַל שֶׁהֶחֱיִיתָנוּ וְקִיַּמְתָּנוּ.
כֵּן תְּחַיֵּנוּ וּתְקַיְּמֵנוּ
וְתֶאֱסֹף גָּלֻיּוֹתֵינוּ
לְחַצְרוֹת קָדְשֶׁךָ
לִשְׁמֹר חֻקֶּיךָ
וְלַעֲשׂוֹת רְצוֹנֶךָ
וּלְעָבְדְּךָ בְּלֵבָב שָׁלֵם
עַל שֶׁאֲנַחְנוּ מוֹדִים לָךְ.
בָּרוּךְ אֵל הַהוֹדָאוֹת.

וְעַל כֻּלָּם יִתְבָּרַךְ וְיִתְרוֹמַם שִׁמְךָ מַלְכֵּנוּ תָּמִיד לְעוֹלָם וָעֶד.

Let all that lives thank You, Selah! and praise Your name in truth,
God, our Savior and Help, Selah!
▾Blessed are You, LORD, whose name is "the Good"
and to whom thanks are due.

On public fast days only, the following is said by the Leader during the Repetition of the Amida, except in a house of mourning. In Israel, on Fast Days, if Kohanim bless the congregation, turn to page 1008.

Our God and God of our fathers, bless us with the threefold blessing in the Torah, written by the hand of Moses Your servant and pronounced by Aaron and his sons the priests, Your holy people, as it is said:

May the LORD bless you and protect you. *Num. 6*
Cong: May it be Your will.
May the LORD make His face shine on you and be gracious to you.
Cong: May it be Your will.
May the LORD turn His face toward you, and grant you peace.
Cong: May it be Your will.

PEACE

שָׁלוֹם רָב Grant great peace[IAB] to Your people Israel for ever, for You are the sovereign LORD of all peace; and may it be good in Your eyes to bless Your people Israel at every time, at every hour, with Your peace.

On fast days:

שִׂים שָׁלוֹם Grant peace, goodness and blessing,
grace, loving-kindness and compassion
to us and all Israel Your people.
Bless us, our Father, all as one,
with the light of Your face,
for by the light of Your face
You have given us, LORD our God,
the Torah of life and love of kindness,
righteousness, blessing, compassion,
life and peace.
May it be good in Your eyes
to bless Your people Israel
at every time, in every hour,
with Your peace.

BIUR TEFILLA • ביאור תפילה

שָׁלוֹם רָב – *Grant great peace.* The most common Ashkenazi practice is, except on a fast day, to change the text of this blessing from *Sim Shalom* said in the morning to *Shalom*

This **BIUR TEFILLA** *continues on page 283.*

וְכֹל הַחַיִּים יוֹדְוּךָ סֶּלָה, וִיהַלְלוּ אֶת שִׁמְךָ בֶּאֱמֶת
הָאֵל יְשׁוּעָתֵנוּ וְעֶזְרָתֵנוּ סֶלָה.
ׄבָּרוּךְ אַתָּה יהוה, הַטּוֹב שִׁמְךָ וּלְךָ נָאֶה לְהוֹדוֹת.

On public fast days only, the following is said by the שליח ציבור *during the* חזרת הש״ץ *except in a house of mourning. In* ארץ ישראל*, on Fast Days, if* כהנים *say* ברכת כהנים *turn to page 1009.*

אֱלֹהֵינוּ וֵאלֹהֵי אֲבוֹתֵינוּ, בָּרְכֵנוּ בַּבְּרָכָה הַמְשֻׁלֶּשֶׁת בַּתּוֹרָה, הַכְּתוּבָה עַל יְדֵי מֹשֶׁה עַבְדֶּךָ, הָאֲמוּרָה מִפִּי אַהֲרֹן וּבָנָיו כֹּהֲנִים, עַם קְדוֹשֶׁיךָ, כָּאָמוּר

במדבר ו
יְבָרֶכְךָ יהוה וְיִשְׁמְרֶךָ: קהל: כֵּן יְהִי רָצוֹן
יָאֵר יהוה פָּנָיו אֵלֶיךָ וִיחֻנֶּךָּ: קהל: כֵּן יְהִי רָצוֹן
יִשָּׂא יהוה פָּנָיו אֵלֶיךָ וְיָשֵׂם לְךָ שָׁלוֹם: קהל: כֵּן יְהִי רָצוֹן

ברכת שלום

שָׁלוֹם רָב עַל יִשְׂרָאֵל עַמְּךָ תָּשִׂים לְעוֹלָם
כִּי אַתָּה הוּא מֶלֶךְ אָדוֹן לְכָל הַשָּׁלוֹם.
וְטוֹב בְּעֵינֶיךָ לְבָרֵךְ אֶת עַמְּךָ יִשְׂרָאֵל
בְּכָל עֵת וּבְכָל שָׁעָה בִּשְׁלוֹמֶךָ.

עאב

On fast days:

שִׂים שָׁלוֹם טוֹבָה וּבְרָכָה
חֵן וָחֶסֶד וְרַחֲמִים
עָלֵינוּ וְעַל כָּל יִשְׂרָאֵל עַמֶּךָ.
בָּרְכֵנוּ אָבִינוּ כֻּלָּנוּ כְּאֶחָד בְּאוֹר פָּנֶיךָ
כִּי בְאוֹר פָּנֶיךָ נָתַתָּ לָּנוּ יהוה אֱלֹהֵינוּ
תּוֹרַת חַיִּים וְאַהֲבַת חֶסֶד
וּצְדָקָה וּבְרָכָה וְרַחֲמִים וְחַיִּים וְשָׁלוֹם.
וְטוֹב בְּעֵינֶיךָ לְבָרֵךְ אֶת עַמְּךָ יִשְׂרָאֵל
בְּכָל עֵת וּבְכָל שָׁעָה בִּשְׁלוֹמֶךָ.

ANI TEFILLA • אני תפילה

שָׁלוֹם רָב – *Grant great peace.* The word *shalom* is related to the word *shalem,* meaning whole or complete. Each of us has a purpose in life, a task that makes us complete. **The day is not yet over. How can I still fulfill my potential today?**

IYUN TEFILLA • עיון תפילה

שָׁלוֹם רָב – *Grant great peace.* Perhaps because it is later in the day, our appreciation of the need for *shalom* – peace, wholeness – is greater than it was this morning, hence we ask now for an abundance of it.

Blessed are You, LORD, who blesses His people Israel with peace.

The following verse concludes the Leader's Repetition of the Amida. Some also say it here as part of the silent Amida.

May the words of my mouth and the meditation of my heart find favor before You, LORD, my Rock and Redeemer. *Ps. 19*

אֱלֹהַי My God, *Berakhot 17a*
guard my tongue from evil and my lips from deceitful speech.
To those who curse me, let my soul be silent;
may my soul be to all like the dust.
Open my heart to Your Torah and let my soul
pursue Your commandments.
As for all who plan evil against me,
swiftly thwart their counsel and frustrate their plans.
Act for the sake of Your name; act for the sake of Your right hand;
act for the sake of Your holiness; act for the sake of Your Torah.
That Your beloved ones may be delivered, *Ps. 60*
save with Your right hand and answer me.
May the words of my mouth and the meditation of my heart *Ps. 19*
find favor before You, LORD, my Rock and Redeemer.

Bow, take three steps back, then bow, first left, then right, then center, while saying:

May He who makes peace in His high places,
make peace for us and all Israel – and say: Amen.

יְהִי רָצוֹן May it be Your will, LORD our God and God of our ancestors,
that the Temple be rebuilt speedily in our days,
and grant us a share in Your Torah.
And there we will serve You with reverence,
as in the days of old and as in former years.
Then the offering of Judah and Jerusalem will be pleasing to the LORD *Mal. 3*
as in the days of old and as in former years.

On days when Taḥanun is not said, the Leader says Full Kaddish on page 290.

---

there is a possibility that they might have been drinking alcohol, hence it is not said in the afternoon (except on a fast day), which in turn precludes repeating its themes in *Sim Shalom*. Hence a different text, namely *Shalom Rav*, is substituted.

בָּרוּךְ אַתָּה יהוה, הַמְבָרֵךְ אֶת עַמּוֹ יִשְׂרָאֵל בַּשָּׁלוֹם.

The following verse concludes the חזרת הש״ץ.
Some also say it here as part of the silent עמידה.

יִהְיוּ לְרָצוֹן אִמְרֵי־פִי וְהֶגְיוֹן לִבִּי לְפָנֶיךָ, יהוה צוּרִי וְגוֹאֲלִי: תהלים יט

אֱלֹהַי ברכות יז.
נְצֹר לְשׁוֹנִי מֵרָע וּשְׂפָתַי מִדַּבֵּר מִרְמָה
וְלִמְקַלְלַי נַפְשִׁי תִדֹּם, וְנַפְשִׁי כֶּעָפָר לַכֹּל תִּהְיֶה.
פְּתַח לִבִּי בְּתוֹרָתֶךָ, וּבְמִצְוֹתֶיךָ תִּרְדֹּף נַפְשִׁי.
וְכָל הַחוֹשְׁבִים עָלַי רָעָה
מְהֵרָה הָפֵר עֲצָתָם וְקַלְקֵל מַחֲשַׁבְתָּם.
עֲשֵׂה לְמַעַן שְׁמֶךָ, עֲשֵׂה לְמַעַן יְמִינֶךָ
עֲשֵׂה לְמַעַן קְדֻשָּׁתֶךָ, עֲשֵׂה לְמַעַן תּוֹרָתֶךָ.
לְמַעַן יֵחָלְצוּן יְדִידֶיךָ, הוֹשִׁיעָה יְמִינְךָ וַעֲנֵנִי: תהלים ס
יִהְיוּ לְרָצוֹן אִמְרֵי־פִי וְהֶגְיוֹן לִבִּי לְפָנֶיךָ, יהוה צוּרִי וְגוֹאֲלִי: תהלים יט

Bow, take three steps back, then bow, first left, then right, then center, while saying:

עֹשֶׂה שָׁלוֹם בִּמְרוֹמָיו
הוּא יַעֲשֶׂה שָׁלוֹם עָלֵינוּ וְעַל כָּל יִשְׂרָאֵל, וְאִמְרוּ אָמֵן.

יְהִי רָצוֹן מִלְּפָנֶיךָ יהוה אֱלֹהֵינוּ וֵאלֹהֵי אֲבוֹתֵינוּ
שֶׁיִּבָּנֶה בֵּית הַמִּקְדָּשׁ בִּמְהֵרָה בְיָמֵינוּ
וְתֵן חֶלְקֵנוּ בְּתוֹרָתֶךָ
וְשָׁם נַעֲבָדְךָ בְּיִרְאָה כִּימֵי עוֹלָם וּכְשָׁנִים קַדְמוֹנִיּוֹת.
וְעָרְבָה לַיהוה מִנְחַת יְהוּדָה וִירוּשָׁלָםִ כִּימֵי עוֹלָם וּכְשָׁנִים קַדְמוֹנִיּוֹת: מלאכי ג

On days when תחנון *is not said, the* שליח ציבור *says* קדיש שלם *on page 291.*

Rav. The wording of the morning's *Sim Shalom* is an extension of the themes recited in the preceding *Birkat Kohanim*. But the *kohanim* never give their blessing when

AVINU MALKENU

On fast days, except days when Taḥanun is not said
(see list on page 288), Avinu Malkenu is said.

The Ark is opened.

אָבִֽינוּ מַלְכֵּֽנוּ Our Father, our King, we have sinned before You.

Our Father, our King, we have no king but You.

Our Father, our King, deal kindly with us for the sake of Your name.

Our Father our King, bless us with a good year.

Our Father, our King, nullify all harsh decrees against us.

Our Father, our King, nullify the plans of those who hate us.

Our Father, our King, thwart the counsel of our enemies.

Our Father, our King, rid us of every oppressor and adversary.

Our Father, our King, close the mouths of our adversaries and accusers.

Our Father, our King, eradicate pestilence, sword, famine, captivity and destruction, iniquity and eradication from the people of Your covenant.

Our Father, our King, withhold the plague from Your heritage.

Our Father, our King, forgive and pardon all our iniquities.

Our Father, our King, wipe away and remove our transgressions and sins from Your sight.

Our Father, our King, erase in Your abundant mercy all records of our sins.

The following nine sentences are said responsively, first by the Leader, then by the congregation:

Our Father, our King, bring us back to You in perfect repentance.

Our Father, our King, send a complete healing to the sick of Your people.

Our Father, our King, tear up the evil decree against us.

Our Father, our King, remember us with a memory of favorable deeds before You.

Our Father, our King, remember us for a good life.

Our Father, our King, remember us for redemption and salvation.

Our Father, our King, remember us for livelihood and sustenance.

אבינו מלכנו

On fast days, except days when תחנון *is not said (see list on page 289),* אבינו מלכנו *is said.*

The ארון קודש *is opened.*

אָבִינוּ מַלְכֵּנוּ, חָטָאנוּ לְפָנֶיךָ.
אָבִינוּ מַלְכֵּנוּ, אֵין לָנוּ מֶלֶךְ אֶלָּא אָתָּה.
אָבִינוּ מַלְכֵּנוּ, עֲשֵׂה עִמָּנוּ לְמַעַן שְׁמֶךָ.
אָבִינוּ מַלְכֵּנוּ, בָּרֵךְ עָלֵינוּ שָׁנָה טוֹבָה.
אָבִינוּ מַלְכֵּנוּ, בַּטֵּל מֵעָלֵינוּ כָּל גְּזֵרוֹת קָשׁוֹת.
אָבִינוּ מַלְכֵּנוּ, בַּטֵּל מַחְשְׁבוֹת שׂוֹנְאֵינוּ.
אָבִינוּ מַלְכֵּנוּ, הָפֵר עֲצַת אוֹיְבֵינוּ.
אָבִינוּ מַלְכֵּנוּ, כַּלֵּה כָּל צַר וּמַשְׂטִין מֵעָלֵינוּ.
אָבִינוּ מַלְכֵּנוּ, סְתֹם פִּיּוֹת מַשְׂטִינֵנוּ וּמְקַטְרְגֵינוּ.
אָבִינוּ מַלְכֵּנוּ, כַּלֵּה דֶּבֶר וְחֶרֶב וְרָעָב וּשְׁבִי וּמַשְׁחִית וְעָוֹן וּשְׁמַד מִבְּנֵי בְרִיתֶךָ.
אָבִינוּ מַלְכֵּנוּ, מְנַע מַגֵּפָה מִנַּחֲלָתֶךָ.
אָבִינוּ מַלְכֵּנוּ, סְלַח וּמְחַל לְכָל עֲוֹנוֹתֵינוּ.
אָבִינוּ מַלְכֵּנוּ, מְחֵה וְהַעֲבֵר פְּשָׁעֵינוּ וְחַטֹּאתֵינוּ מִנֶּגֶד עֵינֶיךָ.
אָבִינוּ מַלְכֵּנוּ, מְחֹק בְּרַחֲמֶיךָ הָרַבִּים כָּל שִׁטְרֵי חוֹבוֹתֵינוּ.

The following nine sentences are said responsively, first by the שליח ציבור*, then by the* קהל*:*

אָבִינוּ מַלְכֵּנוּ, הַחֲזִירֵנוּ בִּתְשׁוּבָה שְׁלֵמָה לְפָנֶיךָ.
אָבִינוּ מַלְכֵּנוּ, שְׁלַח רְפוּאָה שְׁלֵמָה לְחוֹלֵי עַמֶּךָ.
אָבִינוּ מַלְכֵּנוּ, קְרַע רֹעַ גְּזַר דִּינֵנוּ.
אָבִינוּ מַלְכֵּנוּ, זָכְרֵנוּ בְּזִכָּרוֹן טוֹב לְפָנֶיךָ.
אָבִינוּ מַלְכֵּנוּ, זָכְרֵנוּ לְחַיִּים טוֹבִים.
אָבִינוּ מַלְכֵּנוּ, זָכְרֵנוּ לִגְאֻלָּה וִישׁוּעָה.
אָבִינוּ מַלְכֵּנוּ, זָכְרֵנוּ לְפַרְנָסָה וְכַלְכָּלָה.

Our Father, our King, remember us for merit.
Our Father, our King, remember us for pardon and forgiveness.

End of responsive reading.

Our Father, our King, let salvation soon flourish for us.
Our Father, our King, raise the honor of Your people Israel.
Our Father, our King, raise the honor of Your anointed.
Our Father, our King, fill our hands with Your blessings.
Our Father, our King, fill our storehouses with abundance.
Our Father, our King, hear our voice, pity and be compassionate to us.
Our Father, our King, accept, with compassion and favor, our prayer.
Our Father, our King, open the gates of heaven to our prayer.
Our Father, our King, remember that we are dust.
Our Father, our King, please do not turn us away from You empty-handed.
Our Father, our King, may this moment be a moment of compassion and a time of favor before You.
Our Father, our King, have pity on us, our children and our infants.
Our Father, our King, act for the sake of those who were killed for Your holy name.
Our Father, our King, act for the sake of those who were slaughtered for proclaiming Your Unity.
Our Father, our King, act for the sake of those who went through fire and water to sanctify Your name.
Our Father, our King, avenge before our eyes the spilt blood of Your servants.
Our Father, our King, act for Your sake, if not for ours.
Our Father, our King, act for Your sake, and save us.
Our Father, our King, act for the sake of Your abundant compassion.
Our Father, our King, act for the sake of Your great, mighty and awesome name by which we are called.
▸ Our Father, our King, be gracious to us and answer us, though we have no worthy deeds; act with us in charity and loving-kindness and save us.

The Ark is closed.

אָבִינוּ מַלְכֵּנוּ, זָכְרֵנוּ לִזְכֻיּוֹת.
אָבִינוּ מַלְכֵּנוּ, זָכְרֵנוּ לִסְלִיחָה וּמְחִילָה.

End of responsive reading.

אָבִינוּ מַלְכֵּנוּ, הַצְמַח לָנוּ יְשׁוּעָה בְּקָרוֹב.
אָבִינוּ מַלְכֵּנוּ, הָרֵם קֶרֶן יִשְׂרָאֵל עַמֶּךָ.
אָבִינוּ מַלְכֵּנוּ, הָרֵם קֶרֶן מְשִׁיחֶךָ.
אָבִינוּ מַלְכֵּנוּ, מַלֵּא יָדֵינוּ מִבִּרְכוֹתֶיךָ.
אָבִינוּ מַלְכֵּנוּ, מַלֵּא אֲסָמֵינוּ שָׂבָע.
אָבִינוּ מַלְכֵּנוּ, שְׁמַע קוֹלֵנוּ, חוּס וְרַחֵם עָלֵינוּ.
אָבִינוּ מַלְכֵּנוּ, קַבֵּל בְּרַחֲמִים וּבְרָצוֹן אֶת תְּפִלָּתֵנוּ.
אָבִינוּ מַלְכֵּנוּ, פְּתַח שַׁעֲרֵי שָׁמַיִם לִתְפִלָּתֵנוּ.
אָבִינוּ מַלְכֵּנוּ, זְכֹר כִּי עָפָר אֲנָחְנוּ.
אָבִינוּ מַלְכֵּנוּ, נָא אַל תְּשִׁיבֵנוּ רֵיקָם מִלְּפָנֶיךָ.
אָבִינוּ מַלְכֵּנוּ, תְּהֵא הַשָּׁעָה הַזֹּאת שְׁעַת רַחֲמִים וְעֵת רָצוֹן מִלְּפָנֶיךָ.
אָבִינוּ מַלְכֵּנוּ, חֲמֹל עָלֵינוּ וְעַל עוֹלָלֵינוּ וְטַפֵּנוּ.
אָבִינוּ מַלְכֵּנוּ, עֲשֵׂה לְמַעַן הֲרוּגִים עַל שֵׁם קָדְשֶׁךָ.
אָבִינוּ מַלְכֵּנוּ, עֲשֵׂה לְמַעַן טְבוּחִים עַל יִחוּדֶךָ.
אָבִינוּ מַלְכֵּנוּ, עֲשֵׂה לְמַעַן בָּאֵי בָאֵשׁ וּבַמַּיִם עַל קִדּוּשׁ שְׁמֶךָ.
אָבִינוּ מַלְכֵּנוּ, נְקֹם לְעֵינֵינוּ נִקְמַת דַּם עֲבָדֶיךָ הַשָּׁפוּךְ.
אָבִינוּ מַלְכֵּנוּ, עֲשֵׂה לְמַעַנְךָ אִם לֹא לְמַעֲנֵנוּ.
אָבִינוּ מַלְכֵּנוּ, עֲשֵׂה לְמַעַנְךָ וְהוֹשִׁיעֵנוּ.
אָבִינוּ מַלְכֵּנוּ, עֲשֵׂה לְמַעַן רַחֲמֶיךָ הָרַבִּים.
אָבִינוּ מַלְכֵּנוּ, עֲשֵׂה לְמַעַן שִׁמְךָ הַגָּדוֹל הַגִּבּוֹר וְהַנּוֹרָא שֶׁנִּקְרָא עָלֵינוּ.
◄ אָבִינוּ מַלְכֵּנוּ, חָנֵּנוּ וַעֲנֵנוּ, כִּי אֵין בָּנוּ מַעֲשִׂים
עֲשֵׂה עִמָּנוּ צְדָקָה וָחֶסֶד וְהוֹשִׁיעֵנוּ.

The ארון קודש *is closed.*

TAḤANUN

Taḥanun is not said on Erev Shabbat. It is also not said on the following days: Rosh Ḥodesh, Tisha B'Av, Tu B'Av, and the preceding afternoons.

Taḥanun is also not said: on the occasion of a Brit Mila, either where the brit will take place or where the father, Sandek or Mohel are present; if a groom is present (and some say, a bride) on the day of his wedding or during the week of Sheva Berakhot; in a house of mourning.

LOWERING THE HEAD

Say while sitting; in the presence of a Torah scroll say until "in sudden shame," leaning forward and resting one's head on the left arm (unless you are wearing tefillin on the left arm, in which case rest on the right arm out of respect for the tefillin).

וַיֹּאמֶר דָּוִד David said to Gad, "I am in great distress. *II Sam. 24*
Let us fall into God's hand, for His mercy is great;
but do not let me fall into the hand of man."

Compassionate and gracious One, I have sinned before You.
Lord, full of compassion, have compassion on me
and accept my pleas.

Lord, do not rebuke me in Your anger *Ps. 6*
or chastise me in Your wrath.
Be gracious to me, Lord, for I am weak.
Heal me, Lord, for my bones are in agony.
My soul is in anguish, and You, O Lord – how long?
Turn, Lord, set my soul free; save me for the sake of Your love.
For no one remembers You when he is dead.
Who can praise You from the grave? I am weary with my sighing.
Every night I drench my bed, I soak my couch with my tears.
My eye grows dim from grief, worn out because of all my foes.
Leave me, all you evildoers,
for the Lord has heard the sound of my weeping.
The Lord has heard my pleas. The Lord will accept my prayer.
All my enemies will be shamed and utterly dismayed.
They will turn back in sudden shame.

Sit upright.

סדר תחנון

תחנון is not said on ערב שבת. It is also not said on the following days: ראש חודש, תשעה באב, ט״ו באב, and the preceding afternoons.

תחנון is also not said: on the occasion of a ברית מילה, either where the ברית will take place or where the father, סנדק or מוהל are present; if a חתן is present (and some say, a כלה) on the day of his wedding or during the week of שבע ברכות; in a house of mourning.

נפילת אפיים

Say while sitting; in the presence of a ספר תורה say until יֵבֹשׁוּ רָגַע, leaning forward and resting one's head on the left arm (unless you are wearing תפילין on the left arm, in which case rest on the right arm out of respect for the תפילין).

וַיֹּאמֶר דָּוִד אֶל־גָּד, צַר־לִי מְאֹד   שמואל ב׳ כד
נִפְּלָה־נָּא בְיַד־יהוה, כִּי רַבִּים רַחֲמָו, וּבְיַד־אָדָם אַל־אֶפֹּלָה:

רַחוּם וְחַנּוּן, חָטָאתִי לְפָנֶיךָ.
יהוה מָלֵא רַחֲמִים, רַחֵם עָלַי וְקַבֵּל תַּחֲנוּנָי.

יהוה, אַל־בְּאַפְּךָ תוֹכִיחֵנִי, וְאַל־בַּחֲמָתְךָ תְיַסְּרֵנִי: תהלים ו
חָנֵּנִי יהוה, כִּי אֻמְלַל אָנִי, רְפָאֵנִי יהוה, כִּי נִבְהֲלוּ עֲצָמָי:
וְנַפְשִׁי נִבְהֲלָה מְאֹד, וְאַתְּ יהוה, עַד־מָתָי:
שׁוּבָה יהוה, חַלְּצָה נַפְשִׁי, הוֹשִׁיעֵנִי לְמַעַן חַסְדֶּךָ:
כִּי אֵין בַּמָּוֶת זִכְרֶךָ, בִּשְׁאוֹל מִי יוֹדֶה־לָּךְ:
יָגַעְתִּי בְּאַנְחָתִי, אַשְׂחֶה בְכָל־לַיְלָה מִטָּתִי
בְּדִמְעָתִי עַרְשִׂי אַמְסֶה:
עָשְׁשָׁה מִכַּעַס עֵינִי, עָתְקָה בְּכָל־צוֹרְרָי:
סוּרוּ מִמֶּנִּי כָּל־פֹּעֲלֵי אָוֶן, כִּי־שָׁמַע יהוה קוֹל בִּכְיִי:
שָׁמַע יהוה תְּחִנָּתִי, יהוה תְּפִלָּתִי יִקָּח:
יֵבֹשׁוּ וְיִבָּהֲלוּ מְאֹד כָּל־אֹיְבָי, יָשֻׁבוּ יֵבֹשׁוּ רָגַע:

Sit upright.

שׁוֹמֵר יִשְׂרָאֵל Guardian of Israel,
guard the remnant of Israel,
and let not Israel perish, who declare, "Listen, Israel."
Guardian of a unique nation, guard the remnant of a unique people,
and let not that unique nation perish, who proclaim the unity of
Your name [saying], "The LORD is our God, the LORD is One."
Guardian of a holy nation, guard the remnant of that holy people,
and let not the holy nation perish, who three times repeat
the threefold declaration of holiness to the Holy One.
You who are conciliated by calls for compassion and placated by pleas,
be conciliated and placated toward an afflicted generation,
for there is no other help.
Our Father, our King, be gracious to us and answer us,
though we have no worthy deeds;
act with us in charity and loving-kindness and save us.

Stand at ▲.

וַאֲנַחְנוּ We do not know ▲what to do, but our eyes are turned to You. *II Chr. 12*
Remember, LORD, Your compassion and loving-kindness, for they are *Ps. 25*
everlasting. May Your loving-kindness, LORD, be with us, for we have put *Ps. 33*
our hope in You. Do not hold against us the sins of those who came before *Ps. 79*
us. May Your mercies meet us swiftly, for we have been brought very low.
Be gracious to us, LORD, be gracious to us, for we are sated with contempt. *Ps. 123*
In wrath, remember mercy. He knows our nature; He remembers that *Hab. 3* *Ps. 103*
we are dust. ▸ Help us, God of our salvation, for the sake of the glory of *Ps. 79*
Your name. Save us and grant atonement for our sins for Your name's sake.

FULL KADDISH

Leader: יִתְגַּדַּל Magnified and sanctified may His great name be,
in the world He created by His will.
May He establish His kingdom
in your lifetime and in your days,
and in the lifetime of all the house of Israel,
swiftly and soon – and say: Amen.

All: May His great name be blessed for ever and all time.

שׁוֹמֵר יִשְׂרָאֵל, שְׁמֹר שְׁאֵרִית יִשְׂרָאֵל, וְאַל יֹאבַד יִשְׂרָאֵל
הָאוֹמְרִים שְׁמַע יִשְׂרָאֵל.
שׁוֹמֵר גּוֹי אֶחָד, שְׁמֹר שְׁאֵרִית עַם אֶחָד, וְאַל יֹאבַד גּוֹי אֶחָד
הַמְיַחֲדִים שִׁמְךָ, יהוה אֱלֹהֵינוּ יהוה אֶחָד.
שׁוֹמֵר גּוֹי קָדוֹשׁ, שְׁמֹר שְׁאֵרִית עַם קָדוֹשׁ, וְאַל יֹאבַד גּוֹי קָדוֹשׁ
הַמְשַׁלְּשִׁים בְּשָׁלֹשׁ קְדֻשּׁוֹת לְקָדוֹשׁ.
מִתְרַצֶּה בְּרַחֲמִים וּמִתְפַּיֵּס בְּתַחֲנוּנִים, הִתְרַצֵּה וְהִתְפַּיֵּס לְדוֹר עָנִי
כִּי אֵין עוֹזֵר.
אָבִינוּ מַלְכֵּנוּ, חָנֵּנוּ וַעֲנֵנוּ, כִּי אֵין בָּנוּ מַעֲשִׂים
עֲשֵׂה עִמָּנוּ צְדָקָה וָחֶסֶד וְהוֹשִׁיעֵנוּ.

Stand at *.

וַאֲנַחְנוּ לֹא נֵדַע *מַה־נַּעֲשֶׂה, כִּי עָלֶיךָ עֵינֵינוּ: זְכֹר־רַחֲמֶיךָ יהוה דברי הימים ב׳ יב תהלים כה
וַחֲסָדֶיךָ, כִּי מֵעוֹלָם הֵמָּה: יְהִי־חַסְדְּךָ יהוה עָלֵינוּ, כַּאֲשֶׁר יִחַלְנוּ לָךְ: תהלים לג
אַל־תִּזְכָּר־לָנוּ עֲוֹנֹת רִאשֹׁנִים, מַהֵר יְקַדְּמוּנוּ רַחֲמֶיךָ, כִּי דַלּוֹנוּ מְאֹד: תהלים עט
חָנֵּנוּ יהוה חָנֵּנוּ, כִּי־רַב שָׂבַעְנוּ בוּז: בְּרֹגֶז רַחֵם תִּזְכּוֹר: כִּי־הוּא יָדַע תהלים קכג חבקוק ג תהלים קג
יִצְרֵנוּ, זָכוּר כִּי־עָפָר אֲנָחְנוּ: ◂ עָזְרֵנוּ אֱלֹהֵי יִשְׁעֵנוּ עַל־דְּבַר כְּבוֹד־ תהלים עט
שְׁמֶךָ, וְהַצִּילֵנוּ וְכַפֵּר עַל־חַטֹּאתֵינוּ לְמַעַן שְׁמֶךָ:

קדיש שלם

ש״ץ: יִתְגַּדַּל וְיִתְקַדַּשׁ שְׁמֵהּ רַבָּא (קהל: אָמֵן)
בְּעָלְמָא דִּי בְרָא כִרְעוּתֵהּ
וְיַמְלִיךְ מַלְכוּתֵהּ
בְּחַיֵּיכוֹן וּבְיוֹמֵיכוֹן וּבְחַיֵּי דְכָל בֵּית יִשְׂרָאֵל
בַּעֲגָלָא וּבִזְמַן קָרִיב, וְאִמְרוּ אָמֵן. (קהל: אָמֵן)

קהל וש״ץ: יְהֵא שְׁמֵהּ רַבָּא מְבָרַךְ לְעָלַם וּלְעָלְמֵי עָלְמַיָּא.

Leader: Blessed and praised,
glorified and exalted, raised and honored,
uplifted and lauded be
the name of the Holy One, blessed be He,
beyond any blessing,
song, praise and consolation
uttered in the world –
and say: Amen.

May the prayers and pleas of all Israel
be accepted by their Father in heaven –
and say: Amen.

May there be great peace from heaven,
and life for us and all Israel –
and say: Amen.

Bow, take three steps back, as if taking leave of the Divine Presence, then bow, first left, then right, then center, while saying:
May He who makes peace in His high places,
make peace for us and all Israel –
and say: Amen.

Stand while saying Aleinu. Bow at ▾.
עָלֵינוּ It is our duty to praise the Master of all,
and ascribe greatness to the Author of creation,
who has not made us like the nations of the lands
nor placed us like the families of the earth;
who has not made our portion like theirs,
nor our destiny like all their multitudes.
(For they worship vanity and emptiness,
and pray to a god who cannot save.)
▾But we bow in worship
and thank the Supreme King of kings,
the Holy One, blessed be He,

ש״ץ: יִתְבָּרַךְ וְיִשְׁתַּבַּח וְיִתְפָּאַר
וְיִתְרוֹמַם וְיִתְנַשֵּׂא וְיִתְהַדָּר וְיִתְעַלֶּה וְיִתְהַלָּל
שְׁמֵהּ דְּקֻדְשָׁא בְּרִיךְ הוּא (קהל: בְּרִיךְ הוּא)
לְעֵלָּא מִן כָּל בִּרְכָתָא
וְשִׁירָתָא, תֻּשְׁבְּחָתָא וְנֶחֱמָתָא
דַּאֲמִירָן בְּעָלְמָא וְאִמְרוּ אָמֵן. (קהל: אָמֵן)

תִּתְקַבַּל צְלוֹתְהוֹן וּבָעוּתְהוֹן דְּכָל יִשְׂרָאֵל
קֳדָם אֲבוּהוֹן דִּי בִשְׁמַיָּא, וְאִמְרוּ אָמֵן. (קהל: אָמֵן)

יְהֵא שְׁלָמָא רַבָּא מִן שְׁמַיָּא
וְחַיִּים, עָלֵינוּ וְעַל כָּל יִשְׂרָאֵל
וְאִמְרוּ אָמֵן. (קהל: אָמֵן)

Bow, take three steps back, as if taking leave of the Divine Presence, then bow, first left, then right, then center, while saying:

עֹשֶׂה שָׁלוֹם בִּמְרוֹמָיו
הוּא יַעֲשֶׂה שָׁלוֹם עָלֵינוּ
וְעַל כָּל יִשְׂרָאֵל, וְאִמְרוּ אָמֵן. (קהל: אָמֵן)

Stand while saying עָלֵינוּ*. Bow at* ▾.

עָלֵינוּ לְשַׁבֵּחַ לַאֲדוֹן הַכֹּל, לָתֵת גְּדֻלָּה לְיוֹצֵר בְּרֵאשִׁית
שֶׁלֹּא עָשָׂנוּ כְּגוֹיֵי הָאֲרָצוֹת
וְלֹא שָׂמָנוּ כְּמִשְׁפְּחוֹת הָאֲדָמָה
שֶׁלֹּא שָׂם חֶלְקֵנוּ כָּהֶם וְגוֹרָלֵנוּ כְּכָל הֲמוֹנָם.
(שֶׁהֵם מִשְׁתַּחֲוִים לְהֶבֶל וָרִיק וּמִתְפַּלְלִים אֶל אֵל לֹא יוֹשִׁיעַ.)
▾וַאֲנַחְנוּ כּוֹרְעִים וּמִשְׁתַּחֲוִים וּמוֹדִים
לִפְנֵי מֶלֶךְ מַלְכֵי הַמְּלָכִים, הַקָּדוֹשׁ בָּרוּךְ הוּא

who extends the heavens and establishes the earth,
whose throne of glory is in the heavens above,
and whose power's Presence is in the highest of heights.
He is our God; there is no other.
Truly He is our King, there is none else,
as it is written in His Torah:
"You shall know and take to heart this day that the LORD is God, *Deut. 4*
in heaven above and on earth below. There is no other."

Therefore, we place our hope in You, LORD our God,
that we may soon see the glory of Your power,
when You will remove abominations from the earth,
and idols will be utterly destroyed,
when the world will be perfected
under the sovereignty of the Almighty,
when all humanity will call on Your name,
to turn all the earth's wicked toward You.
All the world's inhabitants will realize and know
that to You every knee must bow
and every tongue swear loyalty.
Before You, LORD our God, they will kneel and bow down
and give honor to Your glorious name.
They will all accept the yoke of Your kingdom,
and You will reign over them soon and for ever.
For the kingdom is Yours, and to all eternity You will reign in glory,
as it is written in Your Torah:
"The LORD will reign for ever and ever." *Ex. 15*
▸ And it is said: "Then the LORD shall be King over all the earth; *Zech. 14*
on that day the LORD shall be One and His name One."

Some add:

Have no fear of sudden terror or of the ruin when it overtakes the wicked. *Prov. 3*
Devise your strategy, but it will be thwarted; propose your plan, *Is. 8*
but it will not stand, for God is with us.
When you grow old, I will still be the same. *Is. 46*
When your hair turns gray, I will still carry you.
I made you, I will bear you, I will carry you, and I will rescue you.

שֶׁהוּא נוֹטֶה שָׁמַיִם וְיוֹסֵד אָרֶץ, וּמוֹשַׁב יְקָרוֹ בַּשָּׁמַיִם מִמַּעַל
וּשְׁכִינַת עֻזּוֹ בְּגָבְהֵי מְרוֹמִים.
הוּא אֱלֹהֵינוּ, אֵין עוֹד.
אֱמֶת מַלְכֵּנוּ, אֶפֶס זוּלָתוֹ
כַּכָּתוּב בְּתוֹרָתוֹ
וְיָדַעְתָּ הַיּוֹם וַהֲשֵׁבֹתָ אֶל־לְבָבֶךָ דברים ד
כִּי יהוה הוּא הָאֱלֹהִים בַּשָּׁמַיִם מִמַּעַל וְעַל־הָאָרֶץ מִתָּחַת, אֵין עוֹד:

עַל כֵּן נְקַוֶּה לְּךָ יהוה אֱלֹהֵינוּ, לִרְאוֹת מְהֵרָה בְּתִפְאֶרֶת עֻזֶּךָ
לְהַעֲבִיר גִּלּוּלִים מִן הָאָרֶץ, וְהָאֱלִילִים כָּרוֹת יִכָּרֵתוּן
לְתַקֵּן עוֹלָם בְּמַלְכוּת שַׁדַּי.
וְכָל בְּנֵי בָשָׂר יִקְרְאוּ בִשְׁמֶךָ לְהַפְנוֹת אֵלֶיךָ כָּל רִשְׁעֵי אָרֶץ.
יַכִּירוּ וְיֵדְעוּ כָּל יוֹשְׁבֵי תֵבֵל
כִּי לְךָ תִּכְרַע כָּל בֶּרֶךְ, תִּשָּׁבַע כָּל לָשׁוֹן.
לְפָנֶיךָ יהוה אֱלֹהֵינוּ יִכְרְעוּ וְיִפֹּלוּ, וְלִכְבוֹד שִׁמְךָ יְקָר יִתֵּנוּ
וִיקַבְּלוּ כֻלָּם אֶת עֹל מַלְכוּתֶךָ
וְתִמְלֹךְ עֲלֵיהֶם מְהֵרָה לְעוֹלָם וָעֶד.
כִּי הַמַּלְכוּת שֶׁלְּךָ הִיא וּלְעוֹלְמֵי עַד תִּמְלֹךְ בְּכָבוֹד
כַּכָּתוּב בְּתוֹרָתֶךָ, יהוה יִמְלֹךְ לְעֹלָם וָעֶד: שמות טו
► וְנֶאֱמַר, וְהָיָה יהוה לְמֶלֶךְ עַל־כָּל־הָאָרֶץ זכריה יד
בַּיּוֹם הַהוּא יִהְיֶה יהוה אֶחָד וּשְׁמוֹ אֶחָד:

Some add:

אַל־תִּירָא מִפַּחַד פִּתְאֹם וּמִשֹּׁאַת רְשָׁעִים כִּי תָבֹא: משלי ג
עֻצוּ עֵצָה וְתֻפָר, דַּבְּרוּ דָבָר וְלֹא יָקוּם, כִּי עִמָּנוּ אֵל: ישעיה ח
וְעַד־זִקְנָה אֲנִי הוּא, וְעַד־שֵׂיבָה אֲנִי אֶסְבֹּל ישעיה מו
אֲנִי עָשִׂיתִי וַאֲנִי אֶשָּׂא וַאֲנִי אֶסְבֹּל וַאֲמַלֵּט:

MOURNER'S KADDISH

The following prayer, said by mourners, requires the presence of a minyan.
A transliteration can be found on page 1141.

A transliteration can be found on page 1141.

Mourner: יִתְגַּדַּל Magnified and sanctified
may His great name be,
in the world He created by His will.
May He establish His kingdom
in your lifetime and in your days,
and in the lifetime
of all the house of Israel,
swiftly and soon –
and say: Amen.

All: May His great name be blessed for ever and all time.

Mourner: Blessed and praised,
glorified and exalted,
raised and honored,
uplifted and lauded
be the name of the Holy One,
blessed be He,
beyond any blessing,
song, praise and consolation
uttered in the world –
and say: Amen.

May there be great peace from heaven,
and life for us and all Israel –
and say: Amen.

Bow, take three steps back, as if taking leave of the Divine Presence,
then bow, first left, then right, then center, while saying:

May He who makes peace in His high places,
make peace for us and all Israel –
and say: Amen.

קדיש יתום

The following prayer, said by mourners, requires the presence of a מנין.
A transliteration can be found on page 1141.

אבל: יִתְגַּדַּל וְיִתְקַדַּשׁ שְׁמֵהּ רַבָּא (קהל: אָמֵן)
בְּעָלְמָא דִּי בְרָא כִרְעוּתֵהּ
וְיַמְלִיךְ מַלְכוּתֵהּ
בְּחַיֵּיכוֹן וּבְיוֹמֵיכוֹן וּבְחַיֵּי דְכָל בֵּית יִשְׂרָאֵל
בַּעֲגָלָא וּבִזְמַן קָרִיב
וְאִמְרוּ אָמֵן. (קהל: אָמֵן)

קהל ואבל: יְהֵא שְׁמֵהּ רַבָּא מְבָרַךְ לְעָלַם וּלְעָלְמֵי עָלְמַיָּא.

אבל: יִתְבָּרַךְ וְיִשְׁתַּבַּח וְיִתְפָּאַר
וְיִתְרוֹמַם וְיִתְנַשֵּׂא וְיִתְהַדָּר וְיִתְעַלֶּה וְיִתְהַלָּל
שְׁמֵהּ דְּקֻדְשָׁא בְּרִיךְ הוּא (קהל: בְּרִיךְ הוּא)
לְעֵלָּא מִן כָּל בִּרְכָתָא
וְשִׁירָתָא, תֻּשְׁבְּחָתָא וְנֶחֱמָתָא
דַּאֲמִירָן בְּעָלְמָא
וְאִמְרוּ אָמֵן. (קהל: אָמֵן)

יְהֵא שְׁלָמָא רַבָּא מִן שְׁמַיָּא
וְחַיִּים, עָלֵינוּ וְעַל כָּל יִשְׂרָאֵל
וְאִמְרוּ אָמֵן. (קהל: אָמֵן)

Bow, take three steps back, as if taking leave of the Divine Presence, then bow, first left, then right, then center, while saying:

עֹשֶׂה שָׁלוֹם בִּמְרוֹמָיו
הוּא יַעֲשֶׂה שָׁלוֹם עָלֵינוּ וְעַל כָּל יִשְׂרָאֵל
וְאִמְרוּ אָמֵן. (קהל: אָמֵן)

Ma'ariv for Weekdays

On Motza'ei Shabbat, many congregations recite Psalms 144 and 67 before Ma'ariv (page 340).

וְהוּא רַחוּם He is compassionate.[B] *Ps. 78*
He forgives iniquity and does not destroy.
Repeatedly He suppresses His anger, not rousing His full wrath.
LORD, save! May the King, answer us on the day we call. *Ps. 20*

1.	Introduction	בָּרְכוּ אֶת יהוה	*Bless the LORD*	Calling the community together
2.	First blessing	הַמַּעֲרִיב עֲרָבִים	*Who brings on evenings*	Hashem as Creator and His love for humanity
3.	Second blessing	אַהֲבַת עוֹלָם	*With everlasting love*	Hashem's love of Israel in particular
4.	*Shema*	שְׁמַע יִשְׂרָאֵל	*Listen, Israel*	1. Acceptance of His sovereignty 2. Acceptance of His commandments 3. The exodus from Egypt
5.	Third blessing	אֱמֶת וֶאֱמוּנָה... גָּאַל יִשְׂרָאֵל	*True and faithful... who redeemed Israel*	Hashem as Redeemer
6.	Fourth blessing	הַשְׁכִּיבֵנוּ... הַפּוֹרֵשׂ סֻכַּת שָׁלוֹם...	*Help us lie down... Who spreads a canopy of peace...*	Peace
7.	*Amida*			

BIUR TEFILLA • בִּיאוּר תְּפִלָּה

וְהוּא רַחוּם – *He is compassionate.* A number of reasons are offered for this introduction. One of them simply suggests the possibility that we committed some wrong during the course of the day. This introductory statement declares, before we pray, our belief that Hashem will forgive us. This verse was chosen, it was suggested, because it has 13 words in it, reminiscent of the 13 *Middot* (attributes of forgiveness) of Hashem. In any event, consider it a way to get into the right frame of mind before the *Ḥazan* calls us together; a way of gathering our thoughts and being mindful. Pause a moment, to focus.

מעריב לחול

On מוצאי שבת*, many congregations recite Psalms 144 and 67 before* מעריב *(page 341).*

תהלים עח וְהוּא רַחוּם, יְכַפֵּר עָוֹן וְלֹא־יַשְׁחִית
וְהִרְבָּה לְהָשִׁיב אַפּוֹ, וְלֹא־יָעִיר כָּל־חֲמָתוֹ:
תהלים כ יהוה הוֹשִׁיעָה, הַמֶּלֶךְ יַעֲנֵנוּ בְיוֹם־קָרְאֵנוּ:

INTRODUCTION TO MA'ARIV

Ma'ariv is one of the three prayer times in the Jewish day. The times correspond to certain sacrificial rites that took place during the time of the *Beit HaMikdash* but their origins are said to date back to the times of the three Patriarchs, Avraham, Yitzḥak and Yaakov (*Berakhot* 26b). It has been suggested that the timing of each service also relates to the character and life experience of the Patriarch who established it. Avraham, the bold and assertive pioneer, is associated with the morning, and thus *Shaḥarit*. Yitzḥak, the one who never left Israel, but stayed and worked the Land, is associated with the afternoon and *Minḥa*. Yaakov's life, on the other hand, was filled with trials and tribulations, with uncertainty and clouds of darkness. Yaakov is the one who established *Ma'ariv*.

The phrase the Torah uses is "*vayifga baMakom*" (*Bereshit* 28:11), which in Rabbinic Hebrew could be read to mean, "He bumped into God." There are spiritual experiences we have when we are least expecting them – when we are alone, afraid, thinking of something else altogether. This was Yaakov's vision of prayer. Not everything in the life of the spirit is under our control. The great transformative experiences – love, a sudden sense of beauty, an upsurge of happiness – happen unpredictably and leave us, in Wordsworth's famous words, "surprised by joy." The glory of Yaakov's epiphany is that it happened at night, in the midst of fear and flight (Rabbi J. Sacks).

The nighttime hours are often a time of uncertainty, when the insecurities of our lives rear their heads the most. What better time to search out an encounter with the One who knows us best? Preoccupied with the successes or disappointments of our day, we enter into an intimate conversation with Hashem, finding friendship and support, and, perhaps, a transformative experience.

In terms of structure, the *Amida* lies at the core and climax of *Ma'ariv* as it does in all of the services. Before that lies the prayer popularly known simply as *Shema*, one of the most important in all of Jewish liturgy and life. It is bounded by two blessings on each side, thus forming one large unit consisting of two blessings, *Shema*, two more blessings, and then the *Amida*. The service ends with a number of brief concluding declarations. As in every service, each of the constituent parts is interconnected and related to the overall theme of the service. In short, there is an order or sequence, translated in Hebrew as *seder*, from which the name of this book, *Siddur*, derives.

BLESSINGS OF THE SHEMA

The Leader says the following, bowing at "Bless," standing straight at "the Lord"; the congregation, followed by the Leader, responds, bowing at "Bless," standing straight at "the Lord":

Leader: BLESS
the Lord, the blessed One.

Congregation: Bless the Lord, the blessed One,
for ever and all time.

Leader: Bless the Lord, the blessed One,
for ever and all time.

בָּרוּךְ Blessed are You, Lord our God, King of the Universe,
who by His word brings on evenings,
by His wisdom opens the gates of heaven,
with understanding makes time change and the seasons rotate,
and by His will orders the stars in their constellations in the sky.
He creates day and night,
rolling away the light before the darkness,
and darkness before the light.
▸ He makes the day pass and brings on night,
distinguishing day from night:
the Lord of hosts is His name.
May the living and forever enduring God rule over us for all time.
Blessed are You, Lord,
who brings on evenings.[1]

---

the attributes of day and night together, for both reflect the miracle of creation and its single source, Hashem, whose unity we will declare momentarily. Night and day; sun and stars; past, present, and future are all part of one continuum. The world is whole and there is a pattern and there is a plan. We need only find our place in it.

קריאת שמע וברכותיה

The שליח ציבור *says the following, bowing at* בָּרְכוּ*, standing straight at* ה׳*; the* קהל*, followed by the* שליח ציבור*, responds, bowing at* בָּרוּךְ*, standing straight at* ה׳*:*

ש״ץ: בָּרְכוּ

אֶת יהוה הַמְבֹרָךְ.

קהל: בָּרוּךְ יהוה הַמְבֹרָךְ לְעוֹלָם וָעֶד.

ש״ץ: בָּרוּךְ יהוה הַמְבֹרָךְ לְעוֹלָם וָעֶד.

בָּרוּךְ אַתָּה יהוה אֱלֹהֵינוּ מֶלֶךְ הָעוֹלָם
אֲשֶׁר בִּדְבָרוֹ מַעֲרִיב עֲרָבִים
בְּחָכְמָה פּוֹתֵחַ שְׁעָרִים
וּבִתְבוּנָה מְשַׁנֶּה עִתִּים וּמַחֲלִיף אֶת הַזְּמַנִּים
וּמְסַדֵּר אֶת הַכּוֹכָבִים בְּמִשְׁמְרוֹתֵיהֶם בָּרָקִיעַ כִּרְצוֹנוֹ.
בּוֹרֵא יוֹם וָלָיְלָה, גּוֹלֵל אוֹר מִפְּנֵי חֹשֶׁךְ וְחֹשֶׁךְ מִפְּנֵי אוֹר
◂ וּמַעֲבִיר יוֹם וּמֵבִיא לָיְלָה, וּמַבְדִּיל בֵּין יוֹם וּבֵין לָיְלָה
יהוה צְבָאוֹת שְׁמוֹ.
אֵל חַי וְקַיָּם תָּמִיד, יִמְלֹךְ עָלֵינוּ לְעוֹלָם וָעֶד.
בָּרוּךְ אַתָּה יהוה, הַמַּעֲרִיב עֲרָבִים.[ע]

IYUN TEFILLA • עיון תפילה

הַמַּעֲרִיב עֲרָבִים – *Who brings on evenings.* If in the morning we were conscious of the sun and the beginning of the day, here we are aware of the ending of the day and the descent of darkness which envelops us. The Gemara (*Berakhot* 11b) says that we must recall

אַהֲבַת עוֹלָם With everlasting love
have You loved Your people, the house of Israel.
You have taught us Torah and commandments,
decrees and laws of justice.
Therefore, LORD our God, when we lie down and when we rise up[B]
we will speak of Your decrees, rejoicing in the words of Your Torah
and Your commandments for ever.
▸ For they are our life and the length of our days;
on them will we meditate day and night.[B]
May You never take away Your love from us.
Blessed are You, LORD, who loves His people Israel.

The Shema must be said with intense concentration.
When not with a minyan, say:
God, faithful King!

The following verse should be said aloud, while covering the eyes with the right hand:

Listen, Israel: the LORD is our God, the LORD is One.

Deut. 6

Quietly: Blessed be the name of His glorious kingdom for ever and all time.

וְאָהַבְתָּ Love the LORD your God with all your heart, with all your soul, and with all your might. These words which I command you today shall be on your heart. Teach them repeatedly to your children, speaking of them when you sit at home and when you travel on the way, when you lie down and when you rise. Bind them as a sign on your hand, and they shall be an emblem between your eyes. Write them on the doorposts of your house and gates. Deut. 6

וְהָיָה If you indeed heed My commandments with which I charge you today, to love the LORD your God and worship Him with all your heart Deut. 11

---

to enter the Promised Land, the very first message to the people was the centrality of Torah in their lives and the need to "*meditate upon them day and night*... do not fear and do not lose resolve, for Hashem is with you wherever you will go" (*Yehoshua* 1:8–9). By reciting the *Shema* a second time today, we fulfill that mandate. And in doing so, we pray that Hashem will be with us wherever we will go, physically and emotionally.

אַהֲבַת עוֹלָם בֵּית יִשְׂרָאֵל עַמְּךָ אָהָבְתָּ
תּוֹרָה וּמִצְוֹת, חֻקִּים וּמִשְׁפָּטִים, אוֹתָנוּ לִמַּדְתָּ
עַל כֵּן יהוה אֱלֹהֵינוּ בְּשָׁכְבֵנוּ וּבְקוּמֵנוּ נָשִׂיחַ בְּחֻקֶּיךָ
וְנִשְׂמַח בְּדִבְרֵי תוֹרָתֶךָ וּבְמִצְוֹתֶיךָ לְעוֹלָם וָעֶד
• כִּי הֵם חַיֵּינוּ וְאֹרֶךְ יָמֵינוּ, וּבָהֶם נֶהְגֶּה יוֹמָם וָלָיְלָה.
וְאַהֲבָתְךָ אַל תָּסִיר מִמֶּנּוּ לְעוֹלָמִים.
בָּרוּךְ אַתָּה יהוה, אוֹהֵב עַמּוֹ יִשְׂרָאֵל.

The שמע must be said with intense concentration.
When not with a מנין, say:

אֵל מֶלֶךְ נֶאֱמָן

The following verse should be said aloud, while covering the eyes with the right hand:

דברים ו **שְׁמַע יִשְׂרָאֵל, יהוה אֱלֹהֵינוּ, יהוה | אֶחָד:**

Quietly בָּרוּךְ שֵׁם כְּבוֹד מַלְכוּתוֹ לְעוֹלָם וָעֶד.

דברים ו וְאָהַבְתָּ אֵת יהוה אֱלֹהֶיךָ, בְּכָל־לְבָבְךָ וּבְכָל־נַפְשְׁךָ וּבְכָל־
מְאֹדֶךָ: וְהָיוּ הַדְּבָרִים הָאֵלֶּה, אֲשֶׁר אָנֹכִי מְצַוְּךָ הַיּוֹם, עַל־לְבָבֶךָ:
וְשִׁנַּנְתָּם לְבָנֶיךָ וְדִבַּרְתָּ בָּם, בְּשִׁבְתְּךָ בְּבֵיתֶךָ וּבְלֶכְתְּךָ בַדֶּרֶךְ,
וּבְשָׁכְבְּךָ וּבְקוּמֶךָ: וּקְשַׁרְתָּם לְאוֹת עַל־יָדֶךָ וְהָיוּ לְטֹטָפֹת בֵּין
עֵינֶיךָ: וּכְתַבְתָּם עַל־מְזֻזוֹת בֵּיתֶךָ וּבִשְׁעָרֶיךָ:

דברים יא וְהָיָה אִם־שָׁמֹעַ תִּשְׁמְעוּ אֶל־מִצְוֹתַי אֲשֶׁר אָנֹכִי מְצַוֶּה אֶתְכֶם
הַיּוֹם, לְאַהֲבָה אֶת־יהוה אֱלֹהֵיכֶם וּלְעָבְדוֹ, בְּכָל־לְבַבְכֶם וּבְכָל־

BIUR TEFILLA • ביאור תפילה

בְּשָׁכְבֵנוּ וּבְקוּמֵנוּ – *When we lie down and when we rise up.* These two Hebrew words anticipate the words of the *Shema* and the reason that we recite it twice a day: "when you go to sleep and when you rise up."

וּבָהֶם נֶהְגֶּה יוֹמָם וָלָיְלָה – *On them will we meditate day and night.* The source of this line is a verse from *Yehoshua*. As *Benei Yisrael* were about

and with all your soul, I will give rain in your land in its season, the early and late rain; and you shall gather in your grain, wine and oil. I will give grass in your field for your cattle, and you shall eat and be satisfied. Be careful lest your heart be tempted and you go astray and worship other gods, bowing down to them. Then the LORD's anger will flare against you and He will close the heavens so that there will be no rain. The land will not yield its crops, and you will perish swiftly from the good land that the LORD is giving you. Therefore, set these, My words, on your heart and soul. Bind them as a sign on your hand, and they shall be an emblem between your eyes. Teach them to your children, speaking of them when you sit at home and when you travel on the way, when you lie down and when you rise. Write them on the doorposts of your house and gates, so that you and your children may live long in the land that the LORD swore to your ancestors to give them, for as long as the heavens are above the earth.

וַיֹּאמֶר The LORD spoke[H] to Moses, saying: Speak to the Israelites *Num. 15*
and tell them to make tassels on the corners of their garments for all generations. They shall attach to the tassel at each corner a thread of blue. This shall be your tassel, and you shall see it and remember all of the LORD's commandments and keep them, not straying after your heart and after your eyes, following your own sinful desires. Thus you will be reminded to keep all My commandments, and be holy to your God. I am the LORD your God, who brought you out of the land of Egypt to be your God. I am the LORD your God.

True –

The Leader repeats:

▸ The LORD your God is true –

HILKHOT TEFILLA • הלכות תפילה

וַיֹּאמֶר – *Spoke.* The primary halakhic function of the third paragraph of the *Shema* at this time is to recall the exodus from Egypt. The exodus is the rationale provided for many mitzvot in the Torah. It lies at the heart of our chosenness, and at the heart of our need to be empathetic toward others less fortunate.

נַפְשְׁכֶם: וְנָתַתִּי מְטַר־אַרְצְכֶם בְּעִתּוֹ, יוֹרֶה וּמַלְקוֹשׁ, וְאָסַפְתָּ דְגָנֶךָ וְתִירֹשְׁךָ וְיִצְהָרֶךָ: וְנָתַתִּי עֵשֶׂב בְּשָׂדְךָ לִבְהֶמְתֶּךָ, וְאָכַלְתָּ וְשָׂבָעְתָּ: הִשָּׁמְרוּ לָכֶם פֶּן־יִפְתֶּה לְבַבְכֶם, וְסַרְתֶּם וַעֲבַדְתֶּם אֱלֹהִים אֲחֵרִים וְהִשְׁתַּחֲוִיתֶם לָהֶם: וְחָרָה אַף־יהוה בָּכֶם, וְעָצַר אֶת־הַשָּׁמַיִם וְלֹא־יִהְיֶה מָטָר, וְהָאֲדָמָה לֹא תִתֵּן אֶת־יְבוּלָהּ, וַאֲבַדְתֶּם מְהֵרָה מֵעַל הָאָרֶץ הַטֹּבָה אֲשֶׁר יהוה נֹתֵן לָכֶם: וְשַׂמְתֶּם אֶת־דְּבָרַי אֵלֶּה עַל־לְבַבְכֶם וְעַל־נַפְשְׁכֶם, וּקְשַׁרְתֶּם אֹתָם לְאוֹת עַל־יֶדְכֶם, וְהָיוּ לְטוֹטָפֹת בֵּין עֵינֵיכֶם: וְלִמַּדְתֶּם אֹתָם אֶת־בְּנֵיכֶם לְדַבֵּר בָּם, בְּשִׁבְתְּךָ בְּבֵיתֶךָ וּבְלֶכְתְּךָ בַדֶּרֶךְ, וּבְשָׁכְבְּךָ וּבְקוּמֶךָ: וּכְתַבְתָּם עַל־מְזוּזוֹת בֵּיתֶךָ וּבִשְׁעָרֶיךָ: לְמַעַן יִרְבּוּ יְמֵיכֶם וִימֵי בְנֵיכֶם עַל הָאֲדָמָה אֲשֶׁר נִשְׁבַּע יהוה לַאֲבֹתֵיכֶם לָתֵת לָהֶם, כִּימֵי הַשָּׁמַיִם עַל־הָאָרֶץ:

במדבר טו וַיֹּאמֶר יהוה אֶל־מֹשֶׁה לֵּאמֹר: דַּבֵּר אֶל־בְּנֵי יִשְׂרָאֵל וְאָמַרְתָּ אֲלֵהֶם, וְעָשׂוּ לָהֶם צִיצִת עַל־כַּנְפֵי בִגְדֵיהֶם לְדֹרֹתָם, וְנָתְנוּ עַל־צִיצִת הַכָּנָף פְּתִיל תְּכֵלֶת: וְהָיָה לָכֶם לְצִיצִת, וּרְאִיתֶם אֹתוֹ וּזְכַרְתֶּם אֶת־כָּל־מִצְוֹת יהוה וַעֲשִׂיתֶם אֹתָם, וְלֹא תָתוּרוּ אַחֲרֵי לְבַבְכֶם וְאַחֲרֵי עֵינֵיכֶם, אֲשֶׁר־אַתֶּם זֹנִים אַחֲרֵיהֶם: לְמַעַן תִּזְכְּרוּ וַעֲשִׂיתֶם אֶת־כָּל־מִצְוֹתָי, וִהְיִיתֶם קְדֹשִׁים לֵאלֹהֵיכֶם: אֲנִי יהוה אֱלֹהֵיכֶם, אֲשֶׁר הוֹצֵאתִי אֶתְכֶם מֵאֶרֶץ מִצְרַיִם, לִהְיוֹת לָכֶם לֵאלֹהִים, אֲנִי יהוה אֱלֹהֵיכֶם:

אֱמֶת

The שליח ציבור *repeats:*

‹ יהוה אֱלֹהֵיכֶם אֱמֶת

וֶאֱמוּנָה – and faithful[1] is all this,
and firmly established for us
that He is the LORD our God,
and there is none besides Him,
and that we, Israel, are His people.
He is our King,
who redeems us from the hand of kings
and delivers us from the grasp of all tyrants.
He is our God,
who on our behalf repays our foes
and brings just retribution on our mortal enemies;
who performs great deeds beyond understanding
and wonders beyond number;
who kept us alive, *Ps. 66*
not letting our foot slip;
who led us on the high places of our enemies,
raising our pride above all our foes;
who did miracles for us
and brought vengeance against Pharaoh;
who performed signs and wonders
in the land of Ham's children;
who smote in His wrath
all the firstborn of Egypt,
and brought out His people Israel from their midst
into everlasting freedom;

---

goes to sleep, the soul rises to heaven and although Hashem orders her to return to the body, she does not wish to do so. Hashem responds: "Man placed his faith in Me at night by placing his soul in My hands for safekeeping." Hashem therefore remains faithful to man, protects his soul overnight, and a miracle takes place in the morning when the soul is restored and he awakes feeling refreshed and invigorated, ready to begin a new day. (Rashi)

וֶאֱמוּנָה ע כָּל זֹאת וְקַיָּם עָלֵינוּ
כִּי הוּא יהוה אֱלֹהֵינוּ וְאֵין זוּלָתוֹ
וַאֲנַחְנוּ יִשְׂרָאֵל עַמּוֹ.
הַפּוֹדֵנוּ מִיַּד מְלָכִים
מַלְכֵּנוּ הַגּוֹאֲלֵנוּ מִכַּף כָּל הֶעָרִיצִים.
הָאֵל הַנִּפְרָע לָנוּ מִצָּרֵינוּ
וְהַמְשַׁלֵּם גְּמוּל לְכָל אוֹיְבֵי נַפְשֵׁנוּ.
הָעוֹשֶׂה גְדוֹלוֹת עַד אֵין חֵקֶר
וְנִפְלָאוֹת עַד אֵין מִסְפָּר
תהלים סו הַשָּׂם נַפְשֵׁנוּ בַּחַיִּים
וְלֹא־נָתַן לַמּוֹט רַגְלֵנוּ:
הַמַּדְרִיכֵנוּ עַל בָּמוֹת אוֹיְבֵינוּ
וַיָּרֶם קַרְנֵנוּ עַל כָּל שׂוֹנְאֵינוּ.
הָעוֹשֶׂה לָּנוּ נִסִּים וּנְקָמָה בְּפַרְעֹה
אוֹתוֹת וּמוֹפְתִים בְּאַדְמַת בְּנֵי חָם.
הַמַּכֶּה בְעֶבְרָתוֹ כָּל בְּכוֹרֵי מִצְרָיִם
וַיּוֹצֵא אֶת עַמּוֹ יִשְׂרָאֵל מִתּוֹכָם לְחֵרוּת עוֹלָם.

IYUN TEFILLA • עיון תפילה

וֶאֱמוּנָה – *And faithful.* Just as in the morning there was a blessing on God's presence in history, so too do we say one here. The difference is that the one in the morning refers specifically to the redemption from Egypt which took place in the past. Here, however, in keeping with the theme of the evening, our focus shifts to the future, about redemption yet to come. (*Magen Avraham*)

וֶאֱמוּנָה – *Faithful.* After a long day of work and pressures, there is no person whose soul does not ache. When the person

who led His children through the divided Reed Sea,
plunging their pursuers and enemies into the depths.
When His children saw His might,
they gave praise and thanks to His name,
▸ and willingly accepted His Sovereignty.
Moses and the children of Israel
then sang a song to You
with great joy,
and they all exclaimed:

מִי־כָמֹכָה "Who is like You, LORD, *Ex. 15*
among the mighty?
Who is like You, majestic in holiness,
awesome in praises, doing wonders?"

▸ Your children beheld Your majesty
as You parted the sea before Moses.
"This is my God!" they responded,
and then said:

"The LORD shall reign for ever and ever." *Ex. 15*

▸ And it is said,

"For the LORD has redeemed Jacob *Jer. 31*
and rescued him from a power
stronger than his own."

Blessed are You, LORD,
who redeemed Israel.

הַשְׁכִּיבֵנוּ Help us lie down, O LORD our God, in peace,
and rise up, O our King, to life.
Spread over us Your canopy of peace.
Direct us with Your good counsel,[A]
and save us for the sake of Your name.

הַמַּעֲבִיר בָּנָיו בֵּין גִּזְרֵי יַם סוּף
אֶת רוֹדְפֵיהֶם וְאֶת שׂוֹנְאֵיהֶם בִּתְהוֹמוֹת טִבַּע
וְרָאוּ בָנָיו גְּבוּרָתוֹ, שִׁבְּחוּ וְהוֹדוּ לִשְׁמוֹ
· וּמַלְכוּתוֹ בְּרָצוֹן קִבְּלוּ עֲלֵיהֶם.
מֹשֶׁה וּבְנֵי יִשְׂרָאֵל, לְךָ עָנוּ שִׁירָה בְּשִׂמְחָה רַבָּה
וְאָמְרוּ כֻלָּם

מִי־כָמֹכָה בָּאֵלִם יהוה — שמות טו
מִי כָּמֹכָה נֶאְדָּר בַּקֹּדֶשׁ
נוֹרָא תְהִלֹּת עֹשֵׂה פֶלֶא:

· מַלְכוּתְךָ רָאוּ בָנֶיךָ, בּוֹקֵעַ יָם לִפְנֵי מֹשֶׁה
זֶה אֵלִי עָנוּ, וְאָמְרוּ
יהוה יִמְלֹךְ לְעֹלָם וָעֶד: — שמות טו
· וְנֶאֱמַר
כִּי־פָדָה יהוה אֶת־יַעֲקֹב, וּגְאָלוֹ מִיַּד חָזָק מִמֶּנּוּ: — ירמיהו לא
בָּרוּךְ אַתָּה יהוה, גָּאַל יִשְׂרָאֵל.

הַשְׁכִּיבֵנוּ יהוה אֱלֹהֵינוּ לְשָׁלוֹם
וְהַעֲמִידֵנוּ מַלְכֵּנוּ לְחַיִּים
וּפְרֹשׂ עָלֵינוּ סֻכַּת שְׁלוֹמֶךָ, וְתַקְּנֵנוּ בְּעֵצָה טוֹבָה[א] מִלְּפָנֶיךָ
וְהוֹשִׁיעֵנוּ לְמַעַן שְׁמֶךָ.

ANI TEFILLA • אני תפילה

וְתַקְּנֵנוּ בְּעֵצָה טוֹבָה – *Direct us with Your good counsel.* At night, we are more open to possibilities, more open to divine inspiration. I pray that I will be open to Your direction and advice. (*Iyun Tefilla*, Rabbi Yaakov Tzvi Mecklenburg)

Shield us and remove from us every enemy,
plague, sword, famine and sorrow.
Remove the adversary from before and behind us.[B]
Shelter us in the shadow of Your wings,
for You, God, are our Guardian and Deliverer;
You, God, are a gracious and compassionate King.
▸ Guard our going out and our coming in,
for life and peace, from now and for ever.
Blessed are You, LORD,
who guards His people Israel for ever.

In Israel in some communities outside Israel
the service continues with Half Kaddish on page 314.

בָּרוּךְ Blessed be the LORD for ever. Amen and Amen.[B] *Ps. 89*
Blessed from Zion be the LORD *Ps. 135*
who dwells in Jerusalem. Halleluya!
Blessed be the LORD, God of Israel, *Ps. 72*
who alone does wondrous things.
Blessed be His glorious name for ever,
and may the whole earth be filled with His glory. Amen and Amen.
May the glory of the LORD endure for ever; *Ps. 104*
may the LORD rejoice in His works.
May the name of the LORD be blessed now and for all time. *Ps. 113*
For the sake of His great name *1 Sam. 12*
the LORD will not abandon His people,
for the LORD vowed to make you a people of His own.

---

afraid to remain there after dark; as such, this passage was recited in place of the *Shemoneh Esreh* (Abudarham). In a related vein, it may be that latecomers to the service would have ended up praying after everyone else finished, and so this section was added for everyone to say so that the latecomers could catch up; everyone would pray the *Amida* together, and then be able to leave together (Tosafot). It thus served as a kind of *Pesukei DeZimra* for those who recited it. Although social conditions have changed, the prayer was nevertheless retained, although in Israel and in some Diaspora communities it is omitted and the service continues with *Kaddish*.

וְהָגֵן בַּעֲדֵנוּ, וְהָסֵר מֵעָלֵינוּ אוֹיֵב, דֶּבֶר וְחֶרֶב וְרָעָב וְיָגוֹן
וְהָסֵר שָׂטָן מִלְּפָנֵינוּ וּמֵאַחֲרֵינוּ, וּבְצֵל כְּנָפֶיךָ תַּסְתִּירֵנוּ
כִּי אֵל שׁוֹמְרֵנוּ וּמַצִּילֵנוּ אָתָּה
כִּי אֵל מֶלֶךְ חַנּוּן וְרַחוּם אָתָּה.
› וּשְׁמֹר צֵאתֵנוּ וּבוֹאֵנוּ לְחַיִּים וּלְשָׁלוֹם מֵעַתָּה וְעַד עוֹלָם.
בָּרוּךְ אַתָּה יהוה, שׁוֹמֵר עַמּוֹ יִשְׂרָאֵל לָעַד.

In ארץ ישראל *and in some communities outside* ארץ ישראל *the service continues with* חצי קדיש *on page 315.*

תהלים פט בָּרוּךְ יהוה לְעוֹלָם, אָמֵן וְאָמֵן:
תהלים קלה בָּרוּךְ יהוה מִצִּיּוֹן, שֹׁכֵן יְרוּשָׁלָםִ, הַלְלוּיָהּ:
תהלים עב בָּרוּךְ יהוה אֱלֹהִים אֱלֹהֵי יִשְׂרָאֵל, עֹשֵׂה נִפְלָאוֹת לְבַדּוֹ:
וּבָרוּךְ שֵׁם כְּבוֹדוֹ לְעוֹלָם
וְיִמָּלֵא כְבוֹדוֹ אֶת־כָּל־הָאָרֶץ, אָמֵן וְאָמֵן:
תהלים קד יְהִי כְבוֹד יהוה לְעוֹלָם, יִשְׂמַח יהוה בְּמַעֲשָׂיו:
תהלים קיג יְהִי שֵׁם יהוה מְבֹרָךְ מֵעַתָּה וְעַד־עוֹלָם:
שמואל א, יב כִּי לֹא־יִטֹּשׁ יהוה אֶת־עַמּוֹ בַּעֲבוּר שְׁמוֹ הַגָּדוֹל
כִּי הוֹאִיל יהוה לַעֲשׂוֹת אֶתְכֶם לוֹ לְעָם:

BIUR TEFILLA • ביאור תפילה

בָּרוּךְ יהוה לְעוֹלָם אָמֵן וְאָמֵן – *Blessed be the Lord for ever. Amen and Amen.* The source of this passage is not entirely clear. It contains the four-letter name of Hashem 18 times, corresponding to the 18 blessings of *Shemoneh Esreh*. Its origin is said to have been a substitute for that prayer during Babylonian times, when synagogues were located outside the city and people were

BIUR TEFILLA • ביאור תפילה

וְהָסֵר שָׂטָן מִלְּפָנֵינוּ וּמֵאַחֲרֵינוּ – *Remove the adversary from before and behind us.* The *Satan* is the evil inclination (*Bava Batra* 16a), the disposition that we sometimes have to do what we know in our heart of hearts we should not do. We therefore ask here for help with our own inclinations which, especially at night, can seem to overwhelm us.

When all the people saw [God's wonders] they fell on their faces and said: "The LORD, He is God; the LORD, He is God." *I Kings 18*
Then the LORD shall be King over all the earth; *Zech. 14*
on that day the LORD shall be One and His name One.
May Your love, LORD, be upon us, as we have put our hope in You. *Ps. 33*
Save us, LORD our God, gather us *Ps. 106*
and deliver us from the nations,
to thank Your holy name, and glory in Your praise.
All the nations You made shall come and bow before You, LORD, *Ps. 86*
and pay honor to Your name,
for You are great and You perform wonders:
You alone are God.
We, Your people, the flock of Your pasture, will praise You for ever. *Ps. 79*
For all generations we will relate Your praise.

בָּרוּךְ Blessed is the LORD by day, blessed is the LORD by night.
Blessed is the LORD when we lie down;
blessed is the LORD when we rise.
For in Your hand are the souls of the living and the dead,
[as it is written:] "In His hand is every living soul, *Job 12*
and the breath of all mankind."
Into Your hand I entrust my spirit: *Ps. 31*
You redeemed me, LORD, God of truth.

---

somewhere we forget the reasons that we began the journey, or alternatively we miss important stops along the way. *Tefilla* is a journey. The moment of encounter is upon us. Perhaps what the verse is also telling us is *vayifga baMakom*, not that he encountered the place, but he encountered, *HaMakom*, God. The key to that encounter is the realization that one can return to the spot where "my fathers prayed."

ANI TEFILLA • אני תפילה

Prayer enlightens man about his needs. It tells man the story of hidden hopes and expectations. It teaches him how to behold the vision and how to strive in order to realize this vision, when to be satisfied with what one possesses, when to reach out for more. In a word, man finds his need-awareness, himself, in prayer. (Rabbi J.B. Soloveitchik)

וַיַּרְא כָּל־הָעָם וַיִּפְּלוּ עַל־פְּנֵיהֶם מלכים א, יח
וַיֹּאמְרוּ, יהוה הוּא הָאֱלֹהִים, יהוה הוּא הָאֱלֹהִים:
וְהָיָה יהוה לְמֶלֶךְ עַל־כָּל־הָאָרֶץ זכריה יד
בַּיּוֹם הַהוּא יִהְיֶה יהוה אֶחָד וּשְׁמוֹ אֶחָד:
יְהִי־חַסְדְּךָ יהוה עָלֵינוּ, כַּאֲשֶׁר יִחַלְנוּ לָךְ: תהלים לג
הוֹשִׁיעֵנוּ יהוה אֱלֹהֵינוּ, וְקַבְּצֵנוּ מִן־הַגּוֹיִם תהלים קו
לְהוֹדוֹת לְשֵׁם קָדְשֶׁךָ, לְהִשְׁתַּבֵּחַ בִּתְהִלָּתֶךָ:
כָּל־גּוֹיִם אֲשֶׁר עָשִׂיתָ, יָבוֹאוּ וְיִשְׁתַּחֲווּ לְפָנֶיךָ, אֲדֹנָי תהלים פו
וִיכַבְּדוּ לִשְׁמֶךָ:
כִּי־גָדוֹל אַתָּה וְעֹשֵׂה נִפְלָאוֹת, אַתָּה אֱלֹהִים לְבַדֶּךָ:
וַאֲנַחְנוּ עַמְּךָ וְצֹאן מַרְעִיתֶךָ, נוֹדֶה לְּךָ לְעוֹלָם תהלים עט
לְדוֹר וָדֹר נְסַפֵּר תְּהִלָּתֶךָ:

בָּרוּךְ יהוה בַּיּוֹם, בָּרוּךְ יהוה בַּלָּיְלָה
בָּרוּךְ יהוה בְּשָׁכְבֵנוּ, בָּרוּךְ יהוה בְּקוּמֵנוּ.
כִּי בְיָדְךָ נַפְשׁוֹת הַחַיִּים וְהַמֵּתִים.
אֲשֶׁר בְּיָדוֹ נֶפֶשׁ כָּל־חָי, וְרוּחַ כָּל־בְּשַׂר־אִישׁ: איוב יב
בְּיָדְךָ אַפְקִיד רוּחִי, פָּדִיתָה אוֹתִי יהוה אֵל אֱמֶת: תהלים לא

ANI TEFILLA • אני תפילה

Yaakov, who established *Ma'ariv*, is said to have been journeying from Be'er Sheva to Ḥaran when suddenly "*vayifga bamakom* – he encountered the place" (*Bereshit* 28:10–11). The Gemara (*Ḥullin* 91b) relates that when he reached Ḥaran it occurred to him that along the way "I passed by the place where my fathers had prayed. How could I not have prayed there myself?" And so he returned to that spot, and miraculously the ground between the two places contracted, and that is why the verse immediately says "he encountered the place." Sometimes in our haste to get

Our God in heaven, bring unity to Your name,
establish Your kingdom constantly
and reign over us for ever and all time.

יִרְאוּ May our eyes see, our hearts rejoice,
and our souls be glad in Your true salvation,
when Zion is told, "Your God reigns."
The LORD is King, the LORD was King,
the LORD will be King for ever and all time.
▸ For sovereignty is Yours, and to all eternity You will reign in glory,
for we have no king but You.
Blessed are You, LORD,
the King who in His constant glory will reign over us
and all His creation for ever and all time.

HALF KADDISH

Leader: יִתְגַּדַּל Magnified and sanctified may His great name be,
in the world He created by His will.
May He establish His kingdom
in your lifetime and in your days,
and in the lifetime of all the house of Israel,
swiftly and soon – and say: Amen.

All: May His great name[A] be blessed for ever and all time.

Leader: Blessed and praised, glorified and exalted,
raised and honored, uplifted and lauded
be the name of the Holy One, blessed be He,
beyond any blessing, song, praise and consolation
uttered in the world – and say: Amen.

ANI TEFILLA · אני תפילה

יְהֵא שְׁמֵהּ רַבָּא – *May His great name.* Whoever says *yeheh shemeh raba*... with all his strength, the Heavenly Court rips up any negative decree against him (*Shabbat* 119b). "With all his strength" – with all of His strength, for through the power of one's *tefilla*, one strengthens the hand of Hashem to destroy the decree. (Maharsha)

אֱלֹהֵינוּ שֶׁבַּשָּׁמַיִם, יַחֵד שִׁמְךָ וְקַיֵּם מַלְכוּתְךָ תָּמִיד
וּמְלֹךְ עָלֵינוּ לְעוֹלָם וָעֶד.

יִרְאוּ עֵינֵינוּ וְיִשְׂמַח לִבֵּנוּ, וְתָגֵל נַפְשֵׁנוּ בִּישׁוּעָתְךָ בֶּאֱמֶת
בֶּאֱמֹר לְצִיּוֹן מָלַךְ אֱלֹהָיִךְ.
יהוה מֶלֶךְ, יהוה מָלָךְ, יהוה יִמְלֹךְ לְעֹלָם וָעֶד.
◄ כִּי הַמַּלְכוּת שֶׁלְּךָ הִיא, וּלְעוֹלְמֵי עַד תִּמְלֹךְ בְּכָבוֹד
כִּי אֵין לָנוּ מֶלֶךְ אֶלָּא אָתָּה.
בָּרוּךְ אַתָּה יהוה
הַמֶּלֶךְ בִּכְבוֹדוֹ תָּמִיד, יִמְלֹךְ עָלֵינוּ לְעוֹלָם וָעֶד
וְעַל כָּל מַעֲשָׂיו.

חצי קדיש

ש״ץ: יִתְגַּדַּל וְיִתְקַדַּשׁ שְׁמֵהּ רַבָּא (קהל: אָמֵן)
בְּעָלְמָא דִּי בְרָא כִרְעוּתֵהּ
וְיַמְלִיךְ מַלְכוּתֵהּ
בְּחַיֵּיכוֹן וּבְיוֹמֵיכוֹן וּבְחַיֵּי דְכָל בֵּית יִשְׂרָאֵל
בַּעֲגָלָא וּבִזְמַן קָרִיב, וְאִמְרוּ אָמֵן. (קהל: אָמֵן)

קהל וש״ץ: יְהֵא שְׁמֵהּ רַבָּא[א] מְבָרַךְ לְעָלַם וּלְעָלְמֵי עָלְמַיָּא.

ש״ץ: יִתְבָּרַךְ וְיִשְׁתַּבַּח וְיִתְפָּאַר וְיִתְרוֹמַם וְיִתְנַשֵּׂא
וְיִתְהַדָּר וְיִתְעַלֶּה וְיִתְהַלָּל
שְׁמֵהּ דְּקֻדְשָׁא בְּרִיךְ הוּא (קהל: בְּרִיךְ הוּא)
לְעֵלָּא מִן כָּל בִּרְכָתָא
וְשִׁירָתָא, תֻּשְׁבְּחָתָא וְנֶחֱמָתָא
דַּאֲמִירָן בְּעָלְמָא, וְאִמְרוּ אָמֵן. (קהל: אָמֵן)

THE AMIDA

The following prayer, until "in former years" on page 330, is said silently, standing with feet together. Take three steps forward and at the points indicated by ▾, bend the knees at the first word, bow at the second, and stand straight before saying God's name.

O Lord, open my lips, so that my mouth may declare Your praise. *Ps. 51*

PATRIARCHS

▾בָּרוּךְ▾ Blessed are You, Lord our God and God of our fathers,
God of Abraham, God of Isaac and God of Jacob;
the great, mighty and awesome God, God Most High,
who bestows acts of loving-kindness and creates all,
who remembers the loving-kindness of the fathers
and will bring a Redeemer to their children's children
for the sake of His name, in love.
King, Helper, Savior, Shield:
▾Blessed are You, Lord, Shield of Abraham.

DIVINE MIGHT

אַתָּה גִּבּוֹר You are eternally mighty, Lord.
You give life to the dead
and have great power to save.

In Israel: He causes the dew to fall.

He sustains the living with loving-kindness,
and with great compassion revives the dead.
He supports the fallen, heals the sick, sets captives free,
and keeps His faith with those who sleep in the dust.
Who is like You, Master of might,
and who can compare to You,
O King who brings death and gives life,
and makes salvation grow?
Faithful are You to revive the dead.
Blessed are You, Lord,
who revives the dead.

עמידה

The following prayer, until קַדְמֹנִיּוֹת *on page 331, is said silently, standing with feet together. Take three steps forward and at the points indicated by* ˇ*, bend the knees at the first word, bow at the second, and stand straight before saying God's name.*

אֲדֹנָי, שְׂפָתַי תִּפְתָּח, וּפִי יַגִּיד תְּהִלָּתֶךָ: תהלים נא

אבות

ˇבָּרוּךְ אַתָּה יהוה, אֱלֹהֵינוּ וֵאלֹהֵי אֲבוֹתֵינוּ
אֱלֹהֵי אַבְרָהָם, אֱלֹהֵי יִצְחָק, וֵאלֹהֵי יַעֲקֹב
הָאֵל הַגָּדוֹל הַגִּבּוֹר וְהַנּוֹרָא, אֵל עֶלְיוֹן
גּוֹמֵל חֲסָדִים טוֹבִים, וְקוֹנֵה הַכֹּל
וְזוֹכֵר חַסְדֵי אָבוֹת
וּמֵבִיא גוֹאֵל לִבְנֵי בְנֵיהֶם לְמַעַן שְׁמוֹ בְּאַהֲבָה.
מֶלֶךְ עוֹזֵר וּמוֹשִׁיעַ וּמָגֵן.
ˇבָּרוּךְ אַתָּה יהוה, מָגֵן אַבְרָהָם.

גבורות

אַתָּה גִּבּוֹר לְעוֹלָם, אֲדֹנָי
מְחַיֵּה מֵתִים אַתָּה, רַב לְהוֹשִׁיעַ
בארץ ישראל: מוֹרִיד הַטָּל
מְכַלְכֵּל חַיִּים בְּחֶסֶד, מְחַיֵּה מֵתִים בְּרַחֲמִים רַבִּים
סוֹמֵךְ נוֹפְלִים, וְרוֹפֵא חוֹלִים, וּמַתִּיר אֲסוּרִים
וּמְקַיֵּם אֱמוּנָתוֹ לִישֵׁנֵי עָפָר.
מִי כָמוֹךָ, בַּעַל גְּבוּרוֹת, וּמִי דּוֹמֶה לָּךְ
מֶלֶךְ, מֵמִית וּמְחַיֶּה וּמַצְמִיחַ יְשׁוּעָה.
וְנֶאֱמָן אַתָּה לְהַחֲיוֹת מֵתִים.
בָּרוּךְ אַתָּה יהוה, מְחַיֵּה הַמֵּתִים.

HOLINESS

אַתָּה קָדוֹשׁ You are holy and Your name is holy,
and holy ones praise You daily, Selah!
Blessed are You, Lord, the holy God.

KNOWLEDGE

אַתָּה חוֹנֵן You grace humanity with knowledge
and teach mortals understanding.

On Motza'ei Shabbat say:

אַתָּה חוֹנַנְתָּנוּ You have graced us with the knowledge of Your Torah, and taught us to perform the statutes of Your will. You have distinguished, Lord our God, between sacred and profane, light and darkness, Israel and the nations, and between the seventh day and the six days of work. Our Father, our King, may the days approaching us bring peace; may we be free from all sin, cleansed from all iniquity, holding fast to our reverence of You. And

---

Grace us with the knowledge, understanding
and discernment that come from You.
Blessed are You, Lord, who graciously grants knowledge.

REPENTANCE

הֲשִׁיבֵנוּ Bring us back, our Father, to Your Torah.
Draw us near, our King, to Your service.
Lead us back to You in perfect repentance.
Blessed are You, Lord, who desires repentance.

FORGIVENESS

Strike the left side of the chest at °.

סְלַח לָנוּ Forgive us, our Father,
for we have °sinned.
Pardon us, our King,
for we have °transgressed;
for You pardon and forgive.
Blessed are You, Lord,
the gracious One who repeatedly forgives.

קדושת השם

אַתָּה קָדוֹשׁ וְשִׁמְךָ קָדוֹשׁ
וּקְדוֹשִׁים בְּכָל יוֹם יְהַלְלְוּךָ סֶּלָה.
בָּרוּךְ אַתָּה יהוה, הָאֵל הַקָּדוֹשׁ.

דעת

אַתָּה חוֹנֵן לְאָדָם דַּעַת, וּמְלַמֵּד לֶאֱנוֹשׁ בִּינָה.

On מוצאי שבת *say:*

אַתָּה חוֹנַנְתָּנוּ לְמַדַּע תּוֹרָתֶךָ, וַתְּלַמְּדֵנוּ לַעֲשׂוֹת חֻקֵּי רְצוֹנֶךָ, וַתַּבְדֵּל יהוה אֱלֹהֵינוּ בֵּין קֹדֶשׁ לְחֹל, בֵּין אוֹר לְחֹשֶׁךְ, בֵּין יִשְׂרָאֵל לָעַמִּים, בֵּין יוֹם הַשְּׁבִיעִי לְשֵׁשֶׁת יְמֵי הַמַּעֲשֶׂה. אָבִינוּ מַלְכֵּנוּ, הָחֵל עָלֵינוּ הַיָּמִים הַבָּאִים לִקְרָאתֵנוּ לְשָׁלוֹם, חֲשׂוּכִים מִכָּל חֵטְא וּמְנֻקִּים מִכָּל עָוֹן וּמְדֻבָּקִים בְּיִרְאָתֶךָ. וְ

חָנֵּנוּ מֵאִתְּךָ דֵּעָה בִּינָה וְהַשְׂכֵּל.
בָּרוּךְ אַתָּה יהוה, חוֹנֵן הַדָּעַת.

תשובה

הֲשִׁיבֵנוּ אָבִינוּ לְתוֹרָתֶךָ
וְקָרְבֵנוּ מַלְכֵּנוּ לַעֲבוֹדָתֶךָ
וְהַחֲזִירֵנוּ בִּתְשׁוּבָה שְׁלֵמָה לְפָנֶיךָ.
בָּרוּךְ אַתָּה יהוה, הָרוֹצֶה בִּתְשׁוּבָה.

סליחה

Strike the left side of the chest at °.

סְלַח לָנוּ אָבִינוּ כִּי °חָטָאנוּ
מְחַל לָנוּ מַלְכֵּנוּ כִּי °פָשָׁעְנוּ
כִּי מוֹחֵל וְסוֹלֵחַ אָתָּה.
בָּרוּךְ אַתָּה יהוה, חַנּוּן הַמַּרְבֶּה לִסְלֹחַ.

REDEMPTION

רְאֵה Look on our affliction,
plead our cause,
and redeem us soon for Your name's sake,
for You are a powerful Redeemer.
Blessed are You, LORD,
the Redeemer of Israel.

HEALING

רְפָאֵנוּ Heal us, LORD, and we shall be healed.
Save us and we shall be saved,
for You are our praise.
Bring complete recovery for all our ailments,

The following prayer for a sick person may be said here:
May it be Your will, O LORD my God and God of my ancestors, that You speedily send a complete recovery from heaven, a healing of both soul and body, to the patient (*name*), son/daughter of (*mother's name*) among the other afflicted of Israel.

---

for You, God, King,
are a faithful and compassionate Healer.
Blessed are You, LORD,
Healer of the sick of His people Israel.

PROSPERITY

בָּרֵךְ Bless this year for us, LORD our God,
and all its types of produce for good.
Grant blessing on the face of the earth,
and from its goodness satisfy us,
blessing our year as the best of years.
Blessed are You, LORD,
who blesses the years.

גאולה

רְאֵה בְעָנְיֵנוּ, וְרִיבָה רִיבֵנוּ
וּגְאָלֵנוּ מְהֵרָה לְמַעַן שְׁמֶךָ
כִּי גּוֹאֵל חָזָק אָתָּה.
בָּרוּךְ אַתָּה יהוה, גּוֹאֵל יִשְׂרָאֵל.

רפואה

רְפָאֵנוּ יהוה וְנֵרָפֵא
הוֹשִׁיעֵנוּ וְנִוָּשֵׁעָה
כִּי תְהִלָּתֵנוּ אָתָּה
וְהַעֲלֵה רְפוּאָה שְׁלֵמָה לְכָל מַכּוֹתֵינוּ

The following prayer for a sick person may be said here:

יְהִי רָצוֹן מִלְּפָנֶיךָ יהוה אֱלֹהַי וֵאלֹהֵי אֲבוֹתַי, שֶׁתִּשְׁלַח מְהֵרָה רְפוּאָה שְׁלֵמָה
מִן הַשָּׁמַיִם רְפוּאַת הַנֶּפֶשׁ וּרְפוּאַת הַגּוּף לַחוֹלֶה/לַחוֹלָה *name of patient*
בֶּן/בַּת *mother's name* בְּתוֹךְ שְׁאָר חוֹלֵי יִשְׂרָאֵל.

כִּי אֵל מֶלֶךְ רוֹפֵא נֶאֱמָן וְרַחֲמָן אָתָּה.
בָּרוּךְ אַתָּה יהוה, רוֹפֵא חוֹלֵי עַמּוֹ יִשְׂרָאֵל.

ברכת השנים

בָּרֵךְ עָלֵינוּ יהוה אֱלֹהֵינוּ אֶת הַשָּׁנָה הַזֹּאת
וְאֶת כָּל מִינֵי תְבוּאָתָהּ, לְטוֹבָה
וְתֵן בְּרָכָה עַל פְּנֵי הָאֲדָמָה
וְשַׂבְּעֵנוּ מִטּוּבָהּ
וּבָרֵךְ שְׁנָתֵנוּ כַּשָּׁנִים הַטּוֹבוֹת.
בָּרוּךְ אַתָּה יהוה, מְבָרֵךְ הַשָּׁנִים.

INGATHERING OF EXILES

תְּקַע Sound the great shofar for our freedom,
raise high the banner to gather our exiles,
and gather us together
from the four quarters of the earth.
Blessed are You, Lord,
who gathers the dispersed of His people Israel.

JUSTICE

הָשִׁיבָה Restore our judges as at first,
and our counselors as at the beginning,
and remove from us sorrow and sighing.
May You alone, Lord,
reign over us
with loving-kindness and compassion,
and vindicate us in justice.
Blessed are You, Lord,
the King who loves righteousness and justice.

AGAINST INFORMERS

וְלַמַּלְשִׁינִים For the slanderers
let there be no hope,
and may all wickedness
perish in an instant.
May all Your people's enemies swiftly be cut down.
May You swiftly uproot, crush, cast down
and humble the arrogant swiftly
in our days.
Blessed are You, Lord,
who destroys enemies and humbles the arrogant.

קבוץ גלויות

תְּקַע בְּשׁוֹפָר גָּדוֹל לְחֵרוּתֵנוּ
וְשָׂא נֵס לְקַבֵּץ גָּלֻיּוֹתֵינוּ
וְקַבְּצֵנוּ יַחַד מֵאַרְבַּע כַּנְפוֹת הָאָרֶץ.
בָּרוּךְ אַתָּה יהוה
מְקַבֵּץ נִדְחֵי עַמּוֹ יִשְׂרָאֵל.

השבת המשפט

הָשִׁיבָה שׁוֹפְטֵינוּ כְּבָרִאשׁוֹנָה
וְיוֹעֲצֵינוּ כְּבַתְּחִלָּה
וְהָסֵר מִמֶּנּוּ יָגוֹן וַאֲנָחָה
וּמְלֹךְ עָלֵינוּ אַתָּה יהוה לְבַדְּךָ בְּחֶסֶד וּבְרַחֲמִים
וְצַדְּקֵנוּ בַּמִּשְׁפָּט.
בָּרוּךְ אַתָּה יהוה
מֶלֶךְ אוֹהֵב צְדָקָה וּמִשְׁפָּט.

ברכת המינים

וְלַמַּלְשִׁינִים אַל תְּהִי תִקְוָה
וְכָל הָרִשְׁעָה כְּרֶגַע תֹּאבֵד
וְכָל אוֹיְבֵי עַמְּךָ מְהֵרָה יִכָּרֵתוּ
וְהַזֵּדִים מְהֵרָה תְעַקֵּר וּתְשַׁבֵּר וּתְמַגֵּר וְתַכְנִיעַ
בִּמְהֵרָה בְיָמֵינוּ.
בָּרוּךְ אַתָּה יהוה
שׁוֹבֵר אוֹיְבִים וּמַכְנִיעַ זֵדִים.

THE RIGHTEOUS

עַל הַצַּדִּיקִים To the righteous, the pious,
the elders of Your people the house of Israel,
the remnant of their scholars,
the righteous converts, and to us,
may Your compassion be aroused, LORD our God.
Grant a good reward
to all who sincerely trust in Your name.
Set our lot with them,
so that we may never be ashamed,
for in You we trust.
Blessed are You, LORD,
who is the support and trust of the righteous.

REBUILDING JERUSALEM

וְלִירוּשָׁלַיִם To Jerusalem, Your city,
may You return in compassion,
and may You dwell in it as You promised.
May You rebuild it rapidly in our days
as an everlasting structure,
and install within it soon the throne of David.
Blessed are You, LORD,
who builds Jerusalem.

KINGDOM OF DAVID

אֶת צֶמַח May the offshoot of Your servant David soon flower,
and may his pride be raised high by Your salvation,
for we wait for Your salvation all day.
Blessed are You, LORD,
who makes the glory of salvation flourish.

על הצדיקים

עַל הַצַּדִּיקִים וְעַל הַחֲסִידִים
וְעַל זִקְנֵי עַמְּךָ בֵּית יִשְׂרָאֵל
וְעַל פְּלֵיטַת סוֹפְרֵיהֶם
וְעַל גֵּרֵי הַצֶּדֶק, וְעָלֵינוּ
יֶהֱמוּ רַחֲמֶיךָ יהוה אֱלֹהֵינוּ
וְתֵן שָׂכָר טוֹב לְכָל הַבּוֹטְחִים בְּשִׁמְךָ בֶּאֱמֶת
וְשִׂים חֶלְקֵנוּ עִמָּהֶם
וּלְעוֹלָם לֹא נֵבוֹשׁ כִּי בְךָ בָּטָחְנוּ.
בָּרוּךְ אַתָּה יהוה, מִשְׁעָן וּמִבְטָח לַצַּדִּיקִים.

בניין ירושלים

וְלִירוּשָׁלַיִם עִירְךָ בְּרַחֲמִים תָּשׁוּב
וְתִשְׁכֹּן בְּתוֹכָהּ כַּאֲשֶׁר דִּבַּרְתָּ
וּבְנֵה אוֹתָהּ בְּקָרוֹב בְּיָמֵינוּ בִּנְיַן עוֹלָם
וְכִסֵּא דָוִד מְהֵרָה לְתוֹכָהּ תָּכִין.
בָּרוּךְ אַתָּה יהוה, בּוֹנֵה יְרוּשָׁלָיִם.

משיח בן דוד

אֶת צֶמַח דָּוִד עַבְדְּךָ מְהֵרָה תַצְמִיחַ
וְקַרְנוֹ תָּרוּם בִּישׁוּעָתֶךָ
כִּי לִישׁוּעָתְךָ קִוִּינוּ כָּל הַיּוֹם.
בָּרוּךְ אַתָּה יהוה, מַצְמִיחַ קֶרֶן יְשׁוּעָה.

RESPONSE TO PRAYER

שְׁמַע קוֹלֵנוּ Listen to our voice, LORD our God.
Spare us and have compassion on us,
and in compassion and favor accept our prayer,
for You, God, listen to prayers and pleas.
Do not turn us away, O our King,
empty-handed from Your presence,
for You listen with compassion
to the prayer of Your people Israel.
Blessed are You, LORD, who listens to prayer.

TEMPLE SERVICE

רְצֵה Find favor, LORD our God,
in Your people Israel and their prayer.
Restore the service to Your most holy House,
and accept in love and favor
the fire-offerings of Israel and their prayer.
May the service of Your people Israel always find favor with You.

On Rosh Ḥodesh say:

אֱלֹהֵינוּ Our God and God of our ancestors, may there rise, come, reach, appear, be favored, heard, regarded and remembered before You, our recollection and remembrance, as well as the remembrance of our ancestors, and of the Messiah son of David Your servant, and of Jerusalem Your holy city, and of all Your people the house of Israel – for deliverance and well-being, grace, loving-kindness and compassion, life and peace, on this day of Rosh Ḥodesh. On it remember us, LORD our God, for good; recollect us for blessing, and deliver us for life. In accord with Your promise of salvation and compassion, spare us and be gracious to us; have compassion on us and deliver us, for our eyes are turned to You because You, God, are a gracious and compassionate King.

וְתֶחֱזֶינָה And may our eyes witness Your return
to Zion in compassion.
Blessed are You, LORD, who restores His Presence to Zion.

שומע תפלה

שְׁמַע קוֹלֵנוּ יהוה אֱלֹהֵינוּ
חוּס וְרַחֵם עָלֵינוּ
וְקַבֵּל בְּרַחֲמִים וּבְרָצוֹן אֶת תְּפִלָּתֵנוּ
כִּי אֵל שׁוֹמֵעַ תְּפִלּוֹת וְתַחֲנוּנִים אָתָּה
וּמִלְּפָנֶיךָ מַלְכֵּנוּ רֵיקָם אַל תְּשִׁיבֵנוּ
כִּי אַתָּה שׁוֹמֵעַ תְּפִלַּת עַמְּךָ יִשְׂרָאֵל בְּרַחֲמִים.
בָּרוּךְ אַתָּה יהוה, שׁוֹמֵעַ תְּפִלָּה.

עבודה

רְצֵה יהוה אֱלֹהֵינוּ בְּעַמְּךָ יִשְׂרָאֵל וּבִתְפִלָּתָם
וְהָשֵׁב אֶת הָעֲבוֹדָה לִדְבִיר בֵּיתֶךָ
וְאִשֵּׁי יִשְׂרָאֵל וּתְפִלָּתָם בְּאַהֲבָה תְקַבֵּל בְּרָצוֹן
וּתְהִי לְרָצוֹן תָּמִיד עֲבוֹדַת יִשְׂרָאֵל עַמֶּךָ.

On ראש חודש *say:*

אֱלֹהֵינוּ וֵאלֹהֵי אֲבוֹתֵינוּ, יַעֲלֶה וְיָבוֹא וְיַגִּיעַ, וְיֵרָאֶה וְיֵרָצֶה וְיִשָּׁמַע, וְיִפָּקֵד וְיִזָּכֵר זִכְרוֹנֵנוּ וּפִקְדוֹנֵנוּ וְזִכְרוֹן אֲבוֹתֵינוּ, וְזִכְרוֹן מָשִׁיחַ בֶּן דָּוִד עַבְדֶּךָ, וְזִכְרוֹן יְרוּשָׁלַיִם עִיר קָדְשֶׁךָ, וְזִכְרוֹן כָּל עַמְּךָ בֵּית יִשְׂרָאֵל, לְפָנֶיךָ, לִפְלֵיטָה לְטוֹבָה, לְחֵן וּלְחֶסֶד וּלְרַחֲמִים, לְחַיִּים וּלְשָׁלוֹם בְּיוֹם רֹאשׁ הַחֹדֶשׁ הַזֶּה. זָכְרֵנוּ יהוה אֱלֹהֵינוּ בּוֹ לְטוֹבָה, וּפָקְדֵנוּ בוֹ לִבְרָכָה, וְהוֹשִׁיעֵנוּ בוֹ לְחַיִּים. וּבִדְבַר יְשׁוּעָה וְרַחֲמִים, חוּס וְחָנֵּנוּ וְרַחֵם עָלֵינוּ וְהוֹשִׁיעֵנוּ, כִּי אֵלֶיךָ עֵינֵינוּ, כִּי אֵל מֶלֶךְ חַנּוּן וְרַחוּם אָתָּה.

וְתֶחֱזֶינָה עֵינֵינוּ בְּשׁוּבְךָ לְצִיּוֹן בְּרַחֲמִים.
בָּרוּךְ אַתָּה יהוה, הַמַּחֲזִיר שְׁכִינָתוֹ לְצִיּוֹן.

THANKSGIVING

Bow at the first nine words.

▾מוֹדִים▴ We give thanks to You,
for You are the LORD our God and God of our ancestors
for ever and all time.
You are the Rock of our lives,
Shield of our salvation from generation to generation.
We will thank You and declare Your praise for our lives,
which are entrusted into Your hand; for our souls,
which are placed in Your charge;
for Your miracles which are with us every day;
and for Your wonders and favors
at all times, evening, morning and midday.
You are good – for Your compassion never fails.
You are compassionate – for Your loving-kindnesses never cease.
We have always placed our hope in You.
For all these things may Your name be blessed and exalted, our
King, continually, for ever and all time.
Let all that lives thank You, Selah!
and praise Your name in truth,
God, our Savior and Help, Selah!
▾Blessed are You, LORD, whose name is "the Good"
and to whom thanks are due.

PEACE

שָׁלוֹם רָב Grant great peace to Your people Israel for ever,
for You are the sovereign LORD of all peace;
and may it be good in Your eyes
to bless Your people Israel
at every time, at every hour, with Your peace.
Blessed are You, LORD, who blesses His people Israel with peace.

Some say the following verse:

May the words of my mouth and the meditation of my heart *Ps. 19*
find favor before You, LORD, my Rock and Redeemer.

הודאה

Bow at the first five words.

מוֹדִים אֲנַחְנוּ לָךְ

שָׁאַתָּה הוּא יהוה אֱלֹהֵינוּ וֵאלֹהֵי אֲבוֹתֵינוּ לְעוֹלָם וָעֶד.

צוּר חַיֵּינוּ, מָגֵן יִשְׁעֵנוּ אַתָּה הוּא לְדוֹר וָדוֹר.

נוֹדֶה לְּךָ וּנְסַפֵּר תְּהִלָּתֶךָ

עַל חַיֵּינוּ הַמְּסוּרִים בְּיָדֶךָ

וְעַל נִשְׁמוֹתֵינוּ הַפְּקוּדוֹת לָךְ

וְעַל נִסֶּיךָ שֶׁבְּכָל יוֹם עִמָּנוּ

וְעַל נִפְלְאוֹתֶיךָ וְטוֹבוֹתֶיךָ שֶׁבְּכָל עֵת, עֶרֶב וָבֹקֶר וְצָהֳרָיִם.

הַטּוֹב, כִּי לֹא כָלוּ רַחֲמֶיךָ

וְהַמְרַחֵם, כִּי לֹא תַמּוּ חֲסָדֶיךָ

מֵעוֹלָם קִוִּינוּ לָךְ.

וְעַל כֻּלָּם יִתְבָּרַךְ וְיִתְרוֹמַם שִׁמְךָ מַלְכֵּנוּ תָּמִיד לְעוֹלָם וָעֶד.

וְכֹל הַחַיִּים יוֹדוּךָ סֶּלָה, וִיהַלְלוּ אֶת שִׁמְךָ בֶּאֱמֶת

הָאֵל יְשׁוּעָתֵנוּ וְעֶזְרָתֵנוּ סֶלָה.

בָּרוּךְ אַתָּה יהוה, הַטּוֹב שִׁמְךָ וּלְךָ נָאֶה לְהוֹדוֹת.

ברכת שלום

שָׁלוֹם רָב עַל יִשְׂרָאֵל עַמְּךָ תָּשִׂים לְעוֹלָם

כִּי אַתָּה הוּא מֶלֶךְ אָדוֹן לְכָל הַשָּׁלוֹם.

וְטוֹב בְּעֵינֶיךָ לְבָרֵךְ אֶת עַמְּךָ יִשְׂרָאֵל

בְּכָל עֵת וּבְכָל שָׁעָה בִּשְׁלוֹמֶךָ.

בָּרוּךְ אַתָּה יהוה, הַמְבָרֵךְ אֶת עַמּוֹ יִשְׂרָאֵל בַּשָּׁלוֹם.

Some say the following verse:

יִהְיוּ לְרָצוֹן אִמְרֵי־פִי וְהֶגְיוֹן לִבִּי לְפָנֶיךָ, יהוה צוּרִי וְגֹאֲלִי: תהלים יט

אֱלֹהַי My God, *Berakhot 17a*
guard my tongue from evil and my lips from deceitful speech.
To those who curse me, let my soul be silent;
may my soul be to all like the dust.
Open my heart to Your Torah
and let my soul pursue Your commandments.
As for all who plan evil against me,
swiftly thwart their counsel and frustrate their plans.
Act for the sake of Your name; act for the sake of Your right hand;
act for the sake of Your holiness; act for the sake of Your Torah.
That Your beloved ones may be delivered, *Ps. 60*
save with Your right hand and answer me.
May the words of my mouth *Ps. 19*
and the meditation of my heart find favor before You,
LORD, my Rock and Redeemer.

Bow, take three steps back, then bow, first left, then right, then center, while saying:

May He who makes peace in His high places,
make peace for us and all Israel – and say: Amen.

יְהִי רָצוֹן May it be Your will, LORD our God and God of our ancestors,
that the Temple be rebuilt speedily in our days, and grant us a share in Your Torah.
And there we will serve You with reverence,
as in the days of old and as in former years.
Then the offering of Judah and Jerusalem *Mal. 3*
will be pleasing to the LORD as in the days of old and as in former years.

On Motza'ei Shabbat the Leader continues with Half Kaddish on page 342, then "May the pleasantness" on page 342.

On other evenings the Leader says Full Kaddish:

FULL KADDISH

Leader: יִתְגַּדַּל Magnified and sanctified may His great name be,
in the world He created by His will.
May He establish His kingdom
in your lifetime and in your days,
and in the lifetime of all the house of Israel,
swiftly and soon – and say: Amen.

All: May His great name be blessed for ever and all time.

אֱלֹהַי ברכות יז.

נְצֹר לְשׁוֹנִי מֵרָע וּשְׂפָתַי מִדַּבֵּר מִרְמָה

וְלִמְקַלְלַי נַפְשִׁי תִדֹּם, וְנַפְשִׁי כֶּעָפָר לַכֹּל תִּהְיֶה.

פְּתַח לִבִּי בְּתוֹרָתֶךָ, וּבְמִצְוֹתֶיךָ תִּרְדֹּף נַפְשִׁי.

וְכָל הַחוֹשְׁבִים עָלַי רָעָה

מְהֵרָה הָפֵר עֲצָתָם וְקַלְקֵל מַחֲשַׁבְתָּם.

עֲשֵׂה לְמַעַן שְׁמֶךָ, עֲשֵׂה לְמַעַן יְמִינֶךָ

עֲשֵׂה לְמַעַן קְדֻשָּׁתֶךָ, עֲשֵׂה לְמַעַן תּוֹרָתֶךָ.

לְמַעַן יֵחָלְצוּן יְדִידֶיךָ, הוֹשִׁיעָה יְמִינְךָ וַעֲנֵנִי: תהלים ס

יִהְיוּ לְרָצוֹן אִמְרֵי־פִי וְהֶגְיוֹן לִבִּי לְפָנֶיךָ, יהוה צוּרִי וְגֹאֲלִי: תהלים יט

Bow, take three steps back, then bow, first left, then right, then center, while saying:

עֹשֶׂה שָׁלוֹם בִּמְרוֹמָיו

הוּא יַעֲשֶׂה שָׁלוֹם עָלֵינוּ וְעַל כָּל יִשְׂרָאֵל, וְאִמְרוּ אָמֵן.

יְהִי רָצוֹן מִלְּפָנֶיךָ יהוה אֱלֹהֵינוּ וֵאלֹהֵי אֲבוֹתֵינוּ

שֶׁיִּבָּנֶה בֵּית הַמִּקְדָּשׁ בִּמְהֵרָה בְיָמֵינוּ, וְתֵן חֶלְקֵנוּ בְּתוֹרָתֶךָ

וְשָׁם נַעֲבָדְךָ בְּיִרְאָה כִּימֵי עוֹלָם וּכְשָׁנִים קַדְמוֹנִיּוֹת.

וְעָרְבָה לַיהוה מִנְחַת יְהוּדָה וִירוּשָׁלָםִ כִּימֵי עוֹלָם וּכְשָׁנִים קַדְמוֹנִיּוֹת: מלאכי ג

On מוצאי שבת *the* שליח ציבור *continues with* חצי קדיש *on page 343, then* וִיהִי נֹעַם *on page 343.*

On other evenings the שליח ציבור *says* קדיש שלם*:*

קדיש שלם

ש״ץ: יִתְגַּדַּל וְיִתְקַדַּשׁ שְׁמֵהּ רַבָּא (קהל: אָמֵן)

בְּעָלְמָא דִּי בְרָא כִרְעוּתֵהּ, וְיַמְלִיךְ מַלְכוּתֵהּ

בְּחַיֵּיכוֹן וּבְיוֹמֵיכוֹן וּבְחַיֵּי דְכָל בֵּית יִשְׂרָאֵל

בַּעֲגָלָא וּבִזְמַן קָרִיב, וְאִמְרוּ אָמֵן. (קהל: אָמֵן)

קהל וש״ץ: יְהֵא שְׁמֵהּ רַבָּא מְבָרַךְ לְעָלַם וּלְעָלְמֵי עָלְמַיָּא.

Leader: Blessed and praised, glorified and exalted,
raised and honored, uplifted and lauded be
the name of the Holy One, blessed be He,
beyond any blessing, song, praise and consolation
uttered in the world –
and say: Amen.

May the prayers and pleas of all Israel
be accepted by their Father in heaven –
and say: Amen.

May there be great peace from heaven,
and life for us and all Israel –
and say: Amen.

Bow, take three steps back, as if taking leave of the Divine Presence, then bow, first left, then right, then center, while saying:

May He who makes peace in His high places,
make peace for us and all Israel –
and say: Amen.

On Tisha B'Av, Megillat Eikha is read (page 898).

Stand while saying Aleinu. Bow at ▼.

עָלֵינוּ It is our duty to praise the Master of all,
and ascribe greatness to the Author of creation,
who has not made us like the nations of the lands
nor placed us like the families of the earth;
who has not made our portion like theirs,
nor our destiny like all their multitudes.
(For they worship vanity and emptiness,
and pray to a god who cannot save.)
▼But we bow in worship and thank the Supreme King of kings,
the Holy One, blessed be He,
who extends the heavens and establishes the earth,
whose throne of glory is in the heavens above,
and whose power's Presence is in the highest of heights.

ש״ץ: יִתְבָּרַךְ וְיִשְׁתַּבַּח וְיִתְפָּאַר וְיִתְרוֹמַם וְיִתְנַשֵּׂא
וְיִתְהַדָּר וְיִתְעַלֶּה וְיִתְהַלָּל
שְׁמֵהּ דְּקֻדְשָׁא בְּרִיךְ הוּא (קהל: בְּרִיךְ הוּא)
לְעֵלָּא מִן כָּל בִּרְכָתָא
וְשִׁירָתָא, תֻּשְׁבְּחָתָא וְנֶחֱמָתָא
דַּאֲמִירָן בְּעָלְמָא, וְאִמְרוּ אָמֵן. (קהל: אָמֵן)

תִּתְקַבַּל צְלוֹתְהוֹן וּבָעוּתְהוֹן דְּכָל יִשְׂרָאֵל
קֳדָם אֲבוּהוֹן דִּי בִשְׁמַיָּא, וְאִמְרוּ אָמֵן. (קהל: אָמֵן)

יְהֵא שְׁלָמָא רַבָּא מִן שְׁמַיָּא
וְחַיִּים, עָלֵינוּ וְעַל כָּל יִשְׂרָאֵל, וְאִמְרוּ אָמֵן. (קהל: אָמֵן)

Bow, take three steps back, as if taking leave of the Divine Presence, then bow, first left, then right, then center, while saying:

עֹשֶׂה שָׁלוֹם בִּמְרוֹמָיו
הוּא יַעֲשֶׂה שָׁלוֹם עָלֵינוּ
וְעַל כָּל יִשְׂרָאֵל, וְאִמְרוּ אָמֵן. (קהל: אָמֵן)

On תשעה באב, מגילת איכה *is read (page 899).*

Stand while saying עָלֵינוּ. *Bow at* ▾.

עָלֵינוּ לְשַׁבֵּחַ לַאֲדוֹן הַכֹּל, לָתֵת גְּדֻלָּה לְיוֹצֵר בְּרֵאשִׁית
שֶׁלֹּא עָשָׂנוּ כְּגוֹיֵי הָאֲרָצוֹת, וְלֹא שָׂמָנוּ כְּמִשְׁפְּחוֹת הָאֲדָמָה
שֶׁלֹּא שָׂם חֶלְקֵנוּ כָּהֶם וְגוֹרָלֵנוּ כְּכָל הֲמוֹנָם.
(שֶׁהֵם מִשְׁתַּחֲוִים לְהֶבֶל וָרִיק וּמִתְפַּלְלִים אֶל אֵל לֹא יוֹשִׁיעַ.)
▾וַאֲנַחְנוּ כּוֹרְעִים וּמִשְׁתַּחֲוִים וּמוֹדִים
לִפְנֵי מֶלֶךְ מַלְכֵי הַמְּלָכִים, הַקָּדוֹשׁ בָּרוּךְ הוּא
שֶׁהוּא נוֹטֶה שָׁמַיִם וְיוֹסֵד אָרֶץ
וּמוֹשַׁב יְקָרוֹ בַּשָּׁמַיִם מִמַּעַל, וּשְׁכִינַת עֻזּוֹ בְּגָבְהֵי מְרוֹמִים.

He is our God; there is no other.
Truly He is our King, there is none else,
as it is written in His Torah:
"You shall know and take to heart this day *Deut. 4*
that the LORD is God,
in heaven above and on earth below.
There is no other."

Therefore, we place our hope in You, LORD our God,
that we may soon see the glory of Your power,
when You will remove abominations from the earth,
and idols will be utterly destroyed,
when the world will be perfected
under the sovereignty of the Almighty,
when all humanity will call on Your name,
to turn all the earth's wicked toward You.
All the world's inhabitants will realize and know
that to You every knee must bow and every tongue swear loyalty.
Before You, LORD our God, they will kneel and bow down
and give honor to Your glorious name.
They will all accept the yoke of Your kingdom,
and You will reign over them soon and for ever.
For the kingdom is Yours,
and to all eternity You will reign in glory,
as it is written in Your Torah:
"The LORD will reign for ever and ever." *Ex. 15*
▸ And it is said: "Then the LORD shall be King over all the earth; *Zech. 14*
on that day the LORD shall be One and His name One."

Some add:

Have no fear of sudden terror or of the ruin when it overtakes the wicked. *Prov. 3*
Devise your strategy, but it will be thwarted; propose your plan, *Is. 8*
but it will not stand, for God is with us.
When you grow old, I will still be the same. *Is. 46*
When your hair turns gray, I will still carry you.
I made you, I will bear you, I will carry you, and I will rescue you.

הוּא אֱלֹהֵינוּ, אֵין עוֹד.
אֱמֶת מַלְכֵּנוּ, אֶפֶס זוּלָתוֹ
כַּכָּתוּב בְּתוֹרָתוֹ
וְיָדַעְתָּ הַיּוֹם וַהֲשֵׁבֹתָ אֶל־לְבָבֶךָ דברים ד
כִּי יהוה הוּא הָאֱלֹהִים בַּשָּׁמַיִם מִמַּעַל וְעַל־הָאָרֶץ מִתָּחַת
אֵין עוֹד:

עַל כֵּן נְקַוֶּה לְּךָ יהוה אֱלֹהֵינוּ
לִרְאוֹת מְהֵרָה בְּתִפְאֶרֶת עֻזֶּךָ
לְהַעֲבִיר גִּלּוּלִים מִן הָאָרֶץ, וְהָאֱלִילִים כָּרוֹת יִכָּרֵתוּן
לְתַקֵּן עוֹלָם בְּמַלְכוּת שַׁדַּי.
וְכָל בְּנֵי בָשָׂר יִקְרְאוּ בִשְׁמֶךָ לְהַפְנוֹת אֵלֶיךָ כָּל רִשְׁעֵי אָרֶץ.
יַכִּירוּ וְיֵדְעוּ כָּל יוֹשְׁבֵי תֵבֵל
כִּי לְךָ תִּכְרַע כָּל בֶּרֶךְ, תִּשָּׁבַע כָּל לָשׁוֹן.
לְפָנֶיךָ יהוה אֱלֹהֵינוּ יִכְרְעוּ וְיִפֹּלוּ, וְלִכְבוֹד שִׁמְךָ יְקָר יִתֵּנוּ
וִיקַבְּלוּ כֻלָּם אֶת עֹל מַלְכוּתֶךָ
וְתִמְלֹךְ עֲלֵיהֶם מְהֵרָה לְעוֹלָם וָעֶד.
כִּי הַמַּלְכוּת שֶׁלְּךָ הִיא וּלְעוֹלְמֵי עַד תִּמְלֹךְ בְּכָבוֹד
כַּכָּתוּב בְּתוֹרָתֶךָ, יהוה יִמְלֹךְ לְעֹלָם וָעֶד: שמות טו
◂ וְנֶאֱמַר, וְהָיָה יהוה לְמֶלֶךְ עַל־כָּל־הָאָרֶץ זכריה יד
בַּיּוֹם הַהוּא יִהְיֶה יהוה אֶחָד וּשְׁמוֹ אֶחָד:

Some add:

אַל־תִּירָא מִפַּחַד פִּתְאֹם וּמִשֹּׁאַת רְשָׁעִים כִּי תָבֹא: משלי ג
עֻצוּ עֵצָה וְתֻפָר, דַּבְּרוּ דָבָר וְלֹא יָקוּם, כִּי עִמָּנוּ אֵל: ישעיה ח
וְעַד־זִקְנָה אֲנִי הוּא, וְעַד־שֵׂיבָה אֲנִי אֶסְבֹּל ישעיה מו
אֲנִי עָשִׂיתִי וַאֲנִי אֶשָּׂא וַאֲנִי אֶסְבֹּל וַאֲמַלֵּט:

MOURNER'S KADDISH

The following prayer, said by mourners, requires the presence of a minyan.
A transliteration can be found on page 1141.

Mourner: יִתְגַּדַּל Magnified and sanctified
may His great name be,
in the world He created by His will.
May He establish His kingdom
in your lifetime and in your days,
and in the lifetime of all the house of Israel,
swiftly and soon –
and say: Amen.

All: May His great name be blessed
for ever and all time.

Mourner: Blessed and praised,
glorified and exalted,
raised and honored,
uplifted and lauded
be the name of the Holy One,
blessed be He,
beyond any blessing,
song, praise and consolation
uttered in the world –
and say: Amen.

May there be great peace from heaven,
and life for us and all Israel –
and say: Amen.

Bow, take three steps back, as if taking leave of the Divine Presence,
then bow, first left, then right, then center, while saying:

May He who makes peace in His high places,
make peace for us and all Israel –
and say: Amen.

קדיש יתום

The following prayer, said by mourners, requires the presence of a מנין*.*
A transliteration can be found on *page 1141.*

אבל: יִתְגַּדַּל וְיִתְקַדַּשׁ שְׁמֵהּ רַבָּא (קהל: אָמֵן)
בְּעָלְמָא דִּי בְרָא כִרְעוּתֵהּ
וְיַמְלִיךְ מַלְכוּתֵהּ
בְּחַיֵּיכוֹן וּבְיוֹמֵיכוֹן וּבְחַיֵּי דְכָל בֵּית יִשְׂרָאֵל
בַּעֲגָלָא וּבִזְמַן קָרִיב
וְאִמְרוּ אָמֵן. (קהל: אָמֵן)

קהל ואבל: יְהֵא שְׁמֵהּ רַבָּא מְבָרַךְ לְעָלַם וּלְעָלְמֵי עָלְמַיָּא.

אבל: יִתְבָּרַךְ וְיִשְׁתַּבַּח וְיִתְפָּאַר
וְיִתְרוֹמַם וְיִתְנַשֵּׂא וְיִתְהַדָּר וְיִתְעַלֶּה וְיִתְהַלָּל
שְׁמֵהּ דְּקֻדְשָׁא בְּרִיךְ הוּא (קהל: בְּרִיךְ הוּא)
לְעֵלָּא מִן כָּל בִּרְכָתָא
וְשִׁירָתָא, תֻּשְׁבְּחָתָא וְנֶחֱמָתָא
דַּאֲמִירָן בְּעָלְמָא
וְאִמְרוּ אָמֵן. (קהל: אָמֵן)

יְהֵא שְׁלָמָא רַבָּא מִן שְׁמַיָּא
וְחַיִּים, עָלֵינוּ וְעַל כָּל יִשְׂרָאֵל
וְאִמְרוּ אָמֵן. (קהל: אָמֵן)

Bow, take three steps back, as if taking leave of the Divine Presence, then bow, first left, then right, then center, while saying:

עֹשֶׂה שָׁלוֹם בִּמְרוֹמָיו
הוּא יַעֲשֶׂה שָׁלוֹם עָלֵינוּ וְעַל כָּל יִשְׂרָאֵל
וְאִמְרוּ אָמֵן. (קהל: אָמֵן)

From the second day of Rosh Ḥodesh Elul through Shemini Atzeret (in Israel through Hoshana Raba), the following psalm is said:

לְדָוִד By David. The LORD is my light and my salvation – whom then shall I fear? The LORD is the stronghold of my life – of whom shall I be afraid? When evil men close in on me to devour my flesh, it is they, my enemies and foes, who stumble and fall. Should an army besiege me, my heart would not fear. Should war break out against me, still I would be confident. One thing I ask of the LORD, only this do I seek: to live in the House of the LORD all the days of my life, to gaze on the beauty of the LORD and worship in His Temple. For He will keep me safe in His pavilion on the day of trouble. He will hide me under the cover of His tent. He will set me high upon a rock. Now my head is high above my enemies who surround me. I will sacrifice in His tent with shouts of joy. I will sing and chant praises to the LORD. LORD, hear my voice when I call. Be gracious to me and answer me. On Your behalf my heart says, "Seek My face." Your face, LORD, will I seek. Do not hide Your face from me. Do not turn Your servant away in anger. You have been my help. Do not reject or forsake me, God, my Savior. Were my father and my mother to forsake me, the LORD would take me in. Teach me Your way, LORD, and lead me on a level path, because of my oppressors. Do not abandon me to the will of my foes, for false witnesses have risen against me, breathing violence. ▸ Were it not for my faith that I shall see the LORD's goodness in the land of the living. Hope in the LORD. Be strong and of good courage, and hope in the LORD! *Ps. 27*

Mourner's Kaddish *(on previous page)*

From the second day of ראש חודש אלול *through* שמיני עצרת
(*in* ארץ ישראל *through* הושענא רבה), *the following psalm is said:*

לְדָוִד, יהוה אוֹרִי וְיִשְׁעִי, מִמִּי אִירָא, יהוה מָעוֹז־חַיַּי, מִמִּי אֶפְחָד: תהלים כז
בִּקְרֹב עָלַי מְרֵעִים לֶאֱכֹל אֶת־בְּשָׂרִי, צָרַי וְאֹיְבַי לִי, הֵמָּה כָשְׁלוּ וְנָפָלוּ:
אִם־תַּחֲנֶה עָלַי מַחֲנֶה, לֹא־יִירָא לִבִּי, אִם־תָּקוּם עָלַי מִלְחָמָה, בְּזֹאת
אֲנִי בוֹטֵחַ: אַחַת שָׁאַלְתִּי מֵאֵת־יהוה, אוֹתָהּ אֲבַקֵּשׁ, שִׁבְתִּי בְּבֵית־
יהוה כָּל־יְמֵי חַיַּי, לַחֲזוֹת בְּנֹעַם־יהוה, וּלְבַקֵּר בְּהֵיכָלוֹ: כִּי יִצְפְּנֵנִי
בְּסֻכֹּה בְּיוֹם רָעָה, יַסְתִּרֵנִי בְּסֵתֶר אָהֳלוֹ, בְּצוּר יְרוֹמְמֵנִי: וְעַתָּה יָרוּם
רֹאשִׁי עַל אֹיְבַי סְבִיבוֹתַי, וְאֶזְבְּחָה בְאָהֳלוֹ זִבְחֵי תְרוּעָה, אָשִׁירָה
וַאֲזַמְּרָה לַיהוה: שְׁמַע־יהוה קוֹלִי אֶקְרָא, וְחָנֵּנִי וַעֲנֵנִי: לְךָ אָמַר לִבִּי
בַּקְּשׁוּ פָנָי, אֶת־פָּנֶיךָ יהוה אֲבַקֵּשׁ: אַל־תַּסְתֵּר פָּנֶיךָ מִמֶּנִּי, אַל תַּט־
בְּאַף עַבְדֶּךָ, עֶזְרָתִי הָיִיתָ, אַל־תִּטְּשֵׁנִי וְאַל־תַּעַזְבֵנִי, אֱלֹהֵי יִשְׁעִי:
כִּי־אָבִי וְאִמִּי עֲזָבוּנִי, וַיהוה יַאַסְפֵנִי: הוֹרֵנִי יהוה דַּרְכֶּךָ, וּנְחֵנִי בְּאֹרַח
מִישׁוֹר, לְמַעַן שׁוֹרְרָי: אַל־תִּתְּנֵנִי בְּנֶפֶשׁ צָרָי, כִּי קָמוּ־בִי עֵדֵי־שֶׁקֶר,
וִיפֵחַ חָמָס: ◁ לוּלֵא הֶאֱמַנְתִּי לִרְאוֹת בְּטוּב־יהוה בְּאֶרֶץ חַיִּים: קַוֵּה
אֶל־יהוה, חֲזַק וְיַאֲמֵץ לִבֶּךָ, וְקַוֵּה אֶל־יהוה:

קדיש יתום (*on previous page*)

MOTZA'EI SHABBAT

In many congregations, the following two psalms are sung before Ma'ariv at the end of Shabbat.

לְדָוִד Of David. Blessed is the LORD, my Rock, who trains my hands for war, my fingers for battle. He is my Benefactor, my Fortress, my Stronghold and my Refuge, my Shield in whom I trust, He who subdues nations under me. LORD, what is man that You care for him, what are mortals that You think of them? Man is no more than a breath, his days like a fleeting shadow. LORD, part Your heavens and come down; touch the mountains so that they pour forth smoke. Flash forth lightning and scatter them; shoot Your arrows and panic them. Reach out Your hand from on high; deliver me and rescue me from the mighty waters, from the hands of strangers, whose every word is worthless, whose right hands are raised in falsehood. To You, God, I will sing a new song; to You I will play music on a ten-stringed harp. He who gives salvation to kings, who saved His servant David from the cruel sword: may He deliver me and rescue me from the hands of strangers, whose every word is worthless, whose right hands are raised in falsehood. Then our sons will be like saplings, well nurtured in their youth. Our daughters will be like pillars carved for a palace. Our barns will be filled with every kind of provision. Our sheep will increase by thousands, even tens of thousands in our fields. Our oxen will draw heavy loads. There will be no breach in the walls, no going into captivity, no cries of distress in our streets. Happy are the people for whom this is so; happy are the people whose God is the LORD. *Ps. 144*

לַמְנַצֵּחַ For the conductor of music. With stringed instruments. A psalm, a song. May God be gracious to us and bless us. May He make His face shine on us, Selah. Then will Your way be known on earth, Your salvation among all the nations. Let the peoples praise You, God; let all peoples praise You. Let nations rejoice and sing for joy, for You judge the peoples with equity, and guide the nations of the earth, Selah. Let the peoples praise You, God; let all peoples praise You. The earth has yielded its harvest. May God, our God, bless us. God will bless us, and all the ends of the earth will fear Him. *Ps. 67*

The service continues with Ma'ariv for Weekdays on page 298.

מוצאי שבת

In many congregations, the following two psalms are sung before מעריב *on* מוצאי שבת.

תהלים קמד לְדָוִד, בָּרוּךְ יהוה צוּרִי, הַמְלַמֵּד יָדַי לַקְרָב, אֶצְבְּעוֹתַי לַמִּלְחָמָה: חַסְדִּי וּמְצוּדָתִי מִשְׂגַּבִּי וּמְפַלְטִי לִי, מָגִנִּי וּבוֹ חָסִיתִי, הָרוֹדֵד עַמִּי תַחְתָּי: יהוה מָה־אָדָם וַתֵּדָעֵהוּ, בֶּן־אֱנוֹשׁ וַתְּחַשְּׁבֵהוּ: אָדָם לַהֶבֶל דָּמָה, יָמָיו כְּצֵל עוֹבֵר: יהוה הַט־שָׁמֶיךָ וְתֵרֵד, גַּע בֶּהָרִים וְיֶעֱשָׁנוּ: בְּרוֹק בָּרָק וּתְפִיצֵם, שְׁלַח חִצֶּיךָ וּתְהֻמֵּם: שְׁלַח יָדֶיךָ מִמָּרוֹם, פְּצֵנִי וְהַצִּילֵנִי מִמַּיִם רַבִּים, מִיַּד בְּנֵי נֵכָר: אֲשֶׁר פִּיהֶם דִּבֶּר־שָׁוְא, וִימִינָם יְמִין שָׁקֶר: אֱלֹהִים שִׁיר חָדָשׁ אָשִׁירָה לָּךְ, בְּנֵבֶל עָשׂוֹר אֲזַמְּרָה־לָּךְ: הַנּוֹתֵן תְּשׁוּעָה לַמְּלָכִים, הַפּוֹצֶה אֶת־דָּוִד עַבְדּוֹ מֵחֶרֶב רָעָה: פְּצֵנִי וְהַצִּילֵנִי מִיַּד בְּנֵי נֵכָר, אֲשֶׁר פִּיהֶם דִּבֶּר־שָׁוְא, וִימִינָם יְמִין שָׁקֶר: אֲשֶׁר בָּנֵינוּ כִּנְטִעִים, מְגֻדָּלִים בִּנְעוּרֵיהֶם, בְּנוֹתֵינוּ כְזָוִיֹּת, מְחֻטָּבוֹת תַּבְנִית הֵיכָל: מְזָוֵינוּ מְלֵאִים, מְפִיקִים מִזַּן אֶל־זַן, צֹאונֵנוּ מַאֲלִיפוֹת מְרֻבָּבוֹת בְּחוּצוֹתֵינוּ: אַלּוּפֵינוּ מְסֻבָּלִים, אֵין פֶּרֶץ וְאֵין יוֹצֵאת, וְאֵין צְוָחָה בִּרְחֹבֹתֵינוּ: אַשְׁרֵי הָעָם שֶׁכָּכָה לּוֹ, אַשְׁרֵי הָעָם שֶׁיהוה אֱלֹהָיו:

תהלים סז לַמְנַצֵּחַ בִּנְגִינֹת, מִזְמוֹר שִׁיר: אֱלֹהִים יְחָנֵּנוּ וִיבָרְכֵנוּ, יָאֵר פָּנָיו אִתָּנוּ סֶלָה: לָדַעַת בָּאָרֶץ דַּרְכֶּךָ, בְּכָל־גּוֹיִם יְשׁוּעָתֶךָ: יוֹדוּךָ עַמִּים אֱלֹהִים, יוֹדוּךָ עַמִּים כֻּלָּם: יִשְׂמְחוּ וִירַנְּנוּ לְאֻמִּים, כִּי־תִשְׁפֹּט עַמִּים מִישֹׁר, וּלְאֻמִּים בָּאָרֶץ תַּנְחֵם סֶלָה: יוֹדוּךָ עַמִּים אֱלֹהִים, יוֹדוּךָ עַמִּים כֻּלָּם: אֶרֶץ נָתְנָה יְבוּלָהּ, יְבָרְכֵנוּ אֱלֹהִים אֱלֹהֵינוּ: יְבָרְכֵנוּ אֱלֹהִים, וְיִירְאוּ אוֹתוֹ כָּל־אַפְסֵי־אָרֶץ:

The service continues with מעריב לחול *on page 299.*

MOTZA'EI SHABBAT

At the conclusion of the Amida on Motza'ei Shabbat, the Leader continues with Half Kaddish below, then "May the pleasantness."

HALF KADDISH

Leader: יִתְגַּדַּל Magnified and sanctified may His great name be,
in the world He created by His will.
May He establish His kingdom
in your lifetime and in your days,
and in the lifetime of all the house of Israel,
swiftly and soon – and say: Amen.

All: May His great name be blessed for ever and all time.

Leader: Blessed and praised, glorified and exalted,
raised and honored, uplifted and lauded
be the name of the Holy One, blessed be He,
beyond any blessing, song, praise and consolation
uttered in the world – and say: Amen.

וִיהִי נֹעַם May the pleasantness of the LORD our God be upon us. *Ps. 90*
Establish for us the work of our hands, O establish the work of our hands.

יֹשֵׁב He who lives in the shelter of the Most High dwells in the *Ps. 91*
shadow of the Almighty. I say of the LORD, my Refuge and Stronghold, my God in whom I trust, that He will save you from the fowler's snare and the deadly pestilence. With His pinions He will cover you, and beneath His wings you will find shelter; His faithfulness is an encircling shield. You need not fear terror by night, nor the arrow that flies by day; not the pestilence that stalks in

---

(*Mishkan*) in the desert (*Torat Kohanim Shemini*, and Rashi *Shemot* 39:43). In any event, the implication is perhaps that Hashem lend our work week the pleasantness and satisfaction that comes from successfully completing one's work.

What are your goals for this coming work week?

מוצאי שבת

At the conclusion of the עמידה *on* מוצאי שבת*, the* שליח ציבור *continues with* חצי קדיש *below, then* וִיהִי נֹעַם.

חצי קדיש

ש״ץ: יִתְגַּדַּל וְיִתְקַדַּשׁ שְׁמֵהּ רַבָּא (קהל: אָמֵן)
בְּעָלְמָא דִּי בְרָא כִרְעוּתֵהּ
וְיַמְלִיךְ מַלְכוּתֵהּ
בְּחַיֵּיכוֹן וּבְיוֹמֵיכוֹן וּבְחַיֵּי דְכָל בֵּית יִשְׂרָאֵל
בַּעֲגָלָא וּבִזְמַן קָרִיב, וְאִמְרוּ אָמֵן. (קהל: אָמֵן)

קהל וש״ץ: יְהֵא שְׁמֵהּ רַבָּא מְבָרַךְ לְעָלַם וּלְעָלְמֵי עָלְמַיָּא.

ש״ץ: יִתְבָּרַךְ וְיִשְׁתַּבַּח וְיִתְפָּאַר וְיִתְרוֹמַם וְיִתְנַשֵּׂא
וְיִתְהַדָּר וְיִתְעַלֶּה וְיִתְהַלָּל
שְׁמֵהּ דְּקֻדְשָׁא בְּרִיךְ הוּא (קהל: בְּרִיךְ הוּא)
לְעֵלָּא מִן כָּל בִּרְכָתָא וְשִׁירָתָא, תֻּשְׁבְּחָתָא וְנֶחֱמָתָא
דַּאֲמִירָן בְּעָלְמָא, וְאִמְרוּ אָמֵן. (קהל: אָמֵן)

תהלים צ וִיהִי נֹעַם אֲדֹנָי אֱלֹהֵינוּ עָלֵינוּ וּמַעֲשֵׂה יָדֵינוּ כּוֹנְנָה עָלֵינוּ וּמַעֲשֵׂה
יָדֵינוּ כּוֹנְנֵהוּ:

תהלים צא יֹשֵׁב בְּסֵתֶר עֶלְיוֹן, בְּצֵל שַׁדַּי יִתְלוֹנָן: אֹמַר לַיהוה מַחְסִי וּמְצוּדָתִי,
אֱלֹהַי אֶבְטַח־בּוֹ: כִּי הוּא יַצִּילְךָ מִפַּח יָקוּשׁ, מִדֶּבֶר הַוּוֹת:
בְּאֶבְרָתוֹ יָסֶךְ לָךְ, וְתַחַת־כְּנָפָיו תֶּחְסֶה, צִנָּה וְסֹחֵרָה אֲמִתּוֹ:
לֹא־תִירָא מִפַּחַד לָיְלָה, מֵחֵץ יָעוּף יוֹמָם: מִדֶּבֶר בָּאֹפֶל יַהֲלֹךְ,

---

BIUR TEFILLA · ביאור תפילה

וִיהִי נֹעַם – *May the pleasantness.* This particular line is said to have been the verse which Moshe used to bless Israel after they had completed the building of the Tabernacle

darkness, nor the plague that ravages at noon. A thousand may fall at your side, ten thousand at your right hand, but it will not come near you. You will only look with your eyes and see the punishment of the wicked. Because you said, "The LORD is my Refuge," taking the Most High as your shelter, no harm will befall you, no plague come near your tent, for He will command His angels about you, to guard you in all your ways. They will lift you in their hands, lest your foot stumble on a stone. You will tread on lions and vipers; you will trample on young lions and snakes. [God says:] "Because he loves Me, I will rescue him; I will protect him, because he acknowledges My name. When he calls on Me, I will answer him; I will be with him in distress, I will deliver him and bring him honor.
▸ With long life I will satisfy him and show him My salvation.
With long life I will satisfy him and show him My salvation.

▸ You are the Holy One, enthroned on the praises of Israel. *Ps. 22*
And [the angels] call to one another, saying,
"Holy, holy, holy is the LORD of hosts; *Is. 6*
the whole world is filled with His glory."
And they receive permission from one another, saying: *Targum Yonatan Is. 6*
"Holy in the highest heavens, home of His Presence;
holy on earth, the work of His strength;
holy for ever and all time is the LORD of hosts;
the whole earth is full of His radiant glory."

▸ Then a wind lifted me up *Ezek. 3*
and I heard behind me the sound of a great noise, saying,
"Blessed is the LORD's glory from His place."
Then a wind lifted me up and I heard behind me *Targum Yonatan Ezek. 3*
the sound of a great tempest of those who uttered praise, saying,
"Blessed is the LORD's glory
from the place of the home of His Presence."

The LORD shall reign for ever and all time. *Ex. 15*
The LORD's kingdom is established for ever and all time. *Targum Onkelos Ex. 15*

מִקֶּטֶב יָשׁוּד צָהֳרָיִם: יִפֹּל מִצִּדְּךָ אֶלֶף, וּרְבָבָה מִימִינֶךָ, אֵלֶיךָ
לֹא יִגָּשׁ: רַק בְּעֵינֶיךָ תַבִּיט, וְשִׁלֻּמַת רְשָׁעִים תִּרְאֶה: כִּי־אַתָּה
יהוה מַחְסִי, עֶלְיוֹן שַׂמְתָּ מְעוֹנֶךָ: לֹא־תְאֻנֶּה אֵלֶיךָ רָעָה, וְנֶגַע
לֹא־יִקְרַב בְּאָהֳלֶךָ: כִּי מַלְאָכָיו יְצַוֶּה־לָּךְ, לִשְׁמָרְךָ בְּכָל־דְּרָכֶיךָ:
עַל־כַּפַּיִם יִשָּׂאוּנְךָ, פֶּן־תִּגֹּף בָּאֶבֶן רַגְלֶךָ: עַל־שַׁחַל וָפֶתֶן תִּדְרֹךְ,
תִּרְמֹס כְּפִיר וְתַנִּין: כִּי בִי חָשַׁק וַאֲפַלְּטֵהוּ, אֲשַׂגְּבֵהוּ כִּי־יָדַע
שְׁמִי: יִקְרָאֵנִי וְאֶעֱנֵהוּ, עִמּוֹ אָנֹכִי בְצָרָה, אֲחַלְּצֵהוּ וַאֲכַבְּדֵהוּ:
◂ אֹרֶךְ יָמִים אַשְׂבִּיעֵהוּ, וְאַרְאֵהוּ בִּישׁוּעָתִי:
אֹרֶךְ יָמִים אַשְׂבִּיעֵהוּ, וְאַרְאֵהוּ בִּישׁוּעָתִי:

◂ וְאַתָּה קָדוֹשׁ יוֹשֵׁב תְּהִלּוֹת יִשְׂרָאֵל: תהלים כב
וְקָרָא זֶה אֶל־זֶה וְאָמַר
קָדוֹשׁ, קָדוֹשׁ, קָדוֹשׁ, יהוה צְבָאוֹת, מְלֹא כָל־הָאָרֶץ כְּבוֹדוֹ: ישעיה ו
וּמְקַבְּלִין דֵּין מִן דֵּין וְאָמְרִין תרגום יונתן ישעיה ו
קַדִּישׁ בִּשְׁמֵי מְרוֹמָא עִלָּאָה בֵּית שְׁכִינְתֵהּ
קַדִּישׁ עַל אַרְעָא עוֹבַד גְּבוּרְתֵהּ
קַדִּישׁ לְעָלַם וּלְעָלְמֵי עָלְמַיָּא
יהוה צְבָאוֹת, מַלְיָא כָל אַרְעָא זִיו יְקָרֵהּ.

◂ וַתִּשָּׂאֵנִי רוּחַ, וָאֶשְׁמַע אַחֲרַי קוֹל רַעַשׁ גָּדוֹל יחזקאל ג
בָּרוּךְ כְּבוֹד־יהוה מִמְּקוֹמוֹ:
וּנְטָלַתְנִי רוּחָא, וּשְׁמָעִית בַּתְרַי קָל זִיעַ סַגִּיא, דִּמְשַׁבְּחִין וְאָמְרִין תרגום יונתן יחזקאל ג
בְּרִיךְ יְקָרָא דַיהוה מֵאֲתַר בֵּית שְׁכִינְתֵהּ.

יהוה יִמְלֹךְ לְעֹלָם וָעֶד: שמות טו
יהוה מַלְכוּתֵהּ קָאֵם לְעָלַם וּלְעָלְמֵי עָלְמַיָּא. תרגום אונקלוס שמות טו

יהוה Lord, God of Abraham, Isaac and Yisrael, our ancestors, may *1 Chr. 29*
You keep this for ever so that it forms the thoughts in Your people's
heart, and directs their heart toward You. He is compassionate. He *Ps. 78*
forgives iniquity and does not destroy. Repeatedly He suppresses
His anger, not rousing His full wrath. For You, my Lord, are good *Ps. 86*
and forgiving, abundantly kind to all who call on You. Your righ- *Ps. 119*
teousness is eternally righteous, and Your Torah is truth. Grant *Micah 7*
truth to Jacob, loving-kindness to Abraham, as You promised our
ancestors in ancient times. Blessed is my Lord for day after day He *Ps. 68*
burdens us [with His blessings]; God is our salvation, Selah! The *Ps. 46*
Lord of hosts is with us; the God of Jacob is our refuge, Selah!
Lord of hosts, happy is the one who trusts in You. Lord, save! *Ps. 84* *Ps. 20*
May the King answer us on the day we call.

בָּרוּךְ Blessed is He, our God, who created us for His glory, separating us from those who go astray; who gave us the Torah of truth, planting within us eternal life. May He open our heart to His Torah, imbuing our heart with the love and awe of Him, that we may do His will and serve Him with a perfect heart, so that we neither toil in vain nor give birth to confusion.

יְהִי רָצוֹן May it be Your will, O Lord our God and God of our ancestors, that we keep Your laws in this world, and thus be worthy to live,
see and inherit goodness and blessing in the Messianic Age and in
the life of the World to Come. So that my soul may sing to You and *Ps. 30*
not be silent. Lord, my God, for ever I will thank You. Blessed is *Jer. 17*
the man who trusts in the Lord, whose trust is in the Lord alone.
Trust in the Lord for evermore, for God, the Lord, is an everlast- *Is. 26*
ing Rock. ▸ Those who know Your name trust in You, for You, Lord, *Ps. 9*
do not forsake those who seek You. The Lord desired, for the sake *Is. 42*
of Israel's merit, to make the Torah great and glorious.

יהוה אֱלֹהֵי אַבְרָהָם יִצְחָק וְיִשְׂרָאֵל אֲבֹתֵינוּ, שָׁמְרָה־זֹּאת לְעוֹלָם דברי הימים א׳ כט
לְיֵצֶר מַחְשְׁבוֹת לְבַב עַמֶּךָ, וְהָכֵן לְבָבָם אֵלֶיךָ: וְהוּא רַחוּם יְכַפֵּר תהלים עח
עָוֹן וְלֹא־יַשְׁחִית, וְהִרְבָּה לְהָשִׁיב אַפּוֹ, וְלֹא־יָעִיר כָּל־חֲמָתוֹ:
כִּי־אַתָּה אֲדֹנָי טוֹב וְסַלָּח, וְרַב־חֶסֶד לְכָל־קֹרְאֶיךָ: צִדְקָתְךָ תהלים פו תהלים קיט
צֶדֶק לְעוֹלָם וְתוֹרָתְךָ אֱמֶת: תִּתֵּן אֱמֶת לְיַעֲקֹב, חֶסֶד לְאַבְרָהָם, מיכה ז
אֲשֶׁר־נִשְׁבַּעְתָּ לַאֲבֹתֵינוּ מִימֵי קֶדֶם: בָּרוּךְ אֲדֹנָי יוֹם יוֹם יַעֲמָס־ תהלים סח
לָנוּ, הָאֵל יְשׁוּעָתֵנוּ סֶלָה: יהוה צְבָאוֹת עִמָּנוּ, מִשְׂגָּב לָנוּ אֱלֹהֵי תהלים מו
יַעֲקֹב סֶלָה: יהוה צְבָאוֹת, אַשְׁרֵי אָדָם בֹּטֵחַ בָּךְ: יהוה הוֹשִׁיעָה, תהלים פד תהלים כ
הַמֶּלֶךְ יַעֲנֵנוּ בְיוֹם־קָרְאֵנוּ:

בָּרוּךְ הוּא אֱלֹהֵינוּ שֶׁבְּרָאָנוּ לִכְבוֹדוֹ, וְהִבְדִּילָנוּ מִן הַתּוֹעִים, וְנָתַן לָנוּ תּוֹרַת אֱמֶת, וְחַיֵּי עוֹלָם נָטַע בְּתוֹכֵנוּ. הוּא יִפְתַּח לִבֵּנוּ בְּתוֹרָתוֹ, וְיָשֵׂם בְּלִבֵּנוּ אַהֲבָתוֹ וְיִרְאָתוֹ וְלַעֲשׂוֹת רְצוֹנוֹ וּלְעָבְדוֹ בְּלֵבָב שָׁלֵם, לְמַעַן לֹא נִיגַע לָרִיק וְלֹא נֵלֵד לַבֶּהָלָה.

יְהִי רָצוֹן מִלְּפָנֶיךָ יהוה אֱלֹהֵינוּ וֵאלֹהֵי אֲבוֹתֵינוּ, שֶׁנִּשְׁמֹר חֻקֶּיךָ
בָּעוֹלָם הַזֶּה, וְנִזְכֶּה וְנִחְיֶה וְנִרְאֶה וְנִירַשׁ טוֹבָה וּבְרָכָה, לִשְׁנֵי
יְמוֹת הַמָּשִׁיחַ וּלְחַיֵּי הָעוֹלָם הַבָּא. לְמַעַן יְזַמֶּרְךָ כָבוֹד וְלֹא יִדֹּם, תהלים ל
יהוה אֱלֹהַי, לְעוֹלָם אוֹדֶךָּ: בָּרוּךְ הַגֶּבֶר אֲשֶׁר יִבְטַח בַּיהוה, ירמיה יז
וְהָיָה יהוה מִבְטַחוֹ: בִּטְחוּ בַיהוה עֲדֵי־עַד, כִּי בְּיָהּ יהוה צוּר ישעיה כו
עוֹלָמִים: ‹ וְיִבְטְחוּ בְךָ יוֹדְעֵי שְׁמֶךָ, כִּי לֹא־עָזַבְתָּ דֹרְשֶׁיךָ, יהוה: תהלים ט
יהוה חָפֵץ לְמַעַן צִדְקוֹ, יַגְדִּיל תּוֹרָה וְיַאְדִּיר: ישעיה מב

FULL KADDISH

Leader: יִתְגַּדַּל Magnified and sanctified may His great name be,
in the world He created by His will.
May He establish His kingdom in your lifetime
and in your days,
and in the lifetime of all the house of Israel,
swiftly and soon –
and say: Amen.

All: May His great name be blessed for ever and all time.

Leader: Blessed and praised, glorified and exalted,
raised and honored,
uplifted and lauded be
the name of the Holy One,
blessed be He,
beyond any blessing,
song, praise and consolation uttered in the world –
and say: Amen.

On Tisha B'Av, omit the next verse and continue with "May there be great peace."

May the prayers and pleas of all Israel
be accepted by their Father in heaven –
and say: Amen.

May there be great peace from heaven,
and life for us and all Israel –
and say: Amen.

Bow, take three steps back, as if taking leave of the Divine Presence, then bow, first left, then right, then center, while saying:

May He who makes peace in His high places,
make peace for us and all Israel –
and say: Amen.

קדיש שלם

ש״ץ: יִתְגַּדַּל וְיִתְקַדַּשׁ שְׁמֵהּ רַבָּא (קהל: אָמֵן)
בְּעָלְמָא דִּי בְרָא כִרְעוּתֵהּ
וְיַמְלִיךְ מַלְכוּתֵהּ
בְּחַיֵּיכוֹן וּבְיוֹמֵיכוֹן וּבְחַיֵּי דְכָל בֵּית יִשְׂרָאֵל
בַּעֲגָלָא וּבִזְמַן קָרִיב, וְאִמְרוּ אָמֵן. (קהל: אָמֵן)

קהל וש״ץ: יְהֵא שְׁמֵהּ רַבָּא מְבָרַךְ לְעָלַם וּלְעָלְמֵי עָלְמַיָּא.

ש״ץ: יִתְבָּרַךְ וְיִשְׁתַּבַּח וְיִתְפָּאַר
וְיִתְרוֹמַם וְיִתְנַשֵּׂא וְיִתְהַדָּר וְיִתְעַלֶּה וְיִתְהַלָּל
שְׁמֵהּ דְּקֻדְשָׁא בְּרִיךְ הוּא (קהל: בְּרִיךְ הוּא)
לְעֵלָּא מִן כָּל בִּרְכָתָא
וְשִׁירָתָא, תֻּשְׁבְּחָתָא וְנֶחֱמָתָא
דַּאֲמִירָן בְּעָלְמָא, וְאִמְרוּ אָמֵן. (קהל: אָמֵן)

On תשעה באב, omit the next verse and continue with יְהֵא שְׁלָמָא.

תִּתְקַבַּל צְלוֹתְהוֹן וּבָעוּתְהוֹן דְּכָל יִשְׂרָאֵל
קֳדָם אֲבוּהוֹן דִּי בִשְׁמַיָּא, וְאִמְרוּ אָמֵן. (קהל: אָמֵן)

יְהֵא שְׁלָמָא רַבָּא מִן שְׁמַיָּא
וְחַיִּים, עָלֵינוּ וְעַל כָּל יִשְׂרָאֵל, וְאִמְרוּ אָמֵן. (קהל: אָמֵן)

Bow, take three steps back, as if taking leave of the Divine Presence, then bow, first left, then right, then center, while saying:

עֹשֶׂה שָׁלוֹם בִּמְרוֹמָיו
הוּא יַעֲשֶׂה שָׁלוֹם עָלֵינוּ
וְעַל כָּל יִשְׂרָאֵל, וְאִמְרוּ אָמֵן. (קהל: אָמֵן)

On Tisha B'Av, the following prayers are omitted and the service continues with Aleinu on page 358.

BIBLICAL VERSES OF BLESSING

וְיִתֶּן־לְךָ May God give you dew from heaven and the richness of the earth, and corn and wine in plenty. May peoples serve you and nations bow down to you. Be lord over your brothers, and may your mother's sons bow down to you. A curse on those who curse you, but a blessing on those who bless you. *Gen. 27*

וְאֵל שַׁדַּי May God Almighty bless you; may He make you fruitful and numerous until you become an assembly of peoples. May He give you and your descendants the blessing of Abraham, that you may possess the land where you are now staying, the land God gave to Abraham. *Gen. 28* This comes from the God of your father – may He help you – and from the Almighty – may He bless you with blessings of the heaven above and the blessings of the deep that lies below, the blessings of breast and womb. The blessings of your father surpass the blessings of my fathers to the bounds of the endless hills. May they rest on the head of Joseph, on the brow of the prince among his brothers. *Gen. 49* He will love you and bless you and increase your numbers. He will bless the fruit of your womb and the fruit of your land: your corn, your wine and oil, the calves of your herds and the lambs of your flocks, in the land He swore to your fathers to give you. You will be blessed more than any other people. None of your men or women will be childless, nor any of your livestock without young. The LORD will keep you free from any disease. He will not inflict on you the terrible diseases you knew in Egypt, but He will inflict them on those who hate you. *Deut. 7*

הַמַּלְאָךְ May the angel who rescued me from all harm, bless these boys. May they be called by my name and the names of my fathers Abraham and Isaac, and may they increase greatly on the earth. *Gen. 48* The LORD your God has increased your numbers so that today you are as many as the stars in the sky. May the LORD, God of your fathers, increase you a thousand times, and bless you as He promised you. *Deut. 1*

---

and the land. The subsequent paragraphs contain other blessings for redemption, forgiveness, the absence of shame, the presence of joy, peace and consolation, all worthwhile dreams for the coming week. There is no way to know what the coming days will bring. We can only hope and pray.

What are your hopes and prayers for the coming week?

On תשעה באב*, the following prayers are omitted and the service continues with* עָלֵינוּ *on page 359.*

פסוקי ברכה

וְיִתֶּן־לְךָ הָאֱלֹהִים מִטַּל הַשָּׁמַיִם וּמִשְׁמַנֵּי הָאָרֶץ, וְרֹב דָּגָן וְתִירֹשׁ: יַעַבְדוּךָ בראשית כז
עַמִּים וְיִשְׁתַּחֲוֻ לְךָ לְאֻמִּים, הֱוֵה גְבִיר לְאַחֶיךָ וְיִשְׁתַּחֲווּ לְךָ בְּנֵי אִמֶּךָ,
אֹרְרֶיךָ אָרוּר וּמְבָרְכֶיךָ בָּרוּךְ:

וְאֵל שַׁדַּי יְבָרֵךְ אֹתְךָ וְיַפְרְךָ וְיַרְבֶּךָ, וְהָיִיתָ לִקְהַל עַמִּים: וְיִתֶּן־לְךָ אֶת־ בראשית כח
בִּרְכַּת אַבְרָהָם, לְךָ וּלְזַרְעֲךָ אִתָּךְ, לְרִשְׁתְּךָ אֶת־אֶרֶץ מְגֻרֶיךָ אֲשֶׁר־נָתַן
אֱלֹהִים לְאַבְרָהָם: מֵאֵל אָבִיךָ וְיַעְזְרֶךָּ וְאֵת שַׁדַּי וִיבָרְכֶךָּ, בִּרְכֹת שָׁמַיִם בראשית מט
מֵעָל בִּרְכֹת תְּהוֹם רֹבֶצֶת תָּחַת, בִּרְכֹת שָׁדַיִם וָרָחַם: בִּרְכֹת אָבִיךָ גָּבְרוּ
עַל־בִּרְכֹת הוֹרַי עַד־תַּאֲוַת גִּבְעֹת עוֹלָם, תִּהְיֶיןָ לְרֹאשׁ יוֹסֵף וּלְקָדְקֹד
נְזִיר אֶחָיו: וַאֲהֵבְךָ וּבֵרַכְךָ וְהִרְבֶּךָ, וּבֵרַךְ פְּרִי־בִטְנְךָ וּפְרִי־אַדְמָתֶךָ, דְּגָנְךָ דברים ז
וְתִירֹשְׁךָ וְיִצְהָרֶךָ, שְׁגַר־אֲלָפֶיךָ וְעַשְׁתְּרֹת צֹאנֶךָ, עַל הָאֲדָמָה אֲשֶׁר־נִשְׁבַּע
לַאֲבֹתֶיךָ לָתֶת לָךְ: בָּרוּךְ תִּהְיֶה מִכָּל־הָעַמִּים, לֹא־יִהְיֶה בְךָ עָקָר וַעֲקָרָה
וּבִבְהֶמְתֶּךָ: וְהֵסִיר יהוה מִמְּךָ כָּל־חֹלִי, וְכָל־מַדְוֵי מִצְרַיִם הָרָעִים אֲשֶׁר
יָדַעְתָּ, לֹא יְשִׂימָם בָּךְ, וּנְתָנָם בְּכָל־שֹׂנְאֶיךָ:

הַמַּלְאָךְ הַגֹּאֵל אֹתִי מִכָּל־רָע יְבָרֵךְ אֶת־הַנְּעָרִים, וְיִקָּרֵא בָהֶם שְׁמִי וְשֵׁם בראשית מח
אֲבֹתַי אַבְרָהָם וְיִצְחָק, וְיִדְגּוּ לָרֹב בְּקֶרֶב הָאָרֶץ: יהוה אֱלֹהֵיכֶם הִרְבָּה דברים א
אֶתְכֶם, וְהִנְּכֶם הַיּוֹם כְּכוֹכְבֵי הַשָּׁמַיִם לָרֹב: יהוה אֱלֹהֵי אֲבוֹתֵיכֶם יֹסֵף
עֲלֵיכֶם כָּכֶם אֶלֶף פְּעָמִים, וִיבָרֵךְ אֶתְכֶם כַּאֲשֶׁר דִּבֶּר לָכֶם:

BIUR TEFILLA • ביאור תפילה

וְיִתֶּן־לְךָ – *May God give you.* What follows are a series of extra prayers that are added in some congregations. They are blessings for prosperity for the coming week and are drawn from the source, that is to say, from blessings which appear in chronological order in the Torah. It begins with a blessing given by Yitzḥak to Yaakov (*Bereshit* 27), a blessing by Yaakov to Yosef and his brothers (*Bereshit* 49) and a blessing by Moshe to Israel (*Devarim* 7) all referring to the blessings of children

בָּרוּךְ You will be blessed in the city, and blessed in the field. You will be blessed when you come in, and blessed when you go out. Your basket and your kneading trough will be blessed. The fruit of your womb will be blessed, and the crops of your land, and the young of your livestock, the calves of your herds and the lambs of your flocks. The LORD will send a blessing on your barns, and on everything you put your hand to. The LORD your God will bless you in the land He is giving you. The LORD will open for you the heavens, the storehouse of His bounty, to send rain on your land in season, and to bless all the work of your hands. You will lend to many nations but will borrow from none. For the LORD your God will bless you as He has promised: you will lend to many nations but will borrow from none. You will rule over many nations, but none will rule over you. Happy are you, Israel! Who is like you, a people saved by the LORD? He is your Shield and Helper and your glorious Sword. Your enemies will cower before you, and you will tread on their high places. *Deut. 28* *Deut. 15* *Deut. 33*

מָחִיתִי I have wiped away your transgressions like a cloud, your sins like the morning mist. Return to Me for I have redeemed you. Sing for joy, O heavens, for the LORD has done this; shout aloud, you depths of the earth; burst into song, you mountains, you forests and all your trees, for the LORD has redeemed Jacob, and will glory in Israel. Our Redeemer, the LORD of hosts is His name, the Holy One of Israel. *Is. 44* *Is. 47*

יִשְׂרָאֵל Israel is saved by the LORD with everlasting salvation. You will never be ashamed or disgraced to time everlasting. You will eat your fill and praise the name of the LORD your God, who has worked wonders for you. Never again shall My people be shamed. Then you will know that I am in the midst of Israel, that I am the LORD your God, and there is no other. Never again will My people be shamed. You will go out in joy and be led out in peace. The mountains and hills will burst into song before you, and all the trees of the field will clap their hands. Behold, God is my salvation, I will trust and not be afraid. The LORD, the LORD, is my strength and my song. He has become my salvation. With joy you will draw water from the springs of salvation. On that day you will say, "Thank the LORD, proclaim His name, make His deeds known among the nations." Declare that His name is exalted. Sing to the LORD, for He has done glorious things; let this be known throughout the world. Shout aloud and sing for joy, you who dwell in Zion, for great in your midst is the Holy One of Israel. On that day they will say, "See, this is our God; we set our hope in Him and He saved us. This is the LORD in whom we hoped; let us rejoice and be glad in His salvation." *Is. 45* *Joel 2* *Is. 55* *Is. 12* *Is. 25*

בֵּית Come, house of Jacob: let us walk in the light of the LORD. He will be the sure foundation of your times; a rich store of salvation, wisdom and knowledge – the fear of the LORD is a person's treasure. In everything he did, David was successful, for the LORD was with him. *Is. 2* *Is. 32* *I Sam. 18*

בָּרוּךְ אַתָּה בָּעִיר, וּבָרוּךְ אַתָּה בַּשָּׂדֶה: בָּרוּךְ אַתָּה בְּבֹאֶךָ, וּבָרוּךְ אַתָּה דברים כח
בְּצֵאתֶךָ: בָּרוּךְ טַנְאֲךָ וּמִשְׁאַרְתֶּךָ: בָּרוּךְ פְּרִי־בִטְנְךָ וּפְרִי אַדְמָתְךָ וּפְרִי
בְהֶמְתֶּךָ, שְׁגַר אֲלָפֶיךָ וְעַשְׁתְּרוֹת צֹאנֶךָ: יְצַו יהוה אִתְּךָ אֶת־הַבְּרָכָה
בַּאֲסָמֶיךָ וּבְכֹל מִשְׁלַח יָדֶךָ, וּבֵרַכְךָ בָּאָרֶץ אֲשֶׁר־יהוה אֱלֹהֶיךָ נֹתֵן לָךְ:
יִפְתַּח יהוה לְךָ אֶת־אוֹצָרוֹ הַטּוֹב אֶת־הַשָּׁמַיִם, לָתֵת מְטַר־אַרְצְךָ בְּעִתּוֹ,
וּלְבָרֵךְ אֵת כָּל־מַעֲשֵׂה יָדֶךָ, וְהִלְוִיתָ גּוֹיִם רַבִּים וְאַתָּה לֹא תִלְוֶה: כִּי־יהוה דברים טו
אֱלֹהֶיךָ בֵּרַכְךָ כַּאֲשֶׁר דִּבֶּר־לָךְ, וְהַעֲבַטְתָּ גּוֹיִם רַבִּים וְאַתָּה לֹא תַעֲבֹט,
וּמָשַׁלְתָּ בְּגוֹיִם רַבִּים וּבְךָ לֹא יִמְשֹׁלוּ: אַשְׁרֶיךָ יִשְׂרָאֵל, מִי כָמוֹךָ, עַם דברים לג
נוֹשַׁע בַּיהוה, מָגֵן עֶזְרֶךָ וַאֲשֶׁר־חֶרֶב גַּאֲוָתֶךָ, וְיִכָּחֲשׁוּ אֹיְבֶיךָ לָךְ, וְאַתָּה
עַל־בָּמוֹתֵימוֹ תִדְרֹךְ:

מָחִיתִי כָעָב פְּשָׁעֶיךָ וְכֶעָנָן חַטֹּאותֶיךָ, שׁוּבָה אֵלַי כִּי גְאַלְתִּיךָ: רָנּוּ שָׁמַיִם ישעיה מד
כִּי־עָשָׂה יהוה, הָרִיעוּ תַּחְתִּיּוֹת אָרֶץ, פִּצְחוּ הָרִים רִנָּה, יַעַר וְכָל־עֵץ בּוֹ,
כִּי־גָאַל יהוה יַעֲקֹב וּבְיִשְׂרָאֵל יִתְפָּאָר: גֹּאֲלֵנוּ, יהוה צְבָאוֹת שְׁמוֹ, קְדוֹשׁ ישעיה מז
יִשְׂרָאֵל:

יִשְׂרָאֵל נוֹשַׁע בַּיהוה תְּשׁוּעַת עוֹלָמִים, לֹא־תֵבֹשׁוּ וְלֹא־תִכָּלְמוּ עַד־עוֹלְמֵי ישעיה מה
עַד: וַאֲכַלְתֶּם אָכוֹל וְשָׂבוֹעַ, וְהִלַּלְתֶּם אֶת־שֵׁם יהוה אֱלֹהֵיכֶם אֲשֶׁר־עָשָׂה יואל ב
עִמָּכֶם לְהַפְלִיא, וְלֹא־יֵבֹשׁוּ עַמִּי לְעוֹלָם: וִידַעְתֶּם כִּי בְקֶרֶב יִשְׂרָאֵל
אָנִי, וַאֲנִי יהוה אֱלֹהֵיכֶם וְאֵין עוֹד, וְלֹא־יֵבֹשׁוּ עַמִּי לְעוֹלָם: כִּי־בְשִׂמְחָה ישעיה נה
תֵצֵאוּ וּבְשָׁלוֹם תּוּבָלוּן, הֶהָרִים וְהַגְּבָעוֹת יִפְצְחוּ לִפְנֵיכֶם רִנָּה, וְכָל־עֲצֵי
הַשָּׂדֶה יִמְחֲאוּ־כָף: הִנֵּה אֵל יְשׁוּעָתִי אֶבְטַח, וְלֹא אֶפְחָד, כִּי־עָזִּי וְזִמְרָת ישעיה יב
יָהּ יהוה, וַיְהִי־לִי לִישׁוּעָה: וּשְׁאַבְתֶּם־מַיִם בְּשָׂשׂוֹן, מִמַּעַיְנֵי הַיְשׁוּעָה:
וַאֲמַרְתֶּם בַּיּוֹם הַהוּא, הוֹדוּ לַיהוה קִרְאוּ בִשְׁמוֹ, הוֹדִיעוּ בָעַמִּים עֲלִילֹתָיו,
הַזְכִּירוּ כִּי נִשְׂגָּב שְׁמוֹ: זַמְּרוּ יהוה כִּי גֵאוּת עָשָׂה, מוּדַעַת זֹאת בְּכָל־
הָאָרֶץ: צַהֲלִי וָרֹנִּי יוֹשֶׁבֶת צִיּוֹן, כִּי־גָדוֹל בְּקִרְבֵּךְ קְדוֹשׁ יִשְׂרָאֵל: וְאָמַר ישעיה כה
בַּיּוֹם הַהוּא, הִנֵּה אֱלֹהֵינוּ זֶה קִוִּינוּ לוֹ וְיוֹשִׁיעֵנוּ, זֶה יהוה קִוִּינוּ לוֹ, נָגִילָה
וְנִשְׂמְחָה בִּישׁוּעָתוֹ:

בֵּית יַעֲקֹב לְכוּ וְנֵלְכָה בְּאוֹר יהוה: וְהָיָה אֱמוּנַת עִתֶּיךָ, חֹסֶן יְשׁוּעֹת חָכְמַת ישעיה ב ישעיה לג
וָדָעַת, יִרְאַת יהוה הִיא אוֹצָרוֹ: וַיְהִי דָוִד לְכָל־דְּרָכָו מַשְׂכִּיל, וַיהוה עִמּוֹ: שמואל א׳ יח

פָּדָה He redeemed my soul in peace from the battle waged against me, for the sake *Ps. 55* of the many who were with me. The people said to Saul, "Shall Jonathan die – he *1 Sam. 14* who has brought about this great deliverance in Israel? Heaven forbid! As surely as the LORD lives, not a hair of his head shall fall to the ground, for he did this today with God's help." So the people rescued Jonathan and he did not die. Those *Is. 35* redeemed by the LORD shall return; they will enter Zion singing; everlasting joy will crown their heads. Gladness and joy will overtake them, and sorrow and sighing will flee away.

הָפַכְתָּ You have turned my sorrow into dancing. You have removed my sackcloth *Ps. 30* and clothed me with joy. The LORD your God refused to listen to Balaam; in- *Deut. 23* stead the LORD your God turned the curse into a blessing, for the LORD your God loves you. Then maidens will dance and be glad; so too will young men and *Jer. 31* old together; I will turn their mourning into gladness; I will give them comfort and joy instead of sorrow.

בּוֹרֵא I create the speech of lips: Peace, peace to those far and near, says the LORD, *Is. 57* and I will heal them. Then the spirit came upon Amasai, chief of the captains, *1 Chr. 12* and he said: "We are yours, David! We are with you, son of Jesse! Peace, peace to you, and peace to those who help you; for your God will help you." Then David received them and made them leaders of his troop. And you shall say: "To life! *1 Sam. 25* Peace be to you, peace to your household, and peace to all that is yours!" The *Ps. 29* LORD will give strength to His people; the LORD will bless His people with peace.

אָמַר Rabbi Yoḥanan said: Wherever you find the greatness of the Holy One, *Megilla 31a* blessed be He, there you find His humility. This is written in the Torah, repeated in the Prophets, and stated a third time in the Writings. It is written in the Torah: "For the LORD your God is God of gods and LORD of lords, the great, *Deut. 10* mighty and awe-inspiring God, who shows no favoritism and accepts no bribe." Immediately afterwards it is written, "He upholds the cause of the orphan and widow, and loves the stranger, giving him food and clothing." It is repeated in the

---

be omens for good and for blessing instead (*Tur* 220).

אָמַר רַבִּי יוֹחָנָן – *Rabbi Yoḥanan said.* Herein are extolled the virtues of humility taking Hashem Himself as our role model for, as this passage from the Gemara explains (*Megilla* 31a), this attribute of God is extolled across the entire Bible as evidenced in passages from the Torah, the Prophets and the Writings. Perhaps the reason for this message here is that as we are about to enter into the week, we need to recall that the people who are the weakest in society are deserving of special protection by Hashem, something that we need to emulate or else run the risk of being held accountable. In Hashem's greatness lies His humility. In our humility and sensitivity to the weaker people around us, we may find our greatness.

פָּדָה בְשָׁלוֹם נַפְשִׁי מִקְּרָב־לִי, כִּי־בְרַבִּים הָיוּ עִמָּדִי: וַיֹּאמֶר הָעָם אֶל־ תהלים נה שמואל א׳ יד
שָׁאוּל, הֲיוֹנָתָן יָמוּת אֲשֶׁר עָשָׂה הַיְשׁוּעָה הַגְּדוֹלָה הַזֹּאת בְּיִשְׂרָאֵל,
חָלִילָה, חַי־יהוה אִם־יִפֹּל מִשַּׂעֲרַת רֹאשׁוֹ אַרְצָה, כִּי־עִם־אֱלֹהִים עָשָׂה
הַיּוֹם הַזֶּה, וַיִּפְדּוּ הָעָם אֶת־יוֹנָתָן וְלֹא־מֵת: וּפְדוּיֵי יהוה יְשֻׁבוּן וּבָאוּ צִיּוֹן ישעיה לה
בְּרִנָּה, וְשִׂמְחַת עוֹלָם עַל־רֹאשָׁם, שָׂשׂוֹן וְשִׂמְחָה יַשִּׂיגוּ, וְנָסוּ יָגוֹן וַאֲנָחָה:

הָפַכְתָּ מִסְפְּדִי לְמָחוֹל לִי, פִּתַּחְתָּ שַׂקִּי, וַתְּאַזְּרֵנִי שִׂמְחָה: וְלֹא־אָבָה יהוה תהלים ל דברים כג
אֱלֹהֶיךָ לִשְׁמֹעַ אֶל־בִּלְעָם, וַיַּהֲפֹךְ יהוה אֱלֹהֶיךָ לְּךָ אֶת־הַקְּלָלָה לִבְרָכָה,
כִּי אֲהֵבְךָ יהוה אֱלֹהֶיךָ: אָז תִּשְׂמַח בְּתוּלָה בְּמָחוֹל, וּבַחֻרִים וּזְקֵנִים יַחְדָּו, ירמיה לא
וְהָפַכְתִּי אֶבְלָם לְשָׂשׂוֹן, וְנִחַמְתִּים, וְשִׂמַּחְתִּים מִיגוֹנָם:

בּוֹרֵא נִיב שְׂפָתָיִם, שָׁלוֹם שָׁלוֹם לָרָחוֹק וְלַקָּרוֹב אָמַר יהוה, וּרְפָאתִיו: וְרוּחַ ישעיה נז דברי הימים א׳ יב
לָבְשָׁה אֶת־עֲמָשַׂי רֹאשׁ הַשָּׁלִישִׁים, לְךָ דָוִיד וְעִמְּךָ בֶן־יִשַׁי, שָׁלוֹם שָׁלוֹם
לְךָ וְשָׁלוֹם לְעֹזְרֶךָ, כִּי עֲזָרְךָ אֱלֹהֶיךָ, וַיְקַבְּלֵם דָּוִיד וַיִּתְּנֵם בְּרָאשֵׁי הַגְּדוּד:
וַאֲמַרְתֶּם כֹּה לֶחָי, וְאַתָּה שָׁלוֹם וּבֵיתְךָ שָׁלוֹם וְכֹל אֲשֶׁר־לְךָ שָׁלוֹם: יהוה שמואל א׳ כה תהלים כט
עֹז לְעַמּוֹ יִתֵּן, יהוה יְבָרֵךְ אֶת־עַמּוֹ בַשָּׁלוֹם:

אָמַר רַבִּי יוֹחָנָן: בְּכָל מָקוֹם שֶׁאַתָּה מוֹצֵא גְּדֻלָּתוֹ שֶׁל הַקָּדוֹשׁ בָּרוּךְ הוּא, מגילה לא.
שָׁם אַתָּה מוֹצֵא עַנְוְתָנוּתוֹ. דָּבָר זֶה כָּתוּב בַּתּוֹרָה, וְשָׁנוּי בַּנְּבִיאִים, וּמְשֻׁלָּשׁ
בַּכְּתוּבִים. כָּתוּב בַּתּוֹרָה: כִּי יהוה אֱלֹהֵיכֶם הוּא אֱלֹהֵי הָאֱלֹהִים וַאֲדֹנֵי דברים י
הָאֲדֹנִים, הָאֵל הַגָּדֹל הַגִּבֹּר וְהַנּוֹרָא, אֲשֶׁר לֹא־יִשָּׂא פָנִים וְלֹא יִקַּח שֹׁחַד:
וּכְתִיב בָּתְרֵהּ: עֹשֶׂה מִשְׁפַּט יָתוֹם וְאַלְמָנָה, וְאֹהֵב גֵּר לָתֶת לוֹ לֶחֶם וְשִׂמְלָה:

IYUN TEFILLA • עיון תפילה

פָּדָה... הָפַכְתָּ... בּוֹרֵא נִיב – *He redeemed... You have turned... I create the speech.* The Gemara (*Berakhot* 55b) instructs that when one has a bad dream, one should recite three sets of three verses, each set containing at least one reference to the words redemption, reversal and peace respectively. The siddur uses these themes in each of the following paragraphs, perhaps expressing the hope that just as we pray when we wake with a start that a bad dream ultimately turns out to be a good omen (or a purging of the fears of our inner consciousness) so, too, we hope that whatever ominous things may lie ahead of us in the coming hours and days, they should

Prophets, as it says: "So says the High and Exalted One, who lives for ever and whose name is Holy: I live in a high and holy place, but also with the contrite and lowly in spirit, to revive the spirit of the lowly, and to revive the heart of the contrite." It is stated a third time in the Writings: "Sing to God, make music for His name, extol Him who rides the clouds – the LORD is His name – and exult before Him." Immediately afterwards it is written: "Father of the orphans and Justice of widows, is God in His holy habitation." *Is. 57* *Ps. 68*

יְהִי May the LORD our God be with us, as He was with our ancestors. May He never abandon us or forsake us. You who cleave to the LORD your God are all alive this day. For the LORD will comfort Zion, He will comfort all her ruins; He will make her wilderness like Eden, and her desert like a garden of the LORD. Joy and gladness will be found there, thanksgiving and the sound of singing. It pleased the LORD for the sake of [Israel's] righteousness to make the Torah great and glorious. *1 Kings 8* *Deut. 4* *Is. 51* *Is. 42*

שִׁיר הַמַּעֲלוֹת A song of ascents. Happy are all who fear the LORD, who walk in His ways. When you eat the fruit of your labor, happy and fortunate are you. Your wife shall be like a fruitful vine within your house; your sons like olive saplings around your table. So shall the man who fears the LORD be blessed. May the LORD bless you from Zion; may you see the good of Jerusalem all the days of your life; and may you live to see your children's children. Peace be on Israel! *Ps. 128*

HAVDALA IN THE SYNAGOGUE

Some say the full Havdala on page 370.

The Leader takes the cup of wine in his right hand, and says:

Please pay attention, my masters.

Blessed are You, LORD our God, King of the Universe,
who creates the fruit of the vine.

Holding the spice box, the Leader says:

Blessed are You, LORD our God, King of the Universe,
who creates the various spices.

The Leader smells the spices and puts the spice box down.
He lifts his hands toward the flame of the Havdala candle, and says:

Blessed are You, LORD our God, King of the Universe,
who creates the lights of fire.

He lifts the cup of wine in his right hand, and says:

Blessed are You, LORD our God, King of the Universe, who distinguishes between sacred and secular, between light and darkness, between Israel and the nations, between the seventh day and the six days of work. Blessed are You, LORD, who distinguishes between sacred and secular.

שָׁנוּי בַּנְּבִיאִים, דִּכְתִיב: כִּי כֹה אָמַר רָם וְנִשָּׂא שֹׁכֵן עַד וְקָדוֹשׁ שְׁמוֹ, מָרוֹם ישעיה נז
וְקָדוֹשׁ אֶשְׁכּוֹן, וְאֶת־דַּכָּא וּשְׁפַל־רוּחַ, לְהַחֲיוֹת רוּחַ שְׁפָלִים וּלְהַחֲיוֹת לֵב
נִדְכָּאִים: מְשֻׁלָּשׁ בַּכְּתוּבִים, דִּכְתִיב: שִׁירוּ לֵאלֹהִים, זַמְּרוּ שְׁמוֹ, סֹלּוּ לָרֹכֵב תהלים סח
בָּעֲרָבוֹת בְּיָהּ שְׁמוֹ, וְעִלְזוּ לְפָנָיו: וּכְתִיב בַּתְרֵהּ: אֲבִי יְתוֹמִים וְדַיַּן אַלְמָנוֹת,
אֱלֹהִים בִּמְעוֹן קָדְשׁוֹ:

יְהִי יהוה אֱלֹהֵינוּ עִמָּנוּ כַּאֲשֶׁר הָיָה עִם־אֲבֹתֵינוּ, אַל־יַעַזְבֵנוּ וְאַל־יִטְּשֵׁנוּ: מלכים א׳ ח
וְאַתֶּם הַדְּבֵקִים בַּיהוה אֱלֹהֵיכֶם, חַיִּים כֻּלְּכֶם הַיּוֹם: כִּי־נִחַם יהוה צִיּוֹן, נִחַם דברים ד ישעיה נא
כָּל־חָרְבֹתֶיהָ, וַיָּשֶׂם מִדְבָּרָהּ כְּעֵדֶן וְעַרְבָתָהּ כְּגַן־יהוה, שָׂשׂוֹן וְשִׂמְחָה יִמָּצֵא
בָהּ, תּוֹדָה וְקוֹל זִמְרָה: יהוה חָפֵץ לְמַעַן צִדְקוֹ, יַגְדִּיל תּוֹרָה וְיַאְדִּיר: ישעיה מב

שִׁיר הַמַּעֲלוֹת, אַשְׁרֵי כָּל־יְרֵא יהוה, הַהֹלֵךְ בִּדְרָכָיו: יְגִיעַ כַּפֶּיךָ כִּי תֹאכֵל, תהלים קכח
אַשְׁרֶיךָ וְטוֹב לָךְ: אֶשְׁתְּךָ כְּגֶפֶן פֹּרִיָּה בְּיַרְכְּתֵי בֵיתֶךָ, בָּנֶיךָ כִּשְׁתִלֵי זֵיתִים,
סָבִיב לְשֻׁלְחָנֶךָ: הִנֵּה כִי־כֵן יְבֹרַךְ גָּבֶר יְרֵא יהוה: יְבָרֶכְךָ יהוה מִצִּיּוֹן, וּרְאֵה
בְּטוּב יְרוּשָׁלָםִ, כֹּל יְמֵי חַיֶּיךָ: וּרְאֵה־בָנִים לְבָנֶיךָ, שָׁלוֹם עַל־יִשְׂרָאֵל:

הבדלה בבית הכנסת

Some say the full הבדלה *on page 371.*

The שליח ציבור *takes the cup of wine in his right hand, and says:*

סַבְרִי מָרָנָן

בָּרוּךְ אַתָּה יהוה אֱלֹהֵינוּ מֶלֶךְ הָעוֹלָם, בּוֹרֵא פְּרִי הַגָּפֶן.

Holding the spice box, the שליח ציבור *says:*

בָּרוּךְ אַתָּה יהוה אֱלֹהֵינוּ מֶלֶךְ הָעוֹלָם, בּוֹרֵא מִינֵי בְשָׂמִים.

The שליח ציבור *smells the spices and puts the spice box down.*
He lifts his hands toward the flame of the הבדלה *candle, and says:*

בָּרוּךְ אַתָּה יהוה אֱלֹהֵינוּ מֶלֶךְ הָעוֹלָם, בּוֹרֵא מְאוֹרֵי הָאֵשׁ.

He lifts the cup of wine in his right hand, and says:

בָּרוּךְ אַתָּה יהוה אֱלֹהֵינוּ מֶלֶךְ הָעוֹלָם, הַמַּבְדִּיל בֵּין קֹדֶשׁ לְחֹל, בֵּין אוֹר לְחֹשֶׁךְ, בֵּין יִשְׂרָאֵל לָעַמִּים, בֵּין יוֹם הַשְּׁבִיעִי לְשֵׁשֶׁת יְמֵי הַמַּעֲשֶׂה.
בָּרוּךְ אַתָּה יהוה, הַמַּבְדִּיל בֵּין קֹדֶשׁ לְחֹל.

The commentary on *Havdala* can be found on page 371.

Stand while saying Aleinu. Bow at ▾.

עָלֵינוּ It is our duty to praise the Master of all,
and ascribe greatness to the Author of creation,
who has not made us like the nations of the lands
nor placed us like the families of the earth;
who has not made our portion like theirs,
nor our destiny like all their multitudes.
(For they worship vanity and emptiness,
and pray to a god who cannot save.)
▾But we bow in worship and thank the Supreme King of kings,
the Holy One, blessed be He,
who extends the heavens and establishes the earth,
whose throne of glory is in the heavens above,
and whose power's Presence is in the highest of heights.
He is our God; there is no other.
Truly He is our King, there is none else, as it is written in His Torah:
"You shall know and take to heart this day that the LORD is God, *Deut. 4*
in heaven above and on earth below. There is no other."

Therefore, we place our hope in You, LORD our God,
that we may soon see the glory of Your power,
when You will remove abominations from the earth,
and idols will be utterly destroyed,
when the world will be perfected under the sovereignty of the Almighty,
when all humanity will call on Your name,
to turn all the earth's wicked toward You.
All the world's inhabitants will realize and know
that to You every knee must bow and every tongue swear loyalty.
Before You, LORD our God, they will kneel and bow down
and give honor to Your glorious name.
They will all accept the yoke of Your kingdom,
and You will reign over them soon and for ever.
For the kingdom is Yours, and to all eternity You will reign in glory,
as it is written in Your Torah:
"The LORD will reign for ever and ever." *Ex. 15*
▸ And it is said: "Then the LORD shall be King over all the earth; *Zech. 14*
on that day the LORD shall be One and His name One."

Stand while saying עָלֵינוּ. *Bow at* ▾.

עָלֵינוּ לְשַׁבֵּחַ לַאֲדוֹן הַכֹּל, לָתֵת גְּדֻלָּה לְיוֹצֵר בְּרֵאשִׁית
שֶׁלֹּא עָשָׂנוּ כְּגוֹיֵי הָאֲרָצוֹת, וְלֹא שָׂמָנוּ כְּמִשְׁפְּחוֹת הָאֲדָמָה
שֶׁלֹּא שָׂם חֶלְקֵנוּ כָּהֶם וְגוֹרָלֵנוּ כְּכָל הֲמוֹנָם.
(שֶׁהֵם מִשְׁתַּחֲוִים לְהֶבֶל וָרִיק וּמִתְפַּלְלִים אֶל אֵל לֹא יוֹשִׁיעַ.)
▾וַאֲנַחְנוּ כּוֹרְעִים וּמִשְׁתַּחֲוִים וּמוֹדִים
לִפְנֵי מֶלֶךְ מַלְכֵי הַמְּלָכִים, הַקָּדוֹשׁ בָּרוּךְ הוּא
שֶׁהוּא נוֹטֶה שָׁמַיִם וְיוֹסֵד אָרֶץ
וּמוֹשַׁב יְקָרוֹ בַּשָּׁמַיִם מִמַּעַל
וּשְׁכִינַת עֻזּוֹ בְּגָבְהֵי מְרוֹמִים.
הוּא אֱלֹהֵינוּ, אֵין עוֹד.
אֱמֶת מַלְכֵּנוּ, אֶפֶס זוּלָתוֹ, כַּכָּתוּב בְּתוֹרָתוֹ
דברים ד וְיָדַעְתָּ הַיּוֹם וַהֲשֵׁבֹתָ אֶל־לְבָבֶךָ
כִּי יהוה הוּא הָאֱלֹהִים בַּשָּׁמַיִם מִמַּעַל וְעַל־הָאָרֶץ מִתָּחַת, אֵין עוֹד:

עַל כֵּן נְקַוֶּה לְּךָ יהוה אֱלֹהֵינוּ, לִרְאוֹת מְהֵרָה בְּתִפְאֶרֶת עֻזֶּךָ
לְהַעֲבִיר גִּלּוּלִים מִן הָאָרֶץ, וְהָאֱלִילִים כָּרוֹת יִכָּרֵתוּן
לְתַקֵּן עוֹלָם בְּמַלְכוּת שַׁדַּי.
וְכָל בְּנֵי בָשָׂר יִקְרְאוּ בִשְׁמֶךָ לְהַפְנוֹת אֵלֶיךָ כָּל רִשְׁעֵי אָרֶץ.
יַכִּירוּ וְיֵדְעוּ כָּל יוֹשְׁבֵי תֵבֵל, כִּי לְךָ תִּכְרַע כָּל בֶּרֶךְ, תִּשָּׁבַע כָּל לָשׁוֹן.
לְפָנֶיךָ יהוה אֱלֹהֵינוּ יִכְרְעוּ וְיִפֹּלוּ, וְלִכְבוֹד שִׁמְךָ יְקָר יִתֵּנוּ
וִיקַבְּלוּ כֻלָּם אֶת עֹל מַלְכוּתֶךָ וְתִמְלֹךְ עֲלֵיהֶם מְהֵרָה לְעוֹלָם וָעֶד.
כִּי הַמַּלְכוּת שֶׁלְּךָ הִיא וּלְעוֹלְמֵי עַד תִּמְלֹךְ בְּכָבוֹד
כַּכָּתוּב בְּתוֹרָתֶךָ
שמות טו יהוה יִמְלֹךְ לְעֹלָם וָעֶד:
זכריה יד ◂ וְנֶאֱמַר, וְהָיָה יהוה לְמֶלֶךְ עַל־כָּל־הָאָרֶץ
בַּיּוֹם הַהוּא יִהְיֶה יהוה אֶחָד וּשְׁמוֹ אֶחָד:

Some add:

Have no fear of sudden terror or of the ruin when it overtakes the wicked. *Prov. 3*
Devise your strategy, but it will be thwarted; propose your plan, *Is. 8*
but it will not stand, for God is with us.
When you grow old, I will still be the same. *Is. 46*
When your hair turns gray, I will still carry you.
I made you, I will bear you, I will carry you, and I will rescue you.

MOURNER'S KADDISH

The following prayer, said by mourners, requires the presence of a minyan. A transliteration can be found on page 1141.

Mourner: יִתְגַּדַּל Magnified and sanctified
may His great name be,
in the world He created by His will.
May He establish His kingdom
in your lifetime and in your days,
and in the lifetime of all the house of Israel,
swiftly and soon –
and say: Amen.

All: May His great name be blessed for ever and all time.

Mourner: Blessed and praised, glorified and exalted,
raised and honored, uplifted and lauded
be the name of the Holy One,
blessed be He,
beyond any blessing, song, praise and consolation
uttered in the world –
and say: Amen.

May there be great peace from heaven,
and life for us and all Israel – and say: Amen.

Bow, take three steps back, as if taking leave of the Divine Presence, then bow, first left, then right, then center, while saying:

May He who makes peace in His high places,
make peace for us and all Israel –
and say: Amen.

Some add:

משלי ג אַל־תִּירָא מִפַּחַד פִּתְאֹם וּמִשֹּׁאַת רְשָׁעִים כִּי תָבֹא:

ישעיה ח עֻצוּ עֵצָה וְתֻפָר, דַּבְּרוּ דָבָר וְלֹא יָקוּם, כִּי עִמָּנוּ אֵל:

ישעיה מו וְעַד־זִקְנָה אֲנִי הוּא, וְעַד־שֵׂיבָה אֲנִי אֶסְבֹּל
אֲנִי עָשִׂיתִי וַאֲנִי אֶשָּׂא וַאֲנִי אֶסְבֹּל וַאֲמַלֵּט:

קדיש יתום

The following prayer, said by mourners, requires the presence of a מנין.
A transliteration can be found on page 1141.

אבל: יִתְגַּדַּל וְיִתְקַדַּשׁ שְׁמֵהּ רַבָּא (קהל: אָמֵן)
בְּעָלְמָא דִּי בְרָא כִרְעוּתֵהּ
וְיַמְלִיךְ מַלְכוּתֵהּ
בְּחַיֵּיכוֹן וּבְיוֹמֵיכוֹן וּבְחַיֵּי דְכָל בֵּית יִשְׂרָאֵל
בַּעֲגָלָא וּבִזְמַן קָרִיב, וְאִמְרוּ אָמֵן. (קהל: אָמֵן)

קהל ואבל: יְהֵא שְׁמֵהּ רַבָּא מְבָרַךְ לְעָלַם וּלְעָלְמֵי עָלְמַיָּא.

אבל: יִתְבָּרַךְ וְיִשְׁתַּבַּח וְיִתְפָּאַר
וְיִתְרוֹמַם וְיִתְנַשֵּׂא וְיִתְהַדָּר וְיִתְעַלֶּה וְיִתְהַלָּל
שְׁמֵהּ דְּקֻדְשָׁא בְּרִיךְ הוּא (קהל: בְּרִיךְ הוּא)
לְעֵלָּא מִן כָּל בִּרְכָתָא
וְשִׁירָתָא, תֻּשְׁבְּחָתָא וְנֶחֱמָתָא
דַּאֲמִירָן בְּעָלְמָא, וְאִמְרוּ אָמֵן. (קהל: אָמֵן)

יְהֵא שְׁלָמָא רַבָּא מִן שְׁמַיָּא
וְחַיִּים, עָלֵינוּ וְעַל כָּל יִשְׂרָאֵל, וְאִמְרוּ אָמֵן. (קהל: אָמֵן)

Bow, take three steps back, as if taking leave of the Divine Presence, then bow, first left, then right, then center, while saying:

עֹשֶׂה שָׁלוֹם בִּמְרוֹמָיו
הוּא יַעֲשֶׂה שָׁלוֹם עָלֵינוּ
וְעַל כָּל יִשְׂרָאֵל, וְאִמְרוּ אָמֵן. (קהל: אָמֵן)

From the second day of Rosh Ḥodesh Elul through Shemini Atzeret (in Israel through Hoshana Raba), the following psalm is said:

לְדָוִד By David. The LORD is my light and my salvation – whom then shall I fear? The LORD is the stronghold of my life – of whom shall I be afraid? When evil men close in on me to devour my flesh, it is they, my enemies and foes, who stumble and fall. Should an army besiege me, my heart would not fear. Should war break out against me, still I would be confident. One thing I ask of the LORD, only this do I seek: to live in the House of the LORD all the days of my life, to gaze on the beauty of the LORD and worship in His Temple. For He will keep me safe in His pavilion on the day of trouble. He will hide me under the cover of His tent. He will set me high upon a rock. Now my head is high above my enemies who surround me. I will sacrifice in His tent with shouts of joy. I will sing and chant praises to the LORD. LORD, hear my voice when I call. Be gracious to me and answer me. On Your behalf my heart says, "Seek My face." Your face, LORD, will I seek. Do not hide Your face from me. Do not turn Your servant away in anger. You have been my help. Do not reject or forsake me, God, my Savior. Were my father and my mother to forsake me, the LORD would take me in. Teach me Your way, LORD, and lead me on a level path, because of my oppressors. Do not abandon me to the will of my foes, for false witnesses have risen against me, breathing violence. ▸ Were it not for my faith that I shall see the LORD's goodness in the land of the living. Hope in the LORD. Be strong and of good courage, and hope in the LORD! *Ps. 27*

Mourner's Kaddish (on previous page)

---

but my family did not change. Then I realized: first, I must change myself. (Rabbi Israel Salanter)

How will you change yourself this week? This year?

From the second day of ראש חודש אלול *through* שמיני עצרת
(*in* ארץ ישראל *through* הושענא רבה), *the following psalm is said:*

תהלים כז

לְדָוִד, יהוה אוֹרִי וְיִשְׁעִי, מִמִּי אִירָא, יהוה מָעוֹז־חַיַּי, מִמִּי אֶפְחָד: בִּקְרֹב עָלַי מְרֵעִים לֶאֱכֹל אֶת־בְּשָׂרִי, צָרַי וְאֹיְבַי לִי, הֵמָּה כָשְׁלוּ וְנָפָלוּ: אִם־תַּחֲנֶה עָלַי מַחֲנֶה, לֹא־יִירָא לִבִּי, אִם־תָּקוּם עָלַי מִלְחָמָה, בְּזֹאת אֲנִי בוֹטֵחַ: אַחַת שָׁאַלְתִּי מֵאֵת־יהוה, אוֹתָהּ אֲבַקֵּשׁ, שִׁבְתִּי בְּבֵית־יהוה כָּל־יְמֵי חַיַּי, לַחֲזוֹת בְּנֹעַם־יהוה, וּלְבַקֵּר בְּהֵיכָלוֹ: כִּי יִצְפְּנֵנִי בְּסֻכֹּה בְּיוֹם רָעָה, יַסְתִּרֵנִי בְּסֵתֶר אָהֳלוֹ, בְּצוּר יְרוֹמְמֵנִי: וְעַתָּה יָרוּם רֹאשִׁי עַל אֹיְבַי סְבִיבוֹתַי, וְאֶזְבְּחָה בְאָהֳלוֹ זִבְחֵי תְרוּעָה, אָשִׁירָה וַאֲזַמְּרָה לַיהוה: שְׁמַע־יהוה קוֹלִי אֶקְרָא, וְחָנֵּנִי וַעֲנֵנִי: לְךָ אָמַר לִבִּי בַּקְּשׁוּ פָנָי, אֶת־פָּנֶיךָ יהוה אֲבַקֵּשׁ: אַל־תַּסְתֵּר פָּנֶיךָ מִמֶּנִּי, אַל תַּט־בְּאַף עַבְדֶּךָ, עֶזְרָתִי הָיִיתָ, אַל־תִּטְּשֵׁנִי וְאַל־תַּעַזְבֵנִי, אֱלֹהֵי יִשְׁעִי: כִּי־אָבִי וְאִמִּי עֲזָבוּנִי, וַיהוה יַאַסְפֵנִי: הוֹרֵנִי יהוה דַּרְכֶּךָ, וּנְחֵנִי בְּאֹרַח מִישׁוֹר, לְמַעַן שׁוֹרְרָי: אַל־תִּתְּנֵנִי בְּנֶפֶשׁ צָרָי, כִּי קָמוּ־בִי עֵדֵי־שֶׁקֶר, וִיפֵחַ חָמָס: › לוּלֵא הֶאֱמַנְתִּי לִרְאוֹת בְּטוּב־יהוה בְּאֶרֶץ חַיִּים: קַוֵּה אֶל־יהוה, חֲזַק וְיַאֲמֵץ לִבֶּךָ, וְקַוֵּה אֶל־יהוה:

קדיש יתום (*on previous page*)

ANI TEFILLA • אני תפילה

At first, I wanted to change the world. I tried, but the world did not change. Then I tried to change my town, but the town did not change. Then I tried to change my family,

BLESSING OF THE NEW MOON

Kiddush Levana, the Blessing of the New Moon, is said between the third day and the middle day of each month. If possible, it should be said at the end of Shabbat, under the open sky, and in the presence of a minyan.

הַלְלוּיָהּ Halleluya! Praise the LORD from the heavens, praise Him in the heights. Praise Him, all His angels; praise Him, all His hosts. Praise Him, sun and moon; praise Him, all shining stars. Praise Him, highest heavens and the waters above the heavens. Let them praise the name of the LORD, for He commanded and they were created. He established them for ever and all time, issuing a decree that will never change. *Ps. 148*

כִּי־אֶרְאֶה When I see Your heavens, the work of Your fingers, the moon and the stars which You have set in place: What is man that You are mindful of him, the son of man that You care for him? *Ps. 8*

Look at the moon, then say:

בָּרוּךְ Blessed are You, LORD our God, King of the Universe who by His word created the heavens, and by His breath all their host. He set for them laws and times, so that they should not deviate from their appointed task. They are joyous and glad to perform the will of their Owner, the Worker of truth whose work is truth. To the moon He said that it should renew itself as a crown of beauty for those He carried from the womb [Israel], for they are destined to be renewed like it, and to praise their Creator for the sake of His glorious majesty. Blessed are You, LORD, who renews the months.

The following five verses are each said three times:

Blessed is He who formed you; blessed is He who made you;
blessed is He who owns you; blessed is He who created you.

The following verse is said rising on the toes.

Just as I leap toward you but cannot touch you,
so may none of my enemies be able to touch me to do me harm.

May fear and dread fall upon them; *Ex. 15*
by the power of Your arm may they be still as stone.

May they be still as stone through the power of Your arm,
when dread and fear fall upon them.

קידוש לבנה

קידוש לבנה, the Blessing of the New Moon, is said between the third day and the middle day of each month. If possible, it should be said at the end of שבת, under the open sky, and in the presence of a מנין.

הַלְלוּיָהּ, הַלְלוּ אֶת־יהוה מִן־הַשָּׁמַיִם, הַלְלוּהוּ בַּמְּרוֹמִים: הַלְלוּהוּ תהלים קמח
כָל־מַלְאָכָיו, הַלְלוּהוּ כָּל־צְבָאָו: הַלְלוּהוּ שֶׁמֶשׁ וְיָרֵחַ, הַלְלוּהוּ
כָּל־כּוֹכְבֵי אוֹר: הַלְלוּהוּ שְׁמֵי הַשָּׁמָיִם, וְהַמַּיִם אֲשֶׁר מֵעַל הַשָּׁמָיִם:
יְהַלְלוּ אֶת־שֵׁם יהוה, כִּי הוּא צִוָּה וְנִבְרָאוּ: וַיַּעֲמִידֵם לָעַד לְעוֹלָם,
חָק־נָתַן וְלֹא יַעֲבוֹר:

כִּי־אֶרְאֶה שָׁמֶיךָ מַעֲשֵׂה אֶצְבְּעֹתֶיךָ, יָרֵחַ וְכוֹכָבִים אֲשֶׁר כּוֹנָנְתָּה: תהלים ח
מָה־אֱנוֹשׁ כִּי־תִזְכְּרֶנּוּ, וּבֶן־אָדָם כִּי תִפְקְדֶנּוּ:

Look at the moon, then say:

בָּרוּךְ אַתָּה יהוה אֱלֹהֵינוּ מֶלֶךְ הָעוֹלָם, אֲשֶׁר בְּמַאֲמָרוֹ בָּרָא שְׁחָקִים, וּבְרוּחַ פִּיו כָּל צְבָאָם, חֹק וּזְמַן נָתַן לָהֶם שֶׁלֹּא יְשַׁנּוּ אֶת תַּפְקִידָם. שָׂשִׂים וּשְׂמֵחִים לַעֲשׂוֹת רְצוֹן קוֹנָם, פּוֹעֵל אֱמֶת שֶׁפְּעֻלָּתוֹ אֱמֶת. וְלַלְּבָנָה אָמַר שֶׁתִּתְחַדֵּשׁ, עֲטֶרֶת תִּפְאֶרֶת לַעֲמוּסֵי בָטֶן, שֶׁהֵם עֲתִידִים לְהִתְחַדֵּשׁ כְּמוֹתָהּ וּלְפָאֵר לְיוֹצְרָם עַל שֵׁם כְּבוֹד מַלְכוּתוֹ. בָּרוּךְ אַתָּה יהוה, מְחַדֵּשׁ חֳדָשִׁים.

The following five verses are each said three times:

בָּרוּךְ יוֹצְרֵךְ, בָּרוּךְ עוֹשֵׂךְ, בָּרוּךְ קוֹנֵךְ, בָּרוּךְ בּוֹרְאֵךְ.

The following verse is said rising on the toes.

כְּשֵׁם שֶׁאֲנִי רוֹקֵד כְּנֶגְדֵּךְ וְאֵינִי יָכוֹל לִנְגֹּעַ בָּךְ
כָּךְ לֹא יוּכְלוּ כָּל אוֹיְבַי לִנְגֹּעַ בִּי לְרָעָה.

תִּפֹּל עֲלֵיהֶם אֵימָתָה וָפַחַד, בִּגְדֹל זְרוֹעֲךָ יִדְּמוּ כָּאָבֶן: שמות טו
כָּאָבֶן יִדְּמוּ זְרוֹעֲךָ בִּגְדֹל, וָפַחַד אֵימָתָה עֲלֵיהֶם תִּפֹּל.

David, King of Israel, lives and endures.

Turn to three people and say to each:

Peace upon you.

They respond:

Upon you, peace.

Say three times:

May it be a good sign and a good omen for us and all Israel. Amen.

קוֹל Hark! My beloved! Here he comes, leaping over the mountains, bounding over the hills. My beloved is like a gazelle, like a young deer. There he stands outside our wall, peering in through the windows, gazing through the lattice. *Song. 2*

שִׁיר לַמַּעֲלוֹת A song of ascents. I lift my eyes up to the hills; from where will my help come? My help comes from the LORD, Maker of heaven and earth. He will not let your foot stumble; He who guards you does not slumber. See: the Guardian of Israel neither slumbers nor sleeps. The LORD is your Guardian; the LORD is your Shade at your right hand. The sun will not strike you by day, nor the moon by night. The LORD will guard you from all harm; He will guard your life. The LORD will guard your going and coming, now and for evermore. *Ps. 121*

הַלְלוּיָהּ Halleluya! Praise God in His holy place; praise Him in the heavens of His power. Praise Him for His mighty deeds; praise Him for His surpassing greatness. Praise Him with blasts of the ram's horn; praise Him with the harp and lyre. Praise Him with timbrel and dance; praise Him with strings and flute. Praise Him with clashing cymbals; praise Him with resounding cymbals. Let all that breathes praise the LORD. Halleluya! *Ps. 150*

תָּנָא In the academy of Rabbi Yishmael it was taught: Were the people of Israel privileged to greet the presence of their heavenly Father only once a month, it would have been sufficient for them. Abaye said: Therefore it [the blessing of the moon] should be said standing. Who is this coming up from the desert, leaning on her beloved? *Sanhedrin 42a* *Song. 8*

דָּוִד מֶלֶךְ יִשְׂרָאֵל חַי וְקַיָּם.

Turn to three people and say to each:

שָׁלוֹם עֲלֵיכֶם.

They respond:

עֲלֵיכֶם שָׁלוֹם.

Say three times:

סִימָן טוֹב וּמַזָּל טוֹב יְהֵא לָנוּ וּלְכָל יִשְׂרָאֵל, אָמֵן.

קוֹל דּוֹדִי הִנֵּה־זֶה בָּא, מְדַלֵּג עַל־הֶהָרִים, מְקַפֵּץ עַל־הַגְּבָעוֹת: דּוֹמֶה דוֹדִי לִצְבִי אוֹ לְעֹפֶר הָאַיָּלִים, הִנֵּה־זֶה עוֹמֵד אַחַר כָּתְלֵנוּ, מַשְׁגִּיחַ מִן־הַחַלֹּנוֹת, מֵצִיץ מִן־הַחֲרַכִּים: שיר השירים ב

שִׁיר לַמַּעֲלוֹת, אֶשָּׂא עֵינַי אֶל־הֶהָרִים, מֵאַיִן יָבֹא עֶזְרִי: עֶזְרִי מֵעִם יהוה, עֹשֵׂה שָׁמַיִם וָאָרֶץ: אַל־יִתֵּן לַמּוֹט רַגְלֶךָ, אַל־יָנוּם שֹׁמְרֶךָ: הִנֵּה לֹא־יָנוּם וְלֹא יִישָׁן, שׁוֹמֵר יִשְׂרָאֵל: יהוה שֹׁמְרֶךָ, יהוה צִלְּךָ עַל־יַד יְמִינֶךָ: יוֹמָם הַשֶּׁמֶשׁ לֹא־יַכֶּכָּה, וְיָרֵחַ בַּלָּיְלָה: יהוה יִשְׁמָרְךָ מִכָּל־רָע, יִשְׁמֹר אֶת־נַפְשֶׁךָ: יהוה יִשְׁמָר־צֵאתְךָ וּבוֹאֶךָ, מֵעַתָּה וְעַד־עוֹלָם: תהלים קכא

הַלְלוּיָהּ, הַלְלוּ־אֵל בְּקָדְשׁוֹ, הַלְלוּהוּ בִּרְקִיעַ עֻזּוֹ: הַלְלוּהוּ בִגְבוּרֹתָיו, הַלְלוּהוּ כְּרֹב גֻּדְלוֹ: הַלְלוּהוּ בְּתֵקַע שׁוֹפָר, הַלְלוּהוּ בְּנֵבֶל וְכִנּוֹר: הַלְלוּהוּ בְתֹף וּמָחוֹל, הַלְלוּהוּ בְּמִנִּים וְעוּגָב: הַלְלוּהוּ בְצִלְצְלֵי־שָׁמַע, הַלְלוּהוּ בְּצִלְצְלֵי תְרוּעָה: כֹּל הַנְּשָׁמָה תְּהַלֵּל יָהּ, הַלְלוּיָהּ: תהלים קנ

תָּנָא דְבֵי רַבִּי יִשְׁמָעֵאל: אִלְמָלֵי לֹא זָכוּ יִשְׂרָאֵל אֶלָּא לְהַקְבִּיל פְּנֵי אֲבִיהֶם שֶׁבַּשָּׁמַיִם פַּעַם אַחַת בַּחֹדֶשׁ, דַּיָּם. אָמַר אַבַּיֵּי: הִלְכָּךְ צָרִיךְ לְמֵימְרָא מְעֻמָּד. מִי זֹאת עֹלָה מִן־הַמִּדְבָּר, מִתְרַפֶּקֶת עַל־דּוֹדָהּ: סנהדרין מב. שיר השירים ח

וִיהִי May it be Your will, LORD my God and God of my ancestors, to make good the deficiency of the moon, so that it is no longer in its diminished state. May the light of the moon be like the light of the sun and like the light of the seven days of creation as it was before it was diminished, as it says, "The two great luminaries." And may there *Gen. 1* be fulfilled for us the verse: "They shall seek the LORD their God, and *Hos. 3* David their king." Amen.

לַמְנַצֵּחַ For the conductor of music. With stringed instruments, a psalm. *Ps. 67* A song. May God be gracious to us and bless us. May He make His face shine on us, Selah. Then will Your way be known on earth, Your salvation among all the nations. Let the peoples praise You, God; let all peoples praise You. Let nations rejoice and sing for joy, for You judge the peoples with equity, and guide the nations of the earth, Selah. Let the peoples praise You, God; let all peoples praise You. The earth has yielded its harvest. May God, our God, bless us. God will bless us, and all the ends of the earth will fear Him.

The service continues with Aleinu (page 358)
and Mourner's Kaddish (page 360)
followed by "Good are the radiant stars" below.

All sing:

טוֹבִים Good are the radiant stars our God created;
He formed them with knowledge,
understanding and deliberation.
He gave them strength and might
to rule throughout the world.

Full of splendor, radiating light,
beautiful is their splendor throughout the world.
Glad as they go forth, joyous as they return,
they fulfill with awe their Creator's will.

Glory and honor they give to His name,
jubilation and song at the mention of His majesty.
He called the sun into being and it shone with light.
He looked and fashioned the form of the moon.

וִיהִי רָצוֹן מִלְּפָנֶיךָ יהוה אֱלֹהַי וֵאלֹהֵי אֲבוֹתַי, לְמַלֹּאת פְּגִימַת הַלְּבָנָה וְלֹא יִהְיֶה בָּהּ שׁוּם מִעוּט. וִיהִי אוֹר הַלְּבָנָה כְּאוֹר הַחַמָּה וּכְאוֹר שִׁבְעַת יְמֵי בְרֵאשִׁית, כְּמוֹ שֶׁהָיְתָה קֹדֶם מִעוּטָהּ, שֶׁנֶּאֱמַר: אֶת־שְׁנֵי בראשית א
הַמְּאֹרֹת הַגְּדֹלִים: וְיִתְקַיֵּם בָּנוּ מִקְרָא שֶׁכָּתוּב: וּבִקְשׁוּ אֶת־יהוה הושע ג
אֱלֹהֵיהֶם וְאֵת דָּוִיד מַלְכָּם: אָמֵן.

לַמְנַצֵּחַ בִּנְגִינֹת, מִזְמוֹר שִׁיר: אֱלֹהִים יְחָנֵּנוּ וִיבָרְכֵנוּ, יָאֵר פָּנָיו אִתָּנוּ תהלים סז
סֶלָה: לָדַעַת בָּאָרֶץ דַּרְכֶּךָ, בְּכָל־גּוֹיִם יְשׁוּעָתֶךָ: יוֹדוּךָ עַמִּים אֱלֹהִים, יוֹדוּךָ עַמִּים כֻּלָּם: יִשְׂמְחוּ וִירַנְּנוּ לְאֻמִּים, כִּי־תִשְׁפֹּט עַמִּים מִישֹׁר, וּלְאֻמִּים בָּאָרֶץ תַּנְחֵם סֶלָה: יוֹדוּךָ עַמִּים אֱלֹהִים, יוֹדוּךָ עַמִּים כֻּלָּם: אֶרֶץ נָתְנָה יְבוּלָהּ, יְבָרְכֵנוּ אֱלֹהִים אֱלֹהֵינוּ: יְבָרְכֵנוּ אֱלֹהִים, וְיִירְאוּ אוֹתוֹ כָּל־אַפְסֵי־אָרֶץ:

The service continues with קדיש יתום *(page 359) and* עָלֵינוּ *(page 361) followed by* טוֹבִים מְאוֹרוֹת *below.*

All sing:

טוֹבִים מְאוֹרוֹת שֶׁבָּרָא אֱלֹהֵינוּ
יְצָרָם בְּדַעַת בְּבִינָה וּבְהַשְׂכֵּל
כֹּחַ וּגְבוּרָה נָתַן בָּהֶם
לִהְיוֹת מוֹשְׁלִים בְּקֶרֶב תֵּבֵל.

מְלֵאִים זִיו וּמְפִיקִים נֹגַהּ
נָאֶה זִיוָם בְּכָל הָעוֹלָם
שְׂמֵחִים בְּצֵאתָם וְשָׂשִׂים בְּבוֹאָם
עוֹשִׂים בְּאֵימָה רְצוֹן קוֹנָם.

פְּאֵר וְכָבוֹד נוֹתְנִים לִשְׁמוֹ
צָהֳלָה וְרִנָּה לְזֵכֶר מַלְכוּתוֹ
קָרָא לַשֶּׁמֶשׁ וַיִּזְרַח אוֹר
רָאָה וְהִתְקִין צוּרַת הַלְּבָנָה.

HAVDALA AT HOME

Taking a cup of wine in the right hand, say:

הִנֵּה Behold, God is my salvation. I will trust and not be afraid. *Is. 12*
The LORD, the LORD, is my strength and my song.
He has become my salvation.
With joy you will draw water from the springs of salvation.
Salvation is the LORD's; on Your people is Your blessing, Selah. *Ps. 3*
The LORD of hosts is with us, the God of Jacob is our stronghold, Selah. *Ps. 46*
LORD of hosts: happy is the one who trusts in You. *Ps. 84*
LORD, save! May the King answer us on the day we call. *Ps. 20*
For the Jews there was light and gladness, joy and honor – *Esther 8*
so may it be for us.
I will lift the cup of salvation and call on the name of the LORD. *Ps. 116*

fire was granted as a gift by God for man to join Him in becoming a creator, to continue the act of creation and help perfect the world. Beginning the week by lighting a match is also a way of highlighting the difference between Shabbat whose beginning is marked by the lighting of candles and the cessation of any further "work," and the end of Shabbat which is marked by our relighting a candle to show that "work" is now permitted. Alternatively, it is as if light was created anew (Rashba cited *Be'er Heiteiv* 299:14) and the process of creation begins once again. To see the light cast from the candle is to banish darkness and feel joy at the ability to control one's environment (*Pirkei DeRabbi Eliezer* 20).

And finally, there is a blessing which highlights the differences between light and darkness, the holy and the profane, Israel and the nations. Hopefully these are among the lessons that we have been reminded of over Shabbat, the ones that will help us approach the coming week with the right perspective as creators, as holy beings, and as people with a mission to be a holy light unto the nations.

The order of the blessings seems to go in order of the senses or faculties moving from the lower to the upper portions of our head, i.e., for wine we use our sense of taste, for spices our sense of smell, for light our sense of sight, and for the final blessing we use our intelligence to distinguish between the holy and the mundane (Rabbi Y. Jacobson).

HILKHOT TEFILLA · הלכות תפילה

Havdala is usually said while standing (Rema) although some do sit (*Shulḥan Arukh* 296:6). Although there is a custom to recite it in the synagogue, just we did

This **HILKHOT TEFILLA** *continues on page 373.*

סדר הבדלה בבית

Taking a cup of wine in the right hand, say:

הִנֵּה אֵל יְשׁוּעָתִי אֶבְטַח, וְלֹא אֶפְחָד ישעיה יב
כִּי־עָזִּי וְזִמְרָת יָהּ יהוה, וַיְהִי־לִי לִישׁוּעָה:
וּשְׁאַבְתֶּם־מַיִם בְּשָׂשׂוֹן, מִמַּעַיְנֵי הַיְשׁוּעָה:
לַיהוה הַיְשׁוּעָה, עַל־עַמְּךָ בִרְכָתֶךָ סֶּלָה: תהלים ג
יהוה צְבָאוֹת עִמָּנוּ, מִשְׂגָּב לָנוּ אֱלֹהֵי יַעֲקֹב סֶלָה: תהלים מו
יהוה צְבָאוֹת, אַשְׁרֵי אָדָם בֹּטֵחַ בָּךְ: תהלים פד
יהוה הוֹשִׁיעָה, הַמֶּלֶךְ יַעֲנֵנוּ בְיוֹם־קָרְאֵנוּ: תהלים כ
לַיְּהוּדִים הָיְתָה אוֹרָה וְשִׂמְחָה וְשָׂשֹׂן וִיקָר: כֵּן תִּהְיֶה לָּנוּ. אסתר ח
כּוֹס־יְשׁוּעוֹת אֶשָּׂא, וּבְשֵׁם יהוה אֶקְרָא: תהלים קטז

INTRODUCTION TO HAVDALA

Just as we ushered in the Shabbat with candles and wine, so too do we escort her out. This is an extension of the commandment to "remember the Shabbat and sanctify it" for remembering is as much an obligation as we cross over the threshold from the holy to the mundane as it was when we crossed from the mundane to the holy twenty-five hours ago. (Rambam, *Sefer HaMitzvot* 155). The very name of the ceremony, *Havdala*, derives from the Hebrew word "to separate" or "distinguish."

The Kiddush is preceded by the recitation of some verses that focus on the theme of salvation (mentioned seven times) and the name of Hashem (eight times), as if to say that rescue during the coming week will come from Hashem alone, and only to those who put their faith in Him.

Another blessing is said over fragrant spices, designed to provide consolation and rejuvenation, a kind of counterbalance to the loss of our *neshama yeteira*, the extra soul which helped to animate and spiritualize us over the course of Shabbat (Abudarham). This is to make the departure of Shabbat less abrupt and disconcerting.

Another blessing is then said over a candle with multiple wicks. It is the symbolic representation of our return to the creative process of the week. The Gemara (*Pesaḥim* 54a) relates that after the very first Shabbat, Adam decided to replicate the actions of God and brought two stones, rubbed them together, and created fire. Unlike Prometheus of Greek mythology who defied the gods by stealing fire and giving it to humanity, in the Jewish conception,

When making Havdala for others, add:
Please pay attention, my masters.

Blessed are You, Lord our God, King of the Universe,
who creates the fruit of the vine.

Hold the spice box and say:

Blessed are You, Lord our God, King of the Universe,
who creates the various spices.

Smell the spices and put the spice box down.
Lift the hands toward the flame of the Havdala candle and say:

Blessed are You, Lord our God, King of the Universe,
who creates the lights of fire.

Holding the cup of wine again in the right hand, say:

בָּרוּךְ Blessed are You, Lord our God, King of the Universe,
who distinguishes between sacred and secular,
between light and darkness,
between Israel and the nations,
between the seventh day and the six days of work.
Blessed are You, Lord,
who distinguishes between sacred and secular.

---

one's love for the mitzva or as a symbolic prayer for a week filled with insight and wisdom.

Regarding the blessing over the candle, since one does not recite a blessing of this kind without deriving some resulting benefit, the custom is to hold up one's hands to be able to see them in the light of the candle and thereby use the light that is cast from the flame. Some specifically look at the reflection from their fingernails to see the contrast between shadows and light. Some also look at their fingers in the bent position as if to say that they have been tied down from using fire or "work" during Shabbat, and then stretch them open in the light of the flame in order to show that they are now free again to be used as they wish (Maharam of Rothenburg).

When making הבדלה *for others, add:*

סַבְרִי מָרָנָן

בָּרוּךְ אַתָּה יהוה אֱלֹהֵינוּ מֶלֶךְ הָעוֹלָם
בּוֹרֵא פְּרִי הַגָּפֶן.

Hold the spice box and say:

בָּרוּךְ אַתָּה יהוה אֱלֹהֵינוּ מֶלֶךְ הָעוֹלָם
בּוֹרֵא מִינֵי בְשָׂמִים.

Smell the spices and put the spice box down.
Lift the hands toward the flame of the הבדלה *candle and say:*

בָּרוּךְ אַתָּה יהוה אֱלֹהֵינוּ מֶלֶךְ הָעוֹלָם
בּוֹרֵא מְאוֹרֵי הָאֵשׁ.

Holding the cup of wine again in the right hand, say:

בָּרוּךְ אַתָּה יהוה אֱלֹהֵינוּ מֶלֶךְ הָעוֹלָם
הַמַּבְדִּיל בֵּין קֹדֶשׁ לְחֹל
בֵּין אוֹר לְחֹשֶׁךְ
בֵּין יִשְׂרָאֵל לָעַמִּים
בֵּין יוֹם הַשְּׁבִיעִי לְשֵׁשֶׁת יְמֵי הַמַּעֲשֶׂה.
בָּרוּךְ אַתָּה יהוה, הַמַּבְדִּיל בֵּין קֹדֶשׁ לְחֹל.

---

kiddush on Friday night, the primary obligation is to recite it at home.

The tradition is that the glass is filled to the very brim (some fill it to overflowing) as a sign of impending wealth during the coming week in keeping with the rabbinic adage (*Eiruvin* 65a) that any house that has wine flowing like water is filled with blessing (Rema 296:1).

Similarly some have the custom to dip ones finger in the wine and dab the top of one's eyes or forehead as a sign of

הַמַּבְדִּיל He who distinguishes between sacred and secular,
may He forgive our sins.
May He multiply our offspring and wealth like the sand,
and like the stars at night.

The day has passed like a palm tree's shadow;
I call on God to fulfill what the watchman said: *Is. 21*
"Morning comes, though now it is night."

Your righteousness is as high as Mount Tabor.
May You pass high over my sins.
[Let them be] like yesterday when it has passed, *Ps. 90*
like a watch in the night.

The time of offerings has passed.
Would that I might rest.
I am weary with my sighing, *Ps. 6*
every night I drench [with tears].

Hear my voice; let it not be cast aside.
Open for me the lofty gate.
My head is filled with the dew of dawn, *Song. 5*
my hair with raindrops of the night.

Heed my prayer, revered and awesome God.
When I cry, grant me deliverance at twilight, *Prov. 7*
as the day fades, or in the darkness of the night.

I call to You, Lord: Save me.
Make known to me the path of life.
Rescue me from misery before day turns to night.

Cleanse the defilement of my deeds,
lest those who torment me say,
"Where is the God who made me, *Job 35*
who gives cause for songs in the night?"

We are in Your hands like clay:
please forgive our sins, light and grave.
Day to day they pour forth speech, *Ps. 19*
and night to night [they communicate knowledge].

הַמַּבְדִּיל בֵּין קֹדֶשׁ לְחֹל, חַטֹּאתֵינוּ הוּא יִמְחֹל
זַרְעֵנוּ וְכַסְפֵּנוּ יַרְבֶּה כַחוֹל וְכַכּוֹכָבִים בַּלָּיְלָה.

יוֹם פָּנָה כְּצֵל תֹּמֶר, אֶקְרָא לָאֵל עָלַי גּוֹמֵר
אָמַר שֹׁמֵר, אָתָא בֹקֶר וְגַם־לָיְלָה: ישעיה כא

צִדְקָתְךָ כְּהַר תָּבוֹר, עַל חֲטָאַי עָבוֹר תַּעֲבֹר
כְּיוֹם אֶתְמוֹל כִּי יַעֲבֹר, וְאַשְׁמוּרָה בַלָּיְלָה: תהלים צ

חָלְפָה עוֹנַת מִנְחָתִי, מִי יִתֵּן מְנוּחָתִי
יָגַעְתִּי בְאַנְחָתִי, אַשְׂחֶה בְכָל־לָיְלָה: תהלים ו

קוֹלִי בַּל יֻנְטַל, פְּתַח לִי שַׁעַר הַמְנֻטָּל
שֶׁרֹּאשִׁי נִמְלָא טָל, קְוֻצּוֹתַי רְסִיסֵי לָיְלָה: שיר השירים ה

הֵעָתֵר נוֹרָא וְאָיֹם, אֲשַׁוֵּעַ, תְּנָה פִדְיוֹם
בְּנֶשֶׁף־בְּעֶרֶב יוֹם, בְּאִישׁוֹן לָיְלָה: משלי ז

קְרָאתִיךָ יָהּ, הוֹשִׁיעֵנִי, אֹרַח חַיִּים תּוֹדִיעֵנִי
מִדַּלָּה תְבַצְּעֵנִי, מִיּוֹם עַד לָיְלָה.

טַהֵר טִנּוּף מַעֲשַׂי, פֶּן יֹאמְרוּ מַכְעִיסַי
אַיֵּה אֱלוֹהַּ עֹשָׂי, נֹתֵן זְמִרוֹת בַּלָּיְלָה: איוב לה

נַחְנוּ בְיָדְךָ כַּחֹמֶר, סְלַח נָא עַל קַל וָחֹמֶר
יוֹם לְיוֹם יַבִּיעַ אֹמֶר, וְלַיְלָה לְּלָיְלָה: תהלים יט

SHEMA BEFORE SLEEP AT NIGHT[B]

הֲרֵינִי I hereby forgive anyone who has angered or provoked me or sinned against me, physically or financially or by failing to give me due respect, or in any other matter relating to me, involuntarily or willingly, inadvertently or deliberately, whether in word or deed: let no one incur punishment because of me.

בָּרוּךְ Blessed are You, Lord our God, King of the Universe,
who makes the bonds of sleep fall on my eyes,[IHB]
and slumber on my eye-lids.
May it be Your will, Lord my God and God of my fathers,
that You make me lie down in peace
and arise in peace.
Let not my imagination,
bad dreams or troubling thoughts disturb me.[B]

HILKHOT TEFILLA • הלכות תפילה

הַמַּפִּיל חֶבְלֵי שֵׁנָה עַל עֵינַי – *Who makes the bonds of sleep fall on my eyes.* There are two traditions regarding the sequence of the recitation of the *Shema* and the blessing. Which should be recited first? Which should be one's final prayer before drifting into sleep? Interestingly, the *Mishna Berura* suggests that it is up to each individual to decide according to one's own level of fatigue – if you don't think you can stay awake long enough to say the blessing, say it first; otherwise, leave it for the end. Each of us leaves our consciousness of the previous day and the presence of God in our lives in our own way. Also interesting is that unlike almost all other prayers, this one is in the singular, perhaps because it takes place at a most intimate and personal moment in our day.

BIUR TEFILLA • ביאור תפילה

הַמַּפִּיל חֶבְלֵי שֵׁנָה עַל עֵינַי – *Who makes the bonds of sleep fall on my eyes.* We say a blessing on it because sleep is something that man needs. The Midrash (*Bereshit Raba* 9:6) teaches that "*vehineh tov meod*" (and God saw that it was *very* good) is a reference to sleep. With it, man is able to get up in the morning and pursue Torah (Abudarham). Is this a statement of fact or of thanks?

וְאַל יְבַהֲלוּנִי רַעְיוֹנַי וַחֲלוֹמוֹת רָעִים וְהִרְהוּרִים רָעִים – *Let not my imagination, bad dreams or troubling thoughts disturb me.* One's imagination, bad thoughts and bad dreams can shake one to the core at night, causing one to wake up startled, confused and ill at ease, and subsequently leaving one as tired, if not more so, than when one went to sleep. We pray that our sleep is restful and refreshing.

קריאת שמע על המיטה[ב]

הֲרֵינִי מוֹחֵל לְכָל מִי שֶׁהִכְעִיס וְהִקְנִיט אוֹתִי אוֹ שֶׁחָטָא כְּנֶגְדִּי, בֵּין בְּגוּפִי בֵּין בְּמָמוֹנִי בֵּין בִּכְבוֹדִי בֵּין בְּכָל אֲשֶׁר לִי, בֵּין בְּאֹנֶס בֵּין בְּרָצוֹן, בֵּין בְּשׁוֹגֵג בֵּין בְּמֵזִיד, בֵּין בְּדִבּוּר בֵּין בְּמַעֲשֶׂה, וְלֹא יֵעָנֵשׁ שׁוּם אָדָם בְּסִבָּתִי.

בָּרוּךְ אַתָּה יהוה אֱלֹהֵינוּ מֶלֶךְ הָעוֹלָם
הַמַּפִּיל חֶבְלֵי שֵׁנָה עַל עֵינַי[עה״ב] וּתְנוּמָה עַל עַפְעַפָּי.
וִיהִי רָצוֹן מִלְּפָנֶיךָ, יהוה אֱלֹהַי וֵאלֹהֵי אֲבוֹתַי
שֶׁתַּשְׁכִּיבֵנִי לְשָׁלוֹם וְתַעֲמִידֵנִי לְשָׁלוֹם
וְאַל יְבַהֲלוּנִי רַעְיוֹנַי וַחֲלוֹמוֹת רָעִים וְהִרְהוּרִים רָעִים[ב]

BIUR TEFILLA • ביאור תפילה

קריאת שמע על המיטה – *Shema before sleep at night.* The Gemara (*Berakhot* 4b) says that, separate from what one said in *Ma'ariv*, one should recite the [first paragraph of the] *Shema* again because of its reference to the timing of its recitation, namely, בְּשָׁכְבְּךָ, when you lie down. As a result there is a special recitation of the *Shema* which is said just before one nods off to sleep. In addition, the Gemara elsewhere (*Berakhot* 60b) mentions a blessing that should be said upon going to sleep. At its core, then, "the bedtime *Shema*" consists of a blessing and the recitation of the *Shema*; all of the other paragraphs represent additional prayers that are an expansion of one's request for protection during the night.

IYUN TEFILLA • עיון תפילה

הַמַּפִּיל חֶבְלֵי שֵׁנָה עַל עֵינַי – *Who makes the bonds of sleep fall on my eyes.* Here it sounds like sleep is something cast upon you, against your will. Some of us would like to stay up all night if we could, but the blessing assures us that sleep is a *ḥesed* provided by Hashem for the benefit of our bodies, and our souls. Alternatively, young children have a fear of the dark, as their imaginations run wild about the dangers. As adults, we often have our own fears and trepidations about the day prior, about the night and day ahead. Sleep is cast upon us to teach us that the dark is to be embraced before the dawn of a new day.

Compare the text above with the text of the blessing that we say in the morning:

> בָּרוּךְ אַתָּה יהוה אֱלֹהֵינוּ מֶלֶךְ הָעוֹלָם, הַמַּעֲבִיר שֵׁנָה מֵעֵינַי וּתְנוּמָה מֵעַפְעַפָּי.
>
> Blessed are You, Hashem our God, King of the Universe, who removes sleep from my eyes and slumber from my eyelids.

May my bed be flawless before You.
Enlightten my eyes lest I sleep the sleep of death,[B]
for it is You who illuminates the pupil of the eye.
Blessed are You, LORD, who gives light to the whole world in His glory.[B]

When saying all three paragraphs of Shema, say:
God, faithful King!

The following verse should be said aloud, while covering the eyes with the right hand:

Listen, Israel: the LORD is our God, the LORD is One. *Deut. 6*

Quietly: Blessed be the name of His glorious kingdom for ever and all time.

וְאָהַבְתָּ Love the LORD your God with all your heart, with all your *Deut. 6*
soul, and with all your might. These words which I command you today shall be on your heart. Teach them repeatedly to your children, speaking of them when you sit at home and when you travel on the way, when you lie down and when you rise. Bind them as a sign on your hand, and they shall be an emblem between your eyes. Write them on the doorposts of your house and gates.

וִיהִי May the pleasantness of the LORD our God be upon us. Establish for us *Ps. 90*
the work of our hands, O establish the work of our hands.

יֹשֵׁב He who lives in the shelter of the Most High dwells in the shadow of the *Ps. 91*
Almighty. I say of God, my Refuge and Stronghold, my LORD in whom I trust, that He will save you from the fowler's snare and the deadly pestilence. With His pinions He will cover you, and beneath His wings you will find shelter; His faithfulness is an encircling shield. You need not fear terror by night, nor

---

I will thank Hashem for the restoration of my soul and my reemergence from a state of slumber to a rejuvenated state of being alive.

הַמֵּאִיר לָעוֹלָם כֻּלּוֹ בִּכְבוֹדוֹ – *Who gives light to the whole world in His glory.* The blessing ends on a note of optimism. Dark as it may seem at night, we will awaken in the morning to acknowledge a new day, illuminated both literally and figuratively by the light which Hashem provides. Such a thought brings comfort, peace and rest.

וּתְהֵא מִטָּתִי שְׁלֵמָה לְפָנֶיךָ
וְהָאֵר עֵינַי פֶּן אִישַׁן הַמָּוֶת, כִּי אַתָּה הַמֵּאִיר לְאִישׁוֹן בַּת עָיִן.
בָּרוּךְ אַתָּה יהוה, הַמֵּאִיר לָעוֹלָם כֻּלּוֹ בִּכְבוֹדוֹ.

When saying all three paragraphs of שמע*, say:*

אֵל מֶלֶךְ נֶאֱמָן

The following verse should be said aloud, while covering the eyes with the right hand:

שְׁמַע יִשְׂרָאֵל, יהוה אֱלֹהֵינוּ, יהוה | אֶחָד: דברים ו

Quietly בָּרוּךְ שֵׁם כְּבוֹד מַלְכוּתוֹ לְעוֹלָם וָעֶד.

וְאָהַבְתָּ אֵת יהוה אֱלֹהֶיךָ, בְּכָל־לְבָבְךָ וּבְכָל־נַפְשְׁךָ וּבְכָל־ דברים ו
מְאֹדֶךָ: וְהָיוּ הַדְּבָרִים הָאֵלֶּה, אֲשֶׁר אָנֹכִי מְצַוְּךָ הַיּוֹם, עַל־לְבָבֶךָ:
וְשִׁנַּנְתָּם לְבָנֶיךָ וְדִבַּרְתָּ בָּם, בְּשִׁבְתְּךָ בְּבֵיתֶךָ וּבְלֶכְתְּךָ בַדֶּרֶךְ,
וּבְשָׁכְבְּךָ וּבְקוּמֶךָ: וּקְשַׁרְתָּם לְאוֹת עַל־יָדֶךָ וְהָיוּ לְטֹטָפֹת בֵּין
עֵינֶיךָ: וּכְתַבְתָּם עַל־מְזֻזוֹת בֵּיתֶךָ וּבִשְׁעָרֶיךָ:

וִיהִי נֹעַם אֲדֹנָי אֱלֹהֵינוּ עָלֵינוּ וּמַעֲשֵׂה יָדֵינוּ כּוֹנְנָה עָלֵינוּ וּמַעֲשֵׂה יָדֵינוּ תהלים צ
כּוֹנְנֵהוּ:

יֹשֵׁב בְּסֵתֶר עֶלְיוֹן, בְּצֵל שַׁדַּי יִתְלוֹנָן: אֹמַר לַיהוה מַחְסִי וּמְצוּדָתִי, תהלים צא
אֱלֹהַי אֶבְטַח־בּוֹ: כִּי הוּא יַצִּילְךָ מִפַּח יָקוּשׁ, מִדֶּבֶר הַוּוֹת: בְּאֶבְרָתוֹ
יָסֶךְ לָךְ, וְתַחַת־כְּנָפָיו תֶּחְסֶה, צִנָּה וְסֹחֵרָה אֲמִתּוֹ: לֹא־תִירָא מִפַּחַד

BIUR TEFILLA • ביאור תפילה

וְהָאֵר עֵינַי פֶּן אִישַׁן הַמָּוֶת – *Enlighten my eyes lest I sleep the sleep of death.* Only at the end does one admit to the biggest fear of them all – lest I not awake in the morning. The apprehension of death is not always present, but the possibility is. Here it receives its due mention, a prelude to the celebratory statement in the morning of *Modeh Ani*, wherein

the arrow that flies by day; not the pestilence that stalks in darkness, nor the plague that ravages at noon. A thousand may fall at your side, ten thousand at your right hand, but it will not come near you. You will only look with your eyes and see the punishment of the wicked. Because you said, "The LORD is my Refuge," taking the Most High as your shelter, no harm will befall you, no plague come near your tent, for He will command His angels about you, to guard you in all your ways. They will lift you in their hands, lest your foot stumble on a stone. You will tread on lions and vipers; you will trample on young lions and snakes. [God says:] "Because he loves Me, I will rescue him; I will protect him, because he acknowledges My name. When he calls on Me, I will answer him; I will be with him in distress, I will deliver him and bring him honor. With long life I will satisfy him and show him My salvation.

With long life I will satisfy him and show him My salvation.

יהוה LORD, how numerous are my enemies, how many rise against me. *Ps. 3*
Many say of me: "There is no help for him in God," Selah. But You, LORD, are a shield around me. You are my glory; You raise my head high. I cry aloud to the LORD, and He answers me from His holy mountain, Selah. I lie down to sleep and I wake again, for the LORD supports me. I will not fear the myriad forces ranged against me on all sides. Arise, LORD, save me, O my God; strike all my enemies across the cheek; break the teeth of the wicked. From the LORD comes deliverance; may Your blessing rest upon Your people, Selah.

הַשְׁכִּיבֵנוּ Help us lie down, O LORD our God, in peace, and rise up, O our King, to life. Spread over us Your canopy of peace. Direct us with Your good counsel, and save us for the sake of Your name. Shield us and remove from us every enemy, plague, sword, famine and sorrow. Remove the adversary from before and behind us. Shelter us in the shadow of Your wings, for You, God, are our Guardian and Deliverer; You, God, are a gracious and compassionate King. Guard our going out and our coming in, for life and peace, from now and for ever.

בָּרוּךְ Blessed is the LORD by day, blessed is the LORD by night. Blessed is
the LORD when we lie down; blessed is the LORD when we rise. For in Your
hand are the souls of the living and the dead, [as it is written:] "In His hand *Job 12*
is every living soul, and the breath of all mankind." Into Your hand I entrust *Ps. 31*
my spirit: You redeemed me, LORD, God of truth. Our God in heaven, bring unity to Your name, establish Your kingdom constantly and reign over us for ever and all time.

לָֽיְלָה, מֵחֵץ יָעוּף יוֹמָם: מִדֶּֽבֶר בָּאֹֽפֶל יַהֲלֹךְ, מִקֶּֽטֶב יָשׁוּד צָהֳרָֽיִם:
יִפֹּל מִצִּדְּךָ אֶֽלֶף, וּרְבָבָה מִימִינֶֽךָ, אֵלֶֽיךָ לֹא יִגָּשׁ: רַק בְּעֵינֶֽיךָ תַבִּיט,
וְשִׁלֻּמַת רְשָׁעִים תִּרְאֶה: כִּי־אַתָּה יהוה מַחְסִי, עֶלְיוֹן שַֽׂמְתָּ מְעוֹנֶֽךָ:
לֹא־תְאֻנֶּה אֵלֶֽיךָ רָעָה, וְנֶֽגַע לֹא־יִקְרַב בְּאָהֳלֶֽךָ: כִּי מַלְאָכָיו יְצַוֶּה־לָּךְ,
לִשְׁמָרְךָ בְּכָל־דְּרָכֶֽיךָ: עַל־כַּפַּֽיִם יִשָּׂאֽוּנְךָ, פֶּן־תִּגֹּף בָּאֶֽבֶן רַגְלֶֽךָ: עַל־
שַֽׁחַל וָפֶֽתֶן תִּדְרֹךְ, תִּרְמֹס כְּפִיר וְתַנִּין: כִּי בִי חָשַׁק וַאֲפַלְּטֵֽהוּ, אֲשַׂגְּבֵֽהוּ
כִּי־יָדַע שְׁמִי: יִקְרָאֵֽנִי וְאֶעֱנֵֽהוּ, עִמּוֹ־אָנֹכִי בְצָרָה, אֲחַלְּצֵֽהוּ וַאֲכַבְּדֵֽהוּ:
אֹֽרֶךְ יָמִים אַשְׂבִּיעֵֽהוּ, וְאַרְאֵֽהוּ בִּישׁוּעָתִי:
אֹֽרֶךְ יָמִים אַשְׂבִּיעֵֽהוּ, וְאַרְאֵֽהוּ בִּישׁוּעָתִי:

תהלים ג יהוה מָה־רַבּוּ צָרָי, רַבִּים קָמִים עָלָי: רַבִּים אֹמְרִים לְנַפְשִׁי, אֵין יְשׁוּעָֽתָה
לּוֹ בֵאלֹהִים, סֶֽלָה: וְאַתָּה יהוה מָגֵן בַּעֲדִי, כְּבוֹדִי וּמֵרִים רֹאשִׁי: קוֹלִי
אֶל־יהוה אֶקְרָא, וַיַּעֲנֵֽנִי מֵהַר קָדְשׁוֹ, סֶֽלָה: אֲנִי שָׁכַֽבְתִּי וָאִישָֽׁנָה,
הֱקִיצֽוֹתִי כִּי יהוה יִסְמְכֵֽנִי: לֹא־אִירָא מֵרִבְבוֹת עָם, אֲשֶׁר סָבִיב שָֽׁתוּ
עָלָי: קוּמָה יהוה, הוֹשִׁיעֵֽנִי אֱלֹהַי, כִּי־הִכִּֽיתָ אֶת־כָּל־אֹיְבַי לֶֽחִי, שִׁנֵּי
רְשָׁעִים שִׁבַּֽרְתָּ: לַיהוה הַיְשׁוּעָה, עַל־עַמְּךָ בִרְכָתֶֽךָ סֶּֽלָה:

הַשְׁכִּיבֵֽנוּ, יהוה אֱלֹהֵֽינוּ, לְשָׁלוֹם. וְהַעֲמִידֵֽנוּ, מַלְכֵּֽנוּ, לְחַיִּים. וּפְרֹשׂ עָלֵֽינוּ
סֻכַּת שְׁלוֹמֶֽךָ, וְתַקְּנֵֽנוּ בְּעֵצָה טוֹבָה מִלְּפָנֶֽיךָ, וְהוֹשִׁיעֵֽנוּ לְמַֽעַן שְׁמֶֽךָ. וְהָגֵן
בַּעֲדֵֽנוּ, וְהָסֵר מֵעָלֵֽינוּ אוֹיֵב, דֶּֽבֶר וְחֶֽרֶב וְרָעָב וְיָגוֹן. וְהָסֵר שָׂטָן מִלְּפָנֵֽינוּ
וּמֵאַחֲרֵֽינוּ, וּבְצֵל כְּנָפֶֽיךָ תַּסְתִּירֵֽנוּ, כִּי אֵל שׁוֹמְרֵֽנוּ וּמַצִּילֵֽנוּ אָֽתָּה, כִּי אֵל
מֶֽלֶךְ חַנּוּן וְרַחוּם אָֽתָּה. וּשְׁמֹר צֵאתֵֽנוּ וּבוֹאֵֽנוּ לְחַיִּים וּלְשָׁלוֹם מֵעַתָּה
וְעַד עוֹלָם.

בָּרוּךְ יהוה בַּיּוֹם, בָּרוּךְ יהוה בַּלָּֽיְלָה, בָּרוּךְ יהוה בְּשָׁכְבֵֽנוּ, בָּרוּךְ
איוב יב יהוה בְּקוּמֵֽנוּ. כִּי בְיָדְךָ נַפְשׁוֹת הַחַיִּים וְהַמֵּתִים. אֲשֶׁר בְּיָדוֹ נֶֽפֶשׁ כָּל־
תהלים לא חָי, וְרֽוּחַ כָּל־בְּשַׂר־אִישׁ: בְּיָדְךָ אַפְקִיד רוּחִי, פָּדִֽיתָה אוֹתִי יהוה אֵל
אֱמֶת: אֱלֹהֵֽינוּ שֶׁבַּשָּׁמַֽיִם, יַחֵד שִׁמְךָ וְקַיֵּם מַלְכוּתְךָ תָּמִיד, וּמְלֹךְ עָלֵֽינוּ
לְעוֹלָם וָעֶד.

יִרְאוּ May our eyes see, our hearts rejoice, and our souls be glad in Your true salvation, when Zion is told, "Your God reigns." The LORD is King, the LORD was King, and the LORD will be King for ever and all time. For sovereignty is Yours, and to all eternity You will reign in glory, for we have no king but You.

הַמַּלְאָךְ May the angel who rescued me from all harm, bless these boys. May they be called by my name and the names of my fathers Abraham and Isaac, and may they increase greatly on the earth. *Gen. 48*

וַיֹּאמֶר He said, "If you listen carefully to the voice of the LORD your God and do what is right in His eyes, if you pay attention to His commandments and keep all His statutes, I will not bring on you any of the diseases I brought on the Egyptians, for I am the LORD who heals you." The LORD said to the accuser, "The LORD shall rebuke you, accuser. The LORD who has chosen Jerusalem shall rebuke you! Is not this man a burning stick snatched from the fire?" Look! It is Solomon's bed, escorted by sixty warriors, the noblest of Israel, all of them wearing the sword, experienced in battle, each with his sword at his side, prepared for the terror of the nights. *Ex. 15* *Zech. 3* *Song. 3*

Say three times:

יְבָרֶכְךָ May the LORD bless you and protect you. *Num. 6*
May the LORD make His face shine on you and be gracious to you.
May the LORD turn His face toward you and grant you peace.

Say three times:

הִנֵּה See – the Guardian of Israel *Ps. 121*
neither slumbers nor sleeps.

Say three times:

לִישׁוּעָתְךָ For Your salvation I hope, LORD. *Gen. 49*
I hope, LORD, for Your salvation.
LORD, for Your salvation I hope.

Say three times:

בְּשֵׁם In the name of the LORD, God of Israel:
may Michael be at my right hand,
Gabriel, at my left;
in front of me, Uriel,
behind me, Raphael;
and above my head the Presence of God.

יִרְאוּ עֵינֵינוּ וְיִשְׂמַח לִבֵּנוּ, וְתָגֵל נַפְשֵׁנוּ בִּישׁוּעָתְךָ בֶּאֱמֶת, בֶּאֱמֹר לְצִיּוֹן מָלַךְ אֱלֹהָיִךְ. יהוה מֶלֶךְ, יהוה מָלָךְ, יהוה יִמְלֹךְ לְעוֹלָם וָעֶד. כִּי הַמַּלְכוּת שֶׁלְּךָ הִיא, וּלְעוֹלְמֵי עַד תִּמְלֹךְ בְּכָבוֹד, כִּי אֵין לָנוּ מֶלֶךְ אֶלָּא אָתָּה.

הַמַּלְאָךְ הַגֹּאֵל אֹתִי מִכָּל־רָע יְבָרֵךְ אֶת־הַנְּעָרִים, וְיִקָּרֵא בָהֶם שְׁמִי וְשֵׁם אֲבֹתַי אַבְרָהָם וְיִצְחָק, וְיִדְגּוּ לָרֹב בְּקֶרֶב הָאָרֶץ: בראשית מח

וַיֹּאמֶר אִם־שָׁמוֹעַ תִּשְׁמַע לְקוֹל יהוה אֱלֹהֶיךָ, וְהַיָּשָׁר בְּעֵינָיו תַּעֲשֶׂה, שמות טו
וְהַאֲזַנְתָּ לְמִצְוֹתָיו וְשָׁמַרְתָּ כָּל־חֻקָּיו, כָּל־הַמַּחֲלָה אֲשֶׁר־שַׂמְתִּי בְמִצְרַיִם
לֹא־אָשִׂים עָלֶיךָ, כִּי אֲנִי יהוה רֹפְאֶךָ: וַיֹּאמֶר יהוה אֶל־הַשָּׂטָן, יִגְעַר יהוה זכריה ג
בְּךָ הַשָּׂטָן, וְיִגְעַר יהוה בְּךָ הַבֹּחֵר בִּירוּשָׁלָםִ, הֲלוֹא זֶה אוּד מֻצָּל מֵאֵשׁ:
הִנֵּה מִטָּתוֹ שֶׁלִּשְׁלֹמֹה, שִׁשִּׁים גִּבֹּרִים סָבִיב לָהּ, מִגִּבֹּרֵי יִשְׂרָאֵל: כֻּלָּם שיר השירים ג
אֲחֻזֵי חֶרֶב, מְלֻמְּדֵי מִלְחָמָה, אִישׁ חַרְבּוֹ עַל־יְרֵכוֹ מִפַּחַד בַּלֵּילוֹת:

Say three times:

יְבָרֶכְךָ יהוה וְיִשְׁמְרֶךָ: במדבר ו
יָאֵר יהוה פָּנָיו אֵלֶיךָ וִיחֻנֶּךָּ:
יִשָּׂא יהוה פָּנָיו אֵלֶיךָ וְיָשֵׂם לְךָ שָׁלוֹם:

Say three times:

הִנֵּה לֹא־יָנוּם וְלֹא יִישָׁן שׁוֹמֵר יִשְׂרָאֵל: תהלים קכא

Say three times:

לִישׁוּעָתְךָ קִוִּיתִי יהוה: בראשית מט
קִוִּיתִי יהוה לִישׁוּעָתְךָ
יהוה לִישׁוּעָתְךָ קִוִּיתִי

Say three times:

בְּשֵׁם יהוה אֱלֹהֵי יִשְׂרָאֵל
מִימִינִי מִיכָאֵל, וּמִשְּׂמֹאלִי גַּבְרִיאֵל
וּמִלְּפָנַי אוּרִיאֵל, וּמֵאֲחוֹרַי רְפָאֵל
וְעַל רֹאשִׁי שְׁכִינַת אֵל.

שִׁיר הַמַּעֲלוֹת A song of ascents. Ps. 128
Happy are all who fear the Lord, who walk in His ways.
When you eat the fruit of your labor, happy and fortunate are you.
Your wife shall be like a fruitful vine within your house;
your sons like olive saplings around your table.
So shall the man who fears the Lord be blessed.
May the Lord bless you from Zion;
may you see the good of Jerusalem all the days of your life;
and may you live to see your children's children. Peace be on Israel!

Say three times:

רִגְזוּ Tremble, and do not sin. Ps. 4
Search your heart as you lie on your bed, and be silent. Selah.

אֲדוֹן עוֹלָם Lord of the Universe,
who reigned before the birth of any thing;
when by His will all things were made,
then was His name proclaimed King.
And when all things shall cease to be,
He alone will reign in awe.
He was, He is, and He shall be glorious for evermore.
He is One, there is none else, alone, unique, beyond compare;
Without beginning, without end, His might, His rule are everywhere.
He is my God; my Redeemer lives.
He is the Rock on whom I rely –
my banner and my safe retreat, my cup, my portion when I cry.
Into His hand my soul I place, when I awake and when I sleep.
The Lord is with me, I shall not fear;
body and soul from harm will He keep.

תהלים קכח

שִׁיר הַמַּעֲלוֹת, אַשְׁרֵי כָּל־יְרֵא יהוה, הַהֹלֵךְ בִּדְרָכָיו:
יְגִיעַ כַּפֶּיךָ כִּי תֹאכֵל, אַשְׁרֶיךָ וְטוֹב לָךְ:
אֶשְׁתְּךָ כְּגֶפֶן פֹּרִיָּה בְּיַרְכְּתֵי בֵיתֶךָ
בָּנֶיךָ כִּשְׁתִלֵי זֵיתִים, סָבִיב לְשֻׁלְחָנֶךָ:
הִנֵּה כִי־כֵן יְבֹרַךְ גָּבֶר יְרֵא יהוה:
יְבָרֶכְךָ יהוה מִצִּיּוֹן, וּרְאֵה בְּטוּב יְרוּשָׁלָםִ, כֹּל יְמֵי חַיֶּיךָ:
וּרְאֵה־בָנִים לְבָנֶיךָ, שָׁלוֹם עַל־יִשְׂרָאֵל:

Say three times:

תהלים ד

רִגְזוּ וְאַל־תֶּחֱטָאוּ
אִמְרוּ בִלְבַבְכֶם עַל־מִשְׁכַּבְכֶם, וְדֹמּוּ סֶלָה:

אֲדוֹן עוֹלָם אֲשֶׁר מָלַךְ בְּטֶרֶם כָּל־יְצִיר נִבְרָא.
לְעֵת נַעֲשָׂה בְחֶפְצוֹ כֹּל אֲזַי מֶלֶךְ שְׁמוֹ נִקְרָא.
וְאַחֲרֵי כִּכְלוֹת הַכֹּל לְבַדּוֹ יִמְלֹךְ נוֹרָא.
וְהוּא הָיָה וְהוּא הֹוֶה וְהוּא יִהְיֶה בְּתִפְאָרָה.
וְהוּא אֶחָד וְאֵין שֵׁנִי לְהַמְשִׁיל לוֹ לְהַחְבִּירָה.
בְּלִי רֵאשִׁית בְּלִי תַכְלִית וְלוֹ הָעֹז וְהַמִּשְׂרָה.
וְהוּא אֵלִי וְחַי גּוֹאֲלִי וְצוּר חֶבְלִי בְּעֵת צָרָה.
וְהוּא נִסִּי וּמָנוֹס לִי מְנָת כּוֹסִי בְּיוֹם אֶקְרָא.
בְּיָדוֹ אַפְקִיד רוּחִי בְּעֵת אִישַׁן וְאָעִירָה.
וְעִם רוּחִי גְּוִיָּתִי יהוה לִי וְלֹא אִירָא.

שבת
SHABBAT

Erev Shabbat

EIRUV TEḤUMIN

On Shabbat and Yom Tov it is forbidden to walk more than 2000 cubits (about 3000 feet) beyond the boundary (teḥum) of the town where you live or are staying when the day begins. By placing food sufficient for two meals, before nightfall, at a point within 2000 cubits from the town limits, you confer on that place the status of a dwelling for the next day, and are then permitted to walk 2000 cubits from there.

בָּרוּךְ Blessed are You, LORD our God, King of the Universe,
who has made us holy through His commandments,
and has commanded us about the mitzva of Eiruv.

By this Eiruv may we be permitted to walk from this place,
two thousand cubits in any direction.

EIRUV ḤATZEROT

On Shabbat it is forbidden to carry objects from one private domain to another, or from a private domain into space shared by others, such as a communal staircase, corridor or courtyard. An Eiruv Ḥatzerot is created when each of the Jewish households in a court or apartment block, before Shabbat, places a loaf of bread or matza in one of the homes. The entire court or block then becomes a single private domain within which it is permitted to carry.

בָּרוּךְ Blessed are You, LORD our God, King of the Universe,
who has made us holy through His commandments,
and has commanded us about the mitzva of Eiruv.

By this Eiruv may we be permitted to move,
carry out and carry in from the houses to the courtyard,
or from the courtyard to the houses, or from house to house,
for all the houses within the courtyard.

ערב שבת

עירוב תחומין

On שבת *and* יום טוב *it is forbidden to walk more than 2000 cubits (about 3000 feet) beyond the boundary* (תחום) *of the town where you live or are staying when the day begins. By placing food sufficient for two meals, before nightfall, at a point within 2000 cubits from the town limits, you confer on that place the status of a dwelling for the next day, and are then permitted to walk 2000 cubits from there.*

בָּרוּךְ אַתָּה יהוה אֱלֹהֵינוּ מֶלֶךְ הָעוֹלָם
אֲשֶׁר קִדְּשָׁנוּ בְּמִצְוֹתָיו וְצִוָּנוּ עַל מִצְוַת עֵרוּב.

בְּדֵין עֵרוּבָא יְהֵא שְׁרֵא לִי לְמֵיזַל מֵאַתְרָא הָדֵין
תְּרֵין אַלְפִּין אַמִּין לְכָל רוּחָא.

עירוב חצרות

On שבת *it is forbidden to carry objects from one private domain to another, or from a private domain into space shared by others, such as a communal staircase, corridor or courtyard. An* עירוב חצרות *is created when each of the Jewish households in a court or apartment block, before* שבת*, places a loaf of bread or matza in one of the homes. The entire court or block then becomes a single private domain within which it is permitted to carry.*

בָּרוּךְ אַתָּה יהוה אֱלֹהֵינוּ מֶלֶךְ הָעוֹלָם
אֲשֶׁר קִדְּשָׁנוּ בְּמִצְוֹתָיו וְצִוָּנוּ עַל מִצְוַת עֵרוּב.

בְּדֵין עֵרוּבָא יְהֵא שְׁרֵא לָנָא לְטַלְטוּלֵי
וּלְאַפּוּקֵי וּלְעַיּוּלֵי מִן הַבָּתִּים לֶחָצֵר וּמִן הֶחָצֵר לַבָּתִּים
וּמִבַּיִת לְבַיִת לְכָל הַבָּתִּים שֶׁבֶּחָצֵר.

CANDLE LIGHTING

On Erev Shabbat cover the eyes with the hands after lighting the candles, and say:

בָּרוּךְ Blessed are You, Lord our God, King of the Universe,
who has made us holy through His commandments,
and has commanded us to light the Sabbath light.

Prayer after candle lighting (add the words in parentheses as appropriate):

יְהִי May it be Your will, Lord my God and God of my forebears,
that You give me grace –
me (and my husband/and my father/and my mother/
and my sons and my daughters) and all those close to me,
and give us and all Israel good and long lives.
And remember us with a memory that brings goodness and blessing;
come to us with compassion
and bless us with great blessings.
Build our homes until they are complete,
and allow Your Presence to live among us.
And may I merit to raise children and grandchildren,
each one wise and understanding,
loving the Lord and in awe of God,
people of truth, holy children,
who will cling on to the Lord
and light up the world with Torah
and with good actions,
and with all the kinds of work that serve the Creator.
Please, hear my pleading at this time,
by the merit of Sarah and Rebecca, Rachel and Leah our mothers,
and light our candle that it should never go out,
and light up Your face,
so that we shall be saved, Amen.

הדלקת נרות

On ערב שבת cover the eyes with the hands after lighting the candles, and say:

בָּרוּךְ אַתָּה יהוה אֱלֹהֵינוּ מֶלֶךְ הָעוֹלָם
אֲשֶׁר קִדְּשָׁנוּ בְּמִצְוֹתָיו וְצִוָּנוּ לְהַדְלִיק נֵר שֶׁל שַׁבָּת.

Prayer after candle lighting (add the words in parentheses as appropriate):

יְהִי רָצוֹן מִלְּפָנֶיךָ יהוה אֱלֹהַי וֵאלֹהֵי אֲבוֹתַי
שֶׁתְּחוֹנֵן אוֹתִי (וְאֶת אִישִׁי/ וְאֶת אָבִי/ וְאֶת אִמִּי/
וְאֶת בָּנַי וְאֶת בְּנוֹתַי) וְאֶת כָּל קְרוֹבַי
וְתִתֶּן לָנוּ וּלְכָל יִשְׂרָאֵל חַיִּים טוֹבִים וַאֲרֻכִּים
וְתִזְכְּרֵנוּ בְּזִכְרוֹן טוֹבָה וּבְרָכָה
וְתִפְקְדֵנוּ בִּפְקֻדַּת יְשׁוּעָה וְרַחֲמִים
וּתְבָרְכֵנוּ בְּרָכוֹת גְּדוֹלוֹת
וְתַשְׁלִים בָּתֵּינוּ וְתַשְׁכֵּן שְׁכִינָתְךָ בֵּינֵינוּ.
וְזַכֵּנִי לְגַדֵּל בָּנִים וּבְנֵי בָנִים חֲכָמִים וּנְבוֹנִים
אוֹהֲבֵי יהוה יִרְאֵי אֱלֹהִים
אַנְשֵׁי אֱמֶת זֶרַע קֹדֶשׁ
בַּיהוה דְּבֵקִים
וּמְאִירִים אֶת הָעוֹלָם בַּתּוֹרָה וּבְמַעֲשִׂים טוֹבִים
וּבְכָל מְלֶאכֶת עֲבוֹדַת הַבּוֹרֵא.
אָנָּא שְׁמַע אֶת תְּחִנָּתִי בָּעֵת הַזֹּאת
בִּזְכוּת שָׂרָה וְרִבְקָה וְרָחֵל וְלֵאָה אִמּוֹתֵינוּ
וְהָאֵר נֵרֵנוּ שֶׁלֹּא יִכְבֶּה לְעוֹלָם וָעֶד
וְהָאֵר פָּנֶיךָ וְנִוָּשֵׁעָה. אָמֵן.

Most congregations sing "Beloved of the soul" before the Kabbalat Shabbat service.

יְדִיד Beloved of the soul, Father of compassion,
draw Your servant close to Your will.
Like a deer will Your servant run
and fall prostrate before Your beauty.
To him Your love is sweeter
than honey from the comb, than any taste.

הָדוּר Glorious, beautiful, radiance of the world,
my soul is sick with love for You.
Please, God, heal her now
by showing her Your tender radiance.
Then she will recover her strength and be healed,
Be Your servant for eternity.

One must allow body and mind to let down their defenses, to peel back the facades and concerns of our weekday lives, in order to get in touch with things that matter most. For those who have incorporated Shabbat observance into their lives, the transition is easier and more natural, for the body and the soul come to expect this reprieve. Even so, preparation is still required.

For millennia it has been known that one must embrace this day in order to be embraced by it. To be sure, it will come whether we prepare for it or not, but our experience of it will be enhanced the more we seek to be conscious of its presence. Like any activity in life, the more we anticipate, the more we prepare and ready ourselves, the more meaningful will the encounter be. And so there developed customs designed to put us into the correct frame of mind, to enable us to make the switch that our body and soul so badly crave. That is much of the purpose of this special service known as *Kabbalat Shabbat*, or "receiving the Sabbath."

Almost two thousand years ago the Talmud made reference to greeting the Sabbath as an important guest or as a bride whom the groom goes out to greet in order to escort her to the bridal canopy. But the standardized service that we now use is actually a relatively late composition, attributed to the Kabbalists, the mystics who lived in Tzefat (Safed) in northern Israel in the sixteenth century who created their own ceremonies to welcome the Sabbath into their midst. Led by the influential Rabbi Isaac Luria, known as the Ari (the Lion), or the Ari *zal* (the Ari, may his memory be for a blessing), many would gather in the courtyard of the synagogue or actually go out into the fields reciting psalms and songs to greet the Sabbath, as it were, as she entered one's life. Over the course of time, the ceremony moved indoors – sometimes into a different room of the synagogue since this was not a part of the regular service – and

This **INTRODUCTION** *continues on page 395.*

Most congregations sing יְדִיד נֶפֶשׁ *at this point before* קבלת שבת.

יְדִיד נֶפֶשׁ, אָב הָרַחֲמָן, מְשֹׁךְ עַבְדְּךָ אֶל רְצוֹנָךְ
יָרוּץ עַבְדְּךָ כְּמוֹ אַיָּל, יִשְׁתַּחֲוֶה מוּל הֲדָרָךְ
כִּי יֶעֱרַב לוֹ יְדִידוּתָךְ, מִנֹּפֶת צוּף וְכָל טָעַם.

הָדוּר, נָאֶה, זִיו הָעוֹלָם, נַפְשִׁי חוֹלַת אַהֲבָתָךְ
אָנָּא, אֵל נָא, רְפָא נָא לָהּ, בְּהַרְאוֹת לָהּ נֹעַם זִיוָךְ
אָז תִּתְחַזֵּק וְתִתְרַפֵּא, וְהָיְתָה לָךְ שִׁפְחַת עוֹלָם.

INTRODUCTION TO YEDID NEFESH

This poem was written by Rabbi Elazar Azikri around 1584. Its language is reminiscent of the love poetry of the Song of Songs, an ode to the love between God and Israel. First published as part of the author's own work, it then appeared in a collection of midnight prayers (*Tikkun Ḥatzot*) associated in Kabbalistic circles with the end of the exile and the coming of the Messiah. It subsequently came to be printed as a concluding prayer to Torah study, and then appeared in a number of different but related contexts where one wanted to focus on the love of God and the prayer for redemption. These are precisely the themes one finds in *Kabbalat Shabbat* and so the poem, actually a song, came to be included there by many congregations. Others include it in the songs sung in the afternoon as Shabbat ebbs away.

The present rendition is taken from a manuscript in the author's own hand and thus differs in some ways from those subsequently printed. Consider, for example, the difference in meaning rendered in the second last word in the second stanza which is **שִׁפְחָה**, a maidservant, as opposed to the common version which uses the word **שִׂמְחָה** or happiness.

Read carefully and you will see that this is one of the boldest expressions of the intimate relationship between man and God that is expressed in the siddur. Moreover, unlike so much of the rest of the siddur, this prayer is almost entirely in the singular rather than the plural expressing a particularly personal expression of longing. Most important is the expression it is meant to give to our desire, our passion, our need to be close to the Divine, and if we are not feeling it at the moment, then hopefully we can do so by the end.

INTRODUCTION TO KABBALAT SHABBAT

The transition from a life of the mundane to a life of holiness usually does not happen in a fleeting moment or two. It takes time and a mental shift to another plane.

וָתִיק Ancient of Days, let Your mercy be aroused;
please have pity on Your beloved child.
How long have I yearned
to see the glory of Your strength.
Please, my God, my heart's desire –
hasten; do not hide Yourself.

הִגָּלֵה Reveal Yourself, beloved, and spread over me
the tabernacle of Your peace.
Let the earth shine with Your glory,
let us be overjoyed and rejoice in You.
Hurry, beloved, for the appointed time has come,
and be gracious to me as in the times of old.

Much has been written about the first group of psalms and about the ways in which their themes and language connect with one another and with the service. Suffice it to say here that the overarching theme is praise and thanks to God for creation. We acknowledge His kingship and power which can be both terrifying and awe inspiring, both for us and for the nations of the world. Because the Sabbath marks the climax of creation, we gain perspective on it by looking backwards at the rest of creation and evaluating our place within it, both as individuals and as a nation.

These themes are symbolically alluded to by the very choice of the number of psalms recited; there are six of them corresponding to the six days of the week. The climax will be the realization that comes with the presence of God on Shabbat that is the subject of the song *Lekha Dodi*, the seventh component. It might therefore be helpful to see these psalms as a journey, a recap, as it were, of our week. With each psalm we can move one step closer to the present, the presence that is Shabbat.

For those who are interested in delving further, the first group of psalms are actually quite complex and intriguing from both a literary and theological point of view. The language is highly reminiscent of the language used on Rosh HaShana and Yom Kippur, particularly about God's sovereignty. But there also seems to be some internal structure in which chapters 95 and 96 form a single unit as do chapters 97 and 98. Rav Moshe Lichtenstein describes it thus: "In each group, the first psalm relates to creation itself and the response to it, while the second chapter deals with God's kingship in the world and His judgment of the world. The second psalm of both units focuses not on nature itself, but rather the control and authority over it. If you will, the first of the pair deals with the past, the period of creation itself and that which came into existence at the time, while the second relates to the Almighty's ongoing involvement in the natural world as King and Magistrate. It speaks of the continuing reality resulting from creation, as opposed to the actual moment of creation." (Yet one must also explain

This **OVERVIEW** *continues on page 397.*

וָתִיק, יֶהֱמוּ רַחֲמֶיךָ, וְחוּס נָא עַל בֵּן אוֹהֲבָךְ
כִּי זֶה כַּמֶּה נִכְסֹף נִכְסַף לִרְאוֹת בְּתִפְאֶרֶת עֻזָּךְ
אָנָּא, אֵלִי, מַחְמַד לִבִּי, חוּשָׁה נָּא, וְאַל תִּתְעַלָּם.

הִגָּלֵה נָא וּפְרֹשׂ, חָבִיב, עָלַי אֶת סֻכַּת שְׁלוֹמָךְ
תָּאִיר אֶרֶץ מִכְּבוֹדָךְ, נָגִילָה וְנִשְׂמְחָה בָךְ.
מַהֵר, אָהוּב, כִּי בָא מוֹעֵד, וְחָנֵּנִי כִּימֵי עוֹלָם.

---

then eventually into the main sanctuary itself (*Noheg KeTzon Yosef*, *Magen Avraham*). Since the Shabbat itself has not yet arrived at this point, there were communities that used musical instruments in the service in keeping with the Talmudic dictum (*Shabbat* 30b) that the Divine Presence only descends in a place where there is joy, as it says of the prophet Elisha "And it came to pass when the minstrel played, that the hand of God came upon him" (*Melakhim* II 3:15). Instruments in a synagogue are now eschewed, but an atmosphere of joy still remains the goal.

HILKHOT TEFILLA · הלכות תפילה

Since the standardized *Kabbalat Shabbat* service as we know it is a relatively recent phenomenon (400 years old in a tradition of millennia), there is a custom in many communities that the person leading the service stands in a different place than he would for most other occasions in order to convey that this is not one of the services that is part of a biblical or rabbinic tradition. In some congregations, in order to highlight the difference, he will go back to the usual place at the podium where the leader (*ḥazan*) normally stands for the evening service (*Ma'ariv*) which follows this one.

The beginning of *Kabbalat Shabbat* through the singing of the song *Lekha Dodi* is omitted in many communities in whole or in part when Yom Tov "clashes" with Shabbat. So, for example, when Yom Tov begins on a Friday night, some felt that it would be a slap in the face to Yom Tov, as it were, to have a service which welcomed the Shabbat but ignored the Yom Tov (*Arukh HaShulḥan* 270:3). Some felt that some of the themes of the *Kabbalat Shabbat* service were less in keeping with the themes of Shabbat (e.g. *Alef le'Magen* in *Mateh Efraim* 625). As such, much of *Kabbalat Shabbat* is omitted.

AN OVERVIEW OF THE KABBALAT SHABBAT SERVICE

The structure of the service consists of three parts:

1. Chapters from the book of *Tehillim* (Psalms): 95, 96, 97, 98, 99, 29
2. The poetic song called *Lekha Dodi* (Come, My Beloved)
3. More chapters of *Tehillim*: 92 and 93

Kabbalat Shabbat

Mourners during the week of Shiva leave the synagogue at this point, returning after "Come, my Beloved" on page 424.

Ps. 95

לְכוּ נְרַנְּנָה Come, let us sing for joy to the LORD,
let us shout aloud[B] to the Rock of our salvation.
Let us greet Him with thanksgiving,
shout aloud to Him with songs of praise.
For the LORD is the great God, the King great above all powers.
In His hand are the depths of the earth,
and the mountain peaks are His.
The sea is His, for He made it;
the dry land too, for His hands formed it.
Come, let us bow in worship
and bend the knee before the LORD our Maker.
For He is our God, and we are the people of His pasture,
the flock He tends[I] – today, if you would heed His voice.[I]

---

to the Temple (Ibn Ezra). Or, rather than a call to physical movement, it could be an expression of encouragement to the reader (Radak) to participate spiritually. Alternatively, it could be a call to believe in God and His providence (Meiri). Or, finally, it could be a combination of all of these: to join physically, spiritually, theologically in the community of celebration that is Shabbat.

Allow yourself to relax and join in with those around you.

נְקַדְּמָה פָנָיו – *Let us greet Him.* The word פָּנָיו (*panav*) literally means His face or countenance. In the Torah it is used as an expression when one encountered God in the Tabernacle (*Shemot* 27:21), or before the Holy Ark there (*Shemot* 16:33 and Rashi) or, alternatively, when one stands before the Divine Presence (*Shemot* 33:14). Shabbat too can be such an encounter. One can stand in the presence of the Divine not only in place but also in time.

Imagine yourself there now.

IYUN TEFILLA • עיון תפילה

כִּי הוּא אֱלֹהֵינוּ, וַאֲנַחְנוּ עַם מַרְעִיתוֹ וְצֹאן יָדוֹ – *For He is our God, and we are the people of His pasture, the flock He tends.* This verse parallels the third verse above in that they both give reasons why one should praise Hashem. In the verse above, it was because He is "great...above all powers," that is, He is a universal God. But here it is because we have a special relationship with Him. We can be both universalistic and

This IYUN TEFILLA *continues on page 399.*

קבלת שבת

Mourners during the week of שבעה *leave the* בית כנסת *at this point, returning after* לְכָה דוֹדִי *on page 425.*

לְכוּ נְרַנְּנָה לַיהוה, נָרִיעָה לְצוּר יִשְׁעֵנוּ: תהלים צה
נְקַדְּמָה פָנָיו בְּתוֹדָה, בִּזְמִרוֹת נָרִיעַ לוֹ:
כִּי אֵל גָּדוֹל יהוה, וּמֶלֶךְ גָּדוֹל עַל־כָּל־אֱלֹהִים:
אֲשֶׁר בְּיָדוֹ מֶחְקְרֵי־אָרֶץ, וְתוֹעֲפוֹת הָרִים לוֹ:
אֲשֶׁר־לוֹ הַיָּם וְהוּא עָשָׂהוּ, וְיַבֶּשֶׁת יָדָיו יָצָרוּ:
בֹּאוּ נִשְׁתַּחֲוֶה וְנִכְרָעָה, נִבְרְכָה לִפְנֵי־יהוה עֹשֵׂנוּ:
כִּי הוּא אֱלֹהֵינוּ, וַאֲנַחְנוּ עַם מַרְעִיתוֹ וְצֹאן יָדוֹ
הַיּוֹם אִם־בְּקֹלוֹ תִשְׁמָעוּ:

why the need for both units. Try to find a difference between them.)

In short, what we are supposed to be thinking about and what we may be feeling, are guided not only by what words we say but how they are said as well. Look for common words and expressions, be sensitive to the nuances of difference, but never lose sight of the destination, the holiness of time that is Shabbat.

BIUR TEFILLA · ביאור תפילה

לְכוּ נְרַנְּנָה לַיהוה, נָרִיעָה – *Come, let us sing for joy to the Lord, let us shout aloud.* The psalm begins with a joyful celebratory tone, calling on everyone to join together to sing and shout. From the outset, the goal is to move us away from our work week and recognize that we are about to enter into a different state of mind. That happens not by itself, but by a change in our perspective.

Think joyfulness.

The word **לְכוּ** (*lekhu*) can literally mean to walk, which in this context could mean urging people to walk

ANI TEFILLA · אני תפילה

Imagine a building with a soundproof room in which takes place a party where the music is blaring and people are dancing wildly with reckless abandon. Someone from another planet arrives at that moment and is positioned outside the building. He sees what is going on but cannot hear the sounds nor can he understand what these people are doing. Their actions can look strangely incomprehensible, people gesturing wildly and moving quickly with no apparent purpose. That is the way I sometimes look back upon my week. At the moment, it all seemed to make sense; now, in retrospect, at least some of my actions look foreign and misplaced and I resolve to make next week look different.

Do not harden your hearts as you did at Meribah,
as you did that day at Massah in the desert,[B]
when your ancestors tested and tried Me
though they had seen My deeds.
▸ For forty years I strove with that generation.
I said, "They are a people whose hearts go astray,
who have not understood My ways."
So I swore in My anger,
"They shall not enter My place of rest."

שִׁירוּ Sing to the LORD a new song;[B] Ps. 96
sing to the LORD all the earth.
Sing to the LORD,[A] bless His name;
proclaim his deliverance day after day.

BIUR TEFILLA • ביאור תפילה

Psalm 96. These verses are reminiscent of those that appear with some variations in the book of Chronicles (*Divrei Hayamim* I 16), recited as part of the celebration by David when the Holy Ark was brought to Jerusalem (*Avoda Zara* 24b). Its celebratory tone is in keeping with the spirit of welcoming the Shabbat into one's midst for, like being in the presence of the Ark, or immersed in the unique atmosphere of Jerusalem and the Temple, so, too, we find ourselves now on the verge of an encounter with holiness.

שִׁירוּ לַיהוה שִׁיר חָדָשׁ – *Sing to the LORD a new song.* The phrase "a new song" appears in a few of these psalms. Its purpose is to convey that we believe that God was not like a watchmaker who created the world, wound it up so that it would operate by itself and then walked away. Rather, He is forever involved in creation, each day is a new day of re-creation. As such, each day requires a new song (Malbim). In Judaism, we take nothing for granted. **How can you see your today as a new day? Think of the small things. Sometimes the special can be found in the everyday.**

ANI TEFILLA • אני תפילה

שִׁירוּ לַיהוה שִׁיר חָדָשׁ, שִׁירוּ לַיהוה כָּל־הָאָרֶץ שִׁירוּ לַיהוה – ***Sing** to the LORD a new song; **sing** to the LORD all the earth, **Sing** to the LORD.* Sing! Sing! Sing! That is the message of the first verses of this psalm. Sometimes we sing because we are happy; at other times we are happy because we sing.

אַל־תַּקְשׁוּ לְבַבְכֶם כִּמְרִיבָה, כְּיוֹם מַסָּה בַּמִּדְבָּר:ב
אֲשֶׁר נִסּוּנִי אֲבוֹתֵיכֶם, בְּחָנְוּנִי גַּם רָאוּ פָעֳלִי:
◂ אַרְבָּעִים שָׁנָה אָקוּט בְּדוֹר, וָאֹמַר עַם תֹּעֵי לֵבָב הֵם
וְהֵם לֹא־יָדְעוּ דְרָכָי:
אֲשֶׁר־נִשְׁבַּעְתִּי בְאַפִּי, אִם־יְבֹאוּן אֶל מְנוּחָתִי:

שִׁירוּ לַיהוה שִׁיר חָדָשׁ,ב שִׁירוּ לַיהוה כָּל־הָאָרֶץ: תהלים צו
שִׁירוּ לַיהוה,א בָּרְכוּ שְׁמוֹ, בַּשְּׂרוּ מִיּוֹם־לְיוֹם יְשׁוּעָתוֹ:

particularistic at the same time. To be Jewish means to see yourself as special and unique even as you see yourself as part of humanity at large.

BIUR TEFILLA · ביאור תפילה

אַל־תַּקְשׁוּ לְבַבְכֶם כִּמְרִיבָה, כְּיוֹם מַסָּה בַּמִּדְבָּר – *Do not harden your hearts as you did at Meribah, as you did that day at Massah in the desert.* In a dramatic turn, the psalm shifts from the third person to God Himself speaking, as it were, in the first person, directly to the Jewish people. He admonishes us not to make the same mistakes our ancestors did in the desert: they saw the plagues, the splitting of the sea, the revelation at Sinai. Nevertheless, they lost their faith (cf. *Shemot* 17:7). Supernatural miracles are no guarantor of ongoing belief.

IYUN TEFILLA · עיון תפילה

הַיּוֹם אִם־בְּקֹלוֹ תִשְׁמָעוּ – *Today, if you would heed His voice.* (previous page) The *Midrash Shoḥer Tov* homiletically interprets the word "today" as a reference to the Shabbat day. And so "Rabbi Levi said, 'If the entire Jewish people were to observe even one Shabbat appropriately, then they would be redeemed immediately' (*Yerushalmi Ta'anit* 1:1)." Of course, this isn't a statement just about the nation, but about each of us, today, right now.

ANI TEFILLA · אני תפילה

"Hardening of the heart" is both an intellectual and spiritual malady. It is what prevented Pharaoh from letting the Hebrews leave Egypt. And it is what prevented the Jews from entering the Promised Land. This, despite the fact that the generation of the desert was the first to feel the Divine Presence in its midst. It is as if the psalmist is saying, "You have that opportunity again right now, this evening. Don't make the same mistake. Suspend your intellectual and spiritual doubts. Immerse yourself in My Sabbath, "My place of rest."

Try to do that now. Let go.

Declare His glory among the nations,
His marvels among all peoples.
For great is the LORD and greatly to be praised;
He is awesome beyond all heavenly powers.
For all the gods of the peoples are mere idols:
it was the LORD who made the heavens.
Before Him are majesty and splendor;
there are strength and beauty in His holy place.
Render to the LORD, O families of the peoples;
render to the LORD glory and might.
Render to the LORD the glory due to His name;
bring an offering and come into His courts.
Bow down to the LORD in the splendor of holiness.
Tremble before Him, all the earth.
Say among the nations, "The LORD is King."
The world stands firm, it will not be shaken.
He will judge the peoples with equity.

וּבֹאוּ לְחַצְרוֹתָיו: הִשְׁתַּחֲווּ – *Come into His courts, Bow down.* Like a servant who cannot gain entry to the inner chambers of the palace, one might mistakenly think that one cannot approach God; He is too hidden, too distant. Not so. If one is prepared to simply acknowledge Hashem as Creator of the world, then one's entry to the courtyard is guaranteed. This is because one will perforce "bow" and be humbled by the realization of one's place in the universe.

Think of being somewhere in nature that made you "bow."

ANI TEFILLA • אני תפילה

"The Egyptian, the Babylonian, and the Persian rose, filled the planet with sound and splendor, then faded to dream-stuff and passed away; the Greek and the Roman followed, and made a vast noise, and they are gone; other peoples have sprung up and held their torch high for a time, but it burned out, and they sit in twilight now, or have vanished. The Jew saw them all, beat them all, and is now what he always was, exhibiting no decadence, no infirmities of age, no weakening of his parts, no slowing of his energies, no dulling of his alert and aggressive mind.

All things are mortal but the Jew; all other forces pass, but he remains. What is the secret of his immortality?" (Mark Twain)

Welcome to Shabbat. Welcome to immortality.

סַפְּרוּ בַגּוֹיִם כְּבוֹדוֹ,ב בְּכָל־הָעַמִּים נִפְלְאוֹתָיו:
כִּי גָדוֹל יהוה וּמְהֻלָּל מְאֹד, נוֹרָא הוּא עַל־כָּל־אֱלֹהִים:
כִּי כָּל־אֱלֹהֵי הָעַמִּים אֱלִילִים, וַיהוה שָׁמַיִם עָשָׂה:
הוֹד־וְהָדָר לְפָנָיו, עֹז וְתִפְאֶרֶת בְּמִקְדָּשׁוֹ:
הָבוּ לַיהוה מִשְׁפְּחוֹת עַמִּים,ע הָבוּ לַיהוה כָּבוֹד וָעֹז:
הָבוּ לַיהוהע כְּבוֹד שְׁמוֹ, שְׂאוּ־מִנְחָה וּבֹאוּ לְחַצְרוֹתָיו:
הִשְׁתַּחֲווּע לַיהוה בְּהַדְרַת־קֹדֶשׁ, חִילוּ מִפָּנָיו כָּל־הָאָרֶץ:
אִמְרוּ בַגּוֹיִם יהוה מָלָךְ, אַף־תִּכּוֹן תֵּבֵל בַּל־תִּמּוֹט
יָדִין עַמִּים בְּמֵישָׁרִים:

BIUR TEFILLA • ביאור תפילה

סַפְּרוּ בַגּוֹיִם כְּבוֹדוֹ – *Declare His glory among the nations.* His glory could be a description of God Himself and the miracles He has performed. Alternatively, it could be a reference to the Jewish people: Our very survival against all odds through the millennia is a subject of incredulousness by the nations of the world. In their eyes, we are His glory (Radak).

How might this still be true in our own time?

IYUN TEFILLA • עיון תפילה

הָבוּ לַיהוה מִשְׁפְּחוֹת עַמִּים, הָבוּ לַיהוה כָּבוֹד וָעֹז: הָבוּ לַיהוה – ***Render*** *to the* Lord, *O families of the peoples,* ***render*** *to the* Lord *glory and might,* ***Render*** *to the* Lord. The threefold invitation to "sing…sing… sing" at the beginning of the psalm is paralleled by the threefold call to the nations of the world to "render to Hashem," to come together in unity to recognize that there is but one God, a belief that is one of Judaism's most significant contributions to civilization. One of the byproducts of being filled with happiness is the desire to share it with others. We do so not by trying to impose our will but by sharing our joy. We can share that joy by being joyful. We can also become joyful by allowing ourselves to be drawn in by the joy of others.

Look around you. Whom can you influence?

Who can be made joyful by you? Who can help you be more joyful?

הָבוּ לַיהוה מִשְׁפְּחוֹת עַמִּים – *literally: Bring to the* Lord *the families of the nations.* The midrash homiletically suggests that unlike so many nations of the world, our shared lineage goes back to a time well before the giving of the Torah at Sinai (*Yalkut Shimoni* 684). Our history and our beliefs have been uninterrupted and unparalleled.

▸ Let the heavens rejoice and the earth be glad.
Let the sea roar, and all that is in it;
let the fields be jubilant, and all they contain.
Then the trees of the forest will sing for joy before the LORD,
for He is coming to judge the earth.[1]
He will judge the world with justice,
and the peoples with His faithfulness.

יהוה מָלָךְ The LORD reigns, let the earth be glad.[B] *Ps. 97*
Let the many islands rejoice.
Clouds and thick darkness surround Him;
righteousness and justice are the foundation of His throne.[B]
Fire goes ahead of Him,
consuming His enemies on every side.
His lightning lights up the world;
the earth sees and trembles.
Mountains melt like wax before the LORD,
before the LORD of all the earth.
The heavens proclaim His righteousness,
and all the peoples see His glory.

יהוה מָלָךְ תָּגֵל הָאָרֶץ – *The LORD reigns, let the earth be glad.* This is an imperative directed to us. Sometimes one must be commanded to be positive and optimistic even if one is not feeling it (*Da'at Sofrim*).

עָנָן וַעֲרָפֶל סְבִיבָיו צֶדֶק וּמִשְׁפָּט, מְכוֹן כִּסְאוֹ – *Clouds and thick darkness surround Him; righteousness and justice are the foundation of His throne.* The initial image is one of darkness and foreboding (*Metzuda*). Alternatively, perhaps it is an allusion to the fact that God can be hidden and unfathomable, especially in a world where evil and injustice can seem to get the upper hand so often. Responds the psalmist: If you want to see God, look at acts of kindness and fairness, righteousness and justice (Radak). Therein lies the light that allows one to keep the faith. Think back to one's week.

Where did you see such an act this week? How can you be the agent of such an act this coming week?

◂ יִשְׂמְחוּ הַשָּׁמַיִם וְתָגֵל הָאָֽרֶץ, יִרְעַם הַיָּם וּמְלֹאוֹ:
יַעֲלֹז שָׂדַי וְכָל־אֲשֶׁר־בּוֹ, אָז יְרַנְּנוּ כָּל־עֲצֵי־יָֽעַר:
לִפְנֵי יהוה כִּי בָא, כִּי בָא לִשְׁפֹּט הָאָֽרֶץע
יִשְׁפֹּט־תֵּבֵל בְּצֶֽדֶק, וְעַמִּים בֶּאֱמוּנָתוֹ:

תהלים צז

יהוה מָלָךְ תָּגֵל הָאָֽרֶץ,ב יִשְׂמְחוּ אִיִּים רַבִּים:
עָנָן וַעֲרָפֶל סְבִיבָיו, צֶֽדֶק וּמִשְׁפָּט מְכוֹן כִּסְאוֹ:ב
אֵשׁ לְפָנָיו תֵּלֵךְ, וּתְלַהֵט סָבִיב צָרָיו:
הֵאִֽירוּ בְרָקָיו תֵּבֵל, רָאֲתָה וַתָּחֵל הָאָֽרֶץ:
הָרִים כַּדּוֹנַג נָמַֽסּוּ מִלִּפְנֵי יהוה, מִלִּפְנֵי אֲדוֹן כָּל־הָאָֽרֶץ:
הִגִּֽידוּ הַשָּׁמַיִם צִדְקוֹ, וְרָאוּ כָל־הָעַמִּים כְּבוֹדוֹ:

IYUN TEFILLA • עיון תפילה

כִּי בָא לִשְׁפֹּט הָאָֽרֶץ – *He is coming to judge the earth.* Perhaps this is another reference to the return of the Ark, which contained the laws of the Torah, to Jerusalem as mentioned at the outset. It symbolizes a return of justice to the world, a code of morality that all can share, the guarantee of a measure of universal integrity. For our mission as Jews is not to proselytize but to act as a light unto the nations by the way we live our lives, being the most moral we can be, living Shabbat as it should be.

BIUR TEFILLA • ביאור תפילה

Psalm 97. It has been suggested that this psalm is a continuation of the previous one but in what way is the subject of dispute. Perhaps it is merely a continuation of the description of the kinds of events which must precede God's revelation and the ideal society (Rabbi S. Hirsch). Alternatively, if the previous one was about singing a new song announcing God's reign, here God comes to reveal Himself. There is a description of the reaction of the entire world, the heavens and the earth, the idol worshipers and the righteous, resulting in a world that is more moral and upright. Certainly Shabbat may be seen to be a foretaste and foreshadowing of that world.

All who worship images and boast in idols are put to shame.[AI]
Bow down to Him, all you heavenly powers.
Zion hears and rejoices, and the towns of Judah are glad
because of your judgments, LORD.
For You, LORD, are supreme over all the earth;
You are exalted far above all heavenly powers.
▸ Let those who love the LORD hate evil,[I]
for He protects the lives of his devoted ones,
delivering them from the hand of the wicked.
Light is sown for the righteous,[I] and joy for the upright in heart.
Rejoice in the LORD, you who are righteous,
and give thanks to His holy name.

---

of loving God is the desire to be like God, to imitate His ways, just as a young child wants to be like his parents out of a deep abiding connection with them. The commandment to be like Him is not translated into abstract theological concepts but into concrete practical ones.

> R. Hama son of R. Hanina further said: What means the text: You shall walk after the LORD your God? (*Devarim* 13:5) Is it, then, possible for a human being to literally walk after the Divine Presence; for has it not been said: "For the LORD your God is a devouring fire" (*Devarim* 4:24)? But [the meaning is] to walk after the *attributes* of the Holy One, blessed be He. As He clothes the naked, for it is written: "And the LORD God made for Adam and for his wife coats of skin, and clothed them," (*Bereshit* 3:21), so should you also clothe the naked. The Holy One, blessed be He, visited the sick, for it is written: "And the LORD appeared to him by the oaks of Mamre" (*Bereshit* 18:1), so should you also visit the sick. The Holy One, blessed be He, comforted mourners, for it is written: "And it came to pass after the death of Abraham, that God blessed Isaac his son," (*Bereshit* 25:11), so should you also comfort mourners. The Holy one, blessed be He, buried the dead, for it is written: "And He buried him in the valley," (*Devarim* 34:6), so should you also bury the dead. (*Sotah* 14a)

To love Hashem means to be sensitive to one another's needs.

How can you imitate God this Shabbat?

Alternatively, the "lovers of Hashem" are the non-Jews who return to monotheism (Meiri). Our dream is join forces with all peoples who can share our core values even if they do not share our lifestyle.

אוֹר זָרֻעַ לַצַּדִּיק – *Light is sown for the righteous.* Righteous behavior can be a light which illuminates the world for those around you. Earlier, fire and lightning were mentioned but these are temporary sources of light that can quickly dissipate. Good deeds, however, have the potential to light up small dark corners of the world, one act at time, like seeds that are sown that ultimately bear fruit (*Da'at Sofrim*).

This **IYUN TEFILLA** *continues on page 407.*

יֵבֹשׁוּ כׇּל־עֹבְדֵי פֶסֶל הַמִּתְהַלְלִים בָּאֱלִילִים[אע]
הִשְׁתַּחֲווּ־לוֹ כׇּל־אֱלֹהִים:
שָׁמְעָה וַתִּשְׂמַח צִיּוֹן, וַתָּגֵלְנָה בְּנוֹת יְהוּדָה
לְמַעַן מִשְׁפָּטֶיךָ יהוה:
כִּי־אַתָּה יהוה עֶלְיוֹן עַל־כׇּל־הָאָרֶץ
מְאֹד נַעֲלֵיתָ עַל־כׇּל־אֱלֹהִים:
◂ אֹהֲבֵי יהוה שִׂנְאוּ רָע,[ע] שֹׁמֵר נַפְשׁוֹת חֲסִידָיו
מִיַּד רְשָׁעִים יַצִּילֵם:
אוֹר זָרֻעַ לַצַּדִּיק,[ע] וּלְיִשְׁרֵי־לֵב שִׂמְחָה:
שִׂמְחוּ צַדִּיקִים בַּיהוה, וְהוֹדוּ לְזֵכֶר קׇדְשׁוֹ:

ANI TEFILLA • אני תפילה

יֵבֹשׁוּ כׇּל־עֹבְדֵי פֶסֶל הַמִּתְהַלְלִים בָּאֱלִילִים – *All who worship images and boast in idols are put to shame.* A young man came to his grandfather wanting to understand the dangers of materialism. His grandfather asked him to look outside the window which overlooked the street and asked him what he saw. "I see people of all kinds, walking past the building," he replied. "And now," said the grandfather, "look into this mirror and tell me what you see." The boy was perplexed but did as he was told and responded, "Well, I see myself." "Now you will understand," said the grandfather. "For, in truth, the window pane and the mirror are both made of glass, the only difference being that one of them is covered in silver. But that is the impact of silver, that it has a tendency to make people lose sight of others, and only see themselves."

Shabbat in general, and prayer in particular, are an opportunity to look beyond the self and ask oneself what one sees.

IYUN TEFILLA • עיון תפילה

יֵבֹשׁוּ כׇּל־עֹבְדֵי פֶסֶל הַמִּתְהַלְלִים בָּאֱלִילִים – *All who worship images and boast in idols are put to shame.* Alternatively, "they are praised through idols." People rejoice in their gods – idols, money, materialism, career success – fame, but in our heart of hearts we know that what really counts is to be a good person. Shabbat can be about regaining that perspective, and taking it into the following week.

Resolve to do something different next week.

אֹהֲבֵי יהוה שִׂנְאוּ רָע – *Let those who love the Lord hate evil.* In Jewish life, a major aspect

Ps. 98

מִזְמוֹר A Psalm. Sing a new song to the LORD,[I]
for He has done wondrous things;
He has saved by His right hand and His holy arm.
The LORD has made His salvation known;
He has displayed His righteousness in the sight of the nations.[B]
He remembered His loving-kindness
and faithfulness to the house of Israel;[I]
all the ends of the earth have seen the victory of our LORD.[I]

---

because we are different today than we were yesterday and, hopefully, we are also renewed.

Shake off the old you for a moment or two and feel new again.

זָכַר חַסְדּוֹ וֶאֱמוּנָתוֹ לְבֵית יִשְׂרָאֵל – *He remembered His loving-kindness and faithfulness to the house of Israel.* The words could also homiletically be understood to mean "He remembered the faith of the house of Israel." The Jewish people believed in God at the time of the exodus but the Egyptians did not, yet they saw the same miracles before their very eyes (*Kedushat Levi*). Two people can see the same event and come to very different conclusions. Truth can be difficult to see or it can be staring you in the face.

רָאוּ כָל־אַפְסֵי־אָרֶץ אֵת יְשׁוּעַת אֱלֹהֵינוּ – *All the ends of the earth have seen the victory of our LORD.* Even before the age of telecommunications, the world was aware of the Jewish people. At times there was anti-Semitism in countries where there were not even any Jews. Instead, we pray for the day when Jews are known in the far corners of the globe only for their morality and religiosity. In what way can I make a difference in that mission?

The harp, the trumpets, the songs, the shofar, the shouts for joy are all reminiscent of the coronation of a king. Indeed, much of the language here is reminiscent of that used in the Rosh HaShana services where the theme of God's sovereignty is emphasized most. The clapping of the thunder and the seas, the breaking surf of the ocean, the grandeur of the mountains evoke a world that is in sync with man's own recognition of a force that is greater than the self.

Was there ever a time when you experienced the thunder or the ocean or the view from atop a mountain and felt that there was something bigger than yourself?

ANI TEFILLA • אני תפילה

A young man who thought he did not need a life of Torah and mitzvot once recounted to Rav Noach Weinberg that he was riding along mountain road on his motorcycle, when a big truck came barreling at him. He swerved and went off the road and instinctively he called out to God to save him. "I landed in a bush and was unscathed," said the young man. "So you see, God and I are the best of friends [even without Judaism]." Rav Noach responded: "And who do you think it was who sent the truck?"

תהלים צח

מִזְמוֹר, שִׁירוּ לַיהוה שִׁיר חָדָשׁ כִּי־נִפְלָאוֹת עָשָׂה
הוֹשִׁיעָה־לּוֹ יְמִינוֹ וּזְרוֹעַ קָדְשׁוֹ:
הוֹדִיעַ יהוה יְשׁוּעָתוֹ, לְעֵינֵי הַגּוֹיִם גִּלָּה צִדְקָתוֹ:
זָכַר חַסְדּוֹ וֶאֱמוּנָתוֹ לְבֵית יִשְׂרָאֵל
רָאוּ כָל־אַפְסֵי־אָרֶץ אֵת יְשׁוּעַת אֱלֹהֵינוּ:

What small act of light can you plant today?

In addition, righteous behavior can lead you out of the darkness, for it has a way of changing your perspective.

This could also be interpreted to mean that light is planted within the righteous. Each of us has that spark of light within us that can be uncovered further by our simply making changes in our lives.

How can I enable my inner light to shine brighter today?

This psalm and the next one are often part of the service held on Israel Independence Day, Yom Ha'Atzma'ut.

What themes do you think they that made them an appropriate choice for that day?

BIUR TEFILLA • ביאור תפילה

Psalm 98. If in the previous psalm God was revealed to the world, here there is a celebration of His having been revealed specifically through the restoration of the Jewish people in the eyes of the nations of the world. This, in turn, will have two consequences: it will lead man to a greater knowledge of God and it will enable the Jewish people to fulfill its mission to convey to the rest of the world how God should be worshiped. The glimpse of that future brings joy not only to humankind but to all of creation as the forces of nature all make themselves felt in celebratory terms. In the eyes of the religious personality, the world is one organic whole that lives together and celebrates together.

הוֹדִיעַ יהוה יְשׁוּעָתוֹ, לְעֵינֵי הַגּוֹיִם גִּלָּה צִדְקָתוֹ – *The Lord has made His salvation known; He has displayed His righteousness in the sight of the nations.* He has made His salvation known through his restoration of the Jewish people.

What evidence can you see of this today? In what ways do you think it is acknowledged by the people of the world?

IYUN TEFILLA • עיון תפילה

שִׁירוּ לַיהוה שִׁיר חָדָשׁ – *Sing a new song to the Lord.* We have seen this expression already in Psalm 96. Each fresh insight into life dictates the need for a new song, sometimes for others, sometimes for ourselves. The siddur wants us to take nothing for granted. And even if the words of this new song become familiar and worn, we ourselves change, our realizations grow with each passing minute and week. Our song is new

Shout for joy to the LORD, all the earth;
burst into song,[A] sing with joy, play music.
Play music to the LORD on the harp –
on the harp with the sound of singing.
With trumpets and the sound of the shofar,
shout for joy before the LORD, the King.
▸ Let the sea and all that is in it thunder,
the world and all who live in it.
Let the rivers clap their hands,
the mountains sing together for joy –
before the LORD, for He is coming to judge the earth.
He will judge the world with justice, and the peoples with equity.

יהוה מָלָךְ The LORD reigns, let the peoples tremble. *Ps. 99*
He sits enthroned on the Cherubim, let the earth quake.
Great is the LORD in Zion, He is exalted[B] over all the peoples.
Let them praise Your name, O great and awesome One: He is holy!

BIUR TEFILLA · ביאור תפילה

Psalm 99. The psalm may be divided into three sections. He is the God of all of the nations. He represents justice and righteousness. He answers all who are close to Him. Each section contains the word "exalted" (*ram/romemu*). Each contains some reference to the Temple. And each speaks about His holiness. For holiness and exaltedness can mean set apart, seemingly distant and remote from the everyday. Nevertheless, the theme is exactly the opposite.

וְרָם הוּא – *He is exalted.* The word "exalted" or "on high" (*ram*), which appears three times in this psalm, is a reference to that which is high but disconnected from any foundation, such as the sky, whereas the synonymous "great" (*gadol*) is a reference to that which is high but is rooted in the ground and grows upwards. There are those who say that God is on high, removed from this world, whereas the Jewish people have always seen Him as very much connected to our daily lives here on earth. We may view Him as being beyond our grasp but He is nevertheless very close (Rabbi Mordekhai Benet). For Judaism, religion is not only something otherworldly; it must be in the here and now, of this earth and this life.

הָרִֽיעוּ לַיהוה כָּל־הָאָֽרֶץ, פִּצְחוּ[א] וְרַנְּנוּ וְזַמֵּֽרוּ׃
זַמְּרוּ לַיהוה בְּכִנּוֹר, בְּכִנּוֹר וְקוֹל זִמְרָה׃
בַּחֲצֹצְרוֹת וְקוֹל שׁוֹפָר, הָרִֽיעוּ לִפְנֵי הַמֶּֽלֶךְ יהוה׃
◂ יִרְעַם הַיָּם וּמְלֹאוֹ, תֵּבֵל וְיֹֽשְׁבֵי בָהּ׃
נְהָרוֹת יִמְחֲאוּ־כָף, יַֽחַד הָרִים יְרַנֵּֽנוּ׃
לִפְנֵי יהוה כִּי בָא לִשְׁפֹּט הָאָֽרֶץ
יִשְׁפֹּט־תֵּבֵל בְּצֶֽדֶק, וְעַמִּים בְּמֵישָׁרִים׃

תהלים צט
יהוה מָלָךְ יִרְגְּזוּ עַמִּים, יֹשֵׁב כְּרוּבִים תָּנוּט הָאָֽרֶץ׃
יהוה בְּצִיּוֹן גָּדוֹל, וְרָם[ב] הוּא עַל־כָּל־הָעַמִּים׃
יוֹדוּ שִׁמְךָ גָּדוֹל וְנוֹרָא קָדוֹשׁ הוּא׃

ANI TEFILLA · אני תפילה

פִּצְחוּ – *Burst into song.* The word **פצח** can mean to burst or to crack open. Sometimes one must crack open one's heart to sing. It does not come so easily to everyone or when one is not necessarily in the mood. The siddur encourages us to open ourselves up, to crack our outer layer like the earth's crust so that our inner voice may be heard. **Take a deep breath. Give your soul permission to be heard.**

Once when I was in Auschwitz, I found myself in the presence of the Rebbe of Sanz, Rabbi Yekutiel Halberstam, and I heard him provide some teaching on the verse "Sing a new song to Hashem, for He has done wondrous things; He has saved by His right hand and His holy arm." The Rebbe said whatever he said, first translating each word into Yiddish so all would understand. I couldn't understand at that time exactly what he was saying, but the verse alone awakened such fury within me: What am I hearing from this man?! Where [in Auschwitz] are the "wonders"?! Where is "His arm"?!

Even so, as the years passed and many experiences later, I recalled that event once again and suddenly it occurred to me: was that scene itself not a "wonder"? Is it not an incredible thing that in the midst of the hell of Auschwitz there is a Jew who believes in God and has faith in Him and is heartened by the miracles that He will yet perform? It was this understanding that caused me, albeit very belatedly, to return to Judaism. (Lapid HaEsh, p. 211)

The King in His might loves justice.[I]
You have established equity.[I]
The justice and righteousness in Jacob is Your doing.[I]
Exalt the LORD our God, and bow at His footstool: He is holy!
Moses and Aaron were among His priests;
Samuel was among those who called on His name.[B]
They called on the LORD and He answered them.
▸ He spoke to them in a pillar of cloud;
they observed His testimonies and the statute He gave them.
LORD our God, You answered them.
You were for them a forgiving God,
though You punished their misdeeds.[B]
Exalt the LORD our God and bow at His holy mountain,
for the LORD our God is holy.

---

personalities these three were picked for special mention. It could be because they were priests (*kohanim*) and Levites and thus responsible for the functioning of the Temple which is soon to be mentioned. Or, on a related note, they all heard the voice of God calling out to them from atop the Ark where the cherubim, mentioned in the opening verse of this psalm, were located.

Alternatively, it could be because they represent the three roles of prophecy, priesthood and kingship (Shmuel was the one who anointed Israel's first kings, Shaul and David) (Rabbi Jonathan Sacks).

Furthermore, it could be for their teaching roles; Moshe was responsible for the first Jewish legal system while Aharon was the leader of ritual and, in a later generation, Shmuel traveled around the country doing both. The law has a home in the Temple, but it cannot reside only there.

It could also be because despite their higher status, they too called out in prayer, or because their prayers were answered. Despite the fact that all is decreed from Heaven, there is always room for man's requests to be fulfilled. Change is always possible.

וְנֹקֵם עַל־עֲלִילוֹתָם – *Though You punished their misdeeds.* If this is a reference to Moshe and Aharon and Shmuel, then the implication is clear. Judaism has always recognized that our most illustrious leaders were also human beings replete with their own failings for which they were held accountable (*Bemidbar* 20:12; *Shmuel* I 8:3). They nevertheless provide inspiration in that they were able to become the great people that they were, despite their shortcomings. Could we not do the same?

The more we raise our biblical role models to the status of angels, the more we reduce their stature as great men (Rav Aharon Lichtenstein). We too can overcome our own inclinations.

וְעֹז מֶלֶךְ מִשְׁפָּט אָהֵב, אַתָּה כּוֹנַנְתָּ מֵישָׁרִים
מִשְׁפָּט וּצְדָקָה בְּיַעֲקֹב אַתָּה עָשִׂיתָ:
רוֹמְמוּ יהוה אֱלֹהֵינוּ, וְהִשְׁתַּחֲווּ לַהֲדֹם רַגְלָיו, קָדוֹשׁ הוּא:
מֹשֶׁה וְאַהֲרֹן בְּכֹהֲנָיו, וּשְׁמוּאֵל בְּקֹרְאֵי שְׁמוֹ
קֹרְאִים אֶל־יהוה וְהוּא יַעֲנֵם:
בְּעַמּוּד עָנָן יְדַבֵּר אֲלֵיהֶם, שָׁמְרוּ עֵדֹתָיו וְחֹק נָתַן־לָמוֹ:
יהוה אֱלֹהֵינוּ אַתָּה עֲנִיתָם
אֵל נֹשֵׂא הָיִיתָ לָהֶם, וְנֹקֵם עַל־עֲלִילוֹתָם:
רוֹמְמוּ יהוה אֱלֹהֵינוּ, וְהִשְׁתַּחֲווּ לְהַר קָדְשׁוֹ
כִּי־קָדוֹשׁ יהוה אֱלֹהֵינוּ:

IYUN TEFILLA • עיון תפילה

וְעֹז מֶלֶךְ מִשְׁפָּט אָהֵב – *The King in His might loves justice.* Most sovereigns rule by physical force and power. The God of Israel rules through justice.
How do you use your power with your friends, your family, your employees?

אַתָּה כּוֹנַנְתָּ מֵישָׁרִים – *You have established equity.* A person sees his enemy's donkey suffering under a burden. He goes to help him in keeping with the biblical commandment (*Shemot* 23:5): "And if you see your enemy's donkey crouching under his burden...you shall surely help him." His enemy is overwhelmed by the gesture and they become steadfast friends (*Midrash Shoḥer Tov* 99:5). The word equity can also be understood as *yashrut*, doing the right thing. Following the laws of the Torah leads to doing the right thing, even if it may go against our natural inclination, and peace is the inevitable result.
What acts of justice could I have done this week?

מִשְׁפָּט וּצְדָקָה בְּיַעֲקֹב אַתָּה עָשִׂיתָ – *The justice and righteousness in Jacob is Your doing.* Morality has always been at the center of the Jewish mission to be a light unto the nations. Despite our belief that our system of laws is the most far-reaching and the most ethical, we know that does not make us better than other peoples; it simply gives us more responsibility.
What can I do next week to better live up to that responsibility?
How can I start today?

BIUR TEFILLA • ביאור תפילה

מֹשֶׁה וְאַהֲרֹן בְּכֹהֲנָיו, וּשְׁמוּאֵל בְּקֹרְאֵי שְׁמוֹ – *Moses and Aaron were among His priests; Samuel was among those who called on His name.* It is not clear why of all the biblical

The following psalm is said standing:

מִזְמוֹר לְדָוִד A psalm of David. Ps. 29
Render to the LORD, you angelic powers,
render to the LORD glory and might.
Render to the LORD the glory due to His name.
Bow to the LORD in the beauty of holiness.
The LORD's voice echoes over the waters;
the God of glory thunders;
the LORD is over the mighty waters.
The LORD's voice in power,[I]
the LORD's voice in beauty,[A]
the LORD's voice breaks cedars,[I]
the LORD shatters the cedars of Lebanon.

---

the force of that voice equally. Instead, it says, when standing at Sinai each person heard the voice of revelation according to his or her own ability to be attuned to the sound (*Shemot Raba* 5:9). Spirituality is not a one-size-fits-all phenomenon. Each of us can hear the sound, but each in our own way.
What is your way?

קוֹל יהוה שֹׁבֵר אֲרָזִים – *The LORD's voice breaks cedars.* The cedars of Lebanon are the biblical symbols for great strength and power. Like nuclear energy, God's presence can be felt in the destructive forces that man can harness for the purposes of war and oppression, no less than they can be found in the positive ways in which we use such forces of nature for our benefit. Shabbat is about maintaining our sense of balance between the two.

ANI TEFILLA · אני תפילה

קוֹל יהוה בֶּהָדָר – *The LORD's voice in beauty.* Imagine the voice of beauty in nature. Think about a place where you once heard that voice, the rustling of the leaves, the wind whistling through your hair, the deafening sound of silence. The voice that speaks to you through the beauty of nature is that same voice that speaks to you through the beauty of the Torah, for their origins are the same. As nature is there to sensitize you to your place, so too the voice of the Torah is there to guide you in shaping and developing your human personality (Rabbi S. Hirsch).

What can you do to better hear those voices?

The Ba'al Shem Tov said that no two people have the same abilities. Each person must worship Hashem using his own strengths. If he tries to imitate another person he will not only lose out on his own merit but will not be able to accomplish anything using someone else's talents.
What are your strengths that you can utilize to worship Hashem?

The following psalm is said standing:

תהלים כט

מִזְמוֹר לְדָוִד, הָבוּ לַיהוה בְּנֵי אֵלִים, הָבוּ לַיהוה כָּבוֹד וָעֹז:
הָבוּ לַיהוה כְּבוֹד שְׁמוֹ, הִשְׁתַּחֲווּ לַיהוה בְּהַדְרַת־קֹדֶשׁ:
קוֹל יהוה עַל הַמָּיִם, אֵל־הַכָּבוֹד הִרְעִים, יהוה עַל־מַיִם רַבִּים:
קוֹל־יהוה בַּכֹּחַ, קוֹל יהוה בֶּהָדָר:
קוֹל יהוה שֹׁבֵר אֲרָזִים, וַיְשַׁבֵּר יהוה אֶת־אַרְזֵי הַלְּבָנוֹן:

BIUR TEFILLA · ביאור תפילה

Psalm 29. This psalm breaks the sequence of the preceding Psalms 95-99. Various reasons have been given as to why this particular one was chosen. At its core, it seems to emphasize the presence of Hashem in all of His majesty and power. Too overwhelming to be experienced firsthand, His presence is symbolized by the many references to His voice, both thunderous and beautiful. The word voice (*kol*) appears seven times, which the Talmud (*Berakhot* 29a) says is reminiscent of the seven blessings of the *Amida* prayer we are yet to say where we rendezvous with God most personally. Others note that it has no fewer than eighteen references to God's name, an allusion to the eighteen blessings we say in the weekday *Amida* (*Berakhot* 28b) and, indeed, the midrash goes to great lengths to show how each line corresponds to each one of those blessings (*Shoḥer Tov*).

Still others suggest that the imagery is very reminiscent of the scene at the revelation of Sinai when the Torah was given (*Shemot* 19:16-19; 20:15), described in terms of thunder and lightning and the sounds or voice of God (*Zevaḥim* 116a; *Mekhilta Yitro*). Further, there is a tradition that the giving of the Torah itself took place on Shabbat (*Shabbat* 86b). This explains why the psalm will be recited again in the morning when we remove the Torah from the Ark for public reading.

Any or all of these reasons would account for the prevalent custom that there is to stand when reciting this psalm. The previous psalms have been leading us to this point, preparing us for an encounter with the Divine as we are to welcome the Shabbat. As with the arrival of any important guests, our first impulse is to stand with excitement to greet them. If we have been unable to muster the right intentions until now, our physical act helps guide our thoughts and feelings. Stand to welcome the Shabbat.

IYUN TEFILLA · עיון תפילה

קוֹל־יהוה בַּכֹּחַ – *The Lord's voice in power.* The midrash homiletically opines that the verse should have said in "its" or "His" power which would have suggested that all felt

He makes Lebanon skip like a calf, Sirion like a young wild ox.
The LORD's voice cleaves flames of fire.
The LORD's voice makes the desert quake,
the LORD shakes the desert of Kadesh.
▸ The LORD's voice makes hinds calve and strips the forests bare,
and in His temple all say: "Glory!"
The LORD sat enthroned at the Flood,
the LORD sits enthroned as King for ever.
The LORD will give strength to His people;
the LORD will bless His people with peace.[I]

The following is said in some congregations:

Please, by the power[B] of Your great right hand, set the captive nation free.
Accept Your people's prayer. Strengthen us, purify us, You who are revered.
Please, Mighty One, guard like the pupil of the eye those who seek Your unity.
Bless them, cleanse them, have compassion on them,
grant them Your righteousness always.
Mighty One, Holy One, in Your great goodness guide Your congregation.
Only One, Exalted One, turn to Your people, who proclaim Your holiness.
Accept our plea and heed our cry, You who know all secret thoughts.[I]
Blessed be the name of His glorious kingdom for ever and all time.

---

forbidden to pronounce. The first letter of each word is said to form that name and so these verses were substituted in their place, although there were differing traditions as to how they should be read (*Responsa Rashba* 1:220). Some suggest that the seven verses parallel the seven references to the voice (*kol*) of God mentioned in the previous psalm (*Tikkunei Zohar, tikkun* 21); others suggest that the 42-letter name of God is particularly associated with the mystery of Creation (*Tosafot Ḥagiga* 11b). In any event, its association with these mystical traditions is what also led some congregations to omit the prayer altogether. For others, it is a most sublime introduction to the experience of the prayer which immediately follows.

IYUN TEFILLA · עיון תפילה

וְשַׁמַע צַעֲקָתֵנוּ, יוֹדֵעַ תַּעֲלוּמוֹת – *Heed our cry, You who know all secret thoughts.* Just as our thoughts are internal, so too can be our cry. Just as our thoughts can express our will without our speaking so can the longing of our heart and soul express themselves in a cry even if it cannot be heard (*Sefat Emet*). That is the meaning of the verse, "I will hear them before they speak" (*Yeshayahu* 65:24). Hashem "knows all secret thoughts." We need only open our hearts to speak, or to cry. **Try to open your heart now.**

וַיַּרְקִידֵם כְּמוֹ־עֵגֶל, לְבָנוֹן וְשִׂרְיוֹן כְּמוֹ בֶן־רְאֵמִים:
קוֹל־יהוה חֹצֵב לַהֲבוֹת אֵשׁ:
קוֹל יהוה יָחִיל מִדְבָּר, יָחִיל יהוה מִדְבַּר קָדֵשׁ:
◂ קוֹל יהוה יְחוֹלֵל אַיָּלוֹת וַיֶּחֱשֹׂף יְעָרוֹת
וּבְהֵיכָלוֹ, כֻּלּוֹ אֹמֵר כָּבוֹד:
יהוה לַמַּבּוּל יָשָׁב, וַיֵּשֶׁב יהוה מֶלֶךְ לְעוֹלָם:
יהוה עֹז לְעַמּוֹ יִתֵּן, יהוה יְבָרֵךְ אֶת־עַמּוֹ בַשָּׁלוֹם:[ע]

The following is said in some congregations:

אָנָּא, בְּכֹחַ גְּדֻלַּת יְמִינְךָ, תַּתִּיר צְרוּרָה.
קַבֵּל רִנַּת עַמְּךָ, שַׂגְּבֵנוּ, טַהֲרֵנוּ, נוֹרָא.
נָא גִבּוֹר, דּוֹרְשֵׁי יִחוּדְךָ כְּבָבַת שָׁמְרֵם.
בָּרְכֵם, טַהֲרֵם, רַחֲמֵם, צִדְקָתְךָ תָּמִיד גָּמְלֵם.
חֲסִין קָדוֹשׁ, בְּרֹב טוּבְךָ נַהֵל עֲדָתֶךָ.
יָחִיד גֵּאֶה, לְעַמְּךָ פְּנֵה, זוֹכְרֵי קְדֻשָּׁתֶךָ.
שַׁוְעָתֵנוּ קַבֵּל וּשְׁמַע צַעֲקָתֵנוּ, יוֹדֵעַ תַּעֲלוּמוֹת.[ע]
בָּרוּךְ שֵׁם כְּבוֹד מַלְכוּתוֹ לְעוֹלָם וָעֶד.

BIUR TEFILLA · ביאור תפילה

אָנָּא, בְּכֹחַ – *Please, by the power.* This short prayer seems to interrupt the sequence of six psalms that culminate with the saying of *Lekha Dodi* in the next section. Indeed, that is one reason why some congregations do not recite it at all. The prayer is said to date back to the first century CE and it has a long history in the mystical tradition, appearing in different parts of different services in addition to Friday night. There are essentially seven verses (the eighth has a history of its own) wherein each verse consists of six words, thus totaling 42 words, the same number of letters in one of God's mystical names that we are

IYUN TEFILLA · עיון תפילה

יהוה יְבָרֵךְ אֶת־עַמּוֹ בַשָּׁלוֹם – *The LORD will bless His people with peace.* It is possible that the peace (*shalom*) referred to here is the state where there is no strife among men. But it could also be a reference to the inner peace that comes to the one who has a sense of place in the world, a calmness and security that come with the faith and perspective that lie at the heart of the greeting we give one another this day: *Shabbat Shalom.*

לְכָה דוֹדִי Come, my Beloved,[BH] to greet the bride;
let us welcome the Sabbath.
Come, my Beloved, to greet the bride;
let us welcome the Sabbath.

שָׁמוֹר "Observe" and "Remember" in one act of speech,[B]
The One and Only God made us hear.
The LORD is One and His name is One,
For renown, for splendor, and for praise.
Come, my Beloved, to greet the bride;
let us welcome the Sabbath.

---

go out to greet the "Sabbath Queen" then, we also seek to greet the King and welcome Him into our midst in a way that we do not and usually cannot during the week. As the individual's weekday pain or sorrow recedes so too does that of the nation as a whole and the focus becomes one of optimism for both – the individual and the national entity hoping to be restored (Rabbi S. Hirsch).

The poem is an acrostic wherein the first letter of each stanza forms the name of the author – ShLoMoH HaLeVI שלמה הלוי. It is almost always sung aloud in unison, sometimes accompanied by dancing in the aisles, a far cry from going out into the fields but still a physical act designed to go out to greet one's guest rather than sitting back and waiting passively for the guest to come to you. In some congregations it is said responsively instead.

HILKHOT TEFILLA • הלכות תפילה

לְכָה דוֹדִי – *Come, my Beloved.* Although there is no obligation to stand for this prayer, some have the custom to do so, just as one would when greeting a guest. Others stand only for the last stanza when the guest arrives as it were. In many congregations, one can see both customs going on at the same time for either is appropriate. Do whichever enables you to bring greater meaning.

ANI TEFILLA • אני תפילה

It is told that the Ari, who lived in Tzefat at the same time as Rabbi Alkabetz, said that one should go out into the field, ideally to a mountain top, face the west where the sun was setting and, at the moment it sets, close your eyes, put one hand atop another on your chest and have in mind with great awe and trembling that you are standing before Hashem ready to accept the Shabbat, and sing in a pleasant voice (*Petura DeAbba ot* 17).

Think of yourself atop that mountain. Close your eyes. Sing your heart out.

BIUR TEFILLA • ביאור תפילה

שָׁמוֹר וְזָכוֹר בְּדִבּוּר אֶחָד – *"Observe" and "Remember" in one act of speech.* This is a reference to the two versions of the Ten Commandments found in the Torah. In one (*Shemot* 20:8), it says that we should "Remember the Shabbat day to keep it holy." In the other (*Devarim* 5:12), the

This **BIUR TEFILLA** *continues on page 419.*

לְכָה דוֹדִי[בה] לִקְרַאת כַּלָּה, פְּנֵי שַׁבָּת נְקַבְּלָה.
לְכָה דוֹדִי לִקְרַאת כַּלָּה, פְּנֵי שַׁבָּת נְקַבְּלָה.

שָׁמוֹר וְזָכוֹר בְּדִבּוּר אֶחָד[ב]
הִשְׁמִיעָנוּ אֵל הַמְיֻחָד
יהוה אֶחָד וּשְׁמוֹ אֶחָד
לְשֵׁם וּלְתִפְאֶרֶת וְלִתְהִלָּה.
לְכָה דוֹדִי לִקְרַאת כַּלָּה, פְּנֵי שַׁבָּת נְקַבְּלָה.

BIUR TEFILLA · ביאור תפילה

לְכָה דוֹדִי – *Come, my beloved.* The Talmud relates that "R. Ḥanina robed himself and stood at sunset of Sabbath eve [and] exclaimed, 'Come and let us go forth to welcome the queen Sabbath.' R. Yannai donned his robes on Sabbath eve and exclaimed, 'Come, O bride, Come, O bride!'" (*Shabbat* 119a). Rashi explains that the Shabbat is so called because of the profound sense of love that Israel has for her.

The language of R. Ḥanina "Come let us go forth" and the suggestion of R. Yannai that our relationship to the Shabbat is like that of two lovers, form the basis for this central poem of the Shabbat service. Written by Rabbi Shlomo HaLevi Alkabetz in the sixteenth century in Tzefat (Safed), who was a member of that influential group of mystics mentioned earlier, the song took its language from the biblical *Shir HaShirim* (Song of Songs), the allegorical love song about the relationship between God and the Jewish people:

> I am my beloved's (*dodi*); and his longing is for me. Come, my beloved (*lekha dodi*), let us go to the field...we will get up early and go to the vineyards, to see if the vine has flowered, whether its blossoms have opened out, if the pomegranate buds have burst; and there shall I give you my love. (*Shir HaShirim* 7:11–14)

Already in ancient times, this unique relationship was expressed thus: "As creation unfolded, it became clear that each day had a partner: Sunday had Monday, Tuesday had Wednesday, Thursday had Friday. The Shabbat came to God and said, 'Master of the Universe! Each day has a partner, yet I have none!' God replied: 'The Jewish People (*Knesset Yisrael*) will be your partner'" (*Bereshit Raba* 11:8). As if to say, from the first days of creation itself, the two were wedded to one another, and their destinies were intertwined forever. Every week, that commitment is renewed.

The truth is that of the nine stanzas of the song, only three speak about Shabbat; the others speak about the yearning for redemption, the rebuilding of the *Beit HaMikdash* (Temple) and the longing for the *Shekhina* or Divine Presence, themes which are part and parcel of the Shabbat experience which is described as a taste of the World to Come (*Berakhot* 56b). When we

לִקְרַאת To greet the Sabbath, come let us go,
For of blessing, she is the source.
From the outset, as of old, ordained:
Last in deed, first in thought.

Come, my Beloved, to greet the bride;
let us welcome the Sabbath.

מִקְדַּשׁ Sanctuary of the King, royal city,
Arise, go forth from your ruined state.
Too long have you dwelt in the valley of tears.
He will shower compassion on you.

Come, my Beloved, to greet the bride;
let us welcome the Sabbath.

---

that was created according to the Torah during the six days of Creation and yet man is often considered the ultimate goal of that Creation. Why, then, was Shabbat created last? Perhaps it is because history has proven that man can then come to mistakenly see himself as the ultimate creator and to conduct himself as if he has absolute power. As such, Shabbat was given in order to help us maintain perspective that we too are but creations despite our power to create. Shabbat reminds us to use that power positively and, in that sense, it was the intended goal of creation even if it was not created first.

מִקְדַּשׁ מֶלֶךְ עִיר מְלוּכָה – *Sanctuary of the King, royal city.* The reference is to Jerusalem, and herein begins the focus on her restoration as the symbol of the redemption when Israel and God will be reconnected , so to speak, in the holy city. "R. Yoḥanan said in the name of R. Shimon bar Yoḥai: 'If Israel were to keep two Sabbaths [in succession] according to its laws, then Israel would be redeemed immediately'" (*Shabbat* 118b). In keeping Shabbat we fulfill our national destiny too.

How?

ANI TEFILLA • אני תפילה

"The Talmud (*Shabbat* 118b) says that if the Jews were to observe Shabbat twice in a row, the *Geula* [redemption] would come immediately. If we could observe Shabbat as it should be, the *Geula* would come because there would be no need for *Geula*. That would be *Geula*. That would be redemption. That would be the messianic time" (Elie Wiesel).

לִקְרַאת שַׁבָּת לְכוּ וְנֵלְכָה
כִּי הִיא מְקוֹר הַבְּרָכָה[ע]
מֵרֹאשׁ מִקֶּדֶם נְסוּכָה
סוֹף מַעֲשֶׂה בְּמַחֲשָׁבָה תְּחִלָּה.[ע]
לְכָה דוֹדִי לִקְרַאת כַּלָּה, פְּנֵי שַׁבָּת נְקַבְּלָה.

מִקְדַּשׁ מֶלֶךְ עִיר מְלוּכָה[ע]
קוּמִי צְאִי מִתּוֹךְ הַהֲפֵכָה
רַב לָךְ שֶׁבֶת בְּעֵמֶק הַבָּכָא
וְהוּא יַחֲמֹל עָלַיִךְ חֶמְלָה.
לְכָה דוֹדִי לִקְרַאת כַּלָּה, פְּנֵי שַׁבָּת נְקַבְּלָה.

---

commandment is expressed as "Observe the Shabbat day to keep it holy." The Rabbis explained that the two were expressed by God in a single breath, in a way that the human mouth cannot utter and the ear cannot hear (*Shevuot* 20b). In practical terms it was understood that "observe" (*shamor*) is a reference to the negative commandments regarding Shabbat, the things we are not permitted to do. "Remember" (*zakhor*) on the other hand, encompasses those positive commandments which guide us to making the day special (cf. Ramban on *Shemot* 20:8). Both go hand in hand: the prohibitions make room for us to create the physical and emotional space that are the hallmarks of Shabbat. One without the other is only a shadow of the Shabbat experience, a body without a soul.

Allow yourself to observe and remember.

IYUN TEFILLA • עיון תפילה

כִּי הִיא מְקוֹר הַבְּרָכָה – *For of blessing, she is the source.* Of all of the days of creation, only of the seventh day does it say that God blessed it (*Bereshit* 2:3). Shabbat, then, is a day of blessing. What exactly does that mean? The text does not say. Perhaps it is riches for the one who observes it, or added insight, or added calm, or added food or rest or... (see *Bereshit Raba* 11). The blessing is for each of us to find for ourselves.

Stop for a moment and ask yourself, what blessing do I seek this Shabbat?

סוֹף מַעֲשֶׂה בְּמַחֲשָׁבָה תְּחִלָּה – *Last in deed, first in thought.* Shabbat was the last thing

הִתְנַעֲרִי Shake yourself off, arise from the dust!
Put on your clothes of glory, My people.[B]
Through the son of Jesse the Bethlehemite,
Draw near to my soul and redeem it.

Come, my Beloved, to greet the bride;
let us welcome the Sabbath.

הִתְעוֹרְרִי Wake up, wake up,[H]
For your light has come: rise, shine!
Awake, awake, break out in song,
For the LORD's glory is revealed on you.

Come, my Beloved, to greet the bride;
let us welcome the Sabbath.

לֹא תֵבֹשִׁי Do not be ashamed, do not be confounded.
Why be downcast? Why do you mourn?
In you the needy of My people find shelter,
And the city shall be rebuilt on its hill.

Come, my Beloved, to greet the bride;
let us welcome the Sabbath.

HILKHOT TEFILLA • הלכות תפילה

הִתְעוֹרְרִי הִתְעוֹרְרִי – *Wake up, wake up.* There is an old tradition in many communities to change the melody at some point near the middle of the song. A custom from Frankfurt, Germany, for example, changes it at this stanza where the acrostic of the second part of the author's name begins. They then revert to the first melody for the last stanza which returns to the theme of Shabbat with which the song began (*Divrei Kehillot*). Less complicated is a more widespread custom to change the melody with the sixth stanza (Lo tevoshi – "Do not be ashamed") and, in some communities, that melody is often more upbeat than the one used at the beginning. While numerous reasons have been given for these changes, none is considered authoritative . Nevertheless the custom, like so many others, has taken on a life of its own.

הִתְנַעֲרִי, מֵעָפָר קוּמִי
לִבְשִׁי בִּגְדֵי תִפְאַרְתֵּךְ עַמִּי[ב]
עַל יַד בֶּן יִשַׁי בֵּית הַלַּחְמִי
קָרְבָה אֶל נַפְשִׁי, גְּאָלָהּ.
לְכָה דוֹדִי לִקְרַאת כַּלָּה, פְּנֵי שַׁבָּת נְקַבְּלָה.

הִתְעוֹרְרִי הִתְעוֹרְרִי[ה]
כִּי בָא אוֹרֵךְ קוּמִי אוֹרִי
עוּרִי עוּרִי, שִׁיר דַּבֵּרִי
כְּבוֹד יהוה עָלַיִךְ נִגְלָה.
לְכָה דוֹדִי לִקְרַאת כַּלָּה, פְּנֵי שַׁבָּת נְקַבְּלָה.

לֹא תֵבֹשִׁי וְלֹא תִכָּלְמִי
מַה תִּשְׁתּוֹחֲחִי וּמַה תֶּהֱמִי
בָּךְ יֶחֱסוּ עֲנִיֵּי עַמִּי
וְנִבְנְתָה עִיר עַל תִּלָּהּ.
לְכָה דוֹדִי לִקְרַאת כַּלָּה, פְּנֵי שַׁבָּת נְקַבְּלָה.

BIUR TEFILLA • ביאור תפילה

לִבְשִׁי בִּגְדֵי תִפְאַרְתֵּךְ עַמִּי – *Put on your clothes of glory, My people.* There are those who say that the subject of the sentence is Jerusalem herself (*Iyun Tefilla*, *Barukh She'amar*) because the verb and noun are in the feminine form yet the word "people" is masculine. As such, the phrase "My people" describes the clothes, that is, My people are the clothes of Jerusalem. When they do not act appropriately, then Jerusalem is naked. It is up to us, then, to adorn ourselves with deeds and attitudes that can adorn her.

What can you do a little differently this Shabbat to make "Jerusalem" more beautiful?

וְהָיוּ Those who despoiled you shall be despoiled,
And all who devoured you shall be far away.
Your God will rejoice over you
As a bridegroom rejoices over his bride.
Come, my Beloved, to greet the bride;
let us welcome the Sabbath.

יָמִין Right and left you shall spread out,
And God you will revere.
Through the descendant of Peretz,
We shall rejoice and we shall be glad.
Come, my Beloved, to greet the bride;
let us welcome the Sabbath.

Stand and turn to face the door or the rear (usually western side) of the synagogue, as if to greet the incoming bride, bowing at the words "Enter, O bride!," then turn back to face the front.

בּוֹאִי Come in peace, O crown of her husband;
Come with joy and jubilation,
Among the faithful of the treasured people.
Enter, O bride! Enter, O bride![H]
Come, my Beloved, to greet the bride;
let us welcome the Sabbath.

---

from the west (*Bava Batra* 25a), while others insist that one face the door regardless of where it is, because a guest always comes via the door. Some turn clockwise to do so, others counterclockwise, some bow once at the mention of these final words of the stanza, as one would when royalty appears, while others bow two or three times. All are deeply rooted customs. It is fairly common however, that at the very end one turns back toward the Ark again, and bows slightly once again, this time to indicate having shown no disrespect to the Ark from which one normally does not turn away.

ANI TEFILLA • אני תפילה

The Talmud (*Shabbat* 10a) relates that God said to Moshe, "I have a gift in My treasury that I have been storing in order to give to Israel. Go and tell them." Rabbi Menaḥem Mendel of Kosov reminds us that the true value of a gift is not the gift itself but rather the love that it represents.

וְהָיוּ לִמְשִׁסָּה שֹׁאסָיִךְ
וְרָחֲקוּ כָּל מְבַלְּעָיִךְ
יָשִׂישׂ עָלַיִךְ אֱלֹהָיִךְ
כִּמְשׂוֹשׂ חָתָן עַל כַּלָּה.
לְכָה דוֹדִי לִקְרַאת כַּלָּה, פְּנֵי שַׁבָּת נְקַבְּלָה.

יָמִין וּשְׂמֹאל תִּפְרֹצִי
וְאֶת יהוה תַּעֲרִיצִי
עַל יַד אִישׁ בֶּן פַּרְצִי
וְנִשְׂמְחָה וְנָגִילָה.
לְכָה דוֹדִי לִקְרַאת כַּלָּה, פְּנֵי שַׁבָּת נְקַבְּלָה.

Stand and turn to face the door or the rear (usually western side) of the בית כנסת*, as if to greet the incoming bride, bowing at the words* בּוֹאִי כַלָּה*, then turn back to face the front.*

בּוֹאִי בְשָׁלוֹם עֲטֶרֶת בַּעְלָהּ
גַּם בְּשִׂמְחָה וּבְצָהֳלָה
תּוֹךְ אֱמוּנֵי עַם סְגֻלָּה
בּוֹאִי כַלָּה, בּוֹאִי כַלָּה.ה
לְכָה דוֹדִי לִקְרַאת כַּלָּה, פְּנֵי שַׁבָּת נְקַבְּלָה.

HILKHOT TEFILLA • הלכות תפילה

בּוֹאִי כַלָּה, בּוֹאִי כַלָּה - *Enter, O bride! Enter, O bride!* As we are finally welcoming the Shabbat bride or the Divine Presence into our midst, there is a custom to actually stand up and turn to face the door. As in so many other customs, there are differences in tradition. Since the door is usually in the back of the synagogue, some turn there, the direction of the setting sun. If the door is located elsewhere, then some will still turn to the west, in keeping with a tradition that the *Shekhina* (Divine Presence) comes

Mourners during the week of Shiva return to the synagogue at this point. They are greeted with the following words of consolation:

הַמָּקוֹם May the Almighty comfort you
among the other mourners of Zion and Jerusalem.

מִזְמוֹר A psalm. A song for the Sabbath day.[B] *Ps. 92*
It is good to thank the LORD[B] and sing psalms to Your name,
Most High[B] –

So significant was this psalm considered, that for many it represented that singular moment when the Shabbat actually is accepted by the person praying and the point at which the prohibitions of Shabbat take effect (*Beit Yosef* 261). That is why the mourner was welcomed before this point. It is also the reason why, on a day when all of the preceding paragraphs of *Kabbalat Shabbat* are omitted (e.g. when a Yom Tov ends or its onset or intermediate days coincide with Shabbat), the service still begins here, for this, according to many, marks the official liturgical acceptance of Shabbat.

The midrash relates that Adam was born and sinned on the sixth day of the week toward the very end of the day. And when Shabbat was created and Adam was about to be punished, the Shabbat protested and said, "Master of the Universe, of all of the days of the week, are You going to pick me as the one on which man is to be sentenced to die for the very first time?! You blessed me and decreed that I should be a day of respite and this is it?" And Adam was thereby saved from expulsion. As a result Adam created "A song for the Sabbath day." Whereupon the Shabbat said, don't sing to me, sing instead "It is good to thank Hashem and sing psalms to Your name" (*Midrash Shoḥer Tov* 92).

Why was the argument of Shabbat effective? What does it say about the unique character of the day?

Why is this story said in the name of Adam and not some later personality from the Torah?

What underlying mistaken belief did Adam have singing the song to Shabbat?

What is the correction that Shabbat made?

What are the ideas or lessons that the midrash seeks to convey?

שִׁיר לְיוֹם הַשַּׁבָּת – *A song for the Sabbath day.* A song to be sung on the day of Shabbat (Ibn Ezra).

Alternatively, a song to be sung to the Shabbat day for the benefit I derive from her (Alsheikh).

טוֹב לְהֹדוֹת לַיהוה – *It is good to thank the LORD.* The Shabbat day is particularly suited for thanking God because it is a day when one's body is less encumbered by the demands of the week, thereby freeing up the soul to be heard (Radak).

What does Shabbat make you thankful for?

Alternatively, the word *lehodot* can also mean to acknowledge.

What would you like to acknowledge to God today?

וּלְזַמֵּר לְשִׁמְךָ עֶלְיוֹן – *And sing psalms to Your name, Most High.* Shabbat is particularly conducive to song. Sing.

Mourners during the week of שבעה *return to the* בית כנסת *at this point. They are greeted with the following words of consolation:*

הַמָּקוֹם יְנַחֵם אֶתְכֶם בְּתוֹךְ שְׁאָר אֲבֵלֵי צִיּוֹן וִירוּשָׁלָיִם.

מִזְמוֹר שִׁיר לְיוֹם הַשַּׁבָּת: תהלים צב
טוֹב לְהֹדוֹת לַיהוה, וּלְזַמֵּר לְשִׁמְךָ עֶלְיוֹן:

ANI TEFILLA • אני תפילה

The name of Hashem here is HaMakom, which literally means the Place. This is because God is both immanent and transcendent; "He is the place of the world, but the world is not His place" (Bereshit Raba 68:12). It is a name that is used most often when it is difficult to sense Hashem's Presence, when He seems to be hiding. We thus wish for the mourner that despite his pain and sorrow, his feeling of abandonment and aloneness, that he find the One who can seem distant but is really very close. May Hashem, the Place, comfort him. (Rabbi Joseph B. Soloveitchik)

HILKHOT TEFILLA • הלכות תפילה

The *Kabbalat Shabbat* service is considered so happy and celebratory, that it is deemed to be at odds with the mood of a mourner whose presence at a public event is normally not allowed during the seven days (*shiva*) of mourning. As such, one who is still in that mourning period does not join the congregation for this service. Since Shabbat has not yet actually begun, we take the opportunity to wish him the traditional blessing given in the house of mourning, something which is not permitted on Shabbat itself because its somber message is not in keeping with the atmosphere we seek to create on that day. At this moment, then, now that his public display of mourning is temporarily ending (for public *shiva* is suspended on Shabbat), he is welcomed back into the community and we stand ready to enter into Shabbat together.

BIUR TEFILLA • ביאור תפילה

Psalm 92: This psalm is said no less than three different times over the course of Shabbat, once this evening and twice tomorrow morning. And yet, surprisingly, despite its opening title as "A song for the Sabbath day," there is little mention of the Shabbat within. Rather, it begins by speaking about how great Hashem is, clearly in terms of everything He does, a realization that engenders feelings of happiness, song and music. One might think that such happiness should be tempered by the fact that there is evil in the world and that bad people seem to succeed. Nevertheless, one should know that such success is ephemeral in the larger scheme of things. It thus concludes on a positive and optimistic note. Its future-oriented perspective led the Rabbis to conclude that it refers to an ideal point in the distant future, "which would be entirely Shabbat," a messianic or eschatological point in time (*Rosh HaShana* 31a). Shabbat is a taste of the World to Come.

to tell of Your loving-kindness in the morning
and Your faithfulness at night,
to the music of the ten-stringed lyre and the melody of the harp.
For You have made me rejoice by Your work, O LORD;
I sing for joy at the deeds of Your hands.
How great are Your deeds, LORD,
and how very deep Your thoughts.
A boor cannot know, nor can a fool understand,[I]
that though the wicked spring up like grass
and all evildoers flourish,
it is only that they may be destroyed for ever.
But You, LORD, are eternally exalted.
For behold Your enemies, LORD,
behold Your enemies will perish;
all evildoers will be scattered.
You have raised my pride like that of a wild ox;
I am anointed with fresh oil.
My eyes shall look in triumph on my adversaries,
my ears shall hear the downfall of the wicked who rise against me.[A]
▸ The righteous will flourish like a palm tree
and grow tall like a cedar in Lebanon.
Planted in the LORD's House,
blossoming in our God's courtyards,
they will still bear fruit in old age,
and stay vigorous and fresh,
proclaiming that the LORD is upright:
He is my Rock, in whom there is no wrong.

ANI TEFILLA • אני תפילה

בַּקָּמִים עָלַי מְרֵעִים תִּשְׁמַעְנָה אָזְנָי – *My ears shall hear the downfall of the wicked who rise against me.* In Hebrew we generally refer to "love of Hashem" but "fear of Heaven." Why do we not say "fear of Hashem" or "love of Heaven"? The answer may be that love is a reflection of our feeling of closeness, the kind of intimacy that allows one to address

This **ANI TEFILLA** *continues on page 429.*

לְהַגִּיד בַּבֹּקֶר חַסְדֶּךָ, וֶאֱמוּנָתְךָ בַּלֵּילוֹת:
עֲלֵי־עָשׂוֹר וַעֲלֵי־נָבֶל, עֲלֵי הִגָּיוֹן בְּכִנּוֹר:
כִּי שִׂמַּחְתַּנִי יהוה בְּפָעֳלֶךָ, בְּמַעֲשֵׂי יָדֶיךָ אֲרַנֵּן:
מַה־גָּדְלוּ מַעֲשֶׂיךָ יהוה, מְאֹד עָמְקוּ מַחְשְׁבֹתֶיךָ:
אִישׁ־בַּעַר לֹא יֵדָע, וּכְסִיל לֹא־יָבִין אֶת־זֹאת:[ע]
בִּפְרֹחַ רְשָׁעִים כְּמוֹ עֵשֶׂב, וַיָּצִיצוּ כָּל־פֹּעֲלֵי אָוֶן
לְהִשָּׁמְדָם עֲדֵי־עַד:
וְאַתָּה מָרוֹם לְעֹלָם יהוה:
כִּי הִנֵּה אֹיְבֶיךָ יהוה, כִּי־הִנֵּה אֹיְבֶיךָ יֹאבֵדוּ
יִתְפָּרְדוּ כָּל־פֹּעֲלֵי אָוֶן:
וַתָּרֶם כִּרְאֵים קַרְנִי, בַּלֹּתִי בְּשֶׁמֶן רַעֲנָן:
וַתַּבֵּט עֵינִי בְּשׁוּרָי
בַּקָּמִים עָלַי מְרֵעִים תִּשְׁמַעְנָה אָזְנָי:[א]
◂ צַדִּיק כַּתָּמָר יִפְרָח, כְּאֶרֶז בַּלְּבָנוֹן יִשְׂגֶּה:
שְׁתוּלִים בְּבֵית יהוה, בְּחַצְרוֹת אֱלֹהֵינוּ יַפְרִיחוּ:
עוֹד יְנוּבוּן בְּשֵׂיבָה, דְּשֵׁנִים וְרַעֲנַנִּים יִהְיוּ:
לְהַגִּיד כִּי־יָשָׁר יהוה, צוּרִי, וְלֹא־עַוְלָתָה בּוֹ:

IYUN TEFILLA • עיון תפילה

אִישׁ־בַּעַר לֹא יֵדָע, וּכְסִיל לֹא־יָבִין אֶת־זֹאת – *A boor cannot know, nor can a fool understand.* A boor is a like a brute beast who only comprehends what lies before him. The conceited fool is the one who tenaciously adheres to his views even if they are utterly unjustifiable. The institution of Shabbat presupposes that we are neither, for if either were the case, the lessons that Shabbat is designed to teach would be lost upon us.

How might I use reason to learn those lessons today?

Whoever doesn't know what he doesn't know, knows nothing (Rashba).

Ps. 93

יהוה מָלָךְ The LORD reigns.
He is robed in majesty.
The LORD is robed, girded with strength.
The world is firmly established;
it cannot be moved.
Your throne stands firm as of old;
You are eternal.
Rivers lift up, LORD, rivers lift up their voice,[B]
rivers lift up their crashing waves.
▸ Mightier than the noise of many waters,
than the mighty waves of the sea
is the LORD on high.
Your testimonies are very sure;[I]
holiness adorns Your House, LORD,
for evermore.

What would our lives be like without the oceans and rivers, lakes and streams that help comprise more than 70 percent of the Earth's surface?

IYUN TEFILLA • עיון תפילה

עֵדֹתֶיךָ נֶאֶמְנוּ מְאֹד – *Your testimonies are very sure.* Your laws, among which the Shabbat stands out first and foremost, are constants. They accompany the individual throughout one's life, through all of the changes that life may bring (Rabbi S. Hirsch). They are the anchor that gives one the stability with which to negotiate the turbulent waters and they are the subtle force that imposes calm. Shabbat, and all of the rest of the Torah's laws, are what have kept the Jewish people alive and vibrant for millennia and so it will always be, "for evermore."

ANI TEFILLA • אני תפילה

"Anyone who feels a true bond in his heart, with the life of the nation over many generations, simply will not be able – even if he believes neither in the World to Come nor the Jewish State – to imagine the Jewish People without *Shabbat Malketa* (the Sabbath Queen). It may be said without exaggeration that more than the Jews kept the Sabbath, it was the Sabbath that kept them" (Aḥad HaAm).

תהלים צג

יהוה מָלָךְ, גֵּאוּת לָבֵשׁ, לָבֵשׁ יהוה עֹז הִתְאַזָּר
אַף־תִּכּוֹן תֵּבֵל בַּל־תִּמּוֹט:
נָכוֹן כִּסְאֲךָ מֵאָז, מֵעוֹלָם אָתָּה:
נָשְׂאוּ נְהָרוֹת יהוה, נָשְׂאוּ נְהָרוֹת קוֹלָם
יִשְׂאוּ נְהָרוֹת דָּכְיָם:
◂ מִקֹּלוֹת מַיִם רַבִּים
אַדִּירִים מִשְׁבְּרֵי־יָם, אַדִּיר בַּמָּרוֹם יהוה:
עֵדֹתֶיךָ נֶאֶמְנוּ מְאֹד
לְבֵיתְךָ נַאֲוָה־קֹדֶשׁ
יהוה לְאֹרֶךְ יָמִים:

---

the other by name. Fear, however, conveys a sense of distance in a relationship, like the gap which separates man from the heavens (Rabbi J.B. Soloveitchik). In human affairs, love is probably more favored than fear. But in a relationship with the Divine, both are natural and both are to be embraced.

Do you love more than you fear? Do you fear more than you love? How might you reach a greater level of each?

BIUR TEFILLA • ביאור תפילה

Psalm 93: This short psalm is said to be an extension of the previous one and the pair will be seen again during the *Pesukei DeZimra* section of the service in the morning. In its tight structure it summarizes a number of the themes seen thus far: a God who is eternal, a force in nature and the history of man, the God recognized by all mankind who has a special relationship with Israel, symbolized by the Temple and the laws that govern our lives as Jews.

נָשְׂאוּ נְהָרוֹת יהוה, נָשְׂאוּ נְהָרוֹת קוֹלָם... – *Rivers lift up, Lord, rivers lift up their voice...* The floods may symbolize the rising and falling of nations, each desirous of imposing its will on others or on the world or on God (Radak, Rabbi S. Hirsch). Alternatively, they may be symbols for Hashem's mastery over nature, both the fact that the oceans do not overtake the world, and the fact that they can be harnessed for man's benefit for drinking and irrigation (Malbim).

MOURNER'S KADDISH

The following prayer, said by mourners, requires the presence of a minyan.
A transliteration can be found on page 1141.

Mourner: יִתְגַּדַּל Magnified and sanctified
may His great name be,
in the world He created by His will.
May He establish His kingdom
in your lifetime and in your days,
and in the lifetime of all the house of Israel,
swiftly and soon –
and say: Amen.

All: May His great name be blessed
for ever and all time.

Mourner: Blessed and praised,
glorified and exalted,
raised and honored,
uplifted and lauded
be the name of the Holy One,
blessed be He,
beyond any blessing,
song, praise and consolation
uttered in the world –
and say: Amen.

May there be great peace from heaven,
and life for us and all Israel –
and say: Amen.

Bow, take three steps back, as if taking leave of the Divine Presence,
then bow, first left, then right, then center, while saying:

May He who makes peace in His high places,
make peace for us and all Israel –
and say: Amen.

קדיש יתום

The following prayer, said by mourners, requires the presence of a מנין*.*
A transliteration can be found on page 1141.

אבל: יִתְגַּדַּל וְיִתְקַדַּשׁ שְׁמֵהּ רַבָּא (קהל: אָמֵן)
בְּעָלְמָא דִּי בְרָא כִרְעוּתֵהּ וְיַמְלִיךְ מַלְכוּתֵהּ
בְּחַיֵּיכוֹן וּבְיוֹמֵיכוֹן וּבְחַיֵּי דְכָל בֵּית יִשְׂרָאֵל
בַּעֲגָלָא וּבִזְמַן קָרִיב
וְאִמְרוּ אָמֵן. (קהל: אָמֵן)

קהל ואבל: יְהֵא שְׁמֵהּ רַבָּא מְבָרַךְ לְעָלַם וּלְעָלְמֵי עָלְמַיָּא.

אבל: יִתְבָּרַךְ וְיִשְׁתַּבַּח וְיִתְפָּאַר
וְיִתְרוֹמַם וְיִתְנַשֵּׂא וְיִתְהַדָּר וְיִתְעַלֶּה וְיִתְהַלָּל
שְׁמֵהּ דְּקֻדְשָׁא בְּרִיךְ הוּא (קהל: בְּרִיךְ הוּא)
לְעֵלָּא מִן כָּל בִּרְכָתָא
וְשִׁירָתָא, תֻּשְׁבְּחָתָא וְנֶחֱמָתָא
דַּאֲמִירָן בְּעָלְמָא
וְאִמְרוּ אָמֵן. (קהל: אָמֵן)

יְהֵא שְׁלָמָא רַבָּא מִן שְׁמַיָּא
וְחַיִּים, עָלֵינוּ וְעַל כָּל יִשְׂרָאֵל
וְאִמְרוּ אָמֵן. (קהל: אָמֵן)

Bow, take three steps back, as if taking leave of the Divine Presence, then bow, first left, then right, then center, while saying:

עֹשֶׂה שָׁלוֹם בִּמְרוֹמָיו
הוּא יַעֲשֶׂה שָׁלוֹם עָלֵינוּ וְעַל כָּל יִשְׂרָאֵל
וְאִמְרוּ אָמֵן. (קהל: אָמֵן)

1. בַּמֶּה מַדְלִיקִין With what wicks may we light[1] the Sabbath lamp and with what may we not light? We may not use a wick of cedar bast, or

1. ***Ner with kik oil.*** *Samuel said:*

I asked all the seafarers about it, and they told me that there is a certain bird in the towns of the sea called kik. Rabbi

---

INTRODUCTION TO BAMEH MADLIKIN

The following passages are from the second chapter of the Mishna tractate *Shabbat* and consist of technical discussions about the different kinds of oils and wicks that were acceptable for use in Talmudic times. The reasons for its presence in the service is the subject of dispute leading to some reciting it here, others later on and still others not at all.

Those reasons are fascinating in themselves for, like so many other parts of the Siddur, they lend insight into the history of the Jewish communities through the centuries. One opinion, for example, contends that it was placed here as a kind of filler for the congregation to say so that latecomers could catch up and not be left alone at the end of the service to face perceived perils at the time (*Sefer Haltim*). Another opinion suggests that it was placed here for those who did not want to start eating the Shabbat meal until night fell and so they chose to fill the time in learning Torah in the broadest sense, in this case learning the laws that governed the light in the house (*Baḥ*). Another opinion points to the need to teach the ignorant what oils and wicks can be used (*Roke'aḥ*), although another says that is precisely the reason not to say it at all since we do not use forbidden materials today (*Magen Avraham*). Still another says that this particular mitzva was selected because one of the reasons for lighting candles is to enhance the atmosphere of peace in one's home and this was a theme to be emphasized before returning home to be with one's family (Abudarham). Finally, there is an historical reason that has been suggested; namely, the Sadducees, and later the Karaites, were sects who rejected the validity of the Oral Law, including the interpretation of the biblical verse which said that one may not light a candle in one's home on Shabbat "Do not light a fire in any of your dwellings on the Sabbath day" (*Shemot* 35:3). They interpreted this to mean that no artificial light whatsoever was permitted in one's home on Shabbat, whereas the Rabbis had ruled that one may not actually kindle a flame on Shabbat but there was nothing wrong with having a preexisting flame that lasted into Shabbat. Hence the study of this particular section of the Mishna, part of the Oral Law, that deals with Shabbat lights was selected for study as a reminder of the validity of the Oral Law which goes hand in hand with the Written Law of Torah (*Sefer Haltim*).

Yitzḥak son of Rav Yehuda said: It is cotton-seed oil; Resh Lakish said: Oil from Yona's kikayon (Shabbat 21a).

In Bameh Madlikin, Rav Kook sees a parallel between oil and success, and between the wick and an individual. The loftier kind of success we seek is one which fills a person with inner happiness and raises one's life to a higher plane.

This success is akin to the oil which is drawn through the extent of the wick, fully saturating it. Each Talmudic explanation of the term "kik" hints to a success which remains external to the individual.

א בַּמֶּה מַדְלִיקִין[1] וּבַמָּה אֵין מַדְלִיקִין. אֵין מַדְלִיקִין לֹא בְלֶכֶשׁ, וְלֹא בְחֹסֶן, וְלֹא בְכַלָּךְ, וְלֹא בִּפְתִילַת הָאִידָן, וְלֹא בִּפְתִילַת הַמִּדְבָּר, וְלֹא בִירוֹקָה שֶׁעַל פְּנֵי הַמָּיִם. וְלֹא בְזֶפֶת וְלֹא בְשַׁעֲוָה וְלֹא בְּשֶׁמֶן קִיק וְלֹא בְּשֶׁמֶן שְׂרֵפָה וְלֹא בְאַלְיָה וְלֹא בְחֵלֶב. נַחוּם הַמָּדִי אוֹמֵר: מַדְלִיקִין בְּחֵלֶב מְבֻשָּׁל, וַחֲכָמִים אוֹמְרִים: אֶחָד מְבֻשָּׁל וְאֶחָד שֶׁאֵינוֹ מְבֻשָּׁל, אֵין מַדְלִיקִין בּוֹ.

uncombed flax, or raw silk, or a wick made of willow bast or desert weed, or seaweed. [For oil] we may not use pitch, or wax, or cottonseed oil or [contaminated consecrated] oil that must be destroyed by burning, or fat from sheeps' tails, or tallow. Naḥum the Mede says: We may use boiled tallow. But the sages say: Whether boiled or not boiled, we may not use it.

First, the towns of the sea, though reputably prosperous, were known for their moral corruption. Anyone who pursues success there could be guaranteed that it would not penetrate their inner being nor bring them serenity. True happiness is not found on a distant island, but in the home of every Jew, in a life of modesty, humility and pure-heartedness. The love of family and the Torah awaken the holiest emotions of the heart by the light of the candles in one's home on Shabbat eve.

Second, the cotton plant resembles a grapevine in its form. The grapevine represents happiness, which appears to be internal, but in truth remains external to a person. Ultimately, the heart is empty.

Third, the kikayon of Yona was here today and gone tomorrow. It highlights an ephemeral happiness, which dissipates all too soon. Because there is no inherent connection between material success and an individual, nothing can be harvested in the long term.

1. משנה שבת, פרק שני – *Mishna Shabbat, chapter 2.*

ב אֵין מַדְלִיקִין בְּשֶׁמֶן שְׂרֵפָה בְּיוֹם טוֹב. רַבִּי יִשְׁמָעֵאל אוֹמֵר: אֵין מַדְלִיקִין בְּעִטְרָן מִפְּנֵי כְּבוֹד הַשַּׁבָּת. וַחֲכָמִים מַתִּירִין בְּכָל הַשְּׁמָנִים, בְּשֶׁמֶן שֻׁמְשְׁמִין, בְּשֶׁמֶן אֱגוֹזִים, בְּשֶׁמֶן צְנוֹנוֹת, בְּשֶׁמֶן דָּגִים, בְּשֶׁמֶן פַּקֻּעוֹת, בְּעִטְרָן וּבְנֵפְט. רַבִּי טַרְפוֹן אוֹמֵר: אֵין מַדְלִיקִין אֶלָּא בְּשֶׁמֶן זַיִת בִּלְבָד.

ג כָּל הַיּוֹצֵא מִן הָעֵץ אֵין מַדְלִיקִין בּוֹ, אֶלָּא פִשְׁתָּן. וְכָל הַיּוֹצֵא מִן הָעֵץ אֵינוֹ מִטַּמֵּא טֻמְאַת אֹהָלִים, אֶלָּא פִשְׁתָּן. פְּתִילַת הַבֶּגֶד שֶׁקִּפְּלָהּ וְלֹא הִבְהֲבָהּ, רַבִּי אֱלִיעֶזֶר אוֹמֵר: טְמֵאָה הִיא, וְאֵין מַדְלִיקִין בָּהּ. רַבִּי עֲקִיבָא אוֹמֵר: טְהוֹרָה הִיא, וּמַדְלִיקִין בָּהּ.

ד לֹא יִקֹּב אָדָם שְׁפוֹפֶרֶת שֶׁל בֵּיצָה וִימַלְּאֶנָּה שֶׁמֶן וְיִתְּנֶנָּה עַל פִּי הַנֵּר,

2. [Contaminated consecrated] oil that must be destroyed by burning may not be used for a festival lamp. Rabbi Yishmael says: We may not use tar out of respect for the honor due to the Sabbath. But the sages permit all these oils: sesame oil, nut oil, radish oil, fish oil, gourd oil, tar or naphtha. Rabbi Tarfon, however, says: We may use only olive oil.

3. No product from a tree may be used as a wick for the Sabbath lamp, except flax. Also no product of a tree can contract "tent" uncleanness, except flax. If a wick was made from a cloth that has been twisted but not singed, Rabbi Eliezer declares, it is susceptible to contamination and may not be used for a Sabbath lamp; but Rabbi Akiva says, it is not susceptible to contamination, and may be used for the Sabbath lamp.

4. One may not pierce an eggshell, fill it with oil, and put it over the mouth of a lamp so that the oil may drip from it into the lamp, even if the vessel is of earth-

Rather, what our souls yearn for in earnest from Shabbat can only be acquired through hard work and a pure heart. This inherent happiness spreads naturally to the downhearted. This is the success we seek, and this is the oil we light.

2. Rabbi Tarfon says: We only light with olive oil. *The Shabbat lights allude to the enlightenment of the mind, which comes with the holiness of the day of rest. There are many kinds of oil, and there are many kinds of wisdom. Human wisdom can lead to character refinement and can prepare an individual to bring much good to the world. But the purest olive oil, the enlightenment of the Torah, is reserved for Shabbat. It is impervious to confusion and evil intention. The*

enware, but Rabbi Yehuda permits it. If, however, the potter had originally attached it to the lamp, it is permitted because it constitutes a single vessel. One may not fill a bowl with oil, put it beside a lamp, and put the end of the wick in it so that it draws oil from the bowl; but Rabbi Yehuda permits this.

5. One who extinguishes a lamp because he is afraid of heathens, robbers, or depression, or to enable a sick person to sleep, is not liable [for violating the Sabbath]. If he did it to spare the lamp, or the oil, or the wick, he is liable. Rabbi Yose absolves him in all these cases except that of sparing the wick, because he thereby turns it into charcoal.

6. For three transgressions women may die in childbirth: for being careless in observing the laws of menstruation, separating ḥalla [dough-offering], and lighting the Sabbath light.

בִּשְׁבִיל שֶׁתְּהֵא מְנַטֶּפֶת, וַאֲפִילוּ הִיא שֶׁל חֶרֶס. וְרַבִּי יְהוּדָה מַתִּיר. אֲבָל אִם חִבְּרָהּ הַיּוֹצֵר מִתְּחִלָּה מֻתָּר, מִפְּנֵי שֶׁהוּא כְּלִי אֶחָד. לֹא יְמַלֵּא אָדָם אֶת הַקְּעָרָה שֶׁמֶן וְיִתְּנֶנָּה בְּצַד הַנֵּר וְיִתֵּן רֹאשׁ הַפְּתִילָה בְּתוֹכָהּ, בִּשְׁבִיל שֶׁתְּהֵא שׁוֹאֶבֶת. וְרַבִּי יְהוּדָה מַתִּיר.

ה הַמְכַבֶּה אֶת הַנֵּר מִפְּנֵי שֶׁהוּא מִתְיָרֵא מִפְּנֵי גוֹיִם, מִפְּנֵי לִסְטִים, מִפְּנֵי רוּחַ רָעָה, אוֹ בִשְׁבִיל הַחוֹלֶה שֶׁיִּישַׁן, פָּטוּר. כְּחָס עַל הַנֵּר, כְּחָס עַל הַשֶּׁמֶן, כְּחָס עַל הַפְּתִילָה, חַיָּב. רַבִּי יוֹסֵי פּוֹטֵר בְּכֻלָּן חוּץ מִן הַפְּתִילָה, מִפְּנֵי שֶׁהוּא עוֹשָׂה פֶּחָם.

ו עַל שָׁלֹשׁ עֲבֵרוֹת נָשִׁים מֵתוֹת בִּשְׁעַת לֵדָתָן, עַל שֶׁאֵינָן זְהִירוֹת בַּנִּדָּה, בְּחַלָּה וּבְהַדְלָקַת הַנֵּר.

holiest day is dedicated to the pursuit of the wisdom of the Torah.

6. ***For three transgressions women may die in childbirth.*** *Rav Kook explains that the moment of childbirth signifies the influx of divine energy into a person's home. To bring a new soul into this world, women must first prepare spiritually. The observance of Nidda represents the disruption of a natural animal pattern of sexual engagement in favor of a relationship built on ideals and lofty aspirations. Ḥalla, a portion of dough reserved for the Kohen, shows that a family accepts their interdependence with unique and holy individuals whom they hope will influence their home. The Shabbat lights demonstrate the inner light that a family seeks to reveal in its home through calm interactions. Every heart rests from sadness and anxiety; every simple delight is sanctified and raised up. With these practices, a family is ready to receive the divine light and a new soul.*

7. One should say three things at home on the eve of the Sabbath just before dark: Have you tithed? Have you prepared the Eiruv? Light the Sabbath lamp. If there is doubt whether or not darkness has fallen, we may not tithe the definitely untithed produce, nor immerse [unclean] vessels, nor light the Sabbath lamp. We may tithe produce about which there is a doubt whether it has been tithed or not, we may prepare an Eiruv, and insulate hot food.

ז שְׁלֹשָׁה דְבָרִים צָרִיךְ אָדָם לוֹמַר בְּתוֹךְ בֵּיתוֹ עֶרֶב שַׁבָּת עִם חֲשֵׁכָה: עִשַּׂרְתֶּם, עֵרַבְתֶּם, הַדְלִיקוּ אֶת הַנֵּר. סָפֵק חֲשֵׁכָה סָפֵק אֵינָהּ חֲשֵׁכָה, אֵין מְעַשְּׂרִין אֶת הַוַּדַּאי, וְאֵין מַטְבִּילִין אֶת הַכֵּלִים, וְאֵין מַדְלִיקִין אֶת הַנֵּרוֹת. אֲבָל מְעַשְּׂרִין אֶת הַדְּמַאי, וּמְעָרְבִין וְטוֹמְנִין אֶת הַחַמִּין.

It was taught,[2] Rabbi Ḥanina said: One should examine his clothing on the eve of the Sabbath before nightfall [to ensure that one is not carrying anything], for one may forget and go out. Rabbi Yosef said: This is an important law about the Sabbath [for it is easy to forget, and thus inadvertently violate the holiness of the day].

תַּנְיָא,[2] אָמַר רַבִּי חֲנִינָא: חַיָּב אָדָם לְמַשְׁמֵשׁ בְּגָדָיו בְּעֶרֶב שַׁבָּת עִם חֲשֵׁכָה, שֶׁמָּא יִשְׁכַּח וְיֵצֵא. אָמַר רַב יוֹסֵף: הִלְכְתָא רַבְּתָא לְשַׁבְּתָא.

7. ***One should say three things at home on the eve of Sabbath.*** *Rav Kook emphasizes the importance of attaining certainty that the most important tasks in one's home have been fulfilled. As Shabbat enters and the holiness of Israel shines brightest, the soul which attains certainty that one's home is completely ready shall be engraved with its light.*

Rabbi Ḥanina said: One should examine his clothing. *According to Rav Kook, one of the fundamentals of Shabbat is comparing one's external life with one's inner life. The greater the distance is between the two, the greater the alienation one feels from one's true nature. In our external lives, we are*

2. שבת יב. – *Shabbat 12a.*

אָמַר רַבִּי אֶלְעָזָר,[3] אָמַר רַבִּי חֲנִינָא: תַּלְמִידֵי חֲכָמִים מַרְבִּים שָׁלוֹם בָּעוֹלָם, שֶׁנֶּאֱמַר: וְכָל־בָּנַיִךְ לִמּוּדֵי יהוה, וְרַב שְׁלוֹם בָּנָיִךְ:[4] אַל תִּקְרֵי בָּנָיִךְ, אֶלָּא בּוֹנָיִךְ. שָׁלוֹם רָב לְאֹהֲבֵי תוֹרָתֶךָ, וְאֵין־לָמוֹ מִכְשׁוֹל: יְהִי־שָׁלוֹם בְּחֵילֵךְ, שַׁלְוָה בְּאַרְמְנוֹתָיִךְ. לְמַעַן אַחַי וְרֵעָי אֲדַבְּרָה־נָּא שָׁלוֹם בָּךְ:[5] לְמַעַן בֵּית־יהוה אֱלֹהֵינוּ אֲבַקְשָׁה טוֹב לָךְ:[6] ‹ יהוה עֹז לְעַמּוֹ יִתֵּן, יהוה יְבָרֵךְ אֶת־עַמּוֹ בַשָּׁלוֹם:[7]

Rabbi Elazar said[3] in the name of Rabbi Ḥanina: The disciples of the sages increase peace in the world, as it is said, "And all your children shall be taught of the LORD, and great shall be the peace of your children [*banayikh*]."[4] Read not *banayikh*, "your children," but *bonayikh*, "your builders." Those who love Your Torah have great peace; there is no stumbling block for them. May there be peace within your ramparts, prosperity in your palaces. For the sake of my brothers and friends, I shall say, "Peace be within you."[5] For the sake of the House of the LORD our God, I will seek your good.[6] ▸ May the LORD grant strength to His people; may the LORD bless His people with peace.[7]

constantly pulled by others in many different directions. Shabbat is a process not only of accentuating one's inner life, but also of bringing one's two lives in step with each other. Though one would not violate the spiritual dimension of Shabbat if his clothing is not examined, one would not have achieved a refocusing of one's external life, represented by one's clothing. Therefore, in addition to examining one's clothing, special Shabbat clothing is worn to demonstrate the realignment of one's external life.

Adapted by Rabbi Sarna from Rav Kook, *Olat Re'iyya*. Rabbi Avraham Yitzchak Kook, a renowned Halakhist, Kabbalist, and Jewish thinker was the first Chief Rabbi of Israel.

3. ברכות סד. – *Berakhot 64a*
4. ישעיה נד – *Yeshayahu 54*
5. תהלים קיט – *Tehillim 119*
6. תהלים קכב – *Tehillim 122*
7. תהלים כט – *Tehillim 29*

THE RABBIS' KADDISH

The following prayer, said by mourners, requires the presence of a minyan. A transliteration can be found on page 1140.

Mourner: יִתְגַּדַּל Magnified and sanctified[B]
may His great name be,
in the world He created by His will.
May He establish His kingdom in your lifetime
and in your days,
and in the lifetime of all the house of Israel,
swiftly and soon –
and say: Amen.

All: May His great name be blessed for ever and all time.

Mourner: Blessed and praised,
glorified and exalted,
raised and honored,
uplifted and lauded
be the name of the Holy One,
blessed be He,
beyond any blessing,
song, praise and consolation
uttered in the world –
and say: Amen.

To Israel, to the teachers,
their disciples and their disciples' disciples,
and to all who engage in the study of Torah,
in this (*In Israel add:* holy) place or elsewhere,

BIUR TEFILLA · ביאור תפילה

יִתְגַּדַּל וְיִתְקַדַּשׁ – *Magnified and sanctified. Kaddish* was originally recited after communal learning of homiletic portions of the Oral Law. Since there were many people

This **BIUR TEFILLA** *continues on page 441*

קדיש דרבנן

The following prayer, said by mourners, requires the presence of a מנין.
A transliteration can be found on page 1140.

אבל: יִתְגַּדַּל וְיִתְקַדַּשׁ שְׁמֵהּ רַבָּא (קהל: אָמֵן)
בְּעָלְמָא דִּי בְרָא כִרְעוּתֵהּ
וְיַמְלִיךְ מַלְכוּתֵהּ
בְּחַיֵּיכוֹן וּבְיוֹמֵיכוֹן וּבְחַיֵּי דְכָל בֵּית יִשְׂרָאֵל
בַּעֲגָלָא וּבִזְמַן קָרִיב
וְאִמְרוּ אָמֵן. (קהל: אָמֵן)

קהל ואבל: יְהֵא שְׁמֵהּ רַבָּא מְבָרַךְ לְעָלַם וּלְעָלְמֵי עָלְמַיָּא.

אבל: יִתְבָּרַךְ וְיִשְׁתַּבַּח וְיִתְפָּאַר וְיִתְרוֹמַם וְיִתְנַשֵּׂא
וְיִתְהַדָּר וְיִתְעַלֶּה וְיִתְהַלָּל
שְׁמֵהּ דְּקֻדְשָׁא בְּרִיךְ הוּא (קהל: בְּרִיךְ הוּא)
לְעֵלָּא מִן כָּל בִּרְכָתָא
וְשִׁירָתָא, תֻּשְׁבְּחָתָא וְנֶחֱמָתָא
דַּאֲמִירָן בְּעָלְמָא
וְאִמְרוּ אָמֵן. (קהל: אָמֵן)

עַל יִשְׂרָאֵל וְעַל רַבָּנָן
וְעַל תַּלְמִידֵיהוֹן
וְעַל כָּל תַּלְמִידֵי תַלְמִידֵיהוֹן
וְעַל כָּל מָאן דְּעָסְקִין בְּאוֹרַיְתָא
דִּי בְּאַתְרָא (בארץ ישראל: קַדִּישָׁא) הָדֵין
וְדִי בְּכָל אֲתַר וַאֲתַר

may there come to them
and you great peace,
grace, kindness and compassion,
long life, ample sustenance and deliverance,
from their Father in Heaven –
and say: Amen.

May there be great peace from heaven,
and (good) life for us and all Israel –
and say: Amen.

Bow, take three steps back, as if taking leave of the Divine Presence, then bow, first left, then right, then center, while saying:

May He who makes peace in His high places,
in His compassion make peace
for us and all Israel –
and say: Amen.

Israel, but stayed and worked the Land, is associated with the afternoon and *Minḥa*. Yaakov's life, on the other hand, was filled with trials and tribulations, with uncertainty and clouds of darkness. Yaakov is the one who established *Ma'ariv*.

The phrase the Torah uses is "*vayifga baMakom*," (*Bereshit* 28:11) which in Rabbinic Hebrew could be read to mean, "He bumped into God." There are spiritual experiences we have when we are least expecting them – when we are alone, afraid, thinking of something else altogether. This was Yaakov's vision of prayer. Not everything in the life of the spirit is under our control. The great transformative experiences – love, a sudden sense of beauty, an upsurge of happiness – happen unpredictably and leave us, in Wordsworth's famous words, "surprised by joy." The glory of Yaakov's epiphany is that it happened at night, in the midst of fear and flight (Rabbi J. Sacks).

The nighttime hours are often a time of uncertainty, when the insecurities of our lives rear their heads the most. What better time to search out an encounter with the One who knows us best? Preoccupied with the successes or disappointments of our day, we enter into an intimate conversation with Hashem, finding friendship and support, and, perhaps, a transformative experience.

For more on teffilat Ma'ariv see page 299.

יְהֵא לְהוֹן וּלְכוֹן שְׁלָמָא רַבָּא
חִנָּא וְחִסְדָּא, וְרַחֲמֵי
וְחַיֵּי אֲרִיכֵי, וּמְזוֹנֵי רְוִיחֵי
וּפֻרְקָנָא מִן קֳדָם אֲבוּהוֹן דִּי בִשְׁמַיָּא
וְאִמְרוּ אָמֵן. (קהל: אָמֵן)

יְהֵא שְׁלָמָא רַבָּא מִן שְׁמַיָּא
וְחַיִּים (טוֹבִים) עָלֵינוּ וְעַל כָּל יִשְׂרָאֵל
וְאִמְרוּ אָמֵן. (קהל: אָמֵן)

Bow, take three steps back, as if taking leave of the Divine Presence, then bow, first left, then right, then center, while saying:

עֹשֶׂה שָׁלוֹם בִּמְרוֹמָיו
הוּא יַעֲשֶׂה בְרַחֲמָיו שָׁלוֹם
עָלֵינוּ וְעַל כָּל יִשְׂרָאֵל
וְאִמְרוּ אָמֵן. (קהל: אָמֵן)

---

who did not understand Hebrew, the prayer was composed in Aramaic, the language of the Talmud and the vernacular at the time, so that everyone could understand and participate in the sanctification of God's name (*Tosafot Berakhot* 3b). The original text is preserved even though Aramaic has not really survived as a spoken language of the Jews. I have often wondered what lessons the creators of the prayerbook sought to convey by remaining faithful to the original. **What do you think an answer might be?**

INTRODUCTION TO MA'ARIV

The Gemara (*Berakhot* 26b) explains that each one of the three daily services was established by one of the *Avot*. It has often been suggested that the timing also relates to the character of each of the *Avot*. Avraham, the bold and assertive pioneer, is associated with the morning, and thus *Shaharit*. Yitzhak, the one who never left

Ma'ariv for Shabbat

BLESSINGS OF THE SHEMA

The Leader says the following, bowing at "Bless," standing straight at "the LORD"; the congregation, followed by the Leader, responds, bowing at "Bless," standing straight at "the LORD":

Leader: **BLESS**[B]
the LORD, the blessed One.

Congregation: Bless the LORD, the blessed One,
for ever and all time.

Leader: Bless the LORD, the blessed One,
for ever and all time.

בָּרוּךְ Blessed are You, LORD our God, King of the Universe,
who by His word brings on evenings,
by His wisdom opens the gates of heaven,
with understanding makes time change
and the seasons rotate,
and by His will orders the stars in their constellations in the sky.

---

revelation in Torah. God can be found in both, although in different ways.

בָּרוּךְ – *Blessed.* This opening formula ("Blessed are You...") marks the first of the two blessings before the *Shema* and it concludes at the end of the paragraph with the same formula ("Blessed are You who brings on evenings.") Although the formula appears twice, the prayer itself is actually considered one long blessing with an introduction and conclusion.

ANI TEFILLA • אני תפילה

"The sun descending in the west, / The evening star does shine; / The birds are silent in their nest, / And I must seek for mine." (William Blake)

מעריב לשבת

קריאת שמע וברכותיה

The שליח ציבור *says the following, bowing at* בָּרְכוּ*, standing straight at* ה'*; the* קהל*, followed by the* שליח ציבור*, responds, bowing at* בָּרוּךְ*, standing straight at* ה'*:*

ש״ץ: בָּרְכוּ ב
אֶת יהוה הַמְבֹרָךְ.

קהל: בָּרוּךְ יהוה הַמְבֹרָךְ לְעוֹלָם וָעֶד.

ש״ץ: בָּרוּךְ יהוה הַמְבֹרָךְ לְעוֹלָם וָעֶד.

בָּרוּךְ אַתָּה יהוה אֱלֹהֵינוּ מֶלֶךְ הָעוֹלָם
אֲשֶׁר בִּדְבָרוֹ מַעֲרִיב עֲרָבִים
בְּחָכְמָה פּוֹתֵחַ שְׁעָרִים
וּבִתְבוּנָה מְשַׁנֶּה עִתִּים וּמַחֲלִיף אֶת הַזְּמַנִּים
וּמְסַדֵּר אֶת הַכּוֹכָבִים בְּמִשְׁמְרוֹתֵיהֶם בָּרָקִיעַ כִּרְצוֹנוֹ.

BIUR TEFILLA • ביאור תפילה

בָּרְכוּ – *Bless.* Just as in the morning, as a prelude to the *Shema*, the *Ḥazan* invites us to join together as a single entity to declare our most basic beliefs and allegiance. Let's support one another. We will declare Him One, as one.

בָּרוּךְ – *Bless.* Like in *Shaḥarit*, *Keriat Shema* has two introductory blessings, and as in the morning, the theme of the first is Hashem's revelation in nature, and the theme of the second is Hashem's

He creates day and night,
rolling away the light before the darkness,
and darkness before the light.
▸ He makes the day pass and brings on night,
distinguishing day from night:
the LORD of hosts is His name.
May the living and forever enduring God
rule over us for all time.
Blessed are You, LORD,
who brings on evenings.[I]

אַהֲבַת עוֹלָם With everlasting love[B]
have You loved Your people, the house of Israel.
You have taught us Torah and commandments,
decrees and laws of justice.
Therefore, LORD our God, when we lie down and when we rise up
we will speak of Your decrees,
rejoicing in the words of Your Torah
and Your commandments for ever.
▸ For they are our life and the length of our days;
on them will we meditate day and night.
May You never take away Your love from us.
Blessed are You, LORD,
who loves His people Israel.

---

are You...) is only to be found at the very end of the blessing and not at the beginning. This is a common formulation in the Siddur where the concluding formula from the previous blessing is deemed sufficient to also act as the opening for the next. It is known in halakhic (legal) terminology as *berakha hasemukha leḥaverta*, a blessing [without the opening formula] that is appended to its neighbor [which has the formula at its end].

BIUR TEFILLA • ביאור תפילה

אַהֲבַת עוֹלָם – *With everlasting love.* The previous blessing was universalistic in its focus on God's presence in nature; this blessing moves toward God's relationship with the Jewish people, in particular with the gift of Torah.

בּוֹרֵא יוֹם וָלָיְלָה
גּוֹלֵל אוֹר מִפְּנֵי חֹשֶׁךְ וְחֹשֶׁךְ מִפְּנֵי אוֹר
◂ וּמַעֲבִיר יוֹם וּמֵבִיא לָיְלָה
וּמַבְדִּיל בֵּין יוֹם וּבֵין לָיְלָה
יהוה צְבָאוֹת שְׁמוֹ.
אֵל חַי וְקַיָּם תָּמִיד, יִמְלֹךְ עָלֵינוּ לְעוֹלָם וָעֶד.
בָּרוּךְ אַתָּה יהוה, הַמַּעֲרִיב עֲרָבִים.[ע]

אַהֲבַת עוֹלָם[הב] בֵּית יִשְׂרָאֵל עַמְּךָ אָהָבְתָּ
תּוֹרָה וּמִצְוֹת, חֻקִּים וּמִשְׁפָּטִים, אוֹתָנוּ לִמַּדְתָּ
עַל כֵּן יהוה אֱלֹהֵינוּ בְּשָׁכְבֵנוּ וּבְקוּמֵנוּ נָשִׂיחַ בְּחֻקֶּיךָ
וְנִשְׂמַח בְּדִבְרֵי תוֹרָתֶךָ וּבְמִצְוֹתֶיךָ לְעוֹלָם וָעֶד
◂ כִּי הֵם חַיֵּינוּ וְאֹרֶךְ יָמֵינוּ, וּבָהֶם נֶהְגֶּה יוֹמָם וָלָיְלָה.
וְאַהֲבָתְךָ אַל תָּסִיר מִמֶּנּוּ לְעוֹלָמִים.
בָּרוּךְ אַתָּה יהוה, אוֹהֵב עַמּוֹ יִשְׂרָאֵל.

IYUN TEFILLA • עיון תפילה

הַמַּעֲרִיב עֲרָבִים – *Who brings on evenings.* If in the morning we were conscious of the sun and the beginning of the day, here we are aware of the ending of the day and the descent of darkness which envelops us. The Gemara (*Berakhot* 11b) says that we must recall the attributes of day and night together, for both reflect the miracle of creation and its single source, Hashem, whose unity we will declare momentarily. Night and day; sun and stars; past, present, and future are all part of one continuum. The world is whole and there is a pattern and there is a plan. We need only find our place in it.

HILKHOT TEFILLA • הלכות תפילה

אַהֲבַת עוֹלָם – *With everlasting love.* This marks the beginning of the second blessing prior to the *Shema*. Unlike the first one, here the standard formula (*Barukh ata.../* Blessed

The Shema must be said with intense concentration. In the first paragraph one should accept, with love, the sovereignty of God; in the second, the mitzvot as the will of God. The end of the third paragraph constitutes fulfillment of the mitzva to remember, morning and evening, the exodus from Egypt.

For introduction and further commentary on Shema, see weekday Shaḥarit (pages 120–126), weekday Ma'ariv (pages 303–304) and Shaḥarit for Shabbat (pages 597–600).

When not with a minyan, say:

God, faithful King!

The following verse should be said aloud, while covering the eyes with the right hand:

Listen, Israel:| the LORD is our God, the LORD is One. *Deut. 6*

Quietly: Blessed be the name of His glorious kingdom for ever and all time.

וְאָהַבְתָּ Love the LORD[A] your God with all your heart, with all *Deut. 6*
your soul, and with all your might. These words which I command you today shall be on your heart. Teach them repeatedly to

---

ANI TEFILLA • אני תפילה

Father explained that the reason it is customary to cover one's eyes is a symbolic gesture to indicate that although our sense perceptions may tell that what we are experiencing is bad, we are willing to let our faith supersede and overrule our perception. There are times when we may look at the world and wonder about God or about His mercy or justice in the world, and so we cover our eyes as if to declare that we recognize that our perceptions are not always correct and we rely instead on God's judgment and wisdom. (Rabbi Abraham Twerski)

וְאָהַבְתָּ אֵת יהוה – *Love the LORD.*
Rabbi Moshe Leib of Sassov announced to his disciples that he had learned what it meant to love another from a conversation he overheard between two villagers. One said to the other: "Tell me, dear Ivan, do you love me?" Ivan replied, "I love you very much." The first one responded: "Do you know what causes me pain?" Ivan replied: "How can I know what gives you pain?" The first one responded: "If you do not know what gives me pain, then how can you say that you truly love me?"

"Understand, then," said Rabbi Moshe Leib, "to love, to truly love someone, means to know what brings them pain."

The שמע must be said with intense concentration. In the first paragraph one should accept, with love, the sovereignty of God; in the second, the mitzvot as the will of God. The end of the third paragraph constitutes fulfillment of the mitzva to remember, morning and evening, the exodus from Egypt.

For introduction and further commentary on שמע, see weekday שחרית (pages 120–126), weekday מעריב (pages 303–304) and שחרית for שבת (pages 597–600).

When not with a מנין, say:

אֵל מֶלֶךְ נֶאֱמָן

The following verse should be said aloud, while covering the eyes with the right hand:

שְׁמַע יִשְׂרָאֵל, יהוה אֱלֹהֵינוּ, יהוה ׀ אֶחָד: דברים ו

Quietly בָּרוּךְ שֵׁם כְּבוֹד מַלְכוּתוֹ לְעוֹלָם וָעֶד.

וְאָהַבְתָּ אֵת יהוה אֱלֹהֶיךָ, בְּכָל־לְבָבְךָ וּבְכָל־נַפְשְׁךָ וּבְכָל־ דברים ו
מְאֹדֶךָ: וְהָיוּ הַדְּבָרִים הָאֵלֶּה, אֲשֶׁר אָנֹכִי מְצַוְּךָ הַיּוֹם, עַל־לְבָבֶךָ:

IYUN TEFILLA • עיון תפילה

שְׁמַע יִשְׂרָאֵל – *Listen, Israel.* This statement and paragraph are generally said to comprise *kabbalat ol malkhut shamayim*, accepting upon oneself the yoke of the sovereignty of Heaven. The "yoke of heaven" sounds like such a scary term, but the truth is that yokes are put on animals not for the purpose of hurting them, but for the purpose of enabling them to stay on a path and to achieve a purpose. Similarly, when we declare that we accept the "yoke of heaven," we are not accepting some sort of master that is going to work us to death, we are accepting upon ourselves a King who will lead us to spiritual freedom, give us strength to conquer our weaknesses, and guide us to a common, higher, purpose (Rabbi N. Mindel).

ANI TEFILLA • אני תפילה

Prayer in general is about a dialogue where man and Hashem speak to one another. The fact that one of the parties cannot be "heard" does not mean that the He is not involved in the conversation. Knowing someone is at the other end of the line even if they do not speak, doesn't mean that one is talking to oneself. In Shema, however, that element of dialogue is missing. "It expresses itself more in the form of declaration, confession, profession of faith. Whether this takes the form of soliloquy, in which man declares and challenges himself, or a colloquy – in which he addresses himself to a Thou – is irrelevant. What is important is the fact that if there is a thou in Shema, the thou is not God but a finite being like myself." (Rabbi Joseph B. Soloveitchik)

your children, speaking of them when you sit at home and when you travel on the way, when you lie down and when you rise. Bind them as a sign on your hand, and they shall be an emblem between your eyes. Write them on the doorposts of your house and gates.

וְהָיָה If you indeed heed My commandments with which I charge you today, to love the LORD your God and worship Him with all your heart and with all your soul, I will give rain in your land in its season, the early and late rain; and you shall gather in your grain, wine and oil. I will give grass in your field for your cattle, and you shall eat and be satisfied. Be careful lest your heart be tempted and you go astray and worship other gods, bowing down to them. Then the LORD's anger will flare against you and He will close the heavens so that there will be no rain. The land will not yield its crops, and you will perish swiftly from the good land that the LORD is giving you. Therefore, set these, My words, on your heart and soul. Bind them as a sign on your hand, and they shall be an emblem between your eyes. Teach them to your children, speaking of them when you sit at home and when you travel on the way, when you lie down and when you rise. Write them on the doorposts of your house and gates, so that you and your children may live long in the land that the LORD swore to your ancestors to give them, for as long as the heavens are above the earth. *Deut. 11*

וַיֹּאמֶר The LORD spoke to Moses, saying: Speak to the Israelites and tell them to make tassels on the corners of their garments for all generations. They shall attach to the tassel at each corner a thread of blue. This shall be your tassel, and you shall see it and remember all of the LORD's commandments and keep them, not straying after your heart and after your eyes, following your own sinful desires. Thus you will be reminded to keep all My *Num. 15*

וְשִׁנַּנְתָּם לְבָנֶיךָ וְדִבַּרְתָּ בָּם, בְּשִׁבְתְּךָ בְּבֵיתֶךָ וּבְלֶכְתְּךָ בַדֶּרֶךְ,
וּבְשָׁכְבְּךָ וּבְקוּמֶךָ: וּקְשַׁרְתָּם לְאוֹת עַל־יָדֶךָ וְהָיוּ לְטֹטָפֹת בֵּין
עֵינֶיךָ: וּכְתַבְתָּם עַל־מְזֻזוֹת בֵּיתֶךָ וּבִשְׁעָרֶיךָ:

וְהָיָה אִם־שָׁמֹעַ תִּשְׁמְעוּ אֶל־מִצְוֹתַי אֲשֶׁר אָנֹכִי מְצַוֶּה אֶתְכֶם דברים יא
הַיּוֹם, לְאַהֲבָה אֶת־יהוה אֱלֹהֵיכֶם וּלְעָבְדוֹ, בְּכָל־לְבַבְכֶם וּבְכָל־
נַפְשְׁכֶם: וְנָתַתִּי מְטַר־אַרְצְכֶם בְּעִתּוֹ, יוֹרֶה וּמַלְקוֹשׁ, וְאָסַפְתָּ
דְגָנֶךָ וְתִירֹשְׁךָ וְיִצְהָרֶךָ: וְנָתַתִּי עֵשֶׂב בְּשָׂדְךָ לִבְהֶמְתֶּךָ, וְאָכַלְתָּ
וְשָׂבָעְתָּ: הִשָּׁמְרוּ לָכֶם פֶּן־יִפְתֶּה לְבַבְכֶם, וְסַרְתֶּם וַעֲבַדְתֶּם
אֱלֹהִים אֲחֵרִים וְהִשְׁתַּחֲוִיתֶם לָהֶם: וְחָרָה אַף־יהוה בָּכֶם, וְעָצַר
אֶת־הַשָּׁמַיִם וְלֹא־יִהְיֶה מָטָר, וְהָאֲדָמָה לֹא תִתֵּן אֶת־יְבוּלָהּ,
וַאֲבַדְתֶּם מְהֵרָה מֵעַל הָאָרֶץ הַטֹּבָה אֲשֶׁר יהוה נֹתֵן לָכֶם:
וְשַׂמְתֶּם אֶת־דְּבָרַי אֵלֶּה עַל־לְבַבְכֶם וְעַל־נַפְשְׁכֶם, וּקְשַׁרְתֶּם
אֹתָם לְאוֹת עַל־יֶדְכֶם, וְהָיוּ לְטוֹטָפֹת בֵּין עֵינֵיכֶם: וְלִמַּדְתֶּם
אֹתָם אֶת־בְּנֵיכֶם לְדַבֵּר בָּם, בְּשִׁבְתְּךָ בְּבֵיתֶךָ וּבְלֶכְתְּךָ בַדֶּרֶךְ,
וּבְשָׁכְבְּךָ וּבְקוּמֶךָ: וּכְתַבְתָּם עַל־מְזוּזוֹת בֵּיתֶךָ וּבִשְׁעָרֶיךָ:
לְמַעַן יִרְבּוּ יְמֵיכֶם וִימֵי בְנֵיכֶם עַל הָאֲדָמָה אֲשֶׁר נִשְׁבַּע יהוה
לַאֲבֹתֵיכֶם לָתֵת לָהֶם, כִּימֵי הַשָּׁמַיִם עַל־הָאָרֶץ:

וַיֹּאמֶר יהוה אֶל־מֹשֶׁה לֵּאמֹר: דַּבֵּר אֶל־בְּנֵי יִשְׂרָאֵל וְאָמַרְתָּ במדבר טו
אֲלֵהֶם, וְעָשׂוּ לָהֶם צִיצִת עַל־כַּנְפֵי בִגְדֵיהֶם לְדֹרֹתָם, וְנָתְנוּ
עַל־צִיצִת הַכָּנָף פְּתִיל תְּכֵלֶת: וְהָיָה לָכֶם לְצִיצִת, וּרְאִיתֶם אֹתוֹ
וּזְכַרְתֶּם אֶת־כָּל־מִצְוֹת יהוה וַעֲשִׂיתֶם אֹתָם, וְלֹא תָתֻרוּ אַחֲרֵי
לְבַבְכֶם וְאַחֲרֵי עֵינֵיכֶם, אֲשֶׁר־אַתֶּם זֹנִים אַחֲרֵיהֶם: לְמַעַן תִּזְכְּרוּ

commandments, and be holy to your God. I am the LORD your God, who brought you out of the land of Egypt to be your God. I am the LORD your God.

True[B] –

The Leader repeats:

▸ The LORD your God is true –

וֶאֱמוּנָה – and faithful is all this,[BH]
and firmly established for us
that He is the LORD our God,
and there is none besides Him,
and that we, Israel, are His people.
He is our King,
who redeems us from the hand of kings
and delivers us from the grasp of all tyrants.
He is our God, who on our behalf repays our foes
and brings just retribution on our mortal enemies;
who performs great deeds beyond understanding
and wonders beyond number;
who kept us alive, *Ps. 66*
not letting our foot slip;
who led us on the high places of our enemies,
raising our pride above all our foes;

---

the history of the Jewish people. To be a Jew standing before God means to be cognizant of being a part of an unending continuum of Jewish history, to see oneself as the link in a chain that goes back thousands of years if not beyond. To be a Jew means to belong.

HILKHOT TEFILLA • הלכות תפילה

וֶאֱמוּנָה – *Faithful.* Rav says (*Berakhot* 12a) that whoever does not include the theme of *Emet Ve-Emuna* in the evening prayer does not fulfill his obligation. The assertion is based upon the verse in *Tehillim* (92:3), "I will tell of Your *ḥesed* in the morning and Your *emuna* (faithfulness) at night. The nighttime is all about Hashem's faithfulness...and our faith.

וַעֲשִׂיתֶם אֶת־כׇּל־מִצְוֺתָי, וִהְיִיתֶם קְדֹשִׁים לֵאלֹהֵיכֶם: אֲנִי יְהוָה
אֱלֹהֵיכֶם, אֲשֶׁר הוֹצֵאתִי אֶתְכֶם מֵאֶרֶץ מִצְרַיִם, לִהְיוֹת לָכֶם
לֵאלֹהִים, אֲנִי יְהוָה אֱלֹהֵיכֶם:

אֱמֶת[ב]

The שליח ציבור *repeats:*

‹ יהוה אֱלֹהֵיכֶם אֱמֶת

וֶאֱמוּנָה[בה] כׇּל זֹאת וְקַיָּם עָלֵינוּ
כִּי הוּא יהוה אֱלֹהֵינוּ וְאֵין זוּלָתוֹ
וַאֲנַחְנוּ יִשְׂרָאֵל עַמּוֹ.
הַפּוֹדֵנוּ מִיַּד מְלָכִים
מַלְכֵּנוּ הַגּוֹאֲלֵנוּ מִכַּף כׇּל הֶעָרִיצִים.
הָאֵל הַנִּפְרָע לָנוּ מִצָּרֵינוּ
וְהַמְשַׁלֵּם גְּמוּל לְכׇל אֹיְבֵי נַפְשֵׁנוּ.
הָעוֹשֶׂה גְדוֹלוֹת עַד אֵין חֵקֶר,
וְנִפְלָאוֹת עַד אֵין מִסְפָּר
הַשָּׂם נַפְשֵׁנוּ בַּחַיִּים, וְלֹא־נָתַן לַמּוֹט רַגְלֵנוּ: תהלים סו
הַמַּדְרִיכֵנוּ עַל בָּמוֹת אוֹיְבֵינוּ
וַיָּרֶם קַרְנֵנוּ עַל כׇּל שׂוֹנְאֵינוּ.

BIUR TEFILLA • ביאור תפילה

אֱמֶת – *True.* This word, while technically not part of the biblical passage just recited, is nevertheless appended to the final line of the *Shema* so that the sentence reads "The LORD your God is true."

וֶאֱמוּנָה – *And faithful.* This marks the beginning of the third blessing. If the first blessing was about creation and the second about revelation, the third is about redemption, in this case God's presence in

who did miracles for us
and brought vengeance against Pharaoh;
who performed signs and wonders
in the land of Ham's children;
who smote in His wrath all the firstborn of Egypt,
and brought out His people Israel from their midst
into everlasting freedom;
who led His children through the divided Reed Sea,
plunging their pursuers and enemies into the depths.
When His children saw His might,
they gave praise
and thanks to His name,
▸ and willingly accepted His Sovereignty.
Moses and the children of Israel
then sang a song to You with great joy,
and they all exclaimed:

It is customary to wait for the Leader to reach this point, whereupon the congregation recites this verse aloud, followed by the Leader:

"Who is like You, LORD, among the mighty? *Ex. 15*
Who is like You, majestic in holiness,
awesome in praises, doing wonders?"

▸ Your children beheld Your majesty
as You parted the sea before Moses.
"This is my God!" they responded,
and then said:

Wait for the Leader, then say the following verse aloud, which is then repeated by the Leader.

"The LORD shall reign for ever and ever." *Ex. 15*

▸ And it is said,
"For the LORD has redeemed Jacob *Jer. 31*
and rescued him from a power
stronger than his own."
Blessed are You, LORD,
who redeemed Israel.

הָעוֹשֶׂה לָּֽנוּ נִסִּים וּנְקָמָה בְּפַרְעֹה
אוֹתוֹת וּמוֹפְתִים בְּאַדְמַת בְּנֵי חָם.
הַמַּכֶּה בְעֶבְרָתוֹ כָּל בְּכוֹרֵי מִצְרָֽיִם
וַיּוֹצֵא אֶת עַמּוֹ יִשְׂרָאֵל מִתּוֹכָם לְחֵרוּת עוֹלָם.
הַמַּעֲבִיר בָּנָיו בֵּין גִּזְרֵי יַם סוּף
אֶת רוֹדְפֵיהֶם וְאֶת שׂוֹנְאֵיהֶם בִּתְהוֹמוֹת טִבַּע
וְרָאוּ בָנָיו גְּבוּרָתוֹ, שִׁבְּחוּ וְהוֹדוּ לִשְׁמוֹ
· וּמַלְכוּתוֹ בְּרָצוֹן קִבְּלוּ עֲלֵיהֶם.
מֹשֶׁה וּבְנֵי יִשְׂרָאֵל, לְךָ עָנוּ שִׁירָה בְּשִׂמְחָה רַבָּה
וְאָמְרוּ כֻלָּם

It is customary to wait for the שליח ציבור *to reach this point, whereupon the* קהל *recites this verse aloud, followed by the* שליח ציבור:

מִי־כָמֹֽכָה בָּאֵלִם יהוה שמות טו
מִי כָּמֹֽכָה נֶאְדָּר בַּקֹּֽדֶשׁ
נוֹרָא תְהִלֹּת עֹֽשֵׂה פֶֽלֶא:

· מַלְכוּתְךָ רָאוּ בָנֶֽיךָ, בּוֹקֵֽעַ יָם לִפְנֵי מֹשֶׁה
זֶה אֵלִי עָנוּ, וְאָמְרוּ

Wait for the שליח ציבור*, then say the following verse aloud, which is then repeated by the Leader.*

יהוה יִמְלֹךְ לְעֹלָם וָעֶד: שמות טו

· וְנֶאֱמַר
כִּי־פָדָה יהוה אֶת־יַעֲקֹב, וּגְאָלוֹ מִיַּד חָזָק מִמֶּֽנּוּ: ירמיהו לא
בָּרוּךְ אַתָּה יהוה, גָּאַל יִשְׂרָאֵל.

ANI TEFILLA · אני תפילה

Faith is not the absence of reason, it is a skill in its own right which, when cultivated, allows us to experience the ultimate. *(Rabbi Menaḥem Mendel Schneerson. Cited in Toward a Meaningful Life by Rabbi Simon Jacobson)*

הַשְׁכִּיבֵנוּ Help us lie down,[B] O LORD our God, in peace,
and rise up, O our King, to life.
Spread over us Your canopy of peace.
Direct us with Your good counsel,
and save us for the sake of Your name.
Shield us and remove from us every enemy,
plague, sword, famine and sorrow.
Remove the adversary from before and behind us.
Shelter us in the shadow of Your wings,[A]
for You, God, are our Guardian and Deliverer;
You, God, are a gracious and compassionate King.
▸ Guard our going out and our coming in,
for life and peace, from now and for ever.
Spread over us Your canopy of peace.
Blessed are You, LORD,
who spreads a canopy of peace[B] over us,
over all His people Israel, and over Jerusalem.

---

ness, some by going out in the fields and some by going to work. But on Shabbat, with everyone at home, the Jewish people do not need to be guarded but instead God spreads His blanket of peace over us (Roke'aḥ).

ANI TEFILLA • אני תפילה

וּבְצֵל כְּנָפֶיךָ תַּסְתִּירֵנוּ – *Shelter us in the shadow of Your wings.* Like a mother bird who protects her chicks by gathering them under her wing. The warm embrace of a parent, the feeling of comfort and security that comes with being enveloped, protected and secure. That is what we all long for, no matter how old we are. That is what Hashem provides. Feel enveloped.

ANI TEFILLA • אני תפילה

A man is walking down the road with his young son and they come across a large rock. Says the boy, "Father, do you think that I can move that rock?" The father answers, "If you use all of your strength, I'm sure that you can do it." The boy walks up to the rock and begins to push. He strains and struggles and tries desperately to dislodge it, only to give up in frustration and disappointment. "You were wrong," he said to his father, "I couldn't do it." His father put his arm around him and said, "You didn't use all of your strength – you didn't ask me for help."

הַשְׁכִּיבֵנוּ[ב] יהוה אֱלֹהֵינוּ לְשָׁלוֹם, וְהַעֲמִידֵנוּ מַלְכֵּנוּ לְחַיִּים
וּפְרֹשׂ עָלֵינוּ סֻכַּת שְׁלוֹמֶךָ, וְתַקְּנֵנוּ בְּעֵצָה טוֹבָה מִלְּפָנֶיךָ
וְהוֹשִׁיעֵנוּ לְמַעַן שְׁמֶךָ.
וְהָגֵן בַּעֲדֵנוּ, וְהָסֵר מֵעָלֵינוּ אוֹיֵב, דֶּבֶר וְחֶרֶב וְרָעָב וְיָגוֹן
וְהָסֵר שָׂטָן מִלְּפָנֵינוּ וּמֵאַחֲרֵינוּ, וּבְצֵל כְּנָפֶיךָ תַּסְתִּירֵנוּ[א]
כִּי אֵל שׁוֹמְרֵנוּ וּמַצִּילֵנוּ אָתָּה, כִּי אֵל מֶלֶךְ חַנּוּן וְרַחוּם אָתָּה.
◂ וּשְׁמֹר צֵאתֵנוּ וּבוֹאֵנוּ לְחַיִּים וּלְשָׁלוֹם מֵעַתָּה וְעַד עוֹלָם.
וּפְרֹשׂ עָלֵינוּ סֻכַּת שְׁלוֹמֶךָ.
בָּרוּךְ אַתָּה יהוה
הַפּוֹרֵשׂ סֻכַּת שָׁלוֹם[ב] עָלֵינוּ
וְעַל כָּל עַמּוֹ יִשְׂרָאֵל וְעַל יְרוּשָׁלַיִם.

BIUR TEFILLA • ביאור תפילה

הַשְׁכִּיבֵנוּ – *Help us lie down.* This marks the beginning of the second blessing following the *Shema*. It is considered an extension of the previous one (*Berakhot* 4b) though here the redemption which is requested sounds personal as much as communal. For nighttime can be a period of great uncertainty and insecurity. And so, just as the *tallit* or prayer shawl which is worn in the morning can be seen as a protective cloak, here we ask Hashem Himself to shelter us from the dangers that lurk from our enemies and, perhaps even more daunting, from the negative forces that lie within ourselves.

From what insecurities do you wish for protection this evening?

הַפּוֹרֵשׂ סֻכַּת שָׁלוֹם – *Who spreads a canopy of peace.* The conclusion of this final blessing is different than its parallel in the weekday service. For while we ask for protection from external and internal forces, the truth is that on Shabbat the feeling is that one is already protected to some extent. To what might this be compared? It is similar to a king who has a shepherd who watches his flock. Each day the shepherd remains in the field and stays awake at night to guard his flock. But one night a week, the shepherd brings the flock back home and thus he is able to get a good night's sleep. Similarly, on weekdays, the Guardian of Israel does not sleep because He must guard the Jewish people who go about their busi-

In anticipation of the Amida which is recited while standing, the custom is to stand for this passage, which is said aloud together with the Leader.

וְשָׁמְרוּ The children of Israel must keep the Sabbath,[1] Ex. 31
observing the Sabbath[1] in every generation
as an everlasting covenant.
It is a sign between Me and the children of Israel for ever,
for in six days God made the heavens and the earth,
but on the seventh day He ceased work and refreshed Himself.

HALF KADDISH

Leader: יִתְגַּדַּל Magnified and sanctified may His great name be,
in the world He created by His will.
May He establish His kingdom
in your lifetime and in your days,
and in the lifetime of all the house of Israel,
swiftly and soon – and say: Amen.

All: May His great name[A] be blessed for ever and all time.

Leader: Blessed and praised, glorified and exalted,
raised and honored, uplifted and lauded
be the name of the Holy One, blessed be He,
beyond any blessing, song, praise and consolation
uttered in the world – and say: Amen.

לַעֲשׂוֹת אֶת־הַשַּׁבָּת – *Observing the Sabbath.* Literally the phrase means "to make the Shabbat." The Midrash therefore suggests that whoever keeps the Shabbat, it is as if he actually created the Shabbat (*Mekhilta*). One explanation is because unlike other ritual objects such as a *tallit* or *tefillin*, or the like, Shabbat has no external visible distinguishing characteristics. It can be a day like any other day of the week. The difference lies in what we "make" of it (*Torah Temima*).

ANI TEFILLA • אני תפילה

יְהֵא שְׁמֵהּ רַבָּא – *May His great name.*
Rav Yose said: I was once traveling on the road and I entered one of the ruins of Jerusalem in order to pray.

Eliyahu, of blessed memory, came and guarded the door/waited for me until I completed my *Amida* prayer…

He said, "My son, what sound did you hear in this ruin?" I replied, "I heard a divine voice cooing like a dove and saying: 'Woe to the children, on account of whose sins I destroyed My House and burnt My Temple and exiled them among the nations of the world.'"

This **ANI TEFILLA** *continues on page 459.*

In anticipation of the עמידה *which is recited while standing, the custom is to stand for this passage, which is said aloud together with the* שליח ציבור.

וְשָׁמְרוּ בְנֵי־יִשְׂרָאֵל אֶת־הַשַּׁבָּת שמות לא
לַעֲשׂוֹת אֶת־הַשַּׁבָּת לְדֹרֹתָם בְּרִית עוֹלָם:
בֵּינִי וּבֵין בְּנֵי יִשְׂרָאֵל, אוֹת הִוא לְעֹלָם
כִּי־שֵׁשֶׁת יָמִים עָשָׂה יהוה אֶת־הַשָּׁמַיִם וְאֶת־הָאָרֶץ
וּבַיּוֹם הַשְּׁבִיעִי שָׁבַת וַיִּנָּפַשׁ:

חצי קדיש

ש״ץ: יִתְגַּדַּל וְיִתְקַדַּשׁ שְׁמֵהּ רַבָּא (קהל: אָמֵן)
בְּעָלְמָא דִּי בְרָא כִרְעוּתֵהּ וְיַמְלִיךְ מַלְכוּתֵהּ
בְּחַיֵּיכוֹן וּבְיוֹמֵיכוֹן וּבְחַיֵּי דְכָל בֵּית יִשְׂרָאֵל
בַּעֲגָלָא וּבִזְמַן קָרִיב, וְאִמְרוּ אָמֵן. (קהל: אָמֵן)

קהל וש״ץ: יְהֵא שְׁמֵהּ רַבָּא מְבָרַךְ לְעָלַם וּלְעָלְמֵי עָלְמַיָּא.

ש״ץ: יִתְבָּרַךְ וְיִשְׁתַּבַּח וְיִתְפָּאַר וְיִתְרוֹמַם וְיִתְנַשֵּׂא
וְיִתְהַדָּר וְיִתְעַלֶּה וְיִתְהַלָּל
שְׁמֵהּ דְּקֻדְשָׁא בְּרִיךְ הוּא (קהל: בְּרִיךְ הוּא)
לְעֵלָּא מִן כָּל בִּרְכָתָא וְשִׁירָתָא, תֻּשְׁבְּחָתָא וְנֶחֱמָתָא
דַּאֲמִירָן בְּעָלְמָא, וְאִמְרוּ אָמֵן. (קהל: אָמֵן)

IYUN TEFILLA · עיון תפילה

וְשָׁמְרוּ בְנֵי־יִשְׂרָאֵל אֶת־הַשַּׁבָּת – *The children of Israel must keep the Sabbath.* As we get closer to the *Amida* prayer which is our most intimate encounter with the Divine in the service, we stop to remind ourselves of the theme of the day. For all of the emphasis that there has just been on Hashem's protection of us, we must recall that it is contingent upon our doing our share; in the present case, that means that Hashem will protect us only if we protect the specialness of Shabbat (Abudarham). Perhaps that is a reason for the emphasis on "observing the Sabbath" (literally, "to make the Sabbath"); it is dependent on us.

THE AMIDA

The following prayer, until "in former years" on page 472, is said silently, standing with feet together. Take three steps forward and at the points indicated by ▾, bend the knees at the first word, bow at the second, and stand straight before saying God's name.

O Lord, open my lips, so that my mouth may declare Your praise. Ps. 51

PATRIARCHS

▾Blessed[B] are You, Lord our God and God of our fathers,[I]
God of Abraham, God of Isaac and God of Jacob;
the great, mighty and awesome God, God Most High,

---

the third *Amida* focuses on the extra sacrificial offerings, reminiscent of a celebratory feast; and the middle blessing of the afternoon *Amida* begins with words *ata eḥad*, reminiscent of the word *yiḥud*, the most intimate moment when bride and groom are alone (Abudarham and Shela). All of this, of course, is in keeping with the theme of marriage between Israel and the Shabbat and the Creator as mentioned earlier.

Regardless of what reason one devises, the changing themes of the *Amida* potentially tell us something about the shifting moods of the day. Shabbat is not just one long continuum of sameness but rather a dynamic day with its own rhythms. One needs to help create them, just as much as one needs to be drawn in by them. The siddur is designed to help do that.

Another critical difference between the middle blessings of the *Amida* on Shabbat and the weekday is that those during the week are filled almost entirely with personal requests: petitions for health, wealth, forgiveness and the like. The Talmud Yerushalmi (15:3), however, tells us that on Shabbat all personal requests are forbidden for they are at odds with the spirit of the day (*Shabbat* 21a). Focusing on someone's illness, for example, could lead one to a feeling of sadness (*Tanḥuma, Vayera*). Instead, our focus on Shabbat is more about communal and spiritual concerns than about the things which preoccupy us during the week. The siddur, then, not only is a response to our moods but is also designed to help shape our experience of the day.

BIUR TEFILLA • ביאור תפילה

בָּרוּךְ – *Blessed.* The Hebrew word for blessing, *berakha,* shares a linguistic root with the word *bereikha* which refers to an underground spring of water (*Responsa, Rashba*).

What might be the connection between the two? How might this help direct your intentions or mindset (*kavana*) for the remainder of the prayer?

IYUN TEFILLA • עיון תפילה

אֱלֹהֵינוּ וֵאלֹהֵי אֲבוֹתֵינוּ – *Our God and God of our fathers.* There are two ways to achieve faith: through tradition, the information and experience handed down to us by our parents and ancestors; and the faith that we acquire on our own. It is not enough to base one's commitment

This **IYUN TEFILLA** *continues on page 461.*

עמידה

The following prayer, until קַדְמֹנִיּוֹת *on page 473, is said silently, standing with feet together. Take three steps forward and at the points indicated by* ˅*, bend the knees at the first word, bow at the second, and stand straight before saying God's name.*

אֲדֹנָי, שְׂפָתַי תִּפְתָּח, וּפִי יַגִּיד תְּהִלָּתֶךָ: תהלים נא

אבות

˅בָּרוּךְ˅ אַתָּה יהוה, אֱלֹהֵינוּ וֵאלֹהֵי אֲבוֹתֵינוּ
אֱלֹהֵי אַבְרָהָם, אֱלֹהֵי יִצְחָק, וֵאלֹהֵי יַעֲקֹב
הָאֵל הַגָּדוֹל הַגִּבּוֹר וְהַנּוֹרָא, אֵל עֶלְיוֹן

And he said to me, "By your life and by your head! Not in this moment alone does it so exclaim, but three times each day does it exclaim thus. And more than that, whenever Israel fulfills the will of the *Makom* and goes into the synagogues and schoolhouses and responds: 'May His great name be blessed!' the Holy One, blessed be He, shakes His head and says: 'Happy is the King who is thus praised in this House! Woe to the Father who had to banish His children' – and woe to the children who had to be banished from the table of their father." (*Berakhot* 3a)

INTRODUCTION TO THE AMIDA

This prayer which is the key component of any service, is known by a number of names and has a number of variations. It is known in Rabbinic literature simply as *Tefilla* or "prayer" because it is the ultimate prayer, a most intimate moment between man and his Creator. It is also called the *Amida*, which means "standing," because it is essentially a prayer said like a servant standing before one's master. (The version that is said during the week is also called *Shemoneh Esreh* or "Eighteen" as a reference to the number of blessings it contains. Some popularly also refer to the version said on Shabbat as *Shemoneh Esreh* even though that is technically a misnomer since the number of blessings on Shabbat is reduced to seven. Nevertheless, the one during the week can still be called the *Amida* since one's posture at that time remains the same.)

On Shabbat, the *Amida* is recited on four different occasions. In each case, there are a total of seven blessings and in each case the first three and last three blessings are identical. However, in contrast to all of the weekday services where the middle section is also exactly the same, on Shabbat, the text and theme of the middle section is different for each one of the four versions. There is no one authoritative reason for this so each person may find his or her own meaning. One suggestion comes from the fourteenth-century commentator Abudarham, who suggests that the theme of this evening parallels the wedding ceremony. On Friday night, the middle blessing begins with the words *ata kidashta* (You sanctified), a word reminiscent of the betrothal ceremony (*kiddushin*); in the morning, the initial focus is on happiness (*Yismaḥ Moshe*);

who bestows acts of loving-kindness and creates all,
who remembers the loving-kindness of the fathers
and will bring a Redeemer to their children's children
for the sake of His name, in love.
King, Helper, Savior, Shield:
▾Blessed are You, Lord, Shield of Abraham.

DIVINE MIGHT

אַתָּה גִּבּוֹר You are eternally mighty, Lord.
You give life to the dead and have great power to save.

In Israel: He causes the dew to fall.

He sustains the living with loving-kindness,
and with great compassion revives the dead.
He supports the fallen, heals the sick,
sets captives free,
and keeps His faith with those who sleep in the dust.
Who is like You, Master of might,
and who can compare to You,
O King who brings death and gives life,
and makes salvation grow?
Faithful are You to revive the dead.
Blessed are You, Lord, who revives the dead.

HOLINESS

אַתָּה קָדוֹשׁ You are holy and Your name is holy,
and holy ones praise You daily, Selah!
Blessed are You, Lord, the holy God.

ANI TEFILLA · אני תפילה

Someone once complained to Rav Simḥa Bunim that he had headaches after he prayed. Said Rav Bunim, "What does the head have to do with prayer? Prayer is a service of the heart not a labor of the head."

גּוֹמֵל חֲסָדִים טוֹבִים, וְקוֹנֵה הַכֹּל, וְזוֹכֵר חַסְדֵי אָבוֹת
וּמֵבִיא גוֹאֵל לִבְנֵי בְנֵיהֶם לְמַעַן שְׁמוֹ בְּאַהֲבָה.
מֶלֶךְ עוֹזֵר וּמוֹשִׁיעַ וּמָגֵן.
בָּרוּךְ אַתָּה יהוה, מָגֵן אַבְרָהָם.

גבורות

אַתָּה גִּבּוֹר לְעוֹלָם, אֲדֹנָי
מְחַיֵּה מֵתִים אַתָּה, רַב לְהוֹשִׁיעַ

בארץ ישראל בקיץ: מוֹרִיד הַטָּל

מְכַלְכֵּל חַיִּים בְּחֶסֶד, מְחַיֵּה מֵתִים בְּרַחֲמִים רַבִּים
סוֹמֵךְ נוֹפְלִים, וְרוֹפֵא חוֹלִים, וּמַתִּיר אֲסוּרִים
וּמְקַיֵּם אֱמוּנָתוֹ לִישֵׁנֵי עָפָר.
מִי כָמְוֹךָ, בַּעַל גְּבוּרוֹת, וּמִי דּוֹמֶה לָּךְ
מֶלֶךְ, מֵמִית וּמְחַיֶּה וּמַצְמִיחַ יְשׁוּעָה.
וְנֶאֱמָן אַתָּה לְהַחֲיוֹת מֵתִים.
בָּרוּךְ אַתָּה יהוה, מְחַיֵּה הַמֵּתִים.

קדושת השם

אַתָּה קָדוֹשׁ וְשִׁמְךָ קָדוֹשׁ
וּקְדוֹשִׁים בְּכָל יוֹם יְהַלְלְוּךָ סֶּלָה.
בָּרוּךְ אַתָּה יהוה, הָאֵל הַקָּדוֹשׁ.

---

solely on tradition but, rather, one has to make it one's own. And, though people may not talk about it much, one must continue to do so. We change and develop over time, even once we become adults, and so too, therefore, our relationship with Hashem can also change. But then, like all relationships, it is something we need to work on. Let today's prayer be a next step to a more personal relationship.

HOLINESS OF THE DAY

אַתָּה קִדַּשְׁתָּ You sanctified the seventh day
for Your name's sake,[I]
as the culmination of the creation of heaven and earth.
Of all days, You blessed it;[I]
of all seasons You sanctified it[I] –
and so it is written in Your Torah:[B]

---

exclusively on Shabbat, while another sees it in the light that fills his home on Shabbat, while still another expresses it in terms of the added light that shines from a person's face on Shabbat which is different than the rest of the week (*Bereshit Raba* 11:2). Food, clothing, external light, internal light; these are just some of the options.

What blessing do you wish for yourself this Shabbat?

וְקִדַּשְׁתּוֹ – *You sanctified it.* What does it mean to sanctify something? What does it mean to bless a day? Sanctification means to set something aside for a holy purpose; to use it for something mundane is to deprive it of its special status. We are trained to understand this concept as it relates to objects or rituals, but the Torah here conveys a revolutionary idea, namely, that one can also make time itself holy. Holiness is the space that we make for God in our lives.

How can you use this day to give Him more space?

BIUR TEFILLA · ביאור תפילה

וְכֵן כָּתוּב בְּתוֹרָתְךָ – *And so it is written in Your Torah.* The following verses come from *Bereshit* 2:1-3. The numeration of chapters and verses in the Bible are a non-Jewish invention from the medieval period. Jews, however, had a different way of dividing the text, namely, according to the seven *aliyot* or chapters used for the weekly public recitation of the Torah (*Keriat HaTorah*). It is interesting to note that the verses about Shabbat are numbered in the Bible as the beginning of Chapter 2, whereas according to the Rabbis, in the Torah they are a part of the previous chapter about creation.

What might this signify?

קדושת היום

אַתָּה קִדַּשְׁתָּ אֶת יוֹם הַשְּׁבִיעִי לִשְׁמֶךָ[ע]
תַּכְלִית מַעֲשֵׂה שָׁמַיִם וָאָרֶץ
וּבֵרַכְתּוֹ[ע] מִכָּל הַיָּמִים
וְקִדַּשְׁתּוֹ[ע] מִכָּל הַזְּמַנִּים
וְכֵן כָּתוּב בְּתוֹרָתֶךָ[ב]

IYUN TEFILLA • עיון תפילה

אַתָּה קִדַּשְׁתָּ אֶת יוֹם הַשְּׁבִיעִי לִשְׁמֶךָ – *You sanctified the seventh day for Your name's sake.* A holy person is one who has opened himself up to holiness. A holy place is a place which draws people looking for holiness. A holy time is a time that awakens or invites us to holiness (Rabbi Ḥayyim Vidal). Prayer is about opening one's heart to holiness. The synagogue is a place that draws others like us looking for holiness. Shabbat is a holy time that invites us to do so.

אַתָּה קִדַּשְׁתָּ אֶת יוֹם הַשְּׁבִיעִי לִשְׁמֶךָ – *You sanctified the seventh day for Your name's sake.* Shabbat is a day not only for rest and relaxation, a day to get back to oneself and one's family and friends and community. For if one does not use it as an opportunity to also recognize the role of God then one has missed the essence of the day. From the perspective of Hashem, Shabbat would theoretically remain holy regardless of man's presence. But from the perspective of man, Shabbat is an opportunity not a foregone conclusion. Whether we take advantage of the gift of time to focus on these relationships is dependent upon us.

וּבֵרַכְתּוֹ – *You blessed it.* As the text goes on to prove, this concept comes from the description of Shabbat at the time of its creation. "And God blessed the seventh day and He sanctified it." What does it mean that God blessed the day? The word blessing generally denotes being bestowed with something extra. The Midrash cites the example of the manna in the desert which came in double portions for Shabbat so that the Israelites would not have to collect it on Shabbat itself. Alternatively, says the Midrash, there are those who see the blessing in the special clothes that they wear

וַיְכֻלּוּ Then the heavens and the earth were completed, Gen. 2
and all their array.
With the seventh day, God[B] completed the work He had done.[AB]
He ceased on the seventh day from all the work He had done.
God blessed the seventh day and declared it holy,
because on it He ceased from all His work He had created to do.[B]

אֱלֹהֵינוּ Our God and God of our ancestors,
may You find favor in our rest.[B]
Make us holy through Your commandments
and grant us our share in Your Torah.
Satisfy us with Your goodness, grant us joy in Your salvation,
and purify our hearts to serve You in truth.[I]

What might be the difference between the two?

אֲשֶׁר־בָּרָא אֱלֹהִים לַעֲשׂוֹת – *He had created to do.* The wording is a little awkward and redundant. What does the last phrase mean? It could be that with the Shabbat, He set everything to work on its own, to continue to function in the way it was conceived (Ibn Ezra). Whatever creation was about, with the completion of Shabbat, time as we know it began. This could mean that there was a system of time, a life to our planet, before the one we are familiar with. In any event, the world was set in motion, though the Creator did not walk away.

Alternatively, it is a reference not to the world but to Shabbat. He created the Shabbat day in such a way that it would continue to do the work for which it was intended: the moral and spiritual betterment of mankind (Rabbi S. Hirsch).

How might I permit Shabbat to do its work with me?

רְצֵה בִמְנוּחָתֵנוּ – *Find favor in our rest...* In another example of the relationship between form and content, what follows are seven expressions of our hopes for this Shabbat day that is upon us.

What different meaning do you want to bring to each one of these expressions?

IYUN TEFILLA • עיון תפילה

וְטַהֵר לִבֵּנוּ לְעָבְדְּךָ בֶּאֱמֶת – *Purify our hearts to serve You in truth.* How can we ask God for this? Isn't it up to us what goes on in our hearts? The Gemara explains "Whoever comes to be purified gets assistance from above (*Yoma* 38b). In other words, the first steps must come from us and only then can we expect to get help. Perhaps the same is true for all of the other expressions which precede this one; one needs to invest in Shabbat in order to reap its rewards.

For more commentary on these final three blessings, see *Shaḥarit* (pages 175–186) and *Minḥa* (pages 783–788).

בראשית ב

וַיְכֻלּוּ הַשָּׁמַיִם וְהָאָרֶץ וְכָל־צְבָאָם:
וַיְכַל אֱלֹהִים בַּיּוֹם הַשְּׁבִיעִי מְלַאכְתּוֹ אֲשֶׁר עָשָׂה
וַיִּשְׁבֹּת בַּיּוֹם הַשְּׁבִיעִי מִכָּל־מְלַאכְתּוֹ אֲשֶׁר עָשָׂה:
וַיְבָרֶךְ אֱלֹהִים אֶת־יוֹם הַשְּׁבִיעִי, וַיְקַדֵּשׁ אֹתוֹ
כִּי בוֹ שָׁבַת מִכָּל־מְלַאכְתּוֹ, אֲשֶׁר־בָּרָא אֱלֹהִים לַעֲשׂוֹת:

אֱלֹהֵינוּ וֵאלֹהֵי אֲבוֹתֵינוּ, רְצֵה בִמְנוּחָתֵנוּ.
קַדְּשֵׁנוּ בְּמִצְוֹתֶיךָ, וְתֵן חֶלְקֵנוּ בְּתוֹרָתֶךָ
שַׂבְּעֵנוּ מִטּוּבֶךָ, וְשַׂמְּחֵנוּ בִּישׁוּעָתֶךָ
וְטַהֵר לִבֵּנוּ לְעָבְדְּךָ בֶּאֱמֶת.

BIUR TEFILLA • ביאור תפילה

וַיְכַל אֱלֹהִים בַּיּוֹם הַשְּׁבִיעִי – *With the seventh day, God completed.* Here is but one of many examples where the form of the text reflects its substance – if only we can discern its clues. These next three statements from the Torah contain 35 (5x7) Hebrew words. And the entire creation narrative (*Bereshit* 1–2:3) speaks of seven and its multiples. The word "good" appears seven times, the word "God" 35 times, the word "earth" 21 times, and the words "firmament"/"heavens" 21 times. The opening verse contains seven words, and the complete text 469 (7x67) words. From the very outset, seven dominates, as if to signal from the beginning that the seventh day was the culmination and purpose of creation (Rabbi Jonathan Sacks).

וַיְכַל אֱלֹהִים בַּיּוֹם הַשְּׁבִיעִי מְלַאכְתּוֹ אֲשֶׁר עָשָׂה – *With the seventh day, God completed the work He had done.* The verse seems to imply that the work was actually completed on the seventh day, and yet wasn't the seventh day a day of rest? The answer is that counter-intuitively rest, too, was something that needed to be proactively created (Rashi). This rest was apparently different than just a state of non-exertion which cannot really be said to be a creation.

ANI TEFILLA • אני תפילה

וַיְכַל אֱלֹהִים בַּיּוֹם הַשְּׁבִיעִי מְלַאכְתּוֹ אֲשֶׁר עָשָׂה – *With the seventh day God completed the work He had done.*

Asks the Midrash: "To what may this be compared? To a *ḥuppa*, a wedding canopy. One decorates it and adorns it so that it is most beautiful. What is missing? The bride. So, too, Hashem created the world. What was it missing? Shabbat.

Rabbanan say: To what may this be compared? To a king's beautiful signet ring that was missing his seal. So, too, Hashem created the world. What was it missing? Shabbat" (*Bereshit Raba* 10:10).

What might be the differences in perspective about Shabbat between these two parables?

In love and favor, O Lord our God,
grant us as our heritage Your holy Shabbat,
so that Israel, who sanctify Your name, may find rest on it.
Blessed are You, Lord, who sanctifies the Sabbath.

TEMPLE SERVICE

רְצֵה Find favor, Lord our God, in Your people Israel
and their prayer.
Restore the service[I] to Your most holy House,
and accept in love and favor
the fire-offerings of Israel and their prayer.
May the service of Your people Israel always find favor with You.

On Rosh Ḥodesh, say:

אֱלֹהֵינוּ Our God and God of our ancestors, may there rise, come,[B] reach, appear, be favored, heard, regarded and remembered before You, our recollection and remembrance, as well as the remembrance of our ancestors, and of the Messiah son of David Your servant, and of Jerusalem Your holy city, and of all Your people the house of Israel – for deliverance and well-being, grace, loving-kindness and compassion, life and peace, on this day of Rosh Ḥodesh. On it remember us, Lord our God, for good; recollect us for blessing, and deliver us for life. In accord with Your promise of salvation and compassion, spare us and be gracious to us; have compassion on us and deliver us, for our eyes are turned to You because You, God, are a gracious and compassionate King.

וְתֶחֱזֶינָה And may our eyes witness
Your return to Zion in compassion.
Blessed are You, Lord, who restores His Presence to Zion.

BIUR TEFILLA • ביאור תפילה

יַעֲלֶה וְיָבוֹא – *May there rise, come.* On Rosh Ḥodesh and on Ḥol HaMo'ed (the intermediate days of a festival), this prayer is added "as a supplication of Israel and Jerusalem for the reinstitution of the Temple service and of the sacrifices of the day" (Rashi, *Shabbat* 24a). In truth, however, the passage does not explicitly mention these themes. The Torah ordains that "on your days of rejoicing and your holy days and on your Rosh Ḥodesh, you will blow the trumpets over your offerings that they may to you a

This **BIUR TEFILLA** *continues on page 469.*

וְהַנְחִילֵנוּ, יהוה אֱלֹהֵינוּ, בְּאַהֲבָה וּבְרָצוֹן שַׁבַּת קָדְשֶׁךָ
וְיָנוּחוּ בָהּ יִשְׂרָאֵל מְקַדְּשֵׁי שְׁמֶךָ.
בָּרוּךְ אַתָּה יהוה, מְקַדֵּשׁ הַשַּׁבָּת.

עבודה
רְצֵה יהוה אֱלֹהֵינוּ בְּעַמְּךָ יִשְׂרָאֵל וּבִתְפִלָּתָם
וְהָשֵׁב אֶת הָעֲבוֹדָה[ע] לִדְבִיר בֵּיתֶךָ
וְאִשֵּׁי יִשְׂרָאֵל וּתְפִלָּתָם בְּאַהֲבָה תְקַבֵּל בְּרָצוֹן
וּתְהִי לְרָצוֹן תָּמִיד עֲבוֹדַת יִשְׂרָאֵל עַמֶּךָ.

On ראש חודש, *say:*

אֱלֹהֵינוּ וֵאלֹהֵי אֲבוֹתֵינוּ, יַעֲלֶה וְיָבוֹא[ב] וְיַגִּיעַ, וְיֵרָאֶה וְיֵרָצֶה וְיִשָּׁמַע, וְיִפָּקֵד וְיִזָּכֵר זִכְרוֹנֵנוּ וּפִקְדוֹנֵנוּ וְזִכְרוֹן אֲבוֹתֵינוּ, וְזִכְרוֹן מָשִׁיחַ בֶּן דָּוִד עַבְדֶּךָ, וְזִכְרוֹן יְרוּשָׁלַיִם עִיר קָדְשֶׁךָ, וְזִכְרוֹן כָּל עַמְּךָ בֵּית יִשְׂרָאֵל, לְפָנֶיךָ, לִפְלֵיטָה לְטוֹבָה, לְחֵן וּלְחֶסֶד וּלְרַחֲמִים, לְחַיִּים וּלְשָׁלוֹם בְּיוֹם רֹאשׁ הַחֹדֶשׁ הַזֶּה. זָכְרֵנוּ יהוה אֱלֹהֵינוּ בּוֹ לְטוֹבָה, וּפָקְדֵנוּ בוֹ לִבְרָכָה, וְהוֹשִׁיעֵנוּ בוֹ לְחַיִּים. וּבִדְבַר יְשׁוּעָה וְרַחֲמִים, חוּס וְחָנֵּנוּ וְרַחֵם עָלֵינוּ וְהוֹשִׁיעֵנוּ, כִּי אֵלֶיךָ עֵינֵינוּ, כִּי אֵל מֶלֶךְ חַנּוּן וְרַחוּם אָתָּה.

וְתֶחֱזֶינָה עֵינֵינוּ בְּשׁוּבְךָ לְצִיּוֹן בְּרַחֲמִים.
בָּרוּךְ אַתָּה יהוה, הַמַּחֲזִיר שְׁכִינָתוֹ לְצִיּוֹן.

IYUN TEFILLA · עיון תפילה

וְהָשֵׁב אֶת הָעֲבוֹדָה – *Restore the service.* Why do we long for the restoration of the *Beit HaMikdash* and its sacrifices? Why not just be satisfied with prayers? Imagine being separated from a loved one for years, communicating only through some technological device that can help span the distance. Now imagine that person is in the next room. That feeling of being close to someone you love, someone who loves you, is irreplaceable.

THANKSGIVING

Bow at the first nine words.

▾We give thanks[1] to You,
for You are the LORD our God and God of our ancestors
for ever and all time.
You are the Rock of our lives,
Shield of our salvation from generation to generation.
We will thank You and declare Your praise for our lives,
which are entrusted into Your hand;
for our souls, which are placed in Your charge;
for Your miracles which are with us every day;
and for Your wonders and favors
at all times, evening, morning and midday.
You are good – for Your compassion never fails.
You are compassionate – for Your loving-kindnesses never cease.
We have always placed our hope in You.
For all these things
may Your name be blessed and exalted,
our King, continually, for ever and all time.
Let all that lives thank You, Selah!
and praise Your name in truth,
God, our Savior and Help, Selah!
▾Blessed are You, LORD,
whose name is "the Good" and to whom thanks are due.

---

material things, especially those which he may never attain, prevents a person from being satisfied with what he has. If you can be grateful to God for what you have, then you will be less likely to get as caught up in the obsessions of the material world. What they knew intuitively in the eleventh century took social scientists a thousand years to prove; recent studies show that gratitude can be an antidote for materialism. Grateful people, it turns out, are more satisfied with their lives. When Yaakov's wife Leah gives birth to a fourth son, she is overwhelmed with gratitude (*Bereshit* 29:35): "She conceived again, and bore a son and said 'This time let me ***thank*** (*odeh*) God' and she named the child Yehuda." Yehuda or Judah, thus derives from the word for gratitude and Yehuda/Judah is of course the derivation of the name *Yehudi* or Jew. In other words, to be a Jew means to give thanks.

הודאה

Bow at the first five words.

ימוֹדִים ע אֲנַחְנוּ לָךְ
שָׁאַתָּה הוּא יהוה אֱלֹהֵינוּ וֵאלֹהֵי אֲבוֹתֵינוּ לְעוֹלָם וָעֶד.
צוּר חַיֵּינוּ, מָגֵן יִשְׁעֵנוּ, אַתָּה הוּא לְדוֹר וָדוֹר.
נוֹדֶה לְּךָ וּנְסַפֵּר תְּהִלָּתֶךָ
עַל חַיֵּינוּ הַמְּסוּרִים בְּיָדֶךָ
וְעַל נִשְׁמוֹתֵינוּ הַפְּקוּדוֹת לָךְ
וְעַל נִסֶּיךָ שֶׁבְּכָל יוֹם עִמָּנוּ
וְעַל נִפְלְאוֹתֶיךָ וְטוֹבוֹתֶיךָ שֶׁבְּכָל עֵת, עֶרֶב וָבֹקֶר וְצָהֳרָיִם.
הַטּוֹב, כִּי לֹא כָלוּ רַחֲמֶיךָ,
וְהַמְרַחֵם, כִּי לֹא תַמּוּ חֲסָדֶיךָ
מֵעוֹלָם קִוִּינוּ לָךְ.
וְעַל כֻּלָּם יִתְבָּרַךְ וְיִתְרוֹמַם שִׁמְךָ מַלְכֵּנוּ תָּמִיד לְעוֹלָם וָעֶד.
וְכֹל הַחַיִּים יוֹדְוּךָ סֶּלָה, וִיהַלְלוּ אֶת שִׁמְךָ בֶּאֱמֶת
הָאֵל יְשׁוּעָתֵנוּ וְעֶזְרָתֵנוּ סֶלָה.
יבָּרוּךְ אַתָּה יהוה, הַטּוֹב שִׁמְךָ וּלְךָ נָאֶה לְהוֹדוֹת.

---

memorial before your God" (*Bemidbar* 10:10). Perhaps, then, this prayer is a substitute for the trumpet sound, in *tefilla*, the substitute for the offerings (Rabbi E. Munk).

Alternatively, the prayer is an antidote to forgetting. We ask Hashem to remember but we need to do the same. I remember my poor behavior. I remember the good things I have done and commandments to which I try to adhere. I recall my past and my future, my place in the context of my people and ask myself if I have lived up to my potential. And I ask Hashem to do the same and to find my remembering and my commitment to this day worthy of His ongoing support.

IYUN TEFILLA · עיון תפילה

מוֹדִים – *We give thanks.* The eleventh-century text *Ḥovot HaLevavot* suggests some reasons why ingratitude is so bad. First of all, the constant striving to acquire more

PEACE

שָׁלוֹם רָב Grant great peace[B] to Your people Israel for ever,
for You are the sovereign LORD of all peace;
and may it be good in Your eyes
to bless Your people Israel
at every time, at every hour, with Your peace.
Blessed are You, LORD,
who blesses His people Israel with peace.[I]

Some say the following verse:

May the words of my mouth and the meditation of my heart find favor before You, LORD, my Rock and Redeemer. *Ps. 19*

אֱלֹהַי My God, *Berakhot 17a*
guard my tongue from evil[A]
and my lips from deceitful speech.
To those who curse me, let my soul be silent;
may my soul be to all like the dust.
Open my heart to Your Torah[B]
and let my soul pursue Your commandments.

---

told many stories, some true, some false, about others but he now regretted his behavior in all sincerity. "Tell me," he pleaded, "how can I atone for this once and for all?" The rabbi told him to go home, find a feather pillow, take it to the middle of the town square and cut it open. The man dutifully followed the advice, went home, got a pillow, took it to the town square, cut it open and watched as the feathers were carried in all different directions by the wind. He went back to his rabbi and asked, "Now, Rabbi, what should I do?" Answered the rabbi, "Now, go collect the feathers."

BIUR TEFILLA · ביאור תפילה

פְּתַח לִבִּי בְּתוֹרָתֶךָ – *Open my heart to Your Torah.* In education there is such a thing as "reading readiness" which has been defined as the point at which a person is ready to learn to read and the time during which a person transitions from being a non-reader into a reader. The statement in this prayer is about "Torah readiness."

What is the state of your Torah readiness?

Alternatively, perhaps the phrase could be translated "Open my heart with Your Torah" in which case readiness will only come about when you take the plunge.

Are you ready?

ברכת שלום

שָׁלוֹם רָב[ב] עַל יִשְׂרָאֵל עַמְּךָ תָּשִׂים לְעוֹלָם
כִּי אַתָּה הוּא מֶלֶךְ אָדוֹן לְכָל הַשָּׁלוֹם.
וְטוֹב בְּעֵינֶיךָ לְבָרֵךְ אֶת עַמְּךָ יִשְׂרָאֵל
בְּכָל עֵת וּבְכָל שָׁעָה בִּשְׁלוֹמֶךָ.
בָּרוּךְ אַתָּה יהוה, הַמְבָרֵךְ אֶת עַמּוֹ יִשְׂרָאֵל בַּשָּׁלוֹם.[ע]

Some say the following verse:

תהלים יט

יִהְיוּ לְרָצוֹן אִמְרֵי־פִי וְהֶגְיוֹן לִבִּי לְפָנֶיךָ, יהוה צוּרִי וְגֹאֲלִי:

ברכות יז.

אֱלֹהַי
נְצֹר לְשׁוֹנִי מֵרָע[א] וּשְׂפָתַי מִדַּבֵּר מִרְמָה
וְלִמְקַלְלַי נַפְשִׁי תִדֹּם, וְנַפְשִׁי כֶּעָפָר לַכֹּל תִּהְיֶה.
פְּתַח לִבִּי בְּתוֹרָתֶךָ,[ב] וּבְמִצְוֹתֶיךָ תִּרְדֹּף נַפְשִׁי.

IYUN TEFILLA • עיון תפילה

הַמְבָרֵךְ אֶת עַמּוֹ יִשְׂרָאֵל בַּשָּׁלוֹם – *Who blesses His people Israel with peace.* One of God's names is "Peace" (*Shabbat* 10b). That is one meaning of the greeting *Shalom Aleikhem* – May peace be upon you, that is, May Hashem's name be upon you. Perhaps, too, that is the meaning of the phrase *Shabbat Shalom*. May the peace of Shabbat be upon you; May Hashem be upon you. Without Peace, there is nothing.

BIUR TEFILLA • ביאור תפילה

שָׁלוֹם רָב – *Grant great peace.* The theme of this particular blessing is different than the parallel one in *Shaharit* and *Musaf* because the themes there are tied to the Priestly Blessing (*Birkat Kohanim*) which is generally only recited in the morning.

As night approaches, our fears and insecurities can become larger than life. Perhaps that's one reason that the emphasis here is on "great" peace, for we need more of it during this part of the day.

ANI TEFILLA • אני תפילה

נְצֹר לְשׁוֹנִי מֵרָע – *Guard my tongue from [speaking] evil. A man came to his rabbi to confess that he had spent many years gossiping about other people and that he had*

As for all who plan evil against me,
swiftly thwart their counsel and frustrate their plans.
Act for the sake of Your name;
act for the sake of Your right hand;
act for the sake of Your holiness;
act for the sake of Your Torah.
That Your beloved ones may be delivered, *Ps. 60*
save with Your right hand and answer me.
May the words of my mouth *Ps. 19*
and the meditation of my heart find favor before You,
LORD, my Rock and Redeemer.

Bow and take three steps back as if taking leave of the Divine Presence.

May He who makes peace in His high places,
make peace for us and all Israel –
and say: Amen.

יְהִי רָצוֹן May it be Your will, LORD our God and God of our ancestors,
that the Temple be rebuilt speedily in our days,
and grant us a share in Your Torah.
And there we will serve You with reverence,
as in the days of old and as in former years.
Then the offering of Judah and Jerusalem *Mal. 3*
will be pleasing to the LORD
as in the days of old and as in former years.

וְכָל הַחוֹשְׁבִים עָלַי רָעָה
מְהֵרָה הָפֵר עֲצָתָם וְקַלְקֵל מַחֲשַׁבְתָּם.
עֲשֵׂה לְמַעַן שְׁמֶךָ
עֲשֵׂה לְמַעַן יְמִינֶךָ
עֲשֵׂה לְמַעַן קְדֻשָּׁתֶךָ
עֲשֵׂה לְמַעַן תּוֹרָתֶךָ.
לְמַעַן יֵחָלְצוּן יְדִידֶיךָ, הוֹשִׁיעָה יְמִינְךָ וַעֲנֵנִי: תהלים ס
יִהְיוּ לְרָצוֹן אִמְרֵי־פִי וְהֶגְיוֹן לִבִּי לְפָנֶיךָ, יהוה צוּרִי וְגֹאֲלִי: תהלים יט

Bow and take three steps back as if taking leave of the Divine Presence.

עֹשֶׂה שָׁלוֹם בִּמְרוֹמָיו
הוּא יַעֲשֶׂה שָׁלוֹם עָלֵינוּ וְעַל כָּל יִשְׂרָאֵל
וְאִמְרוּ אָמֵן.

יְהִי רָצוֹן מִלְּפָנֶיךָ יהוה אֱלֹהֵינוּ וֵאלֹהֵי אֲבוֹתֵינוּ
שֶׁיִּבָּנֶה בֵּית הַמִּקְדָּשׁ בִּמְהֵרָה בְיָמֵינוּ
וְתֵן חֶלְקֵנוּ בְּתוֹרָתֶךָ
וְשָׁם נַעֲבָדְךָ בְּיִרְאָה כִּימֵי עוֹלָם וּכְשָׁנִים קַדְמֹנִיּוֹת.
וְעָרְבָה לַיהוה מִנְחַת יְהוּדָה וִירוּשָׁלָיִם כִּימֵי עוֹלָם וּכְשָׁנִים קַדְמֹנִיּוֹת: מלאכי ג

All stand and say:

וַיְכֻלּוּ Then the heavens and the earth were completed,[BH] Gen. 2
and all their array.
With the seventh day, God completed the work He had done.
He ceased on the seventh day from all the work He had done.
God blessed the seventh day
and declared it holy,
because on it He ceased from all His work
He had created to do.

ME'EIN SHEVA

The following until "who sanctifies the Sabbath" on page 478, is omitted when praying with an occasional minyan or alone.

The Leader continues:

בָּרוּךְ Blessed are You, LORD our God and God of our fathers,
God of Abraham, God of Isaac and God of Jacob,
the great, mighty and awesome God,
God Most High, Creator of heaven and earth.

---

testimony in a Jewish court of law. Indeed, there is another law which says that two witnesses are required for the testimony to be valid. Hence, there arose another custom that one might see from time to time: if someone failed to say this paragraph with the congregation because his own *Amida* was prolonged, then once he has finished he joins with some other person to recite this paragraph together, two witnesses bearing testimony to an eternal truth.

ANI TEFILLA • אני תפילה

What makes these verses so significant? The Gemara suggests that "Whoever recites this paragraph, it is as if he is a partner with God in the creation of the world" (*Shabbat* 119b).

What do you think this might mean?

Rav Ḥisda said in Mar Ukba's name: He who prays on the eve of the Sabbath and recites, "and the the heaven and the earth were finished," the two ministering angels who accompany each man place their hands on his head and say to him: Your iniquity is taken away and your sin purged. (*Shabbat* 119b)

All stand and say:

וַיְכֻלּוּ הַשָּׁמַיִם וְהָאָֽרֶץ וְכָל־צְבָאָם: בראשית ב
וַיְכַל אֱלֹהִים בַּיּוֹם הַשְּׁבִיעִי מְלַאכְתּוֹ אֲשֶׁר עָשָׂה
וַיִּשְׁבֹּת בַּיּוֹם הַשְּׁבִיעִי מִכָּל־מְלַאכְתּוֹ אֲשֶׁר עָשָׂה:
וַיְבָֽרֶךְ אֱלֹהִים אֶת־יוֹם הַשְּׁבִיעִי, וַיְקַדֵּשׁ אֹתוֹ
כִּי בוֹ שָׁבַת מִכָּל־מְלַאכְתּוֹ, אֲשֶׁר־בָּרָא אֱלֹהִים, לַעֲשׂוֹת:

ברכה מעין שבע

The following until מְקַדֵּשׁ הַשַּׁבָּת *on page 479,*
is omitted when praying with an occasional מנין *or alone.*

The שליח ציבור *continues:*

בָּרוּךְ אַתָּה יהוה, אֱלֹהֵינוּ וֵאלֹהֵי אֲבוֹתֵינוּ
אֱלֹהֵי אַבְרָהָם, אֱלֹהֵי יִצְחָק, וֵאלֹהֵי יַעֲקֹב
הָאֵל הַגָּדוֹל הַגִּבּוֹר וְהַנּוֹרָא, אֵל עֶלְיוֹן, קֹנֵה שָׁמַיִם וָאָֽרֶץ.

BIUR TEFILLA • ביאור תפילה

וַיְכֻלּוּ הַשָּׁמַיִם וְהָאָֽרֶץ – *Then the heavens and the earth were completed.* This paragraph, which was just recited in the *Amida*, is now recited again by the entire community together and, so important is it, that it will be repeated once again a little later on in *Kiddush*. From historical perspective, this paragraph is not found in the festival *Amida* since the theme here is Shabbat and so, when a festival fell on a Friday night, the paragraph was added after the *Amida* was over so that its message would not be lost (*Tosafot Pesaḥim* 106a). In order not to distinguish from one Shabbat to another, the prayer was added every Friday night. Origins aside, there is much power to a communal declaration of God as Creator (*HaManhig, Shabbat* 6). **Feel its power.**

HILKHOT TEFILLA • הלכות תפילה

וַיְכֻלּוּ הַשָּׁמַיִם וְהָאָֽרֶץ – *Then the heavens and the earth were completed.* The custom is to recite these verses while standing, just as is required of witnesses who give

The congregation then the Leader:

מָגֵן אָבוֹת By His word, He was the Shield of our ancestors.[B]
By His promise, He will revive the dead.
There is none like the holy God
who gives rest to His people on His holy Sabbath day,
for He found them worthy of His favor to give them rest.
Before Him we will come in worship with reverence and awe,
giving thanks to His name daily, continually, with due blessings.
He is God to whom thanks are due, the LORD of peace
who sanctifies the Sabbath and blesses the seventh day,
and in holiness gives rest to a people filled with delight,
in remembrance of the work of creation.

The Leader continues:

אֱלֹהֵינוּ Our God and God of our ancestors,
may You find favor in our rest.
Make us holy through Your commandments
and grant us our share in Your Torah.

---

aloud in order to make sure that everyone could fulfill the mitzva of *Kiddush* (*Talmud Yerushalmi Berakhot* 8:1, *Sefer Ḥaredim*).

What both reasons have in common is the concern for community on this night. To ensure that we act together, on behalf of one another, we share our knowledge and our companionship.

מָגֵן אָבוֹת – *Shield of our ancestors.* This whole section is sometimes referred to as the "abridged seven," a reference to the fact that, as described above, it contains words or phrases which are reminiscent of the words or phrases in each of the seven blessings in the *Amida*. Thus, this particular phrase, "shield of our ancestors," would correspond to the phrase *magen Avraham* or "shield of Abraham" in the *Amida*. Can you find the other six correspondences?

HILKHOT TEFILLA • הלכות תפילה

Because the reasons for the recitation of this prayer are so community driven, it is not recited when praying alone. Similarly, it is not said when services are held in a temporary location or correspondingly, where there is no Torah scroll present. Because of the association between the recitation of this prayer and the protection from danger, there is a custom not to recite it when the first night of Pesaḥ occurs on a Friday night, since that night (often called *Leil Shimurim*) is known to be a particularly auspicious time in its own right for protection by the Guardian of Israel.

The קהל *then the* שליח ציבור:

מָגֵן אָבוֹת בִּדְבָרוֹ, מְחַיֵּה מֵתִים בְּמַאֲמָרוֹ
הָאֵל הַקָּדוֹשׁ שֶׁאֵין כָּמוֹהוּ
הַמֵּנִיחַ לְעַמּוֹ בְּיוֹם שַׁבַּת קָדְשׁוֹ
כִּי בָם רָצָה לְהָנִיחַ לָהֶם
לְפָנָיו נַעֲבֹד בְּיִרְאָה וָפַחַד
וְנוֹדֶה לִשְׁמוֹ בְּכָל יוֹם תָּמִיד, מֵעֵין הַבְּרָכוֹת
אֵל הַהוֹדָאוֹת, אֲדוֹן הַשָּׁלוֹם
מְקַדֵּשׁ הַשַּׁבָּת וּמְבָרֵךְ שְׁבִיעִי
וּמֵנִיחַ בִּקְדֻשָּׁה לְעַם מְדֻשְּׁנֵי עֹנֶג
זֵכֶר לְמַעֲשֵׂה בְרֵאשִׁית.

The שליח ציבור *continues:*

אֱלֹהֵינוּ וֵאלֹהֵי אֲבוֹתֵינוּ, רְצֵה בִמְנוּחָתֵנוּ.
קַדְּשֵׁנוּ בְּמִצְוֹתֶיךָ וְתֵן חֶלְקֵנוּ בְּתוֹרָתֶךָ

BIUR TEFILLA • ביאור תפילה

מָגֵן אָבוֹת – *Shield of our ancestors.* This prayer is very unusual in that if you look carefully, you will see a number of elements of the *Amida* that was just recited, both in themes and in the language used. (Compare and contrast the two. What similarities and differences can you find?) It would thus make it appear that this prayer is a kind of repetition of the *Amida*, a practice which, while mandated for morning and afternoon services, is not at all the practice for the regular *Ma'ariv* service. And so, like many prayers with ancient roots, this one's origins are not entirely clear. One view from the Talmud Bavli suggests that it was placed here in order to accommodate those who came to the synagogue late from outlying areas. They would need extra time to catch up and there was a concern that if they did not, being left alone could leave one in potential peril, and so the service was prolonged with this prayer so that everyone could leave together (*Shabbat* 24b, Rashi). Alternatively, the Talmud Yerushalmi suggests that when there was no wine available, the recitation of the *Amida* could also serve as a substitute for making *Kiddush*, since both share the same themes and language. For illiterate Jews who could not read the *Amida* or *Kiddush*, this blessing was recited

Satisfy us with Your goodness, grant us joy in Your salvation,
and purify our hearts to serve You in truth.
In love and favor, LORD our God,
grant us as our heritage Your holy Sabbath,
so that Israel who sanctify Your name may find rest on it.
Blessed are You, LORD, who sanctifies the Sabbath.

FULL KADDISH

Leader: יִתְגַּדַּל Magnified and sanctified may His great name be,
in the world He created by His will.
May He establish His kingdom
in your lifetime and in your days,
and in the lifetime of all the house of Israel,
swiftly and soon –
and say: Amen.

All: May His great name be blessed for ever and all time.

Leader: Blessed and praised, glorified and exalted,
raised and honored, uplifted and lauded be
the name of the Holy One,
blessed be He,
beyond any blessing,
song, praise and consolation
uttered in the world –
and say: Amen.

May the prayers and pleas of all Israel
be accepted by their Father in heaven –
and say: Amen.

May there be great peace from heaven,
and life for us and all Israel –
and say: Amen.

שַׂבְּעֵנוּ מִטּוּבֶךָ וְשַׂמְּחֵנוּ בִּישׁוּעָתֶךָ
וְטַהֵר לִבֵּנוּ לְעָבְדְּךָ בֶּאֱמֶת.
וְהַנְחִילֵנוּ יהוה אֱלֹהֵינוּ בְּאַהֲבָה וּבְרָצוֹן שַׁבַּת קָדְשֶׁךָ
וְיָנוּחוּ בָהּ יִשְׂרָאֵל מְקַדְּשֵׁי שְׁמֶךָ.
בָּרוּךְ אַתָּה יהוה, מְקַדֵּשׁ הַשַּׁבָּת.

קדיש שלם

ש״ץ: יִתְגַּדַּל וְיִתְקַדַּשׁ שְׁמֵהּ רַבָּא (קהל: אָמֵן)
בְּעָלְמָא דִּי בְרָא כִרְעוּתֵהּ
וְיַמְלִיךְ מַלְכוּתֵהּ
בְּחַיֵּיכוֹן וּבְיוֹמֵיכוֹן וּבְחַיֵּי דְכָל בֵּית יִשְׂרָאֵל
בַּעֲגָלָא וּבִזְמַן קָרִיב, וְאִמְרוּ אָמֵן. (קהל: אָמֵן)

קהל וש״ץ: יְהֵא שְׁמֵהּ רַבָּא מְבָרַךְ לְעָלַם וּלְעָלְמֵי עָלְמַיָּא.

ש״ץ: יִתְבָּרַךְ וְיִשְׁתַּבַּח וְיִתְפָּאַר
וְיִתְרוֹמַם וְיִתְנַשֵּׂא וְיִתְהַדָּר וְיִתְעַלֶּה וְיִתְהַלָּל
שְׁמֵהּ דְּקֻדְשָׁא בְּרִיךְ הוּא (קהל: בְּרִיךְ הוּא)
לְעֵלָּא מִן כָּל בִּרְכָתָא
וְשִׁירָתָא, תֻּשְׁבְּחָתָא וְנֶחֱמָתָא
דַּאֲמִירָן בְּעָלְמָא, וְאִמְרוּ אָמֵן. (קהל: אָמֵן)

תִּתְקַבַּל צְלוֹתְהוֹן וּבָעוּתְהוֹן דְּכָל יִשְׂרָאֵל
קֳדָם אֲבוּהוֹן דִּי בִשְׁמַיָּא, וְאִמְרוּ אָמֵן. (קהל: אָמֵן)

יְהֵא שְׁלָמָא רַבָּא מִן שְׁמַיָּא
וְחַיִּים, עָלֵינוּ וְעַל כָּל יִשְׂרָאֵל, וְאִמְרוּ אָמֵן. (קהל: אָמֵן)

Bow, take three steps back, as if taking leave of the Divine Presence, then bow, first left, then right, then center, while saying:

May He who makes peace in His high places,[1]
make peace for us and all Israel – and say: Amen.

KIDDUSH IN THE SYNAGOGUE

The Leader raises a cup of wine and says:

Please pay attention, my masters.
בָּרוּךְ Blessed are You, LORD our God, King of the Universe,
who creates the fruit of the vine.

בָּרוּךְ Blessed are You, LORD our God, King of the Universe,
who has made us holy with His commandments, has favored us,
and in love and favor given us His holy Sabbath as a heritage,
a remembrance of the work of creation.
It is the first among the holy days of assembly,
a remembrance of the exodus from Egypt.
For You chose us and sanctified us from all the peoples,
and in love and favor gave us Your holy Sabbath as a heritage.
Blessed are You, LORD, who sanctifies the Sabbath.

The wine should be drunk by children under the age of Bar/Bat Mitzva or, if there are none, by the Leader.

INTRODUCTION TO KIDDUSH IN THE SYNAGOGUE

The custom to say *Kiddush* in the synagogue is another vestige of an ancient practice of communal solidarity, though which one in particular may not be clear. There was a time when guests who had no place else to go would stay in the synagogue or nearby for a communal meal. *Kiddush* was recited at this point in the service for all of those who would not be able to have wine in the place they were eating, either because they could not afford it or because it was unavailable (*Pesaḥim* 101, Rashi). Alternatively, or concomitantly, it was considered a kind of folk remedy for the community restoring one's eyesight, physical or spiritual (*Berakhot* 43b, *Seder R. Amram Gaon*).

While there are some communities, especially in Israel, that have abandoned the custom because it is no longer necessary since synagogues are no longer used as hostels, other communities continue the practice in deference to tradition and to the values that it symbolizes. There is, however, one technical complication.

This **INTRODUCTION TO KIDDUSH IN THE SYNAGOGUE** *continues on page 483.*

Bow, take three steps back, as if taking leave of the Divine Presence, then bow, first left, then right, then center, while saying:

עֹשֶׂה שָׁלוֹם בִּמְרוֹמָיו[ע]
הוּא יַעֲשֶׂה שָׁלוֹם עָלֵינוּ וְעַל כָּל יִשְׂרָאֵל, וְאִמְרוּ אָמֵן. (קהל: אָמֵן)

קידוש בבית הכנסת

The שליח ציבור *raises a cup of wine and says:*

סַבְרִי מָרָנָן
בָּרוּךְ אַתָּה יהוה אֱלֹהֵינוּ מֶלֶךְ הָעוֹלָם בּוֹרֵא פְּרִי הַגָּפֶן.

בָּרוּךְ אַתָּה יהוה אֱלֹהֵינוּ מֶלֶךְ הָעוֹלָם
אֲשֶׁר קִדְּשָׁנוּ בְּמִצְוֹתָיו, וְרָצָה בָנוּ
וְשַׁבַּת קָדְשׁוֹ בְּאַהֲבָה וּבְרָצוֹן הִנְחִילָנוּ, זִכָּרוֹן לְמַעֲשֵׂה בְרֵאשִׁית
כִּי הוּא יוֹם תְּחִלָּה לְמִקְרָאֵי קֹדֶשׁ, זֵכֶר לִיצִיאַת מִצְרָיִם
כִּי בָנוּ בָחַרְתָּ וְאוֹתָנוּ קִדַּשְׁתָּ מִכָּל הָעַמִּים
וְשַׁבַּת קָדְשְׁךָ בְּאַהֲבָה וּבְרָצוֹן הִנְחַלְתָּנוּ.
בָּרוּךְ אַתָּה יהוה, מְקַדֵּשׁ הַשַּׁבָּת.

The wine should be drunk by children under the age of בר מצווה *or* בת מצווה *or, if there are none, by the* שליח ציבור.

IYUN TEFILLA • עיון תפילה

עֹשֶׂה שָׁלוֹם בִּמְרוֹמָיו – *May He who makes peace in His high places.* What peace is referred to here? One opinion refers to an ancient view that angels do not serve multiple purposes but rather each has its own single mission "no one angel can have more than one charge" (*Bereshit Raba* 50:2). As such, one might easily imagine them coming into conflict with one another, as each tries to accomplish his one goal even if it were to mean negating the task of another. Nevertheless, such conflicts do not take place for what they have in common is their unswerving devotion to Hashem; they thus recognize the value of the other and avoid any conflict (*Rinat Ḥayyim*). So, too, should it be with man. Perhaps that is a reason that all of our prayer services end with the emphasis on peace. As we are about to take leave the synagogue with a greater appreciation for the role of God in our lives, we commit ourselves to living a more prayerful and peaceful life with our fellow man.

How can I add more peace to my relationships this evening?

Stand while saying Aleinu. Bow at ▾.

עָלֵינוּ It is our duty to praise the Master of all,
and ascribe greatness to the Author of creation,
who has not made us like the nations of the lands
nor placed us like the families of the earth;
who has not made our portion like theirs,
nor our destiny like all their multitudes.
(For they worship vanity and emptiness,
and pray to a god who cannot save.)
▾But we bow in worship and thank the Supreme King of kings,
the Holy One, blessed be He,
who extends the heavens and establishes the earth,
whose throne of glory is in the heavens above,
and whose power's Presence is in the highest of heights.
He is our God; there is no other.
Truly He is our King, there is none else,
as it is written in His Torah:
"You shall know and take to heart this day that the LORD is God, *Deut. 4*
in heaven above and on earth below. There is no other."

---

home" message at the end of every prayer service.

A conflicting tradition suggests that the prayer is even older, having been composed by Moshe's successor, Yehoshua. The initial paragraph of the prayer, which among other things, expresses disgust at the existence and fallacy of idolatry is said to be a reference to Yehoshua's reaction to the paganism he witnessed during the conquest of Canaan. To reconcile those traditions, there are those who say it was written by Rav but he did so from the perspective of Yehoshua as he conquered the Land.

There are two distinct but interrelated themes here. The first paragraph is all about our chosenness in the eyes of Hashem. The second is about why we were chosen: to perfect or repair the world, known in Hebrew as *tikkun olam*. It is a phrase that has commonly been adopted for every cause of social justice, yet those who do so mistakenly omit the rest of the original which reads "to perfect the world under the sovereignty of the Almighty." The American poet and essayist Ralph Waldo Emerson once said, "One man's justice is another's injustice." Only an immutable absolute morality that is based on an unchanging God has a chance of truly repairing the world, else we are left to a world of relativism.

As you prepare to leave the synagogue this evening and reenter the world of human interaction, what can you do to repair the world under the sovereignty of the Almighty?

Stand while saying עָלֵינוּ. *Bow at* *.

עָלֵינוּ לְשַׁבֵּחַ לַאֲדוֹן הַכֹּל, לָתֵת גְּדֻלָּה לְיוֹצֵר בְּרֵאשִׁית
שֶׁלֹּא עָשָׂנוּ כְּגוֹיֵי הָאֲרָצוֹת, וְלֹא שָׂמָנוּ כְּמִשְׁפְּחוֹת הָאֲדָמָה
שֶׁלֹּא שָׂם חֶלְקֵנוּ כָּהֶם וְגוֹרָלֵנוּ כְּכָל הֲמוֹנָם.
(שֶׁהֵם מִשְׁתַּחֲוִים לְהֶבֶל וָרִיק וּמִתְפַּלְלִים אֶל אֵל לֹא יוֹשִׁיעַ.)
*וַאֲנַחְנוּ כּוֹרְעִים וּמִשְׁתַּחֲוִים וּמוֹדִים
לִפְנֵי מֶלֶךְ מַלְכֵי הַמְּלָכִים, הַקָּדוֹשׁ בָּרוּךְ הוּא
שֶׁהוּא נוֹטֶה שָׁמַיִם וְיוֹסֵד אָרֶץ, וּמוֹשַׁב יְקָרוֹ בַּשָּׁמַיִם מִמַּעַל
וּשְׁכִינַת עֻזּוֹ בְּגָבְהֵי מְרוֹמִים.
הוּא אֱלֹהֵינוּ, אֵין עוֹד.
אֱמֶת מַלְכֵּנוּ, אֶפֶס זוּלָתוֹ
כַּכָּתוּב בְּתוֹרָתוֹ, וְיָדַעְתָּ הַיּוֹם וַהֲשֵׁבֹתָ אֶל־לְבָבֶךָ דברים ד
כִּי יהוה הוּא הָאֱלֹהִים בַּשָּׁמַיִם מִמַּעַל וְעַל־הָאָרֶץ מִתָּחַת
אֵין עוֹד:

Kiddush is legally required to be said at the place where one eats a meal (*ein Kiddush ela bemakom seuda*), and parenthetically, that is the reason that one does not fulfill one's obligation with this recitation and must repeat it at one's meal. Also, one is not permitted to eat or drink before saying *Kiddush* at that meal, thus putting the person reciting this *Kiddush* in a technical suspended state where on the one hand, he must say *Kiddush* but on the other not drink from the wine, but if he does not drink from the wine then his blessing is in vain! As a result another custom developed for young children, who would otherwise not be reciting *Kiddush* on their own, to derive the benefit by being the ones to drink the wine.

INTRODUCTION TO ALEINU

Aleinu is one of the oldest prayers in the siddur having been attributed to Rav, the head of one of the largest *yeshivot* in Babylonia (third century). Interestingly, it originally appeared not in the daily service but in the Rosh HaShana *Maḥzor* where it served as an introduction to *malkhiyot*. *Malkhiyot* is that first section of *Shemoneh Esreh* of *Musaf* on Rosh HaShana which declares Hashem's sovereignty in the world above all else. The prayer's ideas were considered so beautifully expressed and so central to the mission of the Jewish People, that it was eventually adopted as the "take

Therefore, we place our hope in You, LORD our God,
that we may soon see the glory of Your power,
when You will remove abominations from the earth,
and idols will be utterly destroyed,
when the world will be perfected under the sovereignty of the Almighty,
when all humanity will call on Your name,
to turn all the earth's wicked toward You.
All the world's inhabitants will realize and know
that to You every knee must bow and every tongue swear loyalty.
Before You, LORD our God, they will kneel and bow down
and give honor to Your glorious name.
They will all accept the yoke of Your kingdom,
and You will reign over them soon and for ever.
For the kingdom is Yours,
and to all eternity You will reign in glory,
as it is written in Your Torah: "The LORD will reign for ever and ever." *Ex. 15*
▸ And it is said: "Then the LORD shall be King over all the earth; *Zech. 14*
on that day the LORD shall be One and His name One."

Some add:

Have no fear of sudden terror or of the ruin when it overtakes the wicked. *Prov. 3*
Devise your strategy, but it will be thwarted; *Is. 8*
propose your plan, but it will not stand, for God is with us.
When you grow old, I will still be the same. *Is. 46*
When your hair turns gray, I will still carry you.
I made you, I will bear you, I will carry you, and I will rescue you.

MOURNER'S KADDISH

The following prayer, said by mourners, requires the presence of a minyan.
A transliteration can be found on page 1141.

Mourner: יִתְגַּדַּל Magnified and sanctified may His great name be,
in the world He created by His will.
May He establish His kingdom
in your lifetime and in your days,
and in the lifetime of all the house of Israel,
swiftly and soon – and say: Amen.

All: May His great name be blessed for ever and all time.

עַל כֵּן נְקַוֶּה לְּךָ יהוה אֱלֹהֵינוּ, לִרְאוֹת מְהֵרָה בְּתִפְאֶרֶת עֻזֶּךָ
לְהַעֲבִיר גִּלּוּלִים מִן הָאָרֶץ, וְהָאֱלִילִים כָּרוֹת יִכָּרֵתוּן
לְתַקֵּן עוֹלָם בְּמַלְכוּת שַׁדַּי.
וְכָל בְּנֵי בָשָׂר יִקְרְאוּ בִשְׁמֶךָ לְהַפְנוֹת אֵלֶיךָ כָּל רִשְׁעֵי אָרֶץ.
יַכִּירוּ וְיֵדְעוּ כָּל יוֹשְׁבֵי תֵבֵל
כִּי לְךָ תִּכְרַע כָּל בֶּרֶךְ, תִּשָּׁבַע כָּל לָשׁוֹן.
לְפָנֶיךָ יהוה אֱלֹהֵינוּ יִכְרְעוּ וְיִפֹּלוּ, וְלִכְבוֹד שִׁמְךָ יְקָר יִתֵּנוּ
וִיקַבְּלוּ כֻלָּם אֶת עֹל מַלְכוּתֶךָ
וְתִמְלֹךְ עֲלֵיהֶם מְהֵרָה לְעוֹלָם וָעֶד.
כִּי הַמַּלְכוּת שֶׁלְּךָ הִיא וּלְעוֹלְמֵי עַד תִּמְלֹךְ בְּכָבוֹד
כַּכָּתוּב בְּתוֹרָתֶךָ, יהוה יִמְלֹךְ לְעֹלָם וָעֶד: שמות טו
◂ וְנֶאֱמַר, וְהָיָה יהוה לְמֶלֶךְ עַל־כָּל־הָאָרֶץ זכריה יד
בַּיּוֹם הַהוּא יִהְיֶה יהוה אֶחָד וּשְׁמוֹ אֶחָד:

Some add:

אַל־תִּירָא מִפַּחַד פִּתְאֹם וּמִשֹּׁאַת רְשָׁעִים כִּי תָבֹא: משלי ג
עֻצוּ עֵצָה וְתֻפָר, דַּבְּרוּ דָבָר וְלֹא יָקוּם, כִּי עִמָּנוּ אֵל: ישעיה ח
וְעַד־זִקְנָה אֲנִי הוּא, וְעַד־שֵׂיבָה אֲנִי אֶסְבֹּל, אֲנִי עָשִׂיתִי וַאֲנִי אֶשָּׂא וַאֲנִי אֶסְבֹּל וַאֲמַלֵּט: ישעיה מו

קדיש יתום

The following prayer, said by mourners, requires the presence of a מנין*.*
A transliteration can be found on page 1141.

אבל: יִתְגַּדַּל וְיִתְקַדַּשׁ שְׁמֵהּ רַבָּא (קהל: אָמֵן)
בְּעָלְמָא דִּי בְרָא כִרְעוּתֵהּ
וְיַמְלִיךְ מַלְכוּתֵהּ
בְּחַיֵּיכוֹן וּבְיוֹמֵיכוֹן וּבְחַיֵּי דְכָל בֵּית יִשְׂרָאֵל
בַּעֲגָלָא וּבִזְמַן קָרִיב, וְאִמְרוּ אָמֵן. (קהל: אָמֵן)

קהל ואבל: יְהֵא שְׁמֵהּ רַבָּא מְבָרַךְ לְעָלַם וּלְעָלְמֵי עָלְמַיָּא.

Mourner: Blessed and praised, glorified and exalted,
raised and honored, uplifted and lauded
be the name of the Holy One,
blessed be He,
beyond any blessing, song, praise and consolation
uttered in the world – and say: Amen.

May there be great peace from heaven,
and life for us and all Israel – and say: Amen.

Bow, take three steps back, as if taking leave of the Divine Presence, then bow, first left, then right, then center, while saying:

May He who makes peace in His high places,
make peace for us and all Israel – and say: Amen.

From the second day of Rosh Ḥodesh Elul until and including Shemini Atzeret, the following psalm is said:

לְדָוִד A psalm of David. The LORD is my light and my salvation – whom *Ps. 27*
then shall I fear? The LORD is the stronghold of my life – of whom shall I be afraid? When evil men close in on me to devour my flesh, it is they, my enemies and foes, who stumble and fall. Should an army besiege me, my heart would not fear. Should war break out against me, still I would be confident. One thing I ask of the LORD, only this do I seek: to live in the House of the LORD all the days of my life, to gaze on the beauty of the LORD and worship in His Temple. For He will keep me safe in His pavilion on the day of trouble. He will hide me under the cover of His tent. He will set me high upon a rock. Now my head is high above my enemies who surround me. I will sacrifice in His tent with shouts of joy. I will sing and chant praises to the LORD. LORD, hear my voice when I call. Be gracious to me and answer me. On Your behalf my heart says, "Seek My face." Your face, LORD, will I seek. Do not hide Your face from me. Do not turn Your servant away in anger. You have been my help. Do not reject or forsake me, God, my Savior. Were my father and my mother to forsake me, the LORD would take me in. Teach me Your way, LORD, and lead me on a level path, because of my oppressors. Do not abandon me to the will of my foes, for false witnesses have risen against me, breathing violence. ▸ Were it not for my faith that I shall see the LORD's goodness in the land of the living. Hope in the LORD. Be strong and of good courage, and hope in the LORD!

Mourner's Kaddish (on previous page)

אבל: יִתְבָּרַךְ וְיִשְׁתַּבַּח וְיִתְפָּאַר
וְיִתְרוֹמַם וְיִתְנַשֵּׂא וְיִתְהַדָּר וְיִתְעַלֶּה וְיִתְהַלָּל
שְׁמֵהּ דְּקֻדְשָׁא בְּרִיךְ הוּא (קהל: בְּרִיךְ הוּא)
לְעֵלָּא מִן כָּל בִּרְכָתָא וְשִׁירָתָא, תֻּשְׁבְּחָתָא וְנֶחֱמָתָא
דַּאֲמִירָן בְּעָלְמָא, וְאִמְרוּ אָמֵן. (קהל: אָמֵן)

יְהֵא שְׁלָמָא רַבָּא מִן שְׁמַיָּא
וְחַיִּים, עָלֵינוּ וְעַל כָּל יִשְׂרָאֵל, וְאִמְרוּ אָמֵן. (קהל: אָמֵן)

Bow, take three steps back, as if taking leave of the Divine Presence, then bow, first left, then right, then center, while saying:

עֹשֶׂה שָׁלוֹם בִּמְרוֹמָיו
הוּא יַעֲשֶׂה שָׁלוֹם עָלֵינוּ וְעַל כָּל יִשְׂרָאֵל, וְאִמְרוּ אָמֵן. (קהל: אָמֵן)

From the second day of ראש חודש אלול *until and including* שמיני עצרת*, the following psalm is said:*

לְדָוִד, יהוה אוֹרִי וְיִשְׁעִי, מִמִּי אִירָא, יהוה מָעוֹז־חַיַּי, מִמִּי אֶפְחָד: בִּקְרֹב תהלים כז
עָלַי מְרֵעִים לֶאֱכֹל אֶת־בְּשָׂרִי, צָרַי וְאֹיְבַי לִי, הֵמָּה כָשְׁלוּ וְנָפָלוּ: אִם־תַּחֲנֶה
עָלַי מַחֲנֶה, לֹא־יִירָא לִבִּי, אִם־תָּקוּם עָלַי מִלְחָמָה, בְּזֹאת אֲנִי בוֹטֵחַ: אַחַת
שָׁאַלְתִּי מֵאֵת־יהוה, אוֹתָהּ אֲבַקֵּשׁ, שִׁבְתִּי בְּבֵית־יהוה כָּל־יְמֵי חַיַּי, לַחֲזוֹת
בְּנֹעַם־יהוה, וּלְבַקֵּר בְּהֵיכָלוֹ: כִּי יִצְפְּנֵנִי בְּסֻכֹּה בְּיוֹם רָעָה, יַסְתִּרֵנִי בְּסֵתֶר
אָהֳלוֹ, בְּצוּר יְרוֹמְמֵנִי: וְעַתָּה יָרוּם רֹאשִׁי עַל אֹיְבַי סְבִיבוֹתַי, וְאֶזְבְּחָה
בְאָהֳלוֹ זִבְחֵי תְרוּעָה, אָשִׁירָה וַאֲזַמְּרָה לַיהוה: שְׁמַע־יהוה קוֹלִי אֶקְרָא,
וְחָנֵּנִי וַעֲנֵנִי: לְךָ אָמַר לִבִּי בַּקְּשׁוּ פָנָי, אֶת־פָּנֶיךָ יהוה אֲבַקֵּשׁ: אַל־תַּסְתֵּר
פָּנֶיךָ מִמֶּנִּי, אַל תַּט־בְּאַף עַבְדֶּךָ, עֶזְרָתִי הָיִיתָ, אַל־תִּטְּשֵׁנִי וְאַל־תַּעַזְבֵנִי,
אֱלֹהֵי יִשְׁעִי: כִּי־אָבִי וְאִמִּי עֲזָבוּנִי, וַיהוה יַאַסְפֵנִי: הוֹרֵנִי יהוה דַּרְכֶּךָ, וּנְחֵנִי
בְּאֹרַח מִישׁוֹר, לְמַעַן שׁוֹרְרָי: אַל־תִּתְּנֵנִי בְּנֶפֶשׁ צָרָי, כִּי קָמוּ־בִי עֵדֵי־שֶׁקֶר,
וִיפֵחַ חָמָס: ‹ לוּלֵא הֶאֱמַנְתִּי לִרְאוֹת בְּטוּב־יהוה בְּאֶרֶץ חַיִּים: קַוֵּה אֶל־
יהוה, חֲזַק וְיַאֲמֵץ לִבֶּךָ, וְקַוֵּה אֶל־יהוה:

קדיש יתום *(on previous page)*

Most congregations sing Yigdal at this point.
In Israel, most congregations sing Adon Olam (page 20).

(page 20)

GREAT

is the living God and praised.
He exists, and His existence is beyond time.

He is One, and there is no unity like His.
Unfathomable, His oneness is infinite.

He has neither bodily form nor substance;
His holiness is beyond compare.

He preceded all that was created.
He was first: there was no beginning to His beginning.

Behold He is Master of the Universe; every creature
shows His greatness and majesty.

The rich flow of His prophecy He gave
to His treasured people in whom He gloried.

Never in Israel has there arisen another like Moses,
a prophet who beheld God's image.

God gave His people a Torah of truth
by the hand of His prophet, most faithful of His House.

God will not alter or change His law
for any other, for eternity.

He sees and knows our secret thoughts;
as soon as something is begun, He foresees its end.

He rewards people with loving-kindness according to their deeds;
He punishes the wicked according to his wickedness.

At the end of days He will send our Messiah,
to redeem those who await His final salvation.

God will revive the dead in His great loving-kindness.
Blessed for evermore is His glorious name!

Most congregations sing יגדל *at this point.*
In ארץ ישראל, *most congregations sing* אדון עולם (*page 21*).

יִגְדַּל

אֱלֹהִים חַי וְיִשְׁתַּבַּח, נִמְצָא וְאֵין עֵת אֶל מְצִיאוּתוֹ.
אֶחָד וְאֵין יָחִיד כְּיִחוּדוֹ, נֶעְלָם וְגַם אֵין סוֹף לְאַחְדּוּתוֹ.
אֵין לוֹ דְּמוּת הַגּוּף וְאֵינוֹ גוּף, לֹא נַעֲרֹךְ אֵלָיו קְדֻשָּׁתוֹ.
קַדְמוֹן לְכָל דָּבָר אֲשֶׁר נִבְרָא, רִאשׁוֹן וְאֵין רֵאשִׁית לְרֵאשִׁיתוֹ.
הִנּוֹ אֲדוֹן עוֹלָם, וְכָל נוֹצָר יוֹרֶה גְדֻלָּתוֹ וּמַלְכוּתוֹ.
שֶׁפַע נְבוּאָתוֹ נְתָנוֹ אֶל־אַנְשֵׁי סְגֻלָּתוֹ וְתִפְאַרְתּוֹ.
לֹא קָם בְּיִשְׂרָאֵל כְּמֹשֶׁה עוֹד נָבִיא וּמַבִּיט אֶת תְּמוּנָתוֹ.
תּוֹרַת אֱמֶת נָתַן לְעַמּוֹ אֵל עַל יַד נְבִיאוֹ נֶאֱמַן בֵּיתוֹ.
לֹא יַחֲלִיף הָאֵל וְלֹא יָמִיר דָּתוֹ לְעוֹלָמִים לְזוּלָתוֹ.
צוֹפֶה וְיוֹדֵעַ סְתָרֵינוּ, מַבִּיט לְסוֹף דָּבָר בְּקַדְמָתוֹ.
גּוֹמֵל לְאִישׁ חֶסֶד כְּמִפְעָלוֹ, נוֹתֵן לְרָשָׁע רָע כְּרִשְׁעָתוֹ.
יִשְׁלַח לְקֵץ יָמִין מְשִׁיחֵנוּ לִפְדּוֹת מְחַכֵּי קֵץ יְשׁוּעָתוֹ.
מֵתִים יְחַיֶּה אֵל בְּרֹב חַסְדּוֹ, בָּרוּךְ עֲדֵי עַד שֵׁם תְּהִלָּתוֹ.

Kiddush and Zemirot for Shabbat Evening

BLESSING THE CHILDREN

On the evenings of Shabbat many have the custom to bless their children.

To sons, say:

יְשִׂמְךָ May God make you like Ephraim and Manasseh.

To daughters, say:

יְשִׂימֵךְ May God make you like Sarah, Rebecca, Rachel and Leah. *Gen. 48*

יְבָרֶכְךָ May the LORD bless you and protect you. *Num. 6*
May the LORD make His face shine on you
and be gracious to you.
May the LORD turn His face toward you
and grant you peace.

---

again ends in the prayer for peace. How is such peace achieved? Perhaps in part through the blessing itself. Rabbi Yaakov Tzvi Mecklenburg noted that during the week parents may come to curse (!) children because of the strife that can occur between them. The blessing is a way for them to reconnect. A somewhat gentler version of this can be found in a contemporary explanation by former Vice-Presidential nominee, Senator Joe Lieberman. "Of all the things that observant Jews do on the Sabbath," he writes, "...I would put blessing your family high on the list. It is a priceless moment of connection that no matter what has happened during the week, the parent feels blessed to have that child... As a parent you know that weeks can go by when you think of your children less as blessings and more as problems to be solved... Stopping to bless your children once a week makes us pause to appreciate how blessed we are to have them in the first place and reminds them of the love we feel for them."

קידוש וזמירות לליל שבת

ברכת הבנים

On ליל שבת *many have the custom to bless their children.*

To sons, say:

יְשִׂמְךָ אֱלֹהִים
כְּאֶפְרַיִם וְכִמְנַשֶּׁה:

To daughters, say:

בראשית מח

יְשִׂימֵךְ אֱלֹהִים
כְּשָׂרָה רִבְקָה רָחֵל וְלֵאָה.

במדבר ו

יְבָרֶכְךָ יהוה וְיִשְׁמְרֶךָ:
יָאֵר יהוה פָּנָיו אֵלֶיךָ וִיחֻנֶּךָּ:
יִשָּׂא יהוה פָּנָיו אֵלֶיךָ וְיָשֵׂם לְךָ שָׁלוֹם:

INTRODUCTION TO BIRKAT HABANIM

The blessing of one's children can be one of the most moving rituals of Shabbat night. The parent puts one hand or two upon the head of one's child and first invokes the blessing that the boys be like Efraim and Menashe while the girls be like the Matriarchs. Why aren't the boys similarly blessed that they should be like the Patriarchs? Perhaps it is because if one looks at all of the sons of the Patriarchs, one will notice that there was always strife between them, always a battle over who would be the bearer of the future. Efraim and Menashe, blessed by their grandfather Yaakov (*Bereshit* 48:14), are the first siblings between whom there is no such rivalry; indeed, the first where the birthright is not contested. What better way to bless one's children, then, than with the blessing of peace (Rabbi Shlomo Riskin)?

This blessing is followed by the tripartite blessing of the *kohanim* (priests) which

Many people sing each of the four verses of the following song three times:

שָׁלוֹם עֲלֵיכֶם Welcome,
ministering angels, angels of the Most High,
from the Supreme King of kings,
the Holy One, blessed be He.

Enter in peace,
angels of peace, angels of the Most High,
from the Supreme King of kings,
the Holy One, blessed be He.

Bless me with peace,
angels of peace, angels of the Most High,
from the Supreme King of kings,
the Holy One, blessed be He.

Go in peace,
angels of peace, angels of the Most High,
from the Supreme King of kings,
the Holy One, blessed be He.

כִּי מַלְאָכָיו He will command His angels about you, *Ps. 91*
to guard you in all your ways.
May the Lord guard your going out and your return, *Ps. 121*
from now and for all time.

---

for Judaism generally rejects any notion of intermediaries between man and God, the song nevertheless spread quickly since its creation around the seventeenth century in Kabbalistic circles. It has thus become a common way to transition from welcoming the Shabbat in the synagogue to welcoming her into one's home.

The motif of the song is clearly peace. It is a hallmark of Shabbat and if one is not yet feeling it then now is the time to let it wash over you. The warm glow of the candles, the camaraderie of friends or family or newly found acquaintances, the festive air of a good meal should individually or all contribute to a different kind of awareness. As one allows the pressures or routines of the week to slip away, peace and a sense of wholeness begin to take their place.

Many people sing each of the four verses of the following song three times:

שָׁלוֹם עֲלֵיכֶם
מַלְאֲכֵי הַשָּׁרֵת, מַלְאֲכֵי עֶלְיוֹן
מִמֶּלֶךְ מַלְכֵי הַמְּלָכִים, הַקָּדוֹשׁ בָּרוּךְ הוּא.

בּוֹאֲכֶם לְשָׁלוֹם
מַלְאֲכֵי הַשָּׁלוֹם, מַלְאֲכֵי עֶלְיוֹן
מִמֶּלֶךְ מַלְכֵי הַמְּלָכִים, הַקָּדוֹשׁ בָּרוּךְ הוּא.

בָּרְכוּנִי לְשָׁלוֹם
מַלְאֲכֵי הַשָּׁלוֹם, מַלְאֲכֵי עֶלְיוֹן
מִמֶּלֶךְ מַלְכֵי הַמְּלָכִים, הַקָּדוֹשׁ בָּרוּךְ הוּא.

צֵאתְכֶם לְשָׁלוֹם
מַלְאֲכֵי הַשָּׁלוֹם, מַלְאֲכֵי עֶלְיוֹן
מִמֶּלֶךְ מַלְכֵי הַמְּלָכִים, הַקָּדוֹשׁ בָּרוּךְ הוּא.

כִּי מַלְאָכָיו יְצַוֶּה־לָּךְ, לִשְׁמָרְךָ בְּכָל־דְּרָכֶיךָ: תהלים צא
יהוה יִשְׁמָר־צֵאתְךָ וּבוֹאֶךָ, מֵעַתָּה וְעַד־עוֹלָם: תהלים קכא

INTRODUCTION TO SHALOM ALEIKHEM

The roots of this song can be found in the Gemara (*Shabbat* 119b). "It was taught by the *tanna* Rabbi Yose son of Yehuda: Two ministering angels accompany a person on Friday night on his way home from the synagogue, one good and one evil. When he arrives at home and finds a lit candle, a set table, and his bed made, the good angel says, "May you have another Shabbat like this one,' and the evil angel is forced to respond 'Amen' against his will. If he does not find the house in this state the evil angel says, 'May you have another Shabbat like this one,' and the good angel is forced to answer 'Amen' against his will."

While there were those who objected to the potentially problematic notion of appealing directly to angels (Vilna Gaon),

אֵשֶׁת־חַיִל A woman of strength, who can find? Her worth is far beyond pearls. *Prov. 31*
Her husband's heart trusts in her, and he has no lack of gain.
She brings him good, not harm, all the days of her life.
She seeks wool and linen, and works with willing hands.
She is like a ship laden with merchandise, bringing her food from afar.
She rises while it is still night, providing food for her household, portions for her maids.
She considers a field and buys it; from her earnings she plants a vineyard.
She girds herself with strength, and braces her arms for her tasks.
She sees that her business goes well; her lamp does not go out at night.
She holds the distaff in her hand, and grasps the spindle with her palms.
She reaches out her palm to the poor, and extends her hand to the needy.
She has no fear for her family when it snows, for all her household is clothed in crimson wool.
She makes elegant coverings; her clothing is fine linen and purple wool.
Her husband is well known in the gates,
where he sits with the elders of the land.
She makes linen garments and sells them, and supplies merchants with sashes.
She is clothed with strength and dignity; she can laugh at the days to come.
She opens her mouth with wisdom,
and the law of kindness is on her tongue.
She watches over the ways of her household,
and never eats the bread of idleness.
Her children rise and call her happy; her husband also praises her:
"Many women have excelled, but you surpass them all."
Charm is deceptive and beauty vain:
it is the God-fearing woman who deserves praise.
Give her the reward she has earned;
let her deeds bring her praise in the gates.

---

which a husband sings to his wife, thus reinforcing the message of the harmony and respect that are supposed to be the hallmark of the home on Shabbat.

At the same time, commentators have understood there to be mystical or allegorical overtones, wherein the subject of the poem is thought to be the human soul, or the Torah or the Matriarchs of the Jewish people, or the *Shekhina* (Divine Presence), or the nation of Israel, or the Shabbat. Pick one and see how it can change the meaning of the poem…and your appreciation for this moment of Shabbat.

אֵֽשֶׁת־חַֽיִל מִי יִמְצָא, וְרָחֹק מִפְּנִינִים מִכְרָהּ: משלי לא
בָּֽטַח בָּהּ לֵב בַּעְלָהּ, וְשָׁלָל לֹא יֶחְסָר:
גְּמָלַֽתְהוּ טוֹב וְלֹא־רָע, כֹּל יְמֵי חַיֶּֽיהָ:
דָּֽרְשָׁה צֶֽמֶר וּפִשְׁתִּים, וַתַּֽעַשׂ בְּחֵֽפֶץ כַּפֶּֽיהָ:
הָיְתָה כָּאֳנִיּוֹת סוֹחֵר, מִמֶּרְחָק תָּבִיא לַחְמָהּ:
וַתָּֽקָם בְּעוֹד לַֽיְלָה, וַתִּתֵּן טֶֽרֶף לְבֵיתָהּ, וְחֹק לְנַעֲרֹתֶֽיהָ:
זָמְמָה שָׂדֶה וַתִּקָּחֵֽהוּ, מִפְּרִי כַפֶּֽיהָ נָֽטְעָה כָּֽרֶם:
חָגְרָה בְעוֹז מָתְנֶֽיהָ, וַתְּאַמֵּץ זְרוֹעֹתֶֽיהָ:
טָֽעֲמָה כִּי־טוֹב סַחְרָהּ, לֹא־יִכְבֶּה בַלַּֽיְלָה נֵרָהּ:
יָדֶֽיהָ שִׁלְּחָה בַכִּישׁוֹר, וְכַפֶּֽיהָ תָּֽמְכוּ פָֽלֶךְ:
כַּפָּהּ פָּרְשָׂה לֶעָנִי, וְיָדֶֽיהָ שִׁלְּחָה לָאֶבְיוֹן:
לֹא־תִירָא לְבֵיתָהּ מִשָּׁלֶג, כִּי כָל־בֵּיתָהּ לָבֻשׁ שָׁנִים:
מַרְבַדִּים עָֽשְׂתָה־לָּהּ, שֵׁשׁ וְאַרְגָּמָן לְבוּשָׁהּ:
נוֹדָע בַּשְּׁעָרִים בַּעְלָהּ, בְּשִׁבְתּוֹ עִם־זִקְנֵי־אָֽרֶץ:
סָדִין עָֽשְׂתָה וַתִּמְכֹּר, וַחֲגוֹר נָֽתְנָה לַכְּנַעֲנִי:
עוֹז־וְהָדָר לְבוּשָׁהּ, וַתִּשְׂחַק לְיוֹם אַחֲרוֹן:
פִּֽיהָ פָּֽתְחָה בְחָכְמָה, וְתֽוֹרַת־חֶֽסֶד עַל־לְשׁוֹנָהּ:
צוֹפִיָּה הֲלִיכוֹת בֵּיתָהּ, וְלֶֽחֶם עַצְלוּת לֹא תֹאכֵל:
קָֽמוּ בָנֶֽיהָ וַיְאַשְּׁרֽוּהָ, בַּעְלָהּ וַיְהַלְלָהּ:
רַבּוֹת בָּנוֹת עָֽשׂוּ חָֽיִל, וְאַתְּ עָלִית עַל־כֻּלָּֽנָה:
שֶֽׁקֶר הַחֵן וְהֶֽבֶל הַיֹּֽפִי, אִשָּׁה יִרְאַת־יהוה הִיא תִתְהַלָּל:
תְּנוּ־לָהּ מִפְּרִי יָדֶֽיהָ, וִיהַלְלֽוּהָ בַשְּׁעָרִים מַעֲשֶֽׂיהָ:

INTRODUCTION TO EISHET ḤAYYIL

Another custom established by the Ari *zal* and his circle was the singing of this final chapter of the book of Proverbs (*Mishlei* 31:10-31), a 22-verse alphabetic acrostic. On its surface, it is a song of praise to the woman of the house in her capacity as homemaker, businesswoman, benefactor, mother and above all, a person whose beliefs permeate and carry her household. As such, it is often interpreted as something

KIDDUSH FOR SHABBAT EVENING

The Shabbat meal begins with the reciting of Kiddush, and is followed by the ritual washing of the hands in preparation for eating the Shabbat loaves.

Quietly: And it was evening, and it was morning – Gen. 1
יוֹם הַשִּׁשִּׁי the sixth day.

Then the heavens and the earth were completed, and all their array. Gen. 2
With the seventh day, God completed the work He had done.
He ceased on the seventh day from all the work He had done.
God blessed the seventh day and declared it holy,
because on it He ceased from all His work He had created to do.

When saying Kiddush for others, add:
Please pay attention, my masters.

Blessed are You, Lord our God, King of the Universe,
who creates the fruit of the vine.

HILKHOT TEFILLA • הלכות תפילה

There is a principle which states that *Kiddush* needs to be recited in the place where the meal is eaten (*ein Kiddush ela bemakom seuda*). As such, there is a custom to incorporate the *Kiddush* into the meal, as it were, by reciting the entire text while seated at the table as a prelude to the meal. Others maintain that the first paragraph is the equivalent of giving testimony to God's creation of the world and so one should stand for the entire *Kiddush*. Still others have the custom to stand for the first paragraph and then sit for the remainder of the *Kiddush*.

Participants are not required to drink from the wine, answering "Amen" to the blessing is sufficient, although there is a custom for the one reciting the *Kiddush* to share the wine from his cup with others (See *Shulḥan Arukh* 271:14).

ANI TEFILLA • אני תפילה

It was the custom of Rabbi David HaLevi, author of the *Turei Zahav* [on *Shulḥan Arukh*] that he would always recite *Kiddush* on Shabbat from a siddur. The reason, he said, apart from the holiness of the letters themselves, was because from time to time there would be a person at the table who did not know the *Kiddush* by heart and that person would be embarrassed to have to use a siddur to recite the words. Rabbi HaLevi himself would therefore use the siddur so that the guest would do so as well without fear of being embarrassed. He would sometimes say to the guest, "Follow along in the siddur just as I do, for to do so is really a very old custom." (*Sha'ar HaHakhana*).

קידוש לליל שבת

The שבת meal begins with the reciting of קידוש, and is followed by the ritual washing of the hands in preparation for eating the חלות.

Quietly וַיְהִי־עֶרֶב וַיְהִי־בֹקֶר   בראשית א

יוֹם הַשִּׁשִּׁי:

וַיְכֻלּוּ הַשָּׁמַיִם וְהָאָרֶץ וְכָל־צְבָאָם: בראשית ב

וַיְכַל אֱלֹהִים בַּיּוֹם הַשְּׁבִיעִי מְלַאכְתּוֹ אֲשֶׁר עָשָׂה

וַיִּשְׁבֹּת בַּיּוֹם הַשְּׁבִיעִי מִכָּל־מְלַאכְתּוֹ אֲשֶׁר עָשָׂה:

וַיְבָרֶךְ אֱלֹהִים אֶת־יוֹם הַשְּׁבִיעִי, וַיְקַדֵּשׁ אֹתוֹ

כִּי בוֹ שָׁבַת מִכָּל־מְלַאכְתּוֹ, אֲשֶׁר־בָּרָא אֱלֹהִים, לַעֲשׂוֹת:

When saying קידוש for others, add:

סַבְרִי מָרָנָן

בָּרוּךְ אַתָּה יהוה אֱלֹהֵינוּ מֶלֶךְ הָעוֹלָם, בּוֹרֵא פְּרִי הַגָּפֶן.

INTRODUCTION TO KIDDUSH

The Ten Commandments (*Shemot* 20:7) mandate that we "remember the Shabbat day to keep it holy." Rather than leaving this as a general and somewhat ambiguous command, tradition informs us that one should "remember it over wine," that is, we should formally remember the Shabbat's presence and holiness by making a ritual declaration to that effect over a cup of wine. We use wine, says one authority, because it enlivens one's heart and the more positive feelings one has toward an act, the more lasting it will be; this is another case where the heart follows one's actions. (*Sefer HaḤinukh*).

The text is made up of three parts: testifying to the rationale for the day as expressed in the first version of the Ten Commandments – the theme of creation; the blessing usually recited before partaking of wine; and the sanctification of the day, which contains the added rationale of the exodus from Egypt which is found in the second version of the Ten Commandments (*Devarim* 5:14). Both aspects, creation and the exodus, are related. The one speaks of the God of creation; the other, the God of redemption. The one reminds man that he is not God; the other describes what can happen in a society where rulers come to see themselves as gods. In that sense, Shabbat is not only a religious institution but a political and moral one as well.

Blessed are You, Lord our God, King of the Universe,
who has made us holy through His commandments,
who has favored us,
and in love and favor gave us His holy Sabbath as a heritage,
a remembrance of the work of creation.
It is the first among the holy days of assembly,
a remembrance of the exodus from Egypt.
For You chose us and sanctified us from all the peoples,
and in love and favor
gave us Your holy Sabbath as a heritage.
Blessed are You, Lord,
who sanctifies the Sabbath.

It is customary for all present to drink of the wine.

---

how the Sabbath preserves time and space for the family against the pressures of the world outside. As we walked away from the school, Penelope turned to me and said, "That Sabbath of yours is saving the parents' marriages." (Rabbi Jonathan Sacks)

ANI TEFILLA • אני תפילה

It was during the last of the Shabbat meals, Seuda Shelishit, that the founder of Ḥabad Hasidism, Rabbi Shneur Zalman of Liadi, asked his assistant to bring in the young Lithuanian peasant who had been standing outside the synagogue door. In answer to the assistant's questioning look, the Rebbe said, "I feel his Jewish soul; he is one of us."

The young man came in and after being asked by the Rebbe about his parentage, explained that he was a foundling, left at the doorstep of a kind Christian couple with no children. But he always felt an affinity toward Jews and Judaism. "You were left by your parents escaping a pogrom and certain death. You are a Jew," said the Rebbe.

The Rebbe went on to give a learned discourse and asked the young man "Do you understand?" "Nyet," he replied. The Rebbe then gave a brilliant analogy, interweaving a moving story with mystical symbolism. Again he asked the young man, "Do you understand?" to which he again replied "Nyet." And then the Rebbe started a melody, a wordless song, filled with heartfelt yearning for the Messiah, suffused with love of Torah and desire to joyously hold on to the departing Shabbat. The disciples danced, and the Russian peasant danced. With tears streaming down his cheeks, the youth turned to the Rebbe and cried out, "Now I understand." (Rabbi Shlomo Riskin)

בָּרוּךְ אַתָּה יהוה אֱלֹהֵינוּ מֶלֶךְ הָעוֹלָם
אֲשֶׁר קִדְּשָׁנוּ בְּמִצְוֹתָיו, וְרָצָה בָנוּ
וְשַׁבַּת קָדְשׁוֹ בְּאַהֲבָה וּבְרָצוֹן הִנְחִילָנוּ
זִכָּרוֹן לְמַעֲשֵׂה בְרֵאשִׁית
כִּי הוּא יוֹם תְּחִלָּה לְמִקְרָאֵי קֹדֶשׁ
זֵכֶר לִיצִיאַת מִצְרָיִם
כִּי בָנוּ בָחַרְתָּ וְאוֹתָנוּ קִדַּשְׁתָּ מִכָּל הָעַמִּים
וְשַׁבַּת קָדְשְׁךָ בְּאַהֲבָה וּבְרָצוֹן הִנְחַלְתָּנוּ.
בָּרוּךְ אַתָּה יהוה, מְקַדֵּשׁ הַשַּׁבָּת.

It is customary for all present to drink of the wine.

INTRODUCTION TO ZEMIROT

Recall that Psalm 92, the song for the Shabbat day, recited toward the end of *Kabbalat Shabbat*, and again during *Pesukei DeZimra*, and again at the end of *Musaf*, begins with the words "A song for the Sabbath day. It is good to thank Hashem and sing songs (*lezamer*) to Your name." Singing is an expression of one's happiness and, instead, sometimes it is a way to achieve a feeling of happiness. That is why singing *zemirot* or hymns are such an indelible part of the Shabbat meal experience.

The *Or Zarua* (*Shabbat* 42:4) points to a midrash (see the *Biur Tefilla* comment on *Kedusha* of *Shaḥarit* on page 610) which implies that there is a spiritual dimension of the songs that puts us in the category of angels. That is possible because on Shabbat we are so divorced from our daily concerns that we can dedicate ourselves to spirituality in a way simply not possible during the week.

The *zemirot* were written by both the famous and the anonymous over the centuries, each focusing on a different theme or aspect of Shabbat.

ANI TEFILLA • אני תפילה

Once, while making a television documentary about the state of the family in Britain, I took Penelope Leach, Britain's leading childcare expert, to see what happened in a Jewish school on Friday morning. The children, as usual, were performing their "mock Shabbat," role-playing what would happen that night at home. Penelope watched fascinated. The five-year-old parents blessed the five-year-old children and welcomed the five-year-old guests. When it was over, she asked one five-year-old boy what he liked most about the Sabbath. "I like it," he said, "because it's the only time Daddy doesn't have to rush off." It was a revealing insight into

ZEMIROT FOR SHABBAT EVENING

כָּל מְקַדֵּשׁ All who fittingly sanctify[B] the seventh day, / All who protect the Sabbath properly from desecration, / Will have great reward in accord with their deed. / "Each in his own camp, each under his own banner." *Num. 1*

Lovers of the LORD, who await the building of the Temple, / Be glad and joyful on the Sabbath as if receiving the gift of God's inheritance, / Raise your hands in holiness and say to God: / "Blessed is the LORD who has given rest to His people Israel." *1 Kings 8*

Seekers of the LORD, offspring of His beloved Abraham,[I] / Who are slow to leave the Sabbath but hasten to enter it, / Who rejoice to keep it and make its *eiruv* – / "This is the day the LORD has made, let us rejoice and be glad in it." *Ps. 118*

Remember Moses' Torah, from which the laws of Sabbath are learned,[B] / Engraved is the seventh day like a bedecked bride between her companions,[I] / The pure inherit it and sanctify it with the words: "All that He had made… / With the seventh day God completed the work He had done." *Gen. 2*

It is a sacred day from beginning to end, / All Jacob's offspring will honor it as the King's word and decree, / Resting on it and rejoicing with delights of food and drink. / "All the congregation of Israel will observe it." *Ex. 12*

Extend Your loving-kindness to those who know You, zealous and retributive God, / Those who keep the seventh day, fulfilling "Remember" and "Observe," / Grant them the joy of Jerusalem rebuilt, make them shine with the light of Your face. / "Fill them with the rich plenty of Your House, give them drink from Your river of delights." *Ps. 36*

Help those who, on the seventh day, rest from plow and harvest, / Who walk slowly, and eat three meals to bless You. / May their righteousness shine like the light of the seven days, / LORD God of Israel, grant completion. *1 Sam. 14*

חֲרוּתָה... כְּכַלָּה בֵּין רֵעוֹתֶיהָ מְשֻׁבָּצָה – *Engraved… like a bedecked bride between her companions.* Shabbat stands out among the other days of the week and its observance is a touchstone of Jewish identity. A Jew who is observant in general is nevertheless popularly known as someone who is "*shomer Shabbat*" (a Shabbat observer), for a commitment to Shabbat is symbolic of a more intimate relationship with God, like a bride and her groom.

BIUR TEFILLA • ביאור תפילה

זִכְרוּ תּוֹרַת מֹשֶׁה בְּמִצְוַת שַׁבָּת גְּרוּסָה – *Remember Moses' Torah, from which the laws of Sabbath are learned.* This could be understood as a reference to the Oral Law which is the source of a wealth of laws and information about Shabbat observance. Both the Oral and the Written Law were given at the same time.

זמירות לליל שבת

כָּל מְקַדֵּשׁ[ב] שְׁבִיעִי כָּרָאוּי לוֹ / כָּל שׁוֹמֵר שַׁבָּת כַּדָּת, מֵחַלְּלוֹ / שְׂכָרוֹ הַרְבֵּה מְאֹד
עַל פִּי פָעֳלוֹ / אִישׁ עַל־מַחֲנֵהוּ וְאִישׁ עַל־דִּגְלוֹ: במדבר א

אוֹהֲבֵי יהוה הַמְחַכִּים לְבִנְיַן אֲרִיאֵל / בְּיוֹם הַשַּׁבָּת שִׂישׂוּ וְשִׂמְחוּ כִּמְקַבְּלֵי מַתַּן
נַחֲלִיאֵל / גַּם שְׂאוּ יְדֵיכֶם קֹדֶשׁ וְאִמְרוּ לָאֵל / בָּרוּךְ יהוה אֲשֶׁר נָתַן מְנוּחָה מלכים א, ח
לְעַמּוֹ יִשְׂרָאֵל:

דּוֹרְשֵׁי יהוה זֶרַע אַבְרָהָם אוֹהֲבוֹ[ע] / הַמְאַחֲרִים לָצֵאת מִן הַשַּׁבָּת וּמְמַהֲרִים
לָבוֹא / וּשְׂמֵחִים לְשָׁמְרוֹ וּלְעָרֵב עֵרוּבוֹ / זֶה־הַיּוֹם עָשָׂה יהוה, נָגִילָה וְנִשְׂמְחָה בוֹ: תהלים קיח

זִכְרוּ תּוֹרַת מֹשֶׁה בְּמִצְוַת שַׁבָּת גְּרוּסָה[ב] / חֲרוּתָה לַיּוֹם הַשְּׁבִיעִי, כְּכַלָּה בֵּין רֵעוֹתֶיהָ
מְשֻׁבָּצָה[ע] / טְהוֹרִים יִירָשׁוּהָ, וִיקַדְּשׁוּהָ בְּמַאֲמַר כָּל אֲשֶׁר עָשָׂה / וַיְכַל אֱלֹהִים בראשית ב
בַּיּוֹם הַשְּׁבִיעִי מְלַאכְתּוֹ אֲשֶׁר עָשָׂה:

יוֹם קָדוֹשׁ הוּא, מִבּוֹאוֹ וְעַד צֵאתוֹ / כָּל זֶרַע יַעֲקֹב יְכַבְּדוּהוּ, כִּדְבַר הַמֶּלֶךְ וְדָתוֹ /
לָנוּחַ בּוֹ וְלִשְׂמֹחַ בְּתַעֲנוּג אָכוֹל וְשָׁתֹה / כָּל־עֲדַת יִשְׂרָאֵל יַעֲשׂוּ אֹתוֹ: שמות יב

מְשֹׁךְ חַסְדְּךָ לְיוֹדְעֶיךָ, אֵל קַנּוֹא וְנוֹקֵם / נוֹטְרֵי יוֹם הַשְּׁבִיעִי זָכוֹר וְשָׁמוֹר לְהָקֵם /
שַׂמְּחֵם בְּבִנְיַן שָׁלֵם, בְּאוֹר פָּנֶיךָ תַּבְהִיקֵם / יִרְוְיֻן מִדֶּשֶׁן בֵּיתֶךָ, וְנַחַל עֲדָנֶיךָ תַשְׁקֵם: תהלים לו

עֲזֹר לַשּׁוֹבְתִים בַּשְּׁבִיעִי, בֶּחָרִישׁ וּבַקָּצִיר עוֹלָמִים / פּוֹסְעִים בּוֹ פְּסִיעָה קְטַנָּה,
סוֹעֲדִים בּוֹ, לְבָרֵךְ שָׁלֹשׁ פְּעָמִים / צִדְקָתָם תַּצְהִיר כְּאוֹר שִׁבְעַת הַיָּמִים / יהוה שמואל א, יד
אֱלֹהֵי יִשְׂרָאֵל, הָבָה תָמִים:

BIUR TEFILLA • ביאור תפילה

כָּל מְקַדֵּשׁ – *All who fittingly sanctify.* This piyut or liturgical poem focuses on keeping the Shabbat, particularly the positive mitzvot associated with it and their reward.

IYUN TEFILLA • עיון תפילה

דּוֹרְשֵׁי יהוה זֶרַע אַבְרָהָם אוֹהֲבוֹ – *Seekers of the Lord, offspring of His beloved Abraham.* All of us long to be touched, most of us long for an encounter with the Divine. As the children of Avraham, we are all "seekers of Hashem" for he himself came to believe in God on his own by searching. We at least have the benefit of thousands of years of tradition.

How will you use that history for your own search?

מְנוּחָה וְשִׂמְחָה Rest and joy,[B] light for all Jews,
Is the Sabbath day, day of delights;
Those who keep and recall it bear witness
That in six days all creation was made.

The highest heavens, land and seas,
The hosts of heaven, high and sublime;
Sea monsters, humans and all wild beasts,
Were created by God, the LORD, who formed all worlds.[I]

It was He who spoke to His treasured people:
"Keep it to make it holy from beginning to end."
The holy Sabbath is His day of delight,
For on it God rested from all His work.

Through the Sabbath commandment
God will give you strength,
Rise, pray to Him, and He will invigorate you.
Recite the Nishmat prayer, and the Kedusha,
Then eat with joy, for He is pleased with you.

With twin loaves,[B] and wine for the Kiddush,
With many delicacies and a willing spirit;
Those who delight in it shall merit great reward:
The coming of the redeemer, and life in the World to Come.

God's creation of this world. The bottom of the letter is open, says the Gemara, to indicate that man is given free will; the world of choices in this world is open to him, so that if he wishes to choose not to conform, he may easily do so. The opening at the side of the *heh*, however, indicates that Heaven always recognizes the possibility of return, to go back under the protective dome and comfort of Heaven if one would only choose to do so.

BIUR TEFILLA • ביאור תפילה

בְּמִשְׁנֶה לֶחֶם – *With twin loaves.* A reference to the two loaves of bread on which the blessing of *HaMotzi* is said before the meal on Shabbat. This is a reminder of the double portion of manna which was collected on Fridays by the Israelites in the desert so that they would not need to perform the labor of collecting it on Shabbat.

Some suggest that this song was intended to be sung on Friday night while others contend it was to be sung on Shabbat after lunch. What "proofs" might one bring for each opinion from the words of the song?

מְנוּחָה וְשִׂמְחָה אוֹר לַיְּהוּדִים
יוֹם שַׁבָּתוֹן, יוֹם מַחֲמַדִּים
שׁוֹמְרָיו וְזוֹכְרָיו הֵמָּה מְעִידִים
כִּי לְשִׁשָּׁה כֹּל בְּרוּאִים וְעוֹמְדִים.

שְׁמֵי שָׁמַיִם, אֶרֶץ וְיַמִּים
כָּל צְבָא מָרוֹם גְּבוֹהִים וְרָמִים
תַּנִּין וְאָדָם וְחַיַּת רְאֵמִים
כִּי בְּיָהּ יהוה צוּר עוֹלָמִים.

הוּא אֲשֶׁר דִּבֶּר לְעַם סְגֻלָּתוֹ
שָׁמוֹר לְקַדְּשׁוֹ מִבּוֹאוֹ עַד צֵאתוֹ
שַׁבַּת קֹדֶשׁ יוֹם חֶמְדָּתוֹ
כִּי בוֹ שָׁבַת אֵל מִכָּל מְלַאכְתּוֹ.

בְּמִצְוַת שַׁבָּת אֵל יַחֲלִיצָךְ
קוּם קְרָא אֵלָיו, יָחִישׁ לְאַמְּצָךְ
נִשְׁמַת כָּל חַי וְגַם נַעֲרִיצָךְ
אֱכֹל בְּשִׂמְחָה כִּי כְבָר רָצָךְ.

בְּמִשְׁנֶה לֶחֶם וְקִדּוּשׁ רַבָּה
בְּרֹב מַטְעַמִּים וְרוּחַ נְדִיבָה
יִזְכּוּ לְרַב טוּב הַמִּתְעַנְּגִים בָּהּ
בְּבִיאַת גּוֹאֵל לְחַיֵּי הָעוֹלָם הַבָּא.

BIUR TEFILLA • ביאור תפילה

מְנוּחָה וְשִׂמְחָה – *Rest and joy.* The song speaks to the testimony Shabbat observance bears to creation in both the upper and lower worlds. In the merit of keeping the positive aspects of the day including praying, eating, making kiddush and the like, man will acquire the World to Come.

IYUN TEFILLA • עיון תפילה

כִּי בְּיָהּ יהוה צוּר עוֹלָמִים – *Were created by God, the Lord, who formed all worlds.* The Gemara (*Menaḥot* 29b) relates that, the name of God used here is comprised of two letters, *yod* and *heh* which represent God's creation respectively of the World to Come and this world. The letter *heh* represents

מַה־יְּדִידוּת How beloved[B] is your rest, Sabbath Queen, / We run to greet you: Come, royal bride, / Dressed in fine robes. We light the light with blessing. / All labors end [as is said:] "You shall do no work."

To savor the delights of fowl, quail and fish.

In advance all kinds of tasty food have been prepared, / Fattened chickens made ready while it was still day. / Varied dishes set out, and fragrant wines to drink, / And special delicacies all three times.

To savor the delights of fowl, quail and fish.

They shall inherit Jacob's heritage, a heritage unbounded, / Rich and poor will honor [the Sabbath] and be worthy of redemption, / If you keep the Sabbath day you will be My special treasure, / Six days shall you labor – and on the seventh let us rejoice.

To savor the delights of fowl, quail and fish.

Your secular concerns are forbidden; so too are calculations. / Reflections are permitted, and arranging matches for girls, / And teaching a child a book, and singing songs of praise, / And meditating on fine words at every place and gathering.

To savor the delights of fowl, quail and fish.

Your walk shall be unhurried; you shall call the Sabbath a delight. / Sleep too is praiseworthy, for it refreshes the spirit. / Therefore my soul yearns for you, to rest in you in love, / As if within a fence of roses: on it son and daughter rest.

To savor the delights of fowl, quail and fish.

A foretaste of the World to Come[B] is the day of Sabbath rest. / All who take delight in it will be worthy of great joy. / They will be delivered with relief from the birthpangs of the Messiah, / May our redemption spring forth, and sadness and sighing flee away.

To savor the delights of fowl, quail and fish.

Shabbat in particular is not simply passive, a state of inactivity, but rather something which each of us must actively create, as it were. On the verse (*Bereshit* 2:1) which says that God finished creation on the seventh day, Rashi cites the midrash which wonders how it is that God could finish creation on that day when in fact He was supposed to have finished creating on the sixth day. One answer offered is that He actually did create something on Shabbat, namely rest. What distinguishes Shabbat rest from pure relaxation is partially outlined in the rest of the song.

מֵעֵין עוֹלָם הַבָּא – *A foretaste of the World to Come.* The Gemara (*Berakhot* 57b) says that Shabbat is one-sixtieth of what the World to Come is like. **What do you think this might mean?**

מַה־יְּדִידוּת[ב] מְנוּחָתֵךְ, אַתְּ שַׁבָּת הַמַּלְכָּה
בְּכֵן נָרוּץ לִקְרָאתֵךְ, בּוֹאִי כַלָּה נְסוּכָה
לְבוּשׁ בִּגְדֵי חֲמוּדוֹת, לְהַדְלִיק נֵר בִּבְרָכָה
וַתֵּכֶל כָּל הָעֲבוֹדוֹת, לֹא תַעֲשׂוּ מְלָאכָה.
לְהִתְעַנֵּג בְּתַעֲנוּגִים בַּרְבּוּרִים וּשְׂלָו וְדָגִים.

מֵעֶרֶב מַזְמִינִים כָּל מִינֵי מַטְעַמִּים
מִבְּעוֹד יוֹם מוּכָנִים תַּרְנְגוֹלִים מְפֻטָּמִים
וְלַעֲרֹךְ בּוֹ כַּמָּה מִינִים, שְׁתוֹת יֵינוֹת מְבֻשָּׂמִים
וְתַפְנוּקֵי מַעֲדַנִּים בְּכָל שָׁלֹשׁ פְּעָמִים.
לְהִתְעַנֵּג בְּתַעֲנוּגִים בַּרְבּוּרִים וּשְׂלָו וְדָגִים.

נַחֲלַת יַעֲקֹב יִירָשׁ, בְּלִי מְצָרִים נַחֲלָה
וִיכַבְּדוּהוּ עָשִׁיר וָרָשׁ, וְתִזְכּוּ לִגְאֻלָּה
יוֹם שַׁבָּת אִם תְּכַבֵּדוּ וִהְיִיתֶם לִי סְגֻלָּה
שֵׁשֶׁת יָמִים תַּעֲבֹדוּ וּבַשְּׁבִיעִי נָגִילָה.
לְהִתְעַנֵּג בְּתַעֲנוּגִים בַּרְבּוּרִים וּשְׂלָו וְדָגִים.

חֲפָצֶיךָ אֲסוּרִים וְגַם לַחְשֹׁב חֶשְׁבּוֹנוֹת
הִרְהוּרִים מֻתָּרִים וּלְשַׁדֵּךְ הַבָּנוֹת
וְתִינוֹק לְלַמְּדוֹ סֵפֶר, לַמְנַצֵּחַ בִּנְגִינוֹת
וְלַהֲגוֹת בְּאִמְרֵי שֶׁפֶר בְּכָל פִּנּוֹת וּמַחֲנוֹת.
לְהִתְעַנֵּג בְּתַעֲנוּגִים בַּרְבּוּרִים וּשְׂלָו וְדָגִים.

הִלּוּכָךְ יְהֵא בְנַחַת, עֹנֶג קְרָא לַשַּׁבָּת
וְהַשֵּׁנָה מְשֻׁבַּחַת כְּדָת נֶפֶשׁ מְשִׁיבַת
בְּכֵן נַפְשִׁי לְךָ עָרְגָה וְלָנוּחַ בְּחִבַּת
כַּשּׁוֹשַׁנִּים סוּגָה, בּוֹ יָנוּחוּ בֵּן וּבַת. לְהִתְעַנֵּג בְּתַעֲנוּגִים בַּרְבּוּרִים וּשְׂלָו וְדָגִים.

מֵעֵין עוֹלָם הַבָּא[ב] יוֹם שַׁבָּת מְנוּחָה
כָּל הַמִּתְעַנְּגִים בָּהּ יִזְכּוּ לְרֹב שִׂמְחָה
מֵחֶבְלֵי מָשִׁיחַ יֻצָּלוּ לִרְוָחָה
פְּדוּתֵנוּ תַצְמִיחַ, וְנָס יָגוֹן וַאֲנָחָה. לְהִתְעַנֵּג בְּתַעֲנוּגִים בַּרְבּוּרִים וּשְׂלָו וְדָגִים.

BIUR TEFILLA • בִּיאוּר תְּפִלָּה

מַה־יְּדִידוּת – *How beloved.* The first stanza contains references to the source and spirit of the *Kabbalat Shabbat* service that was just recited in the synagogue. Rest on

יוֹם זֶה לְיִשְׂרָאֵל This day for Israel[B] is light and joy,
a Sabbath of serenity.
At the assembly at Sinai You decreed the laws,
Sabbath and the festivals – to keep them all my years;
Setting a table before me with courses of fine food – A Sabbath of serenity.
This day, for Israel, is light and joy, a Sabbath of serenity.

Heart's delight to a shattered people,[B]
To suffering spirits, an extra soul.
From troubled hearts may it banish sighs – A Sabbath of serenity.
This day, for Israel, is light and joy, a Sabbath of serenity.

You sanctified and blessed it above all other days.
In six days You finished the making of all worlds.
On it sad souls find quiet and safety – A Sabbath of serenity.
This day, for Israel, is light and joy, a Sabbath of serenity.

All work is forbidden by the revered One's commandment,
I will merit royal glory if I keep the Sabbath day,
Bringing the awesome One a sweetly scented gift – A Sabbath of serenity.
This day, for Israel, is light and joy, a Sabbath of serenity.

Renew our Sanctuary, remember the ruined city.
Bestow Your goodness, Savior, on one who is sad,
Yet still she spends the Sabbath in song and praise – A Sabbath of serenity.
This day, for Israel, is light and joy, a Sabbath of serenity.

---

stanzas might have been inserted later in tribute to him.

Shabbat is a day of light, happiness and rest. Elsewhere we have noted the midrash (*Bereshit Raba* 11) which claims that the added blessing that man receives on Shabbat is an increased glow. This is a theme that has already appeared in the first line of the song *Menuḥa VeSimḥa* which appears above. How might one explain this extra light? Is it the joy that comes from spending time with friends and family? Is it the glow that comes from being more well rested than any other day of the week? Is it the extra soul (*neshama yeteira*) which man receives on this day? Is it just the sheer happiness that comes from observing this day like no other?

חֶמְדַּת הַלְּבָבוֹת לְאֻמָּה שְׁבוּרָה–*Heart's delight to a shattered people.* The stanza contains a number of descriptions of the pains of a diaspora experience and personal angst. **Shabbat can provide a temporary reprieve for those feelings. How?**

יוֹם זֶה לְיִשְׂרָאֵל אוֹרָה וְשִׂמְחָה, שַׁבַּת מְנוּחָה.

צִוִּיתָ פִּקּוּדִים בְּמַעֲמַד סִינַי
שַׁבָּת וּמוֹעֲדִים לִשְׁמֹר בְּכָל שָׁנַי
לַעֲרֹךְ לְפָנַי מַשְׂאֵת וַאֲרוּחָה שַׁבַּת מְנוּחָה.
יוֹם זֶה לְיִשְׂרָאֵל אוֹרָה וְשִׂמְחָה, שַׁבַּת מְנוּחָה.

חֶמְדַּת הַלְּבָבוֹת לְאֻמָּה שְׁבוּרָה
לִנְפָשׁוֹת נִכְאָבוֹת נְשָׁמָה יְתֵרָה
לְנֶפֶשׁ מְצֵרָה יָסִיר אֲנָחָה שַׁבַּת מְנוּחָה.
יוֹם זֶה לְיִשְׂרָאֵל אוֹרָה וְשִׂמְחָה, שַׁבַּת מְנוּחָה.

קִדַּשְׁתָּ בֵּרַכְתָּ אוֹתוֹ מִכָּל יָמִים
בְּשֵׁשֶׁת כִּלִּיתָ מְלֶאכֶת עוֹלָמִים
בּוֹ מָצְאוּ עֲגוּמִים הַשְׁקֵט וּבִטְחָה שַׁבַּת מְנוּחָה.
יוֹם זֶה לְיִשְׂרָאֵל אוֹרָה וְשִׂמְחָה, שַׁבַּת מְנוּחָה.

לְאִסּוּר מְלָאכָה צִוִּיתָנוּ נוֹרָא
אֶזְכֶּה הוֹד מְלוּכָה אִם שַׁבָּת אֶשְׁמְרָה
אַקְרִיב שַׁי לַמּוֹרָא, מִנְחָה מֶרְקָחָה שַׁבַּת מְנוּחָה.
יוֹם זֶה לְיִשְׂרָאֵל אוֹרָה וְשִׂמְחָה, שַׁבַּת מְנוּחָה.

חַדֵּשׁ מִקְדָּשֵׁנוּ, זָכְרָה נֶחֱרֶבֶת
טוּבְךָ, מוֹשִׁיעֵנוּ, תְּנָה לַנֶּעֱצֶבֶת
בְּשַׁבָּת יוֹשֶׁבֶת בְּזֶמֶר וּשְׁבָחָה שַׁבַּת מְנוּחָה.
יוֹם זֶה לְיִשְׂרָאֵל אוֹרָה וְשִׂמְחָה, שַׁבַּת מְנוּחָה.

BIUR TEFILLA • ביאור תפילה

יוֹם זֶה לְיִשְׂרָאֵל – *This day for Israel.* This is yet another liturgical poem whose author is unknown. There is an acrostic in the first refrain and subsequent four stanzas that spells the name Yitzḥak, but there are different versions of the poem which include even more stanzas which would spell Yitzḥak Luria *ḥazak*, that is, the Ari; these

יָהּ רִבּוֹן Master of all worlds, our God, adored,
King of kings, over all the LORD:
Your wondrous deeds to applaud
We sing to You with one accord.
God of all worlds, our God, adored; King of kings, over all, the LORD.

Early and late my praise shall ring,
To You, holy Author of every thing:
Beasts of the field, birds that take wing.
Angels and mortals to You shall sing.
God of all worlds, our God, adored; King of kings, over all, the LORD.

Your great good deeds are vast in scale,
You humble the proud, You lift the frail.
A thousand years would not avail
Of Your works to tell the tale.
God of all worlds, our God, adored; King of kings, over all, the LORD.

Yours is the glory, the greatness too,
From the lion's jaw, Your flock rescue.
Bring Your exiles home to You:
The people You chose, deliver anew.
God of all worlds, our God, adored; King of kings, over all, the LORD.

Come back to Your Temple, Your sacred shrine,
That there in joy our souls may entwine.
In song our voices to combine,
When Jerusalem's beauty again will shine.
God of all worlds, our God, adored; King of kings, over all, the LORD.

---

who was born in Damascus, moved to Tzefat and later became the rabbi of Gaza. The poem is unusual in a few ways beginning with the fact that it is written in Aramaic rather than Hebrew. More importantly, it contains no explicit reference to Shabbat and there is no indication that it was written for that purpose. Yet it's extolling the greatness of Hashem, especially as Creator, and our unique relationship with Him has made it a standard addition to the Friday night tradition.

It is said that the poem was frequently sung during the Holocaust during particularly difficult moments.

What themes can you find that might explain this choice?

יָהּ רִבּוֹן עָלַם וְעָלְמַיָּא
אַנְתְּ הוּא מַלְכָּא מֶלֶךְ מַלְכַיָּא
עוֹבַד גְּבוּרְתָּךְ וְתִמְהַיָּא
שְׁפַר קָדָמָךְ לְהַחֲוָיָא.
יָהּ רִבּוֹן עָלַם וְעָלְמַיָּא, אַנְתְּ הוּא מַלְכָּא מֶלֶךְ מַלְכַיָּא.

שְׁבָחִין אֲסַדֵּר צַפְרָא וְרַמְשָׁא
לָךְ אֱלָהָא קַדִּישָׁא דִּי בְרָא כָּל נַפְשָׁא
עִירִין קַדִּישִׁין וּבְנֵי אֱנָשָׁא
חֵיוַת בָּרָא וְעוֹפֵי שְׁמַיָּא.
יָהּ רִבּוֹן עָלַם וְעָלְמַיָּא, אַנְתְּ הוּא מַלְכָּא מֶלֶךְ מַלְכַיָּא.

רַבְרְבִין עוֹבְדָיךְ וְתַקִּיפִין
מָכֵךְ רָמַיָּא וְזָקֵף כְּפִיפִין
לוּ יְחֵי גְבַר שְׁנִין אַלְפִין
לָא יֵעֹל גְּבוּרְתָּךְ בְּחֻשְׁבְּנַיָּא.
יָהּ רִבּוֹן עָלַם וְעָלְמַיָּא, אַנְתְּ הוּא מַלְכָּא מֶלֶךְ מַלְכַיָּא.

אֱלָהָא דִּי לֵהּ יְקָר וּרְבוּתָא
פְּרֹק יָת עָנָךְ מִפֻּם אַרְיָוָתָא
וְאַפֵּק יָת עַמָּךְ מִגּוֹ גָלוּתָא
עַמָּא דִּי בְחַרְתְּ מִכָּל אֻמַּיָּא.
יָהּ רִבּוֹן עָלַם וְעָלְמַיָּא, אַנְתְּ הוּא מַלְכָּא מֶלֶךְ מַלְכַיָּא.

לְמַקְדְּשָׁךְ תּוּב וּלְקֹדֶשׁ קֻדְשִׁין
אֲתַר דִּי בֵהּ יֶחֱדוּן רוּחִין וְנַפְשִׁין
וִיזַמְּרוּן לָךְ שִׁירִין וְרַחֲשִׁין
בִּירוּשְׁלֵם קַרְתָּא דְשֻׁפְרַיָּא.
יָהּ רִבּוֹן עָלַם וְעָלְמַיָּא, אַנְתְּ הוּא מַלְכָּא מֶלֶךְ מַלְכַיָּא.

BIUR TEFILLA • ביאור תפילה

יָהּ רִבּוֹן – *Master of all.* The acrostic at the beginning of each stanza spells the name Israel, a reference to its author, Rabbi Yisrael Najara, one of the greatest poets,

צָמְאָה נַפְשִׁי My soul thirsts[B] for God, the living God
My heart and flesh will sing joyfully to the living God. Ps. 84
The One God created me, and said "As I live,
no one shall see Me and live."[I]

My soul thirsts for God, the living God
My heart and flesh will sing joyfully
to the living God.

He created all with wisdom, design and deliberation,
Deeply hidden though it is from the eyes of all that live.
His glory is high above all, every mouth makes known His splendor,
Blessed is He in whose hands is the life-force of all that lives.

My soul thirsts for God, the living God
My heart and flesh will sing joyfully
to the living God.

He set apart the quiet one's offspring,[B] to teach them decrees,
Which if one performs them, thereby he shall live.
Who can vindicate himself? We are like specks of dust,
Truly none can vindicate itself before You, nothing that lives.

My soul thirsts for God, the living God
My heart and flesh will sing joyfully
to the living God.

As the body needs water for its survival, so too does the soul need a connection to God. Both body and soul need their sustenance in order to thrive and feel healthy and alive. Indeed, note the motif word חָי *hai*, live or life, which appears twice in the first two lines and once in every line thereafter. The Jewish people lives, as does its faith in God.

הִבְדִּיל נִינֵי תָם – *He set apart the quiet one's offspring.* This is a reference to Yaakov who was known as a *tam* or quiet one (*Bereshit* 25:27).

IYUN TEFILLA • עיון תפילה

אֵל אֶחָד בְּרָאַנִי, וְאָמַר חַי אָנִי, כִּי לֹא יִרְאַנִי הָאָדָם וָחָי – *The One God created me, and said "As I live, no one shall see Me and live."* As sure as I am alive, says God, My word is true (Ibn Ezra on *Shemot* 33:20). And in this case, what is true is that He cannot be seen. The message is clear: God exists, even if we cannot always physically see Him. Even so, my soul knows that He is there. The heart has its reasons, said Pascal, of which reason has no knowledge.

תהלים פד

צָמְאָה נַפְשִׁי לֵאלֹהִים לְאֵל חָי:
לִבִּי וּבְשָׂרִי יְרַנְּנוּ אֶל אֵל־חָי:
אֵל אֶחָד בְּרָאַנִי, וְאָמַר חַי אָנִי
כִּי לֹא יִרְאַנִי הָאָדָם וָחָי.

צָמְאָה נַפְשִׁי לֵאלֹהִים לְאֵל חָי
לִבִּי וּבְשָׂרִי יְרַנְּנוּ אֶל אֵל־חָי.

בָּרָא כֹל בְּחָכְמָה, בְּעֵצָה וּבִמְזִמָּה
מְאֹד נֶעְלָמָה מֵעֵינֵי כָל חָי.
רָם עַל כֹּל כְּבוֹדוֹ, כָּל פֶּה יְחַוֶּה הוֹדוֹ
בָּרוּךְ אֲשֶׁר בְּיָדוֹ נֶפֶשׁ כָּל חָי.

צָמְאָה נַפְשִׁי לֵאלֹהִים לְאֵל חָי
לִבִּי וּבְשָׂרִי יְרַנְּנוּ אֶל אֵל־חָי.

הִבְדִּיל נִינֵי תָם, חֻקִּים לְהוֹרוֹתָם
אֲשֶׁר יַעֲשֶׂה אוֹתָם הָאָדָם וָחָי.
מִי זֶה יִצְטַדָּק, נִמְשַׁל לְאָבָק דָּק
אֱמֶת, כִּי לֹא יִצְדַּק לְפָנֶיךָ כָּל חָי.

צָמְאָה נַפְשִׁי לֵאלֹהִים לְאֵל חָי
לִבִּי וּבְשָׂרִי יְרַנְּנוּ אֶל אֵל־חָי.

BIUR TEFILLA • ביאור תפילה

צָמְאָה נַפְשִׁי – *My soul thirsts.* Aside from its opening line, the first letter of every stanza spells out the name of Rabbi Avraham ibn Ezra, the famous Spanish exegete and poet whose varied interests extended to mathematics and astronomy in the twelfth century.

The first line, based on *Tehillim* 42:3, sets the stage for a focal point of religious life in general and Shabbat in particular. We all long to be touched, we all long for connection. The poet expresses that search in terms of a thirst that yearns to be quenched.

In the heart, the inclination is like a viper's poison,
How then can we return, and be like flesh that lives?
Those who have gone astray, if they wished,
could turn from their way,
Before they go to their rest in the place destined
for all that lives.

My soul thirsts for God, the living God
My heart and flesh will sing joyfully
mto the living God.

For everything, I shall thank You, every mouth
shall declare Your oneness,
You who open Your hand and satisfy all that lives.
Recall the love of ancient times, and revive those
who slumber,
Bring near the days when the Messiah shall live.

My soul thirsts for God, the living God
My heart and flesh will sing joyfully
to the living God.

See who is the true mistress,[B] when the handmaid says,
"No, your son is dead while my son lives."
I will bow face down and spread my hands toward you,
When I open my mouth to say: "The soul of all that lives."

My soul thirsts for God, the living God
My heart and flesh will sing joyfully
to the living God.

---

is Sarah, the handmaid is Hagar, the mother of Yishmael, and the speech she gives is based upon that of the case of the two mothers who came before King Shlomo (*Melakhim* I 20:31).

בְּלֵב יֵצֶר חָשׁוּב כִּדְמוּת חֲמַת עַכְשׁוּב
וְאֵיכָכָה יָשׁוּב הַבָּשָׂר הֶחָי.
נְסוֹגִים אִם אָבוּ, וּמִדַּרְכָּם שָׁבוּ
טֶרֶם יִשְׁכָּבוּ בֵּית מוֹעֵד לְכָל חָי.

צָמְאָה נַפְשִׁי לֵאלֹהִים לְאֵל חָי
לִבִּי וּבְשָׂרִי יְרַנְּנוּ אֶל אֵל־חָי.

עַל כֹּל אֲהוֹדֶךָ, כָּל פֶּה תְּיַחֲדֶךָ
פּוֹתֵחַ אֶת יָדֶךָ וּמַשְׂבִּיעַ לְכָל חָי.
זְכֹר אַהֲבַת קְדוּמִים, וְהַחֲיֵה נִרְדָּמִים
וְקָרֵב הַיָּמִים אֲשֶׁר בֶּן יִשַׁי חָי.

צָמְאָה נַפְשִׁי לֵאלֹהִים לְאֵל חָי
לִבִּי וּבְשָׂרִי יְרַנְּנוּ אֶל אֵל־חָי.

רְאֵה לִגְבֶרֶת אֱמֶת,[ב] שִׁפְחָה נוֹאֶמֶת
לֹא כִי, בְּנֵךְ הַמֵּת וּבְנִי הֶחָי.
אֶקֹּד עַל אַפִּי, וְאֶפְרֹשׂ לְךָ כַּפִּי
עֵת אֶפְתַּח פִּי בְּנִשְׁמַת כָּל חָי.

צָמְאָה נַפְשִׁי לֵאלֹהִים לְאֵל חָי
לִבִּי וּבְשָׂרִי יְרַנְּנוּ אֶל אֵל־חָי.

BIUR TEFILLA • ביאור תפילה

רְאֵה לִגְבֶרֶת אֱמֶת – *See who is the true mistress*... The references in this stanza may be a polemic against the Islamic world where Ibn Ezra first lived. The true mistress

צוּר מִשֶּׁלּוֹ The Rock from whom we have eaten: Bless Him, my faithful friends;
we have sufficed, we have left over, just as the LORD said.

He feeds His world – our Shepherd, our Father,
we have eaten of His bread, His wine we have drunk.
So let us thank His name, let us praise Him with our mouths,
saying, singing: None is holy like the LORD.
The Rock from whom we have eaten: Bless Him, my faithful friends;
we have sufficed, we have left over, just as the LORD said.

With song and sound of thanks, we shall bless our God,
for the gift He gave our fathers: A lovely land.
With food and sustenance He has satisfied our souls.
His kindness overwhelms us: True is the LORD.
The Rock from whom we have eaten: Bless Him, my faithful friends;
we have sufficed, we have left over, just as the LORD said.

Have compassion in Your love for Your people, our Rock,
for Zion, Your home of glory, Temple of our splendor.
The son of David Your servant: may he come and redeem us,
breath of our life, anointed of the LORD.
The Rock from whom we have eaten: Bless Him, my faithful friends;
we have sufficed, we have left over, just as the LORD said.

May the Temple be rebuilt, Zion's city full again;
there we will sing a new song as we go up in joy,
to the Compassionate, the Holy One – may He be blessed and raised on high –
with a full cup of wine, sign of the blessing of the LORD.
The Rock from whom we have eaten: Bless Him, my faithful friends;
we have sufficed, we have left over, just as the LORD said.

Birkat HaMazon can be found on page 976.

---

themes of first three blessings of *Birkat HaMazon*. (See if you can find the language in each that connects them. *Birkat HaMazon* can be found on page 981). The final stanza's reference to a cup of wine alludes to the custom of saying *Birkat HaMazon* over wine which is drunk at the conclusion of the blessing.

The opening is apparently based upon a midrash (*Bereshit Raba* 43:7) in which Avraham, the paradigm of *ḥesed* (kindness) to others is said to have offered food and drink to passersby. At the conclusion of the meal he instructed them to say a blessing of thanks and they inquired to whom it should be directed, whereupon he replied "Bless the God of the world, whose food (מִשֶּׁלּוֹ) we have eaten." In other words, the food we eat is not ours, no matter how hard we worked for it, prepared it, or shared it with others. Rather, everything comes from Hashem, "the Rock from whom we have eaten."

צוּר מִשֶּׁלּוֹ אָכַלְנוּ[ב]   בָּרְכוּ אֱמוּנַי
שָׂבַעְנוּ וְהוֹתַרְנוּ   כִּדְבַר יהוה.

הַזָּן אֶת עוֹלָמוֹ   רוֹעֵנוּ אָבִינוּ
אָכַלְנוּ אֶת לַחְמוֹ   וְיֵינוֹ שָׁתִינוּ
עַל כֵּן נוֹדֶה לִשְׁמוֹ   וּנְהַלְּלוֹ בְּפִינוּ
אָמַרְנוּ וְעָנִינוּ   אֵין קָדוֹשׁ כַּיהוה.
צוּר מִשֶּׁלּוֹ אָכַלְנוּ, בָּרְכוּ אֱמוּנַי, שָׂבַעְנוּ וְהוֹתַרְנוּ כִּדְבַר יהוה.

בְּשִׁיר וְקוֹל תּוֹדָה   נְבָרֵךְ אֱלֹהֵינוּ
עַל אֶרֶץ חֶמְדָּה   שֶׁהִנְחִיל לַאֲבוֹתֵינוּ
מָזוֹן וְצֵידָה   הִשְׂבִּיעַ לְנַפְשֵׁנוּ
חַסְדּוֹ גָּבַר עָלֵינוּ   וֶאֱמֶת יהוה.
צוּר מִשֶּׁלּוֹ אָכַלְנוּ, בָּרְכוּ אֱמוּנַי, שָׂבַעְנוּ וְהוֹתַרְנוּ כִּדְבַר יהוה.

רַחֵם בְּחַסְדֶּךָ   עַל עַמְּךָ צוּרֵנוּ
עַל צִיּוֹן מִשְׁכַּן כְּבוֹדֶךָ   זְבוּל בֵּית תִּפְאַרְתֵּנוּ
בֶּן דָּוִד עַבְדֶּךָ   יָבוֹא וְיִגְאָלֵנוּ
רוּחַ אַפֵּינוּ   מְשִׁיחַ יהוה.
צוּר מִשֶּׁלּוֹ אָכַלְנוּ, בָּרְכוּ אֱמוּנַי, שָׂבַעְנוּ וְהוֹתַרְנוּ כִּדְבַר יהוה.

יִבָּנֶה הַמִּקְדָּשׁ   עִיר צִיּוֹן תְּמַלֵּא
וְשָׁם נָשִׁיר שִׁיר חָדָשׁ   וּבִרְנָנָה נַעֲלֶה
הָרַחֲמָן הַנִּקְדָּשׁ   יִתְבָּרַךְ וְיִתְעַלֶּה
עַל כּוֹס יַיִן מָלֵא   כְּבִרְכַּת יהוה.
צוּר מִשֶּׁלּוֹ אָכַלְנוּ, בָּרְכוּ אֱמוּנַי, שָׂבַעְנוּ וְהוֹתַרְנוּ כִּדְבַר יהוה.

ברכת המזון *can be found on page 977.*

BIUR TEFILLA • ביאור תפילה

צוּר מִשֶּׁלּוֹ אָכַלְנוּ – *The Rock from whom we have eaten.* This song is traditionally the last one sung for the evening as it was apparently intended as a prelude to *Birkat HaMazon*, the blessing said at the conclusion of the meal. The first three stanzas reflect the

A PSALM BEFORE VERSES OF PRAISE

מִזְמוֹר שִׁיר A psalm of David. A song for the dedication of the House. I will exalt You, Lord, for You have lifted me up, and not let my enemies rejoice over me. Lord, my God, I cried to You for help and You healed me. Lord, You lifted my soul from the grave; You spared me from going down to the pit. Sing to the Lord, you His devoted ones, and give thanks to His holy name. For His anger is for a moment, but His favor for a lifetime. At night there may be weeping, but in the morning there is joy. When I felt secure, I said, "I shall never be shaken." Lord, when You favored me, You made me stand firm as a mountain, but when You hid Your face, I was terrified. To You, Lord, I called; I pleaded with my Lord: "What gain would there be if I died and went down to the grave? Can dust thank You? Can it declare Your truth? Hear, Lord, and be gracious to me; Lord, be my help." You have turned my sorrow into dancing. ▸ You have removed my sackcloth and clothed me with joy, so that my soul may sing to You and not be silent. Lord my God, for ever will I thank You. *Ps. 30*

MOURNER'S KADDISH

The following prayer, said by mourners, requires the presence of a minyan.
A transliteration can be found on page 1141.

Mourner: יִתְגַּדַּל Magnified and sanctified may His great name be,
in the world He created by His will.
May He establish His kingdom in your lifetime and in your days,
and in the lifetime of all the house of Israel,
swiftly and soon – and say: Amen.

All: May His great name be blessed for ever and all time.

Mourner: Blessed and praised, glorified and exalted,
raised and honored, uplifted and lauded
be the name of the Holy One, blessed be He,
beyond any blessing, song, praise and consolation
uttered in the world – and say: Amen.

May there be great peace from heaven,
and life for us and all Israel – and say: Amen.

Bow, take three steps back, as if taking leave of the Divine Presence,
then bow, first left, then right, then center, while saying:

May He who makes peace in His high places,
make peace for us and all Israel – and say: Amen.

מזמור לפני פסוקי דזמרה

מִזְמוֹר שִׁיר־חֲנֻכַּת הַבַּיִת לְדָוִד: אֲרוֹמִמְךָ יהוה כִּי דִלִּיתָנִי, וְלֹא־שִׂמַּחְתָּ תהלים ל
אֹיְבַי לִי: יהוה אֱלֹהָי, שִׁוַּעְתִּי אֵלֶיךָ וַתִּרְפָּאֵנִי: יהוה, הֶעֱלִיתָ מִן־שְׁאוֹל
נַפְשִׁי, חִיִּיתַנִי מִיָּרְדִי־בוֹר: זַמְּרוּ לַיהוה חֲסִידָיו, וְהוֹדוּ לְזֵכֶר קָדְשׁוֹ: כִּי
רֶגַע בְּאַפּוֹ, חַיִּים בִּרְצוֹנוֹ, בָּעֶרֶב יָלִין בֶּכִי וְלַבֹּקֶר רִנָּה: וַאֲנִי אָמַרְתִּי
בְשַׁלְוִי, בַּל־אֶמּוֹט לְעוֹלָם: יהוה, בִּרְצוֹנְךָ הֶעֱמַדְתָּה לְהַרְרִי עֹז, הִסְתַּרְתָּ
פָנֶיךָ הָיִיתִי נִבְהָל: אֵלֶיךָ יהוה אֶקְרָא, וְאֶל־אֲדֹנָי אֶתְחַנָּן: מַה־בֶּצַע
בְּדָמִי, בְּרִדְתִּי אֶל שָׁחַת, הֲיוֹדְךָ עָפָר, הֲיַגִּיד אֲמִתֶּךָ: שְׁמַע־יהוה וְחָנֵּנִי,
יהוה הֱיֵה־עֹזֵר לִי: ◂ הָפַכְתָּ מִסְפְּדִי לְמָחוֹל לִי, פִּתַּחְתָּ שַׂקִּי, וַתְּאַזְּרֵנִי
שִׂמְחָה: לְמַעַן יְזַמֶּרְךָ כָבוֹד וְלֹא יִדֹּם, יהוה אֱלֹהַי, לְעוֹלָם אוֹדֶךָּ:

קדיש יתום

The following prayer, said by mourners, requires the presence of a מנין.
A transliteration can be found on page 1141.

אבל: יִתְגַּדַּל וְיִתְקַדַּשׁ שְׁמֵהּ רַבָּא (קהל: אָמֵן)
בְּעָלְמָא דִּי בְרָא כִרְעוּתֵהּ וְיַמְלִיךְ מַלְכוּתֵהּ
בְּחַיֵּיכוֹן וּבְיוֹמֵיכוֹן וּבְחַיֵּי דְכָל בֵּית יִשְׂרָאֵל
בַּעֲגָלָא וּבִזְמַן קָרִיב, וְאִמְרוּ אָמֵן. (קהל: אָמֵן)

קהל ואבל: יְהֵא שְׁמֵהּ רַבָּא מְבָרַךְ לְעָלַם וּלְעָלְמֵי עָלְמַיָּא.

אבל: יִתְבָּרַךְ וְיִשְׁתַּבַּח וְיִתְפָּאַר וְיִתְרוֹמַם וְיִתְנַשֵּׂא
וְיִתְהַדָּר וְיִתְעַלֶּה וְיִתְהַלָּל שְׁמֵהּ דְּקֻדְשָׁא בְּרִיךְ הוּא (קהל: בְּרִיךְ הוּא)
לְעֵלָּא מִן כָּל בִּרְכָתָא וְשִׁירָתָא, תֻּשְׁבְּחָתָא וְנֶחֱמָתָא
דַּאֲמִירָן בְּעָלְמָא, וְאִמְרוּ אָמֵן. (קהל: אָמֵן)

יְהֵא שְׁלָמָא רַבָּא מִן שְׁמַיָּא
וְחַיִּים, עָלֵינוּ וְעַל כָּל יִשְׂרָאֵל, וְאִמְרוּ אָמֵן. (קהל: אָמֵן)

Bow, take three steps back, as if taking leave of the Divine Presence,
then bow, first left, then right, then center, while saying:

עֹשֶׂה שָׁלוֹם בִּמְרוֹמָיו
הוּא יַעֲשֶׂה שָׁלוֹם עָלֵינוּ וְעַל כָּל יִשְׂרָאֵל, וְאִמְרוּ אָמֵן. (קהל: אָמֵן)

PESUKEI DEZIMRA

It is the general custom to stand for this blessing.
Some men also have a custom to hold onto the two front tzitziot of their tallit and kiss them upon conclusion of the prayer, at "songs of praise" (on the next page). From the beginning of this prayer to the end of the Amida, conversation is forbidden.

Some say:

I hereby prepare my mouth to thank, praise and laud my Creator, for the sake of the unification of the Holy One, blessed be He, and His Divine Presence, through that which is hidden and concealed, in the name of all Israel.

BLESSED IS HE WHO SPOKE

and the world came into being, blessed is He.
Blessed is He who creates the universe.
Blessed is He who speaks and acts.
Blessed is He who decrees and fulfills.
Blessed is He who shows compassion to the earth.
Blessed is He who shows compassion to all creatures.
Blessed is He who gives a good reward
to those who fear Him.
Blessed is He who lives for ever and exists to eternity.
Blessed is He who redeems and saves.
Blessed is His name.

HILKHOT TEFILLA • הלכות תפילה

The rationale for standing for this prayer is not clear (*Mishna Berura* 51:1). It may be because as the opening blessing of this section of the siddur (*Pesukei DeZimra*) it parallels the closing blessing of *Yishtabaḥ* (page 577) where the custom is also to stand for other reasons. It could also be related to the tradition that the prayer was found on a note that fell from Heaven (Baḥ 53) and is thus considered so holy as to merit standing for its recitation. Similarly, the holding of the *tzitzit* may be tied to this association of holiness, for there are various Kabbalistic connections between the number of knots and/or strings with Kabbalistic understandings of the ways of Heaven and the names of God (e.g. Responsa *Zikhron Yehuda* 9). At the very least, one sees that the prayer itself is not "just" an introductory blessing, but the portal to a different awareness. Prepare yourself.

פסוקי דזמרה

It is the general custom to stand for this blessing.
Some men also have a custom to hold onto the two front ציציות *of their* טלית *and kiss them upon conclusion of the prayer, at* בַּתִּשְׁבָּחוֹת *(on the next page). From the beginning of this prayer to the end of the* עמידה*, conversation is forbidden.*

Some say:

הֲרֵינִי מְזַמֵּן אֶת פִּי לְהוֹדוֹת וּלְהַלֵּל וּלְשַׁבֵּחַ אֶת בּוֹרְאִי, לְשֵׁם יִחוּד קֻדְשָׁא בְּרִיךְ הוּא וּשְׁכִינְתֵּהּ עַל יְדֵי הַהוּא טָמִיר וְנֶעְלָם בְּשֵׁם כָּל יִשְׂרָאֵל.

בָּרוּךְ שֶׁאָמַר
וְהָיָה הָעוֹלָם, בָּרוּךְ הוּא.
בָּרוּךְ עוֹשֶׂה בְרֵאשִׁית
בָּרוּךְ אוֹמֵר וְעוֹשֶׂה
בָּרוּךְ גּוֹזֵר וּמְקַיֵּם
בָּרוּךְ מְרַחֵם עַל הָאָרֶץ
בָּרוּךְ מְרַחֵם עַל הַבְּרִיּוֹת
בָּרוּךְ מְשַׁלֵּם שָׂכָר טוֹב לִירֵאָיו
בָּרוּךְ חַי לָעַד וְקַיָּם לָנֶצַח
בָּרוּךְ פּוֹדֶה וּמַצִּיל
בָּרוּךְ שְׁמוֹ

For the parts of Pesukei Dezimra that are the same as on weekdays, commentary can be found on pages 65–95.

ANI TEFILLA • אני תפילה

"The more you appreciate your life the more your life appreciates." (Rabbi David Aaron)

Blessed are You, Lord our God, King of the Universe,
God, compassionate Father, extolled by the mouth of His people,
praised and glorified by the tongue of His devoted ones
and those who serve Him.
With the songs of Your servant David
we will praise You, O Lord our God.
With praises and psalms we will magnify and praise You, glorify You,
Speak Your name and proclaim Your kingship,
our King, our God, ▸ the only One, Giver of life to the worlds
the King whose great name is praised and glorified to all eternity.
Blessed are You, Lord, the King extolled with songs of praise.

הודו Thank the Lord, call on His name, make His acts known among the peoples. Sing to Him, make music to Him, tell of all His wonders. Glory in His holy name; let the hearts of those who seek the Lord rejoice. Search out the Lord and His strength; seek His presence at all times. Remember the wonders He has done, His miracles, and the judgments He pronounced. Descendants of Yisrael His servant, sons of Jacob His chosen ones: He is the Lord our God. His judgments are throughout the earth. Remember His covenant for ever, the word He commanded for a thousand generations. He made it with Abraham, vowed it to Isaac, and confirmed it to Jacob as a statute and to Israel as an everlasting covenant, saying, "To you I will give the land of Canaan as your allotted heritage." You were then small in number, few, strangers there, wandering from nation to nation, from one kingdom to another, but He let no man oppress them, and for their sake He rebuked kings: "Do not touch My anointed ones, and do My prophets no harm." Sing to the Lord, all the earth; proclaim His salvation daily. Declare His glory among the nations, His marvels among all the peoples. For great is the Lord and greatly to be praised; He is awesome beyond all heavenly powers. ▸ For all the gods of the peoples are mere idols; it was the Lord who made the heavens. *1 Chr. 16*

Before Him are majesty and splendor; there is strength and beauty in His holy place. Render to the Lord, families of the peoples, render to the Lord honor and might. Render to the Lord the glory

בָּרוּךְ אַתָּה יהוה אֱלֹהֵינוּ מֶלֶךְ הָעוֹלָם
הָאֵל הָאָב הָרַחֲמָן הַמְהֻלָּל בְּפִי עַמּוֹ
מְשֻׁבָּח וּמְפֹאָר בִּלְשׁוֹן חֲסִידָיו וַעֲבָדָיו
וּבְשִׁירֵי דָוִד עַבְדֶּךָ נְהַלֶּלְךָ יהוה אֱלֹהֵינוּ.
בִּשְׁבָחוֹת וּבִזְמִירוֹת, נְגַדֶּלְךָ וּנְשַׁבֵּחֲךָ וּנְפָאֶרְךָ
וְנַזְכִּיר שִׁמְךָ וְנַמְלִיכְךָ מַלְכֵּנוּ אֱלֹהֵינוּ, ◂ יָחִיד חֵי הָעוֹלָמִים
מֶלֶךְ, מְשֻׁבָּח וּמְפֹאָר עֲדֵי עַד שְׁמוֹ הַגָּדוֹל
בָּרוּךְ אַתָּה יהוה, מֶלֶךְ מְהֻלָּל בַּתִּשְׁבָּחוֹת.

דברי הימים א׳ טז

הוֹדוּ לַיהוה קִרְאוּ בִשְׁמוֹ, הוֹדִיעוּ בָעַמִּים עֲלִילֹתָיו: שִׁירוּ לוֹ, זַמְּרוּ־לוֹ, שִׂיחוּ בְּכָל־נִפְלְאוֹתָיו: הִתְהַלְלוּ בְּשֵׁם קָדְשׁוֹ, יִשְׂמַח לֵב מְבַקְשֵׁי יהוה: דִּרְשׁוּ יהוה וְעֻזּוֹ, בַּקְּשׁוּ פָנָיו תָּמִיד: זִכְרוּ נִפְלְאֹתָיו אֲשֶׁר עָשָׂה, מֹפְתָיו וּמִשְׁפְּטֵי־פִיהוּ: זֶרַע יִשְׂרָאֵל עַבְדּוֹ, בְּנֵי יַעֲקֹב בְּחִירָיו: הוּא יהוה אֱלֹהֵינוּ בְּכָל־הָאָרֶץ מִשְׁפָּטָיו: זִכְרוּ לְעוֹלָם בְּרִיתוֹ, דָּבָר צִוָּה לְאֶלֶף דּוֹר: אֲשֶׁר כָּרַת אֶת־אַבְרָהָם, וּשְׁבוּעָתוֹ לְיִצְחָק: וַיַּעֲמִידֶהָ לְיַעֲקֹב לְחֹק, לְיִשְׂרָאֵל בְּרִית עוֹלָם: לֵאמֹר, לְךָ אֶתֵּן אֶרֶץ־כְּנָעַן, חֶבֶל נַחֲלַתְכֶם: בִּהְיוֹתְכֶם מְתֵי מִסְפָּר, כִּמְעַט וְגָרִים בָּהּ: וַיִּתְהַלְּכוּ מִגּוֹי אֶל־גּוֹי, וּמִמַּמְלָכָה אֶל־עַם אַחֵר: לֹא־הִנִּיחַ לְאִישׁ לְעָשְׁקָם, וַיּוֹכַח עֲלֵיהֶם מְלָכִים: אַל־תִּגְּעוּ בִּמְשִׁיחָי, וּבִנְבִיאַי אַל־תָּרֵעוּ: שִׁירוּ לַיהוה כָּל־הָאָרֶץ, בַּשְּׂרוּ מִיּוֹם־אֶל־יוֹם יְשׁוּעָתוֹ: סַפְּרוּ בַגּוֹיִם אֶת־כְּבוֹדוֹ, בְּכָל־הָעַמִּים נִפְלְאֹתָיו: כִּי גָדוֹל יהוה וּמְהֻלָּל מְאֹד, וְנוֹרָא הוּא עַל־כָּל־אֱלֹהִים: ◂ כִּי כָּל־אֱלֹהֵי הָעַמִּים אֱלִילִים, וַיהוה שָׁמַיִם עָשָׂה:

הוֹד וְהָדָר לְפָנָיו, עֹז וְחֶדְוָה בִּמְקֹמוֹ: הָבוּ לַיהוה מִשְׁפְּחוֹת עַמִּים, הָבוּ לַיהוה כָּבוֹד וָעֹז: הָבוּ לַיהוה כְּבוֹד שְׁמוֹ, שְׂאוּ מִנְחָה

due to His name; bring an offering and come before Him; bow down to the Lord in the splendor of holiness. Tremble before Him, all the earth; the world stands firm, it will not be shaken. Let the heavens rejoice and the earth be glad; let them declare among the nations, "The Lord is King." Let the sea roar, and all that is in it; let the fields be jubilant, and all they contain. Then the trees of the forest will sing for joy before the Lord, for He is coming to judge the earth. Thank the Lord for He is good; His loving-kindness is for ever. Say: "Save us, God of our salvation; gather us and rescue us from the nations, to acknowledge Your holy name and glory in Your praise. Blessed is the Lord, God of Israel, from this world to eternity." And let all the people say "Amen" and "Praise the Lord."

▸ Exalt the Lord our God and bow before His footstool: He is *Ps. 99*
holy. Exalt the Lord our God and bow at His holy mountain; for
holy is the Lord our God.

He is compassionate. He forgives iniquity and does not destroy. *Ps. 78*
Repeatedly He suppresses His anger, not rousing His full wrath. You, *Ps. 40*
Lord: do not withhold Your compassion from me. May Your loving-
kindness and truth always guard me. Remember, Lord, Your acts of *Ps. 25*
compassion and love, for they have existed for ever. Ascribe power *Ps. 68*
to God, whose majesty is over Israel and whose might is in the skies.
You are awesome, God, in Your holy places. It is the God of Israel
who gives might and strength to the people, may God be blessed.
God of retribution, Lord, God of retribution, appear. Arise, Judge of *Ps. 94*
the earth, to repay the arrogant their just deserts. Salvation belongs *Ps. 3*
to the Lord; may Your blessing rest upon Your people, Selah! ▸ The *Ps. 46*
Lord of hosts is with us, the God of Jacob is our stronghold, Selah!
Lord of hosts, happy is the one who trusts in You. Lord, save! May *Ps. 84*
the King answer us on the day we call.

Save Your people and bless Your heritage; tend them and carry *Ps. 28*
them for ever. Our soul longs for the Lord; He is our Help and Shield. *Ps. 33*
For in Him our hearts rejoice, for in His holy name we have trusted.
May Your loving-kindness, Lord, be upon us, as we have put our hope
in You. Show us, Lord, Your loving-kindness and grant us Your salva- *Ps. 85*
tion. Arise, help us and redeem us for the sake of Your love. I am the *Ps. 44*

וּבֹאוּ לְפָנָיו, הִשְׁתַּחֲווּ לַיהוה בְּהַדְרַת־קֹדֶשׁ: חִילוּ מִלְּפָנָיו כָּל־
הָאָרֶץ, אַף־תִּכּוֹן תֵּבֵל בַּל־תִּמּוֹט: יִשְׂמְחוּ הַשָּׁמַיִם וְתָגֵל הָאָרֶץ,
וְיֹאמְרוּ בַגּוֹיִם יהוה מָלָךְ: יִרְעַם הַיָּם וּמְלוֹאוֹ, יַעֲלֹץ הַשָּׂדֶה וְכָל־
אֲשֶׁר־בּוֹ: אָז יְרַנְּנוּ עֲצֵי הַיָּעַר, מִלִּפְנֵי יהוה, כִּי־בָא לִשְׁפּוֹט אֶת־
הָאָרֶץ: הוֹדוּ לַיהוה כִּי טוֹב, כִּי לְעוֹלָם חַסְדּוֹ: וְאִמְרוּ, הוֹשִׁיעֵנוּ
אֱלֹהֵי יִשְׁעֵנוּ, וְקַבְּצֵנוּ וְהַצִּילֵנוּ מִן־הַגּוֹיִם, לְהֹדוֹת לְשֵׁם קָדְשֶׁךָ,
לְהִשְׁתַּבֵּחַ בִּתְהִלָּתֶךָ: בָּרוּךְ יהוה אֱלֹהֵי יִשְׂרָאֵל מִן־הָעוֹלָם
וְעַד־הָעֹלָם, וַיֹּאמְרוּ כָל־הָעָם אָמֵן, וְהַלֵּל לַיהוה:

‹ רוֹמְמוּ יהוה אֱלֹהֵינוּ וְהִשְׁתַּחֲווּ לַהֲדֹם רַגְלָיו, קָדוֹשׁ הוּא: תהלים צט
רוֹמְמוּ יהוה אֱלֹהֵינוּ וְהִשְׁתַּחֲווּ לְהַר קָדְשׁוֹ, כִּי־קָדוֹשׁ יהוה אֱלֹהֵינוּ:

וְהוּא רַחוּם, יְכַפֵּר עָוֹן וְלֹא־יַשְׁחִית, וְהִרְבָּה לְהָשִׁיב אַפּוֹ, תהלים עח
וְלֹא־יָעִיר כָּל־חֲמָתוֹ: אַתָּה יהוה לֹא־תִכְלָא רַחֲמֶיךָ מִמֶּנִּי, חַסְדְּךָ תהלים מ
וַאֲמִתְּךָ תָּמִיד יִצְּרוּנִי: זְכֹר־רַחֲמֶיךָ יהוה וַחֲסָדֶיךָ, כִּי מֵעוֹלָם תהלים כה
הֵמָּה: תְּנוּ עֹז לֵאלֹהִים, עַל־יִשְׂרָאֵל גַּאֲוָתוֹ, וְעֻזּוֹ בַּשְּׁחָקִים: תהלים סח
נוֹרָא אֱלֹהִים מִמִּקְדָּשֶׁיךָ, אֵל יִשְׂרָאֵל הוּא נֹתֵן עֹז וְתַעֲצֻמוֹת
לָעָם, בָּרוּךְ אֱלֹהִים: אֵל־נְקָמוֹת יהוה, אֵל נְקָמוֹת הוֹפִיעַ: הִנָּשֵׂא תהלים צד
שֹׁפֵט הָאָרֶץ, הָשֵׁב גְּמוּל עַל־גֵּאִים: לַיהוה הַיְשׁוּעָה, עַל־עַמְּךָ תהלים ג
בִרְכָתֶךָ סֶּלָה: ‹ יהוה צְבָאוֹת עִמָּנוּ, מִשְׂגָּב לָנוּ אֱלֹהֵי יַעֲקֹב תהלים מו
סֶלָה: יהוה צְבָאוֹת, אַשְׁרֵי אָדָם בֹּטֵחַ בָּךְ: יהוה הוֹשִׁיעָה, הַמֶּלֶךְ תהלים פד תהלים כ
יַעֲנֵנוּ בְיוֹם־קָרְאֵנוּ:

הוֹשִׁיעָה אֶת־עַמֶּךָ, וּבָרֵךְ אֶת־נַחֲלָתֶךָ, וּרְעֵם וְנַשְּׂאֵם עַד־ תהלים כח
הָעוֹלָם: נַפְשֵׁנוּ חִכְּתָה לַיהוה, עֶזְרֵנוּ וּמָגִנֵּנוּ הוּא: כִּי־בוֹ יִשְׂמַח תהלים לג
לִבֵּנוּ, כִּי בְשֵׁם קָדְשׁוֹ בָטָחְנוּ: יְהִי־חַסְדְּךָ יהוה עָלֵינוּ, כַּאֲשֶׁר
יִחַלְנוּ לָךְ: הַרְאֵנוּ יהוה חַסְדֶּךָ, וְיֶשְׁעֲךָ תִּתֶּן־לָנוּ: קוּמָה עֶזְרָתָה תהלים פה תהלים מד
לָּנוּ, וּפְדֵנוּ לְמַעַן חַסְדֶּךָ: אָנֹכִי יהוה אֱלֹהֶיךָ הַמַּעַלְךָ מֵאֶרֶץ תהלים פא

LORD your God who brought you up from the land of Egypt: open
your mouth wide and I will fill it. Happy is the people for whom this Ps. 144
is so; happy is the people whose God the LORD. ▸ As for me, I trust in Ps. 13
Your loving-kindness; my heart rejoices in Your salvation. I will sing to
the LORD for He has been good to me.

לַמְנַצֵּחַ For the conductor of music. A psalm of David. The heavens Ps. 19
declare the glory of God; the skies proclaim the work of His hands.[1]
Day to day they pour forth speech; night to night they communicate

---

windows and said, "Stay here for an orbit," about 90 minutes. He gave us that pause because on a flight, you're so busy that unless somebody forces you to take a moment like that, you don't get one. I'm so grateful for that. (Astronaut Tracy Caldwell Dyson)

Look around you. What are you taking for granted?

BIUR TEFILLA • ביאור תפילה

לַמְנַצֵּחַ – *TEHILLIM 19.* This psalm essentially divides into two. The first half praises God and the wonders of creation; the second half praises the Torah and the desire to fulfill it. Described here, then, are "the sources from which one could come to recognize God and worship Him." From nature, one can discern the existence of God, from the Torah one can discern what one should do with that knowledge (Rabbi S. Hirsch). From nature one learns the what, from Torah one learns the why. From the history of mankind one learns over and over again that science is no guarantor of a moral or religious life, and from Torah one cannot learn everything there is to know about how the natural world operates. One needs both to live a balanced life.

IYUN TEFILLA • עיון תפילה

הַשָּׁמַיִם מְסַפְּרִים כְּבוֹד־אֵל, וּמַעֲשֵׂה יָדָיו מַגִּיד הָרָקִיעַ – *The heavens declare the glory of God; the skies proclaim the work of His hands.* One possible reading of this passage is that it is man who is the one who looks at the universe and tells the story. Alternatively, it is the sky, the sun and the moon and the way that they keep to their appointed courses, the working of nature within its boundaries that tells its story all by itself – it is the story told silently without any words. The glory of Hashem is visible, perceivable yet indescribable, like a work of art drawn upon man's heart, a feeling, a thought, that words cannot describe (Radak). The word "*lehagid*," "to declare," is usually used to convey something which someone did not know before, to inform.

What aspect of nature have you never really looked at before?

Look at it now in your mind's eye. Hear its story.

The **IYUN TEFILLA** *continues on page 527.*

מִצְרָיִם, הַרְחֶב־פִּיךָ וַאֲמַלְאֵהוּ: אַשְׁרֵי הָעָם שֶׁכָּכָה לּוֹ, אַשְׁרֵי תהלים קמד
הָעָם שֶׁיהוה אֱלֹהָיו: ‹ וַאֲנִי בְּחַסְדְּךָ בָטַחְתִּי, יָגֵל לִבִּי בִּישׁוּעָתֶךָ, תהלים יג
אָשִׁירָה לַיהוה, כִּי גָמַל עָלָי:

לַמְנַצֵּחַ מִזְמוֹר לְדָוִד: הַשָּׁמַיִם מְסַפְּרִים כְּבוֹד־אֵל, וּמַעֲשֵׂה יָדָיו תהלים יט
מַגִּיד הָרָקִיעַ: ע יוֹם לְיוֹם יַבִּיעַ אֹמֶר, וְלַיְלָה לְּלַיְלָה יְחַוֶּה־דָּעַת: ע

AN INTRODUCTION TO THE ADDITIONAL TEHILLIM OF SHABBAT MORNING

On Shabbat and Yom Tov additional selections of psalms (*Tehillim*) are added to the morning service. There is more time to reflect, more mental space to allow for the messages we want to permeate and penetrate, fewer distractions to drag us away from considering life's priorities.

There are seven new psalms introduced here (in addition to Psalms 92 and 93 which we recited for the first time last evening), one apparently for each day of the week or perhaps, too, an echo of the seven blessings said beneath the marriage canopy at a wedding (Ya'avetz). Unlike the *Tehillim* that were recited last night during Ma'ariv, or like others which will follow in the next section, these particular chapters are not in sequential order as they appear in the book of *Tehillim*. They may instead have some thematic order which includes topics such as Shabbat and the giving of the Torah (which tradition says took place on Shabbat) (*Levush*) or, as another observed, there may be three themes: "the memorial to Creation, the memorial to the exodus from Egypt, and the anticipation of the "world-wide Sabbath to come" (Munk). How these may tie together and which may resonate most will vary with each of us – and sometimes will vary from one Shabbat to the next.

The important thing is that they be said slowly, qualitatively, in a pleasant voice and cadence (*Or Zarua*), else we will have said many words but with little chance to be impacted by them.

ANI TEFILLA · אני תפילה

The first time I glimpsed Earth from space, I stared long and hard… No adjective can convey the feeling of knowing I was one of a small fraction of humans to see it with my own eyes: the richness of the changing colors, the glow of the atmosphere, the opalescence of the sun glinting off the water. It was overwhelming. You have these emotions going through your body because you've worked a lifetime to be there.

It wasn't until the middle of my first flight – day five or six – when my commander brought the rookies onto the flight deck, and asked, "Can you ask Mission Control to turn off all the station's external lights so we can see the outside?" He stuck us in front of the

knowledge.[I] There is no speech, there are no words, their voice is not heard.[B] Yet their music carries throughout the earth, their words to the end of the world. In them He has set a tent for the sun. It emerges like a groom from his marriage chamber, rejoicing like a champion about to run a race. It rises at one end of the heaven and makes its circuit to the other: nothing is hidden from its heat. The LORD's Torah is perfect, refreshing the soul.[B] The LORD's testimony is faithful, making the simple wise. The LORD's precepts are just, gladdening the heart. The LORD's commandment is radiant, giving light to the eyes.[I] The fear of the LORD is pure, enduring for ever.[A] The LORD's judgments are true, altogether righteous.[I] More precious than gold, than much fine gold. They are sweeter than honey,[I] than honey from the comb. Your

---

longer it will stay with you and the more beneficial and satisfying it will be (Radak).

BIUR TEFILLA • ביאור תפילה

אֵין־אֹמֶר וְאֵין דְּבָרִים, בְּלִי נִשְׁמָע קוֹלָם – *There is no speech, there are no words, their voice is not heard.* The messages that nature sends us cannot always be put into words. Sometimes it's alright to just feel something and know it to be true without being able to articulate it. Shabbat can be that kind of day.

תּוֹרַת יהוה תְּמִימָה, מְשִׁיבַת נָפֶשׁ – *The LORD's Torah is perfect, refreshing the soul.* Torah generally refers not only to the Five Books of Moses but to the entire corpus of Jewish law. The Midrash finds a hint to this in the fact that the next verses contain five words each (corresponding to the five books of the Torah); furthermore, a total of six different categories of law (corresponding to the six divisions of the Oral Law, *Sidrei Mishna*) are mentioned, and Hashem's name is attached to each. The written law and the oral law all in essence have the same source and all can be "refreshing" if only one opens one's eyes to them, investing one's soul as well as one's mind.

How can you add to your knowledge of Judaism today?

ANI TEFILLA • אני תפילה

יִרְאַת יהוה טְהוֹרָה, עוֹמֶדֶת לָעַד – *The fear of the LORD is pure, enduring for ever.*

Imagine a tall building in the middle of a crowded area. Someone announces that the building is tilting and it is about to fall, thereby creating a huge panic as people run away to avoid being crushed. One lone person arrives on the scene and quickly realizes that the fault lay not with the structure of the building but with the eyesight of the person who first raised the concern. "Get him to a doctor," said the observer, "for he is clearly about to lose his sight altogether." And so it is with those who would claim that the Torah's laws need to be changed because the structure of the system is faulty. Such people do not realize that the structure is what has kept and will keep the building standing forever. (Ḥafetz Ḥayyim)

How can you change your perspective today?

אֵין־אֹמֶר וְאֵין דְּבָרִים, בְּלִי נִשְׁמָע קוֹלָם: בְּכָל־הָאָרֶץ יָצָא קַוָּם, וּבִקְצֵה תֵבֵל מִלֵּיהֶם, לַשֶּׁמֶשׁ שָׂם־אֹהֶל בָּהֶם: וְהוּא כְּחָתָן יֹצֵא מֵחֻפָּתוֹ, יָשִׂישׂ כְּגִבּוֹר לָרוּץ אֹרַח: מִקְצֵה הַשָּׁמַיִם מוֹצָאוֹ, וּתְקוּפָתוֹ עַל־קְצוֹתָם, וְאֵין נִסְתָּר מֵחַמָּתוֹ: תּוֹרַת יהוה תְּמִימָה, מְשִׁיבַת נָפֶשׁ, עֵדוּת יהוה נֶאֱמָנָה, מַחְכִּימַת פֶּתִי: פִּקּוּדֵי יהוה יְשָׁרִים, מְשַׂמְּחֵי־לֵב, מִצְוַת יהוה בָּרָה, מְאִירַת עֵינָיִם: יִרְאַת יהוה טְהוֹרָה, עוֹמֶדֶת לָעַד, מִשְׁפְּטֵי־יהוה אֱמֶת, צָדְקוּ יַחְדָּו: הַנֶּחֱמָדִים מִזָּהָב וּמִפַּז רָב, וּמְתוּקִים מִדְּבַשׁ וְנֹפֶת צוּפִים: גַּם־

IYUN TEFILLA • עיון תפילה

מִשְׁפְּטֵי־יהוה אֱמֶת, צָדְקוּ יַחְדָּו – *The Lord's judgments are true, altogether righteous.* The Torah's laws of morality go where secular laws dare not. The latter are often predicated on the notion of not interfering with other people's rights. Jewish law is predicated on the notion that one is responsible for other people's welfare. These are two very different views of the world and of social justice. What examples can you think of?

הַנֶּחֱמָדִים מִזָּהָב וּמִפַּז רָב, וּמְתוּקִים מִדְּבַשׁ – *More precious than gold, than much fine gold. They are sweeter than honey.* Material wealth can be stolen or lost whereas one's knowledge of Torah and one's heritage are forever in one's possession. One can give one's money away and be left with nothing, but knowledge can be shared without any loss and can even be enhanced. Money is sweet like honey to its owner but too much of it can make one ill, whereas wisdom, the more it is imbibed, the

יוֹם לְיוֹם יַבִּיעַ אֹמֶר, וְלַיְלָה לְּלַיְלָה יְחַוֶּה־דָּעַת – *Day to day they pour forth speech; night to night they communicate knowledge.* From a purely technical view, watch the globe from outer space via time lapse and see how one day turns into the next seamlessly. Alternatively, each day informs the next; days and nights can have a life of their own, almost animate. They share their beauty with the next day. Life is cumulative. Even as every day is a new creation, a fresh beginning, what we do or say today will inform our tomorrow. Viewed in this way, our Shabbat can inform the rest of our week.

מִצְוַת יהוה בָּרָה, מְאִירַת עֵינָיִם – *The Lord's commandment is radiant, giving light to the eyes.* Here lies the connection between the two sources of knowledge of God. Both the sun and the Torah provide light, both enable us to see through the dark, both provide a new way of taking in the life around us, the one in the natural sphere, the other in the moral sphere. Yet there are also differences: looking for a long time at the sun can make one blind; looking more at the Torah can enable one to keep seeing more.

servant, too, is careful of them, for in observing them there is great reward. Yet who can discern his errors? Cleanse me of hidden faults. Keep Your servant also from willful sins; let them not have dominion over me. Then shall I be blameless, and innocent of grave sin. ▸ May the words of my mouth and the meditation of my heart find favor before You, LORD, my Rock and my Redeemer.

לְדָוִד Of David. When he pretended to be insane before Abimelech, who drove him away, and he left. *Ps. 34*
I will bless the LORD at all times;
His praise will be always on my lips.
My soul will glory in the LORD;
let the lowly hear this and rejoice.
Magnify the LORD with me;
let us exalt His name together.
I sought the LORD, and He answered me;
He saved me from all my fears.
Those who look to Him are radiant;
Their faces are never downcast.
This poor man called, and the LORD heard;
He saved him from all his troubles.

IYUN TEFILLA • עיון תפילה

בְּכָל־עֵת – *At all times.* Everything and everyone was created at just the right point in history. Avraham could not have been born at the time of Adam or vice versa. Each of us is born at a particular time in human history to fulfill our unique role that no one before or after us could do (*Midrash Shoḥer Tov*). The challenge is for us is to discover what that role is. During the week it is sometimes hard to do so. Shabbat presents that opportunity.

What can you do this week to come closer to fulfilling or finding your unique role?

זֶה עָנִי קָרָא - *This poor man called.* The *Zohar* says the prayers of a poor person are more readily accepted than those of other people and that the prayers of others do not appear before God until those of the poor have been presented first. (*Me'am Lo'ez*) What is it about the prayer of the poor that takes precedence? David, King of Israel, calls himself a poor person here.

In what way was he so? Consider yourself poor. Now pray.

עַבְדְּךָ נִזְהָר בָּהֶם, בְּשָׁמְרָם עֵקֶב רָב: שְׁגִיאוֹת מִי־יָבִין, מִנִּסְתָּרוֹת נַקֵּנִי: גַּם מִזֵּדִים חֲשֹׂךְ עַבְדֶּךָ, אַל־יִמְשְׁלוּ־בִי אָז אֵיתָם, וְנִקֵּיתִי מִפֶּשַׁע רָב: • יִהְיוּ לְרָצוֹן אִמְרֵי־פִי וְהֶגְיוֹן לִבִּי לְפָנֶיךָ, יהוה, צוּרִי וְגֹאֲלִי:

לְדָוִד, בְּשַׁנּוֹתוֹ אֶת־טַעְמוֹ לִפְנֵי אֲבִימֶלֶךְ, וַיְגָרְשֵׁהוּ וַיֵּלַךְ: תהלים לד
אֲבָרְכָה אֶת־יהוה בְּכָל־עֵת, תָּמִיד תְּהִלָּתוֹ בְּפִי:
בַּיהוה תִּתְהַלֵּל נַפְשִׁי, יִשְׁמְעוּ עֲנָוִים וְיִשְׂמָחוּ:
גַּדְּלוּ לַיהוה אִתִּי, וּנְרוֹמְמָה שְׁמוֹ יַחְדָּו:
דָּרַשְׁתִּי אֶת־יהוה וְעָנָנִי, וּמִכָּל־מְגוּרוֹתַי הִצִּילָנִי:
הִבִּיטוּ אֵלָיו וְנָהָרוּ, וּפְנֵיהֶם אַל־יֶחְפָּרוּ:
זֶה עָנִי קָרָא, וַיהוה שָׁמֵעַ, וּמִכָּל־צָרוֹתָיו הוֹשִׁיעוֹ:

ANI TEFILLA • אני תפילה

Science is about explanation. Religion is about meaning. Science analyzes, religion integrates. Science breaks things down to their component parts. Religion binds people together in relationships of trust. Science tells us what is. Religion tells us what ought to be. Science describes. Religion beckons, summons, calls. Science sees objects. Religion speaks to us as subjects. (Rabbi J. Sacks)

BIUR TEFILLA • ביאור תפילה

לְדָוִד – *TEHILLIM 34*. The Bible (Shmuel I 21) relates that as David fled for his life from King Shaul, and while he prayed for deliverance, he found himself in the midst of the Pelishtim (Philistines) who thought they recognized him and also sought him harm. David feigned madness and was promptly released whereupon, according to tradition, he composed this psalm. Above all else, then, it is a testimony to the efficacy of prayer, even as each of us is required to be as creative as possible in first helping ourselves.

The psalm is one of those that is an alphabetical **acrostic**. Some say that one letter is missing; others say it really is there. (Can you find it?) Regardless, there are 22 verses, the same number as the letters in the Hebrew alphabet.

The LORD's angel encamps around those who fear Him,
and He rescues them.
Taste and see that the LORD is good;[B]
happy is the man who takes refuge in Him.
Fear the LORD, you His holy ones,
for those who fear Him lack nothing.[I]
Young lions may grow weak and hungry,
but those who seek the LORD
lack no good thing.
Come, my children,
listen to me;
I will teach you the fear of the LORD.
Who desires life,
loving each day to see good?
Then guard your tongue from evil
and your lips from speaking deceit.[I]

ANI TEFILLA • אני תפילה

Rabbi Eliyahu Meir Bloch, the head of the Telz yeshiva in Cleveland, once went to visit a potential donor who was very wealthy. "Explain something to me," said the man. "I really am lacking nothing. I have a house in New York and another in Florida and a summer home in California. I have my own small private jet, a yacht and numerous cars and yet there is one thing I am still missing – happiness. I'm just not happy. And yet, I see you, a person with limited means who travels around the country with your hand out for donations, and yet it seems to me from the look on your face that you are a happy man. Why the difference between us?" Rabbi Bloch answered: "You know that we are both Jews and both of us possess a pure soul that accompanies us all day. Yet we know that we also have a body and that body needs to be fed, needs to be given water in order to survive, else we would shrivel up and die. The same is true of the soul. It too needs to be nourished and fed and that is what I try to do by learning Torah and living a life of mitzvot. Your soul, too, craves attention. Yet you try to satisfy it with houses and cars and boats – material things."

That is why "lions," powerful people can still feel "hungry." The soul cannot be nourished with material things. But "those who seek Hashem" will not lack.

חֹנֶה מַלְאַךְ־יהוה סָבִיב לִירֵאָיו, וַיְחַלְּצֵם:
טַעֲמוּ וּרְאוּ כִּי־טוֹב יהוה, אַשְׁרֵי הַגֶּבֶר יֶחֱסֶה־בּוֹ:
יְראוּ אֶת־יהוה קְדֹשָׁיו, כִּי־אֵין מַחְסוֹר לִירֵאָיו:
כְּפִירִים רָשׁוּ וְרָעֵבוּ, וְדֹרְשֵׁי יהוה לֹא־יַחְסְרוּ כָל־טוֹב:
לְכוּ־בָנִים שִׁמְעוּ־לִי, יִרְאַת יהוה אֲלַמֶּדְכֶם:
מִי־הָאִישׁ הֶחָפֵץ חַיִּים, אֹהֵב יָמִים לִרְאוֹת טוֹב:
נְצֹר לְשׁוֹנְךָ מֵרָע, וּשְׂפָתֶיךָ מִדַּבֵּר מִרְמָה:

BIUR TEFILLA • ביאור תפילה

טַעֲמוּ וּרְאוּ כִּי־טוֹב יהוה – *Taste and see that the Lord is good.* The word "see" can refer to one's eyesight: Look around you and see the actual good aspects of your life that surround you. But it can also mean to understand as in "Can't you see what I mean?"

The word טַעַם in this context can mean to think or to consider. But it can also mean to taste in the sense of an experience that goes beyond the cognitive. We are encouraged to experience a relationship with God not just try to understand it; only by actually living a Jewish life, getting to know it as an insider will we come to see how good and pleasant and fulfilling it can be. One cannot describe a sunset to a person who has been blind since birth. So, too, one cannot explain the beauty of Shabbat until it has been repeatedly experienced.

IYUN TEFILLA • עיון תפילה

כִּי־אֵין מַחְסוֹר לִירֵאָיו – *For those who fear Him lack nothing.* Note that it does not say that those who fear God will have riches; rather, that they will not be wanting. Do not be envious looking at those who have more wealth than you, for as long as you feel that you have enough, you will be satisfied. (*Etz HaDa'at Tov*). A traditional blessing in our family is: "May you always have just enough."

"Who is wealthy?" asks the Mishna in Avot (4:1), "the person who is happy with what he has."

נְצֹר לְשׁוֹנְךָ מֵרָע, וּשְׂפָתֶיךָ מִדַּבֵּר מִרְמָה – *Then guard your tongue from evil and your lips from speaking deceit.* Herein lies a source for the expression *lashon hara*, or gossip, which is forbidden by Jewish law. The path to having one's prayers answered lies not only in the ritual sphere but in the interpersonal as well. To be religious means to strive for wholeness in all facets of one's life, not just in the synagogue, not just on Shabbat.

Turn from evil and do good;[B]
seek peace and pursue it.[B]
The eyes of the LORD are on the righteous
and His ears attentive to their cry;
The LORD's face is set against those who do evil,
to erase their memory from the earth.
The righteous cry out, and the LORD hears them;
delivering them from all their troubles.
The LORD is close to the brokenhearted,
and saves those who are crushed in spirit.
Many troubles may befall the righteous,
but the LORD delivers him from them all;
He protects all his bones,
so that none of them will be broken.
Evil will slay the wicked;
the enemies of the righteous will be condemned.
▸ The LORD redeems His servants;
none who take refuge in Him shall be condemned.

תְּפִלָּה לְמֹשֶׁה A prayer of Moses, the man of God. LORD, You have *Ps. 90*
been our shelter[I] in every generation. Before the mountains were born, before You brought forth the earth and the world, from everlasting to everlasting You are God. You turn men back to dust, saying, "Return, you children of men."[IB] For a thousand years

---

IYUN TEFILLA • עיון תפילה

מָעוֹן אַתָּה – *You have been our shelter.* There are those religions that believe that God is distant and unreachable, a transcendent being who is impossible to approach, with whom one has no connection. There are others that believe that God is immanent, close to man, a part of this world, a part of nature. Judaism believes in neither of these. Rather, God is both distant and near. The world is not His place, yet He is also close to us, watches over us and protects us, His place is in the world (*Midrash Shoḥer Tov, Bereshit Raba* 68:9).

שׁוּבוּ בְנֵי־אָדָם – *Return, you children of men.* Sometimes a person cannot emerge from the doldrums on his own. One needs the kindness and care of others who remind us to return to our former selves (*Menaḥem Tzyion*). Shabbat is an opportunity to spend time with those people and to reach out to others.

The **BIUR TEFILLA** *on psalm 90 is on page 535.*

סוּר מֵרָע וַעֲשֵׂה־טוֹב, בַּקֵּשׁ שָׁלוֹם וְרָדְפֵהוּ: ב
עֵינֵי יהוה אֶל־צַדִּיקִים, וְאָזְנָיו אֶל־שַׁוְעָתָם:
פְּנֵי יהוה בְּעֹשֵׂי רָע, לְהַכְרִית מֵאֶרֶץ זִכְרָם:
צָעֲקוּ וַיהוה שָׁמֵעַ, וּמִכָּל־צָרוֹתָם הִצִּילָם:
קָרוֹב יהוה לְנִשְׁבְּרֵי־לֵב, וְאֶת־דַּכְּאֵי־רוּחַ יוֹשִׁיעַ:
רַבּוֹת רָעוֹת צַדִּיק, וּמִכֻּלָּם יַצִּילֶנּוּ יהוה:
שֹׁמֵר כָּל־עַצְמוֹתָיו, אַחַת מֵהֵנָּה לֹא נִשְׁבָּרָה:
תְּמוֹתֵת רָשָׁע רָעָה, וְשֹׂנְאֵי צַדִּיק יֶאְשָׁמוּ:
◂ פּוֹדֶה יהוה נֶפֶשׁ עֲבָדָיו, וְלֹא יֶאְשְׁמוּ כָּל־הַחֹסִים בּוֹ:

תהלים צ
תְּפִלָּה לְמֹשֶׁה אִישׁ־הָאֱלֹהִים, אֲדֹנָי, מָעוֹן אַתָּה הָיִיתָ לָּנוּ בְּדֹר
וָדֹר: בְּטֶרֶם הָרִים יֻלָּדוּ, וַתְּחוֹלֵל אֶרֶץ וְתֵבֵל, וּמֵעוֹלָם עַד־עוֹלָם
אַתָּה אֵל: תָּשֵׁב אֱנוֹשׁ עַד־דַּכָּא, וַתֹּאמֶר שׁוּבוּ בְנֵי־אָדָם: עב

BIUR TEFILLA • ביאור תפילה

תְּפִלָּה לְמֹשֶׁה – *TEHILLIM 90.* This psalm can be divided into two parts: the fleeting nature of life on the one hand, and the prayer for happiness and satisfaction on the other. It is one of the more sobering of all the psalms in *Tehillim*, yet it can also be hopeful, somber yet joyful, depending upon which part one emphasizes. One tradition suggests that the psalm was written by Moshe specifically before his death and thus serves as both a reflection on life and a mandate for how to live it. Throughout, there is an emphasis on time consciousness, a particularly important theme for the island of time that is Shabbat.

סוּר מֵרָע וַעֲשֵׂה־טוֹב – *Turn from evil and do good.* "Turn from evil" refers to the negative commandments; "do good" refers to the positive commandments (Ibn Ezra). In Jewish society it is not enough to "do no harm." The very definition of morality is where one also proactively seeks to do good.

בַּקֵּשׁ שָׁלוֹם וְרָדְפֵהוּ – *Seek peace and pursue it.* Peace is not simply an ideal to be dreamed about nor is it something that one should just wait for (Rashi); rather, it is something to be actively pursued whether in human relations, in the political sphere (Malbim), or in one's inner life (Seforno).

How can you pursue peace today?

in Your sight are like yesterday[IA] when it has passed, like a watch in the night. You sweep men away; they sleep.[A] In the morning they are like grass newly grown: in the morning it flourishes and is new, but by evening it withers and dries up.[I] For we are consumed by Your anger, terrified by Your fury. You have set our iniquities before You, our secret sins in the light of Your presence. All our days pass away in Your wrath, we spend our years like a sigh. The span of our life is seventy years, or if we are strong, eighty years; but the best of them is trouble and sorrow, for they quickly pass, and we fly away. Who can know the force of Your anger? Your wrath matches the fear due to You. Teach us rightly to number our days, that we may gain a heart of wisdom. Relent, O Lord! How much longer?[I] Be sorry for Your servants.[I]

Until now, one might have thought that life is without meaning given how short and fleeting it is. This could be the stance of the human being before a distant eternal God. But here the verse speaks of "Your servants," which represents another perspective; namely, that of the loyal servant who finds meaning in service. Life's brevity thus leads not to hopelessness but to purpose, not to futility but to meaning (*Da'at Mikra*).

ANI TEFILLA • אני תפילה

כִּי אֶלֶף שָׁנִים בְּעֵינֶיךָ, כְּיוֹם אֶתְמוֹל – *For a thousand years in Your sight are like yesterday.* *A man once pleaded with God to bestow a bit of His abundance upon him. He implored and begged his Creator for long life and wealth. After all, the poor soul figured, God had an abundance of everything; why then, wouldn't He spare something for a Jew in need. He entered a huge, empty synagogue and began to cry."Ribono Shel Olam (Master of the Universe), in the great extent of Your eternity what is a million years?" The man began to tremble. He imagined that he actually heard a response."To Me a million years is but a mere second!" boomed a voice inside his mind. The man continued, "And to the magnitude of Your great bounty, what, may I ask, is a billion dollars?" "A billion dollars is just a mere penny," came the resonating reply. "Then," begged the man, "can I not have just one of your pennies?" "Surely!" came the response. And then a pause. "But you must wait a mere second."*

זְרַמְתָּם, שֵׁנָה יִהְיוּ – *You sweep men away; they sleep.* How often do we feel like we have slept life away? One wakens with a start only to realize with remorse how much time and opportunity have been lost. We sleep about one-third of our lives on earth.

How often can our waking hours be called sleep of a different kind?

How many opportunities did you lose last week? How will this Shabbat and next week be different?

Are you living your eulogy or your resume?

The **ANI TEFILLA** *continues on page 537.*

כִּי אֶלֶף שָׁנִים בְּעֵינֶיךָ, כְּיוֹם אֶתְמוֹל[עא] כִּי יַעֲבֹר, וְאַשְׁמוּרָה בַלָּיְלָה:
זְרַמְתָּם, שֵׁנָה יִהְיוּ,[א] בַּבֹּקֶר כֶּחָצִיר יַחֲלֹף: בַּבֹּקֶר יָצִיץ וְחָלָף,
לָעֶרֶב יְמוֹלֵל וְיָבֵשׁ:[ע] כִּי־כָלִינוּ בְאַפֶּךָ, וּבַחֲמָתְךָ נִבְהָלְנוּ: שַׁתָּ
עֲוֺנֹתֵינוּ לְנֶגְדֶּךָ, עֲלֻמֵנוּ לִמְאוֹר פָּנֶיךָ: כִּי כָל־יָמֵינוּ פָּנוּ בְעֶבְרָתֶךָ,
כִּלִּינוּ שָׁנֵינוּ כְמוֹ־הֶגֶה: יְמֵי־שְׁנוֹתֵינוּ בָהֶם שִׁבְעִים שָׁנָה, וְאִם
בִּגְבוּרֹת שְׁמוֹנִים שָׁנָה, וְרָהְבָּם עָמָל וָאָוֶן, כִּי־גָז חִישׁ וַנָּעֻפָה:
מִי־יוֹדֵעַ עֹז אַפֶּךָ, וּכְיִרְאָתְךָ עֶבְרָתֶךָ, לִמְנוֹת יָמֵינוּ כֵּן הוֹדַע,
וְנָבִא לְבַב חָכְמָה:[א] שׁוּבָה יהוה עַד־מָתָי,[ע] וְהִנָּחֵם עַל־עֲבָדֶיךָ:[ע]

BIUR TEFILLA • ביאור תפילה

שׁוּבוּ בְנֵי־אָדָם – *Return, you children of men.* The juxtaposition of this verse with the one which precedes, led the Rabbis to suggest that repentance was created before the world itself was. The implication is that it is part of the very fabric of creation, it is a natural element. Change is always possible.

IYUN TEFILLA • עיון תפילה

כִּי אֶלֶף שָׁנִים בְּעֵינֶיךָ, כְּיוֹם אֶתְמוֹל – *For a thousand years in Your sight are like yesterday.* Hashem is eternal and time, when measured by man, is relative. There are those who often turn to this verse to suggest that when the Bible speaks of the world being created in six days, it speaks metaphorically, for a day in God's reckoning is very different than a period of 24 hours and could be a thousand years, millions of years or more.

בַּבֹּקֶר יָצִיץ וְחָלָף, לָעֶרֶב יְמוֹלֵל וְיָבֵשׁ – *In the morning it flourishes and is new, but by evening it withers and dries up.* The imagery here is the basis of part of the famous prayer *Untaneh Tokef*, said on the High Holy Days: "Man is founded in dust and ends in dust. He lays down his soul to bring home bread. He is like a broken shard, like grass dried up, like a faded flower, like a fleeting shadow, like a passing cloud, like a breath of wind, like whirling dust, like a dream that slips away." Unfortunately, we tend to think of these things only at times of judgment. Yet every day is an opportunity to begin anew.

How can you treat today as a fresh new beginning?

שׁוּבָה יהוה עַד־מָתָי – *Relent, O Lord! How much longer?* The Rabbis homiletically understand these two verses as a call to man to repent on the day before he dies. Since one does not know that day with any certainty, one must therefore repent every day; hence these two verses say "teach us to number our days," to be conscious of each day as if it were our last, "Return, (*shuvu*) for how long?" until the day of one's death (*Midrash Shoḥer Tov*).

וְהִנָּחֵם עַל־עֲבָדֶיךָ – *Be sorry for Your servants.*

Satisfy us in the morning with Your loving-kindness, that we may sing and rejoice all our days. Grant us joy for as many days as You have afflicted us, for as many years as we saw trouble. Let Your deeds be seen by Your servants, and Your glory by their children. ▸ May the pleasantness of the LORD our God be upon us. Establish for us the work of our hands, O establish the work of our hands.[1]

Ps. 91

יֹשֵׁב בְּסֵתֶר He who lives in the shelter of the Most High dwells in the shadow of the Almighty. I say of the LORD, my Refuge and Stronghold, my God in whom I trust, that He will save you from the fowler's snare and the deadly pestilence.[B] With His pinions He will cover you, and beneath His wings you will find shelter; His faithfulness is an encircling shield. You need not fear terror by night,[B] nor the arrow that flies by day; not the pestilence that stalks in darkness,[B]

---

should accompany him with regard to the various dangers that lurk in his life... a person must be aware of the existential dangers that surround him; he should not live under the false illusion that the world is a tranquil, safe place. On the other hand, this awareness should not embitter him or cause him to live in constant fear. Admittedly, the world is full of all sorts of dangers, but it is not ownerless: God watches over His creatures and treats each according to its needs. A person who trusts in God and makes Him his abode and his refuge will enjoy His protection from all of the dangers in the world. As his trust in God and closeness to Him grow, so God's Divine patronage in his regard will assume deeper and broader significance." (Rabbi Elchanan Samet)

כִּי הוּא יַצִּילְךָ מִפַּח יָקוּשׁ, מִדֶּבֶר הַוּוֹת – *He will save you from the fowler's snare and the deadly pestilence.* The first speaks to the dangers that can come suddenly from one's fellow man, the traps laid by men; the other, comes from nature. Notice how many other such allusions there are in the verses that follow.

לֹא תִירָא, מִפַּחַד לָיְלָה – *You need not fear terror by night.* Fear (*yira*) and terror (*paḥad*) are two different things. The one has a rational basis; the other is irrational bordering on the phobic. To be sure, there are real threats that lurk in the dark of the night. Some come from without, many come from within. The person of faith is able to cope, put them at bay or push them away.

מִדֶּבֶר בָּאֹפֶל יַהֲלֹךְ – *The pestilence that stalks in darkness.* What might be the difference between the pestilence here and the one mentioned above in the third verse?

שַׂבְּעֵנוּ בַבֹּקֶר חַסְדֶּךָ, וּנְרַנְּנָה וְנִשְׂמְחָה בְּכָל־יָמֵינוּ: שַׂמְּחֵנוּ
כִּימוֹת עִנִּיתָנוּ, שְׁנוֹת רָאִינוּ רָעָה: יֵרָאֶה אֶל־עֲבָדֶיךָ פָעֳלֶךָ,
וַהֲדָרְךָ עַל־בְּנֵיהֶם: ‹ וִיהִי נֹעַם אֲדֹנָי אֱלֹהֵינוּ עָלֵינוּ, וּמַעֲשֵׂה
יָדֵינוּ כּוֹנְנָה עָלֵינוּ, וּמַעֲשֵׂה יָדֵינוּ כּוֹנְנֵהוּ:

תהלים צא יֹשֵׁב בְּסֵתֶר עֶלְיוֹן, בְּצֵל שַׁדַּי יִתְלוֹנָן: אֹמַר לַיהוה מַחְסִי וּמְצוּדָתִי,
אֱלֹהַי אֶבְטַח־בּוֹ: כִּי הוּא יַצִּילְךָ מִפַּח יָקוּשׁ, מִדֶּבֶר הַוּוֹת:
בְּאֶבְרָתוֹ יָסֶךְ לָךְ, וְתַחַת־כְּנָפָיו תֶּחְסֶה, צִנָּה וְסֹחֵרָה אֲמִתּוֹ:
לֹא־תִירָא מִפַּחַד לָיְלָה, מֵחֵץ יָעוּף יוֹמָם: מִדֶּבֶר בָּאֹפֶל יַהֲלֹךְ,

---

IYUN TEFILLA • עיון תפילה

וַהֲדָרְךָ עַל־בְּנֵיהֶם... וּמַעֲשֵׂה יָדֵינוּ כּוֹנְנָה עָלֵינוּ – *Your glory by their children... establish for us the work of our hands.* The religious personality knows that life is neither hopeless nor pointless despite one's mortality. One's children, one's contributions to others, can stand for posterity and negate any despondency about the limits of one's life.

– לִמְנוֹת יָמֵינוּ כֵּן הוֹדַע, וְנָבִא לְבַב חָכְמָה
Teach us rightly to number our days, that we may gain a heart of wisdom. Life is short. The days of our lives should not be counted but weighed (Menaḥem Tzyion). Help me not to count my days but to make each day count.

BIUR TEFILLA • ביאור תפילה

יֹשֵׁב בְּסֵתֶר – *TEHILLIM 91.* This psalm is considered by many to be an extension of the one which precedes and, indeed, if you look closely you can find some parallels in language. It too is divided into two parts, though in this case the division is equal – there are eight verses consisting of 56 words in each. The themes in each of the halves sound similar but in truth, one builds on the other. It has been suggested that there are represented here at least two different voices – a husband and wife, or a parent and child, or a teacher and student – and that it should therefore be read as if it was said responsively.

The psalm is known by the Rabbis as "The Song of Mishaps" (*Shir Shel Pega'im*) for it speaks dramatically about the various forces, human and natural, that can appear out of nowhere to upend a person's life.

Our psalm contains a didactic theme: it guides the person – especially if he is young – to the proper awareness that

nor the plague that ravages at noon. A thousand may fall at your side, ten thousand at your right hand, but it will not come near you. You will only look with your eyes and see the punishment of the wicked. Because you said "The LORD is my Refuge,"[B] taking the Most High as your shelter, no harm will befall you, no plague will come near your tent, for He will command His angels about you, to guard you in all your ways. They will lift you in their hands, lest your foot stumble on a stone. You will tread on lions and vipers, you will trample on young lions and snakes. [God says] "Because he loves Me, I will rescue him; I will protect him, because he acknowledges My name. When he calls on Me, I will answer him,[B] I will be with him in distress,[I] I will deliver him and bring him honor.[I]
▸ With long life I will satisfy him, and show him My salvation.
With long life I will satisfy him, and show him My salvation."

When a person is not always conscious of the presence of God in his life, when he is separated from God, then God is also separated from him and then he is exposed to any evil that might befall him (Maimonides, *Guide for the Perplexed* 3:51).

Look around you. Who could benefit from your imitating God today?

ANI TEFILLA • אני תפילה

Eli Wiesel, the Nobel Laureate and famed Holocaust writer, was asked: "Did you lose your God after the Holocaust?" He answered, "God was my friend as a boy. I was a young Hasid, and God accompanied me everywhere. And for a time, after the war, I did not wish to have a relationship with Him. But He never left me completely, and now He is back fully in my life. But the relationship has changed. I have a right to assert my place. It is now more a rapport, not of equals, of course, but of two parties with a real and painful dialogue."

Someone once asked the Ba'al Shem Tov: "Why is it that one who clings to God and knows He is close to him, sometimes experiences a sense of interruption and remoteness?" The Ba'al Shem explained: "When a father sets out to teach his little child to walk, he stands in front of him and holds his two hands on either side of the child to catch him just in case he falls, and the child goes toward his father between his father's outstretched hands. But the moment he is close to his father, his father moves away a little, and holds his hands further apart, and he does this over and over, so that the child may learn to walk."

Believe that He is there, waiting for you to move forward.

מִקֶּטֶב יָשׁוּד צָהֳרָיִם: יִפֹּל מִצִּדְּךָ אֶלֶף, וּרְבָבָה מִימִינֶךָ, אֵלֶיךָ
לֹא יִגָּשׁ: רַק בְּעֵינֶיךָ תַבִּיט, וְשִׁלֻּמַת רְשָׁעִים תִּרְאֶה: כִּי־אַתָּה
יהוה מַחְסִי,ב עֶלְיוֹן שַׂמְתָּ מְעוֹנֶךָ: לֹא־תְאֻנֶּה אֵלֶיךָ רָעָה, וְנֶגַע
לֹא־יִקְרַב בְּאָהֳלֶךָ: כִּי מַלְאָכָיו יְצַוֶּה־לָּךְ, לִשְׁמָרְךָ בְּכָל־דְּרָכֶיךָ:
עַל־כַּפַּיִם יִשָּׂאוּנְךָ, פֶּן־תִּגֹּף בָּאֶבֶן רַגְלֶךָ: עַל־שַׁחַל וָפֶתֶן תִּדְרֹךְ,
תִּרְמֹס כְּפִיר וְתַנִּין: כִּי בִי חָשַׁק וַאֲפַלְּטֵהוּ, אֲשַׂגְּבֵהוּ כִּי־יָדַע
שְׁמִי: יִקְרָאֵנִי וְאֶעֱנֵהוּ,ב עִמּוֹ אָנֹכִי בְצָרָה,ע אֲחַלְּצֵהוּ וַאֲכַבְּדֵהוּ:ע
◂ אֹרֶךְ יָמִים אַשְׂבִּיעֵהוּ, וְאַרְאֵהוּ בִּישׁוּעָתִי:
אֹרֶךְ יָמִים אַשְׂבִּיעֵהוּ, וְאַרְאֵהוּ בִּישׁוּעָתִי:

BIUR TEFILLA • ביאור תפילה

יִקְרָאֵנִי וְאֶעֱנֵהוּ – *When he calls on Me, I will answer him.* Prophecy and prayer are similar. But in prophecy, it is God who initiates the conversation; in prayer, it is man. Man must first call out to God if he ever expects an answer.

כִּי־אַתָּה יהוה מַחְסִי – *Because you said "The Lord is my Refuge" [or "Because You are Hashem my Refuge].* Here is where the second half of the psalm begins. How does it compare and contrast with the parallel verse found in the second line above?

IYUN TEFILLA • עיון תפילה

עִמּוֹ אָנֹכִי בְצָרָה, אֲחַלְּצֵהוּ וַאֲכַבְּדֵהוּ – *I will be with him in distress, I will deliver him and bring him honor.* Herein lies an opportunity for *imitatio Dei*, to imitate the ways of the Creator, by being prepared to participate in the sorrows of others and to declare "I am with him in times of trouble." I will "deliver him" to the extent that I am able by relieving his suffering, I will "bring him honor" by extending my hand in a respectful and honorable way so that he will not be embarrassed (*Menaḥem Tzyion*).

עִמּוֹ אָנֹכִי בְצָרָה – *I will be with him in distress.* Moshe asked God why of all the trees in the world, did He decide to reveal Himself to him for the first time from within a lowly thornbush rather than from a more regal tree. Hashem answered: "My people are suffering in slavery and I should reveal myself from a more exalted tree?" – "I will be with him in distress (*Yalkut Shimoni* 843) .When man suffers, God, as it were, suffers too.

הַלְלוּיָהּ Halleluya! Praise the name of the LORD. Praise Him, you Ps. 135
servants of the LORD who stand in the LORD's House, in the courtyards of the House of our God. Praise the LORD, for the LORD is good;[B] sing praises to His name, for it is lovely. For the LORD has chosen Jacob as His own, Israel as his treasure. For I know that the LORD is great, that our LORD is above all heavenly powers. Whatever pleases the LORD, He does,[I] in heaven and on earth, in the seas and all the depths. He raises clouds from the ends of the earth;[I] He sends lightning with the rain; He brings out the wind from His storehouses. He struck down the firstborn of Egypt, of both man and animals.[B] He sent signs and wonders into your midst, Egypt – against Pharaoh and all his servants. He struck down[I] many nations and slew mighty kings: Siḥon, King of the Amorites,[B] Og, King of Bashan, and all the kingdoms of Canaan, giving their land as a heritage, a heritage for His people Israel. Your name, LORD, endures for ever; Your renown, LORD, for all generations. For the LORD will bring justice to His people, and have compassion on

---

לְסִיחוֹן מֶלֶךְ הָאֱמֹרִי – *Siḥon, king of the Amorites.* This could be a symbolic reference to the 31 kings whom Yehoshua conquered when entering the Promised Land.

IYUN TEFILLA • עיון תפילה

כָּל אֲשֶׁר־חָפֵץ יהוה עָשָׂה – *Whatever pleases the LORD, He does.* God can do whatever He wishes. Alternatively, God does many things that we cannot understand, that are not revealed to us until some point in history or in our lives when their true purpose is discovered.

Can you recall any events in your life that you thought were bad but ultimately turned out for the best?

מַעֲלֶה נְשִׂאִים מִקְצֵה הָאָרֶץ – *He raises clouds from the ends of the earth.* This is an example of God's power. The endless cycle of evaporation and precipitation that keeps us alive is something that we can be oblivious to except when we notice its absence during times of drought. The siddur reminds us that God's power, and our sense of wonder, lies especially in the things that we take for granted.

שֶׁהִכָּה – *He struck down.* Sometimes man needs to be hit with a "smack" in order to wake up to the Divine will. There were numerous smaller, less consequential plagues before the final one, but Pharaoh and the Egyptians did not pay heed. How many of us really do?

הַלְלוּיָהּ, הַלְלוּ אֶת־שֵׁם יהוה, הַלְלוּ עַבְדֵי יהוה: שֶׁעֹמְדִים בְּבֵית תהלים קלה
יהוה, בְּחַצְרוֹת בֵּית אֱלֹהֵינוּ: הַלְלוּיָהּ כִּי־טוֹב יהוה,ב זַמְּרוּ
לִשְׁמוֹ כִּי נָעִים: כִּי־יַעֲקֹב בָּחַר לוֹ יָהּ, יִשְׂרָאֵל לִסְגֻלָּתוֹ: כִּי אֲנִי
יָדַעְתִּי כִּי־גָדוֹל יהוה, וַאֲדֹנֵינוּ מִכָּל־אֱלֹהִים: כֹּל אֲשֶׁר־חָפֵץ יהוה
עָשָׂה,ע בַּשָּׁמַיִם וּבָאָרֶץ, בַּיַּמִּים וְכָל־תְּהֹמוֹת: מַעֲלֶה נְשִׂאִים
מִקְצֵה הָאָרֶץ,ע בְּרָקִים לַמָּטָר עָשָׂה, מוֹצֵא־רוּחַ מֵאוֹצְרוֹתָיו:
שֶׁהִכָּהע בְּכוֹרֵי מִצְרָיִם, מֵאָדָם עַד־בְּהֵמָה:ב שָׁלַח אוֹתֹת וּמֹפְתִים
בְּתוֹכֵכִי מִצְרָיִם, בְּפַרְעֹה וּבְכָל־עֲבָדָיו: שֶׁהִכָּה גּוֹיִם רַבִּים, וְהָרַג
מְלָכִים עֲצוּמִים: לְסִיחוֹן מֶלֶךְ הָאֱמֹרִי,ב וּלְעוֹג מֶלֶךְ הַבָּשָׁן, וּלְכֹל
מַמְלְכוֹת כְּנָעַן: וְנָתַן אַרְצָם נַחֲלָה, נַחֲלָה לְיִשְׂרָאֵל עַמּוֹ: יהוה
שִׁמְךָ לְעוֹלָם, יהוה זִכְרְךָ לְדֹר־וָדֹר: כִּי־יָדִין יהוה עַמּוֹ, וְעַל־

BIUR TEFILLA • ביאור תפילה

הַלְלוּיָהּ – *TEHILLIM 135.* This psalm and the next one form an almost independent unit thematically. Similarly, they appear together at the concluding part of the Passover Seder because of the relevant themes they contain. Here they serve the function of furthering the themes of God's continuing presence in the natural world and the world of man. In the present psalm, one might discern three distinct parts: a call to recognize His Presence; a call to acknowledge His Presence in history; a call to recognize that His is the only Presence. Each part consists of five, seven and nine verses respectively, perhaps reflecting the ever-expanding realization of the Divine in all aspects of our lives that can begin with small steps and grow exponentially.

כִּי־טוֹב יהוה – *For the Lord is good.* Praise Him because He is Good. Alternatively, praise Him because of the good that He does.

Which speaks to you most today?

שֶׁהִכָּה בְּכוֹרֵי מִצְרָיִם, מֵאָדָם עַד־בְּהֵמָה – *He struck down the firstborn of Egypt, of both man and animals.* This is a reference to the last of the ten plagues during the exodus, the one which convinced Pharaoh to free us. At the same time, none of the firstborn of the Israelites was killed, thus making it a miracle within a miracle (Ibn Ezra). Above all else, it could not be dismissed as a mere coincidence or act of nature.

What historical events can you think of which might be seen as natural but within which could also be sensed the miraculous? What event in your personal life could you view in the same way?

His servants. The idols of the nations are silver and gold,[I] the work of human hands.[I] They have mouths, but cannot speak; eyes, but cannot see; ears, but cannot hear; there is no breath in their mouths. Those who make them will become like them: so will all who trust in them. ▸ House of Israel, bless the LORD. House of Aaron, bless the LORD. House of Levi, bless the LORD. You who fear the LORD,[B] bless the LORD. Blessed is the LORD from Zion, He who dwells in Jerusalem. Halleluya!

The custom is to stand for the following psalm.

הודו Thank the LORD for He is good; His loving-kindness is for ever.[A] Ps. 136
Thank the God of gods, His loving-kindness is for ever.
Thank the LORD of lords, His loving-kindness is for ever.

---

the fact that it has 26 verses: there were 26 generations from Adam until the giving of the Torah at Sinai (*Pesahim* 118a); 26 is the *gematria* (numerical equivalent) of God's four-letter name (Abudarham); remove the four verses of introduction and there remain 22 verses, one for each letter of the *Alef-Beit*.

One of the reasons for the search for greater meaning is perhaps the sheer scope and grandeur of the prayer. It speaks of the greatness of Hashem as manifest by the many kindnesses that He has done for the world at large, and then the kindnesses that He has done specifically for the Jewish People, and then concluding once again with all of mankind. Look closely and one will find an almost chronological unfolding of God's involvement in nature and history from the time of creation to Israel's entry into the Promised Land. But the climax, as it were, comes at the very end in a most surprising way.

ANI TEFILLA · אני תפילה

הודוּ לַיהוה כִּי־טוֹב, כִּי לְעוֹלָם חַסְדּוֹ – *Thank the LORD, for He is good, His loving-kindness is for ever.* It is important for a person to give praise to God not for His sake, but as a reminder to oneself. For the more that one can admit to the good things that one has in one's life and acknowledge that they are a result of God's blessing, then the more one is likely to live one's life a particular way and thus the more open one becomes to receiving more of His kindness. (*Da'at Sofrim*)

What are two of the good things in your life that you can acknowledge today?

עֲבָדָיו יִתְנֶחָם: עֲצַבֵּי הַגּוֹיִם כֶּסֶף וְזָהָב, מַעֲשֵׂה יְדֵי אָדָם: פֶּה־
לָהֶם וְלֹא יְדַבֵּרוּ, עֵינַיִם לָהֶם וְלֹא יִרְאוּ: אָזְנַיִם לָהֶם וְלֹא יַאֲזִינוּ,
אַף אֵין־יֶשׁ־רְוּחַ בְּפִיהֶם: כְּמוֹהֶם יִהְיוּ עֹשֵׂיהֶם, כֹּל אֲשֶׁר־בֹּטֵחַ
בָּהֶם: ◂ בֵּית יִשְׂרָאֵל בָּרְכוּ אֶת־יהוה, בֵּית אַהֲרֹן בָּרְכוּ אֶת־
יהוה: בֵּית הַלֵּוִי בָּרְכוּ אֶת־יהוה, יִרְאֵי יהוה בָּרְכוּ אֶת־יהוה:
בָּרוּךְ יהוה מִצִּיּוֹן, שֹׁכֵן יְרוּשָׁלָםִ, הַלְלוּיָהּ:

The custom is to stand for the following psalm.

תהלים קלו

הוֹדוּ לַיהוה כִּי־טוֹב	כִּי לְעוֹלָם חַסְדּוֹ:
הוֹדוּ לֵאלֹהֵי הָאֱלֹהִים	כִּי לְעוֹלָם חַסְדּוֹ:
הוֹדוּ לַאֲדֹנֵי הָאֲדֹנִים	כִּי לְעוֹלָם חַסְדּוֹ:

BIUR TEFILLA • ביאור תפילה

בֵּית יִשְׂרָאֵל...בֵּית אַהֲרֹן...בית הלוי...יִרְאֵי יהוה – *House of Israel... House of Aaron... House of Levi... You who fear the Lord.* In these two verses there are four categories of people mentioned. In the first three, they are referred to as the House of... This is because, like a family, anyone born into it is automatically a member, an organic part of the whole, who accepts upon himself the mission and destiny of that house. So, the priests of the House of Aaron, the Levites and Israel, each a family within a family, accept upon themselves to fulfill the obligations thrust upon them by virtue of their birth as a family. But so too is the demand made of each individual who has "fear of God" in his heart, to actualize it as a Jew and as a human being. (Rabbi S. Hirsch)

IYUN TEFILLA • עיון תפילה

עֲצַבֵּי הַגּוֹיִם כֶּסֶף וְזָהָב – *The idols of the nations are silver and gold.* We tend to look at polytheistic cultures as primitive and naive. But if in ancient times, the idols were made of silver and gold, it sometimes seems that today's idols are often the silver and gold themselves.

מַעֲשֵׂה יְדֵי אָדָם – *The work of human hands.* In Judaism, there are no intermediaries. Everyone can have a direct personal connection with God.

BIUR TEFILLA • ביאור תפילה

תהלים קלו – *TEHILLIM 136.* This particular psalm is referred to as *Hallel Gadol*, (the Great Praise). Many try to find symbolic meanings, each with its own message, in

To the One who alone works great wonders,[I] His loving-kindness is for ever.
Who made the heavens with wisdom,[B] His loving-kindness is for ever.
Who spread the earth upon the waters, His loving-kindness is for ever.
Who made the great lights, His loving-kindness is for ever.
The sun to rule by day, His loving-kindness is for ever.
The moon and the stars to rule by night; His loving-kindness is for ever.
Who struck Egypt through their firstborn, His loving-kindness is for ever.
And brought out Israel from their midst, His loving-kindness is for ever.
With a strong hand and outstretched arm, His loving-kindness is for ever.
Who split the Reed Sea into parts, His loving-kindness is for ever.
And made Israel pass through it, His loving-kindness is for ever.
Casting Pharaoh and his army into the Reed Sea; His loving-kindness is for ever.
Who led His people through the wilderness;[I] His loving-kindness is for ever.
Who struck down great kings, His loving-kindness is for ever.
And slew mighty kings, His loving-kindness is for ever.
Sihon, King of the Amorites, His loving-kindness is for ever.

BIUR TEFILLA • ביאור תפילה

לְעֹשֵׂה הַשָּׁמַיִם בִּתְבוּנָה – *Who made the heavens with wisdom.* He creates the heavens with His own wisdom and insight. Alternatively, He made creation with its own wisdom so that it operates according to its own internal logical principles (*Tehillot Hashem*). Alternatively, if you contemplate the heavens, you will understand that there is a Creator (Rabbi Simcha Bunim). Think of a place where you once saw how awesome the sky was. **Which of these interpretations speaks most to that experience?**

ANI TEFILLA • אני תפילה

Forty-one days after the revelation at Mount Sinai, the Israelites were making a golden calf to worship (Exodus 32). Faith is about seeing the miraculous in the everyday, not about waiting every day for miracles (Rabbi Jonathan Sacks).

לְעֹשֵׂה נִפְלָאוֹת גְּדֹלוֹת לְבַדּוֹ[ע]	כִּי לְעוֹלָם חַסְדּוֹ:
לְעֹשֵׂה הַשָּׁמַיִם בִּתְבוּנָה[ב]	כִּי לְעוֹלָם חַסְדּוֹ:
לְרֹקַע הָאָרֶץ עַל־הַמָּיִם	כִּי לְעוֹלָם חַסְדּוֹ:
לְעֹשֵׂה אוֹרִים גְּדֹלִים	כִּי לְעוֹלָם חַסְדּוֹ:
אֶת־הַשֶּׁמֶשׁ לְמֶמְשֶׁלֶת בַּיּוֹם	כִּי לְעוֹלָם חַסְדּוֹ:
אֶת־הַיָּרֵחַ וְכוֹכָבִים לְמֶמְשְׁלוֹת בַּלָּיְלָה	כִּי לְעוֹלָם חַסְדּוֹ:
לְמַכֵּה מִצְרַיִם בִּבְכוֹרֵיהֶם	כִּי לְעוֹלָם חַסְדּוֹ:
וַיּוֹצֵא יִשְׂרָאֵל מִתּוֹכָם	כִּי לְעוֹלָם חַסְדּוֹ:
בְּיָד חֲזָקָה וּבִזְרוֹעַ נְטוּיָה	כִּי לְעוֹלָם חַסְדּוֹ:
לְגֹזֵר יַם־סוּף לִגְזָרִים	כִּי לְעוֹלָם חַסְדּוֹ:
וְהֶעֱבִיר יִשְׂרָאֵל בְּתוֹכוֹ	כִּי לְעוֹלָם חַסְדּוֹ:
וְנִעֵר פַּרְעֹה וְחֵילוֹ בְיַם־סוּף	כִּי לְעוֹלָם חַסְדּוֹ:
לְמוֹלִיךְ עַמּוֹ בַּמִּדְבָּר[ע]	כִּי לְעוֹלָם חַסְדּוֹ:
לְמַכֵּה מְלָכִים גְּדֹלִים	כִּי לְעוֹלָם חַסְדּוֹ:
וַיַּהֲרֹג מְלָכִים אַדִּירִים	כִּי לְעוֹלָם חַסְדּוֹ:
לְסִיחוֹן מֶלֶךְ הָאֱמֹרִי	כִּי לְעוֹלָם חַסְדּוֹ:

IYUN TEFILLA · עיון תפילה

לְעֹשֵׂה נִפְלָאוֹת גְּדֹלוֹת לְבַדּוֹ – *To the One who alone works great wonders.* God does wonders for us every day, even if we are not always conscious of them. Think of the threats that present themselves, the germs averted, the accidents avoided, the coming together of seemingly random forces of destruction or disaster or illness. These too are wonders which God does "by Himself," without people knowing. (*Meam Loez*)

Take a moment to acknowledge this absence as provided by His Presence.

לְמוֹלִיךְ עַמּוֹ בַּמִּדְבָּר – *Who led His people through the wilderness.* One might think that being forced to enter and live in the desert is anything but a *ḥesed* or act of kindness. Yet the desert is the place where God provided for us and where we learned to be a people. The Torah was given in the desert and not in a specific country to symbolize the fact that anyone could join and acquire the knowledge and commitment of a life enriched by the Torah even if it means that sometimes one needs to travel in a desert to get there.

And Og, King of Bashan,	His loving-kindness is for ever.
And gave their land as a heritage,	His loving-kindness is for ever.
A heritage for His servant Israel;	His loving-kindness is for ever.
Who remembered us in our lowly state,	His loving-kindness is for ever.
And rescued us from our tormentors,	His loving-kindness is for ever.
▸ Who gives food to all flesh,[B]	His loving-kindness is for ever.
Give thanks to the God of heaven.	His loving-kindness is for ever.

רַנְּנוּ Sing joyfully to the LORD, you righteous, for praise from the upright is seemly. Give thanks to the LORD with the harp; make music to Him on the ten-stringed lute. Sing Him a new song,[B] play skillfully with shouts of joy. For the LORD's word is right, and all His deeds are done in faith.[A] He loves righteousness and justice; *Ps. 33*

---

this psalm that opens with three lines of praise and concludes with three expressions of faith and requests for His kindness, thus totaling twenty-two verses altogether – the same number of letters in the Hebrew *Alef-Beit*. The verses in between contain seven elements of praise, and there are seven synonyms for praise throughout. The first three lines of the psalm speak directly to the listener ("Sing...you righteous") whereas the last three lines switch change to first person plural ("our soul..."), which is expressed no fewer than seven times in the Hebrew. Perhaps the allusion to the *Alef-Beit* symbolically represents the complete set of praises that is possible, while the number seven is itself a symbolic representation of completion representing here the Shabbat. The leader invites us to sing His praises, the very call to praise becomes praise itself, and we are drawn in, and we are left feeling ourselves a little more complete and whole.

שִׁירוּ־לוֹ שִׁיר חָדָשׁ – *Sing Him a new song.* Say something completely different (Radak) for every miracle that He does for you (Meiri). Alternatively, sing the same song anew every day (Rabbi Saadia Gaon).

How might your song this week be different from the one you might have sung last week?

ANI TEFILLA • אני תפילה

וְכָל־מַעֲשֵׂהוּ בֶּאֱמוּנָה – *And all of his deeds are done in faith.*

A man once received a wound on his leg. His friend came to console him and said how bad he felt for him. Said the injured man: "I thank God that it was only my leg that was hurt and not my eyes." Some see in misfortunes only the bad while people of faith see Hashem's hand in keeping the glass half-full (*Me'am Loez*).

Make your challenges today into a glass half-full.

וּלְעוֹג מֶלֶךְ הַבָּשָׁן כִּי לְעוֹלָם חַסְדּוֹ:
וְנָתַן אַרְצָם לְנַחֲלָה כִּי לְעוֹלָם חַסְדּוֹ:
נַחֲלָה לְיִשְׂרָאֵל עַבְדּוֹ כִּי לְעוֹלָם חַסְדּוֹ:
שֶׁבְּשִׁפְלֵנוּ זָכַר לָנוּ כִּי לְעוֹלָם חַסְדּוֹ:
וַיִּפְרְקֵנוּ מִצָּרֵינוּ כִּי לְעוֹלָם חַסְדּוֹ:
◂ נֹתֵן לֶחֶם לְכָל־בָּשָׂר [ב] כִּי לְעוֹלָם חַסְדּוֹ:
הוֹדוּ לְאֵל הַשָּׁמָיִם כִּי לְעוֹלָם חַסְדּוֹ:

תהלים לג רַנְּנוּ צַדִּיקִים בַּיהוה, לַיְשָׁרִים נָאוָה תְהִלָּה: הוֹדוּ לַיהוה בְּכִנּוֹר,
בְּנֵבֶל עָשׂוֹר זַמְּרוּ־לוֹ: שִׁירוּ־לוֹ שִׁיר חָדָשׁ, [ב] הֵיטִיבוּ נַגֵּן בִּתְרוּעָה:
כִּי־יָשָׁר דְּבַר־יהוה, וְכָל־מַעֲשֵׂהוּ בֶּאֱמוּנָה: [א] אֹהֵב צְדָקָה וּמִשְׁפָּט,

BIUR TEFILLA • ביאור תפילה

נֹתֵן לֶחֶם לְכָל־בָּשָׂר – *Who gives food to all flesh.* Note the way in which this concluding line stands out. Whereas all of the preceding verses generally speak of the past, this one speaks of the ongoing present. Whereas the others speak of events natural and supernatural in history, this one speaks of the basic staple of daily life. For in the small crumb of bread lies the same revelation of God that was displayed to mankind in general and the Jewish people in particular over the course of time. This morsel contains within it the same *ḥesed*, the same care, the same concern and support from on High. It is up to us to acknowledge it as such.

From here derives the mandate for man to acquire his needs in the most honest way from the hand of God. One's food comes not alone from the social or personal circumstances of one's life, but from Hashem. That is the meaning of the Gemara *Pesaḥim* 118a: "Making a living is as difficult as it was for Hashem to split the Red Sea at the time of the exodus." (Rabbi S. R. Hirsch)

ANI TEFILLA • אני תפילה

Which is a greater miracle, a sheaf of wheat or a loaf of bread?

BIUR TEFILLA • ביאור תפילה

תהלים לג – *TEHILLIM 33.* As we have seen before, sometimes form and content, the medium and message, go hand in hand. That is to say, sometimes in the siddur the way something is said can parallel or complement what is being said. Consider

the earth is full of the LORD's loving-kindness. By the LORD's word the heavens were made, and all their starry host by the breath of His mouth. He gathers the sea waters as a heap, and places the deep in storehouses. Let all the earth fear the LORD, and all the world's inhabitants stand in awe of Him. For He spoke, and it was; He commanded, and it stood firm. The LORD foils the plans of nations; He thwarts the intentions of peoples. The LORD's plans stand for ever, His heart's intents for all generations. Happy is the nation whose God is the LORD, the people He has chosen as His own. From heaven the LORD looks down and sees all mankind; from His dwelling place He oversees all who live on earth. He forms the hearts of all, and discerns all their deeds. No king is saved by the size of his army; no warrior is delivered by great strength. A horse is a vain hope for deliverance; despite its great strength, it cannot save. The eye of the LORD is on those who fear Him, on those who place their hope in His unfailing love, to rescue their soul from death, and keep them alive in famine. Our soul waits for the LORD; He is our Help and Shield. ▸ In Him our hearts rejoice, for we trust in His holy name. Let Your unfailing love be upon us, LORD, as we have put our hope in You.

You in the bad times when our hearts are more broken than they are now and our sense of dependence greater than we might be feeling right now (*Ohel Yaakov*).

IYUN TEFILLA · עיון תפילה

בִּדְבַר יהוה שָׁמַיִם נַעֲשׂוּ – *By the LORD's word the heavens were made.* The reference is to the days of Creation where it says throughout, "And God said let there be..." All of creation took place by Divine command, by an utterance. Creations are the expressions of God's will. From which the Gemara concludes that speech is like action. When a person merely recites the text of *Kiddush* over wine which attests to Creation, then it is as if he becomes a partner of God in the creation of the world (*Shabbat* 119b). Our words have the power to create worlds... or destroy them. **How will I use my words today?**

חֶסֶד יהוה מָלְאָה הָאָרֶץ: בִּדְבַר יהוה שָׁמַיִם נַעֲשׂוּ, וּבְרוּחַ פִּיו כָּל־צְבָאָם: כֹּנֵס כַּנֵּד מֵי הַיָּם, נֹתֵן בְּאוֹצָרוֹת תְּהוֹמוֹת: יִירְאוּ מֵיהוה כָּל־הָאָרֶץ, מִמֶּנּוּ יָגוּרוּ כָּל־יֹשְׁבֵי תֵבֵל: כִּי הוּא אָמַר וַיֶּהִי, הוּא־צִוָּה וַיַּעֲמֹד: יהוה הֵפִיר עֲצַת־גּוֹיִם, הֵנִיא מַחְשְׁבוֹת עַמִּים: עֲצַת יהוה לְעוֹלָם תַּעֲמֹד, מַחְשְׁבוֹת לִבּוֹ לְדֹר וָדֹר: אַשְׁרֵי הַגּוֹי אֲשֶׁר־יהוה אֱלֹהָיו, הָעָם בָּחַר לְנַחֲלָה לוֹ: מִשָּׁמַיִם הִבִּיט יהוה, רָאָה אֶת־כָּל־בְּנֵי הָאָדָם: מִמְּכוֹן־שִׁבְתּוֹ הִשְׁגִּיחַ, אֶל כָּל־יֹשְׁבֵי הָאָרֶץ: הַיֹּצֵר יַחַד לִבָּם, הַמֵּבִין אֶל־כָּל־מַעֲשֵׂיהֶם: אֵין־הַמֶּלֶךְ נוֹשָׁע בְּרָב־חָיִל, גִּבּוֹר לֹא־יִנָּצֵל בְּרָב־כֹּחַ: שֶׁקֶר הַסּוּס לִתְשׁוּעָה, וּבְרֹב חֵילוֹ לֹא יְמַלֵּט: הִנֵּה עֵין יהוה אֶל־יְרֵאָיו, לַמְיַחֲלִים לְחַסְדּוֹ: לְהַצִּיל מִמָּוֶת נַפְשָׁם, וּלְחַיּוֹתָם בָּרָעָב: נַפְשֵׁנוּ חִכְּתָה לַיהוה, עֶזְרֵנוּ וּמָגִנֵּנוּ הוּא: כִּי־בוֹ יִשְׂמַח לִבֵּנוּ, כִּי בְשֵׁם קָדְשׁוֹ בָטָחְנוּ: יְהִי־חַסְדְּךָ יהוה עָלֵינוּ, כַּאֲשֶׁר יִחַלְנוּ לָךְ:

BIUR TEFILLA • ביאור תפילה

יְהִי־חַסְדְּךָ יהוה עָלֵינוּ, כַּאֲשֶׁר יִחַלְנוּ לָךְ – *Let Your unfailing love be upon us, Lord, as we have put our hope in You.* Let Your kindness be upon us because we have been waiting for You.

Alternatively, let Your kindness be upon us to the extent that we have waited for You, i.e., to the same measure that we have put our faith in Him (Ba'al Shem Tov).

Alternatively, be with us [even in good times] to the same extent that we rely upon

אֹהֵב צְדָקָה וּמִשְׁפָּט, חֶסֶד יהוה מָלְאָה הָאָרֶץ – *He loves righteousness and justice; the earth is full of the Lord's loving-kindness.* Hashem loves justice but, says the Radak, He loves loving-kindness more.

What indication is there of this from the verse? What indication is there of this in the Bible?

What indication of this is there in your life?

מִזְמוֹר שִׁיר A psalm. A song for the Sabbath day. It is good to thank *Ps. 92*
the LORD and sing psalms to Your name, Most High – to tell of Your loving-kindness in the morning and Your faithfulness at night,[I] to the music of the ten-stringed lyre and the melody of the harp. For You have made me rejoice by Your work, O LORD; I sing for joy at the deeds of Your hands. How great are Your deeds, LORD, and how very deep Your thoughts. A boor cannot know, nor can a fool understand, that though the wicked spring up like grass and all evildoers flourish, it is only that they may be destroyed for ever. But You, LORD, are eternally exalted. For behold Your enemies, LORD, behold Your enemies will perish; all evildoers will be scattered. You have raised my pride like that of a wild ox; I am anointed with fresh oil. My eyes shall look in triumph on my adversaries, my ears shall hear the downfall of the wicked who rise against me. ▸ The righteous will flourish like a palm tree and grow tall like a cedar in Lebanon.[B] Planted in the LORD's House, blossoming in our God's courtyards, they will still bear fruit in old age, and stay vigorous and fresh, proclaiming that the LORD is upright: He is my Rock, in whom there is no wrong.

Different prayers are recited at different times of the day because our moods are different throughout the day and the ways that we relate to the world around us are different as well. In the evening, we tend to feel more vulnerable and are thus called upon to have faith (*emuna*) that everything will work out. In the morning, when things are bright, there is the most potential to be thankful for the *hesed* that fills one's life. This is especially so on Shabbat when one does not have to put such thoughts aside in order to rush to work. Shabbat morning is different than any other morning of the week.

Take a moment to feel it.

There is more time to reflect upon all of the good things in the world and in your life.

Take a moment to count them.

תהלים צב

מִזְמוֹר שִׁיר לְיוֹם הַשַּׁבָּת: טוֹב לְהֹדוֹת לַיהוה, וּלְזַמֵּר לְשִׁמְךָ
עֶלְיוֹן: לְהַגִּיד בַּבֹּקֶר חַסְדֶּךָ, וֶאֱמוּנָתְךָ בַּלֵּילוֹת: ע עֲלֵי־עָשׂוֹר
וַעֲלֵי־נָבֶל, עֲלֵי הִגָּיוֹן בְּכִנּוֹר: כִּי שִׂמַּחְתַּנִי יהוה בְּפָעֳלֶךָ, בְּמַעֲשֵׂי
יָדֶיךָ אֲרַנֵּן: מַה־גָּדְלוּ מַעֲשֶׂיךָ יהוה, מְאֹד עָמְקוּ מַחְשְׁבֹתֶיךָ:
אִישׁ־בַּעַר לֹא יֵדָע, וּכְסִיל לֹא־יָבִין אֶת־זֹאת: בִּפְרֹחַ רְשָׁעִים
כְּמוֹ עֵשֶׂב, וַיָּצִיצוּ כָּל־פֹּעֲלֵי אָוֶן, לְהִשָּׁמְדָם עֲדֵי־עַד: וְאַתָּה מָרוֹם
לְעֹלָם יהוה: כִּי הִנֵּה אֹיְבֶיךָ יהוה, כִּי־הִנֵּה אֹיְבֶיךָ יֹאבֵדוּ, יִתְפָּרְדוּ
כָּל־פֹּעֲלֵי אָוֶן: וַתָּרֶם כִּרְאֵים קַרְנִי, בַּלֹּתִי בְּשֶׁמֶן רַעֲנָן: וַתַּבֵּט עֵינִי
בְּשׁוּרָי, בַּקָּמִים עָלַי מְרֵעִים תִּשְׁמַעְנָה אָזְנָי: › צַדִּיק כַּתָּמָר יִפְרָח,
כְּאֶרֶז בַּלְּבָנוֹן יִשְׂגֶּה: ב שְׁתוּלִים בְּבֵית יהוה, בְּחַצְרוֹת אֱלֹהֵינוּ
יַפְרִיחוּ: עוֹד יְנוּבוּן בְּשֵׂיבָה, דְּשֵׁנִים וְרַעֲנַנִּים יִהְיוּ: לְהַגִּיד כִּי־
יָשָׁר יהוה, צוּרִי, וְלֹא־עַוְלָתָה בּוֹ:

BIUR TEFILLA • ביאור תפילה

תהלים צב – *TEHILLIM 92.* This is the second time that this psalm is recited on Shabbat. For further commentary, see page 425.

צַדִּיק כַּתָּמָר יִפְרָח, כְּאֶרֶז בַּלְּבָנוֹן יִשְׂגֶּה – *The righteous will flourish like a palm tree and grow tall like a cedar in Lebanon.* Unlike the evil who are compared to grass, the *tzaddik* or righteous person is compared to two of the most exquisite trees in the Middle East – the palm and the cedar. The one is known for its leaves and fruit, the other for its stature, but as the next verse indicates, both must be firmly rooted to grow, just as must one's life in religious faith in order to flourish.

IYUN TEFILLA • עיון תפילה

לְהַגִּיד בַּבֹּקֶר חַסְדֶּךָ, וֶאֱמוּנָתְךָ בַּלֵּילוֹת – *To tell of Your loving-kindness in the morning and Your faithfulness at night.* Jewish prayer is both time-sensitive and sensitive to time.

יהוה מָלָךְ The LORD reigns. He is robed in majesty. The LORD is robed, girded with strength. The world is firmly established; it cannot be moved. Your throne stands firm as of old; You are eternal. Rivers lift up, LORD, rivers lift up their voice, rivers lift up their Crashing waves. ▸ Mightier than the noise of many waters, than the mighty waves of the sea is the LORD on high. Your testimonies are very sure; holiness adorns Your House, LORD, for evermore. *Ps. 93*

יְהִי כְבוֹד May the LORD's glory be for ever; may the LORD rejoice *Ps. 104*
in His works. May the LORD's name be blessed, now and for ever. *Ps. 113*
From the rising of the sun to its setting, may the LORD's name be
praised. The LORD is high above all nations; His glory is above the
heavens. LORD, Your name is for ever. Your renown, LORD, is for all *Ps. 135*
generations. The LORD has established His throne in heaven; His *Ps. 103*
kingdom rules all. Let the heavens rejoice and the earth be glad. Let *1 Chr. 16*
them say among the nations, "The LORD is King." The LORD is King,
the LORD was King, the LORD will be King for ever and all time.
The LORD is King for ever and all time; nations will perish from *Ps. 10*
His land. The LORD foils the plans of nations; He frustrates the *Ps. 33*
intentions of peoples. Many are the intentions in a person's mind, *Prov. 19*
but the LORD's plan prevails. The LORD's plan shall stand for ever, *Ps. 33*
His mind's intent for all generations. For He spoke and it was; He

---

Six days shall you toil in the market; on the seventh day, shall you detach from money matters.

Six days shall you create, drive, create, invent, push, drive; on the seventh day shall you reflect.

Six days shall you be the perfect success; on the seventh day, shall you remember that not everything is in your power.

Six days shall you be a miserable failure; on the seventh day, shall you be on top of the world.

Six days shall you enjoy the blessings of work; on the seventh day shall you understand that being as important as doing. (Blu Greenberg)

יהוה מָלָךְ, גֵּאוּת לָבֵשׁ, לָבֵשׁ יהוה עֹז הִתְאַזָּר, אַף־תִּכּוֹן תֵּבֵל תהלים צג
בַּל־תִּמּוֹט: נָכוֹן כִּסְאֲךָ מֵאָז, מֵעוֹלָם אָתָּה: נָשְׂאוּ נְהָרוֹת יהוה,
נָשְׂאוּ נְהָרוֹת קוֹלָם, יִשְׂאוּ נְהָרוֹת דָּכְיָם: ◂ מִקֹּלוֹת מַיִם רַבִּים,
אַדִּירִים מִשְׁבְּרֵי־יָם, אַדִּיר בַּמָּרוֹם יהוה: עֵדֹתֶיךָ נֶאֶמְנוּ מְאֹד
לְבֵיתְךָ נַאֲוָה־קֹדֶשׁ, יהוה לְאֹרֶךְ יָמִים:

יְהִי כְבוֹד יהוה לְעוֹלָם, יִשְׂמַח יהוה בְּמַעֲשָׂיו: יְהִי שֵׁם יהוה תהלים קד תהלים קיג
מְבֹרָךְ, מֵעַתָּה וְעַד־עוֹלָם: מִמִּזְרַח־שֶׁמֶשׁ עַד־מְבוֹאוֹ, מְהֻלָּל
שֵׁם יהוה: רָם עַל־כָּל־גּוֹיִם יהוה, עַל הַשָּׁמַיִם כְּבוֹדוֹ: יהוה תהלים קלה
שִׁמְךָ לְעוֹלָם, יהוה זִכְרְךָ לְדֹר־וָדֹר: יהוה בַּשָּׁמַיִם הֵכִין כִּסְאוֹ, תהלים קג
וּמַלְכוּתוֹ בַּכֹּל מָשָׁלָה: יִשְׂמְחוּ הַשָּׁמַיִם וְתָגֵל הָאָרֶץ, וְיֹאמְרוּ דברי הימים א׳ טז
בַגּוֹיִם יהוה מָלָךְ: יהוה מֶלֶךְ, יהוה מָלָךְ, יהוה יִמְלֹךְ לְעוֹלָם וָעֶד.
יהוה מֶלֶךְ עוֹלָם וָעֶד, אָבְדוּ גוֹיִם מֵאַרְצוֹ: יהוה הֵפִיר עֲצַת־גּוֹיִם, תהלים י תהלים לג
הֵנִיא מַחְשְׁבוֹת עַמִּים: רַבּוֹת מַחֲשָׁבוֹת בְּלֶב־אִישׁ, וַעֲצַת יהוה משלי יט
הִיא תָקוּם: עֲצַת יהוה לְעוֹלָם תַּעֲמֹד, מַחְשְׁבוֹת לִבּוֹ לְדֹר וָדֹר: תהלים לג

BIUR TEFILLA • ביאור תפילה

תהלים צג – *TEHILLIM 93.* This is the second time that this psalm is recited on Shabbat. For further commentary, see page 429.

This psalm marks the conclusion of the additional psalms that are added on Shabbat morning. What follows is the same service that occurs during weekdays until one gets to the prayer known as *Nishmat* ("The soul") on page 569.

ANI TEFILLA • אני תפילה

Six days shall you be a workaholic; on the seventh day, shall you join the serene company of human beings.

Six days shall you take orders from your boss; on the seventh day, shall you be a master/mistress of your own life.

commanded and it stood firm. For the LORD has chosen Zion; He Ps. 132
desired it for His dwelling. For the LORD has chosen Jacob, Israel Ps. 135
as His special treasure. For the LORD will not abandon His people; Ps. 94
nor will He forsake His heritage. ▸ He is compassionate. He forgives Ps. 78
iniquity and does not destroy. Repeatedly He suppresses His anger,
not rousing His full wrath. LORD, save! May the King answer us on Ps. 20
the day we call.

The line beginning with "You open Your hand" should be said with special concentration, representing as it does the key idea of this psalm, and of Pesukei DeZimra as a whole, that God is the creator and sustainer of all.

אַשְׁרֵי Happy are those who dwell in Your House; Ps. 84
they shall continue to praise You, Selah!
Happy are the people for whom this is so; Ps. 144
happy are the people whose God is the LORD.
A song of praise by David. Ps. 145

א I will elevate You, my God, the King,
and bless Your name for ever and all time.

ב Every day I will bless You,
and praise Your name for ever and all time.

ג Great is the LORD and greatly to be praised;
His greatness is unfathomable.

ד One generation will praise Your works to the next,
and tell of Your mighty deeds.

ה On the glorious splendor of Your majesty I will meditate,
and on the acts of Your wonders.

ו They shall talk of the power of Your awesome deeds,
and I will tell of Your greatness.

ז They shall recite the record of Your great goodness,
and sing with joy of Your righteousness.

ח The LORD is generous and compassionate,
slow to anger and great in loving-kindness.

ט The LORD is good to all,
and His compassion extends to all His works.

י All Your works shall thank You, LORD,
and Your devoted ones shall bless You.

כִּי הוּא אָמַר וַיֶּהִי, הוּא־צִוָּה וַיַּעֲמֹד: כִּי־בָחַר יהוה בְּצִיּוֹן, אִוָּהּ תהלים קלב
לְמוֹשָׁב לוֹ: כִּי־יַעֲקֹב בָּחַר לוֹ יָהּ, יִשְׂרָאֵל לִסְגֻלָּתוֹ: כִּי לֹא־יִטֹּשׁ תהלים קלה תהלים צד
יהוה עַמּוֹ, וְנַחֲלָתוֹ לֹא יַעֲזֹב: ◂ וְהוּא רַחוּם, יְכַפֵּר עָוֹן וְלֹא־יַשְׁחִית, תהלים עח
וְהִרְבָּה לְהָשִׁיב אַפּוֹ, וְלֹא־יָעִיר כָּל־חֲמָתוֹ: יהוה הוֹשִׁיעָה, הַמֶּלֶךְ תהלים כ
יַעֲנֵנוּ בְיוֹם־קָרְאֵנוּ:

The line beginning with פּוֹתֵחַ אֶת יָדֶךָ *should be said with special concentration, representing as it does the key idea of this psalm, and of* פסוקי דזמרה *as a whole, that God is the creator and sustainer of all.*

אַשְׁרֵי יוֹשְׁבֵי בֵיתֶךָ, עוֹד יְהַלְלוּךָ סֶּלָה: תהלים פד
אַשְׁרֵי הָעָם שֶׁכָּכָה לּוֹ, אַשְׁרֵי הָעָם שֶׁיהוה אֱלֹהָיו: תהלים קמד
תְּהִלָּה לְדָוִד תהלים קמה

אֲרוֹמִמְךָ אֱלוֹהַי הַמֶּלֶךְ, וַאֲבָרְכָה שִׁמְךָ לְעוֹלָם וָעֶד:
בְּכָל־יוֹם אֲבָרְכֶךָּ, וַאֲהַלְלָה שִׁמְךָ לְעוֹלָם וָעֶד:
גָּדוֹל יהוה וּמְהֻלָּל מְאֹד, וְלִגְדֻלָּתוֹ אֵין חֵקֶר:
דּוֹר לְדוֹר יְשַׁבַּח מַעֲשֶׂיךָ, וּגְבוּרֹתֶיךָ יַגִּידוּ:
הֲדַר כְּבוֹד הוֹדֶךָ, וְדִבְרֵי נִפְלְאֹתֶיךָ אָשִׂיחָה:
וֶעֱזוּז נוֹרְאֹתֶיךָ יֹאמֵרוּ, וּגְדוּלָּתְךָ אֲסַפְּרֶנָּה:
זֵכֶר רַב־טוּבְךָ יַבִּיעוּ, וְצִדְקָתְךָ יְרַנֵּנוּ:
חַנּוּן וְרַחוּם יהוה, אֶרֶךְ אַפַּיִם וּגְדָל־חָסֶד:
טוֹב־יהוה לַכֹּל, וְרַחֲמָיו עַל־כָּל־מַעֲשָׂיו:
יוֹדוּךָ יהוה כָּל־מַעֲשֶׂיךָ, וַחֲסִידֶיךָ יְבָרְכוּכָה:

Commentary for the *mizmorim* that appear from this page till 561 can be found on pages 79–92.

כ They shall talk of the glory of Your kingship,
and speak of Your might.
ל To make known to mankind His mighty deeds
and the glorious majesty of His kingship.
מ Your kingdom is an everlasting kingdom,
and Your reign is for all generations.
ס The LORD supports all who fall,
and raises all who are bowed down.
ע All raise their eyes to You in hope,
and You give them their food in due season.
פ You open Your hand, and satisfy every living thing with favor.
צ The LORD is righteous in all His ways, and kind in all He does.
ק The LORD is close to all who call on Him,
to all who call on Him in truth.
ר He fulfills the will of those who fear Him;
He hears their cry and saves them.
ש The LORD guards all who love Him,
but all the wicked He will destroy.
ת ▸ My mouth shall speak the praise of the LORD,
and all creatures shall bless His holy name for ever and all time.
We will bless the LORD now and for ever. Halleluya! *Ps. 115*

הַלְלוּיָהּ Halleluya! Praise the LORD, my soul. I will praise the LORD *Ps. 146* all my life; I will sing to my God as long as I live. Put not your trust in princes, or in mortal man who cannot save. His breath expires,| he returns to the earth; on that day his plans come to an end. Happy is he whose help is the God of Jacob, whose hope is in the LORD his God who made heaven and earth, the sea and all they contain; He who keeps faith for ever. He secures justice for the oppressed.| He gives food to the hungry. The LORD sets captives free. The LORD gives sight to the blind. The LORD raises those bowed down. The LORD loves the righteous. The LORD protects the stranger. He gives courage to the orphan and widow. He thwarts the way of the wicked. ▸ The LORD shall reign for ever. He is your God, Zion, for all generations. Halleluya!

כְּבוֹד מַלְכוּתְךָ יֹאמֵרוּ, וּגְבוּרָתְךָ יְדַבֵּרוּ:
לְהוֹדִיעַ לִבְנֵי הָאָדָם גְּבוּרֹתָיו, וּכְבוֹד הֲדַר מַלְכוּתוֹ:
מַלְכוּתְךָ מַלְכוּת כָּל־עֹלָמִים, וּמֶמְשַׁלְתְּךָ בְּכָל־דּוֹר וָדֹר:
סוֹמֵךְ יהוה לְכָל־הַנֹּפְלִים, וְזוֹקֵף לְכָל־הַכְּפוּפִים:
עֵינֵי־כֹל אֵלֶיךָ יְשַׂבֵּרוּ, וְאַתָּה נוֹתֵן־לָהֶם אֶת־אָכְלָם בְּעִתּוֹ:
פּוֹתֵחַ אֶת־יָדֶךָ, וּמַשְׂבִּיעַ לְכָל־חַי רָצוֹן:
צַדִּיק יהוה בְּכָל־דְּרָכָיו, וְחָסִיד בְּכָל־מַעֲשָׂיו:
קָרוֹב יהוה לְכָל־קֹרְאָיו, לְכֹל אֲשֶׁר יִקְרָאֻהוּ בֶאֱמֶת:
רְצוֹן־יְרֵאָיו יַעֲשֶׂה, וְאֶת־שַׁוְעָתָם יִשְׁמַע, וְיוֹשִׁיעֵם:
שׁוֹמֵר יהוה אֶת־כָּל־אֹהֲבָיו, וְאֵת כָּל־הָרְשָׁעִים יַשְׁמִיד:
‹ תְּהִלַּת יהוה יְדַבֶּר פִּי, וִיבָרֵךְ כָּל־בָּשָׂר שֵׁם קָדְשׁוֹ לְעוֹלָם וָעֶד:
וַאֲנַחְנוּ נְבָרֵךְ יָהּ מֵעַתָּה וְעַד־עוֹלָם, הַלְלוּיָהּ: תהלים קטו

תהלים קמו הַלְלוּיָהּ, הַלְלִי נַפְשִׁי אֶת־יהוה: אֲהַלְלָה יהוה בְּחַיָּי, אֲזַמְּרָה
לֵאלֹהַי בְּעוֹדִי: אַל־תִּבְטְחוּ בִנְדִיבִים, בְּבֶן־אָדָם שֶׁאֵין
לוֹ תְשׁוּעָה: תֵּצֵא רוּחוֹ, יָשֻׁב לְאַדְמָתוֹ, בַּיּוֹם הַהוּא אָבְדוּ
עֶשְׁתֹּנֹתָיו: אַשְׁרֵי שֶׁאֵל יַעֲקֹב בְּעֶזְרוֹ, שִׂבְרוֹ עַל־יהוה אֱלֹהָיו:
עֹשֶׂה שָׁמַיִם וָאָרֶץ, אֶת־הַיָּם וְאֶת־כָּל־אֲשֶׁר־בָּם, הַשֹּׁמֵר אֱמֶת
לְעוֹלָם: עֹשֶׂה מִשְׁפָּט לַעֲשׁוּקִים, נֹתֵן לֶחֶם לָרְעֵבִים, יהוה
מַתִּיר אֲסוּרִים: יהוה פֹּקֵחַ עִוְרִים, יהוה זֹקֵף כְּפוּפִים, יהוה
אֹהֵב צַדִּיקִים: יהוה שֹׁמֵר אֶת־גֵּרִים, יָתוֹם וְאַלְמָנָה יְעוֹדֵד,
וְדֶרֶךְ רְשָׁעִים יְעַוֵּת: ‹ יִמְלֹךְ יהוה לְעוֹלָם, אֱלֹהַיִךְ צִיּוֹן לְדֹר
וָדֹר, הַלְלוּיָהּ:

הַלְלוּיָהּ Halleluya! How good it is to sing songs to our God; how pleasant and fitting to praise Him. The LORD rebuilds Jerusalem. He gathers the scattered exiles of Israel. He heals the brokenhearted and binds up their wounds. He counts the number of the stars, calling each by name. Great is our LORD and mighty in power; His understanding has no limit. The LORD gives courage to the humble, but casts the wicked to the ground. Sing to the LORD in thanks; make music to our God on the harp. He covers the sky with clouds. He provides the earth with rain and makes grass grow on the hills. He gives food to the cattle and to the ravens when they cry. He does not take delight in the strength of horses nor pleasure in the fleetness of man. The LORD takes pleasure in those who fear Him, who put their hope in His loving care. Praise the LORD, Jerusalem; sing to your God, Zion, for He has strengthened the bars of your gates and blessed your children in your midst. He has brought peace to your borders, and satisfied you with the finest wheat. He sends His commandment to earth; swiftly runs His word. He spreads snow like fleece, sprinkles frost like ashes, scatters hail like crumbs. Who can stand His cold? He sends His word and melts them; He makes the wind blow and the waters flow. ▸ He has declared His words to Jacob, His statutes and laws to Israel. He has done this for no other nation; such laws they do not know. Halleluya! *Ps. 147*

הַלְלוּיָהּ Halleluya! Praise the LORD from the heavens, praise Him in the heights. Praise Him, all His angels; praise Him, all His hosts. Praise Him, sun and moon; praise Him, all shining stars. Praise Him, highest heavens and the waters above the heavens. Let them praise the name of the LORD, for He commanded and they were created. He established them for ever and all time, issuing a decree that will never change. Praise the LORD from the earth: sea monsters and all the deep seas; fire and hail, snow and mist, storm winds that obey His word; mountains and all *Ps. 148*

הַלְלוּיָהּ, כִּי־טוֹב זַמְּרָה אֱלֹהֵינוּ, כִּי־נָעִים נָאוָה תְהִלָּה: בּוֹנֵה תהלים קמז
יְרוּשָׁלַםִ יהוה, נִדְחֵי יִשְׂרָאֵל יְכַנֵּס: הָרוֹפֵא לִשְׁבוּרֵי לֵב, וּמְחַבֵּשׁ
לְעַצְּבוֹתָם: מוֹנֶה מִסְפָּר לַכּוֹכָבִים, לְכֻלָּם שֵׁמוֹת יִקְרָא: גָּדוֹל
אֲדוֹנֵינוּ וְרַב־כֹּחַ, לִתְבוּנָתוֹ אֵין מִסְפָּר: מְעוֹדֵד עֲנָוִים יהוה,
מַשְׁפִּיל רְשָׁעִים עֲדֵי־אָרֶץ: עֱנוּ לַיהוה בְּתוֹדָה, זַמְּרוּ לֵאלֹהֵינוּ
בְכִנּוֹר: הַמְכַסֶּה שָׁמַיִם בְּעָבִים, הַמֵּכִין לָאָרֶץ מָטָר, הַמַּצְמִיחַ
הָרִים חָצִיר: נוֹתֵן לִבְהֵמָה לַחְמָהּ, לִבְנֵי עֹרֵב אֲשֶׁר יִקְרָאוּ: לֹא
בִגְבוּרַת הַסּוּס יֶחְפָּץ, לֹא־בְשׁוֹקֵי הָאִישׁ יִרְצֶה: רוֹצֶה יהוה
אֶת־יְרֵאָיו, אֶת־הַמְיַחֲלִים לְחַסְדּוֹ: שַׁבְּחִי יְרוּשָׁלַםִ אֶת־יהוה,
הַלְלִי אֱלֹהַיִךְ צִיּוֹן: כִּי־חִזַּק בְּרִיחֵי שְׁעָרָיִךְ, בֵּרַךְ בָּנַיִךְ בְּקִרְבֵּךְ:
הַשָּׂם־גְּבוּלֵךְ שָׁלוֹם, חֵלֶב חִטִּים יַשְׂבִּיעֵךְ: הַשֹּׁלֵחַ אִמְרָתוֹ אָרֶץ,
עַד־מְהֵרָה יָרוּץ דְּבָרוֹ: הַנֹּתֵן שֶׁלֶג כַּצָּמֶר, כְּפוֹר כָּאֵפֶר יְפַזֵּר:
מַשְׁלִיךְ קַרְחוֹ כְפִתִּים, לִפְנֵי קָרָתוֹ מִי יַעֲמֹד: יִשְׁלַח דְּבָרוֹ וְיַמְסֵם,
יַשֵּׁב רוּחוֹ יִזְּלוּ־מָיִם: ‹ מַגִּיד דְּבָרָו לְיַעֲקֹב, חֻקָּיו וּמִשְׁפָּטָיו
לְיִשְׂרָאֵל: לֹא עָשָׂה כֵן לְכָל־גּוֹי, וּמִשְׁפָּטִים בַּל־יְדָעוּם, הַלְלוּיָהּ:

הַלְלוּיָהּ, הַלְלוּ אֶת־יהוה מִן־הַשָּׁמַיִם, הַלְלוּהוּ בַּמְּרוֹמִים: תהלים קמח
הַלְלוּהוּ כָל־מַלְאָכָיו, הַלְלוּהוּ כָּל־צְבָאָו: הַלְלוּהוּ שֶׁמֶשׁ וְיָרֵחַ,
הַלְלוּהוּ כָּל־כּוֹכְבֵי אוֹר: הַלְלוּהוּ שְׁמֵי הַשָּׁמָיִם, וְהַמַּיִם אֲשֶׁר מֵעַל
הַשָּׁמָיִם: יְהַלְלוּ אֶת־שֵׁם יהוה, כִּי הוּא צִוָּה וְנִבְרָאוּ: וַיַּעֲמִידֵם
לָעַד לְעוֹלָם, חָק־נָתַן וְלֹא יַעֲבוֹר: הַלְלוּ אֶת־יהוה מִן־הָאָרֶץ,
תַּנִּינִים וְכָל־תְּהֹמוֹת: אֵשׁ וּבָרָד שֶׁלֶג וְקִיטוֹר, רוּחַ סְעָרָה עֹשָׂה
דְבָרוֹ: הֶהָרִים וְכָל־גְּבָעוֹת, עֵץ פְּרִי וְכָל־אֲרָזִים: הַחַיָּה וְכָל־

hills, fruit trees and all cedars; wild animals and all cattle, creeping things and winged birds; kings of the earth and all nations, princes and all judges on earth; youths and maidens, old and young. ▸ Let them praise the name of the LORD, for His name alone is sublime; His majesty is above earth and heaven. He has raised the pride of His people, for the glory of all His devoted ones, the children of Israel, the people close to Him. Halleluya!

הַלְלוּיָהּ Halleluya! Sing to the LORD a new song, His praise in the assembly of the devoted. Let Israel rejoice in its Maker; let the children of Zion exult in their King. Let them praise His name with dancing; sing praises to Him with timbrel and harp. For the LORD delights in His people; He adorns the humble with salvation. Let the devoted revel in glory; let them sing for joy on their beds. Let high praises of God be in their throats, and a two-edged sword in their hand: to impose retribution on the nations, punishment on the peoples, ▸ binding their kings with chains, their nobles with iron fetters, carrying out the judgment written against them. This is the glory of all His devoted ones. Halleluya! *Ps. 149*

הַלְלוּיָהּ Halleluya! Praise God in His holy place; *Ps. 150*
praise Him in the heavens of His power.
Praise Him for His mighty deeds;
praise Him for His surpassing greatness.
Praise Him with blasts of the shofar;
praise Him with the harp and lyre.
Praise Him with timbrel and dance;
praise Him with strings and flute.
Praise Him with clashing cymbals;
praise Him with resounding cymbals.
▸ Let all that breathes praise the LORD. Halleluya!
Let all that breathes praise the LORD. Halleluya!

בְּהֵמָה, רֶמֶשׂ וְצִפּוֹר כָּנָף: מַלְכֵי־אֶרֶץ וְכָל־לְאֻמִּים, שָׂרִים וְכָל־
שֹׁפְטֵי אָרֶץ: בַּחוּרִים וְגַם־בְּתוּלוֹת, זְקֵנִים עִם־נְעָרִים: ◂ יְהַלְלוּ
אֶת־שֵׁם יהוה, כִּי־נִשְׂגָּב שְׁמוֹ לְבַדּוֹ, הוֹדוֹ עַל־אֶרֶץ וְשָׁמָיִם: וַיָּרֶם
קֶרֶן לְעַמּוֹ, תְּהִלָּה לְכָל־חֲסִידָיו, לִבְנֵי יִשְׂרָאֵל עַם קְרֹבוֹ, הַלְלוּיָהּ:

הַלְלוּיָהּ, שִׁירוּ לַיהוה שִׁיר חָדָשׁ, תְּהִלָּתוֹ בִּקְהַל חֲסִידִים: יִשְׂמַח תהלים קמט
יִשְׂרָאֵל בְּעֹשָׂיו, בְּנֵי־צִיּוֹן יָגִילוּ בְמַלְכָּם: יְהַלְלוּ שְׁמוֹ בְמָחוֹל, בְּתֹף
וְכִנּוֹר יְזַמְּרוּ־לוֹ: כִּי־רוֹצֶה יהוה בְּעַמּוֹ, יְפָאֵר עֲנָוִים בִּישׁוּעָה:
יַעְלְזוּ חֲסִידִים בְּכָבוֹד, יְרַנְּנוּ עַל־מִשְׁכְּבוֹתָם: רוֹמְמוֹת אֵל
בִּגְרוֹנָם, וְחֶרֶב פִּיפִיּוֹת בְּיָדָם: לַעֲשׂוֹת נְקָמָה בַּגּוֹיִם, תּוֹכֵחוֹת
בַּלְאֻמִּים: ◂ לֶאְסֹר מַלְכֵיהֶם בְּזִקִּים, וְנִכְבְּדֵיהֶם בְּכַבְלֵי בַרְזֶל:
לַעֲשׂוֹת בָּהֶם מִשְׁפָּט כָּתוּב, הָדָר הוּא לְכָל־חֲסִידָיו, הַלְלוּיָהּ:

הַלְלוּיָהּ, הַלְלוּ־אֵל בְּקָדְשׁוֹ תהלים קנ
הַלְלוּהוּ בִּרְקִיעַ עֻזּוֹ:
הַלְלוּהוּ בִגְבוּרֹתָיו
הַלְלוּהוּ כְּרֹב גֻּדְלוֹ:
הַלְלוּהוּ בְּתֵקַע שׁוֹפָר
הַלְלוּהוּ בְּנֵבֶל וְכִנּוֹר:
הַלְלוּהוּ בְּתֹף וּמָחוֹל
הַלְלוּהוּ בְּמִנִּים וְעוּגָב:
הַלְלוּהוּ בְצִלְצְלֵי־שָׁמַע
הַלְלוּהוּ בְּצִלְצְלֵי תְרוּעָה:
◂ כֹּל הַנְּשָׁמָה תְּהַלֵּל יָהּ, הַלְלוּיָהּ:
כֹּל הַנְּשָׁמָה תְּהַלֵּל יָהּ, הַלְלוּיָהּ:

בָּרוּךְ Blessed be the LORD for ever. Amen and Amen. *Ps. 89*
Blessed from Zion be the LORD *Ps. 135*
who dwells in Jerusalem. Halleluya!
Blessed be the LORD, God of Israel, *Ps. 72*
who alone does wonders.
▸ Blessed be His glorious name for ever,
and may all the earth be filled with His glory.
Amen and Amen.

Stand until "The soul" on page 568.

וַיְבָרֶךְ David blessed the LORD in front of the entire assembly. David *1 Chr. 29* said, "Blessed are You, LORD, God of our father Yisrael, for ever and ever. Yours, LORD, are the greatness and the power, the glory, majesty and splendor, for everything in heaven and earth is Yours. Yours, LORD, is the kingdom; You are exalted as Head over all. Both riches and honor are in Your gift and You reign over all things. In Your hand are strength and might. It is in Your power to make great and give strength to all. Therefore, our God, we thank You and praise Your glorious name." You alone are the LORD. You *Neh. 9* made the heavens, even the highest heavens, and all their hosts, the earth and all that is on it, the seas and all they contain. You give life to them all, and the hosts of heaven worship You. ▸ You are the LORD God who chose Abram and brought him out of Ur of the Chaldees, changing his name to Abraham. You found his heart faithful toward You, ◂ and You made a covenant with him to give to his descendants the land of the Canaanites, Hittites, Amorites, Perizzites, Jebusites and Girgashites. You fulfilled Your promise for You are righteous. You saw the suffering of our ancestors in Egypt. You heard their cry at the Sea of Reeds. You sent signs and wonders against Pharaoh, all his servants and all the people of his land, because You knew how arrogantly the Egyptians treated them. You created for Yourself renown that remains to this day. ▸ You divided the sea before them, so that they passed through the sea on dry land, but You cast their pursuers into the depths, like a stone into mighty waters.

בָּרוּךְ יהוה לְעוֹלָם, אָמֵן וְאָמֵן: תהלים פט
בָּרוּךְ יהוה מִצִּיּוֹן, שֹׁכֵן יְרוּשָׁלָםִ, הַלְלוּיָהּ: תהלים קלה
בָּרוּךְ יהוה אֱלֹהִים אֱלֹהֵי יִשְׂרָאֵל, עֹשֵׂה נִפְלָאוֹת לְבַדּוֹ: תהלים עב
◂ וּבָרוּךְ שֵׁם כְּבוֹדוֹ לְעוֹלָם, וְיִמָּלֵא כְבוֹדוֹ אֶת־כָּל־הָאָרֶץ
אָמֵן וְאָמֵן:

Stand until נִשְׁמַת *on page 569.*

וַיְבָרֶךְ דָּוִיד אֶת־יהוה לְעֵינֵי כָּל־הַקָּהָל, וַיֹּאמֶר דָּוִיד, בָּרוּךְ אַתָּה יהוה, אֱלֹהֵי יִשְׂרָאֵל אָבִינוּ, מֵעוֹלָם וְעַד־עוֹלָם: לְךָ יהוה הַגְּדֻלָּה וְהַגְּבוּרָה וְהַתִּפְאֶרֶת וְהַנֵּצַח וְהַהוֹד, כִּי־כֹל בַּשָּׁמַיִם וּבָאָרֶץ, לְךָ יהוה הַמַּמְלָכָה וְהַמִּתְנַשֵּׂא לְכֹל לְרֹאשׁ: וְהָעֹשֶׁר וְהַכָּבוֹד מִלְּפָנֶיךָ, וְאַתָּה מוֹשֵׁל בַּכֹּל, וּבְיָדְךָ כֹּחַ וּגְבוּרָה, וּבְיָדְךָ לְגַדֵּל וּלְחַזֵּק לַכֹּל: וְעַתָּה אֱלֹהֵינוּ מוֹדִים אֲנַחְנוּ לָךְ, וּמְהַלְלִים לְשֵׁם תִּפְאַרְתֶּךָ: (דברי הימים א׳ כט)

אַתָּה־הוּא יהוה לְבַדֶּךָ, אַתָּ עָשִׂיתָ אֶת־הַשָּׁמַיִם, שְׁמֵי הַשָּׁמַיִם וְכָל־צְבָאָם, הָאָרֶץ וְכָל־אֲשֶׁר עָלֶיהָ, הַיַּמִּים וְכָל־אֲשֶׁר בָּהֶם, וְאַתָּה מְחַיֶּה אֶת־כֻּלָּם, וּצְבָא הַשָּׁמַיִם לְךָ מִשְׁתַּחֲוִים: ◂ אַתָּה הוּא יהוה הָאֱלֹהִים אֲשֶׁר בָּחַרְתָּ בְּאַבְרָם, וְהוֹצֵאתוֹ מֵאוּר כַּשְׂדִּים, וְשַׂמְתָּ שְׁמוֹ אַבְרָהָם: וּמָצָאתָ אֶת־לְבָבוֹ נֶאֱמָן לְפָנֶיךָ, ◂ וְכָרוֹת עִמּוֹ הַבְּרִית לָתֵת אֶת־אֶרֶץ הַכְּנַעֲנִי הַחִתִּי הָאֱמֹרִי וְהַפְּרִזִּי וְהַיְבוּסִי וְהַגִּרְגָּשִׁי, לָתֵת לְזַרְעוֹ, וַתָּקֶם אֶת־דְּבָרֶיךָ, כִּי צַדִּיק אָתָּה: וַתֵּרֶא אֶת־עֳנִי אֲבֹתֵינוּ בְּמִצְרָיִם, וְאֶת־זַעֲקָתָם שָׁמַעְתָּ עַל־יַם־סוּף: וַתִּתֵּן אֹתֹת וּמֹפְתִים בְּפַרְעֹה וּבְכָל־עֲבָדָיו וּבְכָל־עַם אַרְצוֹ, כִּי יָדַעְתָּ כִּי הֵזִידוּ עֲלֵיהֶם, וַתַּעַשׂ־לְךָ שֵׁם כְּהַיּוֹם הַזֶּה: ◂ וְהַיָּם בָּקַעְתָּ לִפְנֵיהֶם, וַיַּעַבְרוּ בְתוֹךְ־הַיָּם בַּיַּבָּשָׁה, וְאֶת־רֹדְפֵיהֶם הִשְׁלַכְתָּ בִמְצוֹלֹת כְּמוֹ־אֶבֶן, בְּמַיִם עַזִּים: (נחמיה ט)

וַיּוֹשַׁע That day the LORD saved Israel from the hands of the Egyptians, *Ex. 14*
and Israel saw the Egyptians lying dead on the seashore. ▸ When Israel saw the great power the LORD had displayed against the Egyptians, the people feared the LORD, and believed in the LORD and in His servant, Moses.

אָז יָשִׁיר־מֹשֶׁה Then Moses and the Israelites sang this song *Ex. 15*
to the LORD, saying:
I will sing to the LORD, for He has triumphed gloriously;
horse and rider He has hurled into the sea.
The LORD is my strength and song; He has become my salvation.
This is my God, and I will beautify Him,
my father's God, and I will exalt Him.
The LORD is a Master of war; LORD is His name.
Pharaoh's chariots and army He cast into the sea;
the best of his officers drowned in the Sea of Reeds.
The deep waters covered them;
they went down to the depths like a stone.
Your right hand, LORD, is majestic in power.
Your right hand, LORD, shatters the enemy.
In the greatness of Your majesty, You overthrew those who rose against You.
You sent out Your fury; it consumed them like stubble.
By the blast of Your nostrils the waters piled up.
The surging waters stood straight like a wall;
the deeps congealed in the heart of the sea.
The enemy said, "I will pursue. I will overtake. I will divide the spoil.
My desire shall have its fill of them.
I will draw my sword. My hand will destroy them."
You blew with Your wind; the sea covered them.
They sank in the mighty waters like lead.
Who is like You, LORD, among the mighty? Who is like You –
majestic in holiness, awesome in glory, working wonders?
You stretched out Your right hand, the earth swallowed them.
In Your loving-kindness, You led the people You redeemed.
In Your strength, You guided them to Your holy abode.

וַיּוֹשַׁע יהוה בַּיּוֹם הַהוּא אֶת־יִשְׂרָאֵל מִיַּד מִצְרָיִם, וַיַּרְא יִשְׂרָאֵל שמות יד
אֶת־מִצְרַיִם מֵת עַל־שְׂפַת הַיָּם: ◂ וַיַּרְא יִשְׂרָאֵל אֶת־הַיָּד הַגְּדֹלָה
אֲשֶׁר עָשָׂה יהוה בְּמִצְרַיִם, וַיִּירְאוּ הָעָם אֶת־יהוה, וַיַּאֲמִינוּ
בַּיהוה וּבְמֹשֶׁה עַבְדּוֹ:

אָז יָשִׁיר־מֹשֶׁה וּבְנֵי יִשְׂרָאֵל אֶת־הַשִּׁירָה הַזֹּאת לַיהוה, וַיֹּאמְרוּ שמות טו
לֵאמֹר, אָשִׁירָה לַיהוה כִּי־גָאֹה גָּאָה, סוּס
וְרֹכְבוֹ רָמָה בַיָּם: עָזִּי וְזִמְרָת יָהּ וַיְהִי־לִי
לִישׁוּעָה, זֶה אֵלִי וְאַנְוֵהוּ, אֱלֹהֵי
אָבִי וַאֲרֹמְמֶנְהוּ: יהוה אִישׁ מִלְחָמָה, יהוה
שְׁמוֹ: מַרְכְּבֹת פַּרְעֹה וְחֵילוֹ יָרָה בַיָּם, וּמִבְחַר
שָׁלִשָׁיו טֻבְּעוּ בְיַם־סוּף: תְּהֹמֹת יְכַסְיֻמוּ, יָרְדוּ בִמְצוֹלֹת כְּמוֹ־
אָבֶן: יְמִינְךָ יהוה נֶאְדָּרִי בַּכֹּחַ, יְמִינְךָ
יהוה תִּרְעַץ אוֹיֵב: וּבְרֹב גְּאוֹנְךָ תַּהֲרֹס
קָמֶיךָ, תְּשַׁלַּח חֲרֹנְךָ יֹאכְלֵמוֹ כַּקַּשׁ: וּבְרוּחַ
אַפֶּיךָ נֶעֶרְמוּ מַיִם, נִצְּבוּ כְמוֹ־נֵד
נֹזְלִים, קָפְאוּ תְהֹמֹת בְּלֶב־יָם: אָמַר
אוֹיֵב אֶרְדֹּף, אַשִּׂיג, אֲחַלֵּק שָׁלָל, תִּמְלָאֵמוֹ
נַפְשִׁי, אָרִיק חַרְבִּי תּוֹרִישֵׁמוֹ יָדִי: נָשַׁפְתָּ
בְרוּחֲךָ כִּסָּמוֹ יָם, צָלְלוּ כַּעוֹפֶרֶת בְּמַיִם
אַדִּירִים: מִי־כָמֹכָה בָּאֵלִם יהוה, מִי
כָּמֹכָה נֶאְדָּר בַּקֹּדֶשׁ, נוֹרָא תְהִלֹּת עֹשֵׂה
פֶלֶא: נָטִיתָ יְמִינְךָ תִּבְלָעֵמוֹ אָרֶץ: נָחִיתָ
בְחַסְדְּךָ עַם־זוּ גָּאָלְתָּ, נֵהַלְתָּ בְעָזְּךָ אֶל־נְוֵה
קָדְשֶׁךָ: שָׁמְעוּ עַמִּים יִרְגָּזוּן, חִיל

Nations heard and trembled;
terror gripped Philistia's inhabitants.
The chiefs of Edom were dismayed,
Moab's leaders were seized with trembling,
the people of Canaan melted away.
Fear and dread fell upon them.
By the power of Your arm, they were still as stone –
until Your people crossed, LORD,
until the people You acquired crossed over.
You will bring them and plant them on the mountain of Your heritage –
the place, LORD, You made for Your dwelling,
the Sanctuary, LORD, Your hands established.
The LORD will reign for ever and all time.

The LORD will reign for ever and all time.
The LORD's kingship is established for ever and to all eternity.

When Pharaoh's horses, chariots and riders went into the sea,
the LORD brought the waters of the sea back over them,
but the Israelites walked on dry land through the sea.

▸ For kingship is the LORD's and He rules over the nations. *Ps. 22*
Saviors shall go up to Mount Zion to judge Mount Esau, *Ob. 1*
and the LORD's shall be the kingdom.
Then the LORD shall be King over all the earth; *Zech. 14*
on that day the LORD shall be One and His name One,

(as it is written in Your Torah, saying:
Listen, Israel: the LORD is our God, the LORD is One.) *Deut. 6*

---

what seems like the bad. In the midst of crisis, it is hard to see the positive, unless you believe that it too is ultimately for the good. So ingrained is this worldview in Jewish life that it has been given expression in numerous ways, both popular and legal. As early as the first century, there was a sage who was known by the name Nahum ish Gamzu presumably because he would forever say *"gam zu le'tova"* meaning, "this too is for the good," a phrase still used colloquially today. In a similar vein, there is actually a blessing on hearing bad news, not because one ignores its sadness but because one prays that ultimately it is for the good. Judaism by its nature is forever optimistic.

אָחַז יֹשְׁבֵי פְּלָשֶׁת: אָז נִבְהֲלוּ אַלּוּפֵי
אֱדוֹם, אֵילֵי מוֹאָב יֹאחֲזֵמוֹ רָעַד, נָמֹגוּ
כֹּל יֹשְׁבֵי כְנָעַן: תִּפֹּל עֲלֵיהֶם אֵימָתָה
וָפַחַד, בִּגְדֹל זְרוֹעֲךָ יִדְּמוּ כָּאָבֶן, עַד־
יַעֲבֹר עַמְּךָ יהוה, עַד־יַעֲבֹר עַם־זוּ
קָנִיתָ: תְּבִאֵמוֹ וְתִטָּעֵמוֹ בְּהַר נַחֲלָתְךָ, מָכוֹן
לְשִׁבְתְּךָ פָּעַלְתָּ יהוה, מִקְּדָשׁ אֲדֹנָי כּוֹנְנוּ
יָדֶיךָ: יהוה יִמְלֹךְ לְעֹלָם וָעֶד:

יהוה יִמְלֹךְ לְעֹלָם וָעֶד.
יהוה מַלְכוּתֵהּ קָאֵם לְעָלַם וּלְעָלְמֵי עָלְמַיָּא.

כִּי
בָא סוּס פַּרְעֹה בְּרִכְבּוֹ וּבְפָרָשָׁיו בַּיָּם, וַיָּשֶׁב יהוה עֲלֵהֶם אֶת־מֵי
הַיָּם, וּבְנֵי יִשְׂרָאֵל הָלְכוּ בַיַּבָּשָׁה בְּתוֹךְ הַיָּם:

תהלים כב ‹ כִּי לַיהוה הַמְּלוּכָה וּמֹשֵׁל בַּגּוֹיִם:
עובדיה א וְעָלוּ מוֹשִׁעִים בְּהַר צִיּוֹן לִשְׁפֹּט אֶת־הַר עֵשָׂו
וְהָיְתָה לַיהוה הַמְּלוּכָה:
זכריה יד וְהָיָה יהוה לְמֶלֶךְ עַל־כָּל־הָאָרֶץ
בַּיּוֹם הַהוּא יִהְיֶה יהוה אֶחָד וּשְׁמוֹ אֶחָד:
דברים ו (וּבְתוֹרָתְךָ כָּתוּב לֵאמֹר, שְׁמַע יִשְׂרָאֵל, יהוה אֱלֹהֵינוּ יהוה אֶחָד:)

ANI TEFILLA • אני תפילה

Rabbi Levi Yitzḥak of Berditchev said that David thought that one should praise God when good things happen but he couldn't understand why one should do so when bad things happen. But when David saw that he was saved as a result of having to lower himself by acting as if he had lost his senses, he realized that this too was part of God's plan. Hence he said, "I will bless Hashem at all times," during the good and

THE SOUL[B]

of all that lives shall bless Your name,[1] LORD our God,
and the spirit of all flesh shall always glorify
and exalt Your remembrance, our King.
From eternity to eternity You are God.
Without You, we have no King, Redeemer or Savior,
who liberates, rescues, sustains
and shows compassion in every time of trouble and distress.
We have no King but You, God of the first and last,
God of all creatures,[B] Master of all ages,
extolled by a multitude of praises,
who guides His world with loving-kindness
and His creatures with compassion.
The LORD neither slumbers nor sleeps.
He rouses the sleepers and wakens the slumberers.
He makes the dumb speak, sets the bound free,
supports the fallen, and raises those bowed down.

---

think more clearly. We feel more profoundly. Indeed, the word for soul (*neshama*) and breath (*neshima*) are closely related. "In the still silence of the turning world it is as if we hear all that lives sing a song of praise to God who brought the universe into being, sustains it, and guides the destinies of all things" (Rabbi J. Sacks).

Take a deep breath or two, recite the prayer and feel.

IYUN TEFILLA • עיון תפילה

נִשְׁמַת כָּל חַי תְּבָרֵךְ אֶת שִׁמְךָ – *The soul of all that lives will bless Your name.* The constant prayer of our soul is always striving to emerge from concealment to revelation, to spread through all the life-powers of our entire spirit and all the life-powers of our entire body (Rav Kook, *Olat Reiya*). As I read this prayer, I will try to allow my soul to peek out from its hiding place.

BIUR TEFILLA • ביאור תפילה

אֱלֹהֵי הָרִאשׁוֹנִים וְהָאַחֲרוֹנִים, אֱלוֹהַּ כָּל בְּרִיּוֹת אֲדוֹן כָּל תּוֹלָדוֹת – *Literally: God of the first and the last, God of all creations, Master of all nature.* Each phrase represents a different aspect of his dominion: He is the God of man, of animals, of the inanimate (Hida). On this day, our goal is to see ourselves as a part of and not apart from.

נִשְׁמַת[ב]

כָּל חַי תְּבָרֵךְ אֶת שִׁמְךָ,[ע] יהוה אֱלֹהֵינוּ
וְרוּחַ כָּל בָּשָׂר תְּפָאֵר וּתְרוֹמֵם זִכְרְךָ מַלְכֵּנוּ תָּמִיד.
מִן הָעוֹלָם וְעַד הָעוֹלָם אַתָּה אֵל
וּמִבַּלְעָדֶיךָ אֵין לָנוּ מֶלֶךְ גּוֹאֵל וּמוֹשִׁיעַ
פּוֹדֶה וּמַצִּיל וּמְפַרְנֵס וּמְרַחֵם
בְּכָל עֵת צָרָה וְצוּקָה אֵין לָנוּ מֶלֶךְ אֶלָּא אָתָּה.
אֱלֹהֵי הָרִאשׁוֹנִים וְהָאַחֲרוֹנִים, אֱלוֹהַּ כָּל בְּרִיּוֹת
אֲדוֹן כָּל תּוֹלָדוֹת,[ב] הַמְהֻלָּל בְּרֹב הַתִּשְׁבָּחוֹת
הַמְנַהֵג עוֹלָמוֹ בְּחֶסֶד וּבְרִיּוֹתָיו בְּרַחֲמִים.
וַיהוה לֹא יָנוּם וְלֹא יִישָׁן
הַמְעוֹרֵר יְשֵׁנִים וְהַמֵּקִיץ נִרְדָּמִים
וְהַמֵּשִׂיחַ אִלְּמִים וְהַמַּתִּיר אֲסוּרִים
וְהַסּוֹמֵךְ נוֹפְלִים וְהַזּוֹקֵף כְּפוּפִים.

BIUR TEFILLA • ביאור תפילה

נִשְׁמַת – *NISHMAT.*

As the *Psukei DeZimra* section nears its conclusion, as we get closer to the *Amida*, we move ever higher. We just spoke of the emergence of Israel from the splitting of the Sea and of a day when all will go up to Jerusalem, to Mount Zion. Now, on Shabbat and Yom Tov, we can speak as well about the ascendancy of our own soul. During the week, we immerse ourselves as we have these past minutes in God's presence in creation and in history but we do not necessarily have time to linger and pursue their impact upon us. Today, however, we can push ourselves a little further, reaching further inward even as we strive upward.

Hassidic tradition suggests that at this juncture we acquire a small piece of the *neshama yeteira* or "extra soul" that is a hallmark of Shabbat (Arizal, cited in *Petura deAba*). We breathe more deeply. We

To You alone we give thanks:
If our mouths were as full of song as the sea,
and our tongue with jubilation as its myriad waves,
if our lips were full of praise like the spacious heavens,
and our eyes shone like the sun and moon,
if our hands were outstretched like eagles of the sky,
and our feet as swift as hinds –
still we could not thank You enough,
LORD our God and God of our ancestors,
or bless Your name
for even one of the thousand thousands
and myriad myriads of favors
You did for our ancestors and for us.
You redeemed us from Egypt, LORD our God,
and freed us from the house of bondage.
In famine You nourished us;
in times of plenty You sustained us.
You delivered us from the sword, saved us from the plague,
and spared us from serious and lasting illness.
Until now Your mercies have helped us.
Your love has not forsaken us.
May You, LORD our God, never abandon us.[A]

ANI TEFILLA • אני תפילה

מֵחֶרֶב הִצַּלְתָּנוּ... וְאַל תִּטְּשֵׁנוּ... לָנֶצַח – *You delivered us from the sword... May You... never abandon us.* I must share with you what I experienced at a meeting of revering recovering alcoholics. It was a "gratitude meeting," at which one person after another expressed thankfulness for the second chance in life and for all of the wonderful things that happened since giving up drinking. The last person to speak said, "I am now sober for four years, and I wish I could tell you that they have been good. I lost my job when my company downsized. My wife divorced me and took custody of the children. I was unable to pay the mortgage, and the bank foreclosed on my house. Last week, the finance company repossessed my car. But I know that God did not bring me all this way only to walk out on me now." That is what we say in the *Nishmat* prayer... As individuals and as a nation, God did not allow us to survive much travail only to walk out on us now (Rabbi Abraham Twerski).

לְךָ לְבַדְּךָ אֲנַחְנוּ מוֹדִים.
אִלּוּ פִינוּ מָלֵא שִׁירָה כַּיָּם,[ע] וּלְשׁוֹנֵנוּ רִנָּה כַּהֲמוֹן גַּלָּיו
וְשִׂפְתוֹתֵינוּ שֶׁבַח כְּמֶרְחֲבֵי רָקִיעַ
וְעֵינֵינוּ מְאִירוֹת כַּשֶּׁמֶשׁ וְכַיָּרֵחַ
וְיָדֵינוּ פְרוּשׂוֹת כְּנִשְׁרֵי שָׁמָיִם, וְרַגְלֵינוּ קַלּוֹת כָּאַיָּלוֹת
אֵין אֲנַחְנוּ מַסְפִּיקִים לְהוֹדוֹת לְךָ
יהוה אֱלֹהֵינוּ וֵאלֹהֵי אֲבוֹתֵינוּ
וּלְבָרֵךְ אֶת שְׁמֶךָ
עַל אַחַת מֵאָלֶף אֶלֶף אַלְפֵי אֲלָפִים
וְרִבֵּי רְבָבוֹת פְּעָמִים הַטּוֹבוֹת
שֶׁעָשִׂיתָ עִם אֲבוֹתֵינוּ וְעִמָּנוּ.
מִמִּצְרַיִם גְּאַלְתָּנוּ,[ע] יהוה אֱלֹהֵינוּ, וּמִבֵּית עֲבָדִים פְּדִיתָנוּ
בְּרָעָב זַנְתָּנוּ וּבְשָׂבָע כִּלְכַּלְתָּנוּ
מֵחֶרֶב הִצַּלְתָּנוּ וּמִדֶּבֶר מִלַּטְתָּנוּ
וּמֵחֳלָיִים רָעִים וְנֶאֱמָנִים דִּלִּיתָנוּ.
עַד הֵנָּה עֲזָרוּנוּ רַחֲמֶיךָ, וְלֹא עֲזָבוּנוּ חֲסָדֶיךָ
וְאַל תִּטְּשֵׁנוּ, יהוה אֱלֹהֵינוּ, לָנֶצַח.[א]

IYUN TEFILLA • עיון תפילה

אִלּוּ פִינוּ מָלֵא שִׁירָה כַּיָּם – *If our mouths were as full of song as the sea.* Of course, the sea is never really full. Neither should be our appreciation.

מִמִּצְרַיִם גְּאַלְתָּנוּ – *You redeemed us from Egypt.* The word for Egypt (*Mitzrayim*) is often associated with the word *meitzarim* which means straits, a bad or difficult situation. Just as Hashem saved us there, so too does the redemption from Egypt spill easily into other areas of human suffering where we acknowledge His relieving hand: famine, wars, plague, illness.

Perhaps, too, this is the source for a custom ascribed to Rabbi Yehuda HaḤasid (twelfth century) that before one travels on a journey, something that was filled with danger in those days, one should vow to recite this prayer (*Nishmat*) upon arrival at one's destination (*Ḥemdat Yamim*).

Therefore the limbs You formed within us,
the spirit and soul You breathed into our nostrils,
and the tongue You placed in our mouth –
they will thank and bless,[I]
praise and glorify, exalt and esteem,
hallow and do homage to Your name, O our King.
For every mouth shall give thanks to You,
every tongue vow allegiance to You,
every knee shall bend to You,[B]
every upright body shall bow to You,
all hearts shall fear You,
and our innermost being sing praises to Your name,
as is written:

"All my bones shall say:[I] LORD, who is like You? *Ps. 35*
You save the poor from one stronger than him,
the poor and needy from one who would rob him."

Who is like You?
Who is equal to You?
Who can be compared to You?
O great, mighty and awesome God, God Most High,
Maker of heaven and earth.

---

yet others who use their hands and their actions to praise You or bring attention to You. I alone could not do it all but, as a community, we can merge our strengths to form a powerful unified voice (Hatam Sofer). My praise merges with that of others and we become a sum of all our parts. We are a praying community to whom I contribute what I can and from whom I draw the strength I do not have.

כָּל עַצְמֹתַי תֹּאמַרְנָה – *All of my bones will say.* From here one may learn that one should sway one's body during prayer (*Sefer Hassidim*).

BIUR TEFILLA • ביאור תפילה

וְכָל קוֹמָה לְפָנֶיךָ תִשְׁתַּחֲוֶה – *Every upright body shall bow to You.* Rabbi Barukh of Mezbizh said that the meaning is not that every person standing will bow; rather, a person can bow down even if he is standing upright, as long as his heart his broken.

עַל כֵּן אֵבָרִים שֶׁפִּלַּגְתָּ בָּנוּ
וְרוּחַ וּנְשָׁמָה שֶׁנָּפַחְתָּ בְּאַפֵּינוּ
וְלָשׁוֹן אֲשֶׁר שַׂמְתָּ בְּפִינוּ
הֵן הֵם יוֹדוּ וִיבָרְכוּ[ע] וִישַׁבְּחוּ וִיפָאֲרוּ
וִירוֹמְמוּ וְיַעֲרִיצוּ וְיַקְדִּישׁוּ וְיַמְלִיכוּ אֶת שִׁמְךָ מַלְכֵּנוּ
כִּי כָל פֶּה לְךָ יוֹדֶה
וְכָל לָשׁוֹן לְךָ תִשָּׁבַע
וְכָל בֶּרֶךְ לְךָ תִכְרַע
וְכָל קוֹמָה לְפָנֶיךָ תִשְׁתַּחֲוֶה[ב]
וְכָל לְבָבוֹת יִירָאוּךָ
וְכָל קֶרֶב וּכְלָיוֹת יְזַמְּרוּ לִשְׁמֶךָ
כַּדָּבָר שֶׁכָּתוּב

כָּל עַצְמֹתַי תֹּאמַרְנָה[ע] יהוה מִי כָמוֹךָ תהלים לה
מַצִּיל עָנִי מֵחָזָק מִמֶּנּוּ, וְעָנִי וְאֶבְיוֹן מִגֹּזְלוֹ:

מִי יִדְמֶה לָּךְ
וּמִי יִשְׁוֶה לָּךְ
וּמִי יַעֲרָךְ לָךְ
הָאֵל הַגָּדוֹל, הַגִּבּוֹר וְהַנּוֹרָא
אֵל עֶלְיוֹן, קוֹנֵה שָׁמַיִם וָאָרֶץ.

IYUN TEFILLA • עיון תפילה

עַל כֵּן אֵבָרִים שֶׁפִּלַּגְתָּ בָּנוּ וְרוּחַ וּנְשָׁמָה... וְלָשׁוֹן... הֵן הֵם יוֹדוּ וִיבָרְכוּ – *Therefore The limbs You formed within us, the spirit and soul…the tongue...they will thank and bless.* I cannot do it all alone. But there are people standing beside me right now who have great voices or use their voices for positive purpose, there are those who use their intellects and

► We will laud, praise and glorify You and bless Your holy name,
as it is said:

"Of David. Bless the LORD, O my soul, Ps. 103
and all that is within me bless His holy name."

הָאֵל God – in Your absolute power,
Great – in the glory of Your name,
Mighty – for ever,
Awesome[B] – in Your awe-inspiring deeds,
The King – who sits on a throne.
High and lofty

The Leader begins here:

HE INHABITS ETERNITY;
exalted and holy is His name.
And it is written:

Sing joyfully to the LORD, you righteous, Ps. 33
for praise from the upright is seemly.

► By the mouth	of the upright	You shall be praised.
By the words	of the righteous	You shall be blessed.
By the tongue	of the devout	You shall be extolled,
And in the midst	of the holy	You shall be sanctified.

HILKHOT TEFILLA • הלכות תפילה

There is often a change in the *ḥazan* (prayer leader) at this point as we make the transition from the *Psukei DeZimra* section of the service which we are completing, to the next section (called *Birkhot Shema*) which is of greater *halakhic* significance. However, there are different customs about where the new *ḥazan* takes over and different communities chose different lines as the starting point depending upon the theme of the day (e.g. *Kol Bo,* 37). Nowadays, most commonly, on Shabbat, he begins with the words "He inhabits eternity" (שׁוֹכֵן עַד), focusing on His role as Creator; on Yom Tov, he begins "God in Your absolute power" (הָאֵל בְּתַעֲצוּמוֹת עֻזֶּךָ) to emphasize His power

This **HILKHOT TEFILLA** *continues on page 577.*

◂ נְהַלֶּלְךָ וּנְשַׁבֵּחֲךָ וּנְפָאֶרְךָ וּנְבָרֵךְ אֶת שֵׁם קָדְשֶׁךָ
כָּאָמוּר

תהלים קג
לְדָוִד, בָּרְכִי נַפְשִׁי אֶת־יהוה
וְכָל־קְרָבַי אֶת־שֵׁם קָדְשׁוֹ:

הָאֵל בְּתַעֲצוּמוֹת עֻזֶּךָ
הַגָּדוֹל בִּכְבוֹד שְׁמֶךָ
הַגִּבּוֹר לָנֶצַח וְהַנּוֹרָא[ב] בְּנוֹרְאוֹתֶיךָ
הַמֶּלֶךְ הַיּוֹשֵׁב עַל כִּסֵּא
רָם וְנִשָּׂא

The שליח ציבור *begins here:*

שׁוֹכֵן עַד

מָרוֹם וְקָדוֹשׁ שְׁמוֹ
וְכָתוּב

תהלים לג
רַנְּנוּ צַדִּיקִים בַּיהוה, לַיְשָׁרִים נָאוָה תְהִלָּה:

◂ בְּפִי יְשָׁרִים תִּתְהַלָּל
וּבְדִבְרֵי צַדִּיקִים תִּתְבָּרַךְ
וּבִלְשׁוֹן חֲסִידִים תִּתְרוֹמָם
וּבְקֶרֶב קְדוֹשִׁים תִּתְקַדָּשׁ

BIUR TEFILLA • ביאור תפילה

הָאֵל בְּתַעֲצֻמוֹת עֻזֶּךָ... הַגָּדוֹל... הַגִּבּוֹר... וְהַנּוֹרָא – *God – in Your absolute power, Great... Mighty... Awesome.* Look a few lines above for these very same adjectives, though here they are explained. These lines are a kind of midrash on those which precede.

וּבְמַקְהֲלוֹת And in the assemblies
of tens of thousands of Your people, the house of Israel,
with joyous song shall Your name, our King,
be glorified in every generation.
▸ For this is the duty of all creatures before You,
LORD our God and God of our ancestors:
to thank, praise, laud, glorify, exalt,
honor, bless, raise high and acclaim –
even beyond all the words of song and praise
of David, son of Jesse, Your servant, Your anointed.

The custom is to stand from the beginning of "Yishtabaḥ" until after "Barekhu" on page 580.

יִשְׁתַּבַּח May Your name be praised for ever, our King,
the great and holy God, King in heaven and on earth.
For to You, LORD our God and God of our ancestors,
it is right to offer song and praise,
hymn and psalm,
strength and dominion,
eternity, greatness and power,

HILKHOT TEFILLA • הלכות תפילה

The reason for standing probably has less to do with anything intrinsic to the blessing itself (though recall we stood for the opening blessing of *Barukh She'Amar* as well) than to its context. We want to make sure that there is no interruption from one section to another of the prayer service. Parenthetically, that is why the *ḥazan* or leader who takes over for the next upcoming section of the service already does so for this prayer even though the *Psukei DeZimra* section is not yet complete. Since we do not want any interruption between *Yishtabaḥ* and the *Kaddish* and *Barekhu* which follow, for which we have to stand, everyone stands in anticipation of those prayers so that no movement is necessary (Rema 51:7, *Baḥ* 51).

As indicated previously (page 57), Ashkenazic practice is generally to stand for any prayer like *Kaddish* and *Barekhu* which are considered a *davar she-be-kedusha*, an opportunity to publicly sanctify Hashem's Name.

וּבְמַקְהֲלוֹת רִבְבוֹת עַמְּךָ בֵּית יִשְׂרָאֵל
בְּרִנָּה יִתְפָּאַר שִׁמְךָ מַלְכֵּנוּ בְּכָל דּוֹר וָדוֹר
◂ שֶׁכֵּן חוֹבַת כָּל הַיְצוּרִים
לְפָנֶיךָ יהוה אֱלֹהֵינוּ וֵאלֹהֵי אֲבוֹתֵינוּ
לְהוֹדוֹת, לְהַלֵּל, לְשַׁבֵּחַ, לְפָאֵר, לְרוֹמֵם
לְהַדֵּר, לְבָרֵךְ, לְעַלֵּה וּלְקַלֵּס
עַל כָּל דִּבְרֵי שִׁירוֹת וְתִשְׁבְּחוֹת
דָּוִד בֶּן יִשַׁי, עַבְדְּךָ מְשִׁיחֶךָ.

The custom is to stand from the beginning of יִשְׁתַּבַּח *until after* בָּרְכוּ *on page 581.*

יִשְׁתַּבַּח שִׁמְךָ לָעַד, מַלְכֵּנוּ
הָאֵל הַמֶּלֶךְ הַגָּדוֹל וְהַקָּדוֹשׁ בַּשָּׁמַיִם וּבָאָרֶץ
כִּי לְךָ נָאֶה, יהוה אֱלֹהֵינוּ וֵאלֹהֵי אֲבוֹתֵינוּ
שִׁיר וּשְׁבָחָה, הַלֵּל וְזִמְרָה
עֹז וּמֶמְשָׁלָה, נֶצַח, גְּדֻלָּה וּגְבוּרָה

---

symbolized in the Exodus (*Levush*), and on Rosh HaShana and Yom Kippur, he begins with "The King" (הַמֶּלֶךְ) to emphasize Hashem's sovereignty.

ANI TEFILLA • אני תפילה

When I was a child, a group of us were sitting on the ground enjoying one another's company. I was absentmindedly picking at the blades of grass around me when an adult began to yell at me that it was forbidden to tear plants on Shabbat. I recall thinking, "what's the big deal? The world will not come to a crashing end simply because I tore this blade of grass! What difference should it make to God that I do this?" It was only later that I realized that on Shabbat, our task is not to display our ability to control nature but, rather, to display our understanding that we are a part of nature. In this respect, on Shabbat, I am no different than a blade of grass.

song of praise and glory,
holiness and kingship,
▸ blessings and thanks, from now and for ever.
Blessed are You, LORD, God and King,
exalted in praises,
God of thanksgivings,
Master of wonders,
who delights in hymns of song,
King, God, Giver of life to the worlds.

HALF KADDISH

Leader: יִתְגַּדַּל Magnified and sanctified
may His great name be,
in the world He created by His will.
May He establish His kingdom
in your lifetime and in your days,
and in the lifetime of all the house of Israel,
swiftly and soon –
and say: Amen.

All: May His great name be blessed
for ever and all time.

Leader: Blessed and praised,
glorified and exalted,
raised and honored,
uplifted and lauded
be the name of the Holy One,
blessed be He,
beyond any blessing,
song, praise and consolation
uttered in the world –
and say: Amen.

תְּהִלָּה וְתִפְאֶרֶת, קְדֻשָּׁה וּמַלְכוּת
◂ בְּרָכוֹת וְהוֹדָאוֹת, מֵעַתָּה וְעַד עוֹלָם.
בָּרוּךְ אַתָּה יהוה
אֵל מֶלֶךְ גָּדוֹל בַּתִּשְׁבָּחוֹת
אֵל הַהוֹדָאוֹת, אֲדוֹן הַנִּפְלָאוֹת
הַבּוֹחֵר בְּשִׁירֵי זִמְרָה
מֶלֶךְ, אֵל, חֵי הָעוֹלָמִים.

חצי קדיש

ש״ץ: יִתְגַּדַּל וְיִתְקַדַּשׁ שְׁמֵהּ רַבָּא (קהל: אָמֵן)
בְּעָלְמָא דִּי בְרָא כִרְעוּתֵהּ
וְיַמְלִיךְ מַלְכוּתֵהּ
בְּחַיֵּיכוֹן וּבְיוֹמֵיכוֹן וּבְחַיֵּי דְכָל בֵּית יִשְׂרָאֵל
בַּעֲגָלָא וּבִזְמַן קָרִיב
וְאִמְרוּ אָמֵן. (קהל: אָמֵן)

קהל וש״ץ: יְהֵא שְׁמֵהּ רַבָּא מְבָרַךְ לְעָלַם וּלְעָלְמֵי עָלְמַיָּא.

ש״ץ: יִתְבָּרַךְ וְיִשְׁתַּבַּח וְיִתְפָּאַר וְיִתְרוֹמַם וְיִתְנַשֵּׂא
וְיִתְהַדָּר וְיִתְעַלֶּה וְיִתְהַלָּל
שְׁמֵהּ דְּקֻדְשָׁא בְּרִיךְ הוּא (קהל: בְּרִיךְ הוּא)
לְעֵֽלָּא מִן כָּל בִּרְכָתָא
וְשִׁירָתָא, תֻּשְׁבְּחָתָא וְנֶחֱמָתָא
דַּאֲמִירָן בְּעָלְמָא
וְאִמְרוּ אָמֵן. (קהל: אָמֵן)

BLESSINGS OF THE SHEMA

The following blessing and response are said only in the presence of a minyan.

Leader: **BLESS** the LORD, the blessed One.

Congregation: Bless the LORD, the blessed One, for ever and all time.

Leader: Bless the LORD, the blessed One, for ever and all time.

The custom is to sit from this point until the Amida, since the predominant emotion of this section of the prayers is love rather than awe. Conversation is forbidden until after the Amida.

בָּרוּךְ Blessed are You, LORD our God, King of the Universe,
who forms light and creates darkness, makes peace and creates all. *Is. 45*

	NAME		CONTENT	THEME
Blessing 1	יוֹצֵר אוֹר	*Yotzer Or*	Creator of light	Creation
Blessing 2	אַהֲבָה רַבָּה	*Ahava Raba*	Love of Israel as manifest in the giving of the Torah	Revelation
Shema	שְׁמַע יִשְׂרָאֵל	Paragraph 1 Paragraph 2 Paragraph 3		Acceptance of Sovereignty of God Acceptance of the Commandments (revelation) Exodus from Egypt (redemption)
Blessing 3	גָּאַל יִשְׂרָאֵל	*Ga'al Yisrael*	The Exodus from Egypt	Redemption. The one overarching theme of the unit is that there is only one God (*Hashem eḥad*), whose Presence can be felt in all three of the particular domains mentioned in the blessings and in the *Shema*. Think about these themes as we move ever closer to our rendezvous with the One.

קריאת שמע וברכותיה

The following blessing and response are said only in the presence of a מנין.

ש״ץ: **בָּרְכוּ**

אֶת יהוה הַמְבֹרָךְ.

קהל: בָּרוּךְ יהוה הַמְבֹרָךְ לְעוֹלָם וָעֶד.

ש״ץ: בָּרוּךְ יהוה הַמְבֹרָךְ לְעוֹלָם וָעֶד.

The custom is to sit from this point until the עמידה*, since the predominant emotion of this section of the prayers is love rather than awe. Conversation is forbidden until after the* עמידה.

בָּרוּךְ אַתָּה יהוה אֱלֹהֵינוּ מֶלֶךְ הָעוֹלָם
יוֹצֵר אוֹר וּבוֹרֵא חֹשֶׁךְ ישעיה מה
עֹשֶׂה שָׁלוֹם וּבוֹרֵא אֶת הַכֹּל.

Commentary on Barekhu can be found on page 107.

INTRODUCTION TO KERIAT SHEMA AND ITS BLESSINGS

Commentary on Keriat Shema and its blessings can be found on pages 109–135.

The next section of the service has at its center the *Shema*, one of the most significant prayers in all of Jewish liturgy. Its recitation twice a day, in the morning and the evening, is considered a commandment, and like most commandments it is accompanied by blessings. In this particular case, however, the Rabbis mandated that there be two blessings before the *Shema* and one after it (*Berakhot* 11a). Each blessing, moreover, has its own theme, one which is inextricably tied to each of the different themes of the *Shema* itself.

The structure might therefore be described as follows:

All will thank You. All will praise You.
All[B] will declare: Nothing is as holy as the LORD.
All will exalt You, Selah, You who form all –
the God who daily opens the doors of the gates of the East
and cleaves the windows of the sky,
who brings out the sun from its place and the moon from its abode,
giving light to the whole world and its inhabitants
whom He created by the attribute of compassion.
In compassion He gives light to the earth and its inhabitants,
and in His goodness daily, continually, renews the work of creation.
He is the King who alone was exalted since time began,
praised, glorified and raised high from days of old.
Eternal God, in Your great compassion, have compassion on us,
LORD of our strength, Rock of our refuge,
Shield of our salvation, Stronghold of our safety.

אֵין כְּעֶרְכֶּךָ None can be compared to You,
there is none besides You;
None without You.
Who is like You?

▸ None can be compared to You,
LORD our God – in this world.
There is none besides You, our King –
in the life of the World to Come.
There is none but You, our Redeemer –
in the days of the Messiah.
There is none like You, our Savior –
at the resurrection of the dead.

BIUR TEFILLA • ביאור תפילה

הַכֹּל...וְהַכֹּל...וְהַכֹּל – *All...all...all.* The opening blessing of this section spoke of Hashem as the one who "fashions light" and "created all." During the weekday service, the next passage primarily emphasizes the first theme, light. But today, another section is inserted, this one emphasizing the word "all," as indicated by the unusual number of times it appears.

What do you think this is meant to convey and why might it be an appropriate theme for today?

הַכֹּל יוֹדְוּךָ וְהַכֹּל יְשַׁבְּחוּךָ
וְהַכֹּל יֹאמְרוּ אֵין קָדוֹשׁ כַּיהוה
הַכֹּל[ב] יְרוֹמְמוּךָ סֶּלָה, יוֹצֵר הַכֹּל.
הָאֵל הַפּוֹתֵחַ בְּכָל יוֹם דַּלְתוֹת שַׁעֲרֵי מִזְרָח
וּבוֹקֵעַ חַלּוֹנֵי רָקִיעַ
מוֹצִיא חַמָּה מִמְּקוֹמָהּ וּלְבָנָה מִמְּכוֹן שִׁבְתָּהּ
וּמֵאִיר לָעוֹלָם כֻּלּוֹ וּלְיוֹשְׁבָיו שֶׁבָּרָא בְּמִדַּת הָרַחֲמִים.
הַמֵּאִיר לָאָרֶץ וְלַדָּרִים עָלֶיהָ בְּרַחֲמִים
וּבְטוּבוֹ מְחַדֵּשׁ בְּכָל יוֹם תָּמִיד מַעֲשֵׂה בְרֵאשִׁית.
הַמֶּלֶךְ הַמְרוֹמָם לְבַדּוֹ מֵאָז
הַמְשֻׁבָּח וְהַמְפֹאָר וְהַמִּתְנַשֵּׂא מִימוֹת עוֹלָם.
אֱלֹהֵי עוֹלָם, בְּרַחֲמֶיךָ הָרַבִּים רַחֵם עָלֵינוּ
אֲדוֹן עֻזֵּנוּ, צוּר מִשְׂגַּבֵּנוּ, מָגֵן יִשְׁעֵנוּ, מִשְׂגָּב בַּעֲדֵנוּ.

אֵין כְּעֶרְכֶּךָ
וְאֵין זוּלָתֶךָ
אֶפֶס בִּלְתֶּךָ
וּמִי דּוֹמֶה לָּךְ.

› אֵין כְּעֶרְכְּךָ, יהוה אֱלֹהֵינוּ, בָּעוֹלָם הַזֶּה
וְאֵין זוּלָתְךָ, מַלְכֵּנוּ, לְחַיֵּי הָעוֹלָם הַבָּא
אֶפֶס בִּלְתְּךָ, גּוֹאֲלֵנוּ, לִימוֹת הַמָּשִׁיחַ
וְאֵין דּוֹמֶה לְּךָ, מוֹשִׁיעֵנוּ, לִתְחִיַּת הַמֵּתִים.

HILKHOT TEFILLA • הלכות תפילה

Because this entire section is viewed as one indivisible unit, no talking is permitted unless it is an emergency or for the sake of the prayer service itself. See Table of Permitted Responses, page 1128.

אֵל אָדוֹן God, LORD of all creation,[BI]
the Blessed, is blessed by every soul.
His greatness and goodness fill the world;
knowledge and wisdom surround Him.[I]

Exalted above the holy Ḥayyot,
adorned in glory on the Chariot;
Merit and right are before His throne,
kindness and compassion before His glory.

---

with the old question of why did God bring the world into being? The letters of the *Alef-Beit* symbolize the written word of the Torah, the demands of which bring purpose and meaning to our world (Rabbi I. Wohlgemuth).

ANI TEFILLA • אני תפילה

A young illiterate boy came to shul and wanted to pray but had never been taught how to read. And so he simply recited the Alef-Beit over and over again. He then said to God: "I don't know the prayers. All I know are the letters of the Alef-Beit. Please take the letters and turn them into the right words to reflect what I feel in my heart." The Ba'al Shem Tov said that the boy's prayer broke through the gates of heaven, and enabled everyone else's prayers to enter as well.

IYUN TEFILLA • עיון תפילה

גָּדְלוֹ וְטוּבוֹ מָלֵא עוֹלָם, דַּעַת וּתְבוּנָה סוֹבְבִים אוֹתוֹ – *His greatness and goodness fill the world; knowledge and wisdom surround Him.* Hashem cannot be seen but that does not mean that He cannot be perceived. When one views the intricacy of creation, the sheer complexity of all of life down to the most basic unit that science will allow, one cannot help but feel that it is filled with "knowledge and wisdom." They surround Him, even as they leave Him invisible (*Dover Shalom*).

ANI TEFILLA • אני תפילה

A philosopher once came to Rabbi Meir and told him, "I don't believe in God. I feel that the universe came into being by itself, of its own accord, without any outside help." Rabbi Meir did not reply. A few days later, he came to the philosopher, and showed him a beautiful piece of poetry, written in a find hand on smooth white parchment. The philosopher looked at the parchment and admired it. He asked, "Who is the great poet who wrote this lovely poem? Who was the talented scribe who copied it?" Rabbi Meir

This **ANI TEFILLA** *continues on page 587.*

אֵל אָדוֹן עַל כָּל הַמַּעֲשִׂים
בָּרוּךְ וּמְבֹרָךְ בְּפִי כָּל נְשָׁמָה
גָּדְלוֹ וְטוּבוֹ מָלֵא עוֹלָם
דַּעַת וּתְבוּנָה סוֹבְבִים אוֹתוֹ.

הַמִּתְגָּאֶה עַל חַיּוֹת הַקֹּדֶשׁ
וְנֶהְדָּר בְּכָבוֹד עַל הַמֶּרְכָּבָה
זְכוּת וּמִישׁוֹר לִפְנֵי כִסְאוֹ
חֶסֶד וְרַחֲמִים לִפְנֵי כְבוֹדוֹ.

IYUN TEFILLA · עיון תפילה

אֵל אָדוֹן עַל כָּל הַמַּעֲשִׂים – *God, Lord of all creation.* Whereas the weekday prayer has 22 words in alphabetical order to describe this (...אֵל בָּרוּךְ גְּדוֹל דֵּעָה), today we add 22 complete lines, each of which begins with a successive letter of the *Alef-Beit*.

Why are certain prayers constructed this way? There is no one correct answer. One possibility comes from the experience that some of us have had of being in a place that was of such overwhelming beauty, a place that filled us with such awe, that we could not adequately describe it. There is a word here for every letter of the alphabet, but these are just representatives for every word in the entire language that we could possibly use to describe the feelings that we have at this moment. It's not only about what the words mean but about how they help us feel.

Alternatively, the blessing grapples

BIUR TEFILLA · ביאור תפילה

אֵל אָדוֹן עַל כָּל הַמַּעֲשִׂים – *God, Lord of all creation.* Only on Shabbat and Yom Tov is this special hymn added. Its mystical overtones are reminiscent of the vision of the divine chariot recorded in *Yeḥezkel* 1 and are reflected as well in the insistence of some that not a letter of it be changed (*Yesod veShoresh haAvoda*). Yet it also stands on its own as a song of great mystery and splendor inviting all to recognize not only the world's beauty but its dynamism as well. The sun and moon and stars are filled with vitality, they are miracles that dance across the heavens lighting up the sky. So, too, should they have that effect upon us as their "happiness" becomes our own, for on this day in particular we are all creations.

When did you last notice the miracle of the sun? The mystery of the moon? Consider them now.

Good are the radiant stars our God created;
He formed them with knowledge,
understanding, and deliberation.[1]
He gave them strength and might
to rule throughout the world.

Full of splendor, radiating light,
beautiful is their splendor throughout the world.
Glad as they go forth, joyous as they return,
they fulfill with awe their Creator's will.

Glory and honor they give to His name,
jubilation and song at the mention of His majesty.
He called the sun into being and it shone with light.
He looked and fashioned the form of the moon.

All the hosts on high give Him praise;
the Seraphim, Ophanim and holy Ḥayyot
ascribe glory and greatness –

IYUN TEFILLA • עיון תפילה

יְצָרָם בְּדַעַת בְּבִינָה וּבְהַשְׂכֵּל – *He formed them with knowledge, understanding, and deliberation.* If you want to know God, look carefully at all of His creations. As the Rambam (*Yesodei HaTorah* 2:2) says: "What is the path [a person should take] to attain love and fear of Him? When a person contemplates His wondrous and great deeds and creations, and appreciates His infinite wisdom that surpasses all comparison, he will immediately love, praise, and glorify [Him], yearning with tremendous desire to know [God's] great name, as David stated: 'My soul thirsts for Hashem, for the living God' [Psalms 42:3]."

Seen in this light, the siddur may be understood to mean that astronomy, biology, anatomy, and the like can all be used as vehicles for getting to know God better.

When you read about these subjects, do you see them as aspects of human knowledge or as a way to come to a better knowledge of God?

טוֹבִים מְאוֹרוֹת שֶׁבָּרָא אֱלֹהֵינוּ
יְצָרָם בְּדַעַת בְּבִינָה וּבְהַשְׂכֵּל
כֹּחַ וּגְבוּרָה נָתַן בָּהֶם
לִהְיוֹת מוֹשְׁלִים בְּקֶרֶב תֵּבֵל.

מְלֵאִים זִיו וּמְפִיקִים נֹגַהּ
נָאֶה זִיוָם בְּכָל הָעוֹלָם
שְׂמֵחִים בְּצֵאתָם וְשָׂשִׂים בְּבוֹאָם
עוֹשִׂים בְּאֵימָה רְצוֹן קוֹנָם.

פְּאֵר וְכָבוֹד נוֹתְנִים לִשְׁמוֹ
צָהֳלָה וְרִנָּה לְזֵכֶר מַלְכוּתוֹ
קָרָא לַשֶּׁמֶשׁ וַיִּזְרַח אוֹר
רָאָה וְהִתְקִין צוּרַת הַלְּבָנָה.

שֶׁבַח נוֹתְנִים לוֹ כָּל צְבָא מָרוֹם
תִּפְאֶרֶת וּגְדֻלָּה, שְׂרָפִים וְאוֹפַנִּים וְחַיּוֹת הַקֹּדֶשׁ.

---

shook his head and answered, "You are completely wrong. There was no poet. There was no scribe. This is what really happened. The parchment was lying on my desk next to a bottle of ink. A cat accidentally knocked over the bottle, spilling ink all over the parchment. This poem was the result." The philosopher looked at Rabbi Meir in amazement. He said, "But that is impossible! Such a lovely poem! Such perfect script! Such things do not come into being by themselves. There must be an author! There must be a scribe!" Rabbi Meir smiled. He answered the philosopher, "You yourself have said it! How could the universe, which is much more beautiful than any poem, come into being by itself? There must be an Author. There must be a Creator." (Rabbi Aryeh Kaplan citing *Ḥovot Halevavot* 1:6)

לָאֵל To God who rested[I] from all works,
and on the seventh day ascended and sat on His throne of glory.
He robed the day of rest in glory[I]
and called the Sabbath day a delight.[B]
This is the praise of the seventh day,
that on it God rested from all His work.
The seventh day itself gives praise, saying,
"A psalm, a song for the Sabbath day. Ps. 92
It is good to give thanks to the LORD."
Therefore let all He has formed glorify and bless God.
Let them give praise, honor and grandeur to God,
the King, who formed all things
and in His holiness gave a heritage of rest
to His people Israel on the holy Sabbath day.
May Your name, O LORD our God, be sanctified,
and Your renown, O our King, be glorified
in the heavens above and on earth below.
May You be blessed, our Deliverer,
by the praises of Your handiwork,
and by the radiant lights You have made:
may they glorify You. Selah!

---

coming into our midst. In legal terms, this is referred to as part of *kavod Shabbat*, the honor that one is required to give the day in anticipation of its arrival.

When one speaks therefore of wanting to "dress to impress" on this day, who is it that one should be dressing for–oneself? Other people? Shabbat? Hashem?

BIUR TEFILLA • ביאור תפילה

עֹנֶג קָרָא לְיוֹם הַשַּׁבָּת – *And called the Sabbath day a delight. Oneg Shabbat* is not simply a poetic description of the day but a legal term which refers to the commandment to enjoy the day by eating and drinking in its honor. "If you refrain from work on Shabbat...," says the prophet Yeshayahu in the name of Hashem, "if you proclaim the Shabbat day a delight (*oneg*), then I will mount you atop the heights of the world, I will provide you your heritage" (*Yeshayahu* 58:13–14).

לָאֵל אֲשֶׁר שָׁבַת מִכָּל הַמַּעֲשִׂים
בַּיּוֹם הַשְּׁבִיעִי נִתְעַלָּה וְיָשַׁב עַל כִּסֵּא כְבוֹדוֹ.
תִּפְאֶרֶת עָטָה לְיוֹם הַמְּנוּחָה
עֹנֶג קָרָא לְיוֹם הַשַּׁבָּת.
זֶה שֶׁבַח שֶׁלַּיּוֹם הַשְּׁבִיעִי
שֶׁבּוֹ שָׁבַת אֵל מִכָּל מְלַאכְתּוֹ
וְיוֹם הַשְּׁבִיעִי מְשַׁבֵּחַ וְאוֹמֵר
מִזְמוֹר שִׁיר לְיוֹם הַשַּׁבָּת, טוֹב לְהֹדוֹת לַיהוה: תהלים צב
לְפִיכָךְ יְפָאֲרוּ וִיבָרְכוּ לָאֵל כָּל יְצוּרָיו
שֶׁבַח יְקָר וּגְדֻלָּה יִתְּנוּ לָאֵל מֶלֶךְ יוֹצֵר כֹּל
הַמַּנְחִיל מְנוּחָה לְעַמּוֹ יִשְׂרָאֵל בִּקְדֻשָּׁתוֹ בְּיוֹם שַׁבַּת קֹדֶשׁ.
שִׁמְךָ יהוה אֱלֹהֵינוּ יִתְקַדַּשׁ, וְזִכְרְךָ מַלְכֵּנוּ יִתְפָּאַר
בַּשָּׁמַיִם מִמַּעַל וְעַל הָאָרֶץ מִתָּחַת.
תִּתְבָּרַךְ מוֹשִׁיעֵנוּ עַל שֶׁבַח מַעֲשֵׂה יָדֶיךָ
וְעַל מְאוֹרֵי אוֹר שֶׁעָשִׂיתָ, יְפָאֲרוּךָ סֶּלָה.

IYUN TEFILLA • עיון תפילה

לָאֵל אֲשֶׁר שָׁבַת – *To God who rested.* In the midst of this lively description of how the world came into being, the Shabbat of Creation takes center stage, just as she does today. Hashem rested, as it were, not because of fatigue (which is an absurdity) but to remind us that there is something larger than our own lives, something even grander than the cosmos we toil so hard to discover and conquer. The day itself thus testifies to its Creator, it sings to Him "a song sung by the Shabbat day," it pays homage to Him, as do we (see the commentary on *Tehillim* 92 in *Kabbalat Shabbat* on page 425).

תִּפְאֶרֶת עָטָה לְיוֹם הַמְּנוּחָה – *He robed the day of rest in glory.* Just as Hashem "dressed" the day, so, too, do we. Quite literally, our clothes for Shabbat should be different than those we wear during the week, just as we would dress up for any important guest who was

תִּתְבָּרַךְ May You be blessed,
our Rock, King and Redeemer,
Creator of holy beings.
May Your name be praised for ever,
our King, Creator of the ministering angels,
all of whom stand in the universe's heights,
proclaiming together, in awe, aloud,
the words of the living God, the eternal King.
They are all beloved,
all pure,
all mighty,
and all perform in awe and reverence
the will of their Maker.
▸ All open their mouths in holiness and purity,
with song and psalm,
and bless, praise, glorify,
revere, sanctify, and declare the sovereignty of – ◂
The name of the great, mighty
and awesome God and King,
holy is He.
▸ All accept on themselves,
one from another,
the yoke of the kingdom of heaven,
granting permission to one another
to sanctify the One who formed them,
in serene spirit,
pure speech and sweet melody.
All, as one, proclaim His holiness,
saying in awe:

All say aloud: Holy, holy, holy is the LORD of hosts; *Is. 6*
the whole world is filled with His glory.

תִּתְבָּרַךְ
צוּרֵנוּ מַלְכֵּנוּ וְגוֹאֲלֵנוּ, בּוֹרֵא קְדוֹשִׁים
יִשְׁתַּבַּח שִׁמְךָ לָעַד, מַלְכֵּנוּ, יוֹצֵר מְשָׁרְתִים
וַאֲשֶׁר מְשָׁרְתָיו כֻּלָּם עוֹמְדִים בְּרוּם עוֹלָם
וּמַשְׁמִיעִים בְּיִרְאָה יַחַד בְּקוֹל
דִּבְרֵי אֱלֹהִים חַיִּים וּמֶלֶךְ עוֹלָם.
כֻּלָּם אֲהוּבִים
כֻּלָּם בְּרוּרִים
כֻּלָּם גִּבּוֹרִים
וְכֻלָּם עוֹשִׂים בְּאֵימָה וּבְיִרְאָה רְצוֹן קוֹנָם
◂ וְכֻלָּם פּוֹתְחִים אֶת פִּיהֶם בִּקְדֻשָּׁה וּבְטָהֳרָה
בְּשִׁירָה וּבְזִמְרָה
וּמְבָרְכִים וּמְשַׁבְּחִים וּמְפָאֲרִים
◂ וּמַעֲרִיצִים וּמַקְדִּישִׁים וּמַמְלִיכִים
אֶת שֵׁם הָאֵל הַמֶּלֶךְ הַגָּדוֹל, הַגִּבּוֹר וְהַנּוֹרָא
קָדוֹשׁ הוּא.
◂ וְכֻלָּם מְקַבְּלִים עֲלֵיהֶם עֹל מַלְכוּת שָׁמַיִם זֶה מִזֶּה
וְנוֹתְנִים רְשׁוּת זֶה לָזֶה לְהַקְדִּישׁ לְיוֹצְרָם בְּנַחַת רוּחַ
בְּשָׂפָה בְרוּרָה וּבִנְעִימָה
קְדֻשָּׁה כֻּלָּם כְּאֶחָד
עוֹנִים וְאוֹמְרִים בְּיִרְאָה

All say aloud קָדוֹשׁ, קָדוֹשׁ, קָדוֹשׁ יהוה צְבָאוֹת ישעיה ו
מְלֹא כָל־הָאָרֶץ כְּבוֹדוֹ:

▸ Then the Ophanim and the Holy Ḥayyot,
with a roar of noise,
raise themselves toward the Seraphim and,
facing them, give praise, saying:

All say aloud: Blessed is the LORD's glory from His place. *Ezek. 3*

לָאֵל To the blessed God they offer melodies.
To the King, living and eternal God,
they say psalms and proclaim praises.
For it is He alone
who does mighty deeds and creates new things,
who is Master of battles and sows righteousness,
who makes salvation grow and creates cures,
who is is revered in praises, the LORD of wonders,
who in His goodness,
continually renews the work of creation,
day after day, as it is said:
"[Praise] Him who made the great lights, *Ps. 136*
for His love endures for ever."
▸ May You make a new light shine over Zion,
and may we all soon be worthy of its light.
Blessed are You, LORD,
who forms the radiant lights.

אַהֲבָה You have loved us with great love, LORD our God,
and with surpassing compassion
have You had compassion on us.
Our Father, our King,
for the sake of our ancestors who trusted in You,
and to whom You taught the laws of life,
be gracious also to us and teach us.

› וְהָאוֹפַנִּים וְחַיּוֹת הַקֹּדֶשׁ
בְּרַעַשׁ גָּדוֹל מִתְנַשְּׂאִים לְעֻמַּת שְׂרָפִים
לְעֻמָּתָם מְשַׁבְּחִים וְאוֹמְרִים

All say aloud בָּרוּךְ כְּבוֹד־יהוה מִמְּקוֹמוֹ: יחזקאל ג

לָאֵל בָּרוּךְ נְעִימוֹת יִתֵּנוּ, לַמֶּלֶךְ אֵל חַי וְקַיָּם
זְמִירוֹת יֹאמֵרוּ וְתִשְׁבָּחוֹת יַשְׁמִיעוּ
כִּי הוּא לְבַדּוֹ
פּוֹעֵל גְּבוּרוֹת, עוֹשֶׂה חֲדָשׁוֹת
בַּעַל מִלְחָמוֹת, זוֹרֵעַ צְדָקוֹת
מַצְמִיחַ יְשׁוּעוֹת, בּוֹרֵא רְפוּאוֹת
נוֹרָא תְהִלּוֹת, אֲדוֹן הַנִּפְלָאוֹת
הַמְחַדֵּשׁ בְּטוּבוֹ בְּכָל יוֹם תָּמִיד מַעֲשֵׂה בְרֵאשִׁית
כָּאָמוּר
לְעֹשֵׂה אוֹרִים גְּדֹלִים תהלים קלו
כִּי לְעוֹלָם חַסְדּוֹ:
› אוֹר חָדָשׁ עַל צִיּוֹן תָּאִיר וְנִזְכֶּה כֻלָּנוּ מְהֵרָה לְאוֹרוֹ.
בָּרוּךְ אַתָּה יהוה, יוֹצֵר הַמְּאוֹרוֹת.

אַהֲבָה רַבָּה אֲהַבְתָּנוּ, יהוה אֱלֹהֵינוּ
חֶמְלָה גְדוֹלָה וִיתֵרָה חָמַלְתָּ עָלֵינוּ.
אָבִינוּ מַלְכֵּנוּ, בַּעֲבוּר אֲבוֹתֵינוּ שֶׁבָּטְחוּ בְךָ
וַתְּלַמְּדֵם חֻקֵּי חַיִּים, כֵּן תְּחָנֵּנוּ וּתְלַמְּדֵנוּ.

Our Father, compassionate Father, ever compassionate,
have compassion on us.
Instill in our hearts the desire to understand and discern,
to listen, learn and teach, to observe, perform and fulfill
all the teachings of Your Torah in love.
Enlighten our eyes in Your Torah
and let our hearts cling to Your commandments.
Unite our hearts to love and revere Your name,
so that we may never be ashamed.
And because we have trusted in Your holy, great and revered name,
may we be glad and rejoice in Your salvation.

At this point, gather the four tzitziot of the tallit, holding them in the left hand.

Bring us back[H] in peace from the four quarters of the earth
and lead us upright to our land.
▸ For You are a God who performs acts of salvation,
and You chose us from all peoples and tongues,
bringing us close to Your great name for ever in truth,
that we may thank You and proclaim Your oneness in love.
Blessed are You, Lord, who chooses His people Israel in love.[A]

---

the heart (*al levavkhem* – *Hagahot Maimoni*). Still others avoid the custom altogether (Rav Natroni Gaon), suggesting that the *tztizit* need to be seen not necessarily touched.

There are numerous other customs that arose as well including the practice of kissing the *tzitzit* every time the word is mentioned in the third paragraph of *Shema*. All of these customs arose simply because at the very mention of the mitzva itself, in the words of the Rema, one wants to show how beloved it is.

ANI TEFILLA · אני תפילה

הַבּוֹחֵר בְּעַמּוֹ יִשְׂרָאֵל בְּאַהֲבָה – *Who chooses His people Israel in love.* In terms of responsibility to God and doing His will through mitzvot, the concept of Israel means, first of all, me. When one recites in prayer, "Who chooses His people Israel with love," one is not thinking of the Chief Rabbi, but of oneself. When one says, 'You alone will we worship with awe and reverence,' one is also not thinking of any official body at the head of the community, but, again, of oneself. In other words, when one says 'we' in this context, or 'we Jews,' or 'we, the People of Israel,' one means 'I' or, at least, primarily 'I.' As it was once expressed, 'A person should pray in the synagogue as though he were in a forest, with a tree here and a tree there, and feel that he alone is communicating with God in worship' (Rabbi Adin Steinsaltz).

אָבִינוּ, הָאָב הָרַחֲמָן, הַמְרַחֵם
רַחֵם עָלֵינוּ, וְתֵן בְּלִבֵּנוּ לְהָבִין וּלְהַשְׂכִּיל
לִשְׁמֹעַ, לִלְמֹד וּלְלַמֵּד, לִשְׁמֹר וְלַעֲשׂוֹת, וּלְקַיֵּם
אֶת כָּל דִּבְרֵי תַלְמוּד תּוֹרָתֶךָ בְּאַהֲבָה.
וְהָאֵר עֵינֵינוּ בְּתוֹרָתֶךָ, וְדַבֵּק לִבֵּנוּ בְּמִצְוֹתֶיךָ
וְיַחֵד לְבָבֵנוּ לְאַהֲבָה וּלְיִרְאָה אֶת שְׁמֶךָ
וְלֹא נֵבוֹשׁ לְעוֹלָם וָעֶד.
כִּי בְשֵׁם קָדְשְׁךָ הַגָּדוֹל וְהַנּוֹרָא בָּטָחְנוּ
נָגִילָה וְנִשְׂמְחָה בִּישׁוּעָתֶךָ.

At this point, gather the four ציציות *of the* טלית*, holding them in the left hand.*

וַהֲבִיאֵנוּ[ה] לְשָׁלוֹם מֵאַרְבַּע כַּנְפוֹת הָאָרֶץ
וְתוֹלִיכֵנוּ קוֹמְמִיּוּת לְאַרְצֵנוּ.
‹ כִּי אֵל פּוֹעֵל יְשׁוּעוֹת אָתָּה
וּבָנוּ בָחַרְתָּ מִכָּל עַם וְלָשׁוֹן
וְקֵרַבְתָּנוּ לְשִׁמְךָ הַגָּדוֹל סֶלָה, בֶּאֱמֶת
לְהוֹדוֹת לְךָ וּלְיַחֶדְךָ בְּאַהֲבָה.
בָּרוּךְ אַתָּה יהוה, הַבּוֹחֵר בְּעַמּוֹ יִשְׂרָאֵל בְּאַהֲבָה.[א]

HILKHOT TEFILLA · הלכות תפילה

וַהֲבִיאֵנוּ – *Bring us back.* Because *tzitzit* figure prominently in the third paragraph of *Shema* there arose a very old custom to gather the *tzitzit* of all four corners of the *tallit* at this point in the blessing of *Ahava Raba* (which mentions the ingathering from the four corners of the world) and to hold on to them until shortly after the completion of the *Shema*. Others gather only the two front ones (Vilna Gaon), citing the reason that double the 5 knots and 8 strings on each amounts to 26, the numerical equivalent of the Tetragrammaton name of God. Some hold only one of the *tzitzit* since the numerical equivalent of the word is 600 to which one adds the 5 knots and 8 strings to equal 613, the traditional count of all *mitzvot* in the Torah (Mahari Beruna) which one then holds near

The Shema must be said with intense concentration. In the first paragraph one should accept, with love, the sovereignty of God; in the second, the mitzvot as the will of God. The end of the third paragraph constitutes fulfillment of the mitzva to remember, morning and evening, the exodus from Egypt. See laws 71–80.

When not praying with a minyan, say:
God, faithful King!

The following verse should be said aloud, while covering the eyes with the right hand:

Listen, Israel: the LORD is our God, the LORD is One. *Deut. 6*

Quietly: Blessed be the name of His glorious kingdom for ever and all time.[H]

וְאָהַבְתָּ Love the LORD your God with all your heart, with all your soul, and with all your might. These words which I command you today shall be on your heart. Teach them repeatedly to your children, speaking of them when you sit at home and when you travel on the way, when you lie down and when you rise. Bind them as a sign on your hand, and they shall be an emblem between your eyes. Write them on the doorposts of your house and gates. *Deut. 6*

ANI TEFILLA • אני תפילה

It was Friday, a few hours before we boarded the helicopter. Emmanuel asked me, "What would you do if, God forbid, our helicopter were to be hit by a missile and we would have just minutes to live before we crashed?" I answered him: "I don't know. I imagine I would be very sad and scared; I'd close my eyes and wait for it be over as quickly as possible and with as little pain as possible." Emmanuel thought for a moment and said: "What I would do, and what I think you should do, would be to say Shema Yisrael." I looked at him and said, "OK, fine, you'll say Shema Yisrael, but what will that accomplish since in any event in another second the helicopter will crash and we will all die?!" He answered me with one sentence that follows me to this day and I believe will continue to follow me the rest of my life. "If a person has five seconds left to live and there is still significance to his life and aspirations for what comes after it then that means that his life has meaning. But, if on the other hand,

This **ANI TEFILLA** *continues on page 599.*

The שמע *must be said with intense concentration. In the first paragraph one should accept, with love, the sovereignty of God; in the second, the* מצוות *as the will of God. The end of the third paragraph constitutes fulfillment of the* מצווה *to remember, morning and evening, the exodus from Egypt. See laws 71–80.*

When not praying with a מנין*, say:*

אֵל מֶלֶךְ נֶאֱמָן

The following verse should be said aloud, while covering the eyes with the right hand:

שְׁמַע יִשְׂרָאֵל, יהוה אֱלֹהֵינוּ, יהוה | אֶחָד׃ דברים ו

Quietly בָּרוּךְ שֵׁם כְּבוֹד מַלְכוּתוֹ לְעוֹלָם וָעֶד.[ה]

וְאָהַבְתָּ אֵת יהוה אֱלֹהֶיךָ, בְּכָל־לְבָבְךָ וּבְכָל־נַפְשְׁךָ וּבְכָל־ דברים ו
מְאֹדֶךָ׃ וְהָיוּ הַדְּבָרִים הָאֵלֶּה, אֲשֶׁר אָנֹכִי מְצַוְּךָ הַיּוֹם, עַל־לְבָבֶךָ׃
וְשִׁנַּנְתָּם לְבָנֶיךָ וְדִבַּרְתָּ בָּם, בְּשִׁבְתְּךָ בְּבֵיתֶךָ וּבְלֶכְתְּךָ בַדֶּרֶךְ,
וּבְשָׁכְבְּךָ וּבְקוּמֶךָ׃ וּקְשַׁרְתָּם לְאוֹת עַל־יָדֶךָ וְהָיוּ לְטֹטָפֹת בֵּין
עֵינֶיךָ׃ וּכְתַבְתָּם עַל־מְזֻזוֹת בֵּיתֶךָ וּבִשְׁעָרֶיךָ׃

Commentary on Keriat Shema can be found on weekday Shaharit pages 120–126 and Ma'ariv for Shabbat pages 447–450.

HILKHOT TEFILLA • הלכות תפילה

The prevailing custom is to cover one's eyes when one recites the first line of the Shema, primarily to be able to enhance one's concentration (*Berakhot* 13b; *Shulḥan Arukh* 61:4). The reading of this verse is considered by most to be a commandment of Torah origin and is seen as a statement of accepting upon oneself the "the yoke of Heaven," i.e., to accept the God of Israel as one's own. It is actually more of a declaration and, as such, the custom is to say it aloud.

For additional laws and customs, see appendix on laws of daily prayer 71–80.

HILKHOT TEFILLA • הלכות תפילה

בָּרוּךְ שֵׁם כְּבוֹד מַלְכוּתוֹ לְעוֹלָם וָעֶד – *Blessed be the name of His glorious kingdom for ever and all time*. The custom is to recite this verse in a whisper except on Yom Kippur when it is said using the same tone as the first line. A purely technical reason may be that unlike all of the verses of the *Shema* which come from the Torah, this line does not (*Pesaḥim* 56a) and lest one think that it was part of the original text, it is recited quietly.

וְהָיָה If you indeed heed My commandments with which I charge you today, to love the LORD your God and worship Him with all your heart and with all your soul, I will give rain in your land in its season, the early and late rain; and you shall gather in your grain, wine and oil. I will give grass in your field for your cattle, and you shall eat and be satisfied. Be careful lest your heart be tempted and you go astray and worship other gods, bowing down to them. Then the LORD's anger will flare against you and He will close the heavens so that there will be no rain. The land will not yield its crops, and you will perish swiftly from the good land that the LORD is giving you. Therefore, set these, My words, on your heart and soul. Bind them as a sign on your hand, and they shall be an emblem between your eyes. Teach them to your children, speaking of them when you sit at home and when you travel on the way, when you lie down and when you rise. Write them on the doorposts of your house and gates, so that you and your children may live long in the land that the LORD swore to your ancestors to give them, for as long as the heavens are above the earth. *Deut. 11*

Hold the tzitziot in the right hand also (some transfer to the right hand), kissing them at °.

וַיֹּאמֶר The LORD spoke to Moses, saying: Speak to the Israelites and tell them to make °tassels on the corners of their garments for all generations. They shall attach to the °tassel at each corner a thread of blue. This shall be your °tassel, and you shall see it and remember all of the LORD's commandments and keep them, not straying after your heart and after your eyes, following your own sinful desires. Thus you will be reminded to keep all My commandments, and be holy to your God. I am the LORD your *Num. 15*

---

order to satisfy our drives, or to enjoy or live for the moment. Rather, life is one added step on the way to the next."

Lt. Colonel Emmanuel Yehuda Moreno was killed in battle the next day Shabbat, August 19, 2006.

וְהָיָה אִם־שָׁמֹעַ תִּשְׁמְעוּ אֶל־מִצְוֺתַי אֲשֶׁר אָנֹכִי מְצַוֶּה אֶתְכֶם דברים יא
הַיּוֹם, לְאַהֲבָה אֶת־יהוה אֱלֹהֵיכֶם וּלְעָבְדוֹ, בְּכָל־לְבַבְכֶם וּבְכָל־
נַפְשְׁכֶם: וְנָתַתִּי מְטַר־אַרְצְכֶם בְּעִתּוֹ, יוֹרֶה וּמַלְקוֹשׁ, וְאָסַפְתָּ
דְגָנֶךָ וְתִירֹשְׁךָ וְיִצְהָרֶךָ: וְנָתַתִּי עֵשֶׂב בְּשָׂדְךָ לִבְהֶמְתֶּךָ, וְאָכַלְתָּ
וְשָׂבָעְתָּ: הִשָּׁמְרוּ לָכֶם פֶּן־יִפְתֶּה לְבַבְכֶם, וְסַרְתֶּם וַעֲבַדְתֶּם
אֱלֹהִים אֲחֵרִים וְהִשְׁתַּחֲוִיתֶם לָהֶם: וְחָרָה אַף־יהוה בָּכֶם, וְעָצַר
אֶת־הַשָּׁמַיִם וְלֹא־יִהְיֶה מָטָר, וְהָאֲדָמָה לֹא תִתֵּן אֶת־יְבוּלָהּ,
וַאֲבַדְתֶּם מְהֵרָה מֵעַל הָאָרֶץ הַטֹּבָה אֲשֶׁר יהוה נֹתֵן לָכֶם:
וְשַׂמְתֶּם אֶת־דְּבָרַי אֵלֶּה עַל־לְבַבְכֶם וְעַל־נַפְשְׁכֶם, וּקְשַׁרְתֶּם
אֹתָם לְאוֹת עַל־יֶדְכֶם, וְהָיוּ לְטוֹטָפֹת בֵּין עֵינֵיכֶם: וְלִמַּדְתֶּם
אֹתָם אֶת־בְּנֵיכֶם לְדַבֵּר בָּם, בְּשִׁבְתְּךָ בְּבֵיתֶךָ וּבְלֶכְתְּךָ בַדֶּרֶךְ,
וּבְשָׁכְבְּךָ וּבְקוּמֶךָ: וּכְתַבְתָּם עַל־מְזוּזוֹת בֵּיתֶךָ וּבִשְׁעָרֶיךָ: לְמַעַן
יִרְבּוּ יְמֵיכֶם וִימֵי בְנֵיכֶם עַל הָאֲדָמָה אֲשֶׁר נִשְׁבַּע יהוה לַאֲבֹתֵיכֶם
לָתֵת לָהֶם, כִּימֵי הַשָּׁמַיִם עַל־הָאָרֶץ:

Hold the ציציות *in the right hand also (some transfer to the right hand), kissing them at* °.

וַיֹּאמֶר יהוה אֶל־מֹשֶׁה לֵּאמֹר: דַּבֵּר אֶל־בְּנֵי יִשְׂרָאֵל וְאָמַרְתָּ במדבר טו
אֲלֵהֶם, וְעָשׂוּ לָהֶם °צִיצִת עַל־כַּנְפֵי בִגְדֵיהֶם לְדֹרֹתָם, וְנָתְנוּ °עַל־
צִיצִת הַכָּנָף פְּתִיל תְּכֵלֶת: וְהָיָה לָכֶם °לְצִיצִת, וּרְאִיתֶם אֹתוֹ
וּזְכַרְתֶּם אֶת־כָּל־מִצְוֺת יהוה וַעֲשִׂיתֶם אֹתָם, וְלֹא תָתֻרוּ אַחֲרֵי
לְבַבְכֶם וְאַחֲרֵי עֵינֵיכֶם, אֲשֶׁר־אַתֶּם זֹנִים אַחֲרֵיהֶם: לְמַעַן תִּזְכְּרוּ
וַעֲשִׂיתֶם אֶת־כָּל־מִצְוֺתָי, וִהְיִיתֶם קְדֹשִׁים לֵאלֹהֵיכֶם: אֲנִי יהוה

---

a person has five seconds to live and he does not understand the significance of those five seconds, then apparently there is no meaning to his entire life, because we do not live in

God, who brought you out of the land of Egypt to be your God. I am the LORD your God.

°True –

The Leader repeats:

▸ The LORD your God is true[|] –

וְיַצִּיב And firm, established and enduring, right, faithful,
beloved, cherished, delightful, pleasant,
awesome, mighty, perfect, accepted,
good and beautiful
is this faith for us for ever.

True is the eternal God, our King, Rock of Jacob,
Shield of our salvation.
He exists and His name exists
through all generations.
His throne is established,
His kingship and faithfulness endure for ever.

At °, kiss the tzitziot and release them.

His words live and persist,
faithful and desirable
°for ever and all time.
▸ So they were for our ancestors, so they are for us,
and so they will be for our children
and all our generations and for all future generations
of the seed of Israel, Your servants.

---

organs that rabbinic tradition says are in the human body. Reciting each part of the *Shema* carefully will result in the healing of each part of the body. But the truth is that there are only 245 words in the three paragraphs of *Shema*, and so the leader adds the three words at the end in order to round out the number. In Ashkenazic practice, if one is praying alone, since we do not repeat words when it can be avoided, one instead adds the three words "God, faithful King" (*El Melekh ne'eman*) at the beginning of the *Shema* (see page 597 in order to arrive at the required number).

אֱלֹהֵיכֶם, אֲשֶׁר הוֹצֵאתִי אֶתְכֶם מֵאֶרֶץ מִצְרַיִם, לִהְיוֹת לָכֶם לֵאלֹהִים, אֲנִי יהוה אֱלֹהֵיכֶם:

°אֱמֶת[ב]

The שליח ציבור *repeats:*

› יהוה אֱלֹהֵיכֶם אֱמֶת[ה]

וְיַצִּיב, וְנָכוֹן וְקַיָּם, וְיָשָׁר וְנֶאֱמָן
וְאָהוּב וְחָבִיב, וְנֶחְמָד וְנָעִים
וְנוֹרָא וְאַדִּיר, וּמְתֻקָּן וּמְקֻבָּל, וְטוֹב וְיָפֶה
הַדָּבָר הַזֶּה עָלֵינוּ לְעוֹלָם וָעֶד.

אֱמֶת אֱלֹהֵי עוֹלָם מַלְכֵּנוּ
צוּר יַעֲקֹב מָגֵן יִשְׁעֵנוּ
לְדוֹר וָדוֹר הוּא קַיָּם וּשְׁמוֹ קַיָּם
וְכִסְאוֹ נָכוֹן, וּמַלְכוּתוֹ וֶאֱמוּנָתוֹ לָעַד קַיֶּמֶת.

At °, kiss the ציציות *and release them.*

וּדְבָרָיו חָיִים וְקַיָּמִים, נֶאֱמָנִים וְנֶחֱמָדִים
°לָעַד וּלְעוֹלְמֵי עוֹלָמִים
› עַל אֲבוֹתֵינוּ וְעָלֵינוּ
עַל בָּנֵינוּ וְעַל דּוֹרוֹתֵינוּ
וְעַל כָּל דּוֹרוֹת זֶרַע יִשְׂרָאֵל עֲבָדֶיךָ.

HILKHOT TEFILLA · הלכות תפילה

יהוה אֱלֹהֵיכֶם אֱמֶת – *The Lord your God is true.* There is a very old custom in which the leader or *ḥazan* connects the last two words of the *Shema* to the first word of the next paragraph so as to form a single phrase. The source, which is rather mystical, suggests that there are 248 words in the *Keriat Shema* which corresponds to the 248

For the early and the later generations
this faith has proved good and enduring for ever –
True and faithful, an irrevocable law.
True You are the LORD: our God and God of our ancestors,
▸ our King and King of our ancestors,
our Redeemer and Redeemer of our ancestors,
our Maker,
Rock of our salvation,
our Deliverer and Rescuer:
this has ever been Your name.
There is no God but You.

עֶזְרַת You have always been the help of our ancestors,
Shield and Savior of their children after them
in every generation.
Your dwelling is in the heights of the universe,
and Your judgments and righteousness
reach to the ends of the earth.
Happy is the one who obeys Your commandments
and takes to heart Your teaching and Your word.
True You are the Master of Your people
and a mighty King who pleads their cause.
True You are the first and You are the last.
Besides You, we have no king,
redeemer or savior.
From Egypt You redeemed us, LORD our God,
and from the slave-house You delivered us.
All their firstborn You killed,
but Your firstborn You redeemed.
You split the Sea of Reeds
and drowned the arrogant.
You brought Your beloved ones across.
The water covered their foes; *Ps. 106*
not one of them was left.

עַל הָרִאשׁוֹנִים וְעַל הָאַחֲרוֹנִים
דָּבָר טוֹב וְקַיָּם לְעוֹלָם וָעֶד
אֱמֶת וֶאֱמוּנָה, חֹק וְלֹא יַעֲבֹר.
אֱמֶת שָׁאַתָּה הוּא יהוה אֱלֹהֵינוּ וֵאלֹהֵי אֲבוֹתֵינוּ
◂ מַלְכֵּנוּ מֶלֶךְ אֲבוֹתֵינוּ
גּוֹאֲלֵנוּ גּוֹאֵל אֲבוֹתֵינוּ
יוֹצְרֵנוּ צוּר יְשׁוּעָתֵנוּ
פּוֹדֵנוּ וּמַצִּילֵנוּ מֵעוֹלָם שְׁמֶךָ
אֵין אֱלֹהִים זוּלָתֶךָ.

עֶזְרַת אֲבוֹתֵינוּ אַתָּה הוּא מֵעוֹלָם
מָגֵן וּמוֹשִׁיעַ לִבְנֵיהֶם אַחֲרֵיהֶם בְּכָל דּוֹר וָדוֹר.
בְּרוּם עוֹלָם מוֹשָׁבֶךָ
וּמִשְׁפָּטֶיךָ וְצִדְקָתְךָ עַד אַפְסֵי אָרֶץ.
אַשְׁרֵי אִישׁ שֶׁיִּשְׁמַע לְמִצְוֹתֶיךָ
וְתוֹרָתְךָ וּדְבָרְךָ יָשִׂים עַל לִבּוֹ.
אֱמֶת אַתָּה הוּא אָדוֹן לְעַמֶּךָ
וּמֶלֶךְ גִּבּוֹר לָרִיב רִיבָם.
אֱמֶת אַתָּה הוּא רִאשׁוֹן וְאַתָּה הוּא אַחֲרוֹן
וּמִבַּלְעָדֶיךָ אֵין לָנוּ מֶלֶךְ גּוֹאֵל וּמוֹשִׁיעַ.
מִמִּצְרַיִם גְּאַלְתָּנוּ, יהוה אֱלֹהֵינוּ
וּמִבֵּית עֲבָדִים פְּדִיתָנוּ
כָּל בְּכוֹרֵיהֶם הָרַגְתָּ, וּבְכוֹרְךָ גָּאָלְתָּ
וְיַם סוּף בָּקַעְתָּ, וְזֵדִים טִבַּעְתָּ
וִידִידִים הֶעֱבַרְתָּ
וַיְכַסּוּ־מַיִם צָרֵיהֶם, אֶחָד מֵהֶם לֹא נוֹתָר: תהלים קו

For this, the beloved ones praised and exalted God,
the cherished ones sang psalms, songs and praises,
blessings and thanksgivings to the King,
the living and enduring God.
High and exalted, great and awesome,
He humbles the haughty and raises the lowly,
freeing captives and redeeming those in need, helping the poor
and answering His people when they cry out to Him.

Stand in preparation for the Amida. Take three steps back before beginning the Amida.

▸ Praises to God Most High, the Blessed One who is blessed.
Moses and the children of Israel
recited to You a song with great joy,
and they all exclaimed:

"Who is like You, LORD, among the mighty? *Ex. 15*
Who is like You, majestic in holiness,
awesome in praises, doing wonders?"

▸ With a new song, the redeemed people praised
Your name at the seashore.
Together they all gave thanks, proclaimed Your kingship,
and declared:

"The LORD shall reign for ever and ever." *Ex. 15*

Congregants should end the following blessing together with the Leader so as to be able to move directly from the words "redeemed Israel" to the Amida, without the interruption of saying Amen.

▸ צוּר יִשְׂרָאֵל Rock of Israel! Arise to the help of Israel.
Deliver, as You promised, Judah and Israel.

Our Redeemer, the LORD of hosts is His name, *Is. 47*
the Holy One of Israel.

Blessed are You, LORD, who redeemed Israel.

ANI TEFILLA · אני תפילה

"Looking for God is like a drop in the ocean looking for water." (Rabbi David Aaron)

עַל זֹאת שִׁבְּחוּ אֲהוּבִים, וְרוֹמְמוּ אֵל
וְנָתְנוּ יְדִידִים זְמִירוֹת, שִׁירוֹת וְתִשְׁבָּחוֹת
בְּרָכוֹת וְהוֹדָאוֹת לְמֶלֶךְ אֵל חַי וְקַיָּם
רָם וְנִשָּׂא, גָּדוֹל וְנוֹרָא
מַשְׁפִּיל גֵּאִים וּמַגְבִּיהַּ שְׁפָלִים
מוֹצִיא אֲסִירִים, וּפוֹדֶה עֲנָוִים וְעוֹזֵר דַּלִּים
וְעוֹנֶה לְעַמּוֹ בְּעֵת שַׁוְּעָם אֵלָיו.

Stand in preparation for the עמידה*. Take three steps back before beginning the* עמידה*.*

› תְּהִלּוֹת לְאֵל עֶלְיוֹן, בָּרוּךְ הוּא וּמְבֹרָךְ
מֹשֶׁה וּבְנֵי יִשְׂרָאֵל
לְךָ עָנוּ שִׁירָה בְּשִׂמְחָה רַבָּה
וְאָמְרוּ כֻלָּם
מִי־כָמֹכָה בָּאֵלִם, יהוה שמות טו
מִי כָּמֹכָה נֶאְדָּר בַּקֹּדֶשׁ, נוֹרָא תְהִלֹּת, עֹשֵׂה פֶלֶא:
› שִׁירָה חֲדָשָׁה שִׁבְּחוּ גְאוּלִים
לְשִׁמְךָ עַל שְׂפַת הַיָּם
יַחַד כֻּלָּם הוֹדוּ וְהִמְלִיכוּ
וְאָמְרוּ
יהוה יִמְלֹךְ לְעֹלָם וָעֶד: שמות טו

The קהל *should end the following blessing together with the* שליח ציבור
so as to be able to move directly from the words גָּאַל יִשְׂרָאֵל *to*
the עמידה*, without the interruption of saying* אמן*.*

› צוּר יִשְׂרָאֵל, קוּמָה בְּעֶזְרַת יִשְׂרָאֵל
וּפְדֵה כִנְאֻמֶךָ יְהוּדָה וְיִשְׂרָאֵל.
גֹּאֲלֵנוּ יהוה צְבָאוֹת שְׁמוֹ, קְדוֹשׁ יִשְׂרָאֵל: ישעיה מז
בָּרוּךְ אַתָּה יהוה, גָּאַל יִשְׂרָאֵל.

THE AMIDA

The Amida until "in former years" on page 628, is said standing with feet together. The Amida is said silently, following the precedent of Hannah when she prayed for a child (1 Sam. 1:13). If there is a minyan, it is repeated aloud by the Leader. Take three steps forward, as if formally entering the place of the Divine Presence. At the points indicated by ▾, bend the knees at the first word, bow at the second, and stand straight before saying God's name.

O LORD, open my lips, so that my mouth may declare Your praise. *Ps. 51*

PATRIARCHS

▾Blessed are You, LORD[B] our God and God of our fathers,
God of Abraham, God of Isaac and God of Jacob;[I]
the great, mighty and awesome God, God Most High,

STRUCTURE OF THE AMIDA FOR ALL SHABBAT SERVICES

STANDARDIZED FIRST THREE BLESSINGS OF PRAISE

1. אבות – Patriarchs
2. גבורות – Divine Might
3. קדושת שם – Holiness

THE MIDDLE BLESSING – THE HOLINESS OF SHABBAT

4. קדושת היום – Holiness of the day

Consists of: (a) Statement about Shabbat appropriate to the theme of this particular Shabbat service (changes for *Ma'ariv, Shaḥarit, Musaf and Minḥa*). (b) Verses from the Torah that speak about Shabbat. (c) Another thematic statement about Shabbat. (d) The conclusion of the blessing which is the same for every Shabbat service.

STANDARDIZED LAST THREE BLESSINGS OF GRATITUDE

5. עבודה – Temple Service
6. מודים – Thanksgiving
7. שלום – Peace

PRIVATE MEDITATION

אלהי נצור – My God, guard my tongue…

BIUR TEFILLA • ביאור תפילה

בָּרוּךְ אַתָּה יהוה – *Blessed are You, LORD.* The physical act of bowing is both the last preparation for prayer as well as its introduction. The very act of bowing is an act of submission. It is thus both an acknowledgment of before Whom one stands as well as an act of prayer itself (Rabbi H. Vidal). People often make the mistake of rushing through these movements out of rote. It pays to take your time.

IYUN TEFILLA • עיון תפילה

אַבְרָהָם... יִצְחָק... יַעֲקֹב – *Abraham…Isaac…Jacob.* If Moses was so great, why don't we refer to the "God of Moses" just as we refer to God of Abraham, Isaac and Jacob? There is an inherent difference between Abraham and Moses. Abraham searched for God, but God did not react immediately. It was only much later, according to the Midrash, after Abraham had come to believe in Him, that God appeared to

This **IYUN TEFILLA** *continues on page 609.*

עמידה

The עמידה until קַדְמֹנִיּוֹת on page 629, is said standing with feet together. The עמידה is said silently, following the precedent of Hannah when she prayed for a child (שמואל א׳ א, יג). If there is a מנין, it is repeated aloud by the שליח ציבור. Take three steps forward, as if formally entering the place of the Divine Presence. At the points indicated by ˅, bend the knees at the first word, bow at the second, and stand straight before saying God's name.

אֲדֹנָי, שְׂפָתַי תִּפְתָּח, וּפִי יַגִּיד תְּהִלָּתֶךָ: תהלים נא

אבות

˅בָּרוּךְ ˅אַתָּה יהוה, אֱלֹהֵינוּ וֵאלֹהֵי אֲבוֹתֵינוּ
אֱלֹהֵי אַבְרָהָם, אֱלֹהֵי יִצְחָק, וֵאלֹהֵי יַעֲקֹב
הָאֵל הַגָּדוֹל הַגִּבּוֹר וְהַנּוֹרָא, אֵל עֶלְיוֹן

INTRODUCTION TO THE AMIDA

For an overview of the Amida prayer in general, see page 134 (Amida of Shaḥarit for Weekdays).

The first three blessings and the last three blessings of the *Amida* are identical for every version of the *Amida* that there is, both throughout this day and for every other prayer service.

The first blessing, called *Avot* (Patriarchs) is an acknowledgment of the historic relationship that Hashem has had with the Jewish people since the days of our forefathers who brought monotheism to the world.

The second blessing called *Gevurot* (Divine Might) is an acknowledgment of God's power, particularly over nature but also in the affairs of man, for how could we speak to God if we were not ready to first admit to our dependence and inferiority?

The third blessing, called *Kedusha* (Holiness) speaks to God's immanence and transcendence. He is totally beyond us and yet, a close and personal relationship is possible as well.

In sum, our posture is "like a servant who organizes his praise before his master" (*Berakhot* 34a). One speaks to God this way not to engage in small talk, nor to be falsely ingratiating, but rather for us to realize before Whom we stand and to admit as much before Him.

The last three blessings similarly appear in every version of the *Amida* that there is. These blessings are "like a servant who received his allotment from his master and takes his leave" (*Berakhot* 34a). One does not turn one's back on the King, nor does one end the conversation abruptly, rather one leaves with a sense of ongoing commitment going forward, a sense of gratitude for having been heard and a sense of peace, both physical and spiritual.

By bracketing the middle blessing this way, the siddur seeks to help us frame our encounter with the Divine in an appropriate and very Jewish manner. The themes and posture are laid out for us, but what we bring to them, how we internalize them, how we are ultimately impacted by them, is up to each and every one of us in our own way.

who bestows acts of loving-kindness and creates all,
who remembers the loving-kindness of the fathers
and will bring a Redeemer to their children's children
for the sake of His name, in love.
King, Helper, Savior, Shield:
▾Blessed are You, LORD, Shield of Abraham.[I]

DIVINE MIGHT

אַתָּה גִּבּוֹר You are eternally mighty, LORD.
You give life to the dead and have great power to save.

In Israel: He causes the dew to fall.

He sustains the living with loving-kindness,
and with great compassion revives the dead.
He supports the fallen, heals the sick, sets captives free,
and keeps His faith with those who sleep in the dust.
Who is like You, Master of might,
and who can compare to You,
O King who brings death and gives life, and makes salvation grow?
Faithful are You to revive the dead.
Blessed are You, LORD, who revives the dead.[B]

When saying the Amida silently, continue with "You are holy" on page 614.

and then returned. Yitzḥak lived the life of a holy person, named by God, ready for the ultimate sacrifice, he never left the Land of Israel. Yaakov was born in Israel, lived in the Diaspora, returned to Israel, and then died in the Diaspora. His was a life of trials and tribulations, in which God was ever present but not necessarily always heard. We mention each of the Patriarchs perhaps in part because each of them points toward a different path toward interacting with Hashem and with the Land. Paths that speaks to each of us differently, perhaps at different points in our lives, perhaps at different points in our day. The path to faith or the Land isn't always a straight one but, as indicated by the concluding blessing, we all aspire to be like Avraham.

IYUN TEFILLA • עיון תפילה

מְחַיֵּה מֵתִים אַתָּה – *You give life to the dead.* The blessing speaks about Hashem both as one who "brings death," and "gives life." Life and death are both part of living. A seed seems to decompose when it is actually beginning to sprout. What looks like death

This **IYUN TEFILLA** *continues on page 611.*

גּוֹמֵל חֲסָדִים טוֹבִים, וְקֹנֵה הַכֹּל
וְזוֹכֵר חַסְדֵי אָבוֹת
וּמֵבִיא גוֹאֵל לִבְנֵי בְנֵיהֶם לְמַעַן שְׁמוֹ בְּאַהֲבָה.
מֶלֶךְ עוֹזֵר וּמוֹשִׁיעַ וּמָגֵן.
בָּרוּךְ אַתָּה יהוה, מָגֵן אַבְרָהָם.

גבורות

אַתָּה גִּבּוֹר לְעוֹלָם, אֲדֹנָי, מְחַיֵּה מֵתִים אַתָּה, רַב לְהוֹשִׁיעַ
בארץ ישראל בקיץ: מוֹרִיד הַטָּל
מְכַלְכֵּל חַיִּים בְּחֶסֶד, מְחַיֵּה מֵתִים בְּרַחֲמִים רַבִּים
סוֹמֵךְ נוֹפְלִים, וְרוֹפֵא חוֹלִים, וּמַתִּיר אֲסוּרִים
וּמְקַיֵּם אֱמוּנָתוֹ לִישֵׁנֵי עָפָר.
מִי כָמוֹךָ, בַּעַל גְּבוּרוֹת, וּמִי דּוֹמֶה לָּךְ
מֶלֶךְ, מֵמִית וּמְחַיֶּה וּמַצְמִיחַ יְשׁוּעָה.
וְנֶאֱמָן אַתָּה לְהַחֲיוֹת מֵתִים.
בָּרוּךְ אַתָּה יהוה, מְחַיֵּה הַמֵּתִים.

When saying the עמידה *silently, continue with* אַתָּה קָדוֹשׁ *on page 615.*

בָּרוּךְ אַתָּה יהוה, מָגֵן אַבְרָהָם – *Blessed are You, Lord, Shield of Abraham.* Each of the Patriarchs may be seen as representing a different approach to the relationship with God and the Land. Avraham, according to the Rabbis, discovered God on his own, without the benefit of a Jewish education or tradition, boldly charting the path toward faith as a rationalist or a romantic, depending on how one views him. He was born outside the Land, made *aliya*, left for a period

him. Moses was just the opposite. Moses did not search for the Almighty. He was a shepherd for Jethro, and "he hid his face because he feared to look at God (*Shemot* 3:6)." God searched for Moses, and He found him. Abraham, Isaac, and Jacob are the only true forefathers; God's revelation to them came after a long time and many frustrated efforts (Rabbi Joseph B. Soloveitchik). In short, the search for God lies at the heart of our prayer, even if He does not react immediately.

KEDUSHA[B]

During the Leader's Repetition, the following is said standing with feet together, rising on the toes at the words indicated by ▲.

Cong. then Leader: נְקַדֵּשׁ We will sanctify Your name on earth,
as they sanctify it in the highest heavens,
as is written by Your prophet,
"And they [the angels] call to one another saying: *Is. 6*

---

those three clashes of the cymbals," he said, "the entire concert would fall apart, for the essential thing about an orchestra is that every single sound is balanced with another; if one sound is missing, then the entire combination fails."

The Rav said that it was at that moment that he understood the gemara's statement (Berakhot 8a) that whoever has a synagogue in his community and does not attend, is called a bad neighbor.

BIUR TEFILLA · ביאור תפילה

קדושה – *KEDUSHA* (also see the commentary on kedusha on Weekday Shacharit page 143 and on Minḥa of Shabbat on page 777

We have been on a journey moving ever higher, ever closer to an encounter with the Divine, which ideally found its most personal expression in the *Amida*. Now, before we descend, we join together as a community of people who have raised ourselves above ourselves, striving for the summit as a collective. Putting this into words, we adopt the stance of angels, as it were, describing Hashem's awesome distance and His intimate closeness. It is called simply *Kedusha*, holiness, for that is what we describe and it is for that we strive. Apparently in the times of the Geonim, at least in Israel, the *Kedusha* was only said on Shabbat (*Tosafot, Sanhedrin* 37b). To explain this custom, the story is told that the angels had six wings (*Yeshayahu* 6) and each wing would sing a song to *Hashem* on one of the six days of the week. The angels turned to Him and said, "*Hashem*, we only have six wings, and what of the seventh day?" To which He responded, "Don't worry, I have one more wing that can sing before Me, as the verse says: 'From the edge (*kenaf*) of the earth we have heard songs'" (*Yeshayahu* 24:16). The implication is clear: on Shabbat we are that wing.

As in the *Amida* itself, there is a widespread custom to stand with one's feet together as they if they were a single entity, similar to the vision of *Yeḥezkel* (1:7), one of the most mystical in all of *Tanakh* in which he described the angels as: "their legs were as one straight leg." At this moment, we see ourselves as wholly spiritual creatures.

It is as if our feet are bound and our will is not our own (Rabbeinu Baḥye, *Bemidbar* 16:22). One should have in mind the commandment "and I will be sanctified among the children of Israel" (Ḥida 18:13 in the name of Arizal)

קדושה[ב]

During the חזרת הש״ץ*, the following is said standing with feet together, rising on the toes at the words indicated by* •.

then קהל ש״ץ: נְקַדֵּשׁ אֶת שִׁמְךָ בָּעוֹלָם
כְּשֵׁם שֶׁמַּקְדִּישִׁים אוֹתוֹ בִּשְׁמֵי מָרוֹם
כַּכָּתוּב עַל יַד נְבִיאֶךָ:
וְקָרָא זֶה אֶל־זֶה וְאָמַר ישעיה ו

---

is actually the beginning of life. What looks like something bad is actually something good. That is the way Hashem works.

What "bad" can you point to in your life or the life of someone else that really turned out to be "good" in the end?

INTRODUCTION TO *ḤAZARAT HASHATZ* – The Reader's repetition of the *Amida*

The repetition of the *Amida* by the *ḥazan* was established for a very functional reason, namely, to enable those who could not read the prayer to nevertheless fulfill their obligation by listening to the *ḥazan* recite it and answering *amen* to each of its blessings. Such a response is considered tantamount to saying the blessing oneself. In halakhic discourse this is known as *shome'a k'oneh*, the listener is like one who recited it. It is a statement that everyone should be able to participate in communal prayer, regardless of their background or ability.

At the same time, Rabbi Soloveitchik maintained that the repetition had another function, namely, it was a prayer not with the community, but of the community. That is to say, it is another *Amida*, said not by a group of individuals, but by a collective, represented by the *ḥazan*. We pray not just as individuals for ourselves and for others but for the single entity called community. As such, there are some who have the custom to remain standing, feet together, for the entire repetition as if they were saying the *Amida* yet again. Too often some people think of this practice as being repetitious; think of it instead as a totally new prayer, a new opportunity to come together as something larger than oneself.

ANI TEFILLA • אני תפילה

The story is told that Rav Soloveitchik once went to hear the Boston Symphony Orchestra and observed that the harpist worked so hard throughout the performance but the person on cymbals struck the instrument only three times the entire evening. The Rav wondered whether they both got paid the same amount since the amount of effort they expended was certainly not equal, and so he went and asked the cymbalist if it were so. The musician not only confirmed that they were paid the same but that their importance was equal. "Without

Cong. then Leader: ▲Holy, ▲holy, ▲holy[BH] is the LORD of hosts
the whole world is filled with His glory."
Then with a sound of mighty noise,[B] majestic and strong,
they make their voice heard, raising themselves
toward the Seraphim, and facing them say: "Blessed…

Cong. then Leader: ▲"Blessed is the LORD's glory from His place." *Ezek. 3*
Reveal Yourself from Your place,[A] O our King,
and reign over us,
for we are waiting for You.[I]
When will You reign in Zion?
May it be soon in our days,
and may You dwell there for ever and all time.
May You be exalted and sanctified
in the midst of Jerusalem, Your city,
from generation to generation for evermore.
May our eyes see Your kingdom,
as is said in the songs of Your splendor,
written by David your righteous anointed one:

ANI TEFILLA • אני תפילה

מִמְּקוֹמְךָ מַלְכֵּנוּ תוֹפִיעַ – *Reveal Yourself from Your place*. I once heard a convert say that one of the biggest adjustments to Jewish prayer was the absence of some physical representation of God to pray to. When I was a child, I recall wondering what would happen if the ark suddenly opened and God revealed Himself there or somewhere else at the front of the synagogue. How would all of us act differently at that moment?

How would your prayer be different right now if Hashem were suddenly to appear before you?

IYUN TEFILLA • עיון תפילה

כִּי מְחַכִּים אֲנַחְנוּ לָךְ – *For we are waiting for You*. The king is about to arrive. The troops are rallied and preparations are made. The officers make sure that everything is in order and the troops are gathered on the parade grounds in full regalia standing at attention awaiting the arrival of their commander in chief. But the king is delayed and one officer, try as he might, begins to get drowsy and falls asleep on a chair in front of the troops.

This **IYUN TEFILLA** *continues on page 615.*

then קהל ש״ץ: ׳קָדוֹשׁ, ׳קָדוֹשׁ, ׳קָדוֹשׁ, בה יהוה צְבָאוֹת
מְלֹא כָל־הָאָרֶץ כְּבוֹדוֹ:
אָז בְּקוֹל ב רַעַשׁ גָּדוֹל אַדִּיר וְחָזָק, מַשְׁמִיעִים קוֹל
מִתְנַשְּׂאִים לְעֻמַּת שְׂרָפִים
לְעֻמָּתָם בָּרוּךְ יֹאמֵרוּ

then קהל ש״ץ: ׳בָּרוּךְ כְּבוֹד־יהוה מִמְּקוֹמוֹ: יחזקאל ג
מִמְּקוֹמְךָ מַלְכֵּנוּ תוֹפִיעַ א וְתִמְלֹךְ עָלֵינוּ
כִּי מְחַכִּים אֲנַחְנוּ לָךְ ע
מָתַי תִּמְלֹךְ בְּצִיּוֹן, בְּקָרוֹב בְּיָמֵינוּ לְעוֹלָם וָעֶד תִּשְׁכֹּן
תִּתְגַּדַּל וְתִתְקַדַּשׁ בְּתוֹךְ יְרוּשָׁלַיִם עִירְךָ
לְדוֹר וָדוֹר וּלְנֵצַח נְצָחִים.
וְעֵינֵינוּ תִרְאֶינָה מַלְכוּתֶךָ
כַּדָּבָר הָאָמוּר בְּשִׁירֵי עֻזֶּךָ, עַל יְדֵי דָוִד מְשִׁיחַ צִדְקֶךָ

BIUR TEFILLA • ביאור תפילה

קָדוֹשׁ, קָדוֹשׁ, קָדוֹשׁ – *Holy, holy, holy.* When reciting these words, one might have in mind the Aramaic translation that Hashem is holy above, He is holy on earth, and He will be holy forever (see the prayer *U'Va L'Tzion* on page 231 He defies our limitations of space and time.

קָדוֹשׁ, קָדוֹשׁ, קָדוֹשׁ – *Holy, holy, holy.* This is in effect an admission that Hashem is beyond us. We shouldn't get upset that He sometimes seems elusive and untouchable. Were He not, He would not be God.

אָז בְּקוֹל – *Then with a mighty noise.* This *Kedusha* is a little different from the one said during the week, and has echoes of the description of the praise by the angels in the first of the *birkhot Keriat Shema* (page 114).

HILKHOT TEFILLA • הלכות תפילה

קָדוֹשׁ, קָדוֹשׁ, קָדוֹשׁ – *Holy, holy, holy.* Some have the custom here to go up and down on one's tiptoes with the recitation of each one of these words, as if one is reaching higher and higher.

Cong. then Leader: ▲"The LORD shall reign for ever. He is your God, Zion, from generation to generation, Halleluya!" *Ps. 146*

Leader: From generation to generation we will declare Your greatness, and we will proclaim Your holiness for evermore. Your praise, our God, shall not leave our mouth forever, for You, God, are a great and holy King. Blessed are You, LORD, the holy God.

The Leader continues with "Moses rejoiced" below.

HOLINESS

אַתָּה קָדוֹשׁ You are holy[B] and Your name is holy,
and holy ones praise You daily, Selah!
Blessed are You, LORD, the holy God.

HOLINESS OF THE DAY

יִשְׂמַח Moses rejoiced at the gift of his portion[I]
when You called him "faithful servant."
A crown of glory You placed on his head
when he stood before You on Mount Sinai.
He brought down in his hands two tablets of stone
on which was engraved the observance of the Sabbath.
So it is written in Your Torah:

Ten Commandments was especially joyful. Some commentaries point to the Gemara which describes a conversation between Moshe and Hashem atop Mount Sinai: "Hashem said to Moshe: 'I have a wonderful gift from my treasure house and its name is Shabbat. I want to give it to Israel. Go and let them know" (*Shabbat* 10b). It must always be remembered that Shabbat is a gift, not alone an obligation, not alone a yoke, not alone a lifestyle, but a gift.

If you were to look at this day more as a gift, how might it change the way you observe it today?

At the same time, perhaps it is an echo of the tradition that the Torah was given on Shabbat (*Shabbat* 86a). One can then understand Moshe's great joy... and the need for us to follow. Knowing Torah brings one joy.

What about this day generally gives you joy?

How can you make this Shabbat into more of a day of joy?

then קהל ש״ץ: ׳יִמְלֹךְ יהוה לְעוֹלָם, אֱלֹהַיִךְ צִיּוֹן לְדֹר וָדֹר, הַלְלוּיָהּ: תהלים קמו

ש״ץ: לְדוֹר וָדוֹר נַגִּיד גָּדְלֶךָ, וּלְנֵצַח נְצָחִים קְדֻשָּׁתְךָ נַקְדִּישׁ
וְשִׁבְחֲךָ אֱלֹהֵינוּ מִפִּינוּ לֹא יָמוּשׁ לְעוֹלָם וָעֶד
כִּי אֵל מֶלֶךְ גָּדוֹל וְקָדוֹשׁ אָתָּה.
בָּרוּךְ אַתָּה יהוה הָאֵל הַקָּדוֹשׁ.

The שליח ציבור *continues with* יִשְׂמַח מֹשֶׁה *below.*

קדושת השם

אַתָּה קָדוֹשׁ[ב] וְשִׁמְךָ קָדוֹשׁ
וּקְדוֹשִׁים בְּכָל יוֹם יְהַלְלוּךָ סֶּלָה.
בָּרוּךְ אַתָּה יהוה, הָאֵל הַקָּדוֹשׁ.

קדושת היום

יִשְׂמַח מֹשֶׁה בְּמַתְּנַת חֶלְקוֹ[ע]
כִּי עֶבֶד נֶאֱמָן קָרָאתָ לּוֹ
כְּלִיל תִּפְאֶרֶת בְּרֹאשׁוֹ נָתַתָּ לּוֹ
בְּעָמְדוֹ לְפָנֶיךָ עַל הַר סִינַי
וּשְׁנֵי לוּחוֹת אֲבָנִים הוֹרִיד בְּיָדוֹ
וְכָתוּב בָּהֶם שְׁמִירַת שַׁבָּת
וְכֵן כָּתוּב בְּתוֹרָתֶךָ

IYUN TEFILLA • עיון תפילה

יִשְׂמַח מֹשֶׁה בְּמַתְּנַת חֶלְקוֹ – *Moses rejoiced at the gift of his portion.* This passage describes Moshe's happiness at being able to bring the word of God to the Jewish people. In particular, the Rabbis understood that the presence of Shabbat in the

When the king finally appears, he is sympathetic but unforgiving, for what kind of example did this officer set, what did it say about his allegiance and commitment? So, too, with us. With a full heart we say "we are waiting for You" but as time goes on we tire, we sleep, forgetting that at any moment, the King could arrive (Ḥafetz Ḥayyim).

וְשָׁמְרוּ The children of Israel must keep the Sabbath,| Ex. 31
observing the Sabbath in every generation
as an everlasting covenant.
It is a sign between Me and the children of Israel for ever,|
for in six days God made the heavens and the earth,
but on the seventh day
He ceased work and refreshed Himself.|

וּבַיּוֹם הַשְּׁבִיעִי שָׁבַת וַיִּנָּפַשׁ – *But on the seventh day He ceased work and refreshed Himself.* Did God really need to recharge His batteries, as it were? The Gemara (*Beitza* 16a) homiletically learns from here instead that on Shabbat one receives an "added soul" (*neshama yeteira*), often understood as an added measure of spirituality. Rashi explains that in practical terms it means that one has a greater capacity for relaxation and joy, and that even one's eating and drinking on this day have a different dimension.

According to Rabbi Tzaddok of Lublin, the extra soul that we receive on Shabbat is not the same one that returns every week but a totally new one every Shabbat. "Hence, Shabbat is not a comfortably familiar ritual, the spiritual equivalent of a pair of old shoes... Rather, it bespeaks spiritual adventurousness, a pioneering drive, a fascination with the unknown and untried, and readiness to embrace the new as a way to *avodat Hashem* (service of *Hashem*)" (Rabbi Norman Lamm).

How can you engage your *neshama yeteira* (extra soul) this Shabbat?

וַיִּנָּפַשׁ – *He... refreshed Himself.* Shabbat is about refreshing one's soul, creating it anew, reliving being born into a new world. This highlights one of the main differences between the Western notion of relaxing and the Shabbat version of rest; the one is about recreation, the other is about re-creation.

ANI TEFILLA • אני תפילה

The story is told of a fool from Chelm who was so forgetful that before he went to bed he made a list of where everything was so that he could find it all in the morning: my pants are on the chair, my shirt is hanging in the closet, my shoes are near the door, and I, I am lying in bed. When he got up the next morning he consulted the list and found everything – except he could not find himself lying in the bed. Rabbi Ḥanokh Henikh Alexander would tell this story to his followers and when asked why, he responded, "Because we are all like that fool. We are so involved in everyday life that we spend all of our time keeping tabs on our material things, but not enough time asking ourselves 'Where am I?'"

שמות לא

וְשָׁמְרוּ בְנֵי־יִשְׂרָאֵל אֶת־הַשַּׁבָּת
לַעֲשׂוֹת אֶת־הַשַּׁבָּת לְדֹרֹתָם בְּרִית עוֹלָם:
בֵּינִי וּבֵין בְּנֵי יִשְׂרָאֵל אוֹת הִוא לְעֹלָם
כִּי־שֵׁשֶׁת יָמִים עָשָׂה יהוה אֶת־הַשָּׁמַיִם וְאֶת־הָאָרֶץ
וּבַיּוֹם הַשְּׁבִיעִי שָׁבַת וַיִּנָּפַשׁ:

IYUN TEFILLA • עיון תפילה

וְשָׁמְרוּ בְנֵי־יִשְׂרָאֵל אֶת־הַשַּׁבָּת – *The children of Israel must keep the Shabbat.* The Ten Commandments are written twice in the Torah. In one, the commandment is given to "keep the Shabbat" (*Devarim* 5:12); in the other, it is to "remember the Shabbat" (*Shemot* 20:8). But the expression "keep the Shabbat" regarding the seventh day of the week appears seven times throughout the Torah. The expression "remember the Shabbat" appears only once (*Iyun Tefilla*). The siddur here seeks to remind us to observe the day, to keep it and not just to remember it with words. We are good at mouthing our commitments but we must also act upon them.

How will you do a better job of that today?

בֵּינִי וּבֵין בְּנֵי יִשְׂרָאֵל אוֹת הִיא לְעוֹלָם – *It is a sign between Me and the children of Israel for ever.* The Rabbis point to this verse from *Shemot* 31:17 to explain why tefillin are not worn on Shabbat and Yom Tov. For tefillin are also referred to as a "sign" (**אות** *Shemot* 13:9). Thus, donning tefillin is considered disrespectful to the "sign" of Shabbat (*Shulhan Arukh*, 31:1). Shabbat is a connecting link between the Jewish people and Hashem, a distinguishing sign that even the non-Jewish world has come to recognize as one of our most unique characteristics.

בֵּינִי וּבֵין בְּנֵי יִשְׂרָאֵל אוֹת הִיא לְעוֹלָם – *It is a sign between Me and the children of Israel for ever.* "Rabbi Yehoshua ben Levi said: All of the commandments that Hashem gave to Israel were given publicly, except for the Shabbat which was given in private (*Beitza* 16a)." But what does this mean?! Isn't the commandment of Shabbat one of the Ten Commandments that were given in public for all to see and hear? Rather, what the Rabbis meant to say was that the commandment may have been public but the inner essence of Shabbat–its meaning, its taste, its secret–that is what was given in private. That is why it says it is "between me and Israel" (*Rabbeinu Beḥaye*).

How would you define the essence of Shabbat to someone else?

How can you yet experience it yourself today?

וְלֹא You, O LORD our God, did not give it
to the other nations of the world,[I]
nor did You, our King, give it as a heritage
to those who worship idols.
In its rest the uncircumcised do not dwell,
for You gave it in love to Israel Your people,
to the descendants of Jacob whom You chose.
May the people who sanctify the seventh day
all find satisfaction and delight in Your goodness,[B]
for You favored the seventh day
and made it holy,
calling it the most cherished of days,[IA]
a remembrance of the act of creation.

IYUN TEFILLA • עיון תפילה

חֶמְדַּת יָמִים אוֹתוֹ קָרָאתָ – *Calling it the most cherished of days.* What a person does with this day can have an impact on the following week, for your actions generate a sense of blessing that is implanted within you.

Create the opportunities for blessing today that you can take with you into next week.

ANI TEFILLA • אני תפילה

חֶמְדַּת יָמִים אוֹתוֹ קָרָאתָ – *Calling it the most cherished of days.* My grandfather, ז״ל, used to say, "Shabbos! I love the Shabbos! I don't know how the non-Jews survive without it."

What can you do today that will impact the rest of your week?

ANI TEFILLA • אני תפילה

"Mr. Speaker, allow me just one further point. This House should know, it is not necessary to be an observant Jew to appreciate the full historic and sacred aura that enshrines the 'perfect gift' called Shabbat. Its prohibitions are not arbitrary. They provide insulation against corrosive everydayness, they build fences against invasions by the profane, and they enrich the soul by creating a space for sacred time. In a word, one need not be pious to accept the cherished principle of Shabbat. One merely needs to be a proud Jew" (Prime Minister Menachem Begin speaking to the Knesset).

וְלֹא נְתַתּוֹ, יהוה אֱלֹהֵינוּ, לְגוֹיֵי הָאֲרָצוֹת[ע]
וְלֹא הִנְחַלְתּוֹ, מַלְכֵּנוּ, לְעוֹבְדֵי פְסִילִים
וְגַם בִּמְנוּחָתוֹ לֹא יִשְׁכְּנוּ עֲרֵלִים
כִּי לְיִשְׂרָאֵל עַמְּךָ נְתַתּוֹ בְּאַהֲבָה
לְזֶרַע יַעֲקֹב אֲשֶׁר בָּם בָּחָרְתָּ.
עַם מְקַדְּשֵׁי שְׁבִיעִי
כֻּלָּם יִשְׂבְּעוּ וְיִתְעַנְּגוּ מִטּוּבֶךָ[ב]
וּבַשְּׁבִיעִי רָצִיתָ בּוֹ וְקִדַּשְׁתּוֹ
חֶמְדַּת יָמִים אוֹתוֹ קָרָאתָ[עא]
זֵכֶר לְמַעֲשֵׂה בְרֵאשִׁית.

IYUN TEFILLA • עיון תפילה

וְלֹא נְתַתּוֹ, יהוה אֱלֹהֵינוּ, לְגוֹיֵי הָאֲרָצוֹת – *You, O Lord our God, did not give it to the other nations of the world.* Were Shabbat only about rest from fatigue or the eroding impact of the work week, then it would be the property of all mankind, for everyone understands the need to take a break, to recharge one's batteries so that one can return to work refreshed. But Shabbat is not only about that kind of rest; it is about refreshing one's soul, about gaining perspective, about one's relationship with God, with one's family and with oneself. That understanding, that goal, was given to the Jewish people alone.

BIUR TEFILLA • ביאור תפילה

כֻּלָּם יִשְׂבְּעוּ וְיִתְעַנְּגוּ מִטּוּבֶךָ – *All find satisfaction and delight in Your goodness.* Shouldn't it be the reverse – first one experiences the delight or joy (*oneg*) of eating and then one eats and becomes satiated? That is true of physical pleasure: one eats delicious food but then comes to a point at which one cannot eat any more. But in spiritual matters, there is no limit to one's growth and satisfaction. Hence one can be satisfied but still be delighted by more Torah, more song, more Shabbat (*Barukh SheAmar*).

אֱלֹהֵינוּ Our God and God of our ancestors,
find favor in our rest.
Make us holy through Your commandments
and grant us our share in Your Torah.
Satisfy us with Your goodness,
grant us joy in Your salvation,
and purify our hearts to serve You in truth.
In love and favor, LORD our God,
grant us as our heritage Your holy Sabbath,
so that Israel who sanctify Your name may find rest on it.
Blessed are You, LORD,
who sanctifies the Sabbath.

---

commandments, we will come to find our place in Your Torah. Through actions comes understanding.

וְתֵן חֶלְקֵנוּ בְּתוֹרָתֶךָ – *And grant us our share in Your Torah.* There is a mystical tradition which says that every Jewish soul yet to be born stood at Sinai at the time of the revelation. As such, each of us actually owns a share in the Torah for we were there when it was originally given. We need only reclaim our rightful place in its tradition. If so, then the prayer takes on new meaning: Help us to find ourselves. Help us to get in touch with what we already have.

בָּרוּךְ אַתָּה יהוה, מְקַדֵּשׁ הַשַּׁבָּת – *Blessed are You, LORD, who sanctifies the Sabbath.* Shabbat derives its sanctity directly from God. The day itself therefore maintains its holiness regardless of what people do on that day, even if they do not know it is there. But we know that it is there, waiting to be discovered.

ANI TEFILLA • אני תפילה

"The revelation at Sinai, which is our focus in the Sabbath morning service, is about destiny. It is not about what we are. It is about what we are destined to become and how following the commandments Moses received from God on Sinai can help us become that. By telling us how to live, the commandments give us our mission – if we choose to accept it – of bettering, even perfecting, the world God created... I was taught that the Children of Israel became a nation not when they were liberated from slavery, but when the Law was revealed to them on Sinai – because that gave them their reason for being, their national destiny.

This **ANI TEFILLA** *continues on page 623.*

אֱלֹהֵינוּ וֵאלֹהֵי אֲבוֹתֵינוּ, רְצֵה בִמְנוּחָתֵנוּ
קַדְּשֵׁנוּ בְּמִצְוֹתֶיךָ[ע] וְתֵן חֶלְקֵנוּ בְּתוֹרָתֶךָ[ע]
שַׂבְּעֵנוּ מִטּוּבֶךָ וְשַׂמְּחֵנוּ בִּישׁוּעָתֶךָ
וְטַהֵר לִבֵּנוּ לְעָבְדְּךָ בֶּאֱמֶת
וְהַנְחִילֵנוּ, יהוה אֱלֹהֵינוּ, בְּאַהֲבָה וּבְרָצוֹן שַׁבַּת קָדְשֶׁךָ
וְיָנְוּחוּ בוֹ יִשְׂרָאֵל מְקַדְּשֵׁי שְׁמֶךָ.
בָּרוּךְ אַתָּה יהוה, מְקַדֵּשׁ הַשַּׁבָּת.[ע]

IYUN TEFILLA • עיון תפילה

For more commentary on this blessing, see *Ma'ariv* (page 464) and *Musaf* (page 693).

קַדְּשֵׁנוּ בְּמִצְוֹתֶיךָ – *Make us holy through Your commandments.*

In what ways do you wish your life would be more holy?

How could you make the commandments that you already do make your life or your being more holy than you feel it is?

קַדְּשֵׁנוּ בְּמִצְוֹתֶיךָ וְתֵן חֶלְקֵנוּ בְּתוֹרָתֶךָ – *Make us holy through Your commandments and grant us our share in Your Torah.* In most other instances, the order is reversed, we first ask for a part in the Torah and then ask for help in fulfilling commandments. To what may this be compared? When accepting the Torah at Sinai, the Jewish people responded "we will do and we will listen," as if to say, we will commit ourselves to a Jewish life even if there are parts of the system which we do not yet fully understand. It is our prayer that through immersing ourselves in the

ANI TEFILLA • אני תפילה

The story is told of the day when the first train from Minsk to Pinsk rolled into town for its maiden voyage and two men bought tickets to see what it would be like to ride this new invention. Reuven was so amazed by this huge machine that he spent all of his time walking around the train, measuring its wheels, examining the locomotive and the passenger cars. He became so engrossed that he did not notice the final boarding call and the train pulled out of the station leaving him behind on the platform. Shimon, on the other hand, got onto the train as soon as it pulled into the station, thinking that he would come to better understand how it worked while he was on the journey.

When it comes to Shabbat, to prayer, and to other commandments, it pays to get on the train first.

TEMPLE SERVICE[B]

רְצֵה Find favor,[B] Lord our God, in Your people Israel
and their prayer.[B]
Restore the service to Your most holy House,[B]
and accept in love and favor
the fire-offerings[B] of Israel and their prayer.[B]
May the service of Your people Israel
always find favor with You.

On Rosh Hodesh, say:

אֱלֹהֵינוּ Our God and God of our ancestors, may there rise, come,[I] reach, appear, be favored, heard, regarded and remembered before You, our recollection and remembrance, as well as the remembrance of our ancestors, and of the Messiah son of David Your servant, and of Jerusalem Your holy city, and of all Your people the house of Israel – for deliverance and well-being, grace, loving-kindness and compassion, life and peace, on this day of Rosh Hodesh. On it remember us, Lord our God, for good; recollect us for blessing, and deliver us for life. In accord with Your promise of salvation and compassion, spare us and be gracious to us; have compassion on us and deliver us, for our eyes are turned to You because You, God, are a gracious and compassionate King.

וְתֶחֱזֶינָה And may our eyes witness[B] Your return
to Zion in compassion.
Blessed are You, Lord,
who restores His Presence to Zion.[I]

ANI TEFILLA • אני תפילה

Rabbi Refael of Bershad once told that he complained to his teacher Rabbi Pinhas of Koretz that in difficult times it's very hard to have perfect faith in the belief that God watches out for every person. It actually seems as if God is hiding his face from such an unhappy person. What could he do to restore his faith? Rabbi Pinhas answered him: "It ceases to be a hiding if you know that it is hiding."

עבודה[ב]

רְצֵה[ב] יהוה אֱלֹהֵינוּ בְּעַמְּךָ יִשְׂרָאֵל וּבִתְפִלָּתָם[ב]
וְהָשֵׁב אֶת הָעֲבוֹדָה לִדְבִיר בֵּיתֶךָ[ב]
וְאִשֵּׁי[ב] יִשְׂרָאֵל וּתְפִלָּתָם בְּאַהֲבָה תְקַבֵּל בְּרָצוֹן[ב]
וּתְהִי לְרָצוֹן תָּמִיד עֲבוֹדַת יִשְׂרָאֵל עַמֶּךָ.

On ראש חודש*, say:*

אֱלֹהֵינוּ וֵאלֹהֵי אֲבוֹתֵינוּ, יַעֲלֶה וְיָבוֹא[ע] וְיַגִּיעַ, וְיֵרָאֶה וְיֵרָצֶה וְיִשָּׁמַע, וְיִפָּקֵד וְיִזָּכֵר זִכְרוֹנֵנוּ וּפִקְדוֹנֵנוּ וְזִכְרוֹן אֲבוֹתֵינוּ, וְזִכְרוֹן מָשִׁיחַ בֶּן דָּוִד עַבְדֶּךָ, וְזִכְרוֹן יְרוּשָׁלַיִם עִיר קָדְשֶׁךָ, וְזִכְרוֹן כָּל עַמְּךָ בֵּית יִשְׂרָאֵל, לְפָנֶיךָ, לִפְלֵיטָה לְטוֹבָה, לְחֵן וּלְחֶסֶד וּלְרַחֲמִים, לְחַיִּים וּלְשָׁלוֹם בְּיוֹם רֹאשׁ הַחֹדֶשׁ הַזֶּה. זָכְרֵנוּ יהוה אֱלֹהֵינוּ בּוֹ לְטוֹבָה, וּפָקְדֵנוּ בוֹ לִבְרָכָה, וְהוֹשִׁיעֵנוּ בוֹ לְחַיִּים. וּבִדְבַר יְשׁוּעָה וְרַחֲמִים, חוּס וְחָנֵּנוּ וְרַחֵם עָלֵינוּ וְהוֹשִׁיעֵנוּ, כִּי אֵלֶיךָ עֵינֵינוּ, כִּי אֵל מֶלֶךְ חַנּוּן וְרַחוּם אָתָּה.

וְתֶחֱזֶינָה עֵינֵינוּ[ב] בְּשׁוּבְךָ לְצִיּוֹן בְּרַחֲמִים.
בָּרוּךְ אַתָּה יהוה, הַמַּחֲזִיר שְׁכִינָתוֹ לְצִיּוֹן.[ע]

Those same values give each of us a personal destiny. But you can't be passive about your destiny. It isn't fulfilled unless you decide to work to make it happen.

The commandment to observe the Sabbath is… at the heart of our destiny. But the Sabbath doesn't automatically enter our lives. We have to decide to bring it in, to seize that part of our destiny. And that can be difficult."

My religious observance, including my Sabbath observance, has taught me that it's ok to be different… When you choose your own path – whether in faith, politics, or whatever you do – you will not only feel better, but people will respect you for your choice"

(Senator Joe Lieberman, Vice-Presidential candidate, 2000)

THANKSGIVING

Bow at the first nine words.

▼We give thanks to You,
for You are
the Lord our God
and God of our ancestors
for ever and all time.
You are the Rock of our lives,
Shield of our salvation
from generation to generation.
We will thank You and
declare Your praise for our lives,
which are entrusted into Your hand;
for our souls,
which are placed in Your charge;
for Your miracles
which are with us every day;
and for Your wonders and favors
at all times,
evening, morning and midday.
You are good –
for Your compassion never fails.
You are compassionate –
for Your loving-kindnesses never cease.
We have always placed our hope in You.

During the Leader's Repetition, the congregation says quietly:

▼We give thanks to You,
for You are
the Lord our God
and God of our ancestors,
God of all flesh,
who formed us
and formed the universe.
Blessings and thanks
are due to Your great
and holy name
for giving us life
and sustaining us.
May You continue
to give us life
and sustain us;
and may You gather our
exiles to Your holy courts,
to keep Your decrees,
do Your will and serve You
with a perfect heart,
for it is for us
to give You thanks.
Blessed be God
to whom thanksgiving is due.

וְעַל כֻּלָּם For all these things may Your name be blessed and exalted,
our King, continually, for ever and all time.
Let all that lives thank You, Selah!
and praise Your name in truth,
God, our Savior and Help, Selah!
▼Blessed are You, Lord,
whose name is "the Good" and to whom thanks are due.

הודאה

Bow at the first five words.

ˈמוֹדִים אֲנַֽחְנוּ לָךְ
שָׁאַתָּה הוּא
יהוה אֱלֹהֵֽינוּ וֵאלֹהֵי אֲבוֹתֵֽינוּ
לְעוֹלָם וָעֶד.
צוּר חַיֵּֽינוּ, מָגֵן יִשְׁעֵֽנוּ
אַתָּה הוּא לְדוֹר וָדוֹר.
נוֹדֶה לְּךָ וּנְסַפֵּר תְּהִלָּתֶֽךָ
עַל חַיֵּֽינוּ הַמְּסוּרִים בְּיָדֶֽךָ
וְעַל נִשְׁמוֹתֵֽינוּ הַפְּקוּדוֹת לָךְ
וְעַל נִסֶּֽיךָ שֶׁבְּכָל יוֹם עִמָּֽנוּ
וְעַל נִפְלְאוֹתֶֽיךָ[ע] וְטוֹבוֹתֶֽיךָ
שֶׁבְּכָל עֵת, עֶֽרֶב וָבֹֽקֶר וְצָהֳרָֽיִם.
הַטּוֹב, כִּי לֹא כָלוּ רַחֲמֶֽיךָ
וְהַמְרַחֵם, כִּי לֹא תַֽמּוּ חֲסָדֶֽיךָ
מֵעוֹלָם קִוִּֽינוּ לָךְ.

During the חזרת הש״ץ, *the* קהל *says quietly:*

ˈמוֹדִים אֲנַֽחְנוּ לָךְ
שָׁאַתָּה הוּא
יהוה אֱלֹהֵֽינוּ וֵאלֹהֵי אֲבוֹתֵֽינוּ
אֱלֹהֵי כָל בָּשָׂר
יוֹצְרֵֽנוּ, יוֹצֵר בְּרֵאשִׁית.
בְּרָכוֹת וְהוֹדָאוֹת
לְשִׁמְךָ הַגָּדוֹל וְהַקָּדוֹשׁ
עַל שֶׁהֶחֱיִיתָֽנוּ וְקִיַּמְתָּֽנוּ.
כֵּן תְּחַיֵּֽנוּ וּתְקַיְּמֵֽנוּ
וְתֶאֱסֹף גָּלֻיּוֹתֵֽינוּ
לְחַצְרוֹת קָדְשֶֽׁךָ
לִשְׁמֹר חֻקֶּֽיךָ
וְלַעֲשׂוֹת רְצוֹנֶֽךָ וּלְעָבְדְּךָ
בְּלֵבָב שָׁלֵם
עַל שֶׁאֲנַֽחְנוּ מוֹדִים לָךְ.
בָּרוּךְ אֵל הַהוֹדָאוֹת.

וְעַל כֻּלָּם יִתְבָּרַךְ וְיִתְרוֹמַם שִׁמְךָ מַלְכֵּֽנוּ תָּמִיד לְעוֹלָם וָעֶד.
וְכֹל הַחַיִּים יוֹדֽוּךָ סֶּֽלָה
וִיהַלְלוּ אֶת שִׁמְךָ בֶּאֱמֶת
הָאֵל יְשׁוּעָתֵֽנוּ וְעֶזְרָתֵֽנוּ סֶֽלָה.
ˈבָּרוּךְ אַתָּה יהוה, הַטּוֹב שִׁמְךָ וּלְךָ נָאֶה לְהוֹדוֹת.

BIRKAT KOHANIM

The following is said by the Leader during the Repetition of the Amida.
In Israel, if Kohanim bless the congregation, turn to page 1008.

Our God and God of our fathers, bless us with the threefold blessing in the Torah, written by the hand of Moses Your servant and pronounced by Aaron and his sons the priests, Your holy people, as it is said:

May the LORD bless you and protect you. *Num. 6*
Cong: May it be Your will.
May the LORD make His face shine on you and be gracious to you.
Cong: May it be Your will.
May the LORD turn His face toward you, and grant you peace.
Cong: May it be Your will.

PEACE

שִׂים שָׁלוֹם Grant peace, goodness and blessing,
grace, loving-kindness and compassion to us
and all Israel Your people.
Bless us, our Father, all as one, with the light of Your face,
for by the light of Your face You have given us, LORD our God,
the Torah of life and love of kindness,
righteousness, blessing, compassion, life and peace.
May it be good in Your eyes to bless Your people Israel
at every time, in every hour, with Your peace.
Blessed are You, LORD, who blesses His people Israel with peace.

The following verse concludes the Leader's Repetition of the Amida.
Some also say it here as part of the silent Amida.

May the words of my mouth and the meditation of my heart *Ps. 19*
find favor before You, LORD, my Rock and Redeemer.

אֱלֹהַי My God, *Berakhot 17a*
guard my tongue from evil and my lips from deceitful speech.
To those who curse me, let my soul be silent;[A]
may my soul be to all like the dust.

with yourself. When people make you angry or insult you or get on your bad side, there is something to be said for not allowing that to ruin your day or create within you a feeling of

This **ANI TEFILLA** *continues on page 629.*

ברכת כהנים

The following is said by the שליח ציבור *during* חזרת הש״ץ.
In ארץ ישראל, *if* כהנים *say* ברכת כהנים, *turn to page 1009.*

אֱלֹהֵינוּ וֵאלֹהֵי אֲבוֹתֵינוּ, בָּרְכֵנוּ בַּבְּרָכָה הַמְשֻׁלֶּשֶׁת בַּתּוֹרָה, הַכְּתוּבָה עַל יְדֵי מֹשֶׁה עַבְדֶּךָ, הָאֲמוּרָה מִפִּי אַהֲרֹן וּבָנָיו כֹּהֲנִים עַם קְדוֹשֶׁיךָ, כָּאָמוּר

במדבר ו
יְבָרֶכְךָ יהוה וְיִשְׁמְרֶךָ: קהל: כֵּן יְהִי רָצוֹן
יָאֵר יהוה פָּנָיו אֵלֶיךָ וִיחֻנֶּךָּ: קהל: כֵּן יְהִי רָצוֹן
יִשָּׂא יהוה פָּנָיו אֵלֶיךָ וְיָשֵׂם לְךָ שָׁלוֹם: קהל: כֵּן יְהִי רָצוֹן

ברכת שלום

שִׂים שָׁלוֹם טוֹבָה וּבְרָכָה
חֵן וָחֶסֶד וְרַחֲמִים עָלֵינוּ וְעַל כָּל יִשְׂרָאֵל עַמֶּךָ.
בָּרְכֵנוּ אָבִינוּ כֻּלָּנוּ כְּאֶחָד בְּאוֹר פָּנֶיךָ
כִּי בְאוֹר פָּנֶיךָ נָתַתָּ לָּנוּ, יהוה אֱלֹהֵינוּ
תּוֹרַת חַיִּים וְאַהֲבַת חֶסֶד, וּצְדָקָה וּבְרָכָה וְרַחֲמִים וְחַיִּים וְשָׁלוֹם.
וְטוֹב בְּעֵינֶיךָ לְבָרֵךְ אֶת עַמְּךָ יִשְׂרָאֵל
בְּכָל עֵת וּבְכָל שָׁעָה בִּשְׁלוֹמֶךָ.
בָּרוּךְ אַתָּה יהוה, הַמְבָרֵךְ אֶת עַמּוֹ יִשְׂרָאֵל בַּשָּׁלוֹם.

The following verse concludes the חזרת הש״ץ.
Some also say it here as part of the silent עמידה.

תהלים יט
יִהְיוּ לְרָצוֹן אִמְרֵי־פִי וְהֶגְיוֹן לִבִּי לְפָנֶיךָ, יהוה צוּרִי וְגֹאֲלִי:

ברכות יז.
אֱלֹהַי
נְצֹר לְשׁוֹנִי מֵרָע, וּשְׂפָתַי מִדַּבֵּר מִרְמָה
וְלִמְקַלְלַי נַפְשִׁי תִדֹּם,[א] וְנַפְשִׁי כֶּעָפָר לַכֹּל תִּהְיֶה.

ANI TEFILLA • אני תפילה

וְלִמְקַלְלַי נַפְשִׁי תִדֹּם – *To those who curse me, let my soul be silent.* One sees from here that one of the goals of prayer is to imbue you with a sense of serenity, of being at peace

Open my heart to Your Torah
and let my soul pursue Your commandments.
As for all who plan evil against me,
swiftly thwart their counsel and frustrate their plans.
  Act for the sake of Your name;
  act for the sake of Your right hand;
  act for the sake of Your holiness;
  act for the sake of Your Torah.
That Your beloved ones may be delivered,[B] *Ps. 60*
save with Your right hand and answer me.
May the words of my mouth *Ps. 19*
and the meditation of my heart
find favor before You, LORD, my Rock and Redeemer.

Bow, take three steps back, then bow, first left, then right, then center, while saying:

May He who makes peace in His high places,
make peace for us and all Israel –
and say: Amen.

יְהִי רָצוֹן May it be Your will, LORD our God and God of our ancestors,
that the Temple be rebuilt speedily in our days,
and grant us a share in Your Torah.
And there we will serve You with reverence,
as in the days of old and as in former years.
Then the offering of Judah and Jerusalem *Mal. 3*
will be pleasing to the LORD as in the days of old and as in former years.

On Rosh Hodesh the service continues with Hallel on page 842.

---

think of me. It is their pettiness. There are more important things in life to get upset about. Seen in this light, when you walk away from *tefilla*, you walk away transformed.

פְּתַח לִבִּי בְּתוֹרָתֶךָ, וּבְמִצְוֹתֶיךָ תִּרְדֹּף נַפְשִׁי.
וְכָל הַחוֹשְׁבִים עָלַי רָעָה,
מְהֵרָה הָפֵר עֲצָתָם וְקַלְקֵל מַחֲשַׁבְתָּם.
עֲשֵׂה לְמַעַן שְׁמֶךָ
עֲשֵׂה לְמַעַן יְמִינֶךָ
עֲשֵׂה לְמַעַן קְדֻשָּׁתֶךָ
עֲשֵׂה לְמַעַן תּוֹרָתֶךָ.
תהלים ס לְמַעַן יֵחָלְצוּן יְדִידֶיךָ, הוֹשִׁיעָה יְמִינְךָ וַעֲנֵנִי:
תהלים יט יִהְיוּ לְרָצוֹן אִמְרֵי־פִי וְהֶגְיוֹן לִבִּי לְפָנֶיךָ, יהוה צוּרִי וְגֹאֲלִי:

Bow, take three steps back, then bow, first left, then right, then center, while saying:

עֹשֶׂה שָׁלוֹם בִּמְרוֹמָיו
הוּא יַעֲשֶׂה שָׁלוֹם עָלֵינוּ וְעַל כָּל יִשְׂרָאֵל
וְאִמְרוּ אָמֵן.

יְהִי רָצוֹן מִלְּפָנֶיךָ יהוה אֱלֹהֵינוּ וֵאלֹהֵי אֲבוֹתֵינוּ
שֶׁיִּבָּנֶה בֵּית הַמִּקְדָּשׁ בִּמְהֵרָה בְיָמֵינוּ
וְתֵן חֶלְקֵנוּ בְּתוֹרָתֶךָ
וְשָׁם נַעֲבָדְךָ בְּיִרְאָה כִּימֵי עוֹלָם וּכְשָׁנִים קַדְמֹנִיּוֹת.
מלאכי ג וְעָרְבָה לַיהוה מִנְחַת יְהוּדָה וִירוּשָׁלָםִ כִּימֵי עוֹלָם וּכְשָׁנִים קַדְמֹנִיּוֹת:

On ראש חודש *the service continues with* הלל *on page 843.*

anger or resentment or a desire for revenge. Let their taunts not bother me, says this *tefilla*. I am better than that. My self-esteem comes from within me not from what others

FULL KADDISH

Leader: יִתְגַּדַּל Magnified and sanctified may His great name be,
in the world He created by His will.
May He establish His kingdom
in your lifetime and in your days,
and in the lifetime of all the house of Israel,
swiftly and soon –
and say: Amen.

All: May His great name be blessed for ever and all time.

Leader: Blessed and praised,
glorified and exalted,
raised and honored,
uplifted and lauded
be the name of the Holy One,
blessed be He,
beyond any blessing, song,
praise and consolation
uttered in the world –
and say: Amen.

May the prayers and pleas of all Israel
be accepted by their Father in heaven –
and say: Amen.

May there be great peace from heaven,
and life for us and all Israel –
and say: Amen.

Bow, take three steps back, as if taking leave of the Divine Presence, then bow, first left, then right, then center, while saying:

May He who makes peace in His high places,
make peace for us and all Israel –
and say: Amen.

קדיש שלם

ש״ץ: יִתְגַּדַּל וְיִתְקַדַּשׁ שְׁמֵהּ רַבָּא (קהל: אָמֵן)
בְּעָלְמָא דִּי בְרָא כִרְעוּתֵהּ
וְיַמְלִיךְ מַלְכוּתֵהּ
בְּחַיֵּיכוֹן וּבְיוֹמֵיכוֹן וּבְחַיֵּי דְכָל בֵּית יִשְׂרָאֵל
בַּעֲגָלָא וּבִזְמַן קָרִיב, וְאִמְרוּ אָמֵן. (קהל: אָמֵן)

קהל וש״ץ: יְהֵא שְׁמֵהּ רַבָּא מְבָרַךְ לְעָלַם וּלְעָלְמֵי עָלְמַיָּא.

ש״ץ: יִתְבָּרַךְ וְיִשְׁתַּבַּח וְיִתְפָּאַר
וְיִתְרוֹמַם וְיִתְנַשֵּׂא וְיִתְהַדָּר וְיִתְעַלֶּה וְיִתְהַלָּל
שְׁמֵהּ דְּקֻדְשָׁא בְּרִיךְ הוּא (קהל: בְּרִיךְ הוּא)
לְעֵלָּא מִן כָּל בִּרְכָתָא
וְשִׁירָתָא, תֻּשְׁבְּחָתָא וְנֶחֱמָתָא
דַּאֲמִירָן בְּעָלְמָא, וְאִמְרוּ אָמֵן. (קהל: אָמֵן)

תִּתְקַבַּל צְלוֹתְהוֹן וּבָעוּתְהוֹן דְּכָל יִשְׂרָאֵל
קֳדָם אֲבוּהוֹן דִּי בִשְׁמַיָּא, וְאִמְרוּ אָמֵן. (קהל: אָמֵן)

יְהֵא שְׁלָמָא רַבָּא מִן שְׁמַיָּא
וְחַיִּים, עָלֵינוּ וְעַל כָּל יִשְׂרָאֵל, וְאִמְרוּ אָמֵן. (קהל: אָמֵן)

Bow, take three steps back, as if taking leave of the Divine Presence, then bow, first left, then right, then center, while saying:

עֹשֶׂה שָׁלוֹם בִּמְרוֹמָיו
הוּא יַעֲשֶׂה שָׁלוֹם עָלֵינוּ
וְעַל כָּל יִשְׂרָאֵל, וְאִמְרוּ אָמֵן. (קהל: אָמֵן)

REMOVING THE TORAH FROM THE ARK

אֵין־כָּמְוֹךָ There is none like You among the heavenly powers, *Ps. 86*
LORD, and there are no works like Yours.
Your kingdom is an eternal kingdom, *Ps. 145*
and Your dominion is for all generations.

The LORD is King, the LORD was King,
the LORD shall be King for ever and all time.
The LORD will give strength to His people; *Ps. 29*
the LORD will bless His people with peace.

Father of compassion,
favor Zion with Your goodness; rebuild the walls of Jerusalem. *Ps. 51*
For we trust in You alone, King, God, high and exalted,
Master of worlds.

---

physical ascent to the platform where the Torah is read, as well as an echo of the ascent to Mount Sinai where the Torah was given. A minimum of ten verses are read, according to one tradition as a symbolic representation of the Ten Commandments (*Megilla* 21b; *Yerushalmi Taanit* 4:3). A minimum of three people are called up, reminiscent perhaps of Moshe, Aharon and Miriam, under whose watch the Torah was given. Minimally, a *Kohen*, *Levi* and *Yisrael* are called up to the Torah, thus representing the collective of the entire nation. Indeed, the entire procedure is highly reminiscent of the giving of the Torah at Mount Sinai, when the entire Jewish people heard the voice of God communicate with them. This revelation at Sinai was not to a single prophet but to an entire nation of millions, and each parent passed on what they saw and heard to their children who did the same with their children in a chain of tradition that brings us here today. If one ever wanted proof of the truth of Torah and revelation and God, said Rabbi Yehuda HaLevi in the early twelfth century, then this unbroken unending chain of tradition is it.

In addition to the set number of people who are called up on Shabbat and holy days, there is another *aliya* that is added at the end, called *maftir*, or conclusion. This person will also be given the honor of reading from the portion from the *Navi* or book of Prophets that is also read subsequently on this day. He is given an *aliya* for the Torah as well, in deference to the honor of the Torah, lest one think that a reading from the Prophets is equal in status to that of the Torah itself (*Megilla* 23a).

הוצאת ספר תורה

אֵין־כָּמְוֹךָ בָאֱלֹהִים, אֲדֹנָי, וְאֵין כְּמַעֲשֶׂיךָ: תהלים פו
מַלְכוּתְךָ מַלְכוּת כָּל־עֹלָמִים, וּמֶמְשַׁלְתְּךָ בְּכָל־דּוֹר וָדֹר: תהלים קמה

יהוה מֶלֶךְ, יהוה מָלָךְ, יהוה יִמְלֹךְ לְעֹלָם וָעֶד.
יהוה עֹז לְעַמּוֹ יִתֵּן, יהוה יְבָרֵךְ אֶת־עַמּוֹ בַשָּׁלוֹם: תהלים כט

אַב הָרַחֲמִים
הֵיטִיבָה בִרְצוֹנְךָ אֶת־צִיּוֹן תִּבְנֶה חוֹמוֹת יְרוּשָׁלָםִ: תהלים נא
כִּי בְךָ לְבַד בָּטָחְנוּ, מֶלֶךְ אֵל רָם וְנִשָּׂא, אֲדוֹן עוֹלָמִים.

INTRODUCTION TO KERIAT HATORAH

The Gemara (*Berakhot* 8a-b) teaches that one should repeat the weekly portion for oneself three times, twice in the original and once in translation. Today, only the Yemenite community actually maintains this practice, known as *shnayim mikra v'eḥad targum*, in the morning service, replete with a translator. For most others, however, the practice became to find ongoing time during the week to do this review, often using the commentary of Rashi as a replacement for a literal translation (*Shulḥan Arukh* 285:2 and *Mishna Berura*). The entire practice ensures that one has an ongoing intimate relationship with the weekly reading. The Torah is not something that lives in a building, but in the fabric of one's being.

Tradition has it that Moshe himself decreed that there be a regular Torah reading on Shabbat and all holy days (*Soferim* 10:1). The Torah has 54 divisions, or portions, each one called a *parasha*, one for each Shabbat of the year during a leap year. In a non-leap year, some of the portions (*parshiyot*) are doubled up, so that the entire Torah is completed annually, a collective reaffirmation of our identity.

The portion that is read is itself divided into a different number of sections depending on the sanctity of the occasion, and each section is apportioned to a different person in the congregation. On Shabbat there are 7 people called up, on Yom Kippur there are 6, on a *yom tov* there are 5, on Rosh Ḥodesh and Ḥol HaMoed (intermediate days of a festival) there are 4 and during the week there are 3 (*Megilla* 4:1-2). Each division is called an *aliya*, or ascent, a reference to the

The Ark is opened and the congregation stands. All say:

וַיְהִי בִּנְסֹעַ Whenever the Ark set out,[B] Moses would say, *Num. 10*
"Arise, LORD, and may Your enemies be scattered.
May those who hate You flee before You."
For the Torah shall come forth from Zion, *Is. 2*
and the word of the LORD from Jerusalem.
Blessed is He who in His Holiness
gave the Torah to His people Israel.

Blessed is the name of the Master of the Universe. Blessed is Your crown and Your place. May Your favor always be with Your people Israel. Show Your people the salvation of Your right hand in Your Temple. Grant us the gift of Your good light, and accept our prayers in mercy. May it be Your will to prolong our life in goodness. May I be counted among the righteous, so that You will have compassion on me and protect me and all that is mine and all that is Your people Israel's. You feed all; You sustain all; You rule over all; You rule over kings, for sovereignty is Yours. I am a servant of the Holy One, blessed be He, before whom and before whose glorious Torah I bow at all times. Not in man do I trust, nor on any angel do I rely, but on the God of heaven who is the God of truth, whose Torah is truth, whose prophets speak truth, and who abounds in acts of love and truth. ▸ In Him I trust, and to His holy and glorious name I offer praises. May it be Your will to open my heart to the Torah, and to fulfill the wishes of my heart and of the hearts of all Your people Israel for good, for life, and for peace. *Zohar, Vayak-hel*

The Leader takes the Torah scroll in his right arm. Leader then congregation:

Listen, Israel: the LORD is our God, the LORD is One. *Deut. 6*

Leader then congregation:

One is our God; great is our Master; holy is His name.

The Leader turns to face the Ark, bows and says:

Magnify the LORD with me, and let us exalt His name together.[B] *Ps. 34*

BIUR TEFILLA • ביאור תפילה

גַּדְּלוּ לַיהוה אִתִּי וּנְרוֹמְמָה שְׁמוֹ יַחְדָּו – *Magnify the LORD with me and let us exalt His name together.* There is a custom for the one holding the Torah to literally "magnify" and "exalt" the

This **BIUR TEFILLA** *continues on page 637.*

The ארון קודש *is opened and the* קהל *stands. All say:*

וַיְהִי בִּנְסֹעַ הָאָרֹן וַיֹּאמֶר מֹשֶׁה במדבר י
קוּמָה יהוה וְיָפֻצוּ אֹיְבֶיךָ וְיָנֻסוּ מְשַׂנְאֶיךָ מִפָּנֶיךָ:
כִּי מִצִּיּוֹן תֵּצֵא תוֹרָה וּדְבַר־יהוה מִירוּשָׁלָםִ: ישעיה ב
בָּרוּךְ שֶׁנָּתַן תּוֹרָה לְעַמּוֹ יִשְׂרָאֵל בִּקְדֻשָּׁתוֹ.

בְּרִיךְ שְׁמֵהּ דְּמָרֵא עָלְמָא, בְּרִיךְ כִּתְרָךְ וְאַתְרָךְ. יְהֵא רְעוּתָךְ עִם עַמָּךְ יִשְׂרָאֵל לְעָלַם, וּפֻרְקַן יְמִינָךְ אַחֲזִי לְעַמָּךְ בְּבֵית מַקְדְּשָׁךְ, וּלְאַמְטוּיֵי לָנָא מִטּוּב נְהוֹרָךְ, וּלְקַבֵּל צְלוֹתַנָא בְּרַחֲמִין. יְהֵא רַעֲוָא קֳדָמָךְ דְּתוֹרִיךְ לַן חַיִּין בְּטִיבוּ, וְלֶהֱוֵי אֲנָא פְקִידָא בְּגוֹ צַדִּיקַיָּא, לְמִרְחַם עָלַי וּלְמִנְטַר יָתִי וְיָת כָּל דִּי לִי וְדִי לְעַמָּךְ יִשְׂרָאֵל. אַנְתְּ הוּא זָן לְכֹלָּא וּמְפַרְנֵס לְכֹלָּא, אַנְתְּ הוּא שַׁלִּיט עַל כֹּלָּא, אַנְתְּ הוּא דְּשַׁלִּיט עַל מַלְכַיָּא, וּמַלְכוּתָא דִּילָךְ הִיא. אֲנָא עַבְדָּא דְקֻדְשָׁא בְּרִיךְ הוּא, דְּסָגֵדְנָא קַמֵּהּ וּמִקַּמֵּי דִּיקָר אוֹרַיְתֵהּ בְּכָל עִדָּן וְעִדָּן. לָא עַל אֱנָשׁ רָחִיצְנָא וְלָא עַל בַּר אֱלָהִין סָמִיכְנָא, אֶלָּא בֶּאֱלָהָא דִשְׁמַיָּא, דְּהוּא אֱלָהָא קְשׁוֹט, וְאוֹרַיְתֵהּ קְשׁוֹט, וּנְבִיאוֹהִי קְשׁוֹט, וּמַסְגֵּא לְמֶעְבַּד טַבְוָן וּקְשׁוֹט. ◂ בֵּהּ אֲנָא רָחִיץ, וְלִשְׁמֵהּ קַדִּישָׁא יַקִּירָא אֲנָא אֵמַר תֻּשְׁבְּחָן. יְהֵא רַעֲוָא קֳדָמָךְ דְּתִפְתַּח לִבַּאי בְּאוֹרַיְתָא, וְתַשְׁלִים מִשְׁאֲלִין דְּלִבַּאי וְלִבָּא דְכָל עַמָּךְ יִשְׂרָאֵל לְטָב וּלְחַיִּין וְלִשְׁלָם. זוהר ויקהל

The שליח ציבור *takes the* ספר תורה *in his right arm.* שליח ציבור *then* קהל:

שְׁמַע יִשְׂרָאֵל, יהוה אֱלֹהֵינוּ, יהוה אֶחָד: דברים ו

קהל *then* שליח ציבור:

אֶחָד אֱלֹהֵינוּ, גָּדוֹל אֲדוֹנֵינוּ, קָדוֹשׁ שְׁמוֹ.

The שליח ציבור *turns to face the* ארון קודש*, bows and says:*

גַּדְּלוּ לַיהוה אִתִּי וּנְרוֹמְמָה שְׁמוֹ יַחְדָּו: תהלים לד

BIUR TEFILLA • ביאור תפילה

וַיְהִי בִּנְסֹעַ הָאָרֹן – *Whenever the ark set out.* These words (*Bemidbar* 10:35) were recited in the desert whenever the Ark of the Covenant was moved from its resting place. It declares that the Torah will always emerge victorious over its enemies (Rabbi S. R. Hirsch), whether the enemies from without or the forces of doubt from within. As we open the ark for the Torah, so too, do we need to open our minds and our hearts to what it has to tell us.

The Ark is closed. The Leader carries the Torah scroll to the bima and the congregation says:

לְךָ Yours, LORD, are the greatness and the power, the glory and the majesty and splendor, for everything in heaven and earth is Yours. Yours, LORD, is the kingdom; You are exalted as Head over all. *1 Chr. 29*

רוֹמְמוּ Exalt the LORD our God and bow to His footstool; He is holy. Exalt the LORD our God, and bow at His holy mountain, for holy is the LORD our God. *Ps. 99*

Over all may the name of the Supreme King of kings, the Holy One blessed be He, be magnified and sanctified, praised and glorified, exalted and extolled, in the worlds that He has created – this world and the World to Come – in accordance with His will, and the will of those who fear Him, and the will of the whole house of Israel. He is the Rock of worlds, LORD of all creatures, God of all souls, who dwells in the spacious heights and inhabits the high heavens of old. His holiness is over the Ḥayyot and over the throne of glory. Therefore may Your name, LORD our God, be sanctified among us in the sight of all that lives. Let us sing before Him a new song,
as it is written: "Sing to God, make music for His name, extol Him who rides the *Ps. 68*
clouds – the LORD is His name – and exult before Him." And may we see Him eye
to eye when He returns to His abode as it is written: "For they shall see eye to eye *Is. 52*
when the LORD returns to Zion." And it is said: "Then will the glory of the LORD be *Is. 40*
revealed, and all mankind together shall see that the mouth of the LORD has spoken."

Father of mercy, have compassion on the people borne by Him. May He remember the covenant with the mighty (patriarchs), and deliver us from evil times. May He reproach the evil instinct in the people by Him, and graciously grant that we be an eternal remnant. May He fulfill in good measure our requests for salvation and compassion.

ANI TEFILLA · אני תפילה

Prayer is about man reaching out to communicate with God.

Learning Torah is about God reaching out to communicate with man.

"How does one read a chapter of the Bible?" my teacher Nechama Leibowitz, ז״ל, would frequently ask. She would then answer her own question: "Exactly like a young woman who receives a letter from her lover and pours over every period and apostrophe. Why did he write the word *shalom* the way he did, why did he add this word or that, and leave out another? That is the way to read *Tanakh*." Torah, in other words, is a love letter, from Hashem to us. Read it that way. See if it makes a difference.

The שליח ציבור *is closed. The* ארון קודש *carries the* ספר תורה *to the* בימה *and the* קהל *says:*

לְךָ יהוה הַגְּדֻלָּה וְהַגְּבוּרָה וְהַתִּפְאֶרֶת וְהַנֵּצַח וְהַהוֹד, כִּי־כֹל בַּשָּׁמַיִם וּבָאָרֶץ, לְךָ יהוה הַמַּמְלָכָה וְהַמִּתְנַשֵּׂא לְכֹל לְרֹאשׁ: דברי הימים א׳ כט

רוֹמְמוּ יהוה אֱלֹהֵינוּ וְהִשְׁתַּחֲווּ לַהֲדֹם רַגְלָיו, קָדוֹשׁ הוּא: רוֹמְמוּ יהוה אֱלֹהֵינוּ וְהִשְׁתַּחֲווּ לְהַר קָדְשׁוֹ, כִּי־קָדוֹשׁ יהוה אֱלֹהֵינוּ: תהלים צט

עַל הַכֹּל יִתְגַּדַּל וְיִתְקַדַּשׁ וְיִשְׁתַּבַּח וְיִתְפָּאַר וְיִתְרוֹמַם וְיִתְנַשֵּׂא שְׁמוֹ שֶׁל מֶלֶךְ
מַלְכֵי הַמְּלָכִים הַקָּדוֹשׁ בָּרוּךְ הוּא בָּעוֹלָמוֹת שֶׁבָּרָא, הָעוֹלָם הַזֶּה וְהָעוֹלָם
הַבָּא, כִּרְצוֹנוֹ וְכִרְצוֹן יְרֵאָיו וְכִרְצוֹן כָּל בֵּית יִשְׂרָאֵל. צוּר הָעוֹלָמִים, אֲדוֹן כָּל
הַבְּרִיּוֹת, אֱלוֹהַּ כָּל הַנְּפָשׁוֹת, הַיּוֹשֵׁב בְּמֶרְחֲבֵי מָרוֹם, הַשּׁוֹכֵן בִּשְׁמֵי שְׁמֵי קֶדֶם,
קְדֻשָּׁתוֹ עַל הַחַיּוֹת, וּקְדֻשָּׁתוֹ עַל כִּסֵּא הַכָּבוֹד. וּבְכֵן יִתְקַדַּשׁ שִׁמְךָ בָּנוּ יהוה
תהלים סח אֱלֹהֵינוּ לְעֵינֵי כָּל חָי, וְנֹאמַר לְפָנָיו שִׁיר חָדָשׁ, כַּכָּתוּב: שִׁירוּ לֵאלֹהִים זַמְּרוּ
שְׁמוֹ, סֹלּוּ לָרֹכֵב בָּעֲרָבוֹת, בְּיָהּ שְׁמוֹ, וְעִלְזוּ לְפָנָיו: וְנִרְאֵהוּ עַיִן בְּעַיִן בְּשׁוּבוֹ אֶל
ישעיה נב ישעיה מ נָוֵהוּ, כַּכָּתוּב: כִּי עַיִן בְּעַיִן יִרְאוּ בְּשׁוּב יהוה צִיּוֹן: וְנֶאֱמַר: וְנִגְלָה כְּבוֹד יהוה,
וְרָאוּ כָל־בָּשָׂר יַחְדָּו כִּי פִּי יהוה דִּבֵּר:

אַב הָרַחֲמִים הוּא יְרַחֵם עַם עֲמוּסִים, וְיִזְכֹּר בְּרִית אֵיתָנִים, וְיַצִּיל נַפְשׁוֹתֵינוּ מִן הַשָּׁעוֹת הָרָעוֹת, וְיִגְעַר בְּיֵצֶר הָרָע מִן הַנְּשׂוּאִים, וְיָחֹן אוֹתָנוּ לִפְלֵיטַת עוֹלָמִים, וִימַלֵּא מִשְׁאֲלוֹתֵינוּ בְּמִדָּה טוֹבָה יְשׁוּעָה וְרַחֲמִים.

HILKHOT TEFILLA • הלכות תפילה

There is a custom for one to physically approach the Torah as it passes by, if it is possible, and in order to show one's enthusiasm and love, to kiss it either directly or by using one's siddur or tzitzit.

In truth, there is something distorted in having the Torah come to us. Were it physically possible, each of us should go to it.

Torah by raising it up. The Abudarham suggests that this is to symbolize the raising up of the ark to Jerusalem by King David after it had been captured by the Philistines. The prooftext he cites from that story is "Whenever the bearers of the ark walked six paces" they would celebrate with another sacrifice (*Shmuel* II 6:13). Interestingly, the Hebrew phrase we recite here itself has six words. Each step the *ḥazan* takes, therefore, each word we recite, is intended as a celebration of a renewed relationship with a long lost friend. Imagine what it was like for David on that day. Let his excitement inspire you.

The Torah scroll is placed on the bima and the Gabbai calls a Kohen to the Torah.

וְיַעֲזֹר May He help, shield and save all who seek refuge in Him, and let us say: Amen. Let us all render greatness to our God and give honor to the Torah. *Let the Kohen come forward. Arise (*name* son of *father's name*), the Kohen.

**If no Kohen is present, a Levi or Yisrael is called up as follows:*

/As there is no Kohen, arise (*name* son of *father's name*) in place of a Kohen./

Blessed is He who, in His holiness, gave the Torah to His people Israel.

The congregation followed by the Gabbai:

You who cling to the LORD your God are all alive today. *Deut. 4*

...הִיא לַמַּחֲזִיקִים בָּהּ – "It is a tree of life to those who grasp it.") One reason may be purely practical – you need to open the Torah to find the place (*Megilla* 32a). Another suggestion is that it is as if one is actually *receiving* the Torah on Mount Sinai (*Orkhot Ḥayyim*). And yet another suggestion is that there is a need to hold onto any article over which one is reciting a blessing, similar to a *lulav* (*Beit Yosef*). The custom is to keep holding at least one of the handles until one is completely finished with one's *aliya*.

5. The Gemara (*Megilla* 32a) relates a dispute about how one should recite the blessings. Rabbi Meir was concerned that if you look into the *sefer Torah* when reciting the blessings, people might think that the blessings were actually printed inside the Torah and were part of the Torah itself. Those who follow his opinion therefore suggest that one turn one's head to the left (*Magen Avraham* 139:8) or the right (*Arukh HaShulḥan* 139:13), or close one's eyes (*Ḥayyei Adam*), or do anything but look down. Rabbi Yehuda, on the other hand, said that you don't really need to worry about that since most people know the blessings are separate from the Torah itself; therefore, just recite the blessing however you want.
6. Reciting *Barekhu* is in effect an invitation to the community to join with you in learning Torah together, with you as their representative. They, in turn, answer in order to convey their presence and their participation. It is therefore important to recite the words loudly enough so that everyone (or at least a *minyan*'s worth) can hear you.
7. Ideally, each person is supposed to read the Torah portion for his own *aliya*. But if that were always enforced, then some people who could not read it accurately might be embarrassed (Ran), or he might read it with so many errors that those present would not be fulfilling their obligation to hear the Torah reading (Rosh), or a person who could not read Hebrew would never get an *aliya*, nor could a blind person. As such,

This **HILKHOT TEFILLA** *continues on page 641.*

The ספר תורה *is placed on the* שולחן *and the* גבאי *calls a* כהן *to the* תורה.

וְיַעֲזֹר וְיָגֵן וְיוֹשִׁיעַ לְכָל הַחוֹסִים בּוֹ, וְנֹאמַר אָמֵן. הַכֹּל הָבוּ גֹדֶל לֵאלֹהֵינוּ וּתְנוּ כָבוֹד לַתּוֹרָה. *כֹּהֵן קְרַב, יַעֲמֹד (פלוני בֶּן פלוני) **הַכֹּהֵן.**

**If no* כהן *is present, a* לוי *or* ישראל *is called up as follows:*

/**אֵין כָּאן כֹּהֵן, יַעֲמֹד** (פלוני בֶּן פלוני) **בִּמְקוֹם כֹּהֵן.**/

בָּרוּךְ שֶׁנָּתַן תּוֹרָה לְעַמּוֹ יִשְׂרָאֵל בִּקְדֻשָּׁתוֹ.

The קהל *followed by the* גבאי*:*

וְאַתֶּם הַדְּבֵקִים בַּיהוה אֱלֹהֵיכֶם חַיִּים כֻּלְּכֶם הַיּוֹם: דברים ד

HILKHOT TEFILLA • הלכות תפילה

A GUIDE TO GETTING AN ALIYA

1. Getting an *aliya* is a big deal. It's important to recall that the *kavod* (honor) is not only yours but the Torah's. In fact Rabbi Yehuda (*Berakhot* 55a) suggested that, except in certain extenuating circumstances, one's life might be shortened, God forbid, if one turns down an *aliya*. After all, the Torah is described as כִּי הוּא חַיֶּיךָ וְאֹרֶךְ יָמֶיךָ (*Devarim* 30:20) – "Torah is your life and the length of your days." Why would you want to give it up?
2. In order to show your love of the Torah and what an honor it is to get an *aliya*, and in order that everyone else doesn't have to wait unnecessarily long until you get from your seat to the *bima*, the custom is to take the shortest route to the Torah. If you are equidistant from both sides of the *bima*, the custom is to go up on the right side and leave via the left side. This is just because there is a preference in Judaism for the right (*Yoma* 15b). Hence, some halakhic authorities prefer that you always go up the right side even if it is further away from you (*Ḥatam Sofer OḤ 187*). The prophet Yeḥezkel (46:9) noted that in the *Beit HaMikdash* the custom was to enter via one gate and leave via another. Consider this *aliya*, then, a kind of *going up* to the *Beit HaMikdash*.
3. Since you are about to "read" the Torah, it makes sense to see exactly what you are about to "read" before making the blessing. That's why there is a custom for the *ba'al keria* to show you the place where your *aliya* begins. There is another custom to make a motion to touch that spot with one's tallit or some other material and then kiss it in order to display one's love of Torah and one's excitement at this opportunity.
4. There is a custom to hold onto the wooden handles which are called the *Etzei Ḥayyim* or "Trees (lit. wood) of Life." (Recall the verse [*Mishlei* 3:18] עֵץ־חַיִּים

The appropriate Torah portion is read.

The Reader shows the oleh the section to be read. The oleh touches the scroll at that place with the tzitzit of his tallit, which he then kisses. Holding the handles of the scroll, he says:

Oleh: Bless the LORD, the blessed One.

Cong: Bless the LORD, the blessed One,
for ever and all time.

Oleh: Bless the LORD, the blessed One,
for ever and all time.
Blessed are You, LORD our God,
King of the Universe,
who has chosen us from all peoples
and has given us His Torah.
Blessed are You, LORD, Giver of the Torah.

After the reading, the oleh says:

Oleh: Blessed are You, LORD our God,
King of the Universe,
who has given us the Torah of truth,
planting everlasting life in our midst.
Blessed are You, LORD, Giver of the Torah.

---

one does not miss any of the reading (*Magen Avraham* 141:8).

9. When returning to one's seat, the custom is to take the longest route back, as if to symbolize your sadness at leaving the Torah (*Levush*) or lest it look like you are trying to make a hasty getaway (*Arukh HaShulhan*). If the routes are equidistant, then leave from the opposite side you came from.

10. Finally, it is customary for people to wish you a יִישַׁר כֹּחַ (*yishar ko'ah/kohakha*), "may your strength be increased" or "more power to you," to which the traditional reply is בָּרוּךְ תִּהְיֶה (*barukh tihiyeh*), "May you be blessed." In Sepharadi tradition, the greeting is חֲזַק וּבָרוּךְ (*hazak ubarukh*) "may your strength be increased and may you be blessed," to which the traditional reply is חֲזַק וֶאֱמָץ (*hazak ve'ematz*) "Be strong and courageous."

The appropriate תורה *portion is read.*

The קורא *shows the* עולה *the section to be read. The* עולה *touches the scroll at that place with the* ציצית *of his* טלית*, which he then kisses. Holding the handles of the scroll, he says:*

עולה: **בָּרְכוּ אֶת יהוה הַמְבֹרָךְ.**

קהל: בָּרוּךְ יהוה הַמְבֹרָךְ לְעוֹלָם וָעֶד.

עולה: **בָּרוּךְ יהוה הַמְבֹרָךְ לְעוֹלָם וָעֶד.**

בָּרוּךְ אַתָּה יהוה, אֱלֹהֵינוּ מֶלֶךְ הָעוֹלָם

אֲשֶׁר בָּחַר בָּנוּ מִכָּל הָעַמִּים

וְנָתַן לָנוּ אֶת תּוֹרָתוֹ.

בָּרוּךְ אַתָּה יהוה, נוֹתֵן הַתּוֹרָה.

After the קריאת התורה*, the* עולה *says:*

עולה: **בָּרוּךְ אַתָּה יהוה אֱלֹהֵינוּ מֶלֶךְ הָעוֹלָם**

אֲשֶׁר נָתַן לָנוּ תּוֹרַת אֱמֶת

וְחַיֵּי עוֹלָם נָטַע בְּתוֹכֵנוּ.

בָּרוּךְ אַתָּה יהוה, נוֹתֵן הַתּוֹרָה.

---

the custom evolved to have a *ba'al keria*, who would be in charge of the reading and act as a *shaliaḥ* or messenger for the person getting the *aliya*. Nevertheless, there is a custom that the person getting an *aliya* should do his best to read along in a whisper with the *ba'al keria* as if to fulfill his own obligation to read, and so as to reinforce that the blessing he said was on his own reading.

8. Upon completion of the final blessing, the custom is to remain at the *bima* standing beside the *gabbai* until the completion of the next *aliya*. This is considered a fulfillment of giving honor to the Torah by not abandoning it prematurely (*Levush*). While theoretically one could leave once the next person getting an *aliya* is standing in front of the Torah, the custom is to wait until the end of his *aliya* and to try to get back to one's seat before the next *aliya* so that

One who has survived a situation of danger says:

Blessed are You, Lord our God, King of the Universe, who bestows good on the unworthy, who has bestowed on me much good.

The congregation responds:

Amen. May He who bestowed much good on you
continue to bestow on you much good, Selah.

After a Bar Mitzva boy has finished the Torah blessing, his father says aloud:

Blessed is He who has released me from the responsibility for this child.

FOR AN OLEH

May He who blessed our fathers, Abraham, Isaac and Jacob, bless (*name,* son of *father's name*) who has been called up in honor of the All-Present, in honor of the Torah, and in honor of Shabbat. As a reward for this, may the Holy One, blessed be He, protect and deliver him from all trouble and distress, all infection and illness, and send blessing and success to all the work of his hands, together with all Israel, his brethren, and let us say: Amen.

FOR A SICK MAN

May He who blessed our fathers, Abraham, Isaac and Jacob, Moses and Aaron, David and Solomon, bless and heal one who is ill, (*sick person's name,* son of *mother's name*), on whose behalf (*name of the one making the offering*) is making a contribution to charity. As a reward for this, may the Holy One, blessed be He, be filled with compassion for him, to restore his health, cure him, strengthen and revive him, sending him a swift and full recovery from heaven to all his 248 organs and 365 sinews, amongst the other sick ones in Israel, a healing of the spirit and a healing of the body – though on Shabbat it is forbidden to cry out, may healing be quick to come – now, swiftly and soon, and let us say: Amen.

FOR A SICK WOMAN

May He who blessed our fathers, Abraham, Isaac and Jacob, Moses and Aaron, David and Solomon, bless and heal one who is ill, (*sick person's name,* daughter of *mother's name*), on whose behalf (*name of the one making the offering*) is making a contribution to charity. As a reward for this, may the Holy One, blessed be He, be filled with compassion for her, to restore her health, cure her, strengthen and revive her, sending her a swift and full recovery from heaven to all her organs and sinews, amongst the other sick ones in Israel, a healing of the spirit and a healing of the body – though on Shabbat it is forbidden to cry out, may healing be quick to come – now, swiftly and soon, and let us say: Amen.

One who has survived a situation of danger says:

בָּרוּךְ אַתָּה יהוה אֱלֹהֵינוּ מֶלֶךְ הָעוֹלָם הַגּוֹמֵל לְחַיָּבִים טוֹבוֹת שֶׁגְּמָלַנִי כָּל טוֹב.

The קהל *responds:*

אָמֵן. מִי שֶׁגְּמָלְךָ כָּל טוֹב הוּא יִגְמָלְךָ כָּל טוֹב, סֶלָה.

After a בר מצווה *has finished the* תורה *blessing, his father says aloud:*

בָּרוּךְ שֶׁפְּטָרַנִי מֵעָנְשׁוֹ שֶׁלָּזֶה.

מי שברך לעולה לתורה

מִי שֶׁבֵּרַךְ אֲבוֹתֵינוּ אַבְרָהָם יִצְחָק וְיַעֲקֹב, הוּא יְבָרֵךְ אֶת (פלוני בֶּן פלוני), בַּעֲבוּר שֶׁעָלָה לִכְבוֹד הַמָּקוֹם וְלִכְבוֹד הַתּוֹרָה וְלִכְבוֹד הַשַּׁבָּת. בִּשְׂכַר זֶה הַקָּדוֹשׁ בָּרוּךְ הוּא יִשְׁמְרֵהוּ וְיַצִּילֵהוּ מִכָּל צָרָה וְצוּקָה וּמִכָּל נֶגַע וּמַחֲלָה, וְיִשְׁלַח בְּרָכָה וְהַצְלָחָה בְּכָל מַעֲשֵׂה יָדָיו עִם כָּל יִשְׂרָאֵל אֶחָיו, וְנֹאמַר אָמֵן.

מי שברך לחולֶה

מִי שֶׁבֵּרַךְ אֲבוֹתֵינוּ אַבְרָהָם יִצְחָק וְיַעֲקֹב, מֹשֶׁה וְאַהֲרֹן דָּוִד וּשְׁלֹמֹה הוּא יְבָרֵךְ וִירַפֵּא אֶת הַחוֹלֶה (פלוני בֶּן פלונית) בַּעֲבוּר שֶׁ(פלוני בֶּן פלוני) נוֹדֵר צְדָקָה בַּעֲבוּרוֹ. בִּשְׂכַר זֶה הַקָּדוֹשׁ בָּרוּךְ הוּא יִמָּלֵא רַחֲמִים עָלָיו לְהַחֲלִימוֹ וּלְרַפְּאתוֹ וּלְהַחֲזִיקוֹ וּלְהַחֲיוֹתוֹ וְיִשְׁלַח לוֹ מְהֵרָה רְפוּאָה שְׁלֵמָה מִן הַשָּׁמַיִם לִרְמַ״ח אֵבָרָיו וּשְׁסָ״ה גִּידָיו בְּתוֹךְ שְׁאָר חוֹלֵי יִשְׂרָאֵל, רְפוּאַת הַנֶּפֶשׁ וּרְפוּאַת הַגּוּף. שַׁבָּת הִיא מִלִּזְעֹק וּרְפוּאָה קְרוֹבָה לָבוֹא, הַשְׁתָּא בַּעֲגָלָא וּבִזְמַן קָרִיב, וְנֹאמַר אָמֵן.

מי שברך לחולָה

מִי שֶׁבֵּרַךְ אֲבוֹתֵינוּ אַבְרָהָם יִצְחָק וְיַעֲקֹב, מֹשֶׁה וְאַהֲרֹן דָּוִד וּשְׁלֹמֹה הוּא יְבָרֵךְ וִירַפֵּא אֶת הַחוֹלָה (פלונית בַּת פלונית) בַּעֲבוּר שֶׁ(פלוני בֶּן פלוני) נוֹדֵר צְדָקָה בַּעֲבוּרָהּ. בִּשְׂכַר זֶה הַקָּדוֹשׁ בָּרוּךְ הוּא יִמָּלֵא רַחֲמִים עָלֶיהָ לְהַחֲלִימָהּ וּלְרַפְּאתָהּ וּלְהַחֲזִיקָהּ וּלְהַחֲיוֹתָהּ וְיִשְׁלַח לָהּ מְהֵרָה רְפוּאָה שְׁלֵמָה מִן הַשָּׁמַיִם לְכָל אֵבָרֶיהָ וּלְכָל גִּידֶיהָ בְּתוֹךְ שְׁאָר חוֹלֵי יִשְׂרָאֵל, רְפוּאַת הַנֶּפֶשׁ וּרְפוּאַת הַגּוּף. שַׁבָּת הִיא מִלִּזְעֹק וּרְפוּאָה קְרוֹבָה לָבוֹא, הַשְׁתָּא בַּעֲגָלָא וּבִזְמַן קָרִיב, וְנֹאמַר אָמֵן.

FOR A BAR MITZVA

May He who blessed our fathers, Abraham, Isaac and Jacob, bless (*name*, son of *father's name*) who has completed thirteen years and attained the age of the commandments, who has been called to the Torah to give praise and thanks to God, may His name be blessed, for all the good He has bestowed on him. May the Holy One, blessed be He, protect and sustain him and direct his heart to be perfect with God, to walk in His ways and keep the commandments all the days of his life, and let us say: Amen.

FOR A BAT MITZVA

May He who blessed our fathers, Abraham, Isaac and Jacob, Sarah, Rebecca, Rachel and Leah, bless (*name*, daughter of *father's name*) who has completed twelve years and attained the age of the commandments, and gives praise and thanks to God, may His name be blessed, for all the good He has bestowed on her. May the Holy One, blessed be He, protect and sustain her and direct her heart to be perfect with God, to walk in His ways and keep the commandments all the days of her life, and let us say: Amen.

In some congregations, during the week before a yahrzeit,
"God, full of mercy" for a relative is said.

For a male close relative:

אֵל מָלֵא רַחֲמִים God, full of mercy, who dwells on high, grant fitting rest on the wings of the Divine Presence, in the heights of the holy and the pure who shine like the radiance of heaven, to the soul of (*name* son of *father's name*) who has gone to his eternal home, and to this I pledge (without formal vow) to give charity in his memory, may his resting place be in the Garden of Eden. Therefore, Master of compassion, shelter him in the shadow of Your wings forever and bind his soul in the bond of everlasting life. The LORD is his heritage; may he rest in peace, and let us say: Amen.

For a female close relative:

אֵל מָלֵא רַחֲמִים God, full of mercy, who dwells on high, grant fitting rest on the wings of the Divine Presence, in the heights of the holy and the pure who shine like the radiance of heaven, to the soul of (*name* daughter of *father's name*) who has gone to her eternal home, and to this I pledge (without formal vow) to give charity in her memory, may her resting place be in the Garden of Eden. Therefore, Master of compassion, shelter her in the shadow of Your wings forever and bind her soul in the bond of everlasting life. The LORD is her heritage; may she rest in peace, and let us say: Amen.

מי שברך לבר מצווה

מִי שֶׁבֵּרַךְ אֲבוֹתֵינוּ אַבְרָהָם יִצְחָק וְיַעֲקֹב הוּא יְבָרֵךְ אֶת (פלוני בֶּן פלוני) שֶׁמָּלְאוּ לוֹ שְׁלֹשׁ עֶשְׂרֵה שָׁנָה וְהִגִּיעַ לְמִצְוֹת, וְעָלָה לַתּוֹרָה, לָתֵת שֶׁבַח וְהוֹדָיָה לְהַשֵּׁם יִתְבָּרַךְ עַל כָּל הַטּוֹבָה שֶׁגָּמַל אִתּוֹ. יִשְׁמְרֵהוּ הַקָּדוֹשׁ בָּרוּךְ הוּא וִיחַיֵּהוּ, וִיכוֹנֵן אֶת לִבּוֹ לִהְיוֹת שָׁלֵם עִם יהוה וְלָלֶכֶת בִּדְרָכָיו וְלִשְׁמֹר מִצְוֹתָיו כָּל הַיָּמִים, וְנֹאמַר אָמֵן.

מי שברך לבת מצווה

מִי שֶׁבֵּרַךְ אֲבוֹתֵינוּ אַבְרָהָם יִצְחָק וְיַעֲקֹב, שָׂרָה רִבְקָה רָחֵל וְלֵאָה, הוּא יְבָרֵךְ אֶת (פלונית בַּת פלוני) שֶׁמָּלְאוּ לָהּ שְׁתֵּים עֶשְׂרֵה שָׁנָה וְהִגִּיעָה לְמִצְוֹת, וְנוֹתֶנֶת שֶׁבַח וְהוֹדָיָה לְהַשֵּׁם יִתְבָּרַךְ עַל כָּל הַטּוֹבָה שֶׁגָּמַל אִתָּהּ. יִשְׁמְרֶהָ הַקָּדוֹשׁ בָּרוּךְ הוּא וִיחַיֶּהָ, וִיכוֹנֵן אֶת לִבָּהּ לִהְיוֹת שָׁלֵם עִם יהוה וְלָלֶכֶת בִּדְרָכָיו וְלִשְׁמֹר מִצְוֹתָיו כָּל הַיָּמִים, וְנֹאמַר אָמֵן.

In some congregations, during the week before a yahrzeit, אֵל מָלֵא רַחֲמִים *for a relative is said.*

For a male close relative:

אֵל מָלֵא רַחֲמִים, שׁוֹכֵן בַּמְּרוֹמִים, הַמְצֵא מְנוּחָה נְכוֹנָה עַל כַּנְפֵי הַשְּׁכִינָה, בְּמַעֲלוֹת קְדוֹשִׁים וּטְהוֹרִים, כְּזֹהַר הָרָקִיעַ מַזְהִירִים, לְנִשְׁמַת (פלוני בֶּן פלוני) שֶׁהָלַךְ לְעוֹלָמוֹ, בַּעֲבוּר שֶׁבְּלִי נֶדֶר אֶתֵּן צְדָקָה בְּעַד הַזְכָּרַת נִשְׁמָתוֹ, בְּגַן עֵדֶן תְּהֵא מְנוּחָתוֹ. לָכֵן, בַּעַל הָרַחֲמִים יַסְתִּירֵהוּ בְּסֵתֶר כְּנָפָיו לְעוֹלָמִים, וְיִצְרֹר בִּצְרוֹר הַחַיִּים אֶת נִשְׁמָתוֹ, יהוה הוּא נַחֲלָתוֹ, וְיָנְוּחַ בְּשָׁלוֹם עַל מִשְׁכָּבוֹ, וְנֹאמַר אָמֵן.

For a female close relative:

אֵל מָלֵא רַחֲמִים, שׁוֹכֵן בַּמְּרוֹמִים, הַמְצֵא מְנוּחָה נְכוֹנָה עַל כַּנְפֵי הַשְּׁכִינָה, בְּמַעֲלוֹת קְדוֹשִׁים וּטְהוֹרִים, כְּזֹהַר הָרָקִיעַ מַזְהִירִים, לְנִשְׁמַת (פלונית בַּת פלוני) שֶׁהָלְכָה לְעוֹלָמָהּ, בַּעֲבוּר שֶׁבְּלִי נֶדֶר אֶתֵּן צְדָקָה בְּעַד הַזְכָּרַת נִשְׁמָתָהּ, בְּגַן עֵדֶן תְּהֵא מְנוּחָתָהּ. לָכֵן, בַּעַל הָרַחֲמִים יַסְתִּירֶהָ בְּסֵתֶר כְּנָפָיו לְעוֹלָמִים, וְיִצְרֹר בִּצְרוֹר הַחַיִּים אֶת נִשְׁמָתָהּ, יהוה הוּא נַחֲלָתָהּ, וְתָנְוּחַ בְּשָׁלוֹם עַל מִשְׁכָּבָהּ, וְנֹאמַר אָמֵן.

HALF KADDISH

Before Maftir is read, the Reader says Half Kaddish:

Reader: יִתְגַּדַּל Magnified and sanctified may His great name be,
in the world He created by His will.
May He establish His kingdom
in your lifetime and in your days,
and in the lifetime of all the house of Israel,
swiftly and soon –
and say: Amen.

All: May His great name be blessed for ever and all time.

Reader: Blessed and praised,
glorified and exalted,
raised and honored,
uplifted and lauded
be the name of the Holy One,
blessed be He,
beyond any blessing, song,
praise and consolation
uttered in the world –
and say: Amen.

HAGBAHA AND GELILA

The Torah scroll is lifted and the congregation says:

וְזֹאת הַתּוֹרָה This is the Torah *Deut. 4*
that Moses placed before the children of Israel,
at the LORD's commandment, by the hand of Moses. *Num. 9*

Some add: It is a tree of life to those who grasp it, *Prov. 3*
and those who uphold it are happy.
Its ways are ways of pleasantness, and all its paths are peace.
Long life is in its right hand; in its left, riches and honor.
It pleased the LORD for the sake of [Israel's] righteousness, *Is. 42*
to make the Torah great and glorious.

The Torah scroll is bound and covered.

חצי קדיש

Before מפטיר *is read, the* קורא *says* חצי קדיש:

קורא: יִתְגַּדַּל וְיִתְקַדַּשׁ שְׁמֵהּ רַבָּא (קהל: אָמֵן)
בְּעָלְמָא דִּי בְרָא כִרְעוּתֵהּ
וְיַמְלִיךְ מַלְכוּתֵהּ
בְּחַיֵּיכוֹן וּבְיוֹמֵיכוֹן וּבְחַיֵּי דְכָל בֵּית יִשְׂרָאֵל
בַּעֲגָלָא וּבִזְמַן קָרִיב
וְאִמְרוּ אָמֵן. (קהל: אָמֵן)

קהל וקורא: יְהֵא שְׁמֵהּ רַבָּא מְבָרַךְ לְעָלַם וּלְעָלְמֵי עָלְמַיָּא.

קורא: יִתְבָּרַךְ וְיִשְׁתַּבַּח וְיִתְפָּאַר וְיִתְרוֹמַם וְיִתְנַשֵּׂא
וְיִתְהַדָּר וְיִתְעַלֶּה וְיִתְהַלָּל
שְׁמֵהּ דְּקֻדְשָׁא בְּרִיךְ הוּא (קהל: בְּרִיךְ הוּא)
לְעֵלָּא מִן כָּל בִּרְכָתָא
וְשִׁירָתָא, תֻּשְׁבְּחָתָא וְנֶחֱמָתָא
דַּאֲמִירָן בְּעָלְמָא
וְאִמְרוּ אָמֵן. (קהל: אָמֵן)

הגבהה וגלילה

The ספר תורה *is lifted and the* קהל *says:*

וְזֹאת הַתּוֹרָה אֲשֶׁר־שָׂם מֹשֶׁה לִפְנֵי בְּנֵי יִשְׂרָאֵל: דברים ד
עַל־פִּי יהוה בְּיַד מֹשֶׁה: במדבר ט

Some add עֵץ־חַיִּים הִיא לַמַּחֲזִיקִים בָּהּ וְתֹמְכֶיהָ מְאֻשָּׁר: משלי ג
דְּרָכֶיהָ דַרְכֵי־נֹעַם וְכָל־נְתִיבֹתֶיהָ שָׁלוֹם:
אֹרֶךְ יָמִים בִּימִינָהּ, בִּשְׂמֹאולָהּ עֹשֶׁר וְכָבוֹד:
יהוה חָפֵץ לְמַעַן צִדְקוֹ יַגְדִּיל תּוֹרָה וְיַאְדִּיר: ישעיה מב

The ספר תורה *is bound and covered.*

BLESSINGS BEFORE AND AFTER READING THE HAFTARA

Before reading the Haftara, the person called up for Maftir says:

בָּרוּךְ Blessed are You, LORD our God, King of the Universe, who chose good prophets and was pleased with their words, spoken in truth. Blessed are You, LORD, who chose the Torah, His servant Moses, His people Israel, and the prophets of truth and righteousness.

After the Haftara, the person called up for Maftir says the following blessings:

בָּרוּךְ Blessed are You, LORD our God, King of the Universe, Rock of all worlds, righteous for all generations, the faithful God who says and does, speaks and fulfills, all of whose words are truth and righteousness. You are faithful, LORD our God, and faithful are Your words, not one of which returns unfulfilled, for You, God, are a faithful (and compassionate) King. Blessed are You, LORD, faithful in all His words.

---

is called up at the end of the Torah reading to make one blessing before and another after that reading (= two blessings), then two blessings before the *haftara*, then read a minimum of 21 verses from a selection of a book of the Prophets that is related in some way to the weekly Torah portion and then four blessings afterwards for a total of eight blessings.

Finally, there is an opinion which suggests that the public reading from the Prophets is the remnant of an old custom to take time out on Shabbat to do some learning after finishing *Shaḥarit*, something that is more difficult to do during the week when everyone needs to rush off to work (Rashi). Seen in this light, the reading is a way for us to extend our individual and communal commitment to learning beyond that which some may think of as the minimum. In particular, we focus on the books that are too often ignored in education (*Shakh* in *Yoreh De'ah* 245:5), the Prophets, whose prophecies and speeches were written down because they have a message not only for their own time but for future generations as well. The essence of our listening intently to this recitation, then, is our ability to discern and internalize those messages, as has been done for generations of Jews since these words were first uttered.

The Gemara (*Megilla* 14a) informs us that there were far more prophets who lived over the course of biblical times than the ones which we know of. However, the only prophecies that were actually written down were the ones that would be needed for

This **INTRODUCTION TO HAFTARA** *continues on page 651.*

ברכות ההפטרה

Before reading the הפטרה*, the person called up for* מפטיר *says:*

בָּרוּךְ אַתָּה יהוה אֱלֹהֵינוּ מֶלֶךְ הָעוֹלָם אֲשֶׁר בָּחַר בִּנְבִיאִים טוֹבִים, וְרָצָה בְדִבְרֵיהֶם הַנֶּאֱמָרִים בֶּאֱמֶת. בָּרוּךְ אַתָּה יהוה, הַבּוֹחֵר בַּתּוֹרָה וּבְמֹשֶׁה עַבְדּוֹ וּבְיִשְׂרָאֵל עַמּוֹ וּבִנְבִיאֵי הָאֱמֶת וָצֶדֶק.

After the הפטרה*, the person called up for* מפטיר *says the following blessings:*

בָּרוּךְ אַתָּה יהוה אֱלֹהֵינוּ מֶלֶךְ הָעוֹלָם, צוּר כָּל הָעוֹלָמִים, צַדִּיק בְּכָל הַדּוֹרוֹת, הָאֵל הַנֶּאֱמָן, הָאוֹמֵר וְעוֹשֶׂה, הַמְדַבֵּר וּמְקַיֵּם, שֶׁכָּל דְּבָרָיו אֱמֶת וָצֶדֶק. נֶאֱמָן אַתָּה הוּא יהוה אֱלֹהֵינוּ וְנֶאֱמָנִים דְּבָרֶיךָ, וְדָבָר אֶחָד מִדְּבָרֶיךָ אָחוֹר לֹא יָשׁוּב רֵיקָם, כִּי אֵל מֶלֶךְ נֶאֱמָן (וְרַחֲמָן) אָתָּה. בָּרוּךְ אַתָּה יהוה, הָאֵל הַנֶּאֱמָן בְּכָל דְּבָרָיו.

INTRODUCTION TO HAFTARA

In addition to the weekly Torah portion, there is also a tradition to read a relatively short selection, called the *Haftara*, from a book of the Prophets. The exact source for this custom is not definitively known. One opinion has it that it was instituted by Ezra the Scribe in the fifth century BCE once all of the books of the Bible were canonized.

A more widely accepted theory is that there was a time in Jewish history when the public reading of the Torah was banned by the government (perhaps during the time of the Ḥanukka story in the second century BCE or even later during the time of the Roman empire). In order to nevertheless keep echoes of the tradition alive, the community resorted to reading a selection of the Prophets that was related in some way (e.g., in theme or language) to what would have been the Torah portion for that week. They established that the selection be a minimum of 21 verses long (to correspond to the minimum of three verses of the Torah read by each of the seven people who would have gotten an *aliya*) and that there be seven introductory blessings (to correspond to the missing blessings made by the seven people who would have gotten an *aliya*) (*Mishna Berura* 284:2). When the decree was rescinded, the practice nevertheless continued such that today one person

רַחֵם Have compassion on Zion for it is the source of our life, and save the one grieved in spirit swiftly in our days. Blessed are You, LORD, who makes Zion rejoice in her children.

שַׂמְּחֵנוּ Grant us joy, LORD our God, through Elijah the prophet Your servant, and through the kingdom of the house of David Your anointed – may he soon come and make our hearts glad. May no stranger sit on his throne, and may others not continue to inherit his glory, for You promised him by Your holy name that his light would never be extinguished. Blessed are You, LORD, Shield of David.

עַל הַתּוֹרָה For the Torah, for divine worship, for the prophets, and for this Sabbath day which You, LORD our God, have given us for holiness and rest, honor and glory – for all these we thank and bless You, LORD our God, and may Your name be blessed by the mouth of all that lives, continually, for ever and all time. Blessed are You, LORD, who sanctifies the Sabbath.

The following three paragraphs are only said when praying with a minyan (some say the first paragraph without a minyan).

יְקוּם פֻּרְקָן May deliverance arise[B] from heaven, bringing grace, love and compassion, long life, ample sustenance and heavenly help, physical health and enlightenment of mind, living and thriving children who will neither interrupt nor cease from the words of the Torah – to our masters and teachers of the holy communities in the land of Israel and Babylon; to the leaders of assemblies and the leaders of communities in exile; to the heads of academies and to the judges in the gates; to all their disciples and their disciples' disciples, and to

BIUR TEFILLA · ביאור תפילה

יְקוּם פֻּרְקָן – *May deliverance arise.* As indicated by the fact that they are in Aramaic and not Hebrew, these two prayers come from Talmudic and Geonic times (first century and onwards) in Babylonia. They are prayers for leadership, religious as well as lay people, professional as well as voluntary, those who contribute their time as well as those who contribute their money. Without them our communities could not function. Perhaps

This **BIUR TEFILLA** *continues on page 653.*

רַחֵם עַל צִיּוֹן כִּי הִיא בֵּית חַיֵּינוּ, וְלַעֲלוּבַת נֶפֶשׁ תּוֹשִׁיעַ בִּמְהֵרָה בְיָמֵינוּ. בָּרוּךְ אַתָּה יהוה, מְשַׂמֵּחַ צִיּוֹן בְּבָנֶיהָ.

שַׂמְּחֵנוּ יהוה אֱלֹהֵינוּ בְּאֵלִיָּהוּ הַנָּבִיא עַבְדֶּךָ, וּבְמַלְכוּת בֵּית דָּוִד מְשִׁיחֶךָ, בִּמְהֵרָה יָבוֹא וְיָגֵל לִבֵּנוּ. עַל כִּסְאוֹ לֹא יֵשֶׁב זָר, וְלֹא יִנְחֲלוּ עוֹד אֲחֵרִים אֶת כְּבוֹדוֹ, כִּי בְשֵׁם קָדְשְׁךָ נִשְׁבַּעְתָּ לּוֹ שֶׁלֹּא יִכְבֶּה נֵרוֹ לְעוֹלָם וָעֶד. בָּרוּךְ אַתָּה יהוה, מָגֵן דָּוִד.

עַל הַתּוֹרָה וְעַל הָעֲבוֹדָה וְעַל הַנְּבִיאִים וְעַל יוֹם הַשַּׁבָּת הַזֶּה, שֶׁנָּתַתָּ לָּנוּ יהוה אֱלֹהֵינוּ לִקְדֻשָּׁה וְלִמְנוּחָה, לְכָבוֹד וּלְתִפְאָרֶת. עַל הַכֹּל יהוה אֱלֹהֵינוּ אֲנַחְנוּ מוֹדִים לָךְ וּמְבָרְכִים אוֹתָךְ, יִתְבָּרַךְ שִׁמְךָ בְּפִי כָּל חַי תָּמִיד לְעוֹלָם וָעֶד. בָּרוּךְ אַתָּה יהוה, מְקַדֵּשׁ הַשַּׁבָּת.

The following three paragraphs are only said when praying with a מנין *(some say the first paragraph without a* מנין*).*

יְקוּם פֻּרְקָן מִן שְׁמַיָּא, חִנָּא וְחִסְדָּא וְרַחֲמֵי וְחַיֵּי אֲרִיכֵי וּמְזוֹנֵי רְוִיחֵי, וְסִיַּעְתָּא דִשְׁמַיָּא, וּבַרְיוּת גּוּפָא וּנְהוֹרָא מְעַלְּיָא, זַרְעָא חַיָּא וְקַיָּמָא, זַרְעָא דִּי לָא יִפְסֻק וְדִי לָא יִבְטֻל מִפִּתְגָּמֵי אוֹרַיְתָא, לְמָרָנָן וְרַבָּנָן חֲבוּרָתָא קַדִּישָׁתָא דִּי בְאַרְעָא דְיִשְׂרָאֵל וְדִי בְבָבֶל, לְרֵישֵׁי כַלָּה, וּלְרֵישֵׁי גַלְוָתָא, וּלְרֵישֵׁי מְתִיבָתָא, וּלְדַיָּנֵי דְבָבָא, לְכָל תַּלְמִידֵיהוֹן, וּלְכָל תַּלְמִידֵי תַלְמִידֵיהוֹן, וּלְכָל מָאן דְּעָסְקִין בְּאוֹרַיְתָא. מַלְכָּא דְעָלְמָא יְבָרֵךְ יָתְהוֹן, יַפֵּשׁ חַיֵּיהוֹן וְיַסְגֵּא

---

future generations, that is to say, the ones whose messages were timeless. The challenge in following the *Haftara* reading is therefore not only to figure out the connection between the Torah reading and the *Haftara* reading for that particular week, but to figure out the connection between the *Haftara* reading and one's own life.

What message in this week's *Haftara* can you take with you into next week?

all who occupy themselves in study of the Torah. May the King of the Universe bless them, prolonging their lives, increasing their days, and adding to their years. May they be redeemed and delivered from all distress and illness. May our Master in heaven be their help at all times and seasons; and let us say: Amen.

יְקוּם פֻּרְקָן May deliverance arise from heaven, bringing grace, love and compassion, long life, ample sustenance and heavenly help, physical health and enlightenment of mind, living and thriving children who will neither interrupt nor cease from the words of the Torah – to all this holy congregation, great and small, women and children. May the King of the Universe bless you, prolonging your lives, increasing your days, and adding to your years. May you be redeemed and delivered from all distress and illness. May our Master in heaven be your help at all times and seasons; and let us say: Amen.

מִי שֶׁבֵּרַךְ May He who blessed our fathers, Abraham, Isaac and Jacob, bless all this holy congregation, together with all other holy congregations: them, their wives, their sons and daughters, and all that is theirs. May He bless those who unite to form synagogues for prayer and those who come there to pray; those who provide lamps for light and wine for Kiddush and Havdala, food for visitors and charity for the poor, and all who faithfully occupy themselves with the needs of the community. May the Holy One, blessed be He, give them their reward; may He remove from them all illness, grant them complete healing, and forgive all their sins. May He send blessing and success to all the work of their hands, together with all Israel their brethren; and let us say: Amen.

---

paid to religious leadership, and the wisdom and hard work contributed by people who have been prepared to step up to the plate. These are the ones who enable us to support one another, to be welcomed into a new community, to educate our children, to acquire and operate cemeteries and charities, hospitals and free loan societies, social service agencies, and, of course, the very synagogue in which you may now be standing. What kind of contribution can you make to keep this communal infrastructure alive?

יוֹמֵיהוֹן, וְיִתֵּן אַרְכָא לִשְׁנֵיהוֹן, וְיִתְפָּרְקוּן וְיִשְׁתֵּיזְבוּן מִן כָּל עָקָא וּמִן כָּל מַרְעִין בִּישִׁין. מָרַן דִּי בִשְׁמַיָּא יְהֵא בְסַעְדְּהוֹן כָּל זְמַן וְעִדָּן, וְנֹאמַר אָמֵן.

יְקוּם פֻּרְקָן מִן שְׁמַיָּא, חִנָּא וְחִסְדָּא וְרַחֲמֵי וְחַיֵּי אֲרִיכֵי וּמְזוֹנֵי רְוִיחֵי, וְסִיַּעְתָּא דִשְׁמַיָּא, וּבַרְיוּת גּוּפָא וּנְהוֹרָא מְעַלְּיָא, זַרְעָא חַיָּא וְקַיָּמָא, זַרְעָא דִּי לָא יִפְסֻק וְדִי לָא יִבְטֻל מִפִּתְגָּמֵי אוֹרַיְתָא, לְכָל קְהָלָא קַדִּישָׁא הָדֵין, רַבְרְבַיָּא עִם זְעֵרַיָּא, טַפְלָא וּנְשַׁיָּא. מַלְכָּא דְעָלְמָא יְבָרֵךְ יָתְכוֹן, יַפֵּשׁ חַיֵּיכוֹן וְיַסְגֵּא יוֹמֵיכוֹן, וְיִתֵּן אַרְכָא לִשְׁנֵיכוֹן, וְתִתְפָּרְקוּן וְתִשְׁתֵּיזְבוּן מִן כָּל עָקָא וּמִן כָּל מַרְעִין בִּישִׁין. מָרַן דִּי בִשְׁמַיָּא יְהֵא בְסַעְדְּכוֹן כָּל זְמַן וְעִדָּן, וְנֹאמַר אָמֵן.

מִי שֶׁבֵּרַךְ אֲבוֹתֵינוּ אַבְרָהָם יִצְחָק וְיַעֲקֹב, הוּא יְבָרֵךְ אֶת כָּל הַקָּהָל הַקָּדוֹשׁ הַזֶּה עִם כָּל קְהִלּוֹת הַקֹּדֶשׁ, הֵם וּנְשֵׁיהֶם וּבְנֵיהֶם וּבְנוֹתֵיהֶם וְכֹל אֲשֶׁר לָהֶם, וּמִי שֶׁמְּיַחֲדִים בָּתֵּי כְנֵסִיּוֹת לִתְפִלָּה, וּמִי שֶׁבָּאִים בְּתוֹכָם לְהִתְפַּלֵּל, וּמִי שֶׁנּוֹתְנִים נֵר לַמָּאוֹר וְיַיִן לְקִדּוּשׁ וּלְהַבְדָּלָה וּפַת לָאוֹרְחִים וּצְדָקָה לָעֲנִיִּים, וְכָל מִי שֶׁעוֹסְקִים בְּצָרְכֵי צִבּוּר בֶּאֱמוּנָה. הַקָּדוֹשׁ בָּרוּךְ הוּא יְשַׁלֵּם שְׂכָרָם, וְיָסִיר מֵהֶם כָּל מַחֲלָה, וְיִרְפָּא לְכָל גּוּפָם, וְיִסְלַח לְכָל עֲוֹנָם, וְיִשְׁלַח בְּרָכָה וְהַצְלָחָה בְּכָל מַעֲשֵׂי יְדֵיהֶם עִם כָּל יִשְׂרָאֵל אֲחֵיהֶם, וְנֹאמַר אָמֵן.

For surely among the keys to Jewish survival over the millennia have been the value placed on education, the deference

the very use of the foreign language of Aramaic is a testimony to the longevity and consistency of this tradition.

The Prayer for the Welfare of the Canadian Government is on the next page.

PRAYER FOR THE WELFARE OF THE AMERICAN GOVERNMENT

The Leader says the following:

הַנּוֹתֵן תְּשׁוּעָה May He who gives salvation to kings and dominion to princes, whose kingdom is an everlasting kingdom, who delivers His servant David from the evil sword, who makes a way in the sea and a path through the mighty waters, bless and protect, guard and help, exalt, magnify and uplift the President, Vice President and all officials of this land. May the Supreme King of kings in His mercy put into their hearts and the hearts of all their counselors and officials, to deal kindly with us and all Israel. In their days and in ours, may Judah be saved and Israel dwell in safety, and may the Redeemer come to Zion. May this be His will, and let us say: Amen.

PRAYER FOR THE SAFETY OF THE AMERICAN MILITARY

The Leader says the following:

אַדִּיר בַּמָּרוֹם God on high who dwells in might, the King to whom peace belongs, look down from Your holy habitation and bless the soldiers of the American military forces who risk their lives for the sake of peace on earth. Be their shelter and stronghold, and let them not falter. Give them the strength and courage to thwart the plans of the enemy and end the rule of evil. May their enemies be scattered and their foes flee before them, and may they rejoice in Your salvation. Bring them back safely to their homes, as is written: "The LORD *Ps. 121*
will guard you from all harm, He will guard your life. The LORD will guard your going and coming, now and for evermore." And may there be fulfilled for us the verse: "Nation shall not lift up sword against *Is. 2*
nation, nor shall they learn war any more." Let all the inhabitants on earth know that sovereignty is Yours and Your name inspires awe over all You have created – and let us say: Amen.

---

sea, and as the creeping things, that have no ruler over them?' Why is man compared to the fishes of the sea? Just as among fish of the sea, the greater swallow up the smaller ones, so with men; were it not for fear of the government, men would swallow each other alive. This is just what we learned: R. Ḥanina, the Deputy High Priest, said, Pray for the welfare of the government, for were it not for the fear thereof, men would

This **INTRODUCTION** *continues on page 657.*

The Prayer for the Welfare of the Canadian Government is on the next page.

תפילה לשלום המלכות

The שליח ציבור *says the following:*

הַנּוֹתֵן תְּשׁוּעָה לַמְּלָכִים וּמֶמְשָׁלָה לַנְּסִיכִים, מַלְכוּתוֹ מַלְכוּת כָּל עוֹלָמִים, הַפּוֹצֶה אֶת דָּוִד עַבְדּוֹ מֵחֶרֶב רָעָה, הַנּוֹתֵן בַּיָּם דֶּרֶךְ וּבְמַיִם עַזִּים נְתִיבָה, הוּא יְבָרֵךְ וְיִשְׁמֹר וְיִנְצֹר וְיַעֲזֹר וִירוֹמֵם וִיגַדֵּל וִינַשֵּׂא לְמַעְלָה אֶת הַנָּשִׂיא וְאֵת מִשְׁנֵהוּ וְאֶת כָּל שָׂרֵי הָאָרֶץ הַזֹּאת. מֶלֶךְ מַלְכֵי הַמְּלָכִים, בְּרַחֲמָיו יִתֵּן בְּלִבָּם וּבְלֵב כָּל יוֹעֲצֵיהֶם וְשָׂרֵיהֶם לַעֲשׂוֹת טוֹבָה עִמָּנוּ וְעִם כָּל יִשְׂרָאֵל. בִּימֵיהֶם וּבְיָמֵינוּ תִּוָּשַׁע יְהוּדָה, וְיִשְׂרָאֵל יִשְׁכֹּן לָבֶטַח, וּבָא לְצִיּוֹן גּוֹאֵל. וְכֵן יְהִי רָצוֹן, וְנֹאמַר אָמֵן.

תפילה לשלום חיילי צבא ארצות הברית

The שליח ציבור *says the following:*

אַדִּיר בַּמָּרוֹם שׁוֹכֵן בִּגְבוּרָה, מֶלֶךְ שֶׁהַשָּׁלוֹם שֶׁלּוֹ, הַשְׁקִיפָה מִמְּעוֹן קָדְשְׁךָ, וּבָרֵךְ אֶת חַיָּלֵי צְבָא אַרְצוֹת הַבְּרִית, הַמְחָרְפִים נַפְשָׁם בְּלֶכְתָּם לָשִׂים שָׁלוֹם בָּאָרֶץ. הֱיֵה נָא לָהֶם מַחֲסֶה וּמָעוֹז, וְאַל תִּתֵּן לַמּוֹט רַגְלָם, חַזֵּק יְדֵיהֶם וְאַמֵּץ רוּחָם לְהָפֵר עֲצַת אוֹיֵב וּלְהַעֲבִיר מֶמְשֶׁלֶת זָדוֹן, יָפוּצוּ אוֹיְבֵיהֶם וְיָנוּסוּ מְשַׂנְאֵיהֶם מִפְּנֵיהֶם, וְיִשְׂמְחוּ
בִּישׁוּעָתֶךָ. הֲשִׁיבֵם בְּשָׁלוֹם אֶל בֵּיתָם, כַּכָּתוּב בְּדִבְרֵי קָדְשֶׁךָ: יהוה תהלים קכא
יִשְׁמָרְךָ מִכָּל־רָע, יִשְׁמֹר אֶת־נַפְשֶׁךָ: יהוה יִשְׁמָר־צֵאתְךָ וּבוֹאֶךָ,
מֵעַתָּה וְעַד־עוֹלָם: וְקַיֵּם בָּנוּ מִקְרָא שֶׁכָּתוּב: לֹא־יִשָּׂא גוֹי אֶל־גּוֹי ישעיה ב
חֶרֶב, וְלֹא־יִלְמְדוּ עוֹד מִלְחָמָה: וְיֵדְעוּ כָּל יוֹשְׁבֵי תֵבֵל כִּי לְךָ מְלוּכָה יָאתָה, וְשִׁמְךָ נוֹרָא עַל כָּל מַה שֶּׁבָּרָאתָ. וְנֹאמַר אָמֵן.

INTRODUCTION TO THE PRAYER FOR THE GOVERNMENT

Already in biblical times the prophet Yirmiyahu (29:7) instructed "Seek the peace of the city to which I have carried you in exile. Pray to Hashem for it, because in its peace, you shall find peace." And the Gemara (*Avoda Zara* 3a-b) adds: "Rav Judah says in the name of Samuel: Why is it written, (*Ḥavakkuk* 1:14) 'And You make man as the fishes of the

PRAYER FOR THE WELFARE OF THE CANADIAN GOVERNMENT

The Leader says the following:

הַנּוֹתֵן תְּשׁוּעָה May He who gives salvation to kings and dominion to princes, whose kingdom is an everlasting kingdom, who delivers His servant David from the evil sword, who makes a way in the sea and a path through the mighty waters, bless and protect, guard and help, exalt, magnify and uplift the Prime Minister and all the elected and appointed officials of Canada. May the Supreme King of kings in His mercy put into their hearts and the hearts of all their counselors and officials, to deal kindly with us and all Israel. In their days and in ours, may Judah be saved and Israel dwell in safety, and may the Redeemer come to Zion. May this be His will, and let us say: Amen.

PRAYER FOR THE SAFETY OF THE CANADIAN MILITARY FORCES

The Leader says the following:

אַדִּיר בַּמָּרוֹם God on high who dwells in might, the King to whom peace belongs, look down from Your holy habitation and bless the soldiers of the Canadian Forces who risk their lives for the sake of peace on earth. Be their shelter and stronghold, and let them not falter. Give them the strength and courage to thwart the plans of the enemy and end the rule of evil. May their enemies be scattered and their foes flee before them, and may they rejoice in Your salvation. Bring them back safely to their
homes, as is written: "The LORD will guard you from all harm, He will *Ps. 121*
guard your life. The LORD will guard your going and coming, now and
for evermore." And may there be fulfilled for us the verse: "Nation shall *Is. 2*
not lift up sword against nation, nor shall they learn war any more." Let all the inhabitants on earth know that sovereignty is Yours and Your name inspires awe over all You have created – and let us say: Amen.

---

us to thrive as a Jewish community in unprecedented ways in our history, even as it has granted us the rights to see ourselves as proud citizens who can make our own contributions to its development for all of its people.

Think about the most oppressive and repressive regimes under which the Jewish people have lived over time. Then say this blessing with gratitude and hope.

תפילה לשלום המלכות

The שליח ציבור *says the following:*

הַנּוֹתֵן תְּשׁוּעָה לַמְּלָכִים וּמֶמְשָׁלָה לַנְּסִיכִים, מַלְכוּתוֹ מַלְכוּת כָּל עוֹלָמִים, הַפּוֹצֶה אֶת דָּוִד עַבְדּוֹ מֵחֶרֶב רָעָה, הַנּוֹתֵן בַּיָּם דֶּרֶךְ וּבְמַיִם עַזִּים נְתִיבָה, הוּא יְבָרֵךְ וְיִשְׁמֹר וְיִנְצֹר וְיַעֲזֹר וִירוֹמֵם וִיגַדֵּל וִינַשֵּׂא לְמַעְלָה אֶת רֹאשׁ הַמֶּמְשָׁלָה וְאֶת כָּל שָׂרֵי הָאָרֶץ הַזֹּאת. מֶלֶךְ מַלְכֵי הַמְּלָכִים, בְּרַחֲמָיו יִתֵּן בְּלִבָּם וּבְלֵב כָּל יוֹעֲצֵיהֶם וְשָׂרֵיהֶם לַעֲשׂוֹת טוֹבָה עִמָּנוּ וְעִם כָּל יִשְׂרָאֵל. בִּימֵיהֶם וּבְיָמֵינוּ תִּוָּשַׁע יְהוּדָה, וְיִשְׂרָאֵל יִשְׁכֹּן לָבֶטַח, וּבָא לְצִיּוֹן גּוֹאֵל. וְכֵן יְהִי רָצוֹן, וְנֹאמַר אָמֵן.

תפילה לשלום חיילי צבא קנדה

The שליח ציבור *says the following:*

אַדִּיר בַּמָּרוֹם שׁוֹכֵן בִּגְבוּרָה, מֶלֶךְ שֶׁהַשָּׁלוֹם שֶׁלּוֹ, הַשְׁקִיפָה מִמְּעוֹן קָדְשְׁךָ, וּבָרֵךְ אֶת חַיָּלֵי צְבָא קָנָדָה, הַמְחָרְפִים נַפְשָׁם בְּלֶכְתָּם לָשִׂים שָׁלוֹם בָּאָרֶץ. הֱיֵה נָא לָהֶם מַחֲסֶה וּמָעוֹז, וְאַל תִּתֵּן לַמּוֹט רַגְלָם, חַזֵּק יְדֵיהֶם וְאַמֵּץ רוּחָם לְהָפֵר עֲצַת אוֹיֵב וּלְהַעֲבִיר מֶמְשֶׁלֶת זָדוֹן, יָפוּצוּ אוֹיְבֵיהֶם וְיָנוּסוּ מְשַׂנְאֵיהֶם מִפְּנֵיהֶם, וְיִשְׂמְחוּ בִּישׁוּעָתֶךָ.
הֲשִׁיבֵם בְּשָׁלוֹם אֶל בֵּיתָם, כַּכָּתוּב בְּדִבְרֵי קָדְשֶׁךָ: יהוה יִשְׁמָרְךָ תהלים קכא
מִכָּל־רָע, יִשְׁמֹר אֶת־נַפְשֶׁךָ: יהוה יִשְׁמָר־צֵאתְךָ וּבוֹאֶךָ, מֵעַתָּה
וְעַד־עוֹלָם: וְקַיֵּם בָּנוּ מִקְרָא שֶׁכָּתוּב: לֹא־יִשָּׂא גוֹי אֶל־גּוֹי חֶרֶב, ישעיה ב
וְלֹא־יִלְמְדוּ עוֹד מִלְחָמָה: וְיֵדְעוּ כָּל יוֹשְׁבֵי תֵבֵל כִּי לְךָ מְלוּכָה יָאֲתָה, וְשִׁמְךָ נוֹרָא עַל כָּל מַה שֶּׁבָּרָאתָ. וְנֹאמַר אָמֵן.

At the same time, in our own times, many of us have been blessed to live in countries where the governments have provided not only for our physical safety, but have enabled

swallow each other alive." This is the most minimalist view of a prayer for the government, the protection it provides for physical welfare.

PRAYER FOR THE STATE OF ISRAEL[B]

The Leader says the following prayer:

אָבִינוּ שֶׁבַּשָּׁמַיִם Heavenly Father, Israel's Rock and Redeemer,[I] bless the State of Israel, the first flowering of our redemption.[I] Shield it under the wings of Your loving-kindness and spread over it the Tabernacle of Your peace.[I] Send Your light and truth to its leaders, ministers and counselors, and direct them with good counsel before You.

Strengthen the hands of the defenders of our Holy Land; grant them deliverance, our God, and crown them with the crown of victory. Grant peace in the land and everlasting joy to its inhabitants.

As for our brothers, the whole house of Israel, remember them in all the lands of our (*In Israel say:* their) dispersion, and swiftly lead us (*In Israel say:* them) upright to Zion Your city, and Jerusalem Your dwelling place, as is written in the Torah of Moses Your servant:

IYUN TEFILLA • עיון תפילה

צוּר יִשְׂרָאֵל וְגוֹאֲלוֹ – *Israel's Rock and Redeemer.* Note the names of Hashem that are used here. Why were these chosen?

When the Declaration of Independence was being drafted in 1948 there was much controversy over whether to include God's name in the text. Secular Zionists were offended at the notion that the achievements of Zionism should be attributed to God, and Religious Zionists were insistent that they should be. The compromise was to include the term "צוּר יִשְׂרָאֵל," a name of God that can also be interpreted in other ways. Now reflect on why the Chief Rabbis in 1948 chose these two names in their prayer for the state.

רֵאשִׁית צְמִיחַת גְּאֻלָּתֵנוּ – *The first flowering of our redemption.* The phrase which declares that Israel is "the first flowering of our redemption" is one that some have objected to, especially those who would claim that the State of Israel has no religious significance, and they therefore leave out the prayer altogether. Still others have objected to the wish that all Jews eventually settle there. We believe, however, that the modern State, for all of its faults, is the instrument through which Hashem will bring the Jewish people its redemption. For the first time in 2000 years we live in our own sovereign state; that fact alone is cause for thanks and for hope.

סֻכַּת שְׁלוֹמֶךָ – *The Tabernacle of Your peace.* **Why do you think it is called the "*sukka*" of peace? What does a *sukka* represent?**

תפילה לשלום מדינת ישראלב

The שליח ציבור *says the following prayer:*

אָבִינוּ שֶׁבַּשָּׁמַיִם, צוּר יִשְׂרָאֵל וְגוֹאֲלוֹ,ע בָּרֵךְ אֶת מְדִינַת יִשְׂרָאֵל, רֵאשִׁית צְמִיחַת גְּאֻלָּתֵנוּ.ע הָגֵן עָלֶיהָ בְּאֶבְרַת חַסְדֶּךָ וּפְרֹשׂ עָלֶיהָ סֻכַּת שְׁלוֹמֶךָ,ע וּשְׁלַח אוֹרְךָ וַאֲמִתְּךָ לְרָאשֶׁיהָ, שָׂרֶיהָ וְיוֹעֲצֶיהָ, וְתַקְּנֵם בְּעֵצָה טוֹבָה מִלְּפָנֶיךָ.

חַזֵּק אֶת יְדֵי מְגִנֵּי אֶרֶץ קָדְשֵׁנוּ, וְהַנְחִילֵם אֱלֹהֵינוּ יְשׁוּעָה וַעֲטֶרֶת נִצָּחוֹן תְּעַטְּרֵם, וְנָתַתָּ שָׁלוֹם בָּאָרֶץ וְשִׂמְחַת עוֹלָם לְיוֹשְׁבֶיהָ.

וְאֶת אַחֵינוּ כָּל בֵּית יִשְׂרָאֵל, פְּקָד נָא בְּכָל אַרְצוֹת פְּזוּרֵינוּ,
וְתוֹלִיכֵנוּ /בארץ ישראל: פְּזוּרֵיהֶם, וְתוֹלִיכֵם/ מְהֵרָה קוֹמְמִיּוּת לְצִיּוֹן
עִירֶךָ וְלִירוּשָׁלַיִם מִשְׁכַּן שְׁמֶךָ, כַּכָּתוּב בְּתוֹרַת מֹשֶׁה עַבְדֶּךָ:
אִם־יִהְיֶה נִדַּחֲךָ בִּקְצֵה הַשָּׁמָיִם, מִשָּׁם יְקַבֶּצְךָ יהוה אֱלֹהֶיךָ דברים ל

BIUR TEFILLA • ביאור תפילה

תפילה לשלום מדינת ישראל – *PRAYER FOR THE STATE OF ISRAEL.* The Prayer for the State of Israel was written by Chief Rabbis Herzog and Uziel in 1948 (allegedly with some minor revisions made by Noble Laureate Shai Agnon). This prayer is a modern contribution to the ongoing millennial development of the siddur as a microcosm of Jewish history, wherein each generation adds its own concerns and aspirations.

ANI TEFILLA • אני תפילה

Once I sat on the steps by a gate at David's Tower, I placed my two heavy baskets at my side. A group of tourists was standing around their guide and I became their target marker. "You see that man with the baskets? Just right of his head there's an arch from the Roman period. Just right of his head." "But he's moving, he's moving!" I said to myself: redemption will come only if their guide tells them, "You see that arch from the Roman period? It's not important: but next to it, left and down a bit, there sits a man who's bought fruit and vegetables for his family." (Yehuda Amichai, *Tourists*)

"Even if you are scattered to the furthermost lands under the heavens, from there the LORD your God will gather you and take you back. The LORD your God will bring you to the land your ancestors possessed and you will possess it; and He will make you more prosperous and numerous than your ancestors. Then the LORD your God will open up your heart and the heart of your descendants, to love the LORD your God with all your heart and with all your soul, that you may live." *Deut. 30*

Unite our hearts to love and revere Your name and observe all the words of Your Torah, and swiftly send us Your righteous anointed one of the house of David, to redeem those who long for Your salvation.

Appear in Your glorious majesty over all the dwellers on earth, and let all who breathe declare: The LORD God of Israel is King and His kingship has dominion over all. Amen, Selah.

PRAYER FOR ISRAEL'S DEFENSE FORCES[A]

The Leader says the following prayer:

מִי שֶׁבֵּרַךְ May He who blessed our ancestors, Abraham, Isaac and Jacob, bless the members of Israel's Defense Forces and its security services who stand guard over our land and the cities of our

---

this, it simply strengthens our faith, Mr. Chief Justice, that the day will yet come when there will be a Sanhedrin of 71 elders and the Jews from all four corners of the world will come to this place, to hang on your every word. Thank you, thank you, thank you, for your letter. With blessings, appreciation, and profound respect, Nechama Leibowitz."

ANI TEFILLA • אני תפילה

מי שברך לחיילי צה״ל – *PRAYER FOR ISRAEL'S DEFENSE FORCES.*

Rabbi Aryeh Levin saw a young soldier on short furlough from the army. He knew him from the neighborhood in Jerusalem and so he crossed the street in order to extend his hand in greeting. "Shalom aleichem," he said, "please come to my home. I would very much like to drink tea with you and hear about your activities."

This **ANI TEFILLA** *continues on page 663.*

וּמִשָּׁם יִקָּחֶךָ: וֶהֱבִיאֲךָ יהוה אֱלֹהֶיךָ אֶל־הָאָרֶץ אֲשֶׁר־יָרְשׁוּ אֲבֹתֶיךָ וִירִשְׁתָּהּ, וְהֵיטִבְךָ וְהִרְבְּךָ מֵאֲבֹתֶיךָ: וּמָל יהוה אֱלֹהֶיךָ אֶת־לְבָבְךָ וְאֶת־לְבַב זַרְעֶךָ, לְאַהֲבָה אֶת־יהוה אֱלֹהֶיךָ בְּכָל־לְבָבְךָ וּבְכָל־נַפְשְׁךָ, לְמַעַן חַיֶּיךָ:

וְיַחֵד לְבָבֵנוּ לְאַהֲבָה וּלְיִרְאָה אֶת שְׁמֶךָ, וְלִשְׁמֹר אֶת כָּל דִּבְרֵי תוֹרָתֶךָ, וּשְׁלַח לָנוּ מְהֵרָה בֶּן דָּוִד מְשִׁיחַ צִדְקֶךָ, לִפְדּוֹת מְחַכֵּי קֵץ יְשׁוּעָתֶךָ.

וְהוֹפַע בַּהֲדַר גְּאוֹן עֻזֶּךָ עַל כָּל יוֹשְׁבֵי תֵבֵל אַרְצֶךָ וְיֹאמַר כֹּל אֲשֶׁר נְשָׁמָה בְאַפּוֹ, יהוה אֱלֹהֵי יִשְׂרָאֵל מֶלֶךְ וּמַלְכוּתוֹ בַּכֹּל מָשָׁלָה, אָמֵן סֶלָה.

מי שברך לחיילי צה״ל[א]

The שליח ציבור *says the following prayer:*

מִי שֶׁבֵּרַךְ אֲבוֹתֵינוּ אַבְרָהָם יִצְחָק וְיַעֲקֹב הוּא יְבָרֵךְ אֶת חַיָּלֵי צְבָא הַהֲגָנָה לְיִשְׂרָאֵל וְאַנְשֵׁי כֹּחוֹת הַבִּטָּחוֹן, הָעוֹמְדִים

ANI TEFILLA • אני תפילה

Israel Supreme Court justice Tzvi Tal once sent a letter to Nechama Leibowitz with a reference to rabbinic literature (*Tosafot* on *Ḥullin*) that supported something that Nechama had written in one of her books. She wrote back to him: "Had someone told me in my youth in the Diaspora at the beginning of this century (for I am 90 years old) that I would merit to see a Supreme Court in Jerusalem, and that a Chief Justice would send me a reference to the Talmud, my brother, of blessed memory, and I would have thought that this was some sort of legend like the Leviathan that we are told the righteous will eat in the World to Come, the kind of legends that father used to tell us in order to strengthen our Zionist education. Yet this is no legend...for I am holding the envelope in my hands and it clearly says "Israel Supreme Court" on it! Since we have merited

God from the Lebanese border to the Egyptian desert, from the Mediterranean sea to the approach of the Aravah, and wherever else they are, on land, in air and at sea. May the LORD make the enemies who rise against us be struck down before them. May the Holy One, blessed be He, protect and deliver them from all trouble and distress, affliction and illness, and send blessing and success to all the work of their hands. May He subdue our enemies under them and crown them with deliverance and victory. And may there be fulfilled in them the verse, "It is the LORD your God who goes *Deut. 20*
with you to fight for you against your enemies, to deliver you." And let us say: Amen.

PRAYER FOR THOSE BEING HELD IN CAPTIVITY

If Israeli soldiers or civilians are being held in captivity, the Leader says the following:

מִי שֶׁבֵּרַךְ May He who blessed our ancestors, Abraham, Isaac and Jacob, Joseph, Moses and Aaron, David and Solomon, bless, protect and guard the members of Israel's Defense Forces missing in action or held captive, and other captives among our brethren, the whole house of Israel, who are in distress or captivity, as we, the members of this holy congregation, pray on their behalf. May the Holy One, blessed be He, have compassion on them and bring them out from darkness and the shadow of death; may He break their bonds, deliver them from their distress, and bring them swiftly back to
their families' embrace. Give thanks to the LORD for His loving- *Ps. 107*
kindness and for the wonders He does for the children of men; and
may there be fulfilled in them the verse: "Those redeemed by the *Is. 35*
LORD will return; they will enter Zion with singing, and everlasting joy will crown their heads. Gladness and joy will overtake them, and sorrow and sighing will flee away." And let us say: Amen.

---

not look up so high as to notice whether you are wearing a kippa. But I can see your heart – and your heart is big and kind and that's what counts. You are also a soldier placing your life at risk for all of us in Israel. Please drink tea with me; your kippa is probably bigger than mine."

עַל מִשְׁמַר אַרְצֵנוּ וְעָרֵי אֱלֹהֵינוּ, מִגְּבוּל הַלְּבָנוֹן וְעַד מִדְבַּר מִצְרַיִם וּמִן הַיָּם הַגָּדוֹל עַד לְבוֹא הָעֲרָבָה וּבְכָל מָקוֹם שֶׁהֵם, בַּיַּבָּשָׁה, בָּאֲוִיר וּבַיָּם. יִתֵּן יהוה אֶת אוֹיְבֵינוּ הַקָּמִים עָלֵינוּ נִגָּפִים לִפְנֵיהֶם. הַקָּדוֹשׁ בָּרוּךְ הוּא יִשְׁמֹר וְיַצִּיל אֶת חַיָּלֵינוּ מִכָּל צָרָה וְצוּקָה וּמִכָּל נֶגַע וּמַחֲלָה, וְיִשְׁלַח בְּרָכָה וְהַצְלָחָה בְּכָל מַעֲשֵׂי יְדֵיהֶם. יַדְבֵּר שׂוֹנְאֵינוּ תַּחְתֵּיהֶם וִיעַטְּרֵם בְּכֶתֶר
יְשׁוּעָה וּבַעֲטֶרֶת נִצָּחוֹן. וִיקֻיַּם בָּהֶם הַכָּתוּב: כִּי יהוה אֱלֹהֵיכֶם דברים כ
הַהֹלֵךְ עִמָּכֶם לְהִלָּחֵם לָכֶם עִם־אֹיְבֵיכֶם לְהוֹשִׁיעַ אֶתְכֶם: וְנֹאמַר אָמֵן.

מי שברך לשבויים

If Israeli soldiers or civilians are being held in captivity, the שליח ציבור *says the following:*

מִי שֶׁבֵּרַךְ אֲבוֹתֵינוּ אַבְרָהָם יִצְחָק וְיַעֲקֹב, יוֹסֵף מֹשֶׁה וְאַהֲרֹן, דָּוִד וּשְׁלֹמֹה, הוּא יְבָרֵךְ וְיִשְׁמֹר וְיִנְצֹר אֶת נֶעְדְּרֵי צְבָא הַהֲגָנָה לְיִשְׂרָאֵל וּשְׁבוּיָו, וְאֶת כָּל אַחֵינוּ הַנְּתוּנִים בְּצָרָה וּבְשִׁבְיָה, בַּעֲבוּר שֶׁכָּל הַקָּהָל הַקָּדוֹשׁ הַזֶּה מִתְפַּלֵּל בַּעֲבוּרָם. הַקָּדוֹשׁ בָּרוּךְ הוּא יִמָּלֵא רַחֲמִים עֲלֵיהֶם, וְיוֹצִיאֵם מֵחֹשֶׁךְ וְצַלְמָוֶת, וּמוֹסְרוֹתֵיהֶם יְנַתֵּק, וּמִמְּצוּקוֹתֵיהֶם יוֹשִׁיעֵם, וִישִׁיבֵם מְהֵרָה
לְחֵיק מִשְׁפְּחוֹתֵיהֶם. יוֹדוּ לַיהוה חַסְדּוֹ וְנִפְלְאוֹתָיו לִבְנֵי אָדָם: תהלים קז
וִיקֻיַּם בָּהֶם מִקְרָא שֶׁכָּתוּב: וּפְדוּיֵי יהוה יְשֻׁבוּן, וּבָאוּ צִיּוֹן ישעיה לה
בְּרִנָּה, וְשִׂמְחַת עוֹלָם עַל־רֹאשָׁם, שָׂשׂוֹן וְשִׂמְחָה יַשִּׂיגוּ, וְנָסוּ יָגוֹן וַאֲנָחָה: וְנֹאמַר אָמֵן.

Rabbi Levin, in his black hat and black kaftan, took the young man's hand in his own. "Don't you see, he said. I'm a very short man. I see you but I can-

The young soldier said, "I don't think it's right for me to come visit you. I don't wear a kippa anymore.

BLESSING THE NEW MONTH

On the Shabbat before Rosh Ḥodesh, the following is said by the congregation, and repeated by the Leader:

יְהִי רָצוֹן May it be Your will,
Lord our God and God of our fathers,
to renew for us this coming month
for good and blessing.
Grant us long life,
a life of peace,
a life of goodness,
a life of blessing,
a life of sustenance,
a life of physical health,
a life marked by reverence for heaven
and dread of sin,
a life without shame or disgrace,
a life of wealth and honor,
a life in which we have love for the Torah
and reverence for heaven,
a life in which our hearts' desires
are fulfilled for good.
Amen, Selah.

Berakhot 16b

Rosh Ḥodesh can be one day or two days long.

Originally, in order to ensure uniformity, authority for the official declaration of the new month was given to the supreme court of the Land, the Sanhedrin in Jerusalem, which announced the beginning of the month after the testimony of witnesses who had seen the first sliver of the new moon, and then word was subsequently spread to the rest of Israel and beyond with a system of bonfire signals atop the mountains. Although authority was subsequently invested in a calendar system in the fourth century, we maintain the echoes of the earlier system by announcing the days of the new month communally in this prayer to alert people for on this day there are special prayers and observances. We therefore stand, as did the witnesses themselves.

ברכת החודש

On the שבת *before* ראש חודש, *the following is said by the* קהל, *and repeated by the* שליח ציבור:

יְהִי רָצוֹן מִלְּפָנֶיךָ, יהוה אֱלֹהֵינוּ וֵאלֹהֵי אֲבוֹתֵינוּ ברכות טז:
שֶׁתְּחַדֵּשׁ עָלֵינוּ אֶת הַחֹדֶשׁ הַזֶּה לְטוֹבָה וְלִבְרָכָה.
וְתִתֶּן לָנוּ חַיִּים אֲרוּכִים
חַיִּים שֶׁל שָׁלוֹם
חַיִּים שֶׁל טוֹבָה
חַיִּים שֶׁל בְּרָכָה
חַיִּים שֶׁל פַּרְנָסָה
חַיִּים שֶׁל חִלּוּץ עֲצָמוֹת
חַיִּים שֶׁיֵּשׁ בָּהֶם יִרְאַת שָׁמַיִם וְיִרְאַת חֵטְא
חַיִּים שֶׁאֵין בָּהֶם בּוּשָׁה וּכְלִמָּה
חַיִּים שֶׁל עֹשֶׁר וְכָבוֹד
חַיִּים שֶׁתְּהֵא בָנוּ אַהֲבַת תּוֹרָה וְיִרְאַת שָׁמַיִם
חַיִּים שֶׁיִּמָּלְאוּ מִשְׁאֲלוֹת לִבֵּנוּ לְטוֹבָה
אָמֵן סֶלָה.

INTRODUCTION TO BIRKAT HAḤODESH

The following prayer is recited on the Shabbat before Rosh Ḥodesh, the new month in the Hebrew calendar. It is recited standing.

The Jewish calendar is primarily lunar (though not exclusively so). The word month is derived from the word moon, just as the Hebrew word for month, *ḥodesh,* is related to the word *ḥadash*, meaning "new," for the new month begins when a new moon appears. But the moon is not always so easily visible when it first appears thus leaving room for error of a day before being sure of its appearance. Thus,

The new moon is announced, then the Leader takes the Torah scroll in his right arm and says:

מִי שֶׁעָשָׂה May He who performed miracles for our ancestors
and redeemed them from slavery to freedom,
redeem us soon, and gather in our dispersed people
from the four quarters of the earth,
so that all Israel may be united in friendship,[1]
and let us say: Amen.

The Leader, then the congregation:

The new month of (*Hebrew month*) will occur on (*day of week*).
May it come to us and all Israel for good.

The congregation and Leader continue:

Outside Israel:

May the Holy One,
blessed be He,
renew this new month
for us and
for all His people,
the house of Israel,
for life and peace,
gladness and joy,
salvation and consolation;
and let us say: Amen.

In Israel:

May the Holy One, blessed be He,
renew this month
for us and for all His people
the house of Israel, wherever they are,
for good and blessing, gladness and joy,
for salvation and consolation,
livelihood and sustenance,
for life and peace,
good tidings and good news,
for complete healing
and imminent redemption,
and let us say: Amen.

(כָּל יִשְׂרָאֵל לִירוּשָׁלַיִם עִיר הַקֹּדֶשׁ) (*Maḥzor Vitry*). This version has historical echoes of the days when the Sanhedrin in Jerusalem established the month, but it also is a powerful statement that what unites us as a people is the centrality of Jerusalem to our national life. Just look at the variety of Jews walking the streets of Yerushalayim.

חֲבֵרִים כָּל יִשְׂרָאֵל – *All Israel may be united in friendship*. These words symbolize the collectivity of Israel, whom the *Beit Din* (court) represents when it declares the new month. In a similar vein, the *ḥazan* holds the Torah scroll, emblematic of the collective Jewish People. The Torah scroll unifies all our people into this one collective and it is this unification which provides the *ḥazan* with the authority to declare the new month (Rabbi Joseph B. Soloveitchik).

The מולד *is announced, then the* שליח ציבור *takes the* ספר תורה *in his right arm and says:*

מִי שֶׁעָשָׂה נִסִּים לַאֲבוֹתֵינוּ
וְגָאַל אוֹתָם מֵעַבְדוּת לְחֵרוּת
הוּא יִגְאַל אוֹתָנוּ בְּקָרוֹב
וִיקַבֵּץ נִדָּחֵינוּ מֵאַרְבַּע כַּנְפוֹת הָאָרֶץ
חֲבֵרִים כָּל יִשְׂרָאֵל
וְנֹאמַר אָמֵן.

The שליח ציבור*, then the* קהל:

רֹאשׁ חֹדֶשׁ *month* יִהְיֶה בְּיוֹם *day* (*וּבְיוֹם *day*)
הַבָּא עָלֵינוּ וְעַל כָּל יִשְׂרָאֵל לְטוֹבָה.

**if the second day falls on Sunday, then substitute:* וּלְמָחֳרָתוֹ בְּיוֹם

The קהל *and* שליח ציבור *continue:*

In חוץ לארץ *say:*

יְחַדְּשֵׁהוּ
הַקָּדוֹשׁ בָּרוּךְ הוּא
עָלֵינוּ
וְעַל כָּל עַמּוֹ
בֵּית יִשְׂרָאֵל
לְחַיִּים וּלְשָׁלוֹם
לְשָׂשׂוֹן וּלְשִׂמְחָה
לִישׁוּעָה וּלְנֶחָמָה
וְנֹאמַר אָמֵן.

in ארץ ישראל *say:*

יְחַדְּשֵׁהוּ הַקָּדוֹשׁ בָּרוּךְ הוּא
עָלֵינוּ וְעַל כָּל עַמּוֹ בֵּית יִשְׂרָאֵל
בְּכָל מָקוֹם שֶׁהֵם
לְטוֹבָה וְלִבְרָכָה, לְשָׂשׂוֹן וּלְשִׂמְחָה
לִישׁוּעָה וּלְנֶחָמָה
לְפַרְנָסָה וּלְכַלְכָּלָה
לְחַיִּים וּלְשָׁלוֹם
לִשְׁמוּעוֹת טוֹבוֹת וְלִבְשׂוֹרוֹת טוֹבוֹת
וְלִרְפוּאָה שְׁלֵמָה, וְלִגְאֻלָּה קְרוֹבָה,
וְנֹאמַר אָמֵן.

IYUN TEFILLA • עיון תפילה

חֲבֵרִים כָּל יִשְׂרָאֵל – *All Israel may be united in friendship.* An earlier manuscript of this text from the twelfth century reads "all Israel friends to Jerusalem the holy city" (**חֲבֵרִים**

The following is omitted on days when Taḥanun is not said.
It is also omitted on a Shabbat before Rosh Ḥodesh.

אַב הָרַחֲמִים Father of compassion, who dwells on high: may He remember in His compassion the pious, the upright and the blameless – holy communities who sacrificed their lives for the sanctification of God's name. Lovely and pleasant in their lives, in death they were not parted. They were swifter than eagles and stronger than lions to do the will of their Maker and the desire of their Creator. O our God, remember them for good with the other righteous of the world, and may He exact retribution for the shed blood of His servants, as it is written in the Torah of Moses, the man of God: "O nations, *Deut. 32*
acclaim His people, for He will avenge the blood of His servants, wreak vengeance on His foes, and make clean His people's land." And by Your servants, the prophets, it is written: "I shall cleanse their *Joel 4*
blood which I have not yet cleansed, says the Lord who dwells in Zion." And in the holy Writings it says: "Why should the nations *Ps. 79*
say: Where is their God? Before our eyes, may those nations know that You avenge the shed blood of Your servants." And it also says: "For the Avenger of blood remembers them and does not forget the *Ps. 9*
cry of the afflicted." And it further says: "He will execute judgment *Ps. 110*
among the nations, filled with the dead, crushing rulers far and wide. From the brook by the wayside he will drink, then he will hold his head high."

---

not a remnant or a residue escape, even an infant or a suckling in the cradle." They then came and struck those who had remained in their houses – comely young men and comely and lovely young women along with elders. All of them stretched forth their necks. Even manumitted serving men and serving women were killed along with them for the sanctification of the name which is awesome and sublime ... Who rules above and below, Who was and will be. Indeed the Lord of Hosts is His name." (Robert Chazan, *European Jewry and the First Crusade*).

Because of its more somber content, it is not recited on happier occasions, such as Festivals or Rosh Ḥodesh or their related days, which may also coincide with Shabbat. However, most have the custom to continue to recite the prayer during the time from Pesaḥ to Shavuot, regardless of any happier day, even on Rosh Ḥodesh itself, because that is the time of year historically when these horrific events took place.

The following is omitted on days when תחנון *is not said.*
It is also omitted on שבת מברכים.

אַב הָרַחֲמִים שׁוֹכֵן מְרוֹמִים, בְּרַחֲמָיו הָעֲצוּמִים הוּא יִפְקֹד בְּרַחֲמִים
הַחֲסִידִים וְהַיְשָׁרִים וְהַתְּמִימִים, קְהִלּוֹת הַקֹּדֶשׁ שֶׁמָּסְרוּ נַפְשָׁם עַל
קְדֻשַּׁת הַשֵּׁם, הַנֶּאֱהָבִים וְהַנְּעִימִים בְּחַיֵּיהֶם, וּבְמוֹתָם לֹא נִפְרָדוּ,
מִנְּשָׁרִים קַלּוּ וּמֵאֲרָיוֹת גָּבֵרוּ לַעֲשׂוֹת רְצוֹן קוֹנָם וְחֵפֶץ צוּרָם. יִזְכְּרֵם
אֱלֹהֵינוּ לְטוֹבָה עִם שְׁאָר צַדִּיקֵי עוֹלָם, וְיִנְקֹם לְעֵינֵינוּ נִקְמַת דַּם
עֲבָדָיו הַשָּׁפוּךְ, כַּכָּתוּב בְּתוֹרַת מֹשֶׁה אִישׁ הָאֱלֹהִים: הַרְנִינוּ גוֹיִם דברים לב
עַמּוֹ, כִּי דַם־עֲבָדָיו יִקּוֹם, וְנָקָם יָשִׁיב לְצָרָיו, וְכִפֶּר אַדְמָתוֹ עַמּוֹ:
וְעַל יְדֵי עֲבָדֶיךָ הַנְּבִיאִים כָּתוּב לֵאמֹר: וְנִקֵּיתִי, דָּמָם לֹא־נִקֵּיתִי, יואל ד
וַיהוה שֹׁכֵן בְּצִיּוֹן: וּבְכִתְבֵי הַקֹּדֶשׁ נֶאֱמַר: לָמָּה יֹאמְרוּ הַגּוֹיִם אַיֵּה תהלים עט
אֱלֹהֵיהֶם, יִוָּדַע בַּגּוֹיִם לְעֵינֵינוּ נִקְמַת דַּם־עֲבָדֶיךָ הַשָּׁפוּךְ: וְאוֹמֵר:
כִּי־דֹרֵשׁ דָּמִים אוֹתָם זָכָר, לֹא־שָׁכַח צַעֲקַת עֲנָוִים: וְאוֹמֵר: יָדִין בַּגּוֹיִם תהלים קי
מָלֵא גְוִיּוֹת, מָחַץ רֹאשׁ עַל־אֶרֶץ רַבָּה: מִנַּחַל בַּדֶּרֶךְ יִשְׁתֶּה, עַל־כֵּן
יָרִים רֹאשׁ:

INTRODUCTION TO AV HARAḤAMIM

On a day like Shabbat, when we have the time to reflect upon things like who we are and how we got here, there developed a custom to recite a prayer on behalf of martyrs who perished for no other reason than that they were Jews. This prayer finds its roots in the massacres that took place in the Rhine Valley during the period of the First Crusades, when the Jewish communities there were decimated and blood literally ran through the streets.

Consider the words of one chronicler from the town of Worms where the Jewish community divided itself into two groups in order to avoid complete annihilation.

"It came to pass on the tenth of Iyyar, on Sunday, they plotted craftily against them. They took a trampled corpse of theirs, that had been buried thirty days previously and carried it through the city, saying: "Behold what the Jews have done to our comrade. They took a gentile and boiled him in water. They then poured the water into our wells in order to kill us." When the crusaders and burghers heard this, they cried out and gathered – all who bore and unsheathed [a sword], from great to small – saying: "Behold the time has come to avenge him who was crucified, whom their ancestors slew. Now let

אַשְׁרֵי Happy[1] are those who dwell in Your House; Ps. 84
they shall continue to praise You, Selah!
Happy are the people for whom this is so; Ps. 144
happy are the people whose God is the LORD.
A song of praise by David. Ps. 145

א I will elevate You, my God, the King, and bless Your name for ever and all time. ב Every day I will bless You, and praise Your name for ever and all time. ג Great is the LORD and greatly to be praised; His greatness is unfathomable. ד One generation will praise Your works to the next, and tell of Your mighty deeds. ה On the glorious splendor of Your majesty I will meditate, and on the acts of Your wonders. ו They shall talk of the power of Your awesome deeds, and I will tell of Your greatness. ז They shall recite the record of Your great goodness, and sing with joy of Your righteousness. ח The LORD is generous and compassionate, slow to anger and great in loving-kindness. ט The LORD is good to all, and His compassion extends to all His works. י All Your works shall thank You, LORD, and Your devoted ones shall bless You. כ They shall talk of the glory of Your kingship, and speak of Your might. ל To make known to mankind His mighty deeds and the glorious majesty of His kingship. מ Your kingdom is an everlasting kingdom, and Your reign is for all generations. ס The LORD supports all who fall, and raises all who are bowed down. ע All raise their eyes to You in hope, and You give them their food

---

Therefore let each letter of the alphabet represent all of the praises that begin with that letter, of which I will offer just one line as an example." In a certain sense, then, the alphabetic listing of words is designed to convey the impression that all words fall short. It's not only about the meaning of the words but the feeling of the *Alef-Beit*.

ANI TEFILLA • אני תפילה

On the Sabbath, a Jew comes to know himself, not as twenty, or thirty, or sixty years old, but as four thousand years old, the bearer of an eternal witness of which the Sabbath is the sign (Michael S. Kogan).

תהלים פד
אַשְׁרֵי יוֹשְׁבֵי בֵיתֶךָ, עוֹד יְהַלְלוּךָ סֶּלָה:

תהלים קמד
אַשְׁרֵי הָעָם שֶׁכָּכָה לּוֹ, אַשְׁרֵי הָעָם שֶׁיהוה אֱלֹהָיו:

תהלים קמה
תְּהִלָּה לְדָוִד

אֲרוֹמִמְךָ אֱלוֹהַי הַמֶּלֶךְ, וַאֲבָרְכָה שִׁמְךָ לְעוֹלָם וָעֶד:
בְּכָל־יוֹם אֲבָרְכֶךָּ, וַאֲהַלְלָה שִׁמְךָ לְעוֹלָם וָעֶד:
גָּדוֹל יהוה וּמְהֻלָּל מְאֹד, וְלִגְדֻלָּתוֹ אֵין חֵקֶר:
דּוֹר לְדוֹר יְשַׁבַּח מַעֲשֶׂיךָ, וּגְבוּרֹתֶיךָ יַגִּידוּ:
הֲדַר כְּבוֹד הוֹדֶךָ, וְדִבְרֵי נִפְלְאֹתֶיךָ אָשִׂיחָה:
וֶעֱזוּז נוֹרְאֹתֶיךָ יֹאמֵרוּ, וּגְדוּלָּתְךָ אֲסַפְּרֶנָּה:
זֵכֶר רַב־טוּבְךָ יַבִּיעוּ, וְצִדְקָתְךָ יְרַנֵּנוּ:
חַנּוּן וְרַחוּם יהוה, אֶרֶךְ אַפַּיִם וּגְדָל־חָסֶד:
טוֹב־יהוה לַכֹּל, וְרַחֲמָיו עַל־כָּל־מַעֲשָׂיו:
יוֹדוּךָ יהוה כָּל־מַעֲשֶׂיךָ, וַחֲסִידֶיךָ יְבָרְכוּכָה:
כְּבוֹד מַלְכוּתְךָ יֹאמֵרוּ, וּגְבוּרָתְךָ יְדַבֵּרוּ:
לְהוֹדִיעַ לִבְנֵי הָאָדָם גְּבוּרֹתָיו, וּכְבוֹד הֲדַר מַלְכוּתוֹ:
מַלְכוּתְךָ מַלְכוּת כָּל־עֹלָמִים, וּמֶמְשַׁלְתְּךָ בְּכָל־דּוֹר וָדֹר:
סוֹמֵךְ יהוה לְכָל־הַנֹּפְלִים, וְזוֹקֵף לְכָל־הַכְּפוּפִים:
עֵינֵי־כֹל אֵלֶיךָ יְשַׂבֵּרוּ, וְאַתָּה נוֹתֵן־לָהֶם אֶת־אָכְלָם בְּעִתּוֹ:

IYUN TEFILLA • עיון תפילה

אַשְׁרֵי – *Happy.* The Gemara (*Berakhot* 4b) relates that anyone who says this chapter of Psalms three times a day is guaranteed a place in the World to Come (It was recited once in *Pesukei DeZimra*, a second time here, and the third will be during *Minḥa*.) One of the reasons was because it is written as an acrostic, wherein each line begins with another letter of the *Alef-Beit*. It is as if one is saying, "Any praise I give You is incomplete.

in due season. פ You open Your hand, and satisfy every living thing with favor. צ The LORD is righteous in all His ways, and kind in all He does. ק The LORD is close to all who call on Him, to all who call on Him in truth. ר He fulfills the will of those who fear Him; He hears their cry and saves them. ש The LORD guards all who love Him, but all the wicked He will destroy. ת ▸ My mouth shall speak the praise of the LORD, and all creatures shall bless His holy name for ever and all time.
We will bless the LORD now and for ever. Halleluya! *Ps. 115*

RETURNING THE TORAH TO THE ARK

The Ark is opened. All stand.
The Leader takes the Torah scroll and says:

יְהַלְלוּ Let them praise the name of the LORD, *Ps. 148*
for His name alone is sublime.

The congregation responds:

הוֹדוֹ His majesty[H] is above earth and heaven.[I]
He has raised the horn of His people,
for the glory of all His devoted ones,
the children of Israel, the people close to Him.
Halleluya!

---

want to confuse our adoration for the Torah itself with that of its Author. Our respect for it, is essentially our respect for Him. To be sure, the Torah is holy, but it derives its holiness from Hashem and it is He that we honor (Rokeach).

IYUN TEFILLA · עיון תפילה

הודו על־אֶרֶץ וְשָׁמָיִם – *His majesty is above earth and heaven.* Alternatively, "on the earth and heaven." Why does the earth come first? This could mean that, contrary to one's initial thought, Hashem is not only located in heaven, as it were, but is also here on earth, watching over it and us (Meiri 149:13). Alternatively, Hashem is primarily located, as it were, on earth, and through our actions the heavens are influenced (*Shir Hashirim Raba* 8).

פּוֹתֵחַ אֶת־יָדֶךָ, וּמַשְׂבִּיעַ לְכָל־חַי רָצוֹן:
צַדִּיק יהוה בְּכָל־דְּרָכָיו, וְחָסִיד בְּכָל־מַעֲשָׂיו:
קָרוֹב יהוה לְכָל־קֹרְאָיו, לְכֹל אֲשֶׁר יִקְרָאֻהוּ בֶאֱמֶת:
רְצוֹן־יְרֵאָיו יַעֲשֶׂה, וְאֶת־שַׁוְעָתָם יִשְׁמַע, וְיוֹשִׁיעֵם:
שׁוֹמֵר יהוה אֶת־כָּל־אֹהֲבָיו, וְאֵת כָּל־הָרְשָׁעִים יַשְׁמִיד:
› תְּהִלַּת יהוה יְדַבֶּר פִּי, וִיבָרֵךְ כָּל־בָּשָׂר שֵׁם קָדְשׁוֹ לְעוֹלָם וָעֶד:
תהלים קטו וַאֲנַחְנוּ נְבָרֵךְ יָהּ מֵעַתָּה וְעַד־עוֹלָם, הַלְלוּיָהּ:

הכנסת ספר תורה

The ארון קודש *is opened. All stand.*
The שליח ציבור *takes the* ספר תורה *and says:*

תהלים קמח יְהַלְלוּ אֶת־שֵׁם יהוה, כִּי־נִשְׂגָּב שְׁמוֹ, לְבַדּוֹ

The קהל *responds:*

הוֹדוֹ עַל־אֶרֶץ וְשָׁמָיִם:
וַיָּרֶם קֶרֶן לְעַמּוֹ
תְּהִלָּה לְכָל־חֲסִידָיו
לִבְנֵי יִשְׂרָאֵל עַם קְרֹבוֹ
הַלְלוּיָהּ:

HILKHOT TEFILLA • הלכות תפילה

יְהַלְלוּ...הודו – *Let them praise... His majesty.* Two strange details: The *ḥazan* here recites the first part of a verse and the congregation responds with the other part when the custom is generally not to divide verses this way (*Magen Avraham* 51:9). Moreover, the focus of this responsive interaction between the *ḥazan* and the congregation is all about Hashem, as opposed to about the Torah which we are returning to the ark. The reason for these anomalies may be the important principle that we never

While the Torah scroll is being returned to the Ark, say:

מִזְמוֹר לְדָוִד A psalm of David.[B] Render to the LORD, you angelic powers, Ps. 29
render to the LORD glory and might. Render to the LORD the glory due to His name. Bow to the LORD in the beauty of holi-ness. The LORD's voice echoes over the waters; the God of glory thunders; the LORD is over the mighty waters. The LORD's voice in power,[I] the LORD's voice in beauty, the LORD's voice breaks cedars, the LORD shatters the cedars of Lebanon. He makes Lebanon skip like a calf, Sirion like a young wild ox. The LORD's voice cleaves flames of fire. The LORD's voice makes the desert quake, the LORD shakes the desert of Kadesh. The LORD's voice makes hinds calve and strips the forests bare, and in His temple all say: "Glory!" The LORD sat enthroned at the Flood, the LORD sits enthroned as King for ever. The LORD will give strength to His people; the LORD will bless His people with peace.

As the Torah scroll is placed into the Ark, all say:

וּבְנֻחֹה יֹאמַר When the Ark came to rest, Moses would say: "Return, O Num. 10
LORD, to the myriad thousands of Israel." Advance, LORD, to Your resting Ps. 132
place, You and Your mighty Ark. Your priests are clothed in righteousness, and Your devoted ones sing in joy. For the sake of Your servant David,
do not reject Your anointed one. For I give you good instruction; do not Prov. 4
forsake My Torah. It is a tree of life to those who grasp it, and those who Prov. 3
uphold it are happy. Its ways are ways of pleasantness, and all its paths
are peace. ▸ Turn us back, O LORD, to You, and we will return. Renew Lam. 5
our days as of old.

The Ark is closed.

IYUN TEFILLA · עיון תפילה

קוֹל־יהוה בַּכֹּחַ – *The LORD's voice in power.* The first of the Ten Commandments is "I am the LORD your God." The word "your" is written in the singular, not in the plural as one would expect. From here the midrash learns that each individual heard this commandment in his or her own way. It is similar to the manna which fell from heaven, which had the unique property that its taste conformed to the wishes of each person, so too this commandment was understood and experienced differently by each person. That is why David said "Hashem's voice was heard with power/ability" rather than "with His power," for it is in the power of each person individually to hear the voice of God in his or her own way (*Yalkut Shimoni, Yitro* 286).

While the ספר תורה *is being returned to the* ארון קודש*, say:*

תהלים כט
מִזְמוֹר לְדָוִד, הָבוּ לַיהוה בְּנֵי אֵלִים, הָבוּ לַיהוה כָּבוֹד וָעֹז: הָבוּ לַיהוה כְּבוֹד שְׁמוֹ, הִשְׁתַּחֲווּ לַיהוה בְּהַדְרַת־קֹדֶשׁ: קוֹל יהוה עַל־הַמָּיִם, אֵל־הַכָּבוֹד הִרְעִים, יהוה עַל־מַיִם רַבִּים: קוֹל־יהוה בַּכֹּחַ, קוֹל יהוה בֶּהָדָר: קוֹל יהוה שֹׁבֵר אֲרָזִים, וַיְשַׁבֵּר יהוה אֶת־אַרְזֵי הַלְּבָנוֹן: וַיַּרְקִידֵם כְּמוֹ־עֵגֶל, לְבָנוֹן וְשִׂרְיוֹן כְּמוֹ בֶן־רְאֵמִים: קוֹל־יהוה חֹצֵב לַהֲבוֹת אֵשׁ: קוֹל יהוה יָחִיל מִדְבָּר, יָחִיל יהוה מִדְבַּר קָדֵשׁ: קוֹל יהוה יְחוֹלֵל אַיָּלוֹת וַיֶּחֱשֹׂף יְעָרוֹת, וּבְהֵיכָלוֹ, כֻּלּוֹ אֹמֵר כָּבוֹד: יהוה לַמַּבּוּל יָשָׁב, וַיֵּשֶׁב יהוה מֶלֶךְ לְעוֹלָם: יהוה עֹז לְעַמּוֹ יִתֵּן, יהוה יְבָרֵךְ אֶת־עַמּוֹ בַשָּׁלוֹם:

As the ספר תורה *is placed into the* ארון קודש*, all say:*

במדבר י, תהלים קלב
וּבְנֻחֹה יֹאמַר, שׁוּבָה יהוה רִבְבוֹת אַלְפֵי יִשְׂרָאֵל: קוּמָה יהוה
לִמְנוּחָתֶךָ, אַתָּה וַאֲרוֹן עֻזֶּךָ: כֹּהֲנֶיךָ יִלְבְּשׁוּ־צֶדֶק, וַחֲסִידֶיךָ יְרַנֵּנוּ:
משלי ד
בַּעֲבוּר דָּוִד עַבְדֶּךָ אַל־תָּשֵׁב פְּנֵי מְשִׁיחֶךָ: כִּי לֶקַח טוֹב נָתַתִּי
משלי ג
לָכֶם, תּוֹרָתִי אַל־תַּעֲזֹבוּ: עֵץ־חַיִּים הִיא לַמַּחֲזִיקִים בָּהּ, וְתֹמְכֶיהָ
איכה ה
מְאֻשָּׁר: דְּרָכֶיהָ דַרְכֵי־נֹעַם וְכָל־נְתִיבֹתֶיהָ שָׁלוֹם: ‹ הֲשִׁיבֵנוּ יהוה
אֵלֶיךָ וְנָשׁוּבָה, חַדֵּשׁ יָמֵינוּ כְּקֶדֶם:

The ארון קודש *is closed.*

BIUR TEFILLA • ביאור תפילה

מִזְמוֹר לְדָוִד – *A psalm of David.* The psalm is traditionally associated with the giving of the Torah (*Zevaḥim* 116a), perhaps because of its repeated mention of the "voice" of Hashem which was heard at Sinai (HaManhig). The word is mentioned seven times, a number clearly related to Shabbat which objectifies the number of completion, the seventh day of the week and, as mentioned, the day on which according to one tradition the Torah was given. See commentary on this psalm in Kabbalat Shabbat page 413.

HALF KADDISH

Leader: יִתְגַּדַּל Magnified and sanctified
may His great name be,
in the world He created by His will.
May He establish His kingdom
in your lifetime and in your days,
and in the lifetime of all the house of Israel,
swiftly and soon –
and say: Amen.

All: May His great name be blessed
for ever and all time.

Leader: Blessed and praised, glorified and exalted,
raised and honored, uplifted and lauded
be the name of the Holy One,
blessed be He,
beyond any blessing, song,
praise and consolation
uttered in the world –
and say: Amen.

---

took on even greater importance. While animal sacrifices can sometimes feel at odds with contemporary sensibilities (and this from a culture whose overindulgence and waste of food can be an embarrassment to the rest of the world), the world and all of its resources were put on earth by God for man's positive use, as a way of enhancing the world through his own development. And it is God Himself who decreed that the very limited and prescribed use of sacrifices was a way for man and God to bridge the gap between them. The Hebrew word for sacrifice, *korban*, is related to the Hebrew word *karov*, meaning close or proximity. As sacrifices force us to confront the end of a life, finitude, they offer us the possibility of getting closer to the Infinite.

For a general introduction to the Amida, see "Introduction to the Amida" on page 134 in Weekday Shaḥarit. For an overview of the structure of the Amida and further commentary, see page 606 in Shaḥarit.

חצי קדיש

ש״ץ: יִתְגַּדַּל וְיִתְקַדַּשׁ שְׁמֵהּ רַבָּא (קהל: אָמֵן)
בְּעָלְמָא דִּי בְרָא כִרְעוּתֵהּ
וְיַמְלִיךְ מַלְכוּתֵהּ
בְּחַיֵּיכוֹן וּבְיוֹמֵיכוֹן וּבְחַיֵּי דְכָל בֵּית יִשְׂרָאֵל
בַּעֲגָלָא וּבִזְמַן קָרִיב
וְאִמְרוּ אָמֵן. (קהל: אָמֵן)

קהל וש״ץ: יְהֵא שְׁמֵהּ רַבָּא מְבָרַךְ לְעָלַם וּלְעָלְמֵי עָלְמַיָּא.

ש״ץ: יִתְבָּרַךְ וְיִשְׁתַּבַּח וְיִתְפָּאַר וְיִתְרוֹמַם וְיִתְנַשֵּׂא
וְיִתְהַדָּר וְיִתְעַלֶּה וְיִתְהַלָּל
שְׁמֵהּ דְּקֻדְשָׁא בְּרִיךְ הוּא (קהל: בְּרִיךְ הוּא)
לְעֵלָּא מִן כָּל בִּרְכָתָא
וְשִׁירָתָא, תֻּשְׁבְּחָתָא וְנֶחֱמָתָא
דַּאֲמִירָן בְּעָלְמָא
וְאִמְרוּ אָמֵן. (קהל: אָמֵן)

INTRODUCTION TO MUSAF

The number of prayer services generally parallels the daily sacrifices that took place in the *Beit HaMikdash*, there being one for each of the three periods of the day, evening, morning and afternoon (*Berakhot* 26b). On Shabbat and Holy Days, there was another sacrificial service which took place in honor of the day. It was, if you will, an additional service, and hence the name of this prayer, called *Musaf* or addition. Whereas the other prayer services reflect different themes and moods of the day, this one takes as its primary motif the sacrifices themselves. When the *Beit HaMikdash* was destroyed, then the words of the prophet *Hoshea* (14:3), "Instead of bulls we will pay the offering of our lips"

Musaf for Shabbat

THE AMIDA

The Amida until "in former years" on page 704, is said standing with feet together. The Amida is said silently, following the precedent of Hannah when she prayed for a child (1 Sam. 1:13). If there is a minyan, it is repeated aloud by the Leader. Take three steps forward, as if formally entering the place of the Divine Presence. At the points indicated by ▾, bend the knees at the first word, bow at the second, and stand straight before saying God's name.

When I proclaim the LORD's name, give glory to our God. *Deut. 32*
O LORD, open my lips, so that my mouth may declare Your praise. *Ps. 51*

PATRIARCHS

▾Blessed are You, LORD our God and God of our fathers,
God of Abraham, God of Isaac and God of Jacob;
the great, mighty and awesome God, God Most High,
who bestows acts of loving-kindness and creates all,
who remembers the loving-kindness of the fathers
and will bring a Redeemer to their children's children
for the sake of His name, in love.
King, Helper, Savior, Shield:
▾Blessed are You, LORD,
Shield of Abraham.

---

was characterized by the spiritual and physical journeys and travails he endured. We invoke the example of each of them, even as we also say beforehand "our God," for our encounter this morning needs to reflect our own personality and relationship with Him as well as those of our ancestors.

What is your relationship with Hashem today? Which of the Patriarchs does it most resemble?

מָגֵן אַבְרָהָם – *Shield of Abraham.* Why is Avraham singled out from all of the patriarchs we mentioned above? Perhaps because his attribute of loving-kindness is so important. It is through the attribute of kindness that we are able to make room for others and to get in touch with our own ability to be more selfless and to withstand the challenges that life throws our way. Research shows that people who give are happier.

How can you better internalize the values of Avraham?

מוסף לשבת

עמידה

The עמידה *until* קַדְמֹנִיּוֹת *on page 705, is said standing with feet together. The* עמידה *is said silently, following the precedent of Hannah when she prayed for a child (*שמואל א׳ א, יג*). If there is a* מנין*, it is repeated aloud by the* שליח ציבור*. Take three steps forward, as if formally entering the place of the Divine Presence. At the points indicated by* ▾*, bend the knees at the first word, bow at the second, and stand straight before saying God's name.*

כִּי שֵׁם יהוה אֶקְרָא, הָבוּ גֹדֶל לֵאלֹהֵינוּ: דברים לב

אֲדֹנָי, שְׂפָתַי תִּפְתָּח, וּפִי יַגִּיד תְּהִלָּתֶךָ: תהלים נא

אבות

▾בָּרוּךְ אַתָּה יהוה, אֱלֹהֵינוּ וֵאלֹהֵי אֲבוֹתֵינוּ
אֱלֹהֵי אַבְרָהָם, אֱלֹהֵי יִצְחָק, וֵאלֹהֵי יַעֲקֹב
הָאֵל הַגָּדוֹל הַגִּבּוֹר וְהַנּוֹרָא, אֵל עֶלְיוֹן
גּוֹמֵל חֲסָדִים טוֹבִים, וְקוֹנֵה הַכֹּל
וְזוֹכֵר חַסְדֵי אָבוֹת
וּמֵבִיא גוֹאֵל לִבְנֵי בְנֵיהֶם לְמַעַן שְׁמוֹ בְּאַהֲבָה.
מֶלֶךְ עוֹזֵר וּמוֹשִׁיעַ וּמָגֵן.
▾בָּרוּךְ אַתָּה יהוה, מָגֵן אַבְרָהָם.

IYUN TEFILLA · עיון תפילה

אֱלֹהֵי אַבְרָהָם, אֱלֹהֵי יִצְחָק, וֵאלֹהֵי יַעֲקֹב – *God of Abraham, God of Isaac and God of Jacob.* Note that it says "God of…" three times instead of just saying once, "God of the Patriarchs." Many suggest that this is because, based on what we know from the biblical narratives about their lives, each of the patriarchs related to God in his own personal way, though the defining characteristics are left to the reader. Avraham, for example, could be said to have expressed his relationship in terms of loving-kindness for others and through a bold spiritual adventurousness; Yitzḥak's life was characterized by the self-sacrifice he displayed at the *Akeida* (Binding of Isaac) and Yaakov's life

DIVINE MIGHT

אַתָּה גִּבּוֹר You are eternally mighty, LORD.
You give life to the dead and have great power to save.

In Israel: He causes the dew to fall.

He sustains the living with loving-kindness,
and with great compassion revives the dead.
He supports the fallen, heals the sick,
sets captives free,
and keeps His faith with those who sleep in the dust.
Who is like You, Master of might,
and who can compare to You,
O King who brings death and gives life,
and makes salvation grow?
Faithful are You to revive the dead.
Blessed are You, LORD, who revives the dead.

During the Repetition of the Amida, the Leader continues with Kedusha on the next page.

HOLINESS

אַתָּה קָדוֹשׁ You are holy and Your name is holy,
and holy ones praise You daily, Selah!
Blessed are You, LORD,
the holy God.

When saying the Amida silently, continue with "You instituted the Sabbath" on Shabbat and "Long ago You formed" on Rosh Ḥodesh on page 686.

IYUN TEFILLA · עיון תפילה

אַתָּה קָדוֹשׁ – *You are holy.* Rabbi Shimon Schwab wrote that Hashem asks that we separate ourselves from our *yetzer hara* (inclination to act badly) because Hashem is holy (*kadosh*). That is, you can be *kadosh* (holy), because I have placed within you a spark of My own holiness (*kedusha*), namely, the image of God (*tzelem Elohim*) implanted within man, which is the ability of the human being to overpower and separate

This **IYUN TEFILLA** *continues on page 683.*

גבורות

אַתָּה גִּבּוֹר לְעוֹלָם, אֲדֹנָי
מְחַיֵּה מֵתִים אַתָּה, רַב לְהוֹשִׁיעַ

בארץ ישראל בקיץ: מוֹרִיד הַטָּל

מְכַלְכֵּל חַיִּים בְּחֶסֶד, מְחַיֵּה מֵתִים בְּרַחֲמִים רַבִּים
סוֹמֵךְ נוֹפְלִים,ע וְרוֹפֵא חוֹלִים, וּמַתִּיר אֲסוּרִים
וּמְקַיֵּם אֱמוּנָתוֹ לִישֵׁנֵי עָפָר.
מִי כָמְוֹךָ, בַּעַל גְּבוּרוֹת, וּמִי דּוֹמֶה לָּךְ
מֶלֶךְ, מֵמִית וּמְחַיֶּה וּמַצְמִיחַ יְשׁוּעָה.
וְנֶאֱמָן אַתָּה לְהַחֲיוֹת מֵתִים.
בָּרוּךְ אַתָּה יהוה, מְחַיֵּה הַמֵּתִים.

During the חזרת הש״ץ*, the* שליח ציבור *continues with* קדושה *on the next page.*

קדושת השם

אַתָּה קָדוֹשׁע וְשִׁמְךָ קָדוֹשׁ
וּקְדוֹשִׁים בְּכָל יוֹם יְהַלְלוּךָ סֶּלָה.
בָּרוּךְ אַתָּה יהוה, הָאֵל הַקָּדוֹשׁ.

When saying the עמידה *silently, continue with*
תִּכַּנְתָּ שַׁבָּת *on* שבת *and* אַתָּה יָצַרְתָּ *on* ראש חודש *on page 687.*

IYUN TEFILLA • עיון תפילה

סוֹמֵךְ נוֹפְלִים – *He supports the fallen.* Rabbi Avraham Weinberg, a leader of the Hasidim of Slonim, noted that the phrase "who raises those who fall" is written in the present tense and not in the past tense. From here one learns that no matter how many times you may have stumbled or fallen, Hashem is still there every day, in the present, to support you and make sure that you can get up again. Every day brings with it new hope for a fresh beginning.

KEDUSHA[B]

During the Leader's Repetition, the following is said standing with feet together, rising on the toes at the words indicated by ▲.

Cong. then Leader: נַעֲרִיצְךָ We will revere and sanctify You[I]
with the words uttered by the holy Seraphim
who sanctify Your name in the Sanctuary;
as is written by Your prophet:
"They call out to one another, saying: *Is. 6*

Cong. then Leader: ▲Holy, ▲holy, ▲holy is the LORD of hosts;
the whole world is filled with His glory."
His glory fills the universe.[I]
His ministering angels ask each other,
"Where is the place of His glory?"
Those facing them reply "Blessed –

ANI TEFILLA • אני תפילה

As much as we here mimic the angels who sanctify the name of God on high, we must never forget that our goal is to sanctify His name here on earth (Ḥafetz Ḥayyim).

IYUN TEFILLA • עיון תפילה

נַעֲרִיצְךָ וְנַקְדִּישְׁךָ – *We will revere and sanctify You.* To revere God is to have a sense of awe based upon the actions He does. To sanctify Him is based upon His holiness, on that which is hidden from us. The revealed and the hidden can both be sources of faith and inspiration (*Dover Shalom*). In the birth of a baby, for example, or the sprouting of a flower are revealed both the obvious birth and hidden mystery of life.

...כְּבוֹדוֹ מָלֵא עוֹלָם – *His glory fills the universe.* His glory fills the universe, and yet we ask one another where is His place of glory and then we respond His glory is to be found in His place. What to make of this confusing search? One answer is that in the end God cannot really be "found" for He is beyond the limits of our understanding. At the same time, one can find traces of His presence everywhere, if one is only willing to look. Counterintuitively, then, His presence at those moments points to His absence.

קדושה[ב]

During the חזרת הש״ץ, the following is said standing with feet together, rising on the toes at the words indicated by ^.

קהל then ש״ץ: נַעֲרִיצְךָ וְנַקְדִּישְׁךָ[ע] כְּסוֹד שִׂיחַ שַׂרְפֵי קֹדֶשׁ
הַמַּקְדִּישִׁים שִׁמְךָ בַּקֹּדֶשׁ
כַּכָּתוּב עַל יַד נְבִיאֶךָ:
וְקָרָא זֶה אֶל־זֶה וְאָמַר ישעיה ו

קהל then ש״ץ: ^קָדוֹשׁ, ^קָדוֹשׁ, ^קָדוֹשׁ, יהוה צְבָאוֹת
מְלֹא כָל הָאָרֶץ כְּבוֹדוֹ:
כְּבוֹדוֹ מָלֵא עוֹלָם[ע]
מְשָׁרְתָיו שׁוֹאֲלִים זֶה לָזֶה
אַיֵּה מְקוֹם כְּבוֹדוֹ
לְעֻמָּתָם בָּרוּךְ יֹאמֵרוּ

BIUR TEFILLA · ביאור תפילה

קדושה – *KEDUSHA*. This *Kedusha* is referred to as *Kedusha Rabba* or in the language of the Zohar *Kedusha Ila'a* (the High *Kedusha*). While in the other versions (e.g. in *Birkhot Keriat Shema*) we mimic what the angels say and thereby we strive to be like the angels, as it were, here we sing the *kedusha* together with them. For the line of *Shema* is described as being Israel's own *kedusha* (Ḥullin 91b). The midrashic source for this particular version of the *Kedusha* describes the angels surrounding God's throne, responsively answering one another (*Pirkei deRabbi Eliezer* 4) and we now imagine that dialogue with them.

himself from his drives and negative inclinations (*yetzer hara*). Just as the Holy One, Blessed be He, (*HaKadosh Barukh Hu*) is holy and not bound by His nature, He has imbued the human being with a similar power of holiness: that of being able to transcend his own urges and inclinations, and separate himself from them.

What inclination can you try to overcome just once today?

The Ramban says that we can become holy by living a life of balance. How can you make your life a little more balanced today?

Cong. then Leader: ▲"Blessed is the LORD's glory from His place." *Ezek. 3*
From His place may He turn with compassion
and be gracious to the people who proclaim the unity
of His name, morning and evening, every day, continually,
twice each day reciting in love the Shema:

Cong. then Leader: "Listen, Israel, the LORD is our God, the LORD is One." *Deut. 6*
He is our God, He is our Father, He is our King,
He is our Savior – and He, in His compassion,
will let us hear a second time in the presence of all that lives,
His promise to be "Your God." *Num. 15*
"I am the LORD your God."

Leader: And in Your holy Writings it is written:

Cong. then Leader: ▲"The LORD shall reign for ever. He is your God, Zion, *Ps. 146*
from generation to generation, Halleluya!"

Leader: From generation to generation
we will declare Your greatness,
and we will proclaim Your holiness for evermore.
Your praise, our God, shall not leave our mouth forever,
for You, God, are a great and holy King.
Blessed are You, LORD, the holy God.

The Leader continues on the next page with "You instituted the Sabbath" on Shabbat and "Long ago You formed" on Rosh Ḥodesh.

---

recited in the *Musaf* service and as a testament to what belief and commitment can bring to a community (Abudarham, *Levush* 421).

אֲנִי יהוה אֱלֹהֵיכֶם – *I am the LORD your God.* I will be with you in your times of distress (*Pirkei deRabbi Eliezer*).

ANI TEFILLA • אני תפילה

A student of Rav Aaron of Karlin complained that he had not reached the level of spirituality that he really wanted to. "What can I do?" the Rabbi asked. "I have tried but have thus far been unable to find the key that will help you unlock your heart." "The key?!" cried the student. "Who needs a key? Use an axe to open my heart if you have to!" "No need," the Rabbi replied. "Your heart has just opened."

קהל then ש״ץ: ׳בָּרוּךְ כְּבוֹד־יהוה מִמְּקוֹמוֹ: יחזקאל ג

מִמְּקוֹמוֹ הוּא יִפֶן בְּרַחֲמִים וְיָחֹן עַם הַמְיַחֲדִים שְׁמוֹ
עֶרֶב וָבֹקֶר בְּכָל יוֹם תָּמִיד
פַּעֲמַיִם בְּאַהֲבָה שְׁמַע אוֹמְרִים

קהל then ש״ץ: שְׁמַע יִשְׂרָאֵל, יהוה אֱלֹהֵינוּ, יהוה אֶחָד: דברים ו
הוּא אֱלֹהֵינוּ, הוּא אָבִינוּ, הוּא מַלְכֵּנוּ, הוּא מוֹשִׁיעֵנוּ
וְהוּא יַשְׁמִיעֵנוּ בְּרַחֲמָיו שֵׁנִית לְעֵינֵי כָּל חָי
לִהְיוֹת לָכֶם לֵאלֹהִים במדבר טו
אֲנִי יהוה אֱלֹהֵיכֶם:

ש״ץ: וּבְדִבְרֵי קָדְשְׁךָ כָּתוּב לֵאמֹר

קהל then ש״ץ: ׳יִמְלֹךְ יהוה לְעוֹלָם, אֱלֹהַיִךְ צִיּוֹן לְדֹר וָדֹר, הַלְלוּיָהּ: תהלים קמו

ש״ץ: לְדוֹר וָדוֹר נַגִּיד גָּדְלֶךָ
וּלְנֵצַח נְצָחִים קְדֻשָּׁתְךָ נַקְדִּישׁ
וְשִׁבְחֲךָ אֱלֹהֵינוּ מִפִּינוּ לֹא יָמוּשׁ לְעוֹלָם וָעֶד
כִּי אֵל מֶלֶךְ גָּדוֹל וְקָדוֹשׁ אָתָּה.
בָּרוּךְ אַתָּה יהוה, הָאֵל הַקָּדוֹשׁ.

The שליח ציבור *continues on the next page with* תִּכַּנְתָּ שַׁבָּת *on* שבת *and* אַתָּה יָצַרְתָּ *on* ראש חודש.

BIUR TEFILLA · ביאור תפילה

שְׁמַע יִשְׂרָאֵל... אֲנִי יהוה אֱלֹהֵיכֶם – *Listen, Israel... I am the Lord your God.* It is interesting to note that this section begins and ends with the first words and the last words of *Kriat Shema*. There is a tradition from at least the Geonic period that the passage was written in a time of persecution when the recitation of *Kriat Shema* was forbidden and the community surreptitiously inserted a responsive reading of the first and last lines here in order not to give up their statement of belief. The edict was miraculously rescinded as a result but it was kept here as a reminder of the centrality of *Shema* even though it is not

On Shabbat Rosh Ḥodesh say "Long ago You formed" below the line.

HOLINESS OF THE DAY

תִּכַּנְתָּ שַׁבָּת You instituted the Sabbath, You favored its offerings.
You commanded its specific laws
along with the order of its libations.
Those who delight in it inherit eternal glory,

Continue on the top of the next page.

On Shabbat Rosh Ḥodesh:

אַתָּה יָצַרְתָּ Long ago You formed Your world,
completing Your work on the seventh day.
You loved us. You favored us, raising us above all languages.
You made us holy through Your commandments,
brought us near, O our King, to Your service,
and called us by Your great and holy name.

Continue below the line on the next page.

IYUN TEFILLA • עיון תפילה

מְעַנְּגֶיהָ – *Those who delight in it.* Rabbi Yehuda said in Rav's name: "He who delights in the Sabbath is granted his heart's desires, for it is said, 'Delight yourself also in Hashem; And He will give you the desires of your heart' (*Tehillim* 37:3). Now, I do not know what this 'delight' refers to; but when it is said, 'and you shall call the Sabbath a delight" (*Yeshayahu* 58:13), you must say that it refers to the delight of the Sabbath" (*Shabbat* 118b). **What one thing could you do today to make Shabbat more delightful?**

HILKHOT TEFILLA • הלכות תפילה

אַתָּה יָצַרְתָּ עוֹלָמְךָ –*You formed Your world.* Whenever Rosh Ḥodesh (the beginning of a new Hebrew month) occurs on Shabbat, the text of the *Musaf* prayer needs to be changed to accommodate the extra themes of that day. This text, then, replaces the middle blessing that is traditionally said every Shabbat, with each day, as it were, making its own contribution to the content.

IYUN TEFILLA • עיון תפילה

אַתָּה יָצַרְתָּ עוֹלָמְךָ מִקֶּדֶם – *Long ago You formed Your world.* The word *mi-kedem*, long ago, can also be translated more narrowly as in primordial time, literally before the world existed. A midrash (*Bereshit Rabba* 1:9) relates that already in the first century, a philosopher came to Rabban Gamliel to suggest that God had help in the creation of the world from the sources of nature such as the wind and water. This is the ancient version of the debate about the origins of matter and whether it predates God's existence. The prayer here states at the outset that God was the Creator, no matter what science ultimately tells us about how old the universe is or whence derives its most basic elements.

On שבת ראש חודש *say* אַתָּה יָצַרְתָּ *below the line.*

קדושת היום

תִּכַּנְתָּ שַׁבָּת,ב רָצִיתָ קָרְבְּנוֹתֶיהָ
צִוִּיתָ פֵּרוּשֶׁיהָ עִם סִדּוּרֵי נְסָכֶיהָ
מְעַנְּגֶיהָבע לְעוֹלָם כָּבוֹד יִנְחָלוּ

Continue on the top of the next page.

בשבת ראש חודש:

אַתָּה יָצַרְתָּ עוֹלָמְךָה מִקֶּדֶם,ע כִּלִּיתָ מְלַאכְתְּךָ בַּיּוֹם הַשְּׁבִיעִי
אָהַבְתָּ אוֹתָנוּ וְרָצִיתָ בָּנוּ, וְרוֹמַמְתָּנוּ מִכָּל הַלְּשׁוֹנוֹת
וְקִדַּשְׁתָּנוּ בְּמִצְוֹתֶיךָ, וְקֵרַבְתָּנוּ מַלְכֵּנוּ לַעֲבוֹדָתֶךָ
וְשִׁמְךָ הַגָּדוֹל וְהַקָּדוֹשׁ עָלֵינוּ קָרָאתָ.

Continue below the line on the next page.

BIUR TEFILLA • ביאור תפילה

תִּכַּנְתָּ שַׁבָּת... – *You instituted the Sabbath.* Each of the following words begins with a different letter of the Hebrew alphabet but while we have seen such acrostics in the siddur before, this is the only instance in which it is arranged in reverse alphabetical order. Some might suggest that it is a fancy literary device. Others suggest that it has mystical significance: this reverse acrostic is known as **תשר״ק** because these are the last four letters of the *Alef-beit* in reverse order but it also forms a word which means to whistle as in *Zekharia* 10:8 "I will whistle and gather them because I will have redeemed them," thus making this whole paragraph an allusion to the ultimate redemption (*Tur* 286). Another, more philosophical reason, suggests that the form is there to convey that the world was created by Hashem *ex nihilo,* out of absolutely nothing, i.e., contrary to the laws of nature which require that everything be created out of some pre-existing matter. In order to stress this reversal of the law of nature, the wording of the paragraph was reversed (Yaavetz). Regardless of the meaning you decide to bring to it, allow the form to influence your perception of the content.

מְעַנְּגֶיהָ – *Those who delight in it.* "*Oneg*" is the word used to describe the enjoyment of Shabbat including the festive meals which are considered an obligatory part of the day. The prayer thus seems to equate the joy of the sacrifices of the day with the joy of the meals that we are soon to enjoy when the service is shortly over.

מְעַנְּגֶיהָ – *Those who delight in it.* "Those who delight" refers to those who equate Shabbat not with a sense of loss or handicap but with actual gain and true delight (Rabbi S. R. Hirsch).

For you today, is Shabbat an intrusion or an infusion?

those who relish it merit life,[1]
and those who love its teachings have chosen greatness.[B]
Even before Sinai they were commanded about it.
Then You, LORD our God, commanded us to offer on it
the additional offering of the Sabbath in the proper way.

יְהִי רָצוֹן May it be Your will, LORD our God
and God of our ancestors,
to lead us back in joy to our land and to plant us within our borders.
There we will prepare for You our obligatory offerings:
the regular daily offerings in their order,
and the additional offerings according to their laws.

Continue on the top of the next page.

You also gave us in love, LORD our God,
Sabbaths for rest and New Moons for atonement.[1]
But because we and our ancestors sinned against You,
our city was laid waste, our Sanctuary made desolate,
our splendor exiled, and the glory gone from our House of life.
We can no longer fulfill our obligations in Your chosen House,
the great and holy Temple called by Your name,
because of the hand that was stretched out against Your Sanctuary.

May it be Your will, LORD our God and God of our ancestors,
to lead us back in joy to our land, and to plant us within our borders.
There we will prepare for You our obligatory offerings:
the regular daily offerings in their order,
and the additional offerings according to their laws.

Continue below the line on the next page.

IYUN TEFILLA • עיון תפילה

וְרָאשֵׁי חֳדָשִׁים לְכַפָּרָה – *New Moons for atonement.* The identification of the new moon (and the new month) has always held symbolic significance in Judaism. The moon derives its light not by its own merit but through the sun, the source of light. So, too, the Jewish people gets its light from God, not because it is inherently better than any other nation. The waxing and waning of the moon, from its shining bright in its fullness, to its immersion in complete darkness, are often understood in terms of the changing fortunes of the Jewish people and its inconsistent ability to accurately reflect the light of its Maker. The reappearance of the moon is thus a cause for celebration, a period of collective atonement, or at-one-ment with the One who created the world, the moon and the Shabbat.

Use this *Rosh Ḥodesh* to be at one.

טוֹעֲמֶיהָ חַיִּים זָכוּ, וְגַם הָאוֹהֲבִים דְּבָרֶיהָ גְּדֻלָּה בָּחָרוּ.
אָז מִסִּינַי נִצְטַוּוּ עָלֶיהָ
וַתְּצַוֵּנוּ יהוה אֱלֹהֵינוּ לְהַקְרִיב בָּהּ קָרְבַּן מוּסַף שַׁבָּת כָּרָאוּי.
יְהִי רָצוֹן מִלְּפָנֶיךָ, יהוה אֱלֹהֵינוּ וֵאלֹהֵי אֲבוֹתֵינוּ
שֶׁתַּעֲלֵנוּ בְשִׂמְחָה לְאַרְצֵנוּ וְתִטָּעֵנוּ בִּגְבוּלֵנוּ
וְשָׁם נַעֲשֶׂה לְפָנֶיךָ אֶת קָרְבְּנוֹת חוֹבוֹתֵינוּ
תְּמִידִים כְּסִדְרָם וּמוּסָפִים כְּהִלְכָתָם.

Continue on the top of the next page.

וַתִּתֶּן לָנוּ יהוה אֱלֹהֵינוּ בְּאַהֲבָה, שַׁבָּתוֹת לִמְנוּחָה וְרָאשֵׁי חֳדָשִׁים לְכַפָּרָה.
וּלְפִי שֶׁחָטָאנוּ לְפָנֶיךָ אֲנַחְנוּ וַאֲבוֹתֵינוּ
חָרְבָה עִירֵנוּ, וְשָׁמֵם בֵּית מִקְדָּשֵׁנוּ, וְגָלָה יְקָרֵנוּ, וְנִטַּל כָּבוֹד מִבֵּית חַיֵּינוּ
וְאֵין אֲנַחְנוּ יְכוֹלִים לַעֲשׂוֹת חוֹבוֹתֵינוּ בְּבֵית בְּחִירָתֶךָ
בַּבַּיִת הַגָּדוֹל וְהַקָּדוֹשׁ שֶׁנִּקְרָא שִׁמְךָ עָלָיו, מִפְּנֵי הַיָּד שֶׁנִּשְׁתַּלְּחָה בְּמִקְדָּשֶׁךָ.
יְהִי רָצוֹן מִלְּפָנֶיךָ, יהוה אֱלֹהֵינוּ וֵאלֹהֵי אֲבוֹתֵינוּ
שֶׁתַּעֲלֵנוּ בְשִׂמְחָה לְאַרְצֵנוּ וְתִטָּעֵנוּ בִּגְבוּלֵנוּ
וְשָׁם נַעֲשֶׂה לְפָנֶיךָ אֶת קָרְבְּנוֹת חוֹבוֹתֵינוּ
תְּמִידִים כְּסִדְרָם וּמוּסָפִים כְּהִלְכָתָם.

Continue below the line on the next page.

BIUR TEFILLA • ביאור תפילה

וְגַם הָאוֹהֲבִים דְּבָרֶיהָ גְּדֻלָּה בָּחָרוּ – *And those who love its teachings have chosen greatness.* The word *devareha* can also allude to speech, in which case the meaning would be those who love the speech of Shabbat, i.e., that which is permitted to be spoken about on Shabbat (Vilna Gaon). Our desire to protect the atmosphere of Shabbat is so great, our passion to protect its specialness is so intense, that we avoid speaking on Shabbat of "mundane" matters that occupy us during the week. Hence the avoidance of talk about business or other topics that may detract from the spiritual.

What things can you avoid talking about today?

IYUN TEFILLA • עיון תפילה

טוֹעֲמֶיהָ חַיִּים זָכוּ – *Those who relish it merit life.* The word for "relish" can also mean "taste." From here there developed a tradition that it was a "meritorious" act to taste the Shabbat food on Friday afternoon (*Maḥzor Vitry*). Alternatively, it is a reference to those who delight in Shabbat merit eternal life. Or, perhaps, it's both – tasting the food in advance gives one a taste of the world to come!

וְאֶת מוּסַף And the additional offering of this Sabbath day
we will prepare and offer before You in love,
in accord with Your will's commandment,
as You wrote for us in Your Torah through Your servant Moses,
by Your own word, as it is said:

"On the Sabbath day, *Num. 28*
make an offering of two lambs a year old, without blemish,
together with two-tenths[B] of an ephah of fine flour
mixed with oil as a meal-offering, and its appropriate libation.[I]
This is the burnt-offering for every Sabbath,[I]
in addition to the regular daily burnt-offering and its libation."

Continue on the top of the next page.

And the additional offerings of this Sabbath day, and of this New Moon day,
we will prepare and offer before You in love,
in accord with Your will's commandment,
as You wrote for us in Your Torah through Your servant Moses,
by Your own word, as it is said:

"On the Sabbath day, make an offering of two lambs a year old, without blemish, together with two-tenths[B] of an ephah of fine flour mixed with oil as a meal-offering, and its appropriate libation.[I] This is the burnt-offering for every Sabbath,[I] in addition to the regular daily burnt-offering and its libation." *Num. 28*

"And on your new moons, present as a burnt-offering to the Lord two young bulls, one ram, and seven yearling lambs without blemish." *Num. 28*

And their meal-offerings and wine-libations as ordained: three-tenths of an ephah for each bull, two-tenths of an ephah for the ram, one-tenth of an ephah for each lamb, wine for the libations, a male goat for atonement, and two regular daily offerings according to their law.

Continue below the line on the next page.

---

significance wherein each offering represents a different facet of our lives. The showbread, for example, which was baked and replaced for each Shabbat, could represent the food we eat, the flour and oil represent our material possessions and the wine libation symbolizes our happiness (Rabbi S.R. Hirsch). **Think about each one of these things (food, possessions, happiness) and the role that they play in your life. How could you elevate each one of them into something more?**

עֹלַת שַׁבַּת בְּשַׁבַּתּוֹ – *The burnt-offering for every Shabbat.* Unlike other days, even holy days, when a sin offering (*korban ḥatat*) was offered, Shabbat is not a day to be marred by a public display of our failings. It's a day to feel whole.
Focus on the positive in your life right now.

וְאֶת מוּסַף יוֹם הַשַּׁבָּת הַזֶּה
נַעֲשֶׂה וְנַקְרִיב לְפָנֶיךָ בְּאַהֲבָה כְּמִצְוַת רְצוֹנֶךָ
כְּמוֹ שֶׁכָּתַבְתָּ עָלֵינוּ בְּתוֹרָתֶךָ, עַל יְדֵי מֹשֶׁה עַבְדֶּךָ מִפִּי כְבוֹדֶךָ
כָּאָמוּר

וּבְיוֹם הַשַּׁבָּת שְׁנֵי־כְבָשִׂים בְּנֵי־שָׁנָה תְּמִימִם — במדבר כח
וּשְׁנֵי עֶשְׂרֹנִים סֹלֶת מִנְחָה בְּלוּלָה בַשֶּׁמֶן וְנִסְכּוֹ:
עֹלַת שַׁבַּת בְּשַׁבַּתּוֹ, עַל־עֹלַת הַתָּמִיד וְנִסְכָּהּ:

Continue on the top of the next page.

וְאֶת מוּסְפֵי יוֹם הַשַּׁבָּת הַזֶּה וְיוֹם רֹאשׁ הַחֹדֶשׁ הַזֶּה
נַעֲשֶׂה וְנַקְרִיב לְפָנֶיךָ בְּאַהֲבָה כְּמִצְוַת רְצוֹנֶךָ
כְּמוֹ שֶׁכָּתַבְתָּ עָלֵינוּ בְּתוֹרָתֶךָ עַל יְדֵי מֹשֶׁה עַבְדֶּךָ מִפִּי כְבוֹדֶךָ, כָּאָמוּר

וּבְיוֹם הַשַּׁבָּת שְׁנֵי־כְבָשִׂים בְּנֵי־שָׁנָה תְּמִימִם, וּשְׁנֵי עֶשְׂרֹנִים סֹלֶת מִנְחָה — במדבר כח
בְּלוּלָה בַשֶּׁמֶן וְנִסְכּוֹ: עֹלַת שַׁבַּת בְּשַׁבַּתּוֹ, עַל־עֹלַת הַתָּמִיד וְנִסְכָּהּ:

וּבְרָאשֵׁי חָדְשֵׁיכֶם תַּקְרִיבוּ עֹלָה לַיהוה, פָּרִים בְּנֵי־בָקָר שְׁנַיִם, וְאַיִל אֶחָד, — במדבר כח
כְּבָשִׂים בְּנֵי־שָׁנָה שִׁבְעָה, תְּמִימִם:

וּמִנְחָתָם וְנִסְכֵּיהֶם כִּמְדֻבָּר, שְׁלֹשָׁה עֶשְׂרֹנִים לַפָּר, וּשְׁנֵי עֶשְׂרֹנִים לָאָיִל, וְעִשָּׂרוֹן לַכֶּבֶשׂ, וְיַיִן כְּנִסְכּוֹ, וְשָׂעִיר לְכַפֵּר, וּשְׁנֵי תְמִידִים כְּהִלְכָתָם.

Continue below the line on the next page.

BIUR TEFILLA • ביאור תפילה

שְׁנֵי־כְבָשִׂים... וּשְׁנֵי עֶשְׂרֹנִים – *two lambs...with two-tenths.* The number two is significant on this day, in particular because of the double portion of manna that fell in the desert on Friday during the time of the Exodus so that no work would have to be done on Shabbat. That is why we have two loaves of bread on the table at each meal. For Shabbat represents a "double measure" of blessing, and that is what the Musaf service portrays and celebrates (Rabbi E. Munk).

What blessings in your life can you focus more on today?

IYUN TEFILLA • עיון תפילה

סֹלֶת מִנְחָה בְּלוּלָה בַשֶּׁמֶן וְנִסְכּוֹ – *Ephah of fine flour mixed with oil as a meal offering, and its appropriate libation.* The sacrifices are deemed by some to have symbolic

יִשְׂמְחוּ Those who keep the Sabbath and call it a delight
shall rejoice in Your kingship.
The people who sanctify the seventh day shall all be satisfied
and take delight in Your goodness,
for You favored the seventh day and declared it holy.
You called it "most desirable of days"
in remembrance of Creation.

אֱלֹהֵינוּ Our God and God of our ancestors, find favor in our rest.
Make us holy through Your commandments
and grant us our share in Your Torah.

Continue on the top of the next page.

Those who keep the Sabbath and call it a delight shall rejoice in Your kingship.
The people who sanctify the seventh day shall all be satisfied
and take delight in Your goodness,
for You favored the seventh day and declared it holy.
You called it "most desirable of days"
in remembrance of Creation.

Our God and God of our ancestors, find favor in our rest,
and on this Sabbath day renew for us the coming month

Continue below the line on the next page.

רְצֵה בִמְנוּחָתֵנוּ – *Find favor in our rest.* We rest because we are tired. We rest because we need a break. Ultimately, however, on this day we rest because God commanded that we do so. Perhaps part of the prayer here is that to the extent that I may be resting for selfish reasons as well, I pray that it ultimately be seen as a fulfillment of His command.

Alternatively, perhaps there is a play on words here, and the Hebrew word for "our rest," *menuḥateinu,* is supposed to echo the word *minḥateinu*, our offerings. Accept our rest as a sacrifice that we offer up to You.

In what ways might your rest today be a sacrifice?

וְתֵן חֶלְקֵנוּ בְּתוֹרָתֶךָ – *And grant us our share in Your Torah.* The gemara (*Nidda* 30b) suggests that when a baby is in the womb it learns the entire Torah and just before birth an angel comes, touches it on the upper lip (hence the indentation) and the baby forgets all that it learned. One could ask, if the child was going to forget everything it learned, then why was it taught all of that to begin with?! One answer might be so that when we ultimately learn about Torah on our own, we find thoughts and ideas that resonate with us. That is the remnant of the Torah that we learned in the womb. Our soul seeks to reclaim our share.

יִשְׂמְחוּ בְמַלְכוּתְךָ[ע] שׁוֹמְרֵי שַׁבָּת וְקוֹרְאֵי עֹנֶג
עַם מְקַדְּשֵׁי שְׁבִיעִי, כֻּלָּם יִשְׂבְּעוּ וְיִתְעַנְּגוּ מִטּוּבֶךָ
וּבַשְּׁבִיעִי רָצִיתָ בּוֹ וְקִדַּשְׁתּוֹ
חֶמְדַּת יָמִים אוֹתוֹ קָרָאתָ, זֵכֶר לְמַעֲשֵׂה בְרֵאשִׁית.

אֱלֹהֵינוּ וֵאלֹהֵי אֲבוֹתֵינוּ,[ע] רְצֵה בִמְנוּחָתֵנוּ[ע]
קַדְּשֵׁנוּ בְּמִצְוֹתֶיךָ וְתֵן חֶלְקֵנוּ בְּתוֹרָתֶךָ[ע]

Continue on the top of the next page.

יִשְׂמְחוּ בְמַלְכוּתְךָ[ע] שׁוֹמְרֵי שַׁבָּת וְקוֹרְאֵי עֹנֶג
עַם מְקַדְּשֵׁי שְׁבִיעִי, כֻּלָּם יִשְׂבְּעוּ וְיִתְעַנְּגוּ מִטּוּבֶךָ
וּבַשְּׁבִיעִי רָצִיתָ בּוֹ וְקִדַּשְׁתּוֹ
חֶמְדַּת יָמִים אוֹתוֹ קָרָאתָ, זֵכֶר לְמַעֲשֵׂה בְרֵאשִׁית.

אֱלֹהֵינוּ וֵאלֹהֵי אֲבוֹתֵינוּ,[ע] רְצֵה בִמְנוּחָתֵנוּ[ע]
וְחַדֵּשׁ עָלֵינוּ בְּיוֹם הַשַּׁבָּת הַזֶּה אֶת הַחֹדֶשׁ הַזֶּה

Continue below the line on the next page.

IYUN TEFILLA • עיון תפילה

יִשְׂמְחוּ בְמַלְכוּתְךָ – *Shall rejoice in your kingship.* People usually associate holy days as being happy, hence the greeting *Ḥag Same'aḥ*. But happiness is a hallmark of Shabbat as well (*Sifri, Bemidbar* 10:10). There is little room for sadness on Shabbat.

Recall that in *Shaḥarit* it spoke about Moshe being happy when we received the gift of Shabbat. As we move further into the day, we hopefully can now speak about our own joy.

אֱלֹהֵינוּ וֵאלֹהֵי אֲבוֹתֵינוּ – *Our God and God of our ancestors.* Whereas during the week, the *Amida* is filled with as many as 19 different requests many of them quite personal, on Shabbat we tend to forgo these kinds of requests in favor of those that are primarily more communal and national. Here, however, in this paragraph that is repeated in every *Amida* we recite on Shabbat, the focus may in fact be more personal. The difference is that they are entirely of a spiritual nature, in keeping with the focus of the day and the expanded capacity of our souls.

What spiritual requests for yourself can you associate with each of these phrases?

Satisfy us with Your goodness,
grant us joy in Your salvation,
and purify our hearts to serve You in truth.[A]
In love and favor, LORD our God,
grant us as our heritage Your holy Sabbath,[I]
so that Israel who sanctify Your name
may find rest on it.
Blessed are You, LORD,
who sanctifies the Sabbath.

Continue with "Find favor" on the next page.

---

for good and blessing, joy and gladness,
deliverance and consolation, sustenance and support,
life and peace, pardon of sin and forgiveness of iniquity
(*From Marḥeshvan to Adar II in a Jewish leap year:* and atonement of transgression).
For You have chosen Your people Israel from all nations;
You have made known to them Your holy Sabbath,
and instituted for them rules for the New Moon.
Blessed are You, LORD,
who sanctifies the Sabbath, Israel and the New Moons.[B]

Continue with "Find favor" on the next page.

ANI TEFILLA • אני תפילה

The rabbi was deathly ill and the inhabitants of the town declared a communal fast and day of prayer for his speedy recovery. A villager came along and made his way to the local bar where he wanted an alcoholic drink. He was told that none was available because of the fast. And so he made his way to the synagogue and prayed: "Master of Universe, please cure the Holy Rabbi so that I may have my drink."

When the rabbi began to recover he said: "The prayer of the villager was more effective than any of yours for he expressed his greatest longing with the greatest intent for my speedy recovery."

How badly do you want what you are praying for?

BIUR TEFILLA • ביאור תפילה

מְקַדֵּשׁ הַשַּׁבָּת וְיִשְׂרָאֵל וְרָאשֵׁי חֳדָשִׁים – *Who sanctifies the Shabbat, Israel and the New Moons.* The Rabbis inform us that the order here is instructive. Hashem Himself sanctified the Shabbat day as evidenced in the verses from *Bereshit* found in Kiddush "And He blessed the seventh day and sanctified it." The Shabbat is a holy day regardless of whether we observe it or not. But the very first commandment in the Torah appears at the time of the Exodus, when we were told to sanctify each new month. In Talmudic times this meant that men came to the central court (Sanhedrin)

This **BIUR TEFILLA** *continues on page 697.*

שַׂבְּעֵנוּ מִטּוּבֶךָ, וְשַׂמְּחֵנוּ בִּישׁוּעָתֶךָ
וְטַהֵר לִבֵּנוּ לְעָבְדְּךָ בֶּאֱמֶת[א]
וְהַנְחִילֵנוּ יהוה אֱלֹהֵינוּ בְּאַהֲבָה וּבְרָצוֹן שַׁבַּת קָדְשֶׁךָ[ע]
וְיָנוּחוּ בוֹ יִשְׂרָאֵל מְקַדְּשֵׁי שְׁמֶךָ.
בָּרוּךְ אַתָּה יהוה, מְקַדֵּשׁ הַשַּׁבָּת.

Continue with רְצֵה *on the next page.*

לְטוֹבָה וְלִבְרָכָה, לְשָׂשׂוֹן וּלְשִׂמְחָה
לִישׁוּעָה וּלְנֶחָמָה, לְפַרְנָסָה וּלְכַלְכָּלָה
לְחַיִּים וּלְשָׁלוֹם, לִמְחִילַת חֵטְא וְלִסְלִיחַת עָוֹן
(*From* מרחשון *to* אדר שני *in a Jewish leap year* וּלְכַפָּרַת פָּשַׁע)
כִּי בְעַמְּךָ יִשְׂרָאֵל בָּחַרְתָּ מִכָּל הָאֻמּוֹת
וְשַׁבַּת קָדְשְׁךָ לָהֶם הוֹדַעְתָּ, וְחֻקֵּי רָאשֵׁי חֳדָשִׁים לָהֶם קָבָעְתָּ.
בָּרוּךְ אַתָּה יהוה, מְקַדֵּשׁ הַשַּׁבָּת וְיִשְׂרָאֵל וְרָאשֵׁי חֳדָשִׁים.[ב]

Continue with רְצֵה *on the next page.*

ANI TEFILLA • אני תפילה

וְטַהֵר לִבֵּנוּ לְעָבְדְּךָ בֶּאֱמֶת – *And purify our hearts to serve You in truth.*

Which aspects of your life do you do by rote? Which ones do you pray you could do with more feeling and more intention "in truth?"

וְטַהֵר לִבֵּנוּ לְעָבְדְּךָ בֶּאֱמֶת – *And purify our hearts to serve You in truth.*

Rav Aharon of Karlin said to someone: You and I both say the same blessing over an apple before we eat it. But do you see that apple tree outside the window? When I see it, I am so overwhelmed by what a miracle from God it is that I just want to erupt in saying the blessing "bori pri ha-etz" (the blessing said before one eats a fruit), yet I cannot because I cannot partake of its fruit from a distance. So you see, I eat in order to say the blessing, but you say the blessing in order to eat.

IYUN TEFILLA • עיון תפילה

וְהַנְחִילֵנוּ... שַׁבַּת קָדְשֶׁךָ – *Grant us as our heritage Your holy Shabbat.* The word is sometimes translated as "inheritance" rather than "heritage."

What, if any, might be the difference? What might be the difference to you with regard to Shabbat?

TEMPLE SERVICE

רְצֵה Find favor, LORD our God,
in Your people Israel and their prayer.
Restore the service to Your most holy House,
and accept in love and favor
the fire-offerings of Israel and their prayer.
May the service of Your people Israel
always find favor with You.
And may our eyes witness
Your return to Zion in compassion.
Blessed are You, LORD,
who restores His Presence to Zion.

רְצֵה – *Find favor.* We are near spent. We have invested ourselves to the extent possible today in the words that we have uttered. Some days are better than others. Today was a little better or a little worse. Nevertheless, it is the best that we could do for now and we hope that Hashem will accept them. Like the sacrifices that are designed to bring one closer, so too we hope that our prayers have brought us closer to Him ...and He to us.

ANI TEFILLA • אני תפילה

Where Joseph-who-honors-the-Sabbaths lived there was a certain gentile who owned much property. Fortunetellers told him, 'Joseph-who-honors-the-Sabbaths will consume all your property. So he went, sold all his property, and bought a precious stone with the proceeds, which he hid in his turban. As he was crossing a bridge the wind blew it off and cast it into the water, [and] a fish swallowed it. Subsequently the fish was hauled up and brought to market on the eve of Shabbat towards sunset. "Who will buy now that it is so late?" cried the fisherman. "Go and take them to Joseph-who-honors-the-Sabbaths," they were told, "as he is accustomed to buy." So they took it to him. He bought it, opened it, found the jewel therein, and sold it for thirteen roomfuls of gold denarii. A certain old man met him [and] said, "He who lends to the Sabbath, the Sabbath repays him." (*Shabbat* 119a)

עבודה

רְצֵה יהוה אֱלֹהֵינוּ בְּעַמְּךָ יִשְׂרָאֵל וּבִתְפִלָּתָם
וְהָשֵׁב אֶת הָעֲבוֹדָה לִדְבִיר בֵּיתֶךָ
וְאִשֵּׁי יִשְׂרָאֵל וּתְפִלָּתָם בְּאַהֲבָה תְקַבֵּל בְּרָצוֹן
וּתְהִי לְרָצוֹן תָּמִיד עֲבוֹדַת יִשְׂרָאֵל עַמֶּךָ.
וְתֶחֱזֶינָה עֵינֵינוּ בְּשׁוּבְךָ לְצִיּוֹן בְּרַחֲמִים.
בָּרוּךְ אַתָּה יהוה, הַמַּחֲזִיר שְׁכִינָתוֹ לְצִיּוֹן.

---

to testify that they saw the first sliver of the moon and only then was the new month declared, independent of the calculation of a calendrical system which already was known in any event. The slaves of Egypt who had no time consciousness, where every day was the same monotonous routine as the day before, were given the gift of being time-aware and having a hand in the establishment of how the days are counted. On this day, then, when Shabbat meets Rosh Ḥodesh, God and we join together to sanctify our respective views of time, one of the most precious commodities we own.

ANI TEFILLA · אני תפילה

On the day following his bar mitzva, Rabbi Binyamin Kaminetsky was summoned to the office of his father, the great Rabbi Yaakov Kaminetsky. "When I came in, I raised my inquiring eyes towards him, but he said nothing. He simply stepped on a bench and took down a small, carefully wrapped package from the bookcase.

"My father took the package in his hand and said to me, 'Today, now that you're an adult, I want to give you the most precious piece of merchandise in the world. But first, I want you to promise me that you will protect it like your own life!'

"My father untied the strings that bound the package, removed the wrapping, and handed me a watch as a gift! In seeing the look on my face, he said: 'My son, know that Rabbi Israel Salanter used to say that time is life. If we lose time, we lose life!'"

How can you master time today? How can you sanctify it?

For further commentary on these final three blessings, see weekday *Shaḥarit* (pages 175–186), *Ma'ariv of Shabbat* (pages 467–470) and *Minḥa* of Shabbat (pages 783–788).

THANKSGIVING

Bow at the first nine words.

▾ *Bow:* We give thanks to You,
for You are *Stand straight*
the LORD our God
and God of our ancestors
for ever and all time.
You are the Rock of our lives,
Shield of our salvation
from generation to generation.
We will thank You and
declare Your praise for our lives,[A]
which are entrusted into Your hand;
for our souls,
which are placed in Your charge;
for Your miracles
which are with us every day;
and for Your wonders[I] and favors
at all times,
evening, morning and midday.
You are good –
for Your compassion never fails.
You are compassionate –
for Your loving-kindnesses never cease.
We have always placed our hope
in You.

During the Leader's Repetition, the congregation says quietly:

▾ *Bow:* We give thanks to You,
for You are *Stand straight*
the LORD our God
and God of our ancestors,
God of all flesh,
who formed us
and formed the universe.
Blessings and thanks
are due to Your great
and holy name
for giving us life
and sustaining us.
May You continue
to give us life
and sustain us;
and may You gather our
exiles to Your holy courts,
to keep Your decrees,
do Your will
and serve You
with a perfect heart,
for it is for us
to give You thanks.
Blessed be God
to whom thanksgiving
is due.

The text alludes to two men who set out on a trading expedition when a thorn got into [the foot of] one of them who began to blaspheme and to revile. After a time, however, when he heard that his friend's ship had sunk into the sea he began to laud and praise. Hence it is written, 'Your anger is turned away, and You comfort me.' This is indeed in line with what R. Elazar stated: What is implied by the Scriptural text (*Tehillim* 72:18), 'Who does wondrous things alone…?' Even the person for whom a miracle is performed is unaware of the miracle (*Nidda* 31a). **What are some of the miracles that could have happened to you today of which you might be unaware?**

הודאה

Bow at the first five words.

▾מוֹדִים אֲנַחְנוּ לָךְ	*During the* חזרת הש״ץ*, the* קהל *says quietly:*
שָׁאַתָּה הוּא	▾ *Bow* מוֹדִים אֲנַחְנוּ לָךְ
יהוה אֱלֹהֵינוּ וֵאלֹהֵי אֲבוֹתֵינוּ	שָׁאַתָּה הוּא *Stand straight*
לְעוֹלָם וָעֶד.	יהוה אֱלֹהֵינוּ וֵאלֹהֵי אֲבוֹתֵינוּ
צוּר חַיֵּינוּ, מָגֵן יִשְׁעֵנוּ	אֱלֹהֵי כָל בָּשָׂר
אַתָּה הוּא לְדוֹר וָדוֹר.	יוֹצְרֵנוּ, יוֹצֵר בְּרֵאשִׁית.
נוֹדֶה לְּךָ וּנְסַפֵּר תְּהִלָּתֶךָ	בְּרָכוֹת וְהוֹדָאוֹת
עַל חַיֵּינוּ[א] הַמְּסוּרִים בְּיָדֶךָ	לְשִׁמְךָ הַגָּדוֹל וְהַקָּדוֹשׁ
וְעַל נִשְׁמוֹתֵינוּ הַפְּקוּדוֹת לָךְ	עַל שֶׁהֶחֱיִיתָנוּ וְקִיַּמְתָּנוּ.
וְעַל נִסֶּיךָ שֶׁבְּכָל יוֹם עִמָּנוּ	כֵּן תְּחַיֵּנוּ וּתְקַיְּמֵנוּ
וְעַל נִפְלְאוֹתֶיךָ[ע] וְטוֹבוֹתֶיךָ	וְתֶאֱסֹף גָּלֻיּוֹתֵינוּ
שֶׁבְּכָל עֵת, עֶרֶב וָבֹקֶר וְצָהֳרָיִם.	לְחַצְרוֹת קָדְשֶׁךָ
הַטּוֹב, כִּי לֹא כָלוּ רַחֲמֶיךָ	לִשְׁמֹר חֻקֶּיךָ
וְהַמְרַחֵם, כִּי לֹא תַמּוּ חֲסָדֶיךָ	וְלַעֲשׂוֹת רְצוֹנֶךָ וּלְעָבְדְּךָ
מֵעוֹלָם קִוִּינוּ לָךְ.	בְּלֵבָב שָׁלֵם
	עַל שֶׁאֲנַחְנוּ מוֹדִים לָךְ.
	בָּרוּךְ אֵל הַהוֹדָאוֹת.

ANI TEFILLA • אני תפילה

עַל חַיֵּינוּ – *For our lives.*
When was the last time you were truly thankful for just being alive?

How might acknowledgment of this change the way you view today's challenges?

IYUN TEFILLA • עיון תפילה

וְעַל נִפְלְאוֹתֶיךָ – *And for Your wonders.* R. Joseph gave the following exposition: What is the purport of the Scriptural text, (*Yeshayahu* 12:1) 'I will give thanks unto You, O Lord; for though You were angry with me, Your anger is turned away, and You comfort me.'

וְעַל כֻּלָּם For all these things
may Your name be blessed and exalted,
our King, continually, for ever and all time.
Let all that lives thank You, Selah!
and praise Your name in truth,
God, our Savior and Help, Selah!
▾Blessed are You, LORD,
whose name is "the Good"
and to whom thanks are due.

The following is said by the Leader during the Repetition of the Amida.
In Israel, if Kohanim bless the congregation, *turn to page 1008.*

Our God and God of our fathers, bless us with the threefold blessing in the Torah, written by the hand of Moses Your servant and pronounced by Aaron and his sons the priests, Your holy people, as it is said:

May the LORD bless you and protect you. *Num. 6*
Cong: May it be Your will.
May the LORD make His face shine on you and be gracious to you.
Cong: May it be Your will.
May the LORD turn His face toward you, and grant you peace.
Cong: May it be Your will.

---

meant to me. I am 83 years old and I am living alone in one room. My friends are all gone, and my family's gone.

I taught for 50 years and yours is the first "thank you" letter I have ever gotten from a student. Sometimes I wonder what I did with my life. I will read and reread your letter until the day I die.'

He was very emotional on the phone. He said, "She is always the one we talk about at every reunion. She was everyone's favorite teacher. We loved her... But no one ever told her..." (Barbara Glantz)

We do not thank enough, not the people around us who do good things for us, nor God who is forever giving us things, especially the smaller things that we take for granted. But we never tell Him. The Jew takes this opportunity every day. Take it now. Think of something that you have otherwise taken for granted in your life and say Modim, "we thank You."

וְעַל כֻּלָּם יִתְבָּרַךְ וְיִתְרוֹמַם שִׁמְךָ מַלְכֵּנוּ תָּמִיד לְעוֹלָם וָעֶד.
וְכֹל הַחַיִּים יוֹדְוּךָ סֶּלָה
וִיהַלְלוּ אֶת שִׁמְךָ בֶּאֱמֶת
הָאֵל יְשׁוּעָתֵנוּ וְעֶזְרָתֵנוּ סֶלָה.
בָּרוּךְ אַתָּה יהוה
הַטּוֹב שִׁמְךָ וּלְךָ נָאֶה לְהוֹדוֹת.

The following is said by the שליח ציבור *during* חורת הש״ץ.
In ארץ ישראל *if* כהנים *say* ברכת כהנים *turn to page 1009.*

אֱלֹהֵינוּ וֵאלֹהֵי אֲבוֹתֵינוּ, בָּרְכֵנוּ בַבְּרָכָה הַמְשֻׁלֶּשֶׁת בַּתּוֹרָה הַכְּתוּבָה עַל יְדֵי מֹשֶׁה עַבְדֶּךָ, הָאֲמוּרָה מִפִּי אַהֲרֹן וּבָנָיו כֹּהֲנִים עַם קְדוֹשֶׁיךָ, כָּאָמוּר

יְבָרֶכְךָ יהוה וְיִשְׁמְרֶךָ: קהל: כֵּן יְהִי רָצוֹן במדבר ו
יָאֵר יהוה פָּנָיו אֵלֶיךָ וִיחֻנֶּךָּ: קהל: כֵּן יְהִי רָצוֹן
יִשָּׂא יהוה פָּנָיו אֵלֶיךָ וְיָשֵׂם לְךָ שָׁלוֹם: קהל: כֵּן יְהִי רָצוֹן

ANI TEFILLA • אני תפילה

"In my speeches and workshops, I sometimes ask my audiences to shut their eyes and think about someone who, at some point in their lives, has rekindled their inner light. It is always a profound experience for everyone as they remember the joy they received from being appreciated by someone when they needed it most.

After one session, a gentleman thanked me for creating a new awareness. He had immediately thought of his eighth grade literature teacher who had really made an impact on his life. He planned to track her down and thank her.

A few months later he called me to say that he had written his teacher. She had gotten his letter and the following week she sent him her response…

'Dear John,

You will never know how much your letter

PEACE

שִׂים שָׁלוֹם Grant peace, goodness[I] and blessing, grace,
loving-kindness and compassion to us
and all Israel Your people.
Bless us, our Father, all as one,
with the light of Your face,
for by the light of Your face You have given us,
Lord our God, the Torah of life and love of kindness,
righteousness, blessing, compassion, life and peace.
May it be good in Your eyes
to bless Your people Israel
at every time, in every hour, with Your peace.
Blessed are You, Lord,
who blesses His people Israel with peace.

The following verse concludes the Leader's Repetition of the Amida. Some also say it here as part of the silent Amida.

May the words of my mouth and the meditation of my heart
find favor before You, Lord, my Rock and Redeemer. *Ps. 19*

אֱלֹהַי My God,[B] *Berakhot 17a*
guard my tongue from evil and my lips from deceitful speech.
To those who curse me, let my soul be silent;
may my soul be to all like the dust.
Open my heart to Your Torah
and let my soul pursue Your commandments.

BIUR TEFILLA • ביאור תפילה

אֱלֹהַי – *My God.* If we began the *Amida* by referring to God as "our God and the God of my fathers… "here we refer to Him as "my God." Hopefully by this point in the services, there is a little more comfort, a little more intimacy, a little more of a personal relationship that we can take with us when we leave.

ברכת שלום

שִׂים שָׁלוֹם טוֹבָה[ע] וּבְרָכָה
חֵן וָחֶסֶד וְרַחֲמִים עָלֵינוּ וְעַל כָּל יִשְׂרָאֵל עַמֶּךָ.
בָּרְכֵנוּ אָבִינוּ כֻּלָּנוּ כְּאֶחָד בְּאוֹר פָּנֶיךָ
כִּי בְאוֹר פָּנֶיךָ נָתַתָּ לָּנוּ, יהוה אֱלֹהֵינוּ
תּוֹרַת חַיִּים וְאַהֲבַת חֶסֶד
וּצְדָקָה וּבְרָכָה וְרַחֲמִים וְחַיִּים וְשָׁלוֹם.
וְטוֹב בְּעֵינֶיךָ לְבָרֵךְ אֶת עַמְּךָ יִשְׂרָאֵל
בְּכָל עֵת וּבְכָל שָׁעָה בִּשְׁלוֹמֶךָ.
בָּרוּךְ אַתָּה יהוה, הַמְבָרֵךְ אֶת עַמּוֹ יִשְׂרָאֵל בַּשָּׁלוֹם.

The following verse concludes the חזרת הש״ץ.
Some also say it here as part of the silent עמידה.

יִהְיוּ לְרָצוֹן אִמְרֵי־פִי וְהֶגְיוֹן לִבִּי לְפָנֶיךָ, יהוה צוּרִי וְגֹאֲלִי: תהלים יט

אֱלֹהַי[ב] ברכות יז.
נְצֹר לְשׁוֹנִי מֵרָע וּשְׂפָתַי מִדַּבֵּר מִרְמָה
וְלִמְקַלְלַי נַפְשִׁי תִדֹּם, וְנַפְשִׁי כֶּעָפָר לַכֹּל תִּהְיֶה.
פְּתַח לִבִּי בְּתוֹרָתֶךָ, וּבְמִצְוֹתֶיךָ תִּרְדֹּף נַפְשִׁי.

IYUN TEFILLA • עיון תפילה

טוֹבָה – *Goodness.* The word *tov* appears in the account of Creation wherein Hashem says that He saw each of the things that He created and said "it was good." What does that mean? One interpretation suggests that it means that it conformed to its purpose, that is, it was ready to fulfill its role in Creation. When we ask for goodness, then, we ask that we too be able to live up to the task for which we were created. True peace comes from being our true selves, the self that Hashem created and wanted us to be (Rabbi David Aaron).

How can you be your true self today?

As for all who plan evil against me,
swiftly thwart their counsel and frustrate their plans.
Act for the sake of Your name;
act for the sake of Your right hand;
act for the sake of Your holiness;
act for the sake of Your Torah.
That Your beloved ones may be delivered, *Ps. 60*
save with Your right hand and answer me.
May the words of my mouth and the meditation of my heart *Ps. 19*
find favor before You, LORD, my Rock and Redeemer.

Bow, take three steps back, then bow, first left, then right, then center, while saying:

May He who makes peace in His high places,
make peace for us and all Israel –
and say: Amen.

יְהִי רָצוֹן May it be Your will, LORD our God and God of our ancestors,
that the Temple be rebuilt speedily in our days,
and grant us a share in Your Torah.
And there we will serve You with reverence,
as in the days of old and as in former years.
Then the offering of Judah and Jerusalem *Mal. 3*
will be pleasing to the LORD as in the days of old and as in former years.

---

that a person who uses speech for petty purposes, for speaking about others for no purpose, is abusing the power that was given to him and, indeed, may even be said to deny his own uniqueness as a human being as opposed to an animal. We thus conclude the *Amida* with a reminder to use our power of speech not to denigrate others but to raise ourselves up, as friends, as servants of Hashem, as members of the human race who aspire to peaceful coexistence.

What will you do when you hear people talking about other people later today?

ANI TEFILLA • אני תפילה

People with great minds talk about ideas. People with average minds talk about events. And people with small minds, talk about other people (Attributed to Eleanor Roosevelt).

וְכָל הַחוֹשְׁבִים עָלַי רָעָה
מְהֵרָה הָפֵר עֲצָתָם וְקַלְקֵל מַחֲשַׁבְתָּם.
עֲשֵׂה לְמַעַן שְׁמֶךָ
עֲשֵׂה לְמַעַן יְמִינֶךָ
עֲשֵׂה לְמַעַן קְדֻשָּׁתֶךָ
עֲשֵׂה לְמַעַן תּוֹרָתֶךָ.

תהלים ס
לְמַעַן יֵחָלְצוּן יְדִידֶיךָ, הוֹשִׁיעָה יְמִינְךָ וַעֲנֵנִי:

תהלים יט
יִהְיוּ לְרָצוֹן אִמְרֵי־פִי וְהֶגְיוֹן לִבִּי לְפָנֶיךָ, יהוה צוּרִי וְגֹאֲלִי:

Bow, take three steps back, then bow, first left, then right, then center, while saying:

עֹשֶׂה שָׁלוֹם בִּמְרוֹמָיו
הוּא יַעֲשֶׂה שָׁלוֹם עָלֵינוּ וְעַל כָּל יִשְׂרָאֵל
וְאִמְרוּ אָמֵן.

יְהִי רָצוֹן מִלְּפָנֶיךָ יהוה אֱלֹהֵינוּ וֵאלֹהֵי אֲבוֹתֵינוּ
שֶׁיִּבָּנֶה בֵּית הַמִּקְדָּשׁ בִּמְהֵרָה בְיָמֵינוּ
וְתֵן חֶלְקֵנוּ בְּתוֹרָתֶךָ
וְשָׁם נַעֲבָדְךָ בְּיִרְאָה כִּימֵי עוֹלָם וּכְשָׁנִים קַדְמֹנִיּוֹת.

מלאכי ג
וְעָרְבָה לַיהוה מִנְחַת יְהוּדָה וִירוּשָׁלָםִ כִּימֵי עוֹלָם וּכְשָׁנִים קַדְמֹנִיּוֹת:

IYUN TEFILLA · עיון תפילה

יִהְיוּ לְרָצוֹן אִמְרֵי־פִי וְהֶגְיוֹן לִבִּי – *May the words of my mouth and the meditation of my heart find favor.* We began the *Amida* by asking that Hashem open our lips and here we ask that those words, both spoken and unspoken, be found worthy. Words are the tools that we use to achieve our highest ideals, to define and live up to our humanity. Man was made in the image of God which is often understood to be related to our intelligence, that which differentiates us from the animals. Communication is the tool that enables us to use that intelligence to its fullest, to ask and answer questions, to describe abstract thoughts, to speak to God. One might say, therefore,

FULL KADDISH

Leader: יִתְגַּדַּל Magnified and sanctified
may His great name be,
in the world He created by His will.
May He establish His kingdom
in your lifetime and in your days,
and in the lifetime of all the house of Israel,
swiftly and soon –
and say: Amen.

All: May His great name be blessed for ever and all time.

Leader: Blessed and praised,
glorified and exalted,
raised and honored,
uplifted and lauded
be the name of the Holy One,
blessed be He,
beyond any blessing,
song, praise and consolation
uttered in the world –
and say: Amen.

May the prayers and pleas of all Israel
be accepted by their Father in heaven –
and say: Amen.

May there be great peace from heaven,
and life for us and all Israel –
and say: Amen.

Bow, take three steps back, as if taking leave of the Divine Presence, then bow, first left, then right, then center, while saying:

May He who makes peace in His high places,
make peace for us and all Israel –
and say: Amen.

קדיש שלם

ש״ץ: יִתְגַּדַּל וְיִתְקַדַּשׁ שְׁמֵהּ רַבָּא (קהל: אָמֵן)
בְּעָלְמָא דִּי בְרָא כִרְעוּתֵהּ
וְיַמְלִיךְ מַלְכוּתֵהּ
בְּחַיֵּיכוֹן וּבְיוֹמֵיכוֹן וּבְחַיֵּי דְכָל בֵּית יִשְׂרָאֵל
בַּעֲגָלָא וּבִזְמַן קָרִיב
וְאִמְרוּ אָמֵן. (קהל: אָמֵן)

קהל וש״ץ: יְהֵא שְׁמֵהּ רַבָּא מְבָרַךְ לְעָלַם וּלְעָלְמֵי עָלְמַיָּא.

ש״ץ: יִתְבָּרַךְ וְיִשְׁתַּבַּח וְיִתְפָּאַר
וְיִתְרוֹמַם וְיִתְנַשֵּׂא וְיִתְהַדָּר וְיִתְעַלֶּה וְיִתְהַלָּל
שְׁמֵהּ דְּקֻדְשָׁא בְּרִיךְ הוּא (קהל: בְּרִיךְ הוּא)
לְעֵלָּא מִן כָּל בִּרְכָתָא וְשִׁירָתָא, תֻּשְׁבְּחָתָא וְנֶחֱמָתָא
דַּאֲמִירָן בְּעָלְמָא
וְאִמְרוּ אָמֵן. (קהל: אָמֵן)

תִּתְקַבַּל צְלוֹתְהוֹן וּבָעוּתְהוֹן דְּכָל יִשְׂרָאֵל
קֳדָם אֲבוּהוֹן דִּי בִשְׁמַיָּא
וְאִמְרוּ אָמֵן. (קהל: אָמֵן)

יְהֵא שְׁלָמָא רַבָּא מִן שְׁמַיָּא
וְחַיִּים, עָלֵינוּ וְעַל כָּל יִשְׂרָאֵל
וְאִמְרוּ אָמֵן. (קהל: אָמֵן)

Bow, take three steps back, as if taking leave of the Divine Presence, then bow, first left, then right, then center, while saying:

עֹשֶׂה שָׁלוֹם בִּמְרוֹמָיו
הוּא יַעֲשֶׂה שָׁלוֹם עָלֵינוּ וְעַל כָּל יִשְׂרָאֵל
וְאִמְרוּ אָמֵן. (קהל: אָמֵן)

אֵין כֵּאלֹהֵינוּ There is none like our God,[B] none like our LORD,
none like our King, none like our Savior.
Who is like our God? Who is like our LORD?
Who is like our King? Who is like our Savior?
We will thank our God, we will thank our LORD,
we will thank our King, we will thank our Savior.
Blessed is our God, blessed is our LORD,
blessed is our King, blessed is our Savior.
You are our God, You are our LORD,
You are our King, You are our Savior.
You are He to whom our ancestors offered the fragrant incense.

פִּטּוּם הַקְּטֹרֶת The incense mixture[B] consisted of balsam, onycha, galbanum[B] and frankincense, each weighing seventy manehs; myrrh, cassia, spikenard and saffron, each *Keritot 6a*

---

stanzas. The first three are an acrostic: the first letter of each Hebrew line spells out the Hebrew word amen (א־מ־ן). The first word in the next stanza is "Blessed" (*barukh*) and the first word in the next stanza is "You" (*ata*). We thus have the repetition of *amen, barukh ata* (Amen, Blessed are You), a kind of affirmation of the entire prayer service until now.

Alternatively, it has been suggested that each one of the names of Hashem that appears here is revealed in the same chronological order in the Torah – *Elohim* (*Bereshit* 1:1), *Adon* (*Bereshit* 15:2), *Melekh* (*Shemot* 15:18), *Moshia* (*Devarim* 33:29). Perhaps, then, the intention is to remind us of an unfolding revelation of our own that we have had this morning, ending in our ability to address Hashem most directly in the second person, *Blessed are You* (*Dover Shalom*).

פִּטּוּם הַקְּטֹרֶת – *The incense mixture.* This passage is actually a portion of the Talmud (*Keritut* 6a; *Yerushalmi Yoma* 4:5) which describes the composition of the incense that burned in the *Beit HaMikdash* every morning and evening on the smaller altar which was located in the sanctuary (*Shemot* 30:7-9). It is hoped that our recitation of the ingredients will act as a substitute for the real thing, just as we found at the very beginning of the service (see page 47).

The purpose of the incense is not known. Among the various rationales offered: as the sacrifice atoned for the body, the intangible scent of the incense atoned for the intangible soul (*Kli Yakar*); the pleasing aroma of the incense was to draw us into having a pleasing association with the awe one has for the Temple and its service, for the connection between one's sense of smell and one's memory is obvious (*Sefer HaḤinukh*); the incense was offered just before the Menora candles were lit, reminding us that our moral actions (= incense) must be more pleasing to God than our intellectual attainments (= lights of the Menora). "In the Jewish conception of life, genius is no license for non-observation of the laws of morality, but on the contrary, the highest degree of morality is made the test for the highest degree of true intelligence…" (Rabbi S. R. Hirsch);

This **BIUR TEFILLA** *continues on page 711.*

אֵין כֵּאלֹהֵינוּ, אֵין כַּאדוֹנֵינוּ, אֵין כְּמַלְכֵּנוּ, אֵין כְּמוֹשִׁיעֵנוּ.
מִי כֵאלֹהֵינוּ, מִי כַאדוֹנֵינוּ, מִי כְמַלְכֵּנוּ, מִי כְמוֹשִׁיעֵנוּ.
נוֹדֶה לֵאלֹהֵינוּ, נוֹדֶה לַאדוֹנֵינוּ, נוֹדֶה לְמַלְכֵּנוּ, נוֹדֶה לְמוֹשִׁיעֵנוּ.
בָּרוּךְ אֱלֹהֵינוּ, בָּרוּךְ אֲדוֹנֵינוּ, בָּרוּךְ מַלְכֵּנוּ, בָּרוּךְ מוֹשִׁיעֵנוּ.
אַתָּה הוּא אֱלֹהֵינוּ, אַתָּה הוּא אֲדוֹנֵינוּ,
אַתָּה הוּא מַלְכֵּנוּ, אַתָּה הוּא מוֹשִׁיעֵנוּ.
אַתָּה הוּא שֶׁהִקְטִירוּ אֲבוֹתֵינוּ לְפָנֶיךָ אֶת קְטֹרֶת הַסַּמִּים.

פִּטּוּם הַקְּטֹרֶת. הַצֳּרִי, וְהַצִּפֹּרֶן, וְהַחֶלְבְּנָה, וְהַלְּבוֹנָה מִשְׁקַל שִׁבְעִים שִׁבְעִים כריתות ו.
מָנֶה, מֹר, וּקְצִיעָה, שִׁבֹּלֶת נֵרְדְּ, וְכַרְכֹּם מִשְׁקַל שִׁשָּׁה עָשָׂר שִׁשָּׁה עָשָׂר מָנֶה,

INTRODUCTION TO THE CONCLUSION OF THE SERVICE

The service draws to a close with some of the same themes with which it began, messages for us to take with us as we embrace the rest of the Shabbat day. Hopefully by now we feel a little closer to the Divine Presence, and we try to hold on to that feeling through our recollection of the symbolism of the sacrifices, the value of peace, and the commitment to live our lives today in a more prayerful way.

BIUR TEFILLA • ביאור תפילה

אֵין כֵּאלֹהֵינוּ – *There is none like our God.* This prayer dates back to the days of the Geonim, and acts as a kind of introduction to the concluding parts of the service. Interestingly, it was supposed to be recited at the conclusion of the morning service every day, but since the words were supposed to be read very carefully rather than recited quickly by rote, just as the eleven incense ingredients themselves were supposed to be measured out very precisely (lest one omit one on punishment of death), there was a concern that in the rush to get to work, people would not give it the attention it deserved. In Ashkenazi communities outside of Israel, it is thus reserved for Shabbat and Yom Tov only (Rema 132:2). In Sephardic tradition, the daily recitation has been maintained.

Spend a moment enjoying a "Shabbat pace of life" and not needing to rush anywhere. Think about what this passage could mean to you.

On Shabbat and Yom Tov, when people have more time, there is a greater likelihood that they will have the necessary focus. Unfortunately, human nature is such that one often gets restless as the end of a journey nears, and the same can be true for the journey that we have been on this morning. The Ashkenazi custom should thus serve as a reminder that there is still much to be gained in these final moments. We need to hang in there.

The prayer, which is usually sung by everyone together, consists of a series of five

weighing sixteen manehs; twelve manehs of costus, three of aromatic bark; nine of cinnamon; nine kabs of Carsina lye; three seahs and three kabs of Cyprus wine. If Cyprus wine was not available, old white wine might be used. A quarter of a kab of Sodom salt, and a minute amount of a smoke-raising herb. Rabbi Nathan says: Also a minute amount of Jordan amber. If one added honey to the mixture, he rendered it unfit for sacred use. If he omitted any one of its ingredients, he is guilty of a capital offense.

Rabban Shimon ben Gamliel says: "Balsam" refers to the sap that drips from the balsam tree. The Carsina lye was used for bleaching the onycha to improve it. The Cyprus wine was used to soak the onycha in it to make it pungent. Though urine is suitable for this purpose, it is not brought into the Temple out of respect.

These were the psalms which the Levites used to recite[B] in the Temple: *Mishna, Tamid 7*

On the first day of the week they used to say: "The earth is the LORD's and all it contains, the world and all who live in it." *Ps. 24*

On the second day they used to say: "Great is the LORD and greatly to be praised in the city of God, on His holy mountain." *Ps. 48*

On the third day they used to say: "God stands in the divine assembly. Among the judges He delivers judgment." *Ps. 82*

On the fourth day they used to say: "God of retribution, LORD, God of retribution, appear." *Ps. 94*

On the fifth day they used to say: "Sing for joy to God, our strength. Shout aloud to the God of Jacob." *Ps. 81*

On the sixth day they used to say: "The LORD reigns: He is robed in majesty; the LORD is robed, girded with strength; the world is firmly established; it cannot be moved." *Ps. 93*

On the Sabbath they used to say: "A psalm, a song for the Sabbath day" – [meaning] a psalm and song for the time to come, for the day which will be entirely Sabbath and rest for life everlasting. *Ps. 92*

---

ites, a different song for each day of the week. So too do we, except that on this day, when there is a little more time, we recite the source for this custom as it is described in the Mishna (*Tamid* 7:4) which highlights the day and the first line of the chapter of Psalms that comprised the song of that day. In the Shaḥarit for weekday, pages 243–251, each one is explained individually. For now, the overall message is perhaps "that each day has its own character, its own tasks, its own tonality in the symphony of time" (Rabbi J. Sacks). Alternatively, it could serve as an opportunity to reflect quickly upon each day of the week that has just passed, and what we made of it. Or, it could be seen as in introduction to the song of Shabbat that we will recite momentarily; an opportunity to revel in the way that this day is so wonderfully different from the rest of the week.

How was this past week different to the one before it?

How will this Shabbat help bring the rest of your week into focus?

How will this Shabbat help next week be different?

הַקֹּשְׁטְ שְׁנֵים עָשָׂר, קִלּוּפָה שְׁלֹשָׁה, וְקִנָּמוֹן תִּשְׁעָה. בֹּרִית כַּרְשִׁינָה תִּשְׁעָה קַבִּין, יֵין קַפְרִיסִין סְאִין תְּלָת וְקַבִּין תְּלָתָא, וְאִם אֵין לוֹ יֵין קַפְרִיסִין, מֵבִיא חֲמַר חִוַּרְיָן עַתִּיק. מֶלַח סְדוֹמִית רֹבַע, מַעֲלֶה עָשָׁן כָּל שֶׁהוּא. רַבִּי נָתָן הַבַּבְלִי אוֹמֵר: אַף כִּפַּת הַיַּרְדֵּן כָּל שֶׁהוּא, וְאִם נָתַן בָּהּ דְּבַשׁ פְּסָלָהּ, וְאִם חִסֵּר אַחַת מִכָּל סַמָּנֶיהָ, חַיָּב מִיתָה.

רַבָּן שִׁמְעוֹן בֶּן גַּמְלִיאֵל אוֹמֵר: הַצֳּרִי אֵינוֹ אֶלָּא שְׂרָף הַנּוֹטֵף מֵעֲצֵי הַקְּטָף. בֹּרִית כַּרְשִׁינָה שֶׁשָּׁפִין בָּהּ אֶת הַצִּפֹּרֶן כְּדֵי שֶׁתְּהֵא נָאָה, יֵין קַפְרִיסִין שֶׁשּׁוֹרִין בּוֹ אֶת הַצִּפֹּרֶן כְּדֵי שֶׁתְּהֵא עַזָּה, וַהֲלֹא מֵי רַגְלַיִם יָפִין לָהּ, אֶלָּא שֶׁאֵין מַכְנִיסִין מֵי רַגְלַיִם בַּמִּקְדָּשׁ מִפְּנֵי הַכָּבוֹד.

משנה תמיד ז
הַשִּׁיר שֶׁהַלְוִיִּם הָיוּ אוֹמְרִים בְּבֵית הַמִּקְדָּשׁ:

תהלים כד
בַּיּוֹם הָרִאשׁוֹן הָיוּ אוֹמְרִים, לַיהוה הָאָרֶץ וּמְלוֹאָהּ, תֵּבֵל וְיֹשְׁבֵי בָהּ:

תהלים מח
בַּשֵּׁנִי הָיוּ אוֹמְרִים, גָּדוֹל יהוה וּמְהֻלָּל מְאֹד, בְּעִיר אֱלֹהֵינוּ הַר־קָדְשׁוֹ:

תהלים פב
בַּשְּׁלִישִׁי הָיוּ אוֹמְרִים, אֱלֹהִים נִצָּב בַּעֲדַת־אֵל, בְּקֶרֶב אֱלֹהִים יִשְׁפֹּט:

תהלים צד
בָּרְבִיעִי הָיוּ אוֹמְרִים, אֵל־נְקָמוֹת יהוה, אֵל נְקָמוֹת הוֹפִיעַ:

תהלים פא
בַּחֲמִישִׁי הָיוּ אוֹמְרִים, הַרְנִינוּ לֵאלֹהִים עוּזֵּנוּ, הָרִיעוּ לֵאלֹהֵי יַעֲקֹב:

תהלים צג
בַּשִּׁשִּׁי הָיוּ אוֹמְרִים, יהוה מָלָךְ גֵּאוּת לָבֵשׁ
לָבֵשׁ יהוה עֹז הִתְאַזָּר, אַף־תִּכּוֹן תֵּבֵל בַּל־תִּמּוֹט:

תהלים צב
בַּשַּׁבָּת הָיוּ אוֹמְרִים, מִזְמוֹר שִׁיר לְיוֹם הַשַּׁבָּת:
מִזְמוֹר שִׁיר לֶעָתִיד לָבוֹא, לְיוֹם שֶׁכֻּלּוֹ שַׁבָּת וּמְנוּחָה לְחַיֵּי הָעוֹלָמִים.

From the recitation of this passage, then, one can minimally take away the cleansing feeling of atonement, the pleasing smell of spirituality, or the call to moral action. It all depends on you.

וְהַחֶלְבְּנָה – *Galbanum*. This particular spice was known for its horrible smell. It was nevertheless included in the *ketoret*, for rather than causing the mixture to smell worse, it was transformed into something that made the *ketoret* itself smell even more pleasant. The galbanum is symbolic of the sinners among Israel and the *Ketoret* thus teaches us that when all the forces of Israel gather together for a common goal, then the inner sweetness of each of us emerges, such that each of us has a part to play the improvement of the Jewish people and the world (Rabbi A. Y. Kook).

BIUR TEFILLA • ביאור תפילה

הַשִּׁיר שֶׁהַלְוִיִּם הָיוּ אוֹמְרִים – *These were the psalms that the Levites used to recite.* The morning service in the *Beit HaMikdash* was marked by the singing of a song by the Lev-

It was taught in the Academy of Elijah: Whoever studies [Torah] laws every day is assured that he will be destined for the World to Come, as it is said, "The ways of the world are His" – read not, "ways" [*halikhot*] but "laws" [*halakhot*]. *Megilla 28b* *Hab. 3*

Rabbi Elazar said in the name of Rabbi Ḥanina: The disciples of the sages increase peace in the world, as it is said, "And all your children shall be taught of the LORD, and great shall be the peace of your children [*banayikh*]." Read not *banayikh*, "your children," but *bonayikh*, "your builders." Those who love Your Torah have great peace; there is no stumbling block for them. May there be peace within your ramparts, prosperity in your palaces. For the sake of my brothers and friends, I shall say, "Peace be within you." For the sake of the House of the LORD our God, I will seek your good. ▸ May the LORD grant strength to His people; may the LORD bless His people with peace. *Berakhot 64a* *Is. 54* *Ps. 119* *Ps. 122* *Ps. 29*

THE RABBIS' KADDISH

The following prayer, said by mourners, requires the presence of a minyan. A transliteration can be found on page 1140.

Mourner: יִתְגַּדַּל Magnified and sanctified
may His great name be,
in the world He created by His will.
May He establish His kingdom in your lifetime
and in your days,
and in the lifetime of all the house of Israel,
swiftly and soon – and say: Amen.

All: May His great name be blessed for ever and all time.

---

wards is said out of happiness (*Birkei Yosef* 55:1; *Mishna Berura* 55:9).

What is the connection between Torah study and peace? After all, would not disagreements of interpretation and arguments ensue; where will there be peace? There are many who mistakenly think that world peace will be brought about through uniformity of opinions, and therefore when they see scholars exploring wisdom and knowledge of Torah, and different opinions emerging, they believe this causes dispute which is the opposite of peace. The truth is otherwise, that true peace can only emerge through the proliferation of peace, and the proliferation of peace entails seeing all the different aspects and opinions. (Rabbi A. Y. Kook)

תָּנָא דְבֵי אֵלִיָּהוּ:[ע] כָּל הַשּׁוֹנֶה הֲלָכוֹת בְּכָל יוֹם מגילה כח:
מֻבְטָח לוֹ שֶׁהוּא בֶּן עוֹלָם הַבָּא, שֶׁנֶּאֱמַר
הֲלִיכוֹת עוֹלָם לוֹ: אַל תִּקְרֵי הֲלִיכוֹת אֶלָּא הֲלָכוֹת. חבקוק ג

אָמַר רַבִּי אֶלְעָזָר, אָמַר רַבִּי חֲנִינָא: תַּלְמִידֵי חֲכָמִים מַרְבִּים שָׁלוֹם בָּעוֹלָם, ברכות סד.
שֶׁנֶּאֱמַר, וְכָל־בָּנַיִךְ לִמּוּדֵי יהוה, וְרַב שְׁלוֹם בָּנָיִךְ: אַל תִּקְרֵי בָּנָיִךְ, אֶלָּא ישעיה נד
בּוֹנָיִךְ. שָׁלוֹם רָב לְאֹהֲבֵי תוֹרָתֶךָ, וְאֵין־לָמוֹ מִכְשׁוֹל: יְהִי־שָׁלוֹם בְּחֵילֵךְ, תהלים קיט תהלים קכב
שַׁלְוָה בְּאַרְמְנוֹתָיִךְ: לְמַעַן אַחַי וְרֵעָי אֲדַבְּרָה־נָּא שָׁלוֹם בָּךְ: לְמַעַן בֵּית־יהוה
אֱלֹהֵינוּ אֲבַקְשָׁה טוֹב לָךְ: ◂ יהוה עֹז לְעַמּוֹ יִתֵּן, יהוה יְבָרֵךְ אֶת־עַמּוֹ בַשָּׁלוֹם: תהלים כט

קדיש דרבנן

The following prayer, said by mourners, requires the presence of a מנין.
A transliteration can be found on page 1140.

אבל: יִתְגַּדַּל וְיִתְקַדַּשׁ שְׁמֵהּ רַבָּא (קהל: אָמֵן)
בְּעָלְמָא דִּי בְרָא כִרְעוּתֵהּ
וְיַמְלִיךְ מַלְכוּתֵהּ
בְּחַיֵּיכוֹן וּבְיוֹמֵיכוֹן וּבְחַיֵּי דְכָל בֵּית יִשְׂרָאֵל
בַּעֲגָלָא וּבִזְמַן קָרִיב, וְאִמְרוּ אָמֵן. (קהל: אָמֵן)

קהל ואבל: יְהֵא שְׁמֵהּ רַבָּא מְבָרַךְ לְעָלַם וּלְעָלְמֵי עָלְמַיָּא.

IYUN TEFILLA • עיון תפילה

תָּנָא דְבֵי אֵלִיָּהוּ – *In the Academy of Elijah.* In deference to the opinion which says that *Kaddish DeRabbanan* should be recited after rabbinic homiletic (as opposed to purely legal) interpretations from the Oral Law (Rambam; *Magen Avraham* 54) this section of learning concludes with two such teachings. The first praises those who incorporate daily Torah into their lives. The second speaks of the way in which doing so can bring peace to the world. The word *shalom* (peace) is mentioned no fewer than six times, an allusion perhaps to the blessing of peace which we desire for the six days of the week (*Kol Bo*). Such teachings please the heart, and so the Kaddish recited after-

Mourner: Blessed and praised,
glorified and exalted,
raised and honored,
uplifted and lauded
be the name of the Holy One,
blessed be He,
beyond any blessing, song, praise
and consolation uttered in the world –
and say: Amen.

To Israel, to the teachers,
their disciples and their disciples' disciples,
and to all who engage
in the study of Torah,
in this (*in Israel add:* holy) place or elsewhere,
may there come to them and you great peace,
grace, kindness and compassion,
long life, ample sustenance and deliverance,
from their Father in Heaven –
and say: Amen.

May there be great peace from heaven,
and (good) life for us and all Israel –
and say: Amen.

Bow, take three steps back, as if taking leave of the Divine Presence, then bow, first left, then right, then center, while saying:

May He who makes peace
in His high places,
in His compassion make peace
for us and all Israel –
and say: Amen.

אבל: יִתְבָּרַךְ וְיִשְׁתַּבַּח וְיִתְפָּאַר וְיִתְרוֹמַם וְיִתְנַשֵּׂא
וְיִתְהַדָּר וְיִתְעַלֶּה וְיִתְהַלָּל
שְׁמֵהּ דְּקֻדְשָׁא בְּרִיךְ הוּא (קהל: בְּרִיךְ הוּא)
לְעֵלָּא מִן כָּל בִּרְכָתָא
וְשִׁירָתָא, תֻּשְׁבְּחָתָא וְנֶחֱמָתָא
דַּאֲמִירָן בְּעָלְמָא
וְאִמְרוּ אָמֵן. (קהל: אָמֵן)

עַל יִשְׂרָאֵל וְעַל רַבָּנָן
וְעַל תַּלְמִידֵיהוֹן וְעַל כָּל תַּלְמִידֵי תַלְמִידֵיהוֹן
וְעַל כָּל מָאן דְּעָסְקִין בְּאוֹרַיְתָא
דִּי בְּאַתְרָא (בארץ ישראל: קַדִּישָׁא) הָדֵין, וְדִי בְּכָל אֲתַר וַאֲתַר
יְהֵא לְהוֹן וּלְכוֹן שְׁלָמָא רַבָּא
חִנָּא וְחִסְדָּא, וְרַחֲמֵי, וְחַיֵּי אֲרִיכֵי, וּמְזוֹנֵי רְוִיחֵי
וּפֻרְקָנָא מִן קֳדָם אֲבוּהוֹן דִּי בִשְׁמַיָּא
וְאִמְרוּ אָמֵן. (קהל: אָמֵן)

יְהֵא שְׁלָמָא רַבָּא מִן שְׁמַיָּא
וְחַיִּים (טוֹבִים) עָלֵינוּ וְעַל כָּל יִשְׂרָאֵל
וְאִמְרוּ אָמֵן. (קהל: אָמֵן)

Bow, take three steps back, as if taking leave of the Divine Presence, then bow, first left, then right, then center, while saying:

עֹשֶׂה שָׁלוֹם בִּמְרוֹמָיו
הוּא יַעֲשֶׂה בְרַחֲמָיו שָׁלוֹם
עָלֵינוּ וְעַל כָּל יִשְׂרָאֵל
וְאִמְרוּ אָמֵן.

Stand while saying Aleinu. Bow at ▾.

עָלֵינוּ It is our duty to praise the Master of all,
and ascribe greatness to the Author of creation,
who has not made us like the nations of the lands
nor placed us like the families of the earth;
who has not made our portion like theirs,
nor our destiny like all their multitudes.
(For they worship vanity and emptiness,
and pray to a god who cannot save.)
▾But we bow in worship and thank the Supreme King of kings,
the Holy One, blessed be He,
who extends the heavens and establishes the earth,
whose throne of glory is in the heavens above,
and whose power's Presence is in the highest of heights.
He is our God; there is no other.
Truly He is our King, there is none else,
as it is written in His Torah:
"You shall know and take to heart this day that the LORD is God, *Deut. 4*
in heaven above and on earth below. There is no other."

Therefore, we place our hope in You, LORD our God,
that we may soon see the glory of Your power,
when You will remove abominations from the earth,
and idols will be utterly destroyed,
when the world will be perfected
under the sovereignty of the Almighty,
when all humanity will call on Your name,
to turn all the earth's wicked toward You.
All the world's inhabitants will realize and know
that to You every knee must bow and every tongue swear loyalty.
Before You, LORD our God, they will kneel and bow down
and give honor to Your glorious name.
They will all accept the yoke of Your kingdom,
and You will reign over them soon and for ever.
For the kingdom is Yours,
and to all eternity You will reign in glory,
as it is written in Your Torah: "The LORD will reign for ever and ever." *Ex. 15*

Stand while saying עָלֵינוּ. *Bow at* ˙.

עָלֵינוּ לְשַׁבֵּחַ לַאֲדוֹן הַכֹּל, לָתֵת גְּדֻלָּה לְיוֹצֵר בְּרֵאשִׁית
שֶׁלֹּא עָשָׂנוּ כְּגוֹיֵי הָאֲרָצוֹת, וְלֹא שָׂמָנוּ כְּמִשְׁפְּחוֹת הָאֲדָמָה
שֶׁלֹּא שָׂם חֶלְקֵנוּ כָּהֶם וְגוֹרָלֵנוּ כְּכָל הֲמוֹנָם.
(שֶׁהֵם מִשְׁתַּחֲוִים לְהֶבֶל וָרִיק וּמִתְפַּלְלִים אֶל אֵל לֹא יוֹשִׁיעַ.)
˙וַאֲנַחְנוּ כּוֹרְעִים וּמִשְׁתַּחֲוִים וּמוֹדִים
לִפְנֵי מֶלֶךְ מַלְכֵי הַמְּלָכִים, הַקָּדוֹשׁ בָּרוּךְ הוּא
שֶׁהוּא נוֹטֶה שָׁמַיִם וְיוֹסֵד אָרֶץ
וּמוֹשַׁב יְקָרוֹ בַּשָּׁמַיִם מִמַּעַל
וּשְׁכִינַת עֻזּוֹ בְּגָבְהֵי מְרוֹמִים.
הוּא אֱלֹהֵינוּ, אֵין עוֹד.
אֱמֶת מַלְכֵּנוּ, אֶפֶס זוּלָתוֹ
כַּכָּתוּב בְּתוֹרָתוֹ, וְיָדַעְתָּ הַיּוֹם וַהֲשֵׁבֹתָ אֶל־לְבָבֶךָ דברים ד
כִּי יהוה הוּא הָאֱלֹהִים בַּשָּׁמַיִם מִמַּעַל וְעַל־הָאָרֶץ מִתָּחַת
אֵין עוֹד:

עַל כֵּן נְקַוֶּה לְּךָ יהוה אֱלֹהֵינוּ, לִרְאוֹת מְהֵרָה בְּתִפְאֶרֶת עֻזֶּךָ
לְהַעֲבִיר גִּלּוּלִים מִן הָאָרֶץ, וְהָאֱלִילִים כָּרוֹת יִכָּרֵתוּן
לְתַקֵּן עוֹלָם בְּמַלְכוּת שַׁדַּי.
וְכָל בְּנֵי בָשָׂר יִקְרְאוּ בִשְׁמֶךָ לְהַפְנוֹת אֵלֶיךָ כָּל רִשְׁעֵי אָרֶץ.
יַכִּירוּ וְיֵדְעוּ כָּל יוֹשְׁבֵי תֵבֵל
כִּי לְךָ תִּכְרַע כָּל בֶּרֶךְ, תִּשָּׁבַע כָּל לָשׁוֹן.
לְפָנֶיךָ יהוה אֱלֹהֵינוּ יִכְרְעוּ וְיִפֹּלוּ, וְלִכְבוֹד שִׁמְךָ יְקָר יִתֵּנוּ
וִיקַבְּלוּ כֻלָּם אֶת עֹל מַלְכוּתֶךָ
וְתִמְלֹךְ עֲלֵיהֶם מְהֵרָה לְעוֹלָם וָעֶד.
כִּי הַמַּלְכוּת שֶׁלְּךָ הִיא וּלְעוֹלְמֵי עַד תִּמְלֹךְ בְּכָבוֹד
כַּכָּתוּב בְּתוֹרָתֶךָ, יהוה יִמְלֹךְ לְעֹלָם וָעֶד: שמות טו

▸ And it is said: "Then the LORD shall be King over all the earth; on that day the LORD shall be One and His name One." Zech. 14

Some add:

Have no fear of sudden terror or of the ruin when it overtakes the wicked. *Prov. 3*
Devise your strategy, but it will be thwarted; *Is. 8*
propose your plan, but it will not stand, for God is with us.
When you grow old, I will still be the same.
When your hair turns gray, I will still carry you. *Is. 46*
I made you, I will bear you, I will carry you, and I will rescue you.

MOURNER'S KADDISH

The following prayer, said by mourners, requires the presence of a minyan. A transliteration can be found on page 1141.

Mourner: יִתְגַּדַּל Magnified and sanctified
may His great name be,
in the world He created by His will.
May He establish His kingdom
in your lifetime and in your days,
and in the lifetime of all the house of Israel,
swiftly and soon –
and say: Amen.

All: May His great name be blessed
for ever and all time.

Mourner: Blessed and praised, glorified and exalted,
raised and honored, uplifted and lauded
be the name of the Holy One,
blessed be He,

---

unfettered, if man is suspicious, envious, petty, and obscene it is only due to the fact that man is still a heathen, his life pagan, and his cult idolatrous. He has not yet understood and intellectually digested the doctrine of (*Devarim* 6:4) "the Lord our God, the Lord is one" (Rabbi Joseph B. Soloveitchik).

▸ וְנֶאֱמַר, וְהָיָה יהוה לְמֶלֶךְ עַל־כָּל־הָאָרֶץ זכריה יד
בַּיּוֹם הַהוּא יִהְיֶה יהוה אֶחָד וּשְׁמוֹ אֶחָד:ע

Some add:

אַל־תִּירָא מִפַּחַד פִּתְאֹם וּמִשֹּׁאַת רְשָׁעִים כִּי תָבֹא: משלי ג
עֻצוּ עֵצָה וְתֻפָר, דַּבְּרוּ דָבָר וְלֹא יָקוּם, כִּי עִמָּנוּ אֵל: ישעיה ח
וְעַד־זִקְנָה אֲנִי הוּא, וְעַד־שֵׂיבָה אֲנִי אֶסְבֹּל אֲנִי עָשִׂיתִי וַאֲנִי אֶשָּׂא וַאֲנִי אֶסְבֹּל וַאֲמַלֵּט: ישעיה מו

קדיש יתום

The following prayer, said by mourners, requires the presence of a מנין*.*
A transliteration can be found on page 1141.

אבל: יִתְגַּדַּל וְיִתְקַדַּשׁ שְׁמֵהּ רַבָּא (קהל: אָמֵן)
בְּעָלְמָא דִּי בְרָא כִרְעוּתֵהּ
וְיַמְלִיךְ מַלְכוּתֵהּ
בְּחַיֵּיכוֹן וּבְיוֹמֵיכוֹן וּבְחַיֵּי דְכָל בֵּית יִשְׂרָאֵל
בַּעֲגָלָא וּבִזְמַן קָרִיב
וְאִמְרוּ אָמֵן. (קהל: אָמֵן)

קהל ואבל: יְהֵא שְׁמֵהּ רַבָּא מְבָרַךְ לְעָלַם וּלְעָלְמֵי עָלְמַיָּא.

אבל: יִתְבָּרַךְ וְיִשְׁתַּבַּח וְיִתְפָּאַר
וְיִתְרוֹמַם וְיִתְנַשֵּׂא וְיִתְהַדָּר וְיִתְעַלֶּה וְיִתְהַלָּל
שְׁמֵהּ דְּקֻדְשָׁא בְּרִיךְ הוּא (קהל: בְּרִיךְ הוּא)

IYUN TEFILLA • עיון תפילה

בַּיּוֹם הַהוּא יִהְיֶה יהוה אֶחָד וּשְׁמוֹ אֶחָד – *On that day the Lord will be One and His name One.* The conclusion one must derive from this prayer is that heathendom still rules our civilized world. If we are dissatisfied with the many imperfections of our social and moral order, if we encounter injustice, brutality, and cruel, ruthless stupidity, if falsehood, wickedness, violence, and evil forces are still rampant and

beyond any blessing, song, praise and consolation
uttered in the world – and say: Amen.

May there be great peace from heaven,
and life for us and all Israel – and say: Amen.

Bow, take three steps back, as if taking leave of the Divine Presence, then bow, first left, then right, then center, while saying:

May He who makes peace in His high places,
make peace for us and all Israel – and say: Amen.

Many congregations say the Daily Psalm after the Song of Glory, page 726. (In Israel on Shabbat Rosh Ḥodesh, some say Barekhi Nafshi, page 250, as the Daily Psalm.)

Today is the holy Sabbath,
on which the Levites used to say this psalm in the Temple:

מִזְמוֹר A psalm. A song for the Sabbath day.[A] It is good to thank the LORD *Ps. 92*
and sing psalms to Your name, Most High – to tell of Your loving-kindness in the morning and Your faithfulness at night, to the music of the ten-stringed lyre and the melody of the harp. For You have made me rejoice by Your work, O LORD; I sing for joy at the deeds of Your hands. How great are Your deeds, LORD, and how very deep Your thoughts. A boor cannot know, nor can a fool understand, that though the wicked spring up like grass and all evildoers flourish, it is only that they may be destroyed for ever. But You, LORD, are eternally exalted. For behold Your enemies, LORD, behold Your enemies will perish; all evildoers will be scattered. You have raised my pride like that of a wild ox; I am anointed with fresh oil. My eyes shall look in triumph on my adversaries; my ears shall hear the downfall of the wicked who rise against me. The righteous will flourish like a palm

---

Shabbat, and it is the third time we will be reciting it since Friday evening. (See pages 425 in Ma'ariv and 551 in Pesukei deZimra for more commentary). The Malbim informs us that one of the messages of Shabbat is the fact that Hashem is not the watchmaker who created something and then walked away. Rather, he watches out for the world and its inhabitants, and takes care of them every day, albeit operating within the confines of nature when He does so. Shabbat is a day to become more in tune with that Divine Providence (*hashgaḥa pratit*), which is the very theme of this psalm.

Where can you see Hashem's role in your life?

Where do you wish you could see Hashem's role in your life?

לְעֵלָּא מִן כָּל בִּרְכָתָא / בשבת שובה: לְעֵלָּא לְעֵלָּא מִכָּל בִּרְכָתָא/
וְשִׁירָתָא, תֻּשְׁבְּחָתָא וְנֶחֱמָתָא
דַּאֲמִירָן בְּעָלְמָא, וְאִמְרוּ אָמֵן. (קהל: אָמֵן)

יְהֵא שְׁלָמָא רַבָּא מִן שְׁמַיָּא
וְחַיִּים, עָלֵינוּ וְעַל כָּל יִשְׂרָאֵל, וְאִמְרוּ אָמֵן. (קהל: אָמֵן)

Bow, take three steps back, as if taking leave of the Divine Presence, then bow, first left, then right, then center, while saying:

עֹשֶׂה שָׁלוֹם בִּמְרוֹמָיו
הוּא יַעֲשֶׂה שָׁלוֹם עָלֵינוּ
וְעַל כָּל יִשְׂרָאֵל, וְאִמְרוּ אָמֵן.

Many congregations say the שיר של יום *after the* שיר הכבוד*, page 727.*
(In ארץ ישראל *on* שבת ראש חודש*, some say* בָּרְכִי נַפְשִׁי*, page 251, as the* שיר של יום*.)*

הַיּוֹם יוֹם שַׁבַּת קֹדֶשׁ,[א] שֶׁבּוֹ הָיוּ הַלְוִיִּם אוֹמְרִים בְּבֵית הַמִּקְדָּשׁ:

מִזְמוֹר שִׁיר לְיוֹם הַשַּׁבָּת: טוֹב לְהֹדוֹת לַיהוה, וּלְזַמֵּר לְשִׁמְךָ עֶלְיוֹן: תהלים צב
לְהַגִּיד בַּבֹּקֶר חַסְדֶּךָ, וֶאֱמוּנָתְךָ בַּלֵּילוֹת: עֲלֵי־עָשׂוֹר וַעֲלֵי־נָבֶל, עֲלֵי
הִגָּיוֹן בְּכִנּוֹר: כִּי שִׂמַּחְתַּנִי יהוה בְּפָעֳלֶךָ, בְּמַעֲשֵׂי יָדֶיךָ אֲרַנֵּן: מַה־גָּדְלוּ
מַעֲשֶׂיךָ יהוה, מְאֹד עָמְקוּ מַחְשְׁבֹתֶיךָ: אִישׁ־בַּעַר לֹא יֵדָע, וּכְסִיל
לֹא־יָבִין אֶת־זֹאת: בִּפְרֹחַ רְשָׁעִים כְּמוֹ־עֵשֶׂב, וַיָּצִיצוּ כָּל־פֹּעֲלֵי אָוֶן,
לְהִשָּׁמְדָם עֲדֵי־עַד: וְאַתָּה מָרוֹם לְעֹלָם יהוה: כִּי הִנֵּה אֹיְבֶיךָ יהוה,
כִּי־הִנֵּה אֹיְבֶיךָ יֹאבֵדוּ, יִתְפָּרְדוּ כָּל־פֹּעֲלֵי אָוֶן: וַתָּרֶם כִּרְאֵים קַרְנִי,
בַּלֹּתִי בְּשֶׁמֶן רַעֲנָן: וַתַּבֵּט עֵינִי בְּשׁוּרָי, בַּקָּמִים עָלַי מְרֵעִים תִּשְׁמַעְנָה

ANI TEFILLA • אני תפילה

הַיּוֹם יוֹם שַׁבַּת קֹדֶשׁ – *Today is the holy Shabbat.* As mentioned above, in the times of the Beit HaMikdash, a different song was sung on each day of the week to mark that day. The following passage is the psalm for

It is told that one of the Hasidic greats once said that anyone who is not prepared to greet a dog or a tree with the greeting *"Shabbat Shalom"* does not understand what Shabbat is truly all about.

tree and grow tall like a cedar in Lebanon. Planted in the LORD's House,[A] blossoming in our God's courtyards, ▸ they will still bear fruit in old age, and stay vigorous and fresh, proclaiming that the LORD is upright: He is my Rock, in whom there is no wrong. *Mourner's Kaddish on the next page*

On Rosh Ḥodesh, say Barekhi Nafshi on page 250 followed by Mourner's Kaddish.

From the second day of Rosh Ḥodesh Elul through Shemini Atzeret (in Israel through Hoshana Raba), the following psalm is said:

לְדָוִד A psalm of David. The LORD is my light and my salvation – whom then shall I fear? The LORD is the stronghold of my life – of whom shall I be afraid? When evil men close in on me to devour my flesh, it is they, my enemies and foes, who stumble and fall. Should an army besiege me, my heart would not fear. Should war break out against me, still I would be confident. One thing I ask of the LORD, only this do I seek: to live in the House of the LORD all the days of my life, to gaze on the beauty of the LORD and worship in His Temple. For He will keep me safe in His pavilion on the day of trouble. He will hide me under the cover of His tent. He will set me high upon a rock. Now my head is high above my enemies who surround me. I will sacrifice in His tent with shouts of joy. I will sing and chant praises to the LORD. LORD, hear my voice when I call. Be gracious to me and answer me. On Your behalf my heart says, "Seek My face." Your face, LORD, will I seek. Do not hide Your face from me. Do not turn Your servant away in anger. You have been my help. Do not reject or forsake me, God, my Savior. Were my father and my mother to forsake me, the LORD would take me in. Teach me Your way, LORD, and lead me on a level path, because of my oppressors. Do not abandon me to the will of my foes, for false witnesses have risen against me, breathing violence. ▸ Were it not for my faith that I shall see the LORD's goodness in the land of the living. Hope in the LORD. Be strong and of good courage, and hope in the LORD! *Ps. 27*

Mourner's Kaddish on the next page

---

becomes ritually pure again. From here there is a lesson to the person who uproots himself from the roots of his Judaism and attaches himself to things which are impure; namely, that he can always return, he can always replant himself anew in the vineyard that is the Jewish community and he can have a new start in the courtyard of Hashem, leading ultimately to giving fruit to happiness and produce that will gladden his or her own heart as well those of others (*Menaḥem Tzion*).

אָזְנָי: צַדִּיק כַּתָּמָר יִפְרָח, כְּאֶרֶז בַּלְּבָנוֹן יִשְׂגֶּה: שְׁתוּלִים בְּבֵית יהוה,[א]
בְּחַצְרוֹת אֱלֹהֵינוּ יַפְרִיחוּ: ◂ עוֹד יְנוּבוּן בְּשֵׂיבָה, דְּשֵׁנִים וְרַעֲנַנִּים יִהְיוּ:
לְהַגִּיד כִּי־יָשָׁר יהוה, צוּרִי, וְלֹא־עַוְלָתָה בּוֹ: *on the next page* קדיש יתום

On ראש חודש*, say* בָּרְכִי נַפְשִׁי *on page 251 followed by* קדיש יתום.

From the second day of ראש חודש אלול *through* שמיני עצרת
(*in* ארץ ישראל *through* הושענא רבה), *the following psalm is said:*

תהלים כז לְדָוִד, יהוה אוֹרִי וְיִשְׁעִי, מִמִּי אִירָא, יהוה מָעוֹז־חַיַּי, מִמִּי אֶפְחָד:
בִּקְרֹב עָלַי מְרֵעִים לֶאֱכֹל אֶת־בְּשָׂרִי, צָרַי וְאֹיְבַי לִי, הֵמָּה כָשְׁלוּ וְנָפָלוּ:
אִם־תַּחֲנֶה עָלַי מַחֲנֶה, לֹא־יִירָא לִבִּי, אִם־תָּקוּם עָלַי מִלְחָמָה, בְּזֹאת
אֲנִי בוֹטֵחַ: אַחַת שָׁאַלְתִּי מֵאֵת־יהוה, אוֹתָהּ אֲבַקֵּשׁ, שִׁבְתִּי בְּבֵית־
יהוה כָּל־יְמֵי חַיַּי, לַחֲזוֹת בְּנֹעַם־יהוה, וּלְבַקֵּר בְּהֵיכָלוֹ: כִּי יִצְפְּנֵנִי
בְּסֻכֹּה בְּיוֹם רָעָה, יַסְתִּרֵנִי בְּסֵתֶר אָהֳלוֹ, בְּצוּר יְרוֹמְמֵנִי: וְעַתָּה יָרוּם
רֹאשִׁי עַל אֹיְבַי סְבִיבוֹתַי, וְאֶזְבְּחָה בְאָהֳלוֹ זִבְחֵי תְרוּעָה, אָשִׁירָה
וַאֲזַמְּרָה לַיהוה: שְׁמַע־יהוה קוֹלִי אֶקְרָא, וְחָנֵּנִי וַעֲנֵנִי: לְךָ אָמַר לִבִּי
בַּקְּשׁוּ פָנָי, אֶת־פָּנֶיךָ יהוה אֲבַקֵּשׁ: אַל־תַּסְתֵּר פָּנֶיךָ מִמֶּנִּי, אַל תַּט־
בְּאַף עַבְדֶּךָ, עֶזְרָתִי הָיִיתָ, אַל־תִּטְּשֵׁנִי וְאַל־תַּעַזְבֵנִי, אֱלֹהֵי יִשְׁעִי:
כִּי־אָבִי וְאִמִּי עֲזָבוּנִי, וַיהוה יַאַסְפֵנִי: הוֹרֵנִי יהוה דַּרְכֶּךָ, וּנְחֵנִי בְּאֹרַח
מִישׁוֹר, לְמַעַן שׁוֹרְרָי: אַל־תִּתְּנֵנִי בְּנֶפֶשׁ צָרָי, כִּי קָמוּ־בִי עֵדֵי־שֶׁקֶר,
וִיפֵחַ חָמָס: ◂ לוּלֵא הֶאֱמַנְתִּי לִרְאוֹת בְּטוּב־יהוה בְּאֶרֶץ חַיִּים: קַוֵּה
אֶל־יהוה, חֲזַק וְיַאֲמֵץ לִבֶּךָ, וְקַוֵּה אֶל־יהוה: *on the next page* קדיש יתום

ANI TEFILLA • אני תפילה

שְׁתוּלִים בְּבֵית יהוה – *Planted in the Lord's House...* In the days of the Temple, gifts of food were tithed to the priests (*terumah*) and were thereby considered holy, such that they were actually capable of becoming ritually impure. The Mishna (*Terumah* 9:7) relates that if a tithed seedling which has become impure is replanted then it

MOURNER'S KADDISH

The following prayer, said by mourners, requires the presence of a minyan. A transliteration can be found on page 1141.

Mourner: יִתְגַּדַּל Magnified and sanctified
may His great name be,
in the world He created by His will.
May He establish His kingdom
in your lifetime and in your days,
and in the lifetime of all the house of Israel,
swiftly and soon – and say: Amen.

All: May His great name be blessed
for ever and all time.

Mourner: Blessed and praised,
glorified and exalted,
raised and honored,
uplifted and lauded
be the name of the Holy One,
blessed be He,
beyond any blessing,
song, praise and consolation
uttered in the world –
and say: Amen.

May there be great peace from heaven,
and life for us and all Israel –
and say: Amen.

Bow, take three steps back, as if taking leave of the Divine Presence, then bow, first left, then right, then center, while saying:

May He who makes peace in His high places,
make peace for us
and all Israel –
and say: Amen.

קדיש יתום

The following prayer, said by mourners, requires the presence of a מנין.
A transliteration can be found on page 1141.

אבל: יִתְגַּדַּל וְיִתְקַדַּשׁ שְׁמֵהּ רַבָּא (קהל: אָמֵן)
בְּעָלְמָא דִּי בְרָא כִרְעוּתֵהּ
וְיַמְלִיךְ מַלְכוּתֵהּ
בְּחַיֵּיכוֹן וּבְיוֹמֵיכוֹן וּבְחַיֵּי דְכָל בֵּית יִשְׂרָאֵל
בַּעֲגָלָא וּבִזְמַן קָרִיב, וְאִמְרוּ אָמֵן. (קהל: אָמֵן)

קהל ואבל: יְהֵא שְׁמֵהּ רַבָּא מְבָרַךְ לְעָלַם וּלְעָלְמֵי עָלְמַיָּא.

אבל: יִתְבָּרַךְ וְיִשְׁתַּבַּח וְיִתְפָּאַר
וְיִתְרוֹמַם וְיִתְנַשֵּׂא וְיִתְהַדָּר וְיִתְעַלֶּה וְיִתְהַלָּל
שְׁמֵהּ דְּקֻדְשָׁא בְּרִיךְ הוּא (קהל: בְּרִיךְ הוּא)
לְעֵלָּא מִן כָּל בִּרְכָתָא
וְשִׁירָתָא, תֻּשְׁבְּחָתָא וְנֶחֱמָתָא
דַּאֲמִירָן בְּעָלְמָא
וְאִמְרוּ אָמֵן. (קהל: אָמֵן)

יְהֵא שְׁלָמָא רַבָּא מִן שְׁמַיָּא
וְחַיִּים, עָלֵינוּ וְעַל כָּל יִשְׂרָאֵל
וְאִמְרוּ אָמֵן. (קהל: אָמֵן)

Bow, take three steps back, as if taking leave of the Divine Presence,
then bow, first left, then right, then center, while saying:

עֹשֶׂה שָׁלוֹם בִּמְרוֹמָיו
הוּא יַעֲשֶׂה שָׁלוֹם עָלֵינוּ
וְעַל כָּל יִשְׂרָאֵל, וְאִמְרוּ אָמֵן.

SONG OF GLORY

The Ark is opened and all stand.

Leader: I will sing sweet psalms and I will weave songs,[B]
to You for whom my soul longs.

Cong: My soul yearns for the shelter of Your hand,
that all Your mystic secrets I might understand.[B]

Leader: Whenever I speak of Your glory above,
my heart is yearning for Your love.

Cong: So Your glories I will proclaim,
and in songs of love give honor to Your name.

---

to do, and to place a crown upon His head. Beneath the surface, then, may lie mystical allusions that only the initiated can perceive. Here too is a source of its perceived holiness.

As we have seen in other places, there is a swing back and forth between addressing Hashem in the second person ("To You for Whom my soul longs") and then in the third person ("He wore") and then back to the second person again. It is as if after all of our prayers this morning, we feel we have a slightly more intimate relationship with Him than we did when we arrived, yet when we realize the chasm that separates us, we recoil and address Him as King, only to long for that personal connection again before we depart.

The theme in all of its lyrical, mystical beauty is the indescribability of God, His relationship with His people, and ours with Him. As described in the first line and the last "For You my soul will always long."

BIUR TEFILLA • ביאור תפילה

אַנְעִים זְמִירוֹת וְשִׁירִים אֶאֱרֹג – *I will sing sweet psalms and I will weave songs.* Just as the weaver ties strands of thread together, so too will I weave these melodies into one big tapestry of praise to You.

נַפְשִׁי חִמְּדָה... לָדַעַת כָּל רָז סוֹדֶךָ – *My soul yearns... that all your mystic secrets I might understand.* I want to be close to You, to understand You, even as I know that You are impossible to understand, and no matter how many secrets or insights I uncover, there will always be more.

שיר הכבוד

The ארון קודש is opened and all stand.

ש״ץ: אַנְעִים זְמִירוֹת וְשִׁירִים אֶאֱרֹג, כִּי אֵלֶיךָ נַפְשִׁי תַעֲרֹג.

קהל: נַפְשִׁי חָמְדָה בְּצֵל יָדֶךָ, לָדַעַת כָּל רָז סוֹדֶךָ.

ש״ץ: מִדֵּי דַבְּרִי בִּכְבוֹדֶךָ, הוֹמֶה לִבִּי אֶל דּוֹדֶיךָ.

קהל: עַל כֵּן אֲדַבֵּר בְּךָ נִכְבָּדוֹת, וְשִׁמְךָ אֲכַבֵּד בְּשִׁירֵי יְדִידוֹת.

INRODUCTION TO ANIM ZEMIROT אנעים זמרות

Perhaps one can learn something about the inclusion of this prayer in the siddur from those who objected to its recitation. This prayer was considered so holy and uplifting that it was deemed by some inappropriate to be said every day, lest we come to take its content for granted. Rather, said one halakhic authority, we should use as our model the fact that the Kohen Gadol (The High Priest) used to enter the Holy of Holies only once a year on Yom Kippur. So, too, should we recite this particular prayer only on that one day.

Many congregations therefore now limit its recitation to Shabbat and Yom Tov. Because of its content, some recite it at the beginning of the service, while others do so just before the reading of the Torah, while still others leave it for the end of the service, ironically a time when its sanctity can sometimes be overlooked because of its proximity to the close. It is often led by a child below the age of Bar Mitzva, perhaps because it gives him an opportunity to practice his skills in leading the congregation on a prayer that is not really part of the core service. Alternatively, perhaps it is because the innocent faith of a younger child is the stance that we must all take for this most awe inspiring poem.

Attributed Rabbi Yehuda HaḤasid over 800 years ago, the prayer has four lines at the beginning and three lines at the end (in addition to a couple of verses recited afterwards), but at its center is an alphabetical acrostic. The first half of each stanza rhymes with the second half, a scheme that was maintained in the English translation. Variations of the word *rosh* (head) figure prominently (its first letter *reish* is also the only one that receives two lines in the acrostic) as does the word *kavod* (glory), from which the poem derives its name (*Shir HaKavod* / Song of Glory). It is as if the poet is trying to aspire to see the full glory of God, something that even the prophet Moshe was unable

Leader: I will tell of Your glory though I have not seen You,
imagine and describe You, though I have not known You.

Cong: By the hand of Your prophets, through Your servants' mystery,
You gave a glimpse[B] of Your wondrous majesty.

Leader: Recounting Your grandeur and Your glory,
of Your great deeds they told the story.

Cong: They depicted You, though not as You are,
but as You do: Your acts, Your power.

Leader: They represented You in many visions;
through them all You are One without divisions.

Cong: They saw You, now old, then young,
Your head with gray, with black hair hung.

Leader: Aged on the day of judgment, yet on the day of war,
a young warrior with mighty hands they saw.

Cong: Triumph like a helmet He wore on his head;
His right hand and holy arm to victory have led.

Leader: His curls are filled with dew drops of light,
His locks with fragments of the night.

Cong: He will glory in me, for He delights in me;
My diadem of beauty He shall be.

Leader: His head is like pure beaten gold;
Engraved on His brow, His sacred name behold.

Cong: For grace and glory, beauty and renown,
His people have adorned Him with a crown.

Leader: Like a youth's, His hair in locks unfurls;
Its black tresses flowing in curls.

Cong: Jerusalem, His splendor, is the dwelling place of right;
may He prize it as His highest delight.

ANI TEFILLA • אני תפילה

The Maggid of Mezeritch used to say that one can learn three things from a child: always be happy, never be idle, and when you want something, ask for it vigorously.

ש״ץ: אֲסַפְּרָה כְבוֹדְךָ וְלֹא רְאִיתִיךָ, אֲדַמְּךָ אֲכַנְּךָ וְלֹא יְדַעְתִּיךָ.

קהל: בְּיַד נְבִיאֶיךָ בְּסוֹד עֲבָדֶיךָ, דִּמִּיתָ הֲדַר כְּבוֹד הוֹדֶךָ.

ש״ץ: גְּדֻלָּתְךָ וּגְבוּרָתֶךָ, כִּנּוּ לְתֹקֶף פְּעֻלָּתֶךָ.

קהל: דִּמּוּ אוֹתְךָ וְלֹא כְּפִי יֶשְׁךָ, וַיְשַׁוּוּךָ לְפִי מַעֲשֶׂיךָ.

ש״ץ: הִמְשִׁילוּךָ בְּרֹב חֶזְיוֹנוֹת, הִנְּךָ אֶחָד בְּכָל דִּמְיוֹנוֹת.

קהל: וַיֶּחֱזוּ בְךָ זִקְנָה וּבַחֲרוּת, וּשְׂעַר רֹאשְׁךָ בְּשֵׂיבָה וְשַׁחֲרוּת.

ש״ץ: זִקְנָה בְּיוֹם דִּין וּבַחֲרוּת בְּיוֹם קְרָב, כְּאִישׁ מִלְחָמוֹת יָדָיו לוֹ רָב.

קהל: חָבַשׁ כּוֹבַע יְשׁוּעָה בְּרֹאשׁוֹ, הוֹשִׁיעָה לּוֹ יְמִינוֹ וּזְרוֹעַ קָדְשׁוֹ.

ש״ץ: טַלְלֵי אוֹרוֹת רֹאשׁוֹ נִמְלָא, קְוֻצּוֹתָיו רְסִיסֵי לָיְלָה.

קהל: יִתְפָּאֵר בִּי כִּי חָפֵץ בִּי, וְהוּא יִהְיֶה לִּי לַעֲטֶרֶת צְבִי.

ש״ץ: כֶּתֶם טָהוֹר פָּז דְּמוּת רֹאשׁוֹ, וְחַק עַל מֵצַח כְּבוֹד שֵׁם קָדְשׁוֹ.

קהל: לְחֵן וּלְכָבוֹד צְבִי תִפְאָרָה, אֻמָּתוֹ לוֹ עִטְּרָה עֲטָרָה.

ש״ץ: מַחְלְפוֹת רֹאשׁוֹ כְּבִימֵי בְחוּרוֹת, קְוֻצּוֹתָיו תַּלְתַּלִּים שְׁחוֹרוֹת.

קהל: נְוֵה הַצֶּדֶק צְבִי תִפְאַרְתּוֹ, יַעֲלֶה נָּא עַל רֹאשׁ שִׂמְחָתוֹ.

BIUR TEFILLA • ביאור תפילה

דִּמּוּ אוֹתְךָ וְלֹא כְּפִי יֶשְׁךָ, וַיְשַׁוּוּךָ לְפִי מַעֲשֶׂיךָ – *They depicted You, though not as You are, but as You do: Your acts, Your power.* The Bible describes Your deeds. We can discern some of Your characteristics only through Your actions since we can never really perceive You. Deeds that we understand as kind, just, punishing, loving, all give us insight into the contours of who You really are. You can be described as a lion (*Amos* 3:8) or as a panther (*Hoshea* 13:7), yet these are but human perceptions and terms for that which we cannot ever really see (Yaavetz).

בְּיַד נְבִיאֶיךָ... דִּמִּיתָ – *By the hand of Your prophets…You gave a glimpse.* All we know of God is what the Bible tells us. The prophets can describe their visions which are but metaphors or vague shapes seen through the thickness of a veil, but even the greatest prophet of all, Moshe, was told "No man can see Me and live" (*Shemot* 33:20).

Leader: Like a crown in His hand may His treasured people be,
a turban of beauty and of majesty.

Cong: He bore them, carried them, with a crown He adorned them.
They were precious in His sight, and He honored them.

Leader: His glory is on me; my glory is on Him.
He is near to me when I call to Him.[B]

Cong: He is bright and rosy; red will be His dress,
when He comes from Edom, treading the winepress.

Leader: He showed the tefillin-knot to Moses, humble, wise,
when the LORD's likeness was before his eyes.

Cong: He delights in His people; the humble He does raise –
He glories in them; He sits enthroned upon their praise.

Leader: Your first word, Your call to every age, is true:
O seek the people who seek You.

Cong: My many songs please take and hear
and may my hymn of joy to You come near.

Leader: May my praise be a crown for Your head,
and like incense before You, the prayers I have said.

Cong: May a poor man's song be precious in Your eyes,
like a song sung over sacrifice.

Leader: To the One who sustains all, may my blessing take flight:
Creator, Life-Giver, God of right and might.

Cong: And when I offer blessing, to me Your head incline:
accepting it as spice, fragrant and fine.

Leader: May my prayer be to You sweet song.
For You my soul will always long.

The Ark is closed.

Yours, LORD, are the greatness and the power, the glory, the majesty *1 Chr. 29*
and splendor, for everything in heaven and earth is Yours. Yours, LORD,
is the kingdom; You are exalted as Head over all. ▸ Who can tell of the *Ps. 106*
mighty acts of the LORD and make all His praise be heard?

Mourner's Kaddish (page 724)

ש״ץ: סְגֻלָּתוֹ תְּהִי בְיָדוֹ עֲטֶרֶת, וּצְנִיף מְלוּכָה צְבִי תִפְאֶרֶת.
קהל: עֲמוּסִים נְשָׂאָם, עֲטֶרֶת עִנְּדָם, מֵאֲשֶׁר יָקְרוּ בְעֵינָיו כִּבְּדָם.

ש״ץ: פְּאֵרוֹ עָלַי וּפְאֵרִי עָלָיו, וְקָרוֹב אֵלַי בְּקָרְאִי אֵלָיו.ב
קהל: צַח וְאָדֹם לִלְבוּשׁוֹ אָדֹם, פּוּרָה בְדָרְכוֹ בְּבוֹאוֹ מֵאֱדוֹם.

ש״ץ: קֶשֶׁר תְּפִלִּין הֶרְאָה לֶעָנָו, תְּמוּנַת יהוה לְנֶגֶד עֵינָיו.
קהל: רוֹצֶה בְעַמּוֹ עֲנָוִים יְפָאֵר, יוֹשֵׁב תְּהִלּוֹת בָּם לְהִתְפָּאֵר.

ש״ץ: רֹאשׁ דְּבָרְךָ אֱמֶת קוֹרֵא מֵרֹאשׁ דּוֹר וָדוֹר, עַם דּוֹרֶשְׁךָ דְּרֹשׁ.
קהל: שִׁית הֲמוֹן שִׁירַי נָא עָלֶיךָ, וְרִנָּתִי תִּקְרַב אֵלֶיךָ.

ש״ץ: תְּהִלָּתִי תְּהִי לְרֹאשְׁךָ עֲטֶרֶת, וּתְפִלָּתִי תִּכּוֹן קְטֹרֶת.
קהל: תִּיקַר שִׁירַת רָשׁ בְּעֵינֶיךָ, כַּשִּׁיר יוּשַׁר עַל קָרְבָּנֶיךָ.

ש״ץ: בִּרְכָתִי תַעֲלֶה לְרֹאשׁ מַשְׁבִּיר, מְחוֹלֵל וּמוֹלִיד, צַדִּיק כַּבִּיר.
קהל: וּבְבִרְכָתִי תְנַעֲנַע לִי רֹאשׁ, וְאוֹתָהּ קַח לְךָ כִּבְשָׂמִים רֹאשׁ.

ש״ץ: יֶעֱרַב נָא שִׂיחִי עָלֶיךָ, כִּי נַפְשִׁי תַעֲרֹג אֵלֶיךָ.

The ארון קודש *is closed.*

לְךָ יהוה הַגְּדֻלָּה וְהַגְּבוּרָה וְהַתִּפְאֶרֶת וְהַנֵּצַח וְהַהוֹד, כִּי־כֹל בַּשָּׁמַיִם דברי הימים א׳ כט
וּבָאָרֶץ, לְךָ יהוה הַמַּמְלָכָה וְהַמִּתְנַשֵּׂא לְכֹל לְרֹאשׁ: ‹ מִי יְמַלֵּל גְּבוּרוֹת תהלים קו
יהוה, יַשְׁמִיעַ כָּל־תְּהִלָּתוֹ:

קדיש יתום (*page 725*)

BIUR TEFILLA • ביאור תפילה

פְּאֵרוֹ עָלַי וּפְאֵרִי עָלָיו, וְקָרוֹב אֵלַי בְּקָרְאִי אֵלָיו – *His glory is on me; my glory is on Him. He is near to me when I call Him.* The word *pe'er*, glory or adornment, is also an allusion to tefillin (*Berakhot* 11a). The bond between the Jewish people and Hashem is so close that not only do we wear tefillin with His name in them, but He also wears tefillin that bear our name (*Berakhot* 6a). Today, however, the tefillin that adorn our heads are the prayers that we offer up; the praises that we hope, in the end, will be "like a crown for Your head" (תְּהִלָּתִי תְּהִי לְרֹאשְׁךָ עֲטֶרֶת).

LORD OF THE UNIVERSE,[BI]

who reigned before the birth of any thing –

When by His will all things were made
then was His name proclaimed King.

And when all things shall cease to be
He alone will reign in awe.

He was, He is, and He shall be[I]
glorious for evermore.

---

yet He is within reach and knowable. He is distant, yet He is my refuge. These are not contradictions but different aspects of an ongoing relationship. At times we feel one way, other times we feel differently. The bottom line is that we can feel both, and both are normal.

בְּטֶרֶם כָּל־יְצִיר נִבְרָא – *Who reigned before the birth of any thing.* This is a cardinal statement of faith. Hashem existed before the world did, before the raw material of matter. As such, the world was not created from something but from nothing, what is referred to as *creation ex nihilo* (*yesh me-ayin*).

Our minds cannot fathom "nothing." That perhaps is just one of the many reasons that we cannot be God; but that does not mean that such a thing is impossible.

וְאַחֲרֵי כִּכְלוֹת הַכֹּל לְבַדּוֹ יִמְלֹךְ נוֹרָא. וְהוּא הָיָה וְהוּא הֹוֶה וְהוּא יִהְיֶה – And when all things shall cease to be, He alone will reign in awe. *He was, He is, He shall be.* Past, present and future are concepts in time that exist only for us, based upon our human perceptions. In Hashem's view there are no such things. He sees everything.

How might that view change the way my life is seen?

ANI TEFILLA • אני תפילה

My father used to tell the story of a very simple man, just barely literate, who came to a bookstore asking to buy a siddur. The proprietor, realizing that the man had limited knowledge, offered him the simplest siddur, but the man asked for something more elaborate. He continued asking for a more sophisticated siddur until finally the storekeeper offered him the Otzar HaTefillot, a massive volume with numerous pages of commentary. The customer was delighted but the storekeeper could not contain himself and finally asked, "Are you really going to be able to understand this book?" "Not at all," the customer answered. "But I have young children at home and whenever they want to pretend to pray they handle the siddur so roughly that they tear the first pages apart. Since the Adon Olam prayer is always at the

This **ANI TEFILLA** *continues on page 735.*

אֲדוֹן עוֹלָם [בע]

אֲשֶׁר מָלַךְ בְּטֶרֶם כָּל־יְצִיר נִבְרָא.

לְעֵת נַעֲשָׂה בְחֶפְצוֹ כֹּל אֲזַי מֶלֶךְ שְׁמוֹ נִקְרָא.

וְאַחֲרֵי כִּכְלוֹת הַכֹּל לְבַדּוֹ יִמְלֹךְ נוֹרָא.

וְהוּא הָיָה וְהוּא הֹוֶה וְהוּא יִהְיֶה[ע] בְּתִפְאָרָה.

BIUR TEFILLA • ביאור תפילה

אֲדוֹן עוֹלָם – *Lord of the universe.* The word *olam* in Hebrew can have multiple meanings or nuances. The phrase may therefore be translated as "Lord of the Universe" or "Lord of the Earth," denoting one of these places. The word could also conjure up an association with the word "forever," and would thus be translated as "Lord who reigns forever," thus denoting that He is beyond time. Or it could remind one of the word for "hidden" suggesting that Hashem is mysterious and unknowable.

Which of these appeals to you most today?

In any event, learning Hebrew can provide one with added dimensions of understanding and intent.

IYUN TEFILLA • עיון תפילה

אֲדוֹן עוֹלָם – *Lord of the universe.* The author of this famous hymn is unknown (it dates back to the eleventh century or perhaps even hundreds of years earlier), but it has found a firm place in the canon of prayer. It is recited by some individuals on their own before services begin, it is part of the liturgy recited at bedtime (*keriat Shema al ha-mita*) yet it is also commonly sung by the entire congregation at the conclusion of the service on Shabbat and Yom Tov. In some Moroccan communities, it is sung as the bride enters the wedding canopy.

What is its appeal? The first half, actually the first six lines, speak about aspects of God, His essence or who He is to the extent that we can know such a thing, while the other four lines speak about His relationship with man. In short, its theme is His exaltedness on the one hand, and His intimate contact with the world on the other, themes that we will return to over and over again, for they speak to the heart of religious experience and belief: He is far but He is close. He is before time but He is this-worldly. He is beyond our grasp and comprehension,

He is One, there is none else,
alone, unique, beyond compare;

Without beginning, without end,
His might, His rule are everywhere.

He is my God;[I] my Redeemer lives.
He is the Rock on whom I rely[A] –

My banner and my safe retreat,[B]
my cup, my portion when I cry.

Into His hand my soul I place,
when I awake and when I sleep.

The Lord is with me, I shall not fear;
body and soul from harm will He keep.[I]

Alternatively, He is my miracle, meaning, perhaps, that the daily miracles that surround me come from Him.

What miracles can you identify around you thus far today?

IYUN TEFILLA • עיון תפילה

בְּיָדוֹ אַפְקִיד רוּחִי בְּעֵת אִישַׁן וְאָעִירָה. וְעִם רוּחִי גְּוִיָּתִי יהוה לִי וְלֹא אִירָא – *Into His hand my soul I place, when I awake and when I sleep. The Lord is with me, I shall not fear; body and soul from harm will He keep.* R. Alexander said: A person loans an article to someone and it gets returned used and tattered, but *HaKadosh Barukh Hu*, the Holy One Blessed be He, is different. For at night we give Him our souls and He returns them to us in the morning refreshed and like new. We go to bed at night spent and exhausted but we awake ready to begin the day as if we are born anew. And if we have the faith to believe that this will happen every morning, then we must have the faith that it will happen after we die as well (*Shoḥer Tov* 25:2).

It was said in the name of Rav Shrira Gaon and Rav Hai his son that whoever had the proper intention during the recitation of this prayer was assured that his prayers would be answered (*Mateh Moshe*). "The beauty of its form, the easy rhythm of its verse, and the tender passion of its contents have an invigorating effect upon spirit and soul. It strengthens in man that attitude of optimism toward life… (Rabbi E. Munk).

וְהוּא אֶחָד וְאֵין שֵׁנִי לְהַמְשִׁיל לוֹ לְהַחְבִּירָה.
בְּלִי רֵאשִׁית בְּלִי תַכְלִית וְלוֹ הָעֹז וְהַמִּשְׂרָה.
וְהוּא אֵלִיעּ וְחַי גּוֹאֲלִי וְצוּר חֶבְלִי בְּעֵת צָרָה.א
וְהוּא נִסִּי וּמָנוֹס לִיב מְנָת כּוֹסִי בְּיוֹם אֶקְרָא.
בְּיָדוֹ אַפְקִיד רוּחִי בְּעֵת אִישַׁן וְאָעִירָה.
וְעִם רוּחִי גְּוִיָּתִי יהוה לִי וְלֹא אִירָא.ע

Father said, "The many customs and practices that were added to the Torah are there to assure that we keep the Adon Olam [i.e., the Master of the Universe] intact." (Rabbi Abraham Twerski)

beginning, it always gets ripped out but with the Otzar HaTefillot siddur, there are so many pages of commentary at the beginning, the kids will have a long way to go before they ever get to Adon Olam."

ANI TEFILLA • אני תפילה

וְצוּר חֶבְלִי בְּעֵת צָרָה – *He is the Rock on whom I rely.* When I'm in pain, when I'm anxious or hurting, He is a rock. Think of a rock and its properties.

Why is Hashem compared to one?

What support can it provide you with in a time of need?

IYUN TEFILLA • עיון תפילה

וְהוּא אֵלִי – *He is my God.* He knows me personally and He is interested in me, to watch over me. This is what Rav Kook said: "It is as if there was no one else in the world but me." They once asked an educator, "Which child is your favorite?" and he answered, "The one I am with in the moment." Hashem does not play favorites. Each of us who is present with Him is His favorite (Rabbi S. Aviner). Be present.

BIUR TEFILLA • ביאור תפילה

וְהוּא נִסִּי וּמָנוֹס לִי – *My banner and my safe retreat.* A banner was originally a flag on a pole used as the standard of a monarch, an army, or knight. It could be used as an identifying mark, or as a way that others could see the leader, or that outsiders could see one from afar.

How can Hashem be a banner in your life?

Kiddush and Zemirot for Shabbat Day

SHABBAT MORNING KIDDUSH

Some say:

אִם־תָּשִׁיב If you keep your feet from breaking the Sabbath, *Is. 58*
and from pursuing your affairs on My holy day,
if you call the Sabbath a delight, and the LORD's holy day honorable,
and if you honor it by not going your own way
or attending to your own affairs, or speaking idle words,
then you will find joy in the LORD,
and I will cause you to ride on the heights of the earth
and to feast on the inheritance of your father Jacob,
for the mouth of the LORD has spoken.

Most begin Kiddush here.

וְשָׁמְרוּ The children of Israel must keep the Sabbath, *Ex. 31*
observing the Sabbath in every generation
as an everlasting covenant.
It is a sign between Me and the children of Israel for ever,
for in six days the LORD made the heavens and the earth,
but on the seventh day He ceased work
and refreshed Himself.

HILKHOT TEFILLA • הלכות תפילה

Unlike the Kiddush of Friday night, this one has no prescribed text or theme. In theory, one need only recite the blessing over wine in order to fulfill one's obligation. Ironically, it is known in the literature as *Kiddusha Raba* ("The Great Kiddush") despite or perhaps because of its brevity. In practice, however, different customs have developed to introduce the blessing with added passages from Tanakh which highlight one theme or another about the special nature of Shabbat. It is known popularly simply as Kiddush. Some just say the blessing over wine; others add a line or lines of other passages but it is always followed by food in keeping with the principle outlined on Friday evening that kiddush is recited together with one's meal. As to how to conduct oneself at a communal kiddush after services, one should consult with one's rabbi.

קידוש וזמירות ליום שבת

קידושא רבה

Some say:

אִם־תָּשִׁיב מִשַּׁבָּת רַגְלֶךָ עֲשׂוֹת חֲפָצֶךָ בְּיוֹם קָדְשִׁי ישעיה נח
וְקָרָאתָ לַשַּׁבָּת עֹנֶג לִקְדוֹשׁ יהוה מְכֻבָּד
וְכִבַּדְתּוֹ מֵעֲשׂוֹת דְּרָכֶיךָ מִמְּצוֹא חֶפְצְךָ וְדַבֵּר דָּבָר:
אָז תִּתְעַנַּג עַל־יהוה
וְהִרְכַּבְתִּיךָ עַל־בָּמֳתֵי אָרֶץ
וְהַאֲכַלְתִּיךָ נַחֲלַת יַעֲקֹב אָבִיךָ
כִּי פִּי יהוה דִּבֵּר:

Most begin קידוש *here.*

וְשָׁמְרוּ בְנֵי־יִשְׂרָאֵל אֶת־הַשַּׁבָּת שמות לא
לַעֲשׂוֹת אֶת־הַשַּׁבָּת לְדֹרֹתָם בְּרִית עוֹלָם:
בֵּינִי וּבֵין בְּנֵי יִשְׂרָאֵל אוֹת הִוא לְעֹלָם
כִּי־שֵׁשֶׁת יָמִים עָשָׂה יהוה אֶת־הַשָּׁמַיִם וְאֶת־הָאָרֶץ
וּבַיּוֹם הַשְּׁבִיעִי שָׁבַת וַיִּנָּפַשׁ:

INTRODUCTION TO KIDDUSH FOR SHABBAT MORNING

When the Torah commands that one should "Remember the Shabbat *day* to keep it holy," the Rabbis learned that one should recite Kiddush during the day just as one did when the Shabbat arrived in the previous evening (*Pesaḥim* 106a). We are thus reminded once again of the sanctity of the day, appropriately just at the moment when we might fall prey to the assumption that the sumptuous food we are about to eat is solely for our own benefit and pleasure. Kiddush reminds us that we can raise the act of eating from an animalistic drive to a humanizing and holy gesture.

זָכוֹר Remember the Sabbath day[H] to keep it holy. *Ex. 20*
Six days you shall labor and do all your work,
but the seventh day is a Sabbath of the LORD your God;
on it you shall not do any work –
you, your son or daughter,
your male or female slave, or your cattle,
or the stranger within your gates.
For in six days the LORD made heaven and earth
and sea and all that is in them,
and rested on the seventh day;
therefore the LORD blessed the Sabbath day
and declared it holy.

When saying Kiddush for others, add:
Please pay attention, my masters.

בָּרוּךְ Blessed are You, LORD our God,
King of the Universe,
who creates the fruit of the vine.[H]

ANI TEFILLA · אני תפילה

Let me share with you a conversation I had with the director of a large retirement home in Miami. The residents' children all lived far away – New York, Washington, Chicago. There were three categories of children. Some sent a check every month to their parents. Sometimes the son or daughter would include a short note; sometimes, not even that. In any event, the parent knew that the child remembered him every month. Others sent the monthly check straight to the retirement home office. It didn't go direct to the parent but at least they remembered the parents every month. The third type, explained the director, comprised those who made use of a standing bank order, such that the money was sent each month by a teller at the bank without the child having any idea as to whether his parent was even still alive. Everything was conducted automatically. (Rabbi Yehuda Amital)

What kind of relationship do you have with God?

שמות כ

זָכוֹר אֶת־יוֹם הַשַּׁבָּת[ה] לְקַדְּשׁוֹ:
שֵׁשֶׁת יָמִים תַּעֲבֹד, וְעָשִׂיתָ כָּל־מְלַאכְתֶּךָ:
וְיוֹם הַשְּׁבִיעִי שַׁבָּת לַיהוה אֱלֹהֶיךָ
לֹא־תַעֲשֶׂה כָל־מְלָאכָה
אַתָּה וּבִנְךָ וּבִתֶּךָ
עַבְדְּךָ וַאֲמָתְךָ וּבְהֶמְתֶּךָ
וְגֵרְךָ אֲשֶׁר בִּשְׁעָרֶיךָ:
כִּי שֵׁשֶׁת־יָמִים עָשָׂה יהוה אֶת־הַשָּׁמַיִם וְאֶת־הָאָרֶץ
אֶת־הַיָּם וְאֶת־כָּל־אֲשֶׁר־בָּם
וַיָּנַח בַּיּוֹם הַשְּׁבִיעִי
עַל־כֵּן בֵּרַךְ יהוה אֶת־יוֹם הַשַּׁבָּת וַיְקַדְּשֵׁהוּ:

When saying קידוש *for others, add:*

סַבְרִי מָרָנָן

בָּרוּךְ אַתָּה יהוה אֱלֹהֵינוּ מֶלֶךְ הָעוֹלָם
בּוֹרֵא פְּרִי הַגָּפֶן.[ה]

HILKHOT TEFILLA • הלכות תפילה

בּוֹרֵא פְּרִי הַגָּפֶן – *Who creates the fruit of the vine.* The blessings over foods are generally broken down into categories. There is one blessing for all fruits, another for all vegetables. Why does wine get its own specific blessing? The answer, says the Gemara (*Berakhot* 35a), is related to the verse in *Tehillim* 104, "And wine cheers the heart of man." Wine has the special property of lightening one's mood, opening one's heart and soul to the messages of Shabbat.

BIUR TEFILLA • ביאור תפילה

זָכוֹר אֶת־יוֹם הַשַּׁבָּת – *Remember the Shabbat day.* This passage is from *Shemot* 20:7. It is the seventh verse in the chapter, it begins with the seventh letter of the alphabet and it goes on to recall seven people who must rest on the seventh day (*Tur*).

ZEMIROT FOR SHABBAT DAY

בָּרוּךְ Blessed be the LORD who, day by day, carries our burden with salvation and redemption. We will rejoice in His name all day long, and raise our head high in His salvation. For He is a stronghold for the poor and a refuge for the needy.

The LORD's tribes are Israel's testimony: He was distressed in their distress, in their suffering and slavery. Through a pavement of sapphire He showed them the strength of His love, He revealed Himself, lifting them from the depths of the pit. For with the LORD is loving- *Ps. 130*
kindness; He abounds in redemption.

How precious is His loving-kindness; He shelters them under His shade. For their sake He went with them into exile in Babylon. When they went down in ships, He was counted among them. He ensured that they were treated mercifully by those who took them captive. For the LORD will not forsake His people, for the sake of His great name.

In Eilam He placed His throne, to rescue His beloved, to remove from them the stronghold of His rebels. He redeemed His servants from passing under the sword. He raised the pride of His people, for the glory of all His devoted ones. For though He afflicts, He also shows *Lam. 3*
compassion and loving-kindness.

When the he-goat [Greece] extended its power, and the vision of the four ascended to the heights, And in their hearts they intended to destroy those He loved, through His priests He laid low those who rose against Him: The LORD's kindness has not ended nor His *Lam. 3*
compassion ceased.

I was handed over to Edom [Rome] by my quarrelsome friends, who daily sated their appetite with my treasures. His help was with me, supporting my foundations, He will not forsake me all the days of my age. For the LORD does not reject forever. *Lam. 3*

When He comes from Edom with garments stained crimson, there will be slaughter in Botzra, and an execution of traitors, their blood will turn His garments red, in His great strength He will bring the leaders low. With His mighty blast like a day of the east wind. *Is. 27*

When the oppressor from Edom sees how it will be, He will think Botzra to be a refuge like Betzer, giving protection to angels and men, willful and accidental sinners alike. Love the *Ps. 31*
LORD, all His devoted ones: all His faithful ones He will guard.

The Rock in His kindness will command His communities to gather, coming together from the four winds, He will settle them upon the high mountains, He will return with us, gathering the dispersed, for it does not say, "He will bring back" but "He will return" and gather.

Blessed is our God who has bestowed good upon us. In His compassion and abundant kindness, He has done great things for us. Like these and those, may He do yet more for us, to magnify His great, mighty and awesome name, by which we are called.

Blessed is our God who created us for His glory, To praise and laud Him and tell of His majesty, His loving-kindness is greater to us than to any other nation. Therefore with all our heart and soul and might, let us proclaim His kingship and His unity.

---

in stanza two through the first letters of stanza nine. The lack of cohesion with the first and last two stanzas both in form and content lead some to believe that these are later interpolations.

The overall theme speaks to the various

This **BIUR TEFILLA** *continues on page 743.*

זמירות ליום שבת

בָּרוּךְ אֲדֹנָי יוֹם יוֹם, יַעֲמָס לָנוּ יֶשַׁע וּפִדְיוֹם, וּבִשְׁמוֹ נָגִיל כָּל הַיּוֹם, וּבִישׁוּעָתוֹ נָרִים רֹאשׁ עֶלְיוֹן. כִּי הוּא מָעוֹז לַדָּל וּמַחְסֶה לָאֶבְיוֹן.

שִׁבְטֵי יָהּ לְיִשְׂרָאֵל עֵדוּת, בְּצָרָתָם לוֹ צָר בְּסִבְלוּת וּבְעַבְדוּת, בִּלְבְנַת הַסַּפִּיר הֶרְאָם עֹז יְדִידוּת, וְנִגְלָה לְהַעֲלוֹתָם מֵעֹמֶק בּוֹר וָדוּת. כִּי־עִם־יהוה הַחֶסֶד, וְהַרְבֵּה עִמּוֹ פְדוּת: תהלים קל

מַה יָּקָר חַסְדּוֹ בְּצִלּוֹ לְגוֹנְנֵמוֹ, בְּגָלוּת בָּבֶלָה שֻׁלַּח לְמַעֲנֵמוֹ, לְהוֹרִיד בָּרִיחִים נִמְנָה בֵינֵימוֹ, וַיִּתְּנֵם לְרַחֲמִים לִפְנֵי שׁוֹבֵימוֹ. כִּי לֹא יִטֹּשׁ יהוה אֶת עַמּוֹ, בַּעֲבוּר הַגָּדוֹל שְׁמוֹ.

עֵילָם שָׁת כִּסְאוֹ לְהַצִּיל יְדִידָיו, לְהַאֲבִיד מִשָּׁם מָעֻזְנֵי מוֹרְדָיו, מֵעֲבֹר בַּשֶּׁלַח פָּדָה אֶת עֲבָדָיו, קֶרֶן לְעַמּוֹ יָרִים, תְּהִלָּה לְכָל חֲסִידָיו. כִּי אִם־הוֹגָה, וְרִחַם כְּרֹב חֲסָדָו: איכה ג

וּצְפִיר הָעִזִּים הִגְדִּיל עֲצוּמָיו, וְגַם חָזוּת אַרְבַּע עָלוּ לִמְרוֹמָיו, וּבְלִבָּם דִּמּוּ לְהַשְׁחִית אֶת רְחוּמָיו, עַל יְדֵי כֹהֲנָיו מִגֵּר מִתְקוֹמְמָיו. חַסְדֵי יהוה כִּי לֹא־תָמְנוּ, כִּי לֹא כָלוּ רַחֲמָיו: איכה ג

נִסְגַּרְתִּי לֶאֱדוֹם בְּיַד רֵעַי מְדָנַי, שֶׁבְּכָל יוֹם מְמַלְּאִים כְּרֵסָם מֵעֲדָנַי, עֶזְרָתוֹ עִמִּי לִסְמֹךְ אֶת אֲדָנַי, וְלֹא נְטַשְׁתַּנִי כָּל יְמֵי עִדָּנַי. כִּי לֹא יִזְנַח לְעוֹלָם אֲדֹנָי: איכה ג

בְּבוֹאוֹ מֵאֱדוֹם חֲמוּץ בְּגָדִים, זֶבַח לוֹ בְּבָצְרָה וְטֶבַח לוֹ בְּבוֹגְדִים, וְיֵז נִצְחָם מַלְבּוּשָׁיו לְהַאְדִּים, בְּכֹחוֹ הַגָּדוֹל יִבְצֹר רוּחַ נְגִידִים. הָגָה בְּרוּחוֹ הַקָּשָׁה בְּיוֹם קָדִים: ישעיה כז

רְאוֹתוֹ כִּי כֵן אֲדוֹמִי הָעוֹצֵר, יַחְשָׁב לוֹ בָּצְרָה תִּקְלֹט כְּבֶצֶר, וּמַלְאָךְ כְּאָדָם בְּתוֹכָהּ יִנָּצֵר, וּמֵזִיד כַּשּׁוֹגֵג בְּמִקְלָט יֵעָצֵר. אֶהֱבוּ אֶת־יהוה כָּל־חֲסִידָיו, אֱמוּנִים נֹצֵר: תהלים לא

יְצַוֶּה צוּר חַסְדּוֹ קְהִלּוֹתָיו לְקַבֵּץ, מֵאַרְבַּע רוּחוֹת עָדָיו לְהִקָּבֵץ, וּבְהַר מְרוֹם הָרִים אוֹתָנוּ לְהַרְבֵּץ, וְאִתָּנוּ יָשׁוּב נִדָּחִים קוֹבֵץ. יָשִׁיב לֹא נֶאֱמַר, כִּי אִם וְשָׁב וְקִבֵּץ.

בָּרוּךְ הוּא אֱלֹהֵינוּ אֲשֶׁר טוֹב גְּמָלָנוּ, כְּרַחֲמָיו וּכְרֹב חֲסָדָיו הִגְדִּיל לָנוּ, אֵלֶּה וְכָאֵלֶּה יוֹסֵף עִמָּנוּ, לְהַגְדִּיל שְׁמוֹ הַגָּדוֹל הַגִּבּוֹר וְהַנּוֹרָא, שֶׁנִּקְרָא עָלֵינוּ.

בָּרוּךְ הוּא אֱלֹהֵינוּ שֶׁבְּרָאָנוּ לִכְבוֹדוֹ, לְהַלְּלוֹ וּלְשַׁבְּחוֹ וּלְסַפֵּר הוֹדוֹ, מִכָּל אֹם גָּבַר עָלֵינוּ חַסְדּוֹ, לָכֵן בְּכָל לֵב וּבְכָל נֶפֶשׁ וּבְכָל מְאוֹדוֹ, נַמְלִיכוֹ וּנְיַחֲדוֹ.

ביאור תפילה · BIUR TEFILLA

בָּרוּךְ אֲדֹנָי יוֹם יוֹם – *Blessed be the Lord who, day by day.* This poem was written by Shimon HaGadol ben Yitzḥak of Magence in the tenth century, one of the earliest poets of Ashkenazic Jewry. His name can be found hidden in acrostic form beginning

May He to whom peace belongs, send us blessing and peace. From left and right, may Israel have peace. May the Compassionate One bless His people with peace, and may they merit to see children and children's children, occupied with Torah and the commandments, bringing Israel peace. Wondrous Counselor, mighty God, everlasting Father, Prince of peace. *Is. 9*

בָּרוּךְ אֵל עֶלְיוֹן Blessed is God Most High[B] who has given us rest, / To relieve our souls from distress and pain. / May He seek the good of Zion, the outcast city. / How long must she grieve, her spirits downcast?

All who keep the Sabbath, man and woman alike, find favor like an offering made to God.

He who rides the heavens, King of worlds, / Gently told His people to rest, / With tasty food and delicacies of all kinds, / With elegant dress, as at a family feast.

All who keep the Sabbath, man and woman alike, find favor like an offering made to God.

Happy are all who await a double reward / From the One who sees all, though He dwells in dense dark. / He will grant him a heritage in hill and valley, / A heritage and resting place like [Jacob] on whom the sun shone.

All who keep the Sabbath, man and woman alike, find favor like an offering made to God.

Whoever keeps the Sabbath fully, not profaning it, / Shows that he is worthy; holy is his lot. / Happy is he who fulfills the day's duty; / It is like a gift presented to God who fashioned him.

All who keep the Sabbath, man and woman alike, find favor like an offering made to God.

The Rock, my God, called it "Beloved of days." / Happy are the faithful if it is kept intact. / He will set on their head a close-fitting crown. / On them the Rock of Eternity will make His spirit rest.

All who keep the Sabbath, man and woman alike, find favor like an offering made to God.

He who remembers the Sabbath day to keep it holy / Will gain high honor like a diadem on his head. / Therefore let each give to his soul / Delight and joy with which to be exalted.

All who keep the Sabbath, man and woman alike, find favor like an offering made to God.

Let her be holy to you – Sabbath the queen – / Placing a blessing in your home. / In all your dwellings, do no work, / Nor your sons and daughters, your servant or maid.

All who keep the Sabbath, man and woman alike, find favor like an offering made to God.

---

exiled, the Divine Presence went with them…and when the day comes when they will be redeemed and return to the Land, the Divine Presence will return with them."

BIUR TEFILLA · ביאור תפילה

בָּרוּךְ אֵל עֶלְיוֹן – *Blessed is God Most High.* This poem was written by Rabbi Barukh ben Rabbi Shmuel of Mainz (Magence).The acrostic spells only his first name with the word chazak as in בָּרוּךְ חָזָק. "

שֶׁהַשָּׁלוֹם שֶׁלּוֹ יָשִׂים עָלֵינוּ בְּרָכָה וְשָׁלוֹם, מִשְּׂמֹאל וּמִיָּמִין עַל יִשְׂרָאֵל שָׁלוֹם, הָרַחֲמָן הוּא יְבָרֵךְ אֶת עַמּוֹ בַשָּׁלוֹם, וְיִזְכּוּ לִרְאוֹת בָּנִים וּבְנֵי בָנִים, עוֹסְקִים, בַּתּוֹרָה וּבְמִצְוֹת, עַל יִשְׂרָאֵל שָׁלוֹם. פֶּלֶא יוֹעֵץ אֵל גִּבּוֹר אֲבִי־עַד שַׂר־שָׁלוֹם: ישעיה ט

בָּרוּךְ אֵל עֶלְיוֹן, אֲשֶׁר נָתַן מְנוּחָה, לְנַפְשֵׁנוּ פִדְיוֹן מִשֵּׁאת וַאֲנָחָה
וְהוּא יִדְרֹשׁ לְצִיּוֹן, עִיר הַנִּדָּחָה, עַד אָנָה תּוּגְיוֹן נֶפֶשׁ נֶאֱנָחָה.
הַשּׁוֹמֵר שַׁבָּת הַבֵּן עִם הַבַּת, לָאֵל יֵרָצוּ כְּמִנְחָה עַל מַחֲבַת.

רוֹכֵב בָּעֲרָבוֹת, מֶלֶךְ עוֹלָמִים, אֶת עַמּוֹ לִשְׁבֹּת אִזֵּן בַּנְּעִימִים
בְּמַאֲכָלוֹת עֲרֵבוֹת בְּמִינֵי מַטְעַמִּים, בְּמַלְבּוּשֵׁי כָבוֹד זֶבַח מִשְׁפָּחָה.
הַשּׁוֹמֵר שַׁבָּת הַבֵּן עִם הַבַּת, לָאֵל יֵרָצוּ כְּמִנְחָה עַל מַחֲבַת.

וְאַשְׁרֵי כָּל חוֹכֶה לְתַשְׁלוּמֵי כֵפֶל, מֵאֵת כֹּל סוֹכֶה, שׁוֹכֵן בָּעֲרָפֶל
נַחֲלָה לוֹ יִזְכֶּה בָּהָר וּבַשָּׁפֶל, נַחֲלָה וּמְנוּחָה כַּשֶּׁמֶשׁ לוֹ זָרְחָה.
הַשּׁוֹמֵר שַׁבָּת הַבֵּן עִם הַבַּת, לָאֵל יֵרָצוּ כְּמִנְחָה עַל מַחֲבַת.

כָּל שׁוֹמֵר שַׁבָּת כַּדָּת מֵחַלְּלוֹ, הֵן הֶכְשֵׁר חִבַּת קֹדֶשׁ גּוֹרָלוֹ
וְאִם יֵצֵא חוֹבַת הַיּוֹם, אַשְׁרֵי לוֹ, אֶל אֵל אָדוֹן מְחוֹלְלוֹ מִנְחָה הִיא שְׁלוּחָה.
הַשּׁוֹמֵר שַׁבָּת הַבֵּן עִם הַבַּת, לָאֵל יֵרָצוּ כְּמִנְחָה עַל מַחֲבַת.

חֶמְדַּת הַיָּמִים קְרָאוֹ אֵלִי צוּר, וְאַשְׁרֵי לִתְמִימִים אִם יִהְיֶה נָצוּר
כֶּתֶר הִלּוּמִים עַל רֹאשָׁם יָצוּר, צוּר הָעוֹלָמִים, רוּחוֹ בָּם נָחָה.
הַשּׁוֹמֵר שַׁבָּת הַבֵּן עִם הַבַּת, לָאֵל יֵרָצוּ כְּמִנְחָה עַל מַחֲבַת.

זָכוֹר אֶת יוֹם הַשַּׁבָּת לְקַדְּשׁוֹ, קַרְנוֹ כִּי גָבְהָה נֵזֶר עַל רֹאשׁוֹ
עַל כֵּן יִתֵּן הָאָדָם לְנַפְשׁוֹ, עֹנֶג וְגַם שִׂמְחָה בָּהֶם לְמָשְׁחָה.
הַשּׁוֹמֵר שַׁבָּת הַבֵּן עִם הַבַּת, לָאֵל יֵרָצוּ כְּמִנְחָה עַל מַחֲבַת.

קֹדֶשׁ הִיא לָכֶם שַׁבָּת הַמַּלְכָּה, אֶל תּוֹךְ בָּתֵּיכֶם לְהָנִיחַ בְּרָכָה
בְּכָל מוֹשְׁבוֹתֵיכֶם לֹא תַעֲשׂוּ מְלָאכָה, בְּנֵיכֶם וּבְנוֹתֵיכֶם עֶבֶד וְגַם שִׁפְחָה.
הַשּׁוֹמֵר שַׁבָּת הַבֵּן עִם הַבַּת, לָאֵל יֵרָצוּ כְּמִנְחָה עַל מַחֲבַת.

---

with us. As the Gemara relates (*Megilla* 29a) "R. Shimon bar Yoḥai said: 'See how beloved Israel is to the Holy One Blessed be He, for in every place where Israel was exiles that the Jewish people have endured over time. The key to our survival of those and any future exile lies in the knowledge that Hashem has always been

יוֹם זֶה מְכֻבָּד This day is honored[B] above all others,
For on it He who formed worlds found rest.

For six days, do your work
But the seventh day is God's:
On the Sabbath you shall do no work,
For in six days He made all.

This day is honored above all others,
for on it He who formed worlds found rest.

Foremost among sacred days[B]
Is this day of rest, this holy Sabbath.
So let each say Kiddush over wine,
And break bread over two complete loaves.[B]

This day is honored above all others,
for on it He who formed worlds found rest.

Eat choice food, drink sweet wine,
For God will give to those who cleave to Him
Clothes to wear, due portions of bread,
Meat and fish, and all tasty foods.

This day is honored above all others,
for on it He who formed worlds found rest.

...רִאשׁוֹן הוּא לְמִקְרָאֵי קֹדֶשׁ – *Foremost among sacred days...* This is a reference to the verses in *Vayikra* 23:2-3 in which the commandments given to observe each of the holidays is preceded with the command to rest on Shabbat. It is thus the first and foremost among the sacred days and so is also called "*Shabbat Shabbaton*" – the Sabbath of Sabbaths.

עַל שְׁתֵּי לֶחֶם יִבְצְעוּ תְמִימִים – *And break bread over two complete loaves.* The requirement is that the two loaves of bread over which one says the blessing of *HaMotzi* at the beginning of the meal must be whole rather than pre-sliced or cut (*Shulḥan Arukh* 274:1).

Alternatively, it has been suggested that the word "complete" refers not to the bread but to the person who breaks the bread and says kiddush, the person who is thereby whole.

Where else in the poem can you find the similar Hebrew word *tamim* (whole, complete, perfect)? What might be the connection?

יוֹם זֶה מְכֻבָּד מִכָּל יָמִים, כִּי בוֹ שָׁבַת צוּר עוֹלָמִים.

שֵׁשֶׁת יָמִים תַּעֲשֶׂה מְלַאכְתֶּךָ
וְיוֹם הַשְּׁבִיעִי לֵאלֹהֶיךָ
שַׁבָּת לֹא תַעֲשֶׂה בוֹ מְלָאכָה
כִּי כֹל עָשָׂה שֵׁשֶׁת יָמִים.
יוֹם זֶה מְכֻבָּד מִכָּל יָמִים, כִּי בוֹ שָׁבַת צוּר עוֹלָמִים.

רִאשׁוֹן הוּא לְמִקְרָאֵי קֹדֶשׁ
יוֹם שַׁבָּתוֹן יוֹם שַׁבַּת קֹדֶשׁ
עַל כֵּן כָּל אִישׁ בְּיֵינוֹ יְקַדֵּשׁ
עַל שְׁתֵּי לֶחֶם יִבְצְעוּ תְמִימִים.
יוֹם זֶה מְכֻבָּד מִכָּל יָמִים, כִּי בוֹ שָׁבַת צוּר עוֹלָמִים.

אֱכֹל מַשְׁמַנִּים, שְׁתֵה מַמְתַּקִּים
כִּי אֵל יִתֵּן לְכֹל בּוֹ דְבֵקִים
בֶּגֶד לִלְבֹּשׁ, לֶחֶם חֻקִּים
בָּשָׂר וְדָגִים וְכָל מַטְעַמִּים.
יוֹם זֶה מְכֻבָּד מִכָּל יָמִים, כִּי בוֹ שָׁבַת צוּר עוֹלָמִים.

BIUR TEFILLA • ביאור תפילה

יוֹם זֶה מְכֻבָּד – *This day is honored.* The composer is an anonymous person named Yisrael whose name appears in an acrostic in all of the stanzas but the last one which curiously also does not fit entirely with the themes of the previous ones.

The poem focuses on aspects of Shabbat which we are already familiar with from the songs of Friday evening: Hashem's rest on Shabbat, the mandate for us to observe not only the prohibitions against work but to sanctify the day with kiddush and *HaMotzi* (the blessing over bread) and by eating and drinking, and saying *Birkat HaMazon*. The day is thus "honored above all others" not alone by the actions of God, but through the meaning that we human beings bring to it.

On it you shall lack nothing – so eat,
Be satisfied and bless
The Lord your God, whom you love,
For He has blessed you from all peoples.

This day is honored above all others,
for on it He who formed worlds found rest.

The heavens declare His glory
And the earth is full of His loving-kindness.
See all these things His hand has made
For He is the Rock, His work is perfect.

This day is honored above all others,
for on it He who formed worlds found rest.

שַׁבָּת הַיּוֹם Today is the Sabbath of the Lord.
Celebrate greatly with my songs,
Multiply my delicacies,
Keep it like the Lord's command. Today is the Sabbath of the Lord.

Do not travel beyond boundaries,
Do not labor on this day:
Eat, drink, make merry.
This is the day the Lord has made. Today is the Sabbath of the Lord.

If you keep it God will guard you like the pupil of His eye,
You, your son and daughter too.
If you call the Sabbath a delight
Then you will find delight before the Lord.
Today is the Sabbath of the Lord.

Eat rich foods and delicacies, Tasty dishes of many kinds,
Soft-shelled nuts and pomegranates:
Eat, be satisfied and bless the Lord. Today is the Sabbath of the Lord.

Make ready on the table delicious bread,
And make, this day, three meals.
Bless and thank His glorious name.
Take care, observe and do, my sons. Today is the Sabbath of the Lord.

לֹא תֶחְסַר כֹּל בּוֹ, וְאָכַלְתָּ
וְשָׂבָעְתָּ וּבֵרַכְתָּ
אֶת יהוה אֱלֹהֶיךָ אֲשֶׁר אָהַבְתָּ
כִּי בֵרַכְךָ מִכָּל הָעַמִּים.
יוֹם זֶה מְכֻבָּד מִכָּל יָמִים, כִּי בוֹ שָׁבַת צוּר עוֹלָמִים.

הַשָּׁמַיִם מְסַפְּרִים כְּבוֹדוֹ
וְגַם הָאָרֶץ מָלְאָה חַסְדּוֹ
רְאוּ כִּי כָל אֵלֶּה עָשְׂתָה יָדוֹ
כִּי הוּא הַצּוּר פָּעֳלוֹ תָמִים.
יוֹם זֶה מְכֻבָּד מִכָּל יָמִים, כִּי בוֹ שָׁבַת צוּר עוֹלָמִים.

שַׁבָּת הַיּוֹם לַיהוה, מְאֹד צַהֲלוּ בְּרִנּוּנַי
וְגַם הַרְבּוּ מַעֲדַנַּי, אוֹתוֹ לִשְׁמֹר כְּמִצְוַת יהוה.
שַׁבָּת הַיּוֹם לַיהוה.

מֵעֲבֹר דֶּרֶךְ וּגְבוּלִים, מֵעֲשׂוֹת הַיּוֹם פְּעָלִים
לֶאֱכֹל וְלִשְׁתּוֹת בְּהִלּוּלִים, זֶה הַיּוֹם עָשָׂה יהוה.
שַׁבָּת הַיּוֹם לַיהוה.

וְאִם תִּשְׁמְרֶנּוּ, יָהּ יִנְצָרְךָ כְּבָבַת, אַתָּה וּבִנְךָ וְגַם הַבַּת
וְקָרָאתָ עֹנֶג לַשַּׁבָּת, אָז תִּתְעַנַּג עַל יהוה.
שַׁבָּת הַיּוֹם לַיהוה.

אֱכֹל מַשְׁמַנִּים וּמַעֲדַנִּים, וּמַטְעַמִּים הַרְבֵּה מִינִים
אֱגוֹזֵי פֶרֶךְ וְרִמּוֹנִים, וְאָכַלְתָּ וְשָׂבָעְתָּ וּבֵרַכְתָּ אֶת יהוה.
שַׁבָּת הַיּוֹם לַיהוה.

לַעֲרֹךְ בְּשֻׁלְחָן לֶחֶם חֲמוּדוֹת, לַעֲשׂוֹת הַיּוֹם שָׁלֹשׁ סְעוּדוֹת
אֶת הַשֵּׁם הַנִּכְבָּד לְבָרֵךְ וּלְהוֹדוֹת, שִׁקְדוּ וְשִׁמְרוּ וַעֲשׂוּ בָנַי.
שַׁבָּת הַיּוֹם לַיהוה.

יוֹם שַׁבָּתוֹן The day of rest[B] should not be forgotten,
Its memory is like sweet fragrance,

On it the dove found rest, And in it the exhausted rest.

This day is honored by the people of faith.
Parents and children guard it with care.
It was engraved on two tablets of stone,
By the greatness of His power and His unfailing strength.

On it the dove found rest, And in it the exhausted rest.

All came together in a covenant:
"We will do and we will obey," they said as one.
Then they responded, saying, "The LORD is One" –
Blessed is He who gives the weary strength.

On it the dove found rest, And in it the exhausted rest.

He spoke in His holiness on the Mount of Myrrh [Sinai]:
"Remember and observe the seventh day."
And learn together all His commands:
Gird your loins and muster strength.

On it the dove found rest, And in it the exhausted rest.

The people who have wandered like a straying flock –
May He remember the covenant and the oath,
So that no harm should happen to them,
As You swore at the end of Noah's flood.

On it the dove found rest, And in it the exhausted rest.

Who exactly is the dove?

The Gemara (*Shabbat* 49a) points to the verse in *Tehillim* 68:14 "the wings of a dove are coated in silver" and concludes that just as the wings of a dove protect her, so too the mitzvot or commandments protect Israel. In that case, the dove might be the Jewish people who find protective rest in Shabbat.

Alternatively, the *Tikkunei Zohar* 6 22b says that while in exile the Divine Presence did not rest except on Shabbat and holy days, and so the dove is really God's Presence.

Alternatively, it is both man and God, as it were, who share their rest and the peace that comes with it.

יוֹם שַׁבָּתוֹן אֵין לִשְׁכַּחַ, זִכְרוֹ כְּרֵיחַ הַנִּיחֹחַ
יוֹנָה מָצְאָה בוֹ מָנוֹחַ וְשָׁם יָנוּחוּ יְגִיעֵי כֹחַ.

הַיּוֹם נִכְבָּד לִבְנֵי אֱמוּנִים
זְהִירִים לְשָׁמְרוֹ אָבוֹת וּבָנִים
חָקוּק בִּשְׁנֵי לוּחוֹת אֲבָנִים
מֵרֹב אוֹנִים וְאַמִּיץ כֹּחַ. יוֹנָה מָצְאָה בוֹ מָנוֹחַ וְשָׁם יָנוּחוּ יְגִיעֵי כֹחַ.

וּבָאוּ כֻלָּם בִּבְרִית יַחַד
נַעֲשֶׂה וְנִשְׁמַע אָמְרוּ כְּאֶחָד
וּפָתְחוּ וְעָנוּ יהוה אֶחָד
בָּרוּךְ נֹתֵן לַיָּעֵף כֹּחַ. יוֹנָה מָצְאָה בוֹ מָנוֹחַ וְשָׁם יָנוּחוּ יְגִיעֵי כֹחַ.

דִּבֶּר בְּקָדְשׁוֹ בְּהַר הַמֹּר
יוֹם הַשְּׁבִיעִי זָכוֹר וְשָׁמוֹר
וְכָל פִּקּוּדָיו יַחַד לִגְמֹר
חַזֵּק מָתְנַיִם וְאַמֵּץ כֹּחַ. יוֹנָה מָצְאָה בוֹ מָנוֹחַ וְשָׁם יָנוּחוּ יְגִיעֵי כֹחַ.

הָעָם אֲשֶׁר נָע, כַּצֹּאן תָּעָה
יִזְכֹּר לְפָקְדוֹ בְּרִית וּשְׁבוּעָה
לְבַל יַעֲבָר בָּם מִקְרֶה רָעָה
כַּאֲשֶׁר נִשְׁבַּעְתָּ עַל מֵי נֹחַ. יוֹנָה מָצְאָה בוֹ מָנוֹחַ וְשָׁם יָנוּחוּ יְגִיעֵי כֹחַ.

BIUR TEFILLA • ביאור תפילה

יוֹם שַׁבָּתוֹן – *The day of rest*. The author was Rabbi Yehuda HaLevi (d. 1141), one of the foremost poets and philosophers in Jewish history.

The refrain speaks of a dove who found rest on Shabbat, just as can those who are exhausted. The image is most commonly connected to the story of Noaḥ who sent out a dove "on the seventh day" (*Bereshit* 8:12). The dove did not return and thus one can assume that it found a place on land to rest after the travails of the Flood.

שִׁמְרוּ שַׁבְּתוֹתַי Observe My Sabbaths,[B] so that you are nourished and sated,
From the radiance of My blessings,
when you come to rest. Borrow on My account, My children,
Delight in My pleasures: Today is the Sabbath of the LORD.

Borrow on My account, My children,
Delight in My pleasures: Today is the Sabbath of the LORD.

Proclaim freedom from toil, then I will grant My blessing,
joining one to the next,
bringing gladness on My day of joy. Wear clothes of fine linen and wool.
And learn from My elders: Today is the Sabbath of the LORD.

Borrow on My account, My children,
Delight in My pleasures: Today is the Sabbath of the LORD.

Quickly bring the portion, obey Esther's command.[I]
Make a reckoning with the Creator,
He will repay you for the food, and more. Trust in Me, My faithful ones,
And drink wine from My plentiful supply. Today is the Sabbath of the LORD.

Borrow on My account, My children,
Delight in My pleasures: Today is the Sabbath of the LORD.

Today is a day of redemption, if you observe the Sabbath;
Then you will be My special treasure.
Stay [for the night of exile], then pass on. Then you will live before Me.
And be filled from My hidden store. Today is the Sabbath of the LORD.

Borrow on My account, My children,
Delight in My pleasures: Today is the Sabbath of the LORD.

Make my city strong, God, the God most high.
Bring back my Temple,
With joy and words of song. There may my singers chant,
My Levites and my priests.
Then you will delight in the LORD. Today is the Sabbath of the LORD.

Borrow on My account, My children,
Delight in My pleasures: Today is the Sabbath of the LORD.

(*Etz Yosef*) (although the wording of the phrase here is a play on Esther 5:5). The reference to haste is found in the Gemara (*Shabbat* 117b) which encourages one to get up early to prepare for Shabbat as a way of honoring the day, as opposed to leaving everything for the last minute. Alternatively, it could be a reference to *Shabbat* 119a which encourages one not to put off eating the Shabbat meal, but to do so as soon as one can, as a way of honoring the day.

שִׁמְרוּ שַׁבְּתוֹתַי,ב לְמַעַן תִּינְקוּ וּשְׂבַעְתֶּם, מִזִּיו בִּרְכוֹתַי
אֶל הַמְּנוּחָה כִּי בָאתֶם, וּלְווּ עָלַי בָּנַי, וְעִדְנוּ מַעֲדָנַי שַׁבָּת הַיּוֹם לַיהוה.
וּלְווּ עָלַי בָּנַי, וְעִדְנוּ מַעֲדָנַי, שַׁבָּת הַיּוֹם לַיהוה.

לֶעָמֵל קִרְאוּ דְרוֹר, וְנָתַתִּי אֶת בִּרְכָתִי, אִשָּׁה אֶל אֲחוֹתָהּ לִצְרֹר
לְגַלּוֹת עַל יוֹם שִׂמְחָתִי, בִּגְדֵי שֵׁשׁ עִם שָׁנִי, וְהִתְבּוֹנְנוּ מִזְּקֵנַי
שַׁבָּת הַיּוֹם לַיהוה.
וּלְווּ עָלַי בָּנַי, וְעִדְנוּ מַעֲדָנַי, שַׁבָּת הַיּוֹם לַיהוה.

מַהֲרוּ אֶת הַמָּנֶה, לַעֲשׂוֹת אֶת דְּבַר אֶסְתֵּר,ע וְחִשְׁבוּ עִם הַקּוֹנֶה
לְשַׁלֵּם אָכוֹל וְהוֹתֵר, בִּטְחוּ בִי אֱמוּנַי, וּשְׁתוּ יֵין מַשְׁמַנַּי שַׁבָּת הַיּוֹם לַיהוה.
וּלְווּ עָלַי בָּנַי, וְעִדְנוּ מַעֲדָנַי, שַׁבָּת הַיּוֹם לַיהוה.

הִנֵּה יוֹם גְּאֻלָּה, יוֹם שַׁבָּת אִם תִּשְׁמֹרוּ, וִהְיִיתֶם לִי סְגֻלָּה
לִינוּ וְאַחַר תַּעֲבֹרוּ, וְאָז תִּחְיוּ לְפָנַי, וּתְמַלְּאוּ צְפוּנַי שַׁבָּת הַיּוֹם לַיהוה.
וּלְווּ עָלַי בָּנַי, וְעִדְנוּ מַעֲדָנַי, שַׁבָּת הַיּוֹם לַיהוה.

חַזֵּק קִרְיָתִי, אֵל אֱלֹהִים עֶלְיוֹן, וְהָשֵׁב אֶת נָוָתִי
בְּשִׂמְחָה וּבְהִגָּיוֹן, יְשׁוֹרְרוּ שָׁם רְנָנַי, לְוִיַּי וְכֹהֲנַי, אָז תִּתְעַנַּג עַל יהוה
שַׁבָּת הַיּוֹם לַיהוה.
וּלְווּ עָלַי בָּנַי, וְעִדְנוּ מַעֲדָנַי, שַׁבָּת הַיּוֹם לַיהוה.

BIUR TEFILLA • ביאור תפילה

שִׁמְרוּ שַׁבְּתוֹתַי – *Observe My Sabbaths.* Here Hashem calls on the Jewish people to keep the Shabbat, and promises that whatever expenditures they must incur He will repay them in kind. The theme comes from the Gemara (*Beitza* 15b) in which Hashem is quoted as saying "spend what you need to in order to sanctify the day" and then adds "believe in Me." Shabbat has always been a focal point of Jewish life, both in terms of the rhythms of our workweek, and the way that we spend our resources, putting our money as it were, where our values are. In return, as in so many of the other songs which are sung this day, there is the promise of redemption.

IYUN TEFILLA • עיון תפילה

מַהֲרוּ אֶת הַמָּנֶה, לַעֲשׂוֹת אֶת דְּבַר אֶסְתֵּר – *Quickly bring the portion, obey Esther's command.* The Shabbat is sometimes referred to in kabbalistic literature as Esther

כִּי אֶשְׁמְרָה If I keep the Sabbath, God will keep me,[I]
It is an eternal sign between God and me.
It is an eternal sign between God and me.

It is forbidden to engage in business or to travel,[H]
Even to speak about the things we need, or about matters of trade or state.
Instead I will study God's Torah and it will make me wise.[I]
It is an eternal sign between God and me.

On it I always find refreshment for my soul.
See: My Holy One gave the first generation,
A sign, by giving them a double portion on the sixth day.
So may my food be doubled every sixth day!
It is an eternal sign between God and me.

Engraved in God's law is His priests' decree,
To prepare the Show-Bread in His presence.
So, His sages ruled, on it fasting is forbidden, except on sins' Atonement Day.
It is an eternal sign between God and me.

It is a day of honor, a day of delight, with bread and fine wine, meat and fish. On it those who mourn are turned around,
For it is a joyous day and it will bring me joy.
It is an eternal sign between God and me.

Those who desecrate it by working will, in the end, be cut off.
Therefore I cleanse my heart with it as if with soap.[I]
Evening and morning I will pray to God,
Additional and afternoon prayer also, and He will answer me.
It is an eternal sign between God and me.

IYUN TEFILLA • עיון תפילה

אֶהְגֶּה בְּתוֹרַת אֵל וּתְחַכְּמֵנִי – *I will study God's Torah and it will make me wise.* Ibn Ezra, the author of this poem (his first name is formed by an acrostic), writes in his commentary on the Torah (*Shemot* 20:8) that on Shabbat one receives greater wisdom than one might have during the week (*Yalkut Lekaḥ Tov*). Surely being well rested and not having to be in so many other places can help focus one's concentration. No matter what your experience during the week, therefore, the Torah one learns on Shabbat feels different.

עַל כֵּן אֲכַבֵּס בּוֹ לִבִּי כְּבוֹרִית – *Therefore I cleanse my heart with it as if with soap.* Shabbat itself is like a bar of soap that has the potential to cleanse one's soul (Rabbi Meir of Permishlan).

כִּי אֶשְׁמְרָה שַׁבָּת אֵל יִשְׁמְרֵנִי.[ע] אוֹת הִיא לְעוֹלְמֵי עַד בֵּינוֹ וּבֵינִי.

אוֹת הִיא לְעוֹלְמֵי עַד בֵּינוֹ וּבֵינִי.

אָסוּר מְצֹא חֵפֶץ, עֲשׂוֹת דְּרָכִים,[ה] גַּם מִלְּדַבֵּר בּוֹ דִּבְרֵי צְרָכִים
דִּבְרֵי סְחוֹרָה אַף דִּבְרֵי מְלָכִים, אֶהְגֶּה בְּתוֹרַת אֵל וּתְחַכְּמֵנִי.[ע]

אוֹת הִיא לְעוֹלְמֵי עַד בֵּינוֹ וּבֵינִי.

בּוֹ אֶמְצָא תָמִיד נֹפֶשׁ לְנַפְשִׁי, הִנֵּה לְדוֹר רִאשׁוֹן נָתַן קְדוֹשִׁי
מוֹפֵת, בְּתֵת לֶחֶם מִשְׁנֶה בַּשִּׁשִּׁי, כָּכָה בְּכָל שִׁשִּׁי יַכְפִּיל מְזוֹנִי.

אוֹת הִיא לְעוֹלְמֵי עַד בֵּינוֹ וּבֵינִי.

רָשַׁם בְּדַת הָאֵל חֹק אֶל סְגָנָיו, בּוֹ לַעֲרֹךְ לֶחֶם פָּנִים בְּפָנָיו
עַל כֵּן לְהִתְעַנּוֹת בּוֹ עַל פִּי נְבוֹנָיו, אָסוּר, לְבַד מִיּוֹם כִּפּוּר עֲוֹנִי.

אוֹת הִיא לְעוֹלְמֵי עַד בֵּינוֹ וּבֵינִי.

הוּא יוֹם מְכֻבָּד, הוּא יוֹם תַּעֲנוּגִים, לֶחֶם וְיַיִן טוֹב, בָּשָׂר וְדָגִים
הַמִּתְאַבְּלִים בּוֹ אָחוֹר נְסוֹגִים, כִּי יוֹם שְׂמָחוֹת הוּא וּתְשַׂמְּחֵנִי.

אוֹת הִיא לְעוֹלְמֵי עַד בֵּינוֹ וּבֵינִי.

מֵחֵל מְלָאכָה בּוֹ סוֹפוֹ לְהַכְרִית, עַל כֵּן אֲכַבֵּס בּוֹ לִבִּי כְּבוֹרִית[ע]
וְאֶתְפַּלְּלָה אֶל אֵל עַרְבִית וְשַׁחֲרִית, מוּסָף וְגַם מִנְחָה הוּא יַעֲנֵנִי.

אוֹת הִיא לְעוֹלְמֵי עַד בֵּינוֹ וּבֵינִי.

HILKHOT TEFILLA • הלכות תפילה

אָסוּר מְצֹא חֵפֶץ, עֲשׂוֹת דְּרָכִים – *It is forbidden to engage in business or to travel.* One is not permitted to travel beyond certain limits of one's town but neither is one permitted to travel somewhere within the permitted limits if it is to tend to one's possessions or the like (*Eiruvin 38b and Rashi* there).

IYUN TEFILLA • עיון תפילה

כִּי אֶשְׁמְרָה שַׁבָּת אֵל יִשְׁמְרֵנִי – *If I keep the Sabbath, God will keep me.* "Rabbi Yoḥanan said: 'whoever keeps the Shabbat according to its laws, even if he is an idolater, will be forgiven'" (*Shabbat* 118b).

דְּרוֹר יִקְרָא God proclaims freedom[B] to boy and girl,
And guards you like the pupil of His eye.
Your name is pleasant, never will it cease.
Rest and be at ease on the Sabbath day.

Seek my Temple and my hall,
And show me a sign of salvation.
Plant a shoot in my vineyard.[B]
Hear the cry of my people.

Tread the winepress in Botzra,
And in Babylon which overpowered.
Crush my foes in anger and wrath,
Hear my voice on the day I cry.

God, let there be on the desert mountain,
Myrtle, acacia, cypress and box tree.[B]
To one who warns and one who is warned,[B]
Let peace flow like river waters.

Crush those who rise against me, zealous God,
Melting their heart with grief.
Then we will open and fill our mouths,
And tongues with songs of joy to You.

Know what is wisdom for your soul,
And it will be a crown for your head.
Keep your Holy One's command,
Observe your holy Sabbath day.

Birkat HaMazon can be found on page 976.

---

is whole again. Similarly, there is expressed the hope of freedom from our enemies who would prevent us from fulfilling our national aspirations.

נְטַע שׂוֹרֵק בְּתוֹךְ כַּרְמִי – *Plant a shoot in my vineyard.* This is generally a reference to the Messiah.

הֲדַס שִׁטָּה בְּרוֹשׁ תִּדְהָר – *Myrtle, acacia, cypress and box tree.* May these trees provide shade for those who leave the desert of exile on their way to Israel.

וְלַמַּזְהִיר וְלַנִּזְהָר – *To one who warns and one who is warned.* One who warns others about the need to keep the Shabbat, and the one who heeds the warning himself.

דְּרוֹר יִקְרָא לְבֵן עִם בַּת, וְיִנְצָרְכֶם כְּמוֹ בָבַת
נְעִים שִׁמְכֶם וְלֹא יֻשְׁבַּת, שְׁבוּ נוּחוּ בְּיוֹם שַׁבָּת

דְּרֹשׁ נָוִי וְאוּלַמִּי, וְאוֹת יֶשַׁע עֲשֵׂה עִמִּי
נְטַע שׂוֹרֵק בְּתוֹךְ כַּרְמִי, שְׁעֵה שַׁוְעַת בְּנֵי עַמִּי.

דְּרֹךְ פּוּרָה בְּתוֹךְ בָּצְרָה, וְגַם בָּבֶל אֲשֶׁר גָּבְרָה
נְתֹץ צָרַי בְּאַף עֶבְרָה, שְׁמַע קוֹלִי בְּיוֹם אֶקְרָא.

אֱלֹהִים תֵּן בְּמִדְבָּר הָר, הֲדַס שִׁטָּה בְּרוֹשׁ תִּדְהָר
וְלַמַּזְהִיר וְלַנִּזְהָר, שְׁלוֹמִים תֵּן כְּמֵי נָהָר.

הֲדֹךְ קָמַי, אֵל קַנָּא, בְּמוֹג לֵבָב וּבִמְגִנָּה
וְנַרְחִיב פֶּה וּנְמַלְאֶנָּה, לְשׁוֹנֵנוּ לְךָ רִנָּה.

דְּעֵה חָכְמָה לְנַפְשֶׁךָ, וְהִיא כֶתֶר לְרֹאשֶׁךָ
נְצֹר מִצְוַת קְדוֹשֶׁךָ, שְׁמֹר שַׁבַּת קָדְשֶׁךָ.

ברכת המזון *can be found on page 977.*

BIUR TEFILLA • ביאור תפילה

דְּרוֹר יִקְרָא – *God proclaims freedom.* This could be one of the earliest liturgical poems written exclusively about Shabbat. The composer was Dunash ibn Librat, one of the pioneers of Jewish grammar and poetry, a student of Rav Saadia Gaon in the tenth century. The poem speaks to the spiritual freedom and redemption given to us by Hashem with the Shabbat. As a bride and bridegroom take care of one another, so too do the Jews preserve Shabbat, and Shabbat, in turn, protects us from our enemies, as Hashem protects us like the pupil of His eye.

The word "freedom" with which the poem opens goes on to have multiple meanings. It is taken from the law of the jubilee year when "freedom is declared throughout the Land" (*Vayikra* 25:10) when all slaves go free, when property returns to its owners and debts are canceled. Perhaps the allusion in the poem is to a world that

Minḥa for Shabbat

אַשְׁרֵי Happy[1] are those who dwell in Your House; *Ps. 84*
they shall continue to praise You, Selah!

Happy are the people for whom this is so; *Ps. 144*
happy are the people whose God is the LORD.

A song of praise by David. *Ps. 145*

א I will elevate You, my God, the King, and bless Your name for ever and all time. ב Every day I will bless You, and praise Your name for ever and all time. ג Great is the LORD and greatly to be praised; His greatness is unfathomable. ד One generation will praise Your works to the next, and tell of Your mighty deeds. ה On the glorious splendor of Your majesty I will meditate, and on the acts of Your wonders. ו They shall talk of the power of Your awesome deeds, and I will tell of Your greatness. ז They shall recite the record of Your great goodness, and sing with joy of Your righteousness. ח The LORD is generous and compassionate, slow to anger and great in loving-kindness. ט The LORD is good to all, and His compassion extends to all His works. י All Your works shall thank You, LORD, and Your devoted ones shall bless You. כ They shall talk of the glory of Your kingship, and speak of Your might. ל To make known to mankind His mighty deeds and the glorious majesty of His kingship. מ Your kingdom is an everlasting kingdom, and Your reign is for all generations. ס The LORD supports all who fall, and raises all who are bowed down. ע All raise their eyes to You in hope, and You give them their food in due season. פ You open Your hand, and satisfy every living thing with favor. צ The LORD is righteous in all His ways, and

מנחה לשבת

אַשְׁרֵיע יוֹשְׁבֵי בֵיתֶךָ, עוֹד יְהַלְלוּךָ סֶּלָה: תהלים פד
אַשְׁרֵי הָעָם שֶׁכָּכָה לּוֹ, אַשְׁרֵי הָעָם שֶׁיהוה אֱלֹהָיו: תהלים קמד
תְּהִלָּה לְדָוִד תהלים קמה
אֲרוֹמִמְךָ אֱלוֹהַי הַמֶּלֶךְ, וַאֲבָרְכָה שִׁמְךָ לְעוֹלָם וָעֶד:
בְּכָל־יוֹם אֲבָרְכֶךָּ, וַאֲהַלְלָה שִׁמְךָ לְעוֹלָם וָעֶד:
גָּדוֹל יהוה וּמְהֻלָּל מְאֹד, וְלִגְדֻלָּתוֹ אֵין חֵקֶר:
דּוֹר לְדוֹר יְשַׁבַּח מַעֲשֶׂיךָ, וּגְבוּרֹתֶיךָ יַגִּידוּ:
הֲדַר כְּבוֹד הוֹדֶךָ, וְדִבְרֵי נִפְלְאֹתֶיךָ אָשִׂיחָה:
וֶעֱזוּז נוֹרְאֹתֶיךָ יֹאמֵרוּ, וּגְדוּלָּתְךָ אֲסַפְּרֶנָּה:
זֵכֶר רַב־טוּבְךָ יַבִּיעוּ, וְצִדְקָתְךָ יְרַנֵּנוּ:
חַנּוּן וְרַחוּם יהוה, אֶרֶךְ אַפַּיִם וּגְדָל־חָסֶד:
טוֹב־יהוה לַכֹּל, וְרַחֲמָיו עַל־כָּל־מַעֲשָׂיו:
יוֹדוּךָ יהוה כָּל־מַעֲשֶׂיךָ, וַחֲסִידֶיךָ יְבָרְכוּכָה:
כְּבוֹד מַלְכוּתְךָ יֹאמֵרוּ, וּגְבוּרָתְךָ יְדַבֵּרוּ:
לְהוֹדִיעַ לִבְנֵי הָאָדָם גְּבוּרֹתָיו, וּכְבוֹד הֲדַר מַלְכוּתוֹ:
מַלְכוּתְךָ מַלְכוּת כָּל־עֹלָמִים, וּמֶמְשַׁלְתְּךָ בְּכָל־דּוֹר וָדֹר:
סוֹמֵךְ יהוה לְכָל־הַנֹּפְלִים, וְזוֹקֵף לְכָל־הַכְּפוּפִים:
עֵינֵי־כֹל אֵלֶיךָ יְשַׂבֵּרוּ, וְאַתָּה נוֹתֵן־לָהֶם אֶת־אָכְלָם בְּעִתּוֹ:
פּוֹתֵחַ אֶת־יָדֶךָ, וּמַשְׂבִּיעַ לְכָל־חַי רָצוֹן:
צַדִּיק יהוה בְּכָל־דְּרָכָיו, וְחָסִיד בְּכָל־מַעֲשָׂיו:

kind in all He does. ק The LORD is close to all who call on Him, to all who call on Him in truth. ר He fulfills the will of those who fear Him; He hears their cry and saves them. ש The LORD guards all who love Him, but all the wicked He will destroy. ת ▸ My mouth shall speak the praise of the LORD, and all creatures shall bless His holy name for ever and all time.
We will bless the LORD now and for ever. Halleluya! *Ps. 115*

וּבָא לְצִיּוֹן גּוֹאֵל "A redeemer will come to Zion,[B] *Is. 59*
to those of Jacob who repent of their sins," declares the LORD.
"As for Me, this is My covenant with them,"[I] says the LORD.
"My spirit, that is on you,
and My words I have placed in your mouth
will not depart from your mouth,
or from the mouth of your children,
or from the mouth of their descendants from
this time on and for ever," says the LORD.

---

enough, especially for those who for health reasons could not put off getting to lunch (*Kol Bo*).

Regardless of the historical reasons, the overall emphasis seems to be on putting one's faith in God and in His Torah, an appropriate theme for the public reading of the Torah that we are about to perform, and for the *Amida* that we are about to recite.

IYUN TEFILLA • עיון תפילה

וַאֲנִי זֹאת בְּרִיתִי אוֹתָם – *As for Me, this is My covenant with them.* The words can literally be read "this is My covenant to them," as if to say that it is a one-sided affair rather than a two way street. The Ḥafetz Ḥayyim once remarked that this is because in some ways the covenant of living the life of a Jew was forced upon us, and cannot be erased no matter how we might try. This explains why in every generation there are Jews who come back to the fold, who assume a life of greater observance than their parents, for the covenant is something from which one cannot escape.

קָרוֹב יהוה לְכָל־קֹרְאָיו, לְכֹל אֲשֶׁר יִקְרָאֻהוּ בֶאֱמֶת:
רְצוֹן־יְרֵאָיו יַעֲשֶׂה, וְאֶת־שַׁוְעָתָם יִשְׁמַע, וְיוֹשִׁיעֵם:
שׁוֹמֵר יהוה אֶת־כָּל־אֹהֲבָיו, וְאֵת כָּל־הָרְשָׁעִים יַשְׁמִיד:
• תְּהִלַּת יהוה יְדַבֶּר פִּי, וִיבָרֵךְ כָּל־בָּשָׂר שֵׁם קָדְשׁוֹ לְעוֹלָם וָעֶד:
תהלים קטו וַאֲנַחְנוּ נְבָרֵךְ יָהּ מֵעַתָּה וְעַד־עוֹלָם, הַלְלוּיָהּ:

ישעיה נט וּבָא לְצִיּוֹן גּוֹאֵל, וּלְשָׁבֵי פֶשַׁע בְּיַעֲקֹב
נְאֻם יהוה:
וַאֲנִי זֹאת בְּרִיתִי אוֹתָם, אָמַר יהוה
רוּחִי אֲשֶׁר עָלֶיךָ וּדְבָרַי אֲשֶׁר־שַׂמְתִּי בְּפִיךָ
לֹא־יָמוּשׁוּ מִפִּיךָ וּמִפִּי זַרְעֲךָ וּמִפִּי זֶרַע זַרְעֲךָ
אָמַר יהוה, מֵעַתָּה וְעַד־עוֹלָם:

BIUR TEFILLA • ביאור תפילה

וּבָא לְצִיּוֹן גּוֹאֵל – *A redeemer will come to Zion.* Those who come to morning services every day during the week will recognize this prayer as one of the last that is said then. It contains a number of themes and elements: a version of the *Kedusha* that we have seen before in the morning's blessing before the *Shema* and in the repetition of the *Amida* although here it includes an Aramaic translation, verses about redemption, faithfulness, and trust in God, and a blessing thanking God for the Torah and the ability to fulfill the commandments.

While its appearance here in Shabbat afternoon *Minḥa* dates back at least to the times of the Geonim over a thousand years ago, the reason for its institution is not so clear. One theory suggests that Shabbat afternoon was a time when classes would be given and they would be concluded with verses about redemption and holiness of the kind contained in this prayer (Abudarham). Another theory suggests that it was in fact supposed to be said in the morning, just as on any other day, but it was pushed off until the afternoon because the morning service was already long

▸ You are the Holy One, enthroned on the praises of Israel. *Ps. 22*
And [the angels] call to one another, saying, ◂ "Holy, holy, holy
is the Lord of hosts; the whole world is filled with His glory."
And they receive permission from one another, saying: *Targum Yonatan Is. 6*
"Holy in the highest heavens, home of His Presence; holy on earth,
the work of His strength; holy for ever and all time is the Lord of hosts;
the whole earth is full of His radiant glory."

▸ Then a wind lifted me up and I heard behind me the sound of *Ezek. 3*
a great noise, saying, ◂ "Blessed is the Lord's glory from His place."
Then a wind lifted me up and I heard behind me *Targum Yonatan Ezek. 3*
the sound of a great tempest of those who uttered praise, saying,
"Blessed is the Lord's glory from the place of the home of His Presence."

The Lord shall reign for ever and all time. *Ex. 15*
The Lord's kingdom is established for ever and all time. *Targum Onkelos Ex. 15*

יהוה Lord, God of Abraham, Isaac and Yisrael, our ancestors, may *1 Chr. 29*
You keep this for ever so that it forms the thoughts in Your people's
heart, and directs their heart toward You. He is compassionate. He *Ps. 78*
forgives iniquity and does not destroy. Repeatedly He suppresses
His anger, not rousing His full wrath. For You, my Lord, are good *Ps. 86*
and forgiving, abundantly kind to all who call on You. Your righ- *Ps. 119*
teousness is eternally righteous, and Your Torah is truth. Grant *Micah 7*
truth to Jacob, loving-kindness to Abraham, as You promised our
ancestors in ancient times. Blessed is my Lord for day after day He *Ps. 68*
burdens us [with His blessings]; is our salvation, Selah! The Lord *Ps. 46*
of hosts is with us; the God of Jacob is our refuge, Selah! Lord of *Ps. 84*
hosts, happy is the one who trusts in You. Lord, save. May the King *Ps. 20*
answer us on the day we call.

בָּרוּךְ Blessed is He, our God, who created us for His glory, separating us from those who go astray; who gave us the Torah of truth, planting within us eternal life. May He open our heart to His Torah, imbuing our heart with the love and awe of Him, that we may do His will and serve Him with a perfect heart, so that we neither toil in vain nor give birth to confusion.

◂ וְאַתָּה קָדוֹשׁ יוֹשֵׁב תְּהִלּוֹת יִשְׂרָאֵל: וְקָרָא זֶה אֶל־זֶה וְאָמַר ◂ תהלים כב / ישעיה ו
קָדוֹשׁ, קָדוֹשׁ, קָדוֹשׁ, יהוה צְבָאוֹת, מְלֹא כָל־הָאָרֶץ כְּבוֹדוֹ:

וּמְקַבְּלִין דֵּין מִן דֵּין וְאָמְרִין, קַדִּישׁ בִּשְׁמֵי מְרוֹמָא עִלָּאָה בֵּית שְׁכִינְתֵהּ תרגום יונתן ישעיה ו
קַדִּישׁ עַל אַרְעָא עוֹבַד גְּבוּרְתֵהּ, קַדִּישׁ לְעָלַם וּלְעָלְמֵי עָלְמַיָּא
יהוה צְבָאוֹת, מַלְיָא כָל אַרְעָא זִיו יְקָרֵהּ.

◂ וַתִּשָּׂאֵנִי רוּחַ, וָאֶשְׁמַע אַחֲרַי קוֹל רַעַשׁ גָּדוֹל ◂ יחזקאל ג
בָּרוּךְ כְּבוֹד־יהוה מִמְּקוֹמוֹ:

וּנְטָלַתְנִי רוּחָא, וּשְׁמָעִית בַּתְרַי קָל זִיעַ סַגִּיא, דִּמְשַׁבְּחִין וְאָמְרִין תרגום יונתן יחזקאל ג
בְּרִיךְ יְקָרָא דַיהוה מֵאֲתַר בֵּית שְׁכִינְתֵהּ.

יהוה יִמְלֹךְ לְעֹלָם וָעֶד: שמות טו
יהוה מַלְכוּתֵהּ קָאֵם לְעָלַם וּלְעָלְמֵי עָלְמַיָּא. תרגום אונקלוס שמות טו

יהוה אֱלֹהֵי אַבְרָהָם יִצְחָק וְיִשְׂרָאֵל אֲבֹתֵינוּ, שָׁמְרָה־זֹּאת לְעוֹלָם דברי הימים א, כט
לְיֵצֶר מַחְשְׁבוֹת לְבַב עַמֶּךָ, וְהָכֵן לְבָבָם אֵלֶיךָ: וְהוּא רַחוּם יְכַפֵּר תהלים עח
עָוֹן וְלֹא־יַשְׁחִית, וְהִרְבָּה לְהָשִׁיב אַפּוֹ, וְלֹא־יָעִיר כָּל־חֲמָתוֹ: כִּי־ תהלים פו
אַתָּה אֲדֹנָי טוֹב וְסַלָּח, וְרַב־חֶסֶד לְכָל־קֹרְאֶיךָ: צִדְקָתְךָ צֶדֶק תהלים קיט
לְעוֹלָם וְתוֹרָתְךָ אֱמֶת: תִּתֵּן אֱמֶת לְיַעֲקֹב, חֶסֶד לְאַבְרָהָם, אֲשֶׁר־ מיכה ז
נִשְׁבַּעְתָּ לַאֲבֹתֵינוּ מִימֵי קֶדֶם: בָּרוּךְ אֲדֹנָי יוֹם יוֹם יַעֲמָס־לָנוּ, הָאֵל תהלים סח
יְשׁוּעָתֵנוּ סֶלָה: יהוה צְבָאוֹת עִמָּנוּ, מִשְׂגָּב לָנוּ אֱלֹהֵי יַעֲקֹב סֶלָה: תהלים מו
יהוה צְבָאוֹת, אַשְׁרֵי אָדָם בֹּטֵחַ בָּךְ: יהוה הוֹשִׁיעָה, הַמֶּלֶךְ יַעֲנֵנוּ תהלים כ / תהלים פד
בְיוֹם־קָרְאֵנוּ:

בָּרוּךְ הוּא אֱלֹהֵינוּ שֶׁבְּרָאָנוּ לִכְבוֹדוֹ, וְהִבְדִּילָנוּ מִן הַתּוֹעִים, וְנָתַן לָנוּ תּוֹרַת אֱמֶת, וְחַיֵּי עוֹלָם נָטַע בְּתוֹכֵנוּ. הוּא יִפְתַּח לִבֵּנוּ בְּתוֹרָתוֹ, וְיָשֵׂם בְּלִבֵּנוּ אַהֲבָתוֹ וְיִרְאָתוֹ וְלַעֲשׂוֹת רְצוֹנוֹ וּלְעָבְדוֹ בְּלֵבָב שָׁלֵם, לְמַעַן לֹא נִיגַע לָרִיק וְלֹא נֵלֵד לַבֶּהָלָה.

יְהִי רָצוֹן May it be Your will, O LORD our God and God of our ancestors, that we keep Your laws in this world, and thus be worthy to live, see and inherit goodness and blessing in the Messianic Age and in
the life of the World to Come. So that my soul may sing to You and *Ps. 30*
not be silent. LORD, my God, for ever I will thank You. Blessed is *Jer. 17*
the man who trusts in the LORD, whose trust is in the LORD alone.
Trust in the LORD for evermore, for God, the LORD, is an everlasting *Is. 26*
Rock. ▸ Those who know Your name trust in You, for You, LORD, do *Ps. 9*
not forsake those who seek You. The LORD desired, for the sake of *Is. 42*
Israel's merit, to make the Torah great and glorious.

HALF KADDISH

Leader: יִתְגַּדַּל Magnified and sanctified
may His great name be,
in the world He created by His will.
May He establish His kingdom
in your lifetime and in your days,
and in the lifetime of all the house of Israel,
swiftly and soon –
and say: Amen.

All: May His great name be blessed
for ever and all time.

Leader: Blessed and praised, glorified and exalted,
raised and honored,
uplifted and lauded
be the name of the Holy One,
blessed be He,
beyond any blessing,
song, praise and consolation
uttered in the world –
and say: Amen.

יְהִי רָצוֹן מִלְּפָנֶיךָ יהוה אֱלֹהֵינוּ וֵאלֹהֵי אֲבוֹתֵינוּ, שֶׁנִּשְׁמֹר חֻקֶּיךָ
בָּעוֹלָם הַזֶּה, וְנִזְכֶּה וְנִחְיֶה וְנִרְאֶה וְנִירַשׁ טוֹבָה וּבְרָכָה, לִשְׁנֵי
יְמוֹת הַמָּשִׁיחַ וּלְחַיֵּי הָעוֹלָם הַבָּא. לְמַעַן יְזַמֶּרְךָ כָבוֹד וְלֹא יִדֹּם, תהלים ל
יהוה אֱלֹהַי, לְעוֹלָם אוֹדֶךָּ: בָּרוּךְ הַגֶּבֶר אֲשֶׁר יִבְטַח בַּיהוה, וְהָיָה ירמיה יז
יהוה מִבְטַחוֹ: בִּטְחוּ בַיהוה עֲדֵי־עַד, כִּי בְּיָהּ יהוה צוּר עוֹלָמִים: ישעיה כו
› וְיִבְטְחוּ בְךָ יוֹדְעֵי שְׁמֶךָ, כִּי לֹא־עָזַבְתָּ דֹרְשֶׁיךָ, יהוה: יהוה חָפֵץ תהלים ט ישעיה מב
לְמַעַן צִדְקוֹ, יַגְדִּיל תּוֹרָה וְיַאְדִּיר:

חצי קדיש

ש״ץ: יִתְגַּדַּל וְיִתְקַדַּשׁ שְׁמֵהּ רַבָּא (קהל: אָמֵן)
בְּעָלְמָא דִּי בְרָא כִרְעוּתֵהּ
וְיַמְלִיךְ מַלְכוּתֵהּ
בְּחַיֵּיכוֹן וּבְיוֹמֵיכוֹן וּבְחַיֵּי דְכָל בֵּית יִשְׂרָאֵל
בַּעֲגָלָא וּבִזְמַן קָרִיב
וְאִמְרוּ אָמֵן. (קהל: אָמֵן)

קהל וש״ץ: יְהֵא שְׁמֵהּ רַבָּא מְבָרַךְ לְעָלַם וּלְעָלְמֵי עָלְמַיָּא.

ש״ץ: יִתְבָּרַךְ וְיִשְׁתַּבַּח וְיִתְפָּאַר וְיִתְרוֹמַם וְיִתְנַשֵּׂא
וְיִתְהַדָּר וְיִתְעַלֶּה וְיִתְהַלָּל
שְׁמֵהּ דְּקֻדְשָׁא בְּרִיךְ הוּא (קהל: בְּרִיךְ הוּא)
לְעֵלָּא מִן כָּל בִּרְכָתָא
וְשִׁירָתָא, תֻּשְׁבְּחָתָא וְנֶחֱמָתָא
דַּאֲמִירָן בְּעָלְמָא
וְאִמְרוּ אָמֵן. (קהל: אָמֵן)

REMOVING THE TORAH FROM THE ARK

וַאֲנִי As for me, may my prayer come to You,[1] LORD, at a time of favor. O God, in Your great love, answer me with Your faithful salvation. *Ps. 69*

The Ark is opened and the congregation stands. All say:

וַיְהִי בִּנְסֹעַ Whenever the Ark set out, Moses would say, *Num. 10*
"Arise, LORD, and may Your enemies be scattered.[B]
May those who hate You flee before You."
For the Torah shall come forth from Zion, *Is. 2*
and the word of the LORD from Jerusalem.
Blessed is He who in His Holiness
gave the Torah to His people Israel.

Blessed is the name of the Master of the Universe. Blessed is Your crown and Your place. May Your favor always be with Your people Israel. Show Your people the salvation of Your right hand in Your Temple. Grant us the gift of Your good light, and accept our prayers in mercy. May it be Your will to prolong our life in goodness. May I be counted among the righteous, so that You will have compassion on me and protect me and all that is mine and all that is Your people Israel's. You feed all; *Zohar, Vayak-hel*

at *Minḥa*, and on Mondays and Thursdays at *Shaḥarit* – so that we would not go for more than three days without being infused with the lifeblood of our existence that is Torah. And yet, we just finished reading the entire week's portion at the services this morning! Why do we need to read again? Perhaps the gesture is a symbolic one; that our commitment to Torah is never complete or finished. No sooner do we end one portion then we begin the next. On the holiday of Simḥat Torah we complete the last portion in the book of *Devarim* and immediately begin all over again with *Bereshit*. In the Oral Law, the Talmud, every individual tractate begins with page number 2; there is no first page. For Torah learning is as continuous and essential to life as breathing.

For further commentary see pages 633–640.

BIUR TEFILLA • ביאור תפילה

וְיָפֻצוּ אֹיְבֶיךָ וְיָנֻסוּ מְשַׂנְאֶיךָ – *May Your enemies be scattered. May those who hate you flee before You.* What is the difference between enemies and those who hate you? Rashi explains that the latter are the people who hate the Jews, for whoever hates the Jews hates God. In contemporary terms this may mean that when looking for sources of anti-Semitism, one need not resort to theories about the Jews being strangers, about our successes, about our character traits and the like. Rather, the source of animosity against us is our religion.

What evidence can you find for this?

הוצאת ספר תורה

וַאֲנִי תְפִלָּתִי־לְךָ יהוה, עֵת רָצוֹן, אֱלֹהִים בְּרָב־חַסְדֶּךָ עֲנֵנִי בֶּאֱמֶת יִשְׁעֶךָ׃ תהלים סט

The ארון קודש *is opened and the* קהל *stands. All say:*

וַיְהִי בִּנְסֹעַ הָאָרֹן וַיֹּאמֶר מֹשֶׁה במדבר י
קוּמָה יהוה וְיָפֻצוּ אֹיְבֶיךָ וְיָנֻסוּ מְשַׂנְאֶיךָ מִפָּנֶיךָ׃
כִּי מִצִּיּוֹן תֵּצֵא תוֹרָה וּדְבַר־יהוה מִירוּשָׁלָםִ׃ ישעיה ב
בָּרוּךְ שֶׁנָּתַן תּוֹרָה לְעַמּוֹ יִשְׂרָאֵל בִּקְדֻשָּׁתוֹ.

בְּרִיךְ שְׁמֵהּ דְּמָרֵא עָלְמָא, בְּרִיךְ כִּתְרָךְ וְאַתְרָךְ. יְהֵא רְעוּתָךְ עִם עַמָּךְ יִשְׂרָאֵל לְעָלַם, וּפֻרְקַן יְמִינָךְ אַחֲזִי לְעַמָּךְ בְּבֵית מַקְדְּשָׁךְ, וּלְאַמְטוּיֵי לָנָא מִטּוּב נְהוֹרָךְ, וּלְקַבֵּל צְלוֹתָנָא בְּרַחֲמִין. יְהֵא רַעֲוָא קֳדָמָךְ דְּתוֹרִיךְ לָן חַיִּין בְּטִיבוּ, וְלֶהֱוֵי אֲנָא פְקִידָא בְּגוֹ צַדִּיקַיָּא, לְמִרְחַם עָלַי וּלְמִנְטַר יָתִי וְיָת כָּל דִּי לִי וְדִי לְעַמָּךְ יִשְׂרָאֵל. זוהר ויקהל

IYUN TEFILLA • עיון תפילה

וַאֲנִי תְפִלָּתִי־לְךָ – *As for me, may my prayer come to You.* In its original context (*Tehillim* 69:14) this verse is immediately preceded by one which says "I am the taunt of drunkards." The Midrash homiletically suggests that the connection is that in other cultures there may be a custom to drink and revel to excess on a day of celebration, but in Judaism pleasure is tempered by reminding ourselves that it is for the sake of Heaven, and that our physical enjoyment should be an outgrowth of our spirituality (Abudarham). On a day that we have spent in no small measure feasting and relaxing, if we have spent too much of today focused on our own physicality and not enough on our need for spirituality, then this statement provides us with an opportunity to begin to restore the balance.

Yet another rationale is that the verse's reference to "a time of favor" is an apt description of *Minḥa* which was described as such by Eliyahu the prophet atop Mount Carmel (*Melakhim I* 18:36), and is taken here to be particularly associated with the notion of the ultimate redemption, a theme that we will soon focus on in our *Amida* (*Shibbolei HaLeket, Berakhot* 6b).

INTRODUCTION TO KERIAT HATORAH

Tradition has it that the prophet Ezra established the public reading of the first ten verses of the following shabbat's portion of the Torah on a regular basis – on Shabbat

You sustain all; You rule over all; You rule over kings, for sovereignty is Yours. I am a servant of the Holy One, blessed be He, before whom and before whose glorious Torah I bow at all times. Not in man do I trust, nor on any angel do I rely, but on the God of heaven who is the God of truth, whose Torah is truth, whose prophets speak truth, and who abounds in acts of love and truth. ▸ In Him I trust, and to His holy and glorious name I offer praises. May it be Your will to open my heart to the Torah, and to fulfill the wishes of my heart and of the hearts of all Your people Israel for good, for life, and for peace.

The Leader takes the Torah scroll in his right arm, bows toward the Ark and says:

Magnify the LORD with me,
and let us exalt His name together. *Ps. 34*

The Ark is closed. The Leader carries the Torah scroll to the bima and the congregation says:

לְךָ Yours, LORD, are the greatness and the power, the glory and the majesty *1 Chr. 29*
and splendor, for everything in heaven and earth is Yours. Yours, LORD, is the kingdom; You are exalted as Head over all.

רוֹמְמוּ Exalt the LORD our God and bow to His footstool; He is holy. Exalt the *Ps. 99*
LORD our God, and bow at His holy mountain, for holy is the LORD our God.

אַב הָרַחֲמִים May the Father of compassion have compassion on the people borne by Him. May He remember the covenant with the mighty [patriarchs], and deliver us from evil times. May He reproach the evil instinct in the people carried by Him, and graciously grant that we be an everlasting remnant. May He fulfill in good measure our requests for salvation and compassion.

The Torah scroll is placed on the bima and the Gabbai calls a Kohen to the Torah.

וְתִגָּלֶה May His kingship over us be soon revealed and made manifest. May He be gracious to our surviving remnant, the remnant of His people the house of Israel in grace, loving-kindness, compassion and favor, and let us say: Amen. Let us all render greatness to our God and give honor to the Torah. *Let the Kohen come forward. Arise (*name* son of *father's name*), the Kohen.

**If no Kohen is present, a Levi or Yisrael is called up as follows:*

/As there is no Kohen, arise (*name* son of *father's name*) in place of a Kohen./

Blessed is He who, in His holiness, gave the Torah to His people Israel.

The congregation followed by the Gabbai:

You who cling to the LORD your God are all alive today. *Deut. 4*

אַנְתְּ הוּא זָן לְכֹלָּא וּמְפַרְנֵס לְכֹלָּא, אַנְתְּ הוּא שַׁלִּיט עַל כֹּלָּא, אַנְתְּ הוּא דְשַׁלִּיט עַל מַלְכַיָּא, וּמַלְכוּתָא דִּילָךְ הִיא. אֲנָא עַבְדָּא דְקֻדְשָׁא בְּרִיךְ הוּא, דְּסָגֵדְנָא קַמֵּהּ וּמִקַּמֵּי דִּיקַר אוֹרַיְתֵהּ בְּכָל עִדָּן וְעִדָּן. לָא עַל אֱנָשׁ רְחִיצְנָא וְלָא עַל בַּר אֱלָהִין סָמֵיכְנָא, אֶלָּא בֶּאֱלָהָא דִשְׁמַיָּא, דְּהוּא אֱלָהָא קְשׁוֹט, וְאוֹרַיְתֵהּ קְשׁוֹט, וּנְבִיאוֹהִי קְשׁוֹט, וּמַסְגֵּא לְמֶעְבַּד טַבְוָן וּקְשׁוֹט. · בֵּהּ אֲנָא רָחִיץ, וְלִשְׁמֵהּ קַדִּישָׁא יַקִּירָא אֲנָא אֵמַר תֻּשְׁבְּחָן. יְהֵא רַעֲוָא קֳדָמָךְ דְּתִפְתַּח לִבַּאי בְּאוֹרַיְתָא, וְתַשְׁלִים מִשְׁאֲלִין דְּלִבַּאי וְלִבָּא דְכָל עַמָּךְ יִשְׂרָאֵל לְטָב וּלְחַיִּין וְלִשְׁלָם.

The שליח ציבור takes the ספר תורה in his right arm, bows toward the ארון קודש and says:

תהלים לד גַּדְּלוּ לַיהוה אִתִּי וּנְרוֹמְמָה שְׁמוֹ יַחְדָּו:

The ארון קודש is closed. The שליח ציבור carries the ספר תורה to the בימה and the קהל says:

דברי הימים א׳ כט לְךָ יהוה הַגְּדֻלָּה וְהַגְּבוּרָה וְהַתִּפְאֶרֶת וְהַנֵּצַח וְהַהוֹד, כִּי־כֹל בַּשָּׁמַיִם וּבָאָרֶץ: לְךָ יהוה הַמַּמְלָכָה וְהַמִּתְנַשֵּׂא לְכֹל לְרֹאשׁ:

תהלים צט רוֹמְמוּ יהוה אֱלֹהֵינוּ וְהִשְׁתַּחֲווּ לַהֲדֹם רַגְלָיו, קָדוֹשׁ הוּא: רוֹמְמוּ יהוה אֱלֹהֵינוּ וְהִשְׁתַּחֲווּ לְהַר קָדְשׁוֹ, כִּי־קָדוֹשׁ יהוה אֱלֹהֵינוּ:

אַב הָרַחֲמִים הוּא יְרַחֵם עַם עֲמוּסִים, וְיִזְכֹּר בְּרִית אֵיתָנִים, וְיַצִּיל נַפְשׁוֹתֵינוּ מִן הַשָּׁעוֹת הָרָעוֹת, וְיִגְעַר בְּיֵצֶר הָרָע מִן הַנְּשׂוּאִים, וְיָחֹן אוֹתָנוּ לִפְלֵיטַת עוֹלָמִים, וִימַלֵּא מִשְׁאֲלוֹתֵינוּ בְּמִדָּה טוֹבָה יְשׁוּעָה וְרַחֲמִים.

The ספר תורה is placed on the שולחן and the גבאי calls a כהן to the תורה.

וְתִגָּלֶה וְתֵרָאֶה מַלְכוּתוֹ עָלֵינוּ בִּזְמַן קָרוֹב, וְיָחֹן פְּלֵיטָתֵנוּ וּפְלֵיטַת עַמּוֹ בֵּית יִשְׂרָאֵל לְחֵן וּלְחֶסֶד וּלְרַחֲמִים וּלְרָצוֹן וְנֹאמַר אָמֵן. הַכֹּל הָבוּ גֹדֶל לֵאלֹהֵינוּ וּתְנוּ כָבוֹד לַתּוֹרָה. *כֹּהֵן קְרָב, יַעֲמֹד (פלוני בֶּן פלוני) הַכֹּהֵן.

**If no כהן is present, a לוי or ישראל is called up as follows:*

/אֵין כָּאן כֹּהֵן, יַעֲמֹד (פלוני בֶּן פלוני) בִּמְקוֹם כֹּהֵן./

בָּרוּךְ שֶׁנָּתַן תּוֹרָה לְעַמּוֹ יִשְׂרָאֵל בִּקְדֻשָּׁתוֹ.

The קהל followed by the גבאי:

דברים ד וְאַתֶּם הַדְּבֵקִים בַּיהוה אֱלֹהֵיכֶם חַיִּים כֻּלְּכֶם הַיּוֹם:

The appropriate Torah portion is read (pages 1014–1072).

The Reader shows the oleh the section to be read.
The oleh touches the scroll at that place with the tzitzit of his tallit or the fabric belt of the Torah scroll, which he then kisses.
Holding the handles of the scroll, he says:

Oleh: Bless the LORD, the blessed One.

Cong: Bless the LORD, the blessed One,
for ever and all time.

Oleh: Bless the LORD, the blessed One,
for ever and all time.

Blessed are You, LORD our God, King of the Universe,
who has chosen us from all peoples
and has given us His Torah.
Blessed are You, LORD, Giver of the Torah.

After the reading, the oleh says:

Oleh: Blessed are You, LORD our God, King of the Universe,
who has given us the Torah of truth,
planting everlasting life in our midst.
Blessed are You, LORD, Giver of the Torah.

The Torah scroll is lifted and the congregation says:

וְזֹאת הַתּוֹרָה This is the Torah that *Deut. 4*
Moses placed before the children of Israel,
at the LORD's commandment, by the hand of Moses. *Num. 9*

Some add: It is a tree of life to those who grasp it, and those who uphold it are happy. *Prov. 3*
Its ways are ways of pleasantness, and all its paths are peace.
Long life is in its right hand; in its left, riches and honor.
It pleased the LORD for the sake of [Israel's] righteousness, *Is. 42*
to make the Torah great and glorious.

The Torah scroll is bound and covered.

IYUN TEFILLA • עיון תפילה

נוֹתֵן הַתּוֹרָה – *Giver of the Torah.* Both blessings emphasize Hashem as the Giver of the Torah. Surely that is significant only if you are prepared to be a recipient. Prepare to receive the Torah again.

The appropriate תורה *portion is read (pages 1014–1072).*

The קורא *shows the* עולה *the section to be read.*
The עולה *touches the scroll at that place with the* ציצית
of his טלית *or the gartel of the* ספר תורה*, which he then kisses.*
Holding the handles of the scroll, he says:

עולה: **בָּרְכוּ אֶת יהוה הַמְבֹרָךְ.**

קהל: **בָּרוּךְ יהוה הַמְבֹרָךְ לְעוֹלָם וָעֶד.**

עולה: **בָּרוּךְ יהוה הַמְבֹרָךְ לְעוֹלָם וָעֶד.**
בָּרוּךְ אַתָּה יהוה, אֱלֹהֵינוּ מֶלֶךְ הָעוֹלָם
אֲשֶׁר בָּחַר בָּנוּ מִכָּל הָעַמִּים
וְנָתַן לָנוּ אֶת תּוֹרָתוֹ.
בָּרוּךְ אַתָּה יהוה, נוֹתֵן הַתּוֹרָה.

After the קריאת התורה*, the* עולה *says:*

עולה: **בָּרוּךְ אַתָּה יהוה אֱלֹהֵינוּ מֶלֶךְ הָעוֹלָם**
אֲשֶׁר נָתַן לָנוּ תּוֹרַת אֱמֶת
וְחַיֵּי עוֹלָם נָטַע בְּתוֹכֵנוּ.
בָּרוּךְ אַתָּה יהוה, נוֹתֵן הַתּוֹרָה.

The ספר תורה *is lifted and the* קהל *says:*

וְזֹאת הַתּוֹרָה אֲשֶׁר־שָׂם מֹשֶׁה לִפְנֵי בְּנֵי יִשְׂרָאֵל: דברים ד
עַל־פִּי יהוה בְּיַד מֹשֶׁה: במדבר ט

Some add עֵץ־חַיִּים הִיא לַמַּחֲזִיקִים בָּהּ וְתֹמְכֶיהָ מְאֻשָּׁר: משלי ג
דְּרָכֶיהָ דַרְכֵי־נֹעַם וְכָל־נְתִיבֹתֶיהָ שָׁלוֹם:
אֹרֶךְ יָמִים בִּימִינָהּ, בִּשְׂמֹאולָהּ עֹשֶׁר וְכָבוֹד:
יהוה חָפֵץ לְמַעַן צִדְקוֹ יַגְדִּיל תּוֹרָה וְיַאְדִּיר: ישעיה מב

The ספר תורה *is bound and covered.*

The Ark is opened. The Leader takes the Torah scroll and says:

יְהַלְלוּ Let them praise the name of the Lord, *Ps. 148*
for His name alone is sublime.

The congregation responds:

הוֹדוֹ His majesty is above earth and heaven.
He has raised the horn of His people,
for the glory of all His devoted ones,
the children of Israel, the people close to Him. Halleluya!

As the Torah scroll is returned to the Ark say:

לְדָוִד מִזְמוֹר A psalm of David. The earth is the Lord's and all it contains, *Ps. 24* the world and all who live in it. For He founded it on the seas and established it on the streams. Who may climb the mountain of the Lord? Who may stand in His holy place? He who has clean hands and a pure heart, who has not taken My name in vain, or sworn deceitfully. He shall receive blessing from the Lord, and just reward from God, his salvation. This is a generation of those who seek Him, the descendants of Jacob who seek Your presence, Selah! Lift up your heads, O gates; be uplifted, eternal doors, so that the King of glory may enter. Who is the King of glory? It is the Lord, strong and mighty, the Lord mighty in battle. Lift up your heads, O gates; lift them up, eternal doors, so that the King of glory may enter. Who is He, the King of glory? The Lord of hosts, He is the King of glory, Selah!

As the Torah scroll is placed into the Ark, say:

וּבְנֻחֹה יֹאמַר When the Ark came to rest, Moses would say: "Return, *Num. 10*
O Lord, to the myriad thousands of Israel." Advance, Lord, to Your *Ps. 132*
resting place, You and Your mighty Ark. Your priests are clothed in
righteousness, and Your devoted ones sing in joy. For the sake of Your
servant David, do not reject Your anointed one. For I give you good *Prov. 4*
instruction; do not forsake My Torah. It is a tree of life to those who *Prov. 3*
grasp it, and those who uphold it are happy. Its ways are ways of pleas-
antness, and all its paths are peace. ▸ Turn us back, O Lord, to You, and *Lam. 5*
we will return. Renew our days as of old.

The Ark is closed.

The ארון קודש *is opened. The* שליח ציבור *takes the* ספר תורה *and says:*

יְהַלְלוּ אֶת־שֵׁם יהוה, כִּי־נִשְׂגָּב שְׁמוֹ, לְבַדּוֹ תהלים קמח

The קהל *responds:*

הוֹדוֹ עַל־אֶרֶץ וְשָׁמָיִם:
וַיָּרֶם קֶרֶן לְעַמּוֹ, תְּהִלָּה לְכָל־חֲסִידָיו
לִבְנֵי יִשְׂרָאֵל עַם קְרֹבוֹ, הַלְלוּיָהּ:

As the ספר תורה *is returned to the* ארון קודש*, say:*

לְדָוִד מִזְמוֹר, לַיהוה הָאָרֶץ וּמְלוֹאָהּ, תֵּבֵל וְיֹשְׁבֵי בָהּ: כִּי־הוּא עַל־ תהלים כד
יַמִּים יְסָדָהּ, וְעַל־נְהָרוֹת יְכוֹנְנֶהָ: מִי־יַעֲלֶה בְהַר־יהוה, וּמִי־יָקוּם
בִּמְקוֹם קָדְשׁוֹ: נְקִי כַפַּיִם וּבַר־לֵבָב, אֲשֶׁר לֹא־נָשָׂא לַשָּׁוְא נַפְשִׁי
וְלֹא נִשְׁבַּע לְמִרְמָה: יִשָּׂא בְרָכָה מֵאֵת יהוה, וּצְדָקָה מֵאֱלֹהֵי יִשְׁעוֹ:
זֶה דּוֹר דֹּרְשָׁו, מְבַקְשֵׁי פָנֶיךָ, יַעֲקֹב, סֶלָה: שְׂאוּ שְׁעָרִים רָאשֵׁיכֶם,
וְהִנָּשְׂאוּ פִּתְחֵי עוֹלָם, וְיָבוֹא מֶלֶךְ הַכָּבוֹד: מִי זֶה מֶלֶךְ הַכָּבוֹד,
יהוה עִזּוּז וְגִבּוֹר, יהוה גִּבּוֹר מִלְחָמָה: שְׂאוּ שְׁעָרִים רָאשֵׁיכֶם,
וּשְׂאוּ פִּתְחֵי עוֹלָם, וְיָבֹא מֶלֶךְ הַכָּבוֹד: מִי הוּא זֶה מֶלֶךְ הַכָּבוֹד,
יהוה צְבָאוֹת הוּא מֶלֶךְ הַכָּבוֹד, סֶלָה:

As the ספר תורה *is placed into the* ארון קודש*, say:*

וּבְנֻחֹה יֹאמַר, שׁוּבָה יהוה רִבְבוֹת אַלְפֵי יִשְׂרָאֵל: קוּמָה יהוה במדבר י תהלים קלב
לִמְנוּחָתֶךָ, אַתָּה וַאֲרוֹן עֻזֶּךָ: כֹּהֲנֶיךָ יִלְבְּשׁוּ־צֶדֶק, וַחֲסִידֶיךָ יְרַנֵּנוּ:
בַּעֲבוּר דָּוִד עַבְדֶּךָ אַל־תָּשֵׁב פְּנֵי מְשִׁיחֶךָ: כִּי לֶקַח טוֹב נָתַתִּי משלי ד
לָכֶם, תּוֹרָתִי אַל־תַּעֲזֹבוּ: עֵץ־חַיִּים הִיא לַמַּחֲזִיקִים בָּהּ, וְתֹמְכֶיהָ משלי ג
מְאֻשָּׁר: דְּרָכֶיהָ דַרְכֵי־נֹעַם וְכָל־נְתִיבֹתֶיהָ שָׁלוֹם: ‹ הֲשִׁיבֵנוּ יהוה איכה ה
אֵלֶיךָ וְנָשׁוּבָ, חַדֵּשׁ יָמֵינוּ כְּקֶדֶם:

The ארון קודש *is closed.*

HALF KADDISH

Leader: יִתְגַּדַּל Magnified and sanctified may His great name be,
in the world He created by His will.
May He establish His kingdom
in your lifetime and in your days,
and in the lifetime of all the house of Israel,
swiftly and soon –
and say: Amen.

All: May His great name be blessed for ever and all time.

Leader: Blessed and praised, glorified and exalted,
raised and honored, uplifted and lauded
be the name of the Holy One, blessed be He,
beyond any blessing, song, praise and consolation
uttered in the world –
and say: Amen.

THE AMIDA

The Amida, until "in former years" on page 790, is said silently, standing with feet together. If there is a minyan, the Amida is repeated aloud by the Leader. Take three steps forward and at the points indicated by ▾, bend the knees at the first word, bow at the second, and stand straight before saying God's name.

When I proclaim the LORD's name, give glory to our God. *Deut. 32*
O LORD, open my lips, so that my mouth may declare Your praise. *Ps. 51*

PATRIARCHS

▾Blessed are You, LORD our God and God of our fathers,|
God of Abraham, God of Isaac and God of Jacob;
the great, mighty and awesome God, God Most High,

אֱלֹהֵינוּ וֵאלֹהֵי אֲבוֹתֵינוּ – *Our God and God of our fathers.* Did you ever have difficulty relating to the existence of God? Some people find strength in recalling that Hashem has had a historical relationship with the Jewish people going all the way back to the Avot, that is, with our Forefathers, and with our fathers.

What event or phenomenon in Jewish history gives you reason to believe?

חצי קדיש

ש״ץ: יִתְגַּדַּל וְיִתְקַדַּשׁ שְׁמֵהּ רַבָּא (קהל: אָמֵן)
בְּעָלְמָא דִּי בְרָא כִרְעוּתֵהּ וְיַמְלִיךְ מַלְכוּתֵהּ
בְּחַיֵּיכוֹן וּבְיוֹמֵיכוֹן, וּבְחַיֵּי דְכָל בֵּית יִשְׂרָאֵל
בַּעֲגָלָא וּבִזְמַן קָרִיב, וְאִמְרוּ אָמֵן. (קהל: אָמֵן)

קהל וש״ץ: יְהֵא שְׁמֵהּ רַבָּא מְבָרַךְ לְעָלַם וּלְעָלְמֵי עָלְמַיָּא.

ש״ץ: יִתְבָּרַךְ וְיִשְׁתַּבַּח וְיִתְפָּאַר וְיִתְרוֹמַם וְיִתְנַשֵּׂא
וְיִתְהַדָּר וְיִתְעַלֶּה וְיִתְהַלָּל
שְׁמֵהּ דְּקֻדְשָׁא בְּרִיךְ הוּא (קהל: בְּרִיךְ הוּא)
לְעֵלָּא מִן כָּל בִּרְכָתָא
וְשִׁירָתָא, תֻּשְׁבְּחָתָא וְנֶחֱמָתָא
דַּאֲמִירָן בְּעָלְמָא, וְאִמְרוּ אָמֵן. (קהל: אָמֵן)

עמידה

The עמידה, until קַדְמֹנִיּוֹת on page 791, is said silently, standing with feet together. If there is a מנין, the עמידה is repeated aloud by the שליח ציבור. Take three steps forward and at the points indicated by ˚, bend the knees at the first word, bow at the second, and stand straight before saying God's name.

דברים לב — כִּי שֵׁם יהוה אֶקְרָא, הָבוּ גֹדֶל לֵאלֹהֵינוּ:
תהלים נא — אֲדֹנָי, שְׂפָתַי תִּפְתָּח, וּפִי יַגִּיד תְּהִלָּתֶךָ:

אבות

˚בָּרוּךְ אַתָּה יהוה, אֱלֹהֵינוּ וֵאלֹהֵי אֲבוֹתֵינוּ[ע]
אֱלֹהֵי אַבְרָהָם, אֱלֹהֵי יִצְחָק, וֵאלֹהֵי יַעֲקֹב
הָאֵל הַגָּדוֹל הַגִּבּוֹר וְהַנּוֹרָא, אֵל עֶלְיוֹן

IYUN TEFILLA • עיון תפילה

For an overview of the Amida prayer in general, see page 134 . For a discussion of the first and last blessings including more commentary see page 606.

who bestows acts of loving-kindness and creates all,
who remembers the loving-kindness of the fathers
and will bring a Redeemer to their children's children
for the sake of His name, in love.
King, Helper, Savior, Shield:
▾Blessed are You, LORD,
Shield of Abraham.

DIVINE MIGHT

אַתָּה גִּבּוֹר You are eternally mighty, LORD.
You give life to the dead and have great power to save.

In Israel: He causes the dew to fall.

He sustains the living with loving-kindness,
and with great compassion revives the dead.
He supports the fallen, heals the sick,
sets captives free,
and keeps His faith with those who sleep in the dust.
Who is like You, Master of might,
and who can compare to You,
O King who brings death and gives life,
and makes salvation grow?
Faithful are You to revive the dead.
Blessed are You, LORD,
who revives the dead.

When saying the Amida silently, continue with "You are holy" on page 778.

---

not only found God but enabled others to do so as well. Therefore, how could one dare recite this blessing without committing oneself to act like Avraham: to reach out to one's fellow man, to have pity on those in need, to have empathy for others even as one is struggling with one's own life challenges, and to accept with faith that Hashem has one's best interests in mind (*Ye'arot Devash*).

גּוֹמֵל חֲסָדִים טוֹבִים, וְקֹנֵה הַכֹּל
וְזוֹכֵר חַסְדֵי אָבוֹת
וּמֵבִיא גוֹאֵל לִבְנֵי בְנֵיהֶם לְמַעַן שְׁמוֹ בְּאַהֲבָה.
מֶלֶךְ עוֹזֵר וּמוֹשִׁיעַ וּמָגֵן.
׳בָּרוּךְ אַתָּה יהוה, מָגֵן אַבְרָהָם.ע

גבורות

אַתָּה גִּבּוֹר לְעוֹלָם, אֲדֹנָי
מְחַיֵּה מֵתִים אַתָּה, רַב לְהוֹשִׁיעַ
בארץ ישראל בקיץ: מוֹרִיד הַטָּל
מְכַלְכֵּל חַיִּים בְּחֶסֶד, מְחַיֵּה מֵתִים בְּרַחֲמִים רַבִּים
סוֹמֵךְ נוֹפְלִים, וְרוֹפֵא חוֹלִים
וּמַתִּיר אֲסוּרִים
וּמְקַיֵּם אֱמוּנָתוֹ לִישֵׁנֵי עָפָר.
מִי כָמוֹךָ, בַּעַל גְּבוּרוֹת, וּמִי דּוֹמֶה לָּךְ
מֶלֶךְ, מֵמִית וּמְחַיֶּה וּמַצְמִיחַ יְשׁוּעָה.
וְנֶאֱמָן אַתָּה לְהַחֲיוֹת מֵתִים.
בָּרוּךְ אַתָּה יהוה, מְחַיֵּה הַמֵּתִים.

When saying the עמידה *silently, continue with* אַתָּה קָדוֹשׁ *on page 779.*

IYUN TEFILLA • עיון תפילה

מָגֵן אַבְרָהָם – *Shield of Abraham.* Abraham was known for being a person of enormous loving-kindness. And he was the knight of faith, the founder of monotheism who

KEDUSHA[B]

During the Leader's Repetition, the following is said standing with feet together, rising on the toes at the words indicated by ▴.

Cong. then Leader: נְקַדֵּשׁ We will sanctify Your name on earth,
as they sanctify it in the highest heavens,
as is written by Your prophet,
"And they [the angels] call to one another saying: *Is. 6*

Cong. then Leader: ▴Holy, ▴holy, ▴holy is the LORD of hosts
the whole world is filled with His glory."
Those facing them say "Blessed – "

Cong. then Leader: ▴"Blessed is the LORD's glory from His place." *Ezek. 3*
And in Your holy Writings it is written thus:

Cong. then Leader: ▴"The LORD shall reign for ever. *Ps. 146*
He is your God, Zion,
from generation to generation, Halleluya!"

Leader: From generation to generation
we will declare Your greatness,
and we will proclaim Your holiness for evermore.
Your praise, our God, shall not leave our mouth forever,
for You, God, are a great and holy King.
Blessed are You, LORD,
the holy God.

The Leader continues with "You are One" on the next page.

---

from the Land together with Her people. He thus speaks of a time in the present when God's glory, as it were, is blessed "in its place," where it may be in the Diaspora. These two visions, past and present, are then reconciled by a third vision, not of the angels but of man, that one day in the future, to use the words of King David, "Hashem will reign forever" in Zion. (Rabbi I. Wohlgemuth) In this short prayer, therefore, we have a merging of past and present, and a millennia old vision of the future that we recited daily.

קדושה[ב]

During the חורת הש״ץ, *the following is said standing with feet together, rising on the toes at the words indicated by* ˙.

then קהל ש״ץ: נְקַדֵּשׁ אֶת שִׁמְךָ בָּעוֹלָם
כְּשֵׁם שֶׁמַּקְדִּישִׁים אוֹתוֹ בִּשְׁמֵי מָרוֹם
כַּכָּתוּב עַל יַד נְבִיאֶךָ: וְקָרָא זֶה אֶל־זֶה וְאָמַר ישעיה ו

then קהל ש״ץ: ˙קָדוֹשׁ, ˙קָדוֹשׁ, ˙קָדוֹשׁ, יהוה צְבָאוֹת
מְלֹא כָל־הָאָרֶץ כְּבוֹדוֹ:
לְעֻמָּתָם בָּרוּךְ יֹאמֵרוּ

then קהל ש״ץ: ˙בָּרוּךְ כְּבוֹד־יהוה מִמְּקוֹמוֹ: יחזקאל ג
וּבְדִבְרֵי קָדְשְׁךָ כָּתוּב לֵאמֹר

then קהל ש״ץ: ˙יִמְלֹךְ יהוה לְעוֹלָם, אֱלֹהַיִךְ צִיּוֹן לְדֹר וָדֹר, הַלְלוּיָהּ: תהלים קמו

ש״ץ: לְדוֹר וָדוֹר נַגִּיד גָּדְלֶךָ
וּלְנֵצַח נְצָחִים קְדֻשָּׁתְךָ נַקְדִּישׁ
וְשִׁבְחֲךָ אֱלֹהֵינוּ מִפִּינוּ לֹא יָמוּשׁ לְעוֹלָם וָעֶד
כִּי אֵל מֶלֶךְ גָּדוֹל וְקָדוֹשׁ אָתָּה.
בָּרוּךְ אַתָּה יהוה, הָאֵל הַקָּדוֹשׁ.

The שליח ציבור *continues with* אַתָּה אֶחָד *on the next page.*

BIUR TEFILLA • ביאור תפילה

קדושה – *KEDUSHA.*
The line quoted from Yeshayahu's vision (*kadosh, kadosh, kadosh*…) perhaps reflects a time when the kingdom of Judah was strong and independent, and the Hand of God was spread over the Land. As Yeshayahu says in the rest of the verse, "the land is filled with His glory." In the time of Yeḥezkel, however, the Temple was destroyed and the Divine Presence was exiled, as it were,

HOLINESS

אַתָּה קָדוֹשׁ You are holy and Your name is holy,
and holy ones praise You daily, Selah!
Blessed are You, LORD,
the holy God.

HOLINESS OF THE DAY

אַתָּה You are One, Your name is One;
and who is like Your people Israel,
a nation unique on earth?

tionship we have with Shabbat, even as we sense that the day is drawing to a close. It has taken us almost an entire day to get to this point. It pays to stop for a moment to reflect on what we have (and have not yet) accomplished in this relationship thus far.

IYUN TEFILLA • עיון תפילה

אַתָּה אֶחָד... גּוֹי אֶחָד – *You are One... a nation unique.* A midrash relates that the three parties – Israel, Shabbat and Hashem – testify about one another: Israel and Hashem testify that Shabbat is a day of rest. Israel and Shabbat testify about Hashem that He is One. Hashem and Shabbat testify to the uniqueness of Israel in the world (Tosafot, *Ḥagiga* 3a).

Think about each of these. How is each unique? How could that potentially impact your life?

גּוֹי אֶחָד בָּאָרֶץ – *A nation unique on earth.*

In what ways do you think the Jewish people is unique?

The Gemara (*Yevamot* 79) suggests that we are unique in that we are "merciful, bashful and benevolent...

Only he who cultivates these three characteristics is fit to join this nation."

What evidence of this can you point to?

How can you become a greater part of the nation in this way?

In what other ways do you think we might be unique?

ANI TEFILLA • אני תפילה

"Shabbat enshrines a social-ethical principle without peer. Shabbat is one of the loftiest values in all of humanity. It originated with us, the Jews. It is all ours. No other civilization in history knew a day of rest. Ancient Egypt had a great culture whose treasures are on view to this day, yet the Egypt of antiquity did not know a day of rest. The Greeks of old excelled in philosophy and the arts, yet they did not know a day of rest. Rome established mighty empires and instituted a system of law which is relevant to this day, yet they did not know a day of rest. Neither did the civilizations of Assyria, Babylon, Persia, India, China – not one of them knew a day of rest." (Prime Minister Menachem Begin).

קדושת השם

אַתָּה קָדוֹשׁ[ע] וְשִׁמְךָ קָדוֹשׁ
וּקְדוֹשִׁים בְּכָל יוֹם יְהַלְלוּךָ סֶּלָה.
בָּרוּךְ אַתָּה יהוה, הָאֵל הַקָּדוֹשׁ.

קדושת היום

אַתָּה אֶחָד וְשִׁמְךָ אֶחָד
וּמִי כְּעַמְּךָ יִשְׂרָאֵל גּוֹי אֶחָד[ע] בָּאָרֶץ.[ע]

IYUN TEFILLA • עיון תפילה

אַתָּה קָדוֹשׁ – *You are holy.* This is admission that Hashem is beyond us. We shouldn't get upset that He sometimes seems elusive and untouchable. Were He not, He would not be God.

INTRODUCTION TO THE MIDDLE BLESSING, *KEDUSHAT HA-YOM*

We have previously noted that the middle blessing of the *Amida* is unique for each version recited on Shabbat, and different commentaries have discerned different themes that are developed which reflect the different moods of the day

We began on Friday evening by focusing on the Shabbat of the Creation (*Ma'ariv*), then the Shabbat of revelation (*Shaharit*) and the Shabbat of the Temple (*Musaf*). Here we focus on the Shabbat of the ideal future, the day when all of humanity will recognize its value and its Source. This may also explain why, unlike the other versions, in *Minḥa* there are no biblical verses brought as support, for Judaism is otherwise very focused on the here and now of daily life and not on some idealized view of the future. As we have absorbed all of the pleasures and messages of Shabbat during the majority of this past day, however, we allow ourselves to imagine what such an ideal world might look like.

Recall, too, the suggestion that the different versions of the *Amida* might represent different stages in the wedding between ourselves and Shabbat: the betrothal (*Ma'ariv*); the happiness (*Shaḥarit*); the festive meal (*Musaf*); and finally, now, at *Minḥa*, the joining of bride and groom. (The Hebrew term for this uniting is *yiḥud*, a word which is similar to the word *eḥad*, meaning "one," the word we use here to describe Hashem's unity.) Alternatively, whereas in *Ma'ariv* we talked about Hashem sanctifying the day, and in *Shaḥarit* we spoke about our own sanctification of the day, here we speak about our coming together (Rabbi Yaakov M. Ḥarlap). In certain ways, then, this prayer represents the most intimate rela-

Splendor of greatness and a crown of salvation
is the day of rest[I] and holiness You have given Your people.
Abraham will rejoice,
Isaac will sing for joy,
Jacob and his children will find rest in it[B] –
a rest of love and generosity,
a rest of truth and faith,
a rest of peace and tranquility, calm and trust;
a complete rest in which You find favor.
May Your children recognize and know
that their rest comes from You,
and that by their rest they sanctify Your name.

אֱלֹהֵינוּ Our God and God of our ancestors,
find favor in our rest.
Make us holy through Your commandments
and grant us our share in Your Torah.[I]
Satisfy us with Your goodness,
grant us joy in Your salvation,
and purify our hearts to serve You in truth.

ANI TEFILLA • אני תפילה

Meditation, though it begins as something one does at a particular stated time, is also often interpreted as the key to a total way of life. Shabbat, on the other hand, is one day out of seven. It never becomes a complete way of life. It represents the Israelites' recognition that although human beings can catch a glimpse of the pure realm of unity and innocence, they also live in the fractured world of division, greed, and sorrow. Shabbat is Israel's ingenious attempt to live both in history and beyond it, both in time and eternity (Harvey Cox, a preeminent non-Jewish theologian, author and teacher at Harvard Divinity School).

IYUN TEFILLA • עיון תפילה

וְתֵן חֶלְקֵנוּ בְּתוֹרָתֶךָ – *And grant us our share in Your Torah.*

What share would you like to have? To what kind of Torah knowledge do you aspire? What next step could you take to get there?

תִּפְאֶרֶת גְּדֻלָּה וַעֲטֶרֶת יְשׁוּעָה
יוֹם מְנוּחָה[ע] וּקְדֻשָּׁה לְעַמְּךָ נָתָתָּ.
אַבְרָהָם יָגֵל, יִצְחָק יְרַנֵּן, יַעֲקֹב וּבָנָיו יָנְוּחוּ בוֹ[ב]
מְנוּחַת אַהֲבָה וּנְדָבָה
מְנוּחַת אֱמֶת וֶאֱמוּנָה
מְנוּחַת שָׁלוֹם וְשַׁלְוָה וְהַשְׁקֵט וָבֶטַח
מְנוּחָה שְׁלֵמָה שֶׁאַתָּה רוֹצֶה בָּהּ.
יַכִּירוּ בָנֶיךָ וְיֵדְעוּ, כִּי מֵאִתְּךָ הִיא מְנוּחָתָם
וְעַל מְנוּחָתָם יַקְדִּישׁוּ אֶת שְׁמֶךָ.

אֱלֹהֵינוּ וֵאלֹהֵי אֲבוֹתֵינוּ, רְצֵה בִמְנוּחָתֵנוּ
קַדְּשֵׁנוּ בְּמִצְוֹתֶיךָ וְתֵן חֶלְקֵנוּ בְּתוֹרָתֶךָ[ע]
שַׂבְּעֵנוּ מִטּוּבֶךָ וְשַׂמְּחֵנוּ בִּישׁוּעָתֶךָ
וְטַהֵר לִבֵּנוּ לְעָבְדְּךָ בֶּאֱמֶת.

BIUR TEFILLA • ביאור תפילה

מְנוּחָה – *Rest.*

How many times is the word *menuḥa*/ rest mentioned in this one paragraph?

אַבְרָהָם יָגֵל, יִצְחָק יְרַנֵּן, יַעֲקֹב וּבָנָיו יָנְוּחוּ בוֹ – *Abraham will rejoice, Isaac will sing for joy, Jacob and his children will find rest in it.* Why are the *Avot* (Patriarchs) mentioned here? Perhaps because, given the theme here, they were the first to recognize and foster monotheism (*Kol Bo*). Alternatively, note that it is only Yaakov who is mentioned as having sons, us among them, who ultimately embraced the Shabbat. Why does the text not mention the sons of Avraham and Yitzḥak as well (*Beit Yosef*)?

מְנוּחַת אַהֲבָה וּנְדָבָה – *A rest of love and generosity.*

מְנוּחַת אֱמֶת וֶאֱמוּנָה – *A rest of truth and faith.*

מְנוּחַת שָׁלוֹם וְשַׁלְוָה וְהַשְׁקֵט וָבֶטַח – *A rest of peace and tranquility, calm and trust.*

מְנוּחָה שְׁלֵמָה שֶׁאַתָּה רוֹצֶה בָּהּ – *A complete rest in which You find favor.*

How would you define each of these kinds of "rest?"

How have you experienced any of these today?

In love and favor, LORD our God,
grant us as our heritage Your holy Sabbaths,
so that Israel who sanctify Your name may find rest on them.
Blessed are You, LORD, who sanctifies the Sabbath.

TEMPLE SERVICE

רְצֵה Find favor, LORD our God, in Your people Israel and their prayer.
Restore the service to Your most holy House,[B]
and accept in love and favor
the fire-offerings of Israel and their prayer.
May the service of Your people Israel always find favor with You.

On Rosh Ḥodesh, say:

אֱלֹהֵינוּ Our God and God of our ancestors, may there rise, come,[B] reach, appear, be favored, heard, regarded and remembered before You, our recollection and remembrance, as well as the remembrance of our ancestors, and of the Messiah son of David Your servant, and of Jerusalem Your holy city, and of all Your people the house of Israel – for deliverance and well-being, grace, loving-kindness and compassion, life and peace, on this day of Rosh Ḥodesh. On it remember us, LORD our God, for good; recollect us for blessing, and deliver us for life. In accord with Your promise of salvation and compassion, spare us and be gracious to us; have compassion on us and deliver us, for our eyes are turned to You because You, God, are a gracious and compassionate King.

IYUN TEFILLA • עיון תפילה

וְיָבוֹא וְיַגִּיעַ, וְיֵרָאֶה וְיֵרָצֶה וְיִשָּׁמַע, וְיִפָּקֵד וְיִזָּכֵר – *Come, reach, appear, be favored, heard, regarded, and remembered before You.* There are seven expressions here related to Hashem's remembering of us. The Vilna Gaon suggested that these correspond to the Kabbalistic concept of seven spheres which separate us from the spiritual realm (*Ḥagiga* 12b). Remembering, like prayer itself, is a process that does not happen in one fell swoop. It takes time and practice, effort and determination, and not a little courage. With time, however, one can get past each of the veils to ultimately see things that one did not see before.

In return, perhaps, the prayer suggests that we be rewarded in seven ways. Can you find them?

וְהַנְחִילֵנוּ יהוה אֱלֹהֵינוּ בְּאַהֲבָה וּבְרָצוֹן שַׁבְּתוֹת קָדְשֶׁךָ
וְיָנוּחוּ בָם יִשְׂרָאֵל מְקַדְּשֵׁי שְׁמֶךָ.
בָּרוּךְ אַתָּה יהוה, מְקַדֵּשׁ הַשַּׁבָּת.

עבודה

רְצֵה יהוה אֱלֹהֵינוּ בְּעַמְּךָ יִשְׂרָאֵל וּבִתְפִלָּתָם
וְהָשֵׁב אֶת הָעֲבוֹדָה לִדְבִיר בֵּיתֶךָ[ב]
וְאִשֵּׁי יִשְׂרָאֵל וּתְפִלָּתָם בְּאַהֲבָה תְקַבֵּל בְּרָצוֹן
וּתְהִי לְרָצוֹן תָּמִיד עֲבוֹדַת יִשְׂרָאֵל עַמֶּךָ.

On ראש חודש, *say:*

אֱלֹהֵינוּ וֵאלֹהֵי אֲבוֹתֵינוּ, יַעֲלֶה וְיָבוֹא וְיַגִּיעַ, וְיֵרָאֶה וְיֵרָצֶה וְיִשָּׁמַע, וְיִפָּקֵד וְיִזָּכֵר[ע] זִכְרוֹנֵנוּ וּפִקְדוֹנֵנוּ וְזִכְרוֹן אֲבוֹתֵינוּ, וְזִכְרוֹן מָשִׁיחַ בֶּן דָּוִד עַבְדֶּךָ, וְזִכְרוֹן יְרוּשָׁלַיִם עִיר קָדְשֶׁךָ, וְזִכְרוֹן כָּל עַמְּךָ בֵּית יִשְׂרָאֵל, לְפָנֶיךָ, לִפְלֵיטָה לְטוֹבָה, לְחֵן וּלְחֶסֶד וּלְרַחֲמִים, לְחַיִּים וּלְשָׁלוֹם בְּיוֹם רֹאשׁ הַחֹדֶשׁ הַזֶּה. זָכְרֵנוּ יהוה אֱלֹהֵינוּ בּוֹ לְטוֹבָה, וּפָקְדֵנוּ בוֹ לִבְרָכָה, וְהוֹשִׁיעֵנוּ בוֹ לְחַיִּים. וּבִדְבַר יְשׁוּעָה וְרַחֲמִים, חוּס וְחָנֵּנוּ וְרַחֵם עָלֵינוּ וְהוֹשִׁיעֵנוּ, כִּי אֵלֶיךָ עֵינֵינוּ, כִּי אֵל מֶלֶךְ חַנּוּן וְרַחוּם אָתָּה.

BIUR TEFILLA • ביאור תפילה

For more commentary on these final blessings, see *Ma'ariv* (pages 467–470).

לִדְבִיר בֵּיתֶךָ – *Your most holy House.* The *Devir*, or House, is a reference to the Holy of Holies (*Kodesh HaKedoshim*), the innermost sanctuary of the Temple. What took place here? It was not the sacrifices which took place in the outer courtyard. It was not the offering of incense or the lighting of the Menora, which took place within the sanctuary itself. Rather, it was the location of the Holy Ark within which was found the Torah. Our expressed desire for its return in this context, therefore, is not to be able to do the rituals per se, but rather to return to the Source, to stand as close to His Presence as one could on this earth. See yourself there now.

וְתֶחֱזֶינָה And may our eyes witness Your return to Zion in compassion.
Blessed are You, LORD,
who restores His Presence to Zion.

THANKSGIVING

Bow at the first nine words.

We give thanks to You,
for You are the LORD our God
and God of our ancestors
for ever and all time.
You are the Rock of our lives,
Shield of our salvation
from generation to generation.
We will thank You and
declare Your praise for our lives,[A]
which are entrusted into Your hand;
for our souls,
which are placed in Your charge;
for Your miracles
which are with us every day;
and for Your wonders and favors
at all times,
evening, morning and midday.
You are good –
for Your compassion never fails.
You are compassionate –
for Your loving-kindnesses never cease.
We have always placed our hope in You.

During the Leader's Repetition, the congregation says quietly:

We give thanks to You,
for You are the LORD our God
and God of our ancestors,
God of all flesh,
who formed us
and formed the universe.
Blessings and thanks
are due to Your great
and holy name
for giving us life
and sustaining us.
May You continue
to give us life and sustain us;
and may You gather our
exiles to Your holy courts,
to keep Your decrees,
do Your will and serve You
with a perfect heart,
for it is for us
to give You thanks.
Blessed be God
to whom thanksgiving
is due.

IYUN TEFILLA · עיון תפילה

שֶׁבְּכָל עֵת – *Are with us… at all times.* Relationships are all about giving. A relationship that is one sided doesn't work. Both sides need to give to the other. It's like parents who in many ways are more connected to their children than the other way around, because they give more. It's only when the children grow up that they realize how much their parents had given them all of those years.

Think of Hashem as a parent. What has He given you? It is time to give thanks in return.

וְתֶחֱזֶינָה עֵינֵינוּ[ע] בְּשׁוּבְךָ לְצִיּוֹן בְּרַחֲמִים.
בָּרוּךְ אַתָּה יהוה, הַמַּחֲזִיר שְׁכִינָתוֹ לְצִיּוֹן.

הודאה

Bow at the first five words.

מוֹדִים אֲנַחְנוּ לָךְ
שָׁאַתָּה הוּא
יהוה אֱלֹהֵינוּ וֵאלֹהֵי אֲבוֹתֵינוּ
לְעוֹלָם וָעֶד.
צוּר חַיֵּינוּ, מָגֵן יִשְׁעֵנוּ
אַתָּה הוּא לְדוֹר וָדוֹר.
נוֹדֶה לְּךָ וּנְסַפֵּר תְּהִלָּתֶךָ
עַל חַיֵּינוּ[א] הַמְּסוּרִים בְּיָדֶךָ
וְעַל נִשְׁמוֹתֵינוּ הַפְּקוּדוֹת לָךְ
וְעַל נִסֶּיךָ שֶׁבְּכָל יוֹם עִמָּנוּ
וְעַל נִפְלְאוֹתֶיךָ[ע] וְטוֹבוֹתֶיךָ
שֶׁבְּכָל עֵת, עֶרֶב וָבֹקֶר וְצָהֳרָיִם.
הַטּוֹב, כִּי לֹא כָלוּ רַחֲמֶיךָ, וְהַמְרַחֵם,
כִּי לֹא תַמּוּ חֲסָדֶיךָ, מֵעוֹלָם קִוִּינוּ לָךְ.

During the חזרת הש״ץ, *the* קהל *says quietly:*

מוֹדִים אֲנַחְנוּ לָךְ
שָׁאַתָּה הוּא
יהוה אֱלֹהֵינוּ וֵאלֹהֵי אֲבוֹתֵינוּ
אֱלֹהֵי כָל בָּשָׂר
יוֹצְרֵנוּ, יוֹצֵר בְּרֵאשִׁית.
בְּרָכוֹת וְהוֹדָאוֹת
לְשִׁמְךָ הַגָּדוֹל וְהַקָּדוֹשׁ
עַל שֶׁהֶחֱיִיתָנוּ וְקִיַּמְתָּנוּ.
כֵּן תְּחַיֵּנוּ וּתְקַיְּמֵנוּ
וְתֶאֱסֹף גָּלֻיּוֹתֵינוּ
לְחַצְרוֹת קָדְשֶׁךָ
לִשְׁמֹר חֻקֶּיךָ וְלַעֲשׂוֹת רְצוֹנֶךָ
וּלְעָבְדְּךָ בְּלֵבָב שָׁלֵם
עַל שֶׁאֲנַחְנוּ מוֹדִים לָךְ.
בָּרוּךְ אֵל הַהוֹדָאוֹת.

IYUN TEFILLA • עיון תפילה

וְתֶחֱזֶינָה עֵינֵינוּ – *May our eyes witness.* Every Jew is obligated to see him or herself as an Israeli. Even if he was born elsewhere – by historical error – he nonetheless belongs to the Land of Israel. A Jew should always say: "I come from *Eretz Yisrael*!" Rabbi Moshe from Coucy, the author of the *halakhic* work called the *Semag* and one of the Ba`alei Tosafot, would sign his name: "Moshe from the Exile of Jerusalem who is in France." It is true that I am in France, but I am from Jerusalem. When a Jew is asked: "Where are you from," he must therefore respond: I come from *Eretz Yisrael* (Rabbi Meir Yeḥiel of Ostrowiec).

ANI TEFILLA • אני תפילה

מוֹדִים – *We give thanks.*

Name five things that you have to be thankful for today.

וְעַל כֻּלָּם For all these things
may Your name be blessed and exalted, our King,
continually, for ever and all time.
Let all that lives thank You,[B] Selah!
and praise Your name in truth,
God, our Savior and Help, Selah!
▾Blessed are You, LORD,
whose name is "the Good" and to whom thanks are due.

PEACE

שָׁלוֹם רָב Grant great peace to Your people Israel for ever, for You are the sovereign LORD of all peace;[I] and may it be good in Your eyes to bless Your people Israel at every time, at every hour, with Your peace.

In Israel:

שִׂים שָׁלוֹם Grant peace,
goodness and blessing,
grace, loving-kindness and compassion
to us and all Israel Your people.
Bless us, our Father, all as one,
with the light of Your face,
for by the light of Your face
You have given us, LORD our God,
the Torah of life
and love of kindness,
righteousness, blessing, compassion,
life and peace.
May it be good in Your eyes
to bless Your people Israel
at every time, in every hour,
with Your peace.

IYUN TEFILLA • עיון תפילה

כִּי אַתָּה הוּא מֶלֶךְ... לְכָל הַשָּׁלוֹם – *For You are the Sovereign…of all peace.* Peace comes about through shared values and ideals, through a common vision of the world that enables us to put our individual differences aside. The more that we can all come to accept God as the source of those values, the greater the chance for peace. Jealousy, unhealthy competition, egocentrism are the enemies of God, and of peace.

How will I carry those values into my week?

וְעַל כֻּלָּם יִתְבָּרַךְ וְיִתְרוֹמַם שִׁמְךָ מַלְכֵּנוּ תָּמִיד לְעוֹלָם וָעֶד.
וְכֹל הַחַיִּים יוֹדְוּךָ סֶּלָה
וִיהַלְלוּ אֶת שִׁמְךָ בֶּאֱמֶת
הָאֵל יְשׁוּעָתֵנוּ וְעֶזְרָתֵנוּ סֶלָה.
בָּרוּךְ אַתָּה יהוה, הַטּוֹב שִׁמְךָ וּלְךָ נָאֶה לְהוֹדוֹת.

ברכת שלום

שָׁלוֹם רָב עַל יִשְׂרָאֵל עַמְּךָ
תָּשִׂים לְעוֹלָם
כִּי אַתָּה הוּא
מֶלֶךְ אָדוֹן לְכָל הַשָּׁלוֹם.
וְטוֹב בְּעֵינֶיךָ
לְבָרֵךְ אֶת עַמְּךָ יִשְׂרָאֵל
בְּכָל עֵת וּבְכָל שָׁעָה
בִּשְׁלוֹמֶךָ.

In ארץ ישראל:
שִׂים שָׁלוֹם טוֹבָה וּבְרָכָה
חֵן וָחֶסֶד וְרַחֲמִים
עָלֵינוּ וְעַל כָּל יִשְׂרָאֵל עַמֶּךָ.
בָּרְכֵנוּ אָבִינוּ כֻּלָּנוּ כְּאֶחָד בְּאוֹר פָּנֶיךָ
כִּי בְאוֹר פָּנֶיךָ נָתַתָּ לָּנוּ יהוה אֱלֹהֵינוּ
תּוֹרַת חַיִּים וְאַהֲבַת חֶסֶד
וּצְדָקָה וּבְרָכָה וְרַחֲמִים וְחַיִּים וְשָׁלוֹם.
וְטוֹב בְּעֵינֶיךָ לְבָרֵךְ אֶת עַמְּךָ יִשְׂרָאֵל
בְּכָל עֵת וּבְכָל שָׁעָה בִּשְׁלוֹמֶךָ.

ANI TEFILLA • אני תפילה

David is driving in Jerusalem. He's late for a meeting, he's looking for a parking place, and can't find one. In desperation, he turns towards heaven and says: "Lord, if you find me a parking place, I promise that I'll eat only kosher, respect Shabbat and all the holidays." Miraculously, a place opens up just in front of him. He turns his face up to heaven and says, "Never mind, I just found one!"

BIUR TEFILLA • ביאור תפילה

וְכֹל הַחַיִּים יוֹדְוּךָ – *Let all that lives thank You.* This could be understood as "all living things" will thank You. Alternatively, it could mean "all of [my] life" will thank You, which would suggest that the way I live my life will be an acknowledgment of all of the good that You have given me. **What can you do to begin living that way?**

Blessed are You, Lord,
who blesses His people Israel with peace.[|]

The following verse concludes the Leader's Repetition of the Amida. Some also say it here as part of the silent Amida.

May the words of my mouth and the meditation of my heart find favor before You, Lord, my Rock and Redeemer. *Ps. 19*

אֱלֹהַי My God, *Berakhot 17a*
guard my tongue from evil
and my lips from deceitful speech.
To those who curse me, let my soul be silent;
may my soul be to all like the dust.[B]
Open my heart to Your Torah
and let my soul pursue Your commandments.
As for all who plan evil against me,
swiftly thwart their counsel and frustrate their plans.
Act for the sake of Your name;
act for the sake of Your right hand;
act for the sake of Your holiness;
act for the sake of Your Torah.

Another possibility: Let me be selfless to the point of humility. This would be in keeping with our being descendants of Avraham who said (*Bereshit* 18:27) "I am mere dust and ashes." Just because one is selfless and humble does not mean that one is devoid of ego or promise. Recall that Avraham was to become the father of a nation, the one who despite or because of his humility God promised (*Bereshit* 13:16): "I will make your offspring like the dust of the earth."

Alternatively: Let me be humble and maintain perspective on what is important in life. After all, King Solomon said "everything comes from dust and returns to dust" (*Kohelet* 3:20). We come from dust and return to dust. Remembering that life is short and that you are made from dust can help give perspective to the little things that make you crazy during the day.

Another possibility: "Let me not become arrogant if I am praised." It was reported that Rav Shimon Schwab, the former rabbinic leader of the German community known as "Breuer's" in New York City, was honored at a dinner. As he entered the hall, he was heard to be quietly whispering in Hebrew "And may my soul be as dust to all."

בָּרוּךְ אַתָּה יהוה, הַמְבָרֵךְ אֶת עַמּוֹ יִשְׂרָאֵל בַּשָּׁלוֹם.[ע]

The following verse concludes the חזרת הש״ץ.
Some also say it here as part of the silent עמידה.

יִהְיוּ לְרָצוֹן אִמְרֵי־פִי וְהֶגְיוֹן לִבִּי לְפָנֶיךָ, יהוה צוּרִי וְגֹאֲלִי: תהלים יט

אֱלֹהַי ברכות יז.

נְצֹר לְשׁוֹנִי מֵרָע וּשְׂפָתַי מִדַּבֵּר מִרְמָה
וְלִמְקַלְלַי נַפְשִׁי תִדֹּם, וְנַפְשִׁי כֶּעָפָר לַכֹּל תִּהְיֶה.[ב]
פְּתַח לִבִּי בְּתוֹרָתֶךָ, וּבְמִצְוֹתֶיךָ תִּרְדֹּף נַפְשִׁי.
וְכָל הַחוֹשְׁבִים עָלַי רָעָה
מְהֵרָה הָפֵר עֲצָתָם וְקַלְקֵל מַחֲשַׁבְתָּם.
עֲשֵׂה לְמַעַן שְׁמֶךָ
עֲשֵׂה לְמַעַן יְמִינֶךָ
עֲשֵׂה לְמַעַן קְדֻשָּׁתֶךָ
עֲשֵׂה לְמַעַן תּוֹרָתֶךָ.

IYUN TEFILLA • עיון תפילה

הַמְבָרֵךְ אֶת עַמּוֹ יִשְׂרָאֵל בַּשָּׁלוֹם – *Who blesses His people Israel with peace.* The midrash reports that "R. Shimon ben Ḥalafta said: 'Great is peace, for there is no vessel which contains blessings like peace, as it says (*Tehillim* 29:11) 'Hashem will bless His people with peace'" (*Bemidbar Rabba* 11:7). The midrash is actually understanding the phrase to say "in peace" rather than "with peace." All of the blessings that we ask for are contained within peace. Without peace there is nothing.

What can you do to make more peace this week?

BIUR TEFILLA • ביאור תפילה

וְנַפְשִׁי כֶּעָפָר לַכֹּל תִּהְיֶה – *May my soul be to all like the dust.* One possibility: May I be so insignificant that people not notice me to talk about me.

That Your beloved ones may be delivered, Ps. 60
save with Your right hand and answer me.
May the words of my mouth and the meditation of my heart Ps. 19
find favor before You, LORD, my Rock and Redeemer.

Bow, take three steps back, then bow, first left, then right, then center, while saying:

May He who makes peace in His high places,
make peace for us and all Israel – and say: Amen.

יְהִי רָצוֹן May it be Your will, LORD our God and God of our ancestors, that the Temple be rebuilt speedily in our days, and grant us a share in Your Torah. And there we will serve You with reverence, as in the days of old and as in former years. Then the offering of Judah and Jerusalem will be pleasing to the LORD as in the days of old and as in former years. Mal. 3

The following is omitted on days when Tahanun is not said.

צִדְקָתְךָ Your righteousness is an everlasting righteousness,[B] Ps. 119
and Your Torah is truth.
Your righteousness, O God, reaches to the highest heights, Ps. 71
for You have done great things.
O God, who is like You?
Your righteousness is like the mighty mountains;[I] Ps. 36
Your judgments like the great depths.
O LORD, You save both man and beast.

---

coming week. These three statements may therefore be three principles that we need to recall going forward: (1) Hashem taught us to live a life of justice and righteousness. (2) Any deviation from this path would be deserving of our forfeiting our lives, were it not for Hashem's loving-kindness. (3) Despite that, there will be times when the "judgments" of Hashem, the decrees that determine trouble and sorrow, will also be unleashed by Him, for these are what affirm our free will and enable us to meet our potential (Rabbi S. R. Hirsch).

IYUN TEFILLA • עיון תפילה

צִדְקָתְךָ כְּהַרְרֵי־אֵל – *Your righteousness is like the mighty mountains.* Why the comparison to the mountains? Sometimes mountains are covered in darkness and haze and cannot be seen clearly. So, too, Hashem's righteousness is sometimes hard to see, and only becomes visible with the passing of time (*Menahem Tzion*). As the week approaches, we pray that our vision will not be tested.

HILKHOT TEFILLA • הלכות תפילה

If today is a day when *Tahanun* would not be said were it a regular weekday, then the following is not said either.

תהלים ס לְמַעַן יֵחָלְצוּן יְדִידֶיךָ, הוֹשִׁיעָה יְמִינְךָ וַעֲנֵנִי:
תהלים יט יִהְיוּ לְרָצוֹן אִמְרֵי־פִי וְהֶגְיוֹן לִבִּי לְפָנֶיךָ, יהוה צוּרִי וְגוֹאֲלִי:

Bow, take three steps back, then bow, first left, then right, then center, while saying:

עֹשֶׂה שָׁלוֹם בִּמְרוֹמָיו
הוּא יַעֲשֶׂה שָׁלוֹם עָלֵינוּ וְעַל כָּל יִשְׂרָאֵל
וְאִמְרוּ אָמֵן.

יְהִי רָצוֹן מִלְּפָנֶיךָ יהוה אֱלֹהֵינוּ וֵאלֹהֵי אֲבוֹתֵינוּ, שֶׁיִּבָּנֶה בֵּית הַמִּקְדָּשׁ בִּמְהֵרָה בְיָמֵינוּ, וְתֵן חֶלְקֵנוּ בְּתוֹרָתֶךָ, וְשָׁם נַעֲבָדְךָ בְּיִרְאָה כִּימֵי עוֹלָם
מלאכי ג וּכְשָׁנִים קַדְמֹנִיּוֹת. וְעָרְבָה לַיהוה מִנְחַת יְהוּדָה וִירוּשָׁלָיִם כִּימֵי עוֹלָם וּכְשָׁנִים קַדְמֹנִיּוֹת:

The following is omitted on days when תחנון *is not said.*

תהלים קיט צִדְקָתְךָ צֶדֶק לְעוֹלָם וְתוֹרָתְךָ אֱמֶת:
תהלים עא וְצִדְקָתְךָ אֱלֹהִים עַד־מָרוֹם, אֲשֶׁר־עָשִׂיתָ גְדֹלוֹת
אֱלֹהִים, מִי כָמוֹךָ:
תהלים לו צִדְקָתְךָ כְּהַרְרֵי־אֵל, מִשְׁפָּטֶיךָ תְּהוֹם רַבָּה
אָדָם וּבְהֵמָה תוֹשִׁיעַ יהוה:

BIUR TEFILLA • ביאור תפילה

צִדְקָתְךָ צֶדֶק לְעוֹלָם - *Your* righteousness *is an everlasting righteousness.* There are a number of theories about the origin and significance of reciting these three individual verses from *Tehillim*, all of which begin with the same word, for while a single authoritative rationale has been lost to us, the custom goes back over a thousand years, and in Jewish life custom can be a more powerful a force than any rationale. There are those who suggest that the verses are a reference to Yosef, Moshe, and David, each of whom died on Shabbat afternoon, and, "like the words said at a funeral, they are an acceptance of loss as God's just decree" (Rabbi J. Sacks). Yet another suggests some messianic overtones (Abudarham) while still others suggest that it is reminiscent of the supplications that we make to Hashem after the *Amida* on a weekday (*Levush*). Alternatively, perhaps, as *Minḥa* comes to an end, and there is a palpable sense that the Shabbat is ebbing away, our thoughts turn toward the challenges and struggles that lay ahead of us in the

FULL KADDISH

Leader: יִתְגַּדַּל Magnified and sanctified may His great name be,
in the world He created by His will.
May He establish His kingdom
in your lifetime and in your days,
and in the lifetime of all the house of Israel,
swiftly and soon – and say: Amen.

All: May His great name[B] be blessed for ever and all time.

Leader: Blessed and praised, glorified and exalted,
raised and honored, uplifted and lauded be
the name of the Holy One,
blessed be He, beyond any blessing,
song, praise and consolation
uttered in the world – and say: Amen.

May the prayers and pleas of all Israel
be accepted by their Father in heaven – and say: Amen.

May there be great peace from heaven,
and life for us and all Israel – and say: Amen.

Bow, take three steps back, as if taking leave of the Divine Presence, then bow, first left, then right, then center, while saying:

May He who makes peace in His high places,
make peace for us and all Israel – and say: Amen.

BIUR TEFILLA • ביאור תפילה

יְהֵא שְׁמֵהּ רַבָּא – *May His great name.* *Maḥzor Vitry* suggests that the prayer is that His name will one day in the future be complete, i.e., when His enemies are destroyed and the world comes to accept that He is the One God.

The *Tur* (56) says that the prayer is that His name is great now at this moment in time, by virtue of the fact that we are all sanctifying it together.

Of course, one can choose to have only one of these in mind, but there is no reason that they cannot both be true at the same time.

קדיש שלם

ש״ץ: יִתְגַּדַּל וְיִתְקַדַּשׁ שְׁמֵהּ רַבָּא (קהל: אָמֵן)
בְּעָלְמָא דִּי בְרָא כִרְעוּתֵהּ
וְיַמְלִיךְ מַלְכוּתֵהּ
בְּחַיֵּיכוֹן וּבְיוֹמֵיכוֹן וּבְחַיֵּי דְכָל בֵּית יִשְׂרָאֵל
בַּעֲגָלָא וּבִזְמַן קָרִיב, וְאִמְרוּ אָמֵן. (קהל: אָמֵן)

קהל וש״ץ: יְהֵא שְׁמֵהּ רַבָּא מְבָרַךְ לְעָלַם וּלְעָלְמֵי עָלְמַיָּא.

ש״ץ: יִתְבָּרַךְ וְיִשְׁתַּבַּח וְיִתְפָּאַר
וְיִתְרוֹמַם וְיִתְנַשֵּׂא וְיִתְהַדָּר וְיִתְעַלֶּה וְיִתְהַלָּל
שְׁמֵהּ דְּקֻדְשָׁא בְּרִיךְ הוּא (קהל: בְּרִיךְ הוּא)
לְעֵלָּא מִן כָּל בִּרְכָתָא
וְשִׁירָתָא, תֻּשְׁבְּחָתָא וְנֶחֱמָתָא
דַּאֲמִירָן בְּעָלְמָא, וְאִמְרוּ אָמֵן. (קהל: אָמֵן)

תִּתְקַבַּל צְלוֹתְהוֹן וּבָעוּתְהוֹן דְּכָל יִשְׂרָאֵל
קֳדָם אֲבוּהוֹן דִּי בִשְׁמַיָּא, וְאִמְרוּ אָמֵן. (קהל: אָמֵן)

יְהֵא שְׁלָמָא רַבָּא מִן שְׁמַיָּא
וְחַיִּים, עָלֵינוּ וְעַל כָּל יִשְׂרָאֵל, וְאִמְרוּ אָמֵן. (קהל: אָמֵן)

Bow, take three steps back, as if taking leave of the Divine Presence, then bow, first left, then right, then center, while saying:

עֹשֶׂה שָׁלוֹם בִּמְרוֹמָיו
הוּא יַעֲשֶׂה שָׁלוֹם עָלֵינוּ
וְעַל כָּל יִשְׂרָאֵל, וְאִמְרוּ אָמֵן. (קהל: אָמֵן)

Between Pesaḥ and Rosh HaShana some recite Ethics of the Fathers, page 798, at this point.

Stand while saying Aleinu.

עָלֵינוּ It is our duty to praise the Master of all,
and ascribe greatness to the Author of creation,
who has not made us like the nations of the lands
nor placed us like the families of the earth;
who has not made our portion like theirs,
nor our destiny like all their multitudes.
(For they worship vanity and emptiness,
and pray to a god who cannot save.)
▾ *Bow:* But we bow in worship
and thank the Supreme King of kings, the Holy One, blessed be He,
who extends the heavens and establishes the earth,
whose throne of glory is in the heavens above,
and whose power's Presence is in the highest of heights.
He is our God; there is no other.
Truly He is our King, there is none else,
as it is written in His Torah: "You shall know and take to heart this day *Deut. 4*
that the LORD is God, in heaven above and on earth below.
There is no other."

Therefore, we place our hope in You, LORD our God,
that we may soon see the glory of Your power,
when You will remove abominations from the earth,
and idols will be utterly destroyed,
when the world will be perfected under the sovereignty of the Almighty,
when all humanity will call on Your name,
to turn all the earth's wicked toward You.
All the world's inhabitants will realize and know
that to You every knee must bow and every tongue swear loyalty.
Before You, LORD our God, they will kneel and bow down
and give honor to Your glorious name.
They will all accept the yoke of Your kingdom,
and You will reign over them soon and for ever.
For the kingdom is Yours, and to all eternity You will reign in glory,
as it is written in Your Torah: "The LORD will reign for ever and ever." *Ex. 15*

Between פסח *and* ראש השנה *some recite* פרקי אבות*, page 799, at this point.*

Stand while saying עָלֵינוּ*.*

עָלֵינוּ לְשַׁבֵּחַ לַאֲדוֹן הַכֹּל, לָתֵת גְּדֻלָּה לְיוֹצֵר בְּרֵאשִׁית
שֶׁלֹּא עָשָׂנוּ כְּגוֹיֵי הָאֲרָצוֹת, וְלֹא שָׂמָנוּ כְּמִשְׁפְּחוֹת הָאֲדָמָה
שֶׁלֹּא שָׂם חֶלְקֵנוּ כָּהֶם וְגוֹרָלֵנוּ כְּכָל הֲמוֹנָם.
(שֶׁהֵם מִשְׁתַּחֲוִים לְהֶבֶל וָרִיק וּמִתְפַּלְלִים אֶל אֵל לֹא יוֹשִׁיעַ.)
▾ *Bow* וַאֲנַחְנוּ כּוֹרְעִים וּמִשְׁתַּחֲוִים וּמוֹדִים
לִפְנֵי מֶלֶךְ מַלְכֵי הַמְּלָכִים, הַקָּדוֹשׁ בָּרוּךְ הוּא
שֶׁהוּא נוֹטֶה שָׁמַיִם וְיוֹסֵד אָרֶץ, וּמוֹשַׁב יְקָרוֹ בַּשָּׁמַיִם מִמַּעַל
וּשְׁכִינַת עֻזּוֹ בְּגָבְהֵי מְרוֹמִים.
הוּא אֱלֹהֵינוּ, אֵין עוֹד.
אֱמֶת מַלְכֵּנוּ, אֶפֶס זוּלָתוֹ
כַּכָּתוּב בְּתוֹרָתוֹ, וְיָדַעְתָּ הַיּוֹם וַהֲשֵׁבֹתָ אֶל־לְבָבֶךָ דברים ד
כִּי יהוה הוּא הָאֱלֹהִים בַּשָּׁמַיִם מִמַּעַל וְעַל־הָאָרֶץ מִתָּחַת
אֵין עוֹד:

עַל כֵּן נְקַוֶּה לְּךָ יהוה אֱלֹהֵינוּ, לִרְאוֹת מְהֵרָה בְּתִפְאֶרֶת עֻזֶּךָ
לְהַעֲבִיר גִּלּוּלִים מִן הָאָרֶץ, וְהָאֱלִילִים כָּרוֹת יִכָּרֵתוּן
לְתַקֵּן עוֹלָם בְּמַלְכוּת שַׁדַּי.
וְכָל בְּנֵי בָשָׂר יִקְרְאוּ בִשְׁמֶךָ לְהַפְנוֹת אֵלֶיךָ כָּל רִשְׁעֵי אָרֶץ.
יַכִּירוּ וְיֵדְעוּ כָּל יוֹשְׁבֵי תֵבֵל
כִּי לְךָ תִּכְרַע כָּל בֶּרֶךְ, תִּשָּׁבַע כָּל לָשׁוֹן.
לְפָנֶיךָ יהוה אֱלֹהֵינוּ יִכְרְעוּ וְיִפֹּלוּ, וְלִכְבוֹד שִׁמְךָ יְקָר יִתֵּנוּ
וִיקַבְּלוּ כֻלָּם אֶת עֹל מַלְכוּתֶךָ
וְתִמְלֹךְ עֲלֵיהֶם מְהֵרָה לְעוֹלָם וָעֶד.
כִּי הַמַּלְכוּת שֶׁלְּךָ הִיא וּלְעוֹלְמֵי עַד תִּמְלֹךְ בְּכָבוֹד
כַּכָּתוּב בְּתוֹרָתֶךָ, יהוה יִמְלֹךְ לְעֹלָם וָעֶד: שמות טו

▸ And it is said: "Then the LORD shall be King over all the earth; *Zech. 14*
on that day the LORD shall be One and His name One."

Some add:

Have no fear of sudden terror or of the ruin when it overtakes the wicked. *Prov. 3*
Devise your strategy, but it will be thwarted; propose your plan, *Is. 8*
but it will not stand, for God is with us.
When you grow old, I will still be the same. *Is. 46*
When your hair turns gray, I will still carry you.
I made you, I will bear you, I will carry you, and I will rescue you.

MOURNER'S KADDISH

The following prayer, said by mourners, requires the presence of a minyan.
A transliteration can be found on page 1141.

Mourner: יִתְגַּדַּל Magnified and sanctified may His great name be,
in the world He created by His will.
May He establish His kingdom in your lifetime
and in your days,
and in the lifetime of all the house of Israel,
swiftly and soon – and say: Amen.

All: May His great name be blessed for ever and all time.

Mourner: Blessed and praised, glorified and exalted,
raised and honored, uplifted and lauded
be the name of the Holy One, blessed be He,
beyond any blessing, song, praise and consolation
uttered in the world –
and say: Amen.

May there be great peace from heaven,
and life for us and all Israel –
and say: Amen.

Bow, take three steps back, as if taking leave of the Divine Presence,
then bow, first left, then right, then center, while saying:
May He who makes peace in His high places,
make peace for us and all Israel –
and say: Amen.

◂ וְנֶאֱמַר, וְהָיָה יהוה לְמֶלֶךְ עַל־כָּל־הָאָרֶץ זכריה יד
בַּיּוֹם הַהוּא יִהְיֶה יהוה אֶחָד וּשְׁמוֹ אֶחָד:

Some add:

אַל־תִּירָא מִפַּחַד פִּתְאֹם וּמִשֹּׁאַת רְשָׁעִים כִּי תָבֹא: משלי ג
עֻצוּ עֵצָה וְתֻפָר, דַּבְּרוּ דָבָר וְלֹא יָקוּם, כִּי עִמָּנוּ אֵל: ישעיה ח
וְעַד־זִקְנָה אֲנִי הוּא, וְעַד־שֵׂיבָה אֲנִי אֶסְבֹּל אֲנִי עָשִׂיתִי וַאֲנִי אֶשָּׂא וַאֲנִי אֶסְבֹּל וַאֲמַלֵּט: ישעיה מו

קדיש יתום

The following prayer, said by mourners, requires the presence of a מנין.
A transliteration can be found on page 1141.

אבל: יִתְגַּדַּל וְיִתְקַדַּשׁ שְׁמֵהּ רַבָּא (קהל: אָמֵן)
בְּעָלְמָא דִּי בְרָא כִרְעוּתֵהּ
וְיַמְלִיךְ מַלְכוּתֵהּ
בְּחַיֵּיכוֹן וּבְיוֹמֵיכוֹן וּבְחַיֵּי דְכָל בֵּית יִשְׂרָאֵל
בַּעֲגָלָא וּבִזְמַן קָרִיב, וְאִמְרוּ אָמֵן. (קהל: אָמֵן)

קהל ואבל: יְהֵא שְׁמֵהּ רַבָּא מְבָרַךְ לְעָלַם וּלְעָלְמֵי עָלְמַיָּא.

אבל: יִתְבָּרַךְ וְיִשְׁתַּבַּח וְיִתְפָּאַר
וְיִתְרוֹמַם וְיִתְנַשֵּׂא וְיִתְהַדָּר וְיִתְעַלֶּה וְיִתְהַלָּל
שְׁמֵהּ דְּקֻדְשָׁא בְּרִיךְ הוּא (קהל: בְּרִיךְ הוּא)
לְעֵלָּא מִן כָּל בִּרְכָתָא
וְשִׁירָתָא, תֻּשְׁבְּחָתָא וְנֶחֱמָתָא
דַּאֲמִירָן בְּעָלְמָא, וְאִמְרוּ אָמֵן. (קהל: אָמֵן)

יְהֵא שְׁלָמָא רַבָּא מִן שְׁמַיָּא
וְחַיִּים, עָלֵינוּ וְעַל כָּל יִשְׂרָאֵל, וְאִמְרוּ אָמֵן. (קהל: אָמֵן)

Bow, take three steps back, as if taking leave of the Divine Presence, then bow, first left, then right, then center, while saying:

עֹשֶׂה שָׁלוֹם בִּמְרוֹמָיו
הוּא יַעֲשֶׂה שָׁלוֹם עָלֵינוּ, וְעַל כָּל יִשְׂרָאֵל, וְאִמְרוּ אָמֵן.

ETHICS OF THE FATHERS

One of the following chapters is read each Shabbat after Pesaḥ until the Shabbat before Rosh HaShana. On the last three Shabbatot before Rosh HaShana, two chapters are read.

All Israel have a share in the World to Come,[B] as it is said: *Sanhedrin 90a*
"Your people are all righteous; they shall inherit the land for ever; *Is. 60*
they are a shoot of My own planting,
a work of My own hands, that I may be glorified."

CHAPTER I

1. Moses received the Torah at Sinai and handed it on to Yehoshua; Yehoshua to the elders; the elders to the prophets; and the prophets handed it on to the men of the Great Assembly. They (the men of the Great Assembly) said three things: Be careful in judgment; raise up many disciples; and make a fence for the Torah.

Why during this time of year in particular? Again, there is no one reason to be found. Some suggest that this is a period of "spring fever" when one needs reminders about being true to our values of ethics and propriety (*Midrash Shmuel*). Similarly, this period is generally considered a time of semi-mourning in Jewish life, the so-called Omer, which commemorates the death of 12,000 pairs of Rabbi Akiva's students, an event which should move us to further humility and self-improvement.

During this time of year, the days are longer and there is more time to do some learning that one may not be able to do during the week (*HaManhig*). This would explain why the custom to learn this material extends from Pesaḥ all the way to Rosh HaShana.

BIUR TEFILLA · ביאור תפילה

כָּל יִשְׂרָאֵל יֵשׁ לָהֶם חֵלֶק לָעוֹלָם הַבָּא – *All Israel have a share in the World to Come.* The recitation of this brief mishna from the tractate *Sanhedrin* was instituted, according to the twelfth-century Provencal scholar Rabbi Avraham ibn Yarḥi "so as to not question the status of those who are returnees to observant Judaism as well as those who are uneducated. If not for the words in that paragraph, those individuals who may not be as involved in Torah study nor in the appropriate performance of *mitzvot* might lose hope that they will merit entrance into the Next World" (*HaManhig*). The passage thus assures that all Jews have a place, regardless of how much they understand or how many commandments they have or haven't performed in the past. Change is always possible and welcome, even if it is only in small increments.

פרקי אבות

One of the following chapters is read each שבת *after* פסח *until the* שבת *before* ראש השנה*. On the last three* שבתות *before* ראש השנה*, two chapters are read.*

סנהדרין צ. כָּל יִשְׂרָאֵל יֵשׁ לָהֶם חֵלֶק לָעוֹלָם הַבָּא. שֶׁנֶּאֱמַר:
ישעיה ס וְעַמֵּךְ כֻּלָּם צַדִּיקִים, לְעוֹלָם יִירְשׁוּ אָרֶץ
נֵצֶר מַטָּעַי, מַעֲשֵׂה יָדַי לְהִתְפָּאֵר:

פרק ראשון

א מֹשֶׁה קִבֵּל תּוֹרָה מִסִּינַי וּמְסָרָהּ לִיהוֹשֻׁעַ, וִיהוֹשֻׁעַ לִזְקֵנִים, וּזְקֵנִים לִנְבִיאִים, וּנְבִיאִים מְסָרוּהָ לְאַנְשֵׁי כְנֶסֶת הַגְּדוֹלָה. הֵם אָמְרוּ שְׁלֹשָׁה דְבָרִים: הֱווּ מְתוּנִים בַּדִּין, וְהַעֲמִידוּ תַלְמִידִים הַרְבֵּה, וַעֲשׂוּ סְיָג לַתּוֹרָה.

INTRODUCTION TO PIRKEI AVOT

פרקי אבות – *PIRKEI AVOT* (*Chapters [Ethics] of the Fathers*) is an unusual tractate of the Mishna which deals almost entirely with ethical teachings of the Rabbis. Its style is short and concise, making it sometimes difficult to understand without commentary. While the values and virtues of Judaism can be found defined and debated throughout all of Mishna and Talmud, this is the only place where such teachings are gathered in one place to the near exclusion of other kinds of legal material. Hence the rabbinic view which said that, of all of the Oral Law, if one wants to be a pious person one should learn *Avot* (*Bava Kamma* 30a).

There are a number of rationales offered for why this section was traditionally learned on Shabbat afternoon and how often and therefore there were and remain numerous different customs related to its recitation. To cite but a few:

Shabbat afternoon was the time when Moshe died (though there is another tradition which says it was Friday evening) and there is a custom that one does not learn Talmud when a great sage dies but only Mishna as is our custom to this day in a house of mourning. In deference to the very first Mishna in this tractate which mentions Moshe's role in tradition, we restrict our learning to these chapters (*Otzar HaGeonim*). Alternatively, simply the fact that Moshe spent a total of four summer months atop Mount Sinai receiving the Torah, as indicated in the first line, would be enough to merit this selection of learning (Rabbi E. Munk).

A common custom was to do this learning only on Shabbat afternoon between Pesaḥ and Shavuot. This would explain why there is a chapter that was added to the original five chapters of the tractate, for there are six *Shabbatot* between the two holidays.

2. Shimon the Just was one of the last survivors of the Great Assembly. He used to say: On three things the world stands: on the Torah, on divine worship, and on acts of loving-kindness.

3. Antigonos of Sokho received [the Torah tradition] from Shimon the Just. He used to say: Do not be like servants who serve their master on condition of receiving a reward, but be like servants who serve their master not on condition of receiving a reward; and let the fear of Heaven be upon you.

4. Yose ben Yo'ezer of Zereda and Yose ben Yoḥanan of Jerusalem received [the tradition] from them. Yose ben Yo'ezer of Zereda used to say: Let your house be a meeting place for sages; sit in the dust at their feet, and with thirst, drink in their words.

5. Yose ben Yoḥanan of Jerusalem used to say: Let your house be open wide; let the poor join the members of your household; and do not gossip inordinately with women. This was said about one's own wife; all the more so does it apply to another man's wife. Hence the sages say: a man who talks too much with a woman brings trouble on himself, neglects the study of Torah, and in the end will inherit Gehinnom.

6. Yehoshua ben Peraḥya and Nittai the Arbelite received [the tradition] from them. Yehoshua ben Peraḥya used to say: Get yourself a teacher, acquire a companion, and give everyone the benefit of the doubt.

7. Nittai the Arbelite used to say: Keep far from a bad neighbor, do not associate with a bad person, and do not despair of divine retribution.

8. Yehuda ben Tabbai and Shimon ben Shataḥ received [the tradition] from them. Yehuda ben Tabbai used to say: [When sitting as a judge] do not act as an advocate; when the parties to a lawsuit appear before you, regard them both as guilty; but when they leave you, having accepted the verdict, regard them both as innocent.

9. Shimon ben Shataḥ used to say: Examine the witnesses thoroughly, and be careful in your words, lest through them they learn how to lie.

10. Shemaya and Avtalyon received [the tradition] from them. Shemaya used to say: Love work, hate public office, and do not become too intimate with the ruling power.

11. Avtalyon used to say: sages, be careful in what you say, lest you incur the penalty of exile and find yourself banished to a place of evil waters, where your disciples who follow you may drink from them and die, with the result that the name of Heaven will be profaned.

12. Hillel and Shammai received [the tradition] from them. Hillel said: Be among the disciples of Aaron, loving peace and pursuing peace, loving people and drawing them close to the Torah.

ב שִׁמְעוֹן הַצַּדִּיק הָיָה מִשְּׁיָרֵי כְּנֶסֶת הַגְּדוֹלָה. הוּא הָיָה אוֹמֵר: עַל שְׁלֹשָׁה דְּבָרִים הָעוֹלָם עוֹמֵד, עַל הַתּוֹרָה, וְעַל הָעֲבוֹדָה, וְעַל גְּמִילוּת חֲסָדִים.

ג אַנְטִיגְנוֹס אִישׁ סוֹכוֹ קִבֵּל מִשִּׁמְעוֹן הַצַּדִּיק. הוּא הָיָה אוֹמֵר: אַל תִּהְיוּ כַּעֲבָדִים הַמְשַׁמְּשִׁים אֶת הָרַב עַל מְנָת לְקַבֵּל פְּרָס, אֶלָּא הֱווּ כַּעֲבָדִים הַמְשַׁמְּשִׁים אֶת הָרַב שֶׁלֹּא עַל מְנָת לְקַבֵּל פְּרָס, וִיהִי מוֹרָא שָׁמַיִם עֲלֵיכֶם.

ד יוֹסֵי בֶּן יוֹעֶזֶר אִישׁ צְרֵדָה וְיוֹסֵי בֶּן יוֹחָנָן אִישׁ יְרוּשָׁלַיִם קִבְּלוּ מֵהֶם. יוֹסֵי בֶּן יוֹעֶזֶר אִישׁ צְרֵדָה אוֹמֵר: יְהִי בֵיתְךָ בֵּית וַעַד לַחֲכָמִים, וֶהֱוֵי מִתְאַבֵּק בַּעֲפַר רַגְלֵיהֶם, וֶהֱוֵי שׁוֹתֶה בַצָּמָא אֶת דִּבְרֵיהֶם.

ה יוֹסֵי בֶּן יוֹחָנָן אִישׁ יְרוּשָׁלַיִם אוֹמֵר: יְהִי בֵיתְךָ פָּתוּחַ לִרְוָחָה, וְיִהְיוּ עֲנִיִּים בְּנֵי בֵיתֶךָ, וְאַל תַּרְבֶּה שִׂיחָה עִם הָאִשָּׁה. בְּאִשְׁתּוֹ אָמְרוּ, קַל וָחֹמֶר בְּאֵשֶׁת חֲבֵרוֹ. מִכָּאן אָמְרוּ חֲכָמִים: כָּל הַמַּרְבֶּה שִׂיחָה עִם הָאִשָּׁה, גּוֹרֵם רָעָה לְעַצְמוֹ, וּבוֹטֵל מִדִּבְרֵי תוֹרָה, וְסוֹפוֹ יוֹרֵשׁ גֵּיהִנֹּם.

ו יְהוֹשֻׁעַ בֶּן פְּרַחְיָה וְנִתַּאי הָאַרְבֵּלִי קִבְּלוּ מֵהֶם. יְהוֹשֻׁעַ בֶּן פְּרַחְיָה אוֹמֵר: עֲשֵׂה לְךָ רַב, וּקְנֵה לְךָ חָבֵר, וֶהֱוֵי דָן אֶת כָּל הָאָדָם לְכַף זְכוּת.

ז נִתַּאי הָאַרְבֵּלִי אוֹמֵר: הַרְחֵק מִשָּׁכֵן רָע, וְאַל תִּתְחַבֵּר לָרָשָׁע, וְאַל תִּתְיָאֵשׁ מִן הַפֻּרְעָנוּת.

ח יְהוּדָה בֶּן טַבַּאי וְשִׁמְעוֹן בֶּן שָׁטָח קִבְּלוּ מֵהֶם. יְהוּדָה בֶּן טַבַּאי אוֹמֵר: אַל תַּעַשׂ עַצְמְךָ כְּעוֹרְכֵי הַדַּיָּנִין, וּכְשֶׁיִּהְיוּ בַּעֲלֵי הַדִּין עוֹמְדִים לְפָנֶיךָ יִהְיוּ בְעֵינֶיךָ כִּרְשָׁעִים, וּכְשֶׁנִּפְטָרִים מִלְּפָנֶיךָ יִהְיוּ בְעֵינֶיךָ כְּזַכָּאִין, כְּשֶׁקִּבְּלוּ עֲלֵיהֶם אֶת הַדִּין.

ט שִׁמְעוֹן בֶּן שָׁטָח אוֹמֵר: הֱוֵי מַרְבֶּה לַחֲקֹר אֶת הָעֵדִים, וֶהֱוֵי זָהִיר בִּדְבָרֶיךָ, שֶׁמָּא מִתּוֹכָם יִלְמְדוּ לְשַׁקֵּר.

י שְׁמַעְיָה וְאַבְטַלְיוֹן קִבְּלוּ מֵהֶם. שְׁמַעְיָה אוֹמֵר: אֱהֹב אֶת הַמְּלָאכָה, וּשְׂנָא אֶת הָרַבָּנוּת, וְאַל תִּתְוַדַּע לָרָשׁוּת.

יא אַבְטַלְיוֹן אוֹמֵר: חֲכָמִים הִזָּהֲרוּ בְּדִבְרֵיכֶם, שֶׁמָּא תָחוּבוּ חוֹבַת גָּלוּת, וְתִגְלוּ לִמְקוֹם מַיִם הָרָעִים, וְיִשְׁתּוּ הַתַּלְמִידִים הַבָּאִים אַחֲרֵיכֶם וְיָמוּתוּ, וְנִמְצָא שֵׁם שָׁמַיִם מִתְחַלֵּל.

יב הִלֵּל וְשַׁמַּאי קִבְּלוּ מֵהֶם. הִלֵּל אוֹמֵר: הֱוֵי מִתַּלְמִידָיו שֶׁל אַהֲרֹן, אוֹהֵב שָׁלוֹם וְרוֹדֵף שָׁלוֹם, אוֹהֵב אֶת הַבְּרִיּוֹת וּמְקָרְבָן לַתּוֹרָה.

13. He used to say: A name made great is a name destroyed. He who does not increase [his knowledge] loses it. He who does not study deserves to die, and he who makes worldly use of the crown [of Torah] passes away.

14. He used to say: If I am not for myself, who will be for me? And if I am only for myself, what am I? And if not now, when?

15. Shammai used to say: Make your Torah study a fixed habit. Say little and do much; and greet everyone cheerfully.

16. Rabban Gamliel used to say: Get yourself a teacher, avoid doubt, and do not make a habit of giving tithes by guessing.

17. Shimon, his son, used to say: All my life I grew up among sages and I found that nothing is better for a person than silence. Not learning but doing is the main thing; and one who talks too much causes sin.

18. Rabban Shimon ben Gamliel used to say: On three things does the world stand – on truth, justice and peace, as it is said, "Administer truth and the judgment of peace in your gates." *Zech. 8*

Rabbi Ḥananya ben Akashya said:[B] The Holy One, blessed be He, wanted to confer merit on Israel. That is why He gave them a copious Torah and many commandments, as it is said, "It pleased the LORD, for the sake of [Israel's] righteousness, to make the Torah great and glorious." *Makkot 23b* *Is. 42*

If there is a minyan, mourners say the Rabbis' Kaddish (page 712).

* * *

All Israel have a share in the World to Come, as it is said: *Sanhedrin 90a*
"Your people are all righteous; they shall inherit the land for ever; *Is. 60*
they are a shoot of My own planting,
a work of My own hands, that I may be glorified."

CHAPTER 2

1. Rabbi [Judah the Prince] said: What is the right path a person should choose for himself? Whatever is honorable to one who chooses it and honorable in the eyes of others. Be as meticulous in the observance of a minor mitzva as a major one, for you do not know the reward for each mitzva. Against the loss

---

content, this mishna may be understood to mean that, as Maimonides says, "It is a fundamental principle of Jewish faith that if a person fulfills even one of the 613 *mitzvot* fully and properly, without ulterior motive but simply for its own sake and out of love, he merits a share in the World to Come. Therefore Rabbi Ḥananya teaches that there are so many *mitzvot* that it is impossible that a person should not have fulfilled at least one in the course of a lifetime, and thereby merit eternal life."

יג הוּא הָיָה אוֹמֵר: נְגַד שְׁמָא אֲבַד שְׁמֵהּ, וּדְלָא מוֹסִיף יָסוּף, וּדְלָא יָלֵף קְטָלָא
חַיָּב, וּדְאִשְׁתַּמַּשׁ בְּתָגָא חֲלָף.

יד הוּא הָיָה אוֹמֵר: אִם אֵין אֲנִי לִי מִי לִי, וּכְשֶׁאֲנִי לְעַצְמִי מָה אֲנִי, וְאִם לֹא
עַכְשָׁו אֵימָתַי.

טו שַׁמַּאי אוֹמֵר: עֲשֵׂה תוֹרָתְךָ קֶבַע, אֱמֹר מְעַט וַעֲשֵׂה הַרְבֵּה, וֶהֱוֵי מְקַבֵּל אֶת
כָּל הָאָדָם בְּסֵבֶר פָּנִים יָפוֹת.

טז רַבָּן גַּמְלִיאֵל אוֹמֵר: עֲשֵׂה לְךָ רַב, וְהִסְתַּלֵּק מִן הַסָּפֵק, וְאַל תַּרְבֶּה לְעַשֵּׂר
אֻמָּדוֹת.

יז שִׁמְעוֹן בְּנוֹ אוֹמֵר: כָּל יָמַי גָּדַלְתִּי בֵּין הַחֲכָמִים, וְלֹא מָצָאתִי לַגּוּף טוֹב
מִשְּׁתִיקָה, וְלֹא הַמִּדְרָשׁ עִקָּר אֶלָּא הַמַּעֲשֶׂה, וְכָל הַמַּרְבֶּה דְבָרִים מֵבִיא חֵטְא.

יח רַבָּן שִׁמְעוֹן בֶּן גַּמְלִיאֵל אוֹמֵר: עַל שְׁלֹשָׁה דְבָרִים הָעוֹלָם קַיָּם, עַל הַדִּין,
וְעַל הָאֱמֶת, וְעַל הַשָּׁלוֹם. שֶׁנֶּאֱמַר: אֱמֶת וּמִשְׁפַּט שָׁלוֹם שִׁפְטוּ בְּשַׁעֲרֵיכֶם: זכריה ח

רַבִּי חֲנַנְיָא בֶּן עֲקַשְׁיָא אוֹמֵר: רָצָה הַקָּדוֹשׁ בָּרוּךְ הוּא לְזַכּוֹת אֶת יִשְׂרָאֵל, לְפִיכָךְ מכות כג:
הִרְבָּה לָהֶם תּוֹרָה וּמִצְוֹת. שֶׁנֶּאֱמַר: יהוה חָפֵץ לְמַעַן צִדְקוֹ, יַגְדִּיל תּוֹרָה וְיַאְדִּיר: ישעיה מב

If there is a מנין, *mourners say* קדיש דרבנן (*page 713*).

* * *

כָּל יִשְׂרָאֵל יֵשׁ לָהֶם חֵלֶק לָעוֹלָם הַבָּא. שֶׁנֶּאֱמַר: סנהדרין צ.
וְעַמֵּךְ כֻּלָּם צַדִּיקִים, לְעוֹלָם יִירְשׁוּ אָרֶץ ישעיה ס
נֵצֶר מַטָּעַי, מַעֲשֵׂה יָדַי לְהִתְפָּאֵר:

פרק שני

א רַבִּי אוֹמֵר: אֵיזוֹ הִיא דֶרֶךְ יְשָׁרָה שֶׁיָּבֹר לוֹ הָאָדָם, כָּל שֶׁהִיא תִּפְאֶרֶת
לְעֹשֶׂיהָ וְתִפְאֶרֶת לוֹ מִן הָאָדָם. וֶהֱוֵי זָהִיר בְּמִצְוָה קַלָּה כְּבַחֲמוּרָה, שֶׁאֵין

BIUR TEFILLA • ביאור תפילה

רַבִּי חֲנַנְיָא בֶּן עֲקַשְׁיָא אוֹמֵר – *Rabbi Ḥananya ben Akashya said.* This passage is not part of the tractate of *Avot* but is appended at the conclusion of every learning session. From a purely technical point of view, it is because this teaching qualifies as *aggada*, a non-legal teaching, and there is a rule that *Kaddish DeRabbanan* is only recited after the recitation of *aggadic* material and not *halakhic*. But from the point of view of its

that fulfilling a mitzva may entail, reckon its reward, and against the benefit a transgression may bring, reckon the loss it involves. Reflect on three things and you will not fall into transgression: know what is above you – a seeing eye, a hearing ear, and a book in which all your deeds are written.

2. Rabban Gamliel, son of Rabbi Judah the Prince, said: It is good to combine Torah study with a worldly occupation, for the effort involved in both makes one forget sin. Torah study without an occupation will in the end fail and lead to sin. And all who work for the community should do so for the sake of Heaven, for their ancestral merit will support them and their righteousness endures for ever. And as for you [God will say], I count you worthy of great reward as though you yourselves had accomplished it all.

3. Be wary in your dealings with the ruling power, for they only befriend a man when it serves their needs. When it is to their advantage, they appear as friends, but they do not stand by a person in his hour of need.

4. He used to say: Do His will as if it were yours, so that He may do your will as if it were His. Set aside your will for the sake of His, that He may set aside the will of others before yours.

5. Hillel said: Do not separate yourself from the community. Do not be sure of yourself until the day you die. Do not judge your fellow until you have stood in his place. Do not say anything that cannot be understood [at once] in the hope that it will eventually be understood. And do not say, I will study when I have the time, for you may never have the time.

6. He used to say: An uncouth person cannot be sin-fearing, nor can an ignoramus be pious. A shy person cannot learn, nor can an impatient one teach. A person over-occupied in business does not always become wise. In a place where there are no worthy people, strive to be worthy.

7. Seeing a skull floating on the water, he said: "Because you drowned others, they drowned you, and those who drowned you will themselves eventually be drowned."

8. He used to say: The more flesh, the more worms. The more possessions, the more worries. The more wives, the more witchcraft. The more maidservants, the more lewdness. The more menservants, the more robbery. The more Torah, the more life. The more study, the more wisdom. The more counsel, the more understanding. The more charity, the more peace. Whoever acquires a good name acquires something for himself. Whoever acquires for himself words of Torah acquires for himself life in the World to Come.

9. Rabban Yoḥanan ben Zakkai received [the tradition] from Hillel and Shammai. He used to say: If you have learnt much Torah, take no special credit for yourself, for it was for this that you were created.

אַתָּה יוֹדֵעַ מַתַּן שְׂכָרָן שֶׁל מִצְוֹת. וֶהֱוֵי מְחַשֵּׁב הֶפְסֵד מִצְוָה כְּנֶגֶד שְׂכָרָהּ, וּשְׂכַר עֲבֵרָה כְּנֶגֶד הֶפְסֵדָהּ. הִסְתַּכֵּל בִּשְׁלֹשָׁה דְבָרִים, וְאֵין אַתָּה בָא לִידֵי עֲבֵרָה. דַּע מַה לְּמַעְלָה מִמְּךָ, עַיִן רוֹאָה, וְאֹזֶן שׁוֹמַעַת, וְכָל מַעֲשֶׂיךָ בַּסֵּפֶר נִכְתָּבִים.

ב רַבָּן גַּמְלִיאֵל בְּנוֹ שֶׁל רַבִּי יְהוּדָה הַנָּשִׂיא אוֹמֵר: יָפֶה תַּלְמוּד תּוֹרָה עִם דֶּרֶךְ אֶרֶץ, שֶׁיְּגִיעַת שְׁנֵיהֶם מְשַׁכַּחַת עָוֹן. וְכָל תּוֹרָה שֶׁאֵין עִמָּהּ מְלָאכָה, סוֹפָהּ בְּטֵלָה וְגוֹרֶרֶת עָוֹן. וְכָל הָעוֹסְקִים עִם הַצִּבּוּר, יִהְיוּ עוֹסְקִים עִמָּהֶם לְשֵׁם שָׁמַיִם, שֶׁזְּכוּת אֲבוֹתָם מְסַיַּעְתָּם, וְצִדְקָתָם עוֹמֶדֶת לָעַד. וְאַתֶּם, מַעֲלֶה אֲנִי עֲלֵיכֶם שָׂכָר הַרְבֵּה כְּאִלּוּ עֲשִׂיתֶם.

ג הֱווּ זְהִירִין בָּרָשׁוּת, שֶׁאֵין מְקָרְבִין לוֹ לָאָדָם אֶלָּא לְצֹרֶךְ עַצְמָן. נִרְאִין כְּאוֹהֲבִין בִּשְׁעַת הֲנָאָתָן, וְאֵין עוֹמְדִין לוֹ לָאָדָם בִּשְׁעַת דָּחְקוֹ.

ד הוּא הָיָה אוֹמֵר: עֲשֵׂה רְצוֹנוֹ כִּרְצוֹנְךָ, כְּדֵי שֶׁיַּעֲשֶׂה רְצוֹנְךָ כִּרְצוֹנוֹ. בַּטֵּל רְצוֹנְךָ מִפְּנֵי רְצוֹנוֹ, כְּדֵי שֶׁיְּבַטֵּל רְצוֹן אֲחֵרִים מִפְּנֵי רְצוֹנֶךָ.

ה הִלֵּל אוֹמֵר: אַל תִּפְרֹשׁ מִן הַצִּבּוּר, וְאַל תַּאֲמִין בְּעַצְמְךָ עַד יוֹם מוֹתְךָ, וְאַל תָּדִין אֶת חֲבֵרְךָ עַד שֶׁתַּגִּיעַ לִמְקוֹמוֹ. וְאַל תֹּאמַר דָּבָר שֶׁאִי אֶפְשַׁר לִשְׁמֹעַ, שֶׁסּוֹפוֹ לְהִשָּׁמֵעַ. וְאַל תֹּאמַר לִכְשֶׁאֶפָּנֶה אֶשְׁנֶה, שֶׁמָּא לֹא תִפָּנֶה.

ו הוּא הָיָה אוֹמֵר: אֵין בּוּר יְרֵא חֵטְא, וְלֹא עַם הָאָרֶץ חָסִיד, וְלֹא הַבַּיְשָׁן לָמֵד, וְלֹא הַקַּפְּדָן מְלַמֵּד, וְלֹא כָל הַמַּרְבֶּה בִסְחוֹרָה מַחְכִּים. וּבְמָקוֹם שֶׁאֵין אֲנָשִׁים, הִשְׁתַּדֵּל לִהְיוֹת אִישׁ.

ז אַף הוּא רָאָה גֻּלְגֹּלֶת אַחַת שֶׁצָּפָה עַל פְּנֵי הַמָּיִם. אָמַר לָהּ: עַל דַּאֲטֵפְתְּ אַטְפוּךְ, וְסוֹף מְטִיפַיִךְ יְטוּפוּן.

ח הוּא הָיָה אוֹמֵר: מַרְבֶּה בָשָׂר, מַרְבֶּה רִמָּה. מַרְבֶּה נְכָסִים, מַרְבֶּה דְאָגָה. מַרְבֶּה נָשִׁים, מַרְבֶּה כְשָׁפִים. מַרְבֶּה שְׁפָחוֹת, מַרְבֶּה זִמָּה. מַרְבֶּה עֲבָדִים, מַרְבֶּה גָזֵל. מַרְבֶּה תוֹרָה, מַרְבֶּה חַיִּים. מַרְבֶּה יְשִׁיבָה, מַרְבֶּה חָכְמָה. מַרְבֶּה עֵצָה, מַרְבֶּה תְבוּנָה. מַרְבֶּה צְדָקָה, מַרְבֶּה שָׁלוֹם. קָנָה שֵׁם טוֹב, קָנָה לְעַצְמוֹ. קָנָה לוֹ דִבְרֵי תוֹרָה, קָנָה לוֹ חַיֵּי הָעוֹלָם הַבָּא.

ט רַבָּן יוֹחָנָן בֶּן זַכַּאי קִבֵּל מֵהִלֵּל וּמִשַּׁמַּאי. הוּא הָיָה אוֹמֵר: אִם לָמַדְתָּ תּוֹרָה הַרְבֵּה, אַל תַּחֲזִיק טוֹבָה לְעַצְמְךָ, כִּי לְכָךְ נוֹצָרְתָּ.

10. Rabban Yoḥanan ben Zakkai had five [pre-eminent] disciples, namely: Rabbi Eliezer ben Hyrcanus, Rabbi Yehoshua ben Ḥananya, Rabbi Yose the Priest, Rabbi Shimon ben Netanel and Rabbi Elazar ben Arakh.

11. He used to recount their praise: Eliezer ben Hyrcanus: a plastered well that never loses a drop. Yehoshua ben Ḥananya: happy the one who gave him birth. Yose the Priest: a pious man. Shimon ben Netanel: a man who fears sin. Elazar ben Arakh: an ever-flowing spring.

12. He used to say: If all the sages of Israel were in one scale of a balance and Eliezer ben Hyrcanus in the other, he would outweigh them all. However, Abba Saul said in his name: If all the sages of Israel, including Eliezer ben Hyrcanus, were in one scale of a balance, and Elazar ben Arakh in the other, he would outweigh them all.

13. He said to them: Go and see which is the right way to which one should cling. Rabbi Eliezer said: a good eye [generosity of spirit]. Rabbi Yehoshua said: a good companion. Rabbi Yose said: a good neighbor. Rabbi Shimon said: one who considers the consequences. Rabbi Elazar said: a good heart. Then he said to them: I prefer the answer of Elazar ben Arakh, for his view includes all of yours.

14. He said to them: Go and see which is the wrong way one should avoid. Rabbi Eliezer said: an evil eye [envy]. Rabbi Yehoshua said: an evil companion. Rabbi Yose said: an evil neighbor. Rabbi Shimon said: one who borrows and does not repay, for borrowing from a person is like borrowing from God, as it is said, "The wicked borrows and does not repay, but the Righteous *Ps. 37* One is gracious and repays." Rabbi Elazar said: an evil heart. Then he said to them: I prefer the answer of Elazar ben Arakh, for his view includes all of yours.

15. Each of the disciples said three things. Rabbi Eliezer said: Let the honor of your fellow be as precious to you as your own. Do not be easily provoked to anger. Repent one day before you die. [He also said:] Warm yourself by the fire of the sages, but be careful of their glowing coals lest you be burnt; for their bite is the bite of a fox, their sting is the sting of a scorpion, their hiss is the hiss of a serpent, and all their words are like fiery coals.

16. Rabbi Yehoshua said: The evil eye [envy], the evil impulse, and hatred of humankind drive a person out of the world.

17. Rabbi Yose said: Let the property of your fellow be as precious to you as your own. Prepare yourself to study Torah, for it does not come to you as an inheritance. And let all your deeds be for the sake of Heaven.

י חֲמִשָּׁה תַלְמִידִים הָיוּ לְרַבָּן יוֹחָנָן בֶּן זַכַּאי. וְאֵלּוּ הֵן: רַבִּי אֱלִיעֶזֶר בֶּן הוּרְקְנוֹס, רַבִּי יְהוֹשֻׁעַ בֶּן חֲנַנְיָה, רַבִּי יוֹסֵי הַכֹּהֵן, רַבִּי שִׁמְעוֹן בֶּן נְתַנְאֵל, רַבִּי אֶלְעָזָר בֶּן עֲרָךְ.

יא הוּא הָיָה מוֹנֶה שְׁבָחָם: אֱלִיעֶזֶר בֶּן הוּרְקְנוֹס, בּוֹר סוּד שֶׁאֵינוֹ מְאַבֵּד טִפָּה. יְהוֹשֻׁעַ בֶּן חֲנַנְיָה, אַשְׁרֵי יוֹלַדְתּוֹ. יוֹסֵי הַכֹּהֵן, חָסִיד. שִׁמְעוֹן בֶּן נְתַנְאֵל, יְרֵא חֵטְא. אֶלְעָזָר בֶּן עֲרָךְ, כְּמַעְיָן הַמִּתְגַּבֵּר.

יב הוּא הָיָה אוֹמֵר: אִם יִהְיוּ כָּל חַכְמֵי יִשְׂרָאֵל בְּכַף מֹאזְנַיִם, וֶאֱלִיעֶזֶר בֶּן הוּרְקְנוֹס בְּכַף שְׁנִיָּה, מַכְרִיעַ אֶת כֻּלָּם. אַבָּא שָׁאוּל אוֹמֵר מִשְּׁמוֹ: אִם יִהְיוּ כָּל חַכְמֵי יִשְׂרָאֵל בְּכַף מֹאזְנַיִם, וֶאֱלִיעֶזֶר בֶּן הוּרְקְנוֹס אַף עִמָּהֶם, וְאֶלְעָזָר בֶּן עֲרָךְ בְּכַף שְׁנִיָּה, מַכְרִיעַ אֶת כֻּלָּם.

יג אָמַר לָהֶם: צְאוּ וּרְאוּ אֵיזוֹ הִיא דֶּרֶךְ טוֹבָה, שֶׁיִּדְבַּק בָּהּ הָאָדָם. רַבִּי אֱלִיעֶזֶר אוֹמֵר: עַיִן טוֹבָה. רַבִּי יְהוֹשֻׁעַ אוֹמֵר: חָבֵר טוֹב. רַבִּי יוֹסֵי אוֹמֵר: שָׁכֵן טוֹב. רַבִּי שִׁמְעוֹן אוֹמֵר: הָרוֹאֶה אֶת הַנּוֹלָד. רַבִּי אֶלְעָזָר אוֹמֵר: לֵב טוֹב. אָמַר לָהֶם, רוֹאֶה אֲנִי אֶת דִּבְרֵי אֶלְעָזָר בֶּן עֲרָךְ מִדִּבְרֵיכֶם, שֶׁבִּכְלַל דְּבָרָיו דִּבְרֵיכֶם.

יד אָמַר לָהֶם: צְאוּ וּרְאוּ, אֵיזוֹ הִיא דֶּרֶךְ רָעָה, שֶׁיִּתְרַחֵק מִמֶּנָּה הָאָדָם. רַבִּי אֱלִיעֶזֶר אוֹמֵר: עַיִן רָעָה. רַבִּי יְהוֹשֻׁעַ אוֹמֵר: חָבֵר רָע. רַבִּי יוֹסֵי אוֹמֵר: שָׁכֵן רָע. רַבִּי שִׁמְעוֹן אוֹמֵר: הַלֹּוֶה וְאֵינוֹ מְשַׁלֵּם, אֶחָד הַלֹּוֶה מִן הָאָדָם כְּלֹוֶה מִן הַמָּקוֹם, שֶׁנֶּאֱמַר: לֹוֶה רָשָׁע וְלֹא יְשַׁלֵּם, וְצַדִּיק חוֹנֵן וְנוֹתֵן: רַבִּי אֶלְעָזָר תהלים לז
אוֹמֵר: לֵב רָע. אָמַר לָהֶם: רוֹאֶה אֲנִי אֶת דִּבְרֵי אֶלְעָזָר בֶּן עֲרָךְ מִדִּבְרֵיכֶם, שֶׁבִּכְלַל דְּבָרָיו דִּבְרֵיכֶם.

טו הֵם אָמְרוּ שְׁלֹשָׁה דְבָרִים. רַבִּי אֱלִיעֶזֶר אוֹמֵר: יְהִי כְבוֹד חֲבֵרְךָ חָבִיב עָלֶיךָ כְּשֶׁלָּךְ, וְאַל תְּהִי נוֹחַ לִכְעֹס. וְשׁוּב יוֹם אֶחָד לִפְנֵי מִיתָתְךָ. וֶהֱוֵי מִתְחַמֵּם כְּנֶגֶד אוּרָן שֶׁל חֲכָמִים, וֶהֱוֵי זָהִיר בְּגַחַלְתָּן שֶׁלֹּא תִכָּוֶה, שֶׁנְּשִׁיכָתָן נְשִׁיכַת שׁוּעָל, וַעֲקִיצָתָן עֲקִיצַת עַקְרָב, וּלְחִישָׁתָן לְחִישַׁת שָׂרָף, וְכָל דִּבְרֵיהֶם כְּגַחֲלֵי אֵשׁ.

טז רַבִּי יְהוֹשֻׁעַ אוֹמֵר: עַיִן הָרָע וְיֵצֶר הָרָע וְשִׂנְאַת הַבְּרִיּוֹת, מוֹצִיאִין אֶת הָאָדָם מִן הָעוֹלָם.

יז רַבִּי יוֹסֵי אוֹמֵר: יְהִי מָמוֹן חֲבֵרְךָ חָבִיב עָלֶיךָ כְּשֶׁלָּךְ. וְהַתְקֵן עַצְמְךָ לִלְמֹד תּוֹרָה, שֶׁאֵינָהּ יְרֻשָּׁה לָךְ. וְכָל מַעֲשֶׂיךָ יִהְיוּ לְשֵׁם שָׁמָיִם.

18. Rabbi Shimon said: Be meticulous in reciting the Shema and the [Amida] prayer. When you pray, do not do so as a fixed routine, but as a plea for mercy and grace before God, as it is said, "For He is gracious and compassionate, slow to anger, abounding in kindness, and renouncing punishment." Do not be evil in your own eyes. *Joel 2*

19. Rabbi Elazar said: Be diligent in the study of Torah. Know how to answer a heretic. Know for whom you labor and who is your Employer who will pay you the reward of your work.

20. Rabbi Tarfon said: The day is short, the task is great, the laborers are lazy, the reward is much, and the Master insistent.

21. He used to say: It is not for you to complete the task, but neither are you free to stand aside from it. If you have studied much Torah, you will be given great reward, for your Employer will faithfully reward your work. Know, though, that the reward of the righteous is granted in the time to come.

Rabbi Ḥananya ben Akashya said: The Holy One, blessed be He, wanted to confer merit on Israel. That is why He gave them a copious Torah and many commandments, as it is said, "It pleased the LORD, for the sake of [Israel's] righteousness, to make the Torah great and glorious." *Makkot 23b* *Is. 42*

If there is a minyan, mourners say the Rabbis' Kaddish (page 712).

* * *

All Israel have a share in the World to Come, as it is said, *Sanhedrin 90a*
"Your people are all righteous; they shall inherit the land for ever; *Is. 60*
they are a shoot of My own planting,
a work of My own hands, that I may be glorified."

CHAPTER 3

1. Akavya ben Mahalalel said: Reflect on three things and you will avoid transgression: Know where you came from, where you are going, and before whom you will have to give an account and reckoning. "Where you came from" – from a putrid drop. "Where you are going" – to a place of dust, worms and maggots. "And before whom you will have to give an account and reckoning" – before the Supreme King of kings, the Holy One, blessed be He.

2. Rabbi Ḥanina, the deputy High Priest, said: Pray for the welfare of the government, for were it not for fear of it, people would swallow one another alive.

3. Rabbi Ḥanina ben Teradyon said: When two people sit together and no words of Torah pass between them, they are regarded as a company of scoffers, as it is said, "He does not sit in the company of scoffers." But when two people sit together and words of Torah do pass between them, the Divine Presence rests with them, as it is said, "Then those who feared the LORD talked together, *Ps. 1* *Mal. 3*

יח רַבִּי שִׁמְעוֹן אוֹמֵר: הֱוֵי זָהִיר בִּקְרִיאַת שְׁמַע וּבִתְפִלָּה. וּכְשֶׁאַתָּה מִתְפַּלֵּל
אַל תַּעַשׂ תְּפִלָּתְךָ קֶבַע, אֶלָּא רַחֲמִים וְתַחֲנוּנִים לִפְנֵי הַמָּקוֹם, שֶׁנֶּאֱמַר: כִּי יואל ב
חַנּוּן וְרַחוּם הוּא, אֶרֶךְ אַפַּיִם וְרַב־חֶסֶד וְנִחָם עַל־הָרָעָה: וְאַל תְּהִי רָשָׁע
בִּפְנֵי עַצְמֶךָ.

יט רַבִּי אֶלְעָזָר אוֹמֵר: הֱוֵי שָׁקוּד לִלְמֹד תּוֹרָה. וְדַע מַה שֶּׁתָּשִׁיב לְאֶפִּיקוֹרוֹס.
וְדַע לִפְנֵי מִי אַתָּה עָמֵל, וּמִי הוּא בַּעַל מְלַאכְתְּךָ, שֶׁיְּשַׁלֶּם לְךָ שְׂכַר פְּעֻלָּתֶךָ.

כ רַבִּי טַרְפוֹן אוֹמֵר: הַיּוֹם קָצָר, וְהַמְּלָאכָה מְרֻבָּה, וְהַפּוֹעֲלִים עֲצֵלִים, וְהַשָּׂכָר
הַרְבֵּה, וּבַעַל הַבַּיִת דּוֹחֵק.

כא הוּא הָיָה אוֹמֵר: לֹא עָלֶיךָ הַמְּלָאכָה לִגְמֹר, וְלֹא אַתָּה בֶן חוֹרִין לִבָּטֵל מִמֶּנָּה.
אִם לָמַדְתָּ תּוֹרָה הַרְבֵּה, נוֹתְנִין לְךָ שָׂכָר הַרְבֵּה. וְנֶאֱמָן הוּא בַּעַל מְלַאכְתְּךָ,
שֶׁיְּשַׁלֶּם לְךָ שְׂכַר פְּעֻלָּתֶךָ. וְדַע, שֶׁמַּתַּן שְׂכָרָן שֶׁל צַדִּיקִים לֶעָתִיד לָבוֹא.

רַבִּי חֲנַנְיָא בֶּן עֲקַשְׁיָא אוֹמֵר: רָצָה הַקָּדוֹשׁ בָּרוּךְ הוּא לְזַכּוֹת אֶת יִשְׂרָאֵל, לְפִיכָךְ מכות כג:
הִרְבָּה לָהֶם תּוֹרָה וּמִצְוֹת. שֶׁנֶּאֱמַר: יהוה חָפֵץ לְמַעַן צִדְקוֹ, יַגְדִּיל תּוֹרָה וְיַאְדִּיר: ישעיה מב

If there is a מנין*, mourners say* קדיש דרבנן *(page 713).*

* * *

כָּל יִשְׂרָאֵל יֵשׁ לָהֶם חֵלֶק לָעוֹלָם הַבָּא. שֶׁנֶּאֱמַר: סנהדרין צ.
וְעַמֵּךְ כֻּלָּם צַדִּיקִים, לְעוֹלָם יִירְשׁוּ אָרֶץ ישעיה ס
נֵצֶר מַטָּעַי, מַעֲשֵׂה יָדַי לְהִתְפָּאֵר:

פרק שלישי

א עֲקַבְיָא בֶּן מַהֲלַלְאֵל אוֹמֵר: הִסְתַּכֵּל בִּשְׁלֹשָׁה דְבָרִים, וְאֵין אַתָּה בָא לִידֵי
עֲבֵרָה. דַּע מֵאַיִן בָּאתָ, וּלְאָן אַתָּה הוֹלֵךְ, וְלִפְנֵי מִי אַתָּה עָתִיד לִתֵּן דִּין
וְחֶשְׁבּוֹן. מֵאַיִן בָּאתָ, מִטִּפָּה סְרוּחָה. וּלְאָן אַתָּה הוֹלֵךְ, לִמְקוֹם עָפָר, רִמָּה
וְתוֹלֵעָה. וְלִפְנֵי מִי אַתָּה עָתִיד לִתֵּן דִּין וְחֶשְׁבּוֹן, לִפְנֵי מֶלֶךְ מַלְכֵי הַמְּלָכִים,
הַקָּדוֹשׁ בָּרוּךְ הוּא.

ב רַבִּי חֲנִינָא סְגַן הַכֹּהֲנִים אוֹמֵר: הֱוֵי מִתְפַּלֵּל בִּשְׁלוֹמָהּ שֶׁל מַלְכוּת, שֶׁאִלְמָלֵא
מוֹרָאָהּ, אִישׁ אֶת רֵעֵהוּ חַיִּים בְּלָעוֹ.

ג רַבִּי חֲנִינָא בֶּן תְּרַדְיוֹן אוֹמֵר: שְׁנַיִם שֶׁיּוֹשְׁבִין, וְאֵין בֵּינֵיהֶם דִּבְרֵי תוֹרָה, הֲרֵי
זֶה מוֹשַׁב לֵצִים, שֶׁנֶּאֱמַר: וּבְמוֹשַׁב לֵצִים לֹא יָשָׁב: אֲבָל שְׁנַיִם שֶׁיּוֹשְׁבִין, תהלים א

and the LORD listened and heard, and a scroll of remembrance was written before Him concerning those who feared the LORD and cherished His name." This verse tells me about two people; from where can I learn that even one person who sits alone and studies Torah, the Holy One, blessed be He, grants him a reward? From the verse, "Though he sits alone and meditates quietly, *Lam. 3*
He will grant him a reward."

4. Rabbi Shimon said: Three who eat at one table, and do not speak words of Torah, are as if they had eaten of sacrifices of dead idols, as it is said, "For all *Is. 28*
the tables are full of vomit and filth, when God is absent." However, three who eat at one table and speak words of Torah, it is as if they had eaten at God's table, as it is said, "And He spoke to me: This is the table before the LORD." *Ezek. 41*

5. Rabbi Ḥanina ben Ḥakhinai said: One who stays awake at night, travels alone, or turns his mind to idle thoughts, endangers his soul.

6. Rabbi Neḥunya ben HaKanna said: One who takes on himself the yoke of Torah will be spared the yoke of government and the yoke of worldly responsibilities, but one who throws off the yoke of the Torah will bear the yoke of government and the yoke of worldly responsibilities.

7. Rabbi Ḥalafta ben Dosa of Kfar Ḥananya said: When ten people sit together and study Torah, the Divine Presence rests among them, as it is said, "God *Ps. 82*
stands in the divine assembly." How do we know that the same applies to five?
From the verse, "He has founded His group on the earth." And how do we know *Amos 9*
that it applies even to three? From the verse, "He judges among the judges." *Ps. 82*
How do we know that the same applies even to two? From the verse, "Then
those who feared the LORD talked together, and the LORD listened and heard." *Mal. 3*
And how do we know that it applies even to one? From the verse, "In every *Ex. 20*
place where I cause My name to be mentioned, I will come to you and bless you."

8. Rabbi Elazar of Bartota said: Give Him what is His, for you and yours are His. This was also said by David: "For all things come from You, and we have *1 Chr. 29*
given You only what is Yours."

9. Rabbi Jacob said: One who is reviewing his Torah study while walking on the way, and interrupts his study to say, "What a beautiful tree" or "What a beautiful field," is regarded by Scripture as if he had endangered his soul.

10. Rabbi Dostai of Rabbi Yannai said in the name of Rabbi Meir: One who forgets even one thing of his Torah learning, Scripture regards him as if he had endangered his soul, for it is said, "Only take heed and guard your soul very *Deut. 4*
carefully so that you do not forget the things that your eyes saw." One might think that this applies even to one who finds his studies too hard to remember. Therefore the verse adds, "Lest they be removed from your heart all the *Ibid.*
days of your life." Thus, one does not endanger his soul unless he deliberately removes teachings from his heart.

וְיֵשׁ בֵּינֵיהֶם דִּבְרֵי תוֹרָה, שְׁכִינָה שְׁרוּיָה בֵינֵיהֶם, שֶׁנֶּאֱמַר: אָז נִדְבְּרוּ יִרְאֵי מלאכי ג
יהוה אִישׁ אֶל־רֵעֵהוּ, וַיַּקְשֵׁב יהוה וַיִּשְׁמָע, וַיִּכָּתֵב סֵפֶר זִכָּרוֹן לְפָנָיו לְיִרְאֵי
יהוה וּלְחֹשְׁבֵי שְׁמוֹ: אֵין לִי אֶלָּא שְׁנַיִם, מִנַּיִן אֲפִלּוּ אֶחָד שֶׁיּוֹשֵׁב וְעוֹסֵק
בַּתּוֹרָה שֶׁהַקָּדוֹשׁ בָּרוּךְ הוּא קוֹבֵעַ לוֹ שָׂכָר, שֶׁנֶּאֱמַר: יֵשֵׁב בָּדָד וְיִדֹּם כִּי נָטַל איכה ג
עָלָיו:

ד רַבִּי שִׁמְעוֹן אוֹמֵר: שְׁלֹשָׁה שֶׁאָכְלוּ עַל שֻׁלְחָן אֶחָד וְלֹא אָמְרוּ עָלָיו דִּבְרֵי
תוֹרָה, כְּאִלּוּ אָכְלוּ מִזִּבְחֵי מֵתִים, שֶׁנֶּאֱמַר: כִּי כָּל־שֻׁלְחָנוֹת מָלְאוּ קִיא ישעיה כח
צֹאָה בְּלִי מָקוֹם: אֲבָל שְׁלֹשָׁה שֶׁאָכְלוּ עַל שֻׁלְחָן אֶחָד, וְאָמְרוּ עָלָיו דִּבְרֵי
תוֹרָה, כְּאִלּוּ אָכְלוּ מִשֻּׁלְחָנוֹ שֶׁל מָקוֹם, שֶׁנֶּאֱמַר: וַיְדַבֵּר אֵלַי, זֶה הַשֻּׁלְחָן יחזקאל מא
אֲשֶׁר לִפְנֵי יהוה:

ה רַבִּי חֲנִינָא בֶּן חֲכִינַאי אוֹמֵר: הַנֵּעוֹר בַּלַּיְלָה, וְהַמְהַלֵּךְ בַּדֶּרֶךְ יְחִידִי, וְהַמְפַנֶּה
לִבּוֹ לְבַטָּלָה, הֲרֵי זֶה מִתְחַיֵּב בְּנַפְשׁוֹ.

ו רַבִּי נְחוּנְיָא בֶּן הַקָּנָה אוֹמֵר: כָּל הַמְקַבֵּל עָלָיו עֹל תּוֹרָה, מַעֲבִירִין מִמֶּנּוּ עֹל
מַלְכוּת וְעֹל דֶּרֶךְ אֶרֶץ. וְכָל הַפּוֹרֵק מִמֶּנּוּ עֹל תּוֹרָה, נוֹתְנִין עָלָיו עֹל מַלְכוּת
וְעֹל דֶּרֶךְ אֶרֶץ.

ז רַבִּי חֲלַפְתָּא בֶּן דּוֹסָא אִישׁ כְּפַר חֲנַנְיָה אוֹמֵר: עֲשָׂרָה שֶׁיּוֹשְׁבִין וְעוֹסְקִין
בַּתּוֹרָה שְׁכִינָה שְׁרוּיָה בֵינֵיהֶם, שֶׁנֶּאֱמַר: אֱלֹהִים נִצָּב בַּעֲדַת־אֵל: וּמִנַּיִן אֲפִלּוּ תהלים פב
חֲמִשָּׁה, שֶׁנֶּאֱמַר: וַאֲגֻדָּתוֹ עַל־אֶרֶץ יְסָדָהּ: וּמִנַּיִן אֲפִלּוּ שְׁלֹשָׁה, שֶׁנֶּאֱמַר: עמוס ט
בְּקֶרֶב אֱלֹהִים יִשְׁפֹּט: וּמִנַּיִן אֲפִלּוּ שְׁנַיִם, שֶׁנֶּאֱמַר: אָז נִדְבְּרוּ יִרְאֵי יהוה אִישׁ תהלים פב / מלאכי ג
אֶל־רֵעֵהוּ, וַיַּקְשֵׁב יהוה וַיִּשְׁמָע: וּמִנַּיִן אֲפִלּוּ אֶחָד, שֶׁנֶּאֱמַר: בְּכָל־הַמָּקוֹם שמות כ
אֲשֶׁר אַזְכִּיר אֶת־שְׁמִי, אָבוֹא אֵלֶיךָ וּבֵרַכְתִּיךָ:

ח רַבִּי אֶלְעָזָר אִישׁ בַּרְתּוֹתָא אוֹמֵר: תֶּן לוֹ מִשֶּׁלּוֹ, שֶׁאַתָּה וְשֶׁלְּךָ שֶׁלּוֹ. וְכֵן בְּדָוִד
הוּא אוֹמֵר: כִּי־מִמְּךָ הַכֹּל, וּמִיָּדְךָ נָתַנּוּ לָךְ: דברי הימים א׳ כט

ט רַבִּי יַעֲקֹב אוֹמֵר: הַמְהַלֵּךְ בַּדֶּרֶךְ וְשׁוֹנֶה, וּמַפְסִיק מִמִּשְׁנָתוֹ וְאוֹמֵר, מַה
נָּאֶה אִילָן זֶה, מַה נָּאֶה נִיר זֶה, מַעֲלֶה עָלָיו הַכָּתוּב כְּאִלּוּ מִתְחַיֵּב בְּנַפְשׁוֹ.

י רַבִּי דוֹסְתָּאִי בְּרַבִּי יַנַּאי מִשּׁוּם רַבִּי מֵאִיר אוֹמֵר: כָּל הַשּׁוֹכֵחַ דָּבָר אֶחָד
מִמִּשְׁנָתוֹ, מַעֲלֶה עָלָיו הַכָּתוּב כְּאִלּוּ מִתְחַיֵּב בְּנַפְשׁוֹ, שֶׁנֶּאֱמַר: רַק הִשָּׁמֶר דברים ד
לְךָ וּשְׁמֹר נַפְשְׁךָ מְאֹד, פֶּן־תִּשְׁכַּח אֶת־הַדְּבָרִים אֲשֶׁר־רָאוּ עֵינֶיךָ: יָכוֹל אֲפִלּוּ
תָּקְפָה עָלָיו מִשְׁנָתוֹ, תַּלְמוּד לוֹמַר: וּפֶן־יָסוּרוּ מִלְּבָבְךָ כֹּל יְמֵי חַיֶּיךָ: הָא אֵינוֹ שם
מִתְחַיֵּב בְּנַפְשׁוֹ, עַד שֶׁיֵּשֵׁב וִיסִירֵם מִלִּבּוֹ.

11. Rabbi Ḥanina ben Dosa said: For one who puts fear of sin before wisdom, wisdom endures. For one who puts wisdom before fear of sin, wisdom does not endure.

12. He also used to say: For one whose good deeds exceed his wisdom, wisdom endures. For one whose wisdom exceeds his good deeds, wisdom does not endure.

13. He also used to say: In one in whom people delight, God delights. In one in whom people do not delight, God does not delight.

14. Rabbi Dosa ben Harkinas said: Sleeping late in the morning, drinking wine at midday, chattering with children and sitting in gatherings of the ignorant – these drive a person from the world.

15. Rabbi Elazar of Modin said: One who desecrates sacred things, despises the festivals, shames his fellow in public, nullifies the covenant of our father Abraham, or attributes meanings to the Torah contrary to normative law, even though he has to his credit Torah and good deeds, has no share in the World to Come.

16. Rabbi Yishmael said: Be yielding to a superior, pleasing to the young, and receive everyone cheerfully.

17. Rabbi Akiva said: Mocking and frivolity lead to immorality. The oral tradition (*Mesora*) is a fence protecting the Torah; tithes are a fence protecting wealth; vows are a fence protecting abstinence. The fence protecting wisdom is silence.

18. He used to say: Beloved is man, for he was created in the image of God. As a gesture of special love, it was made known to him that he was created in the
image of God, as it is said, "For in the image of God He made man." Beloved *Gen. 9*
are Israel for they are called God's children. As a gesture of special love, it was
made known to them that they are called God's children, as it is said, "You are *Deut. 14*
the children of the Lord your God." Beloved are Israel, for they were given a precious vessel [the Torah]. As a gesture of special love, it was made known to them that they were given the precious vessel through which the world was cre-
ated, as it is said, "I have given you good instruction; do not forsake My Torah." *Prov. 4*

19. All is foreseen, yet freedom of choice is given. The world is judged with goodness, but all depends on the majority of one's deeds.

20. He used to say: All is given on collateral, and a net is spread over all the living. The shop is open, the shopkeeper extends credit, the ledger is open, and the hand records. Whoever wishes to borrow may come and borrow. The collectors regularly make their daily rounds and collect payment from a person, whether he realizes it or not. They have [a record] on which they can rely; the judgment is just; and all is prepared for the banquet.

יא רַבִּי חֲנִינָא בֶּן דּוֹסָא אוֹמֵר: כָּל שֶׁיִּרְאַת חֶטְאוֹ קוֹדֶמֶת לְחָכְמָתוֹ, חָכְמָתוֹ מִתְקַיֶּמֶת. וְכָל שֶׁחָכְמָתוֹ קוֹדֶמֶת לְיִרְאַת חֶטְאוֹ, אֵין חָכְמָתוֹ מִתְקַיֶּמֶת.

יב הוּא הָיָה אוֹמֵר: כָּל שֶׁמַּעֲשָׂיו מְרֻבִּין מֵחָכְמָתוֹ, חָכְמָתוֹ מִתְקַיֶּמֶת. וְכָל שֶׁחָכְמָתוֹ מְרֻבָּה מִמַּעֲשָׂיו, אֵין חָכְמָתוֹ מִתְקַיֶּמֶת.

יג הוּא הָיָה אוֹמֵר: כָּל שֶׁרְוּחַ הַבְּרִיּוֹת נוֹחָה הֵימֶנּוּ, רְוּחַ הַמָּקוֹם נוֹחָה הֵימֶנּוּ. וְכָל שֶׁאֵין רְוּחַ הַבְּרִיּוֹת נוֹחָה הֵימֶנּוּ, אֵין רְוּחַ הַמָּקוֹם נוֹחָה הֵימֶנּוּ.

יד רַבִּי דוֹסָא בֶּן הַרְכִּינָס אוֹמֵר: שֵׁנָה שֶׁל שַׁחֲרִית, וְיַיִן שֶׁל צָהֳרַיִם, וְשִׂיחַת הַיְלָדִים, וִישִׁיבַת בָּתֵּי כְנֵסִיּוֹת שֶׁל עַמֵּי הָאָרֶץ, מוֹצִיאִין אֶת הָאָדָם מִן הָעוֹלָם.

טו רַבִּי אֶלְעָזָר הַמּוֹדָעִי אוֹמֵר: הַמְחַלֵּל אֶת הַקֳּדָשִׁים, וְהַמְבַזֶּה אֶת הַמּוֹעֲדוֹת, וְהַמַּלְבִּין פְּנֵי חֲבֵרוֹ בָּרַבִּים, וְהַמֵּפֵר בְּרִיתוֹ שֶׁל אַבְרָהָם אָבִינוּ, וְהַמְגַלֶּה פָנִים בַּתּוֹרָה שֶׁלֹּא כַהֲלָכָה, אַף עַל פִּי שֶׁיֵּשׁ בְּיָדוֹ תּוֹרָה וּמַעֲשִׂים טוֹבִים, אֵין לוֹ חֵלֶק לָעוֹלָם הַבָּא.

טז רַבִּי יִשְׁמָעֵאל אוֹמֵר: הֱוֵי קַל לְרֹאשׁ וְנְוֹחַ לְתִשְׁחֹרֶת, וֶהֱוֵי מְקַבֵּל אֶת כָּל הָאָדָם בְּשִׂמְחָה.

יז רַבִּי עֲקִיבָא אוֹמֵר: שְׂחוֹק וְקַלּוּת רֹאשׁ מַרְגִּילִין אֶת הָאָדָם לְעֶרְוָה. מָסֹרֶת סְיָג לַתּוֹרָה, מַעְשְׂרוֹת סְיָג לָעֹשֶׁר, נְדָרִים סְיָג לַפְּרִישׁוּת, סְיָג לַחָכְמָה שְׁתִיקָה.

יח הוּא הָיָה אוֹמֵר, חָבִיב אָדָם שֶׁנִּבְרָא בְצֶלֶם, חִבָּה יְתֵרָה נוֹדַעַת לוֹ שֶׁנִּבְרָא
בְּצֶלֶם, שֶׁנֶּאֱמַר: כִּי בְּצֶלֶם אֱלֹהִים עָשָׂה אֶת־הָאָדָם: חֲבִיבִין יִשְׂרָאֵל שֶׁנִּקְרְאוּ בראשית ט
בָנִים לַמָּקוֹם, חִבָּה יְתֵרָה נוֹדַעַת לָהֶם שֶׁנִּקְרְאוּ בָנִים לַמָּקוֹם, שֶׁנֶּאֱמַר: בָּנִים דברים יד
אַתֶּם לַיהוה אֱלֹהֵיכֶם: חֲבִיבִין יִשְׂרָאֵל שֶׁנִּתַּן לָהֶם כְּלִי חֶמְדָּה, חִבָּה יְתֵרָה
נוֹדַעַת לָהֶם שֶׁנִּתַּן לָהֶם כְּלִי חֶמְדָּה שֶׁבּוֹ נִבְרָא הָעוֹלָם, שֶׁנֶּאֱמַר: כִּי לֶקַח משלי ד
טוֹב נָתַתִּי לָכֶם, תּוֹרָתִי אַל־תַּעֲזֹבוּ:

יט הַכֹּל צָפוּי, וְהָרְשׁוּת נְתוּנָה, וּבְטוּב הָעוֹלָם נִדּוֹן, וְהַכֹּל לְפִי רֹב הַמַּעֲשֶׂה.

כ הוּא הָיָה אוֹמֵר: הַכֹּל נָתוּן בָּעֵרָבוֹן, וּמְצוּדָה פְרוּסָה עַל כָּל הַחַיִּים. הֶחָנוּת פְּתוּחָה, וְהַחֶנְוָנִי מַקִּיף, וְהַפִּנְקָס פָּתוּחַ, וְהַיָּד כּוֹתֶבֶת, וְכָל הָרוֹצֶה לִלְווֹת יָבֹא וְיִלְוֶה. וְהַגַּבָּאִין מַחֲזִירִין תָּדִיר בְּכָל יוֹם, וְנִפְרָעִין מִן הָאָדָם מִדַּעְתּוֹ וְשֶׁלֹּא מִדַּעְתּוֹ, וְיֵשׁ לָהֶם עַל מַה שֶּׁיִּסְמֹכוּ. וְהַדִּין, דִּין אֱמֶת. וְהַכֹּל מְתֻקָּן לַסְּעוּדָה.

21. Rabbi Elazar ben Azariah said: If there is no Torah, there is no respect; if there is no respect, there is no Torah. If there is no wisdom, there is no reverence; if there is no reverence, there is no wisdom. If there is no knowledge, there is no understanding; if there is no understanding, there is no knowledge. If there is no flour [sustenance], there is no Torah; if there is no Torah, there is no flour.

22. He used to say: To what may one whose wisdom exceeds his deeds be compared? To a tree with many branches but few roots. When a wind comes, it uproots and overturns it, as it is said, "He shall be like a juniper tree in the desert, *Jer. 17*
which does not sense the coming of good: it is set in the scorched places of the wilderness in a barren, uninhabited land." To what may one whose deeds exceed his wisdom be compared? To a tree with few branches but many roots. Even if all the winds of the world come and blow against it, they cannot dislodge it from its place, as it is said, "He shall be like a tree planted by waters, sending *Jer. 17*
forth its roots by a stream: it does not sense the coming of heat; its leaves are ever fresh; it has no care in a year of drought; it does not cease to bear fruit."

23. Rabbi Elazar ben Ḥisma said: The laws of bird offerings and the calculation of menstrual periods are essential laws; astronomy and mathematics are adjuncts to wisdom.

Rabbi Ḥananya ben Akashya said: The Holy One, blessed be He, wanted to confer *Makkot 23b*
merit on Israel. That is why He gave them a copious Torah and many commandments, as it is said, "It pleased the LORD, for the sake of [Israel's] righteousness, *Is. 42*
to make the Torah great and glorious."

If there is a minyan, mourners say the Rabbis' Kaddish (page 712).

* * *

All Israel have a share in the World to Come, as it is said: *Sanhedrin 90a*
"Your people are all righteous; they shall inherit the land for ever; *Is. 60*
they are a shoot of My own planting,
a work of My own hands, that I may be glorified."

CHAPTER 4

1. Ben Zoma said: Who is wise? One who learns from everyone, as it is said, "From all my teachers I have learned, for Your testimonies are my meditation." Who *Ps. 119*
is strong? One who masters his evil impulse, as it is said, "He who is slow to *Prov. 16*
anger is better than the mighty, and he who rules over his spirit is better than he who conquers a city." Who is rich? One who rejoices in what he has, as it is said, "When you eat from the labor of your hands, you will be happy and all *Ps. 128*
will be well with you." "You will be happy" – in this world, "and all will be well with you"– in the World to Come. Who is honored? One who honors others, as it is said, "Those who honor Me, I will honor; but those who scorn Me will *1 Sam. 2*
be despised."

כא רַבִּי אֶלְעָזָר בֶּן עֲזַרְיָה אוֹמֵר: אִם אֵין תּוֹרָה אֵין דֶּרֶךְ אֶרֶץ, אִם אֵין דֶּרֶךְ
אֶרֶץ אֵין תּוֹרָה. אִם אֵין חָכְמָה אֵין יִרְאָה, אִם אֵין יִרְאָה אֵין חָכְמָה. אִם
אֵין דַּעַת אֵין בִּינָה, אִם אֵין בִּינָה אֵין דַּעַת. אִם אֵין קֶמַח אֵין תּוֹרָה, אִם
אֵין תּוֹרָה אֵין קֶמַח.

כב הוּא הָיָה אוֹמֵר: כָּל שֶׁחָכְמָתוֹ מְרֻבָּה מִמַּעֲשָׂיו, לְמָה הוּא דוֹמֶה, לְאִילָן
שֶׁעֲנָפָיו מְרֻבִּין וְשָׁרָשָׁיו מֻעָטִין, וְהָרוּחַ בָּאָה וְעוֹקַרְתּוֹ וְהוֹפַכְתּוֹ עַל פָּנָיו.
שֶׁנֶּאֱמַר, וְהָיָה כְּעַרְעָר בָּעֲרָבָה, וְלֹא יִרְאֶה כִּי־יָבוֹא טוֹב, וְשָׁכַן חֲרֵרִים ירמיה יז
בַּמִּדְבָּר, אֶרֶץ מְלֵחָה וְלֹא תֵשֵׁב: אֲבָל כָּל שֶׁמַּעֲשָׂיו מְרֻבִּין מֵחָכְמָתוֹ, לְמָה
הוּא דוֹמֶה, לְאִילָן שֶׁעֲנָפָיו מֻעָטִין וְשָׁרָשָׁיו מְרֻבִּין, שֶׁאֲפִלּוּ כָּל הָרוּחוֹת
שֶׁבָּעוֹלָם בָּאוֹת וְנוֹשְׁבוֹת בּוֹ, אֵין מְזִיזִין אוֹתוֹ מִמְּקוֹמוֹ. שֶׁנֶּאֱמַר: וְהָיָה כְּעֵץ ירמיה יז
שָׁתוּל עַל־מַיִם, וְעַל־יוּבַל יְשַׁלַּח שָׁרָשָׁיו, וְלֹא יִרְאֶ כִּי־יָבֹא חֹם, וְהָיָה עָלֵהוּ
רַעֲנָן, וּבִשְׁנַת בַּצֹּרֶת לֹא יִדְאָג, וְלֹא יָמִישׁ מֵעֲשׂוֹת פֶּרִי:

כג רַבִּי אֶלְעָזָר בֶּן חִסְמָא אוֹמֵר: קִנִּין וּפִתְחֵי נִדָּה הֵן הֵן גּוּפֵי הֲלָכוֹת, תְּקוּפוֹת
וְגִימַטְרִיָּאוֹת פַּרְפְּרָאוֹת לַחָכְמָה.

רַבִּי חֲנַנְיָא בֶּן עֲקַשְׁיָא אוֹמֵר: רָצָה הַקָּדוֹשׁ בָּרוּךְ הוּא לְזַכּוֹת אֶת יִשְׂרָאֵל, לְפִיכָךְ מכות כג:
הִרְבָּה לָהֶם תּוֹרָה וּמִצְוֹת. שֶׁנֶּאֱמַר: יהוה חָפֵץ לְמַעַן צִדְקוֹ, יַגְדִּיל תּוֹרָה וְיַאְדִּיר: ישעיה מב

If there is a מנין*, mourners say* קדיש דרבנן *(page 713).*

* * *

כָּל יִשְׂרָאֵל יֵשׁ לָהֶם חֵלֶק לָעוֹלָם הַבָּא. שֶׁנֶּאֱמַר: סנהדרין צ.
וְעַמֵּךְ כֻּלָּם צַדִּיקִים, לְעוֹלָם יִירְשׁוּ אָרֶץ ישעיה ס
נֵצֶר מַטָּעַי, מַעֲשֵׂה יָדַי לְהִתְפָּאֵר:

פרק רביעי

א בֶּן זוֹמָא אוֹמֵר: אֵיזֶהוּ חָכָם, הַלּוֹמֵד מִכָּל אָדָם, שֶׁנֶּאֱמַר: מִכָּל־מְלַמְּדַי תהלים קיט
הִשְׂכַּלְתִּי, כִּי עֵדְוֹתֶיךָ שִׂיחָה לִּי: אֵיזֶהוּ גִבּוֹר, הַכּוֹבֵשׁ אֶת יִצְרוֹ, שֶׁנֶּאֱמַר: טוֹב משלי טז
אֶרֶךְ אַפַּיִם מִגִּבּוֹר וּמֹשֵׁל בְּרוּחוֹ מִלֹּכֵד עִיר: אֵיזֶהוּ עָשִׁיר, הַשָּׂמֵחַ בְּחֶלְקוֹ,
שֶׁנֶּאֱמַר: יְגִיעַ כַּפֶּיךָ כִּי תֹאכֵל אַשְׁרֶיךָ וְטוֹב לָךְ: אַשְׁרֶיךָ בָּעוֹלָם הַזֶּה וְטוֹב תהלים קכח
לָךְ לָעוֹלָם הַבָּא. אֵיזֶהוּ מְכֻבָּד, הַמְכַבֵּד אֶת הַבְּרִיּוֹת, שֶׁנֶּאֱמַר: כִּי־מְכַבְּדַי שמואל א׳ ב
אֲכַבֵּד, וּבֹזַי יֵקָלּוּ:

2. Ben Azzai said: Run to do even a minor mitzva, and flee from sin, for one mitzva leads to another, and one sin leads to another – for the reward of a mitzva is another mitzva, and the recompense of a sin is another sin.
3. He used to say: Despise no one and disdain nothing, for there is no one who does not have his hour and there is nothing that does not have its place.
4. Rabbi Levitas of Yavne said: Have extreme humility of spirit, for the end of mortal man is the worm [the grave].
5. Rabbi Yoḥanan ben Beroka said: Whoever profanes God's name in secret will be punished in public. Profaning the name is the same whether done inadvertently or deliberately.
6. Rabbi Yishmael his son said: One who learns in order to teach will be given the opportunity to learn and teach. One who learns in order to do will be given the opportunity to learn, teach, keep and do.
7. Rabbi Zadok said: Do not separate yourself from the community. [When sitting as a judge] do not act as a lawyer. Do not use [the Torah] as a crown for self-glorification, or as a spade with which to dig. Likewise Hillel used to say: One who makes worldly use of the crown [of the Torah] shall fade away. From this you learn that one who seeks personal benefit from the words of Torah risks destroying his life.
8. Rabbi Yose said: One who honors the Torah will be honored by mankind. One who disgraces the Torah will be disgraced by mankind.
9. Rabbi Yishmael his son said: One who avoids serving as a judge spares himself enmity, robbery and false swearing. One who is over-confident in giving decisions is foolish, wicked and arrogant.
10. He used to say: Do not act as a judge alone, for none may judge alone except the One. Do not say "Accept my view"; for they are permitted, not you.
11. Rabbi Yonatan said: Whoever keeps the Torah when poor will eventually keep it in wealth. Whoever neglects the Torah when wealthy will eventually neglect it in poverty.
12. Rabbi Meir said: Limit your business activities and occupy yourself with Torah. Have humility before everyone. If you neglect the Torah, you will have many excuses to neglect it, but if you labor in the Torah, He has great reward to give you.
13. Rabbi Eliezer ben Jacob said: One who performs a single mitzva acquires for himself an advocate. One who commits a single transgression acquires for himself an accuser. Repentance and good deeds are a shield against punishment.
14. Rabbi Yoḥanan the sandal maker said: Every gathering that meets for the sake of heaven will have an enduring effect. One that is not for the sake of heaven will not have an enduring effect.

ב בֶּן עַזַּאי אוֹמֵר: הֱוֵי רָץ לְמִצְוָה קַלָּה וּבוֹרֵחַ מִן הָעֲבֵרָה. שֶׁמִּצְוָה גּוֹרֶרֶת מִצְוָה, וַעֲבֵרָה גּוֹרֶרֶת עֲבֵרָה. שֶׁשְּׂכַר מִצְוָה מִצְוָה, וּשְׂכַר עֲבֵרָה עֲבֵרָה.

ג הוּא הָיָה אוֹמֵר: אַל תְּהִי בָז לְכָל אָדָם, וְאַל תְּהִי מַפְלִיג לְכָל דָּבָר. שֶׁאֵין לְךָ אָדָם שֶׁאֵין לוֹ שָׁעָה, וְאֵין לְךָ דָבָר שֶׁאֵין לוֹ מָקוֹם.

ד רַבִּי לְוִיטַס אִישׁ יַבְנֶה אוֹמֵר: מְאֹד מְאֹד הֱוֵי שְׁפַל רוּחַ, שֶׁתִּקְוַת אֱנוֹשׁ רִמָּה.

ה רַבִּי יוֹחָנָן בֶּן בְּרוֹקָא אוֹמֵר: כָּל הַמְחַלֵּל שֵׁם שָׁמַיִם בַּסֵּתֶר, נִפְרָעִין מִמֶּנּוּ בַּגָּלוּי. אֶחָד שׁוֹגֵג וְאֶחָד מֵזִיד בְּחִלּוּל הַשֵּׁם.

ו רַבִּי יִשְׁמָעֵאל בְּנוֹ אוֹמֵר: הַלּוֹמֵד עַל מְנָת לְלַמֵּד, מַסְפִּיקִין בְּיָדוֹ לִלְמֹד וּלְלַמֵּד. וְהַלּוֹמֵד עַל מְנָת לַעֲשׂוֹת, מַסְפִּיקִין בְּיָדוֹ לִלְמֹד וּלְלַמֵּד, לִשְׁמֹר וְלַעֲשׂוֹת.

ז רַבִּי צָדוֹק אוֹמֵר: אַל תִּפְרֹשׁ מִן הַצִּבּוּר, וְאַל תַּעַשׂ עַצְמְךָ כְּעוֹרְכֵי הַדַּיָּנִין, וְאַל תַּעֲשֶׂהָ עֲטָרָה לְהִתְגַּדֶּל בָּהּ, וְלֹא קַרְדֹּם לַחְפֹּר בָּהּ. וְכָךְ הָיָה הִלֵּל אוֹמֵר: וּדְאִשְׁתַּמַּשׁ בְּתָגָא חֲלָף. הָא לָמַדְתָּ, כָּל הַנֶּהֱנֶה מִדִּבְרֵי תוֹרָה, נוֹטֵל חַיָּיו מִן הָעוֹלָם.

ח רַבִּי יוֹסֵי אוֹמֵר: כָּל הַמְכַבֵּד אֶת הַתּוֹרָה, גּוּפוֹ מְכֻבָּד עַל הַבְּרִיּוֹת. וְכָל הַמְחַלֵּל אֶת הַתּוֹרָה, גּוּפוֹ מְחֻלָּל עַל הַבְּרִיּוֹת.

ט רַבִּי יִשְׁמָעֵאל בְּנוֹ אוֹמֵר: הַחוֹשֵׂךְ עַצְמוֹ מִן הַדִּין, פּוֹרֵק מִמֶּנּוּ אֵיבָה וְגָזֵל וּשְׁבוּעַת שָׁוְא. וְהַגַּס לִבּוֹ בְּהוֹרָאָה, שׁוֹטֶה, רָשָׁע וְגַס רוּחַ.

י הוּא הָיָה אוֹמֵר: אַל תְּהִי דָן יְחִידִי, שֶׁאֵין דָּן יְחִידִי אֶלָּא אֶחָד. וְאַל תֹּאמַר קַבְּלוּ דַעְתִּי, שֶׁהֵן רַשָּׁאִין וְלֹא אָתָּה.

יא רַבִּי יוֹנָתָן אוֹמֵר: כָּל הַמְקַיֵּם אֶת הַתּוֹרָה מֵעֹנִי, סוֹפוֹ לְקַיְּמָהּ מֵעֹשֶׁר. וְכָל הַמְבַטֵּל אֶת הַתּוֹרָה מֵעֹשֶׁר, סוֹפוֹ לְבַטְּלָהּ מֵעֹנִי.

יב רַבִּי מֵאִיר אוֹמֵר: הֱוֵי מְמַעֵט בְּעֵסֶק וַעֲסֹק בַּתּוֹרָה, וֶהֱוֵי שְׁפַל רוּחַ בִּפְנֵי כָל אָדָם. וְאִם בָּטַלְתָּ מִן הַתּוֹרָה, יֶשׁ לְךָ בְּטֵלִים הַרְבֵּה כְּנֶגְדָּךְ. וְאִם עָמַלְתָּ בַּתּוֹרָה, יֶשׁ לוֹ שָׂכָר הַרְבֵּה לִתֶּן לָךְ.

יג רַבִּי אֱלִיעֶזֶר בֶּן יַעֲקֹב אוֹמֵר: הָעוֹשֶׂה מִצְוָה אַחַת, קוֹנֶה לּוֹ פְּרַקְלִיט אֶחָד. וְהָעוֹבֵר עֲבֵרָה אַחַת, קוֹנֶה לּוֹ קַטֵּגוֹר אֶחָד. תְּשׁוּבָה וּמַעֲשִׂים טוֹבִים, כִּתְרִיס בִּפְנֵי הַפֻּרְעָנוּת.

יד רַבִּי יוֹחָנָן הַסַּנְדְּלָר אוֹמֵר: כָּל כְּנֵסִיָּה שֶׁהִיא לְשֵׁם שָׁמַיִם, סוֹפָהּ לְהִתְקַיֵּם. וְשֶׁאֵינָהּ לְשֵׁם שָׁמַיִם, אֵין סוֹפָהּ לְהִתְקַיֵּם.

15. Rabbi Elazar ben Shammua said: Let your student's honor be as precious to you as your own; let your colleague's honor be like the reverence due to your teacher; and let the reverence you have for your teacher be like the reverence due to Heaven.
16. Rabbi Judah said: Be careful when you study, for an inadvertent error in study is tantamount to an intentional sin.
17. Rabbi Shimon said: There are three crowns: the crown of Torah, the crown of priesthood, and the crown of kingship – but the crown of a good name surpasses them all.
18. Rabbi Nehorai said: Exile yourself to a place of Torah, and do not assume that it will come after you, for your fellow students will ensure that it will remain with you. "Do not rely on your own understanding." *Prov. 3*
19. Rabbi Yannai said: It is not in our power to explain either the peace of the wicked or the suffering of the righteous.
20. Rabbi Matya ben Ḥarash said: Be first in greeting everyone. Be a tail to lions rather than a head to foxes.
21. Rabbi Jacob said: This world is like an antechamber before the World to Come. Prepare yourself in the antechamber so that you may enter the banqueting hall.
22. He used to say: Better one hour of repentance and good deeds in this world than all the life in the World to Come. Better one hour of bliss in the World to Come than the whole life of this world.
23. Rabbi Shimon ben Elazar said: Do not try to placate your fellow in his hour of anger. Do not try to comfort him while his dead lies before him. Do not question him about his vow at the time he is making it. Do not try to see him in his hour of disgrace.
24. Samuel the Younger used to quote: "If your enemy falls, do not rejoice; if he stumbles, let not your heart be glad; lest the LORD see it and be displeased, and divert His wrath from him to you." *Prov. 24*
25. Elisha ben Abuya said: When you learn as a child, what is it like? Like ink written on clean paper. When you learn in old age, what is it like? Like ink written on blotted paper.
26. Rabbi Yose bar Judah of Kfar Bavli said: When you learn from the young, what is it like? Like eating unripe grapes or drinking wine straight from the vat. When you learn from the old, what is it like? Like eating ripe grapes and drinking old wine.
27. Rabbi Meir said: Do not look at the container but at what it contains, for a new flask may contain old wine, and an old flask may not contain anything, even new wine.
28. Rabbi Elazar HaKappar said: Envy, lust, and the seeking of honor, drive a person out of the world.

טו רַבִּי אֶלְעָזָר בֶּן שַׁמּוּעַ אוֹמֵר: יְהִי כְבוֹד תַּלְמִידְךָ חָבִיב עָלֶיךָ כְּשֶׁלָּךְ, וּכְבוֹד חֲבֵרְךָ כְּמוֹרָא רַבָּךְ, וּמוֹרָא רַבָּךְ כְּמוֹרָא שָׁמָיִם.

טז רַבִּי יְהוּדָה אוֹמֵר: הֱוֵי זָהִיר בְּתַלְמוּד, שֶׁשִּׁגְגַת תַּלְמוּד עוֹלָה זָדוֹן.

יז רַבִּי שִׁמְעוֹן אוֹמֵר: שְׁלֹשָׁה כְתָרִים הֵן, כֶּתֶר תּוֹרָה וְכֶתֶר כְּהֻנָּה וְכֶתֶר מַלְכוּת, וְכֶתֶר שֵׁם טוֹב עוֹלֶה עַל גַּבֵּיהֶן.

יח רַבִּי נְהוֹרַאי אוֹמֵר: הֱוֵי גוֹלֶה לִמְקוֹם תּוֹרָה. וְאַל תֹּאמַר שֶׁהִיא תָבוֹא אַחֲרֶיךָ,
שֶׁחֲבֵרֶיךָ יְקַיְּמוּהָ בְיָדֶךָ. וְאֶל־בִּינָתְךָ אַל־תִּשָּׁעֵן: משלי ג

יט רַבִּי יַנַּאי אוֹמֵר: אֵין בְּיָדֵינוּ לֹא מִשַּׁלְוַת הָרְשָׁעִים וְאַף לֹא מִיִּסּוּרֵי הַצַּדִּיקִים.

כ רַבִּי מַתְיָא בֶּן חָרָשׁ אוֹמֵר: הֱוֵי מַקְדִּים בִּשְׁלוֹם כָּל אָדָם, וֶהֱוֵי זָנָב לָאֲרָיוֹת, וְאַל תְּהִי רֹאשׁ לַשּׁוּעָלִים.

כא רַבִּי יַעֲקֹב אוֹמֵר: הָעוֹלָם הַזֶּה דּוֹמֶה לִפְרוֹזְדוֹר בִּפְנֵי הָעוֹלָם הַבָּא. הַתְקֵן עַצְמְךָ בַּפְּרוֹזְדוֹר, כְּדֵי שֶׁתִּכָּנֵס לַטְּרַקְלִין.

כב הוּא הָיָה אוֹמֵר: יָפָה שָׁעָה אַחַת בִּתְשׁוּבָה וּמַעֲשִׂים טוֹבִים בָּעוֹלָם הַזֶּה, מִכֹּל חַיֵּי הָעוֹלָם הַבָּא. וְיָפָה שָׁעָה אַחַת שֶׁל קוֹרַת רוּחַ בָּעוֹלָם הַבָּא, מִכֹּל חַיֵּי הָעוֹלָם הַזֶּה.

כג רַבִּי שִׁמְעוֹן בֶּן אֶלְעָזָר אוֹמֵר: אַל תְּרַצֶּה אֶת חֲבֵרְךָ בִּשְׁעַת כַּעְסוֹ, וְאַל תְּנַחֲמֵהוּ בְּשָׁעָה שֶׁמֵּתוֹ מֻטָּל לְפָנָיו, וְאַל תִּשְׁאַל לוֹ בִּשְׁעַת נִדְרוֹ, וְאַל תִּשְׁתַּדֵּל לִרְאוֹתוֹ בִּשְׁעַת קַלְקָלָתוֹ.

כד שְׁמוּאֵל הַקָּטָן אוֹמֵר: בִּנְפֹל אוֹיִבְךָ אַל־תִּשְׂמָח, וּבִכָּשְׁלוֹ אַל־יָגֵל לִבֶּךָ: פֶּן־ משלי כד
יִרְאֶה יהוה וְרַע בְּעֵינָיו, וְהֵשִׁיב מֵעָלָיו אַפּוֹ:

כה אֱלִישָׁע בֶּן אֲבוּיָה אוֹמֵר: הַלּוֹמֵד יֶלֶד, לְמָה הוּא דוֹמֶה, לִדְיוֹ כְתוּבָה עַל נְיָר חָדָשׁ. וְהַלּוֹמֵד זָקֵן, לְמָה הוּא דוֹמֶה, לִדְיוֹ כְתוּבָה עַל נְיָר מָחוּק.

כו רַבִּי יוֹסֵי בַּר יְהוּדָה אִישׁ כְּפַר הַבַּבְלִי אוֹמֵר: הַלּוֹמֵד מִן הַקְּטַנִּים, לְמָה הוּא דוֹמֶה, לְאוֹכֵל עֲנָבִים קֵהוֹת וְשׁוֹתֶה יַיִן מִגִּתּוֹ. וְהַלּוֹמֵד מִן הַזְּקֵנִים, לְמָה הוּא דוֹמֶה, לְאוֹכֵל עֲנָבִים בְּשׁוּלוֹת וְשׁוֹתֶה יַיִן יָשָׁן.

כז רַבִּי מֵאִיר אוֹמֵר: אַל תִּסְתַּכֵּל בַּקַּנְקַן, אֶלָּא בְּמַה שֶּׁיֵּשׁ בּוֹ. יֵשׁ קַנְקַן חָדָשׁ מָלֵא יָשָׁן, וְיָשָׁן שֶׁאֲפִלּוּ חָדָשׁ אֵין בּוֹ.

כח רַבִּי אֶלְעָזָר הַקַּפָּר אוֹמֵר: הַקִּנְאָה וְהַתַּאֲוָה וְהַכָּבוֹד, מוֹצִיאִין אֶת הָאָדָם מִן הָעוֹלָם.

29. He used to say: Those who are born will one day die, those who die will live again, and the living will be judged. It is for us to know, make known, and confirm that He is God, He is the Maker; He is the Creator; He is the Discerner; He is the Judge; He is the Witness; He is the Plaintiff; and He will deliver the judgment. Blessed is He before whom there is no unrighteousness, no forgetfulness, no favoritism and no taking of bribes; and know that all is according to a strict reckoning. Do not let your evil impulse persuade you that the grave is, for you, a place of refuge: for without your consent you were formed, without your consent you were born, without your consent you live, without your consent you will die, and without your consent you will in the future have to give an account and reckoning before the Supreme King of kings, the Holy One, blessed be He.

Rabbi Ḥananya ben Akashya said: The Holy One, blessed be He, wanted to confer merit on Israel. That is why He gave them a copious Torah and many commandments, as it is said, "It pleased the LORD, for the sake of [Israel's] righteousness, to make the Torah great and glorious." *Makkot 23b* *Is. 42*

If there is a minyan, mourners say the Rabbis' Kaddish (page 712).

* * *

All Israel have a share in the World to Come, as it is said, *Sanhedrin 90a*
"Your people are all righteous; they shall inherit the land for ever; *Is. 60*
they are a shoot of My own planting,
a work of My own hands, that I may be glorified."

CHAPTER 5

1. By ten acts of speech the world was created. What does this teach us? Could not the world have been created by a single act of speech? It is to exact punishment from the wicked who destroy a world created by ten acts of speech, and richly to reward the righteous who sustain the world created by ten acts of speech.
2. There were ten generations from Adam to Noah, to make known how patient God is, for all those generations increasingly provoked Him until He brought on them the waters of the Flood.
3. There were ten generations from Noah to Abraham, to make known how patient God is, for all those generations increasingly provoked Him until Abraham our father came and received the reward which could have been theirs.
4. Abraham our father was tested with ten trials and he withstood all of them, to make known how deep was our father Abraham's love of God.
5. Ten miracles were performed for our ancestors in Egypt, and ten at the Sea. The Holy One, blessed be He, brought ten plagues against the Egyptians in Egypt, and ten at the Sea.

כט הוּא הָיָה אוֹמֵר: הַיִּלּוֹדִים לָמוּת, וְהַמֵּתִים לִחְיוֹת, וְהַחַיִּים לִדּוֹן, לֵידַע וּלְהוֹדִיעַ וּלְהִוָּדַע, שֶׁהוּא אֵל, הוּא הַיּוֹצֵר, הוּא הַבּוֹרֵא, הוּא הַמֵּבִין, הוּא הַדַּיָּן, הוּא הָעֵד, הוּא בַּעַל דִּין, הוּא עָתִיד לָדוּן. בָּרוּךְ הוּא, שֶׁאֵין לְפָנָיו לֹא עַוְלָה וְלֹא שִׁכְחָה, וְלֹא מַשּׂוֹא פָנִים וְלֹא מִקַּח שֹׁחַד, שֶׁהַכֹּל שֶׁלּוֹ. וְדַע, שֶׁהַכֹּל לְפִי הַחֶשְׁבּוֹן. וְאַל יַבְטִיחֲךָ יִצְרְךָ שֶׁהַשְּׁאוֹל בֵּית מָנוֹס לָךְ, שֶׁעַל כָּרְחֲךָ אַתָּה נוֹצָר, וְעַל כָּרְחֲךָ אַתָּה נוֹלָד, וְעַל כָּרְחֲךָ אַתָּה חַי, וְעַל כָּרְחֲךָ אַתָּה מֵת, וְעַל כָּרְחֲךָ אַתָּה עָתִיד לִתֵּן דִּין וְחֶשְׁבּוֹן לִפְנֵי מֶלֶךְ מַלְכֵי הַמְּלָכִים הַקָּדוֹשׁ בָּרוּךְ הוּא.

מכות כג: רַבִּי חֲנַנְיָא בֶּן עֲקַשְׁיָא אוֹמֵר: רָצָה הַקָּדוֹשׁ בָּרוּךְ הוּא לְזַכּוֹת אֶת יִשְׂרָאֵל, לְפִיכָךְ
ישעיה מב הִרְבָּה לָהֶם תּוֹרָה וּמִצְוֹת. שֶׁנֶּאֱמַר: יהוה חָפֵץ לְמַעַן צִדְקוֹ, יַגְדִּיל תּוֹרָה וְיַאְדִּיר:

If there is a מנין*, mourners say* קדיש דרבנן *(page 713).*

(page 713)

* * *

סנהדרין צ. כָּל יִשְׂרָאֵל יֵשׁ לָהֶם חֵלֶק לָעוֹלָם הַבָּא. שֶׁנֶּאֱמַר:
ישעיה ס וְעַמֵּךְ כֻּלָּם צַדִּיקִים, לְעוֹלָם יִירְשׁוּ אָרֶץ
נֵצֶר מַטָּעַי, מַעֲשֵׂה יָדַי לְהִתְפָּאֵר:

פרק חמישי

א בַּעֲשָׂרָה מַאֲמָרוֹת נִבְרָא הָעוֹלָם. וּמַה תַּלְמוּד לוֹמַר, וַהֲלֹא בְּמַאֲמָר אֶחָד יָכוֹל לְהִבָּרְאוֹת, אֶלָּא לְהִפָּרַע מִן הָרְשָׁעִים, שֶׁמְּאַבְּדִין אֶת הָעוֹלָם שֶׁנִּבְרָא בַּעֲשָׂרָה מַאֲמָרוֹת, וְלִתֵּן שָׂכָר טוֹב לַצַּדִּיקִים, שֶׁמְּקַיְּמִין אֶת הָעוֹלָם שֶׁנִּבְרָא בַּעֲשָׂרָה מַאֲמָרוֹת.

ב עֲשָׂרָה דוֹרוֹת מֵאָדָם וְעַד נֹחַ, לְהוֹדִיעַ כַּמָּה אֶרֶךְ אַפַּיִם לְפָנָיו, שֶׁכָּל הַדּוֹרוֹת הָיוּ מַכְעִיסִין וּבָאִין, עַד שֶׁהֵבִיא עֲלֵיהֶם אֶת מֵי הַמַּבּוּל.

ג עֲשָׂרָה דוֹרוֹת מִנֹּחַ וְעַד אַבְרָהָם, לְהוֹדִיעַ כַּמָּה אֶרֶךְ אַפַּיִם לְפָנָיו, שֶׁכָּל הַדּוֹרוֹת הָיוּ מַכְעִיסִין וּבָאִין, עַד שֶׁבָּא אַבְרָהָם אָבִינוּ וְקִבֵּל שְׂכַר כֻּלָּם.

ד עֲשָׂרָה נִסְיוֹנוֹת נִתְנַסָּה אַבְרָהָם אָבִינוּ וְעָמַד בְּכֻלָּם, לְהוֹדִיעַ כַּמָּה חִבָּתוֹ שֶׁל אַבְרָהָם אָבִינוּ.

ה עֲשָׂרָה נִסִּים נַעֲשׂוּ לַאֲבוֹתֵינוּ בְּמִצְרַיִם, וַעֲשָׂרָה עַל הַיָּם. עֶשֶׂר מַכּוֹת הֵבִיא הַקָּדוֹשׁ בָּרוּךְ הוּא עַל הַמִּצְרִיִּים בְּמִצְרַיִם, וְעֶשֶׂר עַל הַיָּם.

6. With ten trials our ancestors tried the patience of the Holy One, blessed be He, in the wilderness, as it is written, "They have tested Me these ten times, *Num. 14* and did not listen to My voice."

7. Ten miracles were performed for our ancestors in the Temple: (1) No woman miscarried from the aroma of the sacrificial meat; (2) the sacrificial meat never became putrid; (3) no fly was seen in the slaughterhouse; (4) the High Priest never suffered ritual pollution on Yom Kippur; (5) rain never extinguished the fire of the wood-pile on the altar; (6) the wind never blew away the column of smoke that rose from the altar; (7) no defect was ever found in the Omer, the Two Loaves, or the Showbread; (8) the people stood crowded together, yet there was ample space when they prostrated themselves; (9) no serpent or scorpion ever harmed anyone in Jerusalem; and (10) no one ever said to his fellow, "There is no room for me to stay overnight in Jerusalem."

8. Ten things were created on the eve of the Sabbath at twilight. They were: (1) the mouth of the earth; (2) the mouth of the well; (3) the mouth of [Balaam's] ass; (4) the rainbow; (5) the manna; (6) the staff; (7) the Shamir; (8) the writing [on the Tablets]; (9) the inscription; and (10) the Tablets. Some say: also the demons, Moses' burial place, and the ram of our father Abraham. And some say: also tongs made with tongs.

9. Seven traits characterize an uncultured person, and seven a sage. A sage: (1) does not speak before one who is wiser than he; (2) does not interrupt the words of his fellow; (3) does not answer impetuously; (4) asks relevant questions and gives appropriate answers; (5) deals with first things first, and last things last; (6) about something he has not heard he says, "I have not heard"; and (7) he acknowledges the truth. The opposites of these characterize an uncultured person.

10. Seven types of punishment come into the world for seven kinds of transgression: (1) If some tithe and others do not, a famine caused by drought occurs, so that some go hungry while others have sufficient. (2) If all decide not to tithe, a famine comes through tumult [of war] as well as drought. (3) If they also decide not to set apart ḥalla, a fatal famine ensues.

11. (4) Pestilence comes to the world for crimes that, according to the Torah, carry the death penalty, but are not the preserve of a human tribunal, and also for violation of the laws relating to produce of the seventh year. (5) The sword comes to the world for delay of justice, the perversion of justice, and for those who give a legal decision in violation of normative Torah law.

12. (6) Wild beasts come to the world because of perjury and the desecration of God's name. (7) Exile comes to the world for idolatry, sexual immorality and bloodshed, and for violating the sabbatical year of the land.

ו עֲשָׂרָה נִסְיוֹנוֹת נִסּוּ אֲבוֹתֵינוּ אֶת הַקָּדוֹשׁ בָּרוּךְ הוּא בַּמִּדְבָּר, שֶׁנֶּאֱמַר:
וַיְנַסּוּ אֹתִי זֶה עֶשֶׂר פְּעָמִים, וְלֹא שָׁמְעוּ בְּקוֹלִי: במדבר יד

ז עֲשָׂרָה נִסִּים נַעֲשׂוּ לַאֲבוֹתֵינוּ בְּבֵית הַמִּקְדָּשׁ. לֹא הִפִּילָה אִשָּׁה מֵרֵיחַ בְּשַׂר הַקֹּדֶשׁ, וְלֹא הִסְרִיחַ בְּשַׂר הַקֹּדֶשׁ מֵעוֹלָם, וְלֹא נִרְאָה זְבוּב בְּבֵית הַמִּטְבְּחַיִם, וְלֹא אֵרַע קֶרִי לְכֹהֵן גָּדוֹל בְּיוֹם הַכִּפּוּרִים, וְלֹא כִבּוּ הַגְּשָׁמִים אֵשׁ שֶׁל עֲצֵי הַמַּעֲרָכָה, וְלֹא נִצְּחָה הָרוּחַ אֶת עַמּוּד הֶעָשָׁן, וְלֹא נִמְצָא פְסוּל בָּעֹמֶר וּבִשְׁתֵּי הַלֶּחֶם וּבְלֶחֶם הַפָּנִים, עוֹמְדִים צְפוּפִים וּמִשְׁתַּחֲוִים רְוָחִים, וְלֹא הִזִּיק נָחָשׁ וְעַקְרָב בִּירוּשָׁלַיִם מֵעוֹלָם, וְלֹא אָמַר אָדָם לַחֲבֵרוֹ: צַר לִי הַמָּקוֹם שֶׁאָלִין בִּירוּשָׁלָיִם.

ח עֲשָׂרָה דְבָרִים נִבְרְאוּ בְּעֶרֶב שַׁבָּת בֵּין הַשְּׁמָשׁוֹת. וְאֵלּוּ הֵן, פִּי הָאָרֶץ, פִּי הַבְּאֵר, פִּי הָאָתוֹן, הַקֶּשֶׁת, וְהַמָּן, וְהַמַּטֶּה, וְהַשָּׁמִיר, הַכְּתָב, וְהַמִּכְתָּב, וְהַלּוּחוֹת. וְיֵשׁ אוֹמְרִים, אַף הַמַּזִּיקִין, וּקְבוּרָתוֹ שֶׁל מֹשֶׁה, וְאֵילוֹ שֶׁל אַבְרָהָם אָבִינוּ. וְיֵשׁ אוֹמְרִים, אַף צְבָת בִּצְבָת עֲשׂוּיָה.

ט שִׁבְעָה דְבָרִים בְּגֹלֶם, וְשִׁבְעָה בְּחָכָם. חָכָם אֵינוֹ מְדַבֵּר לִפְנֵי מִי שֶׁגָּדוֹל מִמֶּנּוּ בְּחָכְמָה, וְאֵינוֹ נִכְנָס לְתוֹךְ דִּבְרֵי חֲבֵרוֹ, וְאֵינוֹ נִבְהָל לְהָשִׁיב, שׁוֹאֵל כָּעִנְיָן וּמֵשִׁיב כַּהֲלָכָה, וְאוֹמֵר עַל רִאשׁוֹן רִאשׁוֹן וְעַל אַחֲרוֹן אַחֲרוֹן, וְעַל מַה שֶּׁלֹּא שָׁמַע אוֹמֵר לֹא שָׁמַעְתִּי, וּמוֹדֶה עַל הָאֱמֶת. וְחִלּוּפֵיהֶן בְּגֹלֶם.

י שִׁבְעָה מִינֵי פֻרְעָנֻיּוֹת בָּאִין לָעוֹלָם עַל שִׁבְעָה גוּפֵי עֲבֵרָה. מִקְצָתָן מְעַשְּׂרִין וּמִקְצָתָן אֵינָן מְעַשְּׂרִין, רָעָב שֶׁל בַּצֹּרֶת בָּא, מִקְצָתָן רְעֵבִים וּמִקְצָתָן שְׂבֵעִים. גָּמְרוּ שֶׁלֹּא לְעַשֵּׂר, רָעָב שֶׁל מְהוּמָה וְשֶׁל בַּצֹּרֶת בָּא. וְשֶׁלֹּא לִטּוֹל אֶת הַחַלָּה, רָעָב שֶׁל כְּלָיָה בָּא.

יא דֶּבֶר בָּא לָעוֹלָם עַל מִיתוֹת הָאֲמוּרוֹת בַּתּוֹרָה שֶׁלֹּא נִמְסְרוּ לְבֵית דִּין, וְעַל פֵּרוֹת שְׁבִיעִית. חֶרֶב בָּאָה לָעוֹלָם עַל עִנּוּי הַדִּין, וְעַל עִוּוּת הַדִּין, וְעַל הַמּוֹרִים בַּתּוֹרָה שֶׁלֹּא כַהֲלָכָה.

יב חַיָּה רָעָה בָּאָה לָעוֹלָם עַל שְׁבוּעַת שָׁוְא וְעַל חִלּוּל הַשֵּׁם. גָּלוּת בָּאָה לָעוֹלָם עַל עֲבוֹדָה זָרָה, וְעַל גִּלּוּי עֲרָיוֹת, וְעַל שְׁפִיכוּת דָּמִים, וְעַל שְׁמִטַּת הָאָרֶץ.

13. At four periods [of the seven-year sabbatical cycle] pestilence increases: in the fourth year, the seventh year, the year following the sabbatical year, and annually at the conclusion of the Festival of Sukkot. In the fourth year, [pestilence increases] because of neglect of the tithe for the poor in the third year; in the seventh year, because of neglect of the tithe for the poor in the sixth year; in the year following the sabbatical year, because of the violation of the laws of the seventh-year produce; and at the conclusion of the Festival of Sukkot, for robbing the poor of their gifts.
14. There are four types of human character: (1) One who says, "What is mine is mine, and what is yours is yours," is an average person, though some say this is a Sodom type. (2) One who says, "What is mine is yours and what is yours is mine," is an ignoramus. (3) One who says, "What is mine is yours and what is yours is yours," is pious. (4) One who says, "What is yours is mine and what is mine is mine," is wicked.
15. There are four types of temperament: (1) One who is easily angered and easily pacified – his loss is cancelled by his gain. (2) One who is hard to anger and hard to pacify – his gain is cancelled by his loss. (3) One who is hard to anger and easily pacified is pious. (4) One who is easily angered and hard to pacify is wicked.
16. There are four types of student: (1) One who learns quickly and forgets quickly – his gain is cancelled by his loss. (2) One who learns slowly and forgets slowly – his loss is cancelled by his gain. (3) One who learns quickly and forgets slowly – his is a happy lot. (4) One who learns slowly and forgets quickly – his is a sad lot.
17. There are four types of donor to charity: (1) One who wishes to give but does not want others to give, begrudges others. (2) One who wants others to give, but does not himself give, begrudges himself. (3) One who gives and wants others to give is pious. (4) One who does not himself give and does not want others to give is wicked.
18. There are four types among those who attend the House of Study: (1) One who goes but does not practice [what he learns] receives a reward for going. (2) One who practices but does not go receives a reward for practicing. (3) One who goes and also practices is pious. (4) One who neither goes nor practices is wicked.
19. There are four types among those who sit before the sages: the sponge, the funnel, the strainer and the sieve. The sponge absorbs everything. The funnel takes in at one end and lets out at the other. The strainer lets out the wine and retains the sediment. The sieve allows the flour dust to pass through and retains the fine flour.
20. If love depends on a specific cause, when the cause ends, so does the love. If love does not depend on a specific cause, then it never ends. What is an example of love depending on a specific cause? The love of Amnon for Tamar. What is an example of love not dependent on a specific cause? The love of David and Jonathan.

יג בְּאַרְבָּעָה פְרָקִים הַדֶּבֶר מִתְרַבֶּה, בָּרְבִיעִית, וּבַשְּׁבִיעִית, וּבְמוֹצָאֵי שְׁבִיעִית, וּבְמוֹצָאֵי הֶחָג שֶׁבְּכָל שָׁנָה וְשָׁנָה. בָּרְבִיעִית, מִפְּנֵי מַעְשַׂר עָנִי שֶׁבַּשְּׁלִישִׁית. בַּשְּׁבִיעִית, מִפְּנֵי מַעְשַׂר עָנִי שֶׁבַּשִּׁשִּׁית. בְּמוֹצָאֵי שְׁבִיעִית, מִפְּנֵי פֵּרוֹת שְׁבִיעִית. בְּמוֹצָאֵי הֶחָג שֶׁבְּכָל שָׁנָה וְשָׁנָה, מִפְּנֵי גֶזֶל מַתְּנוֹת עֲנִיִּים.

יד אַרְבַּע מִדּוֹת בָּאָדָם. הָאוֹמֵר שֶׁלִּי שֶׁלִּי וְשֶׁלְּךָ שֶׁלָּךְ, זוֹ מִדָּה בֵינוֹנִית, וְיֵשׁ אוֹמְרִים, זוֹ מִדַּת סְדוֹם. שֶׁלִּי שֶׁלָּךְ וְשֶׁלְּךָ שֶׁלִּי, עַם הָאָרֶץ. שֶׁלִּי שֶׁלָּךְ וְשֶׁלְּךָ שֶׁלָּךְ, חָסִיד. שֶׁלְּךָ שֶׁלִּי וְשֶׁלִּי שֶׁלִּי, רָשָׁע.

טו אַרְבַּע מִדּוֹת בַּדֵּעוֹת. נוֹחַ לִכְעוֹס וְנוֹחַ לִרְצוֹת, יָצָא הֶפְסֵדוֹ בִּשְׂכָרוֹ. קָשֶׁה לִכְעוֹס וְקָשֶׁה לִרְצוֹת, יָצָא שְׂכָרוֹ בְּהֶפְסֵדוֹ. קָשֶׁה לִכְעוֹס וְנוֹחַ לִרְצוֹת, חָסִיד. נוֹחַ לִכְעוֹס וְקָשֶׁה לִרְצוֹת, רָשָׁע.

טז אַרְבַּע מִדּוֹת בְּתַלְמִידִים. מָהִיר לִשְׁמוֹעַ וּמָהִיר לְאַבֵּד, יָצָא שְׂכָרוֹ בְּהֶפְסֵדוֹ. קָשֶׁה לִשְׁמוֹעַ וְקָשֶׁה לְאַבֵּד, יָצָא הֶפְסֵדוֹ בִּשְׂכָרוֹ. מָהִיר לִשְׁמוֹעַ וְקָשֶׁה לְאַבֵּד, זֶה חֵלֶק טוֹב. קָשֶׁה לִשְׁמוֹעַ וּמָהִיר לְאַבֵּד, זֶה חֵלֶק רָע.

יז אַרְבַּע מִדּוֹת בְּנוֹתְנֵי צְדָקָה. הָרוֹצֶה שֶׁיִּתֵּן וְלֹא יִתְּנוּ אֲחֵרִים, עֵינוֹ רָעָה בְּשֶׁל אֲחֵרִים. יִתְּנוּ אֲחֵרִים וְהוּא לֹא יִתֵּן, עֵינוֹ רָעָה בְּשֶׁלּוֹ. יִתֵּן וְיִתְּנוּ אֲחֵרִים, חָסִיד. לֹא יִתֵּן וְלֹא יִתְּנוּ אֲחֵרִים, רָשָׁע.

יח אַרְבַּע מִדּוֹת בְּהוֹלְכֵי בֵית הַמִּדְרָשׁ. הוֹלֵךְ וְאֵינוֹ עוֹשֶׂה, שְׂכַר הֲלִיכָה בְּיָדוֹ. עוֹשֶׂה וְאֵינוֹ הוֹלֵךְ, שְׂכַר מַעֲשֶׂה בְּיָדוֹ. הוֹלֵךְ וְעוֹשֶׂה, חָסִיד. לֹא הוֹלֵךְ וְלֹא עוֹשֶׂה, רָשָׁע.

יט אַרְבַּע מִדּוֹת בְּיוֹשְׁבִים לִפְנֵי חֲכָמִים, סְפוֹג, וּמַשְׁפֵּךְ, מְשַׁמֶּרֶת, וְנָפָה. סְפוֹג, שֶׁהוּא סוֹפֵג אֶת הַכֹּל. וּמַשְׁפֵּךְ, שֶׁמַּכְנִיס בְּזוֹ וּמוֹצִיא בְזוֹ. מְשַׁמֶּרֶת, שֶׁמּוֹצִיאָה אֶת הַיַּיִן וְקוֹלֶטֶת אֶת הַשְּׁמָרִים. וְנָפָה, שֶׁמּוֹצִיאָה אֶת הַקֶּמַח וְקוֹלֶטֶת אֶת הַסֹּלֶת.

כ כָּל אַהֲבָה שֶׁהִיא תְלוּיָה בְדָבָר, בָּטֵל דָּבָר, בְּטֵלָה אַהֲבָה. וְשֶׁאֵינָהּ תְּלוּיָה בְדָבָר, אֵינָהּ בְּטֵלָה לְעוֹלָם. אֵיזוֹ הִיא אַהֲבָה שֶׁהִיא תְלוּיָה בְדָבָר, זוֹ אַהֲבַת אַמְנוֹן וְתָמָר. וְשֶׁאֵינָהּ תְּלוּיָה בְדָבָר, זוֹ אַהֲבַת דָּוִד וִיהוֹנָתָן.

21. Any dispute for the sake of Heaven will have enduring value, but any dispute not for the sake of Heaven will not have enduring value. What is an example of a dispute for the sake of heaven? The dispute between Hillel and Shammai. What is an example of one not for the sake of heaven? The dispute of Koraḥ and all his company.

22. One who brings merit to the many will not be the cause of sin. One who causes the many to sin will be denied the means to repent. Moses attained merit and brought merit to the many; therefore the merit of the many was attributed to him, as it is said, "He carried out the LORD's righteousness and His ordinances with Israel." Jeroboam, son of Nebat, sinned and caused the many to sin; therefore the sin of the many was attributed to him, as it is said, "For the sins of Jeroboam that he committed and that he caused Israel to commit."

Deut. 33

1 Kings 15

23. Whoever possesses these three traits is one of the disciples of our father Abraham; whoever possesses the three opposite traits is one of the disciples of the wicked Balaam. A generous eye, a modest demeanor and a humble soul are the traits of the disciples of our father Abraham. An evil eye, an arrogant demeanor and an insatiable soul are attributes of the disciples of the wicked Balaam. What is the difference between our father Abraham's disciples and those of the wicked Balaam? Our father Abraham's disciples enjoy this world and inherit the World to Come, as it is said, "That I may cause those who love me to inherit substance and so that I may fill their treasures." The wicked Balaam's disciples inherit Gehinnom and go down to the pit of destruction, as it is said, "But You, God, will bring them down to the pit of destruction; bloodthirsty and deceitful men shall not live out half their days; but I trust in You."

Prov. 8

Ps. 55

24. Judah ben Tema said: Be strong as a leopard, light as an eagle, swift as a gazelle, and brave as a lion, to do the will of your Father in heaven. He used to say: The shameless go to Gehinnom; those who have a sense of shame are destined for the Garden of Eden. May it be Your will, O LORD our God and God of our ancestors that the Temple be speedily rebuilt in our days; and grant us our portion in Your Torah.

25. He used to say: Five years old is the age to begin studying Scripture; ten for Mishna; thirteen for the obligation of the commandments; fifteen for the study of Talmud; eighteen for marriage; twenty for seeking a livelihood; thirty for full strength; forty for understanding; fifty for giving counsel; sixty for old age; seventy for ripe old age; eighty for exceptional strength; and ninety for a bent back; at a hundred, one is as if he were dead and had left and gone from the world.

כא כָּל מַחֲלֹקֶת שֶׁהִיא לְשֵׁם שָׁמַיִם, סוֹפָהּ לְהִתְקַיֵּם. וְשֶׁאֵינָהּ לְשֵׁם שָׁמַיִם, אֵין סוֹפָהּ לְהִתְקַיֵּם. אֵיזוֹ הִיא מַחֲלֹקֶת שֶׁהִיא לְשֵׁם שָׁמַיִם, זוֹ מַחֲלֹקֶת הִלֵּל וְשַׁמַּאי. וְשֶׁאֵינָהּ לְשֵׁם שָׁמַיִם, זוֹ מַחֲלֹקֶת קֹרַח וְכָל עֲדָתוֹ.

כב כָּל הַמְזַכֶּה אֶת הָרַבִּים, אֵין חֵטְא בָּא עַל יָדוֹ. וְכָל הַמַּחֲטִיא אֶת הָרַבִּים, אֵין מַסְפִּיקִין בְּיָדוֹ לַעֲשׂוֹת תְּשׁוּבָה. מֹשֶׁה זָכָה וְזִכָּה אֶת הָרַבִּים, זְכוּת
הָרַבִּים תָּלוּי בּוֹ, שֶׁנֶּאֱמַר: צִדְקַת יהוה עָשָׂה וּמִשְׁפָּטָיו עִם־יִשְׂרָאֵל: יָרָבְעָם דברים לג
בֶּן נְבָט, חָטָא וְהֶחֱטִיא אֶת הָרַבִּים, חֵטְא הָרַבִּים תָּלוּי בּוֹ, שֶׁנֶּאֱמַר: עַל־ מלכים א׳ טו
חַטֹּאות יָרָבְעָם אֲשֶׁר חָטָא וַאֲשֶׁר הֶחֱטִיא אֶת־יִשְׂרָאֵל:

כג כָּל מִי שֶׁיֵּשׁ בּוֹ שְׁלֹשָׁה דְבָרִים הַלָּלוּ, הוּא מִתַּלְמִידָיו שֶׁל אַבְרָהָם אָבִינוּ, וּשְׁלֹשָׁה דְבָרִים אֲחֵרִים, הוּא מִתַּלְמִידָיו שֶׁל בִּלְעָם הָרָשָׁע. עַיִן טוֹבָה, וְרוּחַ נְמוּכָה, וְנֶפֶשׁ שְׁפָלָה, תַּלְמִידָיו שֶׁל אַבְרָהָם אָבִינוּ. עַיִן רָעָה, וְרוּחַ גְּבוֹהָה וְנֶפֶשׁ רְחָבָה, תַּלְמִידָיו שֶׁל בִּלְעָם הָרָשָׁע. מַה בֵּין תַּלְמִידָיו שֶׁל אַבְרָהָם אָבִינוּ לְתַלְמִידָיו שֶׁל בִּלְעָם הָרָשָׁע. תַּלְמִידָיו שֶׁל אַבְרָהָם אָבִינוּ
אוֹכְלִין בָּעוֹלָם הַזֶּה וְנוֹחֲלִין הָעוֹלָם הַבָּא, שֶׁנֶּאֱמַר: לְהַנְחִיל אֹהֲבַי יֵשׁ משלי ח
וְאֹצְרֹתֵיהֶם אֲמַלֵּא: אֲבָל תַּלְמִידָיו שֶׁל בִּלְעָם הָרָשָׁע יוֹרְשִׁין גֵּיהִנָּם וְיוֹרְדִין
לִבְאֵר שַׁחַת, שֶׁנֶּאֱמַר: וְאַתָּה אֱלֹהִים תּוֹרִדֵם לִבְאֵר שַׁחַת, אַנְשֵׁי דָמִים תהלים נה
וּמִרְמָה לֹא־יֶחֱצוּ יְמֵיהֶם, וַאֲנִי אֶבְטַח־בָּךְ:

כד יְהוּדָה בֶּן תֵּימָא אוֹמֵר: הֱוֵי עַז כַּנָּמֵר וְקַל כַּנֶּשֶׁר, רָץ כַּצְּבִי וְגִבּוֹר כָּאֲרִי, לַעֲשׂוֹת רְצוֹן אָבִיךָ שֶׁבַּשָּׁמָיִם. הוּא הָיָה אוֹמֵר: עַז פָּנִים לְגֵיהִנָּם, וּבֹשֶׁת פָּנִים לְגַן עֵדֶן. יְהִי רָצוֹן מִלְּפָנֶיךָ, יהוה אֱלֹהֵינוּ וֵאלֹהֵי אֲבוֹתֵינוּ, שֶׁיִּבָּנֶה בֵּית הַמִּקְדָּשׁ בִּמְהֵרָה בְיָמֵינוּ, וְתֵן חֶלְקֵנוּ בְּתוֹרָתֶךָ.

כה הוּא הָיָה אוֹמֵר: בֶּן חָמֵשׁ שָׁנִים לַמִּקְרָא, בֶּן עֶשֶׂר שָׁנִים לַמִּשְׁנָה, בֶּן שְׁלֹשׁ עֶשְׂרֵה לַמִּצְוֹת, בֶּן חֲמֵשׁ עֶשְׂרֵה לַגְּמָרָא, בֶּן שְׁמוֹנֶה עֶשְׂרֵה לַחֻפָּה, בֶּן עֶשְׂרִים לִרְדּוֹף, בֶּן שְׁלֹשִׁים לַכֹּחַ, בֶּן אַרְבָּעִים לַבִּינָה, בֶּן חֲמִשִּׁים לָעֵצָה, בֶּן שִׁשִּׁים לַזִּקְנָה, בֶּן שִׁבְעִים לַשֵּׂיבָה, בֶּן שְׁמוֹנִים לַגְּבוּרָה, בֶּן תִּשְׁעִים לָשׁוּחַ, בֶּן מֵאָה כְּאִלּוּ מֵת וְעָבַר וּבָטֵל מִן הָעוֹלָם.

26. Ben Bag-Bag said: Turn it [the Torah] over and over, for everything is in it. Reflect on it, grow old and gray in it and do not stir from it, for there is no better portion for you than this. Ben Heh-Heh said: According to the effort is the reward.

Rabbi Ḥananya ben Akashya said: The Holy One, blessed be He, wanted to confer merit on Israel. That is why He gave them a copious Torah and many commandments, as it is said, "It pleased the LORD, for the sake of [Israel's] righteousness, to make the Torah great and glorious." *Makkot 23b* *Is. 42*

If there is a minyan, mourners say the Rabbis' Kaddish (page 712).

* * *

All Israel have a share in the World to Come, as it is said, *Sanhedrin 90a*
"Your people are all righteous; they shall inherit the land for ever; *Is. 60*
they are a shoot of My own planting,
a work of My own hands, that I may be glorified."

CHAPTER 6

The sages taught the following in the style of the Mishna – blessed be He who chose them and their teaching.

1. Rabbi Meir said: Whoever engages in Torah study for its own sake merits many things; moreover, the whole world is worthwhile for his sake alone. He is called friend, beloved, a lover of God and a lover of mankind. He brings joy to God; He brings joy to mankind. [The Torah] clothes him with humility and reverence. It prepares him to be righteous, pious, upright and faithful. It keeps him far from sin and near to virtue. People benefit from his advice and wisdom, understanding and courage, as it is said, "Mine are counsel and wisdom; I am understanding, courage is mine." It gives him sovereignty, dominion and discerning judgment. To him the secrets of the Torah are revealed. He becomes like a never-failing fountain, like a river that never runs dry. He becomes modest and patient; he forgives insults. It makes him great, exalting him above all things. *Prov. 8*

2. Rabbi Yehoshua ben Levi said: Every day a heavenly voice resounds from Mount Horeb, proclaiming and saying: "Woe to mankind for their contempt of the Torah!" For whoever does not occupy himself with the Torah is called reprehensible, as it is said, "Like a gold ring in the snout of a pig is a beautiful woman bereft of sense." It also says, "The tablets were the work of God, and the writing was the writing of God, engraved (*ḥarut*) on the tablets." Read not *ḥarut* ("engraved") but *ḥerut* ("freedom"), for the only person who is truly free is one who occupies himself with Torah study; and whoever occupies himself with Torah study will be exalted, as it is said, "And from Mattana to Naḥaliel, and from Naḥaliel to Bamot." *Prov. 11* *Ex. 32* *Num. 21*

כו בֶּן בַּג בַּג אוֹמֵר: הֲפֹךְ בָּהּ וַהֲפֹךְ בָּהּ דְּכֹלָּא בַהּ, וּבַהּ תֶּחֱזֵי, וְסִיב וּבְלֵה בַהּ, וּמִנַּהּ לָא תְזוּעַ, שֶׁאֵין לְךָ מִדָּה טוֹבָה הֵימֶנָּה. בֶּן הֵא הֵא אוֹמֵר: לְפוּם צַעֲרָא אַגְרָא.

מכות כג: רַבִּי חֲנַנְיָא בֶּן עֲקַשְׁיָא אוֹמֵר: רָצָה הַקָּדוֹשׁ בָּרוּךְ הוּא לְזַכּוֹת אֶת יִשְׂרָאֵל, לְפִיכָךְ
ישעיה מב הִרְבָּה לָהֶם תּוֹרָה וּמִצְוֹת. שֶׁנֶּאֱמַר: יהוה חָפֵץ לְמַעַן צִדְקוֹ, יַגְדִּיל תּוֹרָה וְיַאְדִּיר:

If there is a מנין*, mourners say* קדיש דרבנן *(page 713).*

* * *

סנהדרין צ. כָּל יִשְׂרָאֵל יֵשׁ לָהֶם חֵלֶק לָעוֹלָם הַבָּא. שֶׁנֶּאֱמַר:
ישעיה ס וְעַמֵּךְ כֻּלָּם צַדִּיקִים, לְעוֹלָם יִירְשׁוּ אָרֶץ
נֵצֶר מַטָּעַי, מַעֲשֵׂה יָדַי לְהִתְפָּאֵר:

פרק ששי

שָׁנוּ חֲכָמִים בִּלְשׁוֹן הַמִּשְׁנָה, בָּרוּךְ שֶׁבָּחַר בָּהֶם וּבְמִשְׁנָתָם.

א רַבִּי מֵאִיר אוֹמֵר: כָּל הָעוֹסֵק בַּתּוֹרָה לִשְׁמָהּ, זוֹכֶה לִדְבָרִים הַרְבֵּה. וְלֹא עוֹד, אֶלָּא שֶׁכָּל הָעוֹלָם כֻּלּוֹ כְּדַאי הוּא לוֹ. נִקְרָא רֵעַ, אָהוּב, אוֹהֵב אֶת הַמָּקוֹם, אוֹהֵב אֶת הַבְּרִיּוֹת, מְשַׂמֵּחַ אֶת הַמָּקוֹם, מְשַׂמֵּחַ אֶת הַבְּרִיּוֹת, וּמַלְבַּשְׁתּוֹ עֲנָוָה וְיִרְאָה, וּמַכְשַׁרְתּוֹ לִהְיוֹת צַדִּיק, חָסִיד, יָשָׁר, וְנֶאֱמָן, וּמְרַחַקְתּוֹ מִן הַחֵטְא, וּמְקָרַבְתּוֹ לִידֵי זְכוּת, וְנֶהֱנִין מִמֶּנּוּ עֵצָה וְתוּשִׁיָּה, בִּינָה וּגְבוּרָה,
משלי ח שֶׁנֶּאֱמַר: לִי־עֵצָה וְתוּשִׁיָּה, אֲנִי בִינָה, לִי גְבוּרָה: וְנוֹתֶנֶת לוֹ מַלְכוּת וּמֶמְשָׁלָה, וְחִקּוּר דִּין, וּמְגַלִּין לוֹ רָזֵי תוֹרָה, וְנַעֲשֶׂה כְּמַעְיָן הַמִּתְגַּבֵּר וּכְנָהָר שֶׁאֵינוֹ פוֹסֵק, וְהֹוֶה צָנוּעַ, וְאֶרֶךְ רוּחַ, וּמוֹחֵל עַל עֶלְבּוֹנוֹ, וּמְגַדַּלְתּוֹ וּמְרוֹמַמְתּוֹ עַל כָּל הַמַּעֲשִׂים.

ב אָמַר רַבִּי יְהוֹשֻׁעַ בֶּן לֵוִי: בְּכָל יוֹם וָיוֹם, בַּת קוֹל יוֹצֵאת מֵהַר חוֹרֵב וּמַכְרֶזֶת וְאוֹמֶרֶת, אוֹי לָהֶם לַבְּרִיּוֹת מֵעֶלְבּוֹנָהּ שֶׁל תּוֹרָה, שֶׁכָּל מִי שֶׁאֵינוֹ עוֹסֵק
משלי יא בַּתּוֹרָה נִקְרָא נָזוּף, שֶׁנֶּאֱמַר: נֶזֶם זָהָב בְּאַף חֲזִיר, אִשָּׁה יָפָה וְסָרַת טָעַם:
שמות לב וְאוֹמֵר: וְהַלֻּחֹת מַעֲשֵׂה אֱלֹהִים הֵמָּה, וְהַמִּכְתָּב מִכְתַּב אֱלֹהִים הוּא, חָרוּת עַל־הַלֻּחֹת: אַל תִּקְרָא חָרוּת אֶלָּא חֵרוּת, שֶׁאֵין לְךָ בֶּן חוֹרִין אֶלָּא מִי שֶׁעוֹסֵק בְּתַלְמוּד תּוֹרָה. וְכָל מִי שֶׁעוֹסֵק בְּתַלְמוּד תּוֹרָה, הֲרֵי זֶה מִתְעַלֶּה, שֶׁנֶּאֱמַר:
במדבר כא וּמִמַּתָּנָה נַחֲלִיאֵל, וּמִנַּחֲלִיאֵל בָּמוֹת:

3. Whoever learns from someone else a single chapter, a single law, a single verse, a single word, even a single letter, must treat him with honor, for so we find in the case of David, King of Israel, who learned only two things from Aḥitophel, yet he called him his teacher, his guide, and his close friend, for so it says, "But it is you, my equal, my guide, my close friend." The following inference can be derived: If David, King of Israel, who learned only two things from Aḥitophel, called him his teacher, guide and close friend, how much more must one who learns from someone else a chapter, a law, a verse, a word or even a single letter, treat him with honor! And honor is due only to Torah, as it is written, "The wise shall inherit honor," and "The wholehearted shall attain good," and "good" signifies Torah, as it is said, "I have given you good instruction; do not forsake My Torah."

Ps. 55 *Prov. 3* *Prov. 28* *Prov. 4*

4. This is the way of Torah: Eat bread with salt, drink water by measure, sleep on the ground, live a life of hardship, but toil in the Torah! If you do so, "You will be happy and it will be well with you": "You will be happy" in this world, "and it shall be well with you" in the World to Come.

5. Do not seek greatness for yourself, and do not long for honor. Let your deeds exceed your learning. Do not crave the table of kings, for your table is greater than theirs, your crown is greater than their crown, and your Employer can be relied upon to pay you your labor's reward.

6. The Torah is greater than priesthood and kingship, for kingship is acquired with thirty attainments, and priesthood is endowed with twenty-four [gifts], but the Torah is acquired by forty-eight virtues. They are: study, attentive listening, well-ordered speech, intuitive understanding, awe, reverence, humility, joy, purity, serving the wise, association with colleagues, debate with students, serenity, knowledge of Scripture and Mishna; minimizing time spent on business, worldly matters, pleasure, sleep, small talk or laughter; patience, a kindly heart, faith in the sages, and acceptance of suffering; knowing one's place, being happy with one's lot, restraining one's words, and claiming no credit for oneself; being loved, loving God, loving mankind and loving righteousness, justice and admonishment; shunning honors, avoiding arrogance in one's learning or delight in giving decisions; sharing someone else's burden, giving him the benefit of the doubt, guiding him to truth and peace; concentrating on one's study, asking and answering questions, listening and adding to one's knowledge; learning in order to teach, learning in order to do, making one's teacher wiser, being precise in one's studies, and reporting a saying in the name of the one who said it. For you have learned: Whoever reports a saying in the name of the one who said it brings deliverance to the world, as it is said, "And Esther told the king in the name of Mordekhai."

Esther 2

ג הַלּוֹמֵד מֵחֲבֵרוֹ פֶּרֶק אֶחָד, אוֹ הֲלָכָה אַחַת, אוֹ פָּסוּק אֶחָד, אוֹ דִבּוּר אֶחָד,
אוֹ אֲפִלּוּ אוֹת אַחַת, צָרִיךְ לִנְהָג בּוֹ כָּבוֹד. שֶׁכֵּן מָצִינוּ בְּדָוִד מֶלֶךְ יִשְׂרָאֵל,
שֶׁלֹּא לָמַד מֵאֲחִיתֹפֶל אֶלָּא שְׁנֵי דְבָרִים בִּלְבָד, קְרָאוֹ רַבּוֹ אַלּוּפוֹ וּמְיֻדָּעוֹ,
שֶׁנֶּאֱמַר: וְאַתָּה אֱנוֹשׁ כְּעֶרְכִּי, אַלּוּפִי וּמְיֻדָּעִי: וַהֲלֹא דְבָרִים קַל וָחֹמֶר. וּמָה תהלים נה
דָּוִד מֶלֶךְ יִשְׂרָאֵל, שֶׁלֹּא לָמַד מֵאֲחִיתֹפֶל אֶלָּא שְׁנֵי דְבָרִים בִּלְבָד, קְרָאוֹ רַבּוֹ
אַלּוּפוֹ וּמְיֻדָּעוֹ, הַלּוֹמֵד מֵחֲבֵרוֹ פֶּרֶק אֶחָד, אוֹ הֲלָכָה אַחַת, אוֹ פָּסוּק אֶחָד, אוֹ
דִבּוּר אֶחָד, אוֹ אֲפִלּוּ אוֹת אַחַת, עַל אַחַת כַּמָּה וְכַמָּה שֶׁצָּרִיךְ לִנְהָג בּוֹ כָּבוֹד.
וְאֵין כָּבוֹד אֶלָּא תוֹרָה, שֶׁנֶּאֱמַר: כָּבוֹד חֲכָמִים יִנְחָלוּ: וּתְמִימִים יִנְחֲלוּ־טוֹב: משלי ג
וְאֵין טוֹב אֶלָּא תוֹרָה, שֶׁנֶּאֱמַר: כִּי לֶקַח טוֹב נָתַתִּי לָכֶם, תּוֹרָתִי אַל־תַּעֲזֹבוּ: משלי כח משלי ד

ד כָּךְ הִיא דַּרְכָּהּ שֶׁל תּוֹרָה. פַּת בַּמֶּלַח תֹּאכֵל, וּמַיִם בַּמְּשׂוּרָה תִּשְׁתֶּה, וְעַל
הָאָרֶץ תִּישַׁן, וְחַיֵּי צַעַר תִּחְיֶה, וּבַתּוֹרָה אַתָּה עָמֵל. אִם אַתָּה עוֹשֶׂה כֵּן,
אַשְׁרֶיךָ וְטוֹב לָךְ, אַשְׁרֶיךָ בָּעוֹלָם הַזֶּה, וְטוֹב לָךְ לָעוֹלָם הַבָּא.

ה אַל תְּבַקֵּשׁ גְּדֻלָּה לְעַצְמְךָ, וְאַל תַּחְמֹד כָּבוֹד. יוֹתֵר מִלִּמּוּדְךָ עֲשֵׂה. וְאַל
תִּתְאַוֶּה לְשֻׁלְחָנָם שֶׁל מְלָכִים, שֶׁשֻּׁלְחָנְךָ גָּדוֹל מִשֻּׁלְחָנָם, וְכִתְרְךָ גָּדוֹל
מִכִּתְרָם. וְנֶאֱמָן הוּא בַּעַל מְלַאכְתְּךָ, שֶׁיְּשַׁלֶּם לְךָ שְׂכַר פְּעֻלָּתֶךָ.

ו גְּדוֹלָה תוֹרָה יוֹתֵר מִן הַכְּהֻנָּה וּמִן הַמַּלְכוּת. שֶׁהַמַּלְכוּת נִקְנֵית בִּשְׁלֹשִׁים
מַעֲלוֹת, וְהַכְּהֻנָּה בְּעֶשְׂרִים וְאַרְבַּע, וְהַתּוֹרָה נִקְנֵית בְּאַרְבָּעִים וּשְׁמוֹנָה דְבָרִים.
וְאֵלּוּ הֵן, בְּתַלְמוּד, בִּשְׁמִיעַת הָאֹזֶן, בַּעֲרִיכַת שְׂפָתָיִם, בְּבִינַת הַלֵּב, בְּאֵימָה,
בְּיִרְאָה, בַּעֲנָוָה, בְּשִׂמְחָה, בְּטָהֳרָה, בְּשִׁמּוּשׁ חֲכָמִים, בְּדִקְדּוּק חֲבֵרִים, בְּפִלְפּוּל
הַתַּלְמִידִים, בְּיִשּׁוּב, בְּמִקְרָא, בְּמִשְׁנָה, בְּמִעוּט סְחוֹרָה, בְּמִעוּט דֶּרֶךְ אֶרֶץ,
בְּמִעוּט תַּעֲנוּג, בְּמִעוּט שֵׁנָה, בְּמִעוּט שִׂיחָה, בְּמִעוּט שְׂחוֹק, בְּאֶרֶךְ אַפַּיִם,
בְּלֵב טוֹב, בֶּאֱמוּנַת חֲכָמִים, בְּקַבָּלַת הַיִּסּוּרִין, הַמַּכִּיר אֶת מְקוֹמוֹ, וְהַשָּׂמֵחַ
בְּחֶלְקוֹ, וְהָעוֹשֶׂה סְיָג לִדְבָרָיו, וְאֵינוֹ מַחֲזִיק טוֹבָה לְעַצְמוֹ, אָהוּב, אוֹהֵב אֶת
הַמָּקוֹם, אוֹהֵב אֶת הַבְּרִיּוֹת, אוֹהֵב אֶת הַצְּדָקוֹת, אוֹהֵב אֶת הַמֵּישָׁרִים, אוֹהֵב
אֶת הַתּוֹכָחוֹת, וּמִתְרַחֵק מִן הַכָּבוֹד, וְלֹא מֵגִיס לִבּוֹ בְּתַלְמוּדוֹ, וְאֵינוֹ שָׂמֵחַ
בְּהוֹרָאָה, נוֹשֵׂא בְעֹל עִם חֲבֵרוֹ, וּמַכְרִיעוֹ לְכַף זְכוּת, וּמַעֲמִידוֹ עַל הָאֱמֶת,
וּמַעֲמִידוֹ עַל הַשָּׁלוֹם, וּמִתְיַשֵּׁב לִבּוֹ בְּתַלְמוּדוֹ, שׁוֹאֵל וּמֵשִׁיב, שׁוֹמֵעַ וּמוֹסִיף,
הַלּוֹמֵד עַל מְנָת לְלַמֵּד, וְהַלּוֹמֵד עַל מְנָת לַעֲשׂוֹת, הַמַּחְכִּים אֶת רַבּוֹ, וְהַמְכַוֵּן
אֶת שְׁמוּעָתוֹ, וְהָאוֹמֵר דָּבָר בְּשֵׁם אוֹמְרוֹ. הָא לָמַדְתָּ, כָּל הָאוֹמֵר דָּבָר בְּשֵׁם
אוֹמְרוֹ, מֵבִיא גְאֻלָּה לָעוֹלָם, שֶׁנֶּאֱמַר: וַתֹּאמֶר אֶסְתֵּר לַמֶּלֶךְ בְּשֵׁם מָרְדְּכָי: אסתר ב

7. Great is Torah for it gives life to its practitioners in both this world and the
World to Come, as it is said, "For they are life to those that find them, and *Prov. 4*
healing to all their flesh"; and it says, "It shall be healing for your body and *Prov. 3*
marrow for your bones"; and it says, "It is a tree of life to those who grasp it,
and those who support it shall be happy"; and it says, "They shall be a garland *Prov. 1*
of grace on your head, and pendants for your neck"; and it says, "It will adorn *Prov. 4*
your head with a garland of grace, and bestow on you a crown of glory"; and
it says, "Through me shall your days increase, and years of life shall be added *Prov. 9*
to you"; and it says, "At its right hand is length of days; in its left, riches and *Prov. 3*
honor"; and it says, "For length of days and years of life and peace shall they *Prov. 3*
add to you."

8. Rabbi Shimon ben Menasya said in the name of Rabbi Shimon ben Yoḥai:
Beauty, strength, wealth, honor, wisdom, old age, gray hair, and children are
fitting for the righteous and for the world, as it is said: "Gray hair is a crown *Prov. 16*
of glory; it is attained by the way of righteousness"; and it says, "The crown *Prov. 14*
of the wise is their wealth"; and it says, "Grandchildren are the crown of *Prov. 17*
their elders; the glory of children is their parents"; and it says, "The glory of *Prov. 20*
the young is their strength; the majesty of the old is their gray hair"; and it
says, "Then the moon shall be ashamed and the sun shall be abashed, for the *Is. 24*
Lord of hosts will reign on Mount Zion and in Jerusalem, and glory shall be
before His elders." Rabbi Shimon ben Menasya said: These seven qualities
which the sages attributed to the righteous were all present in Rabbi [Judah
the Prince] and his sons.

9. Rabbi Yose ben Kisma said: Once I was walking along the road when a man
met and greeted me, and I returned his greeting. He said to me, "Rabbi, where
do you come from?" I replied, "I come from a great city of sages and scribes."
He said to me, "Rabbi, if you are willing to live with us in our place I will give
you a million gold dinars, as well as precious stones and pearls." I replied,
"Were you to give me all the silver and gold and precious stones and pearls
in the world, I would not live anywhere except in a place of Torah, for so it
is written in the book of Psalms by David, King of Israel, 'I prefer the Torah *Ps. 119*
of your mouth to thousands of gold and silver pieces.' Furthermore, when a
person departs from this world, neither silver nor gold nor precious stones nor
pearls accompany him, but only Torah and good deeds, as it is said, 'When *Prov. 6*
you walk, it will lead you; when you lie down, it will watch over you; and when
you awake, it will talk with you.' 'When you walk, it will lead you' – in this
world; 'when you lie down, it will watch over you' – in the grave; 'and when
you awake, it will speak for you' – in the World to Come. And it says, 'Mine *Hag. 2*
is the silver, and Mine is the gold, says the Lord of hosts.'"

ז גְּדוֹלָה תוֹרָה, שֶׁהִיא נוֹתֶנֶת חַיִּים לְעוֹשֶׂיהָ בָּעוֹלָם הַזֶּה וּבָעוֹלָם הַבָּא,
שֶׁנֶּאֱמַר: כִּי־חַיִּים הֵם לְמֹצְאֵיהֶם, וּלְכָל־בְּשָׂרוֹ מַרְפֵּא: וְאוֹמֵר: רִפְאוּת תְּהִי משלי ד משלי ג
לְשָׁרֶּךָ, וְשִׁקּוּי לְעַצְמוֹתֶיךָ: וְאוֹמֵר: עֵץ־חַיִּים הִיא לַמַּחֲזִיקִים בָּהּ, וְתֹמְכֶיהָ
מְאֻשָּׁר: וְאוֹמֵר: כִּי לִוְיַת חֵן הֵם לְרֹאשֶׁךָ, וַעֲנָקִים לְגַרְגְּרֹתֶיךָ: וְאוֹמֵר: תִּתֵּן משלי א משלי ד
לְרֹאשְׁךָ לִוְיַת־חֵן, עֲטֶרֶת תִּפְאֶרֶת תְּמַגְּנֶךָּ: וְאוֹמֵר: כִּי־בִי יִרְבּוּ יָמֶיךָ, וְיוֹסִיפוּ משלי ט
לְךָ שְׁנוֹת חַיִּים: וְאוֹמֵר: אֹרֶךְ יָמִים בִּימִינָהּ, בִּשְׂמֹאולָהּ עֹשֶׁר וְכָבוֹד: וְאוֹמֵר: משלי ג
כִּי אֹרֶךְ יָמִים וּשְׁנוֹת חַיִּים וְשָׁלוֹם יוֹסִיפוּ לָךְ: משלי ג

ח רַבִּי שִׁמְעוֹן בֶּן מְנַסְיָא מִשּׁוּם רַבִּי שִׁמְעוֹן בֶּן יוֹחַאי אוֹמֵר: הַנּוֹי, וְהַכֹּחַ,
וְהָעֹשֶׁר, וְהַכָּבוֹד, וְהַחָכְמָה, וְהַזִּקְנָה, וְהַשֵּׂיבָה, וְהַבָּנִים, נָאֶה לַצַּדִּיקִים
וְנָאֶה לָעוֹלָם, שֶׁנֶּאֱמַר: עֲטֶרֶת תִּפְאֶרֶת שֵׂיבָה, בְּדֶרֶךְ צְדָקָה תִּמָּצֵא: וְאוֹמֵר: משלי טז
עֲטֶרֶת חֲכָמִים עָשְׁרָם: וְאוֹמֵר: עֲטֶרֶת זְקֵנִים בְּנֵי בָנִים, וְתִפְאֶרֶת בָּנִים משלי יז משלי יד
אֲבוֹתָם: וְאוֹמֵר: תִּפְאֶרֶת בַּחוּרִים כֹּחָם, וַהֲדַר זְקֵנִים שֵׂיבָה: וְאוֹמֵר: וְחָפְרָה משלי כ ישעיה כד
הַלְּבָנָה וּבוֹשָׁה הַחַמָּה, כִּי־מָלַךְ יהוה צְבָאוֹת בְּהַר צִיּוֹן וּבִירוּשָׁלַיִם, וְנֶגֶד
זְקֵנָיו כָּבוֹד: רַבִּי שִׁמְעוֹן בֶּן מְנַסְיָא אוֹמֵר: אֵלּוּ שֶׁבַע מִדּוֹת שֶׁמָּנוּ חֲכָמִים
לַצַּדִּיקִים, כֻּלָּם נִתְקַיְּמוּ בְּרַבִּי וּבְבָנָיו.

ט אָמַר רַבִּי יוֹסֵי בֶּן קִסְמָא: פַּעַם אַחַת הָיִיתִי מְהַלֵּךְ בַּדֶּרֶךְ, וּפָגַע בִּי אָדָם
אֶחָד, וְנָתַן לִי שָׁלוֹם וְהֶחֱזַרְתִּי לוֹ שָׁלוֹם. אָמַר לִי, רַבִּי, מֵאֵיזֶה מָקוֹם אָתָּה.
אָמַרְתִּי לוֹ, מֵעִיר גְּדוֹלָה שֶׁל חֲכָמִים וְשֶׁל סוֹפְרִים אָנִי. אָמַר לִי, רַבִּי, רְצוֹנְךָ
שֶׁתָּדוּר עִמָּנוּ בִּמְקוֹמֵנוּ, וַאֲנִי אֶתֵּן לְךָ אֶלֶף אֲלָפִים דִּינְרֵי זָהָב וַאֲבָנִים
טוֹבוֹת וּמַרְגָּלִיּוֹת. אָמַרְתִּי לוֹ, אִם אַתָּה נוֹתֵן לִי כָּל כֶּסֶף וְזָהָב וַאֲבָנִים
טוֹבוֹת וּמַרְגָּלִיּוֹת שֶׁבָּעוֹלָם, אֵינִי דָר אֶלָּא בִּמְקוֹם תּוֹרָה, וְכֵן כָּתוּב בְּסֵפֶר
תְּהִלִּים עַל יְדֵי דָוִד מֶלֶךְ יִשְׂרָאֵל: טוֹב־לִי תוֹרַת־פִּיךָ מֵאַלְפֵי זָהָב וָכָסֶף: תהלים קיט
וְלֹא עוֹד, אֶלָּא שֶׁבִּשְׁעַת פְּטִירָתוֹ שֶׁל אָדָם, אֵין מְלַוִּין לוֹ לְאָדָם לֹא כֶסֶף
וְלֹא זָהָב וְלֹא אֲבָנִים טוֹבוֹת וּמַרְגָּלִיּוֹת, אֶלָּא תּוֹרָה וּמַעֲשִׂים טוֹבִים בִּלְבָד,
שֶׁנֶּאֱמַר: בְּהִתְהַלֶּכְךָ תַּנְחֶה אֹתָךְ, בְּשָׁכְבְּךָ תִּשְׁמֹר עָלֶיךָ, וַהֲקִיצוֹתָ הִיא משלי ו
תְשִׂיחֶךָ: בְּהִתְהַלֶּכְךָ תַּנְחֶה אֹתָךְ, בָּעוֹלָם הַזֶּה. בְּשָׁכְבְּךָ תִּשְׁמֹר עָלֶיךָ,
בַּקֶּבֶר. וַהֲקִיצוֹתָ הִיא תְשִׂיחֶךָ, לָעוֹלָם הַבָּא. וְאוֹמֵר: לִי הַכֶּסֶף וְלִי הַזָּהָב, חגי ב
נְאֻם יהוה צְבָאוֹת:

10. Five possessions did the Holy One, blessed be He, declare as His own in His world, and they are: the Torah, heaven and earth, Abraham, Israel and the Temple. How do we know this about the Torah? Because it is written, "The LORD created me at the beginning of His way, as the first of His works in days of old." How do we know it about heaven and earth? Because it is written, "So says the LORD: the heaven is My throne, and the earth is My footstool; what house can you build for Me, and where is the place for My rest?"; and it also says, "How numerous are Your works, LORD; You made them all in wisdom; the earth is full of Your creations." How do we know it about Abraham? Because it is written, "And He blessed him and said, Blessed be Abram of God the Most High, owner of heaven and earth." How do we know it about Israel? Because it is written, "Until Your people pass over, O LORD, until this people You acquired pass over"; and it also says, "As for the holy ones who are on earth and for the mighty, all My delight is in them." How do we know it about the Temple? Because it is written, "Your dwelling place which You, LORD, have made; the Temple, O LORD, which Your hands established"; and it also says, "He brought them to His holy realm, the mountain His right hand had acquired."

Prov. 8 · *Is. 66* · *Ps. 104* · *Gen. 14* · *Ex. 15* · *Ps. 16* · *Ex. 15* · *Ps. 78*

11. All that the Holy One, blessed be He, created in His world, He created solely for His glory, as it is said, "All that is called by My name, it is for My glory that I created it, formed it and made it"; and it also says, "The LORD shall reign for ever and ever."

Is. 43 · *Ex. 15*

Rabbi Ḥananya ben Akashya said: The Holy One, blessed be He, wanted to confer merit on Israel. That is why He gave them a copious Torah and many commandments, as it is said, "It pleased the LORD, for the sake of [Israel's] righteousness, to make the Torah great and glorious."

Makkot 23b · *Is. 42*

If there is a minyan, mourners say the Rabbis' Kaddish (page 712).

י חֲמִשָּׁה קִנְיָנִים קָנָה הַקָּדוֹשׁ בָּרוּךְ הוּא בְּעוֹלָמוֹ. וְאֵלּוּ הֵן, תּוֹרָה קִנְיָן אֶחָד,
שָׁמַיִם וָאָרֶץ קִנְיָן אֶחָד, אַבְרָהָם קִנְיָן אֶחָד, יִשְׂרָאֵל קִנְיָן אֶחָד, בֵּית הַמִּקְדָּשׁ
קִנְיָן אֶחָד. תּוֹרָה מִנַּיִן, דִּכְתִיב: יהוה קָנָנִי רֵאשִׁית דַּרְכּוֹ, קֶדֶם מִפְעָלָיו מֵאָז: משלי ח
שָׁמַיִם וָאָרֶץ מִנַּיִן, דִּכְתִיב: כֹּה אָמַר יהוה הַשָּׁמַיִם כִּסְאִי וְהָאָרֶץ הֲדֹם רַגְלָי, ישעיה סו
אֵי־זֶה בַיִת אֲשֶׁר תִּבְנוּ־לִי, וְאֵי־זֶה מָקוֹם מְנוּחָתִי: וְאוֹמֵר: מָה־רַבּוּ מַעֲשֶׂיךָ תהלים קד
יהוה, כֻּלָּם בְּחָכְמָה עָשִׂיתָ, מָלְאָה הָאָרֶץ קִנְיָנֶךָ: אַבְרָהָם מִנַּיִן, דִּכְתִיב:
וַיְבָרְכֵהוּ וַיֹּאמַר, בָּרוּךְ אַבְרָם לְאֵל עֶלְיוֹן, קֹנֵה שָׁמַיִם וָאָרֶץ: יִשְׂרָאֵל מִנַּיִן, בראשית יד
דִּכְתִיב: עַד־יַעֲבֹר עַמְּךָ יהוה, עַד־יַעֲבֹר עַם־זוּ קָנִיתָ: וְאוֹמֵר: לִקְדוֹשִׁים שמות טו תהלים טז
אֲשֶׁר־בָּאָרֶץ הֵמָּה, וְאַדִּירֵי כָּל־חֶפְצִי־בָם: בֵּית הַמִּקְדָּשׁ מִנַּיִן, דִּכְתִיב: מָכוֹן שמות טו
לְשִׁבְתְּךָ פָּעַלְתָּ יהוה, מִקְּדָשׁ אֲדֹנָי כּוֹנְנוּ יָדֶיךָ: וְאוֹמֵר: וַיְבִיאֵם אֶל־גְּבוּל תהלים עח
קָדְשׁוֹ, הַר־זֶה קָנְתָה יְמִינוֹ:

יא כָּל מַה שֶּׁבָּרָא הַקָּדוֹשׁ בָּרוּךְ הוּא בְּעוֹלָמוֹ, לֹא בְרָאוֹ אֶלָּא לִכְבוֹדוֹ,
שֶׁנֶּאֱמַר: כֹּל הַנִּקְרָא בִשְׁמִי וְלִכְבוֹדִי בְּרָאתִיו, יְצַרְתִּיו אַף־עֲשִׂיתִיו: וְאוֹמֵר: ישעיה מג
יהוה יִמְלֹךְ לְעֹלָם וָעֶד: שמות טו

רַבִּי חֲנַנְיָא בֶּן עֲקַשְׁיָא אוֹמֵר: רָצָה הַקָּדוֹשׁ בָּרוּךְ הוּא לְזַכּוֹת אֶת יִשְׂרָאֵל, לְפִיכָךְ מכות כג:
הִרְבָּה לָהֶם תּוֹרָה וּמִצְוֹת. שֶׁנֶּאֱמַר: יהוה חָפֵץ לְמַעַן צִדְקוֹ, יַגְדִּיל תּוֹרָה וְיַאְדִּיר: ישעיה מב

If there is a מנין, mourners say קדיש דרבנן (page 713).

Seuda Shelishit for Shabbat

מִזְמוֹר לְדָוִד A psalm of David. The LORD is my Shepherd, I shall not want. He makes me lie down in green pastures. He leads me beside the still waters. He refreshes my soul. He guides me in the paths of righteousness for His name's sake. Though I walk through the valley of the shadow of death, I will fear no evil, for You are with me; Your rod and Your staff, they comfort me. You set a table before me in the presence of my enemies; You anoint my head with oil; my cup is filled to overflowing. May goodness and kindness follow me all the days of my life, and may I live in the House of the LORD for evermore. Ps. 23

יְדִיד Beloved of the soul,[A] Father of compassion,
draw Your servant close to Your will.
Like a deer will Your servant run and fall prostrate before Your beauty.
To him Your love is sweeter than honey from the comb, than any taste.

הָדוּר Glorious, beautiful, radiance of the world,
my soul is sick with love for You.
Please, God, heal her now by showing her Your tender radiance.
Then she will recover her strength and be healed,
Be Your servant for eternity.

וָתִיק Ancient of Days, let Your mercy be aroused;
please have pity on Your beloved child.
How long have I yearned to see the glory of Your strength.
Please, my God, my heart's desire – hasten; do not hide Yourself.

הִגָּלֵה Reveal Yourself, beloved, and spread over me
the tabernacle of Your peace.
Let the earth shine with Your glory,
let us be overjoyed and rejoice in You.
Hurry, beloved, for the appointed time has come,
and be gracious to me as in the times of old.

---

he was declared the victor, the young man came to him to ask how it was possible that after having practiced for so long, rehearsed each word and sentence, he had nevertheless lost the competition. "It's true," said the little old man. "You knew every word and every sentence of 'The Lord is my Shepherd.' But you see, the difference is that I know the Shepherd."

Sing as if you know the Shepherd.

יְדִיד נֶפֶשׁ – *Beloved of the soul.* For commentary see page 393.

סעודה שלישית של שבת

תהלים כג
מִזְמוֹר לְדָוִד, יהוה רֹעִי לֹא אֶחְסָר: בִּנְאוֹת דֶּשֶׁא יַרְבִּיצֵנִי, עַל־מֵי מְנֻחוֹת יְנַהֲלֵנִי: נַפְשִׁי יְשׁוֹבֵב, יַנְחֵנִי בְמַעְגְּלֵי־צֶדֶק לְמַעַן שְׁמוֹ: גַּם כִּי־אֵלֵךְ בְּגֵיא צַלְמָוֶת לֹא־אִירָא רָע, כִּי־אַתָּה עִמָּדִי, שִׁבְטְךָ וּמִשְׁעַנְתֶּךָ הֵמָּה יְנַחֲמֻנִי: תַּעֲרֹךְ לְפָנַי שֻׁלְחָן נֶגֶד צֹרְרָי, דִּשַּׁנְתָּ בַשֶּׁמֶן רֹאשִׁי, כּוֹסִי רְוָיָה: אַךְ טוֹב וָחֶסֶד יִרְדְּפוּנִי כָּל־יְמֵי חַיָּי, וְשַׁבְתִּי בְּבֵית־יהוה לְאֹרֶךְ יָמִים:

יְדִיד נֶפֶשׁ,[א] אָב הָרַחֲמָן, מְשֹׁךְ עַבְדְּךָ אֶל רְצוֹנֶךָ
יָרוּץ עַבְדְּךָ כְּמוֹ אַיָּל, יִשְׁתַּחֲוֶה מוּל הֲדָרֶךָ
כִּי יֶעֱרַב לוֹ יְדִידוּתֶךָ, מִנֹּפֶת צוּף וְכָל טָעַם.

הָדוּר, נָאֶה, זִיו הָעוֹלָם, נַפְשִׁי חוֹלַת אַהֲבָתֶךָ
אָנָּא, אֵל נָא, רְפָא נָא לָהּ, בְּהַרְאוֹת לָהּ נֹעַם זִיוֶךָ
אָז תִּתְחַזֵּק וְתִתְרַפֵּא, וְהָיְתָה לָךְ שִׁפְחַת עוֹלָם.

וָתִיק, יֶהֱמוּ רַחֲמֶיךָ, וְחוּס נָא עַל בֵּן אוֹהֲבָךְ
כִּי זֶה כַּמָּה נִכְסֹף נִכְסַף לִרְאוֹת בְּתִפְאֶרֶת עֻזָּךְ
אָנָּא, אֵלִי, מַחְמַד לִבִּי, חוּשָׁה נָּא, וְאַל תִּתְעַלָּם.

הִגָּלֵה נָא וּפְרֹשׂ, חָבִיב, עָלַי אֶת סֻכַּת שְׁלוֹמָךְ
תָּאִיר אֶרֶץ מִכְּבוֹדָךְ, נָגִילָה וְנִשְׂמְחָה בָּךְ.
מַהֵר, אָהוּב, כִּי בָא מוֹעֵד, וְחָנֵּנִי כִּימֵי עוֹלָם.

ANI TEFILLA • אני תפילה

The story is told about a poetry reading contest in Britain wherein contestants were required to provide a dramatic reading of the 23rd Psalm – "The Lord is my Shepherd, I shall not lack anything." One young British contestant, a well-rehearsed orator, gave a brilliant performance filled with all of the right enunciation and intonation. He was better than any of his predecessors and it was clear to all that he would be declared the victor. Until a little old Jewish man with a European accent got up and though there were initial giggles and murmurs, his rendition of the psalm touched their hearts and some were actually moved to tears. When

אֵל מִסְתַּתֵּר God hides Himself[B] in the beauty of concealment, His wisdom opaque to all human thought; / Cause of causes, adorned with the highest crown, they [the angels] give You, LORD, a crown.

In the beginning was Your primordial Torah, inscribed with Your hermetic wisdom. Where can it be found? It is hidden. Wisdom begins in awe of the LORD.

Wider than a river, like never-ending streams, deep waters, that only an understanding man can draw, / its outcomes are the fifty gates of understanding. The faithful are guarded by the LORD.

Great God, all eyes are turned toward You. Your great kindness is higher than the heavens. / God of Abraham, remember Your servant, I will tell of the LORD's kindness, sing praises to the LORD.

Sublime, majestic in strength and might, who brings forth unparalleled light, "Awe of Isaac," make our judgment light. Forever, LORD, is Your might.

Who is like You, God, doing great deeds, Mighty One of Jacob, awesome in praise, Splendor of Israel, who listens to prayers, LORD who listens to those in need.

God, may the merit of the fathers be our shield. Eternal One of Israel, redeem us from distress. / Draw us, raise us, from the pit of exile, that we may loudly sing in service at the House of the LORD.

From right and left the prophets were inspired, finding within them Eternity and Glory, / known by the names of Yakhin and Boaz, and all your children shall be learned of the LORD.

Foundation, the Righteous, is hidden in Seven, the sign of the covenant to the world. Source of blessing, Righteous, Foundation of the world, righteous are You, LORD.

Restore, please, David and Solomon's kingdom, with the crown with which his mother crowned it. / The congregation of Israel is sweetly called a bride, a crown of splendor in the hand of the LORD.

Mighty One, unite the ten Sefirot as one. Those who divide them from the LORD will see no light. / Together they shine like sapphire. Bring my song close to You, the LORD.

Birkat HaMazon can be found on page 976.

Moshe Cordevero, a central figure in the development of the Kabbala in Tzefat in the sixteenth century. Each of the first ten stanzas is based on one of the mystical *sefirot*, the divine emanations or attributes through which Hashem is revealed.

אֵל מִסְתַּתֵּר[ב] בְּשַׁפְרִיר חֶבְיוֹן, הַשֵּׂכֶל הַנֶּעְלָם מִכָּל רַעְיוֹן
עִלַּת הָעִלּוֹת מְכֻתָּר בְּכֶתֶר עֶלְיוֹן, כֶּתֶר יִתְּנוּ לְךָ יהוה.

בְּרֵאשִׁית תּוֹרָתְךָ הַקְּדוּמָה, רְשׁוּמָה חָכְמָתְךָ הַסְּתוּמָה
מֵאַיִן תִּמָּצֵא וְהִיא נֶעְלָמָה, רֵאשִׁית חָכְמָה יִרְאַת יהוה.

רְחוֹבוֹת הַנָּהָר נַחֲלֵי אֱמוּנָה, מַיִם עֲמֻקִּים יִדְלֵם אִישׁ תְּבוּנָה
תּוֹצְאוֹתֶיהָ חֲמִשִּׁים שַׁעֲרֵי בִינָה, אֱמוּנִים נוֹצֵר יהוה.

הָאֵל הַגָּדוֹל עֵינֵי כֹל נֶגְדֶּךָ, רַב חֶסֶד גָּדוֹל עַל הַשָּׁמַיִם חַסְדֶּךָ
אֱלֹהֵי אַבְרָהָם זְכֹר לְעַבְדֶּךָ, חַסְדֵי יהוה אַזְכִּיר תְּהִלּוֹת יהוה.

מָרוֹם נֶאְדָּר בְּכֹחַ וּגְבוּרָה, מוֹצִיא אוֹרָה מֵאֵין תְּמוּרָה
פַּחַד יִצְחָק מִשְׁפָּטֵנוּ הָאִירָה, אַתָּה גִּבּוֹר לְעוֹלָם יהוה.

מִי אֵל כָּמוֹךָ עוֹשֶׂה גְדוֹלוֹת, אֲבִיר יַעֲקֹב נוֹרָא תְהִלּוֹת
תִּפְאֶרֶת יִשְׂרָאֵל שׁוֹמֵעַ תְּפִלּוֹת, כִּי שׁוֹמֵעַ אֶל אֶבְיוֹנִים יהוה.

יָהּ, זְכוּת אָבוֹת יָגֵן עָלֵינוּ, נֵצַח יִשְׂרָאֵל, מִצָּרוֹתֵינוּ גְּאָלֵנוּ
וּמִבּוֹר גָּלוּת דְּלֵנוּ וְהַעֲלֵנוּ, לְנַצֵּחַ עַל מְלֶאכֶת בֵּית יהוה.

מִיָּמִין וּמִשְּׂמֹאל יְנִיקַת הַנְּבִיאִים, נֵצַח וָהוֹד מֵהֶם נִמְצָאִים
יָכִין וּבֹעַז בְּשֵׁם נִקְרָאִים, וְכָל בָּנַיִךְ לִמּוּדֵי יהוה.

יְסוֹד צַדִּיק בְּשִׁבְעָה נֶעְלָם, אוֹת בְּרִית הוּא לְעוֹלָם
מַעְיַן הַבְּרָכָה צַדִּיק יְסוֹד עוֹלָם, צַדִּיק אַתָּה יהוה.

נָא הָקֵם מַלְכוּת דָּוִד וּשְׁלֹמֹה, בָּעֲטָרָה שֶׁעִטְּרָה לוֹ אִמּוֹ
כְּנֶסֶת יִשְׂרָאֵל כַּלָּה קְרוּאָה בִּנְעִימָה, עֲטֶרֶת תִּפְאֶרֶת בְּיַד יהוה.

חָזָק מְיַחֵד כְּאֶחָד עֶשֶׂר סְפִירוֹת, וּמַפְרִיד אַלּוּף לֹא יִרְאֶה מְאוֹרוֹת
סַפִּיר גִּזְרָתָם יַחַד מְאִירוֹת, תִּקְרַב רִנָּתִי לְפָנֶיךָ יהוה.

ברכת המזון *can be found on page 977.*

BIUR TEFILLA • ביאור תפילה

אֵל מִסְתַּתֵּר – *God hides Himself.* The poem was written by Avraham Maimin, as indicated by the first letter of each stanza which spells his name. He was a student of Rabbi

ימים מיוחדים

SPECIAL DAYS

Hallel

On Rosh Hodesh Half Hallel is said. See laws 161–162.

בָּרוּךְ Blessed are You, LORD our God, King of the Universe,
who has made us holy through His commandments
and has commanded us to recite the Hallel.

הַלְלוּיָהּ Halleluya! Servants of the LORD,[A] give praise; praise the name Ps. 113
of the LORD. Blessed be the name of the LORD now and for evermore.
From the rising of the sun to its setting, may the LORD's name be
praised. High is the LORD above all nations; His glory is above the

---

new month as a new start, filled with hope for emerging from the limitations that may hold us back, and with the promise that Hashem is ever-present to help us out.

What are your hopes for the coming month?

HILKHOT TEFILLA • הלכות תפילה

Each holiday has its own historical derivation and halakhic status, and this helps determine how much of Hallel is required. The core consists of six successive chapters of *Tehillim* (113–118) with a blessing at the beginning and at the end. Sometimes, the first parts of some of those chapters are omitted, resulting in two versions referred to as "Full Hallel" and "Half/Skipped Hallel." Full Hallel is generally recited for events of great national import, such as Pesah, Shavuot, Sukkot and Hanukka, and, by the decree of the Chief Rabbinate of Israel, on Yom HaAtzma'ut and Yom Yerushalayim as well. Similarly, the shortened version is recited on Rosh Hodesh which, while not a holiday in the classic sense, was nevertheless commemorated with the celebration of seeing the new moon.

ANI TEFILLA • אני תפילה

הַלְלוּיָהּ הַלְלוּ עַבְדֵי יהוה – *Halleluya! Servants of the LORD, give praise.* The first three verses speak of Hashem's presence in time – for eternity and in a single day.

The middle three verses speak of Hashem's presence in space – in the universe, and on earth.

The last three verses, speak of Hashem's presence in the lives of man – helping the poor and the childless.

Where can you feel Hashem's presence most today?

סדר הלל

On ראש חודש, הלל בדילוג *is said. See laws 161–162.*

בָּרוּךְ אַתָּה יהוה אֱלֹהֵינוּ מֶלֶךְ הָעוֹלָם
אֲשֶׁר קִדְּשָׁנוּ בְּמִצְוֹתָיו וְצִוָּנוּ לִקְרֹא אֶת הַהַלֵּל.

הַלְלוּיָהּ, הַלְלוּ עַבְדֵי יהוה,א הַלְלוּ אֶת־שֵׁם יהוה: יְהִי שֵׁם תהלים קיג
יהוה מְבֹרָךְ, מֵעַתָּה וְעַד־עוֹלָם: מִמִּזְרַח־שֶׁמֶשׁ עַד־מְבוֹאוֹ,
מְהֻלָּל שֵׁם יהוה: רָם עַל־כָּל־גּוֹיִם יהוה, עַל הַשָּׁמַיִם כְּבוֹדוֹ: מִי

AN INTRODUCTION TO HALLEL

The Talmud (*Pesaḥim* 117a) brings a number of opinions regarding the ancient roots of Hallel. There are those who suggest that it was recited by Moshe and *Benei Yisrael* at the splitting of the Sea, by Yehoshua and *Benei Yisrael* when faced by the kings of Canaan, and by Mordekhai and Esther when they were facing Haman, to name but three occasions. In short, say the sages, it was to be said whenever the Jewish people were redeemed from some potential calamity. In Rabbinic literature it is called *Hallel Mitzri*, or the Egyptian Hallel, based upon the reference in the second paragraph to the exodus from Egypt. The prayer marks our deliverance, often by seemingly supernatural means, throughout our history. "That is why we say it on Yom HaAtzma'ut and Yom Yerushalayim, the two most transformative events of modern Jewish history, in the faith that it is not human beings alone who shape the destiny of our people, but God working in and through His children" (Rabbi J. Sacks). In Hallel, we praise God's presence in world events, past and present.

Rosh Ḥodesh is not that exact same kind of holy day. Rather, Rosh Ḥodesh marks the beginning of a new month. Recall that the very first commandment that the Israelites were given in Egypt was to sanctify the new moon (*Shemot* 12:1), in effect to enable the measurement and marking of time, and establish the calendar. Each new month is thus not only a natural astrological event, but a psychological and theological one as well. On a national level, the fate of the Jewish people has been compared to the waxing and waning of the moon, from periods of darkness to periods when it fills the world with its reflected light. On a personal level, Rosh Ḥodesh represents a new beginning, one that is filled with optimism about the opportunities for growth and personal enlightenment. As such, we celebrate every

heavens. Who is like the LORD our God, who sits enthroned so high, yet turns so low to see the heavens and the earth? ▸ He raises the poor from the dust and the needy from the refuse heap, giving them a place alongside princes, the princes of His people. He makes the woman in a childless house a happy mother of children. Halleluya!

בְּצֵאת When Israel came out[I] of Egypt, the house of Jacob from a people of foreign tongue, Judah became His sanctuary, Israel His dominion. The sea saw and fled; the Jordan turned back. The mountains skipped like rams, the hills like lambs. ▸ Why was it, sea, that you fled? Jordan, why did you turn back? Why, mountains, did you skip like rams, and you, hills, like lambs? It was at the presence of the LORD, Creator of the earth, at the presence of the God of Jacob, who turned the rock into a pool of water, flint into a flowing spring. Ps. 114

יהוה זְכָרָנוּ The LORD remembers us and will bless us. He will bless the house of Israel. He will bless the house of Aaron. He will bless those who fear the LORD, small and great alike. May the LORD give you increase: you and your children. May you be blessed by the LORD, Maker of heaven and earth. ▸ The heavens are the LORD's, but the earth He has given over to mankind.[B] It is not the dead who praise the LORD,[A] nor those who go down to the silent grave. But we will bless the LORD, now and for ever. Halleluya!

BIUR TEFILLA • ביאור תפילה

וְהָאָרֶץ נָתַן לִבְנֵי־אָדָם – *But the earth He has given over to mankind.* "He gave the earth to man," not as a present but as a trust to be guarded and protected. Hashem gave the planet to mankind, not to be used and abused, but to be developed and nurtured. The Torah gives us the earth as a resource for our use (*Bereshit* 1:28), but also with the responsibility to protect and conserve it (ibid. 2:15). Our challenge is to find the appropriate balance between these two (Rabbi J.B. Soloveitchik).

ANI TEFILLA • אני תפילה

לֹא הַמֵּתִים יְהַלְלוּ־יָהּ – *It is not the dead who praise the LORD.* True, life can be filled with tragedy, and the existence of death, natural as it may be, is still a reason for sadness. Yet knowing that such things exist should also be a reminder that every day presents a new opportunity to praise and thank Hashem for life, and for the things that we have. Even if one has a day when one might feel "down" and want to be in "silence," we

This **ANI TEFILLA** *continues on page 847.*

כַּיהוה אֱלֹהֵינוּ, הַמַּגְבִּיהִי לָשָׁבֶת: הַמַּשְׁפִּילִי לִרְאוֹת, בַּשָּׁמַיִם וּבָאָרֶץ: ‹ מְקִימִי מֵעָפָר דָּל, מֵאַשְׁפֹּת יָרִים אֶבְיוֹן: לְהוֹשִׁיבִי עִם־נְדִיבִים, עִם נְדִיבֵי עַמּוֹ: מוֹשִׁיבִי עֲקֶרֶת הַבַּיִת, אֵם־הַבָּנִים שְׂמֵחָה, הַלְלוּיָהּ:

תהלים קיד בְּצֵאת יִשְׂרָאֵל[ע] מִמִּצְרָיִם, בֵּית יַעֲקֹב מֵעַם לֹעֵז: הָיְתָה יְהוּדָה לְקָדְשׁוֹ, יִשְׂרָאֵל מַמְשְׁלוֹתָיו: הַיָּם רָאָה וַיָּנֹס, הַיַּרְדֵּן יִסֹּב לְאָחוֹר: הֶהָרִים רָקְדוּ כְאֵילִים, גְּבָעוֹת כִּבְנֵי־צֹאן: ‹ מַה־לְּךָ הַיָּם כִּי תָנוּס, הַיַּרְדֵּן תִּסֹּב לְאָחוֹר: הֶהָרִים תִּרְקְדוּ כְאֵילִים, גְּבָעוֹת כִּבְנֵי־צֹאן: מִלִּפְנֵי אָדוֹן חוּלִי אָרֶץ, מִלִּפְנֵי אֱלוֹהַּ יַעֲקֹב: הַהֹפְכִי הַצּוּר אֲגַם־מָיִם, חַלָּמִישׁ לְמַעְיְנוֹ־מָיִם:

יהוה זְכָרָנוּ יְבָרֵךְ, יְבָרֵךְ אֶת־בֵּית יִשְׂרָאֵל, יְבָרֵךְ אֶת־בֵּית אַהֲרֹן: יְבָרֵךְ יִרְאֵי יהוה, הַקְּטַנִּים עִם־הַגְּדֹלִים: יֹסֵף יהוה עֲלֵיכֶם, עֲלֵיכֶם וְעַל־בְּנֵיכֶם: בְּרוּכִים אַתֶּם לַיהוה, עֹשֵׂה שָׁמַיִם וָאָרֶץ: ‹ הַשָּׁמַיִם שָׁמַיִם לַיהוה, וְהָאָרֶץ נָתַן לִבְנֵי־אָדָם:[ב] לֹא הַמֵּתִים יְהַלְלוּ־יָהּ,[א] וְלֹא כָּל־יֹרְדֵי דוּמָה: וַאֲנַחְנוּ נְבָרֵךְ יָהּ, מֵעַתָּה וְעַד־עוֹלָם, הַלְלוּיָהּ:

IYUN TEFILLA • עיון תפילה

בְּצֵאת יִשְׂרָאֵל – *When Israel came out.* Hashem is Master both of nature and of human history. No sooner is Israel freed from Egypt, than the entire natural world responds. The "sea saw and fled" by splitting for the Israelites; similarly "the Jordan [River] turned back" when they crossed over into the Promised Land. The natural world is thus a partner in the historical process. The inanimate world of seas and rivers, mountains and hills, comes alive when seen as part of the continuum of history, at least forty years of which is compressed here into one unified vision.

Have you ever felt in sync with nature? Imagine the whole world that way.

מָה־אָשִׁיב How can I repay the LORD[A] for all His goodness to me? I will lift the cup of salvation and call on the name of the LORD. I will fulfill my vows to the LORD in the presence of all His people. Grievous in the LORD's sight is the death of His devoted ones. Truly, LORD, I am Your servant;[IA] I am Your servant, the son of Your maidservant. You set me free from my chains. ▸ To You I shall bring a thanksgiving-offering and call on the LORD by name. I will fulfill my vows to the LORD in the presence of all His people, in the courts of the House of the LORD, in your midst, Jerusalem. Halleluya!

הַלְלוּ Praise the LORD,[I] all nations; acclaim Him, all you peoples; Ps. 117
for His loving-kindness to us is strong,
and the LORD's faithfulness is everlasting.
Halleluya!

---

that he had followed the Rebbe's advice but to no avail. The Rebbe asked him, "Which Ana Hashem did you recite?" The Hasid answered, "Ana Hashem hoshia na" ("Hashem, please, save us" [see page 853]) *The Rebbe responded, "No, you misunderstood. I wasn't referring to that phrase but to the one which says "Ana Hashem ki ani avdekha" (Please Hashem, for I am Your servant). First one must commit oneself to the King's service; only then can one presume to call on Him for help.*

IYUN TEFILLA · עיון תפילה

הַלְלוּ אֶת־יהוה – *Praise the LORD.*

The shortest of all of the psalms, a mere two verses. The psalmist speaks of the universal significance of Israel's history. It is not Israel alone, but all the nations, who will see in the story of this people, something beyond mere history. "The Jew is the emblem of eternity. He whom neither slaughter nor torture of thousands of years could destroy, he whom neither fire nor sword nor inquisition was able to wipe off the face of the earth, he who was the first to produce the oracles of God, who has been for so long the guardian of prophecy and transmitted it to the rest of the world – such a nation cannot be destroyed. The Jew is everlasting as eternity itself" (Tolstoy). (Rabbi J. Sacks)

Sometimes non-Jews see the miracle of our survival more clearly than we ourselves do (*Pesaḥim* 118b and Rashi).

מָה־אָשִׁיב לַיהוה,[א] כׇּל־תַּגְמוּלוֹהִי עָלָי: כּוֹס־יְשׁוּעוֹת אֶשָּׂא,
וּבְשֵׁם יהוה אֶקְרָא: נְדָרַי לַיהוה אֲשַׁלֵּם, נֶגְדָה־נָּא לְכׇל־עַמּוֹ:
יָקָר בְּעֵינֵי יהוה, הַמָּוְתָה לַחֲסִידָיו: אָנָּה יהוה כִּי־אֲנִי עַבְדֶּךָ,[עא]
אֲנִי־עַבְדְּךָ בֶּן־אֲמָתֶךָ, פִּתַּחְתָּ לְמוֹסֵרָי: · לְךָ־אֶזְבַּח זֶבַח תּוֹדָה,
וּבְשֵׁם יהוה אֶקְרָא: נְדָרַי לַיהוה אֲשַׁלֵּם, נֶגְדָה־נָּא לְכׇל־עַמּוֹ:
בְּחַצְרוֹת בֵּית יהוה, בְּתוֹכֵכִי יְרוּשָׁלָםִ, הַלְלוּיָהּ:

הַלְלוּ אֶת־יהוה[ע] כׇּל־גּוֹיִם, שַׁבְּחוּהוּ כׇּל־הָאֻמִּים: תהלים קיז
כִּי גָבַר עָלֵינוּ חַסְדּוֹ, וֶאֱמֶת־יהוה לְעוֹלָם
הַלְלוּיָהּ:

---

are reminded that life in its totality is indeed beautiful and worth singing about.

Look around you now. What can you see that is life affirming?

ANI TEFILLA · אני תפילה

מָה־אָשִׁיב לַיהוה – *How can I repay the* Lord. How can I possibly thank Hashem for everything I have? The answer: I can't. For no matter how difficult daily circumstances may be, I still have my life, which Judaism maintains is a supreme gift. The good always, always, outweighs the bad.

IYUN TEFILLA · עיון תפילה

אָנָּה יהוה כִּי־אֲנִי עַבְדֶּךָ – *Truly,* Lord, *I am Your servant.* I have come to serve You from two directions. First, I am Your servant; I try to do my best on my own, finding my own faith and my own way. Second, I am a product of my mother, whose traditions and teachings shaped me in becoming a Jew. I am thus a servant in my own right and the child of a servant (Radak). Both of those free me from (physical, social, intellectual or spiritual) chains that would otherwise tie me down. For that I am thankful.

ANI TEFILLA · אני תפילה

אָנָּה יְהוָה כִּי־אֲנִי עַבְדֶּךָ – *Truly,* Lord, *I am Your servant.*
A Hasid came to his Rebbe and asked for direction about how he might get help from Hashem. The Rebbe advised him to say the phrase that begins with the words "Ana Hashem" with all of his strength and devotion. The Hasid returned one day and complained

The following verses are chanted by the Leader. At the end of each verse, the congregation responds, "Thank the Lord for He is good; His loving-kindness is for ever."

הודו Thank the Lord for He is good;[B]	His loving-kindness is for ever.	Ps. 118
Let Israel say	His loving-kindness is for ever.	
Let the house of Aaron say	His loving-kindness is for ever.	
Let those who fear the Lord say	His loving-kindness is for ever.	

מִן־הַמֵּצַר In my distress I called on the Lord.[A] The Lord answered me and set me free. The Lord is with me; I will not be afraid. What can man do to me? The Lord is with me. He is my Helper. I will see the downfall of my enemies. It is better to take refuge in the Lord than to trust in man. It is better to take refuge in the Lord than to trust in princes. The nations all surrounded me, but in the Lord's name I drove them off. They surrounded me on every side, but in the Lord's name I drove them off. They surrounded me like bees,[A] they attacked me as fire attacks brushwood, but in the Lord's name I drove them off. They thrust so hard against me, I nearly fell, but the Lord came to my help. The Lord is my strength and my song; He has become

ANI TEFILLA • אני תפילה

מִן־הַמֵּצַר קָרָאתִי יָּהּ – *In my distress I called on the Lord.*

There were times when I thought my world was crashing around me, when I could not understand why this was happening to me, to my family, to people that I cared about. At those moments, I took strength from the belief that there must be a bigger plan, that Hashem had something in mind that I just couldn't see right now. That belief doesn't always take away the pain of the moment, but it gives one enough perspective to take it in stride and to move on with a sense of optimism. Though I sometimes find myself confined in narrow "straits" (metzar), my knowing that Hashem is there enables me to realize that there is a bigger, more "expansive" (merḥav) picture.

סַבּוּנִי כִדְבֹרִים – *They surrounded me like bees.*

Sometimes those who attack us appear as a forest fire that burns the brush all around us; we see them coming but cannot get out of the way. Sometimes they appear as bees, attractive in color, full of life, bearing sweet honey for us, but if we let our guard down they sting us and quickly move off. Either way, my faith provides me with perspective that makes me strong and resilient.

The following verses are chanted by the שליח ציבור.
At the end of each verse, the קהל *responds:* הוֹדוּ לַיהוה כִּי־טוֹב, כִּי לְעוֹלָם חַסְדּוֹ.

הוֹדוּ לַיהוה כִּי־טוֹב[ב] כִּי לְעוֹלָם חַסְדּוֹ: תהלים קיח
יֹאמַר־נָא יִשְׂרָאֵל כִּי לְעוֹלָם חַסְדּוֹ:
יֹאמְרוּ־נָא בֵית־אַהֲרֹן כִּי לְעוֹלָם חַסְדּוֹ:
יֹאמְרוּ־נָא יִרְאֵי יהוה כִּי לְעוֹלָם חַסְדּוֹ:

מִן־הַמֵּצַר קָרָֽאתִי יָּהּ,[א] עָנָֽנִי בַמֶּרְחָב יָהּ: יהוה לִי לֹא אִירָא,
מַה־יַּעֲשֶׂה לִי אָדָם: יהוה לִי בְּעֹזְרָי, וַאֲנִי אֶרְאֶה בְשֹׂנְאָי: טוֹב
לַחֲסוֹת בַּיהוה, מִבְּטֹחַ בָּאָדָם: טוֹב לַחֲסוֹת בַּיהוה, מִבְּטֹחַ
בִּנְדִיבִים: כָּל־גּוֹיִם סְבָבֽוּנִי, בְּשֵׁם יהוה כִּי אֲמִילַם: סַבּֽוּנִי גַם־
סְבָבֽוּנִי, בְּשֵׁם יהוה כִּי אֲמִילַם: סַבּֽוּנִי כִדְבֹרִים,[א] דֹּעֲכוּ כְּאֵשׁ
קוֹצִים, בְּשֵׁם יהוה כִּי אֲמִילַם: דָּחֹה דְחִיתַֽנִי לִנְפֹּל, וַיהוה עֲזָרָֽנִי:

BIUR TEFILLA · ביאור תפילה

הוֹדוּ לַיהוה כִּי־טוֹב – *Thank the Lord for He is good.* The word *hodu* (thank) is related to the name Yehuda, whose mother, Leah, named him thus because she "thanked God" for his birth (*Bereshit* 29:35). The name "Jew" or "*Yehudi*" also comes from the name Yehuda (Judah). The implication is clear: to be a Jew means to be thankful.

הוֹדוּ לַיהוה כִּי־טוֹב – *Thank the Lord for He is good.* The last three of the groups mentioned here are the ones (referred to in Psalm 115 above) who were called upon to have faith that Hashem would protect and help them. It has been suggested that here there are four groups, the first being all of mankind, and that there is a closeness-to-God hierarchy of sorts from one group to the next (Rashbam). The greater the constant sense that everything comes from God, the more one knows that everything is a gift, the more one knows how fortunate one really is, the more thankful one can be.

How fortunate do you feel today? Give thanks.

הוֹדוּ לַיהוה כִּי־טוֹב – *Thank the Lord for He is good.* There are two possibilities for what "good" describes. One could be: "Thank God because He is good." Alternatively, "Thank God because all is good" (Ibn Ezra). The two are separate but certainly related. Have one or both in mind.

my salvation. Sounds of song and salvation resound in the tents of the righteous: "The LORD's right hand has done mighty deeds. The LORD's right hand is lifted high. The LORD's right hand has done mighty deeds." I will not die but live, and tell what the LORD has done. The LORD has chastened me severely, but He has not given me over to death. ▸ Open for me the gates of righteousness that I may enter them and thank the LORD. This is the gateway to the LORD; through it, the righteous shall enter.

אוֹדְךָ I will thank You, for You answered me,[B]
and became my salvation.
I will thank You, for You answered me,
and became my salvation.

The stone the builders rejected[I]
has become the main cornerstone.
The stone the builders rejected
has become the main cornerstone.

This is the LORD's doing; it is wondrous in our eyes.
This is the LORD's doing; it is wondrous in our eyes.

This is the day the LORD has made;
let us rejoice and be glad in it.
This is the day the LORD has made;
let us rejoice and be glad in it.

IYUN TEFILLA · עיון תפילה

אֶבֶן מָאֲסוּ הַבּוֹנִים – *The stone the builders rejected.* There are those who say that the "foundation stone rejected by the builders" is a reference to King David himself who, before he was anointed, was essentially misunderstood by his family, not unlike the way that Yosef was misunderstood by his brothers. David wasn't even considered to be a candidate for leadership. Nevertheless, he went on to become the cornerstone of Jewish sovereignty. One day a shepherd, the next a king of Israel (*Da'at Soferim*). We ignore the strengths of those around us just as we ourselves are sometimes ignored. But Hashem is aware of the potential in each of us, and for that I give thanks.

עָזִּי וְזִמְרָת יָהּ, וַיְהִי־לִי לִישׁוּעָה: קוֹל רִנָּה וִישׁוּעָה בְּאָהֳלֵי צַדִּיקִים, יְמִין יהוה עֹשָׂה חָיִל: יְמִין יהוה רוֹמֵמָה, יְמִין יהוה עֹשָׂה חָיִל: לֹא־אָמוּת כִּי־אֶחְיֶה, וַאֲסַפֵּר מַעֲשֵׂי יָהּ: יַסֹּר יִסְּרַנִּי יָּהּ, וְלַמָּוֶת לֹא נְתָנָנִי: › פִּתְחוּ־לִי שַׁעֲרֵי־צֶדֶק, אָבֹא־בָם אוֹדֶה יָהּ: זֶה־הַשַּׁעַר לַיהוה, צַדִּיקִים יָבֹאוּ בוֹ:

אוֹדְךָ כִּי עֲנִיתָנִי,ב וַתְּהִי־לִי לִישׁוּעָה:
אוֹדְךָ כִּי עֲנִיתָנִי, וַתְּהִי־לִי לִישׁוּעָה:

אֶבֶן מָאֲסוּ הַבּוֹנִים,ע הָיְתָה לְרֹאשׁ פִּנָּה:
אֶבֶן מָאֲסוּ הַבּוֹנִים, הָיְתָה לְרֹאשׁ פִּנָּה:

מֵאֵת יהוה הָיְתָה זֹּאת, הִיא נִפְלָאת בְּעֵינֵינוּ:
מֵאֵת יהוה הָיְתָה זֹּאת, הִיא נִפְלָאת בְּעֵינֵינוּ:

זֶה־הַיּוֹם עָשָׂה יהוה, נָגִילָה וְנִשְׂמְחָה בוֹ:
זֶה־הַיּוֹם עָשָׂה יהוה, נָגִילָה וְנִשְׂמְחָה בוֹ:

BIUR TEFILLA • ביאור תפילה

אוֹדְךָ כִּי עֲנִיתָנִי – *I will thank You, for You answered me.* Although the following nine verses are part of the same preceding Psalm 118, they are treated differently in that each one of them is repeated. This is because, when looking at the structure of the entire psalm, one notices that all of the verses are coupled, in that the theme or language of one is repeated, in one form or another, in the following verse. That is not the case, however, in these nine verses, each of which stands alone according to many commentators. And so it was decided that, in keeping with the rhythm, tone and theme of the psalm as a whole, each of these verses should be repeated in order to maintain the pattern (Rashi, *Sukka* 38a). The Gemara (*Pesaḥim* 119a) relates that there is also a conversational quality about these verses that lends itself to responsive reading or singing, as may have been done in the *Beit HaMikdash*.

Leader followed by congregation:

אָנָּא LORD, please, save us.[B]
LORD, please, save us.
LORD, please, grant us success.
LORD, please, grant us success.

בָּרוּךְ Blessed is one who comes in the name of the LORD;[I]
we bless you from the House of the LORD.
Blessed is one who comes in the name of the LORD;
we bless you from the House of the LORD.

The LORD is God; He has given us light. Bind the festival offering with thick cords [and bring it] to the horns of the altar.
The LORD is God; He has given us light. Bind the festival offering with thick cords [and bring it] to the horns of the altar.

You are my God and I will thank You; You are my God, I will exalt You.
You are my God and I will thank You; You are my God, I will exalt You.

Thank the LORD for He is good; His loving-kindness is for ever.[A]
Thank the LORD for He is good; His loving-kindness is for ever.

יְהַלְלוּךָ All Your works will praise You, LORD our God, and Your devoted ones – the righteous who do Your will, together with all Your people the house of Israel – will joyously thank, bless, praise, glorify, exalt, revere, sanctify, and proclaim the sovereignty of Your name, our King. ▸ For it is good to thank You and fitting to sing psalms to Your name, for from eternity to eternity You are God. Blessed are You, LORD, King who is extolled with praises.

On Rosh Ḥodesh the service continues with Full Kaddish on page 630 .

IYUN TEFILLA • עיון תפילה

בָּרוּךְ הַבָּא בְּשֵׁם יהוה – *Blessed is one who comes in the name of the LORD.* The blessing is given to those who show up. One cannot expect blessings if one does not first do one's part (*Me'am Loez*).

ANI TEFILLA • אני תפילה

הוֹדוּ לַיהוה כִּי־טוֹב, כִּי לְעוֹלָם חַסְדּוֹ – *Thank the LORD for He is good; His loving-kindness is for ever.* The chapter ends with the exact same phrase with which it began but, hopefully, we can now say it with added meaning.

קהל *followed by* שליח ציבור:

אָנָּא יהוה הוֹשִׁיעָה נָּא:[ב]

אָנָּא יהוה הוֹשִׁיעָה נָּא:

אָנָּא יהוה הַצְלִיחָה נָא:

אָנָּא יהוה הַצְלִיחָה נָא:

בָּרוּךְ הַבָּא בְּשֵׁם יהוה,[ע] **בֵּרַכְנוּכֶם מִבֵּית יהוה:**
בָּרוּךְ הַבָּא בְּשֵׁם יהוה, בֵּרַכְנוּכֶם מִבֵּית יהוה:

אֵל יהוה וַיָּאֶר לָנוּ, אִסְרוּ־חַג בַּעֲבֹתִים עַד־קַרְנוֹת הַמִּזְבֵּחַ:
אֵל יהוה וַיָּאֶר לָנוּ, אִסְרוּ־חַג בַּעֲבֹתִים עַד־קַרְנוֹת הַמִּזְבֵּחַ:

אֵלִי אַתָּה וְאוֹדֶךָּ, אֱלֹהַי אֲרוֹמְמֶךָּ:
אֵלִי אַתָּה וְאוֹדֶךָּ, אֱלֹהַי אֲרוֹמְמֶךָּ:

הוֹדוּ לַיהוה כִּי־טוֹב,[א] **כִּי לְעוֹלָם חַסְדּוֹ:**
הוֹדוּ לַיהוה כִּי־טוֹב, כִּי לְעוֹלָם חַסְדּוֹ:

יְהַלְלוּךָ יהוה אֱלֹהֵינוּ כָּל מַעֲשֶׂיךָ, וַחֲסִידֶיךָ צַדִּיקִים עוֹשֵׂי רְצוֹנֶךָ, וְכָל עַמְּךָ בֵּית יִשְׂרָאֵל בְּרִנָּה יוֹדוּ וִיבָרְכוּ וִישַׁבְּחוּ וִיפָאֲרוּ וִירוֹמְמוּ וְיַעֲרִיצוּ וְיַקְדִּישׁוּ וְיַמְלִיכוּ אֶת שִׁמְךָ מַלְכֵּנוּ, • כִּי לְךָ טוֹב לְהוֹדוֹת וּלְשִׁמְךָ נָאֶה לְזַמֵּר, כִּי מֵעוֹלָם וְעַד עוֹלָם אַתָּה אֵל. בָּרוּךְ אַתָּה יהוה, מֶלֶךְ מְהֻלָּל בַּתִּשְׁבָּחוֹת.

On ראש חודש *the service continues with* קדיש שלם *on page 631.*

BIUR TEFILLA • ביאור תפילה

אָנָּא יהוה הוֹשִׁיעָה נָּא – *Lord, please, save us. Yeshua* refers to being freed from things which constrict us (Malbim) or, alternatively, it could be a reference to the personal happiness associated with being alive (Rabbi S.R. Hirsch).

Hatzlaḥa, on the other hand, refers to success in our endeavors. Help from above, however, only comes about if we put in the effort to begin with.

Which speaks to you more today?

Musaf for Rosh Hodesh

THE AMIDA

The following prayer, until "in former years" on page 868, is said silently, standing with feet together. If there is a minyan, the Amida is repeated aloud by the Leader. Take three steps forward and at the points indicated by ▾, bend the knees at the first word, bow at the second, and stand straight before saying God's name.

When I proclaim the LORD's name, give glory to our God. *Deut. 32*
O LORD, open my lips, so that my mouth may declare Your praise. *Ps. 51*

PATRIARCHS

▾בָּרוּךְ▾ Blessed are You, LORD our God and God of our fathers,
God of Abraham, God of Isaac and God of Jacob;
the great, mighty and awesome God, God Most High,
who bestows acts of loving-kindness and creates all,
who remembers the loving-kindness of the fathers and will bring
a Redeemer to their children's children
for the sake of His name, in love.
King, Helper, Savior, Shield:
▾Blessed are You, LORD, Shield of Abraham.

DIVINE MIGHT

אַתָּה גִּבּוֹר You are eternally mighty, LORD.
You give life to the dead and have great power to save.

---

to be declared by man and not by nature. It is about man finding the moon, not about the moon finding man.

Why should this be so? Perhaps because the feeling of renewal does not happen by itself. It is up to us to start anew, it is up to us to see old things in a new light.

> Each time the moon finds the sun again, each time it receives its rays of light afresh, God wants His people to find Him again, to be illuminated with fresh rays of His light, wherever and however, in running their course, they have had to pass through periods of darkness and obscurity. (Rabbi S.R. Hirsch)

Noticing the fresh birth of the new moon is supposed to induce within each of us a similar rejuvenation. When Israel was in Egypt, they were slaves who had no sense of time, since each day was virtually identical to the next: boring, mundane, and wearying. Hence, the very first mitzva we are given as a people is time-consciousness, the ability to master time by the way we mark it and live it.

מוסף לראש חודש

עמידה

The following prayer, until קַדְמֹנִיּוֹת *on page 869, is said silently, standing with feet together. If there is a* מנין, *the* עמידה *is repeated aloud by the* שליח ציבור. *Take three steps forward and at the points indicated by* ׳, *bend the knees at the first word, bow at the second, and stand straight before saying God's name.*

דברים לב כִּי שֵׁם יהוה אֶקְרָא, הָבוּ גֹדֶל לֵאלֹהֵינוּ:
תהלים נא אֲדֹנָי, שְׂפָתַי תִּפְתָּח, וּפִי יַגִּיד תְּהִלָּתֶךָ:

אבות

׳בָּרוּךְ אַתָּה יהוה, אֱלֹהֵינוּ וֵאלֹהֵי אֲבוֹתֵינוּ
אֱלֹהֵי אַבְרָהָם, אֱלֹהֵי יִצְחָק, וֵאלֹהֵי יַעֲקֹב
הָאֵל הַגָּדוֹל הַגִּבּוֹר וְהַנּוֹרָא, אֵל עֶלְיוֹן
גּוֹמֵל חֲסָדִים טוֹבִים, וְקֹנֵה הַכֹּל, וְזוֹכֵר חַסְדֵי אָבוֹת
וּמֵבִיא גוֹאֵל לִבְנֵי בְנֵיהֶם לְמַעַן שְׁמוֹ בְּאַהֲבָה.
מֶלֶךְ עוֹזֵר וּמוֹשִׁיעַ וּמָגֵן.
׳בָּרוּךְ אַתָּה יהוה, מָגֵן אַבְרָהָם.

גבורות

אַתָּה גִּבּוֹר לְעוֹלָם, אֲדֹנָי
מְחַיֵּה מֵתִים אַתָּה, רַב לְהוֹשִׁיעַ

INTRODUCTION TO MUSAF ROSH ḤODESH

In the times of the *Beit HaMikdash*, Rosh Ḥodesh had to be declared by the court on the basis of testimony from two witnesses who actually saw the appearance of the first sliver of the moon. This does not mean that the Rabbis did not know how to calculate a real calendar; rather, the Torah mandated that it was only Rosh Ḥodesh if the moon was sighted and the court verified the testimony of witnesses. Indeed, if everyone saw the moon but the court did not yet have time to rule before the next day, then the new month was postponed a day, even though everyone knew it was already Rosh Ḥodesh the previous day (*Rosh HaShana* 25b). In short, the new month was

In Israel: He causes the dew to fall.

He sustains the living with loving-kindness,
and with great compassion revives the dead.
He supports the fallen, heals the sick, sets captives free,
and keeps His faith with those who sleep in the dust.
Who is like You, Master of might,
and who can compare to You,
O King who brings death and gives life,
and makes salvation grow?
Faithful are You to revive the dead.
Blessed are You, Lord, who revives the dead.

When saying the Amida silently, continue with "You are holy" on the next page.

KEDUSHA

During the Leader's Repetition, the following is said standing with feet together, rising on the toes at the words indicated by ▴.

Cong. then Leader: נְקַדֵּשׁ We will sanctify Your name on earth,
as they sanctify it in the highest heavens,
as is written by Your prophet,
"And they [the angels] call to one another saying: *Is. 6*

Cong. then Leader: ▴Holy, ▴holy, ▴holy is the Lord of hosts
the whole world is filled with His glory."
Those facing them say "Blessed – "

Cong. then Leader: ▴"Blessed is the Lord's glory from His place." *Ezek. 3*
And in Your holy Writings it is written thus:

Cong. then Leader: ▴"The Lord shall reign for ever. He is your God, Zion, *Ps. 146*
from generation to generation, Halleluya!"

Leader: From generation to generation we will declare Your greatness,
and we will proclaim Your holiness for evermore.
Your praise, our God, shall not leave our mouth forever,
for You, God, are a great and holy King.
Blessed are You, Lord, the holy God.

The Leader continues with "You have given New Moons" on the next page.

בארץ ישראל בקיץ: מוֹרִיד הַטָּל

מְכַלְכֵּל חַיִּים בְּחֶסֶד, מְחַיֵּה מֵתִים בְּרַחֲמִים רַבִּים
סוֹמֵךְ נוֹפְלִים, וְרוֹפֵא חוֹלִים
וּמַתִּיר אֲסוּרִים
וּמְקַיֵּם אֱמוּנָתוֹ לִישֵׁנֵי עָפָר.
מִי כָמְוֹךָ, בַּעַל גְּבוּרוֹת, וּמִי דּוֹמֶה לָּךְ
מֶלֶךְ, מֵמִית וּמְחַיֶּה וּמַצְמִיחַ יְשׁוּעָה.
וְנֶאֱמָן אַתָּה לְהַחֲיוֹת מֵתִים.
בָּרוּךְ אַתָּה יהוה, מְחַיֵּה הַמֵּתִים.

When saying the עמידה silently, continue with אַתָּה קָדוֹשׁ on the next page.

קדושה

During the חזרת הש״ץ, the following is said standing with feet together, rising on the toes at the words indicated by ˄.

then קהל ש״ץ: נְקַדֵּשׁ אֶת שִׁמְךָ בָּעוֹלָם, כְּשֵׁם שֶׁמַּקְדִּישִׁים אוֹתוֹ בִּשְׁמֵי מָרוֹם
כַּכָּתוּב עַל יַד נְבִיאֶךָ: וְקָרָא זֶה אֶל־זֶה וְאָמַר ישעיה ו

then קהל ש״ץ: ˄קָדוֹשׁ, ˄קָדוֹשׁ, ˄קָדוֹשׁ, יהוה צְבָאוֹת, מְלֹא כָל־הָאָרֶץ כְּבוֹדוֹ:
לְעֻמָּתָם בָּרוּךְ יֹאמֵרוּ

then קהל ש״ץ: ˄בָּרוּךְ כְּבוֹד־יהוה מִמְּקוֹמוֹ: יחזקאל ג
וּבְדִבְרֵי קָדְשְׁךָ כָּתוּב לֵאמֹר

then קהל ש״ץ: ˄יִמְלֹךְ יהוה לְעוֹלָם, אֱלֹהַיִךְ צִיּוֹן לְדֹר וָדֹר, הַלְלוּיָהּ: תהלים קמו

ש״ץ: לְדוֹר וָדוֹר נַגִּיד גָּדְלֶךָ, וּלְנֵצַח נְצָחִים קְדֻשָּׁתְךָ נַקְדִּישׁ
וְשִׁבְחֲךָ אֱלֹהֵינוּ מִפִּינוּ לֹא יָמוּשׁ לְעוֹלָם וָעֶד
כִּי אֵל מֶלֶךְ גָּדוֹל וְקָדוֹשׁ אָתָּה.
בָּרוּךְ אַתָּה יהוה הָאֵל הַקָּדוֹשׁ.

The שליח ציבור continues with רָאשֵׁי חֳדָשִׁים on the next page.

HOLINESS

אַתָּה קָדוֹשׁ You are holy and Your name is holy,
and holy ones praise You daily, Selah!
Blessed are You, LORD, the holy God.

HOLINESS OF THE DAY

רָאשֵׁי חֳדָשִׁים You have given New Moons to Your people
as a time of atonement[I] for all their offspring.[B]
They would bring You offerings of goodwill,
and goats as sin-offerings for atonement.
May it serve as a remembrance for them all,
and a deliverance of their lives from the hand of the enemy.[B]
May You establish a new altar in Zion,
and may we offer on it the New Moon burnt-offering,
and prepare goats in favor.
May we all rejoice in the Temple service,
and may the songs of David Your servant,
be heard in Your city,
chanted before Your altar.
Bestow on them everlasting love,
and remember the covenant of the fathers for their children.

---

root of the sin which *Musaf* of Rosh Ḥodesh serves to correct. Hence it is called *zeman kapara*, a time for atonement. Perhaps it behooves us all, therefore, to consider on this day how we can avoid the sin of lack of awareness, whether of God or of our fellow man.

What can I do differently this month?

BIUR TEFILLA • ביאור תפילה

תּוֹלְדוֹתָם – *Their offspring.*
There are those who say that this is a reference to all of the days of the months, the "offspring" of the month mentioned at the beginning (*Kuzari* 3:5). But there are also those who say it should be taken literally to refer to children, and that Rosh Ḥodesh is therefore a particularly auspicious time to pray for the welfare of infants (*Da'at Zekenim*).

שׂוֹנֵא – *The enemy.* Who is the enemy who causes our downfall? There are those who say it is the enemy who attacks the Land of Israel (Ya'avetz). Others say it is the evil inclination which attacks us all (Abudarham).

קדושת השם

אַתָּה קָדוֹשׁ וְשִׁמְךָ קָדוֹשׁ
וּקְדוֹשִׁים בְּכָל יוֹם יְהַלְלוּךָ סֶּלָה.
בָּרוּךְ אַתָּה יהוה, הָאֵל הַקָּדוֹשׁ.

קדושת היום

רָאשֵׁי חֳדָשִׁים לְעַמְּךָ נָתָתָּ
זְמַן כַּפָּרָה[ע] לְכָל תּוֹלְדוֹתָם[ב]
בִּהְיוֹתָם מַקְרִיבִים לְפָנֶיךָ זִבְחֵי רָצוֹן
וּשְׂעִירֵי חַטָּאת לְכַפֵּר בַּעֲדָם.
זִכָּרוֹן לְכֻלָּם יִהְיוּ, וּתְשׁוּעַת נַפְשָׁם מִיַּד שׂוֹנֵא.[ב]
מִזְבֵּחַ חָדָשׁ בְּצִיּוֹן תָּכִין
וְעוֹלַת רֹאשׁ חֹדֶשׁ נַעֲלֶה עָלָיו
וּשְׂעִירֵי עִזִּים נַעֲשֶׂה בְרָצוֹן
וּבַעֲבוֹדַת בֵּית הַמִּקְדָּשׁ נִשְׂמַח כֻּלָּנוּ
וּבְשִׁירֵי דָוִד עַבְדְּךָ הַנִּשְׁמָעִים בְּעִירֶךָ
הָאֲמוּרִים לִפְנֵי מִזְבְּחֶךָ.
אַהֲבַת עוֹלָם תָּבִיא לָהֶם, וּבְרִית אָבוֹת לַבָּנִים תִּזְכֹּר.

IYUN TEFILLA • עיון תפילה

זְמַן כַּפָּרָה – *A time of atonement.* As will be mentioned later on, a part of the ritual was bringing a sacrifice known as a sin-offering or *ḥatat*. The Gemara (*Shevuot* 2a, 9a) explains that this was intended to atone for the possibility that someone had entered into the *Beit HaMikdash,* or had eaten the meat of offerings, in a defiled state. In the present case, it particularly means that he did so without being conscious of the fact that he had sinned. There are times, in other words, when we are so oblivious or ignorant or insensitive, that we may have committed wrongs which, unbeknownst to us, affect not only ourselves but others as well. This lack of awareness lies at the

וַהֲבִיאֵנוּ Bring us back, with song,
to Zion Your city,
and to Jerusalem Your Sanctuary with everlasting joy.
There we will prepare for You our obligatory offerings:
the regular daily offerings in their order,
and the additional offerings according to their law.

וְאֶת מוּסַף The additional offering of this New Moon day[B]
we will prepare and offer to You
with love according to Your will's commandment,
as You have written for us in Your Torah
by Your own word, through Your servant Moses,
as it is said:

"On your new moons,
present as a burnt-offering to the LORD,
two young bulls, one ram,
and seven yearling lambs
without blemish." *Num. 28*

וּמִנְחָתָם And their meal-offerings
and wine-libations as ordained:
three-tenths of an ephah for each bull,
two-tenths of an ephah for the ram,
one-tenth of an ephah for each lamb,
wine for the libations,
a male goat for atonement,
and two regular daily offerings
according to their law.

---

casion. Each is therefore worthy of its own special offering to Hashem to mark the significance of the day. This is the service called *Musaf* or "Addition," which on every Shabbat and festival was added to the regular daily sacrificial rite in the time of the *Beit HaMikdash*. Today, in the absence of the *Beit HaMikdash*, we substitute prayers for our sacrifices, as the prophet Hoshea said (14:3): וּנְשַׁלְּמָה פָרִים שְׂפָתֵינוּ – "We will offer in place of bullocks [the prayer of] our lips."

וַהֲבִיאֵנוּ לְצִיּוֹן עִירְךָ בְּרִנָּה
וְלִירוּשָׁלַיִם בֵּית מִקְדָּשְׁךָ בְּשִׂמְחַת עוֹלָם
וְשָׁם נַעֲשֶׂה לְפָנֶיךָ אֶת קָרְבְּנוֹת חוֹבוֹתֵינוּ
תְּמִידִים כְּסִדְרָם וּמוּסָפִים כְּהִלְכָתָם.

וְאֶת מוּסַף יוֹם רֹאשׁ הַחֹדֶשׁ הַזֶּה[ב]
נַעֲשֶׂה וְנַקְרִיב לְפָנֶיךָ בְּאַהֲבָה כְּמִצְוַת רְצוֹנֶךָ
כְּמוֹ שֶׁכָּתַבְתָּ עָלֵינוּ בְּתוֹרָתֶךָ
עַל יְדֵי מֹשֶׁה עַבְדֶּךָ מִפִּי כְבוֹדֶךָ
כָּאָמוּר
וּבְרָאשֵׁי חָדְשֵׁיכֶם תַּקְרִיבוּ עֹלָה לַיהוה במדבר כח
פָּרִים בְּנֵי־בָקָר שְׁנַיִם
וְאַיִל אֶחָד
כְּבָשִׂים בְּנֵי־שָׁנָה שִׁבְעָה
תְּמִימִם:

וּמִנְחָתָם וְנִסְכֵּיהֶם כִּמְדֻבָּר
שְׁלֹשָׁה עֶשְׂרֹנִים לַפָּר
וּשְׁנֵי עֶשְׂרֹנִים לָאָיִל
וְעִשָּׂרוֹן לַכֶּבֶשׂ
וְיַיִן כְּנִסְכּוֹ, וְשָׂעִיר לְכַפֵּר
וּשְׁנֵי תְמִידִים כְּהִלְכָתָם.

BIUR TEFILLA · ביאור תפילה

מוּסַף יוֹם רֹאשׁ הַחוֹדֶשׁ הַזֶּה – *The additional offering of this New Moon day.* Every holy day has its own special religious significance rooted in a historical event or special oc-

אֱלֹהֵינוּ O God and God of our ancestors,
renew for us the coming month for
good and blessing, joy and gladness,
deliverance and consolation,
sustenance and support,
life and peace,
pardon of sin and forgiveness of iniquity
For You have chosen Your people Israel from all nations,
and have instituted for them rules for the New Moon.
Blessed are You, LORD, who sanctifies Israel and the New Moons.[1]

TEMPLE SERVICE

רְצֵה Find favor, LORD our God,
in Your people Israel and their prayer.
Restore the service to Your most holy House,
and accept in love and favor
the fire-offerings of Israel and their prayer.
May the service of Your people Israel always find favor with You
And may our eyes witness Your return to Zion in compassion.
Blessed are You, LORD, who restores His Presence to Zion.

ANI TEFILLA · אני תפילה

Alexander Herzen (an eighteenth-century Russian writer and thinker) said about the Slavs that they had no history, only geography. The Jews, he said, had the reverse: a great deal of history but all too little geography. Much time, but little space.

What have Jews done with their time? What will you do with yours?

Where does hope come from? It comes from a certain idea about time. So, at any rate, argues Thomas Cahill in his book, *The Gifts of the Jews*. Cahill, a Catholic historian, argues that we owe to the Hebrew Bible one of the great concepts of Western civilization – the idea of linear time. It is in the biblical narrative that, for the first time, we encounter the notion that time itself is the setting of the human journey toward a destination – the Promised Land, the messianic age, the kingdom of heaven. It was this sense of traveling that gave the West its distinctive orientation to the future. (Rabbi J. Sacks)

What are your hopes for the future?

אֱלֹהֵינוּ וֵאלֹהֵי אֲבוֹתֵינוּ
חַדֵּשׁ עָלֵינוּ אֶת הַחֹדֶשׁ הַזֶּה
לְטוֹבָה וְלִבְרָכָה
לְשָׂשׂוֹן וּלְשִׂמְחָה
לִישׁוּעָה וּלְנֶחָמָה
לְפַרְנָסָה וּלְכַלְכָּלָה
לְחַיִּים וּלְשָׁלוֹם
לִמְחִילַת חֵטְא וְלִסְלִיחַת עָוֹן
כִּי בְעַמְּךָ יִשְׂרָאֵל בָּחַרְתָּ מִכָּל הָאֻמּוֹת
וְחֻקֵּי רָאשֵׁי חֳדָשִׁים לָהֶם קָבָעְתָּ.
בָּרוּךְ אַתָּה יהוה, מְקַדֵּשׁ יִשְׂרָאֵל וְרָאשֵׁי חֳדָשִׁים.ע

עבודה

רְצֵה יהוה אֱלֹהֵינוּ בְּעַמְּךָ יִשְׂרָאֵל וּבִתְפִלָּתָם
וְהָשֵׁב אֶת הָעֲבוֹדָה לִדְבִיר בֵּיתֶךָ
וְאִשֵּׁי יִשְׂרָאֵל וּתְפִלָּתָם בְּאַהֲבָה תְקַבֵּל בְּרָצוֹן
וּתְהִי לְרָצוֹן תָּמִיד עֲבוֹדַת יִשְׂרָאֵל עַמֶּךָ.
וְתֶחֱזֶינָה עֵינֵינוּ בְּשׁוּבְךָ לְצִיּוֹן בְּרַחֲמִים.
בָּרוּךְ אַתָּה יהוה, הַמַּחֲזִיר שְׁכִינָתוֹ לְצִיּוֹן.

IYUN TEFILLA • עיון תפילה

מְקַדֵּשׁ יִשְׂרָאֵל וְרָאשֵׁי חֳדָשִׁים – *Who sanctifies Israel and the New Moons.* The Gemara (*Beitza* 17a) suggests that the order here is instructive. God sanctifies Israel first, as it were, and because of that Israel can then sanctify the new moon. Unlike Shabbat, which would be a holy day regardless of our efforts, since God Himself established it, the sanctity of other holy days like Rosh Ḥodesh is dependent upon us. Time is what we make of it.

THANKSGIVING

Bow at the first nine words.

מוֹדִים We give thanks to You,
for You are the LORD our God
and God of our ancestors
for ever and all time.
You are the Rock of our lives,
Shield of our salvation
from generation to generation.
We will thank You and
declare Your praise for our lives,
which are entrusted into Your hand;
for our souls,
which are placed in Your charge;
for Your miracles
which are with us every day;
and for Your wonders and favors
at all times, evening,
morning and midday.
You are good –
for Your compassion never fails.
You are compassionate –
for Your loving-kindnesses never cease.
We have always placed our hope in You.

During the Leader's Repetition, the congregation says quietly:

מוֹדִים We give thanks to You,
for You are the
LORD our God
and God of our ancestors,
God of all flesh,
who formed us
and formed the universe.
Blessings and thanks
are due to Your great
and holy name for giving us
life and sustaining us.
May You continue
to give us life and sustain us;
and may You gather our
exiles to Your holy courts,
to keep Your decrees,
do Your will and serve You
with a perfect heart,
for it is for us
to give You thanks.
Blessed be God to whom
thanksgiving is due.

וְעַל כֻּלָּם For all these things may Your name be blessed and exalted,
our King, continually, for ever and all time.
Let all that lives thank You, Selah! and praise Your name in truth,
God, our Savior and Help, Selah!
Blessed are You, LORD, whose name is "the Good"
and to whom thanks are due.

When saying the Amida silently, continue with "Grant peace" on the next page.

הודאה

Bow at the first five words.

ימוֹדִים אֲנַחְנוּ לָךְ
שָׁאַתָּה הוּא יהוה אֱלֹהֵינוּ
וֵאלֹהֵי אֲבוֹתֵינוּ לְעוֹלָם וָעֶד.
צוּר חַיֵּינוּ, מָגֵן יִשְׁעֵנוּ
אַתָּה הוּא לְדוֹר וָדוֹר.
נוֹדֶה לְּךָ וּנְסַפֵּר תְּהִלָּתֶךָ
עַל חַיֵּינוּ הַמְּסוּרִים בְּיָדֶךָ
וְעַל נִשְׁמוֹתֵינוּ הַפְּקוּדוֹת לָךְ
וְעַל נִסֶּיךָ שֶׁבְּכָל יוֹם עִמָּנוּ
וְעַל נִפְלְאוֹתֶיךָ וְטוֹבוֹתֶיךָ
שֶׁבְּכָל עֵת, עֶרֶב וָבֹקֶר וְצָהֳרָיִם.
הַטּוֹב, כִּי לֹא כָלוּ רַחֲמֶיךָ
וְהַמְרַחֵם, כִּי לֹא תַמּוּ חֲסָדֶיךָ
מֵעוֹלָם קִוִּינוּ לָךְ.

During the חזרת הש״ץ, *the* קהל *says quietly:*

ימוֹדִים אֲנַחְנוּ לָךְ
שָׁאַתָּה הוּא יהוה אֱלֹהֵינוּ
וֵאלֹהֵי אֲבוֹתֵינוּ
אֱלֹהֵי כָל בָּשָׂר
יוֹצְרֵנוּ, יוֹצֵר בְּרֵאשִׁית.
בְּרָכוֹת וְהוֹדָאוֹת
לְשִׁמְךָ הַגָּדוֹל וְהַקָּדוֹשׁ
עַל שֶׁהֶחֱיִיתָנוּ וְקִיַּמְתָּנוּ.
כֵּן תְּחַיֵּנוּ וּתְקַיְּמֵנוּ
וְתֶאֱסֹף גָּלֻיּוֹתֵינוּ
לְחַצְרוֹת קָדְשֶׁךָ
לִשְׁמֹר חֻקֶּיךָ וְלַעֲשׂוֹת רְצוֹנֶךָ
וּלְעָבְדְּךָ בְּלֵבָב שָׁלֵם
עַל שֶׁאֲנַחְנוּ מוֹדִים לָךְ.
בָּרוּךְ אֵל הַהוֹדָאוֹת.

וְעַל כֻּלָּם יִתְבָּרַךְ וְיִתְרוֹמַם שִׁמְךָ מַלְכֵּנוּ תָּמִיד לְעוֹלָם וָעֶד.
וְכֹל הַחַיִּים יוֹדְוּךָ סֶּלָה
וִיהַלְלוּ אֶת שִׁמְךָ בֶּאֱמֶת
הָאֵל יְשׁוּעָתֵנוּ וְעֶזְרָתֵנוּ סֶלָה.
יבָּרוּךְ אַתָּה יהוה, הַטּוֹב שִׁמְךָ וּלְךָ נָאֶה לְהוֹדוֹת.

When saying the עמידה *silently, continue with* שִׂים שָׁלוֹם *on the next page.*

The following is said by the Leader during the Repetition of the Amida.
In Israel, if Kohanim bless the congregation, *turn to page 1008.*

Our God and God of our fathers, bless us with the threefold blessing in the Torah, written by the hand of Moses Your servant and pronounced by Aaron and his sons the priests, Your holy people, as it is said:

May the LORD bless you and protect you. *Num. 6*
Cong: May it be Your will.
May the LORD make His face shine on you and be gracious to you.
Cong: May it be Your will.
May the LORD turn His face toward you, and grant you peace.
Cong: May it be Your will.

The Leader continues with "Grant peace" below.

PEACE

שִׂים שָׁלוֹם Grant peace, goodness and blessing,
grace, loving-kindness and compassion
to us and all Israel Your people.
Bless us, our Father, all as one, with the light of Your face,
for by the light of Your face You have given us, LORD our God,
the Torah of life and love of kindness,
righteousness, blessing, compassion, life and peace.
May it be good in Your eyes to bless Your people Israel
at every time, in every hour, with Your peace.
Blessed are You, LORD,
who blesses His people Israel with peace.

The following verse concludes the Leader's Repetition of the Amida.
Some also say it here as part of the silent Amida.

May the words of my mouth and the meditation of my heart *Ps. 19*
find favor before You, LORD, my Rock and Redeemer.

אֱלֹהַי My God, guard my tongue from evil *Berakhot 17a*
and my lips from deceitful speech.
To those who curse me, let my soul be silent;
may my soul be to all like the dust.

The following is said by the שליח ציבור *during the* חזרת הש״ץ.
In ארץ ישראל*, if* כהנים *say* ברכת כהנים*, turn to page 1009.*

אֱלֹהֵינוּ וֵאלֹהֵי אֲבוֹתֵינוּ, בָּרְכֵנוּ בַּבְּרָכָה הַמְשֻׁלֶּשֶׁת בַּתּוֹרָה, הַכְּתוּבָה עַל יְדֵי מֹשֶׁה עַבְדֶּךָ, הָאֲמוּרָה מִפִּי אַהֲרֹן וּבָנָיו כֹּהֲנִים עַם קְדוֹשֶׁיךָ, כָּאָמוּר

במדבר ו
יְבָרֶכְךָ יהוה וְיִשְׁמְרֶךָ: קהל: כֵּן יְהִי רָצוֹן
יָאֵר יהוה פָּנָיו אֵלֶיךָ וִיחֻנֶּךָּ: קהל: כֵּן יְהִי רָצוֹן
יִשָּׂא יהוה פָּנָיו אֵלֶיךָ וְיָשֵׂם לְךָ שָׁלוֹם: קהל: כֵּן יְהִי רָצוֹן

The שליח ציבור *continues with* שִׂים שָׁלוֹם *below.*

ברכת שלום

שִׂים שָׁלוֹם טוֹבָה וּבְרָכָה
חֵן וָחֶסֶד וְרַחֲמִים עָלֵינוּ וְעַל כָּל יִשְׂרָאֵל עַמֶּךָ.
בָּרְכֵנוּ אָבִינוּ כֻּלָּנוּ כְּאֶחָד בְּאוֹר פָּנֶיךָ
כִּי בְאוֹר פָּנֶיךָ נָתַתָּ לָּנוּ יהוה אֱלֹהֵינוּ
תּוֹרַת חַיִּים וְאַהֲבַת חֶסֶד
וּצְדָקָה וּבְרָכָה וְרַחֲמִים וְחַיִּים וְשָׁלוֹם.
וְטוֹב בְּעֵינֶיךָ לְבָרֵךְ אֶת עַמְּךָ יִשְׂרָאֵל
בְּכָל עֵת וּבְכָל שָׁעָה בִּשְׁלוֹמֶךָ.
בָּרוּךְ אַתָּה יהוה, הַמְבָרֵךְ אֶת עַמּוֹ יִשְׂרָאֵל בַּשָּׁלוֹם.

The following verse concludes the חזרת הש״ץ.
Some also say it here as part of the silent עמידה.

תהלים יט
יִהְיוּ לְרָצוֹן אִמְרֵי־פִי וְהֶגְיוֹן לִבִּי לְפָנֶיךָ, יהוה צוּרִי וְגֹאֲלִי:

ברכות יז.
אֱלֹהַי
נְצֹר לְשׁוֹנִי מֵרָע וּשְׂפָתַי מִדַּבֵּר מִרְמָה
וְלִמְקַלְלַי נַפְשִׁי תִדֹּם, וְנַפְשִׁי כֶּעָפָר לַכֹּל תִּהְיֶה.

Open my heart to Your Torah
and let my soul pursue Your commandments.
As for all who plan evil against me,
swiftly thwart their counsel and frustrate their plans.
Act for the sake of Your name;
act for the sake of Your right hand;
act for the sake of Your holiness;
act for the sake of Your Torah.
That Your beloved ones may be delivered, *Ps. 60*
save with Your right hand and answer me.
May the words of my mouth and the meditation of my heart *Ps. 19*
find favor before You, LORD, my Rock and Redeemer.

Bow, take three steps back, then bow, first left, then right, then center, while saying:

May He who makes peace in His high places,
make peace for us and all Israel – and say: Amen.

יְהִי רָצוֹן May it be Your will, LORD our God and God of our ancestors,
that the Temple be rebuilt speedily in our days, and grant us a share in Your Torah.
And there we will serve You with reverence,
as in the days of old and as in former years.
Then the offering of Judah and Jerusalem *Mal. 3*
will be pleasing to the LORD as in the days of old and as in former years.

After the Leader's Repetition, the service continues with Full Kaddish (page 234), followed by Aleinu (page 236), the Daily Psalm (page 242) and Barekhi Nafshi (page 250).

פְּתַח לִבִּי בְּתוֹרָתֶךָ, וּבְמִצְוֹתֶיךָ תִּרְדֹּף נַפְשִׁי.
וְכָל הַחוֹשְׁבִים עָלַי רָעָה
מְהֵרָה הָפֵר עֲצָתָם וְקַלְקֵל מַחֲשַׁבְתָּם.
עֲשֵׂה לְמַעַן שְׁמֶךָ
עֲשֵׂה לְמַעַן יְמִינֶךָ
עֲשֵׂה לְמַעַן קְדֻשָּׁתֶךָ
עֲשֵׂה לְמַעַן תּוֹרָתֶךָ.
לְמַעַן יֵחָלְצוּן יְדִידֶיךָ, הוֹשִׁיעָה יְמִינְךָ וַעֲנֵנִי: תהלים ס
יִהְיוּ לְרָצוֹן אִמְרֵי־פִי וְהֶגְיוֹן לִבִּי לְפָנֶיךָ, יהוה צוּרִי וְגֹאֲלִי: תהלים יט

Bow, take three steps back, then bow, first left, then right, then center, while saying:

עֹשֶׂה שָׁלוֹם בִּמְרוֹמָיו
הוּא יַעֲשֶׂה שָׁלוֹם עָלֵינוּ וְעַל כָּל יִשְׂרָאֵל, וְאִמְרוּ אָמֵן.

יְהִי רָצוֹן מִלְּפָנֶיךָ יהוה אֱלֹהֵינוּ וֵאלֹהֵי אֲבוֹתֵינוּ
שֶׁיִּבָּנֶה בֵּית הַמִּקְדָּשׁ בִּמְהֵרָה בְיָמֵינוּ, וְתֵן חֶלְקֵנוּ בְּתוֹרָתֶךָ
וְשָׁם נַעֲבָדְךָ בְּיִרְאָה כִּימֵי עוֹלָם וּכְשָׁנִים קַדְמֹנִיּוֹת.
וְעָרְבָה לַיהוה מִנְחַת יְהוּדָה וִירוּשָׁלָיִם כִּימֵי עוֹלָם וּכְשָׁנִים קַדְמֹנִיּוֹת: מלאכי ג

After the חזרת הש״ץ, *the service continues with* קדיש שלם *(page 235),*
followed by עָלֵינוּ *(page 237),* שיר של יום *(page 243) and* בָּרְכִי נַפְשִׁי *(page 251).*

Seliḥot

Seliḥot are said on Fast Days. On Tisha B'Av, Kinot are said instead.

SELIḤOT FOR THE SEVENTEENTH OF TAMMUZ

סְלַח לָנוּ Forgive us, our Father, for in our great foolishness we have blundered. Pardon us, our King, for our iniquities are many.

אֵל אֶרֶךְ You are a God slow to anger, You are called the Master of Compassion, and You have taught the way of repentance. May You remember today and every day the greatness of Your compassion and kindness, for the sake of the descendants of Your beloved ones. Turn toward us in compassion, for You are the Master of Compassion. We come before You in plea and prayer, as You in ancient times showed the humble one [Moses]. Turn from Your fierce anger, as is written in Your Torah. In the shadow of Your wings may we shelter and abide, as on the day when the LORD descended in the cloud. ▸ Disregard transgression and erase guilt as on the day You stood with him [Moses] there. Hear our cry and heed our word, as on the day You proclaimed in the name of the LORD, and there it is written:

Congregation then Leader:

And the LORD passed by before him and proclaimed: Ex. 34

All say aloud:

יהוה The LORD, the LORD, compassionate and gracious God, slow to anger, abounding in loving-kindness and truth, extending loving-kindness to a thousand generations, forgiving iniquity, rebellion and sin, and absolving [the guilty who repent]. Forgive us our iniquity and our sin, and take us as Your inheritance.

Continue:

סְלַח לָנוּ Forgive us, our Father, for we have sinned. Pardon us, our King, for we
have transgressed. For You, LORD, are good and forgiving, abounding in loving- Ps. 86
kindness to all who call on You.

And do not let Him rest, until He establishes, until He makes Jerusalem the Is. 62
praise of all the earth. For in You there is a wellspring of life; in Your light shall Ps. 36
we see light. Our God, we are ashamed of our actions, distraught at our sins.

כְּרַחֵם As a father has compassion for his children,
so, LORD, have compassion for us.
Salvation is the LORD's; on Your people is Your blessing, Selah! Ps. 3
The LORD of hosts is with us, the God of Jacob is our stronghold, Selah! Ps. 46
LORD of hosts, happy is the one who trusts in You. Ps. 84
LORD, save! May the King answer us on the day we call. Ps. 20

סליחות

סליחות *are said on Fast Days. On* תשעה באב, קינות *are said instead.*

סליחות לשבעה עשר בתמוז

סְלַח לָנוּ, אָבִינוּ, כִּי בְּרֹב אִוַּלְתֵּנוּ שָׁגִינוּ. מְחַל לָנוּ, מַלְכֵּנוּ, כִּי רַבּוּ עֲוֹנֵינוּ.

אֵל אֶרֶךְ אַפַּיִם אַתָּה, וּבַעַל הָרַחֲמִים נִקְרֵאתָ, וְדֶרֶךְ תְּשׁוּבָה הוֹרֵיתָ. גְּדֻלַּת רַחֲמֶיךָ וַחֲסָדֶיךָ, תִּזְכֹּר הַיּוֹם וּבְכָל יוֹם לְזֶרַע יְדִידֶיךָ. תֵּפֶן אֵלֵינוּ בְּרַחֲמִים, כִּי אַתָּה הוּא בַּעַל הָרַחֲמִים. בְּתַחֲנוּן וּבִתְפִלָּה פָּנֶיךָ נְקַדֵּם, כְּהוֹדַעְתָּ לֶעָנָו מִקֶּדֶם. מֵחֲרוֹן אַפְּךָ שׁוּב, כְּמוֹ בְּתוֹרָתְךָ כָּתוּב. וּבְצֵל כְּנָפֶיךָ נֶחֱסֶה וְנִתְלוֹנָן, כְּיוֹם וַיֵּרֶד יהוה בֶּעָנָן. ‹ תַּעֲבֹר עַל פֶּשַׁע וְתִמְחֶה אָשָׁם, כְּיוֹם וַיִּתְיַצֵּב עִמּוֹ שָׁם. תַּאֲזִין שַׁוְעָתֵנוּ וְתַקְשִׁיב מֶנּוּ מַאֲמָר, כְּיוֹם וַיִּקְרָא בְשֵׁם יהוה, וְשָׁם נֶאֱמַר

קהל *then* שליח ציבור:

וַיַּעֲבֹר יהוה עַל־פָּנָיו וַיִּקְרָא שמות לד

All say aloud:

יהוה, יהוה, אֵל רַחוּם וְחַנּוּן, אֶרֶךְ אַפַּיִם, וְרַב־חֶסֶד וֶאֱמֶת: נֹצֵר חֶסֶד לָאֲלָפִים, נֹשֵׂא עָוֹן וָפֶשַׁע וְחַטָּאָה, וְנַקֵּה: וְסָלַחְתָּ לַעֲוֹנֵנוּ וּלְחַטָּאתֵנוּ, וּנְחַלְתָּנוּ:

Continue:

סְלַח לָנוּ אָבִינוּ כִּי חָטָאנוּ, מְחַל לָנוּ מַלְכֵּנוּ כִּי פָשָׁעְנוּ. כִּי־אַתָּה אֲדֹנָי טוֹב תהלים פו
וְסַלָּח, וְרַב־חֶסֶד לְכָל־קֹרְאֶיךָ:

וְאַל־תִּתְּנוּ דֳמִי לוֹ, עַד־יְכוֹנֵן וְעַד־יָשִׂים אֶת־יְרוּשָׁלַםִ תְּהִלָּה בָּאָרֶץ: כִּי־ ישעיה סב תהלים לו
עִמְּךָ מְקוֹר חַיִּים, בְּאוֹרְךָ נִרְאֶה־אוֹר: אֱלֹהֵינוּ, בֹּשְׁנוּ בְּמַעֲשֵׂינוּ וְנִכְלַמְנוּ בַּעֲוֹנֵינוּ.

כְּרַחֵם אָב עַל בָּנִים, כֵּן תְּרַחֵם יהוה עָלֵינוּ.
לַיהוה הַיְשׁוּעָה, עַל־עַמְּךָ בִרְכָתֶךָ סֶּלָה: תהלים ג
יהוה צְבָאוֹת עִמָּנוּ, מִשְׂגָּב לָנוּ אֱלֹהֵי יַעֲקֹב סֶלָה: תהלים מו
יהוה צְבָאוֹת, אַשְׁרֵי אָדָם בֹּטֵחַ בָּךְ: תהלים פד
יהוה הוֹשִׁיעָה, הַמֶּלֶךְ יַעֲנֵנוּ בְיוֹם־קָרְאֵנוּ: תהלים כ

▸ Forgive, please, this people's iniquity, *Num. 14*
in the abundance of Your kindness,
and as You have forgiven this people from the time of Egypt until now,
and there it is written:

Congregation then Leader:

And the LORD said, I have forgiven as you asked.

Continue:

הַטֵּה Give ear, my God and hear; open Your eyes and see our desolation, and *Dan. 9* the city that bears Your name, for it is not on the strength of our righteousness that we throw down our pleadings before You, but on the strength of Your great compassion. LORD, hear me; LORD, forgive; LORD, listen and act and do not delay – for Your sake, my God; for Your city and Your people bear Your name.

Our God and God of our fathers:

אָתָנוּ We come before You, Former of the winds.
In our many iniquities our sighs have grown heavy;
the decrees against us powerful and our screams so many –
for on the Seventeenth of Tammuz,
the Tablets were smashed.

We have been exiled from the House of Your choosing;
our judgment was sealed, the decree laid down.
And the light has darkened over us –
for on the Seventeenth of Tammuz,
the Torah scroll was burnt.

Our enemies destroyed the Sanctuary,
the Divine Presence fled from Its corner,
and we were yielded up to the hands of the wanton,
to be consumed –
for on the Seventeenth of Tammuz,
an idol was set up in the Temple.

We were scattered from city to city,
and old and young of us were seized.
The place of our delight was destroyed,
and fire raged through her –
for on the Seventeenth of Tammuz
the city was broken through.

‹ סְלַח־נָא לַעֲוֹן הָעָם הַזֶּה כְּגֹדֶל חַסְדֶּךָ במדבר יד
וְכַאֲשֶׁר נָשָׂאתָה לָעָם הַזֶּה מִמִּצְרַיִם וְעַד־הֵנָּה:
וְשָׁם נֶאֱמַר

שליח ציבור then קהל:

וַיֹּאמֶר יהוה, סָלַחְתִּי כִּדְבָרֶךָ:

Continue:

הַטֵּה אֱלֹהַי אָזְנְךָ וּשְׁמָע, פְּקַח עֵינֶיךָ וּרְאֵה שֹׁמְמֹתֵינוּ וְהָעִיר אֲשֶׁר־נִקְרָא שִׁמְךָ עָלֶיהָ, כִּי לֹא עַל־צִדְקֹתֵינוּ אֲנַחְנוּ מַפִּילִים תַּחֲנוּנֵינוּ לְפָנֶיךָ, כִּי עַל־רַחֲמֶיךָ הָרַבִּים: אֲדֹנָי שְׁמָעָה, אֲדֹנָי סְלָחָה, אֲדֹנָי הַקְשִׁיבָה וַעֲשֵׂה אַל־תְּאַחַר, לְמַעַנְךָ אֱלֹהַי, כִּי־שִׁמְךָ נִקְרָא עַל־עִירְךָ וְעַל־עַמֶּךָ: דניאל ט

אֱלֹהֵינוּ וֵאלֹהֵי אֲבוֹתֵינוּ

אָתָנוּ לְךָ יוֹצֵר רוּחוֹת
בְּרוֹב עֲוֹנֵינוּ כָּבְדוּ אֲנָחוֹת
גְּזֵרוֹת עָצְמוּ וְרַבּוּ צְרִיחוֹת
כִּי בְּשִׁבְעָה עָשָׂר בְּתַמּוּז נִשְׁתַּבְּרוּ הַלֻּחוֹת.

גָּלִינוּ מִבֵּית הַבְּחִירָה
דִּינֵנוּ נֶחְתַּם וְנִגְזְרָה גְּזֵרָה
וְחָשַׁךְ בַּעֲדֵנוּ אוֹרָה
כִּי בְּשִׁבְעָה עָשָׂר בְּתַמּוּז נִשְׂרְפָה הַתּוֹרָה.

הָרְסוּ אוֹיְבֵינוּ הַהֵיכָל
וּבָרְחָה שְׁכִינָה מִזָּוִית הֵיכָל
וְנִמְסַרְנוּ בִּידֵי זֵדִים לְהִתְאַכָּל
כִּי בְּשִׁבְעָה עָשָׂר בְּתַמּוּז הָעֳמַד צֶלֶם בַּהֵיכָל.

זֹרוּנוּ מֵעִיר אֶל עִיר
וְנִלְכַּד מִמֶּנּוּ רַב וְצָעִיר
חָרְבָה מְשׂוֹשֵׂנוּ וְאֵשׁ בָּהּ הִבְעִיר
כִּי בְּשִׁבְעָה עָשָׂר בְּתַמּוּז הָבְקְעָה הָעִיר.

The lethal foe took hold of our Temple, and the cherubs,
bride and bridegroom were deprived of all their ornament.
Because we angered You
we were given up to destruction –
for on the Seventeenth of Tammuz,
the daily offering ceased.

All glory and praise there ended.
The enemy drew his sword
and brandished its point against us;
small children and babies were prepared for the slaughter –
for on the Seventeenth of Tammuz,
the offerings and sacrifices ceased.

We rebelled against the One who inhabits the Heavens,
and so we were dispersed to all the corners of the world.
All our dancing was turned to lament –
for on the Seventeenth of Tammuz,
the Temple service ended.

We acted obstinately with You
in the discord of tongues,
and so our own tongue has learnt lamentation;
we have been abandoned in countless numbers –
for on the Seventeenth of Tammuz,
sin decided our destiny.

We have been dispersed and found no relief,
and so our sighs have multiplied within us;
Rock, see how our souls have been bowed low –
and turn our Seventeenth of Tammuz
into gladness and joy.

We have been obstinate
and many calamities have met us;
and so we have been yielded up to the plunder,
have been pushed into the mud.
See, Lord, and release us from disaster –
and turn our Seventeenth of Tammuz
into joy and gladness.

טָפַשׁ מִקְדָּשֵׁנוּ צַר הַמַּשְׁמִיד
וְנָטַל מֵחָתָן וְכַלָּה אֶצְעָדָה וְצָמִיד
יַעַן כִּעַסְנוּךָ נִתַּנּוּ לְהַשְׁמִיד
כִּי בְּשִׁבְעָה עָשָׂר בְּתַמּוּז בָּטַל הַתָּמִיד.

כָּלָה מֶנּוּ כָּל הוֹד וָשֶׁבַח
חַרְבּוֹ שָׁלַף אוֹיֵב עָלֵינוּ לָאֶבַח
לִהְיוֹת עוֹלָלִים וְיוֹנְקִים מוּכָנִים לַטֶּבַח
כִּי בְּשִׁבְעָה עָשָׂר בְּתַמּוּז בָּטְלוּ עוֹלָה וָזֶבַח.

מָרַדְנוּ לְשׁוֹכֵן מְעוֹנוֹת
לָכֵן נִתְפַּזַּרְנוּ בְּכָל פִּנּוֹת
נֶהְפַּךְ מְחוֹלֵנוּ לְקִינוֹת
כִּי בְּשִׁבְעָה עָשָׂר בְּתַמּוּז בָּטְלוּ קָרְבָּנוֹת.

סָרַרְנוּ לְפָנֶיךָ מֵרִיב לְשׁוֹנוֹת
לָכֵן לָמְדָה לְשׁוֹנֵנוּ לוֹמַר קִינוֹת
עֲזַבְנוּ בְּלִי לְהִמָּנוֹת
כִּי בְּשִׁבְעָה עָשָׂר בְּתַמּוּז גָּרְמוּ לָנוּ עֲוֹנוֹת.

פֹּזַּרְנוּ בְּלִי מְצוֹא רְוָחָה
לָכֵן רָבְתָה בָּנוּ אֲנָחָה
צוּר רְאֵה נַפְשֵׁנוּ כִּי שָׁחָה
וְשִׁבְעָה עָשָׂר בְּתַמּוּז הֲפָךְ לָנוּ לְשָׂשׂוֹן וּלְשִׂמְחָה.

קְשִׁינוּ עֹרֶף וְרָבְתָה בָּנוּ אָסוֹן
לָכֵן נִתַּנּוּ לִמְשִׁסָּה וְרִפְשׁוֹן
רְאֵה יהוה וְחַלְּצֵנוּ מֵאָסוֹן
וְשִׁבְעָה עָשָׂר בְּתַמּוּז הֲפָךְ לָנוּ לְשִׂמְחָה וּלְשָׂשׂוֹן.

▸ Turn to us, You who reside on High,
and gather in our scattered ones from the very ends of the earth.
Say to Zion, "Come, get up," –
and turn our Seventeenth of Tammuz
to a day of salvation and comfort.

אֵל מֶלֶךְ God, King who sits upon a throne of compassion, who acts with loving-kindness, who pardons the iniquities of His people, passing them before Him in order; who forgives sinners and pardons transgressors; who performs righteousness with all flesh and spirit, do not repay their bad actions in kind. ▸ God, You taught us to speak thirteen attributes: recall for us today the covenant of the thirteen attributes, as You in ancient times showed the humble one [Moses], as is written: The LORD descended in the cloud and stood with him there, and proclaimed in the name of the LORD.

Congregation then Leader:

And the LORD passed by before him and proclaimed: *Ex. 34*

All say aloud:

יהוה The LORD, the LORD, compassionate and gracious God, slow to anger, abounding in loving-kindness and truth, extending loving-kindness to a thousand generations, forgiving iniquity, rebellion and sin, and absolving [the guilty who repent]. Forgive us our iniquity and our sin, and take us as Your inheritance.

Continue:

סְלַח לָנוּ Forgive us, our Father, for we have sinned. Pardon us, our King, for we have transgressed. For You, LORD, are good and forgiving, abounding in loving-kindness to all who call on You. *Ps. 86*

God, do not rest, do not be silent and do not be still, for Your enemies clamor and those who hate You hold their heads high. God of retribution, LORD; God of retribution, appear *Ps. 83* *Ps. 94*

כְּרַחֵם As a father has compassion for his children,
so, LORD, have compassion for us.
Salvation is the LORD's; on Your people is Your blessing, Selah! *Ps. 3*
The LORD of hosts is with us, the God of Jacob is our stronghold, Selah! *Ps. 46*
LORD of hosts: happy is the one who trusts in You. *Ps. 84*
LORD, save! May the King answer us on the day we call. *Ps. 20*

› שְׁעֵנוּ שׁוֹכֵן רוּמָה
וְקַבֵּץ נְפוּצוֹתֵינוּ מִקַּצְווֹת אֲדָמָה
תֹּאמַר לְצִיּוֹן קוּמָה
וְשִׁבְעָה עָשָׂר בְּתַמּוּז הֲפָךְ לָנוּ לְיוֹם יְשׁוּעָה וְנֶחָמָה.

אֵל מֶלֶךְ יוֹשֵׁב עַל כִּסֵּא רַחֲמִים, מִתְנַהֵג בַּחֲסִידוּת. מוֹחֵל עֲוֹנוֹת עַמּוֹ, מַעֲבִיר רִאשׁוֹן רִאשׁוֹן. מַרְבֶּה מְחִילָה לְחַטָּאִים, וּסְלִיחָה לְפוֹשְׁעִים. עֹשֶׂה צְדָקוֹת עִם כָּל בָּשָׂר וָרוּחַ, לֹא כְרָעָתָם תִּגְמֹל. › אֵל, הוֹרֵיתָ לָּנוּ לוֹמַר שְׁלֹשׁ עֶשְׂרֵה, וּזְכָר לָנוּ הַיּוֹם בְּרִית שְׁלֹשׁ עֶשְׂרֵה, כְּמוֹ שֶׁהוֹדַעְתָּ לֶעָנָו מִקֶּדֶם, כְּמוֹ שֶׁכָּתוּב: וַיֵּרֶד יהוה בֶּעָנָן, וַיִּתְיַצֵּב עִמּוֹ שָׁם, וַיִּקְרָא בְשֵׁם, יהוה:

שליח ציבור then קהל:

וַיַּעֲבֹר יהוה עַל־פָּנָיו וַיִּקְרָא שמות לד

All say aloud:

יהוה, יהוה, אֵל רַחוּם וְחַנּוּן, אֶרֶךְ אַפַּיִם, וְרַב־חֶסֶד וֶאֱמֶת: נֹצֵר חֶסֶד לָאֲלָפִים, נֹשֵׂא עָוֹן וָפֶשַׁע וְחַטָּאָה, וְנַקֵּה: וְסָלַחְתָּ לַעֲוֹנֵנוּ וּלְחַטָּאתֵנוּ, וּנְחַלְתָּנוּ:

Continue:

סְלַח לָנוּ אָבִינוּ כִּי חָטָאנוּ, מְחַל לָנוּ מַלְכֵּנוּ כִּי פָשָׁעְנוּ. כִּי־אַתָּה אֲדֹנָי טוֹב תהלים פו
וְסַלָּח, וְרַב־חֶסֶד לְכָל־קֹרְאֶיךָ:

אֱלֹהִים אַל־דֳּמִי־לָךְ, אַל־תֶּחֱרַשׁ וְאַל־תִּשְׁקֹט אֵל: כִּי־הִנֵּה אוֹיְבֶיךָ יֶהֱמָיוּן, תהלים פג
וּמְשַׂנְאֶיךָ נָשְׂאוּ רֹאשׁ: אֵל־נְקָמוֹת יהוה, אֵל נְקָמוֹת הוֹפִיעַ: תהלים צד

כְּרַחֵם אָב עַל בָּנִים, כֵּן תְּרַחֵם יהוה עָלֵינוּ.
לַיהוה הַיְשׁוּעָה, עַל־עַמְּךָ בִרְכָתֶךָ סֶּלָה: תהלים ג
יהוה צְבָאוֹת עִמָּנוּ, מִשְׂגָּב לָנוּ אֱלֹהֵי יַעֲקֹב סֶלָה: תהלים מו
יהוה צְבָאוֹת, אַשְׁרֵי אָדָם בֹּטֵחַ בָּךְ: תהלים פד
יהוה הוֹשִׁיעָה, הַמֶּלֶךְ יַעֲנֵנוּ בְיוֹם־קָרְאֵנוּ: תהלים כ

Our God and God of our fathers:

אֲמָרֵר It is bitterly that I weep, over the Hand raised against our ruins.
I blasphemed Him in His House,
in my unfaithfulness and thieving.
The Holy Presence broke out and fled,
flew ten stretches and rose up to the seventh Heaven.

God cut me off, tormented me, burnt me, in the fourth month.
He closed the time set for Him to break those young boys,
who were like boughs just sprouting.
He shot us with His arrows twice, melted and weakened us,
as heedless women wept for Tammuz in the Temple.
He condemned me and became Enemy to me,
then, in the month of Tammuz.

Five traps were laid for me, deep in the Scripture of sufferings sent.
Those people overcame me for my impurity
on the seventeenth of the month.
For I was ensnared like a wretched bride,
unfaithful beneath a wedding canopy of peace and success.
I did not wait for Moses, my shepherd, until the sixth hour,
and the Tablets were smashed.

From His hand was I ornamented
with jewelry of fine gold, brooch and bracelet.
They flowed away on the day of His rage,
when I corrupted my way, and denounced my faith.
I broke off the order of His service and the constant supplies of the altar –
from the Chamber of the Lambs, the daily offering is ended.

Israel is crumbled to pieces, scattered, storm battered, oppressed.
Likened to a ship without a captain, tossed about like a boat.
You have taken her by the head for her sins,
exposed her twice over to mourning and moaning.
Her enemies waged war on her on this day,
and the city was broken through again.

She fled out like a chased gazelle to hide, when none sought her.
They sharpened their tongues, they made her like a lamb,
and left her wool and milk for all takers.
She cries out for the cherished thing with which she was crowned:
the beloved of her eyes eluded her as Apostomus burnt the Torah.

אֱלֹהֵינוּ וֵאלֹהֵי אֲבוֹתֵינוּ

אֱמָרֵר בִּבְכִי מִפְּנֵי יָד שְׁלוּחָה בְּעִי.
בְּנָאֲצִי בְּתוֹךְ בֵּיתוֹ בִּבְגָדַי וְקָבְעִי.
גָּח וּבָרַח וְנָסַע עֶשֶׂר וְעָלָה לַשְּׁבִיעִי.
דָּמַי הֱצִיקָנִי הִשִּׂיקָנִי בַּחֹדֶשׁ הָרְבִיעִי.

הֵבִיא מוֹעֵד בִּמְלֵאָתוֹ לִשְׁבֹּר בַּחוּרַי גְּמוּז.
וְרִבָּה בוֹ פַּעֲמַיִם בְּמִסְמוּס וּמִזְמוּז.
וְבוּלוֹ כְּשָׂר שֶׁאֲנָנוֹת מְבַכּוֹת אֶת הַתַּמּוּז.
חִיְּבַנִי וְאִיְּבַנִי אֱזַי בְּיֶרַח תַּמּוּז.

טָמְנוּ פַּחִים חֲמִשָּׁה בְּמִקְרָא תְּלָאוֹת מְשֻׁלָּחוֹת.
יָכְלוּ לִי בְּשִׁבְעָה עָשָׂר בּוֹ בַּאֲלִיחוֹת.
כִּי נוֹקַשְׁתִּי כְּכַלָּה עֲלוּבָה בְּחֻפַּת שַׁלְוָה וְהַצְלָחוֹת.
לְרוֹעִי לֹא הִמְתַּנְתִּי שֵׁשׁ, וְנִשְׁתַּבְּרוּ הַלֻּחוֹת.

מִיָּדוֹ עֲדֵיתִי חֲלִי כֶתֶם, אֶצְעָדָה וְצָמִיד.
נִגְּרוֹת בְּיוֹם אַפּוֹ, כְּשִׁחַתִּי דְּרָכַי לְהַשְׁמִיד.
סֵדֶר עֲבוֹדָתוֹ וְקֵיץ מִזְבְּחוֹ קִצַּתִּי לְהַעֲמִיד.
עַל כֵּן מִלִּשְׁכַּת הַטְּלָאִים בֻּטַּל הַתָּמִיד.

פּוֹר הִתְפּוֹרְרָה וְנִתְפַּזְּרָה סֹעֲרָה עֲנִיָּה.
צִי נִמְשְׁלָה מִבְּלִי חוֹבֵל, וְנִטְרְפָה כָּאֳנִיָּה.
קָחְתָה בְּחַטָּאתָהּ בְּרֹאשָׁהּ, וּבְכֶפֶל תַּאֲנִיָּה וַאֲנִיָּה.
רִיבוּהָ צָרֶיהָ כְּהַיּוֹם, וְהָבְקְעָה הָעִיר בַּשְּׁנִיָּה.

שִׁלְּחָה כִּצְבִי מֻדָּח מֵאֵין דּוֹרֵשׁ לְהַסְתִּירָה.
שְׁנָנוּ לְשׁוֹנָם וּנְתָנוּהָ כְּשֶׂה, צְמִרָהּ וַחֲלָבָהּ לְהַתִּירָה.
תִּצְעַק עַל כְּלִי חֶמְדָּה שֶׁבּוֹ נִכְתָּרָה.
תַּחֲמוּד עֵינֶיהָ נִצַּל כְּשָׂרַף אַפּוֹסְטְמוֹס הַתּוֹרָה.

A fool cursed those oppressed and broken to vex them;
he taunted abject people: "They shall be consumed;"
"God shall hide His face from seeing."
When idols were placed in the Temple,
God avenged one's hand at the hand of the other, a disgusting item consumed.
This, at the time when He gathered anguish over us;
for an image was set up in the Sanctuary of God.

Miserable and plagued are these children, who were once the very first.
Their troubles have come close on one another's heels these many years;
stricken as if by the stings of bees and scorpions.
They think their hope is gone,
that as they sit in this darkness they have no more chance.

▸ Zealous God, in Your restraint toward those who incite You
they have flourished fat and succulent.
Raise up those who still await You;
let them stand firm always,
like something planted, or carved out with love.
It is on fast days that truth and peace are hewn out.
May they become forever times of joy and celebration – festive days.

אֵל מֶלֶךְ God, King who sits upon a throne of compassion, who acts with loving-kindness, who pardons the iniquities of His people, passing them before Him in order; who forgives sinners and pardons transgressors; who performs righteousness with all flesh and spirit, do not repay their bad actions in kind. ▸ God, You taught us to speak thirteen attributes: recall for us today the covenant of the thirteen attributes, as You in ancient times showed the humble one [Moses], as is written: The LORD descended in the cloud and stood with him there, and proclaimed in the name of the LORD:

Congregation then Leader:

And the LORD passed by before him and proclaimed: *Ex. 34*

All say aloud:

יהוה The LORD, the LORD, compassionate and gracious God, slow to anger, abounding in loving-kindness and truth, extending loving-kindness to a thousand generations, forgiving iniquity, rebellion and sin, and absolving [the guilty who repent]. Forgive us our iniquity and our sin, and take us as Your inheritance.

חֵרֶף עֲשׁוּקִים וּרְצוּצִים בַּעֲבוּר הַרְעִימָם סָכָל.
יְרוּדִים בְּוֹהֲיָה לֶאֱכֹל וּבְהַסְתֵּר פָּנִים מִלְּהִסְתַּכָּל.
יַד הִשְׁלִים מִכְּנַף שְׁקוּצִים נֶאֱכָל.
עֵת צָרָה כְּהִתְכַּנֵּס וְהָעֳמַד צֶלֶם בְּהֵיכָל.

דְּוּוִים סְגוּפִים בָּנִים הָיוּ מִקֶּדֶם רִאשׁוֹנִים.
סְמוּכוֹת צָרוֹתֵיהֶם זוֹ לְזוֹ כַּמָּה שָׁנִים.
לוּקִים כַּאֲשֶׁר תַּעֲשֶׂינָה הַדְּבוֹרִים, וְהָעַקְרַבִּים שׁוֹנִים.
הוֹגִים אָבַד שִׂבְרָם וּבָטֵל סִכּוּיָם בְּאִישׁוֹנִים.

› אֵל קַנָּא, בְּהִתְאַפֵּק בִּמְקַנְאֶיךָ דְּשֵׁנִים וְרַטֻבִּים.
מְחַכִּים תָּקִים עוֹמְדִים לְעוֹלָמִים, כִּנְטִיעִים מְחֻטָּבִים בַּאֲהָבִים.
הָאֱמֶת וְהַשָּׁלוֹם בְּצוֹמוֹת חֲטוּבִים.
נֵצַח הֱיוֹתָם לְשִׂמְחָה וּלְשָׂשׂוֹן וּלְמוֹעֲדִים טוֹבִים.

אֵל מֶלֶךְ יוֹשֵׁב עַל כִּסֵּא רַחֲמִים, מִתְנַהֵג בַּחֲסִידוּת. מוֹחֵל עֲוֹנוֹת עַמּוֹ, מַעֲבִיר רִאשׁוֹן רִאשׁוֹן. מַרְבֶּה מְחִילָה לְחַטָּאִים, וּסְלִיחָה לְפוֹשְׁעִים. עֹשֶׂה צְדָקוֹת עִם כָּל בָּשָׂר וָרוּחַ, לֹא כְרָעָתָם תִּגְמֹל. › אֵל, הוֹרֵיתָ לָּנוּ לוֹמַר שְׁלֹשׁ עֶשְׂרֵה, וּזְכָר לָנוּ הַיּוֹם בְּרִית שְׁלֹשׁ עֶשְׂרֵה, כְּמוֹ שֶׁהוֹדַעְתָּ לֶעָנָו מִקֶּדֶם, כְּמוֹ שֶׁכָּתוּב: וַיֵּרֶד יהוה בֶּעָנָן, וַיִּתְיַצֵּב עִמּוֹ שָׁם, וַיִּקְרָא בְשֵׁם, יהוה:

שליח ציבור then קהל:

שמות לד — וַיַּעֲבֹר יהוה עַל־פָּנָיו וַיִּקְרָא

All say aloud:

יהוה, יהוה, אֵל רַחוּם וְחַנּוּן, אֶרֶךְ אַפַּיִם, וְרַב־חֶסֶד וֶאֱמֶת: נֹצֵר חֶסֶד לָאֲלָפִים, נֹשֵׂא עָוֹן וָפֶשַׁע וְחַטָּאָה, וְנַקֵּה: וְסָלַחְתָּ לַעֲוֹנֵנוּ וּלְחַטָּאתֵנוּ, וּנְחַלְתָּנוּ:

Continue:

סְלַח לָנוּ Forgive us, our Father, for we have sinned. Pardon us, our King, for we have transgressed. For You, LORD, are good and forgiving, abounding in loving-kindness to all who call on You. *Ps. 86*

The following is said responsively:

Turn to this prisoner who has been yielded up,
to the hand of Babylon and then of Seir;
to You he has been calling all these years,
and he pleads like a small child,
on the day the enemy prevailed and the city was broken through.

And so I bow myself and strike my hands together,
on this day of five disasters that scattered me about,
for at the time of the golden calf, the Tablets left me.
And the daily offering was annulled,
and they brought me away in a cage.
And an idol was placed in the Sanctuary that was my crowning glory,
and I was deprived of His counsel.
The meal-offering was ended, and Your Law –
the foe sent it up in flames,
on the day the enemy prevailed and the city was broken through.

I tremble terribly, I stand horrified, on the day the LORD pushed me aside,
And Sennacherib, the Viper of the north, swept me away like a deluge.
My light grew dark, and Sheshakh [Babylon] too, tossed me about like a ball.
And the hunter stretched out his hand, and the goat of Greece,
the hairy one of Rome,
on the day the enemy prevailed and the city was broken through.

The glory of my heart, my Stronghold, will Your rage fume forever?
Will You not see this weary nation, blackened as if by the furnace?
Close, with the descendant of Peretz, the breach in my fence,
and, from among the thorns, pick out the lily.
Build the Temple, and return the borders of the Carmel and of Bashan.
And open Your eyes, exact vengeance from Etzer and Dishan.
Judge a people struck dumb, so that the damages be paid,
by the one who destroys, the one who burns –
on the day the enemy prevailed and the city was broken through.

Continue:

סְלַח לָנוּ אָבִינוּ כִּי חָטָאנוּ, מְחַל לָנוּ מַלְכֵּנוּ כִּי פָשָׁעְנוּ. כִּי־אַתָּה אֲדֹנָי טוֹב תהלים פו
וְסַלָּח, וְרַב־חֶסֶד לְכָל־קֹרְאֶיךָ:

The following is said responsively:

שְׁעֵה נֶאֱסַר, אֲשֶׁר נִמְסַר, בְּיַד בָּבֶל וְגַם שֵׂעִיר.
לְךָ יֶהֱמֶה, זֶה כַּמֶּה, וְיִתְחַנֵּן כְּבֶן צָעִיר.
יוֹם גָּבַר הָאוֹיֵב וַתִּבָּקַע הָעִיר.

לְזֹאת אִכַּף, וְאֶסְפֹּק כַּף, בְּיוֹם חֲמִשָּׁה פְּזָרוּנִי.
וְעַל רֶגֶל הָעֵגֶל, הַלֻּחוֹת יְצָאוּנִי.
וְגַם הִשְׁמִיד הַתָּמִיד, וּבַסּוּגַר הֱבִיאָנִי.
וְהוּשַׂם אֱלִיל בְּהֵיכַל כְּלִיל, וּמֵעֲצָתוֹ כְּלָאַנִי.
וְהַמִּנְחָה הוּנָחָה, וְדָתְךָ, צָר בָּאֵשׁ הִבְעִיר.
יוֹם גָּבַר הָאוֹיֵב וַתִּבָּקַע הָעִיר.

מְאֹד אֶתְחַל, וְאֶתְחַלְחַל, בְּיוֹם שַׁדַּי דְּחָפַנִי.
וְהַשְּׁפִיפוֹן מִצָּפוֹן, כְּשִׁבֹּלֶת שְׁטָפַנִי.
מְאוֹר חָשַׁךְ, וְגַם שֵׁשַׁךְ, כְּמוֹ כַדּוּר צְנָפַנִי.
וְהַצַּיָּד שָׁלַח יָד, וְהַצָּפִיר וְהַשָּׂעִיר.
יוֹם גָּבַר הָאוֹיֵב וַתִּבָּקַע הָעִיר.

הוֹד לִבִּי וּמִשְׂגַּבִּי, הֲלָעַד אַפְּךָ יֶעְשַׁן.
הֲלֹא תִרְאֶה עַם נִלְאֶה, אֲשֶׁר הָשְׁחַר כְּמוֹ כִבְשָׁן.
גְּדֹר פִּרְצִי בְּבֶן פַּרְצִי, וּמֵחֶדֶק לְקֹט שׁוֹשָׁן.
בְּנֵה בֵּית זְבוּל, וְהָשֵׁב גְּבוּל הַכַּרְמֶל וְהַבָּשָׁן.
וְעַיִן פְּקַח, וְנָקָם קַח מֵאֵצֶר וּמִדִּישָׁן.
שְׁפֹט אִלֵּם, וְאָז יְשַׁלֵּם הַמַּבְעֶה וְהַמַּבְעִיר.
יוֹם גָּבַר הָאוֹיֵב וַתִּבָּקַע הָעִיר.

Continue:

אֵל מֶלֶךְ God, King who sits upon a throne of compassion, who acts with loving-kindness, who pardons the iniquities of His people, passing them before Him in order; who forgives sinners and pardons transgressors; who performs righteousness with all flesh and spirit, do not repay their bad actions in kind. God, You taught us to speak thirteen attributes: recall for us today the covenant of the thirteen attributes, as You in ancient times showed the humble one [Moses], as is written: The LORD descended in the cloud and stood with him there, and proclaimed in the name of the LORD:

Congregation then Leader:

And the LORD passed by before him and proclaimed: *Ex. 34*

All say aloud:

יהוה The LORD, the LORD, compassionate and gracious God, slow to anger, abounding in loving-kindness and truth, extending loving-kindness to a thousand generations, forgiving iniquity, rebellion and sin, and absolving [the guilty who repent]. Forgive us our iniquity and our sin, and take us as Your inheritance.

Continue:

סְלַח לָנוּ Forgive us, our Father, for we have sinned. Pardon us, our King, for we have transgressed. For You, LORD, are good and forgiving, abounding in loving-kindness to all who call on You. *Ps. 86*

זְכֹר Remember, LORD, Your compassion and loving-kindness, *Ps. 25*
for they are everlasting. Remember us, LORD, in favoring Your people;
redeem us with Your salvation.

זְכֹר Remember Your congregation, the one that You acquired long ago, *Ps. 74*
the tribe of Your inheritance that You redeemed,
this Mount Zion that You have dwelt in.

זְכֹר Remember, LORD, the fondness of Jerusalem; do not forever forget the
love of Zion. You shall rise up and have compassion for Zion, *Ps. 102*
for now it is right to be gracious, for the time has come.

זְכֹר Remember, LORD, what the Edomites did on the day Jerusalem fell. *Ps. 137*
They said, "Tear it down, tear it down to its very foundations!"

זְכֹר Remember Abraham, Isaac and Jacob, to whom You swore by Your *Ex. 32*
own self, when You said to them, "I shall make Your descendants
as numerous as the stars in the sky, and I shall give all this Land that
I spoke of to your descendants, and they shall inherit it forever."

זְכֹר Remember Your servants, Abraham, Isaac and Jacob; do not attend to *Deut. 9*
the stubbornness of this people, to their wickedness or sinfulness.

Continue:

אֵל מֶלֶךְ יוֹשֵׁב עַל כִּסֵּא רַחֲמִים, מִתְנַהֵג בַּחֲסִידוּת. מוֹחֵל עֲוֹנוֹת עַמּוֹ, מַעֲבִיר רִאשׁוֹן רִאשׁוֹן. מַרְבֶּה מְחִילָה לְחַטָּאִים, וּסְלִיחָה לְפוֹשְׁעִים. עֹשֶׂה צְדָקוֹת עִם כָּל בָּשָׂר וָרוּחַ, לֹא כְרָעָתָם תִּגְמֹל. › אֵל, הוֹרֵיתָ לָנוּ לוֹמַר שְׁלֹשׁ עֶשְׂרֵה, וּזְכָר לָנוּ הַיּוֹם בְּרִית שְׁלֹשׁ עֶשְׂרֵה, כְּמוֹ שֶׁהוֹדַעְתָּ לֶעָנָו מִקֶּדֶם, כְּמוֹ שֶׁכָּתוּב: וַיֵּרֶד יהוה בֶּעָנָן, וַיִּתְיַצֵּב עִמּוֹ שָׁם, וַיִּקְרָא בְשֵׁם, יהוה:

שליח ציבור then קהל:

שמות לד וַיַּעֲבֹר יהוה עַל־פָּנָיו וַיִּקְרָא

All say aloud:

יהוה, יהוה, אֵל רַחוּם וְחַנּוּן, אֶרֶךְ אַפַּיִם, וְרַב־חֶסֶד וֶאֱמֶת: נֹצֵר חֶסֶד לָאֲלָפִים, נֹשֵׂא עָוֹן וָפֶשַׁע וְחַטָּאָה, וְנַקֵּה: וְסָלַחְתָּ לַעֲוֹנֵנוּ וּלְחַטָּאתֵנוּ, וּנְחַלְתָּנוּ:

Continue:

תהלים פו סְלַח לָנוּ אָבִינוּ כִּי חָטָאנוּ, מְחַל לָנוּ מַלְכֵּנוּ כִּי פָשָׁעְנוּ. כִּי־אַתָּה אֲדֹנָי טוֹב וְסַלָּח, וְרַב־חֶסֶד לְכָל־קֹרְאֶיךָ:

תהלים כה זְכֹר־רַחֲמֶיךָ יהוה וַחֲסָדֶיךָ, כִּי מֵעוֹלָם הֵמָּה:

זָכְרֵנוּ יהוה בִּרְצוֹן עַמֶּךָ, פָּקְדֵנוּ בִּישׁוּעָתֶךָ.

תהלים עד זְכֹר עֲדָתְךָ קָנִיתָ קֶּדֶם, גָּאַלְתָּ שֵׁבֶט נַחֲלָתֶךָ

הַר־צִיּוֹן זֶה שָׁכַנְתָּ בּוֹ:

זְכֹר יהוה חִבַּת יְרוּשָׁלָיִם, אַהֲבַת צִיּוֹן אַל תִּשְׁכַּח לָנֶצַח.

תהלים קב אַתָּה תָקוּם תְּרַחֵם צִיּוֹן, כִּי־עֵת לְחֶנְנָהּ, כִּי־בָא מוֹעֵד:

תהלים קלז זְכֹר יהוה לִבְנֵי אֱדוֹם אֵת יוֹם יְרוּשָׁלָיִם

הָאֹמְרִים עָרוּ עָרוּ, עַד הַיְסוֹד בָּהּ:

שמות לב זְכֹר לְאַבְרָהָם לְיִצְחָק וּלְיִשְׂרָאֵל עֲבָדֶיךָ, אֲשֶׁר נִשְׁבַּעְתָּ לָהֶם בָּךְ

וַתְּדַבֵּר אֲלֵהֶם, אַרְבֶּה אֶת־זַרְעֲכֶם כְּכוֹכְבֵי הַשָּׁמָיִם

וְכָל־הָאָרֶץ הַזֹּאת אֲשֶׁר אָמַרְתִּי אֶתֵּן לְזַרְעֲכֶם, וְנָחֲלוּ לְעֹלָם:

דברים ט זְכֹר לַעֲבָדֶיךָ לְאַבְרָהָם לְיִצְחָק וּלְיַעֲקֹב

אַל־תֵּפֶן אֶל־קְשִׁי הָעָם הַזֶּה וְאֶל־רִשְׁעוֹ וְאֶל־חַטָּאתוֹ:

אַל־נָא Please, do not hold against us the sin
that we committed so foolishly, that we have sinned. *Num. 12*
We have sinned, our Rock; forgive us, our Creator.

Some say responsively (all continue with "Remember the covenant" on the next page):

אֵל נָא God, please, heal please, the diseases of this fruitful vine,
ashamed, disgraced and miserable are her fruits.
Redeem her from destruction and from the seeping wound;
answer us as You answered our father Abraham on Mount Moriah –
We have sinned, our Rock;
forgive us, our Creator.

Let the flags of the people redeemed by Your revealed arm,
be spared from plague; let them not be cut down,
and answer our call, and desire the creations of Your hands.
Answer us as You answered our fathers at the Reed Sea –
We have sinned, our Rock;
forgive us, our Creator.

Reveal now the merit of Abraham and Sarah,
the rock from which we were hewn.
Spare us from rage and lead us on a straight path.
Clear our impurity, and open our eyes to the light of Your Torah.
Answer us as You answered Joshua at Gilgal –
We have sinned, our Rock;
forgive us, our Creator.

LORD, witness the ashes of bound Isaac; make our cure spring up.
Put an end to plunder and brokenness, tempest and storm.
Teach us and make us wise with Your perfect word.
Answer us as You answered Samuel at Mitzpah –
We have sinned, our Rock;
forgive us, our Creator.

Jacob who emerged perfect from the womb – do not let his roots dry up.
Cleanse us of all stain and blemish, and do not have us wither.
Help us and we shall be saved,
and receive of Your ways of kindness.
Answer us as You answered Elijah on Mount Carmel –
We have sinned, our Rock;
forgive us, our Creator.

אַל־נָא תָשֵׁת עָלֵינוּ חַטָּאת אֲשֶׁר נוֹאַלְנוּ וַאֲשֶׁר חָטָאנוּ: במדבר יב
חָטָאנוּ צוּרֵנוּ, סְלַח לָנוּ יוֹצְרֵנוּ.

Some say responsively (all continue with זְכָר לָנוּ בְּרִית *on the next page):*

אֵל נָא, רְפָא נָא תַּחֲלוּאֵי גֶּפֶן פּוֹרִיָּה
בּוֹשָׁה וְחָפְרָה, וְאֻמְלַל פִּרְיָהּ
גָּאֳלֶנָּה מִשַּׁחַת וּמִמַּכָּה טְרִיָּה.
עֲנֵנוּ כְּשֶׁעָנִיתָ לְאַבְרָהָם אָבִינוּ בְּהַר הַמּוֹרִיָּה.
חָטָאנוּ צוּרֵנוּ, סְלַח לָנוּ יוֹצְרֵנוּ.

דְּגָלֵי עַם, פְּדוּיֵי בִּזְרוֹעַ חָשׂוּף
הַצֵּל מִנֶּגֶף וְאַל יִהְיוּ לִשְׂסוּף
וְתַעֲנֶה קְרִיאָתֵנוּ וּלְמַעֲשֵׂה יָדֶיךָ תִּכְסֹף
עֲנֵנוּ כְּשֶׁעָנִיתָ לַאֲבוֹתֵינוּ עַל יַם סוּף.
חָטָאנוּ צוּרֵנוּ, סְלַח לָנוּ יוֹצְרֵנוּ.

זְכוּת צוּר חֻצַּב הַיּוֹם לָנוּ תְגַל
חָשְׂכֵנוּ מֵאֱנֹף וּנְחֵנוּ בְּיֹשֶׁר מַעְגָּל
טַהֵר טֻמְאָתֵנוּ וְלִמְאוֹר תּוֹרָתְךָ עֵינֵינוּ גַל
עֲנֵנוּ כְּשֶׁעָנִיתָ לִיהוֹשֻׁעַ בַּגִּלְגָּל.
חָטָאנוּ צוּרֵנוּ, סְלַח לָנוּ יוֹצְרֵנוּ.

יָהּ, רְאֵה דֶּשֶׁן עָקוּד, וְהַצְמַח לָנוּ תְרוּפָה
כַּלֵּה שֹׁד וָשֶׁבֶר, סַעַר וְסוּפָה
לַמְּדֵנוּ וְחַכְּמֵנוּ אִמְרָתְךָ הַצְּרוּפָה
עֲנֵנוּ כְּשֶׁעָנִיתָ לִשְׁמוּאֵל בַּמִּצְפָּה.
חָטָאנוּ צוּרֵנוּ, סְלַח לָנוּ יוֹצְרֵנוּ.

מְתֹמָם מְרַחֵם, שָׁרָשָׁיו אַל תְּקַמֵּל
נַקֵּנוּ מִכֶּתֶם וְשֶׁמֶץ, וְלֹא נֶאֱמַל
סַעֲדֵנוּ וְנִוָּשֵׁעָה, וְאָרְחוֹת חֲסָדֶיךָ נִגָּמֵל
עֲנֵנוּ כְּשֶׁעָנִיתָ לְאֵלִיָּהוּ בְּהַר הַכַּרְמֶל.
חָטָאנוּ צוּרֵנוּ, סְלַח לָנוּ יוֹצְרֵנוּ.

Strengthen us by the righteousness of Moses, drawn from water,
and atone our crimes, wanton or foolish.
Free us from the terror of death that thrusts us back,
rule for our salvation; do not let us melt away in our sins.
Answer us as You answered Jonah in the belly of the fish –
We have sinned, our Rock;
forgive us, our Creator.

Remember Your devoted Aaron's sanctity,
for the sake of Israel of the pleasing steps.
Awaken Your compassion, for we are doubly stricken.
Return us resolutely to our awe of You, do not expose us.
Answer us as You answered David, and Solomon his son in Jerusalem –
We have sinned, our Rock;
forgive us, our Creator.

On the Fast of Esther add:
Answer those who call You; listen out from Your residence.
Hear the cry of those who call out to You, You who listen to the destitute.
Have compassion for Your children, as a father has for his.
Answer us as You answered Mordekhai and Esther:
and on a fifty-cubit gallows they hanged father and sons –
We have sinned, our Rock.
Forgive us, our Creator.

All continue:

זְכֹר Remember the covenant of our fathers, as You have said,
"I shall remember My covenant with Jacob, and My covenant with Isaac, and I shall remember My covenant with Abraham, and I shall remember the Land." *Lev. 26*

זְכֹר Remember the covenant of the early ones, as You have said,
"I shall remember for them the covenant of the early ones, those I took out of the Land of Egypt before the eyes of the nations, in order to be their God: I am the LORD." *Lev. 26*

עֲשֵׂה Deal kindly with us as You have promised, "Even so, when they are in the land of their enemies I shall not reject them and shall not detest them to the point of destruction, to the point of breaking My covenant with them, for I am the LORD their God." Restore our fortunes, and have compassion for us as is written, "And God shall restore your fortunes and have compassion for you, and shall return and gather you in from all the nations among whom the LORD *Lev. 26* *Deut. 30*

עוֹדְדֵנוּ בְּצֶדֶק מָשׁוּי מִמַּיִם, וְכַפֵּר זָדוֹן וּמִשְׁוּגָה
פְּדֵנוּ מִמְּהוּמַת מָוֶת, וְאָחוֹר בַּל נִסּוֹגָה
צַוֵּה יְשׁוּעָתֵנוּ, וּבַעֲוֹנוֹתֵינוּ אַל נִתְמוֹגְגָה
עֲנֵנוּ כְּשֶׁעָנִיתָ לְיוֹנָה בִּמְעֵי הַדָּגָה.
חָטָאנוּ צוּרֵנוּ, סְלַח לָנוּ יוֹצְרֵנוּ.

קְדֻשַּׁת אִישׁ חֲסִידֶךָ זְכֹר לְיֹפַת פְּעָמַיִם
רַחֲמֶיךָ תְּעוֹרֵר כִּי לָקִינוּ בְּכִפְלַיִם
שׁוּבֵנוּ תֹּקֶף לְיִרְאָתֶךָ וְלֹא נֶחֱשַׂף שׁוּלַיִם
עֲנֵנוּ כְּשֶׁעָנִיתָ לְדָוִד וְלִשְׁלֹמֹה בְנוֹ בִּירוּשָׁלַיִם.
חָטָאנוּ צוּרֵנוּ, סְלַח לָנוּ יוֹצְרֵנוּ.

On תענית אסתר *add:*

תַּעֲנֶה לְקוֹרְאֶיךָ, וְהַסְכֵּת מִמְּעוֹנִים
תִּשְׁמַע שַׁוְעַת צוֹעֲקֶיךָ, שׁוֹמֵעַ אֶל אֶבְיוֹנִים
תְּרַחֵם עַל בָּנֶיךָ כְּרַחֵם אָב עַל בָּנִים
עֲנֵנוּ כְּמוֹ שֶׁעָנִיתָ לְמָרְדְּכַי וְאֶסְתֵּר
וְתָלוּ עַל עֵץ־חֲמִשִּׁים הָאָב עִם בָּנִים.
חָטָאנוּ צוּרֵנוּ, סְלַח לָנוּ יוֹצְרֵנוּ.

All continue:

זְכָר לָנוּ בְּרִית אָבוֹת כַּאֲשֶׁר אָמַרְתָּ: וְזָכַרְתִּי אֶת־בְּרִיתִי יַעֲקוֹב ויקרא כו
וְאַף אֶת־בְּרִיתִי יִצְחָק וְאַף אֶת־בְּרִיתִי אַבְרָהָם אֶזְכֹּר
וְהָאָרֶץ אֶזְכֹּר:

זְכָר לָנוּ בְּרִית רִאשׁוֹנִים כַּאֲשֶׁר אָמַרְתָּ: וְזָכַרְתִּי לָהֶם בְּרִית רִאשֹׁנִים ויקרא כו
אֲשֶׁר הוֹצֵאתִי־אֹתָם מֵאֶרֶץ מִצְרַיִם לְעֵינֵי הַגּוֹיִם
לִהְיוֹת לָהֶם לֵאלֹהִים, אֲנִי יהוה:

עֲשֵׂה עִמָּנוּ כְּמָה שֶׁהִבְטַחְתָּנוּ: וְאַף גַּם־זֹאת בִּהְיוֹתָם בְּאֶרֶץ אֹיְבֵיהֶם, ויקרא כו
לֹא־מְאַסְתִּים וְלֹא־גְעַלְתִּים לְכַלֹּתָם, לְהָפֵר בְּרִיתִי אִתָּם, כִּי אֲנִי יהוה
אֱלֹהֵיהֶם: הָשֵׁב שְׁבוּתֵנוּ וְרַחֲמֵנוּ כְּמָה שֶׁכָּתוּב: וְשָׁב יהוה אֱלֹהֶיךָ אֶת־ דברים ל

has scattered you." Gather those of us who have been distanced, as is written,
"If your distanced ones are at the very ends of the heavens, from there shall *Deut. 30*
the LORD your God gather you; from there shall He bring You." Wipe out our
crimes as if they were a cloud, as if they were a haze, as is written, "I have wiped *Is. 44*
out your crimes like a cloud, and as a haze your sins; come back to Me for I have
redeemed you." Wipe out our crimes for Your sake, as You have said, "I, I am the *Is. 43*
one who shall wipe out your crimes for My sake, and I shall not recall your sins."
Whiten our sins as snow and as wool, as is written, "Come now, let us reason *Is. 1*
together, says the LORD; If your sins are like scarlet, they shall be whitened like
snow; should they be as red as crimson, they shall become like wool." Throw
over us pure waters and purify us, as is written, "I shall throw pure waters over *Ezek. 36*
you and you shall be pure. I shall purify you of all your impurities and of all your
idolatry." Have compassion for us and do not destroy us, as is written, "For the *Deut. 4*
LORD your God is a compassionate God; He will not cease to hold you and
He will not destroy you, and will not forget the covenant of your fathers that
He pledged to them." Circumcise our hearts to love Your name, as is written,
"And the LORD will circumcise your heart and the heart of your descendants to *Deut. 30*
love the LORD your God with all your heart and with all your soul, so that you
shall live." Let us find You when we seek You, as is written, "And if from there *Deut. 4*
you seek the LORD your God, you shall find Him, when you seek Him out with
all your heart and with all your soul." Bring us to Your holy mountain, and let
us rejoice in Your house of prayer, as is written, "I shall bring them to My holy *Is. 56*
mountain, and I shall make them rejoice in My house of prayer; their offerings
and their sacrifices will be accepted, desired on My altar, for My House will be
called a house of prayer for all peoples."

The Ark is opened. The following until ◂ is said responsively, verse by verse:

שְׁמַע קוֹלֵנוּ Listen to our voice, LORD our God. Spare us and have compassion
on us, and in compassion and favor accept our prayer. Turn us back, O LORD, *Lam. 5*
to You, and we will return. Renew our days as of old. Do not cast us away from
You, and do not take Your holy spirit from us. Do not cast us away in our old
age; when our strength is gone do not desert us.◂ Do not desert us, LORD; our
God, do not be distant from us. Give us a sign of good things, and those who
hate us shall see it and be ashamed, for You, LORD, will help us and console us.
Hear our speech, LORD, consider our thoughts. May the words of our mouths
and the thoughts within our hearts be pleasing to You, LORD, our Rock and
our Redeemer. For it is You, LORD, that we have longed for; You shall answer
us, LORD our God.

The Ark is closed.

שְׁבוּתְךָ וְרִחֲמֶךָ, וְשָׁב וְקִבֶּצְךָ מִכָּל־הָעַמִּים אֲשֶׁר הֱפִיצְךָ יהוה אֱלֹהֶיךָ
שָׁמָּה: קַבֵּץ נִדָּחֵינוּ כְּמָה שֶׁכָּתוּב: אִם־יִהְיֶה נִדַּחֲךָ בִּקְצֵה הַשָּׁמָיִם, מִשָּׁם דברים ל
יְקַבֶּצְךָ יהוה אֱלֹהֶיךָ וּמִשָּׁם יִקָּחֶךָ: מְחֵה פְשָׁעֵינוּ כָּעָב וְכֶעָנָן כְּמָה שֶׁכָּתוּב:
מָחִיתִי כָעָב פְּשָׁעֶיךָ וְכֶעָנָן חַטֹּאותֶיךָ, שׁוּבָה אֵלַי כִּי גְאַלְתִּיךָ: מְחֵה פְשָׁעֵינוּ ישעיה מד
לְמַעַנְךָ כַּאֲשֶׁר אָמַרְתָּ: אָנֹכִי אָנֹכִי הוּא מֹחֶה פְשָׁעֶיךָ לְמַעֲנִי, וְחַטֹּאתֶיךָ ישעיה מג
לֹא אֶזְכֹּר: הַלְבֵּן חֲטָאֵינוּ כַּשֶּׁלֶג וְכַצֶּמֶר כְּמָה שֶׁכָּתוּב: לְכוּ־נָא וְנִוָּכְחָה ישעיה א
יֹאמַר יהוה, אִם־יִהְיוּ חֲטָאֵיכֶם כַּשָּׁנִים כַּשֶּׁלֶג יַלְבִּינוּ, אִם־יַאְדִּימוּ כַתּוֹלָע
כַּצֶּמֶר יִהְיוּ: זְרֹק עָלֵינוּ מַיִם טְהוֹרִים וְטַהֲרֵנוּ כְּמָה שֶׁכָּתוּב: וְזָרַקְתִּי עֲלֵיכֶם יחזקאל לו
מַיִם טְהוֹרִים וּטְהַרְתֶּם, מִכֹּל טֻמְאוֹתֵיכֶם וּמִכָּל־גִּלּוּלֵיכֶם אֲטַהֵר אֶתְכֶם:
רַחֵם עָלֵינוּ וְאַל תַּשְׁחִיתֵנוּ כְּמָה שֶׁכָּתוּב: כִּי אֵל רַחוּם יהוה אֱלֹהֶיךָ, לֹא דברים ד
יַרְפְּךָ וְלֹא יַשְׁחִיתֶךָ, וְלֹא יִשְׁכַּח אֶת־בְּרִית אֲבוֹתֶיךָ אֲשֶׁר נִשְׁבַּע לָהֶם: מוֹל
אֶת לְבָבֵנוּ לְאַהֲבָה אֶת שְׁמֶךָ כְּמָה שֶׁכָּתוּב: וּמָל יהוה אֱלֹהֶיךָ אֶת־לְבָבְךָ דברים ל
וְאֶת־לְבַב זַרְעֶךָ, לְאַהֲבָה אֶת־יהוה אֱלֹהֶיךָ בְּכָל־לְבָבְךָ וּבְכָל־נַפְשְׁךָ, לְמַעַן
חַיֶּיךָ: הִמָּצֵא לָנוּ בְּבַקָּשָׁתֵנוּ כְּמָה שֶׁכָּתוּב: וּבִקַּשְׁתֶּם מִשָּׁם אֶת־יהוה דברים ד
אֱלֹהֶיךָ וּמָצָאתָ, כִּי תִדְרְשֶׁנּוּ בְּכָל־לְבָבְךָ וּבְכָל־נַפְשֶׁךָ: תְּבִיאֵנוּ אֶל הַר
קָדְשֶׁךָ וְשַׂמְּחֵנוּ בְּבֵית תְּפִלָּתֶךָ כְּמָה שֶׁכָּתוּב: וַהֲבִיאוֹתִים אֶל־הַר קָדְשִׁי ישעיה נו
וְשִׂמַּחְתִּים בְּבֵית תְּפִלָּתִי, עוֹלֹתֵיהֶם וְזִבְחֵיהֶם לְרָצוֹן עַל־מִזְבְּחִי, כִּי בֵיתִי
בֵּית־תְּפִלָּה יִקָּרֵא לְכָל־הָעַמִּים:

The ארון קודש is opened. The following until ▸ is said responsively, verse by verse:

שְׁמַע קוֹלֵנוּ, יהוה אֱלֹהֵינוּ, חוּס וְרַחֵם עָלֵינוּ וְקַבֵּל בְּרַחֲמִים וּבְרָצוֹן אֶת
תְּפִלָּתֵנוּ. הֲשִׁיבֵנוּ יהוה אֵלֶיךָ וְנָשׁוּבָה, חַדֵּשׁ יָמֵינוּ כְּקֶדֶם: אַל תַּשְׁלִיכֵנוּ איכה ה
מִלְּפָנֶיךָ, וְרוּחַ קָדְשְׁךָ אַל תִּקַּח מִמֶּנּוּ. אַל תַּשְׁלִיכֵנוּ לְעֵת זִקְנָה, כִּכְלוֹת
כֹּחֵנוּ אַל תַּעַזְבֵנוּ.▸ אַל תַּעַזְבֵנוּ יהוה, אֱלֹהֵינוּ אַל תִּרְחַק מִמֶּנּוּ. עֲשֵׂה
עִמָּנוּ אוֹת לְטוֹבָה, וְיִרְאוּ שׂוֹנְאֵינוּ וְיֵבֹשׁוּ, כִּי אַתָּה יהוה עֲזַרְתָּנוּ וְנִחַמְתָּנוּ.
אֲמָרֵינוּ הַאֲזִינָה יהוה, בִּינָה הֲגִיגֵנוּ. יִהְיוּ לְרָצוֹן אִמְרֵי פִינוּ וְהֶגְיוֹן לִבֵּנוּ
לְפָנֶיךָ, יהוה צוּרֵנוּ וְגוֹאֲלֵנוּ. כִּי לְךָ יהוה הוֹחָלְנוּ, אַתָּה תַעֲנֶה אֲדֹנָי אֱלֹהֵינוּ.

The ארון קודש is closed.

CONFESSION

אֱלֹהֵינוּ Our God and God of our fathers,
let our prayer come before You, and do not hide Yourself from our plea,
for we are not so arrogant or obstinate as to say before You,
LORD, our God and God of our fathers,
we are righteous and have not sinned,
for in truth, we and our fathers have sinned.

Strike the left side of the chest with the right fist while saying each of the sins.

אָשַׁמְנוּ We have been guilty, we have acted treacherously, we have robbed, we have spoken slander. We have acted perversely, we have acted wickedly, we have acted presumptuously, we have been violent, we have framed lies. We have given bad advice, we have deceived, we have scorned, we have rebelled, we have provoked, we have turned away, we have committed iniquity, we have transgressed, we have persecuted, we have been obstinate. We have acted wickedly, we have corrupted, we have acted abominably, we have strayed, we have led others astray.

סַרְנוּ We have turned away from Your commandments, and good laws, to no avail, for You are just in all that has befallen us, for You have acted faithfully *Neh. 9*
while we have done wickedly.

הִרְשַׁעְנוּ We have been wicked and we have done wrong, and so we have not been saved. Place it in our hearts to abandon the way of wickedness, and hasten our salvation, as is written by Your prophet, "Let each wicked person *Is. 55*
abandon his ways, each man of iniquity his thoughts, and let him come back to the LORD and He will have compassion for him; back to our God for He will forgive abundantly."

מְשִׁיחַ Your righteous anointed one said to You, "Who can discern his own *Ps. 19*
mistakes? Cleanse me of my hidden faults." Cleanse us, LORD our God, of all our sins, and purify us of all our impurities and throw clear waters over us to purify us, as was written by Your prophet, "I shall throw clear waters over you *Ezek. 36*
and you shall be pure. I shall purify you of all your impurities and of all your idolatry." Your people, Your inheritance, famished of Your good, thirsting for Your loving-kindness, craving Your salvation – they shall recognize and know that compassion and forgiveness belong to the LORD our God.

On days when Taḥanun is not said continue with Avinu Malkenu on page 188 followed by Half Kaddish (page 208).

וידוי

אֱלֹהֵינוּ וֵאלֹהֵי אֲבוֹתֵינוּ
תָּבֹא לְפָנֶיךָ תְּפִלָּתֵנוּ, וְאַל תִּתְעַלַּם מִתְּחִנָּתֵנוּ.
שֶׁאֵין אֲנוּ עַזֵּי פָנִים וּקְשֵׁי עֹרֶף לוֹמַר לְפָנֶיךָ
יהוה אֱלֹהֵינוּ וֵאלֹהֵי אֲבוֹתֵינוּ, צַדִּיקִים אֲנַחְנוּ וְלֹא חָטָאנוּ.
אֲבָל אֲנַחְנוּ וַאֲבוֹתֵינוּ חָטָאנוּ.

Strike the left side of the chest with the right fist while saying each of the sins.

אָשַׁמְנוּ, בָּגַדְנוּ, גָּזַלְנוּ, דִּבַּרְנוּ דֹפִי. הֶעֱוִינוּ, וְהִרְשַׁעְנוּ, זַדְנוּ, חָמַסְנוּ, טָפַלְנוּ שֶׁקֶר. יָעַצְנוּ רָע, כִּזַּבְנוּ, לַצְנוּ, מָרַדְנוּ, נִאַצְנוּ, סָרַרְנוּ, עָוִינוּ, פָּשַׁעְנוּ, צָרַרְנוּ, קִשִּׁינוּ עֹרֶף. רָשַׁעְנוּ, שִׁחַתְנוּ, תִּעַבְנוּ, תָּעִינוּ, תִּעְתָּעְנוּ.

סַרְנוּ מִמִּצְוֹתֶיךָ וּמִמִּשְׁפָּטֶיךָ הַטּוֹבִים, וְלֹא שָׁוָה לָנוּ. וְאַתָּה צַדִּיק עַל נחמיה ט
כָּל־הַבָּא עָלֵינוּ, כִּי־אֱמֶת עָשִׂיתָ וַאֲנַחְנוּ הִרְשָׁעְנוּ.

הִרְשַׁעְנוּ וּפָשַׁעְנוּ לָכֵן לֹא נוֹשָׁעְנוּ. וְתֵן בְּלִבֵּנוּ לַעֲזֹב דֶּרֶךְ רֶשַׁע, וְחִישׁ
לָנוּ יֶשַׁע, כַּכָּתוּב עַל יַד נְבִיאֶךָ: יַעֲזֹב רָשָׁע דַּרְכּוֹ וְאִישׁ אָוֶן מַחְשְׁבֹתָיו, ישעיה נה
וְיָשֹׁב אֶל־יהוה וִירַחֲמֵהוּ וְאֶל־אֱלֹהֵינוּ כִּי־יַרְבֶּה לִסְלוֹחַ:

מְשִׁיחַ צִדְקֶךָ אָמַר לְפָנֶיךָ: שְׁגִיאוֹת מִי־יָבִין, מִנִּסְתָּרוֹת נַקֵּנִי: נַקֵּנוּ יהוה תהלים יט
אֱלֹהֵינוּ מִכָּל פְּשָׁעֵינוּ וְטַהֲרֵנוּ מִכָּל טֻמְאוֹתֵינוּ וּזְרֹק עָלֵינוּ מַיִם טְהוֹרִים
וְטַהֲרֵנוּ, כַּכָּתוּב עַל יַד נְבִיאֶךָ: וְזָרַקְתִּי עֲלֵיכֶם מַיִם טְהוֹרִים וּטְהַרְתֶּם, יחזקאל לו
מִכֹּל טֻמְאוֹתֵיכֶם וּמִכָּל־גִּלּוּלֵיכֶם אֲטַהֵר אֶתְכֶם: עַמְּךָ וְנַחֲלָתְךָ רְעֵבֵי
טוּבְךָ, צְמֵאֵי חַסְדְּךָ, תְּאֵבֵי יִשְׁעֶךָ. יַכִּירוּ וְיֵדְעוּ, כִּי לַיהוה אֱלֹהֵינוּ
הָרַחֲמִים וְהַסְּלִיחוֹת.

On days when תחנון *is not said continue with* אבינו מלכנו *on page 189 followed by* חצי קדיש *(page 209).*

אֵל רַחוּם Compassionate God is Your name; Gracious God is Your name. We are called by Your name; LORD, act for the sake of Your name. Act for the sake of Your truth. Act for the sake of Your covenant. Act for the sake of Your greatness and glory. Act for the sake of Your Law. Act for the sake of Your majesty. Act for the sake of Your promise. Act for the sake of Your remembrance. Act for the sake of Your loving-kindness. Act for the sake of Your goodness. Act for the sake of Your oneness. Act for the sake of Your honor. Act for the sake of Your wisdom. Act for the sake of Your kingship. Act for the sake of Your eternity. Act for the sake of Your mystery. Act for the sake of Your might. Act for the sake of Your splendor. Act for the sake of Your righteousness. Act for the sake of Your holiness. Act for the sake of Your great compassion. Act for the sake of Your Presence. Act for the sake of Your praise. Act for the sake of those who loved You, who now dwell in the dust. Act for the sake of Abraham, Isaac and Jacob. Act for the sake of Moses and Aaron. Act for the sake of David and Solomon. Act for the sake of Jerusalem, Your holy city. Act for the sake of Zion, the dwelling place of Your glory. Act for the sake of the desolate site of Your Temple. Act for the sake of the ruins of Your altar. Act for the sake of those killed in sanctification of Your name. Act for the sake of those slaughtered over Your unity. Act for the sake of those who have gone through fire and water in sanctification of Your name. Act for the sake of suckling infants who have not sinned. Act for the sake of little ones just weaned who have done no wrong. Act for the sake of schoolchildren. Act for Your own sake if not for ours. Act for Your own sake, and save us.

עֲנֵנוּ Answer us, LORD, answer us. Answer us, our God, answer us. Answer us, our Father, answer us. Answer us, our Creator, answer us. Answer us, our Redeemer, answer us. Answer us, You who seek us, answer us. Answer us, God who is faithful, answer us. Answer us, You who are ancient and kind, answer us. Answer us, You who are pure and upright, answer us. Answer us, You who are alive and remain, answer us. Answer us, You who are good and do good, answer us. Answer us, You who know our impulses, answer us. Answer us, You who conquer rage, answer us. Answer us, You who clothe Yourself in righteousness, answer us. Answer us, Supreme King of kings, answer us. Answer us, You who are awesome and elevated, answer us. Answer us, You who forgive and pardon, answer us. Answer us, You who answer in times of trouble, answer us. Answer us, You who redeem and save, answer us. Answer us, You who are righteous and straightforward, answer us. Answer us, You who are close to those who call, answer us. Answer us, You who are compassionate and gracious, answer us. Answer us, You who listen to the destitute, answer us. Answer us, You who support the innocent, answer us. Answer us, God of our fathers, answer us. Answer us, God of Abraham, answer us. Answer us, Terror of Isaac, answer us. Answer us, Champion of Jacob, answer us. Answer us, Help of the tribes, answer us. Answer us, Stronghold of the mothers, answer us. Answer us, You who are slow to anger, answer us. Answer us, You who are lightly appeased, answer us. Answer us, You who answer at times of favor, answer us. Answer us, Father of orphans, answer us. Answer us, Justice of widows, answer us.

אֵל רַחוּם שְׁמֶךָ. אֵל חַנּוּן שְׁמֶךָ. בָּנוּ נִקְרָא שְׁמֶךָ. יהוה עֲשֵׂה לְמַעַן שְׁמֶךָ. עֲשֵׂה לְמַעַן אֲמִתָּךְ. עֲשֵׂה לְמַעַן בְּרִיתָךְ. עֲשֵׂה לְמַעַן גָּדְלָךְ וְתִפְאַרְתָּךְ. עֲשֵׂה לְמַעַן דָּתָךְ. עֲשֵׂה לְמַעַן הוֹדָךְ. עֲשֵׂה לְמַעַן וִעוּדָךְ. עֲשֵׂה לְמַעַן זִכְרָךְ. עֲשֵׂה לְמַעַן חַסְדָּךְ. עֲשֵׂה לְמַעַן טוּבָךְ. עֲשֵׂה לְמַעַן יִחוּדָךְ. עֲשֵׂה לְמַעַן כְּבוֹדָךְ. עֲשֵׂה לְמַעַן לִמּוּדָךְ. עֲשֵׂה לְמַעַן מַלְכוּתָךְ. עֲשֵׂה לְמַעַן נִצְחָךְ. עֲשֵׂה לְמַעַן סוֹדָךְ. עֲשֵׂה לְמַעַן עֻזָּךְ. עֲשֵׂה לְמַעַן פְּאֵרָךְ. עֲשֵׂה לְמַעַן צִדְקָתָךְ. עֲשֵׂה לְמַעַן קְדֻשָּׁתָךְ. עֲשֵׂה לְמַעַן רַחֲמֶיךָ הָרַבִּים. עֲשֵׂה לְמַעַן שְׁכִינָתָךְ. עֲשֵׂה לְמַעַן תְּהִלָּתָךְ. עֲשֵׂה לְמַעַן אוֹהֲבֶיךָ שׁוֹכְנֵי עָפָר. עֲשֵׂה לְמַעַן אַבְרָהָם יִצְחָק וְיַעֲקֹב. עֲשֵׂה לְמַעַן מֹשֶׁה וְאַהֲרֹן. עֲשֵׂה לְמַעַן דָּוִד וּשְׁלֹמֹה. עֲשֵׂה לְמַעַן יְרוּשָׁלַיִם עִיר קָדְשֶׁךָ. עֲשֵׂה לְמַעַן צִיּוֹן מִשְׁכַּן כְּבוֹדֶךָ. עֲשֵׂה לְמַעַן שִׁמְמוֹת הֵיכָלֶךָ. עֲשֵׂה לְמַעַן הֲרִיסוּת מִזְבְּחֶךָ. עֲשֵׂה לְמַעַן הֲרוּגִים עַל שֵׁם קָדְשֶׁךָ. עֲשֵׂה לְמַעַן טְבוּחִים עַל יִחוּדֶךָ. עֲשֵׂה לְמַעַן בָּאֵי בָאֵשׁ וּבַמַּיִם עַל קִדּוּשׁ שְׁמֶךָ. עֲשֵׂה לְמַעַן יוֹנְקֵי שָׁדַיִם שֶׁלֹּא חָטְאוּ. עֲשֵׂה לְמַעַן גְּמוּלֵי חָלָב שֶׁלֹּא פָשְׁעוּ. עֲשֵׂה לְמַעַן תִּינוֹקוֹת שֶׁל בֵּית רַבָּן. עֲשֵׂה לְמַעַנְךָ אִם לֹא לְמַעֲנֵנוּ. עֲשֵׂה לְמַעַנְךָ וְהוֹשִׁיעֵנוּ.

עֲנֵנוּ יהוה עֲנֵנוּ. עֲנֵנוּ אֱלֹהֵינוּ עֲנֵנוּ. עֲנֵנוּ אָבִינוּ עֲנֵנוּ. עֲנֵנוּ בּוֹרְאֵנוּ עֲנֵנוּ. עֲנֵנוּ גּוֹאֲלֵנוּ עֲנֵנוּ. עֲנֵנוּ דּוֹרְשֵׁנוּ עֲנֵנוּ. עֲנֵנוּ הָאֵל הַנֶּאֱמָן עֲנֵנוּ. עֲנֵנוּ וָתִיק וְחָסִיד עֲנֵנוּ. עֲנֵנוּ זַךְ וְיָשָׁר עֲנֵנוּ. עֲנֵנוּ חַי וְקַיָּם עֲנֵנוּ. עֲנֵנוּ טוֹב וּמֵטִיב עֲנֵנוּ. עֲנֵנוּ יוֹדֵעַ יֵצֶר עֲנֵנוּ. עֲנֵנוּ כּוֹבֵשׁ כְּעָסִים עֲנֵנוּ. עֲנֵנוּ לוֹבֵשׁ צְדָקוֹת עֲנֵנוּ. עֲנֵנוּ מֶלֶךְ מַלְכֵי הַמְּלָכִים עֲנֵנוּ. עֲנֵנוּ נוֹרָא וְנִשְׂגָּב עֲנֵנוּ. עֲנֵנוּ סוֹלֵחַ וּמוֹחֵל עֲנֵנוּ. עֲנֵנוּ עוֹנֶה בְּעֵת צָרָה עֲנֵנוּ. עֲנֵנוּ פּוֹדֶה וּמַצִּיל עֲנֵנוּ. עֲנֵנוּ צַדִּיק וְיָשָׁר עֲנֵנוּ. עֲנֵנוּ קָרוֹב לְקוֹרְאָיו עֲנֵנוּ. עֲנֵנוּ רַחוּם וְחַנּוּן עֲנֵנוּ. עֲנֵנוּ שׁוֹמֵעַ אֶל אֶבְיוֹנִים עֲנֵנוּ. עֲנֵנוּ תּוֹמֵךְ תְּמִימִים עֲנֵנוּ. עֲנֵנוּ אֱלֹהֵי אֲבוֹתֵינוּ עֲנֵנוּ. עֲנֵנוּ אֱלֹהֵי אַבְרָהָם עֲנֵנוּ. עֲנֵנוּ פַּחַד יִצְחָק עֲנֵנוּ. עֲנֵנוּ אֲבִיר יַעֲקֹב עֲנֵנוּ. עֲנֵנוּ עֶזְרַת הַשְּׁבָטִים עֲנֵנוּ. עֲנֵנוּ מִשְׂגַּב אִמָּהוֹת עֲנֵנוּ. עֲנֵנוּ קָשֶׁה לִכְעֹס עֲנֵנוּ. עֲנֵנוּ רַךְ לִרְצוֹת עֲנֵנוּ. עֲנֵנוּ עוֹנֶה בְּעֵת רָצוֹן עֲנֵנוּ. עֲנֵנוּ אֲבִי יְתוֹמִים עֲנֵנוּ. עֲנֵנוּ דַּיַּן אַלְמָנוֹת עֲנֵנוּ.

מִי שֶׁעָנָה The One who answered Abraham our father on Mount Moriah – answer us.
The One who answered Isaac his son, when he was bound upon the altar – answer us.
The One who answered Jacob in Beth-El – answer us.
The One who answered Joseph in prison – answer us.
The One who answered our fathers at the Reed Sea – answer us.
The One who answered Moses at Horeb – answer us.
The One who answered Aaron over his firepan – answer us.
The One who answered Pinehas when he stood up from among the congregation – answer us.
The One who answered Joshua at Gilgal – answer us.
The One who answered Samuel at Mitzpah – answer us.
The One who answered David and Solomon his son in Jerusalem – answer us.
The One who answered Elijah on Mount Carmel – answer us.
The One who answered Elisha at Jericho – answer us.
The One who answered Jonah in the belly of the fish – answer us.
The One who answered Hezekiah the king of Judah in his illness – answer us.
The One who answered Hananiah, Mishael and Azariah in the furnace of fire – answer us.
The One who answered Daniel in the lions' den – answer us.
The One who answered Mordekhai and Esther in Shushan the capital city – answer us.
The One who answered Ezra in his exile – answer us.
The One who answered so many righteous, devoted, innocent and upright people – answer us.

רַחֲמָנָא Loving God, who answers the oppressed: answer us.
Loving God, who answers the broken hearted: answer us.
Loving God, who answers those of humbled spirit: answer us.
Loving God, answer us.
Loving God, spare; Loving God, release; Loving God, save us.
Loving God, have compassion for us now, swiftly, at a time soon coming.

Continue with "Avinu Malkenu" on page 188.

מִי שֶׁעָנָה לְאַבְרָהָם אָבִינוּ בְּהַר הַמּוֹרִיָּה, הוּא יַעֲנֵנוּ.
מִי שֶׁעָנָה לְיִצְחָק בְּנוֹ כְּשֶׁנֶּעֱקַד עַל גַּבֵּי הַמִּזְבֵּחַ, הוּא יַעֲנֵנוּ.
מִי שֶׁעָנָה לְיַעֲקֹב בְּבֵית אֵל, הוּא יַעֲנֵנוּ.
מִי שֶׁעָנָה לְיוֹסֵף בְּבֵית הָאֲסוּרִים, הוּא יַעֲנֵנוּ.
מִי שֶׁעָנָה לַאֲבוֹתֵינוּ עַל יַם סוּף, הוּא יַעֲנֵנוּ.
מִי שֶׁעָנָה לְמשֶׁה בְּחוֹרֵב, הוּא יַעֲנֵנוּ.
מִי שֶׁעָנָה לְאַהֲרֹן בַּמַּחְתָּה, הוּא יַעֲנֵנוּ.
מִי שֶׁעָנָה לְפִינְחָס בְּקוּמוֹ מִתּוֹךְ הָעֵדָה, הוּא יַעֲנֵנוּ.
מִי שֶׁעָנָה לִיהוֹשֻׁעַ בַּגִּלְגָּל, הוּא יַעֲנֵנוּ.
מִי שֶׁעָנָה לִשְׁמוּאֵל בַּמִּצְפָּה, הוּא יַעֲנֵנוּ.
מִי שֶׁעָנָה לְדָוִד וּשְׁלֹמֹה בְנוֹ בִּירוּשָׁלָיִם, הוּא יַעֲנֵנוּ.
מִי שֶׁעָנָה לְאֵלִיָּהוּ בְּהַר הַכַּרְמֶל, הוּא יַעֲנֵנוּ.
מִי שֶׁעָנָה לֶאֱלִישָׁע בִּירִיחוֹ, הוּא יַעֲנֵנוּ.
מִי שֶׁעָנָה לְיוֹנָה בִּמְעֵי הַדָּגָה, הוּא יַעֲנֵנוּ.
מִי שֶׁעָנָה לְחִזְקִיָּהוּ מֶלֶךְ יְהוּדָה בְּחָלְיוֹ, הוּא יַעֲנֵנוּ.
מִי שֶׁעָנָה לַחֲנַנְיָה מִישָׁאֵל וַעֲזַרְיָה בְּתוֹךְ כִּבְשַׁן הָאֵשׁ, הוּא יַעֲנֵנוּ.
מִי שֶׁעָנָה לְדָנִיֵּאל בְּגוֹב הָאֲרָיוֹת, הוּא יַעֲנֵנוּ.
מִי שֶׁעָנָה לְמָרְדְּכַי וְאֶסְתֵּר בְּשׁוּשַׁן הַבִּירָה, הוּא יַעֲנֵנוּ.
מִי שֶׁעָנָה לְעֶזְרָא בַּגּוֹלָה, הוּא יַעֲנֵנוּ.
מִי שֶׁעָנָה לְכָל הַצַּדִּיקִים וְהַחֲסִידִים וְהַתְּמִימִים וְהַיְשָׁרִים, הוּא יַעֲנֵנוּ.

רַחֲמָנָא דְּעָנֵי לַעֲנִיֵּי עֲנֵינָן.
רַחֲמָנָא דְּעָנֵי לִתְבִירֵי לִבָּא עֲנֵינָן.
רַחֲמָנָא דְּעָנֵי לְמַכִּיכֵי רוּחָא עֲנֵינָן.
רַחֲמָנָא עֲנֵינָן.
רַחֲמָנָא חוּס, רַחֲמָנָא פְּרוֹק, רַחֲמָנָא שֵׁיזִב.
רַחֲמָנָא רַחֵם עֲלָן, הַשְׁתָּא בַּעֲגָלָא וּבִזְמַן קָרִיב.

Continue with אבינו מלכנו *on page 189.*

Tisha B'Av

MA'ARIV FOR TISHA B'AV

On Motza'ei Shabbat, the Leader says the following:

Blessed is He who separates
beween the sacred and the secular.

The Leader then removes his shoes.

The Sevice for Ma'ariv is said until Full Kaddish after Amida, pages 298–330. Then the congregation sits on the floor, and the Leader chants Eikha.

1 How does the city sit solitary, that was full of people! how is she become like a widow! she that was great among the nations, and princess among the provinces, how is she become a vassal! She weeps sore in the night, and her tears are on her cheeks: among all her lovers she has none to comfort her: all her friends have dealt treacherously with her, they have become her enemies. Judah is gone into exile because of affliction, and because of great servitude: she dwells among the nations, she finds no rest: all her persecutors overtook her within the straits. The ways of Zion do mourn, because none come to the solemn assembly: all her gates are desolate: her priests sigh, her virgins are afflicted, and she is in bitterness. Her adversaries have become the chief, her enemies prosper; for the Lord has afflicted her for the multitude of her transgressions: her infants are gone into captivity before the enemy. And from the daughter of Zion all her splendor is departed: her princes are become like harts that find no pasture, and they are gone without strength before the pursuer. Jerusalem remembers in the days of her affliction and of her miseries all her pleasant things that she had in the days of old, when her people fell into the hand of the enemy, and none did help her: the adversaries saw her, and gloated at her destruction. Jerusalem has grievously sinned; therefore she is become loathsome: all that honored her despise her, because they have seen her nakedness: she herself also sighs, and turns backward. Her filthiness was in her skirts; she took no thought of her last end; therefore she came down astonishingly: she has no comforter. O Lord, behold my affliction: for the enemy has magnified himself. The adversary has spread out his hand upon all her pleasant things: for she has seen that heathen nations invade her sanctuary, those whom You did forbid to enter into Your congregation. All her people sigh, they seek bread; they have given their pleasant things for food to relieve the soul: see, O Lord, and consider; how abject I am become. Is it nothing to you, all you that pass by? behold, and see if there is any pain like my pain, which is done to me, with which the Lord has afflicted me in the day of His fierce anger. From above He has sent fire into my bones, and it prevails against them: He has

תשעה באב

מעריב לתשעה באב

On מוצאי שבת*, the* שליח ציבור *says the following:*

בָּרוּךְ הַמַּבְדִּיל בֵּין קֹדֶשׁ לְחוֹל

The שליח ציבור *then removes his shoes.*

The Sevice for מעריב *is said until* קדיש שלם *after* עמידה*,* *pages 299–331.*
Then the קהל *sits on the floor, and the* שליח ציבור *chants* איכה.

א אֵיכָה ׀ יָשְׁבָה בָדָד הָעִיר רַבָּתִי עָם הָיְתָה כְּאַלְמָנָה רַבָּתִי בַגּוֹיִם
שָׂרָתִי בַּמְּדִינוֹת הָיְתָה לָמַס: בָּכוֹ תִבְכֶּה בַּלַּיְלָה וְדִמְעָתָהּ עַל לֶחֱיָהּ
אֵין־לָהּ מְנַחֵם מִכָּל־אֹהֲבֶיהָ כָּל־רֵעֶיהָ בָּגְדוּ בָהּ הָיוּ לָהּ לְאֹיְבִים:
גָּלְתָה יְהוּדָה מֵעֹנִי וּמֵרֹב עֲבֹדָה הִיא יָשְׁבָה בַגּוֹיִם לֹא מָצְאָה מָנוֹחַ
כָּל־רֹדְפֶיהָ הִשִּׂיגוּהָ בֵּין הַמְּצָרִים: דַּרְכֵי צִיּוֹן אֲבֵלוֹת מִבְּלִי בָּאֵי מוֹעֵד
כָּל־שְׁעָרֶיהָ שׁוֹמֵמִין כֹּהֲנֶיהָ נֶאֱנָחִים בְּתוּלֹתֶיהָ נּוּגוֹת וְהִיא מַר־לָהּ:
הָיוּ צָרֶיהָ לְרֹאשׁ אֹיְבֶיהָ שָׁלוּ כִּי־יְהוָה הוֹגָהּ עַל־רֹב פְּשָׁעֶיהָ עוֹלָלֶיהָ
הָלְכוּ שְׁבִי לִפְנֵי־צָר: וַיֵּצֵא מִן בַּת־צִיּוֹן כָּל־הֲדָרָהּ הָיוּ שָׂרֶיהָ כְּאַיָּלִים מִבַּת־
לֹא־מָצְאוּ מִרְעֶה וַיֵּלְכוּ בְלֹא־כֹחַ לִפְנֵי רוֹדֵף: זָכְרָה יְרוּשָׁלַ͏ִם יְמֵי עָנְיָהּ
וּמְרוּדֶיהָ כֹּל מַחֲמֻדֶיהָ אֲשֶׁר הָיוּ מִימֵי קֶדֶם בִּנְפֹל עַמָּהּ בְּיַד־צָר וְאֵין
עוֹזֵר לָהּ רָאוּהָ צָרִים שָׂחֲקוּ עַל־מִשְׁבַּתֶּהָ: חֵטְא חָטְאָה יְרוּשָׁלַ͏ִם
עַל־כֵּן לְנִידָה הָיָתָה כָּל־מְכַבְּדֶיהָ הִזִּילוּהָ כִּי־רָאוּ עֶרְוָתָהּ גַּם־הִיא
נֶאֶנְחָה וַתָּשָׁב אָחוֹר: טֻמְאָתָהּ בְּשׁוּלֶיהָ לֹא זָכְרָה אַחֲרִיתָהּ וַתֵּרֶד
פְּלָאִים אֵין מְנַחֵם לָהּ רְאֵה יְהוָה אֶת־עָנְיִי כִּי הִגְדִּיל אוֹיֵב: יָדוֹ פָּרַשׂ
צָר עַל כָּל־מַחֲמַדֶּיהָ כִּי־רָאֲתָה גוֹיִם בָּאוּ מִקְדָּשָׁהּ אֲשֶׁר צִוִּיתָה לֹא־
יָבֹאוּ בַקָּהָל לָךְ: כָּל־עַמָּהּ נֶאֱנָחִים מְבַקְּשִׁים לֶחֶם נָתְנוּ מחמודיהם מַחֲמַדֵּיהֶם
בְּאֹכֶל לְהָשִׁיב נָפֶשׁ רְאֵה יְהוָה וְהַבִּיטָה כִּי הָיִיתִי זוֹלֵלָה: לוֹא אֲלֵיכֶם
כָּל־עֹבְרֵי דֶרֶךְ הַבִּיטוּ וּרְאוּ אִם־יֵשׁ מַכְאוֹב כְּמַכְאֹבִי אֲשֶׁר עוֹלַל
לִי אֲשֶׁר הוֹגָה יְהוָה בְּיוֹם חֲרוֹן אַפּוֹ: מִמָּרוֹם שָׁלַח־אֵשׁ בְּעַצְמֹתַי

spread a net for my feet, He has turned me back: He has made me desolate and faint all the day. The yoke of my transgressions is fastened on by His hand: they are knit together, and come up upon my neck: He has made my strength to fall, the LORD has delivered me into the hands of those against whom I am not able to rise up. The LORD has spurned all my mighty men in the midst of me: He has called an assembly against me to crush my young men: the LORD has trodden the virgin, the daughter of Judah, as in a winepress. For these things I weep; my eye, my eye runs down with water, because the Comforter that should relieve my soul is far from me: my children are desolate, because the enemy has prevailed. Zion spreads out her hands, and there is none to comfort her: the LORD has commanded against Jacob, adversaries round about him: Jerusalem is like a menstruous woman among them. The LORD is righteous; for I have rebelled against His word: hear, I pray you, all the peoples, and behold my pain: my virgins and my young men are gone into captivity. I called for my lovers, but they deceived me: my priests and my elders perished in the city, while they sought food for themselves to relieve their souls. Behold, O LORD; for I am in distress: my bowels are troubled; my heart is turned within me; for I have grievously rebelled: abroad the sword bereaves, at home it is like death. They have heard that I sigh: there is none to comfort me: all my enemies have heard of my trouble; they are glad that You have done it: You will bring the day that You have called, and they shall be like me. Let all their wickedness come before You; and do to them as You have done
to me for all my transgressions: for my sighs are many, and my heart is faint.
2 How has the LORD covered the daughter of Zion with a cloud in His anger, and
cast down from heaven to earth the beauty of Israel, and remembered not His footstool in the day of His anger! The LORD has swallowed up without pity all the habitations of Jacob: He has thrown down in His wrath the strongholds of the daughter of Judah; He has brought them down to the ground: He has profaned the kingdom and its princes. He has cut off in His fierce anger all the horn of Israel: He has drawn back His right hand from before the enemy, and He has burned against Jacob like a flaming fire, which devours round about. He has bent His bow like an enemy: with His right hand set like an adversary, He has slain all that were pleasant to the eye: in the tent of the daughter of Zion, He has poured out His fury like fire. The LORD was like an enemy: He has swallowed up Israel, He has swallowed up all her palaces: He has destroyed its strongholds, and has increased in the daughter of Judah mourning and lamentation. And He has stripped His tabernacle, as if it were a garden: He has destroyed His place of assembly: the LORD has caused the appointed seasons and sabbaths to be forgotten in Zion, and has spurned in the indignation of His anger both king and priest. The LORD has cast off His altar, He has abhorred His Sanctuary, He has given up into the hand of the enemy the walls of her palaces; they have made a noise in the house of the LORD, as in the day of a solemn assembly. The LORD has purposed

וַיִּרְדֶּנָּה פָּרַשׂ רֶשֶׁת לְרַגְלַי הֱשִׁיבַנִי אָחוֹר נְתָנַנִי שֹׁמֵמָה כָּל־הַיּוֹם דָּוָה׃
נִשְׂקַד עֹל פְּשָׁעַי בְּיָדוֹ יִשְׂתָּרְגוּ עָלוּ עַל־צַוָּארִי הִכְשִׁיל כֹּחִי נְתָנַנִי
אֲדֹנָי בִּידֵי לֹא־אוּכַל קוּם׃ סִלָּה כָל־אַבִּירַי ׀ אֲדֹנָי בְּקִרְבִּי קָרָא עָלַי
מוֹעֵד לִשְׁבֹּר בַּחוּרָי גַּת דָּרַךְ אֲדֹנָי לִבְתוּלַת בַּת־יְהוּדָה׃ עַל־אֵלֶּה ׀
אֲנִי בוֹכִיָּה עֵינִי ׀ עֵינִי יֹרְדָה מַּיִם כִּי־רָחַק מִמֶּנִּי מְנַחֵם מֵשִׁיב נַפְשִׁי
הָיוּ בָנַי שׁוֹמֵמִים כִּי גָבַר אוֹיֵב׃ פֵּרְשָׂה צִיּוֹן בְּיָדֶיהָ אֵין מְנַחֵם לָהּ
צִוָּה יְהוָה לְיַעֲקֹב סְבִיבָיו צָרָיו הָיְתָה יְרוּשָׁלִַם לְנִדָּה בֵּינֵיהֶם׃ צַדִּיק
הוּא יְהוָה כִּי פִיהוּ מָרִיתִי שִׁמְעוּ־נָא כָל־עמים וּרְאוּ מַכְאֹבִי בְּתוּלֹתַי (הָעַמִּים)
וּבַחוּרַי הָלְכוּ בַשֶּׁבִי׃ קָרָאתִי לַמְאַהֲבַי הֵמָּה רִמּוּנִי כֹּהֲנַי וּזְקֵנַי בָּעִיר
גָּוָעוּ כִּי־בִקְשׁוּ אֹכֶל לָמוֹ וְיָשִׁיבוּ אֶת־נַפְשָׁם׃ רְאֵה יְהוָה כִּי־צַר־לִי
מֵעַי חֳמַרְמָרוּ נֶהְפַּךְ לִבִּי בְּקִרְבִּי כִּי מָרוֹ מָרִיתִי מִחוּץ שִׁכְּלָה־חֶרֶב
בַּבַּיִת כַּמָּוֶת׃ שָׁמְעוּ כִּי נֶאֱנָחָה אָנִי אֵין מְנַחֵם לִי כָּל־אֹיְבַי שָׁמְעוּ
רָעָתִי שָׂשׂוּ כִּי אַתָּה עָשִׂיתָ הֵבֵאתָ יוֹם־קָרָאתָ וְיִהְיוּ כָמֹנִי׃ תָּבֹא כָל־
רָעָתָם לְפָנֶיךָ וְעוֹלֵל לָמוֹ כַּאֲשֶׁר עוֹלַלְתָּ לִי עַל כָּל־פְּשָׁעָי כִּי־רַבּוֹת
אַנְחֹתַי וְלִבִּי דַוָּי׃

ב אֵיכָה יָעִיב בְּאַפּוֹ ׀ אֲדֹנָי אֶת־בַּת־צִיּוֹן הִשְׁלִיךְ מִשָּׁמַיִם אֶרֶץ תִּפְאֶרֶת
יִשְׂרָאֵל וְלֹא־זָכַר הֲדֹם־רַגְלָיו בְּיוֹם אַפּוֹ׃ בִּלַּע אֲדֹנָי לא חָמַל אֵת (וְלֹא)
כָּל־נְאוֹת יַעֲקֹב הָרַס בְּעֶבְרָתוֹ מִבְצְרֵי בַת־יְהוּדָה הִגִּיעַ לָאָרֶץ חִלֵּל
מַמְלָכָה וְשָׂרֶיהָ׃ גָּדַע בָּחֳרִי־אַף כֹּל קֶרֶן יִשְׂרָאֵל הֵשִׁיב אָחוֹר יְמִינוֹ
מִפְּנֵי אוֹיֵב וַיִּבְעַר בְּיַעֲקֹב כְּאֵשׁ לֶהָבָה אָכְלָה סָבִיב׃ דָּרַךְ קַשְׁתּוֹ
כְּאוֹיֵב נִצָּב יְמִינוֹ כְּצָר וַיַּהֲרֹג כֹּל מַחֲמַדֵּי־עָיִן בְּאֹהֶל בַּת־צִיּוֹן שָׁפַךְ
כָּאֵשׁ חֲמָתוֹ׃ הָיָה אֲדֹנָי ׀ כְּאוֹיֵב בִּלַּע יִשְׂרָאֵל בִּלַּע כָּל־אַרְמְנוֹתֶיהָ
שִׁחֵת מִבְצָרָיו וַיֶּרֶב בְּבַת־יְהוּדָה תַּאֲנִיָּה וַאֲנִיָּה׃ וַיַּחְמֹס כַּגַּן שֻׂכּוֹ שִׁחֵת
מֹעֲדוֹ שִׁכַּח יְהוָה ׀ בְּצִיּוֹן מוֹעֵד וְשַׁבָּת וַיִּנְאַץ בְּזַעַם־אַפּוֹ מֶלֶךְ וְכֹהֵן׃
זָנַח אֲדֹנָי ׀ מִזְבְּחוֹ נִאֵר מִקְדָּשׁוֹ הִסְגִּיר בְּיַד־אוֹיֵב חוֹמֹת אַרְמְנוֹתֶיהָ
קוֹל נָתְנוּ בְּבֵית־יְהוָה כְּיוֹם מוֹעֵד׃ חָשַׁב יְהוָה ׀ לְהַשְׁחִית חוֹמַת בַּת־

to destroy the wall of the daughter of Zion: He has stretched out a line, He has not withdrawn His hand from destroying: therefore He made the rampart and the wall to lament; they languish together. Her gates are sunk into the ground; He has destroyed and broken her bars: her king and her princes are among the nations: there is no Torah; her prophets also find no vision from the LORD. The elders of the daughter of Zion sit upon the ground, and keep silence: they have cast up dust upon their heads; they have girded themselves with sackcloth: the virgins of Jerusalem hang down their heads to the ground. My eyes fail with tears, my bowels are troubled, my liver is poured upon the earth, for the breach of the daughter of my people; because the children and the sucklings swoon in the broad places of the city. They say to their mothers, Where is corn and wine? when they swoon like wounded men in the broad places of the city, when their soul is poured out into their mothers' bosom. What shall I take to witness for you? what shall I liken to you, O daughter of Jerusalem? what shall I equal to you, that I may comfort you, O virgin daughter of Zion? for your breach is great like the sea: who can heal you? Your prophets have seen for you vain and foolish visions: and they have not exposed your iniquity, to restore your captivity; but have prophesied for you burdens of falsehood and deceit. All that pass by clap their hands at you; they hiss and wag their head at the daughter of Jerusalem, saying, Is this the city that men call The perfection of beauty, The joy of the whole earth? All your enemies have opened their mouth against you: they hiss and gnash the teeth: they say, We have swallowed her up: certainly this is the day that we have looked for; we have found it, we have seen it. The LORD has done that which He devised; He has fulfilled His word that He commanded in the days of old: He has thrown down without pity: and He has caused the enemy to rejoice over you, He has raised up the horn of your adversaries. Their heart cried to the LORD. O wall of the daughter of Zion, let tears run down like a river day and night: give yourself no rest; let not the apple of your eye cease. Arise, cry out in the night: in the beginning of the watches pour out your heart like water before the face of the LORD: lift up your hands toward Him for the life of your young children, that faint for hunger at the head of every street. Behold, O LORD, and consider to whom You have done this. Shall the women eat their fruit, their cherished babes? shall priest and prophet be slain in the Sanctuary of the LORD? Young and old lie on the ground in the streets: my virgins and my young men are fallen by the sword; You have slain them in the day of Your anger; You have killed, and not pitied. You have called as in the day of a solemn assembly, my terrors round about, so that in the day of the LORD's anger none escaped or remained: those that I have cherished and brought up my enemy has consumed.

3 I am the man who has seen affliction by the rod of His wrath. He has led me, and
brought me into darkness, but not into light. Surely He is turned against me; He
turns His hand against me all the day. He has made my flesh and my skin to waste

צִיּוֹן נָטָה קָו לֹא־הֵשִׁיב יָדוֹ מִבַּלֵּעַ וַיַּאֲבֶל־חֵל וְחוֹמָה יַחְדָּו אֻמְלָלוּ׃
טָבְעוּ בָאָרֶץ שְׁעָרֶיהָ אִבַּד וְשִׁבַּר בְּרִיחֶיהָ מַלְכָּהּ וְשָׂרֶיהָ בַגּוֹיִם אֵין
תּוֹרָה גַּם־נְבִיאֶיהָ לֹא־מָצְאוּ חָזוֹן מֵיהוָה׃ יֵשְׁבוּ לָאָרֶץ יִדְּמוּ זִקְנֵי
בַת־צִיּוֹן הֶעֱלוּ עָפָר עַל־רֹאשָׁם חָגְרוּ שַׂקִּים הוֹרִידוּ לָאָרֶץ רֹאשָׁן
בְּתוּלֹת יְרוּשָׁלָ‍ִם׃ כָּלוּ בַדְּמָעוֹת עֵינַי חֳמַרְמְרוּ מֵעַי נִשְׁפַּךְ לָאָרֶץ
כְּבֵדִי עַל־שֶׁבֶר בַּת־עַמִּי בֵּעָטֵף עוֹלֵל וְיוֹנֵק בִּרְחֹבוֹת קִרְיָה׃ לְאִמֹּתָם
יֹאמְרוּ אַיֵּה דָּגָן וָיָיִן בְּהִתְעַטְּפָם כֶּחָלָל בִּרְחֹבוֹת עִיר בְּהִשְׁתַּפֵּךְ נַפְשָׁם
אֶל־חֵיק אִמֹּתָם׃ מָה־אעודך מָה אֲדַמֶּה־לָּךְ הַבַּת יְרוּשָׁלַ‍ִם מָה אֲעִידֵךְ
אַשְׁוֶה־לָּךְ וַאֲנַחֲמֵךְ בְּתוּלַת בַּת־צִיּוֹן כִּי־גָדוֹל כַּיָּם שִׁבְרֵךְ מִי יִרְפָּא־
לָךְ׃ נְבִיאַיִךְ חָזוּ לָךְ שָׁוְא וְתָפֵל וְלֹא־גִלּוּ עַל־עֲוֺנֵךְ לְהָשִׁיב שביתך
וַיֶּחֱזוּ לָךְ מַשְׂאוֹת שָׁוְא וּמַדּוּחִים׃ סָפְקוּ עָלַיִךְ כַּפַּיִם כָּל־עֹבְרֵי דֶרֶךְ שְׁבוּתֵךְ
שָׁרְקוּ וַיָּנִעוּ רֹאשָׁם עַל־בַּת יְרוּשָׁלָ‍ִם הֲזֹאת הָעִיר שֶׁיֹּאמְרוּ כְּלִילַת
יֹפִי מָשׂוֹשׂ לְכָל־הָאָרֶץ׃ פָּצוּ עָלַיִךְ פִּיהֶם כָּל־אֹיְבַיִךְ שָׁרְקוּ וַיַּחַרְקוּ־שֵׁן
אָמְרוּ בִּלָּעְנוּ אַךְ זֶה הַיּוֹם שֶׁקִּוִּינֻהוּ מָצָאנוּ רָאִינוּ׃ עָשָׂה יְהוָה אֲשֶׁר
זָמָם בִּצַּע אֶמְרָתוֹ אֲשֶׁר צִוָּה מִימֵי־קֶדֶם הָרַס וְלֹא חָמָל וַיְשַׂמַּח עָלַיִךְ
אוֹיֵב הֵרִים קֶרֶן צָרָיִךְ׃ צָעַק לִבָּם אֶל־אֲדֹנָי חוֹמַת בַּת־צִיּוֹן הוֹרִידִי
כַנַּחַל דִּמְעָה יוֹמָם וָלַיְלָה אַל־תִּתְּנִי פוּגַת לָךְ אַל־תִּדֹּם בַּת־עֵינֵךְ׃
קוּמִי ׀ רֹנִּי בַלַּיְלָה לְרֹאשׁ אַשְׁמֻרוֹת שִׁפְכִי כַמַּיִם לִבֵּךְ נֹכַח פְּנֵי אֲדֹנָי
שְׂאִי אֵלָיו כַּפַּיִךְ עַל־נֶפֶשׁ עוֹלָלַיִךְ הָעֲטוּפִים בְּרָעָב בְּרֹאשׁ כָּל־חוּצוֹת׃
רְאֵה יְהוָה וְהַבִּיטָה לְמִי עוֹלַלְתָּ כֹּה אִם־תֹּאכַלְנָה נָשִׁים פִּרְיָם עֹלֲלֵי
טִפֻּחִים אִם־יֵהָרֵג בְּמִקְדַּשׁ אֲדֹנָי כֹּהֵן וְנָבִיא׃ שָׁכְבוּ לָאָרֶץ חוּצוֹת
נַעַר וְזָקֵן בְּתוּלֹתַי וּבַחוּרַי נָפְלוּ בֶחָרֶב הָרַגְתָּ בְּיוֹם אַפֶּךָ טָבַחְתָּ לֹא
חָמָלְתָּ׃ תִּקְרָא כְיוֹם מוֹעֵד מְגוּרַי מִסָּבִיב וְלֹא הָיָה בְּיוֹם אַף־יְהוָה
פָּלִיט וְשָׂרִיד אֲשֶׁר־טִפַּחְתִּי וְרִבִּיתִי אֹיְבִי כִלָּם׃
ג אֲנִי הַגֶּבֶר רָאָה עֳנִי בְּשֵׁבֶט עֶבְרָתוֹ׃ אוֹתִי נָהַג וַיֹּלַךְ חֹשֶׁךְ וְלֹא־אוֹר׃
אַךְ בִּי יָשֻׁב יַהֲפֹךְ יָדוֹ כָּל־הַיּוֹם׃ בִּלָּה בְשָׂרִי וְעוֹרִי שִׁבַּר עַצְמוֹתָי׃

away; He has broken my bones. He has built a mound against me, and has beset me round about at head and hell. He has set me in dark places, as those who are long ago dead. He has hedged me about, so that I cannot get out: He has made my chain heavy. Even when I cry and call for help, He stops up my prayer. He has enclosed my ways with hewn stone, He has made my paths crooked. He is to me like a bear lying in wait, and like a lion in secret places. He has turned aside my ways, and pulled me in pieces: He has made me desolate. He has bent his bow, and set me as a mark for the arrow. He has caused the arrows of his quiver to enter into my reins. I am become a derision to all my people; and their song all the day. He has filled me with bitterness, He has sated me with wormwood. He has also broken my teeth with gravel stones, He has pressed me down into the ashes. My soul is far removed from peace: I have forgotten prosperity. And I said, My strength and my hope are perished from the Lord. Remember my affliction and my misery, the wormwood and the gall. My soul has them still in remembrance, and is bowed down within me. This I recall to my mind, therefore I have hope: that the Lord's steadfast love has not ceased, and that His compassions do not fail. They are new every morning: great is Your faithfulness. The Lord is my portion, says my soul; therefore I will hope in Him. The Lord is good to those who wait for Him, to the soul that seeks Him. It is good that a man should quietly hope for the salvation of the Lord. It is good for a man that he bear the yoke in his youth. Let him sit alone and keep silence, because he has taken it upon him. Let him put his mouth in the dust; perhaps there may be hope. Let him offer his cheek to him who strikes him; let him take his fill of insult. For the Lord will not cast off for ever: but though He may cause grief, yet will He have compassion according to the abundance of His steadfast love. For He does not willingly afflict or grieve the children of men. To crush under foot all the prisoners of the earth, to turn aside the right of a man before the face of the Most High, to subvert a man in his cause, the Lord approves not. Who is he that says, and it comes to pass, when the Lord commands it not? Out of the mouth of the Most High do not both good and evil come? Why then does a living man complain, a man for the punishment of his sins? Let us search and try our ways, and turn back to the Lord. Let us lift up our heart with our hands to God in the heavens. We have transgressed and have rebelled: You have not pardoned. You have covered with anger, and pursued us: You have slain, You have not pitied. You have covered yourself with a cloud, so that prayer should not pass through. You have made us offscouring and refuse in the midst of the people. All our enemies have opened their mouths wide against us. Fear and the pit are come upon us, desolation and destruction. My eye runs down with rivers of water for the breach of the daughter of my people. My eye trickles down, and ceases not, without any intermission, till the Lord shall look down, and behold from heaven. My eye affects my soul because of all the daughters of my city. They chased me sore, like a bird, those

בָּנָה עָלַי וַיַּקַּף רֹאשׁ וּתְלָאָה׃ בְּמַחֲשַׁכִּים הוֹשִׁיבַנִי כְּמֵתֵי עוֹלָם׃
גָּדַר בַּעֲדִי וְלֹא אֵצֵא הִכְבִּיד נְחָשְׁתִּי׃ גַּם כִּי אֶזְעַק וַאֲשַׁוֵּעַ שָׂתַם
תְּפִלָּתִי׃ גָּדַר דְּרָכַי בְּגָזִית נְתִיבֹתַי עִוָּה׃ דֹּב אֹרֵב הוּא לִי אריה אֲרִי
בְּמִסְתָּרִים׃ דְּרָכַי סוֹרֵר וַיְפַשְּׁחֵנִי שָׂמַנִי שֹׁמֵם׃ דָּרַךְ קַשְׁתּוֹ וַיַּצִּיבֵנִי
כַּמַּטָּרָא לַחֵץ׃ הֵבִיא בְּכִלְיוֹתָי בְּנֵי אַשְׁפָּתוֹ׃ הָיִיתִי שְּׂחֹק לְכָל־עַמִּי
נְגִינָתָם כָּל־הַיּוֹם׃ הִשְׂבִּיעַנִי בַמְּרוֹרִים הִרְוַנִי לַעֲנָה׃ וַיַּגְרֵס בֶּחָצָץ
שִׁנָּי הִכְפִּישַׁנִי בָּאֵפֶר׃ וַתִּזְנַח מִשָּׁלוֹם נַפְשִׁי נָשִׁיתִי טוֹבָה׃ וָאֹמַר אָבַד
נִצְחִי וְתוֹחַלְתִּי מֵיהוה׃ זְכָר־עָנְיִי וּמְרוּדִי לַעֲנָה וָרֹאשׁ׃ זָכוֹר תִּזְכּוֹר
ותשיח עָלַי נַפְשִׁי׃ זֹאת אָשִׁיב אֶל־לִבִּי עַל־כֵּן אוֹחִיל׃ חַסְדֵי יהוה וְתָשׁוֹחַ
כִּי לֹא־תָמְנוּ כִּי לֹא־כָלוּ רַחֲמָיו׃ חֲדָשִׁים לַבְּקָרִים רַבָּה אֱמוּנָתֶךָ׃
חֶלְקִי יהוה אָמְרָה נַפְשִׁי עַל־כֵּן אוֹחִיל לוֹ׃ טוֹב יהוה לְקֹוָו לְנֶפֶשׁ
תִּדְרְשֶׁנּוּ׃ טוֹב וְיָחִיל וְדוּמָם לִתְשׁוּעַת יהוה׃ טוֹב לַגֶּבֶר כִּי־יִשָּׂא
עֹל בִּנְעוּרָיו׃ יֵשֵׁב בָּדָד וְיִדֹּם כִּי נָטַל עָלָיו׃ יִתֵּן בֶּעָפָר פִּיהוּ אוּלַי יֵשׁ
תִּקְוָה׃ יִתֵּן לְמַכֵּהוּ לֶחִי יִשְׂבַּע בְּחֶרְפָּה׃ כִּי לֹא יִזְנַח לְעוֹלָם אֲדֹנָי׃
כִּי אִם־הוֹגָה וְרִחַם כְּרֹב חֲסָדָו׃ כִּי לֹא עִנָּה מִלִּבּוֹ וַיַּגֶּה בְּנֵי־אִישׁ׃
לְדַכֵּא תַּחַת רַגְלָיו כֹּל אֲסִירֵי אָרֶץ׃ לְהַטּוֹת מִשְׁפַּט־גָּבֶר נֶגֶד פְּנֵי
עֶלְיוֹן׃ לְעַוֵּת אָדָם בְּרִיבוֹ אֲדֹנָי לֹא רָאָה׃ מִי זֶה אָמַר וַתֶּהִי אֲדֹנָי
לֹא צִוָּה׃ מִפִּי עֶלְיוֹן לֹא תֵצֵא הָרָעוֹת וְהַטּוֹב׃ מַה־יִּתְאוֹנֵן אָדָם
חָי גֶּבֶר עַל־חֲטָאָו׃ נַחְפְּשָׂה דְרָכֵינוּ וְנַחְקֹרָה וְנָשׁוּבָה עַד־יהוה׃
נִשָּׂא לְבָבֵנוּ אֶל־כַּפָּיִם אֶל־אֵל בַּשָּׁמָיִם׃ נַחְנוּ פָשַׁעְנוּ וּמָרִינוּ אַתָּה
לֹא סָלָחְתָּ׃ סַכֹּתָה בָאַף וַתִּרְדְּפֵנוּ הָרַגְתָּ לֹא חָמָלְתָּ׃ סַכֹּתָה בֶעָנָן
לָךְ מֵעֲבוֹר תְּפִלָּה׃ סְחִי וּמָאוֹס תְּשִׂימֵנוּ בְּקֶרֶב הָעַמִּים׃ פָּצוּ עָלֵינוּ
פִּיהֶם כָּל־אֹיְבֵינוּ׃ פַּחַד וָפַחַת הָיָה לָנוּ הַשֵּׁאת וְהַשָּׁבֶר׃ פַּלְגֵי־מַיִם
תֵּרַד עֵינִי עַל־שֶׁבֶר בַּת־עַמִּי׃ עֵינִי נִגְּרָה וְלֹא תִדְמֶה מֵאֵין הֲפֻגוֹת׃
עַד־יַשְׁקִיף וְיֵרֶא יהוה מִשָּׁמָיִם׃ עֵינִי עוֹלְלָה לְנַפְשִׁי מִכֹּל בְּנוֹת עִירִי׃
צוֹד צָדוּנִי כַּצִּפּוֹר אֹיְבַי חִנָּם׃ צָמְתוּ בַבּוֹר חַיָּי וַיַּדּוּ־אֶבֶן בִּי׃ צָפוּ־מַיִם

who hate me without cause. They have cut off my life in the dungeon, and have cast stones upon me. Waters flowed over my head; then I said, I am cut off. I called upon Your name, O Lord, out of the nethermost pit. You have heard my voice: hide not Your ear at my sighing, at my cry. You did draw near in the day that I called upon You: You did say, Fear not. O Lord, You have pleaded the causes of my soul; You have redeemed my life. O Lord, You have seen my wrong: judge my cause. You have seen all their vengeance and all their devices against me. You have heard their insult, O Lord, and all their devices against me; the lips of those who rose up against me, and their muttering against me all the day. Behold their sitting down, and their rising up; I am their song. Render to them a recompense, O Lord, according to the work of their hands. Give them sorrow of heart; Your curse be on them! Pursue them in anger and destroy them from under the heavens of the Lord.

4 How is the gold become dim! how is the most fine gold changed! the hallowed stones are poured out at the top of every street. The precious sons of Zion, comparable to fine gold, how are they esteemed as earthen pitchers, the work of the hands of the potter! Even the jackals draw out the breast, they give suck to their young ones: the daughter of my people is become cruel, like the ostriches in the wilderness. The tongue of the sucking child cleaves to the roof of his mouth for thirst: the young children ask bread, and no man gives it to them. They that did feed on dainties are desolate in the streets: they that were brought up in scarlet embrace dunghills. For the doom of the daughter of my people is greater than the sin of Sodom, that was overthrown as in a moment, no hands being laid upon her. Her Nazirites were purer than snow, they were whiter than milk, they were more ruddy in body than rubies, their polishing was as of sapphire: now their visage is blacker than coal; they are not known in the streets: their skin is shriveled upon their bones; it is withered, it is become like a stick. Those slain with the sword are better than those slain with hunger: for when pierced through, the former do ooze with the produce of the fields. Hands of compassionate women have boiled their own children: they were their food in the destruction of the daughter of my people. The Lord has accomplished His fury; He has poured out His fierce anger, and has kindled a fire in Zion and it has devoured its foundations. The kings of the earth, and all the inhabitants of the world, would not have believed that the adversary and the enemy would enter the gates of Jerusalem. It was for the sins of her prophets, and the iniquities of her priests, who shed the blood of the just in the midst of her. They wandered blind through the streets, polluted with blood, so that none could touch their garments. Away! unclean! they cried at them; away! away! do not touch. So they fled, and wandered away: among the nations it was said, They shall no longer sojourn here. The anger of the Lord has divided them; He will no more regard them: they respected not the persons of the priests, they were not gracious to the elders. As for us, our eyes do yet fail for our vain

עַל־רֹאשִׁי אָמַרְתִּי נִגְזָרְתִּי׃ קָרָאתִי שִׁמְךָ יְהוָה מִבּוֹר תַּחְתִּיּוֹת׃ קוֹלִי
שָׁמָעְתָּ אַל־תַּעְלֵם אָזְנְךָ לְרַוְחָתִי לְשַׁוְעָתִי׃ קָרַבְתָּ בְּיוֹם אֶקְרָאֶךָּ
אָמַרְתָּ אַל־תִּירָא׃ רַבְתָּ אֲדֹנָי רִיבֵי נַפְשִׁי גָּאַלְתָּ חַיָּי׃ רָאִיתָה יְהוָה
עַוָּתָתִי שָׁפְטָה מִשְׁפָּטִי׃ רָאִיתָה כָּל־נִקְמָתָם כָּל־מַחְשְׁבֹתָם לִי׃
שָׁמַעְתָּ חֶרְפָּתָם יְהוָה כָּל־מַחְשְׁבֹתָם עָלָי׃ שִׂפְתֵי קָמַי וְהֶגְיוֹנָם עָלַי
כָּל־הַיּוֹם׃ שִׁבְתָּם וְקִימָתָם הַבִּיטָה אֲנִי מַנְגִּינָתָם׃ תָּשִׁיב לָהֶם גְּמוּל
יְהוָה כְּמַעֲשֵׂה יְדֵיהֶם׃ תִּתֵּן לָהֶם מְגִנַּת־לֵב תַּאֲלָתְךָ לָהֶם׃ תִּרְדֹּף
בְּאַף וְתַשְׁמִידֵם מִתַּחַת שְׁמֵי יְהוָה׃

ד אֵיכָה יוּעַם זָהָב יִשְׁנֶא הַכֶּתֶם הַטּוֹב תִּשְׁתַּפֵּכְנָה אַבְנֵי־קֹדֶשׁ בְּרֹאשׁ
כָּל־חוּצוֹת׃ בְּנֵי צִיּוֹן הַיְקָרִים הַמְסֻלָּאִים בַּפָּז אֵיכָה נֶחְשְׁבוּ לְנִבְלֵי־
חֶרֶשׂ מַעֲשֵׂה יְדֵי יוֹצֵר׃ גַּם־תנין חָלְצוּ שַׁד הֵינִיקוּ גּוּרֵיהֶן בַּת־עַמִּי תַּנִּים
לְאַכְזָר כי ענים בַּמִּדְבָּר׃ דָּבַק לְשׁוֹן יוֹנֵק אֶל־חִכּוֹ בַּצָּמָא עוֹלָלִים כַּיְעֵנִים
שָׁאֲלוּ לֶחֶם פֹּרֵשׂ אֵין לָהֶם׃ הָאֹכְלִים לְמַעֲדַנִּים נָשַׁמּוּ בַּחוּצוֹת
הָאֱמֻנִים עֲלֵי תוֹלָע חִבְּקוּ אַשְׁפַּתּוֹת׃ וַיִּגְדַּל עֲוֺן בַּת־עַמִּי מֵחַטַּאת
סְדֹם הַהֲפוּכָה כְמוֹ־רָגַע וְלֹא־חָלוּ בָהּ יָדָיִם׃ זַכּוּ נְזִירֶיהָ מִשֶּׁלֶג צַחוּ
מֵחָלָב אָדְמוּ עֶצֶם מִפְּנִינִים סַפִּיר גִּזְרָתָם׃ חָשַׁךְ מִשְּׁחוֹר תָּאֳרָם לֹא
נִכְּרוּ בַּחוּצוֹת צָפַד עוֹרָם עַל־עַצְמָם יָבֵשׁ הָיָה כָעֵץ׃ טוֹבִים הָיוּ
חַלְלֵי־חֶרֶב מֵחַלְלֵי רָעָב שֶׁהֵם יָזוּבוּ מְדֻקָּרִים מִתְּנוּבֹת שָׂדָי׃ יְדֵי
נָשִׁים רַחֲמָנִיּוֹת בִּשְּׁלוּ יַלְדֵיהֶן הָיוּ לְבָרוֹת לָמוֹ בְּשֶׁבֶר בַּת־עַמִּי׃ כִּלָּה
יְהוָה אֶת־חֲמָתוֹ שָׁפַךְ חֲרוֹן אַפּוֹ וַיַּצֶּת־אֵשׁ בְּצִיּוֹן וַתֹּאכַל יְסוֹדֹתֶיהָ׃ לֹא
הֶאֱמִינוּ מַלְכֵי־אֶרֶץ וכל יֹשְׁבֵי תֵבֵל כִּי יָבֹא צַר וְאוֹיֵב בְּשַׁעֲרֵי יְרוּשָׁלִָם׃ כֹּל
מֵחַטֹּאת נְבִיאֶיהָ עֲוֺנֹת כֹּהֲנֶיהָ הַשֹּׁפְכִים בְּקִרְבָּהּ דַּם צַדִּיקִים׃ נָעוּ
עִוְרִים בַּחוּצוֹת נְגֹאֲלוּ בַּדָּם בְּלֹא יוּכְלוּ יִגְּעוּ בִּלְבֻשֵׁיהֶם׃ סוּרוּ טָמֵא
קָרְאוּ לָמוֹ סוּרוּ סוּרוּ אַל־תִּגָּעוּ כִּי נָצוּ גַּם־נָעוּ אָמְרוּ בַּגּוֹיִם לֹא יוֹסִפוּ
לָגוּר׃ פְּנֵי יְהוָה חִלְּקָם לֹא יוֹסִיף לְהַבִּיטָם פְּנֵי כֹהֲנִים לֹא נָשָׂאוּ זקנים וּזְקֵנִים
לֹא חָנָנוּ׃ עודינה תִּכְלֶינָה עֵינֵינוּ אֶל־עֶזְרָתֵנוּ הָבֶל בְּצִפִּיָּתֵנוּ צִפִּינוּ עוֹדֵינוּ

help: in our watching we have watched for a nation that could not save. They hunt our steps, that we cannot walk in our broad places: our end is near, our days are fulfilled; for our end is come. Our pursuers were swifter than the vultures in the sky: they chased us upon the mountains, they lay in wait for us in the wilderness. The breath of our nostrils, the anointed of the LORD, was taken in their pits, of whom we said, Under His shadow we shall live among the nations. Rejoice and be glad, O daughter of Edom, that dwells in the land of Utz; the cup shall also pass over to you: you shall be drunken, and strip yourself bare. The punishment of your iniquity is accomplished, O daughter of Zion; He will no more carry you away into exile: He will visit your iniquity, O daughter of Edom; He will uncover your sins.

5 Remember, O LORD, what is come upon us: consider, and behold our insult. Our inheritance is turned over to strangers, our houses to aliens. We are become orphans and fatherless, our mothers are like widows. We have drunk our water for money; our own wood is sold to us. We are pursued to our necks: we labor, and have no rest. We have given the hand to Egypt, and to Ashshur, to be satisfied with bread. Our fathers have sinned, and are no more; but we bear their iniquities. Servants rule over us: there is none to deliver us out of their hand. We get our bread with the peril of our lives because of the sword of the wilderness. Our skin is hot like an oven because of the burning famine. Women are ravished in Zion, and maidens in the cities of Judah. Princes are hanged by their hand: the faces of elders are not honored. Young men drag the millstone, and youths stumble under the wood. The elders have ceased from the gate, the young men from their music. The joy of our heart is ceased; our dance is turned into mourning. The crown is fallen from our head: woe to us, that we have sinned! For this our heart is faint; for these things our eyes are dim. Because of the mountain of Zion, which is desolate, foxes prowl over it. You, O LORD, are enthroned forever; Your throne is from generation to generation. Why do You forget us forever, why do You so long forsake us? Turn us to You, O LORD, and we shall be turned; renew our days as of old: unless You have utterly rejected us; and are exceedingly angry against us.

Turn us to You, O LORD, and we shall be turned;
renew our days as of old.

The congregation continues to sit on the floor while the Kinot are said.
For Kinot at Ma'ariv see pages 910–922. For Kinot at Shaharit see pages 924-954.

אֶל־גּוֹי לֹא יוֹשִׁעַ: צָדוּ צְעָדֵינוּ מִלֶּכֶת בִּרְחֹבֹתֵינוּ קָרַב קִצֵּנוּ מָלְאוּ
יָמֵינוּ כִּי־בָא קִצֵּנוּ: קַלִּים הָיוּ רֹדְפֵינוּ מִנִּשְׁרֵי שָׁמָיִם עַל־הֶהָרִים דְּלָקֻנוּ
בַּמִּדְבָּר אָרְבוּ לָנוּ: רוּחַ אַפֵּינוּ מְשִׁיחַ יהוה נִלְכַּד בִּשְׁחִיתוֹתָם אֲשֶׁר
אָמַרְנוּ בְּצִלּוֹ נִחְיֶה בַגּוֹיִם: שִׂישִׂי וְשִׂמְחִי בַּת־אֱדוֹם יושבתי בְּאֶרֶץ יוֹשֶׁבֶת
עוּץ גַּם־עָלַיִךְ תַּעֲבָר־כּוֹס תִּשְׁכְּרִי וְתִתְעָרִי: תַּם־עֲוֹנֵךְ בַּת־צִיּוֹן לֹא
יוֹסִיף לְהַגְלוֹתֵךְ פָּקַד עֲוֹנֵךְ בַּת־אֱדוֹם גִּלָּה עַל־חַטֹּאתָיִךְ:
ה זְכֹר יהוה מֶה־הָיָה לָנוּ הַבִּיטָה וּרְאֵה אֶת־חֶרְפָּתֵנוּ: נַחֲלָתֵנוּ נֶהֶפְכָה
לְזָרִים בָּתֵּינוּ לְנָכְרִים: יְתוֹמִים הָיִינוּ אין אָב אִמֹּתֵינוּ כְּאַלְמָנוֹת: וְאֵין
מֵימֵינוּ בְּכֶסֶף שָׁתִינוּ עֵצֵינוּ בִּמְחִיר יָבֹאוּ: עַל צַוָּארֵנוּ נִרְדָּפְנוּ יָגַעְנוּ
לֹא הוּנַח־לָנוּ: מִצְרַיִם נָתַנּוּ יָד אַשּׁוּר לִשְׂבֹּעַ לָחֶם: אֲבֹתֵינוּ חָטְאוּ וְלֹא
אינם אנחנו עֲוֹנֹתֵיהֶם סָבָלְנוּ: עֲבָדִים מָשְׁלוּ בָנוּ פֹּרֵק אֵין מִיָּדָם: וְאֵינָם וַאֲנַחְנוּ
בְּנַפְשֵׁנוּ נָבִיא לַחְמֵנוּ מִפְּנֵי חֶרֶב הַמִּדְבָּר: עוֹרֵנוּ כְּתַנּוּר נִכְמָרוּ
מִפְּנֵי זַלְעֲפוֹת רָעָב: נָשִׁים בְּצִיּוֹן עִנּוּ בְּתֻלֹת בְּעָרֵי יְהוּדָה: שָׂרִים
בְּיָדָם נִתְלוּ פְּנֵי זְקֵנִים לֹא נֶהְדָּרוּ: בַּחוּרִים טְחוֹן נָשָׂאוּ וּנְעָרִים בָּעֵץ
כָּשָׁלוּ: זְקֵנִים מִשַּׁעַר שָׁבָתוּ בַּחוּרִים מִנְּגִינָתָם: שָׁבַת מְשׂוֹשׂ לִבֵּנוּ
נֶהְפַּךְ לְאֵבֶל מְחֹלֵנוּ: נָפְלָה עֲטֶרֶת רֹאשֵׁנוּ אוֹי־נָא לָנוּ כִּי חָטָאנוּ:
עַל־זֶה הָיָה דָוֶה לִבֵּנוּ עַל־אֵלֶּה חָשְׁכוּ עֵינֵינוּ: עַל הַר־צִיּוֹן שֶׁשָּׁמֵם
שׁוּעָלִים הִלְּכוּ־בוֹ: אַתָּה יהוה לְעוֹלָם תֵּשֵׁב כִּסְאֲךָ לְדֹר וָדוֹר: לָמָּה
לָנֶצַח תִּשְׁכָּחֵנוּ תַּעַזְבֵנוּ לְאֹרֶךְ יָמִים: הֲשִׁיבֵנוּ יהוה ׀ אֵלֶיךָ וְנָשׁוּבָה
חַדֵּשׁ יָמֵינוּ כְּקֶדֶם: כִּי אִם־מָאֹס מְאַסְתָּנוּ קָצַפְתָּ עָלֵינוּ עַד־מְאֹד:

הֲשִׁיבֵנוּ יהוה ׀ אֵלֶיךָ וְנָשׁוּבָה חַדֵּשׁ יָמֵינוּ כְּקֶדֶם:

The קהל continues to sit on the floor while the קינות are said.
For קינות at מעריב see pages 911–923. For קינות at שחרית see pages 925–955.

KINOT FOR MA'ARIV

The structure of this kina is based on the fifth chapter of Eikha. The first eighteen verses are rhyming couplets, corresponding to the first eighteen verses of the chapter. The first stich of each couplet is the opening phrase of the verse in Eikha, while the second expands the idea expressed in that verse. Each stich ends with an expression of lament ("Oh!" or "Oh! What has become of us!"). The last four lines are the last four verses of the Megilla.

זְכֹר Remember, God, what has happened to us, Oh!
See and take heed of our shame,
Oh! What has become of us! *Lam. 5*

נַחֲלָתֵנוּ Our possessions have been turned over to foreigners, Oh!
Our homes to strangers,
Oh! What has become of us!

יְתוֹמִים We have become orphans with no father, Oh!
Our mothers lament in the month of Av,
Oh! What has become of us!

מֵימֵינוּ We were forced to purchase water, Oh!
Because we dishonored the water libation,
Oh! What has become of us!

עַל We were hounded at our necks, Oh!
Because we hounded others hatefully,
Oh! What has become of us!

מִצְרַיִם We extended our hands to Egypt for help, Oh!
But Assyria grasped us as a hunter would his prey,
Oh! What has become of us!

אֲבֹתֵינוּ Our fathers sinned and are no longer, Oh!
But we suffer for their sins,
Oh! What has become of us!

עֲבָדִים Slaves rule over us, Oh!
Because we failed to free our slaves,
Oh! What has become of us!

בְּנַפְשֵׁנוּ We must risk our lives to obtain our bread, Oh!
Because we prevented our hands from giving to the poor,
Oh! What has become of us!

קינות למעריב

The structure of this קינה *is based on the fifth chapter of* איכה*. The first eighteen verses are rhyming couplets, corresponding to the first eighteen verses of the chapter. The first stich of each couplet is the opening phrase of the verse in* איכה*, while the second expands the idea expressed in that verse. Each stich ends with an expression of lament ("Oh!" or "Oh! What has become of us!"). The last four lines are the last four verses of the Megilla.*

זְכֹר יהוה מֶה־הָיָה לָנוּ, אוֹי.
הַבִּיטָה וּרְאֵה אֶת־חֶרְפָּתֵנוּ. אוֹי מֶה הָיָה לָנוּ. איכה ה

נַחֲלָתֵנוּ נֶהֶפְכָה לְזָרִים, אוֹי.
בָּתֵּינוּ לְנָכְרִים. אוֹי מֶה הָיָה לָנוּ.

יְתוֹמִים הָיִינוּ וְאֵין אָב, אוֹי.
וְאִמּוֹתֵינוּ מְקוֹנְנוֹת בְּחֹדֶשׁ אָב. אוֹי מֶה הָיָה לָנוּ.

מֵימֵינוּ בְּכֶסֶף שָׁתִינוּ, אוֹי.
כִּי נִסּוּךְ הַמַּיִם בָּזִינוּ. אוֹי מֶה הָיָה לָנוּ.

עַל צַוָּארֵנוּ נִרְדָּפְנוּ, אוֹי.
כִּי שִׂנְאַת חִנָּם רָדַפְנוּ. אוֹי מֶה הָיָה לָנוּ.

מִצְרַיִם נָתַנּוּ יָד, אוֹי.
וְאַשּׁוּר צָדֵנוּ כְּצַיָּד. אוֹי מֶה הָיָה לָנוּ.

אֲבֹתֵינוּ חָטְאוּ וְאֵינָם, אוֹי.
וַאֲנַחְנוּ סוֹבְלִים אֶת עֲוֹנָם. אוֹי מֶה הָיָה לָנוּ.

עֲבָדִים מָשְׁלוּ בָנוּ, אוֹי.
כִּי שִׁלּוּחַ עֲבָדִים בִּטַּלְנוּ. אוֹי מֶה הָיָה לָנוּ.

בְּנַפְשֵׁנוּ נָבִיא לַחְמֵנוּ, אוֹי.
כִּי קָפַצְנוּ מֵעָנִי יָדֵנוּ. אוֹי מֶה הָיָה לָנוּ.

עוֹרֵנוּ Our skin has shriveled as from an oven's heat, Oh!
Because we exchanged His glory for scandal,
Oh! What has become of us!

נָשִׁים Our enemies violated women in Zion, Oh!
Because we each defiled our neighbor's wife,
Oh! What has become of us!

שָׂרִים Our princes were hung by their hands, Oh!
Because they robbed and cheated the poor,
Oh! What has become of us!

בַּחוּרִים Our young men were forced to carry millstones, Oh!
Because they frequented the house of the harlot,
Oh! What has become of us!

זְקֵנִים Our elders were dislodged from the gates of judgment, Oh!
Because they perverted justice for the widow and orphan,
Oh! What has become of us!

שָׁבַת Joy was dispelled from our heart, Oh!
Because we abandoned our pilgrimages to Jerusalem,
Oh! What has become of us!

נָפְלָה The crown has fallen from our heads, Oh!
For our Holy Temple has been burnt,
Oh! What has become of us!

עַל It is for this that our hearts are pained, Oh!
For the honor of our cherished House is gone,
Oh! What has become of us!

עַל Thus is Mount Zion desolate, Oh!
For an abominable idol has been placed on it,
Oh! What has become of us!

אַתָּה But You, O Lord, are enthroned forever,
Your throne endures through the ages.
Why have You forgotten us utterly, forsaken us for all time?
Take us back, O Lord, to Yourself, and let us come back;
renew our days as of old!
For truly, You have rejected us, bitterly raged against us. *Lam. 5*
Take us back, O Lord, to Yourself, and let us come back;
renew our days as of old! *Lam. 5*

עוֹרֵנוּ כְּתַנּוּר נִכְמָרוּ, אוֹי.
כִּי כְבוֹדָם בְּקָלוֹן הֵמִירוּ. אוֹי מֶה הָיָה לָנוּ.

נָשִׁים בְּצִיּוֹן עִנּוּ, אוֹי.
כִּי אֵשֶׁת אִישׁ טִמְּאוּ וְזִנּוּ. אוֹי מֶה הָיָה לָנוּ.

שָׂרִים בְּיָדָם נִתְלוּ, אוֹי.
כִּי גְּזֵלַת הֶעָנִי חָמְסוּ וְגָזְלוּ. אוֹי מֶה הָיָה לָנוּ.

בַּחוּרִים טְחוֹן נָשָׂאוּ, אוֹי.
כִּי בְּבֵית זוֹנָה נִמְצָאוּ. אוֹי מֶה הָיָה לָנוּ.

זְקֵנִים מִשַּׁעַר שָׁבָתוּ, אוֹי.
כִּי מִשְׁפַּט יָתוֹם וְאַלְמָנָה עִוְּתוּ. אוֹי מֶה הָיָה לָנוּ.

שָׁבַת מְשׂוֹשׂ לִבֵּנוּ, אוֹי.
כִּי נִבְטְלוּ עוֹלֵי רְגָלֵינוּ. אוֹי מֶה הָיָה לָנוּ.

נָפְלָה עֲטֶרֶת רֹאשֵׁנוּ, אוֹי.
כִּי נִשְׂרַף בֵּית מִקְדָּשֵׁנוּ. אוֹי מֶה הָיָה לָנוּ.

עַל זֶה הָיָה דָוֶה לִבֵּנוּ, אוֹי.
כִּי נֻטַּל כְּבוֹד בֵּית מַאֲוַיֵּינוּ. אוֹי מֶה הָיָה לָנוּ.

עַל הַר צִיּוֹן שֶׁשָּׁמֵם, אוֹי.
כִּי נִתַּן עָלָיו שִׁקּוּץ מְשׁוֹמֵם. אוֹי מֶה הָיָה לָנוּ.

אַתָּה יהוה לְעוֹלָם תֵּשֵׁב, כִּסְאֲךָ לְדוֹר וָדוֹר:
לָמָּה לָנֶצַח תִּשְׁכָּחֵנוּ, תַּעַזְבֵנוּ לְאֹרֶךְ יָמִים:
הֲשִׁיבֵנוּ יהוה אֵלֶיךָ וְנָשׁוּב, חַדֵּשׁ יָמֵינוּ כְּקֶדֶם:
איכה ה כִּי אִם־מָאֹס מְאַסְתָּנוּ, קָצַפְתָּ עָלֵינוּ עַד־מְאֹד:
איכה ה הֲשִׁיבֵנוּ יהוה אֵלֶיךָ וְנָשׁוּבָ, חַדֵּשׁ יָמֵינוּ כְּקֶדֶם:

On Motza'ei Shabbat, the following kina is read.
On all other nights continue with Kina on the next page.
If Tisha B'Av begins on Motza'ei Shabbat, the prayer "May the Pleasantness" and Psalm 91 (usually recited on Motza'ei Shabbat) are not said (Geonim, quoted in the Tur, O.Ḥ. 559).

אֵיךְ How from the mouth of boys and girls,
much sadness is now voiced instead of gleeful songs.
"May the Pleasantness" is omitted this Motza'ei Shabbat.

אוֹי Oh! The decree is decreed with such anger, even rage.
His wrath is kindled against us and burns with a fiery flame.
"May the Pleasantness" is omitted this Motza'ei Shabbat.

אוֹי Oh! They have defaced our homes and have defiled our virgins.
Distorted are our faces; blackened like a scorched skillet.
"May the Pleasantness" is omitted this Motza'ei Shabbat.

אוֹי Oh! The foe has so seized us that even our princes have fallen;
precious sons of Zion, cherished like the pupil of the eye. *Lam. 4*
"May the Pleasantness" is omitted this Motza'ei Shabbat.

אוֹי Oh! The crown is fallen; His turned back has triumphed.
Beauty and glory are suspended;
the Divine Presence has recoiled from her beloved.
"May the Pleasantness" is omitted this Motza'ei Shabbat.

אוֹי Oh! The Menora is taken,
together with the frankincense and the stone Sanhedrin chamber.
The land flowing with milk and honey now mourns.
"May the Pleasantness" is omitted this Motza'ei Shabbat.

On מוצאי שבת, the following קינה is read.
On all other nights continue with קינה on the next page.
If תשעה באב begins on מוצאי שבת, the prayer "וִיהִי נֹעַם" and תהלים צא (usually recited on מוצאי שבת) are not said (Geonim, quoted in the Tur, O.Ḥ. 559).

אֵיךְ מִפִּי בֵן וּבַת / הֲגוֹת קִינוֹת רַבַּת.
תְּמוּר שִׁירִים וְחֶדְוַת:
וִיהִי נֹעַם נִשְׁבַּת. בְּמוֹצָאֵי שַׁבָּת:

אוֹי כִּי נִגְזְרָה גְּזֵרָה / בְּחֳרִי אַף וְגַם בְּעֶבְרָה.
וְאַפּוֹ בָּנוּ חָרָה / וּבָעֲרָה חֲמָתוֹ כְּלַבַּת:
וִיהִי נֹעַם נִשְׁבַּת. בְּמוֹצָאֵי שַׁבָּת:

אוֹי כִּי בָתֵּינוּ שַׁמּוּ / וּבְתוּלוֹתֵינוּ עֻנּוּ.
וּפָנֵינוּ נִשְׁתַּנּוּ / וְגַם הָשְׁחֲרוּ כְּמַחֲבַת.
וִיהִי נֹעַם נִשְׁבַּת. בְּמוֹצָאֵי שַׁבָּת:

אוֹי כִּי שַׁדּוּנוּ צָרִים / וְגַם נָפְלוּ בִּי שָׂרִים.
בְּנֵי צִיּוֹן הַיְקָרִים / הָיוּ נְצוּרִים כְּבָבַת: איכה ד
וִיהִי נֹעַם נִשְׁבַּת. בְּמוֹצָאֵי שַׁבָּת:

אוֹי כִּי נָפְלָה עֲטֶרֶת / וְגָבְרָה כָּתֵף סוֹרֶרֶת.
וְחָדַל הוֹד וְתִפְאֶרֶת / צִמְצוּם שֶׁכֶן חִבַּת:
וִיהִי נֹעַם נִשְׁבַּת. בְּמוֹצָאֵי שַׁבָּת:

אוֹי כִּי נִטְּלָה מְנוֹרָה / וּקְטֹרֶת לְבוֹנָה הַטְּהוֹרָה.
וְנִבְזֶה גָּזִית מְיֻקָּרָה / אֲבֵלָה אֶרֶץ זָבַת:
וִיהִי נֹעַם נִשְׁבַּת. בְּמוֹצָאֵי שַׁבָּת:

This kina emphasizes the especial quality of mourning particular to the night of Tisha B'Av, based on the Talmud in Sanhedrin 104b, "Whoever weeps at night – his voice is heard." Some have attributed it to Rabbi Elazar HaKalir, one of Israel's earliest and most prolific liturgical poets (paytanim). Others have pointed out that its form is heavily influenced by later Spanish-Jewish poetry.

בְּלֵיל Tonight, my children weep and wail.
Tonight, my Sanctuary was ruined and my palaces burned.
The entire house of Israel expresses my agony,
and cries for the fire God kindled. *Lev. 10*

Tonight, my children weep and wail.

בְּלֵיל Tonight, cry bitterly, O waif who has lost it all.
She lives alienated from her Father's home;
has left His home, the door shut behind her.
Gone into captivity, devoured by every mouth;
cast that day into a consuming flame,
a glowing ember lit by the LORD.

Tonight, my children weep and wail.

בְּלֵיל Tonight, the wheel of fortune spun to doom,
my first and second Houses destroyed.
She is not to be pitied, this wayward woman, *Jer. 31*
drunk with toxic waters swelling her belly.
Cast out of her home, she has forgotten past happiness.
Hate had the upper hand over love.
She is like a living widow, a deserted woman.
"And Zion said, 'The LORD has forsaken me.'" *Is. 49*

Tonight, my children weep and wail.

בְּלֵיל Tonight, I am dejected, the lights dimmed.
My House destroyed, the priestly watches discontinued.
Tonight, woe surrounds me, winds about me.
He summoned an assembly of five harsh decrees.
Tears shed in vain set the pattern forever.
The LORD brought it all about as predestined. *I Kings 12*

Tonight, my children weep and wail.

בְּלֵיל Tonight, five appalling tragedies occurred.
A decree against our ancestors, denying them the Land;
afflicting them with oppressing pain and worse,
a day destined for harm and hurt.
The enemy stood and shrieked horribly,
"Attack! For this is the day that God foretold!"

Tonight, my children weep and wail.

This קינה *emphasizes the especial quality of mourning particular to the night of* תשעה באב*, based on the Talmud in Sanhedrin 104b, "Whoever weeps at night – his voice is heard." Some have attributed it to Rabbi Elazar HaKalir, one of Israel's earliest and most prolific liturgical poets (paytanim). Others have pointed out that its form is heavily influenced by later Spanish-Jewish poetry.*

בְּלֵיל זֶה יִבְכָּיוּן וְיֵלִילוּ בָּנַי / לֵיל חָרַב קָדְשִׁי וְנִשְׂרְפוּ אַרְמוֹנַי.
וְכָל בֵּית יִשְׂרָאֵל יֶהְגּוּ בִיגוֹנַי / וְיִבְכּוּ אֶת הַשְּׂרֵפָה אֲשֶׁר שָׂרַף יהוה: ויקרא י
בְּלֵיל זֶה יִבְכָּיוּן וְיֵלִילוּ בָּנָי:

בְּלֵיל זֶה תְּיֵלִיל מַר עֲנִיָּה נֶחְדֶּלֶת / וּמִבֵּית אָבִיהָ בְּחַיִּים מֻבְדֶּלֶת.
וְיָצְאָה מִבֵּיתוֹ וְנִסְגַּר הַדֶּלֶת / וְהָלְכָה בַּשִּׁבְיָה, בְּכָל פֶּה נֶאֱכֶלֶת.
בְּיוֹם שְׁלָחָהּ, בְּאֵשׁ בּוֹעֶרֶת וְאוֹכֶלֶת / וְאֵשׁ עִם גַּחֶלֶת יָצְאָה מֵאֵת יהוה:
בְּלֵיל זֶה יִבְכָּיוּן וְיֵלִילוּ בָּנָי:

בְּלֵיל זֶה הַגַּלְגַּל סִבֵּב הַחוֹבָה / רִאשׁוֹן גַּם שֵׁנִי, בֵּיתִי נֶחֱרָבָה.
וְעוֹד לֹא רֻחֲמָה בַּת הַשּׁוֹבֵבָה / הִשְׁקְתָה מֵי רֹאשׁ, וְאֶת בִּטְנָהּ צָבָה. ירמיהו לא
וְשִׁלְּחָהּ מִבֵּיתוֹ, וְגַם נָשְׂתָה טוֹבָה / גְּדוֹלָה הַשִּׂנְאָה מֵאֵת אֲשֶׁר אֲהֵבָהּ.
וּבְאַלְמְנוּת חַיּוּת כְּאִשָּׁה נֶעֱזָבָה / וַתֹּאמֶר צִיּוֹן עֲזָבַנִי יהוה: ישעיה מט
בְּלֵיל זֶה יִבְכָּיוּן וְיֵלִילוּ בָּנָי:

בְּלֵיל זֶה קָדַרְתִּי וְחָשְׁכוּ הַמְּאוֹרוֹת / לְחֻרְבַּן בֵּית קָדְשִׁי, וּבִטּוּל מִשְׁמָרוֹת.
בְּלֵיל זֶה סַבּוּנִי, אֲפָפוּנִי צָרוֹת / וְגַם קָרָא מוֹעֵד, בְּדִין חָמֵשׁ גְּזֵרוֹת.
בְּכִי חִנָּם בָּכוּ, וְנִקְבַּע לַדּוֹרוֹת / יַעַן כִּי הָיְתָה סִבָּה מֵאֵת יהוה: מלכים א יב
בְּלֵיל זֶה יִבְכָּיוּן וְיֵלִילוּ בָּנָי:

בְּלֵיל זֶה, אֵרְעוּ בוֹ חָמֵשׁ מְאֹרָעוֹת / גָּזַר עַל אָבוֹת, בִּפְרֹעַ פְּרָעוֹת.
וְדָבְקוּ בוֹ צָרוֹת מְצֵרוֹת וְגַם רָעוֹת / יוֹם מוּכָן הָיָה, בִּפְגֹעַ פְּגָעוֹת.
וְהֶעֱמִיד הָאוֹיֵב, וְהֵרִים קוֹל זְוָעוֹת / קוּם, כִּי זֶה הַיּוֹם אֲשֶׁר אָמַר יהוה:
בְּלֵיל זֶה יִבְכָּיוּן וְיֵלִילוּ בָּנָי:

This kina was written by Rabbi Solomon ibn Gabirol (Spain, 1021–1058). In Ezekiel chapter 23, the kingdoms of Israel and Judea are depicted as two unfaithful wives, Ohola and Oholiva. This kina is written as a conversation between them, and concludes with a prayer to God to have mercy on them.

שׁוֹמְרוֹן Samaria [the ten tribes of Israel, "Ohola"] proclaimed,
"My sins have caught up with me! My children have left me for another land!"
And Oholiva [Jerusalem, Judah] screamed in response,
"My palaces are in flames!" And Zion said, "The LORD has forsaken me." *Is. 49*

לֹא [Samaria answered,] "You cannot equate your plight to mine!
Can your downfall compare to my collapse?
I, Ohola, acted with spite and treachery;
my betrayal opposed me, and my rebellion accused me.
In a few short days, I paid my debt, and the Assyrian king devoured my fruits.
He stripped me bare of my treasures and jewels,
and carried off my captives to Halah and Habor.
So be still, Oholiva, don't cry as I do; your years endured, but my years did not!"
And Oholiva screamed in response, "My palaces are in flames!"
"The LORD has forsaken me."

מְשִׁיבָה Oholiva responded, "I, too, was perverse
and betrayed the Companion of my Youth just as you did.
So be still, Ohola, as I recall my anguish.
You wandered but once; while I, many times.
I was entrapped by Chaldean hands
and descended to Babylon as a destitute prisoner.
The Temple of which I was so proud was burned.
After seventy years in Babylon, I was remembered
and returned to Zion to found my Temple yet again.
But this time, too, I was not long entrenched
before Rome snatched me, and I was almost no more,
for my multitudes were scattered to distant lands."
And Oholiva screamed in response, "My palaces are in flames!"
And Zion said, "The LORD has forsaken me."

הַחוֹמֵל He who pities the poor, take pity on their plight!
See their desolation and lengthy exile.
Do not be implacably angry, but remember their lowliness.
Remember not their foolish iniquities forever.
Mend their fissures, soothe their grief, for You are their Hope and their Hero.
Renew our days like the days long gone,
as You have spoken, "The LORD rebuilds Jerusalem." *Ps. 147*

This קינה *was written by Rabbi Solomon ibn Gabirol (Spain, 1021–1058). In Ezekiel chapter 23, the kingdoms of Israel and Judea are depicted as two unfaithful wives, Ohola and Oholiva. This* קינה *is written as a conversation between them, and concludes with a prayer to God to have mercy on them.*

שׁוֹמְרוֹן קוֹל תִּתֵּן, מְצָאוּנִי עֲוֹנַי / לְאֶרֶץ אַחֶרֶת יָצְאוּנִי בָנַי.
וְאָהֳלִיבָה תִּזְעַק נִשְׂרְפוּ אַרְמוֹנַי / וַתֹּאמֶר צִיּוֹן עֲזָבַנִי יהוה: ישעיה מט

לֹא לָךְ אָהֳלִיבָה, חֲשׁוֹב עָנְיֵךְ כְּעָנְיִי / הֲתַמְשִׁילִי שִׁבְרֵךְ לְשִׁבְרִי וּלְחָלְיִי.
אֲנִי אָהֳלָה, סוּרָה בָּגַדְתִּי בְקָשְׁיִי / וְקָם עָלַי כַּחֲשִׁי, וְעָנָה בִי מֶרְיִי.
וּלְמִקְצַת הַיָּמִים שִׁלַּמְתִּי נִשְׁיִי / וְתִגְלַת פִּלְאֶסֶר אָכַל אֶת פִּרְיִי.
חֲמוּדוֹתַי הִפְשִׁיט, וְהִצִּיל אֶת עֶדְיִי / וְלַחֲלַח וְחָבוֹר נָשָׂא אֶת שִׁבְיִי.
דֹּמִּי אָהֳלִיבָה, וְאַל תִּבְכִּי כְּבִכְיִי / שְׁנוֹתַיִךְ אָרְכוּ, וְלֹא אָרְכוּ שָׁנַי:
וְאָהֳלִיבָה תִּזְעַק נִשְׂרְפוּ אַרְמוֹנַי / וַתֹּאמֶר צִיּוֹן עֲזָבַנִי יהוה:

מְשִׁיבָה אָהֳלִיבָה, אֲנִי כֵּן נֶעֱקַשְׁתִּי / וּבְאַלּוּף נְעוּרַי כְּאָהֳלָה בָּגַדְתִּי.
דֹּמִּי אָהֳלָה, כִּי יְגוֹנִי זָכַרְתִּי / נָדַדְתְּ אַתְּ אַחַת, וְרַבּוֹת נָדַדְתִּי.
הִנֵּה בְּיַד כַּשְׂדִּים פְּעָמִים נִלְכַּדְתִּי / וּשְׁבִיָּה עֲנִיָּה לְבָבֶל יָרַדְתִּי.
וְנִשְׂרַף הַהֵיכָל אֲשֶׁר בּוֹ נִכְבַּדְתִּי / וּלְשִׁבְעִים שָׁנָה בְּבָבֶל נִפְקַדְתִּי.
וְשַׁבְתִּי לְצִיּוֹן עוֹד, וְהֵיכָל יִסַּדְתִּי / גַּם זֹאת הַפַּעַם, מְעַט לֹא עָמַדְתִּי.
עַד לְקָחַנִי אֱדוֹם, וּכְמְעַט אָבַדְתִּי / וְעַל כָּל הָאֲרָצוֹת נָפוֹצוּ הֲמוֹנַי:
וְאָהֳלִיבָה תִּזְעַק נִשְׂרְפוּ אַרְמוֹנַי / וַתֹּאמֶר צִיּוֹן עֲזָבַנִי יהוה:

הַחוֹמֵל עַל דַּל, חֲמוֹל עַל דַּלּוּתָם / וּרְאֵה שׁוֹמְמוּתָם וְאֹרֶךְ גָּלוּתָם.
וְאַל תִּקְצֹף עַד מְאֹד, וּרְאֵה שִׁפְלוּתָם / וְאַל לָעַד תִּזְכֹּר עֲוֹנָם וְסִכְלוּתָם.
רְפָא נָא אֶת שִׁבְרָם, וְנַחֵם אֲבֵלוּתָם / כִּי אַתָּה סִבְרָם וְאַתָּה אֱיָלוּתָם.
חַדֵּשׁ יָמֵינוּ כִּימֵי קַדְמוֹנַי / כְּנָאֳמָךְ: בּוֹנֵה יְרוּשָׁלַםִ יהוה: תהלים קמז

This kina, which concludes the night kinot, is a very ancient one. It is framed by verses of pleading for the redemption and rebuilding of Jerusalem. Each of the twelve signs of the Zodiac is mentioned, based on the Talmud (Ḥagiga 5b) which describes how, after the destruction of the Temples, even the heavenly hosts joined in mourning with Israel.

עַד How long must Zion cry and Jerusalem mourn?
Pity Zion, rebuild the walls of Jerusalem! *Ps. 102*

א Then, because of our sins, the Sanctuary was destroyed;
because of our sins, the Temple was burned.
ב Jerusalem's heavenly counterpart arranged to mourn,
while the stars in the sky lamented.
ג Jacob's tribes wept bitterly.
The constellations dripped tears.
ד The banners of Jeshurun were shrouded.
Pleiades and Orion dimmed their glow.
ה Forefathers pleaded, but God would not hear;
children wailed, but Father did not respond.
ו Moses' protest was sounded on high, *Song. 2*
but the Faithful Shepherd turned a deaf ear.
ז The sacred seed [the Jews] wore sackcloth;
the angels in heaven donned sackcloth too.
ח The sun darkened, the moon was dim,
the stars and planets withheld their shine.
ט Aries [corresponding to Nisan], first in the constellations, wept bitterly,
for her lambs were led to slaughter.
י Taurus [corresponding to Iyar] bellowed up above,
for we were pursued from behind.
כ Gemini [corresponding to Sivan] seemed torn asunder,
for the blood of brothers was spilled like water.
ל Cancer [corresponding to Tammuz] clambered to the shore
while we were faint with thirst.
מ The heavens trembled at Leo's [corresponding to Av] roar,
but our roaring prayers never reached those heavens.
נ Young virgins were killed and also young lads.
No wonder that Virgo [corresponding to Elul] is darkened in gloom.
ס Libra [corresponding to Tishrei] tipped her scales, yet prayed
for those who chose death over a life of woe.
ע Scorpio [corresponding to Ḥeshvan] was overcome with fear and shuddering,
for the Protector Himself condemned us to sword and hunger.

This קינה, which concludes the night kinot, is a very ancient one. It is framed by verses of pleading for the redemption and rebuilding of Jerusalem. Each of the twelve signs of the Zodiac is mentioned, based on the Talmud (Ḥagiga 5b) which describes how, after the destruction of the Temples, even the heavenly hosts joined in mourning with Israel.

עַד אָנָה בְּכִיָּה בְּצִיּוֹן, וּמִסְפֵּד בִּירוּשָׁלָיִם.
תְּרַחֵם צִיּוֹן וְתִבְנֶה חוֹמוֹת יְרוּשָׁלָיִם: תהלים קב

אָז בַּחֲטָאֵינוּ חָרַב מִקְדָּשׁ / וּבַעֲוֹנוֹתֵינוּ נִשְׂרַף הֵיכָל.
בְּאֶרֶץ חֲבֵרָה לָהּ, קָשְׁרָה מִסְפֵּד / וּצְבָא הַשָּׁמַיִם נָשְׂאוּ קִינָה.
גַּם בָּכוּ בְּמֶרֶר שִׁבְטֵי יַעֲקֹב / וְאַף מַזָּלוֹת יִזְּלוּ דִמְעָה.
דִּגְלֵי יְשֻׁרוּן חָפוּ רֹאשָׁם / וְכִימָה וּכְסִיל קָדְרוּ פְנֵיהֶם.
הֶעְתִּירוּ אָבוֹת, וְאֵל כְּלֹא שׁוֹמֵעַ / צָעֲקוּ בָנִים וְלֹא עָנָה אָב.
וְקוֹל הַתּוֹר נִשְׁמַע בַּמָּרוֹם / וְרוֹעֶה נֶאֱמָן לֹא הִטָּה אֹזֶן. שיר השירים ב
זֶרַע קֹדֶשׁ לָבְשׁוּ שַׂקִּים / וּצְבָא הַשָּׁמַיִם גַּם הֵם, שַׂק הוּשַׂם כְּסוּתָם.
חָשַׁךְ הַשֶּׁמֶשׁ וְיָרֵחַ קָדַר / וְכוֹכָבִים וּמַזָּלוֹת אָסְפוּ נָגְהָם.
טָלֶה רִאשׁוֹן בָּכָה בְּמַר נֶפֶשׁ / עַל כִּי כְבָשָׂיו לַטֶּבַח הוּבָלוּ.
יְלָלָה הִשְׁמִיעַ שׁוֹר בַּמְּרוֹמִים / כִּי עַל צַוָּארֵנוּ נִרְדַּפְנוּ כֻּלָּנוּ.
כּוֹכַב תְּאוֹמִים נִרְאָה חָלוּק / כִּי דַם אַחִים נִשְׁפַּךְ כַּמָּיִם.
לָאָרֶץ בִּקֵּשׁ לִנְפּוֹל סַרְטָן / כִּי הִתְעַלַּפְנוּ מִפְּנֵי צָמָא.
מָרוֹם נִבְעַת מִקּוֹל אַרְיֵה / כִּי שַׁאֲגָתֵנוּ לֹא עָלְתָה לַמָּרוֹם.
נֶהֶרְגוּ בְתוּלוֹת וְגַם בַּחוּרִים / עַל כֵּן בְּתוּלָה קָדְרָה פָנֶיהָ.
סִבֵּב מֹאזְנַיִם וּבִקֵּשׁ תְּחִנָּה / כִּי נִבְחַר לָמוֹ מָוֶת מֵחַיִּים.
עַקְרָב לָבַשׁ פַּחַד וּרְעָדָה / כִּי בְּחֶרֶב וּבְרָעָב שְׁפָטָנוּ צוּרֵנוּ.

פ Our eyes overflowed with streams of tears;
the hope of Sagittarius' [corresponding to Kislev] rainbow was denied us.

צ Water flowed plentifully above our head,
but even Aquarius' [corresponding to Shevat] bucket left our palates dry.

ק The sacrifices we offered were not accepted;
under Capricorn [corresponding to Tevet],
the goats, the sin-offerings, ended.

ר When compassionate mothers cooked their own children,
Pisces [corresponding to Adar] averted her eyes.

ש We ignored the Sabbath with our wayward hearts,
so God ignored whatever merits we had.

ת You will one day again take up Zion's cause with zeal,
and once more illuminate the populous city
with the light of Your splendor.

The congregation stands and the Leader says the following:

תְּרַחֵם Pity Zion as You have spoken.
Make her firm as You gave Your word.
תְּמַהֵר Hasten salvation, hurry redemption.
And return to Jerusalem with great compassion.

כַּכָּתוּב As is written by the hand of Your prophet: "Therefore, thus says the LORD: I have returned to Jerusalem with mercies, My House shall be rebuilt in it, says the LORD of hosts, and a line shall be stretched forth over Jerusalem." And it is said: "Proclaim further, saying, Thus says the LORD of hosts: My cities shall again overflow with prosperity; and the LORD shall yet comfort Zion, and shall yet choose Jerusalem." And it is said: "For the LORD shall comfort Zion: He will comfort all her waste places; and He will make her wilderness like Eden, and her desert like the garden of the LORD; joy and gladness shall be found in it, thanksgiving, and the voice of melody." *Zech. 1* *Is. 51*

The service continues with "You are the Holy One" on page 344. This is usually said only on Motza'ei Shabbat, but is said on Tisha B'Av regardless of the day of the week. "May the pleasantness," usually said on Motza'ei Shabbat, is not said on Tisha B'Av.

פַּלְגֵי מַיִם הוֹרִידוּ דִמְעָה כַּנַּחַל / כִּי אוֹת בַּקֶּשֶׁת לֹא נִתַּן לָנוּ.
צָפוּ מַיִם עַל רֹאשֵׁנוּ / וּבִדְלִי מָלֵא חִכֵּנוּ יָבֵשׁ.
קָרְבְּנוּ קָרְבָּן וְלֹא נִתְקַבַּל / וּגְדִי פֶּסַק שְׂעִיר חַטָּאתֵנוּ.
רַחֲמָנִיּוֹת בִּשְּׁלוּ יַלְדֵיהֶן / וּמַזַּל דָּגִים הֶעְלִים עֵינָיו.
שָׁכַחְנוּ שַׁבָּת בְּלִבּוֹת שׁוֹבָבִים / שַׁדַּי שְׁכַח כָּל צִדְקוֹתֵינוּ.
תְּקַנֵּא לְצִיּוֹן קִנְאָה גְדוֹלָה / וְתָאִיר לְרַבָּתִי עָם מְאוֹר נָגְהֶךָ.

The קהל *stands and the* שליח ציבור *says the following:*

תְּרַחֵם צִיּוֹן כַּאֲשֶׁר אָמַרְתָּ / וּתְכוֹנְנֶהָ כַּאֲשֶׁר דִּבַּרְתָּ /
תְּמַהֵר יְשׁוּעָה וְתָחִישׁ גְּאֻלָּה / וְתָשׁוּב לִירוּשָׁלַיִם בְּרַחֲמִים רַבִּים:

כַּכָּתוּב עַל יַד נְבִיאֶךָ:
זכריה א לָכֵן כֹּה־אָמַר יהוה, שַׁבְתִּי לִירוּשָׁלַםִ בְּרַחֲמִים
בֵּיתִי יִבָּנֶה בָּהּ, נְאֻם יהוה צְבָאוֹת, וְקָו יִנָּטֶה עַל־יְרוּשָׁלָםִ:
וְנֶאֱמַר:
עוֹד קְרָא לֵאמֹר, כֹּה אָמַר יהוה צְבָאוֹת
עוֹד תְּפוּצֶנָה עָרַי מִטּוֹב, וְנִחַם יהוה עוֹד אֶת־צִיּוֹן
וּבָחַר עוֹד בִּירוּשָׁלָםִ:
וְנֶאֱמַר:
ישעיה נא כִּי־נִחַם יהוה צִיּוֹן, נִחַם כָּל־חָרְבֹתֶיהָ
וַיָּשֶׂם מִדְבָּרָהּ כְּעֵדֶן, וְעַרְבָתָהּ כְּגַן־יהוה
שָׂשׂוֹן וְשִׂמְחָה יִמָּצֵא בָהּ, תּוֹדָה וְקוֹל זִמְרָה:

The service continues with וְאַתָּה קָדוֹשׁ *on page 345. This is usually said only on* מוצאי שבת*, but is said on* תשעה באב *regardless of the day of the week.* ויהי נעם*, usually said on* מוצאי שבת*, is not said on* תשעה באב.

KINOT FOR SHAḤARIT

After the Torah scroll is returned to the Ark, the congregation sits on the floor and recites kinot.

This kina by HaKalir is based on Eikha 2:20, and describes the horrors experienced at the time of the siege and the subsequent pillaging of the city. It is arranged in alphabetical order, each line opening with the feminine verb form and ending with "Woe is me!" echoing Job 10:15: "If I have done evil, woe is me!" The last stanza also hints at the source in Eikha, with God reminding the people of their own sins, which were the cause of the calamity.

אִם As I recall,

אִם women eating their own fruit, their coddled babes,
Woe is me!

אִם the compassionate cooking their own children,
once preciously measured ounce by ounce,
Woe is me!

אִם the braids of their head torn from them,
after being tied to racing horses,
Woe is me!

אִם the tongues of infants, stuck to their palates, parched with thirst,
Woe is me!

אִם women wailing to each other, "Come, let us cook our squealing children,"
Woe is me!

אִם the two encountering each other, saying, "Give me your child,"
[the child] hidden, already cut into sections,
Woe is me!

אִם children encountering their parents' flesh in caves and pits,
Woe is me!

אִם condemned maidens, upon their mother's laps, swollen with hunger,
Woe is me!

אִם the souls of babes expiring in the village streets, swollen with hunger,
Woe is me!

אִם burdened with miscarriage and shriveled breasts,
a mother collapsed over her children,
Woe is me!

אִם eight hundred shield-bearers, humbled and exiled to
Arabia to be executed,
Woe is me!

קינות לשחרית

After the סֵפֶר תּוֹרָה *is returned to the* אָרוֹן*, the* קָהָל *sits on the floor and recites* קִינוֹת*.*

This קינה *by HaKalir is based on Eikha 2:20, and describes the horrors experienced at the time of the siege and the subsequent pillaging of the city. It is arranged in alphabetical order, each line opening with the feminine verb form and ending with "Woe is me!" echoing Job 10:15: "If I have done evil, woe is me!" The last stanza also hints at the source in* איכה*, with God reminding the people of their own sins, which were the cause of the calamity.*

אִם־תֹּאכַלְנָה נָשִׁים פִּרְיָם, עֹלְלֵי טִפֻּחִים.
אַלְלַי לִי:
אִם תְּבַשֵּׁלְנָה רַחֲמָנִיּוֹת יַלְדֵיהֶן, הַמְדוּדִים טְפָחִים טְפָחִים.
אַלְלַי לִי:
אִם תְּגַזֵּנָה פְּאַת רֹאשָׁם, וְתִקָּשַׁרְנָה לְסוּסִים פּוֹרְחִים.
אַלְלַי לִי:
אִם תִּדְבַּק לְשׁוֹן יוֹנֵק לְחֵךְ, בְּצִמְאוֹן צְחִיחִים.
אַלְלַי לִי:
אִם תְּהֻמְנָה זוֹ לְעֻמַּת זוֹ, בּוֹאִי וּנְבַשֵּׁל אֶת בָּנֵינוּ צוֹרְחִים.
אַלְלַי לִי:
אִם תִּוָּעַדְנָה זוֹ לְזוֹ, תְּנִי בְנֵךְ, וְהוּא חָבוּי מְנֻתָּח נְתָחִים נְתָחִים.
אַלְלַי לִי:
אִם תְּזֻמֵּנָּה בְּשַׂר אָבוֹת לַבָּנִים, בִּמְעָרוֹת וְשִׁיחִים.
אַלְלַי לִי:
אִם תְּחַיֶּבְנָה בָּנוֹת, אֶל חֵיק אִמּוֹתָם נִתְפָּחִים.
אַלְלַי לִי:
אִם תָּטֹסְנָה רוּחוֹת עוֹלָלִים בִּרְחוֹבוֹת קִרְיָה תְּפוּחִים.
אַלְלַי לִי:
אִם תִּיקַרְנָה בְּשִׁכּוּל רֶחֶם וְצִמּוּק שָׁדַיִם, וְאֵם עַל בָּנִים שְׁחִים.
אַלְלַי לִי:
אִם תְּכַשֵּׁלְנָה שְׁמוֹנֶה מֵאוֹת מָגִנִּים, בַּעֲרַב אֲלוּחִים.
אַלְלַי לִי:

אַם their spirits enflamed by salty food and empty swollen flasks,
Woe is me!

אַם reduced from a thousand to a hundred, from a hundred to ten,
and then to a sorrowful single one,
Woe is me!

אַם eighty thousand budding priests, fleeing behind the Temple's curtains,
Woe is me!

אַם to be burned alive like cut kindling wood,
Woe is me!

אַם eighty thousand murdered priests, hacked to death on
account of the death of an innocent one,
Woe is me!

אַם those who breathed their last, punctured by the odor
of the fruits of the field,
Woe is me!

אַם heaped on one stone, nine large measures of crushed children's brains,
Woe is me!

אַם three hundred infants, hung and strung on one long tree branch,
Woe is me!

אַם gentle and delicate damsels, led away in chains
by the chief executioner,
Woe is me!

אַם elegant princesses, violated by the roadside,
Woe is me!

אַם young lads and lasses, faint with parching thirst,
Woe is me!

וְרוּחַ The Holy Spirit thunders against them.
Woe to the wicked of the Jewish people!
They inform others about what has befallen them,
but do not inform others about what they have done.
They give voice to the fact that women eat their children,
but, to the fact that they killed a prophet and a priest in the Temple,
they do not give voice.

אִם תְּלַהֵטְנָה רוּחָם בְּמִינֵי מְלוּחִים וְנוֹדוֹת נְפוּחִים.
אַלְלַי לִי:

אִם תְּמַעֵטְנָה מֵאֶלֶף מֵאָה, וּמִמֵּאָה עֲשָׂרָה, עַד אֶחָד לְמַפָּחִים.
אַלְלַי לִי:

אִם תְּנַסֵּנָה לְמָסַךְ הֵיכָל, שְׁמוֹנִים אֶלֶף כֹּהֲנִים פְּרָחִים.
אַלְלַי לִי:

אִם תִּשָּׂרַפְנָה שָׁם כָּל אוֹתָן הַנְּפָשׁוֹת, כְּקוֹצִים כְּסוּחִים.
אַלְלַי לִי:

אִם תֵּעָרַפְנָה עַל דַּם נָקִי, שְׁמוֹנִים אֶלֶף כֹּהֲנִים נִרְצָחִים.
אַלְלַי לִי:

אִם תִּפַּחְנָה נְפָשׁוֹת מְדֻקָּרִים, מֵרֵיחַ תְּנוּבוֹת שִׂיחִים.
אַלְלַי לִי:

אִם תִּצָּבַרְנָה עַל אֶבֶן אַחַת, תִּשְׁעָה קַבִּין מוֹחֵי יְלָדִים מֻנָּחִים.
אַלְלַי לִי:

אִם תְּקַעְנָה שְׁלֹשׁ מֵאוֹת יוֹנְקִים, עַל שׂוֹכָה אַחַת מְתוּחִים.
אַלְלַי לִי:

אִם תֵּרָאֶינָה רַכּוֹת וַעֲנֻגּוֹת, כְּבוּלוֹת עַל יַד רַב הַטַּבָּחִים.
אַלְלַי לִי:

אִם תִּשָּׁכַבְנָה בֵּין שְׁפַתַּיִם, בְּנוֹת מְלָכִים מְשֻׁבָּחִים.
אַלְלַי לִי:

אִם תִּתְעַלַּפְנָה הַבְּתוּלוֹת וְהַבַּחוּרִים, בְּצִמְאוֹן צְחִיחִים.
אַלְלַי לִי:

וְרוּחַ הַקֹּדֶשׁ לְמוּלָם מַרְעִים / הוֹי עַל כָּל שְׁכֵנַי הָרָעִים
מַה שֶּׁהִקְרָאָם מוֹדִיעִים / וְאֵת אֲשֶׁר עָשׂוּ לֹא מוֹדִיעִים
אִם־תֹּאכַלְנָה נָשִׁים פִּרְיָם, מַשְׁמִיעִים
אִם־יֵהָרֵג בְּמִקְדַּשׁ אֲדֹנָי כֹּהֵן וְנָבִיא, לֹא מַשְׁמִיעִים:

This kina describes the martyrdom of the Aseret Harugei Malkhut, the ten sages who were martyred by the Romans in the middle of the second century CE. *The theme was a common one among paytanim, appearing as early as the tenth century (Seder Rav Sa'adia Gaon). The lines form an acrostic, first of the alphabet, and then of the author's name, "Meir ben Yeḥiel ḥazak ve'ematz, Yiḥeh ben Yeḥiel," identifying him as Rabbi Meir ben Yeḥiel, an Ashkenazic rabbi of the early thirteenth century.*

א Cedars of Lebanon, masters of Torah,
ב shield bearers in Mishna and Gemara,
ג powerful heroes, toiling in purity:
ד Their blood is spilled like water, and their strength, sapped.
ה They are ten holy ones, martyred by the kingdom.
ו For them, I cry, and my eyes flow with tears.

ז When I remember this, I cry a great and bitter cry.
ח Israel's delight, holy vessels, a wreath and a crown,
ט pure of heart, holiest of holy, slaughtered in horrible death.

י They cast lots to determine who would first be chosen for the sword.
כ When the lot fell upon Rabban Shimon [ben Gamliel],
he stretched his neck and cried, accepting the decree.
ל The executioner turned to Rabban Shimon,
killing him with pent-up fury.

מ The descendant of Aaron [Rabbi Yishma'el]
begged to be allowed to grieve for the prince.
נ [Rabbi Yishma'el] took [Rabban Shimon's]
head and placed it upon his knees, as if it were a pure Menora.
ש Placing his eyes upon his eyes, and his mouth upon his
mouth with sincere love,
ע he proclaimed, "A mouth, vigorous with Torah,
פ suddenly condemned to a horrible and freakish death!"

צ [The prelate] ordered to flay his head with a sharpened razor.
ק He fulfilled with his skin the saying,
"Get down, that we may walk over you!" *Is. 51*
ר The villain did the flaying, and as he reached the place of the special
commandment of tefillin,
ש [Rabbi Yishma'el] let out a scream, causing the world
to shake and the earth to tremble.
ת "His merit will stand for all generations,"
said the voice of God in His glory.

This קינה *describes the martyrdom of the Aseret Harugei Malkhut, the ten sages who were martyred by the Romans in the middle of the second century CE. The theme was a common one among paytanim, appearing as early as the tenth century (Seder Rav Sa'adia Gaon). The lines form an acrostic, first of the alphabet, and then of the author's name, "*מאיר בן יחיאל חזק ואמץ, יחיה בן יחיאל*," identifying him as Rabbi Meir ben Yeḥiel, an Ashkenazic rabbi of the early thirteenth century.*

אַרְזֵי הַלְּבָנוֹן, אַדִּירֵי הַתּוֹרָה.
בַּעֲלֵי תְרִיסִין בְּמִשְׁנָה וּבִגְמָרָא.
גִּבּוֹרֵי כֹחַ, עֲמֵלֶיהָ בְּטָהֳרָה.
דָּמָם נִשְׁפַּךְ כַּמַּיִם, וְנָשְׁתָה גְבוּרָה.
הִנָּם קְדוֹשֵׁי הֲרוּגֵי מַלְכוּת, עֲשָׂרָה.
וְעַל אֵלֶּה אֲנִי בוֹכִיָּה, וְעֵינִי נִגְּרָה:

זֹאת בְּזָכְרִי, אֶזְעַק זְעָקָה גְּדוֹלָה וּמָרָה.
חֶמְדַּת יִשְׂרָאֵל, כְּלֵי הַקֹּדֶשׁ, נֵזֶר וַעֲטָרָה.
טְהוֹרֵי לֵב, קְדוֹשֵׁי קָדָשִׁים, שְׁחִיטָתָן בְּמִיתָה חֲמוּרָה:

יַדּוּ גוֹרָל, מִי רִאשׁוֹן לַחֶרֶב בְּרוּרָה.
כְּנִפֹּל גּוֹרָל עַל רַבָּן שִׁמְעוֹן, פָּשַׁט צַוָּארוֹ וּבָכָה כִּנְגְזָרָה גְּזֵרָה.
לְרַבָּן שִׁמְעוֹן חָזַר הַהֶגְמוֹן, לְהָרְגוֹ בְּנֶפֶשׁ נְצוּרָה:

מִזֶּרַע אַהֲרֹן שָׁאַל בְּבַקָּשָׁה לִבְכּוֹת עַל בֶּן הַגְּבִירָה.
נָטַל אֶת רֹאשׁוֹ, וּנְתָנוֹ עַל אַרְכֻּבּוֹתָיו, מְנוֹרָה הַטְּהוֹרָה.
שָׂם עֵינָיו עַל עֵינָיו, וּפִיו עַל פִּיו בְּאַהֲבָה גְּמוּרָה.
עָנָה וְאָמַר, פֶּה הַמִּתְגַּבֵּר בַּתּוֹרָה.
פִּתְאוֹם נִקְנְסָה עָלָיו מִיתָה מְשֻׁנָּה וַחֲמוּרָה:

צִוָּה לְהַפְשִׁיט אֶת רֹאשׁוֹ הַמֶּלֶךְ, בְּתַעַר הַשְּׂכִירָה.
קִיֵּם בְּעוֹרוֹ, אָמְרוּ לְנַפְשֵׁךְ, שְׁחִי וְנַעֲבֹרָה. ישעיה נא
רָשָׁע הַפּוֹשֵׁט, עֵת הִגִּיעַ לִמְקוֹם תְּפִלִּין, מִצְוָה בָּרָה.
שִׁמַּע צְעָקָה, וְנִזְדַּעְזַע עוֹלָם, וְאֶרֶץ הִתְפּוֹרְרָה.
תַּעֲמֹד זְכוּתוֹ לְדוֹרוֹת, קוֹל יהוה בֶּהָדָרָה:

מֵאַחֲרָיו Afterwards, they brought Rabbi Akiva, uprooter of mountains, who ground one against the other with his intellect. / They combed his flesh with an iron comb to break it. / His soul departed with the word "One," and a heavenly voice said, / "Rabbi Akiva, you are fortunate; your body is pure in every manner of purity."

בֶּן Rabbi Yehuda ben Bava, they brought in with a broken heart and a warning, / killed at age seventy by the cursed evil kingdom. / He fasted frequently, was clean and pious, and was diligent in his work.

חֲנַנְיָא After him was Rabbi Ḥananya ben Teradyon, assembler of great crowds at Zion's gate. / Sitting and teaching, a Torah scroll at his side, they enveloped him with bundles of twigs / and set them afire, winding the Torah scroll around him and lighting a bonfire. / They attached moistened bits of wool to his heart to prolong his agony.

חָסִיד The pious Rabbi Yeshevav the Scribe was killed by this nation of Gomorrah. / They cast him, threw him to the dogs, so that he was never properly buried. / A heavenly voice declared that there was nothing in the Torah of Moses that he did not observe.

אֶת Rabbi Ḥanina ben Ḥakhinai, and after him, Rabbi Ḥutzpit, on that wrathful day. / Birds flying overhead were singed as if torched by the breath of his mouth.

צַדִּיק The righteous Rabbi Elazar ben Shamua was killed with a chisel. / It was Sabbath eve, the time for Kiddush, and as he recited it, / they drew the sword upon him, not permitting him to live to finish it. / His soul departed *Gen. 2*
at the words "God created," the Creator and Sculptor of forms.

הִנֵּה On and on, these villains tortured and threatened. / Stoning, burning, killing, and choking; who can assess [this calamity]? / Of the remnants, lions consumed those scattered sheep! / Eaten in a sacred place like the sin-offering and guilt-offering leaving no trace, / the special offerings of breast and thigh, lion and cub devoured. / May it be good in the eyes of God to never again punish us. / Make firm the tottering knees, O Jacob's *Jer. 10*
Portion, and Deliverer in troubled times.

לְצֶדֶק "The King shall reign in righteousness." / "Your days of mourning shall *Is. 32*
cease." / By His light, we shall journey forward. *Is. 60*

מֵאַחֲרָיו הֵבִיאוּ אֶת רַבִּי עֲקִיבָא, עוֹקֵר הָרִים וְטוֹחֲנָן זוֹ בְּזוֹ בִּסְבָרָה.
אֶת בְּשָׂרוֹ מְסָרְקִין, בְּמַסְרֵק הַבַּרְזֶל לְהִשְׁתַּבְּרָה.
יָצְתָה נִשְׁמָתוֹ בְּאֶחָד, וּבַת קוֹל אָמְרָה.
רַבִּי עֲקִיבָא, אַשְׁרֶיךָ, גּוּפְךָ טָהוֹר בְּכָל מִינֵי טָהֳרָה:

בֶּן בָּבָא רַבִּי יְהוּדָה אַחֲרָיו הֵבִיאוּ, בְּשִׁבְרוֹן לֵב וְאַזְהָרָה.
נֶהֱרַג בֶּן שִׁבְעִים שָׁנָה, בִּידֵי רִשְׁעָה אֲרוּרָה.
יוֹשֵׁב בְּתַעֲנִית הָיָה, נָקִי וְחָסִיד בִּמְלַאכְתּוֹ לְמַהֵרָה:

חֲנַנְיָא בֶּן תְּרַדְיוֹן אַחֲרָיו, מַקְהִיל קְהִלּוֹת בְּצִיּוֹן שְׁעָרָה.
יוֹשֵׁב וְדוֹרֵשׁ, וְסֵפֶר תּוֹרָה עִמּוֹ, וְהִקִּיפוּהוּ בַּחֲבִילֵי זְמוֹרָה.
אֶת הָאוּר הִצִּיתוּ בָהֶם, וּכְרָכוּהוּ בְּסֵפֶר תּוֹרָה, וּבָעֲרוּ בוֹ הַבְעָרָה.
לְלִבּוֹ סְפוֹגִין שֶׁל צֶמֶר הִנִּיחוּ, שֶׁלֹּא יָמוּת מְהֵרָה:

חָסִיד רַבִּי יֶשֵׁבָב הַסּוֹפֵר, הֲרָגוּהוּ עִם עֲמוֹרָה.
זְרָקוּהוּ וְהִשְׁלִיכוּהוּ לַכְּלָבִים, וְלֹא הֻקְבַּר בִּקְבוּרָה.
קוֹל בַּת יָצְאָה עָלָיו, שֶׁלֹּא הִנִּיחַ כְּלוּם מִתּוֹרַת מֹשֶׁה לְשָׁמְרָה:

אֶת רַבִּי חֲנִינָא בֶּן חֲכִינַאי, וְאַחֲרָיו רַבִּי חֻצְפִּית, בְּיוֹם עֶבְרָה.
מִיַּד עוֹף הַפּוֹרֵחַ, בַּהֲבַל פִּיו נִשְׂרַף כִּבִמְדוּרָה:

צַדִּיק, רַבִּי אֶלְעָזָר בֶּן שַׁמּוּעַ, בָּאַחֲרוֹנָה נֶהֱרַג בְּמַדְקֵרָה.
יוֹם עֶרֶב שַׁבָּת הָיָה, זְמַן קִדּוּשׁ, וַיְקַדֵּשׁ וַיִּקְרָא.
חֶרֶב שָׁלְפוּ עָלָיו, וְלֹא הִנִּיחוּהוּ בַּחַיִּים, לְסַיֵּם וּלְגָמְרָה.
יָצְתָה נִשְׁמָתוֹ בְּבָרָא אֱלֹהִים, יוֹצֵר וְצָר צוּרָה: בראשית ב

הִנֵּה כָּהֵנָּה וְכָהֵנָּה, הוֹסִיפוּ בְּנֵי עַוְלָה לְעַנּוֹת בִּגְעָרָה.
בִּסְקִילָה, שְׂרֵפָה, הֶרֶג וְחֶנֶק, מִי יוּכַל לְשַׁעֲרָה.
נוֹתֶרֶת מִמֶּנָּה יֹאכְלוּ אֲרָיוֹת, שֶׂה פְזוּרָה.
יֹאכְלוּהָ בְּמָקוֹם קָדוֹשׁ, כַּחַטָּאת וְכָאָשָׁם, לְאַבֵּד זִכְרָהּ.
חֲזֵה הַתְּנוּפָה וְשׁוֹק הַתְּרוּמָה, טָרְפוּ אַרְיֵה וְהַכְּפִירָה.
יִיטַב בְּעֵינֵי יהוה, וְלֹא יוֹסִיף עוֹד לְיַסְּרָה.
אַמֵּץ בִּרְכַּיִם כּוֹשְׁלוֹת, חֵלֶק יַעֲקֹב, וּמוֹשִׁיעַ בְּעֵת צָרָה: ירמיה י

לְצֶדֶק יִמְלָךְ מֶלֶךְ / וְשָׁלְמוּ יְמֵי אֶבְלֵךְ / לְאוֹרוֹ נִסַּע וְנֵלֵךְ: ישעיה לב ישעיה ס

This kina, of uncertain authorship, is based on a story in Gittin 58a, and is found (with slight variations) in both Ashkenazic and Oriental liturgy..

וְאֶת My Temple – my sins destroyed it!
I let my tears stream down my cheeks.
On this day, I will raise a woeful cry.
And I mourn from year to year.

אֵבֶל With an aggrieved heart, impossible to console,
of all injuries, my pain is unique,
over the son and daughter of Rabbi Yishma'el, the High Priest.
Their memory is like a fire in my heart.
And I mourn from year to year.

עֵת Held captive in the possession of two different masters
who dwelled nearby one another,
and as they discussed various matters,
one related, "Of Zion's captives,
I purchased a maid, clothed in scarlet,
like the moon in radiance and beauty,
and in appearance like Keziah and Jemima.
And I mourn from year to year.

רֵעֵהוּ His comrade responded with double the praise.
"I, too, visited Jerusalem's captives,
and purchased a slave-boy with beautiful eyes
like the sun in full force, at noon,
and like the moon in its fullness.
And I mourn from year to year.

This קינה*, of uncertain authorship, is based on a story in Gittin 58a, and is found (with slight variations) in both Ashkenazic and Oriental liturgy. .*

וְאֶת נָוִי, חַטָּאתִי הִשְׁמִימָה
וְדִמְעָתִי, עַל לֶחְיִי אַזְרִימָה.
וּבְיוֹם זֶה, נְהִי נִהְיָה אָרִימָה.
וְאָהֵימָה מִיָּמִים יָמִימָה:

אֲבֵל לֵב, וְנִחוּם חָדַל חָדוֹל
וּמִכָּל כְּאֵב, צִירִי נִבְדַּל בָּדוֹל.
עַל בֵּן וּבַת רַבִּי יִשְׁמָעֵאל כֹּהֵן גָּדוֹל
זִכְרָם, יְקוֹד בִּלְבָבִי אָשִׂימָה.
וְאָהֵימָה מִיָּמִים יָמִימָה:

עֵת נִשְׁבּוּ, וְנָפְלוּ לִשְׁנֵי אֲדוֹנִים
וְהֵם שְׁכֵנִים, זֶה לְעֻמַּת זֶה חוֹנִים.
וַיְסַפְּרוּ זֶה לָזֶה עִנְיָנִים
זֶה אָמַר, מִשִּׁבְיַת צִיּוֹנִים.
שָׁבִיתִי שִׁפְחָה לְבוּשַׁת שָׁנִים
כַּלְּבָנָה בְּזִיו וְקַלַסְתֵּר פָּנִים.
וּבְתֹאַר, כִּקְצִיעָה וִימִימָה.
וְאָהֵימָה מִיָּמִים יָמִימָה:

רֵעֵהוּ סִפֵּר לוֹ בִּכְפָלַיִם
הֵן אֲנִי בָא מִשְּׁבִי יְרוּשָׁלָיִם.
שָׁבִיתִי עֶבֶד יְפֵה עֵינַיִם
כַּשֶּׁמֶשׁ, בְּתָקְפּוֹ עֵת צָהֳרַיִם.
וְסַהַר, עֵת זְמַנָּהּ הִשְׁלִימָה.
וְאָהֵימָה מִיָּמִים יָמִימָה:

בֹּא "Let us mate them and evenly split
the offspring, sure to be like stars in the sky."
Hearing this makes one's ears ring!
Recalling this, I rend my garments.
And I mourn from year to year.

כְּהִסְכִּימוּ Together, they both agreed to this,
and that night, coupled them into one room.
The slave-masters stood outside with identical intention,
while the slaves cried, embittered, and frightened.
Until dawn, their crying did not abate.
And I mourn from year to year.

זֶה One lamented with a feverish and melted heart,
"How will a grandson of Aaron marry a slave-girl?"
And she, too, wailed, "Because of a villain's transaction,
will a daughter of Yokheved marry a slave?"
Woe that He, who does what He says, has thus decreed!
Over this, the celestial constellations weep!
And I mourn from year to year.

אוֹר With the break of dawn, they recognized one another
and overpowered each other, crying, "Oh, brother!" "Oh, sister!"
They embraced and clung to each other
until their souls departed with one last breath.
And I mourn from year to year.

לְזֹאת For this, Jeremiah lamented in horror.
This horrid decree, I will forever bemoan.
In my heart burns a fire, a scorching flame.
For the son and daughter, I will deliver a powerful lament!
And I mourn from year to year.

בֹּא וּנְזְוָּגֵם, וְנַחַלְקָה בְּנָתַיִם
בְּוְלָדוֹת, כְּמוֹ כּוֹכְבֵי שָׁמַיִם.
לְשֵׁמַע זֹאת, תִּצַלְנָה אָזְנַיִם
לְזֵכֶר זֹאת, אֶת מַדַּי אַפְרִימָה.
וְאָהֵימָה מִיָּמִים יָמִימָה:

כְּהִסְכִּימוּ עַל זֹאת שְׁנֵיהֶם יַחַד
לָעֶרֶב זִוּגוּם בְּחֶדֶר אֶחָד.
וְהָאֲדוֹנִים בַּחוּץ, לִבָּם כְּאֶחָד
וְהֵם בּוֹכִים בְּמַר נֶפֶשׁ, וָפַחַד.
עַד בֹּקֶר, בְּכִיָּתָם לֹא הִדְמִימָה.
וְאָהֵימָה מִיָּמִים יָמִימָה:

זֶה יִסְפֹּד, בִּיקוֹד לֵבָב יִמְסֶה
נִין אַהֲרֹן, אֵיךְ לְשִׁפְחָה יְהִי נוֹשֵׂא.
וְהִיא גַם הִיא, תְּיַלֵּל בְּתִגְרַת שׁוֹסֶה
בַּת יוֹכֶבֶד, אֵיךְ לְעֶבֶד תִּנָּשֵׂא.
אוֹי כִּי זֹאת גָּזַר אוֹמֵר וְעוֹשֶׂה
לְזֹאת יִבְכּוּ עָשׁ, כְּסִיל וְכִימָה.
וְאָהֵימָה מִיָּמִים יָמִימָה:

אוֹר בֹּקֶר, זֶה אֶת זֶה כְּהִכִּירוּ.
הוֹי אָחִי, וְהוֹי אָחוֹת, הִגְבִּירוּ.
וְנִתְחַבְּקוּ יַחַד וְנִתְחַבָּרוּ
עַד יָצְאָה נִשְׁמָתָם בִּנְשִׁימָה.
וְאָהֵימָה מִיָּמִים יָמִימָה:

לְזֹאת יְקוֹנֵן יִרְמְיָה בִּשְׁאִיָּה
גְּזֵרָה זוֹ, תָּמִיד אֲנִי בּוֹכִיָּה.
וּבִלְבָבִי יֵקַד יְקוֹד וּכְוִיָּה
עַל בֵּן וּבַת מִסְפֵּד רַב אַנְהִימָה.
וְאָהֵימָה מִיָּמִים יָמִימָה:

This kina, by Rabbi Kalonymos ben Yehuda of Speyer, laments the massacres perpetrated by the Crusaders in 1096, which destroyed the most prominent Jewish communities of the Rhineland. Some have suggested that Rabbi Kalonymos wrote a kina eulogizing the martyrs of his own community only, with the stanzas about Worms and Mainz being written by other paytanim (similar stanzas were written about the martyrs of Cologne and Frankfurt).

מִי Would that my head were water, and my eyes a fountain of tears, / and I would cry all my days and nights / for the corpses of my babes and infants, and the aged of my community. / I ask you to respond, "Oh! Woe! Alas!" / And weep a weeping, much weeping. *Jer. 8*

For the house of Israel and the people
of the LORD who have fallen by sword.

וְדָמוֹעַ My eyes flow with tears, and I will betake myself to the fields to weep, / and ask others stunned and embittered to join in my wailing / for the beautiful maidens and delicate lads, / wrapped in their schoolbooks and led to slaughter. / Their bodies, rosier than rubies, sapphire, or turquoise, / were slung and trampled like mud in the streets. / "Stay away! They are unclean," shouted the enemy about them. *Jer. 13* *Lam. 4* *Lam. 4*

For the house of Israel and the people
of the LORD who have fallen by sword.

וְתֵרֵד Let my eyes flow with tears, I will wail and shake my head. / I will eulogize [the Torah] with weeping and with sackcloth. / She is more dear than fine gold, more precious than gold, / her glory inward, the glory of all precious vessels. / I have seen her torn, bereaved, and desolate. / Torah, Scripture, Mishna, and Aggada: / raise your voice, lament, and tell this tale. / Where are Torah, Talmud, and students? / The place is in ruin, no one there! *Jer. 13* *Is. 49*

For the house of Israel and the people
of the LORD who have fallen by sword.

וְעַפְעַפַּי My eyelids flow with water, dripping tears. / I weep bitterly for the murdered of Speyer. / It happened on the eighth day of the second month [Iyar] on the day of rest. / "Rest" was transposed to "tempest" destructive. / Handsome youths and dignified elders were killed. / They assembled, all agreeing to be martyred, / testifying to the unity of God's name, courageously. / Mighty men, who do His bidding speedily. / My priests and my young men, all ten expired. *Ezek. 23* *Ps. 103*

For the house of Israel and the people
of the LORD who have fallen by sword.

This קינה, by Rabbi Kalonymos ben Yehuda of Speyer, laments the massacres perpetrated by the Crusaders in 1096, which destroyed the most prominent Jewish communities of the Rhineland. Some have suggested that Rabbi Kalonymos wrote a kina eulogizing the martyrs of his own community only, with the stanzas about Worms and Mainz being written by other paytanim (similar stanzas were written about the martyrs of Cologne and Frankfurt).

מִי יִתֵּן רֹאשִׁי מַיִם, וְעֵינִי מְקוֹר נוֹזְלִי. ירמיה ח
וְאֶבְכֶּה כָּל יְמוֹתַי וְלֵילִי / אֶת חַלְלֵי טַפִּי וְעוֹלָלַי, וִישִׁישֵׁי קְהָלִי.
וְאַתֶּם עֲנוּ אֲבוֹי, אוֹי וְאַלְלַי / וּבְכוּ בֶּכֶה רַב, וְהֶרֶב.
עַל בֵּית יִשְׂרָאֵל וְעַל עַם יהוה, כִּי נָפְלוּ בֶּחָרֶב:

וְדָמוֹעַ תִּדְמַע עֵינִי, וְאֵלְכָה לִּי שְׂדֵה בוֹכִים / וַאֲבַכֶּה עִמִּי מָרֵי לֵבָב ירמיה יג
הַנְּבוּכִים.
עַל בְּתוּלוֹת הַיָּפוֹת, וִילָדִים הָרַכִּים / בְּסִפְרֵיהֶם נִכְרָכִים, וְלַטֶּבַח נִמְשָׁכִים.
אָדְמוּ עֶצֶם מִפְּנִינִים, סַפִּירִים וְנָפָכִים / כְּמוֹ טִיט חוּצוֹת, נְדָשִׁים וְנִשְׁלָכִים. איכה ד
סוּרוּ טָמֵא, קָרְאוּ לָמוֹ מִלִּקְרֵב. איכה ד
עַל בֵּית יִשְׂרָאֵל וְעַל עַם יהוה, כִּי נָפְלוּ בֶּחָרֶב:

וְתֵרַד עֵינִי דִּמְעָה, וְאֵילִילָה וְאָנוּדָה / וְלִבְכִּי וְלַחֲגֹר שַׂק, אֶקְרָא לְהַסְפִּידָה. ירמיה יג
מִפָּז יְקָרָה, וּמִזָּהָב חֲמוּדָה / פְּנִימָה כְּבוּדָה, כְּבוֹד כָּל כְּלֵי חֶמְדָּה.
רְאִיתִיהָ קְרוּעָה, שְׁכוּלָה וְגַלְמוּדָה / הַתּוֹרָה וְהַמִּקְרָא וְהַמִּשְׁנָה וְהָאַגָּדָה. ישעיה מט
עֲנוּ וְקוֹנְנוּ זֹאת לְהַגִּידָה / אֵי תוֹרָה וְתַלְמוּד וְהַלּוֹמְדָהּ.
הֲלֹא הַמָּקוֹם מֵאֵין יוֹשֵׁב חָרֵב.
עַל בֵּית יִשְׂרָאֵל וְעַל עַם יהוה, כִּי נָפְלוּ בֶּחָרֶב:

וְעַפְעַפַּי יִזְּלוּ מַיִם, דֶּמַע לְהַגִּירָה / וַאֲקוֹנֵן מַר, עַל הֲרוּגֵי אַשְׁפִּירָא.
בַּשֵּׁנִי בִּשְׁמוֹנָה בוֹ, בְּיוֹם מַרְגּוֹעַ, הַקְּרָה / מַרְגּוֹעַי לְרִגּוּעַי, נֶחְלְפוּ לְהַבְעִירָה.
נֶהֶרְגוּ בַּחוּרֵי חֶמֶד, וִישִׁישֵׁי הֲדָרָה / נֶאֶסְפוּ יַחַד, נַפְשָׁם הִשְׁלִימוּ בְּמוֹרָא. יחזקאל כג
עַל יִחוּד שֵׁם הַמְיֻחָד, יִחֲדוּ בִּגְבוּרָה / גִּבּוֹרֵי כֹחַ, עֹשֵׂי דְבָרוֹ לְמַהֲרָה. תהלים קג
וְכֹהֲנֵי וְעַלְמֵי נִגְּעוּ, כֻּלָּהֶם עֲשָׂרָה.
עַל בֵּית יִשְׂרָאֵל וְעַל עַם יהוה, כִּי נָפְלוּ בֶּחָרֶב:

וּבְמַר In my bitter agony and grief, I will compose a dirge. / Holy congregations! Their massacre I remember today. / The community of Worms, special and unique. / Giants of the earth, innocent and pure! / Twice, they sanctified the One Name in awe, / cleansed once on the twenty-third of the month Ziv [Iyar], / And on [the first day of] the third month [Sivan], as they chanted Hallel, / they made a pact to be martyred for the love [of God]. / I will moan for them with a torrent of tears of woe, / all deserving to be endowed with majestic crowns! *I Kings 6*

For the house of Israel and the people
of the LORD who have fallen by sword.

וְעַל And upon the great of the wonderful community of Mainz, / swifter than eagles and stronger than lions, / they too consented in unison to sanctify the awesome One Name. / For them, I will scream a piercing scream with bitter soul, / as if for the destruction of both Temples, razed today, / and for the destruction of minor temples [synagogues] and study halls of Torah!

For the house of Israel and the people
of the LORD who have fallen by sword.

בַּחֹדֶשׁ On the third day of the third month [Sivan], these were added to my sorrow and curse. / That month was transformed into one of agony and trouble / on the day the Law was given, when I hoped to be spared in her merit. / On the very day she was given, she departed. / Gone back on high to her original home, / with her "containers" and her "pouches," those who searched her and studied her. / Her disciples and her students in darkness as in light!

For the house of Israel and the people
of the LORD who have fallen by sword.

שִׂימוּ Take this to heart, and compose a bitter eulogy. / Their murder is worthy of mourning and placing ash, / equal to the burning of the House of our God, the porch and the Palace, / because it is improper to add a day of breach and conflagration, / and wrong to advance the date; rather, to postpone it. / Therefore, today [Tisha B'Av], I will arouse my grief / and lament, and wail, and cry with bitter soul, / with sighs weighing heavily from dawn to dusk,

For the house of Israel and the people
of the LORD who have fallen by sword.

וּבְמַר יְגוֹנִי וְעָצְבִּי, יְלֵל אַחְבִּירָה / קְהִלּוֹת הַקֹּדֶשׁ, הֲרִיגָתָם הַיּוֹם בְּזָכְרָה.
קְהַל וּוֹרְמַיְזָא, בְּחוּנָה וּבְחוּרָה / גְּאוֹנֵי אֶרֶץ, וּנְקִיֵּי טָהֳרָה.
פַּעֲמַיִם, קִדְּשׁוּ שֵׁם הַמְיֻחָד בְּמוֹרָא / בְּעֶשְׂרִים וּשְׁלֹשָׁה בְּחֹדֶשׁ זִיו, מלכים א ו
לְטָהֳרָה / וּבְחֹדֶשׁ הַשְּׁלִישִׁי, בִּקְרִיאַת הַלֵּל לְשׁוֹרְרָה.
הִשְׁלִימוּ נַפְשָׁם בְּאַהֲבָה קְשׁוּרָה / אֶהֱמֶה עֲלֵיהֶם בִּבְכִי יְלֵל לְחַשְׁרָה.
כְּלוּלֵי כֶתֶר, עַל רֹאשָׁם לַעֲטָרָה.
עַל בֵּית יִשְׂרָאֵל וְעַל עַם יהוה, כִּי נָפְלוּ בֶּחָרֶב:

וְעַל אַדִּירֵי קְהַל מַגֶּנְצָא הַהֲדוּרָה / מִנְּשָׁרִים קַלּוּ, מֵאֲרָיוֹת לְהִתְגַּבְּרָה.
הִשְׁלִימוּ נַפְשָׁם עַל יִחוּד שֵׁם הַנּוֹרָא / וַעֲלֵיהֶם זַעֲקַת שֶׁבֶר אֶזְעַק, בְּנֶפֶשׁ מָרָה.
עַל שְׁנֵי מִקְדָּשַׁי, יְסוֹדָם כְּהַיּוֹם עֶרְעָרָה / וְעַל חָרְבוֹת מְעַט מִקְדָּשַׁי, וּמִדְרְשֵׁי הַתּוֹרָה.
עַל בֵּית יִשְׂרָאֵל וְעַל עַם יהוה, כִּי נָפְלוּ בֶּחָרֶב:

בַּחֹדֶשׁ הַשְּׁלִישִׁי בַּשְּׁלִישִׁי, נוֹסַף לְדַאֲבוֹן וּמְאֵרָה / הַחֹדֶשׁ אֲשֶׁר נֶהְפַּךְ לְיָגוֹן וְצָרָה.
בְּיוֹם מַתַּן דָּת, שִׁבַּרְתִּי לְהִתְאַשְּׁרָה / וּבְיוֹם נְתִינָתָהּ, כְּמוֹ כֵן אָז חָזְרָה.
עָלְתָה לָהּ לַמָּרוֹם, לִמְקוֹם מְדוֹרָהּ / עִם תִּיקָהּ וְנַרְתִּקָהּ, וְהַדּוֹרְשָׁהּ וְחוֹקְרָהּ.
לוֹמְדֶיהָ וְשׁוֹנֶיהָ בְּאִישׁוֹן, כְּמוֹ אוֹרָה.
עַל בֵּית יִשְׂרָאֵל וְעַל עַם יהוה, כִּי נָפְלוּ בֶּחָרֶב:

שִׂימוּ נָא עַל לְבַבְכֶם, מִסְפֵּד מַר לְקָשְׁרָה / כִּי שְׁקוּלָה הֲרִיגָתָם, לְהִתְאַבֵּל וּלְהִתְעַפְּרָה / כִּשְׂרֵפַת בֵּית אֱלֹהֵינוּ, הָאוּלָם וְהַבִּירָה.
וְכִי אֵין לְהוֹסִיף מוֹעֵד שֶׁבֶר וְתַבְעֵרָה / וְאֵין לְהַקְדִּים, זוּלָתִי לְאַחְרָה.
תַּחַת כֵּן, הַיּוֹם לִוְיָתִי אֲעוֹרְרָה / וְאֶסְפְּדָה וְאֵילִילָה, וְאֶבְכֶּה בְּנֶפֶשׁ מָרָה.
וְאַנְחָתִי כְּבֵדָה, מִבֹּקֶר וְעַד עָרֶב.
עַל בֵּית יִשְׂרָאֵל וְעַל עַם יהוה, כִּי נָפְלוּ בֶּחָרֶב:

עַל For these, I cry and moan moans, / and summon the lamenters and wise Lam. 1
women. / "Alas," and "Alack," they all murmur. / Does any wound compare
to my wound? / Outside, the sword murders, and indoors, there is terror! /
My corpses, killed by the sword, lie strewn, nude and naked. / Bodies lying Is. 5
like refuse for wild beasts and animals. / Nursing child and aged man, lads Deut. 32
and lasses / were teased by my oppressors and endured great shame. /
"Where is their God? The Rock they trusted in" until death? / Let Him Deut. 32
come and rescue and resurrect their souls! / Mighty God, who like You
forgives bundles of sins? / You are silent and restrained; why do You not
gird Yourself with fury? / When my mockers say to me, "If He is a God, Judges 6
let Him do battle!"

For the house of Israel and the people
of the LORD who have fallen by sword.

עֵינִי My eyes, my eyes, flow with tears. Our singing has turned into mourning. / Lam. 1 Lam. 5
My flute accompanies mourners, without respite and never abating. / Who Job 30
will approach me consolingly, and who will encourage me to awaken? /
Wrath issues forth, and a tempest arrives. / The attacking foe devours me Jer. 30 Num. 10
and panics me, / breaks my bones, strews them and scatters them. / He Lam. 3 Lam. 1
has hacked down my great ones, the navel and nucleus. / My wound is fatal, Jer. 15
none to heal or cure. / That is why I say, "Let me be, I will weep bitterly." / Is. 22
Shedding tears until my cheeks shrivel,

For the house of Israel and the people
of the LORD who have fallen by sword.

This kina, its author unknown, is also written in the Sephardic style. With short, succinct phrases, it contrasts the glorious euphoria of the exodus from Egypt with the tragedy and destruction of the exile from Jerusalem. Each of the twenty-three alphabetic stanzas is made of two internally rhyming lines. In each stanza, the second line echoes and contrasts the detail of the first. While the first line emphasizes the close bond between God and His people, the second gives a sense of separation, with a joyous coda of return to Jerusalem.

א A fire burns within me as I recall,
When I left Egypt.
I will invoke lamentations so that I will remember,
When I left Jerusalem.

עַל אֵלֶּה אֲנִי בוֹכִיָּה, וְלִבִּי נוֹהֵם נְהִימוֹת / וְאֶקְרָא לַמְקוֹנְנוֹת, וְאֶל הַחֲכָמוֹת. איכה א
אֱלִי וְאַלְיָה, כֻּלָּם הוֹמוֹת / הֲיֵשׁ מַכְאוֹב לְמַכְאוֹבִי לְדַמּוֹת.
מִחוּץ תְּשַׁכֶּל חֶרֶב, וּמֵחֲדָרִים אֵימוֹת / חֲלָלַי, חַלְלֵי חֶרֶב, מוּטָלִים עֲרֻמִּים וַעֲרֻמּוֹת.
נִבְלָתָם כַּסּוּחָה, לְחַיַּת אֶרֶץ וְלִבְהֵמוֹת / יוֹנֵק עִם אִישׁ שֵׂיבָה, עֲלָמִים וַעֲלָמוֹת. ישעיה ה דברים לב
מִתְעַתְּעִים בְּמוֹ מוֹנַי, וּמַרְבִּים כְּלִמּוֹת / אֵי אֱלֹהֵימוֹ אָמְרוּ, צוּר חָסָיוּ בוֹ עַד מוֹת / יָבוֹא וְיוֹשִׁיעַ, וְיַחֲזִיר נְשָׁמוֹת. דברים לב
חֲסִין יָהּ, מִי כָמוֹךָ, נוֹשֵׂא בָּאֲלֻמּוֹת / תֶּחֱשֶׁה וְתִתְאַפַּק, וְלֹא תַחְגֹּר חֵמוֹת.
בֶּאֱמֹר אֵלַי מַלְעִיגַי, אִם אֱלֹהִים הוּא, יָרֶב. שופטים ו
עַל בֵּית יִשְׂרָאֵל וְעַל עַם יהוה, כִּי נָפְלוּ בֶּחָרֶב:

עֵינִי עֵינִי יֹרְדָה מַּיִם, כִּי נֶהְפַּךְ לְאֵבֶל מְשׂוֹרֵר / וְעֻגָּבִי לְקוֹל בּוֹכִים, מִלְּהָפֵג וּלְקָרֵר. איכה א איכה ה איוב ל
מִי יָנוּד לִי, וְאֵין מַחֲזִיק לְהִתְעוֹרֵר / חֵמָה בִּי יָצְאָה, וְסַעַר מִתְגּוֹרֵר. ירמיה ל
אֲכָלַנִי, הֲמָמַנִי, הַצַּר הַצּוֹרֵר / שִׁבַּר עַצְמוֹתַי, זוֹרֵר וּמְפָרֵר / סִלָּה כָל אַבִּירַי, הַטַּבּוּר וְהַשֹּׁרֶר. במדבר י איכה ג איכה א
מַכָּתִי אֲנוּשָׁה, בְּאֵין מַתְעִיל וּמְזוֹרֵר / רְטִיָּה וּמָזוֹר אֵין לְבָרֵר. ירמיה טו
עַל כֵּן אָמַרְתִּי, שְׁעוּ מֶנִּי, אֲמָרֵר / בַּבֶּכִי, דִּמְעָתִי עַל לֶחְיִי לְצָרֵב. ישעיה כב
עַל בֵּית יִשְׂרָאֵל וְעַל עַם יהוה, כִּי נָפְלוּ בֶּחָרֶב:

This קינה, its author unknown, is also written in the Sephardic style. With short, succinct phrases, it contrasts the glorious euphoria of the exodus from Egypt with the tragedy and destruction of the exile from Jerusalem. Each of the twenty-three alphabetic stanzas is made of two internally rhyming lines. In each stanza, the second line echoes and contrasts the detail of the first. While the first line emphasizes the close bond between God and His people, the second gives a sense of separation, with a joyous coda of return to Jerusalem.

אֵשׁ תּוּקַד בְּקִרְבִּי / בְּהַעֲלוֹתִי עַל לִבִּי. בְּצֵאתִי מִמִּצְרָיִם:
וְקִינִים אָעִירָה / לְמַעַן אַזְכִּירָה. בְּצֵאתִי מִירוּשָׁלָיִם:

א Then Moses sang an unforgettable song, *Ex. 15*
When I left Egypt.
Whereas Jeremiah lamented and wailed a woeful wail, *Mic. 2*
When I left Jerusalem.

ב My House was founded and the divine cloud dwelled there,
When I left Egypt.
But God's wrath descended upon me like a cloud,
When I left Jerusalem.

ג The waves of the sea raised themselves and stood erect like a wall,
When I left Egypt.
The foe flooded me, overflowing my head,
When I left Jerusalem.

ד A heavenly harvest and water from a rock,
When I left Egypt.
Bitter grass and wormwood and bitter waters,
When I left Jerusalem.

ה Morning and evening roundabout Mount Horeb,
When I left Egypt.
Summoned to mourning by the rivers of Babylon, *Ps. 137*
When I left Jerusalem.

ו A vision of God's glory like a consuming fire before me,
When I left Egypt. *Ex. 24*
A sharpened sword let loose to slaughter,
When I left Jerusalem.

ז Sacrificial offerings and meal-offerings and the anointing oil,
When I left Egypt.
God's treasure led away like lambs to the slaughter,
When I left Jerusalem.

ח Festivals and Sabbaths and signs and wonders,
When I left Egypt.
Fast days and mourning and vain pursuits,
When I left Jerusalem.

ט Wondrous tents around four banners,
When I left Egypt.
Tents of Ishmaelites and encampments of the uncircumcised,
When I left Jerusalem.

אָז יָשִׁיר מֹשֶׁה / שִׁיר לֹא יִנָּשֶׁה. בְּצֵאתִי מִמִּצְרָיִם: שמות טו
וַיְקוֹנֵן יִרְמְיָה / וְנָהָה נְהִי נִהְיָה. בְּצֵאתִי מִירוּשָׁלָיִם: מיכה ב

בֵּיתִי הִתְכּוֹנַן / וְשָׁכַן הֶעָנָן. בְּצֵאתִי מִמִּצְרָיִם:
וַחֲמַת אֵל שָׁכְנָה / עָלַי כַּעֲנָנָה. בְּצֵאתִי מִירוּשָׁלָיִם:

גַּלֵּי יָם רָמוּ / וְכַחוֹמָה קָמוּ. בְּצֵאתִי מִמִּצְרָיִם:
זֵידוֹנִים שָׁטְפוּ / וְעַל רֹאשִׁי צָפוּ. בְּצֵאתִי מִירוּשָׁלָיִם:

דְּגַן שָׁמַיִם / וּמִצּוּר מַיִם. בְּצֵאתִי מִמִּצְרָיִם:
לַעֲנָה וּמְרוֹרִים / וּמַיִם הַמָּרִים. בְּצֵאתִי מִירוּשָׁלָיִם:

הַשְׁכֵּם וְהַעֲרֵב / סְבִיבוֹת הַר חוֹרֵב. בְּצֵאתִי מִמִּצְרָיִם:
קוֹרֵא אֶל אֵבֶל / עַל נַהֲרוֹת בָּבֶל. בְּצֵאתִי מִירוּשָׁלָיִם: תהלים קלז

וּמַרְאֵה כְּבוֹד יהוה / כְּאֵשׁ אוֹכֶלֶת לְפָנַי. בְּצֵאתִי מִמִּצְרָיִם: שמות כד
וְחֶרֶב לְטוּשָׁה / וּלְטֶבַח נְטוּשָׁה. בְּצֵאתִי מִירוּשָׁלָיִם:

זֶבַח וּמִנְחָה / וְשֶׁמֶן הַמִּשְׁחָה. בְּצֵאתִי מִמִּצְרָיִם:
סְגֻלַּת אֵל לְקוּחָה / כַּצֹּאן לַטִּבְחָה. בְּצֵאתִי מִירוּשָׁלָיִם:

חַגִּים וְשַׁבָּתוֹת / וּמוֹפְתִים וְאוֹתוֹת. בְּצֵאתִי מִמִּצְרָיִם:
תַּעֲנִית וָאֵבֶל / וּרְדֹף הַהֶבֶל. בְּצֵאתִי מִירוּשָׁלָיִם:

טוֹבוּ אֹהָלִים / לְאַרְבָּעָה דְּגָלִים. בְּצֵאתִי מִמִּצְרָיִם:
אָהֳלֵי יִשְׁמְעֵאלִים / וּמַחֲנוֹת עֲרֵלִים. בְּצֵאתִי מִירוּשָׁלָיִם:

י Jubilee and Sabbatical year and a tranquil land,
When I left Egypt.
Sold beyond reclaim, forever severed,
When I left Jerusalem.

כ The Ark and its cover and gemstones of remembrance,
When I left Egypt.
Slingstones and tools of destruction,
When I left Jerusalem.

ל Levites and Aaron's kin and seventy elders,
When I left Egypt.
Oppressors and persecutors, slave merchants and purchasers,
When I left Jerusalem.

מ Moses cared for us and Aaron guided us,
When I left Egypt.
Nebuchadnezzar and the Emperor Hadrian,
When I left Jerusalem.

נ We waged war and God was there,
When I left Egypt.
Distant from us and utterly absent,
When I left Jerusalem.

ס The folds of the Tabernacle curtain
and the rows of bread on the Tabernacle Table,
When I left Egypt.
Fury vented, enveloping me,
When I left Jerusalem.

ע Burnt-offerings and peace-offerings and fragrant fiery sacrifices,
When I left Egypt.
Stabbed by the sword were the precious sons of Zion, *Lam. 4*
When I left Jerusalem.

פ Decorated turbans fastened in reverence,
When I left Egypt.
Shrieking and blaring trumpets and cries of horror,
When I left Jerusalem.

צ The gold frontlet and power and pride,
When I left Egypt.
The crown is cast down and assistance gone,
When I left Jerusalem.

יוֹבֵל וּשְׁמִטָּה / וְאֶרֶץ שׁוֹקֶטָה. בְּצֵאתִי מִמִּצְרָיִם:
מָכוּר לִצְמִיתוּת / וְכָרוּת לִכְרִיתוּת. בְּצֵאתִי מִירוּשָׁלָיִם:

כַּפֹּרֶת וְאָרוֹן / וְאַבְנֵי זִכָּרוֹן. בְּצֵאתִי מִמִּצְרָיִם:
וְאַבְנֵי הַקֶּלַע / וּכְלֵי הַבֶּלַע. בְּצֵאתִי מִירוּשָׁלָיִם:

לְוִיִּם וְאַהֲרוֹנִים / וְשִׁבְעִים זְקֵנִים. בְּצֵאתִי מִמִּצְרָיִם:
נוֹגְשִׂים וּמוֹנִים / וּמוֹכְרִים וְקוֹנִים. בְּצֵאתִי מִירוּשָׁלָיִם:

מֹשֶׁה יִרְעֵנוּ / וְאַהֲרֹן יַנְחֵנוּ. בְּצֵאתִי מִמִּצְרָיִם:
נְבוּכַדְנֶאצַּר / וְאַדְרִיאָנוּס קֵיסָר. בְּצֵאתִי מִירוּשָׁלָיִם:

נֶעֱרַךְ מִלְחָמָה / וַיהוה שָׁמָּה. בְּצֵאתִי מִמִּצְרָיִם:
רָחַק מִמֶּנּוּ / וְהִנֵּה אֵינֶנּוּ. בְּצֵאתִי מִירוּשָׁלָיִם:

סִתְרֵי פָּרֹכֶת / וְסִדְרֵי מַעֲרֶכֶת. בְּצֵאתִי מִמִּצְרָיִם:
חֵמָה נִתֶּכֶת / עָלַי סוֹכֶכֶת בְּצֵאתִי מִירוּשָׁלָיִם:

עוֹלוֹת וּזְבָחִים / וְאִשֵּׁי נִיחוֹחִים. בְּצֵאתִי מִמִּצְרָיִם:
בְּחֶרֶב מְדֻקָּרִים / בְּנֵי צִיּוֹן הַיְקָרִים. בְּצֵאתִי מִירוּשָׁלָיִם: איכה ד

פְּאֵרֵי מִגְבָּעוֹת / לְכָבוֹד נִקְבָּעוֹת. בְּצֵאתִי מִמִּצְרָיִם:
שְׁרִיקוֹת וּתְרוּעוֹת / לְקָלוֹן וּזְוָעוֹת. בְּצֵאתִי מִירוּשָׁלָיִם:

צִיץ הַזָּהָב / וְהַמְשֵׁל וָרַהַב. בְּצֵאתִי מִמִּצְרָיִם:
הָשְׁלַךְ הַנֵּזֶר / וְאָפֵס הָעֵזֶר. בְּצֵאתִי מִירוּשָׁלָיִם:

ק Holiness and prophecy and God's glory visible,
When I left Egypt.
Defiled and polluted and the spirit of profanity,
When I left Jerusalem.

ר Song and salvation and trumpets sounding blasts,
When I left Egypt.
The screaming of babes and the gasping of corpses,
When I left Jerusalem.

ש The Table and the Menora, burnt-offerings and incense,
When I left Egypt.
Idol and abomination, graven images and pagan monuments,
When I left Jerusalem.

ת The Torah and its message and precious vessels,
When I left Egypt.
Happiness and joy; gone are sorrow and sighing,
When I return to Jerusalem.

This famous piyut by Rabbi Yehuda HaLevi, was widely copied and emulated throughout the ages, and seen as the ultimate expression of the Jewish people's longing for their homeland. There are several notable differences between the Ashkenazic and Sephardic versions. The Sephardic tradition has widely been considered more authentic, often quoted in Torah and academic circles, and is therefore printed here, in a departure from the otherwise Ashkenazic presentation of the kinot.

צִיּוֹן Zion, surely you will inquire after the well-being of your imprisoned ones, those who seek your well-being and are the remnant of your flock. / From west, east, north, and south, promote the well-being of the distant and the close, from every direction. / As well as the well-being of those bound by longing, shedding tears like the dew on Mount Hermon, wishing to shed them on your mountains. *Ps. 133*

לִבְכּוֹת Like a jackal, I cry for your anguish, and when I dream of the return of your captives, I am a harp for your songs. / My heart is to Bethel and yearns excessively for Peniel and for Maḥanayim, and all the places where your pure ones pray. / There the Divine Presence resides close by, and there your Creator opened up the gates of heaven opposite your gates. / And the glory of God alone was your light, and not the sun, the moon, or starlight. / I choose to pour out my soul at that place where God's spirit is poured upon your chosen ones. / You are the royal palace and God's throne, and how do slaves now sit on the thrones of your noblemen? / Would that I could wander among the places where God was revealed to your seers and envoys. / Who can make wings for me so that I can roam afar and move my ruptured heart to your ruptured hills? *Ps. 55*

קְדֻשָּׁה וּנְבוּאָה / וּכְבוֹד יהוה נִרְאָה. בְּצֵאתִי מִמִּצְרָיִם:
נִגְאָלָה וּמוֹרָאָה / וְרוּחַ הַטֻּמְאָה. בְּצֵאתִי מִירוּשָׁלָיִם:

רִנָּה וִישׁוּעָה / וַחֲצוֹצְרוֹת הַתְּרוּעָה. בְּצֵאתִי מִמִּצְרָיִם:
זַעֲקַת עוֹלָל / וְנַאֲקַת חָלָל. בְּצֵאתִי מִירוּשָׁלָיִם:

שֻׁלְחָן וּמְנוֹרָה / וְכָלִיל וּקְטוֹרָה. בְּצֵאתִי מִמִּצְרָיִם:
אֱלִיל וְתוֹעֵבָה / וּפֶסֶל וּמַצֵּבָה. בְּצֵאתִי מִירוּשָׁלָיִם:

תּוֹרָה וּתְעוּדָה / וּכְלֵי הַחֶמְדָּה. בְּצֵאתִי מִמִּצְרָיִם:
שָׂשׂוֹן וְשִׂמְחָה / וְנָס יָגוֹן וַאֲנָחָה. בְּשׁוּבִי לִירוּשָׁלָיִם:

This famous פיוט *by Rabbi Yehuda HaLevi, was widely copied and emulated throughout the ages, and seen as the ultimate expression of the Jewish people's longing for their homeland. There are several notable differences between the Ashkenazic and Sephardic versions. The Sephardic tradition has widely been considered more authentic, often quoted in Torah and academic circles, and is therefore printed here, in a departure from the otherwise Ashkenazic presentation of the* קינות.

צִיּוֹן, הֲלֹא תִשְׁאֲלִי לִשְׁלוֹם אֲסִירַיִךְ, דּוֹרְשֵׁי שְׁלוֹמֵךְ, וְהֵם יֶתֶר עֲדָרָיִךְ:
מִיָּם וּמִזְרָח וּמִצָּפוֹן וְתֵימָן, שְׁלוֹם רָחוֹק וְקָרוֹב, שְׂאִי מִכֹּל עֲבָרָיִךְ:
וּשְׁלוֹם אֲסִיר תַּאֲוָה, נוֹתֵן דְּמָעָיו כְּטַל חֶרְמוֹן, וְנִכְסָף לְרִדְתָּם עַל הֲרָרָיִךְ: תהלים קלג

לִבְכּוֹת עֱנוּתֵךְ אֲנִי תַנִּים, וְעֵת אֶחֱלֹם שִׁיבַת שְׁבוּתֵךְ, אֲנִי כִנּוֹר לְשִׁירָיִךְ:
לִבִּי לְבֵית אֵל, וְלִפְנִיאֵל מְאֹד יֶהֱמֶה, וּלְמַחֲנַיִם, וְכָל פִּגְעֵי טְהוֹרָיִךְ:
שָׁם הַשְּׁכִינָה שְׁכֵנָה לָךְ, וְהַיּוֹצְרֵךְ פָּתַח לְמוּל שַׁעֲרֵי שַׁחַק, שְׁעָרָיִךְ:
וּכְבוֹד יהוה לְבַד הָיָה מְאוֹרֵךְ, וְאֵין שֶׁמֶשׁ וְסַהַר וְכוֹכָבִים מְאִירָיִךְ:
אֶבְחַר לְנַפְשִׁי לְהִשְׁתַּפֵּךְ, בְּמָקוֹם אֲשֶׁר רוּחַ אֱלֹהִים שְׁפוּכָה, עַל בְּחִירָיִךְ:
אַתְּ בֵּית מְלוּכָה, וְאַתְּ כִּסֵּא יהוה, וְאֵיךְ יֵשְׁבוּ עֲבָדִים עֲלֵי כִסְאוֹת גְּבִירָיִךְ:
מִי יִתְּנֵנִי מְשׁוֹטֵט, בַּמְּקוֹמוֹת אֲשֶׁר נִגְלוּ אֱלֹהִים לְחוֹזַיִךְ וְצִירָיִךְ:
מִי יַעֲשֶׂה לִּי כְנָפַיִם וְאַרְחִיק נְדֹד, אָנִיד לְבִתְרֵי לְבָבִי בֵּין בְּתָרָיִךְ: תהלים נה

אֶפּוֹל I will fall to my face upon your land and treasure your stones and cherish your soil. / I will even stand near the graves of my forefathers and be transfixed in Hebron at the site of your prestigious graves. / I will pass through your forest and your Carmel, and I will stand at your Gilead, and I will be awestruck at your Mount Abarim. / Mount Abarim and Mount Hor, where there lie the two great lights; your luminaries and your teachers. / Your souls come alive [from] the air of your land, and from the flowing myrrh of the dust of your soil, and the dripping honey of your rivers.

יִנְעַם It would be pleasant for me to walk naked and barefoot upon the desolate *Is. 20*
ruins that were once your shrines. / In the place of your Ark, now buried, and in the place of the cherubs who once dwelled in your innermost chambers. / I will shear myself, cast off my crown of glory, and curse the day that your saints were defiled in a profane land. / How can I enjoy eating and drinking when I behold dogs dragging your young lions? / Or how can the daylight be sweet to my eyes when I still see, in the mouths of ravens, the corpses of your eaglets? / The cup of agony, slow down! Let up a bit, for already my innards are full and my soul, embittered. / When I remember Ohola [Samaria], I absorb your poison, and I remember Oholiva [Jerusalem] and suck dry your dregs.

צִיּוֹן Zion, perfectly beautiful, with love and grace you were bound long ago, *Lam. 2*
and bound to you are the souls of your comrades. / Those are the ones who rejoice in your tranquility, and who are anguished by your ruin, and who weep for your tragedy. / From the prisoner's dungeon, they yearn for you and bow, each one of them from his place, toward your gates. / The flocks of your multitudes, which have been exiled and dispersed from mountain to hill, have not forgotten your walls. / They hold fast to your skirts and struggle to rise and grasp the branches of your palm tree. / Shinar [Babylon] and Pathros [Egypt], can their greatness compare to yours? And can their vain faith be likened to your perfect faith and light? / To whom can they compare your anointed one? And to whom, your prophets? And to whom, your Levites and singers? / They will fade and totally vanish, these pagan kingdoms, but your power is forever, and your crowns for all generations.

אִוָּךְ Your God has preferred you as an abode, and happy is the man who will choose to draw near and dwell in your courtyards. / Happy is he who waits and is privileged to witness the rising of your light, and upon whom your dawn will break, / To witness the success of your chosen ones, and to delight in your joy, when you return to your past youth.

אֶפּוֹל לְאַפַּי עֲלֵי אַרְצֵךְ, וְאֶרְצֶה אֲבָנַיִךְ מְאֹד, וַאֲחוֹנֵן אֶת עֲפָרָיִךְ:
אַף כִּי בְעָמְדִי עֲלֵי קִבְרוֹת אֲבוֹתַי, וְאֶשְׁתּוֹמֵם בְּחֶבְרוֹן עֲלֵי מִבְחַר קְבָרָיִךְ:
אֶעְבֹּר בְּיַעְרֵךְ וְכַרְמִלֵּךְ וְאֶעְמֹד בְּגִלְעָדֵךְ וְאֶשְׁתּוֹמְמָה אֶל הַר עֲבָרָיִךְ:
הַר הָעֲבָרִים וְהֹר הָהָר, אֲשֶׁר שָׁם שְׁנֵי אוֹרִים גְּדוֹלִים, מְאִירַיִךְ וּמוֹרָיִךְ:
חַיֵּי נְשָׁמוֹת אֲוִיר אַרְצֵךְ, וּמִמָּר דְּרוֹר אַבְקַת עֲפָרֵךְ, וְנֹפֶת צוּף נְהָרָיִךְ:

יִנְעַם לְנַפְשִׁי, הֲלֹךְ עָרֹם וְיָחֵף, עֲלֵי חָרְבוֹת שְׁמָמָה, אֲשֶׁר הָיוּ דְּבִירָיִךְ: ישעיה כ
בִּמְקוֹם אֲרוֹנֵךְ אֲשֶׁר נִגְנַז, וּבִמְקוֹם כְּרוּבַיִךְ, אֲשֶׁר שָׁכְנוּ חַדְרֵי חֲדָרָיִךְ:
אָגֹז וְאַשְׁלִיךְ פְּאֵר נִזְרִי, וְאֶקֹּב זְמַן, חִלֵּל בְּאֶרֶץ טְמֵאָה אֶת נְזִירָיִךְ:
אֵיךְ יֶעֱרַב לִי אֲכֹל וּשְׁתוֹת, בְּעֵת אֶחֱזֶה כִּי יִסְחֲבוּ הַכְּלָבִים אֶת כְּפִירָיִךְ:
אוֹ אֵיךְ מְאוֹר יוֹם יְהִי מָתוֹק לְעֵינַי, בְּעוֹד אֶרְאֶה בְּפִי עוֹרְבִים פִּגְרֵי נְשָׁרָיִךְ:
כּוֹס הַיְגוֹנִים, לְאַט. הַרְפִּי מְעַט, כִּי כְבָר מָלְאוּ כְסָלַי וְנַפְשִׁי מַמְּרוֹרָיִךְ:
עֵת אֶזְכְּרָה אָהֳלָה אֶשְׁתֶּה חֲמָתֵךְ, וְאֶזְכֹּר אָהֳלִיבָה וְאֶמְצֶה אֶת שְׁמָרָיִךְ:

צִיּוֹן כְּלִילַת יֳפִי, אַהֲבָה וְחֵן תִּקְשְׁרִי מֵאָז, וּבָךְ נִקְשְׁרוּ נַפְשׁוֹת חֲבֵרָיִךְ: איכה ב
הֵם הַשְּׂמֵחִים לְשַׁלְוָתֵךְ, וְהַכּוֹאֲבִים עַל שׁוֹמְמוּתֵךְ, וּבוֹכִים עַל שְׁבָרָיִךְ:
מִבּוֹר שְׁבִי שׁוֹאֲפִים נֶגְדֵּךְ, וּמִשְׁתַּחֲוִים אִישׁ מִמְּקוֹמוֹ אֱלֵי נֹכַח שְׁעָרָיִךְ:
עֶדְרֵי הֲמוֹנֵךְ, אֲשֶׁר גָּלוּ וְנִתְפַּזְּרוּ מֵהַר לְגִבְעָה, וְלֹא שָׁכְחוּ גְדֵרָיִךְ:
הַמַּחֲזִיקִים בְּשׁוּלַיִךְ, וּמִתְאַמְּצִים לַעֲלוֹת וְלֶאֱחֹז בְּסַנְסִנֵּי תְמָרָיִךְ:
שִׁנְעָר וּפַתְרוֹס הֲיַעַרְכוּךְ בְּגָדְלָם, וְאִם הֶבְלָם יְדַמּוּ לְתֻמַּיִךְ וְאוּרָיִךְ:
אֶל מִי יְדַמּוּ מְשִׁיחַיִךְ, וְאֶל מִי נְבִיאַיִךְ, וְאֶל מִי לְוִיַּיִךְ וְשָׁרָיִךְ:
יִשְׁנֶה וְיַחֲלֹף כְּלִיל, כָּל־מַמְלְכוֹת הָאֱלִיל, חָסְנֵךְ לְעוֹלָם, לְדוֹר וָדוֹר נְזָרָיִךְ:

אִוָּךְ לְמוֹשָׁב אֱלֹהָיִךְ. וְאַשְׁרֵי אֱנוֹשׁ, יִבְחַר יְקָרֵב וְיִשְׁכֹּן בַּחֲצֵרָיִךְ:
אַשְׁרֵי מְחַכֶּה, וְיַגִּיעַ וְיִרְאֶה עֲלוֹת אוֹרֵךְ, וְיִבָּקְעוּ עָלָיו שְׁחָרָיִךְ:
לִרְאוֹת בְּטוֹבַת בְּחִירַיִךְ, וְלַעֲלֹז בְּשִׂמְחָתֵךְ, בְּשׁוּבֵךְ אֱלֵי קַדְמַת נְעוּרָיִךְ:

This elegy addresses the Torah rather than Zion or the Jewish people. It was written by the Maharam of Rothenburg (1215–1293) to commemorate the burning of the Talmud in Paris in 1242.

שַׁאֲלִי Inquire, consumed in fire, after the well-being of your mourners, who so strongly desire to reside in your dwellings, / who yearn for the earth of the Amos 2
land [Israel], and who are pained and shocked by the conflagration of your scrolls. / They walk in darkness, unillumined, but hope for the light of day to Is. 50
shine upon them and upon you; / and inquire, too, of the welfare of that sighing man, crying with a broken heart, constantly bemoaning your pangs of torment! / Who wails like jackals and ostriches, and calls for a bitter eulogy on your behalf.

אֵיכָה How can that which was given in a [divine] consuming fire, be consumed by a fire kindled by mortals? And [how can] those intruders not be scorched by your embers? / Until when, O pampered one [Rome], will you dwell in great tranquility, while the faces of my flowers are covered by thorns? / [How long] will you sit in arrogance, judging the sons of God with such harsh judgments and presenting them to your tribunals, / and decree to burn the fiery Law and statutes [Torah and Talmud]? Happy is He who will repay you in kind!

צוּרִי Did my Protector present you in the presence of torches and fire, so that, at your end, you would be set on fire from below? / Sinai! Is this why you were chosen by God, higher mountains rejected, and your borders favored? / Were you to be an omen that the Torah would be reduced and lowered from its glory? Can I make such a comparison? / A comparison to a king who cried at his son's wedding feast, knowing that his son would die; is that what you [Sinai] stand for? / Instead of a noble gown, Sinai, cover yourself in a garment of sackcloth, wear a widow's clothes, change your dress!

אוֹרִיד I will shed enough tears for a river to reach the graves of your two noble princes, / Moses, and Aaron on Mount Hor, and will ask them, "Has a new Torah been given? Is that why the [old] scrolls were burned?" / In [Sivan] the third month [was the Torah given], and the connected fourth month [Tammuz] already saw the destruction of your treasure and all your beautiful wreaths. / The tablets shattered [in Tammuz], and the wrong-doing redoubled with the fiery destruction of the radiant Torah. Is this how you were doubly compensated?

אֶתְמַהּ I wondered how my palate could ever again savor food, after I witnessed how all of your treasured possessions were gathered / in the open square like an apostate town, and [how] the divine treasure was burned by those who were banned from entering your community. / I cannot find a clear path; turned to grief are those straight paths of yours! / It is sweeter to my mouth

This elegy addresses the Torah rather than Zion or the Jewish people. It was written by the Maharam of Rothenburg (1215–1293) to commemorate the burning of the Talmud in Paris in 1242.

שַׁאֲלִי, שְׂרוּפָה בָאֵשׁ, לִשְׁלוֹם אֲבֵלָיִךְ. הַמִּתְאַוִּים שְׁכֹן בַּחֲצַר זְבוּלָיִךְ:
הַשּׁוֹאֲפִים בַּעֲפַר אֶרֶץ, וְהַכּוֹאֲבִים הַמִּשְׁתּוֹמְמִים עֲלֵי מוֹקֵד גְּוִילָיִךְ: עמוס ב
הוֹלְכִים חֲשֵׁכִים וְאֵין נֹגַהּ, וְקוֹוִים לְאוֹר יוֹמָם, עֲלֵיהֶם אֲשֶׁר יִזְרַח וְעָלָיִךְ: ישעיה נ
וּשְׁלוֹם אֱנוֹשׁ נֶאֱנָח, בּוֹכֶה בְּלֵב נִשְׁבָּר, תָּמִיד מְקוֹנֵן עֲלֵי צִירֵי חֲבָלָיִךְ:
וַיִּתְאוֹנֵן כְּתַנִּים וּבְנוֹת יַעֲנָה, וַיִּקְרָא מִסְפֵּד מַר בִּגְלָלָיִךְ:

אֵיכָה נְתוּנָה בְּאֵשׁ אוֹכְלָה, תְּאֻכַּל בְּאֵשׁ בָּשָׂר, וְלֹא נִכְווּ זָרִים בְּגַחֲלָיִךְ:
עַד אָן עֲדִינָה, תְּהִי שׁוֹכְנָה בְּרֹב הַשְׁקֵט, וּפְנֵי פְרָחַי הֲלֹא כָסוּ חֲרֻלָּיִךְ:
תֵּשֵׁב בְּרֹב גַּאֲוָה לִשְׁפֹּט בְּנֵי אֵל בְּכָל הַמִּשְׁפָּטִים, וְתָבִיא בִּפְלִילָיִךְ:
עוֹד תִּגְזֹר לִשְׂרֹף דָּת אֵשׁ וְחֻקִּים, וְלָכֵן אַשְׁרֵי שֶׁיְּשַׁלֶּם לָךְ גְּמוּלָיִךְ:

צוּרִי, בְּלַפִּיד וְאֵשׁ הַלְבַעֲבוּר זֶה נְתָנֵךְ, כִּי בְאַחֲרִיתֵךְ תְּלַהֵט אֵשׁ בְּשׁוּלָיִךְ:
סִינַי, הֲעַל כֵּן בְּךָ בָּחַר אֱלֹהִים, וּמָאַס בִּגְדוֹלִים וְזָרַח בִּגְבוּלָיִךְ:
לִהְיוֹת לְמוֹפֵת, לְדָת כִּי תִתְמַעֵט וְתֵרֵד מִכְּבוּדָהּ. וְהֵן אֶמְשֹׁל מְשָׁלָיִךְ:
מָשָׁל לְמֶלֶךְ אֲשֶׁר בָּכָה לְמִשְׁתֵּה בְנוֹ, צָפָה אֲשֶׁר יִגְוַע. כֵּן אַתְּ בְּמִלָּיִךְ:
תַּחַת מְעִיל, תִּתְכַּס סִינַי לְבוּשֵׁךְ בְּשַׂק, תַּעְטֶה לְבוּשׁ אַלְמְנוּת,
תַּחֲלִיף שְׂמָלָיִךְ:

אוֹרִיד דְּמָעוֹת, עֲדֵי יִהְיוּ כְנַחַל, וְיַגִּיעוּ לְקִבְרוֹת שְׁנֵי שָׂרֵי אֲצִילָיִךְ:
מֹשֶׁה וְאַהֲרֹן בְּהֹר הָהָר. וְאֶשְׁאַל, הֲיֵשׁ תּוֹרָה חֲדָשָׁה, בְּכֵן נִשְׂרְפוּ גְלִילָיִךְ:
חֹדֶשׁ שְׁלִישִׁי, וְהָקְשַׁר הָרְבִיעִי לְהַשְׁחִית חֶמְדָּתֵךְ, וְכָל יְפִי כְלִילָיִךְ:
גָּדַע לְלוּחוֹת, וְעוֹד שָׁנָה בְּאִוַּלְתּוֹ, לִשְׂרֹף בְּאֵשׁ דָּת. הֲזֶה תַּשְׁלוּם כְּפֵלָיִךְ:

אֶתְמַהּ לְנַפְשִׁי. וְאֵיךְ יֶעֱרַב לְחִכִּי אֲכֹל, אַחֲרֵי רְאוֹתִי אֲשֶׁר אָסְפוּ שְׁלָלָיִךְ:
אֶל תּוֹךְ רְחוֹבָהּ כְּנִדַּחַת, וְשָׂרְפוּ שְׁלַל עֶלְיוֹן, אֲשֶׁר תִּמְאַס לָבוֹא קְהָלָיִךְ:
לֹא אֵדְעָה לִמְצֹא דֶּרֶךְ סְלוּלָה, הֲכִי הָיוּ אֲבֵלוֹת נְתִיב יֹשֶׁר מְסִלָּיִךְ:
יִמְתַּק בְּפִי מִדְּבַשׁ, לִמְסֹךְ בְּמַשְׁקֶה דְּמָעוֹת. וּלְרַגְלִי, הֱיוֹת כָּבוּל כְּבָלָיִךְ:

than honey, to dilute my drink with tears, and to chain my feet in your chains. I find it pleasing to fetch all my tears until they are gone, for all those who cling to the hem of your robes. / But my tears dry up as they run down my cheeks, for my compassion is in a fever over the departure of your Master! / He took His pouch of silver and went on a distant journey, and with Him fled your [protective] shadows! / And I, bereaved and forlorn, remained alone without them, like a mast atop the mountains of your towers. / No longer will I listen to the voices of your singers, for severed are the strings of your timbrels and flutes. / I will dress and cover myself with sackcloth, for very precious to me, greater and more numerous than sand, are the souls of your victims. / I am very puzzled by the light of day which shines upon all, but remains dark for me and for you.

וַעֲקִי Cry in a bitter voice to your Rock about your breach and your illness. Perhaps He will remember the love of your betrothed! / Gird yourself in a sack garment because of the fire which tore you to shreds and flattened your hills! / For as long as your suffering lasted will your Rock console you. And He will bring back from captivity the tribes of Jeshurun and will lift up your lowly ones! / You will again adorn yourself in scarlet and take up the timbrel, march in a circle, and rejoice in your dances! / My heart will be uplifted when my Rock is again a light for you, when He will illuminate your darkness and dispel your gloom! *Jer. 31*

At this point, many congregations say one or more of the kinot in memory of the victims of the Holocaust (page 956).

The following kina is said standing and recited responsively with the Leader.

This elegy, the only one which is chanted to a melody, closes the kinot. The first stanza, often repeated as a refrain, calls upon Zion to weep, comparing her to woman in the pangs of childbirth, and to a young wife bereaved of her husband. The eleven subsequent stanzas follow a fixed form: rhyming couplets which include an alphabetic acrostic, with each stich detailing one of the calamities of the Destruction.

אֱלִי Lament, Zion and her cities, like a woman in her labor pains,
like a maiden girt in sackcloth for the husband of her youth. *Joel 1*

עֲלֵי For the palace now deserted because of the sin of the sheep of her flocks,
and for the intrusion of God's blasphemers
into the chambers of her sanctuary.

יֶעֱרַב לְעֵינַי, שְׁאֹב מֵימֵי דְמָעַי, עֲדֵי כָלוּ לְכָל מַחֲזִיק בִּכְנַף מְעִילָיִךְ:
אַךְ יֶחֱרְבוּ בְּרִדְתָּם עַל לְחָיַי, עֲבוּר כִּי נִכְמְרוּ רַחֲמַי לְנֹדֹד בְּעָלָיִךְ:
לָקַח צְרוֹר כַּסְפּוֹ, הָלַךְ בְּדֶרֶךְ לְמֵרָחוֹק, וְעִמּוֹ הֲלֹא נָסוּ צְלָלָיִךְ:
וַאֲנִי כְשָׁכוּל וְגַלְמוּד נִשְׁאַרְתִּי לְבַד מֵהֶם, כְּתֹרֶן בְּרֹאשׁ הַר מִגְדָּלָיִךְ:
לֹא אֶשְׁמַע עוֹד לְקוֹל שָׁרִים וְשָׁרוֹת, עֲלֵי כִּי נִתְּקוּ מֵיתְרֵי תֻפֵּי חֲלִילָיִךְ:
אֶלְבַּשׁ וְאֶתְכַּס בְּשַׂק, כִּי לִי מְאֹד יָקְרוּ. עָצְמוּ כְחוֹל יִרְבְּיוּן נַפְשׁוֹת חֲלָלָיִךְ:
אֶתְמַהּ מְאֹד עַל מְאוֹר הַיּוֹם, אֲשֶׁר יִזְרַח אֶל כֹּל, אֲבָל יֶחְשַׁךְ אֵלַי וְאֵלָיִךְ:

זַעֲקִי בְקוֹל מַר לְצוּר, עַל שִׁבְרוֹנֵךְ וְעַל חָלְיֵךְ. וְלוּ יִזְכֹּר אַהֲבַת כְּלוּלָיִךְ:
חִגְרִי לְבוּשׁ שַׂק, עֲלֵי הַהַבְעָרָה אֲשֶׁר יָצְאָה לְחֵלֶק, וְסָפְדָה אֶת תְּלוּלָיִךְ:
כִּימוֹת עֱנוּתֵךְ יְנַחֵמֵךְ צוּר, וְיָשִׁיב שְׁבוּת שִׁבְטֵי יְשֻׁרוּן, וְיָרִים אֶת שְׁפָלָיִךְ:
עוֹד תַּעֲדִי בַּעֲדִי שָׁנִי. וְתֹף תִּקְחִי, תֵּלְכִי בְמָחוֹל וְצַהֲלִי בִּמְחוֹלָיִךְ: ירמיה לא
יָרוּם לְבָבִי, בְּעֵת צוּרִי לְאוֹר לָךְ, וְיַגִּיהַּ לְחָשְׁכֵךְ וְיָאִירוּ אֲפֵלָיִךְ:

At this point, many congregations say one or more of the קינות *in memory of the victims of the Holocaust* *(page 957)*.

The following קינה *is said standing and recited responsively with the* שליח ציבור.

This elegy, the only one which is chanted to a melody, closes the kinot. The first stanza, often repeated as a refrain, calls upon Zion to weep, comparing her to woman in the pangs of childbirth, and to a young wife bereaved of her husband. The eleven subsequent stanzas follow a fixed form: rhyming couplets which include an alphabetic acrostic, with each stich detailing one of the calamities of the Destruction.

אֱלִי צִיּוֹן וְעָרֶיהָ / כְּמוֹ אִשָּׁה בְּצִירֶיהָ.
וְכִבְתוּלָה חֲגוּרַת שַׂק / עַל בַּעַל נְעוּרֶיהָ: יואל א

עֲלֵי אַרְמוֹן אֲשֶׁר נִטַּשׁ / בְּאַשְׁמַת צֹאן עֲדָרֶיהָ.
וְעַל בִּיאַת מְחָרְפֵי אֵל / בְּתוֹךְ מִקְדַּשׁ חֲדָרֶיהָ:

עֲלֵי For the exile of God's servants, the sweet singers of her songs,
and for their blood which has been spilled like the waters of her rivers.

עֲלֵי For the lyrics of her dances, now silenced in her cities,
and for the council now devastated,
and the abolition of her high courts.

עֲלֵי For her daily sacrifices and the redemption of her first born,
and for the defilement of the Temple vessels
and the altar of her incense.

עֲלֵי For the little children of her kings, the sons of David, her princes,
and for their beauty which was darkened
when she was divested of her crowns.

עֲלֵי For the glory that was dispelled at the time her shrines were destroyed,
and for the oppressor who tormented
and placed sackcloth around her waist.

עֲלֵי For the wounds and many blows with which her sainted ones were struck,
and for the smashing upon the rock of her babes, her young ones.

עֲלֵי For the joy of her enemy rejoicing over her downfall,
and for the torture of those once free, her noblemen, her pious ones.

עֲלֵי For the sin which diverted her footsteps from the cleared path,
and for her numerous communities, tarnished and charred.

עֲלֵי For the voices of those who mocked her as her corpses mounted,
and to the scoffing mob in the very midst of her Temple courtyards.

עֲלֵי For Your name which is desecrated in the mouth
of those who stand against her,
and for the prayer which they shout to You, "Hear and heed her words!"

אֱלִי Lament, Zion and her cities, like a woman in her labor pains,
like a maiden girt in sackcloth for the husband of her youth.

עֲלֵי גָלוּת מְשָׁרְתֵי אֵל / מַנְעִימֵי שִׁיר זְמָרֶיהָ.
וְעַל דָּמָם אֲשֶׁר שֻׁפַּךְ / כְּמוֹ מֵימֵי יְאוֹרֶיהָ:

עֲלֵי הֶגְיוֹן מְחוֹלֶיהָ / אֲשֶׁר דָּמַם בְּעָרֶיהָ.
וְעַל וַעַד אֲשֶׁר שָׁמֵם / וּבִטּוּל סַנְהֶדְרֶיהָ:

עֲלֵי זִבְחֵי תְמִידֶיהָ / וּפִדְיוֹנֵי בְכוֹרֶיהָ.
וְעַל חִלּוּל כְּלֵי הֵיכָל / וּמִזְבַּח קְטוֹרֶיהָ:

עֲלֵי טַפֵּי מְלָכֶיהָ / בְּנֵי דָוִד גְּבִירֶיהָ.
וְעַל יָפְיָם אֲשֶׁר חָשַׁךְ / בְּעֵת סָרוּ כְתָרֶיהָ:

עֲלֵי כָבוֹד אֲשֶׁר גָּלָה / בְּעֵת חָרְבַּן דְּבִירֶיהָ.
וְעַל לוֹחֵץ אֲשֶׁר לָחַץ / וְשָׂם שַׂקִּים חֲגוֹרֶיהָ:

עֲלֵי מַחַץ וְרֹב מַכּוֹת / אֲשֶׁר הֻכּוּ נְזִירֶיהָ.
וְעַל נִפּוּץ אֱלֵי סֶלַע / עוֹלָלֶיהָ נְעָרֶיהָ:

עֲלֵי שִׂמְחַת אוֹיְבֶיהָ / בְּשָׂחֲקָם עַל שְׁבָרֶיהָ.
וְעַל עִנּוּי בְּנֵי חוֹרִין / נְדִיבֶיהָ טְהוֹרֶיהָ:

עֲלֵי פֶשַׁע אֲשֶׁר עָוְתָה / סְלֹל דֶּרֶךְ אֲשׁוּרֶיהָ:
וְעַל צִבְאוֹת קְהָלֶיהָ / שְׁזוּפֶיהָ שְׁחֹרֶיהָ:

עֲלֵי קוֹלוֹת מְחָרְפֶיהָ / בְּעֵת רַבּוּ פְגָרֶיהָ.
וְעַל רִגְשַׁת מְגַדְּפֶיהָ / בְּתוֹךְ מִשְׁכַּן חֲצֵרֶיהָ:

עֲלֵי שִׁמְךָ אֲשֶׁר חֻלַּל / בְּפִי קָמֵי מְצֵרֶיהָ.
וְעַל תַּחַן יְצַוְּחוּ לָךְ / קְשֹׁב וּשְׁמַע אֲמָרֶיהָ:

אֱלִי צִיּוֹן וְעָרֶיהָ / כְּמוֹ אִשָּׁה בְּצִירֶיהָ.
וְכִבְתוּלָה חֲגוּרַת שַׂק / עַל בַּעַל נְעוּרֶיהָ:

KINOT IN COMMEMORATION OF THE HOLOCAUST

Elegy on the Ḥurban by Rabbi Shimon Schwab

הַזּוֹכֵר He, mindful of those who are mindful of Him,
each generation and its sainted martyrs, ever since first He chose us;
may He remember the fate that befell the last generation.
Woe! What has befallen us!
All who were swept away in the deluge of blood,
whose lives were lost, drowned in the valleys of tears –
may God remember them in the lands of eternal life.
May their memory be a blessing.

שְׂאוּ Lift up your hands to Him – alas, O ye heavens!
Alas for the best among Yisrael's tribes,
communities, congregations, towns and districts,
brotherhoods, institutions, houses of God!
Would that streams could flow from my eyes, joining the torrents of tears
already shed for the millions of dead consumed in the fires of terror and ruin.

וְעַל For the princes of Torah, pillars of tradition, for the flower of priestly youth,
for the scholars, the teachers, men and women,
and for the precious young in the houses of study.
The pious daughters, grandfathers, grandmothers,
and their progeny, infants newborn,
all of them – thousands upon thousands,beloved in life, in death not divided.

אֶת Search Thou for their blood!
Remember each driven leaf, each life wiped out in the Holocaust –
six million struck dead by lightning, in the storm that felled fully one-third
of the precious stock from the vineyard so dearly beloved by Thee.
O Avenger of innocent blood, erase not the tale of their pain
from the record Thou hast inscribed.

זְכֹר Remember each moan, each heart-rending scream as they went to the slaughter;
rivers of blood, tear-drenched faces – let them not be forgotten!
The shrieks, the groans, the piercing cries as wild dogs tore into soft flesh –
Remember them! Count them! Gather them up in Thy bond
until the day of Thy vengeance for the shame of downtrodden.

בְּמַחֲנוֹת Camps of barbarians: pain and disease, anguish of ravaged souls,
insults and sneers, spittle and shame, searing wounds from merciless whips;
hunger, thirst, madness, torture –
the stumbling of the faint whose strength was gone;
death-rattle of each life draining away in agony –
far be it from Thee ever to forget!

קינות על קדושי השואה

Elegy on the Ḥurban by Rabbi Shimon Schwab

הַזּוֹכֵר מַזְכִּירָיו, דּוֹר דּוֹר וּקְדוֹשָׁיו, מֵעֵת אֲשֶׁר אָז בְּחַרְתָּנוּ
יִזְכּוֹר דֵּרָאוֹן, שֶׁל דּוֹר אַחֲרוֹן, אוֹיָה מֶה הָיָה לָנוּ
שְׁטוּפֵי מַבּוּל דָּם, שֶׁמָּסְרוּ נַפְשׁוֹתָם, כָּל שְׁקוּעֵי עִמְקֵי הַבָּכָא
יִפְקְדֵם אֱלֹהִים, בְּאַרְצוֹת הַחַיִּים, וַעֲדֵי עַד זִכְרָם לִבְרָכָה.

שְׂאוּ אֵלָיו כַּפַּיִם, אֲהָהּ אִי שָׁמַיִם, הוֹי עַל מֵיטַב שִׁבְטֵי יִשְׂרָאֵל
עֵדוֹת וּקְהִלּוֹת, עָרִים וּגְלִילוֹת, חֲבוּרוֹת, מוֹסָדוֹת, כָּל מוֹעֲדֵי אֵל
מִי יִתֵּן פַּלְגֵי מַיִם, תֵּרַדְנָה עֵינַיִם, אֶל אַשְׁדּוֹת נַחֲלֵי הַדְּמָעוֹת
עֲלֵי אַלְפֵי אֲלָפִים, גּוּפִים נִשְׂרָפִים, בְּמוֹ אֵשׁ הַחֻרְבָּן וּזְוָעוֹת.

וְעַל שָׂרֵי הַתּוֹרָה, וּמַחֲזִיקֵי מְסוֹרָה, וְעַל פִּרְחֵי הַכְּהֻנָּה הַצְּעִירִים
וְעַל חוֹבְשֵׁי מִדְרָשׁוֹת, מוֹרִים וּמוֹרוֹת, תִּינוֹקוֹת בֵּית רַבָּן יַקִּירִים
עַל בָּנוֹת בּוֹטְחוֹת, סָבִים וְסָבוֹת, וְעַל זַרְעָם וְטַפָּם שֶׁיָּלְדוּ
וְגַם לְרַבּוֹת, רִבְבוֹת, נֶאֱהָבִים בַּחַיִּים, בְּמוֹתָם לֹא נִפְרָדוּ.

אֶת דָּמָם דְּרשׁ, כִּי תִשָּׂא אֶת רֹאשׁ, שֶׁל כָּל נִדָּף לֶעָלִים הַטְּרוּפִים
כָּל נַפְשׁוֹת מֵת, בִּימֵי שֶׁבֶר וָשֵׁאת, שִׁשָּׁה אַלְפֵי פְּעָמִים אֲלָפִים
שְׁלִישִׁיָּה לְבָעֵר, בְּבְרַק זַעַם סוֹעֵר, מִכַּרְמֵי הַחֶמֶד אֲהַבְתָּ
גּוֹאֵל הַדָּם, נָא זְכֹר צַעֲרָם, אַל תִּמְחֶה מִסֵּפֶר כָּתָבְתָּ.

זְכוֹר הַנְּאָקוֹת, וְרַעַשׁ צְעָקוֹת, אָז יוּבְלוּ לָרֶצַח
יְאוֹרֵי דְּמֵיהֶם, וְדִמְעוֹת פְּנֵיהֶם, לֹא תִשָּׁכַחְנָה לָנֶצַח
כָּל חִיל וּגְנִיחָה, וּנְהִי צְרִיחָה, מִשְׁדּוּדֵי לַהֲקוֹת הַכְּלָבִים
זְכוֹר וּסְפוֹר, בְּנֹאדְךָ צְרוֹר, עַד עֵת נְקֹם עֶלְבּוֹן עֲלוּבִים.

בְּמַחֲנוֹת הַפְּרָאִים, כְּאֵב וּנְגָעִים, וּפַחֵי נְפָשׁוֹת עֲגוּמוֹת
חֲרָפוֹת וּצְחוֹק, כְּלִמּוֹת וָרֹק, פִּצְעֵי הַכָּאוֹת אֲיֻמּוֹת
וּרְעָבוֹן, צִמָּאוֹן, שִׁגָּעוֹן, עִצָּבוֹן, וְכִשָּׁלוֹן נֶחֱלָשִׁים בְּלִי כֹחַ
וְכָל נַאֲקוֹת חָלָל, מִכָּל יָחִיד אֻמְלָל, חָלִילָה לְךָ מִלִּשְׁכֹּחַ.

וְתִימְרוֹת The chimneys – thick smoke from the furnaces,
bones and limbs piled high, halls of poison –
moans and screams of multitudes
choking in gas chambers; the stench of corpses;
dead bundles of skin and bones, food for the soil of the hangmen;
how the tormentors turned human fat into soap,
and skin into ornaments for their women!

וּקְרִיצַת Flicks of the fingers of brutal taskmasters:
To the right – slave labor! To the left – the shadow of death!
Shots of the savage marksmen
felling the hapless who dug their own graves,
to be buried, bodies still twitching in final agony.
Our sisters raped, our daughters made barren;
draughts of poison from evil physicians,
fugitives hiding in holes and bunkers,
their children abandoned in soul-snatchers' homes!

שֶׂה Lambs without blemish –
blood of our captive children offered upon the great altar –
Alas, Thy loving servants' lifeless flesh!
Who could count the saintly flock?
May their light be unfailing, for they have stood Thy test;
They hallowed thy Name; proclaiming, "Shema Yisrael!"
They gave up their lives for God so that He might gather them in.
Believing in His justice until the last,
singing Ani Ma'amin, proud hymn of eternal faith.

וּבְכֵן We are still here: a people bereft, bewildered like orphans,
no graves at which to pray;
no tombstones at which to shed the tears from our seared hearts.
The blood of their sacrifice their only memorial,
blood which will seethe forever, never to be forgotten;
the mountains of ashes their last offering –
the ash-heaps at the altars their tribute for all time to come.

מִי Who could retell Yisrael's pain – minds dazed with grief,
shattered remnants of former glory;
its greatness crushed – O living, merciful God!
Comfort Thy flock which yearns for Thee.
Cause a new light to shine, rays of new glory,
and may the spirit of God rest upon us once more.

וְתִימְרוֹת עָשָׁן, וְקִיטוֹר מִכִּבְשָׁן, תִּלֵּי תִלִּים עֲצָמוֹת וְגִידִים
וְחַדְרֵי הָרַעַל, קוֹל שְׁאָגוֹת מִקָּהָל, הַנֶּחֱנָקִים תּוֹךְ תָּאֵי הָאֵדִים
וְסִרְחוֹן גּוּפוֹת, וּגְוִיּוֹת סְגוּפוֹת, גַּלַּל דֹּמֶן אַדְמַת נוֹאֲצִים
אֵיךְ הָפְכוּ טוֹרְפֵיהֶם, לְבוֹרִית חֶלְבֵיהֶם, וְעוֹר אִישׁ לְקִשּׁוּטֵי הַנָּשִׁים.

וּקְרִיצַת אֶצְבָּעוֹת, שֶׁל רָאשֵׁי הַפְּרָעוֹת, לִימִין שִׁעְבּוּד פֶּרֶךְ, צַלְמָוֶת לִשְׂמֹאל
וְאֵיךְ יָרוּ יְרִיּוֹת, עַל חוֹפְרֵי הַבּוֹרוֹת, בְּיִסּוּרֵי חִבּוּט קֶבֶר הוֹרִידוּם שְׁאוֹל
אֵיךְ עִנּוּ אַחְיוֹתֵינוּ, וְסֵרְסוּ בְּנוֹתֵינוּ, כּוֹסוֹת תַּרְעֵלָה מִידֵי רוֹפְאִים אַכְזָרִים
וּפְלִיטֵי הַשְּׂרִידִים, בִּמְחִלּוֹת וּסְתָרִים, וְטִמְיוֹן יְלָדִים בְּבָתֵּי שְׁמָד כְּמָרִים.

שֶׂה תָמִים לְעוֹלָה, דַּם בְּנֵי הַגּוֹלָה, הוֹי אֲרִיאֵל מִנִּבְלַת חֲסִידֶיךָ
צֹאן קָדָשִׁים מִי יִמְנֶה, אֲשֶׁר אִשָּׁם לֹא תִכְבֶּה, בְּחוּנֶיךָ הָיוּ מְקַדְּשֵׁי שְׁמֶךָ
בְּקוֹל שְׁמַע יִשְׂרָאֵל, מָסְרוּ נֶפֶשׁ לָאֵל, שֶׁהוּא יַאַסְפֵם, וְעַד יוֹם אַחֲרוֹן
הִצְדִּיקוּ דִין, וְאַף אֲנִי מַאֲמִין עָנוּ, וְשָׁרוּ שִׁירַת בִּטָּחוֹן.

וּבְכֵן נִשְׁאַר עַם, כְּיָתוֹם נִדְהָם, בְּלִי קְבָרִים לְהִשְׁתַּטֵּחַ
וְלֹא מַצֵּבוֹת, אֵיפֹה לִבְכּוֹת, יְבָבוֹת לֵבָב רוֹתֵחַ
רַק נִסְכֵי הַדָּם, אַזְכָּרוֹתָם, תּוֹסְסִים בְּלִי שׁוֹכֵחַ
וְהָרֵי אֶפְרֵי עֲקֵדָתָם, תְּרוּמוֹת דִּשְׁנֵי מִזְבֵּחַ.

מִי יְמַלֵּל, צַעַר יִשְׂרָאֵל, אֲשֶׁר דַּעְתּוֹ מִכְּאֵב נִטְרֶפֶת
וּשְׁאֵרִית הַפְּאֵר, כִּמְעַט מִזְּעֵיר, וְאֵיךְ קוֹמָתָהּ הַיּוֹם נִכְפֶּפֶת
אֵל חַי מְרַחֵם, עֲדָתְךָ נַחֵם, אֲשֶׁר לְךָ מְאֹד נִכְסֶפֶת
אוֹר חָדָשׁ תַּזְרִיחַ, קַרְנֵי הוֹד תַּצְמִיחַ, וְרוּחַ אֱלֹהִים מְרַחֶפֶת.

In Memory of the Martyrs of the European Ḥurban
by Rabbi Shlomo Halberstam, the Bobover Rebbe

זִכְרוּ Always remember, and mourn all of Israel,
let your voices be heard on high.
For Germany has destroyed our nation in the furious days of the war,
with cruel and unusual deaths, by hunger and thirst;
do not forget for all generations, until we merit consolation.

צַעֲקָתָם Their shouts and their cries, crowded into cattle cars
like sheep to the slaughter, led to the crematoria.
Let the sound of their pleas forever reverberate
before the One who dwells on high,
as they shouted out "Shema Yisrael" and martyred themselves for the
Master of all Masters.

רָאשֵׁי Revered teachers of Yeshivot and their prize students, and the multitudes
of the nation,
were enslaved, inhumanly tortured, and murdered with no compunction.
The blood of young children cries out to You from the ground;
avenge the infants and the women! Spare no soul among Your enemies.

עַל For the burning of countless houses of study and prayer,
tens of thousands of Torah scrolls and Torah scholars,
we will eulogize with songs of desolation.
They set fire to sanctuaries of God, set the pyres as we looked on.
The arsonists must pay for their arson!
He will pass judgment on the nations so full of corpses.

זַעֲקוּ Cry out, Heaven and Earth, for the thousands of towns,
fortresses of Torah,
each European country and its communities,
observers of our sacred tradition,
for the righteous, the elders, the devout who clung to their pure faith.
From the day we were exiled from our homeland we have not experienced
such catastrophe.

רַחֵם Have mercy on the remnants of our nation. Look down from heaven
upon the holy camps, ten times the number of those
redeemed from Egypt.
Re-establish our Holy Sanctuary, redouble our solace:
Lift us up, and bring us to Zion and Jerusalem.

In Memory of the Martyrs of the European Ḥurban
by Rabbi Shlomo Halberstam, the Bobover Rebbe

זִכְרוּ נָא וְקוֹנְנוּ כָּל יִשְׂרָאֵל, קוֹלְכֶם יִשָּׁמַע בָּרָמָה
כִּי הִשְׁמִידָה גֶּרְמַנְיָה אֶת עַמֵּנוּ בִּימֵי זַעַם הַמִּלְחָמָה
בְּמִיתוֹת מְשֻׁנּוֹת אַכְזָרִיּוֹת, בְּרָעָב וּבְצָמָא
אַל תִּשְׁכְּחוּ בְּכָל הַדּוֹרוֹת, עֲדֵי תִּזְכּוּ לִרְאוֹת בְּנֶחָמָה

צַעֲקָתָם וּבְכִיּוֹתֵיהֶם, צְפוּפִים וּסְגוּרִים בַּקְּרוֹנִים
כַּצֹּאן לַטֶּבַח יוּבָלוּ לִשְׂרֵפָה בַּכִּבְשׁוֹנִים
קוֹל שַׁוְעָם יִזָּכֵר תָּמִיד לִפְנֵי שׁוֹכֵן מְעוֹנִים
בְּקָרְאָם שְׁמַע יִשְׂרָאֵל, מָסְרוּ נַפְשָׁם לַאֲדוֹנֵי הָאֲדוֹנִים

רָאשֵׁי יְשִׁיבוֹת וְתַלְמִידֵיהֶם, וַהֲמוֹנֵי עַמְּךָ שָׁמָּה
הֶעֱבִידוּם בְּעִנּוּיִים קָשִׁים, וַהֲרָגוּם בְּיָד רָמָה
דְּמֵי יְלָדִים רַכִּים צוֹעֲקִים אֵלֶיךָ מִן הָאֲדָמָה
נְקֹם נִקְמַת טַף וְנָשִׁים, לֹא תְחַיֶּה כָּל נְשָׁמָה

עַל שְׂרֵפַת אַלְפֵי מִדְרָשׁוֹת וּבָתֵּי כְנֵסִיּוֹת
רִבְבוֹת סִפְרֵי תוֹרָה וְלוֹמְדֶיהָ, נְקוֹנֵן בִּשְׁאִיּוֹת
שִׁלְּחוּ בָאֵשׁ מִקְדְּשֵׁי אֵל, הִצִּיתוּ וְעֵינֵינוּ צוֹפִיּוֹת
יְשַׁלֵּם הַמַּבְעִיר אֶת הַבְּעֵרָה, יָדִין בַּגּוֹיִם מָלֵא גְוִיּוֹת

זַעֲקוּ שָׁמַיִם וַאֲדָמָה עַל אַלְפֵי עֲיָרוֹת מִבְצְרֵי תוֹרָה
אַרְצוֹת אֵירוֹפָּה וּקְהִלּוֹתֶיהָ, נוֹחֲלֵי וּמְקַיְּמֵי מְסוֹרָה
צַדִּיקִים זְקֵנִים וַחֲסִידִים, דְּבֵקֵי אֱמוּנָה טְהוֹרָה
מִיּוֹם גָּלִינוּ מֵאַרְצֵנוּ, לֹא הָיָה כָּזֶה כִּלָּיוֹן נוֹרָא

רַחֵם עַל שְׁאֵרִיתֵנוּ, הַבֵּט נָא מִשָּׁמַיִם
לְמַחֲנוֹת הַקְּדוֹשִׁים, פִּי עֶשֶׂר כְּיוֹצְאֵי מִצְרַיִם
קוֹמֵם בֵּית קָדְשֵׁנוּ, וְנַחֲמֵנוּ בְּכִפְלַיִם
רוֹמְמֵנוּ, וַהֲבִיאֵנוּ לְצִיּוֹן וִירוּשָׁלַיִם.

Eli, Eli (Lament, Lament)
by Yehuda Leib Bialer

אֵלִי Lament, lament, my soul; cry out
and mourn, O Daughter of Israel,
in eulogy, in howls of grief,
for the flames have consumed Israel.

עַל For the genocide, so carefully planned;
O pangs of grief for the cascades of blood –
none were spared, not old, not young;
all were sacrificed – holy and pure.

עַל For the newborn babes, for the nursing infants,
crushed and dismembered against the cruel stones.
For their blood that flowed in the apathetic streets,
as helpless parents looked on in defeat.

עַל For the holy communities, wiped away;
for the houses of prayer and study,
consumed in flames, in burning pyres,
majestic centers of Jewish life.

עֲלֵי For the generations that were cut down,
blood of the fathers with blood of the sons.
In the killing fields of Auschwitz they were expunged,
in the furnaces of the crematoria.

עֲלֵי For the imprisoned, O God, clothed only in rags,
expiring in droves, in multitudes;
in Treblinka and Majdanek,
their bones were scattered, left to rot.

Eli, Eli (Lament, Lament)
by Yehuda Leib Bialer

אֱלִי, אֱלִי, נַפְשִׁי, בְּכִי
וְזַעֲקִי, בַּת יִשְׂרָאֵל
מִסְפֵּד שְׂאִי וְהִתְיַפְּחִי
אָכְלָה הָאֵשׁ בְּיִשְׂרָאֵל.

עַל טֶבַח עָם, אֲשֶׁר הוּכַּן
יִסּוּרֵי שְׁכוֹל, אַשְׁדּוֹת דָּמִים
זָקֵן גַּם טַף לֹא רֻחַם
עַל עֲקֵדָה קָרְבָּן תָּמִים.

עַל עוֹלָלִים, גְּמוּלֵי חָלָב
הַמְרֻטָּשִׁים לְפִי צוּרִים
וְעַל דָּמָם, אֲשֶׁר זָב
בְּרֹאשׁ חוּצוֹת לְעֵין הוֹרִים.

עַל הַקְּהִלּוֹת הַשּׁוֹמֵמוֹת
וְעַל חֻרְבַּן מִקְדְּשֵׁי אֵל
יְקוּדֵי לַהַב שַׁלְהָבוֹת
עָרֵי פְּאֵר בְּיִשְׂרָאֵל.

עֲלֵי דוֹרוֹת אֲשֶׁר נִגְדְּעוּ
דְּמֵי אָבוֹת עַל דְּמֵי בָנִים
בְּגֵיא אוֹשְׁוִיץ תַּמּוּ גָוָעוּ
עֲלֵי מוֹקְדוֹת הַכִּבְשָׁנִים

עֲלֵי כְּלוּאִים, חֲגוּרֵי שַׂק
הַנְּמַקִּים בְּרִבְבוֹתֵיהֶם
בִּטְרֶבְּלִינְקִי וּמֵידַנֶק
וְאֵין מְלַקֵּט עַצְמוֹתֵיהֶם.

עֲלֵי For the cattle cars, crammed with human cargo
that were cushioned with nothing but tar and chalk.
Bleached by thirst, their souls parched and dry,
they called for water; no hand reached out.

עֲלֵי For the young girls whose strength gave out,
young wives who took their own lives.
The ninety-three pure souls who acted as one,
preferred a pure death to a life of shame.

עֲלֵי For those frozen in fields of snow,
young children in their mothers' arms.
For the martyrs whose wailing could be heard,
buried alive in the communal graves.

עֲלֵי For the sacred scrolls defiled and torn,
stained by the Nazi hands – those profaners of God.
They lay in tatters, disgraced and abused;
none came to protect their dignity.

עֲלֵי For the righteous ones, the humblest ones,
the noble ones, immersed in Torah.
In the poisoned chambers their voices were stilled;
all is dark, even the sacred Menora.

עֲלֵי For the cadets, the nation's youth,
the front lines of battle, lions of rebellion:
In the face of the wicked, the spillers of their blood,
they breathed fire, poured out their wrath.

עַל By the rivers of blood and tears,
vengeance yet burned in their hearts.
In the battle of the ghetto, fearless and true,
their courage shone through, a beacon of valor.

עֲלֵי קְרוֹנוֹת, צְפוּפֵי אָדָם
אֲשֶׁר רֻפְּדוּ גָּפְרִית וָסִיד
צְחֵי צָמָא, כִּכְלוֹת נַפְשָׁם
צָעֲקוּ מַיִם וְאֵין מוֹשִׁיעַ.

עֲלֵי בָנוֹת, אֲשֶׁר עֻלְּפוּ
רְעִיּוֹת בְּנַפְשָׁן שָׁלְחוּ יָדָן
צ"ג הַטְּהוֹרוֹת יַחְדָּו נִסְפּוּ
וְלֹא חֻלַּל תֹּם כְּבוֹדָן.

עֲלֵי קְפוּאִים בִּשְׂדוֹת שְׁלָגִים
יְלָדִים רַכִּים בְּחֵיק אִמָּהוֹת
וְעַל קְדוֹשִׁים הַשּׁוֹאֲגִים
קְבוּרֵי חַיִּים מִתּוֹךְ בּוֹרוֹת.

עֲלֵי גְוִילִים הַמְחֻלָּלִים
בִּידֵי נָאצִים מְנַאֲצֵי אֵל
טְרוּפִים, קְרוּעִים וּמְגֹאָלִים
בֵּין אַשְׁפַּתּוֹת וְאֵין גּוֹאֵל.

עַל צַדִּיקִים, עֲנָוֵי עוֹלָם
נְדִיבֵי עָם, הוֹגֵי תוֹרָה
בְּתָאֵי רַעַל נֶחֱנַק קוֹלָם
נָפְלָה, כָּבְתָה הַמְּנוֹרָה.

עֲלֵי נֹעַר פִּרְחֵי הָעָם
חֲלוּצֵי קְרָב, כְּפִירֵי מְרִי
מוּל זֵדוֹנִים שׁוֹפְכֵי הַדָּם
הִשְׁתַּלְהֲבוּ רִשְׁפֵּי חֳרִי.

עַל נַהֲרוֹת דָּם וּבְכִי
נִקְמַת בְּרִית בַּלֵּב שְׁמוּרָה
בְּקְרָב גֵּטוֹ לְלֹא רֶהִי
נֶחְשַׂף הָעֹז טְמִיר גְּבוּרָה.

עֲלֵי For the sanctity of God and Nation,
in the name of the blood of the innocent,
they steeled themselves, and gave their lives,
they fought and fell, a heroic death.

עֲלֵה Arise, Hero, on an eternal mount,
as the everlasting light of the new dawn,
each drop of blood, each sacrifice,
will be remembered for all time.

עַל For the decimation of a nation we raise a dirge,
bound up in sorrow, cloaked in destruction.
Will hatred's shadow forever reign?
Will the struggle never end?

רְאֵה See, O God, how my skin has shriveled;
my heart is broken as my enemies rise up.
Hear my plea, provide a haven;
Save my soul from the murderous mob.

אֱלִי Lament, lament, my soul; cry out
and mourn, O Daughter of Israel,
in eulogy, in howls of grief,
for the flames have consumed Israel.

עֲלֵי קִדּוּשׁ הַשֵּׁם וָעָם
וְעַל נִקְמַת דַּם טְהוֹרִים
בְּתַעֲצוּמוֹת מָסְרוּ נַפְשָׁם
לָחֲמוּ, נָפְלוּ הַגִּבּוֹרִים.

עֲלֵה גִּבּוֹר עַל בָּמֳתֵי עַד
כְּנֵר תָּמִיד בְּהוֹד זָרְחִים
כָּל נֶטֶף דָּם, קָרְבַּן לְשַׁד
נִזְכֹּר עַד נֵצַח נְצָחִים.

עַל שֶׁבֶר עַם נִשָּׂא קִינָה
כְּבוּלֵי יָגוֹן, עֲטוּיֵי שׁוֹאָה
הֲלָנֶצַח תַּאֲפִיל שִׁנְאָה
וְלֹא תִפְרֹשׁ הַנְּגֹהָה?

רְאֵה, אֱלֹהִים, עוֹרִי צָפַד
נָפַל לִבִּי, שׂוֹנְאַי קָמִים
הַקְשִׁיבָה שַׁוְעִי, חִישָׁה מִפְלָט
הַצִּילָה נַפְשִׁי מֵאַנְשֵׁי דָמִים.

אֱלִי, אֱלִי, נַפְשִׁי, בְּכִי
וְזַעֲקִי, בַּת יִשְׂרָאֵל
מִסְפֵּד שְׂאִי וְהִתְיַפְּחִי
אָכְלָה הָאֵשׁ בְּיִשְׂרָאֵל.

In Memory of Our Six Million Martyrs Who Perished during 1939–1945
by Rabbi Abraham Rosenfeld

א Alas, how You have cast down the glory from our heads.
א Alas, how You have kept Your face hidden from us.
א Alas, how You have grown angry and refused to show compassion.

ב With a broken, heavy heart, on a day of fasting and commemoration,
ב we have come before You to eulogize and shed tears,
in elegies and wailing,
ב as we recall the martyrs of the Holocaust, 1939–1945.

ג You have smashed the glory of Jacob that You once loved.
ג You have cut down those men of stature and
laid low those who were once high.
ג You rendered our vines desolate and left our figs trees
to be ravaged.

ד Our bones stuck to our skin and flesh.
ד You abased our lives into the dirt.
ד Our souls have given out from sorrow and groaning.

ה The beloved ones, the pleasing ones, the honest and the innocent
ה were loaded up into cattle cars like sheep.
ה The heat was stifling and the doorways were sealed.

ו Pious individuals sat silent on the ground
ו asking what their sin was,
ו and why judgment was passed without any pity.

ז Recall the screams of the humble,
ז the shouts of the orphans, the lonely and abandoned,
ז the mocking of the wise, and their beloved students.

ח Soldiers, mighty heads of households,
ח murdered and pierced, they fell by the millions,
ח bringing shame and desolation upon the nations.

In Memory of Our Six Million Martyrs Who Perished during 1939–1945
by Rabbi Abraham Rosenfeld

אֵיכָה תִּפְאַרְתֵּנוּ מֵרָאשֵׁינוּ הִשְׁלַכְתָּ
אֵיכָה פָּנֶיךָ מִמֶּנּוּ הִסְתַּרְתָּ
אֵיכָה קָצַפְתָּ וְלֹא חָמַלְתָּ:

בְּלֵב נִשְׁבָּר וְנִדְכֶּה, בְּיוֹם צוֹם וַעֲצָרָה
בָּאנוּ לְפָנֶיךָ לִסְפֹּד וְלִבְכּוֹת בְּקִינָה וּבִילָלָה
בְּזָכְרֵנוּ אֶת קְדוֹשֵׁי הַשּׁוֹאָה תרצ״ט-תש״ה:

גְּאוֹן יַעֲקֹב אֲשֶׁר אָהַבְתָּ שִׁבַּרְתָּ.
גִּדַּעְתָּ רָמֵי הַקּוֹמָה, וְהַגְּבֹהִים הִשְׁפַּלְתָּ
גְּפָנֵנוּ לְשַׁמָּה וּתְאֵנָתֵנוּ לִקְצָפָה שַׂמְתָּ:

דָּבְקוּ עֲצָמֵינוּ לְעוֹרֵנוּ וּבְשָׂרֵנוּ
דַּכֹּה דִּכִּיתָ לָאָרֶץ חַיֵּינוּ
דָּלְפָה מִתּוּגָה וַאֲנָחָה נַפְשֵׁנוּ:

הַנֶּאֱהָבִים וְהַנְּעִימִים, הַיְשָׁרִים וְהַתְּמִימִים
הָטְעֲנוּ בִּקְרוֹנוֹת כִּכְבָשִׂים וּבְקָרִים
הַחֹם מְחַנֵּק, וְהַפְּתָחִים חֲתוּמִים:

וְתִיקִים יוֹשְׁבִים עַל הָאָרֶץ דּוֹמְמִים
וּמֶה הָיְתָה חַטָּאתָם, הֵם שׁוֹאֲלִים
וְלָמָּה נִגְזַר הַדִּין בְּלִי רַחֲמִים:

זְכוֹר תִּזְכֹּר אֶת צַעֲקַת הָעֲנָוִים
זַעֲקַת הַיְתוֹמִים הַגַּלְמוּדִים וְהַנֶּעֱזָבִים
וְלִזּוּל חֲכָמִים, וְתַלְמִידֵיהֶם הָאֲהוּבִים:

חֲיָלִים רָאשֵׁי בֵּית אָבוֹת גִּבּוֹרִים
חֲלָלִים וּמְדֻקָּרִים נָפְלוּ מִלְיוֹנִים
חֶרְפָּה וּמְשַׁמָּה הָיְתָה לַגּוֹיִם:

ט We nurtured and multiplied, but the cruel one destroyed them.
ט They tore our young like wolves to spill their blood.
ט Whoever plotted the slaughter of six million?

י Life has been lowered into the afterlife,
to the sounds of "Shema Yisrael" and "Ani Ma'amin."
י Their souls gave out as they were adorned with tallit and tefillin.
י May the murderers be shamed and embarrassed
and become non-existent.

כ Our remnants and hearts have given out over the ruin of our lot.
כ We all raise our voices in lament as half our nation was lost.
כ For the Holocaust was equal to the burning of the House of our God.

ל To Auschwitz, Buchenwald, Bergen-Belsen, Dachau,
Majdanek and Treblinka,
ל they were taken away and pressed into gas chambers,
and burnt in the flames of the furnaces in shame.
ל The holy martyrs fought and fell as heroes in the Warsaw Ghetto.

מ From every corner their dried blood screams.
מ When shall an end be put to these mortal dangers?
מ Till when must we eulogize the holy martyrs in bitter lamentations?

נ The Nazis disgraced our covenant and Torah.
נ Those who shame You, fell upon us, and we cry our hearts
out in fasting.
נ The crown of our heads has fallen, woe is our heritage.

ס The Torah scrolls were torn to pieces and defiled in their hands.
ס They scraped the flesh off our remnants,
and turned their skin into adornments.
ס Lament and don sackcloth, sing the praises of the martyrs
and their children.

ע Our eyes run with the blood of tears,
ע for the burning of the synagogues,
ע and the destruction of the schools and study halls.

פ They smashed our congregations and destroyed our communities.
פ Fear and trembling took hold of us.
פ Our faces were covered with shame in our time of trouble.

טַפֵּחְנוּ וְרִבִּינוּ, הָאַכְזָר כִּלָּם וַהֲשְׁמָם
טָרוֹף טָרְפוּ כִּזְאֵבִים לִשְׁפֹּךְ דָּמָם
טֶבַח שֵׁשׁ מֵאוֹת רִבּוֹא מִי זָמָם:

יָרְדוּ חַיִּים שְׁאוֹלָה, בִּשְׁמַע יִשְׂרָאֵל וּבַאֲנִי מַאֲמִין
יָצְאוּ נִשְׁמוֹתֵיהֶם מְעֻטָּרִין בְּטַלִּית וּתְפִלִּין
יֵבֹשׁוּ וְיִכָּלְמוּ וְיִהְיוּ כְאַיִן הָרוֹצְחִין:

כָּלָה שְׁאֵרֵנוּ וּלְבָבֵנוּ עַל שֶׁבֶר חֶלְקֵנוּ
כֻּלָּנוּ נוֹשְׂאִים קִינָה בְּאָבְדַן חֲצִי עַמֵּנוּ
כִּי שְׁקוּלָה הַשּׁוֹאָה כִּשְׂרֵפַת בֵּית אֱלֹהֵינוּ:

לְאוֹשְׁוִיץ בּוּכֶנְוַלְד, בֶּרְגֶן־בֶּלְזֶן, דַּאכַאוּ, מַיְדָנֶק וּטְרֶבְּלִינְקָה
לָקְחוּ וְהָדְחֲקוּ בְּחַדְרֵי גָז, וְנִשְׂרְפוּ בְּמוֹקְדוֹת הַכִּבְשָׁנִים בְּחֶרְפָּה
לָחֲמוּ הַקְּדוֹשִׁים הַטְּהוֹרִים, וְנָפְלוּ כַּגִּבּוֹרִים בְּגֵיטוֹ וַרְשָׁה:

מִכָּל פִּנָּה זוֹעֲקִים דְּמֵיהֶם הַקְּרוּשִׁים
מָתַי יָבוֹא קֵץ לַפְּגָעִים הָאֲנוּשִׁים
מִסְפֵּד מַר וְקִינָה שְׂאוּ עַל הַקְּדוֹשִׁים:

נָאֲצוּ הַנּוֹאֲצִים אֶת הַבְּרִית וְאֶת תּוֹרָתֵנוּ
נָפְלוּ עָלֵינוּ מְחָרְפֶיךָ, וַנִּבְכֶּה בַּצּוֹם נַפְשֵׁנוּ
נָפְלָה עֲטֶרֶת רֹאשֵׁנוּ, אוֹי נָא לְנַחֲלָתֵנוּ:

סִפְרֵי תוֹרָה לִגְזָרִים קָרְעוּ וְטִמְּאוּ בִּידֵיהֶם
סָרְקוּ בְּשַׂר שְׁאֵרֵינוּ, וְעוֹרָם הָפְכוּ לְקִשּׁוּטֵיהֶם
סִפְדוּ וְחִגְרוּ שַׂק, וְהֵילִילוּ עֲלֵיהֶם וְעַל טַפֵּיהֶם:

עֵינֵינוּ זוֹלְגוֹת דָּם דְּמָעוֹת
עַל שְׂרֵפַת בָּתֵּי כְנֵסִיּוֹת
עַל הֲרִיסַת יְשִׁיבוֹת וּבָתֵּי מִדְרָשׁוֹת:

פָּרְצוּ קְהִלּוֹתֵינוּ וְהָרְסוּ עֲדָתֵנוּ
פַּחַד קְרָאָנוּ וּרְעָדָה אֲחָזָתְנוּ
פָּנֵינוּ כִּסְּתָה כְלִמָּה בְּצָרוֹתֵינוּ:

צ They escaped to the wilderness in a time of want and famine.
צ Those modest by nature tried their hand,
צ but their voices were heard like the screams by the Sea of Reeds.

ק Relatives, friends, beloved ones, the pious and honest,
ק the holy and pure, they shine with the brilliance of heaven.
ק Receive them and hide them in the folds of Your wings forever.

ר O compassionate One, recall the remnants of Your heritage with pity.
ר Master of the universe, remove all worry and sorrow
from the heart of Your nation.
ר In Your anger, uproot the evil of the nations of the world
and those who hate Israel.

ש Free the captives and break open the prison for those who are bound.
ש Anoint us with joyous ointment in place of mourning.
ש Bring peace and calm to us and our land.

ת Raise up our glory and hasten our redemption in our days.
ת May the plains of Jordan rejoice and may our
State of Israel bloom like a desert rose.
ת Bless us by the grace of Abraham, Isaac and Jacob, our forefathers.

The service continues with "Ashrei" on page 224.

צִיָּה עָרְקוּ בְּחֶסֶר וּבְכָפָן
צְנוּעוֹת בְּנַפְשָׁן שָׁלְחוּ יָדָן
צְעָקָה בְּיַם סוּף נִשְׁמַע קוֹלָן:

קְרוֹבִים וִידִידִים חֲבִיבִים, חֲסִידִים וִישָׁרִים
קְדוֹשִׁים וּטְהוֹרִים, כְּזֹהַר הָרָקִיעַ מַזְהִירִים
קַבְּלֵם וְהַסְתִּירֵם בְּסֵתֶר כְּנָפֶיךָ לְעוֹלָמִים:

רַחוּם, זְכֹר בְּרַחֲמֶיךָ אֶת שְׂרִידֵי נַחֲלָתֶךָ
רִבּוֹן הָעוֹלָמִים, הָסֵר דְּאָגָה וְתוּגָה מֵעַמֶּךָ
רִשְׁעַת הַגּוֹיִם וְשׂוֹנְאֵי יִשְׂרָאֵל תְּעַקֵּר בְּזַעְמֶךָ:

שְׁבוּיִם הַדְרֵר, וּפְקַח קוֹחַ לַאֲסוּרֵנוּ
שֶׁמֶן שָׂשׂוֹן תַּחַת אֵבֶל תְּעַטְּרֵנוּ
שָׁלוֹם וְשַׁלְוָה תָּשִׂים לָנוּ וּלְאַרְצֵנוּ:

תָּרִים קַרְנֵנוּ וְתָחִישׁ גְּאֻלָּתֵנוּ בִּמְהֵרָה בְיָמֵינוּ
תָּגֵל עֲרָבָה וְתִפְרַח כַּחֲבַצֶּלֶת יִשְׂרָאֵל מְדִינָתֵנוּ
תְּבָרְכֵנוּ בְּבִרְכַּת אַבְרָהָם יִצְחָק וְיַעֲקֹב אֲבוֹתֵינוּ:

The service continues with אַשְׁרֵי *on page 225.*

סדר ברכות

GIVING THANKS

THE MEAL AND ITS BLESSINGS

On washing hands before eating bread:

Blessed are You, Lord our God, King of the Universe,
who has made us holy through His commandments,
and has commanded us about washing hands.

Before eating bread:

Blessed are You, Lord our God, King of the Universe,
who brings forth bread from the earth.

BIRKAT HAMAZON / GRACE AFTER MEALS

On days when Taḥanun is said:

עַל־נַהֲרוֹת By the rivers of Babylon we sat and wept as we remembered Zion. There on the willow trees we hung up our harps, for there our captors asked us for songs, our tormentors, for amusement, said: "Sing us one of the songs of Zion!" How can we sing the Lord's song on foreign soil? If I forget you, Jerusalem, may my right hand forget its skill. May my tongue cling to the roof of my mouth if I do not remember you, if I do not set Jerusalem above my highest joy. Remember, Lord, what the Edomites did on the day Jerusalem fell. They said, "Tear it down, tear it down to its very foundations!" Daughter of Babylon, doomed to destruction, happy is he who repays you for what you have done to us, who seizes your infants and dashes them against the rocks. *Ps. 137*

On Shabbat and on days when Taḥanun is omitted (see list on page 194):

שִׁיר הַמַּעֲלוֹת A song of ascents. When the Lord brought back the exiles of Zion we were like people who dream. Then were our mouths filled with laughter, and our tongues with songs of joy. Then was it said among the nations, "The Lord has done great things for them." The Lord did do great things for us and we rejoiced. Bring back our exiles, Lord, like *Ps. 126*

---

special opportunity, when we sit together in a group, to have a *zimmun* – a calling together of everyone who has eaten in the same place. Rabbi S.R. Hirsch suggests one possible rationale: When we recognize Hashem as the Provider, Preserver, Sustainer of us all, whose goodness enables us all to live and remain alive, we acknowledge that He is near to all of us, and so there is no reason to be envious of another's wealth. *Birkat HaMazon* is thus the great equalizer, reminding us that Hashem gives to each of us what is good and beneficial for us at any particular time. It makes us thankful, gives us perspective, and draws us closer to one another.

סדר סעודה וברכותיה

On washing hands before eating bread:

בָּרוּךְ אַתָּה יהוה אֱלֹהֵינוּ מֶלֶךְ הָעוֹלָם
אֲשֶׁר קִדְּשָׁנוּ בְּמִצְוֹתָיו וְצִוָּנוּ עַל נְטִילַת יָדָיִם.

Before eating bread:

בָּרוּךְ אַתָּה יהוה אֱלֹהֵינוּ מֶלֶךְ הָעוֹלָם
הַמּוֹצִיא לֶחֶם מִן הָאָרֶץ.

ברכת המזון

On days when תחנון *is said:*

תהלים קלז עַל־נַהֲרוֹת בָּבֶל, שָׁם יָשַׁבְנוּ גַּם־בָּכִינוּ, בְּזָכְרֵנוּ אֶת־צִיּוֹן: עַל־עֲרָבִים בְּתוֹכָהּ תָּלִינוּ כִּנֹּרוֹתֵינוּ: כִּי שָׁם שְׁאֵלוּנוּ שׁוֹבֵינוּ דִּבְרֵי־שִׁיר וְתוֹלָלֵינוּ שִׂמְחָה, שִׁירוּ לָנוּ מִשִּׁיר צִיּוֹן: אֵיךְ נָשִׁיר אֶת־שִׁיר־יהוה עַל אַדְמַת נֵכָר: אִם־אֶשְׁכָּחֵךְ יְרוּשָׁלָםִ, תִּשְׁכַּח יְמִינִי: תִּדְבַּק לְשׁוֹנִי לְחִכִּי אִם־לֹא אֶזְכְּרֵכִי, אִם־לֹא אַעֲלֶה אֶת־יְרוּשָׁלַםִ עַל רֹאשׁ שִׂמְחָתִי: זְכֹר יהוה לִבְנֵי אֱדוֹם אֵת יוֹם יְרוּשָׁלָםִ, הָאֹמְרִים עָרוּ עָרוּ עַד הַיְסוֹד בָּהּ: בַּת־בָּבֶל הַשְּׁדוּדָה, אַשְׁרֵי שֶׁיְשַׁלֶּם־לָךְ אֶת־גְּמוּלֵךְ שֶׁגָּמַלְתְּ לָנוּ: אַשְׁרֵי שֶׁיֹּאחֵז, וְנִפֵּץ אֶת־עֹלָלַיִךְ אֶל־הַסָּלַע:

On שבת *and on days when* תחנון *is omitted (see list on page 195):*

תהלים קכו שִׁיר הַמַּעֲלוֹת, בְּשׁוּב יהוה אֶת־שִׁיבַת צִיּוֹן, הָיִינוּ כְּחֹלְמִים: אָז יִמָּלֵא שְׂחוֹק פִּינוּ וּלְשׁוֹנֵנוּ רִנָּה, אָז יֹאמְרוּ בַגּוֹיִם הִגְדִּיל יהוה לַעֲשׂוֹת עִם־אֵלֶּה: הִגְדִּיל יהוה לַעֲשׂוֹת עִמָּנוּ, הָיִינוּ שְׂמֵחִים: שׁוּבָה יהוה

INTRODUCTION TO BIRKAT HAMAZON

The Torah mandated that we say a blessing after our meal, apparently because it is precisely when our stomachs are full that we have a tendency to forget where the meal ultimately came from (*Devarim* 8:12–18). We tend to be very thankful at those moments when we are in need; we tend to forget to be thankful when the need has passed. *Berakhot* are a reminder not to forget.

In this particular mitzva there is also a

streams in a dry land. May those who sowed in tears, reap in joy. May one who goes out weeping, carrying a bag of seed, come back with songs of joy, carrying his sheaves.

Some say:

תְּהִלַּת My mouth shall speak the praise of God, and all creatures shall bless *Ps. 145*
His holy name for ever and all time. We will bless God now and for ever. *Ps. 115*
Halleluya! Thank the LORD for He is good; His loving-kindness is for *Ps. 136*
ever. Who can tell of the LORD's mighty acts and make all His praise *Ps. 106*
be heard?

ZIMMUN / INVITATION

When three or more men say Birkat HaMazon together, the following zimmun is said. When three or more women say Birkat HaMazon, substitute "Friends" for "Gentlemen." The leader should ask permission from those with precedence to lead the Birkat HaMazon.

Leader Gentlemen, let us say grace.

Others May the name of the LORD be blessed from now and for ever. *Ps. 113*

Leader May the name of the LORD be blessed from now and for ever.
With your permission, (my father and teacher / my mother and teacher / the Kohanim present / our teacher the Rabbi / the master of this house / the mistress of this house)
my masters and teachers,
let us bless (*in a minyan:* our God,) the One
from whose food we have eaten.

Others Blessed be (*in a minyan:* our God,) the One
from whose food we have eaten, and by whose goodness we live.

**People present who have not taken part in the meal say:*
*Blessed be (*in a minyan:* our God,) the One
whose name is continually blessed for ever and all time.

Leader Blessed be (*in a minyan:* our God,) the One
from whose food we have eaten, and by whose goodness we live.
Blessed be He, and blessed be His name.

אֶת־שְׁבִיתֵנוּ, כַּאֲפִיקִים בַּנֶּגֶב: הַזֹּרְעִים בְּדִמְעָה בְּרִנָּה יִקְצֹרוּ: הָלוֹךְ יֵלֵךְ וּבָכֹה נֹשֵׂא מֶשֶׁךְ־הַזָּרַע, בֹּא־יָבֹא בְרִנָּה נֹשֵׂא אֲלֻמֹּתָיו:

Some say:

תְּהִלַּת יהוה יְדַבֶּר פִּי, וִיבָרֵךְ כָּל־בָּשָׂר שֵׁם קָדְשׁוֹ לְעוֹלָם וָעֶד: וַאֲנַחְנוּ תהלים קמה תהלים קטו
נְבָרֵךְ יָהּ מֵעַתָּה וְעַד־עוֹלָם, הַלְלוּיָהּ: הוֹדוּ לַיהוה כִּי־טוֹב, כִּי לְעוֹלָם תהלים קלו
חַסְדּוֹ: מִי יְמַלֵּל גְּבוּרוֹת יהוה, יַשְׁמִיעַ כָּל־תְּהִלָּתוֹ: תהלים קו

סדר הזימון

When three or more men say ברכת המזון *together, the following* זימון *is said.*
When three or more women say ברכת המזון*, substitute* חֲבֵרוֹתַי *for* רַבּוֹתַי.
The leader should ask permission from those with precedence to lead the ברכת המזון.

Leader רַבּוֹתַי, נְבָרֵךְ.

Others יְהִי שֵׁם יהוה מְבֹרָךְ מֵעַתָּה וְעַד־עוֹלָם: תהלים קיג

Leader יְהִי שֵׁם יהוה מְבֹרָךְ מֵעַתָּה וְעַד־עוֹלָם:
בִּרְשׁוּת (אָבִי מוֹרִי / אִמִּי מוֹרָתִי / כֹּהֲנִים / מוֹרֵנוּ הָרַב / בַּעַל הַבַּיִת הַזֶּה / בַּעֲלַת הַבַּיִת הַזֶּה)
מָרָנָן וְרַבָּנָן וְרַבּוֹתַי
נְבָרֵךְ (במנין: אֱלֹהֵינוּ) שֶׁאָכַלְנוּ מִשֶּׁלּוֹ.

Others בָּרוּךְ (במנין: אֱלֹהֵינוּ) שֶׁאָכַלְנוּ מִשֶּׁלּוֹ וּבְטוּבוֹ חָיִינוּ.

**People present who have not taken part in the meal say:*
*בָּרוּךְ (במנין: אֱלֹהֵינוּ) וּמְבֹרָךְ שְׁמוֹ תָּמִיד לְעוֹלָם וָעֶד.

Leader בָּרוּךְ (במנין: אֱלֹהֵינוּ) שֶׁאָכַלְנוּ מִשֶּׁלּוֹ וּבְטוּבוֹ חָיִינוּ.
בָּרוּךְ הוּא וּבָרוּךְ שְׁמוֹ.

BLESSING OF NOURISHMENT

בָּרוּךְ Blessed are You, LORD our God, King of the Universe,
who in His goodness feeds the whole world
with grace, kindness and compassion.[B]
He gives food to all living things,
for His kindness is for ever.
Because of His continual great goodness,
we have never lacked food,
nor may we ever lack it,[A]
for the sake of His great name.
For He is God who feeds and sustains all,
does good to all,
and prepares food for all creatures He has created.
Blessed are You, LORD,
who feeds all.[A]

BLESSING OF LAND

נוֹדֶה We thank You,[A] LORD our God,
for having granted as a heritage to our ancestors
a desirable, good and spacious land;
for bringing us out, LORD our God, from the land of Egypt,
freeing us from the house of slavery;

ANI TEFILLA • אני תפילה

לֹא חָסַר לָנוּ וְאַל יֶחְסַר לָנוּ מָזוֹן לְעוֹלָם וָעֶד – *We have never lacked food, nor may we ever lack it.* The premise of the blessing is that Hashem provides sufficient food for the entire world. As such, the fact that some people do not have enough to eat is not a failure of God, but the failure of man.

הַזָּן אֶת הַכֹּל – *Who feeds all.* There is a motif word that is repeated six times in this paragraph. What is the word and what might be the significance?

נוֹדֶה לְּךָ – *We thank You.* There is one word that appears in this blessing no less than ten times! What is the word and what is its significance?

ברכת הזן

בָּרוּךְ אַתָּה יהוה אֱלֹהֵינוּ מֶלֶךְ הָעוֹלָם
הַזָּן אֶת הָעוֹלָם כֻּלּוֹ בְּטוּבוֹ
בְּחֵן בְּחֶסֶד וּבְרַחֲמִים[ב]
הוּא נוֹתֵן לֶחֶם לְכָל בָּשָׂר
כִּי לְעוֹלָם חַסְדּוֹ.
וּבְטוּבוֹ הַגָּדוֹל, תָּמִיד לֹא חָסַר לָנוּ
וְאַל יֶחְסַר לָנוּ מָזוֹן לְעוֹלָם וָעֶד[א]
בַּעֲבוּר שְׁמוֹ הַגָּדוֹל.
כִּי הוּא אֵל זָן וּמְפַרְנֵס לַכֹּל וּמֵטִיב לַכֹּל
וּמֵכִין מָזוֹן לְכָל בְּרִיּוֹתָיו אֲשֶׁר בָּרָא.
בָּרוּךְ אַתָּה יהוה, הַזָּן אֶת הַכֹּל.[א]

ברכת הארץ

נוֹדֶה לְּךָ,[א] יהוה אֱלֹהֵינוּ
עַל שֶׁהִנְחַלְתָּ לַאֲבוֹתֵינוּ אֶרֶץ חֶמְדָּה טוֹבָה וּרְחָבָה
וְעַל שֶׁהוֹצֵאתָנוּ יהוה אֱלֹהֵינוּ מֵאֶרֶץ מִצְרַיִם
וּפְדִיתָנוּ מִבֵּית עֲבָדִים

BIUR TEFILLA • ביאור תפילה

בְּחֵן בְּחֶסֶד וּבְרַחֲמִים – *With grace, kindness and compassion.* What might each of these three terms represent? Where does each manifest itself in your life?

The terms might refer to the different kinds of support that one needs from Hashem at different points in one's life (Rabbi Yosef Albo).

Alternatively, they might refer to different kinds of help depending on the merits of the receiver (Rabbi S.R. Hirsch).

Alternatively, they might refer to different people's economic status (*Arukh HaShulḥan*).

for Your covenant which You sealed in our flesh;
for Your Torah which You taught us;
for Your laws which You made known to us;
for the life, grace and kindness You have bestowed on us;
and for the food by which You continually feed and sustain us,
every day, every season, every hour.
For all this, LORD our God, we thank and bless You.
May Your name be blessed continually
by the mouth of all that lives,
for ever and all time –
for so it is written:
"You will eat and be satisfied, *Deut. 8*
then you shall bless the LORD your God
for the good land He has given you."
Blessed are You, LORD,
for the land and for the food.[I]

BLESSING FOR JERUSALEM

רַחֶם נָא Have compassion, please, LORD our God,
on Israel Your people,[B]
on Jerusalem Your city,
on Zion the dwelling place of Your glory,
on the royal house of David Your anointed,
and on the great and holy House that bears Your name.

(a) The Gemara (*Berakhot* 49a) says that the ending or signature of a blessing may not have two different themes in it. Yet here there are two mentioned. How might they be seen as the same?

(b) What might be the connection between those two things and all of the others? For which should we be grateful?

What reason can you suggest for the order of the eight things that are listed for which we should be grateful?

BIUR TEFILLA • ביאור תפילה

רַחֵם נָא, יהוה אֱלֹהֵינוּ, עַל יִשְׂרָאֵל עַמֶּךָ – *Have compassion, please, LORD our God, on Israel Your people.* Commentators have tried to explain the connection between the requests for the restoration of the *Beit HaMikdash* and the request that our food and material needs be provided. One suggestion cites the Gemara (*Ḥagiga* 27a) which says that the Altar in the *Beit*

This **BIUR TEFILLA** *continues on page 985.*

וְעַל בְּרִיתְךָ שֶׁחָתַמְתָּ בִּבְשָׂרֵנוּ
וְעַל תּוֹרָתְךָ שֶׁלִּמַּדְתָּנוּ
וְעַל חֻקֶּיךָ שֶׁהוֹדַעְתָּנוּ
וְעַל חַיִּים חֵן וָחֶסֶד שֶׁחוֹנַנְתָּנוּ
וְעַל אֲכִילַת מָזוֹן שָׁאַתָּה זָן וּמְפַרְנֵס אוֹתָנוּ תָּמִיד
בְּכָל יוֹם וּבְכָל עֵת וּבְכָל שָׁעָה.
וְעַל הַכֹּל, יהוה אֱלֹהֵינוּ
אֲנַחְנוּ מוֹדִים לָךְ וּמְבָרְכִים אוֹתָךְ
יִתְבָּרַךְ שִׁמְךָ בְּפִי כָּל חַי תָּמִיד לְעוֹלָם וָעֶד
כַּכָּתוּב:
דברים ח וְאָכַלְתָּ וְשָׂבָעְתָּ, וּבֵרַכְתָּ אֶת־יהוה אֱלֹהֶיךָ
עַל־הָאָרֶץ הַטֹּבָה אֲשֶׁר נָתַן־לָךְ:
בָּרוּךְ אַתָּה יהוה, עַל הָאָרֶץ וְעַל הַמָּזוֹן.[ע]

ברכת ירושלים

רַחֵם נָא, יהוה אֱלֹהֵינוּ
עַל יִשְׂרָאֵל עַמֶּךָ[ב]
וְעַל יְרוּשָׁלַיִם עִירֶךָ
וְעַל צִיּוֹן מִשְׁכַּן כְּבוֹדֶךָ
וְעַל מַלְכוּת בֵּית דָּוִד מְשִׁיחֶךָ
וְעַל הַבַּיִת הַגָּדוֹל וְהַקָּדוֹשׁ שֶׁנִּקְרָא שִׁמְךָ עָלָיו.

IYUN TEFILLA • עיון תפילה

עַל הָאָרֶץ וְעַל הַמָּזוֹן – *For the land and for the food*. The blessing enumerates a number of things for which we should be grateful: the Land, the Exodus, the covenant represented by Brit Mila, the Torah, the laws, the life, favor and *ḥesed* that Hashem bestowed upon us, our never-ending supply of food, and for everything. Yet the blessing's signature relates only to the Land and food.

Our God, our Father,
tend us, feed us, sustain us and support us,
relieve us and send us relief,
LORD our God, swiftly from all our troubles.
Please, LORD our God, do not make us dependent
on the gifts or loans of other people,
but only on Your full, open, holy and generous hand
so that we may suffer neither shame nor humiliation
for ever and all time.

On Shabbat, say:

רְצֵה Favor and strengthen us, LORD our God,
through Your commandments,
especially through the commandment of the seventh day,
this great and holy Sabbath.
For it is, for You, a great and holy day.
On it we cease work and rest in love
in accord with Your will's commandment.
May it be Your will, LORD our God,
to grant us rest without distress, grief, or lament on our day of rest.
May You show us the consolation of Zion Your city,
and the rebuilding of Jerusalem Your holy city,
for You are the Master of salvation and consolation.

On Rosh Ḥodesh, say:

אֱלֹהֵינוּ Our God and God of our ancestors,
may there rise, come, reach, appear,
be favored, heard, regarded and remembered before You,
our recollection and remembrance,
as well as the remembrance of our ancestors,
and of the Messiah son of David Your servant,
and of Jerusalem Your holy city,
and of all Your people the house of Israel –

---

that it is because one has guests at one's table. How does this explain the Gemara's statement?

Can you suggest another connection between the themes of the *Beit HaMikdash* and the request for food?

אֱלֹהֵינוּ, אָבִינוּ
רְעֵנוּ, זוּנֵנוּ, פַּרְנְסֵנוּ וְכַלְכְּלֵנוּ
וְהַרְוִיחֵנוּ, וְהַרְוַח לָנוּ יהוה אֱלֹהֵינוּ מְהֵרָה מִכָּל צָרוֹתֵינוּ.
וְנָא אַל תַּצְרִיכֵנוּ, יהוה אֱלֹהֵינוּ
לֹא לִידֵי מַתְּנַת בָּשָׂר וָדָם וְלֹא לִידֵי הַלְוָאָתָם
כִּי אִם לְיָדְךָ הַמְּלֵאָה, הַפְּתוּחָה, הַקְּדוֹשָׁה וְהָרְחָבָה
שֶׁלֹּא נֵבוֹשׁ וְלֹא נִכָּלֵם לְעוֹלָם וָעֶד.

On שבת*, say:*

רְצֵה וְהַחֲלִיצֵנוּ, יהוה אֱלֹהֵינוּ, בְּמִצְוֹתֶיךָ
וּבְמִצְוַת יוֹם הַשְּׁבִיעִי הַשַּׁבָּת הַגָּדוֹל וְהַקָּדוֹשׁ הַזֶּה
כִּי יוֹם זֶה גָּדוֹל וְקָדוֹשׁ הוּא לְפָנֶיךָ
לִשְׁבָּת בּוֹ, וְלָנוּחַ בּוֹ בְּאַהֲבָה כְּמִצְוַת רְצוֹנֶךָ
וּבִרְצוֹנְךָ הָנִיחַ לָנוּ, יהוה אֱלֹהֵינוּ
שֶׁלֹּא תְהֵא צָרָה וְיָגוֹן וַאֲנָחָה בְּיוֹם מְנוּחָתֵנוּ
וְהַרְאֵנוּ, יהוה אֱלֹהֵינוּ, בְּנֶחָמַת צִיּוֹן עִירֶךָ
וּבְבִנְיַן יְרוּשָׁלַיִם עִיר קָדְשֶׁךָ
כִּי אַתָּה הוּא בַּעַל הַיְשׁוּעוֹת וּבַעַל הַנֶּחָמוֹת.

On ראש חודש*, say:*

אֱלֹהֵינוּ וֵאלֹהֵי אֲבוֹתֵינוּ
יַעֲלֶה וְיָבוֹא וְיַגִּיעַ, וְיֵרָאֶה וְיֵרָצֶה וְיִשָּׁמַע
וְיִפָּקֵד וְיִזָּכֵר זִכְרוֹנֵנוּ וּפִקְדוֹנֵנוּ
וְזִכְרוֹן אֲבוֹתֵינוּ
וְזִכְרוֹן מָשִׁיחַ בֶּן דָּוִד עַבְדֶּךָ
וְזִכְרוֹן יְרוּשָׁלַיִם עִיר קָדְשֶׁךָ
וְזִכְרוֹן כָּל עַמְּךָ בֵּית יִשְׂרָאֵל

HaMikdash atoned for the sins of mankind but, in its absence, the table where a person eats has the same impact. How might this connection be understood? Rashi suggests

for deliverance and well-being,
grace, loving-kindness and compassion,
life and peace, on this day of Rosh Ḥodesh.
On it remember us, LORD our God, for good;
recollect us for blessing, and deliver us for life.
In accord with Your promise of salvation and compassion,
spare us and be gracious to us;
have compassion on us and deliver us,
for our eyes are turned to You because You are God,
gracious and compassionate.

וּבְנֵה And may Jerusalem the holy city be rebuilt soon, in our time.
Blessed are You, LORD, who in His compassion
will rebuild Jerusalem. Amen.[B]

BLESSING OF GOD'S GOODNESS

בָּרוּךְ Blessed are You, LORD our God, King of the Universe –
God our Father, our King, our Sovereign,
our Creator, our Redeemer, our Maker,
our Holy One, the Holy One of Jacob.
He is our Shepherd, Israel's Shepherd,
the good King who does good to all.
Every day He has done, is doing, and will do good to us.[B]
He has acted, is acting, and will always act kindly toward us for ever,
granting us grace, kindness and compassion,
relief and rescue, prosperity, blessing, redemption and comfort,
sustenance and support, compassion, life, peace and all good things,
and of all good things may He never let us lack.[B]

---

while the third blessing about the rebuilding of Yerushalayim is in the future tense (Rabbi Munk). Here, we refer to Hashem's goodness toward us in all three tenses.

וּמִכָּל טוּב לְעוֹלָם אַל יְחַסְּרֵנוּ – *And of all good things may He never let us lack.* This is the end of the fourth blessing which is why it is appropriate to answer Amen when it is recited in a group. Despite its length, it does not end in the formula of *Barukh ata* because the entire blessing consists of one theme, which is the criteria for having only one blessing formula at the beginning (Rashi on *Berakhot* 49a).

לְפָנֶיךָ, לִפְלֵיטָה לְטוֹבָה, לְחֵן וּלְחֶסֶד וּלְרַחֲמִים
לְחַיִּים וּלְשָׁלוֹם בְּיוֹם רֹאשׁ הַחֹדֶשׁ הַזֶּה.
זָכְרֵנוּ יהוה אֱלֹהֵינוּ בּוֹ לְטוֹבָה
וּפָקְדֵנוּ בוֹ לִבְרָכָה, וְהוֹשִׁיעֵנוּ בוֹ לְחַיִּים.
וּבִדְבַר יְשׁוּעָה וְרַחֲמִים, חוּס וְחָנֵּנוּ וְרַחֵם עָלֵינוּ, וְהוֹשִׁיעֵנוּ
כִּי אֵלֶיךָ עֵינֵינוּ, כִּי אֵל חַנּוּן וְרַחוּם אָתָּה.

וּבְנֵה יְרוּשָׁלַיִם עִיר הַקֹּדֶשׁ בִּמְהֵרָה בְיָמֵינוּ.
בָּרוּךְ אַתָּה יהוה, בּוֹנֵה בְרַחֲמָיו יְרוּשָׁלָיִם, אָמֵן.[ב]

ברכת הטוב והמטיב

בָּרוּךְ אַתָּה יהוה אֱלֹהֵינוּ מֶלֶךְ הָעוֹלָם
הָאֵל אָבִינוּ, מַלְכֵּנוּ, אַדִּירֵנוּ
בּוֹרְאֵנוּ, גּוֹאֲלֵנוּ, יוֹצְרֵנוּ, קְדוֹשֵׁנוּ, קְדוֹשׁ יַעֲקֹב
רוֹעֵנוּ, רוֹעֵה יִשְׂרָאֵל, הַמֶּלֶךְ הַטּוֹב וְהַמֵּטִיב לַכֹּל
שֶׁבְּכָל יוֹם וָיוֹם
הוּא הֵטִיב, הוּא מֵטִיב, הוּא יֵיטִיב לָנוּ[ב]
הוּא גְמָלָנוּ, הוּא גוֹמְלֵנוּ, הוּא יִגְמְלֵנוּ לָעַד
לְחֵן וּלְחֶסֶד וּלְרַחֲמִים, וּלְרֶוַח, הַצָּלָה וְהַצְלָחָה
בְּרָכָה וִישׁוּעָה, נֶחָמָה, פַּרְנָסָה וְכַלְכָּלָה
וְרַחֲמִים וְחַיִּים וְשָׁלוֹם וְכָל טוֹב
וּמִכָּל טוּב לְעוֹלָם אַל יְחַסְּרֵנוּ.[ב]

BIUR TEFILLA • ביאור תפילה

אָמֵן – *Amen.* Answering "Amen" to one's own blessing is rare. In this case it serves as a marker to separate the end of the three blessings which are from the Torah and the beginning of the fourth blessing which is *deRabbanan*, instituted by the Rabbis.

הוּא הֵטִיב, הוּא מֵטִיב, הוּא יֵיטִיב לָנוּ – *He has done, is doing, and will do good to us.* The first blessing is in the present tense, thanking Hashem for the food which He gives us; the second is in the past, thanking Hashem for the gifts of the Land;

ADDITIONAL REQUESTS

הָרַחֲמָן May the Compassionate One[A]
reign over us for ever and all time.

May the Compassionate One
be blessed in heaven and on earth.

May the Compassionate One
be praised from generation to generation,
be glorified by us to all eternity,
and honored among us for ever and all time.

May the Compassionate One
grant us an honorable livelihood.

May the Compassionate One
break the yoke from our neck and lead us upright to our land.

May the Compassionate One
send us many blessings to this house
and this table at which we have eaten.

May the Compassionate One
send us Elijah the prophet –
may he be remembered for good –
to bring us good tidings of salvation and consolation.

May the Compassionate One
bless the State of Israel, first flowering of our redemption.

May the Compassionate One
bless the members of Israel's Defense Forces,
who stand guard over our land.

---

is that since one's table is like an altar where atonement is granted, then the table is a particularly good place to have one's prayers heard, assuming one conducted oneself appropriately at the meal (*Piskei Teshuvot* 189:2).

What prayer would you like to add today?

בקשות נוספות

הָרַחֲמָן[א] הוּא יִמְלֹךְ עָלֵינוּ לְעוֹלָם וָעֶד.

הָרַחֲמָן הוּא יִתְבָּרַךְ בַּשָּׁמַיִם וּבָאָרֶץ.

הָרַחֲמָן הוּא יִשְׁתַּבַּח לְדוֹר דּוֹרִים
וְיִתְפָּאַר בָּנוּ לָעַד וּלְנֵצַח נְצָחִים
וְיִתְהַדַּר בָּנוּ לָעַד וּלְעוֹלְמֵי עוֹלָמִים.

הָרַחֲמָן הוּא יְפַרְנְסֵנוּ בְּכָבוֹד.

הָרַחֲמָן הוּא יִשְׁבֹּר עֻלֵּנוּ מֵעַל צַוָּארֵנוּ
וְהוּא יוֹלִיכֵנוּ קוֹמְמִיּוּת לְאַרְצֵנוּ.

הָרַחֲמָן הוּא יִשְׁלַח לָנוּ בְּרָכָה מְרֻבָּה בַּבַּיִת הַזֶּה
וְעַל שֻׁלְחָן זֶה שֶׁאָכַלְנוּ עָלָיו.

הָרַחֲמָן הוּא יִשְׁלַח לָנוּ אֶת אֵלִיָּהוּ הַנָּבִיא זָכוּר לַטּוֹב
וִיבַשֶּׂר לָנוּ בְּשׂוֹרוֹת טוֹבוֹת יְשׁוּעוֹת וְנֶחָמוֹת.

הָרַחֲמָן הוּא יְבָרֵךְ אֶת מְדִינַת יִשְׂרָאֵל
רֵאשִׁית צְמִיחַת גְּאֻלָּתֵנוּ.

הָרַחֲמָן הוּא יְבָרֵךְ אֶת חַיָּלֵי צְבָא הַהֲגָנָה לְיִשְׂרָאֵל
הָעוֹמְדִים עַל מִשְׁמַר אַרְצֵנוּ.

ANI TEFILLA • אני תפילה

הָרַחֲמָן – *The Compassionate One*. This series of eight short requests are a later addition but they make room for one to add one's own related personal requests. The rationale

A guest says:

יְהִי רָצוֹן May it be Your will that the master of this house shall not suffer shame in this world, nor humiliation in the World to Come. May all he owns prosper greatly, and may his and our possessions be successful and close to hand. Let not the Accuser hold sway over his deeds or ours, and may no thought of sin, iniquity or transgression enter him or us from now and for evermore.

הָרַחֲמָן May the Compassionate One bless –

When eating at one's own table, say (include the words in parentheses that apply):
me, (my wife/husband, / my father, my teacher / my mother, my teacher/ my children,) and all that is mine,

A guest at someone else's table says (include the words in parentheses that apply):
the master of this house, him (and his wife, the mistress of this house / and his children,) and all that is his,

Children at their parents' table say (include the words in parentheses that apply):
my father, my teacher, (master of this house,) and my mother, my teacher, (mistress of this house,) them, their household, their children, and all that is theirs.

For all other guests, add:
and all the diners here,

אוֹתָנוּ – together with us and all that is ours.
Just as our forefathers
Abraham, Isaac and Jacob were blessed in all, from all, with all,[1]
so may He bless all of us together
with a complete blessing,
and let us say: Amen.

---

eaten from *everything*" (27:33); "for Hashem has been kind to me [Yaakov] and I have *everything* [I need]" (33:11). From here the Gemara (*Bava Batra* 17a) concludes that the *yetzer hara*, the evil inclination, had no power over the *Avot*. **What do you think the Gemara means by this? What is a lesson I can take away from here whenever I say this?**

A guest says:

יְהִי רָצוֹן שֶׁלֹּא יֵבוֹשׁ בַּעַל הַבַּיִת בָּעוֹלָם הַזֶּה, וְלֹא יִכָּלֵם לָעוֹלָם הַבָּא, וְיַצְלִיחַ מְאֹד בְּכָל נְכָסָיו, וְיִהְיוּ נְכָסָיו וּנְכָסֵינוּ מֻצְלָחִים וּקְרוֹבִים לָעִיר, וְאַל יִשְׁלֹט שָׂטָן לֹא בְּמַעֲשֵׂה יָדָיו וְלֹא בְּמַעֲשֵׂה יָדֵינוּ. וְאַל יִזְדַּקֵּר לֹא לְפָנָיו וְלֹא לְפָנֵינוּ שׁוּם דְּבַר הִרְהוּר חֵטְא עֲבֵירָה וְעָוֹן, מֵעַתָּה וְעַד עוֹלָם.

הָרַחֲמָן הוּא יְבָרֵךְ

When eating at one's own table, say (include the words in parentheses that apply):

אוֹתִי (וְאֶת אִשְׁתִּי / וְאֶת בַּעֲלִי / וְאֶת אָבִי מוֹרִי /
וְאֶת אִמִּי מוֹרָתִי / וְאֶת זַרְעִי) וְאֶת כָּל אֲשֶׁר לִי.

A guest at someone else's table says (include the words in parentheses that apply):

אֶת בַּעַל הַבַּיִת הַזֶּה, אוֹתוֹ (וְאֶת אִשְׁתּוֹ בַּעֲלַת הַבַּיִת הַזֶּה /
וְאֶת זַרְעוֹ) וְאֶת כָּל אֲשֶׁר לוֹ.

Children at their parents' table say (include the words in parentheses that apply):

אֶת אָבִי מוֹרִי (בַּעַל הַבַּיִת הַזֶּה), וְאֶת אִמִּי מוֹרָתִי (בַּעֲלַת הַבַּיִת הַזֶּה), אוֹתָם וְאֶת בֵּיתָם וְאֶת זַרְעָם וְאֶת כָּל אֲשֶׁר לָהֶם

For all other guests, add:

וְאֶת כָּל הַמְסֻבִּין כָּאן

אוֹתָנוּ וְאֶת כָּל אֲשֶׁר לָנוּ
כְּמוֹ שֶׁנִּתְבָּרְכוּ אֲבוֹתֵינוּ
אַבְרָהָם יִצְחָק וְיַעֲקֹב, בַּכֹּל, מִכֹּל, כֹּל[ע]
כֵּן יְבָרֵךְ אוֹתָנוּ כֻּלָּנוּ יַחַד בִּבְרָכָה שְׁלֵמָה, וְנֹאמַר אָמֵן.

IYUN TEFILLA • עיון תפילה

בַּכֹּל, מִכֹּל, כֹּל – *In all, from all, with all.* Each of these words is a reference to one of the *Avot*: "And Hashem blessed Avraham with *everything*" (*Bereshit* 24:1); "and I [Yitzḥak] have

בַּמָּרוֹם On high, may grace be invoked for them and for us,
as a safeguard of peace.
May we receive a blessing from the Lord
and a just reward from the God of our salvation,
and may we find grace and good favor in the eyes of God and man.

On Shabbat: May the Compassionate One let us inherit the time, that will be entirely Shabbat and rest for life everlasting.

On Rosh Ḥodesh: May the Compassionate One renew this month for us, for good and blessing.

הָרַחֲמָן May the Compassionate One make us worthy
of the Messianic Age and life in the World to Come.
He gives great / *On Shabbat and Rosh Ḥodesh:* He is a tower of / *II Sam. 22*
salvation to His king, showing kindness to His anointed,
to David and his descendants for ever.
He who makes peace in His high places,
may He make peace for us and all Israel,
and let us say: Amen.

יְראוּ Fear the Lord, you His holy ones; *Ps. 34*
those who fear Him lack nothing.[A]
Young lions may grow weak and hungry,
but those who seek the Lord lack no good thing.
Thank the Lord for He is good; *Ps. 118*
His loving-kindness is for ever.
You open Your hand, and satisfy every living thing with favor. *Ps. 145*
Blessed is the person who trusts in the Lord, *Jer. 17*
whose trust is in the Lord alone.
Once I was young, and now I am old, *Ps. 37*
yet I have never watched a righteous man forsaken
or his children begging for bread.
The Lord will give His people strength. *Ps. 29*
The Lord will bless His people with peace.

If Birkat HaMazon was made on a cup of wine, then the blessing over wine is made and the majority of the cup is drunk, after which Al HaMiḥya, on the next page, is said. If Seuda Shelishit continues after sunset, then the blessing is not said, and the cup of wine is saved for Havdala.

בַּמָּרוֹם יְלַמְּדוּ עֲלֵיהֶם וְעָלֵינוּ זְכוּת, שֶׁתְּהֵא לְמִשְׁמֶֽרֶת שָׁלוֹם
וְנִשָּׂא בְרָכָה מֵאֵת יהוה וּצְדָקָה מֵאֱלֹהֵי יִשְׁעֵנוּ
וְנִמְצָא חֵן וְשֵֽׂכֶל טוֹב בְּעֵינֵי אֱלֹהִים וְאָדָם.

בשבת: הָרַחֲמָן הוּא יַנְחִילֵֽנוּ יוֹם שֶׁכֻּלּוֹ שַׁבָּת וּמְנוּחָה לְחַיֵּי הָעוֹלָמִים.
בראש חודש: הָרַחֲמָן הוּא יְחַדֵּשׁ עָלֵינוּ אֶת הַחֹֽדֶשׁ הַזֶּה לְטוֹבָה וְלִבְרָכָה.

הָרַחֲמָן הוּא יְזַכֵּֽנוּ לִימוֹת הַמָּשִֽׁיחַ וּלְחַיֵּי הָעוֹלָם הַבָּא
מַגְדִּל/ On שבת and ראש חודש מִגְדּוֹל/ יְשׁוּעוֹת מַלְכּוֹ שמואל ב׳ כב
וְעֹֽשֶׂה־חֶֽסֶד לִמְשִׁיחוֹ, לְדָוִד וּלְזַרְעוֹ עַד־עוֹלָם:
עֹשֶׂה שָׁלוֹם בִּמְרוֹמָיו
הוּא יַעֲשֶׂה שָׁלוֹם עָלֵינוּ וְעַל כָּל יִשְׂרָאֵל, וְאִמְרוּ אָמֵן.

יְראוּ אֶת־יהוה קְדֹשָׁיו, כִּי־אֵין מַחְסוֹר לִירֵאָיו:[א] תהלים לד
כְּפִירִים רָשׁוּ וְרָעֵֽבוּ, וְדֹרְשֵׁי יהוה לֹא־יַחְסְרוּ כָל־טוֹב:
הוֹדוּ לַיהוה כִּי־טוֹב, כִּי לְעוֹלָם חַסְדּוֹ: תהלים קיח
פּוֹתֵֽחַ אֶת־יָדֶֽךָ, וּמַשְׂבִּֽיעַ לְכָל־חַי רָצוֹן: תהלים קמה
בָּרוּךְ הַגֶּֽבֶר אֲשֶׁר יִבְטַח בַּיהוה, וְהָיָה יהוה מִבְטַחוֹ: ירמיה יז
נַֽעַר הָיִֽיתִי גַּם־זָקַֽנְתִּי, וְלֹא־רָאִֽיתִי צַדִּיק נֶעֱזָב וְזַרְעוֹ מְבַקֶּשׁ־לָֽחֶם: תהלים לז
יהוה עֹז לְעַמּוֹ יִתֵּן, יהוה יְבָרֵךְ אֶת־עַמּוֹ בַשָּׁלוֹם: תהלים כט

If ברכת המזון *was made on a cup of wine, then* בּוֹרֵא פְּרִי הַגָּפֶן *is said and the majority of the cup is drunk, after which* ברכה מעין שלוש, *on the next page, is said. If* סעודה שלישית *continues after* שקיעה, *then the* ברכה *is not said, and the cup of wine is saved for* הבדלה.

ANI TEFILLA • אני תפילה

יְראוּ אֶת־יהוה קְדֹשָׁיו, כִּי־אֵין מַחְסוֹר לִירֵאָיו – *Fear the Lord, you His holy ones; those who fear Him lack nothing.* The blessing claims that those who fear or believe in Hashem are not lacking anything, yet we know that there are God-fearing people who are poor or who have needs. How might this seeming contradiction be reconciled?

Before eating food, other than bread or matza, made from the five species of grain (wheat, barley, rye, oats and spelt), or rice:

Blessed are You, the LORD our God, King of the Universe, who creates the various kinds of nourishment.

Before drinking wine or grape juice:

Blessed are You, LORD our God, King of the Universe, who creates the fruit of the vine.

Before eating fruit that grows on trees:

Blessed are You, LORD our God, King of the Universe, who creates the fruit of the tree.

Before eating vegetables, or fruit that does not grow on trees:

Blessed are You, LORD our God, King of the Universe, who creates the fruit of the ground.

Before eating other food or drinking other liquids:

Blessed are You, LORD our God, King of the Universe, by whose word all things came to be.

Before eating fruit for the first time in a season, the following is said. This blessing is also said when buying or wearing a new garment of significant value (e.g. a dress or suit); entering a new home for the first time; or hearing personal good news.

Blessed are You, LORD our God, King of the Universe, who has given us life, sustained us, and brought us to this time.

BLESSING AFTER FOOD – AL HAMIḤYA

Grace after eating from the "seven species" of produce with which Israel is blessed: food made from the five grains (but not bread); wine or grape juice; grapes, figs, pomegranates, olives, or dates.

בָּרוּךְ Blessed are You, LORD our God, King of the Universe,

After grain products (but not bread or matza):
for the nourishment and sustenance,

After wine or grape juice:
for the vine and the fruit of the vine,

After grapes, figs, olives, pomegranates or dates:
for the tree and the fruit of the tree,

After grain products (but not bread or matza), and wine or grape juice:
for the nourishment and sustenance and for the vine and the fruit of the vine,

and for the produce of the field; for the desirable, good and spacious land that You willingly gave as heritage to our ancestors, that they might eat of its fruit and be satisfied with its goodness. Have compassion, please, LORD

Before eating food, other than bread or מצה*,*
made from the five species of grain (wheat, barley, rye, oats and spelt), or rice:

בָּרוּךְ אַתָּה יהוה אֱלֹהֵינוּ מֶלֶךְ הָעוֹלָם, בּוֹרֵא מִינֵי מְזוֹנוֹת.

Before drinking wine or grape juice:

בָּרוּךְ אַתָּה יהוה אֱלֹהֵינוּ מֶלֶךְ הָעוֹלָם, בּוֹרֵא פְּרִי הַגָּפֶן.

Before eating fruit that grows on trees:

בָּרוּךְ אַתָּה יהוה אֱלֹהֵינוּ מֶלֶךְ הָעוֹלָם, בּוֹרֵא פְּרִי הָעֵץ.

Before eating vegetables, or fruit that does not grow on trees:

בָּרוּךְ אַתָּה יהוה אֱלֹהֵינוּ מֶלֶךְ הָעוֹלָם, בּוֹרֵא פְּרִי הָאֲדָמָה.

Before eating other food or drinking other liquids:

בָּרוּךְ אַתָּה יהוה אֱלֹהֵינוּ מֶלֶךְ הָעוֹלָם, שֶׁהַכֹּל נִהְיָה בִּדְבָרוֹ.

Before eating fruit for the first time in a season, the following שֶׁהֶחֱיָנוּ *is said. This blessing is also said when buying or wearing a new garment of significant value (e.g. a dress or suit); entering a new home for the first time; or hearing personal good news.*

בָּרוּךְ אַתָּה יהוה אֱלֹהֵינוּ מֶלֶךְ הָעוֹלָם
שֶׁהֶחֱיָנוּ וְקִיְּמָנוּ וְהִגִּיעָנוּ לַזְּמַן הַזֶּה.

ברכה מעין שלוש

Grace after eating from the "seven species" of produce with which Israel is blessed: food made from the five grains (but not bread); wine or grape juice; grapes, figs, pomegranates, olives, or dates.

בָּרוּךְ אַתָּה יהוה אֱלֹהֵינוּ מֶלֶךְ הָעוֹלָם, עַל

After grain products (but not bread or מצה*):*
הַמִּחְיָה וְעַל הַכַּלְכָּלָה

After wine or grape juice:
הַגֶּפֶן וְעַל פְּרִי הַגֶּפֶן

After grapes, figs, olives, pomegranates or dates:
הָעֵץ וְעַל פְּרִי הָעֵץ

After grain products (but not bread or מצה*), and wine or grape juice:*

הַמִּחְיָה וְעַל הַכַּלְכָּלָה וְעַל הַגֶּפֶן וְעַל פְּרִי הַגֶּפֶן

וְעַל תְּנוּבַת הַשָּׂדֶה וְעַל אֶרֶץ חֶמְדָּה טוֹבָה וּרְחָבָה, שֶׁרָצִיתָ וְהִנְחַלְתָּ לַאֲבוֹתֵינוּ לֶאֱכֹל מִפִּרְיָהּ וְלִשְׂבֹּעַ מִטּוּבָהּ. רַחֶם נָא יהוה אֱלֹהֵינוּ עַל יִשְׂרָאֵל עַמֶּךָ וְעַל יְרוּשָׁלַיִם עִירֶךָ וְעַל צִיּוֹן מִשְׁכַּן כְּבוֹדֶךָ וְעַל מִזְבְּחֶךָ וְעַל הֵיכָלֶךָ.

our God, on Israel Your people, on Jerusalem, Your city, on Zion the home of Your glory, on Your altar and Your Temple. May You rebuild Jerusalem, the holy city swiftly in our time, and may You bring us back there, rejoicing in its rebuilding, eating from its fruit, satisfied by its goodness, and blessing You for it in holiness and purity.

On Shabbat: Be pleased to refresh us on this Sabbath Day.
On Rosh Ḥodesh: Remember us for good on this day of the New Moon.

For You, God, are good and do good to all and we thank You for the land

After grain products (but not bread or matza):	*After wine or grape juice:*	*After grapes, figs, olives, pomegranates or dates:*
and for the nourishment. Blessed are You, LORD, for the land and for the nourishment.	and for the fruit of the vine. Blessed are You, LORD, for the land and for the fruit of the vine.	and for the fruit. Blessed are You, LORD, for the land and for the fruit.

After grain products (but not bread or matza), and wine or grape juice:
and for the nourishment and for the fruit of the vine.
Blessed are You, LORD, for the land and for the nourishment
and the fruit of the vine.

BLESSING AFTER FOOD – BOREH NEFASHOT

After food or drink that does not require Birkat HaMazon or Al HaMiḥya – such as meat, fish, dairy products, vegetables, beverages, or fruit other than grapes, figs, pomegranates, olives or dates – say:

בָּרוּךְ Blessed are You, LORD our God, King of the Universe, who creates the many forms of life and their needs. For all You have created to sustain the life of all that lives, blessed be He, Giver of life to the worlds.

The second opinion, however, sees this as one long blessing whose theme is Hashem's provision of our needs. As such, a comma after וְחֶסְרוֹנָן is unnecessary.

In any event, one sees that for all the focus on the spiritual, Judaism acknowledges the importance of the physical. The need to eat is a basic drive, no different from any other animal on the planet. But rather than succumbing to our bestial instincts, Judaism constantly raises the act of eating to a spiritual activity.

Have you ever seen people eating in a way that is more animalistic than human? How might the recitation of this blessing help me maintain my humanity?

וּבְנֵה יְרוּשָׁלַיִם עִיר הַקֹּדֶשׁ בִּמְהֵרָה בְיָמֵינוּ, וְהַעֲלֵנוּ לְתוֹכָהּ וְשַׂמְּחֵנוּ בְּבִנְיָנָהּ וְנֹאכַל מִפִּרְיָהּ וְנִשְׂבַּע מִטּוּבָהּ, וּנְבָרֶכְךָ עָלֶיהָ בִּקְדֻשָּׁה וּבְטָהֳרָה.

בשבת: וּרְצֵה וְהַחֲלִיצֵנוּ בְּיוֹם הַשַּׁבָּת הַזֶּה

בראש חודש: וְזָכְרֵנוּ לְטוֹבָה בְּיוֹם רֹאשׁ הַחֹדֶשׁ הַזֶּה

כִּי אַתָּה יהוה טוֹב וּמֵטִיב לַכֹּל, וְנוֹדֶה לְּךָ עַל הָאָרֶץ

After grain products (but not bread or מצה*):*

וְעַל הַמִּחְיָה.
בָּרוּךְ אַתָּה יהוה עַל הָאָרֶץ וְעַל הַמִּחְיָה.

After wine or grape juice:

וְעַל פְּרִי הַגָּפֶן.*
בָּרוּךְ אַתָּה יהוה עַל הָאָרֶץ וְעַל פְּרִי הַגָּפֶן.*

After grapes, figs, olives, pomegranates or dates:

וְעַל הַפֵּרוֹת.**
בָּרוּךְ אַתָּה יהוה עַל הָאָרֶץ וְעַל הַפֵּרוֹת.**

After grain products (but not bread or מצה*), and wine or grape juice:*

וְעַל הַמִּחְיָה וְעַל פְּרִי הַגָּפֶן.*
בָּרוּךְ אַתָּה יהוה, עַל הָאָרֶץ וְעַל הַמִּחְיָה וְעַל פְּרִי הַגָּפֶן.*

**If the wine is from* ארץ ישראל*, then substitute* גַּפְנָהּ *for* הַגָּפֶן.
***If the fruit is from* ארץ ישראל*, then substitute* פֵּרוֹתֶיהָ *for* הַפֵּרוֹת.

בורא נפשות

After food or drink that does not require ברכת המזון *or* מעין שלוש *– such as meat, fish, dairy products, vegetables, beverages, or fruit other than grapes, figs, pomegranates, olives or dates – say:*

בָּרוּךְ אַתָּה יהוה אֱלֹהֵינוּ מֶלֶךְ הָעוֹלָם, בּוֹרֵא נְפָשׁוֹת רַבּוֹת וְחֶסְרוֹנָן, עַל כָּל מַה שֶּׁבָּרָאתָ, לְהַחֲיוֹת בָּהֶם נֶפֶשׁ כָּל חָי. בָּרוּךְ חֵי הָעוֹלָמִים.

BOREH NEFASHOT

There is a dispute among the Rishonim as to whether the text of the blessing is interpreted as having two themes or just one. According to the first opinion, there should be a comma after the word **וְחֶסְרוֹנָן** (needs). We thank Hashem for the fact that He created us (**בּוֹרֵא נְפָשׁוֹת**) and we acknowledge our deficiencies, that is, our need for bread and water, the staples that we need in order to survive. The second part of the blessing, referring to "all You have created," is therefore a reference to all other kinds of foods from which we derive pleasure, even if they are not staples. Alternatively, we thank Hashem even if we do not have those staples.

BLESSINGS

BLESSINGS ON MITZVOT

In Israel on separating teruma and first tithe (if there is doubt as to whether the teruma and first tithe have been taken, the following blessing is not said, but the subsequent declaration is):

Blessed are You, LORD our God, King of the Universe,
who has made us holy through His commandments,
and has commanded us to separate *terumot* and tithes.

Whatever [of the allocated portion] is more than one in a hundred of everything here, is hereby declared to be *teruma gedola* [the priestly portion] and is the northern portion. The one in a hundred that remains here, together with nine equal portions on the upper side of this produce are declared to be the first [levitical] tithe. The one in a hundred I have made first tithe is hereby declared to be *terumat maaser* [the tithe-of-the-tithe set aside for the priests]. Nine other equal portions on the lower side of the produce are declared to be second tithe, but if this produce must have the tithe of the poor separated from it, let them be the tithe of the poor.

In Israel on separating and redeeming the second tithe (if there is doubt as to whether the second tithe has been taken, the following blessing is not said, but the subsequent declaration is):

Blessed are You, LORD our God, King of the Universe,
who has made us holy through His commandments,
and has commanded us about the redemption of the second tithe.

This second tithe, together with its additional fifth, is hereby redeemed by one *peruta* of the coins I have set aside for the redemption of the second tithe.

On taking ḥalla:

Blessed are You, LORD our God, King of the Universe,
who has made us holy through His commandments,
and has commanded us to set aside ḥalla from the dough.

On redeeming fourth-year fruit:

Blessed are You, LORD our God, King of the Universe,
who has made us holy through His commandments,
and has commanded us about the redemption of fruit of the fourth year.

The Rabbis tell us that we should recite 100 blessings a day. If you imagine a 16-hour day, that would amount to a blessing about every ten minutes. While it is true that in practical terms, lots of those are clumped together (consider how many blessings we say in an average morning *Shaḥarit*), the point is that *Ḥazal* wanted us to be ever conscious of the miracle and Origin of life. *Berakhot* are about not taking life for granted. They take the ordinary and remind us of the extraordinary. They focus on the physical and make it spiritual.

ברכות

ברכות המצוות

In ארץ ישראל *on separating* תרומה *and* מעשר ראשון *(if there is doubt as to whether the* תרומה *and* מעשר ראשון *have been taken, the following blessing is not said, but the subsequent declaration is):*

בָּרוּךְ אַתָּה יהוה אֱלֹהֵינוּ מֶלֶךְ הָעוֹלָם, אֲשֶׁר קִדְּשָׁנוּ בְּמִצְוֹתָיו וְצִוָּנוּ לְהַפְרִישׁ תְּרוּמוֹת וּמַעַשְׂרוֹת.

מַה שֶּׁהוּא יוֹתֵר מֵאֶחָד מִמֵּאָה מִן הַכֹּל שֶׁיֵּשׁ כָּאן, הֲרֵי הוּא תְּרוּמָה גְדוֹלָה בִּצְפוֹנוֹ, וְהָאֶחָד מִמֵּאָה שֶׁנִּשְׁאַר כָּאן עִם תִּשְׁעָה חֲלָקִים כָּמוֹהוּ בְּצַד הָעֶלְיוֹן שֶׁל הַפֵּרוֹת הַלָּלוּ, הֲרֵי הֵם מַעֲשֵׂר רִאשׁוֹן. אוֹתוֹ הָאֶחָד מִמֵּאָה שֶׁעֲשִׂיתִיו מַעֲשֵׂר רִאשׁוֹן הֲרֵי הוּא תְּרוּמַת מַעֲשֵׂר. עוֹד תִּשְׁעָה חֲלָקִים כָּאֵלֶּה בְּצַד הַתַּחְתּוֹן שֶׁל הַפֵּרוֹת הֲרֵי הֵם מַעֲשֵׂר שֵׁנִי, וְאִם הֵם חַיָּבִים בְּמַעֲשַׂר עָנִי, הֲרֵי הֵם מַעֲשַׂר עָנִי.

In ארץ ישראל *on separating and redeeming the* מעשר שני *(if there is doubt as to whether the* מעשר שני *has been taken, the following blessing is not said, but the subsequent declaration is):*

בָּרוּךְ אַתָּה יהוה אֱלֹהֵינוּ מֶלֶךְ הָעוֹלָם, אֲשֶׁר קִדְּשָׁנוּ בְּמִצְוֹתָיו וְצִוָּנוּ עַל פִּדְיוֹן מַעֲשֵׂר שֵׁנִי.

מַעֲשֵׂר שֵׁנִי זֶה, הוּא וְחֻמְשׁוֹ, הֲרֵי הוּא מְחֻלָּל עַל פְּרוּטָה אַחַת מִן הַמַּטְבֵּעַ שֶׁיִּחַדְתִּי לְפִדְיוֹן מַעֲשֵׂר שֵׁנִי.

On taking חלה*:*

בָּרוּךְ אַתָּה יהוה אֱלֹהֵינוּ מֶלֶךְ הָעוֹלָם, אֲשֶׁר קִדְּשָׁנוּ בְּמִצְוֹתָיו וְצִוָּנוּ לְהַפְרִישׁ חַלָּה מִן הָעִסָּה.

On redeeming נטע רבעי*:*

בָּרוּךְ אַתָּה יהוה אֱלֹהֵינוּ מֶלֶךְ הָעוֹלָם, אֲשֶׁר קִדְּשָׁנוּ בְּמִצְוֹתָיו וְצִוָּנוּ עַל פִּדְיוֹן נֶטַע רְבָעִי.

INTRODUCTION TO BERAKHOT

A *berakha* is a kind of meditation, a reflective phrase designed to help us focus on the here and now, on an aspect of our lives that we might otherwise take for granted. It reminds us of the incredible miracle of nature or life that lies before us. It reminds us of the "Wow!" And it reminds us of the Ultimate Source.

On fixing a mezuza to the doorpost:

Blessed are You, LORD our God, King of the Universe,
who has made us holy through His commandments,
and has commanded us to affix the mezuza.

On making a protective railing around one's roof, or a fence around a pit:

Blessed are You, LORD our God, King of the Universe,
who has made us holy through His commandments,
and has commanded us to to affix a guard-rail.

On immersing utensils made by or bought from a gentile:

Blessed are You, LORD our God, King of the Universe,
who has made us holy through His commandments,
and has commanded us about immersing a vessel (vessels).

BLESSINGS ON PLEASURES, SIGHTS AND SOUNDS

On wearing new clothes:

Blessed are You, LORD our God, King of the Universe,
who clothes the naked.

On smelling fragrant shrubs or trees:

Blessed are You, LORD our God, King of the Universe,
who creates fragrant trees.

On smelling fragrant herbs, grasses or flowers:

Blessed are You, LORD our God, King of the Universe,
who creates fragrant plants.

On smelling fragrant fruit:

Blessed are You, LORD our God, King of the Universe,
who gives pleasant fragrance to fruits.

On smelling persimmon oil:

Blessed are You, LORD our God, King of the Universe,
who creates pleasing perfume.

On all other scents:

Blessed are You, LORD our God, King of the Universe,
who creates the various spices.

On fixing a מזוזה *to the doorpost:*

בָּרוּךְ אַתָּה יהוה אֱלֹהֵינוּ מֶלֶךְ הָעוֹלָם, אֲשֶׁר קִדְּשָׁנוּ בְּמִצְוֹתָיו
וְצִוָּנוּ לִקְבֹּעַ מְזוּזָה.

On making a protective railing around one's roof, or a fence around a pit:

בָּרוּךְ אַתָּה יהוה אֱלֹהֵינוּ מֶלֶךְ הָעוֹלָם, אֲשֶׁר קִדְּשָׁנוּ בְּמִצְוֹתָיו
וְצִוָּנוּ לַעֲשׂוֹת מַעֲקֶה.

On immersing utensils made by or bought from a gentile:

בָּרוּךְ אַתָּה יהוה אֱלֹהֵינוּ מֶלֶךְ הָעוֹלָם, אֲשֶׁר קִדְּשָׁנוּ בְּמִצְוֹתָיו
וְצִוָּנוּ עַל טְבִילַת כֶּלִי (כֵּלִים).

ברכות הנהנין, הראייה והשמיעה

On wearing new clothes:

בָּרוּךְ אַתָּה יהוה אֱלֹהֵינוּ מֶלֶךְ הָעוֹלָם
מַלְבִּישׁ עֲרֻמִּים.

On smelling fragrant shrubs or trees:

בָּרוּךְ אַתָּה יהוה אֱלֹהֵינוּ מֶלֶךְ הָעוֹלָם
בּוֹרֵא עֲצֵי בְשָׂמִים.

On smelling fragrant herbs, grasses or flowers:

בָּרוּךְ אַתָּה יהוה אֱלֹהֵינוּ מֶלֶךְ הָעוֹלָם
בּוֹרֵא עִשְׂבֵי בְשָׂמִים.

On smelling fragrant fruit:

בָּרוּךְ אַתָּה יהוה אֱלֹהֵינוּ מֶלֶךְ הָעוֹלָם
הַנּוֹתֵן רֵיחַ טוֹב בַּפֵּרוֹת.

On smelling persimmon oil:

בָּרוּךְ אַתָּה יהוה אֱלֹהֵינוּ מֶלֶךְ הָעוֹלָם
בּוֹרֵא שֶׁמֶן עָרֵב.

On all other scents:

בָּרוּךְ אַתָּה יהוה אֱלֹהֵינוּ מֶלֶךְ הָעוֹלָם
בּוֹרֵא מִינֵי בְשָׂמִים.

On seeing the wonders of nature, such as lightning, and on the 28-year solar cycle:
Blessed are You, LORD our God, King of the Universe,
Author of creation.

On hearing thunder or experiencing a hurricane:
Blessed are You, LORD our God, King of the Universe,
whose power and might fill the world.

On seeing a rainbow:
Blessed are You, LORD our God, King of the Universe,
who remembers the covenant, is faithful to the covenant,
and fulfills His word.

On seeing the ocean or the Mediterranean Sea for the first time in thirty days:
Blessed are You, LORD our God, King of the Universe,
who has made the great sea.

On seeing trees blossoming for the first time in the year:
Blessed are You, LORD our God, King of the Universe,
who has withheld nothing from His world,
but has created in it beautiful creatures and trees
for human beings to enjoy.

On seeing beautiful scenes of nature:
Blessed are You, LORD our God, King of the Universe,
who has [created] such things in His world.

On seeing unusual people or animals:
Blessed are You, LORD our God, King of the Universe,
who makes [all] creatures different.

On hearing good news from which others as well as oneself will benefit:
Blessed are You, LORD our God, King of the Universe,
who is good and does good.

---

not plan to do this. Yet the words flowed from my lips... It was a religious reaction to viewing the majesty of God's creation. When I recited the blessing upon seeing the sea, I did so with emotion and deep feeling. I experienced the words of the benediction "Blessed be He who wrought creation." Not all the blessings that I recite are said with such concentration. It was more than simply a blessing; it was an encounter with the Creator. I felt that the Shekhina [Divine Presence] was hidden in the darkness and vastness of the sea. The experience welled out of me. (Rav Soloveitchik)

On seeing the wonders of nature, such as lightning, and ברכת החמה:

בָּרוּךְ אַתָּה יהוה אֱלֹהֵינוּ מֶלֶךְ הָעוֹלָם, עוֹשֶׂה מַעֲשֵׂה בְרֵאשִׁית.

On hearing thunder or experiencing a hurricane:

בָּרוּךְ אַתָּה יהוה אֱלֹהֵינוּ מֶלֶךְ הָעוֹלָם, שֶׁכֹּחוֹ וּגְבוּרָתוֹ מָלֵא עוֹלָם.

On seeing a rainbow:

בָּרוּךְ אַתָּה יהוה אֱלֹהֵינוּ מֶלֶךְ הָעוֹלָם
זוֹכֵר הַבְּרִית וְנֶאֱמָן בִּבְרִיתוֹ וְקַיָּם בְּמַאֲמָרוֹ.

On seeing the ocean or the Mediterranean Sea for the first time in thirty days:

בָּרוּךְ אַתָּה יהוה אֱלֹהֵינוּ מֶלֶךְ הָעוֹלָם, שֶׁעָשָׂה אֶת הַיָּם הַגָּדוֹל.

On seeing trees blossoming for the first time in the year:

בָּרוּךְ אַתָּה יהוה אֱלֹהֵינוּ מֶלֶךְ הָעוֹלָם, שֶׁלֹּא חִסַּר בְּעוֹלָמוֹ כְּלוּם
וּבָרָא בוֹ בְּרִיּוֹת טוֹבוֹת וְאִילָנוֹת טוֹבִים לְהַנּוֹת בָּהֶם בְּנֵי אָדָם.

On seeing beautiful scenes of nature:

בָּרוּךְ אַתָּה יהוה אֱלֹהֵינוּ מֶלֶךְ הָעוֹלָם, שֶׁכָּכָה לוֹ בְּעוֹלָמוֹ.

On seeing unusual people or animals:

בָּרוּךְ אַתָּה יהוה אֱלֹהֵינוּ מֶלֶךְ הָעוֹלָם, מְשַׁנֶּה הַבְּרִיּוֹת.

On hearing good news from which others as well as oneself will benefit:

בָּרוּךְ אַתָּה יהוה אֱלֹהֵינוּ מֶלֶךְ הָעוֹלָם, הַטּוֹב וְהַמֵּטִיב.

ANI TEFILLA • אני תפילה

I remember how enthused I was the first time I saw the Baltic Sea. I was born in Russia and never saw a major body of water in my youth… I remember that the water was blue, deeply blue. From afar it looked like a blue forest. It resembles the aboriginal forests near Pruzhana, where I was born. When I came close and realized it was the Baltic Sea, I was overwhelmed by its beauty. Spontaneously I began to recite the Psalm, "Bless the Lord, O my soul" [Barekhi Nafshi, Psalm 104 that is recited on Rosh Ḥodesh]. I did

On hearing bad news, and said by a mourner before the ritual tearing of the garment:
Blessed are You, LORD our God, King of the Universe,
the true Judge.[A]

On seeing an outstanding Torah scholar:
Blessed are You, LORD our God, King of the Universe,
who has shared of His wisdom with those who revere Him.

On seeing an outstanding secular scholar:
Blessed are You, LORD our God, King of the Universe,
who has given of His wisdom with human beings.

On seeing a Monarch or Head of State:
Blessed are You, LORD our God, King of the Universe,
who has given of His glory to human beings.

On seeing 600,000 Jews together in Israel:
Blessed are You, LORD our God, King of the Universe,
who knows all secrets.

On seeing Jewish settlements in Israel:
Blessed are You, LORD our God, King of the Universe,
who establishes the border of the widow.

On seeing the place where miracles occurred to the Jewish people:
Blessed are You, LORD our God, King of the Universe,
who performed miracles for our ancestors in this place.

On seeing the place where miracles occurred to oneself or one's family (insert the relevant words):
Blessed are You, LORD our God, King of the Universe,
who performed a miracle for me (my father / my mother / my ancestors)
in this place.

---

and moved them all to Canada to start all over again, leaving behind all the members of his extended family. "How was I to know," he said, "that years later our enemies would come and destroy everyone I left behind, but I was left alive with my wife and children? Only then did I understand the Gemara's admonition that 'A person is obligated to say a blessing over the bad things that happen [like losing all of my money,] just like he is to say a blessing over the good.' For what seems to us like bad in the moment, may indeed be part of a bigger plan of HaKadosh Barukh Hu of which one is not and may not ever be aware."

On hearing bad news, and said by a mourner before the ritual tearing of the garment:

בָּרוּךְ אַתָּה יהוה אֱלֹהֵינוּ מֶלֶךְ הָעוֹלָם, דַּיַּן הָאֱמֶת.[א]

On seeing an outstanding Torah scholar:

בָּרוּךְ אַתָּה יהוה אֱלֹהֵינוּ מֶלֶךְ הָעוֹלָם, שֶׁחָלַק מֵחָכְמָתוֹ לִירֵאָיו.

On seeing an outstanding secular scholar:

בָּרוּךְ אַתָּה יהוה אֱלֹהֵינוּ מֶלֶךְ הָעוֹלָם, שֶׁנָּתַן מֵחָכְמָתוֹ לְבָשָׂר וָדָם.

On seeing a Monarch or Head of State:

בָּרוּךְ אַתָּה יהוה אֱלֹהֵינוּ מֶלֶךְ הָעוֹלָם, שֶׁנָּתַן מִכְּבוֹדוֹ לְבָשָׂר וָדָם.

On seeing 600,000 Jews together in ארץ ישראל:

בָּרוּךְ אַתָּה יהוה אֱלֹהֵינוּ מֶלֶךְ הָעוֹלָם, חֲכַם הָרָזִים.

On seeing Jewish settlements in ארץ ישראל:

בָּרוּךְ אַתָּה יהוה אֱלֹהֵינוּ מֶלֶךְ הָעוֹלָם
מַצִּיב גְּבוּל אַלְמָנָה.

On seeing the place where miracles occurred to the Jewish people:

בָּרוּךְ אַתָּה יהוה אֱלֹהֵינוּ מֶלֶךְ הָעוֹלָם
שֶׁעָשָׂה נִסִּים לַאֲבוֹתֵינוּ בַּמָּקוֹם הַזֶּה.

On seeing the place where miracles occurred to oneself or one's family (insert the relevant words):

בָּרוּךְ אַתָּה יהוה אֱלֹהֵינוּ מֶלֶךְ הָעוֹלָם
שֶׁעָשָׂה לִּי (לְאָבִי/לְאִמִּי/לַאֲבוֹתַי) נֵס בַּמָּקוֹם הַזֶּה.

ANI TEFILLA • אני תפילה

דַּיַּן הָאֱמֶת – *The true Judge.*
My grandfather, ז״ל, emigrated from Eastern Europe without his wife and child in order to make some money, since the economy in Poland then was so poor. But after a few years, World War I broke out and he could not get back home and so he was separated from his family for eight years! Upon his return with his hard-earned savings, he invested it all but, unfortunately, did so unwisely and lost it all. "And for this," he said, "I am supposed to thank God?!" So he picked up his immediate family

ADDITIONAL BLESSINGS

After relieving oneself and washing one's hands, say:

Blessed are You, Lord our God, King of the Universe, who formed man in wisdom and created in him many orifices and cavities. It is revealed and known before the throne of Your glory that were one of them to be ruptured or blocked, it would be impossible to survive and stand before You. Blessed are You, Lord, Healer of all flesh who does wondrous deeds.

On visiting a cemetery, or seeing a Jewish grave, for the first time in thirty days:

Blessed are You, Lord our God, King of the Universe, who formed you in judgment, who nourished and sustained you in judgment, who brought death on you in judgment, who knows the number of you all in judgment, and who in the future will restore you to life in judgment. Blessed are You, Lord, who revives the dead.

You are eternally mighty, Lord. You give life to the dead and have great power to save. He sustains the living with loving-kindness, and with great compassion revives the dead. He supports the fallen, heals the sick, sets captives free, and keeps His faith with those who sleep in the dust. Who is like You, Master of might, and who can compare to You, O King who brings death and gives life, and makes salvation grow? Faithful are You to revive the dead.

In special cases of urgency only, the following short form of the Amida may be said. First say the first three blessings of the Amida from "O Lord" on page 136 until "the holy God" page 144, then say:

הֲבִינֵנוּ Grant us understanding, Lord our God, to know Your ways. Sensitize our hearts so that we may revere You, and forgive us so that we may be redeemed. Keep us far from suffering and satisfy us with the pastures of Your land. Gather our scattered people from the four quarters of the earth. May those who go astray be judged according to Your will: raise Your hand against the wicked. May the righteous rejoice in the rebuilding of Your city, the restoration of Your Temple, the flowering of Your servant David's glory, and the radiant light of the son of Jesse, Your anointed. May You answer us even before we call. Blessed are You, Lord, who hears prayer.

Continue with the final three blessings from "Find favor" on page 174 until the end.

In extreme cases where there is no time to say the abbreviated Amida above, one may say the following. However, if prayer is then possible at a later time, one should say the complete Amida.

צָרְכֵי The needs of Your people Israel are many, and their patience is thin. May it be Your will, Lord our God and God of our ancestors, to give each one of them enough to sustain him, and to every single body, all that it lacks – and perform what is right in Your eyes. Blessed are You, Lord, who listens to prayer.

ברכות נוספות

After relieving oneself and washing one's hands, say:

בָּרוּךְ אַתָּה יהוה אֱלֹהֵינוּ מֶלֶךְ הָעוֹלָם, אֲשֶׁר יָצַר אֶת הָאָדָם בְּחָכְמָה, וּבָרָא בוֹ נְקָבִים נְקָבִים, חֲלוּלִים חֲלוּלִים. גָּלוּי וְיָדוּעַ לִפְנֵי כִסֵּא כְבוֹדֶךָ, שֶׁאִם יִפָּתֵחַ אֶחָד מֵהֶם אוֹ יִסָּתֵם אֶחָד מֵהֶם, אִי אֶפְשָׁר לְהִתְקַיֵּם וְלַעֲמֹד לְפָנֶיךָ. בָּרוּךְ אַתָּה יהוה, רוֹפֵא כָל בָּשָׂר וּמַפְלִיא לַעֲשׂוֹת.

On visiting a cemetery, or seeing a Jewish grave, for the first time in thirty days:

בָּרוּךְ אַתָּה יהוה אֱלֹהֵינוּ מֶלֶךְ הָעוֹלָם, אֲשֶׁר יָצַר אֶתְכֶם בַּדִּין, וְזָן וְכִלְכֵּל אֶתְכֶם בַּדִּין, וְהֵמִית אֶתְכֶם בַּדִּין, וְיוֹדֵעַ מִסְפַּר כֻּלְּכֶם בַּדִּין, וְהוּא עָתִיד לְהַחֲיוֹתְכֶם וּלְקַיֵּם אֶתְכֶם בַּדִּין. בָּרוּךְ אַתָּה יהוה, מְחַיֵּה הַמֵּתִים.

אַתָּה גִּבּוֹר לְעוֹלָם אֲדֹנָי, מְחַיֵּה מֵתִים אַתָּה, רַב לְהוֹשִׁיעַ, מְכַלְכֵּל חַיִּים בְּחֶסֶד, מְחַיֵּה מֵתִים בְּרַחֲמִים רַבִּים, סוֹמֵךְ נוֹפְלִים, וְרוֹפֵא חוֹלִים, וּמַתִּיר אֲסוּרִים, וּמְקַיֵּם אֱמוּנָתוֹ לִישֵׁנֵי עָפָר. מִי כָמוֹךָ בַּעַל גְּבוּרוֹת וּמִי דּוֹמֶה לָּךְ, מֶלֶךְ מֵמִית וּמְחַיֶּה וּמַצְמִיחַ יְשׁוּעָה, וְנֶאֱמָן אַתָּה לְהַחֲיוֹת מֵתִים.

In special cases of urgency only, the following short form of the עמידה *may be said. First say the first three* ברכות *of the* עמידה *from* אֲדֹנָי, שְׂפָתַי תִּפְתָּח *on page 137 until* הַקָּדוֹשׁ *on page 145, then say:*

הֲבִינֵנוּ יהוה אֱלֹהֵינוּ לָדַעַת דְּרָכֶיךָ, וּמוֹל אֶת לְבָבֵנוּ לְיִרְאָתֶךָ, וְתִסְלַח לָנוּ לִהְיוֹת גְּאוּלִים, וְרַחֲקֵנוּ מִמַּכְאוֹב, וְדַשְּׁנֵנוּ בִּנְאוֹת אַרְצֶךָ, וּנְפוּצוֹתֵינוּ מֵאַרְבַּע תְּקַבֵּץ, וְהַתּוֹעִים עַל דַּעְתְּךָ יִשָּׁפֵטוּ, וְעַל הָרְשָׁעִים תָּנִיף יָדֶךָ, וְיִשְׂמְחוּ צַדִּיקִים בְּבִנְיַן עִירֶךָ וּבְתִקּוּן הֵיכָלֶךָ, וּבִצְמִיחַת קֶרֶן לְדָוִד עַבְדֶּךָ וּבַעֲרִיכַת נֵר לְבֶן יִשַׁי מְשִׁיחֶךָ, טֶרֶם נִקְרָא אַתָּה תַעֲנֶה. בָּרוּךְ אַתָּה יהוה, שׁוֹמֵעַ תְּפִלָּה.

Continue with the final three ברכות*, from* רְצֵה *on page 175 until the end.*

In extreme cases where there is no time to say the abbreviated עמידה *above, one may say the following. However, if prayer is then possible at a later time, one should say the complete* עמידה.

צָרְכֵי עַמְּךָ יִשְׂרָאֵל מְרֻבִּים וְדַעְתָּם קְצָרָה. יְהִי רָצוֹן מִלְּפָנֶיךָ יהוה אֱלֹהֵינוּ וֵאלֹהֵי אֲבוֹתֵינוּ, שֶׁתִּתֵּן לְכָל אֶחָד וְאֶחָד כְּדֵי פַרְנָסָתוֹ, וּלְכָל גְּוִיָּה וּגְוִיָּה דֵּי מַחְסוֹרָהּ, וְהַטּוֹב בְּעֵינֶיךָ עֲשֵׂה. בָּרוּךְ אַתָּה יהוה, שׁוֹמֵעַ תְּפִלָּה.

BIRKAT KOHANIM IN ISRAEL

In Israel, the following is said by the Leader during the Repetition of the Amida when Kohanim bless the congregation. If there is more than one Kohen, a member of the congregation calls: (*See laws 95–102.*)

Kohanim!

The Kohanim respond:

Blessed are You, Lord our God, King of the Universe, who has made us holy with the holiness of Aaron, and has commanded us to bless His people Israel with love.

The Leader calls word by word, followed by the Kohanim:

יְבָרֶכְךָ May the LORD bless you and protect you. (*Cong:* Amen.) *Num. 6*
May the LORD make His face shine on you
and be gracious to you. (*Cong:* Amen.)
May the LORD turn His face toward you,
and grant you peace. (*Cong:* Amen.)

The congregation says:

אַדִּיר Majestic One on high who dwells in power: You are peace and Your name is peace. May it be Your will to bestow on us and on Your people the house of Israel, life and blessing as a safeguard for peace.

The Kohanim say:

רִבּוֹנוֹ Master of the Universe: we have done what You have decreed for us. So too may You deal with us as You have promised us. Look down from Your holy dwelling place, from heaven, and bless Your people Israel and the land You have given us as You promised on oath to our ancestors, a land flowing with milk and honey. *Deut. 26*

Go to Blessing of Peace,
on weekdays for Shaharit on page 180 and for Minha on page 280,
and on Shabbat for Shaharit on page 626 and for Musaf on page 700.

ברכת כהנים בארץ ישראל

In ארץ ישראל*, the following is said by the* שליח ציבור *during the* חזרת הש״ץ *when* כהנים *say* ברכת כהנים*. If there is more than one* כהן*, a member of the* קהל *calls: (See laws 95–102.)*

כֹּהֲנִים

The כהנים *respond:*

בָּרוּךְ אַתָּה יהוה אֱלֹהֵינוּ מֶלֶךְ הָעוֹלָם, אֲשֶׁר קִדְּשָׁנוּ בִּקְדֻשָּׁתוֹ שֶׁל אַהֲרֹן וְצִוָּנוּ לְבָרֵךְ אֶת עַמּוֹ יִשְׂרָאֵל בְּאַהֲבָה.

The שליח ציבור *calls word by word, followed by the* כהנים*:*

יְבָרֶכְךָ יהוה וְיִשְׁמְרֶךָ: קהל: אָמֵן במדבר ו

יָאֵר יהוה פָּנָיו אֵלֶיךָ וִיחֻנֶּךָּ: קהל: אָמֵן

יִשָּׂא יהוה פָּנָיו אֵלֶיךָ וְיָשֵׂם לְךָ שָׁלוֹם: קהל: אָמֵן

The קהל *says:*

אַדִּיר בַּמָּרוֹם שׁוֹכֵן בִּגְבוּרָה, אַתָּה שָׁלוֹם וְשִׁמְךָ שָׁלוֹם. יְהִי רָצוֹן שֶׁתָּשִׂים עָלֵינוּ וְעַל כָּל עַמְּךָ בֵּית יִשְׂרָאֵל חַיִּים וּבְרָכָה לְמִשְׁמֶרֶת שָׁלוֹם.

The כהנים *say:*

רִבּוֹנוֹ שֶׁל עוֹלָם, עָשִׂינוּ מַה שֶּׁגָּזַרְתָּ עָלֵינוּ, אַף אַתָּה עֲשֵׂה עִמָּנוּ כְּמוֹ שֶׁהִבְטַחְתָּנוּ. הַשְׁקִיפָה מִמְּעוֹן קָדְשְׁךָ מִן־הַשָּׁמַיִם, וּבָרֵךְ אֶת־עַמְּךָ אֶת־יִשְׂרָאֵל, וְאֵת הָאֲדָמָה אֲשֶׁר נָתַתָּה לָנוּ, כַּאֲשֶׁר נִשְׁבַּעְתָּ לַאֲבֹתֵינוּ, אֶרֶץ זָבַת חָלָב וּדְבָשׁ: דברים כו

Go to ברכת שלום*,*
on weekdays for שחרית *on page 181 and for* מנחה *on page 281,*
and on שבת *for* שחרית *on page 627 and for* מוסף *on page 701.*

THE TRAVELER'S PRAYER

If one intends to return home on the same day, add the words in parentheses:

יְהִי רָצוֹן May it be Your will,
Lord our God and God of our fathers,
to lead us to peace, direct our steps to peace,
guide us to peace, and bring us to our desired destination in life,
joy and peace
(and bring us back to our home in peace).
Rescue us from any enemy or ambush on the way,
and from all afflictions that trouble the world.
Send blessing to the work of our hands,
and let us find grace, kindness and compassion
from You and from all who see us.
Hear our pleas,
for You are a God who hears prayer and pleas.
Blessed are You, Lord, who listens to prayer.

May the Lord guard your going out and your return, *Ps. 121*
from now and for all time.

Repeat three times:

וַיַּעֲקֹב And Jacob went on his way *Gen. 32*
and angels of God met him.
When he saw them, Jacob said, "This is God's camp"
and he named the place Maḥanaim [two camps].

Repeat three times:

יְבָרֶכְךָ May the Lord bless you and protect you. *Num. 6*
May the Lord make His face shine on you and be gracious to you.
May the Lord turn His face toward you and grant you peace.

שִׁיר לַמַּעֲלוֹת A song of ascents. I lift my eyes up to the hills; from where will my help come? My help comes from the Lord, Maker of heaven and earth. He will not let your foot stumble; He who guards you does not slumber. See: the Guardian of Israel neither slumbers nor sleeps. The Lord is your Guardian; the Lord is your Shade at your right hand. The sun will not strike you by day, nor the moon by night. The Lord will guard you from all harm; He will guard your life. The Lord will guard your going and coming, now and for evermore. *Ps. 121*

תפילת הדרך

If one intends to return home on the same day, add the words in parentheses:

יְהִי רָצוֹן מִלְּפָנֶיךָ, יהוה אֱלֹהֵינוּ וֵאלֹהֵי אֲבוֹתֵינוּ
שֶׁתּוֹלִיכֵנוּ לְשָׁלוֹם, וְתַצְעִידֵנוּ לְשָׁלוֹם, וְתַדְרִיכֵנוּ לְשָׁלוֹם
וְתַגִּיעֵנוּ לִמְחוֹז חֶפְצֵנוּ לְחַיִּים וּלְשִׂמְחָה וּלְשָׁלוֹם
(וְתַחֲזִירֵנוּ לְבֵיתֵנוּ לְשָׁלוֹם)
וְתַצִּילֵנוּ מִכַּף כָּל אוֹיֵב וְאוֹרֵב בַּדֶּרֶךְ
וּמִכָּל מִינֵי פֻּרְעָנִיּוֹת הַמִּתְרַגְּשׁוֹת לָבוֹא לָעוֹלָם
וְתִשְׁלַח בְּרָכָה בְּמַעֲשֵׂה יָדֵינוּ
וְתִתְּנֵנוּ לְחֵן וּלְחֶסֶד וּלְרַחֲמִים בְּעֵינֶיךָ וּבְעֵינֵי כָל רוֹאֵינוּ
וְתִשְׁמַע קוֹל תַּחֲנוּנֵינוּ
כִּי אֵל שׁוֹמֵעַ תְּפִלָּה וְתַחֲנוּן אָתָּה.
בָּרוּךְ אַתָּה יהוה, שׁוֹמֵעַ תְּפִלָּה.

תהלים קכא יהוה יִשְׁמָר־צֵאתְךָ וּבוֹאֶךָ, מֵעַתָּה וְעַד־עוֹלָם:

Repeat three times:

בראשית לב וְיַעֲקֹב הָלַךְ לְדַרְכּוֹ, וַיִּפְגְּעוּ־בוֹ מַלְאֲכֵי אֱלֹהִים:
וַיֹּאמֶר יַעֲקֹב כַּאֲשֶׁר רָאָם, מַחֲנֵה אֱלֹהִים זֶה
וַיִּקְרָא שֵׁם־הַמָּקוֹם הַהוּא מַחֲנָיִם:

Repeat three times:

במדבר ו יְבָרֶכְךָ יהוה וְיִשְׁמְרֶךָ:
יָאֵר יהוה פָּנָיו אֵלֶיךָ וִיחֻנֶּךָּ:
יִשָּׂא יהוה פָּנָיו אֵלֶיךָ וְיָשֵׂם לְךָ שָׁלוֹם:

תהלים קכא שִׁיר לַמַּעֲלוֹת, אֶשָּׂא עֵינַי אֶל־הֶהָרִים, מֵאַיִן יָבֹא עֶזְרִי: עֶזְרִי מֵעִם יהוה, עֹשֵׂה שָׁמַיִם וָאָרֶץ: אַל־יִתֵּן לַמּוֹט רַגְלֶךָ, אַל־יָנוּם שֹׁמְרֶךָ: הִנֵּה לֹא־יָנוּם וְלֹא יִישָׁן, שׁוֹמֵר יִשְׂרָאֵל: יהוה שֹׁמְרֶךָ, יהוה צִלְּךָ עַל־יַד יְמִינֶךָ: יוֹמָם הַשֶּׁמֶשׁ לֹא־יַכֶּכָּה, וְיָרֵחַ בַּלָּיְלָה: יהוה יִשְׁמָרְךָ מִכָּל־רָע, יִשְׁמֹר אֶת־נַפְשֶׁךָ: יהוה יִשְׁמָר־צֵאתְךָ וּבוֹאֶךָ, מֵעַתָּה וְעַד־עוֹלָם:

קריאת התורה
TORAH READINGS

קריאת התורה מבהעלותך ועד כי תבוא לשחרית ומנחה של שבת ולימי שני וחמישי

THE READING OF THE TORAH BEHA'ALOTEKHA – KI-TAVO FOR SHAHARIT AND MINHA OF SHABBAT AND FOR MONDAYS AND THURSDAYS

The aliyot for Minha of Shabbat, Mondays and Thursdays are marked with an opening asterisk. The end of the Yisrael aliya is marked with two asterisks.

בהעלותך

ח וידבר יהוה אל־משה לאמר: דבר אל־אהרן ואמרת אליו בהעלתך את־ א ב
הנרת אל־מול פני המנורה יאירו שבעת הנרות: ויעש כן אהרן אל־מול ג
פני המנורה העלה נרתיה כאשר צוה יהוה את־משה: וזה מעשה המנרה ד
מקשה זהב עד־ירכה עד־פרחה מקשה הוא כמראה אשר הראה יהוה
את־משה כן עשה את־המנרה:
לוי *וידבר יהוה אל־משה לאמר: קח את־הלוים מתוך בני ישראל וטהרת ה ו
אתם: וכה־תעשה להם לטהרם הזה עליהם מי חטאת והעבירו תער ז
על־כל־בשרם וכבסו בגדיהם והטהרו: ולקחו פר בן־בקר ומנחתו סלת ח
בלולה בשמן ופר־שני בן־בקר תקח לחטאת: והקרבת את־הלוים לפני ט
ישראל אהל מועד והקהלת את־כל־עדת בני ישראל: והקרבת את־הלוים לפני י
יהוה וסמכו בני־ישראל את־ידיהם על־הלוים: והניף אהרן את־הלוים יא
תנופה לפני יהוה מאת בני ישראל והיו לעבד את־עבדת יהוה: והלוים יב
יסמכו את־ידיהם על ראש הפרים ועשה את־האחד חטאת ואת־האחד
עלה ליהוה לכפר על־הלוים: והעמדת את־הלוים לפני אהרן ולפני בניו יג
והנפת אתם תנופה ליהוה: והבדלת את־הלוים מתוך בני ישראל והיו לי יד
שני הלוים:** ואחרי־כן יבאו הלוים לעבד את־אהל מועד וטהרת אתם והנפת טו
אתם תנופה: כי נתנים נתנים המה לי מתוך בני ישראל תחת פטרת כל־ טז
רחם בכור כל מבני ישראל לקחתי אתם לי: כי לי כל־בכור בבני ישראל יז
באדם ובבהמה ביום הכתי כל־בכור בארץ מצרים הקדשתי אתם לי: ואקח יח
את־הלוים תחת כל־בכור בבני ישראל: ואתנה את־הלוים נתנים | לאהרן יט

וּלְבָנָיו מִתּוֹךְ בְּנֵי יִשְׂרָאֵל לַעֲבֹד אֶת־עֲבֹדַת בְּנֵי־יִשְׂרָאֵל בְּאֹהֶל מוֹעֵד וּלְכַפֵּר
עַל־בְּנֵי יִשְׂרָאֵל וְלֹא יִהְיֶה בִּבְנֵי יִשְׂרָאֵל נֶגֶף בְּגֶשֶׁת בְּנֵי־יִשְׂרָאֵל אֶל־הַקֹּדֶשׁ׃
כ וַיַּעַשׂ מֹשֶׁה וְאַהֲרֹן וְכָל־עֲדַת בְּנֵי־יִשְׂרָאֵל לַלְוִיִּם כְּכֹל אֲשֶׁר־צִוָּה יהוה אֶת־
כא מֹשֶׁה לַלְוִיִּם כֵּן־עָשׂוּ לָהֶם בְּנֵי יִשְׂרָאֵל׃ וַיִּתְחַטְּאוּ הַלְוִיִּם וַיְכַבְּסוּ בִּגְדֵיהֶם וַיָּנֶף
כב אַהֲרֹן אֹתָם תְּנוּפָה לִפְנֵי יהוה וַיְכַפֵּר עֲלֵיהֶם אַהֲרֹן לְטַהֲרָם׃ וְאַחֲרֵי־כֵן בָּאוּ
הַלְוִיִּם לַעֲבֹד אֶת־עֲבֹדָתָם בְּאֹהֶל מוֹעֵד לִפְנֵי אַהֲרֹן וְלִפְנֵי בָנָיו כַּאֲשֶׁר צִוָּה
כג יהוה אֶת־מֹשֶׁה עַל־הַלְוִיִּם כֵּן עָשׂוּ לָהֶם׃ וַיְדַבֵּר יהוה אֶל־מֹשֶׁה
כד לֵּאמֹר׃ זֹאת אֲשֶׁר לַלְוִיִּם מִבֶּן חָמֵשׁ וְעֶשְׂרִים שָׁנָה וָמַעְלָה יָבוֹא לִצְבֹא צָבָא
כה בַּעֲבֹדַת אֹהֶל מוֹעֵד׃ וּמִבֶּן חֲמִשִּׁים שָׁנָה יָשׁוּב מִצְּבָא הָעֲבֹדָה וְלֹא יַעֲבֹד
כו עוֹד׃ וְשֵׁרֵת אֶת־אֶחָיו בְּאֹהֶל מוֹעֵד לִשְׁמֹר מִשְׁמֶרֶת וַעֲבֹדָה לֹא יַעֲבֹד כָּכָה
תַּעֲשֶׂה לַלְוִיִּם בְּמִשְׁמְרֹתָם׃
ט א וַיְדַבֵּר יהוה אֶל־מֹשֶׁה בְמִדְבַּר־סִינַי בַּשָּׁנָה הַשֵּׁנִית לְצֵאתָם מֵאֶרֶץ מִצְרַיִם שלישי
ב ג בַּחֹדֶשׁ הָרִאשׁוֹן לֵאמֹר׃ וְיַעֲשׂוּ בְנֵי־יִשְׂרָאֵל אֶת־הַפָּסַח בְּמוֹעֲדוֹ׃ בְּאַרְבָּעָה
עָשָׂר־יוֹם בַּחֹדֶשׁ הַזֶּה בֵּין הָעַרְבַּיִם תַּעֲשׂוּ אֹתוֹ בְּמֹעֲדוֹ כְּכָל־חֻקֹּתָיו וּכְכָל־
ד ה מִשְׁפָּטָיו תַּעֲשׂוּ אֹתוֹ׃ וַיְדַבֵּר מֹשֶׁה אֶל־בְּנֵי יִשְׂרָאֵל לַעֲשֹׂת הַפָּסַח׃ וַיַּעֲשׂוּ
אֶת־הַפֶּסַח בָּרִאשׁוֹן בְּאַרְבָּעָה עָשָׂר יוֹם לַחֹדֶשׁ בֵּין הָעַרְבַּיִם בְּמִדְבַּר סִינָי
ו כְּכֹל אֲשֶׁר צִוָּה יהוה אֶת־מֹשֶׁה כֵּן עָשׂוּ בְּנֵי יִשְׂרָאֵל׃ וַיְהִי אֲנָשִׁים אֲשֶׁר הָיוּ
טְמֵאִים לְנֶפֶשׁ אָדָם וְלֹא־יָכְלוּ לַעֲשֹׂת־הַפֶּסַח בַּיּוֹם הַהוּא וַיִּקְרְבוּ לִפְנֵי מֹשֶׁה
ז וְלִפְנֵי אַהֲרֹן בַּיּוֹם הַהוּא׃ וַיֹּאמְרוּ הָאֲנָשִׁים הָהֵמָּה אֵלָיו אֲנַחְנוּ טְמֵאִים לְנֶפֶשׁ
אָדָם לָמָּה נִגָּרַע לְבִלְתִּי הַקְרִיב אֶת־קָרְבַּן יהוה בְּמֹעֲדוֹ בְּתוֹךְ בְּנֵי יִשְׂרָאֵל׃
ח וַיֹּאמֶר אֲלֵהֶם מֹשֶׁה עִמְדוּ וְאֶשְׁמְעָה מַה־יְצַוֶּה יהוה לָכֶם׃
ט י וַיְדַבֵּר יהוה אֶל־מֹשֶׁה לֵּאמֹר׃ דַּבֵּר אֶל־בְּנֵי יִשְׂרָאֵל לֵאמֹר אִישׁ אִישׁ כִּי־
יִהְיֶה טָמֵא ׀ לָנֶפֶשׁ אוֹ בְדֶרֶךְ רְחֹקָה לָכֶם אוֹ לְדֹרֹתֵיכֶם וְעָשָׂה פֶסַח לַיהוה׃
יא בַּחֹדֶשׁ הַשֵּׁנִי בְּאַרְבָּעָה עָשָׂר יוֹם בֵּין הָעַרְבַּיִם יַעֲשׂוּ אֹתוֹ עַל־מַצּוֹת וּמְרֹרִים
יב יֹאכְלֻהוּ׃ לֹא־יַשְׁאִירוּ מִמֶּנּוּ עַד־בֹּקֶר וְעֶצֶם לֹא יִשְׁבְּרוּ־בוֹ כְּכָל־חֻקַּת הַפֶּסַח
יג יַעֲשׂוּ אֹתוֹ׃ וְהָאִישׁ אֲשֶׁר־הוּא טָהוֹר וּבְדֶרֶךְ לֹא־הָיָה וְחָדַל לַעֲשׂוֹת הַפֶּסַח
וְנִכְרְתָה הַנֶּפֶשׁ הַהִוא מֵעַמֶּיהָ כִּי ׀ קָרְבַּן יהוה לֹא הִקְרִיב בְּמֹעֲדוֹ חֶטְאוֹ יִשָּׂא
יד הָאִישׁ הַהוּא׃ וְכִי־יָגוּר אִתְּכֶם גֵּר וְעָשָׂה פֶסַח לַיהוה כְּחֻקַּת הַפֶּסַח וּכְמִשְׁפָּטוֹ
טו כֵּן יַעֲשֶׂה חֻקָּה אַחַת יִהְיֶה לָכֶם וְלַגֵּר וּלְאֶזְרַח הָאָרֶץ׃ וּבְיוֹם הָקִים רביעי

אֶת־הַמִּשְׁכָּ֔ן כִּסָּ֤ה הֶֽעָנָן֙ אֶת־הַמִּשְׁכָּ֔ן לְאֹ֖הֶל הָעֵדֻ֑ת וּבָעֶ֜רֶב יִהְיֶ֧ה עַֽל־הַמִּשְׁכָּ֛ן
כְּמַרְאֵה־אֵ֖שׁ עַד־בֹּֽקֶר׃ כֵּ֚ן יִהְיֶ֣ה תָמִ֔יד הֶעָנָ֖ן יְכַסֶּ֑נּוּ וּמַרְאֵה־אֵ֖שׁ לָֽיְלָה׃ וּלְפִ֞י טז יז
הֵעָלֹ֤ת הֶֽעָנָן֙ מֵעַ֣ל הָאֹ֔הֶל וְאַ֣חֲרֵי כֵ֔ן יִסְע֖וּ בְּנֵ֣י יִשְׂרָאֵ֑ל וּבִמְק֗וֹם אֲשֶׁ֤ר יִשְׁכָּן־שָׁם֙
הֶֽעָנָ֔ן שָׁ֥ם יַחֲנ֖וּ בְּנֵ֥י יִשְׂרָאֵֽל׃ עַל־פִּ֣י יְהֹוָ֗ה יִסְעוּ֙ בְּנֵ֣י יִשְׂרָאֵ֔ל וְעַל־פִּ֥י יְהֹוָ֖ה יַחֲנ֑וּ יח
כָּל־יְמֵ֗י אֲשֶׁ֨ר יִשְׁכֹּ֧ן הֶעָנָ֛ן עַל־הַמִּשְׁכָּ֖ן יַחֲנֽוּ׃ וּבְהַאֲרִ֧יךְ הֶעָנָ֛ן עַל־הַמִּשְׁכָּ֖ן יָמִ֣ים יט
רַבִּ֑ים וְשָׁמְר֧וּ בְנֵֽי־יִשְׂרָאֵ֛ל אֶת־מִשְׁמֶ֥רֶת יְהֹוָ֖ה וְלֹ֥א יִסָּֽעוּ׃ וְיֵ֞שׁ אֲשֶׁ֨ר יִהְיֶ֧ה הֶעָנָ֛ן כ
יָמִ֥ים מִסְפָּ֖ר עַל־הַמִּשְׁכָּ֑ן עַל־פִּ֤י יְהֹוָה֙ יַחֲנ֔וּ וְעַל־פִּ֥י יְהֹוָ֖ה יִסָּֽעוּ׃ וְיֵ֞שׁ אֲשֶׁ֣ר יִהְיֶ֔ה כא
הֶעָנָן֙ מֵעֶ֣רֶב עַד־בֹּ֔קֶר וְנַעֲלָ֧ה הֶעָנָ֛ן בַּבֹּ֖קֶר וְנָסָ֑עוּ א֚וֹ יוֹמָ֣ם וָלַ֔יְלָה וְנַעֲלָ֥ה הֶעָנָ֖ן
וְנָסָֽעוּ׃ אֽוֹ־יֹמַ֣יִם אוֹ־חֹ֣דֶשׁ אוֹ־יָמִ֗ים בְּהַאֲרִ֨יךְ הֶעָנָ֤ן עַל־הַמִּשְׁכָּן֙ לִשְׁכֹּ֣ן עָלָ֔יו כב
יַחֲנ֥וּ בְנֵֽי־יִשְׂרָאֵ֖ל וְלֹ֣א יִסָּ֑עוּ וּבְהֵעָלֹת֖וֹ יִסָּֽעוּ׃ עַל־פִּ֤י יְהֹוָה֙ יַחֲנ֔וּ וְעַל־פִּ֥י יְהֹוָ֖ה כג
יִסָּ֑עוּ אֶת־מִשְׁמֶ֤רֶת יְהֹוָה֙ שָׁמָ֔רוּ עַל־פִּ֥י יְהֹוָ֖ה בְּיַד־מֹשֶֽׁה׃
ט וַיְדַבֵּ֥ר יְהֹוָ֖ה אֶל־מֹשֶׁ֥ה לֵּאמֹֽר׃ עֲשֵׂ֣ה לְךָ֗ שְׁתֵּי֙ חֲצוֹצְרֹ֣ת כֶּ֔סֶף מִקְשָׁ֖ה תַּעֲשֶׂ֣ה י א ב
אֹתָ֑ם וְהָי֤וּ לְךָ֙ לְמִקְרָ֣א הָֽעֵדָ֔ה וּלְמַסַּ֖ע אֶת־הַֽמַּחֲנֽוֹת׃ וְתָקְע֖וּ בָּהֵ֑ן וְנֽוֹעֲד֤וּ ג
אֵלֶ֙יךָ֙ כָּל־הָ֣עֵדָ֔ה אֶל־פֶּ֖תַח אֹ֥הֶל מוֹעֵֽד׃ וְאִם־בְּאַחַ֖ת יִתְקָ֑עוּ וְנֽוֹעֲד֤וּ אֵלֶ֙יךָ֙ ד
הַנְּשִׂיאִ֔ים רָאשֵׁ֖י אַלְפֵ֥י יִשְׂרָאֵֽל׃ וּתְקַעְתֶּ֖ם תְּרוּעָ֑ה וְנָֽסְעוּ֙ הַֽמַּחֲנ֔וֹת הַחֹנִ֖ים ה
קֵֽדְמָה׃ וּתְקַעְתֶּ֤ם תְּרוּעָה֙ שֵׁנִ֔ית וְנָֽסְעוּ֙ הַֽמַּחֲנ֔וֹת הַחֹנִ֖ים תֵּימָ֑נָה תְּרוּעָ֥ה יִתְקְע֖וּ ו
לְמַסְעֵיהֶֽם׃ וּבְהַקְהִ֖יל אֶת־הַקָּהָ֑ל תִּתְקְע֖וּ וְלֹ֥א תָרִֽיעוּ׃ וּבְנֵ֤י אַהֲרֹן֙ הַכֹּ֣הֲנִ֔ים ז ח
יִתְקְע֖וּ בַּחֲצֹצְר֑וֹת וְהָי֥וּ לָכֶ֛ם לְחֻקַּ֥ת עוֹלָ֖ם לְדֹרֹתֵיכֶֽם׃ וְכִֽי־תָבֹ֨אוּ מִלְחָמָ֜ה ט
בְּאַרְצְכֶ֗ם עַל־הַצַּר֙ הַצֹּרֵ֣ר אֶתְכֶ֔ם וַהֲרֵעֹתֶ֖ם בַּחֲצֹצְר֑וֹת וְנִזְכַּרְתֶּ֗ם לִפְנֵי֙ יְהֹוָ֣ה
אֱלֹֽהֵיכֶ֔ם וְנוֹשַׁעְתֶּ֖ם מֵאֹֽיְבֵיכֶֽם׃ וּבְי֨וֹם שִׂמְחַתְכֶ֥ם וּֽבְמוֹעֲדֵיכֶם֮ וּבְרָאשֵׁ֣י חָדְשֵׁיכֶם֒ י
וּתְקַעְתֶּ֣ם בַּחֲצֹֽצְרֹ֔ת עַ֚ל עֹלֹ֣תֵיכֶ֔ם וְעַ֖ל זִבְחֵ֣י שַׁלְמֵיכֶ֑ם וְהָי֨וּ לָכֶ֤ם לְזִכָּרוֹן֙ לִפְנֵ֣י
אֱלֹהֵיכֶ֔ם אֲנִ֖י יְהֹוָ֥ה אֱלֹהֵיכֶֽם׃
חמישי וַיְהִ֞י בַּשָּׁנָ֧ה הַשֵּׁנִ֛ית בַּחֹ֥דֶשׁ הַשֵּׁנִ֖י בְּעֶשְׂרִ֣ים בַּחֹ֑דֶשׁ נַעֲלָה֙ הֶֽעָנָ֔ן מֵעַ֖ל מִשְׁכַּ֥ן יא
הָעֵדֻֽת׃ וַיִּסְע֧וּ בְנֵי־יִשְׂרָאֵ֛ל לְמַסְעֵיהֶ֖ם מִמִּדְבַּ֣ר סִינָ֑י וַיִּשְׁכֹּ֥ן הֶעָנָ֖ן בְּמִדְבַּ֥ר יב
פָּארָֽן׃ וַיִּסְע֖וּ בָּרִאשֹׁנָ֑ה עַל־פִּ֥י יְהֹוָ֖ה בְּיַד־מֹשֶֽׁה׃ וַיִּסַּ֞ע דֶּ֣גֶל מַחֲנֵ֧ה בְנֵי־יְהוּדָ֛ה יג יד
בָּרִאשֹׁנָ֖ה לְצִבְאֹתָ֑ם וְעַ֨ל־צְבָא֔וֹ נַחְשׁ֖וֹן בֶּן־עַמִּֽינָדָֽב׃ וְעַ֨ל־צְבָ֔א מַטֵּ֖ה בְּנֵ֣י טו
יִשָּׂשכָ֑ר נְתַנְאֵ֖ל בֶּן־צוּעָֽר׃ וְעַ֨ל־צְבָ֔א מַטֵּ֖ה בְּנֵ֣י זְבוּלֻ֑ן אֱלִיאָ֖ב בֶּן־חֵלֹֽן׃ וְהוּרַ֖ד טז יז
הַמִּשְׁכָּ֑ן וְנָסְע֤וּ בְנֵֽי־גֵרְשׁוֹן֙ וּבְנֵ֣י מְרָרִ֔י נֹשְׂאֵ֖י הַמִּשְׁכָּֽן׃ וְנָסַ֗ע דֶּ֚גֶל מַחֲנֵ֣ה רְאוּבֵ֔ן יח
לְצִבְאֹתָ֑ם וְעַל־צְבָא֔וֹ אֱלִיצ֖וּר בֶּן־שְׁדֵיאֽוּר׃ וְעַ֨ל־צְבָ֔א מַטֵּ֖ה בְּנֵ֣י שִׁמְע֑וֹן יט

כ כא שלמיאל בן־צורישדי: ועל־צבא מטה בני־גד אליסף בן־דעואל: ונסעו
כב הקהתים נשאי המקדש והקימו את־המשכן עד־באם: ונסע דגל מחנה
כג בני־אפרים לצבאתם ועל־צבאו אלישמע בן־עמיהוד: ועל־צבא מטה
כד בני מנשה גמליאל בן־פדהצור: ועל־צבא מטה בני בנימן אבידן בן־
כה גדעוני: ונסע דגל מחנה בני־דן מאסף לכל־המחנת לצבאתם ועל־צבאו
כו כז אחיעזר בן־עמישדי: ועל־צבא מטה בני אשר פגעיאל בן־עכרן: ועל־
כח צבא מטה בני נפתלי אחירע בן־עינן: אלה מסעי בני־ישראל לצבאתם
כט ויסעו: ויאמר משה לחבב בן־רעואל המדיני חתן משה נסעים ׀
אנחנו אל־המקום אשר אמר יהוה אתו אתן לכם לכה אתנו והטבנו לך
ל כי־יהוה דבר־טוב על־ישראל: ויאמר אליו לא אלך כי אם־אל־ארצי ואל־
לא מולדתי אלך: ויאמר אל־נא תעזב אתנו כי ׀ על־כן ידעת חנתנו במדבר
לב והיית לנו לעינים: והיה כי־תלך עמנו והיה ׀ הטוב ההוא אשר ייטיב יהוה
לג עמנו והטבנו לך: ויסעו מהר יהוה דרך שלשת ימים וארון ברית־יהוה
לד נסע לפניהם דרך שלשת ימים לתור להם מנוחה: וענן יהוה עליהם יומם
לה בנסעם מן־המחנה: ׆ ויהי בנסע הארן ויאמר משה קומה ׀ ששי
לו יהוה ויפצו איביך וינסו משנאיך מפניך: ובנחה יאמר שובה יהוה רבבות
אלפי ישראל: ׆

יא א ויהי העם כמתאננים רע באזני יהוה וישמע יהוה ויחר אפו ותבער־בם אש
ב יהוה ותאכל בקצה המחנה: ויצעק העם אל־משה ויתפלל משה אל־יהוה
ג ותשקע האש: ויקרא שם־המקום ההוא תבערה כי־בערה בם אש יהוה:
ד והאספסף אשר בקרבו התאוו תאוה וישבו ויבכו גם בני ישראל ויאמרו מי
ה יאכלנו בשר: זכרנו את־הדגה אשר־נאכל במצרים חנם את הקשאים ואת
ו האבטחים ואת־החציר ואת־הבצלים ואת־השומים: ועתה נפשנו יבשה
ז ח אין כל בלתי אל־המן עינינו: והמן כזרע־גד הוא ועינו כעין הבדלח: שטו
העם ולקטו וטחנו ברחים או דכו במדכה ובשלו בפרור ועשו אתו עגות
ט והיה טעמו כטעם לשד השמן: וברדת הטל על־המחנה לילה ירד המן
י עליו: וישמע משה את־העם בכה למשפחתיו איש לפתח אהלו ויחר־אף
יא יהוה מאד ובעיני משה רע: ויאמר משה אל־יהוה למה הרעת לעבדך
יב ולמה לא־מצתי חן בעיניך לשום את־משא כל־העם הזה עלי: האנכי הריתי

את כל־העם הזה אם־אנכי ילדתיהו כי־תאמר אלי שאהו בחיקך כאשר
ישא האמן את־הינק על האדמה אשר נשבעת לאבתיו: מאין לי בשר לתת יג
לכל־העם הזה כי־יבכו עלי לאמר תנה־לנו בשר ונאכלה: לא־אוכל אנכי יד
לבדי לשאת את־כל־העם הזה כי כבד ממני: ואם־ככה | את־עשה לי הרגני טו
נא הרג אם־מצאתי חן בעיניך ואל־אראה ברעתי:
י ויאמר יהוה אל־משה אספה־לי שבעים איש מזקני ישראל אשר ידעת טז
כי־הם זקני העם ושטריו ולקחת אתם אל־אהל מועד והתיצבו שם עמך:
וירדתי ודברתי עמך שם ואצלתי מן־הרוח אשר עליך ושמתי עליהם ונשאו יז
אתך במשא העם ולא־תשא אתה לבדך: ואל־העם תאמר התקדשו למחר יח
ואכלתם בשר כי בכיתם באזני יהוה לאמר מי יאכלנו בשר כי־טוב לנו
במצרים ונתן יהוה לכם בשר ואכלתם: לא יום אחד תאכלון ולא יומים יט
ולא | חמשה ימים ולא עשרה ימים ולא עשרים יום: עד | חדש ימים עד כ
אשר־יצא מאפכם והיה לכם לזרא יען כי־מאסתם את־יהוה אשר בקרבכם
ותבכו לפניו לאמר למה זה יצאנו ממצרים: ויאמר משה שש־מאות אלף כא
רגלי העם אשר אנכי בקרבו ואתה אמרת בשר אתן להם ואכלו חדש
ימים: הצאן ובקר ישחט להם ומצא להם אם את־כל־דגי הים יאסף להם כב
ומצא להם:
יא ויאמר יהוה אל־משה היד יהוה תקצר עתה תראה היקרך דברי אם־לא: כג
ויצא משה וידבר אל־העם את דברי יהוה ויאסף שבעים איש מזקני העם כד
ויעמד אתם סביבת האהל: וירד יהוה | בענן וידבר אליו ויאצל מן־הרוח כה
אשר עליו ויתן על־שבעים איש הזקנים ויהי כנוח עליהם הרוח ויתנבאו
ולא יספו: וישארו שני־אנשים | במחנה שם האחד | אלדד ושם השני מידד כו
ותנח עלהם הרוח והמה בכתבים ולא יצאו האהלה ויתנבאו במחנה:
וירץ הנער ויגד למשה ויאמר אלדד ומידד מתנבאים במחנה: ויען כז כח
יהושע בן־נון משרת משה מבחריו ויאמר אדני משה כלאם: ויאמר לו כט
משה המקנא אתה לי ומי יתן כל־עם יהוה נביאים כי־יתן יהוה את־רוחו
שביעי עליהם: ויאסף משה אל־המחנה הוא וזקני ישראל: ורוח נסע | מאת יהוה ל לא
ויגז שלוים מן־הים ויטש על־המחנה כדרך יום כה וכדרך יום כה סביבות
המחנה וכאמתים על־פני הארץ: ויקם העם כל־היום ההוא וכל־הלילה לב

וְכֹל ׀ י֣וֹם הַֽמׇּחֳרָ֗ת וַיַּֽאַסְפוּ֙ אֶת־הַשְּׂלָ֔ו הַמַּמְעִ֕יט אָסַ֖ף עֲשָׂרָ֣ה חֳמָרִ֑ים וַיִּשְׁטְח֤וּ
לג לָהֶם֙ שָׁט֔וֹחַ סְבִיב֖וֹת הַֽמַּחֲנֶֽה׃ הַבָּשָׂ֗ר עוֹדֶ֙נּוּ֙ בֵּ֣ין שִׁנֵּיהֶ֔ם טֶ֖רֶם יִכָּרֵ֑ת וְאַ֤ף יְהוָה֙
לד חָרָ֣ה בָעָ֔ם וַיַּ֤ךְ יְהוָה֙ בָּעָ֔ם מַכָּ֖ה רַבָּ֥ה מְאֹֽד׃ וַיִּקְרָ֛א אֶת־שֵֽׁם־הַמָּק֥וֹם הַה֖וּא
לה קִבְר֣וֹת הַֽתַּאֲוָ֑ה כִּי־שָׁם֙ קָֽבְר֔וּ אֶת־הָעָ֖ם הַמִּתְאַוִּֽים׃ מִקִּבְר֧וֹת הַֽתַּאֲוָ֛ה נָסְע֥וּ
הָעָ֖ם חֲצֵר֑וֹת וַיִּהְי֖וּ בַּחֲצֵרֽוֹת׃

יב א וַתְּדַבֵּ֨ר מִרְיָ֤ם וְאַהֲרֹן֙ בְּמֹשֶׁ֔ה עַל־אֹד֛וֹת הָאִשָּׁ֥ה הַכֻּשִׁ֖ית אֲשֶׁ֣ר לָקָ֑ח כִּֽי־
ב אִשָּׁ֥ה כֻשִׁ֖ית לָקָֽח׃ וַיֹּאמְר֗וּ הֲרַ֤ק אַךְ־בְּמֹשֶׁה֙ דִּבֶּ֣ר יְהוָ֔ה הֲלֹ֖א גַּם־בָּ֣נוּ
ג דִבֵּ֑ר וַיִּשְׁמַ֖ע יְהוָֽה׃ וְהָאִ֥ישׁ מֹשֶׁ֖ה עָנָ֣ו מְאֹ֑ד מִכֹּל֙ הָֽאָדָ֔ם אֲשֶׁ֖ר עַל־פְּנֵ֥י
ד הָאֲדָמָֽה׃ וַיֹּ֨אמֶר יְהוָ֜ה פִּתְאֹ֗ם אֶל־מֹשֶׁ֤ה וְאֶֽל־אַהֲרֹן֙ וְאֶל־מִרְיָ֔ם
ה צְא֥וּ שְׁלׇשְׁתְּכֶ֖ם אֶל־אֹ֣הֶל מוֹעֵ֑ד וַיֵּצְא֖וּ שְׁלׇשְׁתָּֽם׃ וַיֵּ֤רֶד יְהוָה֙ בְּעַמּ֣וּד עָנָ֔ן
ו וַֽיַּעֲמֹ֖ד פֶּ֣תַח הָאֹ֑הֶל וַיִּקְרָא֙ אַהֲרֹ֣ן וּמִרְיָ֔ם וַיֵּצְא֖וּ שְׁנֵיהֶֽם׃ וַיֹּ֖אמֶר שִׁמְעוּ־נָ֣א
דְבָרָ֑י אִם־יִֽהְיֶה֙ נְבִ֣יאֲכֶ֔ם יְהוָ֗ה בַּמַּרְאָה֙ אֵלָ֣יו אֶתְוַדָּ֔ע בַּחֲל֖וֹם אֲדַבֶּר־בּֽוֹ׃
ז ח לֹא־כֵ֖ן עַבְדִּ֣י מֹשֶׁ֑ה בְּכׇל־בֵּיתִ֖י נֶאֱמָ֥ן הֽוּא׃ פֶּ֣ה אֶל־פֶּ֞ה אֲדַבֶּר־בּ֗וֹ וּמַרְאֶה֙
וְלֹ֣א בְחִידֹ֔ת וּתְמֻנַ֥ת יְהוָ֖ה יַבִּ֑יט וּמַדּ֙וּעַ֙ לֹ֣א יְרֵאתֶ֔ם לְדַבֵּ֖ר בְּעַבְדִּ֥י בְמֹשֶֽׁה׃
ט י וַיִּֽחַר־אַ֧ף יְהוָ֛ה בָּ֖ם וַיֵּלַֽךְ׃ וְהֶעָנָ֗ן סָ֚ר מֵעַ֣ל הָאֹ֔הֶל וְהִנֵּ֥ה מִרְיָ֖ם מְצֹרַ֣עַת כַּשָּׁ֑לֶג
יא וַיִּ֧פֶן אַהֲרֹ֛ן אֶל־מִרְיָ֖ם וְהִנֵּ֥ה מְצֹרָֽעַת׃ וַיֹּ֥אמֶר אַהֲרֹ֖ן אֶל־מֹשֶׁ֑ה בִּ֣י אֲדֹנִ֔י אַל־נָ֨א
יב תָשֵׁ֤ת עָלֵ֙ינוּ֙ חַטָּ֔את אֲשֶׁ֥ר נוֹאַ֖לְנוּ וַאֲשֶׁ֥ר חָטָֽאנוּ׃ אַל־נָ֥א תְהִ֖י כַּמֵּ֑ת אֲשֶׁ֤ר
יג בְּצֵאתוֹ֙ מֵרֶ֣חֶם אִמּ֔וֹ וַיֵּאָכֵ֖ל חֲצִ֥י בְשָׂרֽוֹ׃ וַיִּצְעַ֣ק מֹשֶׁ֔ה אֶל־יְהוָ֖ה לֵאמֹ֑ר אֵ֕ל נָ֛א
רְפָ֥א נָ֖א לָֽהּ׃
מפטיר יד וַיֹּ֨אמֶר יְהוָ֜ה אֶל־מֹשֶׁ֗ה וְאָבִ֙יהָ֙ יָרֹ֤ק יָרַק֙ בְּפָנֶ֔יהָ הֲלֹ֥א תִכָּלֵ֖ם שִׁבְעַ֣ת יָמִ֑ים
טו תִּסָּגֵ֞ר שִׁבְעַ֤ת יָמִים֙ מִח֣וּץ לַֽמַּחֲנֶ֔ה וְאַחַ֖ר תֵּאָסֵֽף׃ וַתִּסָּגֵ֥ר מִרְיָ֛ם מִח֥וּץ לַֽמַּחֲנֶ֖ה
טז שִׁבְעַ֣ת יָמִ֑ים וְהָעָם֙ לֹ֣א נָסַ֔ע עַד־הֵאָסֵ֖ף מִרְיָֽם׃ וְאַחַ֛ר נָסְע֥וּ הָעָ֖ם מֵחֲצֵר֑וֹת
וַֽיַּחֲנ֖וּ בְּמִדְבַּ֥ר פָּארָֽן׃

יב שלח יג א ב וַיְדַבֵּ֥ר יְהוָ֖ה אֶל־מֹשֶׁ֥ה לֵּאמֹֽר׃ שְׁלַח־לְךָ֣ אֲנָשִׁ֗ים וְיָתֻ֙רוּ֙ אֶת־אֶ֣רֶץ כְּנַ֔עַן
אֲשֶׁר־אֲנִ֥י נֹתֵ֖ן לִבְנֵ֣י יִשְׂרָאֵ֑ל אִ֣ישׁ אֶחָד֩ אִ֨ישׁ אֶחָ֜ד לְמַטֵּ֤ה אֲבֹתָיו֙ תִּשְׁלָ֔חוּ כֹּ֖ל
ג נָשִׂ֥יא בָהֶֽם׃ וַיִּשְׁלַ֨ח אֹתָ֥ם מֹשֶׁ֛ה מִמִּדְבַּ֥ר פָּארָ֖ן עַל־פִּ֣י יְהוָ֑ה כֻּלָּ֣ם אֲנָשִׁ֔ים רָאשֵׁ֥י
לוי ד ה בְּנֵֽי־יִשְׂרָאֵ֖ל הֵֽמָּה׃ *וְאֵ֖לֶּה שְׁמוֹתָ֑ם לְמַטֵּ֣ה רְאוּבֵ֔ן שַׁמּ֖וּעַ בֶּן־זַכּֽוּר׃ לְמַטֵּ֣ה
ו ז שִׁמְע֔וֹן שָׁפָ֖ט בֶּן־חוֹרִֽי׃ לְמַטֵּ֣ה יְהוּדָ֔ה כָּלֵ֖ב בֶּן־יְפֻנֶּֽה׃ לְמַטֵּ֣ה יִשָּׂשכָ֔ר יִגְאָ֖ל
ח ט בֶּן־יוֹסֵֽף׃ לְמַטֵּ֥ה אֶפְרָ֖יִם הוֹשֵׁ֥עַ בִּן־נֽוּן׃ לְמַטֵּ֥ה בִנְיָמִ֖ן פַּלְטִ֥י בֶּן־רָפֽוּא׃ לְמַטֵּ֥ה

זְבוּלֻ֔ן גַּדִּיאֵ֖ל בֶּן־סוֹדִֽי׃ לְמַטֵּ֥ה יוֹסֵ֖ף לְמַטֵּ֣ה מְנַשֶּׁ֑ה גַּדִּ֖י בֶּן־סוּסִֽי׃ לְמַטֵּ֣ה דָ֔ן יא יב
עַמִּיאֵ֖ל בֶּן־גְּמַלִּֽי׃ לְמַטֵּ֣ה אָשֵׁ֔ר סְת֖וּר בֶּן־מִיכָאֵֽל׃ לְמַטֵּ֣ה נַפְתָּלִ֔י נַחְבִּ֖י בֶּן־ יג יד
וׇפְסִֽי׃ לְמַטֵּ֣ה גָ֔ד גְּאוּאֵ֖ל בֶּן־מָכִֽי׃ אֵ֤לֶּה שְׁמוֹת֙ הָֽאֲנָשִׁ֔ים אֲשֶׁר־שָׁלַ֥ח מֹשֶׁ֖ה טו טז
ישראל לָת֣וּר אֶת־הָאָ֑רֶץ וַיִּקְרָ֥א מֹשֶׁ֛ה לְהוֹשֵׁ֥עַ בִּן־נ֖וּן יְהוֹשֻֽׁעַ׃ *וַיִּשְׁלַ֤ח אֹתָם֙ מֹשֶׁ֔ה יז
לָת֖וּר אֶת־אֶ֣רֶץ כְּנָ֑עַן וַיֹּ֣אמֶר אֲלֵהֶ֗ם עֲל֥וּ זֶה֙ בַּנֶּ֔גֶב וַעֲלִיתֶ֖ם אֶת־הָהָֽר׃ וּרְאִיתֶ֥ם יח
אֶת־הָאָ֖רֶץ מַה־הִ֑וא וְאֶת־הָעָם֙ הַיֹּשֵׁ֣ב עָלֶ֔יהָ הֶחָזָ֥ק הוּא֙ הֲרָפֶ֔ה הַמְעַ֥ט ה֖וּא
אִם־רָֽב׃ וּמָ֣ה הָאָ֗רֶץ אֲשֶׁר־הוּא֙ יֹשֵׁ֣ב בָּ֔הּ הֲטוֹבָ֥ה הִ֖וא אִם־רָעָ֑ה וּמָ֣ה הֶֽעָרִ֗ים יט
אֲשֶׁר־הוּא֙ יוֹשֵׁ֣ב בָּהֵ֔נָּה הַבְּמַֽחֲנִ֖ים אִ֥ם בְּמִבְצָרִֽים׃ וּמָ֣ה הָ֠אָרֶץ הַשְּׁמֵנָ֨ה הִ֜וא כ
אִם־רָזָ֗ה הֲיֵֽשׁ־בָּ֥הּ עֵץ֙ אִם־אַ֔יִן וְהִ֨תְחַזַּקְתֶּ֔ם וּלְקַחְתֶּ֖ם מִפְּרִ֣י הָאָ֑רֶץ וְהַ֨יָּמִ֔ים
שני יְמֵ֖י בִּכּוּרֵ֥י עֲנָבִֽים׃** וַֽיַּעֲל֖וּ וַיָּתֻ֣רוּ אֶת־הָאָ֑רֶץ מִמִּדְבַּר־צִ֥ן עַד־רְחֹ֖ב לְבֹ֥א כא
חֲמָֽת׃ וַיַּעֲל֣וּ בַנֶּגֶב֮ וַיָּבֹ֣א עַד־חֶבְרוֹן֒ וְשָׁ֤ם אֲחִימַן֙ שֵׁשַׁ֣י וְתַלְמַ֔י יְלִידֵ֖י הָעֲנָ֑ק כב
וְחֶבְר֗וֹן שֶׁ֤בַע שָׁנִים֙ נִבְנְתָ֔ה לִפְנֵ֖י צֹ֥עַן מִצְרָֽיִם׃ וַיָּבֹ֜אוּ עַד־נַ֣חַל אֶשְׁכֹּ֗ל וַיִּכְרְת֨וּ כג
מִשָּׁ֤ם זְמוֹרָה֙ וְאֶשְׁכּ֤וֹל עֲנָבִים֙ אֶחָ֔ד וַיִּשָּׂאֻ֥הוּ בַמּ֖וֹט בִּשְׁנָ֑יִם וּמִן־הָרִמֹּנִ֖ים וּמִן־
הַתְּאֵנִֽים׃ לַמָּק֣וֹם הַה֔וּא קָרָ֖א נַ֣חַל אֶשְׁכּ֑וֹל עַ֚ל אֹד֣וֹת הָֽאֶשְׁכּ֔וֹל אֲשֶׁר־כָּרְת֥וּ כד
מִשָּׁ֖ם בְּנֵ֥י יִשְׂרָאֵֽל׃ וַיָּשֻׁ֖בוּ מִתּ֣וּר הָאָ֑רֶץ מִקֵּ֖ץ אַרְבָּעִ֥ים יֽוֹם׃ וַיֵּלְכ֡וּ וַיָּבֹ֣אוּ אֶל־ כה כו
מֹשֶׁ֨ה וְאֶֽל־אַהֲרֹ֜ן וְאֶל־כׇּל־עֲדַ֧ת בְּנֵֽי־יִשְׂרָאֵ֛ל אֶל־מִדְבַּ֥ר פָּארָ֖ן קָדֵ֑שָׁה וַיָּשִׁ֨יבוּ
אֹתָ֤ם דָּבָר֙ וְאֶת־כׇּל־הָ֣עֵדָ֔ה וַיַּרְא֖וּם אֶת־פְּרִ֥י הָאָֽרֶץ׃ וַיְסַפְּרוּ־לוֹ֙ וַיֹּ֣אמְר֔וּ בָּ֕אנוּ כז
אֶל־הָאָ֖רֶץ אֲשֶׁ֣ר שְׁלַחְתָּ֑נוּ וְ֠גַ֠ם זָבַ֨ת חָלָ֥ב וּדְבַ֛שׁ הִ֖וא וְזֶה־פִּרְיָֽהּ׃ אֶ֚פֶס כִּֽי־עַ֣ז כח
הָעָ֔ם הַיֹּשֵׁ֖ב בָּאָ֑רֶץ וְהֶעָרִ֗ים בְּצֻר֤וֹת גְּדֹלֹת֙ מְאֹ֔ד וְגַם־יְלִדֵ֥י הָעֲנָ֖ק רָאִ֥ינוּ שָֽׁם׃
עֲמָלֵ֥ק יוֹשֵׁ֖ב בְּאֶ֣רֶץ הַנֶּ֑גֶב וְ֠הַחִתִּ֠י וְהַיְבוּסִ֤י וְהָֽאֱמֹרִי֙ יוֹשֵׁ֣ב בָּהָ֔ר וְהַֽכְּנַעֲנִי֙ יֹשֵׁ֣ב כט
עַל־הַיָּ֔ם וְעַ֖ל יַ֥ד הַיַּרְדֵּֽן׃ וַיַּ֧הַס כָּלֵ֛ב אֶת־הָעָ֖ם אֶל־מֹשֶׁ֑ה וַיֹּ֗אמֶר עָלֹ֤ה נַעֲלֶה֙ ל
וְיָרַ֣שְׁנוּ אֹתָ֔הּ כִּֽי־יָכ֥וֹל נוּכַ֖ל לָֽהּ׃ וְהָ֨אֲנָשִׁ֜ים אֲשֶׁ֤ר עָל֣וּ עִמּוֹ֙ אָֽמְר֔וּ לֹ֥א נוּכַ֖ל לא
לַעֲל֣וֹת אֶל־הָעָ֑ם כִּֽי־חָזָ֥ק ה֖וּא מִמֶּֽנּוּ׃ וַיֹּצִ֜יאוּ דִּבַּ֤ת הָאָ֙רֶץ֙ אֲשֶׁ֣ר תָּר֣וּ אֹתָ֔הּ אֶל־ לב
בְּנֵ֥י יִשְׂרָאֵ֖ל לֵאמֹ֑ר הָאָ֡רֶץ אֲשֶׁר֩ עָבַ֨רְנוּ בָ֜הּ לָת֣וּר אֹתָ֗הּ אֶ֣רֶץ אֹכֶ֤לֶת יוֹשְׁבֶ֙יהָ֙
ה֔וּא וְכׇל־הָעָ֛ם אֲשֶׁר־רָאִ֥ינוּ בְתוֹכָ֖הּ אַנְשֵׁ֥י מִדּֽוֹת׃ וְשָׁ֣ם רָאִ֗ינוּ אֶת־הַנְּפִילִ֛ים בְּנֵ֥י לג
עֲנָ֖ק מִן־הַנְּפִלִ֑ים וַנְּהִ֤י בְעֵינֵ֙ינוּ֙ כַּחֲגָבִ֔ים וְכֵ֥ן הָיִ֖ינוּ בְּעֵינֵיהֶֽם׃ וַתִּשָּׂא֙ כׇּל־הָ֣עֵדָ֔ה א יד
וַֽיִּתְּנ֖וּ אֶת־קוֹלָ֑ם וַיִּבְכּ֥וּ הָעָ֖ם בַּלַּ֥יְלָה הַהֽוּא׃ וַיִּלֹּ֙נוּ֙ עַל־מֹשֶׁ֣ה וְעַֽל־אַהֲרֹ֔ן כֹּ֖ל ב
בְּנֵ֣י יִשְׂרָאֵ֑ל וַיֹּאמְר֨וּ אֲלֵהֶ֜ם כׇּל־הָעֵדָ֗ה לוּ־מַ֙תְנוּ֙ בְּאֶ֣רֶץ מִצְרַ֔יִם א֛וֹ בַּמִּדְבָּ֥ר
הַזֶּ֖ה לוּ־מָֽתְנוּ׃ וְלָמָ֣ה יְ֠הֹוָ֠ה מֵבִ֨יא אֹתָ֜נוּ אֶל־הָאָ֤רֶץ הַזֹּאת֙ לִנְפֹּ֣ל בַּחֶ֔רֶב נָשֵׁ֤ינוּ ג

ד וְטַפֵּ֖נוּ יִהְי֣וּ לָבַ֑ז הֲל֧וֹא ט֛וֹב לָ֖נוּ שׁ֥וּב מִצְרָֽיְמָה׃ וַיֹּאמְר֖וּ אִ֣ישׁ אֶל־אָחִ֑יו נִתְּנָ֥ה
ה רֹ֖אשׁ וְנָשׁ֥וּבָה מִצְרָֽיְמָה׃ וַיִּפֹּ֥ל מֹשֶׁ֛ה וְאַהֲרֹ֖ן עַל־פְּנֵיהֶ֑ם לִפְנֵ֕י כָּל־קְהַ֖ל עֲדַ֥ת בְּנֵ֥י
ו יִשְׂרָאֵֽל׃ וִיהוֹשֻׁ֣עַ בִּן־נ֗וּן וְכָלֵב֙ בֶּן־יְפֻנֶּ֔ה מִן־הַתָּרִ֖ים אֶת־הָאָ֑רֶץ קָרְע֖וּ בִּגְדֵיהֶֽם׃
ז וַיֹּ֣אמְר֔וּ אֶל־כָּל־עֲדַ֥ת בְּנֵי־יִשְׂרָאֵ֖ל לֵאמֹ֑ר הָאָ֗רֶץ אֲשֶׁ֨ר עָבַ֤רְנוּ בָהּ֙ לָת֣וּר אֹתָ֔הּ
ח טוֹבָ֥ה הָאָ֖רֶץ מְאֹ֥ד מְאֹֽד׃ אִם־חָפֵ֥ץ בָּ֙נוּ֙ יהוה וְהֵבִ֤יא אֹתָ֙נוּ֙ אֶל־הָאָ֣רֶץ הַזֹּ֔את שלישי
ט וּנְתָנָ֖הּ לָ֑נוּ אֶ֕רֶץ אֲשֶׁר־הִ֛וא זָבַ֥ת חָלָ֖ב וּדְבָֽשׁ׃ אַ֣ךְ בַּיהוה֮ אַל־תִּמְרֹ֒דוּ֒ וְאַתֶּ֗ם
אַל־תִּֽירְאוּ֙ אֶת־עַ֣ם הָאָ֔רֶץ כִּ֥י לַחְמֵ֖נוּ הֵ֑ם סָ֣ר צִלָּ֞ם מֵעֲלֵיהֶ֛ם וַיהוה אִתָּ֖נוּ אַל־
י תִּירָאֻֽם׃ וַיֹּֽאמְרוּ֙ כָּל־הָ֣עֵדָ֔ה לִרְגּ֥וֹם אֹתָ֖ם בָּאֲבָנִ֑ים וּכְב֣וֹד יהוה נִרְאָה֙ בְּאֹ֣הֶל
מוֹעֵ֔ד אֶֽל־כָּל־בְּנֵ֖י יִשְׂרָאֵֽל׃
יא וַיֹּ֤אמֶר יהוה֙ אֶל־מֹשֶׁ֔ה עַד־אָ֥נָה יְנַאֲצֻ֖נִי הָעָ֣ם הַזֶּ֑ה וְעַד־אָ֙נָה֙ לֹא־יַאֲמִ֣ינוּ בִ֔י יג
יב בְּכֹל֙ הָֽאֹת֔וֹת אֲשֶׁ֥ר עָשִׂ֖יתִי בְּקִרְבּֽוֹ׃ אַכֶּ֥נּוּ בַדֶּ֖בֶר וְאוֹרִשֶׁ֑נּוּ וְאֶֽעֱשֶׂה֙ אֹֽתְךָ֔ לְגוֹי־
יג גָּד֥וֹל וְעָצ֖וּם מִמֶּֽנּוּ׃ וַיֹּ֥אמֶר מֹשֶׁ֖ה אֶל־יהוה וְשָֽׁמְע֣וּ מִצְרַ֔יִם כִּֽי־הֶעֱלִ֧יתָ בְכֹחֲךָ֛
יד אֶת־הָעָ֥ם הַזֶּ֖ה מִקִּרְבּֽוֹ׃ וְאָמְר֗וּ אֶל־יוֹשֵׁב֮ הָאָ֣רֶץ הַזֹּאת֒ שָֽׁמְעוּ֙ כִּֽי־אַתָּ֣ה יהוה
בְּקֶ֖רֶב הָעָ֣ם הַזֶּ֑ה אֲשֶׁר־עַ֨יִן בְּעַ֜יִן נִרְאָ֣ה ׀ אַתָּ֣ה יהוה וַעֲנָֽנְךָ֙ עֹמֵ֣ד עֲלֵהֶ֔ם וּבְעַמֻּ֣ד
טו עָנָ֗ן אַתָּ֨ה הֹלֵ֤ךְ לִפְנֵיהֶם֙ יוֹמָ֔ם וּבְעַמּ֥וּד אֵ֖שׁ לָֽיְלָה׃ וְהֵמַתָּ֛ה אֶת־הָעָ֥ם הַזֶּ֖ה כְּאִ֣ישׁ
טז אֶחָ֑ד וְאָֽמְרוּ֙ הַגּוֹיִ֔ם אֲשֶׁר־שָׁמְע֥וּ אֶֽת־שִׁמְעֲךָ֖ לֵאמֹֽר׃ מִבִּלְתִּ֞י יְכֹ֣לֶת יהוה
יז לְהָבִיא֙ אֶת־הָעָ֣ם הַזֶּ֔ה אֶל־הָאָ֖רֶץ אֲשֶׁר־נִשְׁבַּ֣ע לָהֶ֑ם וַיִּשְׁחָטֵ֖ם בַּמִּדְבָּֽר׃ וְעַתָּ֕ה
יח יִגְדַּל־נָ֖א כֹּ֣חַ אֲדֹנָ֑י כַּאֲשֶׁ֥ר דִּבַּ֖רְתָּ לֵאמֹֽר׃ יהוה אֶ֤רֶךְ אַפַּ֙יִם֙ וְרַב־חֶ֔סֶד נֹשֵׂ֥א
עָוֺ֖ן וָפָ֑שַׁע וְנַקֵּה֙ לֹ֣א יְנַקֶּ֔ה פֹּקֵ֞ד עֲוֺ֣ן אָבוֹת֙ עַל־בָּנִ֔ים עַל־שִׁלֵּשִׁ֖ים וְעַל־רִבֵּעִֽים׃
יט סְלַח־נָ֗א לַעֲוֺ֛ן הָעָ֥ם הַזֶּ֖ה כְּגֹ֣דֶל חַסְדֶּ֑ךָ וְכַאֲשֶׁ֤ר נָשָׂ֙אתָה֙ לָעָ֣ם הַזֶּ֔ה מִמִּצְרַ֖יִם
כ כא וְעַד־הֵֽנָּה׃ וַיֹּ֣אמֶר יהוה סָלַ֖חְתִּי כִּדְבָרֶֽךָ׃ וְאוּלָ֖ם חַי־אָ֑נִי וְיִמָּלֵ֥א כְבוֹד־יהוה
כב אֶת־כָּל־הָאָֽרֶץ׃ כִּ֣י כָל־הָֽאֲנָשִׁ֗ים הָרֹאִ֤ים אֶת־כְּבֹדִי֙ וְאֶת־אֹ֣תֹתַ֔י אֲשֶׁר־עָשִׂ֥יתִי
כג בְמִצְרַ֖יִם וּבַמִּדְבָּ֑ר וַיְנַסּ֣וּ אֹתִ֗י זֶ֚ה עֶ֣שֶׂר פְּעָמִ֔ים וְלֹ֥א שָׁמְע֖וּ בְּקוֹלִֽי׃ אִם־יִרְאוּ֙
כד אֶת־הָאָ֔רֶץ אֲשֶׁ֥ר נִשְׁבַּ֖עְתִּי לַאֲבֹתָ֑ם וְכָל־מְנַאֲצַ֖י לֹ֥א יִרְאֽוּהָ׃ וְעַבְדִּ֣י כָלֵ֗ב עֵ֚קֶב
הָֽיְתָ֞ה ר֤וּחַ אַחֶ֙רֶת֙ עִמּ֔וֹ וַיְמַלֵּ֖א אַחֲרָ֑י וַהֲבִיאֹתִ֗יו אֶל־הָאָ֙רֶץ֙ אֲשֶׁר־בָּ֣א שָׁ֔מָּה
כה וְזַרְע֖וֹ יוֹרִשֶֽׁנָּה׃ וְהָעֲמָלֵקִ֥י וְהַכְּנַעֲנִ֖י יוֹשֵׁ֣ב בָּעֵ֑מֶק מָחָ֗ר פְּנ֨וּ וּס֥עוּ לָכֶ֛ם הַמִּדְבָּ֖ר
דֶּ֥רֶךְ יַם־סֽוּף׃
כו כז וַיְדַבֵּ֣ר יהוה אֶל־מֹשֶׁ֥ה וְאֶֽל־אַהֲרֹ֖ן לֵאמֹֽר׃ עַד־מָתַ֗י לָעֵדָ֤ה הָֽרָעָה֙ הַזֹּ֔את אֲשֶׁ֛ר רביעי
הֵ֥מָּה מַלִּינִ֖ים עָלָ֑י אֶת־תְּלֻנּ֞וֹת בְּנֵ֣י יִשְׂרָאֵ֗ל אֲשֶׁ֨ר הֵ֧מָּה מַלִּינִ֛ים עָלַ֖י שָׁמָֽעְתִּי׃

כח אֱמֹר אֲלֵהֶם חַי־אָנִי נְאֻם־יְהוָֹה אִם־לֹא כַּאֲשֶׁר דִּבַּרְתֶּם בְּאָזְנָי כֵּן אֶעֱשֶׂה
כט לָכֶם׃ בַּמִּדְבָּר הַזֶּה יִפְּלוּ פִגְרֵיכֶם וְכָל־פְּקֻדֵיכֶם לְכָל־מִסְפַּרְכֶם מִבֶּן עֶשְׂרִים
ל שָׁנָה וָמָעְלָה אֲשֶׁר הֲלִינֹתֶם עָלָי׃ אִם־אַתֶּם תָּבֹאוּ אֶל־הָאָרֶץ אֲשֶׁר נָשָׂאתִי
לא אֶת־יָדִי לְשַׁכֵּן אֶתְכֶם בָּהּ כִּי אִם־כָּלֵב בֶּן־יְפֻנֶּה וִיהוֹשֻׁעַ בִּן־נוּן׃ וְטַפְּכֶם אֲשֶׁר
אֲמַרְתֶּם לָבַז יִהְיֶה וְהֵבֵיאתִי אֹתָם וְיָדְעוּ אֶת־הָאָרֶץ אֲשֶׁר מְאַסְתֶּם בָּהּ׃
לב לג וּפִגְרֵיכֶם אַתֶּם יִפְּלוּ בַּמִּדְבָּר הַזֶּה׃ וּבְנֵיכֶם יִהְיוּ רֹעִים בַּמִּדְבָּר אַרְבָּעִים שָׁנָה
לד וְנָשְׂאוּ אֶת־זְנוּתֵיכֶם עַד־תֹּם פִּגְרֵיכֶם בַּמִּדְבָּר׃ בְּמִסְפַּר הַיָּמִים אֲשֶׁר־תַּרְתֶּם
אֶת־הָאָרֶץ אַרְבָּעִים יוֹם יוֹם לַשָּׁנָה יוֹם לַשָּׁנָה תִּשְׂאוּ אֶת־עֲוֺנֹתֵיכֶם אַרְבָּעִים
לה שָׁנָה וִידַעְתֶּם אֶת־תְּנוּאָתִי׃ אֲנִי יְהוָֹה דִּבַּרְתִּי אִם־לֹא ׀ זֹאת אֶעֱשֶׂה לְכָל־
לו הָעֵדָה הָרָעָה הַזֹּאת הַנּוֹעָדִים עָלָי בַּמִּדְבָּר הַזֶּה יִתַּמּוּ וְשָׁם יָמֻתוּ׃ וְהָאֲנָשִׁים
אֲשֶׁר־שָׁלַח מֹשֶׁה לָתוּר אֶת־הָאָרֶץ וַיָּשֻׁבוּ וילונו עָלָיו אֶת־כָּל־הָעֵדָה לְהוֹצִיא וַיַּלִּינוּ
לז דִבָּה עַל־הָאָרֶץ׃ וַיָּמֻתוּ הָאֲנָשִׁים מוֹצִאֵי דִבַּת־הָאָרֶץ רָעָה בַּמַּגֵּפָה לִפְנֵי יְהוָֹה׃
לח וִיהוֹשֻׁעַ בִּן־נוּן וְכָלֵב בֶּן־יְפֻנֶּה חָיוּ מִן־הָאֲנָשִׁים הָהֵם הַהֹלְכִים לָתוּר אֶת־
לט הָאָרֶץ׃ וַיְדַבֵּר מֹשֶׁה אֶת־הַדְּבָרִים הָאֵלֶּה אֶל־כָּל־בְּנֵי יִשְׂרָאֵל וַיִּתְאַבְּלוּ הָעָם
מ מְאֹד׃ וַיַּשְׁכִּמוּ בַבֹּקֶר וַיַּעֲלוּ אֶל־רֹאשׁ־הָהָר לֵאמֹר הִנֶּנּוּ וְעָלִינוּ אֶל־הַמָּקוֹם
מא אֲשֶׁר־אָמַר יְהוָֹה כִּי חָטָאנוּ׃ וַיֹּאמֶר מֹשֶׁה לָמָּה זֶּה אַתֶּם עֹבְרִים אֶת־פִּי
מב יְהוָֹה וְהִוא לֹא תִצְלָח׃ אַל־תַּעֲלוּ כִּי אֵין יְהוָֹה בְּקִרְבְּכֶם וְלֹא תִּנָּגְפוּ לִפְנֵי
מג אֹיְבֵיכֶם׃ כִּי הָעֲמָלֵקִי וְהַכְּנַעֲנִי שָׁם לִפְנֵיכֶם וּנְפַלְתֶּם בֶּחָרֶב כִּי־עַל־כֵּן שַׁבְתֶּם
מד מֵאַחֲרֵי יְהוָֹה וְלֹא־יִהְיֶה יְהוָֹה עִמָּכֶם׃ וַיַּעְפִּלוּ לַעֲלוֹת אֶל־רֹאשׁ הָהָר וַאֲרוֹן
מה בְּרִית־יְהוָֹה וּמֹשֶׁה לֹא־מָשׁוּ מִקֶּרֶב הַמַּחֲנֶה׃ וַיֵּרֶד הָעֲמָלֵקִי וְהַכְּנַעֲנִי הַיֹּשֵׁב
בָּהָר הַהוּא וַיַּכּוּם וַיַּכְּתוּם עַד־הַחָרְמָה׃
טו א ב וַיְדַבֵּר יְהוָֹה אֶל־מֹשֶׁה לֵּאמֹר׃ דַּבֵּר אֶל־בְּנֵי יִשְׂרָאֵל וְאָמַרְתָּ אֲלֵהֶם כִּי תָבֹאוּ יד
ג אֶל־אֶרֶץ מוֹשְׁבֹתֵיכֶם אֲשֶׁר אֲנִי נֹתֵן לָכֶם׃ וַעֲשִׂיתֶם אִשֶּׁה לַיהוָֹה עֹלָה אוֹ־זֶבַח
לְפַלֵּא־נֶדֶר אוֹ בִנְדָבָה אוֹ בְּמֹעֲדֵיכֶם לַעֲשׂוֹת רֵיחַ נִיחֹחַ לַיהוָֹה מִן־הַבָּקָר
ד אוֹ מִן־הַצֹּאן׃ וְהִקְרִיב הַמַּקְרִיב קָרְבָּנוֹ לַיהוָֹה מִנְחָה סֹלֶת עִשָּׂרוֹן בָּלוּל
ה בִּרְבִעִית הַהִין שָׁמֶן׃ וְיַיִן לַנֶּסֶךְ רְבִיעִית הַהִין תַּעֲשֶׂה עַל־הָעֹלָה אוֹ לַזָּבַח
ו לַכֶּבֶשׂ הָאֶחָד׃ אוֹ לָאַיִל תַּעֲשֶׂה מִנְחָה סֹלֶת שְׁנֵי עֶשְׂרֹנִים בְּלוּלָה בַשֶּׁמֶן
ז ח שְׁלִשִׁית הַהִין׃ וְיַיִן לַנֶּסֶךְ שְׁלִשִׁית הַהִין תַּקְרִיב רֵיחַ־נִיחֹחַ לַיהוָֹה׃ *וְכִי־ חמישי
ט תַעֲשֶׂה בֶן־בָּקָר עֹלָה אוֹ־זָבַח לְפַלֵּא־נֶדֶר אוֹ־שְׁלָמִים לַיהוָֹה׃ וְהִקְרִיב עַל־

י בֶּן־הַבָּקָ֖ר מִנְחָ֑ה סֹ֚לֶת שְׁלֹשָׁ֣ה עֶשְׂרֹנִ֔ים בָּל֥וּל בַּשֶּׁ֖מֶן חֲצִ֥י הַהִֽין׃ וְיַ֛יִן תַּקְרִ֥יב
יא לַנֶּ֖סֶךְ חֲצִ֣י הַהִ֑ין אִשֵּׁ֥ה רֵֽיחַ־נִיחֹ֖חַ לַֽיהוָֽה׃ כָּ֣כָה יֵעָשֶׂ֗ה לַשּׁוֹר֙ הָֽאֶחָ֔ד א֖וֹ לָאַ֣יִל
יב הָאֶחָ֑ד אֽוֹ־לַשֶּׂ֥ה בַכְּבָשִׂ֖ים א֥וֹ בָעִזִּֽים׃ כַּמִּסְפָּ֖ר אֲשֶׁ֣ר תַּעֲשׂ֑וּ כָּ֛כָה תַּעֲשׂ֥וּ לָאֶחָ֖ד
יג כְּמִסְפָּרָֽם׃ כָּל־הָאֶזְרָ֥ח יַעֲשֶׂה־כָּ֖כָה אֶת־אֵ֑לֶּה לְהַקְרִ֛יב אִשֵּׁ֥ה רֵֽיחַ־נִיחֹ֖חַ
יד לַֽיהוָֽה׃ וְכִֽי־יָג֨וּר אִתְּכֶ֜ם גֵּ֗ר א֤וֹ אֲשֶֽׁר־בְּתֽוֹכְכֶם֙ לְדֹרֹ֣תֵיכֶ֔ם וְעָשָׂ֛ה אִשֵּׁ֥ה רֵֽיחַ־
טו נִיחֹ֖חַ לַֽיהוָ֑ה כַּאֲשֶׁ֥ר תַּעֲשׂ֖וּ כֵּ֥ן יַעֲשֶֽׂה׃ הַקָּהָ֕ל חֻקָּ֥ה אַחַ֛ת לָכֶ֖ם וְלַגֵּ֣ר הַגָּ֑ר חֻקַּ֤ת
טז עוֹלָם֙ לְדֹרֹ֣תֵיכֶ֔ם כָּכֶ֛ם כַּגֵּ֥ר יִהְיֶ֖ה לִפְנֵ֥י יְהוָֽה׃ תּוֹרָ֥ה אַחַ֛ת וּמִשְׁפָּ֥ט אֶחָ֖ד יִהְיֶ֣ה
לָכֶ֑ם וְלַגֵּ֖ר הַגָּ֥ר אִתְּכֶֽם׃
יז יח וַיְדַבֵּ֥ר יְהוָ֖ה אֶל־מֹשֶׁ֥ה לֵּאמֹֽר׃ דַּבֵּר֙ אֶל־בְּנֵ֣י יִשְׂרָאֵ֔ל וְאָמַרְתָּ֖ אֲלֵהֶ֑ם בְּבֹֽאֲכֶם֙ ששי
יט אֶל־הָאָ֔רֶץ אֲשֶׁ֥ר אֲנִ֛י מֵבִ֥יא אֶתְכֶ֖ם שָֽׁמָּה׃ וְהָיָ֕ה בַּאֲכָלְכֶ֖ם מִלֶּ֣חֶם הָאָ֑רֶץ תָּרִ֥ימוּ
כ תְרוּמָ֖ה לַיהוָֽה׃ רֵאשִׁית֙ עֲרִסֹ֣תֵכֶ֔ם חַלָּ֖ה תָּרִ֣ימוּ תְרוּמָ֑ה כִּתְרוּמַ֣ת גֹּ֔רֶן כֵּ֖ן תָּרִ֥ימוּ
כא כב אֹתָֽהּ׃ מֵרֵאשִׁית֙ עֲרִסֹ֣תֵיכֶ֔ם תִּתְּנ֥וּ לַיהוָ֖ה תְּרוּמָ֑ה לְדֹרֹ֖תֵיכֶֽם׃ וְכִ֣י
כג תִשְׁגּ֔וּ וְלֹ֣א תַעֲשׂ֔וּ אֵ֥ת כָּל־הַמִּצְוֺ֖ת הָאֵ֑לֶּה אֲשֶׁר־דִּבֶּ֥ר יְהוָ֖ה אֶל־מֹשֶֽׁה׃ אֵת֩
כָּל־אֲשֶׁ֨ר צִוָּ֤ה יְהוָה֙ אֲלֵיכֶ֔ם בְּיַד־מֹשֶׁ֑ה מִן־הַיּ֞וֹם אֲשֶׁ֨ר צִוָּ֧ה יְהוָ֛ה וָהָ֖לְאָה
כד לְדֹרֹתֵיכֶֽם׃ וְהָיָ֗ה אִ֣ם מֵעֵינֵ֣י הָעֵדָה֮ נֶֽעֶשְׂתָ֣ה לִשְׁגָגָה֒ וְעָשׂ֣וּ כָל־הָעֵדָ֡ה פַּ֣ר
בֶּן־בָּקָר֩ אֶחָ֨ד לְעֹלָ֜ה לְרֵ֤יחַ נִיחֹ֙חַ֙ לַֽיהוָ֔ה וּמִנְחָת֥וֹ וְנִסְכּ֖וֹ כַּמִּשְׁפָּ֑ט וּשְׂעִיר־
כה עִזִּ֥ים אֶחָ֖ד לְחַטָּֽת׃ וְכִפֶּ֣ר הַכֹּהֵ֗ן עַֽל־כָּל־עֲדַ֛ת בְּנֵ֥י יִשְׂרָאֵ֖ל וְנִסְלַ֣ח לָהֶ֑ם
כִּֽי־שְׁגָגָ֣ה הִ֔וא וְהֵ֡ם הֵבִ֣יאוּ אֶת־קָרְבָּנָם֩ אִשֶּׁ֨ה לַֽיהוָ֜ה וְחַטָּאתָ֛ם לִפְנֵ֥י יְהוָ֖ה
כו עַל־שִׁגְגָתָֽם׃ וְנִסְלַ֗ח לְכָל־עֲדַת֙ בְּנֵ֣י יִשְׂרָאֵ֔ל וְלַגֵּ֖ר הַגָּ֣ר בְּתוֹכָ֑ם כִּ֥י לְכָל־הָעָ֖ם
כז בִּשְׁגָגָֽה׃ וְאִם־נֶ֥פֶשׁ אַחַ֖ת תֶּחֱטָ֣א בִשְׁגָגָ֑ה וְהִקְרִ֛יבָה עֵ֥ז בַּת־שְׁנָתָ֖הּ שביעי
כח לְחַטָּֽאת׃ וְכִפֶּ֣ר הַכֹּהֵ֗ן עַל־הַנֶּ֛פֶשׁ הַשֹּׁגֶ֥גֶת בְּחֶטְאָ֥ה בִשְׁגָגָ֖ה לִפְנֵ֣י יְהוָ֑ה לְכַפֵּ֥ר
כט עָלָ֖יו וְנִסְלַ֥ח לֽוֹ׃ הָֽאֶזְרָח֙ בִּבְנֵ֣י יִשְׂרָאֵ֔ל וְלַגֵּ֖ר הַגָּ֣ר בְּתוֹכָ֑ם תּוֹרָ֤ה אַחַת֙ יִהְיֶ֣ה
ל לָכֶ֔ם לָעֹשֶׂ֖ה בִּשְׁגָגָֽה׃ וְהַנֶּ֜פֶשׁ אֲשֶׁר־תַּעֲשֶׂ֣ה ׀ בְּיָ֣ד רָמָ֗ה מִן־הָֽאֶזְרָח֙ וּמִן־הַגֵּ֔ר
לא אֶת־יְהוָ֖ה ה֣וּא מְגַדֵּ֑ף וְנִכְרְתָ֛ה הַנֶּ֥פֶשׁ הַהִ֖וא מִקֶּ֥רֶב עַמָּֽהּ׃ כִּ֤י דְבַר־יְהוָה֙ בָּזָ֔ה
וְאֶת־מִצְוָת֖וֹ הֵפַ֑ר הִכָּרֵ֧ת ׀ תִּכָּרֵ֛ת הַנֶּ֥פֶשׁ הַהִ֖וא עֲוֺנָ֥הּ בָֽהּ׃
לב לג וַיִּהְי֥וּ בְנֵֽי־יִשְׂרָאֵ֖ל בַּמִּדְבָּ֑ר וַֽיִּמְצְא֗וּ אִ֛ישׁ מְקֹשֵׁ֥שׁ עֵצִ֖ים בְּי֥וֹם הַשַּׁבָּֽת׃ וַיַּקְרִ֣יבוּ
אֹת֔וֹ הַמֹּצְאִ֥ים אֹת֖וֹ מְקֹשֵׁ֣שׁ עֵצִ֑ים אֶל־מֹשֶׁה֙ וְאֶל־אַֽהֲרֹ֔ן וְאֶ֖ל כָּל־הָעֵדָֽה׃
לד לה וַיַּנִּ֥יחוּ אֹת֖וֹ בַּמִּשְׁמָ֑ר כִּ֚י לֹ֣א פֹרַ֔שׁ מַה־יֵּעָשֶׂ֖ה לֽוֹ׃ וַיֹּ֤אמֶר יְהוָה֙ אֶל־
לו מֹשֶׁ֔ה מ֥וֹת יוּמַ֖ת הָאִ֑ישׁ רָג֨וֹם אֹת֤וֹ בָאֲבָנִים֙ כָּל־הָ֣עֵדָ֔ה מִח֖וּץ לַֽמַּחֲנֶֽה׃ וַיֹּצִ֨יאוּ

אֹתוֹ כׇּל־הָעֵדָה אֶל־מִחוּץ לַמַּחֲנֶה וַיִּרְגְּמוּ אֹתוֹ בָּאֲבָנִים וַיָּמֹת כַּאֲשֶׁר צִוָּה
יהוה אֶת־מֹשֶׁה׃
מפטיר וַיֹּאמֶר יהוה אֶל־מֹשֶׁה לֵּאמֹר׃ דַּבֵּר אֶל־בְּנֵי יִשְׂרָאֵל וְאָמַרְתָּ אֲלֵהֶם וְעָשׂוּ לז לח
לָהֶם צִיצִת עַל־כַּנְפֵי בִגְדֵיהֶם לְדֹרֹתָם וְנָתְנוּ עַל־צִיצִת הַכָּנָף פְּתִיל תְּכֵלֶת׃
וְהָיָה לָכֶם לְצִיצִת וּרְאִיתֶם אֹתוֹ וּזְכַרְתֶּם אֶת־כׇּל־מִצְוֺת יהוה וַעֲשִׂיתֶם לט
אֹתָם וְלֹא תָתֻרוּ אַחֲרֵי לְבַבְכֶם וְאַחֲרֵי עֵינֵיכֶם אֲשֶׁר־אַתֶּם זֹנִים אַחֲרֵיהֶם׃
לְמַעַן תִּזְכְּרוּ וַעֲשִׂיתֶם אֶת־כׇּל־מִצְוֺתָי וִהְיִיתֶם קְדֹשִׁים לֵאלֹהֵיכֶם׃ אֲנִי מ מא
יהוה אֱלֹהֵיכֶם אֲשֶׁר הוֹצֵאתִי אֶתְכֶם מֵאֶרֶץ מִצְרַיִם לִהְיוֹת לָכֶם לֵאלֹהִים
אֲנִי יהוה אֱלֹהֵיכֶם׃

קורח
טו
וַיִּקַּח קֹרַח בֶּן־יִצְהָר בֶּן־קְהָת בֶּן־לֵוִי וְדָתָן וַאֲבִירָם בְּנֵי אֱלִיאָב וְאוֹן בֶּן־ א
פֶּלֶת בְּנֵי רְאוּבֵן׃ וַיָּקֻמוּ לִפְנֵי מֹשֶׁה וַאֲנָשִׁים מִבְּנֵי־יִשְׂרָאֵל חֲמִשִּׁים וּמָאתָיִם ב
נְשִׂיאֵי עֵדָה קְרִאֵי מוֹעֵד אַנְשֵׁי־שֵׁם׃ וַיִּקָּהֲלוּ עַל־מֹשֶׁה וְעַל־אַהֲרֹן וַיֹּאמְרוּ ג
אֲלֵהֶם רַב־לָכֶם כִּי כׇל־הָעֵדָה כֻּלָּם קְדֹשִׁים וּבְתוֹכָם יהוה וּמַדּוּעַ תִּתְנַשְּׂאוּ
לוי עַל־קְהַל יהוה׃ *וַיִּשְׁמַע מֹשֶׁה וַיִּפֹּל עַל־פָּנָיו׃ וַיְדַבֵּר אֶל־קֹרַח וְאֶל־כׇּל־ ד ה
עֲדָתוֹ לֵאמֹר בֹּקֶר וְיֹדַע יהוה אֶת־אֲשֶׁר־לוֹ וְאֶת־הַקָּדוֹשׁ וְהִקְרִיב אֵלָיו וְאֵת
אֲשֶׁר יִבְחַר־בּוֹ יַקְרִיב אֵלָיו׃ זֹאת עֲשׂוּ קְחוּ־לָכֶם מַחְתּוֹת קֹרַח וְכׇל־עֲדָתוֹ׃ ו
וּתְנוּ־בָהֵן ׀ אֵשׁ וְשִׂימוּ עֲלֵיהֶן ׀ קְטֹרֶת לִפְנֵי יהוה מָחָר וְהָיָה הָאִישׁ אֲשֶׁר־ ז
ישראל יִבְחַר יהוה הוּא הַקָּדוֹשׁ רַב־לָכֶם בְּנֵי לֵוִי׃ *וַיֹּאמֶר מֹשֶׁה אֶל־קֹרַח שִׁמְעוּ־ ח
נָא בְּנֵי לֵוִי׃ הַמְעַט מִכֶּם כִּי־הִבְדִּיל אֱלֹהֵי יִשְׂרָאֵל אֶתְכֶם מֵעֲדַת יִשְׂרָאֵל ט
לְהַקְרִיב אֶתְכֶם אֵלָיו לַעֲבֹד אֶת־עֲבֹדַת מִשְׁכַּן יהוה וְלַעֲמֹד לִפְנֵי הָעֵדָה
לְשָׁרְתָם׃ וַיַּקְרֵב אֹתְךָ וְאֶת־כׇּל־אַחֶיךָ בְנֵי־לֵוִי אִתָּךְ וּבִקַּשְׁתֶּם גַּם־כְּהֻנָּה׃ י
תַּלִּינוּ לָכֵן אַתָּה וְכׇל־עֲדָתְךָ הַנֹּעָדִים עַל־יהוה וְאַהֲרֹן מַה־הוּא כִּי תלונו עָלָיו׃ יא
וַיִּשְׁלַח מֹשֶׁה לִקְרֹא לְדָתָן וְלַאֲבִירָם בְּנֵי אֱלִיאָב וַיֹּאמְרוּ לֹא נַעֲלֶה׃ הַמְעַט יב יג
כִּי הֶעֱלִיתָנוּ מֵאֶרֶץ זָבַת חָלָב וּדְבַשׁ לַהֲמִיתֵנוּ בַּמִּדְבָּר כִּי־תִשְׂתָּרֵר עָלֵינוּ
שני גַּם־הִשְׂתָּרֵר׃** אַף לֹא אֶל־אֶרֶץ זָבַת חָלָב וּדְבַשׁ הֲבִיאֹתָנוּ וַתִּתֶּן־לָנוּ יד
נַחֲלַת שָׂדֶה וָכָרֶם הַעֵינֵי הָאֲנָשִׁים הָהֵם תְּנַקֵּר לֹא נַעֲלֶה׃ וַיִּחַר לְמֹשֶׁה מְאֹד טו
וַיֹּאמֶר אֶל־יהוה אַל־תֵּפֶן אֶל־מִנְחָתָם לֹא חֲמוֹר אֶחָד מֵהֶם נָשָׂאתִי וְלֹא
הֲרֵעֹתִי אֶת־אַחַד מֵהֶם׃ וַיֹּאמֶר מֹשֶׁה אֶל־קֹרַח אַתָּה וְכׇל־עֲדָתְךָ הֱיוּ לִפְנֵי טז
יהוה אַתָּה וָהֵם וְאַהֲרֹן מָחָר׃ וּקְחוּ ׀ אִישׁ מַחְתָּתוֹ וּנְתַתֶּם עֲלֵיהֶם קְטֹרֶת יז

וְהִקְרַבְתֶּם לִפְנֵי יְהוָה אִישׁ מַחְתָּתוֹ חֲמִשִּׁים וּמָאתַיִם מַחְתֹּת וְאַתָּה וְאַהֲרֹן
יח אִישׁ מַחְתָּתוֹ: וַיִּקְחוּ אִישׁ מַחְתָּתוֹ וַיִּתְּנוּ עֲלֵיהֶם אֵשׁ וַיָּשִׂימוּ עֲלֵיהֶם קְטֹרֶת
יט וַיַּעַמְדוּ פֶּתַח אֹהֶל מוֹעֵד וּמֹשֶׁה וְאַהֲרֹן: וַיַּקְהֵל עֲלֵיהֶם קֹרַח אֶת־כָּל־הָעֵדָה
כ אֶל־פֶּתַח אֹהֶל מוֹעֵד וַיֵּרָא כְבוֹד־יְהוָה אֶל־כָּל־הָעֵדָה: וַיְדַבֵּר שלישי
כא יְהוָה אֶל־מֹשֶׁה וְאֶל־אַהֲרֹן לֵאמֹר: הִבָּדְלוּ מִתּוֹךְ הָעֵדָה הַזֹּאת וַאֲכַלֶּה אֹתָם
כב כְּרָגַע: וַיִּפְּלוּ עַל־פְּנֵיהֶם וַיֹּאמְרוּ אֵל אֱלֹהֵי הָרוּחֹת לְכָל־בָּשָׂר הָאִישׁ אֶחָד
כג כד יֶחֱטָא וְעַל כָּל־הָעֵדָה תִּקְצֹף: וַיְדַבֵּר יְהוָה אֶל־מֹשֶׁה לֵּאמֹר: דַּבֵּר
כה אֶל־הָעֵדָה לֵאמֹר הֵעָלוּ מִסָּבִיב לְמִשְׁכַּן־קֹרַח דָּתָן וַאֲבִירָם: וַיָּקָם מֹשֶׁה וַיֵּלֶךְ
כו אֶל־דָּתָן וַאֲבִירָם וַיֵּלְכוּ אַחֲרָיו זִקְנֵי יִשְׂרָאֵל: וַיְדַבֵּר אֶל־הָעֵדָה לֵאמֹר סוּרוּ נָא
מֵעַל אָהֳלֵי הָאֲנָשִׁים הָרְשָׁעִים הָאֵלֶּה וְאַל־תִּגְּעוּ בְּכָל־אֲשֶׁר לָהֶם פֶּן־תִּסָּפוּ
כז בְּכָל־חַטֹּאתָם: וַיֵּעָלוּ מֵעַל מִשְׁכַּן־קֹרַח דָּתָן וַאֲבִירָם מִסָּבִיב וְדָתָן וַאֲבִירָם
כח יָצְאוּ נִצָּבִים פֶּתַח אָהֳלֵיהֶם וּנְשֵׁיהֶם וּבְנֵיהֶם וְטַפָּם: וַיֹּאמֶר מֹשֶׁה בְּזֹאת תֵּדְעוּן
כט כִּי־יְהוָה שְׁלָחַנִי לַעֲשׂוֹת אֵת כָּל־הַמַּעֲשִׂים הָאֵלֶּה כִּי־לֹא מִלִּבִּי: אִם־כְּמוֹת
כָּל־הָאָדָם יְמֻתוּן אֵלֶּה וּפְקֻדַּת כָּל־הָאָדָם יִפָּקֵד עֲלֵיהֶם לֹא יְהוָה שְׁלָחָנִי:
ל וְאִם־בְּרִיאָה יִבְרָא יְהוָה וּפָצְתָה הָאֲדָמָה אֶת־פִּיהָ וּבָלְעָה אֹתָם וְאֶת־כָּל־
אֲשֶׁר לָהֶם וְיָרְדוּ חַיִּים שְׁאֹלָה וִידַעְתֶּם כִּי נִאֲצוּ הָאֲנָשִׁים הָאֵלֶּה אֶת־יְהוָה:
לא וַיְהִי כְּכַלֹּתוֹ לְדַבֵּר אֵת כָּל־הַדְּבָרִים הָאֵלֶּה וַתִּבָּקַע הָאֲדָמָה אֲשֶׁר תַּחְתֵּיהֶם:
לב וַתִּפְתַּח הָאָרֶץ אֶת־פִּיהָ וַתִּבְלַע אֹתָם וְאֶת־בָּתֵּיהֶם וְאֵת כָּל־הָאָדָם אֲשֶׁר
לג לְקֹרַח וְאֵת כָּל־הָרְכוּשׁ: וַיֵּרְדוּ הֵם וְכָל־אֲשֶׁר לָהֶם חַיִּים שְׁאֹלָה וַתְּכַס עֲלֵיהֶם
לד הָאָרֶץ וַיֹּאבְדוּ מִתּוֹךְ הַקָּהָל: וְכָל־יִשְׂרָאֵל אֲשֶׁר סְבִיבֹתֵיהֶם נָסוּ לְקֹלָם כִּי
לה אָמְרוּ פֶּן־תִּבְלָעֵנוּ הָאָרֶץ: וְאֵשׁ יָצְאָה מֵאֵת יְהוָה וַתֹּאכַל אֵת הַחֲמִשִּׁים
יז א וּמָאתַיִם אִישׁ מַקְרִיבֵי הַקְּטֹרֶת: וַיְדַבֵּר יְהוָה אֶל־מֹשֶׁה לֵּאמֹר:
ב אֱמֹר אֶל־אֶלְעָזָר בֶּן־אַהֲרֹן הַכֹּהֵן וְיָרֵם אֶת־הַמַּחְתֹּת מִבֵּין הַשְּׂרֵפָה וְאֶת־
ג הָאֵשׁ זְרֵה־הָלְאָה כִּי קָדֵשׁוּ: אֵת מַחְתּוֹת הַחַטָּאִים הָאֵלֶּה בְּנַפְשֹׁתָם וְעָשׂוּ
אֹתָם רִקֻּעֵי פַחִים צִפּוּי לַמִּזְבֵּחַ כִּי־הִקְרִיבֻם לִפְנֵי־יְהוָה וַיִּקְדָּשׁוּ וְיִהְיוּ לְאוֹת
ד לִבְנֵי יִשְׂרָאֵל: וַיִּקַּח אֶלְעָזָר הַכֹּהֵן אֵת מַחְתּוֹת הַנְּחֹשֶׁת אֲשֶׁר הִקְרִיבוּ
ה הַשְּׂרֻפִים וַיְרַקְּעוּם צִפּוּי לַמִּזְבֵּחַ: זִכָּרוֹן לִבְנֵי יִשְׂרָאֵל לְמַעַן אֲשֶׁר לֹא־יִקְרַב
אִישׁ זָר אֲשֶׁר לֹא מִזֶּרַע אַהֲרֹן הוּא לְהַקְטִיר קְטֹרֶת לִפְנֵי יְהוָה וְלֹא־יִהְיֶה
כְקֹרַח וְכַעֲדָתוֹ כַּאֲשֶׁר דִּבֶּר יְהוָה בְּיַד־מֹשֶׁה לוֹ:

וַיִּלֹּנוּ כָּל־עֲדַת בְּנֵי־יִשְׂרָאֵל מִמָּחֳרָת עַל־מֹשֶׁה וְעַל־אַהֲרֹן לֵאמֹר אַתֶּם הֲמִתֶּם ו
אֶת־עַם יהוה: וַיְהִי בְּהִקָּהֵל הָעֵדָה עַל־מֹשֶׁה וְעַל־אַהֲרֹן וַיִּפְנוּ אֶל־אֹהֶל ז
מוֹעֵד וְהִנֵּה כִסָּהוּ הֶעָנָן וַיֵּרָא כְּבוֹד יהוה: וַיָּבֹא מֹשֶׁה וְאַהֲרֹן אֶל־פְּנֵי אֹהֶל ח
רביעי מוֹעֵד: *וַיְדַבֵּר יהוה אֶל־מֹשֶׁה לֵּאמֹר: הֵרֹמּוּ מִתּוֹךְ הָעֵדָה הַזֹּאת ט י
וַאֲכַלֶּה אֹתָם כְּרָגַע וַיִּפְּלוּ עַל־פְּנֵיהֶם: וַיֹּאמֶר מֹשֶׁה אֶל־אַהֲרֹן קַח אֶת־ יא
הַמַּחְתָּה וְתֶן־עָלֶיהָ אֵשׁ מֵעַל הַמִּזְבֵּחַ וְשִׂים קְטֹרֶת וְהוֹלֵךְ מְהֵרָה אֶל־הָעֵדָה
וְכַפֵּר עֲלֵיהֶם כִּי־יָצָא הַקֶּצֶף מִלִּפְנֵי יהוה הֵחֵל הַנָּגֶף: וַיִּקַּח אַהֲרֹן כַּאֲשֶׁר ׀ יב
דִּבֶּר מֹשֶׁה וַיָּרָץ אֶל־תּוֹךְ הַקָּהָל וְהִנֵּה הֵחֵל הַנֶּגֶף בָּעָם וַיִּתֵּן אֶת־הַקְּטֹרֶת
וַיְכַפֵּר עַל־הָעָם: וַיַּעֲמֹד בֵּין־הַמֵּתִים וּבֵין הַחַיִּים וַתֵּעָצַר הַמַּגֵּפָה: וַיִּהְיוּ הַמֵּתִים יג יד
בַּמַּגֵּפָה אַרְבָּעָה עָשָׂר אֶלֶף וּשְׁבַע מֵאוֹת מִלְּבַד הַמֵּתִים עַל־דְּבַר־קֹרַח: וַיָּשָׁב טו
אַהֲרֹן אֶל־מֹשֶׁה אֶל־פֶּתַח אֹהֶל מוֹעֵד וְהַמַּגֵּפָה נֶעֱצָרָה:
חמישי טז וַיְדַבֵּר יהוה אֶל־מֹשֶׁה לֵּאמֹר: דַּבֵּר ׀ אֶל־בְּנֵי יִשְׂרָאֵל וְקַח מֵאִתָּם מַטֶּה מַטֶּה טז יז
לְבֵית אָב מֵאֵת כָּל־נְשִׂיאֵהֶם לְבֵית אֲבֹתָם שְׁנֵים עָשָׂר מַטּוֹת אִישׁ אֶת־שְׁמוֹ
תִּכְתֹּב עַל־מַטֵּהוּ: וְאֵת שֵׁם אַהֲרֹן תִּכְתֹּב עַל־מַטֵּה לֵוִי כִּי מַטֶּה אֶחָד לְרֹאשׁ יח
בֵּית אֲבוֹתָם: וְהִנַּחְתָּם בְּאֹהֶל מוֹעֵד לִפְנֵי הָעֵדוּת אֲשֶׁר אִוָּעֵד לָכֶם שָׁמָּה: יט
וְהָיָה הָאִישׁ אֲשֶׁר אֶבְחַר־בּוֹ מַטֵּהוּ יִפְרָח וַהֲשִׁכֹּתִי מֵעָלַי אֶת־תְּלֻנּוֹת בְּנֵי כ
יִשְׂרָאֵל אֲשֶׁר הֵם מַלִּינִם עֲלֵיכֶם: וַיְדַבֵּר מֹשֶׁה אֶל־בְּנֵי יִשְׂרָאֵל וַיִּתְּנוּ אֵלָיו ׀ כא
כָּל־נְשִׂיאֵיהֶם מַטֶּה לְנָשִׂיא אֶחָד מַטֶּה לְנָשִׂיא אֶחָד לְבֵית אֲבֹתָם שְׁנֵים עָשָׂר
מַטּוֹת וּמַטֵּה אַהֲרֹן בְּתוֹךְ מַטּוֹתָם: וַיַּנַּח מֹשֶׁה אֶת־הַמַּטֹּת לִפְנֵי יהוה בְּאֹהֶל כב
הָעֵדֻת: וַיְהִי מִמָּחֳרָת וַיָּבֹא מֹשֶׁה אֶל־אֹהֶל הָעֵדוּת וְהִנֵּה פָּרַח מַטֵּה־אַהֲרֹן כג
לְבֵית לֵוִי וַיֹּצֵא פֶרַח וַיָּצֵץ צִיץ וַיִּגְמֹל שְׁקֵדִים: וַיֹּצֵא מֹשֶׁה אֶת־כָּל־הַמַּטֹּת כד
מִלִּפְנֵי יהוה אֶל־כָּל־בְּנֵי יִשְׂרָאֵל וַיִּרְאוּ וַיִּקְחוּ אִישׁ מַטֵּהוּ:
ששי וַיֹּאמֶר יהוה אֶל־מֹשֶׁה הָשֵׁב אֶת־מַטֵּה אַהֲרֹן לִפְנֵי הָעֵדוּת לְמִשְׁמֶרֶת לְאוֹת כה
לִבְנֵי־מֶרִי וּתְכַל תְּלוּנֹּתָם מֵעָלַי וְלֹא יָמֻתוּ: וַיַּעַשׂ מֹשֶׁה כַּאֲשֶׁר צִוָּה יהוה כו
אֹתוֹ כֵּן עָשָׂה:
וַיֹּאמְרוּ בְּנֵי יִשְׂרָאֵל אֶל־מֹשֶׁה לֵאמֹר הֵן גָּוַעְנוּ אָבַדְנוּ כֻּלָּנוּ אָבָדְנוּ: כֹּל כז כח
הַקָּרֵב ׀ הַקָּרֵב אֶל־מִשְׁכַּן יהוה יָמוּת הַאִם תַּמְנוּ לִגְוֹעַ: וַיֹּאמֶר א
יהוה אֶל־אַהֲרֹן אַתָּה וּבָנֶיךָ וּבֵית־אָבִיךָ אִתָּךְ תִּשְׂאוּ אֶת־עֲוֺן הַמִּקְדָּשׁ וְאַתָּה
וּבָנֶיךָ אִתָּךְ תִּשְׂאוּ אֶת־עֲוֺן כְּהֻנַּתְכֶם: וְגַם אֶת־אַחֶיךָ מַטֵּה לֵוִי שֵׁבֶט אָבִיךָ ב

הַקְרֵב אִתָּךְ וְיִלָּווּ עָלֶיךָ וִישָׁרְתוּךָ וְאַתָּה וּבָנֶיךָ אִתָּךְ לִפְנֵי אֹהֶל הָעֵדֻת׃
ג וְשָׁמְרוּ מִשְׁמַרְתְּךָ וּמִשְׁמֶרֶת כָּל־הָאֹהֶל אַךְ אֶל־כְּלֵי הַקֹּדֶשׁ וְאֶל־הַמִּזְבֵּחַ לֹא
ד יִקְרָבוּ וְלֹא־יָמֻתוּ גַם־הֵם גַּם־אַתֶּם׃ וְנִלְווּ עָלֶיךָ וְשָׁמְרוּ אֶת־מִשְׁמֶרֶת אֹהֶל
ה מוֹעֵד לְכֹל עֲבֹדַת הָאֹהֶל וְזָר לֹא־יִקְרַב אֲלֵיכֶם׃ וּשְׁמַרְתֶּם אֵת מִשְׁמֶרֶת
ו הַקֹּדֶשׁ וְאֵת מִשְׁמֶרֶת הַמִּזְבֵּחַ וְלֹא־יִהְיֶה עוֹד קֶצֶף עַל־בְּנֵי יִשְׂרָאֵל׃ וַאֲנִי
הִנֵּה לָקַחְתִּי אֶת־אֲחֵיכֶם הַלְוִיִּם מִתּוֹךְ בְּנֵי יִשְׂרָאֵל לָכֶם מַתָּנָה נְתֻנִים לַיהוָה
ז לַעֲבֹד אֶת־עֲבֹדַת אֹהֶל מוֹעֵד׃ וְאַתָּה וּבָנֶיךָ אִתְּךָ תִּשְׁמְרוּ אֶת־כְּהֻנַּתְכֶם
לְכָל־דְּבַר הַמִּזְבֵּחַ וּלְמִבֵּית לַפָּרֹכֶת וַעֲבַדְתֶּם עֲבֹדַת מַתָּנָה אֶתֵּן אֶת־כְּהֻנַּתְכֶם
וְהַזָּר הַקָּרֵב יוּמָת׃
ח וַיְדַבֵּר יְהוָה אֶל־אַהֲרֹן וַאֲנִי הִנֵּה נָתַתִּי לְךָ אֶת־מִשְׁמֶרֶת תְּרוּמֹתָי לְכָל־
ט קָדְשֵׁי בְנֵי־יִשְׂרָאֵל לְךָ נְתַתִּים לְמָשְׁחָה וּלְבָנֶיךָ לְחָק־עוֹלָם׃ זֶה יִהְיֶה לְךָ
מִקֹּדֶשׁ הַקֳּדָשִׁים מִן־הָאֵשׁ כָּל־קָרְבָּנָם לְכָל־מִנְחָתָם וּלְכָל־חַטָּאתָם וּלְכָל־
י אֲשָׁמָם אֲשֶׁר יָשִׁיבוּ לִי קֹדֶשׁ קָדָשִׁים לְךָ הוּא וּלְבָנֶיךָ׃ בְּקֹדֶשׁ הַקֳּדָשִׁים
יא תֹּאכְלֶנּוּ כָּל־זָכָר יֹאכַל אֹתוֹ קֹדֶשׁ יִהְיֶה־לָּךְ׃ וְזֶה־לְּךָ תְּרוּמַת מַתָּנָם לְכָל־
תְּנוּפֹת בְּנֵי יִשְׂרָאֵל לְךָ נְתַתִּים וּלְבָנֶיךָ וְלִבְנֹתֶיךָ אִתְּךָ לְחָק־עוֹלָם כָּל־טָהוֹר
יב בְּבֵיתְךָ יֹאכַל אֹתוֹ׃ כֹּל חֵלֶב יִצְהָר וְכָל־חֵלֶב תִּירוֹשׁ וְדָגָן רֵאשִׁיתָם אֲשֶׁר־
יג יִתְּנוּ לַיהוָה לְךָ נְתַתִּים׃ בִּכּוּרֵי כָּל־אֲשֶׁר בְּאַרְצָם אֲשֶׁר־יָבִיאוּ לַיהוָה לְךָ
יד טו יִהְיֶה כָּל־טָהוֹר בְּבֵיתְךָ יֹאכְלֶנּוּ׃ כָּל־חֵרֶם בְּיִשְׂרָאֵל לְךָ יִהְיֶה׃ כָּל־פֶּטֶר
רֶחֶם לְכָל־בָּשָׂר אֲשֶׁר־יַקְרִיבוּ לַיהוָה בָּאָדָם וּבַבְּהֵמָה יִהְיֶה־לָּךְ אַךְ ׀ פָּדֹה
טז תִפְדֶּה אֵת בְּכוֹר הָאָדָם וְאֵת בְּכוֹר־הַבְּהֵמָה הַטְּמֵאָה תִּפְדֶּה׃ וּפְדוּיָו מִבֶּן־
חֹדֶשׁ תִּפְדֶּה בְּעֶרְכְּךָ כֶּסֶף חֲמֵשֶׁת שְׁקָלִים בְּשֶׁקֶל הַקֹּדֶשׁ עֶשְׂרִים גֵּרָה הוּא׃
יז אַךְ בְּכוֹר־שׁוֹר אוֹ־בְכוֹר כֶּשֶׂב אוֹ־בְכוֹר עֵז לֹא תִפְדֶּה קֹדֶשׁ הֵם אֶת־דָּמָם
יח תִּזְרֹק עַל־הַמִּזְבֵּחַ וְאֶת־חֶלְבָּם תַּקְטִיר אִשֶּׁה לְרֵיחַ נִיחֹחַ לַיהוָה׃ וּבְשָׂרָם
יט יִהְיֶה־לָּךְ כַּחֲזֵה הַתְּנוּפָה וּכְשׁוֹק הַיָּמִין לְךָ יִהְיֶה׃ כֹּל ׀ תְּרוּמֹת הַקֳּדָשִׁים
אֲשֶׁר יָרִימוּ בְנֵי־יִשְׂרָאֵל לַיהוָה נָתַתִּי לְךָ וּלְבָנֶיךָ וְלִבְנֹתֶיךָ אִתְּךָ לְחָק־עוֹלָם
כ בְּרִית מֶלַח עוֹלָם הִוא לִפְנֵי יְהוָה לְךָ וּלְזַרְעֲךָ אִתָּךְ׃ וַיֹּאמֶר יְהוָה אֶל־אַהֲרֹן
בְּאַרְצָם לֹא תִנְחָל וְחֵלֶק לֹא־יִהְיֶה לְךָ בְּתוֹכָם אֲנִי חֶלְקְךָ וְנַחֲלָתְךָ בְּתוֹךְ בְּנֵי
כא יִשְׂרָאֵל׃ וְלִבְנֵי לֵוִי הִנֵּה נָתַתִּי כָּל־מַעֲשֵׂר בְּיִשְׂרָאֵל לְנַחֲלָה חֵלֶף שביעי
כב עֲבֹדָתָם אֲשֶׁר־הֵם עֹבְדִים אֶת־עֲבֹדַת אֹהֶל מוֹעֵד׃ וְלֹא־יִקְרְבוּ עוֹד בְּנֵי יִשְׂרָאֵל

כג אל־אהל מועד לשאת חטא למות: ועבד הלוי הוא את־עבדת אהל מועד
והם ישאו עונם חקת עולם לדרתיכם ובתוך בני ישראל לא ינחלו נחלה:
כד כי את־מעשר בני־ישראל אשר ירימו ליהוה תרומה נתתי ללוים לנחלה
על־כן אמרתי להם בתוך בני ישראל לא ינחלו נחלה:
כה כו יז וידבר יהוה אל־משה לאמר: ואל־הלוים תדבר ואמרת אלהם כי־תקחו
מאת בני־ישראל את־המעשר אשר נתתי לכם מאתם בנחלתכם והרמתם
כז ממנו תרומת יהוה מעשר מן־המעשר: ונחשב לכם תרומתכם כדגן מן־
כח הגרן וכמלאה מן־היקב: כן תרימו גם־אתם תרומת יהוה מכל מעשרתיכם
אשר תקחו מאת בני ישראל ונתתם ממנו את־תרומת יהוה לאהרן הכהן:
כט מכל מתנתיכם תרימו את כל־תרומת יהוה מכל־חלבו את־מקדשו ממנו:
ל ואמרת אלהם בהרימכם את־חלבו ממנו ונחשב ללוים כתבואת גרן מפטיר
לא וכתבואת יקב: ואכלתם אתו בכל־מקום אתם וביתכם כי־שכר הוא לכם
לב חלף עבדתכם באהל מועד: ולא־תשאו עליו חטא בהרימכם את־חלבו
ממנו ואת־קדשי בני־ישראל לא תחללו ולא תמותו:

The Maftir for Shabbat Rosh Hodesh, page 1030

יט א ב וידבר יהוה אל־משה ואל־אהרן לאמר: זאת חקת התורה אשר־צוה יהוה חקת
לאמר דבר ׀ אל־בני ישראל ויקחו אליך פרה אדמה תמימה אשר אין־בה
ג מום אשר לא־עלה עליה על: ונתתם אתה אל־אלעזר הכהן והוציא אתה
ד אל־מחוץ למחנה ושחט אתה לפניו: ולקח אלעזר הכהן מדמה באצבעו
ה והזה אל־נכח פני אהל־מועד מדמה שבע פעמים: ושרף את־הפרה לעיניו
ו את־ערה ואת־בשרה ואת־דמה על־פרשה ישרף: ולקח הכהן עץ ארז
ז ואזוב ושני תולעת והשליך אל־תוך שרפת הפרה: *וכבס בגדיו הכהן לוי
ח ורחץ בשרו במים ואחר יבא אל־המחנה וטמא הכהן עד־הערב: והשרף
ט אתה יכבס בגדיו במים ורחץ בשרו במים וטמא עד־הערב: ואסף ׀ איש
טהור את אפר הפרה והניח מחוץ למחנה במקום טהור והיתה לעדת בני־
י ישראל למשמרת למי נדה חטאת הוא: *וכבס האסף את־אפר הפרה ישראל
את־בגדיו וטמא עד־הערב והיתה לבני ישראל ולגר הגר בתוכם לחקת
יא יב עולם: הנגע במת לכל־נפש אדם וטמא שבעת ימים: הוא יתחטא־בו ביום
השלישי וביום השביעי יטהר ואם־לא יתחטא ביום השלישי וביום השביעי
יג לא יטהר: כל־הנגע במת בנפש האדם אשר־ימות ולא יתחטא את־משכן

יהוה טִמֵּא וְנִכְרְתָה הַנֶּפֶשׁ הַהִוא מִיִּשְׂרָאֵל כִּי מֵי נִדָּה לֹא־זֹרַק עָלָיו טָמֵא
יד יִהְיֶה עוֹד טֻמְאָתוֹ בוֹ: זֹאת הַתּוֹרָה אָדָם כִּי־יָמוּת בְּאֹהֶל כָּל־הַבָּא אֶל־הָאֹהֶל
טו וְכָל־אֲשֶׁר בָּאֹהֶל יִטְמָא שִׁבְעַת יָמִים: וְכֹל כְּלִי פָתוּחַ אֲשֶׁר אֵין־צָמִיד פָּתִיל
טז עָלָיו טָמֵא הוּא: וְכֹל אֲשֶׁר־יִגַּע עַל־פְּנֵי הַשָּׂדֶה בַּחֲלַל־חֶרֶב אוֹ בְמֵת אוֹ־בְעֶצֶם
יז אָדָם אוֹ בְקָבֶר יִטְמָא שִׁבְעַת יָמִים: וְלָקְחוּ לַטָּמֵא מֵעֲפַר שְׂרֵפַת הַחַטָּאת
יח וְנָתַן עָלָיו מַיִם חַיִּים אֶל־כֶּלִי:** וְלָקַח אֵזוֹב וְטָבַל בַּמַּיִם אִישׁ טָהוֹר וְהִזָּה שני
עַל־הָאֹהֶל וְעַל־כָּל־הַכֵּלִים וְעַל־הַנְּפָשׁוֹת אֲשֶׁר הָיוּ־שָׁם וְעַל־הַנֹּגֵעַ בַּעֶצֶם
יט אוֹ בֶחָלָל אוֹ בַמֵּת אוֹ בַקָּבֶר: וְהִזָּה הַטָּהֹר עַל־הַטָּמֵא בַּיּוֹם הַשְּׁלִישִׁי וּבַיּוֹם
כ הַשְּׁבִיעִי וְחִטְּאוֹ בַּיּוֹם הַשְּׁבִיעִי וְכִבֶּס בְּגָדָיו וְרָחַץ בַּמַּיִם וְטָהֵר בָּעָרֶב: וְאִישׁ
אֲשֶׁר־יִטְמָא וְלֹא יִתְחַטָּא וְנִכְרְתָה הַנֶּפֶשׁ הַהִוא מִתּוֹךְ הַקָּהָל כִּי אֶת־מִקְדַּשׁ
כא יהוה טִמֵּא מֵי נִדָּה לֹא־זֹרַק עָלָיו טָמֵא הוּא: וְהָיְתָה לָהֶם לְחֻקַּת עוֹלָם
כב וּמַזֵּה מֵי־הַנִּדָּה יְכַבֵּס בְּגָדָיו וְהַנֹּגֵעַ בְּמֵי הַנִּדָּה יִטְמָא עַד־הָעָרֶב: וְכֹל אֲשֶׁר־
יִגַּע־בּוֹ הַטָּמֵא יִטְמָא וְהַנֶּפֶשׁ הַנֹּגַעַת תִּטְמָא עַד־הָעָרֶב:
כ א וַיָּבֹאוּ בְנֵי־יִשְׂרָאֵל כָּל־הָעֵדָה מִדְבַּר־צִן בַּחֹדֶשׁ הָרִאשׁוֹן וַיֵּשֶׁב הָעָם בְּקָדֵשׁ
ב וַתָּמָת שָׁם מִרְיָם וַתִּקָּבֵר שָׁם: וְלֹא־הָיָה מַיִם לָעֵדָה וַיִּקָּהֲלוּ עַל־מֹשֶׁה וְעַל־
ג אַהֲרֹן: וַיָּרֶב הָעָם עִם־מֹשֶׁה וַיֹּאמְרוּ לֵאמֹר וְלוּ גָוַעְנוּ בִּגְוַע אַחֵינוּ לִפְנֵי יהוה:
ד וְלָמָה הֲבֵאתֶם אֶת־קְהַל יהוה אֶל־הַמִּדְבָּר הַזֶּה לָמוּת שָׁם אֲנַחְנוּ וּבְעִירֵנוּ:
ה וְלָמָה הֶעֱלִיתֻנוּ מִמִּצְרַיִם לְהָבִיא אֹתָנוּ אֶל־הַמָּקוֹם הָרָע הַזֶּה לֹא ׀ מְקוֹם
ו זֶרַע וּתְאֵנָה וְגֶפֶן וְרִמּוֹן וּמַיִם אַיִן לִשְׁתּוֹת: וַיָּבֹא מֹשֶׁה וְאַהֲרֹן מִפְּנֵי הַקָּהָל אֶל־
פֶּתַח אֹהֶל מוֹעֵד וַיִּפְּלוּ עַל־פְּנֵיהֶם וַיֵּרָא כְבוֹד־יהוה אֲלֵיהֶם:
ז ח *וַיְדַבֵּר יהוה אֶל־מֹשֶׁה לֵּאמֹר: קַח אֶת־הַמַּטֶּה וְהַקְהֵל אֶת־הָעֵדָה אַתָּה שלישי / שני /
וְאַהֲרֹן אָחִיךָ וְדִבַּרְתֶּם אֶל־הַסֶּלַע לְעֵינֵיהֶם וְנָתַן מֵימָיו וְהוֹצֵאתָ לָהֶם מַיִם
ט מִן־הַסֶּלַע וְהִשְׁקִיתָ אֶת־הָעֵדָה וְאֶת־בְּעִירָם: וַיִּקַּח מֹשֶׁה אֶת־הַמַּטֶּה מִלִּפְנֵי
י יהוה כַּאֲשֶׁר צִוָּהוּ: וַיַּקְהִלוּ מֹשֶׁה וְאַהֲרֹן אֶת־הַקָּהָל אֶל־פְּנֵי הַסָּלַע וַיֹּאמֶר
יא לָהֶם שִׁמְעוּ־נָא הַמֹּרִים הֲמִן־הַסֶּלַע הַזֶּה נוֹצִיא לָכֶם מָיִם: וַיָּרֶם מֹשֶׁה
אֶת־יָדוֹ וַיַּךְ אֶת־הַסֶּלַע בְּמַטֵּהוּ פַּעֲמָיִם וַיֵּצְאוּ מַיִם רַבִּים וַתֵּשְׁתְּ הָעֵדָה
יב וּבְעִירָם: וַיֹּאמֶר יהוה אֶל־מֹשֶׁה וְאֶל־אַהֲרֹן יַעַן לֹא־הֶאֱמַנְתֶּם
בִּי לְהַקְדִּישֵׁנִי לְעֵינֵי בְּנֵי יִשְׂרָאֵל לָכֵן לֹא תָבִיאוּ אֶת־הַקָּהָל הַזֶּה אֶל־הָאָרֶץ
יג אֲשֶׁר־נָתַתִּי לָהֶם: הֵמָּה מֵי מְרִיבָה אֲשֶׁר־רָבוּ בְנֵי־יִשְׂרָאֵל אֶת־יהוה וַיִּקָּדֵשׁ

רביעי יח בָּם: וַיִּשְׁלַח מֹשֶׁה מַלְאָכִים מִקָּדֵשׁ אֶל־מֶלֶךְ אֱדוֹם כֹּה אָמַר אָחִיךָ יד
יִשְׂרָאֵל אַתָּה יָדַעְתָּ אֵת כָּל־הַתְּלָאָה אֲשֶׁר מְצָאָתְנוּ: וַיֵּרְדוּ אֲבֹתֵינוּ מִצְרַיְמָה טו
וַנֵּשֶׁב בְּמִצְרַיִם יָמִים רַבִּים וַיָּרֵעוּ לָנוּ מִצְרַיִם וְלַאֲבֹתֵינוּ: וַנִּצְעַק אֶל־יהוה טז
וַיִּשְׁמַע קֹלֵנוּ וַיִּשְׁלַח מַלְאָךְ וַיֹּצִאֵנוּ מִמִּצְרָיִם וְהִנֵּה אֲנַחְנוּ בְקָדֵשׁ עִיר קְצֵה
גְבוּלֶךָ: נַעְבְּרָה־נָּא בְאַרְצֶךָ לֹא נַעֲבֹר בְּשָׂדֶה וּבְכֶרֶם וְלֹא נִשְׁתֶּה מֵי בְאֵר יז
דֶּרֶךְ הַמֶּלֶךְ נֵלֵךְ לֹא נִטֶּה יָמִין וּשְׂמֹאול עַד אֲשֶׁר־נַעֲבֹר גְּבֻלֶךָ: וַיֹּאמֶר אֵלָיו יח
אֱדוֹם לֹא תַעֲבֹר בִּי פֶּן־בַּחֶרֶב אֵצֵא לִקְרָאתֶךָ: וַיֹּאמְרוּ אֵלָיו בְּנֵי־יִשְׂרָאֵל יט
בַּמְסִלָּה נַעֲלֶה וְאִם־מֵימֶיךָ נִשְׁתֶּה אֲנִי וּמִקְנַי וְנָתַתִּי מִכְרָם רַק אֵין־דָּבָר בְּרַגְלַי
אֶעֱבֹרָה: וַיֹּאמֶר לֹא תַעֲבֹר וַיֵּצֵא אֱדוֹם לִקְרָאתוֹ בְּעַם כָּבֵד וּבְיָד חֲזָקָה: וַיְמָאֵן | כ כא
אֱדוֹם נְתֹן אֶת־יִשְׂרָאֵל עֲבֹר בִּגְבֻלוֹ וַיֵּט יִשְׂרָאֵל מֵעָלָיו:
חמישי / שלישי / *וַיִּסְעוּ מִקָּדֵשׁ וַיָּבֹאוּ בְנֵי־יִשְׂרָאֵל כָּל־הָעֵדָה הֹר הָהָר: וַיֹּאמֶר יהוה אֶל־מֹשֶׁה כב כג
וְאֶל־אַהֲרֹן בְּהֹר הָהָר עַל־גְּבוּל אֶרֶץ־אֱדוֹם לֵאמֹר: יֵאָסֵף אַהֲרֹן אֶל־עַמָּיו כד
כִּי לֹא יָבֹא אֶל־הָאָרֶץ אֲשֶׁר נָתַתִּי לִבְנֵי יִשְׂרָאֵל עַל אֲשֶׁר־מְרִיתֶם אֶת־פִּי
לְמֵי מְרִיבָה: קַח אֶת־אַהֲרֹן וְאֶת־אֶלְעָזָר בְּנוֹ וְהַעַל אֹתָם הֹר הָהָר: וְהַפְשֵׁט כה כו
אֶת־אַהֲרֹן אֶת־בְּגָדָיו וְהִלְבַּשְׁתָּם אֶת־אֶלְעָזָר בְּנוֹ וְאַהֲרֹן יֵאָסֵף וּמֵת שָׁם:
וַיַּעַשׂ מֹשֶׁה כַּאֲשֶׁר צִוָּה יהוה וַיַּעֲלוּ אֶל־הֹר הָהָר לְעֵינֵי כָּל־הָעֵדָה: וַיַּפְשֵׁט כז כח
מֹשֶׁה אֶת־אַהֲרֹן אֶת־בְּגָדָיו וַיַּלְבֵּשׁ אֹתָם אֶת־אֶלְעָזָר בְּנוֹ וַיָּמָת אַהֲרֹן שָׁם
בְּרֹאשׁ הָהָר וַיֵּרֶד מֹשֶׁה וְאֶלְעָזָר מִן־הָהָר: וַיִּרְאוּ כָּל־הָעֵדָה כִּי גָוַע אַהֲרֹן כט
וַיִּבְכּוּ אֶת־אַהֲרֹן שְׁלֹשִׁים יוֹם כֹּל בֵּית יִשְׂרָאֵל: וַיִּשְׁמַע הַכְּנַעֲנִי א כא
מֶלֶךְ־עֲרָד יֹשֵׁב הַנֶּגֶב כִּי בָּא יִשְׂרָאֵל דֶּרֶךְ הָאֲתָרִים וַיִּלָּחֶם בְּיִשְׂרָאֵל וַיִּשְׁבְּ |
מִמֶּנּוּ שֶׁבִי: וַיִּדַּר יִשְׂרָאֵל נֶדֶר לַיהוה וַיֹּאמַר אִם־נָתֹן תִּתֵּן אֶת־הָעָם הַזֶּה ב
בְּיָדִי וְהַחֲרַמְתִּי אֶת־עָרֵיהֶם: וַיִּשְׁמַע יהוה בְּקוֹל יִשְׂרָאֵל וַיִּתֵּן אֶת־הַכְּנַעֲנִי ג
וַיַּחֲרֵם אֶתְהֶם וְאֶת־עָרֵיהֶם וַיִּקְרָא שֵׁם־הַמָּקוֹם חָרְמָה:
וַיִּסְעוּ מֵהֹר הָהָר דֶּרֶךְ יַם־סוּף לִסְבֹב אֶת־אֶרֶץ אֱדוֹם וַתִּקְצַר נֶפֶשׁ־הָעָם ד
בַּדָּרֶךְ: וַיְדַבֵּר הָעָם בֵּאלֹהִים וּבְמֹשֶׁה לָמָה הֶעֱלִיתֻנוּ מִמִּצְרַיִם לָמוּת בַּמִּדְבָּר ה
כִּי אֵין לֶחֶם וְאֵין מַיִם וְנַפְשֵׁנוּ קָצָה בַּלֶּחֶם הַקְּלֹקֵל: וַיְשַׁלַּח יהוה בָּעָם אֵת ו
הַנְּחָשִׁים הַשְּׂרָפִים וַיְנַשְּׁכוּ אֶת־הָעָם וַיָּמָת עַם־רָב מִיִּשְׂרָאֵל: וַיָּבֹא הָעָם אֶל־ ז
מֹשֶׁה וַיֹּאמְרוּ חָטָאנוּ כִּי־דִבַּרְנוּ בַיהוה וָבָךְ הִתְפַּלֵּל אֶל־יהוה וְיָסֵר מֵעָלֵינוּ
אֶת־הַנָּחָשׁ וַיִּתְפַּלֵּל מֹשֶׁה בְּעַד הָעָם: וַיֹּאמֶר יהוה אֶל־מֹשֶׁה עֲשֵׂה לְךָ שָׂרָף ח

ט וְשִׂים אֹתוֹ עַל־נֵס וְהָיָה כָּל־הַנָּשׁוּךְ וְרָאָה אֹתוֹ וָחָי׃ וַיַּעַשׂ מֹשֶׁה נְחַשׁ נְחֹשֶׁת
וַיְשִׂמֵהוּ עַל־הַנֵּס וְהָיָה אִם־נָשַׁךְ הַנָּחָשׁ אֶת־אִישׁ וְהִבִּיט אֶל־נְחַשׁ הַנְּחֹשֶׁת
יא וָחָי׃ *וַיִּסְעוּ בְּנֵי יִשְׂרָאֵל וַיַּחֲנוּ בְּאֹבֹת׃ וַיִּסְעוּ מֵאֹבֹת וַיַּחֲנוּ בְּעִיֵּי הָעֲבָרִים ששי
יב בַּמִּדְבָּר אֲשֶׁר עַל־פְּנֵי מוֹאָב מִמִּזְרַח הַשָּׁמֶשׁ׃ מִשָּׁם נָסָעוּ וַיַּחֲנוּ בְּנַחַל זָרֶד׃
יג מִשָּׁם נָסָעוּ וַיַּחֲנוּ מֵעֵבֶר אַרְנוֹן אֲשֶׁר בַּמִּדְבָּר הַיֹּצֵא מִגְּבֻל הָאֱמֹרִי כִּי אַרְנוֹן
יד גְּבוּל מוֹאָב בֵּין מוֹאָב וּבֵין הָאֱמֹרִי׃ עַל־כֵּן יֵאָמַר בְּסֵפֶר מִלְחֲמֹת יהוה אֶת־
טו וָהֵב בְּסוּפָה וְאֶת־הַנְּחָלִים אַרְנוֹן׃ וְאֶשֶׁד הַנְּחָלִים אֲשֶׁר נָטָה לְשֶׁבֶת עָר
טז וְנִשְׁעַן לִגְבוּל מוֹאָב׃ וּמִשָּׁם בְּאֵרָה הִוא הַבְּאֵר אֲשֶׁר אָמַר יהוה לְמֹשֶׁה אֱסֹף
יז אֶת־הָעָם וְאֶתְּנָה לָהֶם מָיִם׃ אָז יָשִׁיר יִשְׂרָאֵל אֶת־הַשִּׁירָה הַזֹּאת
יח עֲלִי בְאֵר עֱנוּ־לָהּ׃ בְּאֵר חֲפָרוּהָ שָׂרִים כָּרוּהָ נְדִיבֵי הָעָם בִּמְחֹקֵק בְּמִשְׁעֲנֹתָם
יט כ וּמִמִּדְבָּר מַתָּנָה׃ וּמִמַּתָּנָה נַחֲלִיאֵל וּמִנַּחֲלִיאֵל בָּמוֹת׃ וּמִבָּמוֹת הַגַּיְא אֲשֶׁר
בִּשְׂדֵה מוֹאָב רֹאשׁ הַפִּסְגָּה וְנִשְׁקָפָה עַל־פְּנֵי הַיְשִׁימֹן׃
כא כב *וַיִּשְׁלַח יִשְׂרָאֵל מַלְאָכִים אֶל־סִיחֹן מֶלֶךְ־הָאֱמֹרִי לֵאמֹר׃ אֶעְבְּרָה בְאַרְצֶךָ שביעי / רביעי /
לֹא נִטֶּה בְּשָׂדֶה וּבְכֶרֶם לֹא נִשְׁתֶּה מֵי בְאֵר בְּדֶרֶךְ הַמֶּלֶךְ נֵלֵךְ עַד אֲשֶׁר־נַעֲבֹר
כג גְּבֻלֶךָ׃ וְלֹא־נָתַן סִיחֹן אֶת־יִשְׂרָאֵל עֲבֹר בִּגְבֻלוֹ וַיֶּאֱסֹף סִיחֹן אֶת־כָּל־עַמּוֹ
כד וַיֵּצֵא לִקְרַאת יִשְׂרָאֵל הַמִּדְבָּרָה וַיָּבֹא יָהְצָה וַיִּלָּחֶם בְּיִשְׂרָאֵל׃ וַיַּכֵּהוּ יִשְׂרָאֵל
לְפִי־חָרֶב וַיִּירַשׁ אֶת־אַרְצוֹ מֵאַרְנֹן עַד־יַבֹּק עַד־בְּנֵי עַמּוֹן כִּי עַז גְּבוּל בְּנֵי
כה עַמּוֹן׃ וַיִּקַּח יִשְׂרָאֵל אֵת כָּל־הֶעָרִים הָאֵלֶּה וַיֵּשֶׁב יִשְׂרָאֵל בְּכָל־עָרֵי הָאֱמֹרִי
כו בְּחֶשְׁבּוֹן וּבְכָל־בְּנֹתֶיהָ׃ כִּי חֶשְׁבּוֹן עִיר סִיחֹן מֶלֶךְ הָאֱמֹרִי הִוא וְהוּא נִלְחַם
כז בְּמֶלֶךְ מוֹאָב הָרִאשׁוֹן וַיִּקַּח אֶת־כָּל־אַרְצוֹ מִיָּדוֹ עַד־אַרְנֹן׃ עַל־כֵּן יֹאמְרוּ
כח הַמֹּשְׁלִים בֹּאוּ חֶשְׁבּוֹן תִּבָּנֶה וְתִכּוֹנֵן עִיר סִיחוֹן׃ כִּי־אֵשׁ יָצְאָה מֵחֶשְׁבּוֹן לֶהָבָה
כט מִקִּרְיַת סִיחֹן אָכְלָה עָר מוֹאָב בַּעֲלֵי בָּמוֹת אַרְנֹן׃ אוֹי־לְךָ מוֹאָב אָבַדְתָּ
ל עַם־כְּמוֹשׁ נָתַן בָּנָיו פְּלֵיטִם וּבְנֹתָיו בַּשְּׁבִית לְמֶלֶךְ אֱמֹרִי סִיחוֹן׃ וַנִּירָם אָבַד
לא חֶשְׁבּוֹן עַד־דִּיבֹן וַנַּשִּׁים עַד־נֹפַח אֲשֶׁר עַד־מֵידְבָא׃ וַיֵּשֶׁב יִשְׂרָאֵל בְּאֶרֶץ
לב הָאֱמֹרִי׃ וַיִּשְׁלַח מֹשֶׁה לְרַגֵּל אֶת־יַעְזֵר וַיִּלְכְּדוּ בְּנֹתֶיהָ ויירש אֶת־הָאֱמֹרִי [וַיּוֹרֶשׁ]
לג אֲשֶׁר־שָׁם׃ וַיִּפְנוּ וַיַּעֲלוּ דֶּרֶךְ הַבָּשָׁן וַיֵּצֵא עוֹג מֶלֶךְ־הַבָּשָׁן לִקְרָאתָם הוּא
לד וְכָל־עַמּוֹ לַמִּלְחָמָה אֶדְרֶעִי׃ וַיֹּאמֶר יהוה אֶל־מֹשֶׁה אַל־תִּירָא אֹתוֹ כִּי בְיָדְךָ מפטיר
נָתַתִּי אֹתוֹ וְאֶת־כָּל־עַמּוֹ וְאֶת־אַרְצוֹ וְעָשִׂיתָ לּוֹ כַּאֲשֶׁר עָשִׂיתָ לְסִיחֹן מֶלֶךְ
לה הָאֱמֹרִי אֲשֶׁר יוֹשֵׁב בְּחֶשְׁבּוֹן׃ וַיַּכּוּ אֹתוֹ וְאֶת־בָּנָיו וְאֶת־כָּל־עַמּוֹ עַד־בִּלְתִּי

The Maftir for Shabbat Rosh Hodesh, page 1030

כב א הִשְׁאִיר־לוֹ שָׂרִיד וַיִּירְשׁוּ אֶת־אַרְצוֹ׃ וַיִּסְעוּ בְּנֵי יִשְׂרָאֵל וַיַּחֲנוּ בְּעַרְבוֹת מוֹאָב
בלק יט ב מֵעֵבֶר לְיַרְדֵּן יְרֵחוֹ׃ וַיַּרְא בָּלָק בֶּן־צִפּוֹר אֵת כָּל־אֲשֶׁר־עָשָׂה
ג יִשְׂרָאֵל לָאֱמֹרִי׃ וַיָּגָר מוֹאָב מִפְּנֵי הָעָם מְאֹד כִּי רַב־הוּא וַיָּקָץ מוֹאָב מִפְּנֵי
ד בְּנֵי יִשְׂרָאֵל׃ וַיֹּאמֶר מוֹאָב אֶל־זִקְנֵי מִדְיָן עַתָּה יְלַחֲכוּ הַקָּהָל אֶת־כָּל־
סְבִיבֹתֵינוּ כִּלְחֹךְ הַשּׁוֹר אֵת יֶרֶק הַשָּׂדֶה וּבָלָק בֶּן־צִפּוֹר מֶלֶךְ לְמוֹאָב בָּעֵת
ה הַהִוא׃ *וַיִּשְׁלַח מַלְאָכִים אֶל־בִּלְעָם בֶּן־בְּעוֹר פְּתוֹרָה אֲשֶׁר עַל־הַנָּהָר אֶרֶץ לוי
בְּנֵי־עַמּוֹ לִקְרֹא־לוֹ לֵאמֹר הִנֵּה עַם יָצָא מִמִּצְרַיִם הִנֵּה כִסָּה אֶת־עֵין הָאָרֶץ
ו וְהוּא יֹשֵׁב מִמֻּלִי׃ וְעַתָּה לְכָה־נָּא אָרָה־לִּי אֶת־הָעָם הַזֶּה כִּי־עָצוּם הוּא מִמֶּנִּי
אוּלַי אוּכַל נַכֶּה־בּוֹ וַאֲגָרְשֶׁנּוּ מִן־הָאָרֶץ כִּי יָדַעְתִּי אֵת אֲשֶׁר־תְּבָרֵךְ מְבֹרָךְ
ז וַאֲשֶׁר תָּאֹר יוּאָר׃ וַיֵּלְכוּ זִקְנֵי מוֹאָב וְזִקְנֵי מִדְיָן וּקְסָמִים בְּיָדָם וַיָּבֹאוּ אֶל־
ח בִּלְעָם וַיְדַבְּרוּ אֵלָיו דִּבְרֵי בָלָק׃ *וַיֹּאמֶר אֲלֵיהֶם לִינוּ פֹה הַלַּיְלָה וַהֲשִׁבֹתִי ישראל
ט אֶתְכֶם דָּבָר כַּאֲשֶׁר יְדַבֵּר יְהוָה אֵלָי וַיֵּשְׁבוּ שָׂרֵי־מוֹאָב עִם־בִּלְעָם׃ וַיָּבֹא
י אֱלֹהִים אֶל־בִּלְעָם וַיֹּאמֶר מִי הָאֲנָשִׁים הָאֵלֶּה עִמָּךְ׃ וַיֹּאמֶר בִּלְעָם אֶל־
יא הָאֱלֹהִים בָּלָק בֶּן־צִפֹּר מֶלֶךְ מוֹאָב שָׁלַח אֵלָי׃ הִנֵּה הָעָם הַיֹּצֵא מִמִּצְרַיִם
וַיְכַס אֶת־עֵין הָאָרֶץ עַתָּה לְכָה קָבָה־לִּי אֹתוֹ אוּלַי אוּכַל לְהִלָּחֶם בּוֹ וְגֵרַשְׁתִּיו׃
יב וַיֹּאמֶר אֱלֹהִים אֶל־בִּלְעָם לֹא תֵלֵךְ עִמָּהֶם לֹא תָאֹר אֶת־הָעָם כִּי בָרוּךְ הוּא׃**
יג וַיָּקָם בִּלְעָם בַּבֹּקֶר וַיֹּאמֶר אֶל־שָׂרֵי בָלָק לְכוּ אֶל־אַרְצְכֶם כִּי מֵאֵן יְהוָה לְתִתִּי שני / חמישי /
יד לַהֲלֹךְ עִמָּכֶם׃ וַיָּקוּמוּ שָׂרֵי מוֹאָב וַיָּבֹאוּ אֶל־בָּלָק וַיֹּאמְרוּ מֵאֵן בִּלְעָם הֲלֹךְ
טו טז עִמָּנוּ׃ וַיֹּסֶף עוֹד בָּלָק שְׁלֹחַ שָׂרִים רַבִּים וְנִכְבָּדִים מֵאֵלֶּה׃ וַיָּבֹאוּ אֶל־בִּלְעָם
יז וַיֹּאמְרוּ לוֹ כֹּה אָמַר בָּלָק בֶּן־צִפּוֹר אַל־נָא תִמָּנַע מֵהֲלֹךְ אֵלָי׃ כִּי־כַבֵּד אֲכַבֶּדְךָ
יח מְאֹד וְכֹל אֲשֶׁר־תֹּאמַר אֵלַי אֶעֱשֶׂה וּלְכָה־נָּא קָבָה־לִּי אֵת הָעָם הַזֶּה׃ וַיַּעַן
בִּלְעָם וַיֹּאמֶר אֶל־עַבְדֵי בָלָק אִם־יִתֶּן־לִי בָלָק מְלֹא בֵיתוֹ כֶּסֶף וְזָהָב לֹא
יט אוּכַל לַעֲבֹר אֶת־פִּי יְהוָה אֱלֹהָי לַעֲשׂוֹת קְטַנָּה אוֹ גְדוֹלָה׃ וְעַתָּה שְׁבוּ נָא
כ בָזֶה גַּם־אַתֶּם הַלָּיְלָה וְאֵדְעָה מַה־יֹּסֵף יְהוָה דַּבֵּר עִמִּי׃ וַיָּבֹא אֱלֹהִים ׀ אֶל־
בִּלְעָם לַיְלָה וַיֹּאמֶר לוֹ אִם־לִקְרֹא לְךָ בָּאוּ הָאֲנָשִׁים קוּם לֵךְ אִתָּם וְאַךְ
כא אֶת־הַדָּבָר אֲשֶׁר־אֲדַבֵּר אֵלֶיךָ אֹתוֹ תַעֲשֶׂה׃ וַיָּקָם בִּלְעָם בַּבֹּקֶר וַיַּחֲבֹשׁ אֶת־ שלישי
כב אֲתֹנוֹ וַיֵּלֶךְ עִם־שָׂרֵי מוֹאָב׃ וַיִּחַר־אַף אֱלֹהִים כִּי־הוֹלֵךְ הוּא וַיִּתְיַצֵּב מַלְאַךְ
כג יְהוָה בַּדֶּרֶךְ לְשָׂטָן לוֹ וְהוּא רֹכֵב עַל־אֲתֹנוֹ וּשְׁנֵי נְעָרָיו עִמּוֹ׃ וַתֵּרֶא הָאָתוֹן
אֶת־מַלְאַךְ יְהוָה נִצָּב בַּדֶּרֶךְ וְחַרְבּוֹ שְׁלוּפָה בְּיָדוֹ וַתֵּט הָאָתוֹן מִן־הַדֶּרֶךְ וַתֵּלֶךְ

כד בשדה ויך בלעם את־האתון להטתה הדרך: ויעמד מלאך יהוה במשעול
כה הכרמים גדר מזה וגדר מזה: ותרא האתון את־מלאך יהוה ותלחץ אל־
כו הקיר ותלחץ את־רגל בלעם אל־הקיר ויסף להכתה: ויוסף מלאך־יהוה
כז עבור ויעמד במקום צר אשר אין־דרך לנטות ימין ושמאול: ותרא האתון
את־מלאך יהוה ותרבץ תחת בלעם ויחר־אף בלעם ויך את־האתון במקל:
כח ויפתח יהוה את־פי האתון ותאמר לבלעם מה־עשיתי לך כי הכיתני זה
כט שלש רגלים: ויאמר בלעם לאתון כי התעללת בי לו יש־חרב בידי כי עתה
ל הרגתיך: ותאמר האתון אל־בלעם הלוא אנכי אתנך אשר־רכבת עלי
לא מעודך עד־היום הזה ההסכן הסכנתי לעשות לך כה ויאמר לא: ויגל יהוה
את־עיני בלעם וירא את־מלאך יהוה נצב בדרך וחרבו שלפה בידו ויקד
לב וישתחו לאפיו: ויאמר אליו מלאך יהוה על־מה הכית את־אתנך זה שלוש
לג רגלים הנה אנכי יצאתי לשטן כי־ירט הדרך לנגדי: ותראני האתון ותט
לפני זה שלש רגלים אולי נטתה מפני כי עתה גם־אתכה הרגתי ואותה
לד החייתי: ויאמר בלעם אל־מלאך יהוה חטאתי כי לא ידעתי כי אתה נצב
לה לקראתי בדרך ועתה אם־רע בעיניך אשובה לי: ויאמר מלאך יהוה אל־
בלעם לך עם־האנשים ואפס את־הדבר אשר־אדבר אליך אתו תדבר
לו וילך בלעם עם־שרי בלק: וישמע בלק כי־בא בלעם ויצא לקראתו אל־
לז עיר מואב אשר על־גבול ארנן אשר בקצה הגבול: ויאמר בלק אל־בלעם
הלא שלח שלחתי אליך לקרא־לך למה לא־הלכת אלי האמנם לא אוכל
לח כבדך: ויאמר בלעם אל־בלק הנה־באתי אליך עתה היכל אוכל דבר
לט מאומה הדבר אשר ישים אלהים בפי אתו אדבר: וילך בלעם עם־בלק (רביעי /ששי/)
מ ויבאו קרית חצות: ויזבח בלק בקר וצאן וישלח לבלעם ולשרים אשר
מא אתו: ויהי בבקר ויקח בלק את־בלעם ויעלהו במות בעל וירא משם קצה
כג א העם: ויאמר בלעם אל־בלק בנה־לי בזה שבעה מזבחת והכן לי בזה
ב שבעה פרים ושבעה אילים: ויעש בלק כאשר דבר בלעם ויעל בלק ובלעם
ג פר ואיל במזבח: ויאמר בלעם לבלק התיצב על־עלתך ואלכה אולי יקרה
ד יהוה לקראתי ודבר מה־יראני והגדתי לך וילך שפי: ויקר אלהים אל־
בלעם ויאמר אליו את־שבעת המזבחת ערכתי ואעל פר ואיל במזבח:
ה ו וישם יהוה דבר בפי בלעם ויאמר שוב אל־בלק וכה תדבר: וישב אליו

ז וְהִנֵּה נִצָּב עַל־עֹלָתוֹ הוּא וְכָל־שָׂרֵי מוֹאָב׃ וַיִּשָּׂא מְשָׁלוֹ וַיֹּאמַר מִן־אֲרָם יַנְחֵנִי
בָלָק מֶלֶךְ־מוֹאָב מֵהַרְרֵי־קֶדֶם לְכָה אָרָה־לִּי יַעֲקֹב וּלְכָה זֹעֲמָה יִשְׂרָאֵל׃
ח ט מָה אֶקֹּב לֹא קַבֹּה אֵל וּמָה אֶזְעֹם לֹא זָעַם יהוה׃ כִּי־מֵרֹאשׁ צֻרִים אֶרְאֶנּוּ
י וּמִגְּבָעוֹת אֲשׁוּרֶנּוּ הֶן־עָם לְבָדָד יִשְׁכֹּן וּבַגּוֹיִם לֹא יִתְחַשָּׁב׃ מִי מָנָה עֲפַר כ
יַעֲקֹב וּמִסְפָּר אֶת־רֹבַע יִשְׂרָאֵל תָּמֹת נַפְשִׁי מוֹת יְשָׁרִים וּתְהִי אַחֲרִיתִי כָּמֹהוּ׃
יא וַיֹּאמֶר בָּלָק אֶל־בִּלְעָם מֶה עָשִׂיתָ לִי לָקֹב אֹיְבַי לְקַחְתִּיךָ וְהִנֵּה בֵּרַכְתָּ בָרֵךְ׃
יב יג וַיַּעַן וַיֹּאמַר הֲלֹא אֵת אֲשֶׁר יָשִׂים יהוה בְּפִי אֹתוֹ אֶשְׁמֹר לְדַבֵּר׃ וַיֹּאמֶר אֵלָיו חמישי
בָּלָק לְךָ־נָּא אִתִּי אֶל־מָקוֹם אַחֵר אֲשֶׁר תִּרְאֶנּוּ מִשָּׁם אֶפֶס קָצֵהוּ תִרְאֶה
יד וְכֻלּוֹ לֹא תִרְאֶה וְקָבְנוֹ־לִי מִשָּׁם׃ וַיִּקָּחֵהוּ שְׂדֵה צֹפִים אֶל־רֹאשׁ הַפִּסְגָּה וַיִּבֶן
טו שִׁבְעָה מִזְבְּחֹת וַיַּעַל פָּר וָאַיִל בַּמִּזְבֵּחַ׃ וַיֹּאמֶר אֶל־בָּלָק הִתְיַצֵּב כֹּה עַל־עֹלָתֶךָ
טז וְאָנֹכִי אִקָּרֶה כֹּה׃ וַיִּקָּר יהוה אֶל־בִּלְעָם וַיָּשֶׂם דָּבָר בְּפִיו וַיֹּאמֶר שׁוּב אֶל־בָּלָק
יז וְכֹה תְדַבֵּר׃ וַיָּבֹא אֵלָיו וְהִנּוֹ נִצָּב עַל־עֹלָתוֹ וְשָׂרֵי מוֹאָב אִתּוֹ וַיֹּאמֶר לוֹ בָּלָק
יח מַה־דִּבֶּר יהוה׃ וַיִּשָּׂא מְשָׁלוֹ וַיֹּאמַר קוּם בָּלָק וּשְׁמָע הַאֲזִינָה עָדַי בְּנוֹ צִפֹּר׃
יט לֹא אִישׁ אֵל וִיכַזֵּב וּבֶן־אָדָם וְיִתְנֶחָם הַהוּא אָמַר וְלֹא יַעֲשֶׂה וְדִבֶּר וְלֹא
כ כא יְקִימֶנָּה׃ הִנֵּה בָרֵךְ לָקָחְתִּי וּבֵרֵךְ וְלֹא אֲשִׁיבֶנָּה׃ לֹא־הִבִּיט אָוֶן בְּיַעֲקֹב וְלֹא־
כב רָאָה עָמָל בְּיִשְׂרָאֵל יהוה אֱלֹהָיו עִמּוֹ וּתְרוּעַת מֶלֶךְ בּוֹ׃ אֵל מוֹצִיאָם מִמִּצְרָיִם
כג כְּתוֹעֲפֹת רְאֵם לוֹ׃ כִּי לֹא־נַחַשׁ בְּיַעֲקֹב וְלֹא־קֶסֶם בְּיִשְׂרָאֵל כָּעֵת יֵאָמֵר לְיַעֲקֹב
כד וּלְיִשְׂרָאֵל מַה־פָּעַל אֵל׃ הֶן־עָם כְּלָבִיא יָקוּם וְכַאֲרִי יִתְנַשָּׂא לֹא יִשְׁכַּב עַד־
כה יֹאכַל טֶרֶף וְדַם־חֲלָלִים יִשְׁתֶּה׃ וַיֹּאמֶר בָּלָק אֶל־בִּלְעָם גַּם־קֹב לֹא תִקֳּבֶנּוּ
כו גַּם־בָּרֵךְ לֹא תְבָרְכֶנּוּ׃ וַיַּעַן בִּלְעָם וַיֹּאמֶר אֶל־בָּלָק הֲלֹא דִּבַּרְתִּי אֵלֶיךָ לֵאמֹר
כז כֹּל אֲשֶׁר־יְדַבֵּר יהוה אֹתוֹ אֶעֱשֶׂה׃ וַיֹּאמֶר בָּלָק אֶל־בִּלְעָם לְכָה־נָּא אֶקָּחֲךָ ששי
כח אֶל־מָקוֹם אַחֵר אוּלַי יִישַׁר בְּעֵינֵי הָאֱלֹהִים וְקַבֹּתוֹ לִי מִשָּׁם׃ וַיִּקַּח בָּלָק / שביעי /
כט אֶת־בִּלְעָם רֹאשׁ הַפְּעוֹר הַנִּשְׁקָף עַל־פְּנֵי הַיְשִׁימֹן׃ וַיֹּאמֶר בִּלְעָם אֶל־בָּלָק
ל בְּנֵה־לִי בָזֶה שִׁבְעָה מִזְבְּחֹת וְהָכֵן לִי בָּזֶה שִׁבְעָה פָרִים וְשִׁבְעָה אֵילִים׃ וַיַּעַשׂ
כד א בָּלָק כַּאֲשֶׁר אָמַר בִּלְעָם וַיַּעַל פָּר וָאַיִל בַּמִּזְבֵּחַ׃ וַיַּרְא בִּלְעָם כִּי טוֹב בְּעֵינֵי
יהוה לְבָרֵךְ אֶת־יִשְׂרָאֵל וְלֹא־הָלַךְ כְּפַעַם־בְּפַעַם לִקְרַאת נְחָשִׁים וַיָּשֶׁת אֶל־
ב הַמִּדְבָּר פָּנָיו׃ וַיִּשָּׂא בִלְעָם אֶת־עֵינָיו וַיַּרְא אֶת־יִשְׂרָאֵל שֹׁכֵן לִשְׁבָטָיו וַתְּהִי
ג עָלָיו רוּחַ אֱלֹהִים׃ וַיִּשָּׂא מְשָׁלוֹ וַיֹּאמַר נְאֻם בִּלְעָם בְּנוֹ בְעֹר וּנְאֻם הַגֶּבֶר שְׁתֻם
ד ה הָעָיִן׃ נְאֻם שֹׁמֵעַ אִמְרֵי־אֵל אֲשֶׁר מַחֲזֵה שַׁדַּי יֶחֱזֶה נֹפֵל וּגְלוּי עֵינָיִם׃ מַה־טֹּבוּ

ו אֹהָלֶיךָ יַעֲקֹב מִשְׁכְּנֹתֶיךָ יִשְׂרָאֵל: כִּנְחָלִים נִטָּיוּ כְּגַנֹּת עֲלֵי נָהָר כַּאֲהָלִים נָטַע
ז יהוה כַּאֲרָזִים עֲלֵי־מָיִם: יִזַּל־מַיִם מִדָּלְיָו וְזַרְעוֹ בְּמַיִם רַבִּים וְיָרֹם מֵאֲגַג מַלְכּוֹ
ח וְתִנַּשֵּׂא מַלְכֻתוֹ: אֵל מוֹצִיאוֹ מִמִּצְרַיִם כְּתוֹעֲפֹת רְאֵם לוֹ יֹאכַל גּוֹיִם צָרָיו
ט וְעַצְמֹתֵיהֶם יְגָרֵם וְחִצָּיו יִמְחָץ: כָּרַע שָׁכַב כַּאֲרִי וּכְלָבִיא מִי יְקִימֶנּוּ מְבָרְכֶיךָ
י בָרוּךְ וְאֹרְרֶיךָ אָרוּר: וַיִּחַר־אַף בָּלָק אֶל־בִּלְעָם וַיִּסְפֹּק אֶת־כַּפָּיו וַיֹּאמֶר בָּלָק
יא אֶל־בִּלְעָם לָקֹב אֹיְבַי קְרָאתִיךָ וְהִנֵּה בֵּרַכְתָּ בָרֵךְ זֶה שָׁלֹשׁ פְּעָמִים: וְעַתָּה
יב בְּרַח־לְךָ אֶל־מְקוֹמֶךָ אָמַרְתִּי כַּבֵּד אֲכַבֶּדְךָ וְהִנֵּה מְנָעֲךָ יהוה מִכָּבוֹד: וַיֹּאמֶר
בִּלְעָם אֶל־בָּלָק הֲלֹא גַּם אֶל־מַלְאָכֶיךָ אֲשֶׁר־שָׁלַחְתָּ אֵלַי דִּבַּרְתִּי לֵאמֹר:
יג אִם־יִתֶּן־לִי בָלָק מְלֹא בֵיתוֹ כֶּסֶף וְזָהָב לֹא אוּכַל לַעֲבֹר אֶת־פִּי יהוה לַעֲשׂוֹת
יד טוֹבָה אוֹ רָעָה מִלִּבִּי אֲשֶׁר־יְדַבֵּר יהוה אֹתוֹ אֲדַבֵּר: וְעַתָּה הִנְנִי הוֹלֵךְ לְעַמִּי שביעי
טו לְכָה אִיעָצְךָ אֲשֶׁר יַעֲשֶׂה הָעָם הַזֶּה לְעַמְּךָ בְּאַחֲרִית הַיָּמִים: וַיִּשָּׂא מְשָׁלוֹ
טז וַיֹּאמַר נְאֻם בִּלְעָם בְּנוֹ בְעֹר וּנְאֻם הַגֶּבֶר שְׁתֻם הָעָיִן: נְאֻם שֹׁמֵעַ אִמְרֵי־
יז אֵל וְיֹדֵעַ דַּעַת עֶלְיוֹן מַחֲזֵה שַׁדַּי יֶחֱזֶה נֹפֵל וּגְלוּי עֵינָיִם: אֶרְאֶנּוּ וְלֹא עַתָּה
אֲשׁוּרֶנּוּ וְלֹא קָרוֹב דָּרַךְ כּוֹכָב מִיַּעֲקֹב וְקָם שֵׁבֶט מִיִּשְׂרָאֵל וּמָחַץ פַּאֲתֵי מוֹאָב
יח וְקַרְקַר כָּל־בְּנֵי־שֵׁת: וְהָיָה אֱדוֹם יְרֵשָׁה וְהָיָה יְרֵשָׁה שֵׂעִיר אֹיְבָיו וְיִשְׂרָאֵל
יט כ עֹשֶׂה חָיִל: וְיֵרְדְּ מִיַּעֲקֹב וְהֶאֱבִיד שָׂרִיד מֵעִיר: וַיַּרְא אֶת־עֲמָלֵק וַיִּשָּׂא מְשָׁלוֹ
כא וַיֹּאמַר רֵאשִׁית גּוֹיִם עֲמָלֵק וְאַחֲרִיתוֹ עֲדֵי אֹבֵד: וַיַּרְא אֶת־הַקֵּינִי וַיִּשָּׂא מְשָׁלוֹ
כב וַיֹּאמַר אֵיתָן מוֹשָׁבֶךָ וְשִׂים בַּסֶּלַע קִנֶּךָ: כִּי אִם־יִהְיֶה לְבָעֵר קָיִן עַד־מָה אַשּׁוּר
כג כד תִּשְׁבֶּךָּ: וַיִּשָּׂא מְשָׁלוֹ וַיֹּאמַר אוֹי מִי יִחְיֶה מִשֻּׂמוֹ אֵל: וְצִים מִיַּד כִּתִּים וְעִנּוּ
כה אַשּׁוּר וְעִנּוּ־עֵבֶר וְגַם־הוּא עֲדֵי אֹבֵד: וַיָּקָם בִּלְעָם וַיֵּלֶךְ וַיָּשָׁב לִמְקֹמוֹ וְגַם־
בָּלָק הָלַךְ לְדַרְכּוֹ:

ה א ב וַיֵּשֶׁב יִשְׂרָאֵל בַּשִּׁטִּים וַיָּחֶל הָעָם לִזְנוֹת אֶל־בְּנוֹת מוֹאָב: וַתִּקְרֶאןָ לָעָם כא
ג לְזִבְחֵי אֱלֹהֵיהֶן וַיֹּאכַל הָעָם וַיִּשְׁתַּחֲווּ לֵאלֹהֵיהֶן: וַיִּצָּמֶד יִשְׂרָאֵל לְבַעַל
ד פְּעוֹר וַיִּחַר־אַף יהוה בְּיִשְׂרָאֵל: וַיֹּאמֶר יהוה אֶל־מֹשֶׁה קַח אֶת־כָּל־רָאשֵׁי
הָעָם וְהוֹקַע אוֹתָם לַיהוה נֶגֶד הַשָּׁמֶשׁ וְיָשֹׁב חֲרוֹן אַף־יהוה מִיִּשְׂרָאֵל:
ה וַיֹּאמֶר מֹשֶׁה אֶל־שֹׁפְטֵי יִשְׂרָאֵל הִרְגוּ אִישׁ אֲנָשָׁיו הַנִּצְמָדִים לְבַעַל פְּעוֹר:
ו וְהִנֵּה אִישׁ מִבְּנֵי יִשְׂרָאֵל בָּא וַיַּקְרֵב אֶל־אֶחָיו אֶת־הַמִּדְיָנִית לְעֵינֵי מֹשֶׁה
ז וּלְעֵינֵי כָּל־עֲדַת בְּנֵי־יִשְׂרָאֵל וְהֵמָּה בֹכִים פֶּתַח אֹהֶל מוֹעֵד: וַיַּרְא פִּינְחָס מפטיר
ח בֶּן־אֶלְעָזָר בֶּן־אַהֲרֹן הַכֹּהֵן וַיָּקָם מִתּוֹךְ הָעֵדָה וַיִּקַּח רֹמַח בְּיָדוֹ: וַיָּבֹא אַחַר

אִישׁ־יִשְׂרָאֵל אֶל־הַקֻּבָּה וַיִּדְקֹר אֶת־שְׁנֵיהֶם אֵת אִישׁ יִשְׂרָאֵל וְאֶת־הָאִשָּׁה
אֶל־קֳבָתָהּ וַתֵּעָצַר הַמַּגֵּפָה מֵעַל בְּנֵי יִשְׂרָאֵל׃ וַיִּהְיוּ הַמֵּתִים בַּמַּגֵּפָה אַרְבָּעָה ט
וְעֶשְׂרִים אָלֶף׃

פינחס כב וַיְדַבֵּר יהוה אֶל־מֹשֶׁה לֵּאמֹר׃ פִּינְחָס בֶּן־אֶלְעָזָר בֶּן־אַהֲרֹן הַכֹּהֵן הֵשִׁיב י יא
אֶת־חֲמָתִי מֵעַל בְּנֵי־יִשְׂרָאֵל בְּקַנְאוֹ אֶת־קִנְאָתִי בְּתוֹכָם וְלֹא־כִלִּיתִי אֶת־
לוי בְּנֵי־יִשְׂרָאֵל בְּקִנְאָתִי׃ לָכֵן אֱמֹר הִנְנִי נֹתֵן לוֹ אֶת־בְּרִיתִי שָׁלוֹם׃ *וְהָיְתָה לּוֹ יב יג
וּלְזַרְעוֹ אַחֲרָיו בְּרִית כְּהֻנַּת עוֹלָם תַּחַת אֲשֶׁר קִנֵּא לֵאלֹהָיו וַיְכַפֵּר עַל־בְּנֵי
יִשְׂרָאֵל׃ וְשֵׁם אִישׁ יִשְׂרָאֵל הַמֻּכֶּה אֲשֶׁר הֻכָּה אֶת־הַמִּדְיָנִית זִמְרִי בֶּן־סָלוּא יד
נְשִׂיא בֵית־אָב לַשִּׁמְעֹנִי׃ וְשֵׁם הָאִשָּׁה הַמֻּכָּה הַמִּדְיָנִית כָּזְבִּי בַת־צוּר רֹאשׁ טו
אֻמּוֹת בֵּית־אָב בְּמִדְיָן הוּא׃

ישראל *וַיְדַבֵּר יהוה אֶל־מֹשֶׁה לֵּאמֹר׃ צָרוֹר אֶת־הַמִּדְיָנִים וְהִכִּיתֶם אוֹתָם׃ טז יז
כִּי־צֹרְרִים הֵם לָכֶם בְּנִכְלֵיהֶם אֲשֶׁר־נִכְּלוּ לָכֶם עַל־דְּבַר פְּעוֹר וְעַל־דְּבַר יח
כָּזְבִּי בַת־נְשִׂיא מִדְיָן אֲחֹתָם הַמֻּכָּה בְיוֹם־הַמַּגֵּפָה עַל־דְּבַר פְּעוֹר׃ וַיְהִי א כו
אַחֲרֵי הַמַּגֵּפָה

וַיֹּאמֶר יהוה אֶל־מֹשֶׁה וְאֶל אֶלְעָזָר בֶּן־אַהֲרֹן הַכֹּהֵן לֵאמֹר׃ שְׂאוּ אֶת־ ב
רֹאשׁ ׀ כָּל־עֲדַת בְּנֵי־יִשְׂרָאֵל מִבֶּן עֶשְׂרִים שָׁנָה וָמַעְלָה לְבֵית אֲבֹתָם כָּל־
יֹצֵא צָבָא בְּיִשְׂרָאֵל׃ וַיְדַבֵּר מֹשֶׁה וְאֶלְעָזָר הַכֹּהֵן אֹתָם בְּעַרְבֹת מוֹאָב עַל־ ג
יַרְדֵּן יְרֵחוֹ לֵאמֹר׃ מִבֶּן עֶשְׂרִים שָׁנָה וָמָעְלָה כַּאֲשֶׁר צִוָּה יהוה אֶת־מֹשֶׁה ד
שני וּבְנֵי יִשְׂרָאֵל הַיֹּצְאִים מֵאֶרֶץ מִצְרָיִם׃** רְאוּבֵן בְּכוֹר יִשְׂרָאֵל בְּנֵי רְאוּבֵן ה
חֲנוֹךְ מִשְׁפַּחַת הַחֲנֹכִי לְפַלּוּא מִשְׁפַּחַת הַפַּלֻּאִי׃ לְחֶצְרֹן מִשְׁפַּחַת הַחֶצְרוֹנִי ו
לְכַרְמִי מִשְׁפַּחַת הַכַּרְמִי׃ אֵלֶּה מִשְׁפְּחֹת הָרְאוּבֵנִי וַיִּהְיוּ פְקֻדֵיהֶם שְׁלֹשָׁה ז
וְאַרְבָּעִים אֶלֶף וּשְׁבַע מֵאוֹת וּשְׁלֹשִׁים׃ וּבְנֵי פַלּוּא אֱלִיאָב׃ וּבְנֵי אֱלִיאָב נְמוּאֵל ח ט
קְרִיאֵי וְדָתָן וַאֲבִירָם הוּא־דָתָן וַאֲבִירָם קרואי הָעֵדָה אֲשֶׁר הִצּוּ עַל־מֹשֶׁה וְעַל־
אַהֲרֹן בַּעֲדַת־קֹרַח בְּהַצֹּתָם עַל־יהוה׃ וַתִּפְתַּח הָאָרֶץ אֶת־פִּיהָ וַתִּבְלַע אֹתָם י
וְאֶת־קֹרַח בְּמוֹת הָעֵדָה בַּאֲכֹל הָאֵשׁ אֵת חֲמִשִּׁים וּמָאתַיִם אִישׁ וַיִּהְיוּ לְנֵס׃
וּבְנֵי־קֹרַח לֹא־מֵתוּ׃ בְּנֵי שִׁמְעוֹן לְמִשְׁפְּחֹתָם לִנְמוּאֵל מִשְׁפַּחַת יא יב
הַנְּמוּאֵלִי לְיָמִין מִשְׁפַּחַת הַיָּמִינִי לְיָכִין מִשְׁפַּחַת הַיָּכִינִי׃ לְזֶרַח מִשְׁפַּחַת יג
הַזַּרְחִי לְשָׁאוּל מִשְׁפַּחַת הַשָּׁאוּלִי׃ אֵלֶּה מִשְׁפְּחֹת הַשִּׁמְעֹנִי שְׁנַיִם וְעֶשְׂרִים יד
אֶלֶף וּמָאתָיִם׃ בְּנֵי גָד לְמִשְׁפְּחֹתָם לִצְפוֹן מִשְׁפַּחַת הַצְּפוֹנִי לְחַגִּי טו

טו מִשְׁפַּחַת הַחַגִּי לְשׁוּנִי מִשְׁפַּחַת הַשּׁוּנִי׃ לְאָזְנִי מִשְׁפַּחַת הָאָזְנִי לְעֵרִי מִשְׁפַּחַת
יז יח הָעֵרִי׃ לַאֲרוֹד מִשְׁפַּחַת הָאֲרוֹדִי לְאַרְאֵלִי מִשְׁפַּחַת הָאַרְאֵלִי׃ אֵלֶּה מִשְׁפְּחֹת
יט בְּנֵי־גָד לִפְקֻדֵיהֶם אַרְבָּעִים אֶלֶף וַחֲמֵשׁ מֵאוֹת׃ בְּנֵי יְהוּדָה עֵר וְאוֹנָן
כ וַיָּמָת עֵר וְאוֹנָן בְּאֶרֶץ כְּנָעַן׃ וַיִּהְיוּ בְנֵי־יְהוּדָה לְמִשְׁפְּחֹתָם לְשֵׁלָה מִשְׁפַּחַת
כא הַשֵּׁלָנִי לְפֶרֶץ מִשְׁפַּחַת הַפַּרְצִי לְזֶרַח מִשְׁפַּחַת הַזַּרְחִי׃ וַיִּהְיוּ בְנֵי־פֶרֶץ לְחֶצְרֹן
כב מִשְׁפַּחַת הַחֶצְרֹנִי לְחָמוּל מִשְׁפַּחַת הֶחָמוּלִי׃ אֵלֶּה מִשְׁפְּחֹת יְהוּדָה לִפְקֻדֵיהֶם
כג שִׁשָּׁה וְשִׁבְעִים אֶלֶף וַחֲמֵשׁ מֵאוֹת׃ בְּנֵי יִשָּׂשכָר לְמִשְׁפְּחֹתָם תּוֹלָע
כד מִשְׁפַּחַת הַתּוֹלָעִי לְפֻוָה מִשְׁפַּחַת הַפּוּנִי׃ לְיָשׁוּב מִשְׁפַּחַת הַיָּשֻׁבִי לְשִׁמְרֹן
כה מִשְׁפַּחַת הַשִּׁמְרֹנִי׃ אֵלֶּה מִשְׁפְּחֹת יִשָּׂשכָר לִפְקֻדֵיהֶם אַרְבָּעָה וְשִׁשִּׁים אֶלֶף
כו וּשְׁלֹשׁ מֵאוֹת׃ בְּנֵי זְבוּלֻן לְמִשְׁפְּחֹתָם לְסֶרֶד מִשְׁפַּחַת הַסַּרְדִּי
כז לְאֵלוֹן מִשְׁפַּחַת הָאֵלֹנִי לְיַחְלְאֵל מִשְׁפַּחַת הַיַּחְלְאֵלִי׃ אֵלֶּה מִשְׁפְּחֹת הַזְּבוּלֹנִי
כח לִפְקֻדֵיהֶם שִׁשִּׁים אֶלֶף וַחֲמֵשׁ מֵאוֹת׃ בְּנֵי יוֹסֵף לְמִשְׁפְּחֹתָם מְנַשֶּׁה
כט וְאֶפְרָיִם׃ בְּנֵי מְנַשֶּׁה לְמָכִיר מִשְׁפַּחַת הַמָּכִירִי וּמָכִיר הוֹלִיד אֶת־גִּלְעָד לְגִלְעָד
ל מִשְׁפַּחַת הַגִּלְעָדִי׃ אֵלֶּה בְּנֵי גִלְעָד אִיעֶזֶר מִשְׁפַּחַת הָאִיעֶזְרִי לְחֵלֶק מִשְׁפַּחַת
לא לב הַחֶלְקִי׃ וְאַשְׂרִיאֵל מִשְׁפַּחַת הָאַשְׂרִאֵלִי וְשֶׁכֶם מִשְׁפַּחַת הַשִּׁכְמִי׃ וּשְׁמִידָע
לג מִשְׁפַּחַת הַשְּׁמִידָעִי וְחֵפֶר מִשְׁפַּחַת הַחֶפְרִי׃ וּצְלָפְחָד בֶּן־חֵפֶר לֹא־הָיוּ לוֹ
לד בָּנִים כִּי אִם־בָּנוֹת וְשֵׁם בְּנוֹת צְלָפְחָד מַחְלָה וְנֹעָה חָגְלָה מִלְכָּה וְתִרְצָה׃ אֵלֶּה
לה מִשְׁפְּחֹת מְנַשֶּׁה וּפְקֻדֵיהֶם שְׁנַיִם וַחֲמִשִּׁים אֶלֶף וּשְׁבַע מֵאוֹת׃ אֵלֶּה
בְנֵי־אֶפְרַיִם לְמִשְׁפְּחֹתָם לְשׁוּתֶלַח מִשְׁפַּחַת הַשֻּׁתַלְחִי לְבֶכֶר מִשְׁפַּחַת הַבַּכְרִי
לו לז לְתַחַן מִשְׁפַּחַת הַתַּחֲנִי׃ וְאֵלֶּה בְּנֵי שׁוּתָלַח לְעֵרָן מִשְׁפַּחַת הָעֵרָנִי׃ אֵלֶּה
מִשְׁפְּחֹת בְּנֵי־אֶפְרַיִם לִפְקֻדֵיהֶם שְׁנַיִם וּשְׁלֹשִׁים אֶלֶף וַחֲמֵשׁ מֵאוֹת אֵלֶּה בְנֵי־
לח יוֹסֵף לְמִשְׁפְּחֹתָם׃ בְּנֵי בִנְיָמִן לְמִשְׁפְּחֹתָם לְבֶלַע מִשְׁפַּחַת הַבַּלְעִי
לט לְאַשְׁבֵּל מִשְׁפַּחַת הָאַשְׁבֵּלִי לַאֲחִירָם מִשְׁפַּחַת הָאֲחִירָמִי׃ לִשְׁפוּפָם מִשְׁפַּחַת
מ הַשּׁוּפָמִי לְחוּפָם מִשְׁפַּחַת הַחוּפָמִי׃ וַיִּהְיוּ בְנֵי־בֶלַע אַרְדְּ וְנַעֲמָן מִשְׁפַּחַת
מא הָאַרְדִּי לְנַעֲמָן מִשְׁפַּחַת הַנַּעֲמִי׃ אֵלֶּה בְנֵי־בִנְיָמִן לְמִשְׁפְּחֹתָם וּפְקֻדֵיהֶם
מב חֲמִשָּׁה וְאַרְבָּעִים אֶלֶף וְשֵׁשׁ מֵאוֹת׃ אֵלֶּה בְנֵי־דָן לְמִשְׁפְּחֹתָם
מג לְשׁוּחָם מִשְׁפַּחַת הַשּׁוּחָמִי אֵלֶּה מִשְׁפְּחֹת דָּן לְמִשְׁפְּחֹתָם׃ כָּל־מִשְׁפְּחֹת
מד הַשּׁוּחָמִי לִפְקֻדֵיהֶם אַרְבָּעָה וְשִׁשִּׁים אֶלֶף וְאַרְבַּע מֵאוֹת׃ בְּנֵי
אָשֵׁר לְמִשְׁפְּחֹתָם לְיִמְנָה מִשְׁפַּחַת הַיִּמְנָה לְיִשְׁוִי מִשְׁפַּחַת הַיִּשְׁוִי לִבְרִיעָה

מִשְׁפַּחַת הַבְּרִיעִי: לִבְנֵי בְרִיעָה לְחֶבֶר מִשְׁפַּחַת הַחֶבְרִי לְמַלְכִּיאֵל מִשְׁפַּחַת מה
הַמַּלְכִּיאֵלִי: וְשֵׁם בַּת־אָשֵׁר שָׂרַח: אֵלֶּה מִשְׁפְּחֹת בְּנֵי־אָשֵׁר לִפְקֻדֵיהֶם שְׁלֹשָׁה מו מז
וַחֲמִשִּׁים אֶלֶף וְאַרְבַּע מֵאוֹת: בְּנֵי נַפְתָּלִי לְמִשְׁפְּחֹתָם לְיַחְצְאֵל מח
מִשְׁפַּחַת הַיַּחְצְאֵלִי לְגוּנִי מִשְׁפַּחַת הַגּוּנִי: לְיֵצֶר מִשְׁפַּחַת הַיִּצְרִי לְשִׁלֵּם מט
מִשְׁפַּחַת הַשִּׁלֵּמִי: אֵלֶּה מִשְׁפְּחֹת נַפְתָּלִי לְמִשְׁפְּחֹתָם וּפְקֻדֵיהֶם חֲמִשָּׁה נ
וְאַרְבָּעִים אֶלֶף וְאַרְבַּע מֵאוֹת: אֵלֶּה פְּקוּדֵי בְּנֵי יִשְׂרָאֵל שֵׁשׁ־מֵאוֹת אֶלֶף נא
וָאָלֶף שְׁבַע מֵאוֹת וּשְׁלֹשִׁים:
שלישי כג *וַיְדַבֵּר יְהוָה אֶל־מֹשֶׁה לֵּאמֹר: לָאֵלֶּה תֵּחָלֵק הָאָרֶץ בְּנַחֲלָה בְּמִסְפַּר שֵׁמוֹת: נב נג
לָרַב תַּרְבֶּה נַחֲלָתוֹ וְלַמְעַט תַּמְעִיט נַחֲלָתוֹ אִישׁ לְפִי פְקֻדָיו יֻתַּן נַחֲלָתוֹ: אַךְ־ נד נה
בְּגוֹרָל יֵחָלֵק אֶת־הָאָרֶץ לִשְׁמוֹת מַטּוֹת־אֲבֹתָם יִנְחָלוּ: עַל־פִּי הַגּוֹרָל תֵּחָלֵק נו
נַחֲלָתוֹ בֵּין רַב לִמְעָט: וְאֵלֶּה פְקוּדֵי הַלֵּוִי לְמִשְׁפְּחֹתָם לְגֵרְשׁוֹן נז
מִשְׁפַּחַת הַגֵּרְשֻׁנִּי לִקְהָת מִשְׁפַּחַת הַקְּהָתִי לִמְרָרִי מִשְׁפַּחַת הַמְּרָרִי: אֵלֶּה ׀ נח
מִשְׁפְּחֹת לֵוִי מִשְׁפַּחַת הַלִּבְנִי מִשְׁפַּחַת הַחֶבְרֹנִי מִשְׁפַּחַת הַמַּחְלִי מִשְׁפַּחַת
הַמּוּשִׁי מִשְׁפַּחַת הַקָּרְחִי וּקְהָת הוֹלִד אֶת־עַמְרָם: וְשֵׁם ׀ אֵשֶׁת עַמְרָם יוֹכֶבֶד נט
בַּת־לֵוִי אֲשֶׁר יָלְדָה אֹתָהּ לְלֵוִי בְּמִצְרָיִם וַתֵּלֶד לְעַמְרָם אֶת־אַהֲרֹן וְאֶת־מֹשֶׁה
וְאֵת מִרְיָם אֲחֹתָם: וַיִּוָּלֵד לְאַהֲרֹן אֶת־נָדָב וְאֶת־אֲבִיהוּא אֶת־אֶלְעָזָר וְאֶת־ ס
אִיתָמָר: וַיָּמָת נָדָב וַאֲבִיהוּא בְּהַקְרִיבָם אֵשׁ־זָרָה לִפְנֵי יְהוָה: וַיִּהְיוּ פְקֻדֵיהֶם סא סב
שְׁלֹשָׁה וְעֶשְׂרִים אֶלֶף כָּל־זָכָר מִבֶּן־חֹדֶשׁ וָמָעְלָה כִּי ׀ לֹא הָתְפָּקְדוּ בְּתוֹךְ בְּנֵי
יִשְׂרָאֵל כִּי לֹא־נִתַּן לָהֶם נַחֲלָה בְּתוֹךְ בְּנֵי יִשְׂרָאֵל: אֵלֶּה פְּקוּדֵי מֹשֶׁה וְאֶלְעָזָר סג
הַכֹּהֵן אֲשֶׁר פָּקְדוּ אֶת־בְּנֵי יִשְׂרָאֵל בְּעַרְבֹת מוֹאָב עַל יַרְדֵּן יְרֵחוֹ: וּבְאֵלֶּה לֹא־ סד
הָיָה אִישׁ מִפְּקוּדֵי מֹשֶׁה וְאַהֲרֹן הַכֹּהֵן אֲשֶׁר פָּקְדוּ אֶת־בְּנֵי יִשְׂרָאֵל בְּמִדְבַּר
סִינָי: כִּי־אָמַר יְהוָה לָהֶם מוֹת יָמֻתוּ בַּמִּדְבָּר וְלֹא־נוֹתַר מֵהֶם אִישׁ כִּי אִם־ סה
כָּלֵב בֶּן־יְפֻנֶּה וִיהוֹשֻׁעַ בִּן־נוּן: וַתִּקְרַבְנָה בְּנוֹת צְלָפְחָד בֶּן־חֵפֶר א כ
בֶּן־גִּלְעָד בֶּן־מָכִיר בֶּן־מְנַשֶּׁה לְמִשְׁפְּחֹת מְנַשֶּׁה בֶן־יוֹסֵף וְאֵלֶּה שְׁמוֹת בְּנֹתָיו
מַחְלָה נֹעָה וְחָגְלָה וּמִלְכָּה וְתִרְצָה: וַתַּעֲמֹדְנָה לִפְנֵי מֹשֶׁה וְלִפְנֵי אֶלְעָזָר הַכֹּהֵן ב
וְלִפְנֵי הַנְּשִׂיאִם וְכָל־הָעֵדָה פֶּתַח אֹהֶל־מוֹעֵד לֵאמֹר: אָבִינוּ מֵת בַּמִּדְבָּר ג
וְהוּא לֹא־הָיָה בְּתוֹךְ הָעֵדָה הַנּוֹעָדִים עַל־יְהוָה בַּעֲדַת־קֹרַח כִּי־בְחֶטְאוֹ מֵת
וּבָנִים לֹא־הָיוּ לוֹ: לָמָּה יִגָּרַע שֵׁם־אָבִינוּ מִתּוֹךְ מִשְׁפַּחְתּוֹ כִּי אֵין לוֹ בֵּן תְּנָה־לָּנוּ ד
אֲחֻזָּה בְּתוֹךְ אֲחֵי אָבִינוּ: וַיַּקְרֵב מֹשֶׁה אֶת־מִשְׁפָּטָן לִפְנֵי יְהוָה: ה

ו ז ★ויאמר יהוה אל־משה לאמר: כן בנות צלפחד דברת נתן תתן להם אחזת רביעי
ח נחלה בתוך אחי אביהם והעברת את־נחלת אביהן להן: ואל־בני ישראל
ט תדבר לאמר איש כי־ימות ובן אין לו והעברתם את־נחלתו לבתו: ואם־
י אין לו בת ונתתם את־נחלתו לאחיו: ואם־אין לו אחים ונתתם את־נחלתו
יא לאחי אביו: ואם־אין אחים לאביו ונתתם את־נחלתו לשארו הקרב אליו
ממשפחתו וירש אתה והיתה לבני ישראל לחקת משפט כאשר צוה יהוה
את־משה:
יב ויאמר יהוה אל־משה עלה אל־הר העברים הזה וראה את־הארץ אשר
יג נתתי לבני ישראל: וראיתה אתה ונאספת אל־עמיך גם־אתה כאשר נאסף
יד אהרן אחיך: כאשר מריתם פי במדבר־צן במריבת העדה להקדישני במים
טו לעיניהם הם מי־מריבת קדש מדבר־צן: וידבר משה אל־יהוה כד
טז יז לאמר: יפקד יהוה אלהי הרוחת לכל־בשר איש על־העדה: אשר־יצא
לפניהם ואשר יבא לפניהם ואשר יוציאם ואשר יביאם ולא תהיה עדת
יח יהוה כצאן אשר אין־להם רעה: ויאמר יהוה אל־משה קח־לך את־יהושע
יט בן־נון איש אשר־רוח בו וסמכת את־ידך עליו: והעמדת אתו לפני אלעזר
כ הכהן ולפני כל־העדה וצויתה אתו לעיניהם: ונתתה מהודך עליו למען
כא ישמעו כל־עדת בני ישראל: ולפני אלעזר הכהן יעמד ושאל לו במשפט
האורים לפני יהוה על־פיו יצאו ועל־פיו יבאו הוא וכל־בני־ישראל אתו
כב וכל־העדה: ויעש משה כאשר צוה יהוה אתו ויקח את־יהושע ויעמדהו
כג לפני אלעזר הכהן ולפני כל־העדה: ויסמך את־ידיו עליו ויצוהו כאשר
דבר יהוה ביד־משה:
ח א ב ★וידבר יהוה אל־משה לאמר: צו את־בני ישראל ואמרת אלהם את־קרבני חמישי (קריאה לראש חודש
ג לחמי לאשי ריח ניחחי תשמרו להקריב לי במועדו: ואמרת להם זה האשה כח:א–טו)
אשר תקריבו ליהוה כבשים בני־שנה תמימם שנים ליום עלה תמיד:
ד את־הכבש אחד תעשה בבקר ואת הכבש השני תעשה בין הערבים:
ה ו ועשירית האיפה סלת למנחה בלולה בשמן כתית רביעת ההין: עלת
ז תמיד העשיה בהר סיני לריח ניחח אשה ליהוה: ונסכו רביעת ההין לכבש
ח האחד בקדש הסך נסך שכר ליהוה: ואת הכבש השני תעשה בין הערבים
כמנחת הבקר וכנסכו תעשה אשה ריח ניחח ליהוה:

(מפטיר לשבת ראש חודש כח:ח–טו)

וּבְיוֹם הַשַּׁבָּת שְׁנֵי־כְבָשִׂים בְּנֵי־שָׁנָה תְּמִימִם וּשְׁנֵי עֶשְׂרֹנִים סֹלֶת מִנְחָה בְּלוּלָה ט
בַשֶּׁמֶן וְנִסְכּוֹ׃ עֹלַת שַׁבַּת בְּשַׁבַּתּוֹ עַל־עֹלַת הַתָּמִיד וְנִסְכָּהּ׃ י
וּבְרָאשֵׁי חָדְשֵׁיכֶם תַּקְרִיבוּ עֹלָה לַיהוָה פָּרִים בְּנֵי־בָקָר שְׁנַיִם וְאַיִל אֶחָד יא
כְּבָשִׂים בְּנֵי־שָׁנָה שִׁבְעָה תְּמִימִם׃ וּשְׁלֹשָׁה עֶשְׂרֹנִים סֹלֶת מִנְחָה בְּלוּלָה יב
בַשֶּׁמֶן לַפָּר הָאֶחָד וּשְׁנֵי עֶשְׂרֹנִים סֹלֶת מִנְחָה בְּלוּלָה בַשֶּׁמֶן לָאַיִל הָאֶחָד׃
וְעִשָּׂרֹן עִשָּׂרוֹן סֹלֶת מִנְחָה בְּלוּלָה בַשֶּׁמֶן לַכֶּבֶשׂ הָאֶחָד עֹלָה רֵיחַ נִיחֹחַ יג
אִשֶּׁה לַיהוָה׃ וְנִסְכֵּיהֶם חֲצִי הַהִין יִהְיֶה לַפָּר וּשְׁלִישִׁת הַהִין לָאַיִל וּרְבִיעִת יד
הַהִין לַכֶּבֶשׂ יָיִן זֹאת עֹלַת חֹדֶשׁ בְּחָדְשׁוֹ לְחָדְשֵׁי הַשָּׁנָה׃ וּשְׂעִיר עִזִּים אֶחָד טו
ששי לְחַטָּאת לַיהוָה עַל־עֹלַת הַתָּמִיד יֵעָשֶׂה וְנִסְכּוֹ׃ וּבַחֹדֶשׁ הָרִאשׁוֹן טז
בְּאַרְבָּעָה עָשָׂר יוֹם לַחֹדֶשׁ פֶּסַח לַיהוָה׃ וּבַחֲמִשָּׁה עָשָׂר יוֹם לַחֹדֶשׁ הַזֶּה חָג יז
שִׁבְעַת יָמִים מַצּוֹת יֵאָכֵל׃ בַּיּוֹם הָרִאשׁוֹן מִקְרָא־קֹדֶשׁ כָּל־מְלֶאכֶת עֲבֹדָה יח
לֹא תַעֲשׂוּ׃ וְהִקְרַבְתֶּם אִשֶּׁה עֹלָה לַיהוָה פָּרִים בְּנֵי־בָקָר שְׁנַיִם וְאַיִל אֶחָד יט
וְשִׁבְעָה כְבָשִׂים בְּנֵי שָׁנָה תְּמִימִם יִהְיוּ לָכֶם׃ וּמִנְחָתָם סֹלֶת בְּלוּלָה בַשָּׁמֶן כ
שְׁלֹשָׁה עֶשְׂרֹנִים לַפָּר וּשְׁנֵי עֶשְׂרֹנִים לָאַיִל תַּעֲשׂוּ׃ עִשָּׂרוֹן עִשָּׂרוֹן תַּעֲשֶׂה לַכֶּבֶשׂ כא
הָאֶחָד לְשִׁבְעַת הַכְּבָשִׂים׃ וּשְׂעִיר חַטָּאת אֶחָד לְכַפֵּר עֲלֵיכֶם׃ מִלְּבַד עֹלַת כב כג
הַבֹּקֶר אֲשֶׁר לְעֹלַת הַתָּמִיד תַּעֲשׂוּ אֶת־אֵלֶּה׃ כָּאֵלֶּה תַּעֲשׂוּ לַיּוֹם שִׁבְעַת יָמִים כד
לֶחֶם אִשֵּׁה רֵיחַ־נִיחֹחַ לַיהוָה עַל־עוֹלַת הַתָּמִיד יֵעָשֶׂה וְנִסְכּוֹ׃ וּבַיּוֹם הַשְּׁבִיעִי כה
כה מִקְרָא־קֹדֶשׁ יִהְיֶה לָכֶם כָּל־מְלֶאכֶת עֲבֹדָה לֹא תַעֲשׂוּ׃ וּבְיוֹם כו
הַבִּכּוּרִים בְּהַקְרִיבְכֶם מִנְחָה חֲדָשָׁה לַיהוָה בְּשָׁבֻעֹתֵיכֶם מִקְרָא־קֹדֶשׁ יִהְיֶה
לָכֶם כָּל־מְלֶאכֶת עֲבֹדָה לֹא תַעֲשׂוּ׃ וְהִקְרַבְתֶּם עוֹלָה לְרֵיחַ נִיחֹחַ לַיהוָה כז
פָּרִים בְּנֵי־בָקָר שְׁנַיִם אַיִל אֶחָד שִׁבְעָה כְבָשִׂים בְּנֵי שָׁנָה׃ וּמִנְחָתָם סֹלֶת כח
בְּלוּלָה בַשָּׁמֶן שְׁלֹשָׁה עֶשְׂרֹנִים לַפָּר הָאֶחָד שְׁנֵי עֶשְׂרֹנִים לָאַיִל הָאֶחָד׃ עִשָּׂרוֹן כט
עִשָּׂרוֹן לַכֶּבֶשׂ הָאֶחָד לְשִׁבְעַת הַכְּבָשִׂים׃ שְׂעִיר עִזִּים אֶחָד לְכַפֵּר עֲלֵיכֶם׃ ל
מִלְּבַד עֹלַת הַתָּמִיד וּמִנְחָתוֹ תַּעֲשׂוּ תְּמִימִם יִהְיוּ־לָכֶם וְנִסְכֵּיהֶם׃ לא
וּבַחֹדֶשׁ הַשְּׁבִיעִי בְּאֶחָד לַחֹדֶשׁ מִקְרָא־קֹדֶשׁ יִהְיֶה לָכֶם כָּל־מְלֶאכֶת עֲבֹדָה א כט
לֹא תַעֲשׂוּ יוֹם תְּרוּעָה יִהְיֶה לָכֶם׃ וַעֲשִׂיתֶם עֹלָה לְרֵיחַ נִיחֹחַ לַיהוָה פַּר ב
בֶּן־בָּקָר אֶחָד אַיִל אֶחָד כְּבָשִׂים בְּנֵי־שָׁנָה שִׁבְעָה תְּמִימִם׃ וּמִנְחָתָם סֹלֶת ג
בְּלוּלָה בַשָּׁמֶן שְׁלֹשָׁה עֶשְׂרֹנִים לַפָּר שְׁנֵי עֶשְׂרֹנִים לָאָיִל׃ וְעִשָּׂרוֹן אֶחָד לַכֶּבֶשׂ ד
הָאֶחָד לְשִׁבְעַת הַכְּבָשִׂים׃ וּשְׂעִיר־עִזִּים אֶחָד חַטָּאת לְכַפֵּר עֲלֵיכֶם׃ מִלְּבַד ה ו

עֹלַת הַחֹדֶשׁ וּמִנְחָתָהּ וְעֹלַת הַתָּמִיד וּמִנְחָתָהּ וְנִסְכֵּיהֶם כְּמִשְׁפָּטָם לְרֵיחַ
ז נִיחֹחַ אִשֶּׁה לַיהוָה׃ וּבֶעָשׂוֹר לַחֹדֶשׁ הַשְּׁבִיעִי הַזֶּה מִקְרָא־קֹדֶשׁ
ח יִהְיֶה לָכֶם וְעִנִּיתֶם אֶת־נַפְשֹׁתֵיכֶם כָּל־מְלָאכָה לֹא תַעֲשׂוּ׃ וְהִקְרַבְתֶּם עֹלָה
לַיהוָה רֵיחַ נִיחֹחַ פַּר בֶּן־בָּקָר אֶחָד אַיִל אֶחָד כְּבָשִׂים בְּנֵי־שָׁנָה שִׁבְעָה
ט תְּמִימִם יִהְיוּ לָכֶם׃ וּמִנְחָתָם סֹלֶת בְּלוּלָה בַשָּׁמֶן שְׁלֹשָׁה עֶשְׂרֹנִים לַפָּר שְׁנֵי
י עֶשְׂרֹנִים לָאַיִל הָאֶחָד׃ עִשָּׂרוֹן עִשָּׂרוֹן לַכֶּבֶשׂ הָאֶחָד לְשִׁבְעַת הַכְּבָשִׂים׃
יא שְׂעִיר־עִזִּים אֶחָד חַטָּאת מִלְּבַד חַטַּאת הַכִּפֻּרִים וְעֹלַת הַתָּמִיד וּמִנְחָתָהּ
יב וְנִסְכֵּיהֶם׃ וּבַחֲמִשָּׁה עָשָׂר יוֹם לַחֹדֶשׁ הַשְּׁבִיעִי מִקְרָא־קֹדֶשׁ יִהְיֶה שביעי
יג לָכֶם כָּל־מְלֶאכֶת עֲבֹדָה לֹא תַעֲשׂוּ וְחַגֹּתֶם חַג לַיהוָה שִׁבְעַת יָמִים׃ וְהִקְרַבְתֶּם
עֹלָה אִשֵּׁה רֵיחַ נִיחֹחַ לַיהוָה פָּרִים בְּנֵי־בָקָר שְׁלֹשָׁה עָשָׂר אֵילִם שְׁנָיִם כְּבָשִׂים
יד בְּנֵי־שָׁנָה אַרְבָּעָה עָשָׂר תְּמִימִם יִהְיוּ׃ וּמִנְחָתָם סֹלֶת בְּלוּלָה בַשָּׁמֶן שְׁלֹשָׁה
עֶשְׂרֹנִים לַפָּר הָאֶחָד לִשְׁלֹשָׁה עָשָׂר פָּרִים שְׁנֵי עֶשְׂרֹנִים לָאַיִל הָאֶחָד לִשְׁנֵי
טו טז הָאֵילִם׃ וְעִשָּׂרוֹן עִשָּׂרוֹן לַכֶּבֶשׂ הָאֶחָד לְאַרְבָּעָה עָשָׂר כְּבָשִׂים׃ וּשְׂעִיר־עִזִּים
יז אֶחָד חַטָּאת מִלְּבַד עֹלַת הַתָּמִיד מִנְחָתָהּ וְנִסְכָּהּ׃ וּבַיּוֹם הַשֵּׁנִי פָּרִים
בְּנֵי־בָקָר שְׁנֵים עָשָׂר אֵילִם שְׁנָיִם כְּבָשִׂים בְּנֵי־שָׁנָה אַרְבָּעָה עָשָׂר תְּמִימִם׃
יח יט וּמִנְחָתָם וְנִסְכֵּיהֶם לַפָּרִים לָאֵילִם וְלַכְּבָשִׂים בְּמִסְפָּרָם כַּמִּשְׁפָּט׃ וּשְׂעִיר־
כ עִזִּים אֶחָד חַטָּאת מִלְּבַד עֹלַת הַתָּמִיד וּמִנְחָתָהּ וְנִסְכֵּיהֶם׃ וּבַיּוֹם
הַשְּׁלִישִׁי פָּרִים עַשְׁתֵּי־עָשָׂר אֵילִם שְׁנָיִם כְּבָשִׂים בְּנֵי־שָׁנָה אַרְבָּעָה עָשָׂר
כא תְּמִימִם׃ וּמִנְחָתָם וְנִסְכֵּיהֶם לַפָּרִים לָאֵילִם וְלַכְּבָשִׂים בְּמִסְפָּרָם כַּמִּשְׁפָּט׃
כב כג וּשְׂעִיר חַטָּאת אֶחָד מִלְּבַד עֹלַת הַתָּמִיד וּמִנְחָתָהּ וְנִסְכָּהּ׃ וּבַיּוֹם
הָרְבִיעִי פָּרִים עֲשָׂרָה אֵילִם שְׁנָיִם כְּבָשִׂים בְּנֵי־שָׁנָה אַרְבָּעָה עָשָׂר תְּמִימִם׃
כד כה מִנְחָתָם וְנִסְכֵּיהֶם לַפָּרִים לָאֵילִם וְלַכְּבָשִׂים בְּמִסְפָּרָם כַּמִּשְׁפָּט׃ וּשְׂעִיר־עִזִּים
כו אֶחָד חַטָּאת מִלְּבַד עֹלַת הַתָּמִיד מִנְחָתָהּ וְנִסְכָּהּ׃ וּבַיּוֹם הַחֲמִישִׁי
כז פָּרִים תִּשְׁעָה אֵילִם שְׁנָיִם כְּבָשִׂים בְּנֵי־שָׁנָה אַרְבָּעָה עָשָׂר תְּמִימִם׃ וּמִנְחָתָם
כח וְנִסְכֵּיהֶם לַפָּרִים לָאֵילִם וְלַכְּבָשִׂים בְּמִסְפָּרָם כַּמִּשְׁפָּט׃ וּשְׂעִיר חַטָּאת אֶחָד
כט מִלְּבַד עֹלַת הַתָּמִיד וּמִנְחָתָהּ וְנִסְכָּהּ׃ וּבַיּוֹם הַשִּׁשִּׁי פָּרִים שְׁמֹנָה
ל אֵילִם שְׁנָיִם כְּבָשִׂים בְּנֵי־שָׁנָה אַרְבָּעָה עָשָׂר תְּמִימִם׃ וּמִנְחָתָם וְנִסְכֵּיהֶם
לא לַפָּרִים לָאֵילִם וְלַכְּבָשִׂים בְּמִסְפָּרָם כַּמִּשְׁפָּט׃ וּשְׂעִיר חַטָּאת אֶחָד מִלְּבַד
לב עֹלַת הַתָּמִיד מִנְחָתָהּ וּנְסָכֶיהָ׃ וּבַיּוֹם הַשְּׁבִיעִי פָּרִים שִׁבְעָה אֵילִם

שְׁנַ֥יִם כְּבָשִׂ֛ים בְּנֵי־שָׁנָ֥ה אַרְבָּעָ֥ה עָשָׂ֖ר תְּמִימִֽם׃ וּמִנְחָתָ֣ם וְנִסְכֵּהֶ֡ם לַפָּרִ֞ים לג
לָאֵילִ֧ם וְלַכְּבָשִׂ֛ים בְּמִסְפָּרָ֖ם כְּמִשְׁפָּטָֽם׃ וּשְׂעִ֥יר חַטָּ֖את אֶחָ֑ד מִלְּבַד֙ עֹלַ֣ת לד
מפטיר הַתָּמִ֔יד מִנְחָתָ֖הּ וְנִסְכָּֽהּ׃ בַּיּוֹם֙ הַשְּׁמִינִ֔י עֲצֶ֖רֶת תִּהְיֶ֣ה לָכֶ֑ם כָּל־ לה
מְלֶ֥אכֶת עֲבֹדָ֖ה לֹ֥א תַעֲשֽׂוּ׃ וְהִקְרַבְתֶּ֨ם עֹלָ֜ה אִשֵּׁ֨ה רֵ֤יחַ נִיחֹ֙חַ֙ לַֽיהוָ֔ה פַּ֥ר אֶחָ֖ד לו
אַ֣יִל אֶחָ֑ד כְּבָשִׂ֧ים בְּנֵי־שָׁנָ֛ה שִׁבְעָ֖ה תְּמִימִֽם׃ מִנְחָתָ֣ם וְנִסְכֵּיהֶ֡ם לַפָּ֠ר לָאַ֧יִל לז
וְלַכְּבָשִׂ֛ים בְּמִסְפָּרָ֖ם כַּמִּשְׁפָּֽט׃ וּשְׂעִ֥יר חַטָּ֖את אֶחָ֑ד מִלְּבַד֙ עֹלַ֣ת הַתָּמִ֔יד לח
וּמִנְחָתָ֖הּ וְנִסְכָּֽהּ׃ אֵ֛לֶּה תַּעֲשׂ֥וּ לַיהוָ֖ה בְּמוֹעֲדֵיכֶ֑ם לְבַ֨ד מִנִּדְרֵיכֶ֜ם וְנִדְבֹתֵיכֶ֗ם לט
לְעֹלֹתֵיכֶם֙ וּלְמִנְחֹ֣תֵיכֶ֔ם וּלְנִסְכֵּיכֶ֖ם וּלְשַׁלְמֵיכֶֽם׃ וַיֹּ֥אמֶר מֹשֶׁ֖ה אֶל־בְּנֵ֣י יִשְׂרָאֵ֑ל ל א
כְּכֹ֛ל אֲשֶׁר־צִוָּ֥ה יְהוָ֖ה אֶת־מֹשֶֽׁה׃

מטות כו וַיְדַבֵּ֤ר מֹשֶׁה֙ אֶל־רָאשֵׁ֣י הַמַּטּ֔וֹת לִבְנֵ֥י יִשְׂרָאֵ֖ל לֵאמֹ֑ר זֶ֣ה הַדָּבָ֔ר אֲשֶׁ֖ר צִוָּ֥ה ב
יְהוָֽה׃ אִישׁ֩ כִּֽי־יִדֹּ֨ר נֶ֜דֶר לַֽיהוָ֗ה אֽוֹ־הִשָּׁ֤בַע שְׁבֻעָה֙ לֶאְסֹ֤ר אִסָּר֙ עַל־נַפְשׁ֔וֹ לֹ֥א ג
יַחֵ֖ל דְּבָר֑וֹ כְּכָל־הַיֹּצֵ֥א מִפִּ֖יו יַעֲשֶֽׂה׃ וְאִשָּׁ֕ה כִּֽי־תִדֹּ֥ר נֶ֖דֶר לַֽיהוָ֑ה וְאָסְרָ֥ה אִסָּ֛ר ד
בְּבֵ֥ית אָבִ֖יהָ בִּנְעֻרֶֽיהָ׃ וְשָׁמַ֨ע אָבִ֜יהָ אֶת־נִדְרָ֗הּ וֶֽאֱסָרָהּ֙ אֲשֶׁ֣ר אָסְרָ֣ה עַל־ ה
נַפְשָׁ֔הּ וְהֶחֱרִ֥ישׁ לָ֖הּ אָבִ֑יהָ וְקָ֙מוּ֙ כָּל־נְדָרֶ֔יהָ וְכָל־אִסָּ֛ר אֲשֶׁר־אָסְרָ֥ה עַל־נַפְשָׁ֖הּ
יָקֽוּם׃ וְאִם־הֵנִ֨יא אָבִ֣יהָ אֹתָהּ֮ בְּי֣וֹם שָׁמְעוֹ֒ כָּל־נְדָרֶ֙יהָ֙ וֶֽאֱסָרֶ֔יהָ אֲשֶׁר־אָסְרָ֥ה ו
עַל־נַפְשָׁ֖הּ לֹ֣א יָק֑וּם וַֽיהוָה֙ יִסְלַח־לָ֔הּ כִּֽי־הֵנִ֥יא אָבִ֖יהָ אֹתָֽהּ׃ וְאִם־הָי֤וֹ תִֽהְיֶה֙ ז
לְאִ֔ישׁ וּנְדָרֶ֖יהָ עָלֶ֑יהָ א֚וֹ מִבְטָ֣א שְׂפָתֶ֔יהָ אֲשֶׁ֥ר אָסְרָ֖ה עַל־נַפְשָֽׁהּ׃ וְשָׁמַ֥ע ח
אִישָׁ֛הּ בְּי֥וֹם שָׁמְע֖וֹ וְהֶחֱרִ֣ישׁ לָ֑הּ וְקָ֣מוּ נְדָרֶ֗יהָ וֶֽאֱסָרֶ֛הָ אֲשֶׁר־אָסְרָ֥ה עַל־נַפְשָׁ֖הּ
יָקֻֽמוּ׃ וְ֠אִם בְּי֨וֹם שְׁמֹ֣עַ אִישָׁהּ֮ יָנִ֣יא אוֹתָהּ֒ וְהֵפֵ֗ר אֶת־נִדְרָהּ֙ אֲשֶׁ֣ר עָלֶ֔יהָ וְאֵת֙ ט
לוי מִבְטָ֣א שְׂפָתֶ֔יהָ אֲשֶׁ֥ר אָסְרָ֖ה עַל־נַפְשָׁ֑הּ וַֽיהוָ֖ה יִֽסְלַֽח־לָֽהּ׃ *וְנֵ֥דֶר אַלְמָנָ֖ה י
וּגְרוּשָׁ֑ה כֹּ֛ל אֲשֶׁר־אָסְרָ֥ה עַל־נַפְשָׁ֖הּ יָק֥וּם עָלֶֽיהָ׃ וְאִם־בֵּ֥ית אִישָׁ֖הּ נָדָ֑רָה יא
אוֹ־אָסְרָ֥ה אִסָּ֛ר עַל־נַפְשָׁ֖הּ בִּשְׁבֻעָֽה׃ וְשָׁמַ֤ע אִישָׁהּ֙ וְהֶחֱרִ֣שׁ לָ֔הּ לֹ֥א הֵנִ֖יא יב
אֹתָ֑הּ וְקָ֙מוּ֙ כָּל־נְדָרֶ֔יהָ וְכָל־אִסָּ֛ר אֲשֶׁר־אָסְרָ֥ה עַל־נַפְשָׁ֖הּ יָקֽוּם׃ וְאִם־הָפֵר֩ יג
יָפֵ֨ר אֹתָ֥ם ׀ אִישָׁהּ֮ בְּי֣וֹם שָׁמְעוֹ֒ כָּל־מוֹצָ֨א שְׂפָתֶ֧יהָ לִנְדָרֶ֛יהָ וּלְאִסַּ֥ר נַפְשָׁ֖הּ לֹ֣א
ישראל יָק֑וּם אִישָׁ֣הּ הֲפֵרָ֔ם וַֽיהוָ֖ה יִֽסְלַֽח־לָֽהּ׃ *כָּל־נֵ֛דֶר וְכָל־שְׁבֻ֥עַת אִסָּ֖ר לְעַנֹּ֣ת נָ֑פֶשׁ יד
אִישָׁ֥הּ יְקִימֶ֖נּוּ וְאִישָׁ֥הּ יְפֵרֶֽנּוּ׃ וְאִם־הַחֲרֵשׁ֩ יַחֲרִ֨ישׁ לָ֥הּ אִישָׁהּ֮ מִיּ֣וֹם אֶל־יוֹם֒ טו
וְהֵקִים֙ אֶת־כָּל־נְדָרֶ֔יהָ א֥וֹ אֶת־כָּל־אֱסָרֶ֖יהָ אֲשֶׁ֣ר עָלֶ֑יהָ הֵקִ֣ים אֹתָ֔ם כִּֽי־הֶחֱרִ֥שׁ
לָ֖הּ בְּי֥וֹם שָׁמְעֽוֹ׃ וְאִם־הָפֵ֥ר יָפֵ֛ר אֹתָ֖ם אַחֲרֵ֣י שָׁמְע֑וֹ וְנָשָׂ֖א אֶת־עֲוֺנָֽהּ׃ אֵ֣לֶּה טז יז

הַחֻקִּים אֲשֶׁר צִוָּה יהוה אֶת־מֹשֶׁה בֵּין אִישׁ לְאִשְׁתּוֹ בֵּין־אָב לְבִתּוֹ בִּנְעֻרֶיהָ
בֵּית אָבִיהָ:**
לא א ב *וַיְדַבֵּר יהוה אֶל־מֹשֶׁה לֵּאמֹר: נְקֹם נִקְמַת בְּנֵי יִשְׂרָאֵל מֵאֵת הַמִּדְיָנִים אַחַר כז שני
ג תֵּאָסֵף אֶל־עַמֶּיךָ: וַיְדַבֵּר מֹשֶׁה אֶל־הָעָם לֵאמֹר הֵחָלְצוּ מֵאִתְּכֶם אֲנָשִׁים
ד לַצָּבָא וְיִהְיוּ עַל־מִדְיָן לָתֵת נִקְמַת־יהוה בְּמִדְיָן: אֶלֶף לַמַּטֶּה אֶלֶף לַמַּטֶּה
ה לְכֹל מַטּוֹת יִשְׂרָאֵל תִּשְׁלְחוּ לַצָּבָא: וַיִּמָּסְרוּ מֵאַלְפֵי יִשְׂרָאֵל אֶלֶף לַמַּטֶּה
ו שְׁנֵים־עָשָׂר אֶלֶף חֲלוּצֵי צָבָא: וַיִּשְׁלַח אֹתָם מֹשֶׁה אֶלֶף לַמַּטֶּה לַצָּבָא אֹתָם
וְאֶת־פִּינְחָס בֶּן־אֶלְעָזָר הַכֹּהֵן לַצָּבָא וּכְלֵי הַקֹּדֶשׁ וַחֲצֹצְרוֹת הַתְּרוּעָה בְּיָדוֹ:
ז ח וַיִּצְבְּאוּ עַל־מִדְיָן כַּאֲשֶׁר צִוָּה יהוה אֶת־מֹשֶׁה וַיַּהַרְגוּ כָּל־זָכָר: וְאֶת־מַלְכֵי מִדְיָן
הָרְגוּ עַל־חַלְלֵיהֶם אֶת־אֱוִי וְאֶת־רֶקֶם וְאֶת־צוּר וְאֶת־חוּר וְאֶת־רֶבַע חֲמֵשֶׁת
ט מַלְכֵי מִדְיָן וְאֵת בִּלְעָם בֶּן־בְּעוֹר הָרְגוּ בֶּחָרֶב: וַיִּשְׁבּוּ בְנֵי־יִשְׂרָאֵל אֶת־נְשֵׁי
י מִדְיָן וְאֶת־טַפָּם וְאֵת כָּל־בְּהֶמְתָּם וְאֶת־כָּל־מִקְנֵהֶם וְאֶת־כָּל־חֵילָם בָּזָזוּ: וְאֵת
יא כָּל־עָרֵיהֶם בְּמוֹשְׁבֹתָם וְאֵת כָּל־טִירֹתָם שָׂרְפוּ בָּאֵשׁ: וַיִּקְחוּ אֶת־כָּל־הַשָּׁלָל
יב וְאֵת כָּל־הַמַּלְקוֹחַ בָּאָדָם וּבַבְּהֵמָה: וַיָּבִאוּ אֶל־מֹשֶׁה וְאֶל־אֶלְעָזָר הַכֹּהֵן
וְאֶל־עֲדַת בְּנֵי־יִשְׂרָאֵל אֶת־הַשְּׁבִי וְאֶת־הַמַּלְקוֹחַ וְאֶת־הַשָּׁלָל אֶל־הַמַּחֲנֶה
יג אֶל־עַרְבֹת מוֹאָב אֲשֶׁר עַל־יַרְדֵּן יְרֵחוֹ: וַיֵּצְאוּ מֹשֶׁה וְאֶלְעָזָר הַכֹּהֵן שלישי / שני /
יד וְכָל־נְשִׂיאֵי הָעֵדָה לִקְרָאתָם אֶל־מִחוּץ לַמַּחֲנֶה: וַיִּקְצֹף מֹשֶׁה עַל פְּקוּדֵי הֶחָיִל
טו שָׂרֵי הָאֲלָפִים וְשָׂרֵי הַמֵּאוֹת הַבָּאִים מִצְּבָא הַמִּלְחָמָה: וַיֹּאמֶר אֲלֵיהֶם מֹשֶׁה
טז הַחִיִּיתֶם כָּל־נְקֵבָה: הֵן הֵנָּה הָיוּ לִבְנֵי יִשְׂרָאֵל בִּדְבַר בִּלְעָם לִמְסָר־מַעַל בַּיהוה
יז עַל־דְּבַר פְּעוֹר וַתְּהִי הַמַּגֵּפָה בַּעֲדַת יהוה: וְעַתָּה הִרְגוּ כָל־זָכָר בַּטָּף וְכָל־
יח אִשָּׁה יֹדַעַת אִישׁ לְמִשְׁכַּב זָכָר הֲרֹגוּ: וְכֹל הַטַּף בַּנָּשִׁים אֲשֶׁר לֹא־יָדְעוּ מִשְׁכַּב
יט זָכָר הַחֲיוּ לָכֶם: וְאַתֶּם חֲנוּ מִחוּץ לַמַּחֲנֶה שִׁבְעַת יָמִים כֹּל הֹרֵג נֶפֶשׁ וְכֹל ׀
כ נֹגֵעַ בֶּחָלָל תִּתְחַטְּאוּ בַּיּוֹם הַשְּׁלִישִׁי וּבַיּוֹם הַשְּׁבִיעִי אַתֶּם וּשְׁבִיכֶם: וְכָל־בֶּגֶד
כא וְכָל־כְּלִי־עוֹר וְכָל־מַעֲשֵׂה עִזִּים וְכָל־כְּלִי־עֵץ תִּתְחַטָּאוּ: וַיֹּאמֶר
אֶלְעָזָר הַכֹּהֵן אֶל־אַנְשֵׁי הַצָּבָא הַבָּאִים לַמִּלְחָמָה זֹאת חֻקַּת הַתּוֹרָה אֲשֶׁר־
כב צִוָּה יהוה אֶת־מֹשֶׁה: אַךְ אֶת־הַזָּהָב וְאֶת־הַכָּסֶף אֶת־הַנְּחֹשֶׁת אֶת־הַבַּרְזֶל
כג אֶת־הַבְּדִיל וְאֶת־הָעֹפָרֶת: כָּל־דָּבָר אֲשֶׁר־יָבֹא בָאֵשׁ תַּעֲבִירוּ בָאֵשׁ וְטָהֵר אַךְ
כד בְּמֵי נִדָּה יִתְחַטָּא וְכֹל אֲשֶׁר לֹא־יָבֹא בָּאֵשׁ תַּעֲבִירוּ בַּמָּיִם: וְכִבַּסְתֶּם בִּגְדֵיכֶם

רביעי כח בַּיּוֹם הַשְּׁבִיעִי וּטְהַרְתֶּם וְאַחַר תָּבֹאוּ אֶל־הַמַּחֲנֶה: וַיֹּאמֶר יְהוָה כה
אֶל־מֹשֶׁה לֵּאמֹר: שָׂא אֵת רֹאשׁ מַלְקוֹחַ הַשְּׁבִי בָּאָדָם וּבַבְּהֵמָה אַתָּה וְאֶלְעָזָר כו
הַכֹּהֵן וְרָאשֵׁי אֲבוֹת הָעֵדָה: וְחָצִיתָ אֶת־הַמַּלְקוֹחַ בֵּין תֹּפְשֵׂי הַמִּלְחָמָה כז
הַיֹּצְאִים לַצָּבָא וּבֵין כָּל־הָעֵדָה: וַהֲרֵמֹתָ מֶכֶס לַיהוָה מֵאֵת אַנְשֵׁי הַמִּלְחָמָה כח
הַיֹּצְאִים לַצָּבָא אֶחָד נֶפֶשׁ מֵחֲמֵשׁ הַמֵּאוֹת מִן־הָאָדָם וּמִן־הַבָּקָר וּמִן־
הַחֲמֹרִים וּמִן־הַצֹּאן: מִמַּחֲצִיתָם תִּקָּחוּ וְנָתַתָּה לְאֶלְעָזָר הַכֹּהֵן תְּרוּמַת יְהוָה: כט
וּמִמַּחֲצִת בְּנֵי־יִשְׂרָאֵל תִּקַּח ׀ אֶחָד ׀ אָחֻז מִן־הַחֲמִשִּׁים מִן־הָאָדָם מִן־הַבָּקָר ל
מִן־הַחֲמֹרִים וּמִן־הַצֹּאן מִכָּל־הַבְּהֵמָה וְנָתַתָּה אֹתָם לַלְוִיִּם שֹׁמְרֵי מִשְׁמֶרֶת
מִשְׁכַּן יְהוָה: וַיַּעַשׂ מֹשֶׁה וְאֶלְעָזָר הַכֹּהֵן כַּאֲשֶׁר צִוָּה יְהוָה אֶת־מֹשֶׁה: וַיְהִי לא לב
הַמַּלְקוֹחַ יֶתֶר הַבָּז אֲשֶׁר בָּזְזוּ עַם הַצָּבָא צֹאן שֵׁשׁ־מֵאוֹת אֶלֶף וְשִׁבְעִים אֶלֶף
וַחֲמֵשֶׁת אֲלָפִים: וּבָקָר שְׁנַיִם וְשִׁבְעִים אָלֶף: וַחֲמֹרִים אֶחָד וְשִׁשִּׁים אָלֶף: וְנֶפֶשׁ לג לד לה
אָדָם מִן־הַנָּשִׁים אֲשֶׁר לֹא־יָדְעוּ מִשְׁכַּב זָכָר כָּל־נֶפֶשׁ שְׁנַיִם וּשְׁלֹשִׁים אָלֶף:
וַתְּהִי הַמֶּחֱצָה חֵלֶק הַיֹּצְאִים בַּצָּבָא מִסְפַּר הַצֹּאן שְׁלֹשׁ־מֵאוֹת אֶלֶף וּשְׁלֹשִׁים לו
אֶלֶף וְשִׁבְעַת אֲלָפִים וַחֲמֵשׁ מֵאוֹת: וַיְהִי הַמֶּכֶס לַיהוָה מִן־הַצֹּאן שֵׁשׁ מֵאוֹת לז
חָמֵשׁ וְשִׁבְעִים: וְהַבָּקָר שִׁשָּׁה וּשְׁלֹשִׁים אָלֶף וּמִכְסָם לַיהוָה שְׁנַיִם וְשִׁבְעִים: לח
וַחֲמֹרִים שְׁלֹשִׁים אֶלֶף וַחֲמֵשׁ מֵאוֹת וּמִכְסָם לַיהוָה אֶחָד וְשִׁשִּׁים: וְנֶפֶשׁ אָדָם לט מ
שִׁשָּׁה עָשָׂר אָלֶף וּמִכְסָם לַיהוָה שְׁנַיִם וּשְׁלֹשִׁים נָפֶשׁ: וַיִּתֵּן מֹשֶׁה אֶת־מֶכֶס מא
חמישי תְּרוּמַת יְהוָה לְאֶלְעָזָר הַכֹּהֵן כַּאֲשֶׁר צִוָּה יְהוָה אֶת־מֹשֶׁה: וּמִמַּחֲצִית בְּנֵי מב
יִשְׂרָאֵל אֲשֶׁר חָצָה מֹשֶׁה מִן־הָאֲנָשִׁים הַצֹּבְאִים: וַתְּהִי מֶחֱצַת הָעֵדָה מִן־ מג
הַצֹּאן שְׁלֹשׁ־מֵאוֹת אֶלֶף וּשְׁלֹשִׁים אֶלֶף שִׁבְעַת אֲלָפִים וַחֲמֵשׁ מֵאוֹת: וּבָקָר מד
שִׁשָּׁה וּשְׁלֹשִׁים אָלֶף: וַחֲמֹרִים שְׁלֹשִׁים אֶלֶף וַחֲמֵשׁ מֵאוֹת: וְנֶפֶשׁ אָדָם שִׁשָּׁה מה מו
עָשָׂר אָלֶף: וַיִּקַּח מֹשֶׁה מִמַּחֲצִת בְּנֵי־יִשְׂרָאֵל אֶת־הָאָחֻז אֶחָד מִן־הַחֲמִשִּׁים מז
מִן־הָאָדָם וּמִן־הַבְּהֵמָה וַיִּתֵּן אֹתָם לַלְוִיִּם שֹׁמְרֵי מִשְׁמֶרֶת מִשְׁכַּן יְהוָה כַּאֲשֶׁר
צִוָּה יְהוָה אֶת־מֹשֶׁה: וַיִּקְרְבוּ אֶל־מֹשֶׁה הַפְּקֻדִים אֲשֶׁר לְאַלְפֵי הַצָּבָא שָׂרֵי מח
הָאֲלָפִים וְשָׂרֵי הַמֵּאוֹת: וַיֹּאמְרוּ אֶל־מֹשֶׁה עֲבָדֶיךָ נָשְׂאוּ אֶת־רֹאשׁ אַנְשֵׁי מט
הַמִּלְחָמָה אֲשֶׁר בְּיָדֵנוּ וְלֹא־נִפְקַד מִמֶּנּוּ אִישׁ: וַנַּקְרֵב אֶת־קָרְבַּן יְהוָה אִישׁ נ
אֲשֶׁר מָצָא כְלִי־זָהָב אֶצְעָדָה וְצָמִיד טַבַּעַת עָגִיל וְכוּמָז לְכַפֵּר עַל־נַפְשֹׁתֵינוּ
לִפְנֵי יְהוָה: וַיִּקַּח מֹשֶׁה וְאֶלְעָזָר הַכֹּהֵן אֶת־הַזָּהָב מֵאִתָּם כֹּל כְּלִי מַעֲשֶׂה: נא
וַיְהִי ׀ כָּל־זְהַב הַתְּרוּמָה אֲשֶׁר הֵרִימוּ לַיהוָה שִׁשָּׁה עָשָׂר אֶלֶף שְׁבַע־מֵאוֹת נב

נג וַחֲמִשִּׁים שָׁקֶל מֵאֵת שָׂרֵי הָאֲלָפִים וּמֵאֵת שָׂרֵי הַמֵּאוֹת׃ אַנְשֵׁי הַצָּבָא בָּזְזוּ
נד אִישׁ לוֹ׃ וַיִּקַּח מֹשֶׁה וְאֶלְעָזָר הַכֹּהֵן אֶת־הַזָּהָב מֵאֵת שָׂרֵי הָאֲלָפִים וְהַמֵּאוֹת
וַיָּבִאוּ אֹתוֹ אֶל־אֹהֶל מוֹעֵד זִכָּרוֹן לִבְנֵי־יִשְׂרָאֵל לִפְנֵי יהוה׃

לב א וּמִקְנֶה ׀ רַב הָיָה לִבְנֵי רְאוּבֵן וְלִבְנֵי־גָד עָצוּם מְאֹד וַיִּרְאוּ אֶת־אֶרֶץ יַעְזֵר כט ששי / שלישי
ב וְאֶת־אֶרֶץ גִּלְעָד וְהִנֵּה הַמָּקוֹם מְקוֹם מִקְנֶה׃ וַיָּבֹאוּ בְנֵי־גָד וּבְנֵי רְאוּבֵן וַיֹּאמְרוּ
ג אֶל־מֹשֶׁה וְאֶל־אֶלְעָזָר הַכֹּהֵן וְאֶל־נְשִׂיאֵי הָעֵדָה לֵאמֹר׃ עֲטָרוֹת וְדִיבֹן וְיַעְזֵר
ד וְנִמְרָה וְחֶשְׁבּוֹן וְאֶלְעָלֵה וּשְׂבָם וּנְבוֹ וּבְעֹן׃ הָאָרֶץ אֲשֶׁר הִכָּה יהוה לִפְנֵי עֲדַת
ה יִשְׂרָאֵל אֶרֶץ מִקְנֶה הִוא וְלַעֲבָדֶיךָ מִקְנֶה׃ וַיֹּאמְרוּ אִם־מָצָאנוּ חֵן
בְּעֵינֶיךָ יֻתַּן אֶת־הָאָרֶץ הַזֹּאת לַעֲבָדֶיךָ לַאֲחֻזָּה אַל־תַּעֲבִרֵנוּ אֶת־הַיַּרְדֵּן׃
ו וַיֹּאמֶר מֹשֶׁה לִבְנֵי־גָד וְלִבְנֵי רְאוּבֵן הַאַחֵיכֶם יָבֹאוּ לַמִּלְחָמָה וְאַתֶּם תֵּשְׁבוּ פֹה׃
ז וְלָמָּה תנואון אֶת־לֵב בְּנֵי יִשְׂרָאֵל מֵעֲבֹר אֶל־הָאָרֶץ אֲשֶׁר־נָתַן לָהֶם יהוה׃ תְנִיאוּן
ח ט כֹּה עָשׂוּ אֲבֹתֵיכֶם בְּשָׁלְחִי אֹתָם מִקָּדֵשׁ בַּרְנֵעַ לִרְאוֹת אֶת־הָאָרֶץ׃ וַיַּעֲלוּ
עַד־נַחַל אֶשְׁכּוֹל וַיִּרְאוּ אֶת־הָאָרֶץ וַיָּנִיאוּ אֶת־לֵב בְּנֵי יִשְׂרָאֵל לְבִלְתִּי־בֹא
י אֶל־הָאָרֶץ אֲשֶׁר־נָתַן לָהֶם יהוה׃ וַיִּחַר־אַף יהוה בַּיּוֹם הַהוּא וַיִּשָּׁבַע לֵאמֹר׃
יא אִם־יִרְאוּ הָאֲנָשִׁים הָעֹלִים מִמִּצְרַיִם מִבֶּן עֶשְׂרִים שָׁנָה וָמַעְלָה אֵת הָאֲדָמָה
יב אֲשֶׁר נִשְׁבַּעְתִּי לְאַבְרָהָם לְיִצְחָק וּלְיַעֲקֹב כִּי לֹא־מִלְאוּ אַחֲרָי׃ בִּלְתִּי כָּלֵב בֶּן־
יג יְפֻנֶּה הַקְּנִזִּי וִיהוֹשֻׁעַ בִּן־נוּן כִּי מִלְאוּ אַחֲרֵי יהוה׃ וַיִּחַר־אַף יהוה בְּיִשְׂרָאֵל
וַיְנִעֵם בַּמִּדְבָּר אַרְבָּעִים שָׁנָה עַד־תֹּם כָּל־הַדּוֹר הָעֹשֶׂה הָרַע בְּעֵינֵי יהוה׃
יד וְהִנֵּה קַמְתֶּם תַּחַת אֲבֹתֵיכֶם תַּרְבּוּת אֲנָשִׁים חַטָּאִים לִסְפּוֹת עוֹד עַל חֲרוֹן
טו אַף־יהוה אֶל־יִשְׂרָאֵל׃ כִּי תְשׁוּבֻן מֵאַחֲרָיו וְיָסַף עוֹד לְהַנִּיחוֹ בַּמִּדְבָּר וְשִׁחַתֶּם
טז לְכָל־הָעָם הַזֶּה׃ וַיִּגְּשׁוּ אֵלָיו וַיֹּאמְרוּ גִּדְרֹת צֹאן נִבְנֶה לְמִקְנֵנוּ פֹּה
יז וְעָרִים לְטַפֵּנוּ׃ וַאֲנַחְנוּ נֵחָלֵץ חֻשִׁים לִפְנֵי בְּנֵי יִשְׂרָאֵל עַד אֲשֶׁר אִם־הֲבִיאֹנֻם
יח אֶל־מְקוֹמָם וְיָשַׁב טַפֵּנוּ בְּעָרֵי הַמִּבְצָר מִפְּנֵי יֹשְׁבֵי הָאָרֶץ׃ לֹא נָשׁוּב אֶל־בָּתֵּינוּ
יט עַד הִתְנַחֵל בְּנֵי יִשְׂרָאֵל אִישׁ נַחֲלָתוֹ׃ כִּי לֹא נִנְחַל אִתָּם מֵעֵבֶר לַיַּרְדֵּן וָהָלְאָה
כִּי בָאָה נַחֲלָתֵנוּ אֵלֵינוּ מֵעֵבֶר הַיַּרְדֵּן מִזְרָחָה׃
כ וַיֹּאמֶר אֲלֵיהֶם מֹשֶׁה אִם־תַּעֲשׂוּן אֶת־הַדָּבָר הַזֶּה אִם־תֵּחָלְצוּ לִפְנֵי יהוה שביעי / רביעי
כא לַמִּלְחָמָה׃ וְעָבַר לָכֶם כָּל־חָלוּץ אֶת־הַיַּרְדֵּן לִפְנֵי יהוה עַד הוֹרִישׁוֹ אֶת־
כב אֹיְבָיו מִפָּנָיו׃ וְנִכְבְּשָׁה הָאָרֶץ לִפְנֵי יהוה וְאַחַר תָּשֻׁבוּ וִהְיִיתֶם נְקִיִּם מֵיהוה
כג וּמִיִּשְׂרָאֵל וְהָיְתָה הָאָרֶץ הַזֹּאת לָכֶם לַאֲחֻזָּה לִפְנֵי יהוה׃ וְאִם־לֹא תַעֲשׂוּן

כד כֵּן הִנֵּה חֲטָאתֶם לַיהוָה וּדְעוּ חַטַּאתְכֶם אֲשֶׁר תִּמְצָא אֶתְכֶם: בְּנוּ־לָכֶם
כה עָרִים לְטַפְּכֶם וּגְדֵרֹת לְצֹנַאֲכֶם וְהַיֹּצֵא מִפִּיכֶם תַּעֲשׂוּ: וַיֹּאמֶר בְּנֵי־גָד וּבְנֵי
כו רְאוּבֵן אֶל־מֹשֶׁה לֵאמֹר עֲבָדֶיךָ יַעֲשׂוּ כַּאֲשֶׁר אֲדֹנִי מְצַוֶּה: טַפֵּנוּ נָשֵׁינוּ מִקְנֵנוּ
כז וְכָל־בְּהֶמְתֵּנוּ יִהְיוּ־שָׁם בְּעָרֵי הַגִּלְעָד: וַעֲבָדֶיךָ יַעַבְרוּ כָּל־חֲלוּץ צָבָא לִפְנֵי
כח יְהוָה לַמִּלְחָמָה כַּאֲשֶׁר אֲדֹנִי דֹּבֵר: וַיְצַו לָהֶם מֹשֶׁה אֵת אֶלְעָזָר הַכֹּהֵן וְאֵת
כט יְהוֹשֻׁעַ בִּן־נוּן וְאֶת־רָאשֵׁי אֲבוֹת הַמַּטּוֹת לִבְנֵי יִשְׂרָאֵל: וַיֹּאמֶר מֹשֶׁה אֲלֵהֶם
אִם־יַעַבְרוּ בְנֵי־גָד וּבְנֵי־רְאוּבֵן ׀ אִתְּכֶם אֶת־הַיַּרְדֵּן כָּל־חָלוּץ לַמִּלְחָמָה לִפְנֵי
ל יְהוָה וְנִכְבְּשָׁה הָאָרֶץ לִפְנֵיכֶם וּנְתַתֶּם לָהֶם אֶת־אֶרֶץ הַגִּלְעָד לַאֲחֻזָּה: וְאִם־
לא לֹא יַעַבְרוּ חֲלוּצִים אִתְּכֶם וְנֹאחֲזוּ בְתֹכְכֶם בְּאֶרֶץ כְּנָעַן: וַיַּעֲנוּ בְנֵי־גָד וּבְנֵי
לב רְאוּבֵן לֵאמֹר אֵת אֲשֶׁר דִּבֶּר יְהוָה אֶל־עֲבָדֶיךָ כֵּן נַעֲשֶׂה: נַחְנוּ נַעֲבֹר חֲלוּצִים
לג לִפְנֵי יְהוָה אֶרֶץ כְּנָעַן וְאִתָּנוּ אֲחֻזַּת נַחֲלָתֵנוּ מֵעֵבֶר לַיַּרְדֵּן: וַיִּתֵּן לָהֶם ׀ מֹשֶׁה
לִבְנֵי־גָד וְלִבְנֵי רְאוּבֵן וְלַחֲצִי ׀ שֵׁבֶט ׀ מְנַשֶּׁה בֶן־יוֹסֵף אֶת־מַמְלֶכֶת סִיחֹן מֶלֶךְ
הָאֱמֹרִי וְאֶת־מַמְלֶכֶת עוֹג מֶלֶךְ הַבָּשָׁן הָאָרֶץ לְעָרֶיהָ בִּגְבֻלֹת עָרֵי הָאָרֶץ
לד לה סָבִיב: וַיִּבְנוּ בְנֵי־גָד אֶת־דִּיבֹן וְאֶת־עֲטָרֹת וְאֵת עֲרֹעֵר: וְאֶת־עַטְרֹת שׁוֹפָן
לו וְאֶת־יַעְזֵר וְיָגְבְּהָה: וְאֶת־בֵּית נִמְרָה וְאֶת־בֵּית הָרָן עָרֵי מִבְצָר וְגִדְרֹת צֹאן:
לז לח וּבְנֵי רְאוּבֵן בָּנוּ אֶת־חֶשְׁבּוֹן וְאֶת־אֶלְעָלֵא וְאֵת קִרְיָתָיִם: וְאֶת־נְבוֹ וְאֶת־בַּעַל
מְעוֹן מוּסַבֹּת שֵׁם וְאֶת־שִׂבְמָה וַיִּקְרְאוּ בְשֵׁמֹת אֶת־שְׁמוֹת הֶעָרִים אֲשֶׁר בָּנוּ:
לט וַיֵּלְכוּ בְּנֵי מָכִיר בֶּן־מְנַשֶּׁה גִּלְעָדָה וַיִּלְכְּדֻהָ וַיּוֹרֶשׁ אֶת־הָאֱמֹרִי אֲשֶׁר־בָּהּ:
מפטיר מ מא *וַיִּתֵּן מֹשֶׁה אֶת־הַגִּלְעָד לְמָכִיר בֶּן־מְנַשֶּׁה וַיֵּשֶׁב בָּהּ: וְיָאִיר בֶּן־מְנַשֶּׁה הָלַךְ
מב וַיִּלְכֹּד אֶת־חַוֹּתֵיהֶם וַיִּקְרָא אֶתְהֶן חַוֹּת יָאִיר: וְנֹבַח הָלַךְ וַיִּלְכֹּד אֶת־קְנָת
וְאֶת־בְּנֹתֶיהָ וַיִּקְרָא לָה נֹבַח בִּשְׁמוֹ:

מסעי ל לג א אֵלֶּה מַסְעֵי בְנֵי־יִשְׂרָאֵל אֲשֶׁר יָצְאוּ מֵאֶרֶץ מִצְרַיִם לְצִבְאֹתָם בְּיַד־מֹשֶׁה
ב וְאַהֲרֹן: וַיִּכְתֹּב מֹשֶׁה אֶת־מוֹצָאֵיהֶם לְמַסְעֵיהֶם עַל־פִּי יְהוָה וְאֵלֶּה מַסְעֵיהֶם
ג לְמוֹצָאֵיהֶם: וַיִּסְעוּ מֵרַעְמְסֵס בַּחֹדֶשׁ הָרִאשׁוֹן בַּחֲמִשָּׁה עָשָׂר יוֹם לַחֹדֶשׁ
הָרִאשׁוֹן מִמָּחֳרַת הַפֶּסַח יָצְאוּ בְנֵי־יִשְׂרָאֵל בְּיָד רָמָה לְעֵינֵי כָּל־מִצְרָיִם:
לוי ד *וּמִצְרַיִם מְקַבְּרִים אֵת אֲשֶׁר הִכָּה יְהוָה בָּהֶם כָּל־בְּכוֹר וּבֵאלֹהֵיהֶם עָשָׂה
ה ו יְהוָה שְׁפָטִים: וַיִּסְעוּ בְנֵי־יִשְׂרָאֵל מֵרַעְמְסֵס וַיַּחֲנוּ בְּסֻכֹּת: וַיִּסְעוּ מִסֻּכֹּת
ישראל (ברוב הקהילות) ז וַיַּחֲנוּ בְאֵתָם אֲשֶׁר בִּקְצֵה הַמִּדְבָּר: *וַיִּסְעוּ מֵאֵתָם וַיָּשָׁב עַל־פִּי הַחִירֹת אֲשֶׁר
ח עַל־פְּנֵי בַּעַל צְפוֹן וַיַּחֲנוּ לִפְנֵי מִגְדֹּל: וַיִּסְעוּ מִפְּנֵי הַחִירֹת וַיַּעַבְרוּ בְתוֹךְ־הַיָּם

ט הַמִּדְבָּ֑רָה וַיֵּ֨לְכ֜וּ דֶּ֣רֶךְ שְׁלֹ֤שֶׁת יָמִים֙ בְּמִדְבַּ֣ר אֵתָ֔ם וַֽיַּחֲנ֖וּ בְּמָרָֽה׃ וַיִּסְעוּ֙ מִמָּרָ֔ה
וַיָּבֹ֖אוּ אֵילִ֑מָה וּ֠בְאֵילִם שְׁתֵּ֤ים עֶשְׂרֵה֙ עֵינֹ֥ת מַ֛יִם וְשִׁבְעִ֥ים תְּמָרִ֖ים וַיַּחֲנוּ־שָֽׁם׃
י יא וַיִּסְע֖וּ מֵאֵילִ֑ם וַֽיַּחֲנ֖וּ עַל־יַם־סֽוּף׃** וַיִּסְע֖וּ מִיַּם־ס֑וּף וַֽיַּחֲנ֖וּ בְּמִדְבַּר־סִֽין׃ שני
יב יג יד וַיִּסְע֖וּ מִמִּדְבַּר־סִ֑ין וַֽיַּחֲנ֖וּ בְּדָפְקָֽה׃ וַיִּסְע֖וּ מִדָּפְקָ֑ה וַֽיַּחֲנ֖וּ בְּאָלֽוּשׁ׃ וַיִּסְע֖וּ
טו מֵאָל֑וּשׁ וַֽיַּחֲנוּ֙ בִּרְפִידִ֔ם וְלֹא־הָ֨יָה שָׁ֥ם מַ֛יִם לָעָ֖ם לִשְׁתּֽוֹת׃ וַיִּסְע֖וּ מֵרְפִידִ֑ם וַֽיַּחֲנ֖וּ
טז יז בְּמִדְבַּ֥ר סִינָֽי׃ וַיִּסְע֖וּ מִמִּדְבַּ֣ר סִינָ֑י וַֽיַּחֲנ֖וּ בְּקִבְרֹ֥ת הַֽתַּאֲוָֽה׃ וַיִּסְע֖וּ מִקִּבְרֹ֣ת
יח יט הַֽתַּאֲוָ֑ה וַֽיַּחֲנ֖וּ בַּחֲצֵרֹֽת׃ וַיִּסְע֖וּ מֵחֲצֵרֹ֑ת וַֽיַּחֲנ֖וּ בְּרִתְמָֽה׃ וַיִּסְע֖וּ מֵרִתְמָ֑ה וַֽיַּחֲנ֖וּ
כ כא בְּרִמֹּ֥ן פָּֽרֶץ׃ וַיִּסְע֖וּ מֵרִמֹּ֣ן פָּ֑רֶץ וַֽיַּחֲנ֖וּ בְּלִבְנָֽה׃ וַיִּסְע֖וּ מִלִּבְנָ֑ה וַֽיַּחֲנ֖וּ בְּרִסָּֽה׃
כב כג כד וַיִּסְע֖וּ מֵרִסָּ֑ה וַֽיַּחֲנ֖וּ בִּקְהֵלָֽתָה׃ וַיִּסְע֖וּ מִקְּהֵלָ֑תָה וַֽיַּחֲנ֖וּ בְּהַר־שָֽׁפֶר׃ וַיִּסְע֖וּ
כה כו מֵהַר־שָׁ֑פֶר וַֽיַּחֲנ֖וּ בַּחֲרָדָֽה׃ וַיִּסְע֖וּ מֵחֲרָדָ֑ה וַֽיַּחֲנ֖וּ בְּמַקְהֵלֹֽת׃ וַיִּסְע֖וּ מִמַּקְהֵלֹ֑ת
כז כח וַֽיַּחֲנ֖וּ בְּתָֽחַת׃ וַיִּסְע֖וּ מִתָּ֑חַת וַֽיַּחֲנ֖וּ בְּתָֽרַח׃ וַיִּסְע֖וּ מִתָּ֑רַח וַֽיַּחֲנ֖וּ בְּמִתְקָֽה׃
כט ל לא וַיִּסְע֖וּ מִמִּתְקָ֑ה וַֽיַּחֲנ֖וּ בְּחַשְׁמֹנָֽה׃ וַיִּסְע֖וּ מֵחַשְׁמֹנָ֑ה וַֽיַּחֲנ֖וּ בְּמֹסֵרֽוֹת׃ וַיִּסְע֖וּ
לב לג מִמֹּסֵר֑וֹת וַֽיַּחֲנ֖וּ בִּבְנֵ֥י יַעֲקָֽן׃ וַיִּסְע֖וּ מִבְּנֵ֣י יַעֲקָ֑ן וַֽיַּחֲנ֖וּ בְּחֹ֥ר הַגִּדְגָּֽד׃ וַיִּסְע֖וּ מֵחֹ֣ר
לד לה הַגִּדְגָּ֑ד וַֽיַּחֲנ֖וּ בְּיָטְבָֽתָה׃ וַיִּסְע֖וּ מִיָּטְבָ֑תָה וַֽיַּחֲנ֖וּ בְּעַבְרֹנָֽה׃ וַיִּסְע֖וּ מֵעַבְרֹנָ֑ה
לו לז וַֽיַּחֲנ֖וּ בְּעֶצְיֹ֥ן גָּֽבֶר׃ וַיִּסְע֖וּ מֵעֶצְיֹ֣ן גָּ֑בֶר וַיַּחֲנ֥וּ בְמִדְבַּר־צִ֖ן הִ֥וא קָדֵֽשׁ׃ וַיִּסְע֖וּ
לח מִקָּדֵ֑שׁ וַֽיַּחֲנוּ֙ בְּהֹ֣ר הָהָ֔ר בִּקְצֵ֖ה אֶ֥רֶץ אֱדֽוֹם׃ וַיַּ֩עַל֩ אַהֲרֹ֨ן הַכֹּהֵ֜ן אֶל־הֹ֥ר הָהָ֛ר
עַל־פִּ֥י יהוה וַיָּ֣מָת שָׁ֑ם בִּשְׁנַ֣ת הָֽאַרְבָּעִ֗ים לְצֵ֤את בְּנֵֽי־יִשְׂרָאֵל֙ מֵאֶ֣רֶץ מִצְרַ֔יִם
לט בַּחֹ֥דֶשׁ הַחֲמִישִׁ֖י בְּאֶחָ֥ד לַחֹֽדֶשׁ׃ וְאַהֲרֹ֕ן בֶּן־שָׁלֹ֧שׁ וְעֶשְׂרִ֛ים וּמְאַ֖ת שָׁנָ֑ה בְּמֹת֖וֹ
מ בְּהֹ֥ר הָהָֽר׃ וַיִּשְׁמַ֗ע הַֽכְּנַעֲנִי֙ מֶ֣לֶךְ עֲרָ֔ד וְהֽוּא־יֹשֵׁ֥ב בַּנֶּ֖גֶב בְּאֶ֣רֶץ
מא מב כְּנָ֑עַן בְּבֹ֖א בְּנֵ֥י יִשְׂרָאֵֽל׃ וַיִּסְע֖וּ מֵהֹ֣ר הָהָ֑ר וַֽיַּחֲנ֖וּ בְּצַלְמֹנָֽה׃ וַיִּסְע֖וּ מִצַּלְמֹנָ֑ה
מג מד וַֽיַּחֲנ֖וּ בְּפוּנֹֽן׃ וַיִּסְע֖וּ מִפּוּנֹ֑ן וַֽיַּחֲנ֖וּ בְּאֹבֹֽת׃ וַיִּסְע֖וּ מֵאֹבֹ֑ת וַֽיַּחֲנ֛וּ בְּעִיֵּ֥י הָעֲבָרִ֖ים
מה מו בִּגְב֥וּל מוֹאָֽב׃ וַיִּסְע֖וּ מֵעִיִּ֑ים וַֽיַּחֲנ֖וּ בְּדִיבֹ֥ן גָּֽד׃ וַיִּסְע֖וּ מִדִּיבֹ֣ן גָּ֑ד וַֽיַּחֲנ֖וּ בְּעַלְמֹ֥ן
מז מח דִּבְלָתָֽיְמָה׃ וַיִּסְע֖וּ מֵעַלְמֹ֣ן דִּבְלָתָ֑יְמָה וַֽיַּחֲנ֛וּ בְּהָרֵ֥י הָעֲבָרִ֖ים לִפְנֵ֥י נְבֽוֹ׃ וַיִּסְע֖וּ
מט מֵהָרֵ֣י הָעֲבָרִ֑ים וַֽיַּחֲנוּ֙ בְּעַרְבֹ֣ת מוֹאָ֔ב עַ֖ל יַרְדֵּ֥ן יְרֵחֽוֹ׃ וַיַּחֲנ֤וּ עַל־הַיַּרְדֵּן֙ מִבֵּ֣ית
נ הַיְשִׁמֹ֔ת עַ֖ד אָבֵ֣ל הַשִּׁטִּ֑ים בְּעַרְבֹ֖ת מוֹאָֽב׃ *וַיְדַבֵּ֥ר יהוה אֶל־מֹשֶׁ֑ה שלישי / חמישי / (ישראל במעט קהילות)
נא בְּעַרְבֹ֣ת מוֹאָ֔ב עַל־יַרְדֵּ֥ן יְרֵח֖וֹ לֵאמֹֽר׃ דַּבֵּר֙ אֶל־בְּנֵ֣י יִשְׂרָאֵ֔ל וְאָמַרְתָּ֖ אֲלֵהֶ֑ם
נב כִּ֥י אַתֶּ֛ם עֹבְרִ֥ים אֶת־הַיַּרְדֵּ֖ן אֶל־אֶ֥רֶץ כְּנָֽעַן׃ וְהוֹרַשְׁתֶּ֞ם אֶת־כָּל־יֹשְׁבֵ֤י הָאָ֙רֶץ֙
מִפְּנֵיכֶ֔ם וְאִ֨בַּדְתֶּ֔ם אֵ֖ת כָּל־מַשְׂכִּיֹּתָ֑ם וְאֵ֨ת כָּל־צַלְמֵ֤י מַסֵּֽכֹתָם֙ תְּאַבֵּ֔דוּ וְאֵ֥ת
נג כָּל־בָּמוֹתָ֖ם תַּשְׁמִֽידוּ׃ וְהוֹרַשְׁתֶּ֥ם אֶת־הָאָ֖רֶץ וִישַׁבְתֶּם־בָּ֑הּ כִּ֥י לָכֶ֛ם נָתַ֥תִּי

אֶת־הָאָ֖רֶץ לָרֶ֥שֶׁת אֹתָֽהּ׃** וְהִתְנַחַלְתֶּם֩ אֶת־הָאָ֨רֶץ בְּגוֹרָ֜ל לְמִשְׁפְּחֹתֵיכֶ֗ם נד
לָרַ֞ב תַּרְבּ֣וּ אֶת־נַחֲלָת֗וֹ וְלַמְעַט֙ תַּמְעִ֣יט אֶת־נַחֲלָת֔וֹ אֶל֩ אֲשֶׁר־יֵ֨צֵא ל֥וֹ שָׁ֛מָּה
הַגּוֹרָ֖ל ל֣וֹ יִהְיֶ֑ה לְמַטּ֥וֹת אֲבֹתֵיכֶ֖ם תִּתְנֶחָֽלוּ׃ וְאִם־לֹ֨א תוֹרִ֜ישׁוּ אֶת־יֹשְׁבֵ֣י נה
הָאָרֶץ֮ מִפְּנֵיכֶם֒ וְהָיָ֗ה אֲשֶׁ֤ר תּוֹתִ֙ירוּ֙ מֵהֶ֔ם לְשִׂכִּים֙ בְּעֵ֣ינֵיכֶ֔ם וְלִצְנִינִ֖ם בְּצִדֵּיכֶ֑ם
וְצָרֲר֣וּ אֶתְכֶ֔ם עַל־הָאָ֕רֶץ אֲשֶׁ֥ר אַתֶּ֖ם יֹשְׁבִ֥ים בָּֽהּ׃ וְהָיָ֗ה כַּאֲשֶׁ֥ר דִּמִּ֛יתִי לַעֲשׂ֥וֹת נו
לָהֶ֖ם אֶעֱשֶׂ֥ה לָכֶֽם׃

לד וַיְדַבֵּ֥ר יְהוָ֖ה אֶל־מֹשֶׁ֥ה לֵּאמֹֽר׃ צַ֞ו אֶת־בְּנֵ֤י יִשְׂרָאֵל֙ וְאָמַרְתָּ֣ אֲלֵהֶ֔ם כִּֽי־אַתֶּ֥ם א ב
בָּאִ֖ים אֶל־הָאָ֣רֶץ כְּנָ֑עַן זֹ֣את הָאָ֗רֶץ אֲשֶׁ֨ר תִּפֹּ֤ל לָכֶם֙ בְּנַחֲלָ֔ה אֶ֥רֶץ כְּנַ֖עַן
לִגְבֻלֹתֶֽיהָ׃ וְהָיָ֨ה לָכֶ֧ם פְּאַת־נֶ֛גֶב מִמִּדְבַּר־צִ֖ן עַל־יְדֵ֣י אֱד֑וֹם וְהָיָ֤ה לָכֶם֙ גְּב֣וּל ג
נֶ֔גֶב מִקְצֵ֥ה יָם־הַמֶּ֖לַח קֵֽדְמָה׃ וְנָסַ֣ב לָכֶם֩ הַגְּב֨וּל מִנֶּ֜גֶב לְמַעֲלֵ֤ה עַקְרַבִּים֙ ד
וְהָיוּ וְעָ֣בַר צִ֔נָה והיה תּוֹצְאֹתָ֔יו מִנֶּ֖גֶב לְקָדֵ֣שׁ בַּרְנֵ֑עַ וְיָצָ֥א חֲצַר־אַדָּ֖ר וְעָבַ֥ר עַצְמֹֽנָה׃
וְנָסַ֧ב הַגְּב֛וּל מֵעַצְמ֖וֹן נַ֣חְלָה מִצְרָ֑יִם וְהָי֥וּ תוֹצְאֹתָ֖יו הַיָּֽמָּה׃ וּגְב֣וּל יָ֔ם וְהָיָ֥ה ה ו
לָכֶ֛ם הַיָּ֥ם הַגָּד֖וֹל וּגְב֑וּל זֶֽה־יִהְיֶ֥ה לָכֶ֖ם גְּב֥וּל יָֽם׃ וְזֶה־יִהְיֶ֥ה לָכֶ֖ם גְּב֣וּל צָפ֑וֹן ז
מִן־הַיָּם֙ הַגָּדֹ֔ל תְּתָא֥וּ לָכֶ֖ם הֹ֥ר הָהָֽר׃ מֵהֹ֣ר הָהָ֔ר תְּתָא֖וּ לְבֹ֣א חֲמָ֑ת וְהָי֛וּ ח
תּוֹצְאֹ֥ת הַגְּבֻ֖ל צְדָֽדָה׃ וְיָצָ֤א הַגְּבֻל֙ זִפְרֹ֔נָה וְהָי֥וּ תוֹצְאֹתָ֖יו חֲצַ֣ר עֵינָ֑ן זֶה־יִהְיֶ֥ה ט
לָכֶ֖ם גְּב֥וּל צָפֽוֹן׃ וְהִתְאַוִּיתֶ֥ם לָכֶ֖ם לִגְב֣וּל קֵ֑דְמָה מֵחֲצַ֥ר עֵינָ֖ן שְׁפָֽמָה׃ וְיָרַ֨ד י יא
הַגְּבֻ֧ל מִשְּׁפָ֛ם הָרִבְלָ֖ה מִקֶּ֣דֶם לָעָ֑יִן וְיָרַ֣ד הַגְּבֻ֔ל וּמָחָ֛ה עַל־כֶּ֥תֶף יָם־כִּנֶּ֖רֶת
קֵֽדְמָה׃ וְיָרַ֤ד הַגְּבוּל֙ הַיַּרְדֵּ֔נָה וְהָי֥וּ תוֹצְאֹתָ֖יו יָ֣ם הַמֶּ֑לַח זֹאת֩ תִּהְיֶ֨ה לָכֶ֥ם יב
הָאָ֛רֶץ לִגְבֻלֹתֶ֖יהָ סָבִֽיב׃ וַיְצַ֣ו מֹשֶׁ֔ה אֶת־בְּנֵ֥י יִשְׂרָאֵ֖ל לֵאמֹ֑ר זֹ֣את הָאָ֗רֶץ אֲשֶׁ֨ר יג
תִּתְנַחֲל֤וּ אֹתָהּ֙ בְּגוֹרָ֔ל אֲשֶׁר֙ צִוָּ֣ה יְהוָ֔ה לָתֵ֛ת לְתִשְׁעַ֥ת הַמַּטּ֖וֹת וַחֲצִ֥י הַמַּטֶּֽה׃
כִּ֣י לָקְח֞וּ מַטֵּ֨ה בְנֵ֤י הָראוּבֵנִי֙ לְבֵ֣ית אֲבֹתָ֔ם וּמַטֵּ֥ה בְנֵֽי־הַגָּדִ֖י לְבֵ֣ית אֲבֹתָ֑ם יד
וַחֲצִי֙ מַטֵּ֣ה מְנַשֶּׁ֔ה לָקְח֖וּ נַחֲלָתָֽם׃ שְׁנֵ֥י הַמַּטּ֖וֹת וַחֲצִ֣י הַמַּטֶּ֑ה לָקְח֣וּ נַחֲלָתָ֗ם טו
מֵעֵ֛בֶר לְיַרְדֵּ֥ן יְרֵח֖וֹ קֵ֥דְמָה מִזְרָֽחָה׃

רביעי / ששי *וַיְדַבֵּ֥ר יְהוָ֖ה אֶל־מֹשֶׁ֥ה לֵּאמֹֽר׃ אֵ֚לֶּה שְׁמ֣וֹת הָאֲנָשִׁ֔ים אֲשֶׁר־יִנְחֲל֥וּ לָכֶ֖ם טז יז
אֶת־הָאָ֑רֶץ אֶלְעָזָר֙ הַכֹּהֵ֔ן וִיהוֹשֻׁ֖עַ בִּן־נֽוּן׃ וְנָשִׂ֧יא אֶחָ֛ד נָשִׂ֥יא אֶחָ֖ד מִמַּטֶּ֑ה יח
תִּקְח֖וּ לִנְחֹ֥ל אֶת־הָאָֽרֶץ׃ וְאֵ֖לֶּה שְׁמ֣וֹת הָאֲנָשִׁ֑ים לְמַטֵּה֙ יְהוּדָ֔ה כָּלֵ֖ב בֶּן־יְפֻנֶּֽה׃ יט
וּלְמַטֵּה֙ בְּנֵ֣י שִׁמְע֔וֹן שְׁמוּאֵ֖ל בֶּן־עַמִּיהֽוּד׃ לְמַטֵּ֣ה בִנְיָמִ֔ן אֱלִידָ֖ד בֶּן־כִּסְלֽוֹן׃ כ כא
וּלְמַטֵּ֥ה בְנֵי־דָ֖ן נָשִׂ֑יא בֻּקִּ֖י בֶּן־יָגְלִֽי׃ לִבְנֵ֣י יוֹסֵ֔ף לְמַטֵּ֥ה בְנֵֽי־מְנַשֶּׁ֖ה נָשִׂ֑יא כב כג
חַנִּיאֵ֖ל בֶּן־אֵפֹֽד׃ וּלְמַטֵּ֥ה בְנֵֽי־אֶפְרַ֖יִם נָשִׂ֑יא קְמוּאֵ֖ל בֶּן־שִׁפְטָֽן׃ וּלְמַטֵּ֧ה כד כה

כו בְּנֵי־זְבוּלֻן נָשִׂיא אֱלִיצָפָן בֶּן־פַּרְנָךְ׃ וּלְמַטֵּה בְנֵי־יִשָּׂשכָר נָשִׂיא פַּלְטִיאֵל
כז כח בֶּן־עַזָּן׃ וּלְמַטֵּה בְנֵי־אָשֵׁר נָשִׂיא אֲחִיהוּד בֶּן־שְׁלֹמִי׃ וּלְמַטֵּה בְנֵי־נַפְתָּלִי
כט נָשִׂיא פְּדַהְאֵל בֶּן־עַמִּיהוּד׃ אֵלֶּה אֲשֶׁר צִוָּה יהוה לְנַחֵל אֶת־בְּנֵי־יִשְׂרָאֵל
בְּאֶרֶץ כְּנָעַן׃

לה א ב *וַיְדַבֵּר יהוה אֶל־מֹשֶׁה בְּעַרְבֹת מוֹאָב עַל־יַרְדֵּן יְרֵחוֹ לֵאמֹר׃ צַו אֶת־בְּנֵי חמישי
יִשְׂרָאֵל וְנָתְנוּ לַלְוִיִּם מִנַּחֲלַת אֲחֻזָּתָם עָרִים לָשָׁבֶת וּמִגְרָשׁ לֶעָרִים סְבִיבֹתֵיהֶם
ג תִּתְּנוּ לַלְוִיִּם׃ וְהָיוּ הֶעָרִים לָהֶם לָשָׁבֶת וּמִגְרְשֵׁיהֶם יִהְיוּ לִבְהֶמְתָּם וְלִרְכֻשָׁם
ד וּלְכֹל חַיָּתָם׃ וּמִגְרְשֵׁי הֶעָרִים אֲשֶׁר תִּתְּנוּ לַלְוִיִּם מִקִּיר הָעִיר וָחוּצָה אֶלֶף
ה אַמָּה סָבִיב׃ וּמַדֹּתֶם מִחוּץ לָעִיר אֶת־פְּאַת־קֵדְמָה אַלְפַּיִם בָּאַמָּה וְאֶת־
פְּאַת־נֶגֶב אַלְפַּיִם בָּאַמָּה וְאֶת־פְּאַת־יָם ׀ אַלְפַּיִם בָּאַמָּה וְאֵת פְּאַת צָפוֹן
ו אַלְפַּיִם בָּאַמָּה וְהָעִיר בַּתָּוֶךְ זֶה יִהְיֶה לָהֶם מִגְרְשֵׁי הֶעָרִים׃ וְאֵת הֶעָרִים
אֲשֶׁר תִּתְּנוּ לַלְוִיִּם אֵת שֵׁשׁ־עָרֵי הַמִּקְלָט אֲשֶׁר תִּתְּנוּ לָנֻס שָׁמָּה הָרֹצֵחַ
ז וַעֲלֵיהֶם תִּתְּנוּ אַרְבָּעִים וּשְׁתַּיִם עִיר׃ כָּל־הֶעָרִים אֲשֶׁר תִּתְּנוּ לַלְוִיִּם אַרְבָּעִים
ח וּשְׁמֹנֶה עִיר אֶתְהֶן וְאֶת־מִגְרְשֵׁיהֶן׃ וְהֶעָרִים אֲשֶׁר תִּתְּנוּ מֵאֲחֻזַּת בְּנֵי־יִשְׂרָאֵל
מֵאֵת הָרַב תַּרְבּוּ וּמֵאֵת הַמְעַט תַּמְעִיטוּ אִישׁ כְּפִי נַחֲלָתוֹ אֲשֶׁר יִנְחָלוּ יִתֵּן
מֵעָרָיו לַלְוִיִּם׃

ט י *וַיְדַבֵּר יהוה אֶל־מֹשֶׁה לֵּאמֹר׃ דַּבֵּר אֶל־בְּנֵי יִשְׂרָאֵל וְאָמַרְתָּ אֲלֵהֶם כִּי אַתֶּם לב ששי / שביעי
יא עֹבְרִים אֶת־הַיַּרְדֵּן אַרְצָה כְּנָעַן׃ וְהִקְרִיתֶם לָכֶם עָרִים עָרֵי מִקְלָט תִּהְיֶינָה
יב לָכֶם וְנָס שָׁמָּה רֹצֵחַ מַכֵּה־נֶפֶשׁ בִּשְׁגָגָה׃ וְהָיוּ לָכֶם הֶעָרִים לְמִקְלָט מִגֹּאֵל
יג וְלֹא יָמוּת הָרֹצֵחַ עַד־עָמְדוֹ לִפְנֵי הָעֵדָה לַמִּשְׁפָּט׃ וְהֶעָרִים אֲשֶׁר תִּתֵּנוּ שֵׁשׁ־
יד עָרֵי מִקְלָט תִּהְיֶינָה לָכֶם׃ אֵת ׀ שְׁלֹשׁ הֶעָרִים תִּתְּנוּ מֵעֵבֶר לַיַּרְדֵּן וְאֵת שְׁלֹשׁ
טו הֶעָרִים תִּתְּנוּ בְּאֶרֶץ כְּנָעַן עָרֵי מִקְלָט תִּהְיֶינָה׃ לִבְנֵי יִשְׂרָאֵל וְלַגֵּר וְלַתּוֹשָׁב
בְּתוֹכָם תִּהְיֶינָה שֵׁשׁ־הֶעָרִים הָאֵלֶּה לְמִקְלָט לָנוּס שָׁמָּה כָּל־מַכֵּה־נֶפֶשׁ
טז יז בִּשְׁגָגָה׃ וְאִם־בִּכְלִי בַרְזֶל ׀ הִכָּהוּ וַיָּמֹת רֹצֵחַ הוּא מוֹת יוּמַת הָרֹצֵחַ׃ וְאִם
יח בְּאֶבֶן יָד אֲשֶׁר־יָמוּת בָּהּ הִכָּהוּ וַיָּמֹת רֹצֵחַ הוּא מוֹת יוּמַת הָרֹצֵחַ׃ אוֹ בִּכְלִי
יט עֵץ־יָד אֲשֶׁר־יָמוּת בּוֹ הִכָּהוּ וַיָּמֹת רֹצֵחַ הוּא מוֹת יוּמַת הָרֹצֵחַ׃ גֹּאֵל הַדָּם
כ הוּא יָמִית אֶת־הָרֹצֵחַ בְּפִגְעוֹ־בוֹ הוּא יְמִתֶנּוּ׃ וְאִם־בְּשִׂנְאָה יֶהְדָּפֶנּוּ אוֹ־
כא הִשְׁלִיךְ עָלָיו בִּצְדִיָּה וַיָּמֹת׃ אוֹ בְאֵיבָה הִכָּהוּ בְיָדוֹ וַיָּמֹת מוֹת־יוּמַת הַמַּכֶּה
כב רֹצֵחַ הוּא גֹּאֵל הַדָּם יָמִית אֶת־הָרֹצֵחַ בְּפִגְעוֹ־בוֹ׃ וְאִם־בְּפֶתַע בְּלֹא־אֵיבָה

כג הָדָפוֹ אוֹ־הִשְׁלִיךְ עָלָיו כָּל־כְּלִי בְּלֹא צְדִיָּה׃ אוֹ בְכָל־אֶבֶן אֲשֶׁר־יָמוּת בָּהּ בְּלֹא
כד רְאוֹת וַיַּפֵּל עָלָיו וַיָּמֹת וְהוּא לֹא־אוֹיֵב לוֹ וְלֹא מְבַקֵּשׁ רָעָתוֹ׃ וְשָׁפְטוּ הָעֵדָה
כה בֵּין הַמַּכֶּה וּבֵין גֹּאֵל הַדָּם עַל הַמִּשְׁפָּטִים הָאֵלֶּה׃ וְהִצִּילוּ הָעֵדָה אֶת־הָרֹצֵחַ
מִיַּד גֹּאֵל הַדָּם וְהֵשִׁיבוּ אֹתוֹ הָעֵדָה אֶל־עִיר מִקְלָטוֹ אֲשֶׁר־נָס שָׁמָּה וְיָשַׁב בָּהּ
כו עַד־מוֹת הַכֹּהֵן הַגָּדֹל אֲשֶׁר־מָשַׁח אֹתוֹ בְּשֶׁמֶן הַקֹּדֶשׁ׃ וְאִם־יָצֹא יֵצֵא הָרֹצֵחַ
כז אֶת־גְּבוּל עִיר מִקְלָטוֹ אֲשֶׁר יָנוּס שָׁמָּה׃ וּמָצָא אֹתוֹ גֹּאֵל הַדָּם מִחוּץ לִגְבוּל
כח עִיר מִקְלָטוֹ וְרָצַח גֹּאֵל הַדָּם אֶת־הָרֹצֵחַ אֵין לוֹ דָּם׃ כִּי בְעִיר מִקְלָטוֹ יֵשֵׁב
עַד־מוֹת הַכֹּהֵן הַגָּדֹל וְאַחֲרֵי־מוֹת הַכֹּהֵן הַגָּדֹל יָשׁוּב הָרֹצֵחַ אֶל־אֶרֶץ אֲחֻזָּתוֹ׃
כט ל וְהָיוּ אֵלֶּה לָכֶם לְחֻקַּת מִשְׁפָּט לְדֹרֹתֵיכֶם בְּכֹל מוֹשְׁבֹתֵיכֶם׃ כָּל־מַכֵּה־נֶפֶשׁ
לא לְפִי עֵדִים יִרְצַח אֶת־הָרֹצֵחַ וְעֵד אֶחָד לֹא־יַעֲנֶה בְנֶפֶשׁ לָמוּת׃ וְלֹא־תִקְחוּ
לב כֹפֶר לְנֶפֶשׁ רֹצֵחַ אֲשֶׁר־הוּא רָשָׁע לָמוּת כִּי־מוֹת יוּמָת׃ וְלֹא־תִקְחוּ כֹפֶר
לג לָנוּס אֶל־עִיר מִקְלָטוֹ לָשׁוּב לָשֶׁבֶת בָּאָרֶץ עַד־מוֹת הַכֹּהֵן׃ וְלֹא־תַחֲנִיפוּ אֶת־
הָאָרֶץ אֲשֶׁר אַתֶּם בָּהּ כִּי הַדָּם הוּא יַחֲנִיף אֶת־הָאָרֶץ וְלָאָרֶץ לֹא־יְכֻפַּר לַדָּם
לד אֲשֶׁר שֻׁפַּךְ־בָּהּ כִּי־אִם בְּדַם שֹׁפְכוֹ׃ וְלֹא תְטַמֵּא אֶת־הָאָרֶץ אֲשֶׁר אַתֶּם יֹשְׁבִים
בָּהּ אֲשֶׁר אֲנִי שֹׁכֵן בְּתוֹכָהּ כִּי אֲנִי יְהוָה שֹׁכֵן בְּתוֹךְ בְּנֵי יִשְׂרָאֵל׃
שביעי לו א וַיִּקְרְבוּ רָאשֵׁי הָאָבוֹת לְמִשְׁפַּחַת בְּנֵי־גִלְעָד בֶּן־מָכִיר בֶּן־מְנַשֶּׁה מִמִּשְׁפְּחֹת
ב בְּנֵי יוֹסֵף וַיְדַבְּרוּ לִפְנֵי מֹשֶׁה וְלִפְנֵי הַנְּשִׂאִים רָאשֵׁי אָבוֹת לִבְנֵי יִשְׂרָאֵל׃ וַיֹּאמְרוּ
אֶת־אֲדֹנִי צִוָּה יְהוָה לָתֵת אֶת־הָאָרֶץ בְּנַחֲלָה בְּגוֹרָל לִבְנֵי יִשְׂרָאֵל וַאדֹנִי
ג צֻוָּה בַיהוָה לָתֵת אֶת־נַחֲלַת צְלָפְחָד אָחִינוּ לִבְנֹתָיו׃ וְהָיוּ לְאֶחָד מִבְּנֵי שִׁבְטֵי
בְנֵי־יִשְׂרָאֵל לְנָשִׁים וְנִגְרְעָה נַחֲלָתָן מִנַּחֲלַת אֲבֹתֵינוּ וְנוֹסַף עַל נַחֲלַת הַמַּטֶּה
ד אֲשֶׁר תִּהְיֶינָה לָהֶם וּמִגֹּרַל נַחֲלָתֵנוּ יִגָּרֵעַ׃ וְאִם־יִהְיֶה הַיֹּבֵל לִבְנֵי יִשְׂרָאֵל
וְנוֹסְפָה נַחֲלָתָן עַל נַחֲלַת הַמַּטֶּה אֲשֶׁר תִּהְיֶינָה לָהֶם וּמִנַּחֲלַת מַטֵּה אֲבֹתֵינוּ
ה יִגָּרַע נַחֲלָתָן׃ וַיְצַו מֹשֶׁה אֶת־בְּנֵי יִשְׂרָאֵל עַל־פִּי יְהוָה לֵאמֹר כֵּן מַטֵּה בְנֵי־יוֹסֵף
ו דֹּבְרִים׃ זֶה הַדָּבָר אֲשֶׁר־צִוָּה יְהוָה לִבְנוֹת צְלָפְחָד לֵאמֹר לַטּוֹב בְּעֵינֵיהֶם
ז תִּהְיֶינָה לְנָשִׁים אַךְ לְמִשְׁפַּחַת מַטֵּה אֲבִיהֶם תִּהְיֶינָה לְנָשִׁים׃ וְלֹא־תִסֹּב
נַחֲלָה לִבְנֵי יִשְׂרָאֵל מִמַּטֶּה אֶל־מַטֶּה כִּי אִישׁ בְּנַחֲלַת מַטֵּה אֲבֹתָיו יִדְבְּקוּ
ח בְּנֵי יִשְׂרָאֵל׃ וְכָל־בַּת יֹרֶשֶׁת נַחֲלָה מִמַּטּוֹת בְּנֵי יִשְׂרָאֵל לְאֶחָד מִמִּשְׁפַּחַת
מַטֵּה אָבִיהָ תִּהְיֶה לְאִשָּׁה לְמַעַן יִירְשׁוּ בְּנֵי יִשְׂרָאֵל אִישׁ נַחֲלַת אֲבֹתָיו׃
ט וְלֹא־תִסֹּב נַחֲלָה מִמַּטֶּה לְמַטֶּה אַחֵר כִּי־אִישׁ בְּנַחֲלָתוֹ יִדְבְּקוּ מַטּוֹת בְּנֵי

יא יִשְׂרָאֵל: כַּאֲשֶׁר צִוָּה יהוה אֶת־מֹשֶׁה כֵּן עָשׂוּ בְּנוֹת צְלׇפְחָד: וַתִּהְיֶינָה מַחְלָה מפטיר
יב תִרְצָה וְחׇגְלָה וּמִלְכָּה וְנֹעָה בְּנוֹת צְלׇפְחָד לִבְנֵי דֹדֵיהֶן לְנָשִׁים: מִמִּשְׁפְּחֹת
יג בְּנֵי־מְנַשֶּׁה בֶן־יוֹסֵף הָיוּ לְנָשִׁים וַתְּהִי נַחֲלָתָן עַל־מַטֵּה מִשְׁפַּחַת אֲבִיהֶן: אֵלֶּה
הַמִּצְוֺת וְהַמִּשְׁפָּטִים אֲשֶׁר צִוָּה יהוה בְּיַד־מֹשֶׁה אֶל־בְּנֵי יִשְׂרָאֵל בְּעַרְבֹת
מוֹאָב עַל יַרְדֵּן יְרֵחוֹ:

The Maftir for Shabbat Rosh Hodesh, *page 1030*

א דברים

א א אֵלֶּה הַדְּבָרִים אֲשֶׁר דִּבֶּר מֹשֶׁה אֶל־כׇּל־יִשְׂרָאֵל בְּעֵבֶר הַיַּרְדֵּן בַּמִּדְבָּר בָּעֲרָבָה
ב מוֹל סוּף בֵּין־פָּארָן וּבֵין־תֹּפֶל וְלָבָן וַחֲצֵרֹת וְדִי זָהָב: אַחַד עָשָׂר יוֹם מֵחֹרֵב
ג דֶּרֶךְ הַר־שֵׂעִיר עַד קָדֵשׁ בַּרְנֵעַ: וַיְהִי בְּאַרְבָּעִים שָׁנָה בְּעַשְׁתֵּי־עָשָׂר חֹדֶשׁ
בְּאֶחָד לַחֹדֶשׁ דִּבֶּר מֹשֶׁה אֶל־בְּנֵי יִשְׂרָאֵל כְּכֹל אֲשֶׁר צִוָּה יהוה אֹתוֹ אֲלֵהֶם:
ד *אַחֲרֵי הַכֹּתוֹ אֵת סִיחֹן מֶלֶךְ הָאֱמֹרִי אֲשֶׁר יוֹשֵׁב בְּחֶשְׁבּוֹן וְאֵת עוֹג מֶלֶךְ לוי
ה הַבָּשָׁן אֲשֶׁר־יוֹשֵׁב בְּעַשְׁתָּרֹת בְּאֶדְרֶעִי: בְּעֵבֶר הַיַּרְדֵּן בְּאֶרֶץ מוֹאָב הוֹאִיל
ו מֹשֶׁה בֵּאֵר אֶת־הַתּוֹרָה הַזֹּאת לֵאמֹר: יהוה אֱלֹהֵינוּ דִּבֶּר אֵלֵינוּ בְּחֹרֵב לֵאמֹר
ז רַב־לָכֶם שֶׁבֶת בָּהָר הַזֶּה: פְּנוּ ׀ וּסְעוּ לָכֶם וּבֹאוּ הַר הָאֱמֹרִי וְאֶל־כׇּל־שְׁכֵנָיו
בָּעֲרָבָה בָהָר וּבַשְּׁפֵלָה וּבַנֶּגֶב וּבְחוֹף הַיָּם אֶרֶץ הַכְּנַעֲנִי וְהַלְּבָנוֹן עַד־הַנָּהָר
ח הַגָּדֹל נְהַר־פְּרָת: *רְאֵה נָתַתִּי לִפְנֵיכֶם אֶת־הָאָרֶץ בֹּאוּ וּרְשׁוּ אֶת־הָאָרֶץ ישראל
אֲשֶׁר נִשְׁבַּע יהוה לַאֲבֹתֵיכֶם לְאַבְרָהָם לְיִצְחָק וּלְיַעֲקֹב לָתֵת לָהֶם וּלְזַרְעָם
ט אַחֲרֵיהֶם: וָאֹמַר אֲלֵכֶם בָּעֵת הַהִוא לֵאמֹר לֹא־אוּכַל לְבַדִּי שְׂאֵת אֶתְכֶם:
י יא יהוה אֱלֹהֵיכֶם הִרְבָּה אֶתְכֶם וְהִנְּכֶם הַיּוֹם כְּכוֹכְבֵי הַשָּׁמַיִם לָרֹב: *יהוה אֱלֹהֵי שני
אֲבוֹתֵכֶם יֹסֵף עֲלֵיכֶם כָּכֶם אֶלֶף פְּעָמִים וִיבָרֵךְ אֶתְכֶם כַּאֲשֶׁר דִּבֶּר לָכֶם:**
יב יג אֵיכָה אֶשָּׂא לְבַדִּי טׇרְחֲכֶם וּמַשַּׂאֲכֶם וְרִיבְכֶם: הָבוּ לָכֶם אֲנָשִׁים חֲכָמִים וּנְבֹנִים
יד וִידֻעִים לְשִׁבְטֵיכֶם וַאֲשִׂימֵם בְּרָאשֵׁיכֶם: וַתַּעֲנוּ אֹתִי וַתֹּאמְרוּ טוֹב־הַדָּבָר
טו אֲשֶׁר־דִּבַּרְתָּ לַעֲשׂוֹת: וָאֶקַּח אֶת־רָאשֵׁי שִׁבְטֵיכֶם אֲנָשִׁים חֲכָמִים וִידֻעִים
וָאֶתֵּן אֹתָם רָאשִׁים עֲלֵיכֶם שָׂרֵי אֲלָפִים וְשָׂרֵי מֵאוֹת וְשָׂרֵי חֲמִשִּׁים וְשָׂרֵי
טז עֲשָׂרֹת וְשֹׁטְרִים לְשִׁבְטֵיכֶם: וָאֲצַוֶּה אֶת־שֹׁפְטֵיכֶם בָּעֵת הַהִוא לֵאמֹר שָׁמֹעַ
יז בֵּין־אֲחֵיכֶם וּשְׁפַטְתֶּם צֶדֶק בֵּין־אִישׁ וּבֵין־אָחִיו וּבֵין גֵּרוֹ: לֹא־תַכִּירוּ פָנִים
בַּמִּשְׁפָּט כַּקָּטֹן כַּגָּדֹל תִּשְׁמָעוּן לֹא תָגוּרוּ מִפְּנֵי־אִישׁ כִּי הַמִּשְׁפָּט לֵאלֹהִים
יח הוּא וְהַדָּבָר אֲשֶׁר יִקְשֶׁה מִכֶּם תַּקְרִבוּן אֵלַי וּשְׁמַעְתִּיו: וָאֲצַוֶּה אֶתְכֶם בָּעֵת
יט הַהִוא אֵת כׇּל־הַדְּבָרִים אֲשֶׁר תַּעֲשׂוּן: וַנִּסַּע מֵחֹרֵב וַנֵּלֶךְ אֵת כׇּל־הַמִּדְבָּר

הַגָּדוֹל֙ וְהַנּוֹרָ֣א הַה֔וּא אֲשֶׁ֣ר רְאִיתֶ֔ם דֶּ֖רֶךְ הַ֣ר הָֽאֱמֹרִ֑י כַּאֲשֶׁ֥ר צִוָּ֛ה יְהֹוָ֥ה אֱלֹהֵ֖ינוּ
כ אֹתָ֑נוּ וַנָּבֹ֕א עַ֖ד קָדֵ֥שׁ בַּרְנֵֽעַ׃ וָאֹמַ֖ר אֲלֵכֶ֑ם בָּאתֶם֙ עַד־הַ֣ר הָֽאֱמֹרִ֔י אֲשֶׁר־יְהֹוָ֥ה
כא אֱלֹהֵ֖ינוּ נֹתֵ֥ן לָֽנוּ׃ רְ֠אֵה נָתַ֨ן יְהֹוָ֧ה אֱלֹהֶ֛יךָ לְפָנֶ֖יךָ אֶת־הָאָ֑רֶץ עֲלֵ֣ה רֵ֡שׁ כַּאֲשֶׁר֩
שלישי כב דִּבֶּ֨ר יְהֹוָ֜ה אֱלֹהֵ֤י אֲבֹתֶ֙יךָ֙ לָ֔ךְ אַל־תִּירָ֖א וְאַל־תֵּחָֽת׃ וַתִּקְרְב֣וּן אֵלַי֮ כֻּלְּכֶם֒
וַתֹּאמְר֗וּ נִשְׁלְחָ֤ה אֲנָשִׁים֙ לְפָנֵ֔ינוּ וְיַחְפְּרוּ־לָ֖נוּ אֶת־הָאָ֑רֶץ וְיָשִׁ֤בוּ אֹתָ֙נוּ֙ דָּבָ֔ר
כג אֶת־הַדֶּ֙רֶךְ֙ אֲשֶׁ֣ר נַעֲלֶה־בָּ֔הּ וְאֵת֙ הֶֽעָרִ֔ים אֲשֶׁ֥ר נָבֹ֖א אֲלֵיהֶֽן׃ וַיִּיטַ֥ב בְּעֵינַ֖י
כד הַדָּבָ֑ר וָאֶקַּ֤ח מִכֶּם֙ שְׁנֵ֣ים עָשָׂ֣ר אֲנָשִׁ֔ים אִ֥ישׁ אֶחָ֖ד לַשָּֽׁבֶט׃ וַיִּפְנוּ֙ וַיַּעֲל֣וּ הָהָ֔רָה
כה וַיָּבֹ֖אוּ עַד־נַ֣חַל אֶשְׁכֹּ֑ל וַֽיְרַגְּל֖וּ אֹתָֽהּ׃ וַיִּקְח֤וּ בְיָדָם֙ מִפְּרִ֣י הָאָ֔רֶץ וַיּוֹרִ֖דוּ אֵלֵ֑ינוּ
כו וַיָּשִׁ֨בוּ אֹתָ֤נוּ דָבָר֙ וַיֹּ֣אמְר֔וּ טוֹבָ֣ה הָאָ֔רֶץ אֲשֶׁר־יְהֹוָ֥ה אֱלֹהֵ֖ינוּ נֹתֵ֥ן לָֽנוּ׃ וְלֹ֥א
כז אֲבִיתֶ֖ם לַעֲלֹ֑ת וַתַּמְר֕וּ אֶת־פִּ֥י יְהֹוָ֖ה אֱלֹהֵיכֶֽם׃ וַתֵּרָגְנ֤וּ בְאָהֳלֵיכֶם֙ וַתֹּאמְר֔וּ
בְּשִׂנְאַ֤ת יְהֹוָה֙ אֹתָ֔נוּ הוֹצִיאָ֖נוּ מֵאֶ֣רֶץ מִצְרָ֑יִם לָתֵ֥ת אֹתָ֛נוּ בְּיַ֥ד הָאֱמֹרִ֖י
כח לְהַשְׁמִידֵֽנוּ׃ אָנָ֣ה ׀ אֲנַ֣חְנוּ עֹלִ֗ים אַחֵ֨ינוּ֙ הֵמַ֤סּוּ אֶת־לְבָבֵ֙נוּ֙ לֵאמֹ֔ר עַ֣ם גָּד֤וֹל
כט וָרָם֙ מִמֶּ֔נּוּ עָרִ֛ים גְּדֹלֹ֥ת וּבְצוּרֹ֖ת בַּשָּׁמָ֑יִם וְגַם־בְּנֵ֥י עֲנָקִ֖ים רָאִ֥ינוּ שָֽׁם׃ וָאֹמַ֖ר
ל אֲלֵכֶ֑ם לֹא־תַעַרְצ֥וּן וְלֹא־תִֽירְא֖וּן מֵהֶֽם׃ יְהֹוָ֤ה אֱלֹהֵיכֶם֙ הַהֹלֵ֣ךְ לִפְנֵיכֶ֔ם ה֖וּא
לא יִלָּחֵ֣ם לָכֶ֑ם כְּ֠כֹל אֲשֶׁ֨ר עָשָׂ֧ה אִתְּכֶ֛ם בְּמִצְרַ֖יִם לְעֵינֵיכֶֽם׃ וּבַמִּדְבָּר֙ אֲשֶׁ֣ר רָאִ֔יתָ
אֲשֶׁ֤ר נְשָׂאֲךָ֙ יְהֹוָ֣ה אֱלֹהֶ֔יךָ כַּאֲשֶׁ֥ר יִשָּׂא־אִ֖ישׁ אֶת־בְּנ֑וֹ בְּכָל־הַדֶּ֙רֶךְ֙ אֲשֶׁ֣ר הֲלַכְתֶּ֔ם
לב עַד־בֹּאֲכֶ֖ם עַד־הַמָּק֥וֹם הַזֶּֽה׃ וּבַדָּבָ֖ר הַזֶּ֑ה אֵֽינְכֶם֙ מַֽאֲמִינִ֔ם בַּיהֹוָ֖ה אֱלֹהֵיכֶֽם׃
לג הַהֹלֵ֨ךְ לִפְנֵיכֶ֜ם בַּדֶּ֗רֶךְ לָת֥וּר לָכֶ֛ם מָק֖וֹם לַחֲנֹֽתְכֶ֑ם בָּאֵ֣שׁ ׀ לַ֗יְלָה לַרְאֹֽתְכֶם֙
לד בַּדֶּ֙רֶךְ֙ אֲשֶׁ֣ר תֵּֽלְכוּ־בָ֔הּ וּבֶעָנָ֖ן יוֹמָֽם׃ וַיִּשְׁמַ֥ע יְהֹוָ֖ה אֶת־ק֣וֹל דִּבְרֵיכֶ֑ם וַיִּקְצֹ֖ף
לה וַיִּשָּׁבַ֥ע לֵאמֹֽר׃ אִם־יִרְאֶ֥ה אִישׁ֙ בָּאֲנָשִׁ֣ים הָאֵ֔לֶּה הַדּ֥וֹר הָרָ֖ע הַזֶּ֑ה אֵ֚ת הָאָ֣רֶץ
לו הַטּוֹבָ֔ה אֲשֶׁ֣ר נִשְׁבַּ֔עְתִּי לָתֵ֖ת לַאֲבֹתֵיכֶֽם׃ זוּלָתִ֞י כָּלֵ֤ב בֶּן־יְפֻנֶּה֙ ה֣וּא יִרְאֶ֔נָּה
לז וְלֽוֹ־אֶתֵּ֧ן אֶת־הָאָ֛רֶץ אֲשֶׁ֥ר דָּֽרַךְ־בָּ֖הּ וּלְבָנָ֑יו יַ֕עַן אֲשֶׁ֥ר מִלֵּ֖א אַחֲרֵ֥י יְהֹוָֽה׃ גַּם־
לח בִּי֙ הִתְאַנַּ֣ף יְהֹוָ֔ה בִּגְלַלְכֶ֖ם לֵאמֹ֑ר גַּם־אַתָּ֖ה לֹא־תָבֹ֥א שָֽׁם׃ יְהוֹשֻׁ֤עַ בִּן־נוּן֙
רביעי לט הָעֹמֵ֣ד לְפָנֶ֔יךָ ה֖וּא יָ֣בֹא שָׁ֑מָּה אֹת֣וֹ חַזֵּ֔ק כִּי־ה֖וּא יַנְחִלֶ֥נָּה אֶת־יִשְׂרָאֵֽל׃ וְטַפְּכֶם֩
אֲשֶׁ֨ר אֲמַרְתֶּ֜ם לָבַ֣ז יִהְיֶ֗ה וּ֠בְנֵיכֶם אֲשֶׁ֨ר לֹא־יָדְע֤וּ הַיּוֹם֙ ט֣וֹב וָרָ֔ע הֵ֖מָּה יָבֹ֣אוּ
מ שָׁ֑מָּה וְלָהֶ֣ם אֶתְּנֶ֔נָּה וְהֵ֖ם יִירָשֽׁוּהָ׃ וְאַתֶּ֖ם פְּנ֣וּ לָכֶ֑ם וּסְע֥וּ הַמִּדְבָּ֖רָה דֶּ֥רֶךְ יַם־
מא סֽוּף׃ וַתַּעֲנ֣וּ ׀ וַתֹּאמְר֣וּ אֵלַ֗י חָטָ֘אנוּ֮ לַיהֹוָה֒ אֲנַ֤חְנוּ נַעֲלֶה֙ וְנִלְחַ֔מְנוּ כְּכֹ֥ל אֲשֶׁר־
צִוָּ֖נוּ יְהֹוָ֣ה אֱלֹהֵ֑ינוּ וַתַּחְגְּר֗וּ אִ֚ישׁ אֶת־כְּלֵ֣י מִלְחַמְתּ֔וֹ וַתָּהִ֖ינוּ לַעֲלֹ֥ת הָהָֽרָה׃
מב וַיֹּ֨אמֶר יְהֹוָ֜ה אֵלַ֗י אֱמֹ֤ר לָהֶם֙ לֹ֣א תַֽעֲלוּ֙ וְלֹֽא־תִלָּ֣חֲמ֔וּ כִּ֥י אֵינֶ֖נִּי בְּקִרְבְּכֶ֑ם וְלֹ֣א

מג תִּנָּגְפוּ לִפְנֵי אֹיְבֵיכֶם: וָאֲדַבֵּר אֲלֵיכֶם וְלֹא שְׁמַעְתֶּם וַתַּמְרוּ אֶת־פִּי יהוה וַתָּזִדוּ
מד וַתַּעֲלוּ הָהָרָה: וַיֵּצֵא הָאֱמֹרִי הַיֹּשֵׁב בָּהָר הַהוּא לִקְרַאתְכֶם וַיִּרְדְּפוּ אֶתְכֶם
מה כַּאֲשֶׁר תַּעֲשֶׂינָה הַדְּבֹרִים וַיַּכְּתוּ אֶתְכֶם בְּשֵׂעִיר עַד־חָרְמָה: וַתָּשֻׁבוּ וַתִּבְכּוּ
מו לִפְנֵי יהוה וְלֹא־שָׁמַע יהוה בְּקֹלְכֶם וְלֹא הֶאֱזִין אֲלֵיכֶם: וַתֵּשְׁבוּ בְקָדֵשׁ יָמִים
ב א רַבִּים כַּיָּמִים אֲשֶׁר יְשַׁבְתֶּם: וַנֵּפֶן וַנִּסַּע הַמִּדְבָּרָה דֶּרֶךְ יַם־סוּף כַּאֲשֶׁר דִּבֶּר
ב יהוה אֵלָי וַנָּסָב אֶת־הַר־שֵׂעִיר יָמִים רַבִּים: וַיֹּאמֶר יהוה אֵלַי ב חמישי
ג ד לֵאמֹר: רַב־לָכֶם סֹב אֶת־הָהָר הַזֶּה פְּנוּ לָכֶם צָפֹנָה: וְאֶת־הָעָם צַו לֵאמֹר
אַתֶּם עֹבְרִים בִּגְבוּל אֲחֵיכֶם בְּנֵי־עֵשָׂו הַיֹּשְׁבִים בְּשֵׂעִיר וְיִירְאוּ מִכֶּם וְנִשְׁמַרְתֶּם
ה מְאֹד: אַל־תִּתְגָּרוּ בָם כִּי לֹא־אֶתֵּן לָכֶם מֵאַרְצָם עַד מִדְרַךְ כַּף־רָגֶל כִּי־יְרֻשָּׁה
ו לְעֵשָׂו נָתַתִּי אֶת־הַר שֵׂעִיר: אֹכֶל תִּשְׁבְּרוּ מֵאִתָּם בַּכֶּסֶף וַאֲכַלְתֶּם וְגַם־מַיִם
ז תִּכְרוּ מֵאִתָּם בַּכֶּסֶף וּשְׁתִיתֶם: כִּי יהוה אֱלֹהֶיךָ בֵּרַכְךָ בְּכֹל מַעֲשֵׂה יָדֶךָ יָדַע
לֶכְתְּךָ אֶת־הַמִּדְבָּר הַגָּדֹל הַזֶּה זֶה ׀ אַרְבָּעִים שָׁנָה יהוה אֱלֹהֶיךָ עִמָּךְ לֹא
ח חָסַרְתָּ דָּבָר: וַנַּעֲבֹר מֵאֵת אַחֵינוּ בְנֵי־עֵשָׂו הַיֹּשְׁבִים בְּשֵׂעִיר מִדֶּרֶךְ הָעֲרָבָה
ט מֵאֵילַת וּמֵעֶצְיֹן גָּבֶר וַנֵּפֶן וַנַּעֲבֹר דֶּרֶךְ מִדְבַּר מוֹאָב: וַיֹּאמֶר יהוה
אֵלַי אַל־תָּצַר אֶת־מוֹאָב וְאַל־תִּתְגָּר בָּם מִלְחָמָה כִּי לֹא־אֶתֵּן לְךָ מֵאַרְצוֹ
י יְרֻשָּׁה כִּי לִבְנֵי־לוֹט נָתַתִּי אֶת־עָר יְרֻשָּׁה: הָאֵמִים לְפָנִים יָשְׁבוּ בָהּ עַם גָּדוֹל
יא וְרַב וָרָם כָּעֲנָקִים: רְפָאִים יֵחָשְׁבוּ אַף־הֵם כָּעֲנָקִים וְהַמֹּאָבִים יִקְרְאוּ לָהֶם
יב אֵמִים: וּבְשֵׂעִיר יָשְׁבוּ הַחֹרִים לְפָנִים וּבְנֵי עֵשָׂו יִירָשׁוּם וַיַּשְׁמִידוּם מִפְּנֵיהֶם
וַיֵּשְׁבוּ תַּחְתָּם כַּאֲשֶׁר עָשָׂה יִשְׂרָאֵל לְאֶרֶץ יְרֻשָּׁתוֹ אֲשֶׁר־נָתַן יהוה לָהֶם:
יג יד עַתָּה קֻמוּ וְעִבְרוּ לָכֶם אֶת־נַחַל זָרֶד וַנַּעֲבֹר אֶת־נַחַל זָרֶד: וְהַיָּמִים אֲשֶׁר־
הָלַכְנוּ ׀ מִקָּדֵשׁ בַּרְנֵעַ עַד אֲשֶׁר־עָבַרְנוּ אֶת־נַחַל זֶרֶד שְׁלֹשִׁים וּשְׁמֹנֶה שָׁנָה
עַד־תֹּם כָּל־הַדּוֹר אַנְשֵׁי הַמִּלְחָמָה מִקֶּרֶב הַמַּחֲנֶה כַּאֲשֶׁר נִשְׁבַּע יהוה לָהֶם:
טו טז וְגַם יַד־יהוה הָיְתָה בָּם לְהֻמָּם מִקֶּרֶב הַמַּחֲנֶה עַד תֻּמָּם: וַיְהִי כַאֲשֶׁר־תַּמּוּ
יז כָּל־אַנְשֵׁי הַמִּלְחָמָה לָמוּת מִקֶּרֶב הָעָם: וַיְדַבֵּר יהוה אֵלַי לֵאמֹר:
יח יט אַתָּה עֹבֵר הַיּוֹם אֶת־גְּבוּל מוֹאָב אֶת־עָר: וְקָרַבְתָּ מוּל בְּנֵי עַמּוֹן אַל־תְּצֻרֵם
וְאַל־תִּתְגָּר בָּם כִּי לֹא־אֶתֵּן מֵאֶרֶץ בְּנֵי־עַמּוֹן לְךָ יְרֻשָּׁה כִּי לִבְנֵי־לוֹט נְתַתִּיהָ
כ יְרֻשָּׁה: אֶרֶץ־רְפָאִים תֵּחָשֵׁב אַף־הִוא רְפָאִים יָשְׁבוּ־בָהּ לְפָנִים וְהָעַמֹּנִים
כא יִקְרְאוּ לָהֶם זַמְזֻמִּים: עַם גָּדוֹל וְרַב וָרָם כָּעֲנָקִים וַיַּשְׁמִידֵם יהוה מִפְּנֵיהֶם
כב וַיִּירָשֻׁם וַיֵּשְׁבוּ תַחְתָּם: כַּאֲשֶׁר עָשָׂה לִבְנֵי עֵשָׂו הַיֹּשְׁבִים בְּשֵׂעִיר אֲשֶׁר הִשְׁמִיד

אֶת־הַחֹרִי֙ מִפְּנֵיהֶ֔ם וַיִּירָשֻׁ֖ם וַיֵּשְׁב֥וּ תַחְתָּ֖ם עַ֥ד הַיּ֖וֹם הַזֶּֽה׃ וְהָעַוִּ֛ים הַיֹּשְׁבִ֥ים כג
בַּחֲצֵרִ֖ים עַד־עַזָּ֑ה כַּפְתֹּרִים֙ הַיֹּצְאִ֣ים מִכַּפְתֹּ֔ר הִשְׁמִידֻ֖ם וַיֵּשְׁב֥וּ תַחְתָּֽם׃ ק֣וּמוּ כד
סְּע֗וּ וְעִבְרוּ֮ אֶת־נַ֣חַל אַרְנֹן֒ רְאֵ֣ה נָתַ֣תִּי בְ֠יָדְךָ אֶת־סִיחֹ֨ן מֶֽלֶךְ־חֶשְׁבּ֧וֹן הָֽאֱמֹרִ֛י
וְאֶת־אַרְצ֖וֹ הָחֵ֣ל רָ֑שׁ וְהִתְגָּ֥ר בּ֖וֹ מִלְחָמָֽה׃ הַיּ֣וֹם הַזֶּ֗ה אָחֵל֙ תֵּ֤ת פַּחְדְּךָ֙ וְיִרְאָ֣תְךָ֔ כה
עַל־פְּנֵי֙ הָֽעַמִּ֔ים תַּ֖חַת כָּל־הַשָּׁמָ֑יִם אֲשֶׁ֤ר יִשְׁמְעוּן֙ שִׁמְעֲךָ֔ וְרָגְז֥וּ וְחָל֖וּ מִפָּנֶֽיךָ׃
וָאֶשְׁלַ֤ח מַלְאָכִים֙ מִמִּדְבַּ֣ר קְדֵמ֔וֹת אֶל־סִיח֖וֹן מֶ֣לֶךְ חֶשְׁבּ֑וֹן דִּבְרֵ֥י שָׁל֖וֹם לֵאמֹֽר׃ כו
אֶעְבְּרָ֣ה בְאַרְצֶ֔ךָ בַּדֶּ֥רֶךְ בַּדֶּ֖רֶךְ אֵלֵ֑ךְ לֹ֥א אָס֖וּר יָמִ֥ין וּשְׂמֹֽאול׃ אֹ֣כֶל בַּכֶּ֤סֶף כז כח
תַּשְׁבִּרֵ֙נִי֙ וְאָכַ֔לְתִּי וּמַ֛יִם בַּכֶּ֥סֶף תִּתֶּן־לִ֖י וְשָׁתִ֑יתִי רַ֖ק אֶעְבְּרָ֥ה בְרַגְלָֽי׃ כַּאֲשֶׁ֨ר כט
עָֽשׂוּ־לִ֜י בְּנֵ֣י עֵשָׂ֗ו הַיֹּֽשְׁבִים֙ בְּשֵׂעִ֔יר וְהַמּ֣וֹאָבִ֔ים הַיֹּשְׁבִ֖ים בְּעָ֑ר עַ֤ד אֲשֶׁר־אֶֽעֱבֹר֙
אֶת־הַיַּרְדֵּ֔ן אֶל־הָאָ֕רֶץ אֲשֶׁר־יְהוָ֥ה אֱלֹהֵ֖ינוּ נֹתֵ֥ן לָֽנוּ׃ וְלֹ֣א אָבָ֗ה סִיחֹן֙ מֶ֣לֶךְ ל
חֶשְׁבּ֔וֹן הַעֲבִרֵ֖נוּ בּ֑וֹ כִּֽי־הִקְשָׁה֩ יְהוָ֨ה אֱלֹהֶ֜יךָ אֶת־רוּח֗וֹ וְאִמֵּץ֙ אֶת־לְבָב֔וֹ לְמַ֛עַן
ששי ג תִּתּ֥וֹ בְיָדְךָ֖ כַּיּ֥וֹם הַזֶּֽה׃ וַיֹּ֤אמֶר יְהוָה֙ אֵלַ֔י רְאֵ֗ה הַחִלֹּ֙תִי֙ תֵּ֣ת לְפָנֶ֔יךָ לא
אֶת־סִיחֹ֖ן וְאֶת־אַרְצ֑וֹ הָחֵ֣ל רָ֔שׁ לָרֶ֖שֶׁת אֶת־אַרְצֽוֹ׃ וַיֵּצֵ֨א סִיחֹ֜ן לִקְרָאתֵ֗נוּ ה֛וּא לב
וְכָל־עַמּ֖וֹ לַמִּלְחָמָ֑ה יָֽהְצָה׃ וַֽיִּתְּנֵ֛הוּ יְהוָ֥ה אֱלֹהֵ֖ינוּ לְפָנֵ֑ינוּ וַנַּ֥ךְ אֹת֛וֹ וְאֶת־בָּנָ֖ו לג
וְאֶת־כָּל־עַמּֽוֹ׃ וַנִּלְכֹּ֤ד אֶת־כָּל־עָרָיו֙ בָּעֵ֣ת הַהִ֔וא וַנַּחֲרֵם֙ אֶת־כָּל־עִ֣יר מְתִ֔ם לד
וְהַנָּשִׁ֖ים וְהַטָּ֑ף לֹ֥א הִשְׁאַ֖רְנוּ שָׂרִֽיד׃ רַ֥ק הַבְּהֵמָ֖ה בָּזַ֣זְנוּ לָ֑נוּ וּשְׁלַ֥ל הֶעָרִ֖ים אֲשֶׁ֥ר לה
לָכָֽדְנוּ׃ מֵעֲרֹעֵ֞ר אֲשֶׁ֨ר עַל־שְׂפַת־נַ֜חַל אַרְנֹ֗ן וְהָעִ֨יר אֲשֶׁ֤ר בַּנַּ֙חַל֙ וְעַד־הַגִּלְעָ֔ד לו
לֹ֤א הָֽיְתָה֙ קִרְיָ֔ה אֲשֶׁ֥ר שָׂגְבָ֖ה מִמֶּ֑נּוּ אֶת־הַכֹּ֕ל נָתַ֛ן יְהוָ֥ה אֱלֹהֵ֖ינוּ לְפָנֵֽינוּ׃ רַ֛ק לז
אֶל־אֶ֥רֶץ בְּנֵֽי־עַמּ֖וֹן לֹ֣א קָרָ֑בְתָּ כָּל־יַ֞ד נַ֤חַל יַבֹּק֙ וְעָרֵ֣י הָהָ֔ר וְכֹ֥ל אֲשֶׁר־צִוָּ֖ה
יְהוָ֥ה אֱלֹהֵֽינוּ׃ וַנֵּ֣פֶן וַנַּ֔עַל דֶּ֖רֶךְ הַבָּשָׁ֑ן וַיֵּצֵ֣א עוֹג֩ מֶֽלֶךְ־הַבָּשָׁ֨ן לִקְרָאתֵ֜נוּ ה֧וּא א ג
וְכָל־עַמּ֛וֹ לַמִּלְחָמָ֖ה אֶדְרֶֽעִי׃ וַיֹּ֨אמֶר יְהוָ֤ה אֵלַי֙ אַל־תִּירָ֣א אֹת֔וֹ כִּ֣י בְיָדְךָ֞ נָתַ֧תִּי ב
אֹת֛וֹ וְאֶת־כָּל־עַמּ֖וֹ וְאֶת־אַרְצ֑וֹ וְעָשִׂ֣יתָ לּ֔וֹ כַּאֲשֶׁ֣ר עָשִׂ֗יתָ לְסִיחֹן֙ מֶ֣לֶךְ הָֽאֱמֹרִ֔י
אֲשֶׁ֥ר יוֹשֵׁ֖ב בְּחֶשְׁבּֽוֹן׃ וַיִּתֵּן֩ יְהוָ֨ה אֱלֹהֵ֜ינוּ בְּיָדֵ֗נוּ גַּ֛ם אֶת־ע֥וֹג מֶֽלֶךְ־הַבָּשָׁ֖ן וְאֶת־ ג
כָּל־עַמּ֑וֹ וַנַּכֵּ֕הוּ עַד־בִּלְתִּ֥י הִשְׁאִֽיר־ל֖וֹ שָׂרִֽיד׃ וַנִּלְכֹּ֤ד אֶת־כָּל־עָרָיו֙ בָּעֵ֣ת הַהִ֔וא ד
לֹ֤א הָֽיְתָה֙ קִרְיָ֔ה אֲשֶׁ֥ר לֹא־לָקַ֖חְנוּ מֵאִתָּ֑ם שִׁשִּׁ֥ים עִיר֙ כָּל־חֶ֣בֶל אַרְגֹּ֔ב מַמְלֶ֖כֶת
ע֥וֹג בַּבָּשָֽׁן׃ כָּל־אֵ֜לֶּה עָרִ֧ים בְּצֻר֛וֹת חוֹמָ֥ה גְבֹהָ֖ה דְּלָתַ֣יִם וּבְרִ֑יחַ לְבַ֛ד מֵעָרֵ֥י ה
הַפְּרָזִ֖י הַרְבֵּ֥ה מְאֹֽד׃ וַנַּחֲרֵ֣ם אוֹתָ֔ם כַּאֲשֶׁ֣ר עָשִׂ֔ינוּ לְסִיחֹ֖ן מֶ֣לֶךְ חֶשְׁבּ֑וֹן הַחֲרֵם֙ ו
כָּל־עִ֣יר מְתִ֔ם הַנָּשִׁ֖ים וְהַטָּֽף׃ וְכָל־הַבְּהֵמָ֛ה וּשְׁלַ֥ל הֶעָרִ֖ים בַּזּ֥וֹנוּ לָֽנוּ׃ וַנִּקַּ֞ח ז ח
בָּעֵ֣ת הַהִ֗וא אֶת־הָאָ֔רֶץ מִיַּ֕ד שְׁנֵי֙ מַלְכֵ֣י הָֽאֱמֹרִ֔י אֲשֶׁ֖ר בְּעֵ֣בֶר הַיַּרְדֵּ֑ן מִנַּ֥חַל

ט אַרְנֹן עַד־הַר חֶרְמוֹן׃ צִידֹנִים יִקְרְאוּ לְחֶרְמוֹן שִׂרְיֹן וְהָאֱמֹרִי יִקְרְאוּ־לוֹ שְׂנִיר׃
י כֹּל ׀ עָרֵי הַמִּישֹׁר וְכָל־הַגִּלְעָד וְכָל־הַבָּשָׁן עַד־סַלְכָה וְאֶדְרֶעִי עָרֵי מַמְלֶכֶת
יא עוֹג בַּבָּשָׁן׃ כִּי רַק־עוֹג מֶלֶךְ הַבָּשָׁן נִשְׁאַר מִיֶּתֶר הָרְפָאִים הִנֵּה עַרְשׂוֹ עֶרֶשׂ
בַּרְזֶל הֲלֹה הִוא בְּרַבַּת בְּנֵי עַמּוֹן תֵּשַׁע אַמּוֹת אָרְכָּהּ וְאַרְבַּע אַמּוֹת רָחְבָּהּ
יב בְּאַמַּת־אִישׁ׃ וְאֶת־הָאָרֶץ הַזֹּאת יָרַשְׁנוּ בָּעֵת הַהִוא מֵעֲרֹעֵר אֲשֶׁר־עַל־נַחַל
יג אַרְנֹן וַחֲצִי הַר־הַגִּלְעָד וְעָרָיו נָתַתִּי לָראוּבֵנִי וְלַגָּדִי׃ וְיֶתֶר הַגִּלְעָד וְכָל־
הַבָּשָׁן מַמְלֶכֶת עוֹג נָתַתִּי לַחֲצִי שֵׁבֶט הַמְנַשֶּׁה כֹּל חֶבֶל הָאַרְגֹּב לְכָל־הַבָּשָׁן
יד הַהוּא יִקָּרֵא אֶרֶץ רְפָאִים׃ יָאִיר בֶּן־מְנַשֶּׁה לָקַח אֶת־כָּל־חֶבֶל אַרְגֹּב עַד־
גְּבוּל הַגְּשׁוּרִי וְהַמַּעֲכָתִי וַיִּקְרָא אֹתָם עַל־שְׁמוֹ אֶת־הַבָּשָׁן חַוֺּת יָאִיר עַד הַיּוֹם
טו טז הַזֶּה׃ *וּלְמָכִיר נָתַתִּי אֶת־הַגִּלְעָד׃ וְלָראוּבֵנִי וְלַגָּדִי נָתַתִּי מִן־הַגִּלְעָד וְעַד־ שביעי
יז נַחַל אַרְנֹן תּוֹךְ הַנַּחַל וּגְבֻל וְעַד יַבֹּק הַנַּחַל גְּבוּל בְּנֵי עַמּוֹן׃ וְהָעֲרָבָה וְהַיַּרְדֵּן
יח וּגְבֻל מִכִּנֶּרֶת וְעַד יָם הָעֲרָבָה יָם הַמֶּלַח תַּחַת אַשְׁדֹּת הַפִּסְגָּה מִזְרָחָה׃ וָאֲצַו
אֶתְכֶם בָּעֵת הַהִוא לֵאמֹר יְהוָה אֱלֹהֵיכֶם נָתַן לָכֶם אֶת־הָאָרֶץ הַזֹּאת לְרִשְׁתָּהּ
יט חֲלוּצִים תַּעַבְרוּ לִפְנֵי אֲחֵיכֶם בְּנֵי־יִשְׂרָאֵל כָּל־בְּנֵי־חָיִל׃ רַק נְשֵׁיכֶם וְטַפְּכֶם
כ וּמִקְנֵכֶם יָדַעְתִּי כִּי־מִקְנֶה רַב לָכֶם יֵשְׁבוּ בְּעָרֵיכֶם אֲשֶׁר נָתַתִּי לָכֶם׃ עַד אֲשֶׁר־ מפטיר
יָנִיחַ יְהוָה ׀ לַאֲחֵיכֶם כָּכֶם וְיָרְשׁוּ גַם־הֵם אֶת־הָאָרֶץ אֲשֶׁר יְהוָה אֱלֹהֵיכֶם נֹתֵן
כא לָהֶם בְּעֵבֶר הַיַּרְדֵּן וְשַׁבְתֶּם אִישׁ לִירֻשָּׁתוֹ אֲשֶׁר נָתַתִּי לָכֶם׃ וְאֶת־יְהוֹשׁוּעַ
צִוֵּיתִי בָּעֵת הַהִוא לֵאמֹר עֵינֶיךָ הָרֹאֹת אֵת כָּל־אֲשֶׁר עָשָׂה יְהוָה אֱלֹהֵיכֶם
לִשְׁנֵי הַמְּלָכִים הָאֵלֶּה כֵּן־יַעֲשֶׂה יְהוָה לְכָל־הַמַּמְלָכוֹת אֲשֶׁר אַתָּה עֹבֵר שָׁמָּה׃
כב כג לֹא תִּירָאוּם כִּי יְהוָה אֱלֹהֵיכֶם הוּא הַנִּלְחָם לָכֶם׃ וָאֶתְחַנַּן אֶל־ ד ואתחנן
יְהוָה בָּעֵת הַהִוא לֵאמֹר׃ אֲדֹנָי יֱהוִה אַתָּה הַחִלּוֹתָ לְהַרְאוֹת אֶת־עַבְדְּךָ
אֶת־גָּדְלְךָ וְאֶת־יָדְךָ הַחֲזָקָה אֲשֶׁר מִי־אֵל בַּשָּׁמַיִם וּבָאָרֶץ אֲשֶׁר־יַעֲשֶׂה
כד כְמַעֲשֶׂיךָ וְכִגְבוּרֹתֶךָ׃ אֶעְבְּרָה־נָּא וְאֶרְאֶה אֶת־הָאָרֶץ הַטּוֹבָה אֲשֶׁר בְּעֵבֶר
כה הַיַּרְדֵּן הָהָר הַטּוֹב הַזֶּה וְהַלְּבָנֹן׃ *וַיִּתְעַבֵּר יְהוָה בִּי לְמַעַנְכֶם וְלֹא שָׁמַע אֵלָי לוי
כו וַיֹּאמֶר יְהוָה אֵלַי רַב־לָךְ אַל־תּוֹסֶף דַּבֵּר אֵלַי עוֹד בַּדָּבָר הַזֶּה׃ עֲלֵה ׀ רֹאשׁ
הַפִּסְגָּה וְשָׂא עֵינֶיךָ יָמָּה וְצָפֹנָה וְתֵימָנָה וּמִזְרָחָה וּרְאֵה בְעֵינֶיךָ כִּי־לֹא
כז תַעֲבֹר אֶת־הַיַּרְדֵּן הַזֶּה׃ וְצַו אֶת־יְהוֹשֻׁעַ וְחַזְּקֵהוּ וְאַמְּצֵהוּ כִּי־הוּא יַעֲבֹר
כח לִפְנֵי הָעָם הַזֶּה וְהוּא יַנְחִיל אוֹתָם אֶת־הָאָרֶץ אֲשֶׁר תִּרְאֶה׃ וַנֵּשֶׁב בַּגָּיְא מוּל
בֵּית פְּעוֹר׃

וְעַתָּה יִשְׂרָאֵל שְׁמַע אֶל־הַחֻקִּים וְאֶל־הַמִּשְׁפָּטִים אֲשֶׁר אָנֹכִי מְלַמֵּד אֶתְכֶם ד א
לַעֲשׂוֹת לְמַעַן תִּחְיוּ וּבָאתֶם וִירִשְׁתֶּם אֶת־הָאָרֶץ אֲשֶׁר יהוה אֱלֹהֵי אֲבֹתֵיכֶם
נֹתֵן לָכֶם: לֹא תֹסִפוּ עַל־הַדָּבָר אֲשֶׁר אָנֹכִי מְצַוֶּה אֶתְכֶם וְלֹא תִגְרְעוּ מִמֶּנּוּ ב
לִשְׁמֹר אֶת־מִצְוֹת יהוה אֱלֹהֵיכֶם אֲשֶׁר אָנֹכִי מְצַוֶּה אֶתְכֶם: עֵינֵיכֶם הָרֹאוֹת ג
אֵת אֲשֶׁר־עָשָׂה יהוה בְּבַעַל פְּעוֹר כִּי כָל־הָאִישׁ אֲשֶׁר הָלַךְ אַחֲרֵי בַעַל־פְּעוֹר
הִשְׁמִידוֹ יהוה אֱלֹהֶיךָ מִקִּרְבֶּךָ: וְאַתֶּם הַדְּבֵקִים בַּיהוה אֱלֹהֵיכֶם חַיִּים כֻּלְּכֶם ד
(שני (ישראל הַיּוֹם: *רְאֵה ׀ לִמַּדְתִּי אֶתְכֶם חֻקִּים וּמִשְׁפָּטִים כַּאֲשֶׁר צִוַּנִי יהוה אֱלֹהָי לַעֲשׂוֹת ה
כֵּן בְּקֶרֶב הָאָרֶץ אֲשֶׁר אַתֶּם בָּאִים שָׁמָּה לְרִשְׁתָּהּ: וּשְׁמַרְתֶּם וַעֲשִׂיתֶם כִּי ו
הִוא חָכְמַתְכֶם וּבִינַתְכֶם לְעֵינֵי הָעַמִּים אֲשֶׁר יִשְׁמְעוּן אֵת כָּל־הַחֻקִּים הָאֵלֶּה
וְאָמְרוּ רַק עַם־חָכָם וְנָבוֹן הַגּוֹי הַגָּדוֹל הַזֶּה: כִּי מִי־גוֹי גָּדוֹל אֲשֶׁר־לוֹ אֱלֹהִים ז
קְרֹבִים אֵלָיו כַּיהוה אֱלֹהֵינוּ בְּכָל־קָרְאֵנוּ אֵלָיו: וּמִי גּוֹי גָּדוֹל אֲשֶׁר־לוֹ חֻקִּים ח
וּמִשְׁפָּטִים צַדִּיקִם כְּכֹל הַתּוֹרָה הַזֹּאת אֲשֶׁר אָנֹכִי נֹתֵן לִפְנֵיכֶם הַיּוֹם: **רַק ט
הִשָּׁמֶר לְךָ וּשְׁמֹר נַפְשְׁךָ מְאֹד פֶּן־תִּשְׁכַּח אֶת־הַדְּבָרִים אֲשֶׁר־רָאוּ עֵינֶיךָ וּפֶן־
יָסוּרוּ מִלְּבָבְךָ כֹּל יְמֵי חַיֶּיךָ וְהוֹדַעְתָּם לְבָנֶיךָ וְלִבְנֵי בָנֶיךָ: יוֹם אֲשֶׁר עָמַדְתָּ י
לִפְנֵי יהוה אֱלֹהֶיךָ בְּחֹרֵב בֶּאֱמֹר יהוה אֵלַי הַקְהֶל־לִי אֶת־הָעָם וְאַשְׁמִעֵם
אֶת־דְּבָרָי אֲשֶׁר יִלְמְדוּן לְיִרְאָה אֹתִי כָּל־הַיָּמִים אֲשֶׁר הֵם חַיִּים עַל־הָאֲדָמָה
וְאֶת־בְּנֵיהֶם יְלַמֵּדוּן: וַתִּקְרְבוּן וַתַּעַמְדוּן תַּחַת הָהָר וְהָהָר בֹּעֵר בָּאֵשׁ עַד־ יא
לֵב הַשָּׁמַיִם חֹשֶׁךְ עָנָן וַעֲרָפֶל: וַיְדַבֵּר יהוה אֲלֵיכֶם מִתּוֹךְ הָאֵשׁ קוֹל דְּבָרִים יב
אַתֶּם שֹׁמְעִים וּתְמוּנָה אֵינְכֶם רֹאִים זוּלָתִי קוֹל: וַיַּגֵּד לָכֶם אֶת־בְּרִיתוֹ אֲשֶׁר יג
צִוָּה אֶתְכֶם לַעֲשׂוֹת עֲשֶׂרֶת הַדְּבָרִים וַיִּכְתְּבֵם עַל־שְׁנֵי לֻחוֹת אֲבָנִים: וְאֹתִי יד
צִוָּה יהוה בָּעֵת הַהִוא לְלַמֵּד אֶתְכֶם חֻקִּים וּמִשְׁפָּטִים לַעֲשֹׂתְכֶם אֹתָם בָּאָרֶץ
אֲשֶׁר אַתֶּם עֹבְרִים שָׁמָּה לְרִשְׁתָּהּ: וְנִשְׁמַרְתֶּם מְאֹד לְנַפְשֹׁתֵיכֶם כִּי לֹא רְאִיתֶם טו
כָּל־תְּמוּנָה בְּיוֹם דִּבֶּר יהוה אֲלֵיכֶם בְּחֹרֵב מִתּוֹךְ הָאֵשׁ: פֶּן־תַּשְׁחִתוּן וַעֲשִׂיתֶם טז
לָכֶם פֶּסֶל תְּמוּנַת כָּל־סָמֶל תַּבְנִית זָכָר אוֹ נְקֵבָה: תַּבְנִית כָּל־בְּהֵמָה אֲשֶׁר יז
בָּאָרֶץ תַּבְנִית כָּל־צִפּוֹר כָּנָף אֲשֶׁר תָּעוּף בַּשָּׁמָיִם: תַּבְנִית כָּל־רֹמֵשׂ בָּאֲדָמָה יח
תַּבְנִית כָּל־דָּגָה אֲשֶׁר־בַּמַּיִם מִתַּחַת לָאָרֶץ: וּפֶן־תִּשָּׂא עֵינֶיךָ הַשָּׁמַיְמָה יט
וְרָאִיתָ אֶת־הַשֶּׁמֶשׁ וְאֶת־הַיָּרֵחַ וְאֶת־הַכּוֹכָבִים כֹּל צְבָא הַשָּׁמַיִם וְנִדַּחְתָּ
וְהִשְׁתַּחֲוִיתָ לָהֶם וַעֲבַדְתָּם אֲשֶׁר חָלַק יהוה אֱלֹהֶיךָ אֹתָם לְכֹל הָעַמִּים תַּחַת
כָּל־הַשָּׁמָיִם: וְאֶתְכֶם לָקַח יהוה וַיּוֹצִא אֶתְכֶם מִכּוּר הַבַּרְזֶל מִמִּצְרָיִם לִהְיוֹת כ

כא לוֹ לְעַם נַחֲלָה כַּיּוֹם הַזֶּה: וַיהוָה הִתְאַנַּף־בִּי עַל־דִּבְרֵיכֶם וַיִּשָּׁבַע לְבִלְתִּי
עָבְרִי אֶת־הַיַּרְדֵּן וּלְבִלְתִּי־בֹא אֶל־הָאָרֶץ הַטּוֹבָה אֲשֶׁר יהוָה אֱלֹהֶיךָ נֹתֵן
כב לְךָ נַחֲלָה: כִּי אָנֹכִי מֵת בָּאָרֶץ הַזֹּאת אֵינֶנִּי עֹבֵר אֶת־הַיַּרְדֵּן וְאַתֶּם עֹבְרִים
כג וִירִשְׁתֶּם אֶת־הָאָרֶץ הַטּוֹבָה הַזֹּאת: הִשָּׁמְרוּ לָכֶם פֶּן־תִּשְׁכְּחוּ אֶת־בְּרִית
יהוָה אֱלֹהֵיכֶם אֲשֶׁר כָּרַת עִמָּכֶם וַעֲשִׂיתֶם לָכֶם פֶּסֶל תְּמוּנַת כֹּל אֲשֶׁר צִוְּךָ
כד יהוָה אֱלֹהֶיךָ: כִּי יהוָה אֱלֹהֶיךָ אֵשׁ אֹכְלָה הוּא אֵל קַנָּא:
כה כִּי־תוֹלִיד בָּנִים וּבְנֵי בָנִים וְנוֹשַׁנְתֶּם בָּאָרֶץ וְהִשְׁחַתֶּם וַעֲשִׂיתֶם פֶּסֶל תְּמוּנַת (קריאה לתשעה באב
כו כֹּל וַעֲשִׂיתֶם הָרַע בְּעֵינֵי־יהוָה אֱלֹהֶיךָ לְהַכְעִיסוֹ: הַעִידֹתִי בָכֶם הַיּוֹם אֶת־ ד:כה-מ)
הַשָּׁמַיִם וְאֶת־הָאָרֶץ כִּי־אָבֹד תֹּאבֵדוּן מַהֵר מֵעַל הָאָרֶץ אֲשֶׁר אַתֶּם עֹבְרִים
אֶת־הַיַּרְדֵּן שָׁמָּה לְרִשְׁתָּהּ לֹא־תַאֲרִיכֻן יָמִים עָלֶיהָ כִּי הִשָּׁמֵד תִּשָּׁמֵדוּן:
כז וְהֵפִיץ יהוָה אֶתְכֶם בָּעַמִּים וְנִשְׁאַרְתֶּם מְתֵי מִסְפָּר בַּגּוֹיִם אֲשֶׁר יְנַהֵג יהוָה
כח אֶתְכֶם שָׁמָּה: וַעֲבַדְתֶּם־שָׁם אֱלֹהִים מַעֲשֵׂה יְדֵי אָדָם עֵץ וָאֶבֶן אֲשֶׁר לֹא־
כט יִרְאוּן וְלֹא יִשְׁמְעוּן וְלֹא יֹאכְלוּן וְלֹא יְרִיחֻן: וּבִקַּשְׁתֶּם מִשָּׁם אֶת־יהוָה אֱלֹהֶיךָ
ל וּמָצָאתָ כִּי תִדְרְשֶׁנּוּ בְּכָל־לְבָבְךָ וּבְכָל־נַפְשֶׁךָ: בַּצַּר לְךָ וּמְצָאוּךָ כֹּל הַדְּבָרִים
לא הָאֵלֶּה בְּאַחֲרִית הַיָּמִים וְשַׁבְתָּ עַד־יהוָה אֱלֹהֶיךָ וְשָׁמַעְתָּ בְּקֹלוֹ: כִּי אֵל רַחוּם
יהוָה אֱלֹהֶיךָ לֹא יַרְפְּךָ וְלֹא יַשְׁחִיתֶךָ וְלֹא יִשְׁכַּח אֶת־בְּרִית אֲבֹתֶיךָ אֲשֶׁר
לב נִשְׁבַּע לָהֶם: כִּי שְׁאַל־נָא לְיָמִים רִאשֹׁנִים אֲשֶׁר־הָיוּ לְפָנֶיךָ לְמִן־הַיּוֹם אֲשֶׁר
בָּרָא אֱלֹהִים ׀ אָדָם עַל־הָאָרֶץ וּלְמִקְצֵה הַשָּׁמַיִם וְעַד־קְצֵה הַשָּׁמָיִם הֲנִהְיָה
לג כַּדָּבָר הַגָּדוֹל הַזֶּה אוֹ הֲנִשְׁמַע כָּמֹהוּ: הֲשָׁמַע עָם קוֹל אֱלֹהִים מְדַבֵּר מִתּוֹךְ־
לד הָאֵשׁ כַּאֲשֶׁר־שָׁמַעְתָּ אַתָּה וַיֶּחִי: אוֹ ׀ הֲנִסָּה אֱלֹהִים לָבוֹא לָקַחַת לוֹ גוֹי
מִקֶּרֶב גּוֹי בְּמַסֹּת בְּאֹתֹת וּבְמוֹפְתִים וּבְמִלְחָמָה וּבְיָד חֲזָקָה וּבִזְרוֹעַ נְטוּיָה
וּבְמוֹרָאִים גְּדֹלִים כְּכֹל אֲשֶׁר־עָשָׂה לָכֶם יהוָה אֱלֹהֵיכֶם בְּמִצְרַיִם לְעֵינֶיךָ:
לה לו אַתָּה הָרְאֵתָ לָדַעַת כִּי יהוָה הוּא הָאֱלֹהִים אֵין עוֹד מִלְבַדּוֹ: מִן־הַשָּׁמַיִם
הִשְׁמִיעֲךָ אֶת־קֹלוֹ לְיַסְּרֶךָּ וְעַל־הָאָרֶץ הֶרְאֲךָ אֶת־אִשּׁוֹ הַגְּדוֹלָה וּדְבָרָיו
לז שָׁמַעְתָּ מִתּוֹךְ הָאֵשׁ: וְתַחַת כִּי אָהַב אֶת־אֲבֹתֶיךָ וַיִּבְחַר בְּזַרְעוֹ אַחֲרָיו
לח וַיּוֹצִאֲךָ בְּפָנָיו בְּכֹחוֹ הַגָּדֹל מִמִּצְרָיִם: לְהוֹרִישׁ גּוֹיִם גְּדֹלִים וַעֲצֻמִים מִמְּךָ
לט מִפָּנֶיךָ לַהֲבִיאֲךָ לָתֶת־לְךָ אֶת־אַרְצָם נַחֲלָה כַּיּוֹם הַזֶּה: וְיָדַעְתָּ הַיּוֹם וַהֲשֵׁבֹתָ
אֶל־לְבָבֶךָ כִּי יהוָה הוּא הָאֱלֹהִים בַּשָּׁמַיִם מִמַּעַל וְעַל־הָאָרֶץ מִתָּחַת אֵין
מ עוֹד: וְשָׁמַרְתָּ אֶת־חֻקָּיו וְאֶת־מִצְוֹתָיו אֲשֶׁר אָנֹכִי מְצַוְּךָ הַיּוֹם אֲשֶׁר יִיטַב

The Haftara for Tisha B'Av, page 1096

לְךָ וּלְבָנֶיךָ אַחֲרֶיךָ וּלְמַעַן תַּאֲרִיךְ יָמִים עַל־הָאֲדָמָה אֲשֶׁר יְהוָה אֱלֹהֶיךָ נֹתֵן
לְךָ כָּל־הַיָּמִים׃
שלישי ה מא מב *אָז יַבְדִּיל מֹשֶׁה שָׁלֹשׁ עָרִים בְּעֵבֶר הַיַּרְדֵּן מִזְרְחָה שָׁמֶשׁ׃ לָנֻס שָׁמָּה רוֹצֵחַ
אֲשֶׁר יִרְצַח אֶת־רֵעֵהוּ בִּבְלִי־דַעַת וְהוּא לֹא־שֹׂנֵא לוֹ מִתְּמֹל שִׁלְשֹׁם וְנָס
מג אֶל־אַחַת מִן־הֶעָרִים הָאֵל וָחָי׃ אֶת־בֶּצֶר בַּמִּדְבָּר בְּאֶרֶץ הַמִּישֹׁר לָראוּבֵנִי
מד וְאֶת־רָאמֹת בַּגִּלְעָד לַגָּדִי וְאֶת־גּוֹלָן בַּבָּשָׁן לַמְנַשִּׁי׃ וְזֹאת הַתּוֹרָה אֲשֶׁר־
מה שָׂם מֹשֶׁה לִפְנֵי בְּנֵי יִשְׂרָאֵל׃ אֵלֶּה הָעֵדֹת וְהַחֻקִּים וְהַמִּשְׁפָּטִים אֲשֶׁר דִּבֶּר
מו מֹשֶׁה אֶל־בְּנֵי יִשְׂרָאֵל בְּצֵאתָם מִמִּצְרָיִם׃ בְּעֵבֶר הַיַּרְדֵּן בַּגַּיְא מוּל בֵּית פְּעוֹר
בְּאֶרֶץ סִיחֹן מֶלֶךְ הָאֱמֹרִי אֲשֶׁר יוֹשֵׁב בְּחֶשְׁבּוֹן אֲשֶׁר הִכָּה מֹשֶׁה וּבְנֵי יִשְׂרָאֵל
מז בְּצֵאתָם מִמִּצְרָיִם׃ וַיִּירְשׁוּ אֶת־אַרְצוֹ וְאֶת־אֶרֶץ ׀ עוֹג מֶלֶךְ־הַבָּשָׁן שְׁנֵי מַלְכֵי
מח הָאֱמֹרִי אֲשֶׁר בְּעֵבֶר הַיַּרְדֵּן מִזְרַח שָׁמֶשׁ׃ מֵעֲרֹעֵר אֲשֶׁר עַל־שְׂפַת־נַחַל
מט אַרְנֹן וְעַד־הַר שִׂיאֹן הוּא חֶרְמוֹן׃ וְכָל־הָעֲרָבָה עֵבֶר הַיַּרְדֵּן מִזְרָחָה וְעַד יָם
הָעֲרָבָה תַּחַת אַשְׁדֹּת הַפִּסְגָּה׃
רביעי ה א וַיִּקְרָא מֹשֶׁה אֶל־כָּל־יִשְׂרָאֵל וַיֹּאמֶר אֲלֵהֶם שְׁמַע יִשְׂרָאֵל אֶת־הַחֻקִּים
וְאֶת־הַמִּשְׁפָּטִים אֲשֶׁר אָנֹכִי דֹּבֵר בְּאָזְנֵיכֶם הַיּוֹם וּלְמַדְתֶּם אֹתָם וּשְׁמַרְתֶּם
ב ג לַעֲשֹׂתָם׃ יְהוָה אֱלֹהֵינוּ כָּרַת עִמָּנוּ בְּרִית בְּחֹרֵב׃ לֹא אֶת־אֲבֹתֵינוּ כָּרַת יְהוָה
ד אֶת־הַבְּרִית הַזֹּאת כִּי אִתָּנוּ אֲנַחְנוּ אֵלֶּה פֹה הַיּוֹם כֻּלָּנוּ חַיִּים׃ פָּנִים ׀ בְּפָנִים
ה דִּבֶּר יְהוָה עִמָּכֶם בָּהָר מִתּוֹךְ הָאֵשׁ׃ אָנֹכִי עֹמֵד בֵּין־יְהוָה וּבֵינֵיכֶם בָּעֵת
הַהִוא לְהַגִּיד לָכֶם אֶת־דְּבַר יְהוָה כִּי יְרֵאתֶם מִפְּנֵי הָאֵשׁ וְלֹא־עֲלִיתֶם בָּהָר
ו לֵאמֹר׃ אָנֹכִי יְהוָה אֱלֹהֶיךָ אֲשֶׁר הוֹצֵאתִיךָ מֵאֶרֶץ מִצְרַיִם מִבֵּית For Ta'am Elyon see page 1077.
ז ח עֲבָדִים׃ לֹא־יִהְיֶה לְךָ אֱלֹהִים אֲחֵרִים עַל־פָּנָי׃ לֹא־תַעֲשֶׂה לְךָ פֶסֶל כָּל־תְּמוּנָה
ט אֲשֶׁר בַּשָּׁמַיִם מִמַּעַל וַאֲשֶׁר בָּאָרֶץ מִתָּחַת וַאֲשֶׁר בַּמַּיִם מִתַּחַת לָאָרֶץ׃ לֹא־
תִשְׁתַּחֲוֶה לָהֶם וְלֹא תָעָבְדֵם כִּי אָנֹכִי יְהוָה אֱלֹהֶיךָ אֵל קַנָּא פֹּקֵד עֲוֺן אָבוֹת
י עַל־בָּנִים וְעַל־שִׁלֵּשִׁים וְעַל־רִבֵּעִים לְשֹׂנְאָי׃ וְעֹשֶׂה חֶסֶד לַאֲלָפִים לְאֹהֲבַי
מִצְוֹתָי יא וּלְשֹׁמְרֵי מצותו׃ לֹא תִשָּׂא אֶת־שֵׁם־יְהוָה אֱלֹהֶיךָ לַשָּׁוְא כִּי לֹא
יב יְנַקֶּה יְהוָה אֵת אֲשֶׁר־יִשָּׂא אֶת־שְׁמוֹ לַשָּׁוְא׃ שָׁמוֹר אֶת־יוֹם הַשַּׁבָּת
יג לְקַדְּשׁוֹ כַּאֲשֶׁר צִוְּךָ יְהוָה אֱלֹהֶיךָ׃ שֵׁשֶׁת יָמִים תַּעֲבֹד וְעָשִׂיתָ כָּל־מְלַאכְתֶּךָ׃
יד וְיוֹם הַשְּׁבִיעִי שַׁבָּת לַיהוָה אֱלֹהֶיךָ לֹא תַעֲשֶׂה כָל־מְלָאכָה אַתָּה ׀ וּבִנְךָ־וּבִתֶּךָ
וְעַבְדְּךָ־וַאֲמָתֶךָ וְשׁוֹרְךָ וַחֲמֹרְךָ וְכָל־בְּהֶמְתֶּךָ וְגֵרְךָ אֲשֶׁר בִּשְׁעָרֶיךָ לְמַעַן

טו יָנוּחַ עַבְדְּךָ וַאֲמָתְךָ כָּמוֹךָ: וְזָכַרְתָּ כִּי עֶבֶד הָיִיתָ בְּאֶרֶץ מִצְרַיִם וַיֹּצִאֲךָ יְהוָה
אֱלֹהֶיךָ מִשָּׁם בְּיָד חֲזָקָה וּבִזְרֹעַ נְטוּיָה עַל־כֵּן צִוְּךָ יְהוָה אֱלֹהֶיךָ לַעֲשׂוֹת אֶת־
טז יוֹם הַשַּׁבָּת: כַּבֵּד אֶת־אָבִיךָ וְאֶת־אִמֶּךָ כַּאֲשֶׁר צִוְּךָ יְהוָה אֱלֹהֶיךָ
לְמַעַן ׀ יַאֲרִיכֻן יָמֶיךָ וּלְמַעַן יִיטַב לָךְ עַל הָאֲדָמָה אֲשֶׁר־יְהוָה אֱלֹהֶיךָ נֹתֵן
יז לָךְ: לֹא תִרְצָח וְלֹא
תִנְאָף וְלֹא תִגְנֹב וְלֹא־
יח תַעֲנֶה בְרֵעֲךָ עֵד שָׁוְא: וְלֹא
תַחְמֹד אֵשֶׁת רֵעֶךָ וְלֹא
תִתְאַוֶּה בֵּית רֵעֶךָ שָׂדֵהוּ וְעַבְדּוֹ וַאֲמָתוֹ שׁוֹרוֹ וַחֲמֹרוֹ וְכֹל אֲשֶׁר
יט לְרֵעֶךָ: אֶת־הַדְּבָרִים הָאֵלֶּה דִּבֶּר יְהוָה אֶל־כָּל־קְהַלְכֶם בָּהָר מִתּוֹךְ חמישי
הָאֵשׁ הֶעָנָן וְהָעֲרָפֶל קוֹל גָּדוֹל וְלֹא יָסָף וַיִּכְתְּבֵם עַל־שְׁנֵי לֻחֹת אֲבָנִים וַיִּתְּנֵם
כ אֵלָי: וַיְהִי כְּשָׁמְעֲכֶם אֶת־הַקּוֹל מִתּוֹךְ הַחֹשֶׁךְ וְהָהָר בֹּעֵר בָּאֵשׁ וַתִּקְרְבוּן אֵלַי
כא כָּל־רָאשֵׁי שִׁבְטֵיכֶם וְזִקְנֵיכֶם: וַתֹּאמְרוּ הֵן הֶרְאָנוּ יְהוָה אֱלֹהֵינוּ אֶת־כְּבֹדוֹ
וְאֶת־גָּדְלוֹ וְאֶת־קֹלוֹ שָׁמַעְנוּ מִתּוֹךְ הָאֵשׁ הַיּוֹם הַזֶּה רָאִינוּ כִּי־יְדַבֵּר אֱלֹהִים
כב אֶת־הָאָדָם וָחָי: וְעַתָּה לָמָּה נָמוּת כִּי תֹאכְלֵנוּ הָאֵשׁ הַגְּדֹלָה הַזֹּאת אִם־
כג יֹסְפִים ׀ אֲנַחְנוּ לִשְׁמֹעַ אֶת־קוֹל יְהוָה אֱלֹהֵינוּ עוֹד וָמָתְנוּ: כִּי מִי כָל־בָּשָׂר
כד אֲשֶׁר שָׁמַע קוֹל אֱלֹהִים חַיִּים מְדַבֵּר מִתּוֹךְ־הָאֵשׁ כָּמֹנוּ וַיֶּחִי: קְרַב אַתָּה
וּשְׁמָע אֵת כָּל־אֲשֶׁר יֹאמַר יְהוָה אֱלֹהֵינוּ וְאַתְּ ׀ תְּדַבֵּר אֵלֵינוּ אֵת כָּל־אֲשֶׁר
כה יְדַבֵּר יְהוָה אֱלֹהֵינוּ אֵלֶיךָ וְשָׁמַעְנוּ וְעָשִׂינוּ: וַיִּשְׁמַע יְהוָה אֶת־קוֹל דִּבְרֵיכֶם
בְּדַבֶּרְכֶם אֵלָי וַיֹּאמֶר יְהוָה אֵלַי שָׁמַעְתִּי אֶת־קוֹל דִּבְרֵי הָעָם הַזֶּה אֲשֶׁר
כו דִּבְּרוּ אֵלֶיךָ הֵיטִיבוּ כָּל־אֲשֶׁר דִּבֵּרוּ: מִי־יִתֵּן וְהָיָה לְבָבָם זֶה לָהֶם לְיִרְאָה
אֹתִי וְלִשְׁמֹר אֶת־כָּל־מִצְוֺתַי כָּל־הַיָּמִים לְמַעַן יִיטַב לָהֶם וְלִבְנֵיהֶם לְעֹלָם:
כז כח לֵךְ אֱמֹר לָהֶם שׁוּבוּ לָכֶם לְאָהֳלֵיכֶם: וְאַתָּה פֹּה עֲמֹד עִמָּדִי וַאֲדַבְּרָה אֵלֶיךָ
אֵת כָּל־הַמִּצְוָה וְהַחֻקִּים וְהַמִּשְׁפָּטִים אֲשֶׁר תְּלַמְּדֵם וְעָשׂוּ בָאָרֶץ אֲשֶׁר אָנֹכִי
כט נֹתֵן לָהֶם לְרִשְׁתָּהּ: וּשְׁמַרְתֶּם לַעֲשׂוֹת כַּאֲשֶׁר צִוָּה יְהוָה אֱלֹהֵיכֶם אֶתְכֶם
ל לֹא תָסֻרוּ יָמִין וּשְׂמֹאל: בְּכָל־הַדֶּרֶךְ אֲשֶׁר צִוָּה יְהוָה אֱלֹהֵיכֶם אֶתְכֶם תֵּלֵכוּ
ו א לְמַעַן תִּחְיוּן וְטוֹב לָכֶם וְהַאֲרַכְתֶּם יָמִים בָּאָרֶץ אֲשֶׁר תִּירָשׁוּן: וְזֹאת הַמִּצְוָה
הַחֻקִּים וְהַמִּשְׁפָּטִים אֲשֶׁר צִוָּה יְהוָה אֱלֹהֵיכֶם לְלַמֵּד אֶתְכֶם לַעֲשׂוֹת בָּאָרֶץ
ב אֲשֶׁר אַתֶּם עֹבְרִים שָׁמָּה לְרִשְׁתָּהּ: לְמַעַן תִּירָא אֶת־יְהוָה אֱלֹהֶיךָ לִשְׁמֹר

אֶת־כָּל־חֻקֹּתָיו וּמִצְוֺתָיו אֲשֶׁר אָנֹכִי מְצַוֶּךָ אַתָּה וּבִנְךָ וּבֶן־בִּנְךָ כֹּל יְמֵי
ג חַיֶּיךָ וּלְמַעַן יַאֲרִכֻן יָמֶיךָ: וְשָׁמַעְתָּ יִשְׂרָאֵל וְשָׁמַרְתָּ לַעֲשׂוֹת אֲשֶׁר יִיטַב
לְךָ וַאֲשֶׁר תִּרְבּוּן מְאֹד כַּאֲשֶׁר דִּבֶּר יהוה אֱלֹהֵי אֲבֹתֶיךָ לָךְ אֶרֶץ זָבַת חָלָב
וּדְבָשׁ:
ששי ד ה שְׁמַע יִשְׂרָאֵל יהוה אֱלֹהֵינוּ יהוה ׀ אֶחָד: וְאָהַבְתָּ אֵת יהוה אֱלֹהֶיךָ בְּכָל־
ו לְבָבְךָ וּבְכָל־נַפְשְׁךָ וּבְכָל־מְאֹדֶךָ: וְהָיוּ הַדְּבָרִים הָאֵלֶּה אֲשֶׁר אָנֹכִי מְצַוְּךָ
ז הַיּוֹם עַל־לְבָבֶךָ: וְשִׁנַּנְתָּם לְבָנֶיךָ וְדִבַּרְתָּ בָּם בְּשִׁבְתְּךָ בְּבֵיתֶךָ וּבְלֶכְתְּךָ
ח בַדֶּרֶךְ וּבְשָׁכְבְּךָ וּבְקוּמֶךָ: וּקְשַׁרְתָּם לְאוֹת עַל־יָדֶךָ וְהָיוּ לְטֹטָפֹת בֵּין עֵינֶיךָ:
ט י וּכְתַבְתָּם עַל־מְזֻזוֹת בֵּיתֶךָ וּבִשְׁעָרֶיךָ: וְהָיָה כִּי־יְבִיאֲךָ ׀ יהוה
אֱלֹהֶיךָ אֶל־הָאָרֶץ אֲשֶׁר נִשְׁבַּע לַאֲבֹתֶיךָ לְאַבְרָהָם לְיִצְחָק וּלְיַעֲקֹב לָתֶת
יא לָךְ עָרִים גְּדֹלֹת וְטֹבֹת אֲשֶׁר לֹא־בָנִיתָ: וּבָתִּים מְלֵאִים כָּל־טוּב אֲשֶׁר לֹא־
מִלֵּאתָ וּבֹרֹת חֲצוּבִים אֲשֶׁר לֹא־חָצַבְתָּ כְּרָמִים וְזֵיתִים אֲשֶׁר לֹא־נָטָעְתָּ
יב וְאָכַלְתָּ וְשָׂבָעְתָּ: הִשָּׁמֶר לְךָ פֶּן־תִּשְׁכַּח אֶת־יהוה אֲשֶׁר הוֹצִיאֲךָ מֵאֶרֶץ
יג מִצְרַיִם מִבֵּית עֲבָדִים: אֶת־יהוה אֱלֹהֶיךָ תִּירָא וְאֹתוֹ תַעֲבֹד וּבִשְׁמוֹ תִּשָּׁבֵעַ:
יד טו לֹא תֵלְכוּן אַחֲרֵי אֱלֹהִים אֲחֵרִים מֵאֱלֹהֵי הָעַמִּים אֲשֶׁר סְבִיבוֹתֵיכֶם: כִּי
אֵל קַנָּא יהוה אֱלֹהֶיךָ בְּקִרְבֶּךָ פֶּן־יֶחֱרֶה אַף־יהוה אֱלֹהֶיךָ בָּךְ וְהִשְׁמִידְךָ
טז מֵעַל פְּנֵי הָאֲדָמָה: לֹא תְנַסּוּ אֶת־יהוה אֱלֹהֵיכֶם כַּאֲשֶׁר נִסִּיתֶם
יז בַּמַּסָּה: שָׁמוֹר תִּשְׁמְרוּן אֶת־מִצְוֺת יהוה אֱלֹהֵיכֶם וְעֵדֹתָיו וְחֻקָּיו אֲשֶׁר צִוָּךְ:
יח וְעָשִׂיתָ הַיָּשָׁר וְהַטּוֹב בְּעֵינֵי יהוה לְמַעַן יִיטַב לָךְ וּבָאתָ וְיָרַשְׁתָּ אֶת־הָאָרֶץ
יט הַטֹּבָה אֲשֶׁר־נִשְׁבַּע יהוה לַאֲבֹתֶיךָ: לַהֲדֹף אֶת־כָּל־אֹיְבֶיךָ מִפָּנֶיךָ כַּאֲשֶׁר
כ דִּבֶּר יהוה: כִּי־יִשְׁאָלְךָ בִנְךָ מָחָר לֵאמֹר מָה הָעֵדֹת וְהַחֻקִּים
כא וְהַמִּשְׁפָּטִים אֲשֶׁר צִוָּה יהוה אֱלֹהֵינוּ אֶתְכֶם: וְאָמַרְתָּ לְבִנְךָ עֲבָדִים הָיִינוּ
כב לְפַרְעֹה בְּמִצְרָיִם וַיֹּצִיאֵנוּ יהוה מִמִּצְרַיִם בְּיָד חֲזָקָה: וַיִּתֵּן יהוה אוֹתֹת וּמֹפְתִים
כג גְּדֹלִים וְרָעִים ׀ בְּמִצְרַיִם בְּפַרְעֹה וּבְכָל־בֵּיתוֹ לְעֵינֵינוּ: וְאוֹתָנוּ הוֹצִיא מִשָּׁם
כד לְמַעַן הָבִיא אֹתָנוּ לָתֶת לָנוּ אֶת־הָאָרֶץ אֲשֶׁר נִשְׁבַּע לַאֲבֹתֵינוּ: וַיְצַוֵּנוּ יהוה
לַעֲשׂוֹת אֶת־כָּל־הַחֻקִּים הָאֵלֶּה לְיִרְאָה אֶת־יהוה אֱלֹהֵינוּ לְטוֹב לָנוּ כָּל־
כה הַיָּמִים לְחַיֹּתֵנוּ כְּהַיּוֹם הַזֶּה: וּצְדָקָה תִּהְיֶה־לָּנוּ כִּי־נִשְׁמֹר לַעֲשׂוֹת אֶת־כָּל־
שביעי ז א הַמִּצְוָה הַזֹּאת לִפְנֵי יהוה אֱלֹהֵינוּ כַּאֲשֶׁר צִוָּנוּ: כִּי יְבִיאֲךָ יהוה
אֱלֹהֶיךָ אֶל־הָאָרֶץ אֲשֶׁר־אַתָּה בָא־שָׁמָּה לְרִשְׁתָּהּ וְנָשַׁל גּוֹיִם־רַבִּים ׀ מִפָּנֶיךָ

הַחִתִּי וְהַגִּרְגָּשִׁי וְהָאֱמֹרִי וְהַכְּנַעֲנִי וְהַפְּרִזִּי וְהַחִוִּי וְהַיְבוּסִי שִׁבְעָה גוֹיִם רַבִּים
ב וַעֲצוּמִים מִמֶּךָּ׃ וּנְתָנָם יהוה אֱלֹהֶיךָ לְפָנֶיךָ וְהִכִּיתָם הַחֲרֵם תַּחֲרִים אֹתָם
ג לֹא־תִכְרֹת לָהֶם בְּרִית וְלֹא תְחָנֵּם׃ וְלֹא תִתְחַתֵּן בָּם בִּתְּךָ לֹא־תִתֵּן לִבְנוֹ
ד וּבִתּוֹ לֹא־תִקַּח לִבְנֶךָ׃ כִּי־יָסִיר אֶת־בִּנְךָ מֵאַחֲרַי וְעָבְדוּ אֱלֹהִים אֲחֵרִים
ה וְחָרָה אַף־יהוה בָּכֶם וְהִשְׁמִידְךָ מַהֵר׃ כִּי אִם־כֹּה תַעֲשׂוּ לָהֶם מִזְבְּחֹתֵיהֶם
ו תִּתֹּצוּ וּמַצֵּבֹתָם תְּשַׁבֵּרוּ וַאֲשֵׁירֵהֶם תְּגַדֵּעוּן וּפְסִילֵיהֶם תִּשְׂרְפוּן בָּאֵשׁ׃ כִּי עַם
קָדוֹשׁ אַתָּה לַיהוה אֱלֹהֶיךָ בְּךָ בָּחַר ׀ יהוה אֱלֹהֶיךָ לִהְיוֹת לוֹ לְעַם סְגֻלָּה
ז מִכֹּל הָעַמִּים אֲשֶׁר עַל־פְּנֵי הָאֲדָמָה׃ לֹא מֵרֻבְּכֶם מִכָּל־הָעַמִּים חָשַׁק יהוה
ח בָּכֶם וַיִּבְחַר בָּכֶם כִּי־אַתֶּם הַמְעַט מִכָּל־הָעַמִּים׃ כִּי מֵאַהֲבַת יהוה אֶתְכֶם
וּמִשָּׁמְרוֹ אֶת־הַשְּׁבֻעָה אֲשֶׁר נִשְׁבַּע לַאֲבֹתֵיכֶם הוֹצִיא יהוה אֶתְכֶם בְּיָד חֲזָקָה
ט וַיִּפְדְּךָ מִבֵּית עֲבָדִים מִיַּד פַּרְעֹה מֶלֶךְ־מִצְרָיִם׃ וְיָדַעְתָּ כִּי־יהוה אֱלֹהֶיךָ הוּא מפטיר
הָאֱלֹהִים הָאֵל הַנֶּאֱמָן שֹׁמֵר הַבְּרִית וְהַחֶסֶד לְאֹהֲבָיו וּלְשֹׁמְרֵי מִצְוֺתָו לְאֶלֶף
י דּוֹר׃ וּמְשַׁלֵּם לְשֹׂנְאָיו אֶל־פָּנָיו לְהַאֲבִידוֹ לֹא יְאַחֵר לְשֹׂנְאוֹ אֶל־פָּנָיו יְשַׁלֶּם־
יא לוֹ׃ וְשָׁמַרְתָּ אֶת־הַמִּצְוָה וְאֶת־הַחֻקִּים וְאֶת־הַמִּשְׁפָּטִים אֲשֶׁר אָנֹכִי מְצַוְּךָ
הַיּוֹם לַעֲשׂוֹתָם׃

יב וְהָיָה ׀ עֵקֶב תִּשְׁמְעוּן אֵת הַמִּשְׁפָּטִים הָאֵלֶּה וּשְׁמַרְתֶּם וַעֲשִׂיתֶם אֹתָם וְשָׁמַר ז עקב
יג יהוה אֱלֹהֶיךָ לְךָ אֶת־הַבְּרִית וְאֶת־הַחֶסֶד אֲשֶׁר נִשְׁבַּע לַאֲבֹתֶיךָ׃ וַאֲהֵבְךָ
וּבֵרַכְךָ וְהִרְבֶּךָ וּבֵרַךְ פְּרִי־בִטְנְךָ וּפְרִי־אַדְמָתֶךָ דְּגָנְךָ וְתִירֹשְׁךָ וְיִצְהָרֶךָ שְׁגַר־
יד אֲלָפֶיךָ וְעַשְׁתְּרֹת צֹאנֶךָ עַל הָאֲדָמָה אֲשֶׁר־נִשְׁבַּע לַאֲבֹתֶיךָ לָתֶת לָךְ׃ בָּרוּךְ
טו תִּהְיֶה מִכָּל־הָעַמִּים לֹא־יִהְיֶה בְךָ עָקָר וַעֲקָרָה וּבִבְהֶמְתֶּךָ׃ וְהֵסִיר יהוה
מִמְּךָ כָּל־חֹלִי וְכָל־מַדְוֵי מִצְרַיִם הָרָעִים אֲשֶׁר יָדַעְתָּ לֹא יְשִׂימָם בָּךְ וּנְתָנָם
טז בְּכָל־שֹׂנְאֶיךָ׃ וְאָכַלְתָּ אֶת־כָּל־הָעַמִּים אֲשֶׁר יהוה אֱלֹהֶיךָ נֹתֵן לָךְ לֹא־תָחוֹס
יז עֵינְךָ עֲלֵיהֶם וְלֹא תַעֲבֹד אֶת־אֱלֹהֵיהֶם כִּי־מוֹקֵשׁ הוּא לָךְ׃ כִּי
יח תֹאמַר בִּלְבָבְךָ רַבִּים הַגּוֹיִם הָאֵלֶּה מִמֶּנִּי אֵיכָה אוּכַל לְהוֹרִישָׁם׃ לֹא תִירָא
יט מֵהֶם זָכֹר תִּזְכֹּר אֵת אֲשֶׁר־עָשָׂה יהוה אֱלֹהֶיךָ לְפַרְעֹה וּלְכָל־מִצְרָיִם׃ הַמַּסֹּת
הַגְּדֹלֹת אֲשֶׁר־רָאוּ עֵינֶיךָ וְהָאֹתֹת וְהַמֹּפְתִים וְהַיָּד הַחֲזָקָה וְהַזְּרֹעַ הַנְּטוּיָה
אֲשֶׁר הוֹצִאֲךָ יהוה אֱלֹהֶיךָ כֵּן־יַעֲשֶׂה יהוה אֱלֹהֶיךָ לְכָל־הָעַמִּים אֲשֶׁר־אַתָּה
כ יָרֵא מִפְּנֵיהֶם׃ וְגַם אֶת־הַצִּרְעָה יְשַׁלַּח יהוה אֱלֹהֶיךָ בָּם עַד־אֲבֹד הַנִּשְׁאָרִים
כא וְהַנִּסְתָּרִים מִפָּנֶיךָ׃ לֹא תַעֲרֹץ מִפְּנֵיהֶם כִּי־יהוה אֱלֹהֶיךָ בְּקִרְבֶּךָ אֵל גָּדוֹל

לוי כב ונורא: *ונשל יהוה אלהיך את־הגוים האל מפניך מעט מעט לא תוכל
כג כלתם מהר פן־תרבה עליך חית השדה: ונתנם יהוה אלהיך לפניך והמם
כד מהומה גדלה עד השמדם: ונתן מלכיהם בידך והאבדת את־שמם מתחת
כה השמים לא־יתיצב איש בפניך עד השמדך אתם: פסילי אלהיהם תשרפון
באש לא־תחמד כסף וזהב עליהם ולקחת לך פן תוקש בו כי תועבת
כו יהוה אלהיך הוא: ולא־תביא תועבה אל־ביתך והיית חרם כמהו שקץ ׀
תשקצנו ותעב ׀ תתעבנו כי־חרם הוא:
ח א כל־המצוה אשר אנכי מצוך היום תשמרון לעשות למען תחיון ורביתם
ב ובאתם וירשתם את־הארץ אשר־נשבע יהוה לאבתיכם: וזכרת את־כל־
הדרך אשר הוליכך יהוה אלהיך זה ארבעים שנה במדבר למען ענתך
ג לנסתך לדעת את־אשר בלבבך התשמר מצותו אם־לא: ויענך וירעבך
ויאכלך את־המן אשר לא־ידעת ולא ידעון אבתיך למען הודיעך כי לא על־
ישראל ד הלחם לבדו יחיה האדם כי על־כל־מוצא פי־יהוה יחיה האדם: *שמלתך
ה לא בלתה מעליך ורגלך לא בצקה זה ארבעים שנה: וידעת עם־לבבך כי
ו כאשר ייסר איש את־בנו יהוה אלהיך מיסרך: ושמרת את־מצות יהוה
ז אלהיך ללכת בדרכיו וליראה אתו: כי יהוה אלהיך מביאך אל־ארץ טובה
ח ארץ נחלי מים עינת ותהמת יצאים בבקעה ובהר: ארץ חטה ושערה וגפן
ט ותאנה ורמון ארץ־זית שמן ודבש: ארץ אשר לא במסכנת תאכל־בה לחם
י לא־תחסר כל בה ארץ אשר אבניה ברזל ומהרריה תחצב נחשת: ואכלת
שני יא ושבעת וברכת את־יהוה אלהיך על־הארץ הטבה אשר נתן־לך: ** השמר
לך פן־תשכח את־יהוה אלהיך לבלתי שמר מצותיו ומשפטיו וחקתיו אשר
יב יג אנכי מצוך היום: פן־תאכל ושבעת ובתים טבים תבנה וישבת: ובקרך
יד וצאנך ירבין וכסף וזהב ירבה־לך וכל אשר־לך ירבה: ורם לבבך ושכחת
טו את־יהוה אלהיך המוציאך מארץ מצרים מבית עבדים: המוליכך במדבר ׀
הגדל והנורא נחש ׀ שרף ועקרב וצמאון אשר אין־מים המוציא לך מים
טז מצור החלמיש: המאכלך מן במדבר אשר לא־ידעון אבתיך למען ענתך
יז ולמען נסתך להיטבך באחריתך: ואמרת בלבבך כחי ועצם ידי עשה לי
יח את־החיל הזה: וזכרת את־יהוה אלהיך כי הוא הנתן לך כח לעשות חיל
למען הקים את־בריתו אשר־נשבע לאבתיך כיום הזה:

יט וְהָיָה אִם־שָׁכֹחַ תִּשְׁכַּח אֶת־יְהוָה אֱלֹהֶיךָ וְהָלַכְתָּ אַחֲרֵי אֱלֹהִים אֲחֵרִים
כ וַעֲבַדְתָּם וְהִשְׁתַּחֲוִיתָ לָהֶם הַעִדֹתִי בָכֶם הַיּוֹם כִּי אָבֹד תֹּאבֵדוּן׃ כַּגּוֹיִם
אֲשֶׁר יְהוָה מַאֲבִיד מִפְּנֵיכֶם כֵּן תֹּאבֵדוּן עֵקֶב לֹא תִשְׁמְעוּן בְּקוֹל יְהוָה
אֱלֹהֵיכֶם׃

ט א שְׁמַע יִשְׂרָאֵל אַתָּה עֹבֵר הַיּוֹם אֶת־הַיַּרְדֵּן לָבֹא לָרֶשֶׁת גּוֹיִם גְּדֹלִים וַעֲצֻמִים ח
ב מִמֶּךָּ עָרִים גְּדֹלֹת וּבְצֻרֹת בַּשָּׁמָיִם׃ עַם־גָּדוֹל וָרָם בְּנֵי עֲנָקִים אֲשֶׁר אַתָּה
ג יָדַעְתָּ וְאַתָּה שָׁמַעְתָּ מִי יִתְיַצֵּב לִפְנֵי בְּנֵי עֲנָק׃ וְיָדַעְתָּ הַיּוֹם כִּי יְהוָה אֱלֹהֶיךָ
הוּא־הָעֹבֵר לְפָנֶיךָ אֵשׁ אֹכְלָה הוּא יַשְׁמִידֵם וְהוּא יַכְנִיעֵם לְפָנֶיךָ וְהוֹרַשְׁתָּם
ד וְהַאֲבַדְתָּם מַהֵר כַּאֲשֶׁר דִּבֶּר יְהוָה לָךְ׃ אַל־תֹּאמַר בִּלְבָבְךָ בַּהֲדֹף יְהוָה שלישי
אֱלֹהֶיךָ אֹתָם ׀ מִלְּפָנֶיךָ לֵאמֹר בְּצִדְקָתִי הֱבִיאַנִי יְהוָה לָרֶשֶׁת אֶת־הָאָרֶץ
ה הַזֹּאת וּבְרִשְׁעַת הַגּוֹיִם הָאֵלֶּה יְהוָה מוֹרִישָׁם מִפָּנֶיךָ׃ לֹא בְצִדְקָתְךָ וּבְיֹשֶׁר
לְבָבְךָ אַתָּה בָא לָרֶשֶׁת אֶת־אַרְצָם כִּי בְּרִשְׁעַת ׀ הַגּוֹיִם הָאֵלֶּה יְהוָה אֱלֹהֶיךָ
מוֹרִישָׁם מִפָּנֶיךָ וּלְמַעַן הָקִים אֶת־הַדָּבָר אֲשֶׁר נִשְׁבַּע יְהוָה לַאֲבֹתֶיךָ לְאַבְרָהָם
ו לְיִצְחָק וּלְיַעֲקֹב׃ וְיָדַעְתָּ כִּי לֹא בְצִדְקָתְךָ יְהוָה אֱלֹהֶיךָ נֹתֵן לְךָ אֶת־הָאָרֶץ
ז הַטּוֹבָה הַזֹּאת לְרִשְׁתָּהּ כִּי עַם־קְשֵׁה־עֹרֶף אָתָּה׃ זְכֹר אַל־תִּשְׁכַּח אֵת אֲשֶׁר־
הִקְצַפְתָּ אֶת־יְהוָה אֱלֹהֶיךָ בַּמִּדְבָּר לְמִן־הַיּוֹם אֲשֶׁר־יָצָאתָ ׀ מֵאֶרֶץ מִצְרַיִם
ח עַד־בֹּאֲכֶם עַד־הַמָּקוֹם הַזֶּה מַמְרִים הֱיִיתֶם עִם־יְהוָה׃ וּבְחֹרֵב הִקְצַפְתֶּם
ט אֶת־יְהוָה וַיִּתְאַנַּף יְהוָה בָּכֶם לְהַשְׁמִיד אֶתְכֶם׃ בַּעֲלֹתִי הָהָרָה לָקַחַת לוּחֹת
הָאֲבָנִים לוּחֹת הַבְּרִית אֲשֶׁר־כָּרַת יְהוָה עִמָּכֶם וָאֵשֵׁב בָּהָר אַרְבָּעִים יוֹם
י וְאַרְבָּעִים לַיְלָה לֶחֶם לֹא אָכַלְתִּי וּמַיִם לֹא שָׁתִיתִי׃ וַיִּתֵּן יְהוָה אֵלַי אֶת־
שְׁנֵי לוּחֹת הָאֲבָנִים כְּתֻבִים בְּאֶצְבַּע אֱלֹהִים וַעֲלֵיהֶם כְּכָל־הַדְּבָרִים אֲשֶׁר
יא דִּבֶּר יְהוָה עִמָּכֶם בָּהָר מִתּוֹךְ הָאֵשׁ בְּיוֹם הַקָּהָל׃ וַיְהִי מִקֵּץ אַרְבָּעִים יוֹם
יב וְאַרְבָּעִים לַיְלָה נָתַן יְהוָה אֵלַי אֶת־שְׁנֵי לֻחֹת הָאֲבָנִים לֻחוֹת הַבְּרִית׃ וַיֹּאמֶר
יְהוָה אֵלַי קוּם רֵד מַהֵר מִזֶּה כִּי שִׁחֵת עַמְּךָ אֲשֶׁר הוֹצֵאתָ מִמִּצְרָיִם סָרוּ
יג מַהֵר מִן־הַדֶּרֶךְ אֲשֶׁר צִוִּיתִם עָשׂוּ לָהֶם מַסֵּכָה׃ וַיֹּאמֶר יְהוָה אֵלַי לֵאמֹר
יד רָאִיתִי אֶת־הָעָם הַזֶּה וְהִנֵּה עַם־קְשֵׁה־עֹרֶף הוּא׃ הֶרֶף מִמֶּנִּי וְאַשְׁמִידֵם
טו וְאֶמְחֶה אֶת־שְׁמָם מִתַּחַת הַשָּׁמָיִם וְאֶעֱשֶׂה אוֹתְךָ לְגוֹי־עָצוּם וָרָב מִמֶּנּוּ׃ וָאֵפֶן
טז וָאֵרֵד מִן־הָהָר וְהָהָר בֹּעֵר בָּאֵשׁ וּשְׁנֵי לוּחֹת הַבְּרִית עַל שְׁתֵּי יָדָי׃ וָאֵרֶא
וְהִנֵּה חֲטָאתֶם לַיהוָה אֱלֹהֵיכֶם עֲשִׂיתֶם לָכֶם עֵגֶל מַסֵּכָה סַרְתֶּם מַהֵר מִן־

יז הַדֶּרֶךְ אֲשֶׁר־צִוָּה יהוה אֶתְכֶם׃ וָאֶתְפֹּשׂ בִּשְׁנֵי הַלֻּחֹת וָאַשְׁלִכֵם מֵעַל שְׁתֵּי
יח יָדָי וָאֲשַׁבְּרֵם לְעֵינֵיכֶם׃ וָאֶתְנַפַּל לִפְנֵי יהוה כָּרִאשֹׁנָה אַרְבָּעִים יוֹם וְאַרְבָּעִים
לַיְלָה לֶחֶם לֹא אָכַלְתִּי וּמַיִם לֹא שָׁתִיתִי עַל כָּל־חַטַּאתְכֶם אֲשֶׁר חֲטָאתֶם
יט לַעֲשׂוֹת הָרַע בְּעֵינֵי יהוה לְהַכְעִיסוֹ׃ כִּי יָגֹרְתִּי מִפְּנֵי הָאַף וְהַחֵמָה אֲשֶׁר קָצַף
כ יהוה עֲלֵיכֶם לְהַשְׁמִיד אֶתְכֶם וַיִּשְׁמַע יהוה אֵלַי גַּם בַּפַּעַם הַהִוא׃ וּבְאַהֲרֹן
כא הִתְאַנַּף יהוה מְאֹד לְהַשְׁמִידוֹ וָאֶתְפַּלֵּל גַּם־בְּעַד אַהֲרֹן בָּעֵת הַהִוא׃ וְאֶת־
חַטַּאתְכֶם אֲשֶׁר־עֲשִׂיתֶם אֶת־הָעֵגֶל לָקַחְתִּי וָאֶשְׂרֹף אֹתוֹ ׀ בָּאֵשׁ וָאֶכֹּת
אֹתוֹ טָחוֹן הֵיטֵב עַד אֲשֶׁר־דַּק לְעָפָר וָאַשְׁלִךְ אֶת־עֲפָרוֹ אֶל־הַנַּחַל הַיֹּרֵד
כב מִן־הָהָר׃ וּבְתַבְעֵרָה וּבְמַסָּה וּבְקִבְרֹת הַתַּאֲוָה מַקְצִפִים הֱיִיתֶם אֶת־יהוה׃
כג וּבִשְׁלֹחַ יהוה אֶתְכֶם מִקָּדֵשׁ בַּרְנֵעַ לֵאמֹר עֲלוּ וּרְשׁוּ אֶת־הָאָרֶץ אֲשֶׁר נָתַתִּי
לָכֶם וַתַּמְרוּ אֶת־פִּי יהוה אֱלֹהֵיכֶם וְלֹא הֶאֱמַנְתֶּם לוֹ וְלֹא שְׁמַעְתֶּם בְּקֹלוֹ׃
כד כה מַמְרִים הֱיִיתֶם עִם־יהוה מִיּוֹם דַּעְתִּי אֶתְכֶם׃ וָאֶתְנַפַּל לִפְנֵי יהוה אֶת־
אַרְבָּעִים הַיּוֹם וְאֶת־אַרְבָּעִים הַלַּיְלָה אֲשֶׁר הִתְנַפָּלְתִּי כִּי־אָמַר יהוה לְהַשְׁמִיד
כו אֶתְכֶם׃ וָאֶתְפַּלֵּל אֶל־יהוה וָאֹמַר אֲדֹנָי יהוה אַל־תַּשְׁחֵת עַמְּךָ וְנַחֲלָתְךָ אֲשֶׁר
כז פָּדִיתָ בְּגָדְלֶךָ אֲשֶׁר־הוֹצֵאתָ מִמִּצְרַיִם בְּיָד חֲזָקָה׃ זְכֹר לַעֲבָדֶיךָ לְאַבְרָהָם
כח לְיִצְחָק וּלְיַעֲקֹב אַל־תֵּפֶן אֶל־קְשִׁי הָעָם הַזֶּה וְאֶל־רִשְׁעוֹ וְאֶל־חַטָּאתוֹ׃ פֶּן־
יֹאמְרוּ הָאָרֶץ אֲשֶׁר הוֹצֵאתָנוּ מִשָּׁם מִבְּלִי יְכֹלֶת יהוה לַהֲבִיאָם אֶל־הָאָרֶץ
כט אֲשֶׁר־דִּבֶּר לָהֶם וּמִשִּׂנְאָתוֹ אוֹתָם הוֹצִיאָם לַהֲמִתָם בַּמִּדְבָּר׃ וְהֵם עַמְּךָ
וְנַחֲלָתֶךָ אֲשֶׁר הוֹצֵאתָ בְּכֹחֲךָ הַגָּדֹל וּבִזְרֹעֲךָ הַנְּטוּיָה׃
י א בָּעֵת הַהִוא אָמַר יהוה אֵלַי פְּסָל־לְךָ שְׁנֵי־לוּחֹת אֲבָנִים כָּרִאשֹׁנִים וַעֲלֵה ט רביעי
ב אֵלַי הָהָרָה וְעָשִׂיתָ לְּךָ אֲרוֹן עֵץ׃ וְאֶכְתֹּב עַל־הַלֻּחֹת אֶת־הַדְּבָרִים אֲשֶׁר
ג הָיוּ עַל־הַלֻּחֹת הָרִאשֹׁנִים אֲשֶׁר שִׁבַּרְתָּ וְשַׂמְתָּם בָּאָרוֹן׃ וָאַעַשׂ אֲרוֹן עֲצֵי
שִׁטִּים וָאֶפְסֹל שְׁנֵי־לֻחֹת אֲבָנִים כָּרִאשֹׁנִים וָאַעַל הָהָרָה וּשְׁנֵי הַלֻּחֹת בְּיָדִי׃
ד וַיִּכְתֹּב עַל־הַלֻּחֹת כַּמִּכְתָּב הָרִאשׁוֹן אֵת עֲשֶׂרֶת הַדְּבָרִים אֲשֶׁר דִּבֶּר יהוה
ה אֲלֵיכֶם בָּהָר מִתּוֹךְ הָאֵשׁ בְּיוֹם הַקָּהָל וַיִּתְּנֵם יהוה אֵלָי׃ וָאֵפֶן וָאֵרֵד מִן־
הָהָר וָאָשִׂם אֶת־הַלֻּחֹת בָּאָרוֹן אֲשֶׁר עָשִׂיתִי וַיִּהְיוּ שָׁם כַּאֲשֶׁר צִוַּנִי יהוה׃
ו וּבְנֵי יִשְׂרָאֵל נָסְעוּ מִבְּאֵרֹת בְּנֵי־יַעֲקָן מוֹסֵרָה שָׁם מֵת אַהֲרֹן וַיִּקָּבֵר שָׁם
ז וַיְכַהֵן אֶלְעָזָר בְּנוֹ תַּחְתָּיו׃ מִשָּׁם נָסְעוּ הַגֻּדְגֹּדָה וּמִן־הַגֻּדְגֹּדָה יָטְבָתָה אֶרֶץ
ח נַחֲלֵי מָיִם׃ בָּעֵת הַהִוא הִבְדִּיל יהוה אֶת־שֵׁבֶט הַלֵּוִי לָשֵׂאת אֶת־אֲרוֹן

ט בְּרִית־יְהוָה לַעֲמֹד לִפְנֵי יְהוָה לְשָׁרְתוֹ וּלְבָרֵךְ בִּשְׁמוֹ עַד הַיּוֹם הַזֶּה׃ עַל־כֵּן
לֹא־הָיָה לְלֵוִי חֵלֶק וְנַחֲלָה עִם־אֶחָיו יְהוָה הוּא נַחֲלָתוֹ כַּאֲשֶׁר דִּבֶּר יְהוָה
י אֱלֹהֶיךָ לוֹ׃ וְאָנֹכִי עָמַדְתִּי בָהָר כַּיָּמִים הָרִאשֹׁנִים אַרְבָּעִים יוֹם וְאַרְבָּעִים
יא לָיְלָה וַיִּשְׁמַע יְהוָה אֵלַי גַּם בַּפַּעַם הַהִוא לֹא־אָבָה יְהוָה הַשְׁחִיתֶךָ׃ וַיֹּאמֶר
יְהוָה אֵלַי קוּם לֵךְ לְמַסַּע לִפְנֵי הָעָם וְיָבֹאוּ וְיִירְשׁוּ אֶת־הָאָרֶץ אֲשֶׁר־נִשְׁבַּעְתִּי
לַאֲבֹתָם לָתֵת לָהֶם׃
יב וְעַתָּה יִשְׂרָאֵל מָה יְהוָה אֱלֹהֶיךָ שֹׁאֵל מֵעִמָּךְ כִּי אִם־לְיִרְאָה אֶת־יְהוָה אֱלֹהֶיךָ חמישי
לָלֶכֶת בְּכָל־דְּרָכָיו וּלְאַהֲבָה אֹתוֹ וְלַעֲבֹד אֶת־יְהוָה אֱלֹהֶיךָ בְּכָל־לְבָבְךָ וּבְכָל־
יג נַפְשֶׁךָ׃ לִשְׁמֹר אֶת־מִצְוֹת יְהוָה וְאֶת־חֻקֹּתָיו אֲשֶׁר אָנֹכִי מְצַוְּךָ הַיּוֹם לְטוֹב
יד טו לָךְ׃ הֵן לַיהוָה אֱלֹהֶיךָ הַשָּׁמַיִם וּשְׁמֵי הַשָּׁמָיִם הָאָרֶץ וְכָל־אֲשֶׁר־בָּהּ׃ רַק
בַּאֲבֹתֶיךָ חָשַׁק יְהוָה לְאַהֲבָה אוֹתָם וַיִּבְחַר בְּזַרְעָם אַחֲרֵיהֶם בָּכֶם מִכָּל־
טז הָעַמִּים כַּיּוֹם הַזֶּה׃ וּמַלְתֶּם אֵת עָרְלַת לְבַבְכֶם וְעָרְפְּכֶם לֹא תַקְשׁוּ עוֹד׃
יז כִּי יְהוָה אֱלֹהֵיכֶם הוּא אֱלֹהֵי הָאֱלֹהִים וַאֲדֹנֵי הָאֲדֹנִים הָאֵל הַגָּדֹל הַגִּבֹּר
יח וְהַנּוֹרָא אֲשֶׁר לֹא־יִשָּׂא פָנִים וְלֹא יִקַּח שֹׁחַד׃ עֹשֶׂה מִשְׁפַּט יָתוֹם וְאַלְמָנָה
יט וְאֹהֵב גֵּר לָתֶת לוֹ לֶחֶם וְשִׂמְלָה׃ וַאֲהַבְתֶּם אֶת־הַגֵּר כִּי־גֵרִים הֱיִיתֶם בְּאֶרֶץ
כ כא מִצְרָיִם׃ אֶת־יְהוָה אֱלֹהֶיךָ תִּירָא אֹתוֹ תַעֲבֹד וּבוֹ תִדְבָּק וּבִשְׁמוֹ תִּשָּׁבֵעַ׃ הוּא
תְהִלָּתְךָ וְהוּא אֱלֹהֶיךָ אֲשֶׁר־עָשָׂה אִתְּךָ אֶת־הַגְּדֹלֹת וְאֶת־הַנּוֹרָאֹת הָאֵלֶּה
כב אֲשֶׁר רָאוּ עֵינֶיךָ׃ בְּשִׁבְעִים נֶפֶשׁ יָרְדוּ אֲבֹתֶיךָ מִצְרָיְמָה וְעַתָּה שָׂמְךָ יְהוָה
א א אֱלֹהֶיךָ כְּכוֹכְבֵי הַשָּׁמַיִם לָרֹב׃ וְאָהַבְתָּ אֵת יְהוָה אֱלֹהֶיךָ וְשָׁמַרְתָּ מִשְׁמַרְתּוֹ
ב וְחֻקֹּתָיו וּמִשְׁפָּטָיו וּמִצְוֹתָיו כָּל־הַיָּמִים׃ וִידַעְתֶּם הַיּוֹם כִּי ׀ לֹא אֶת־בְּנֵיכֶם
אֲשֶׁר לֹא־יָדְעוּ וַאֲשֶׁר לֹא־רָאוּ אֶת־מוּסַר יְהוָה אֱלֹהֵיכֶם אֶת־גָּדְלוֹ אֶת־יָדוֹ
ג הַחֲזָקָה וּזְרֹעוֹ הַנְּטוּיָה׃ וְאֶת־אֹתֹתָיו וְאֶת־מַעֲשָׂיו אֲשֶׁר עָשָׂה בְּתוֹךְ מִצְרָיִם
ד לְפַרְעֹה מֶלֶךְ־מִצְרַיִם וּלְכָל־אַרְצוֹ׃ וַאֲשֶׁר עָשָׂה לְחֵיל מִצְרַיִם לְסוּסָיו וּלְרִכְבּוֹ
אֲשֶׁר הֵצִיף אֶת־מֵי יַם־סוּף עַל־פְּנֵיהֶם בְּרָדְפָם אַחֲרֵיכֶם וַיְאַבְּדֵם יְהוָה עַד
ה ו הַיּוֹם הַזֶּה׃ וַאֲשֶׁר עָשָׂה לָכֶם בַּמִּדְבָּר עַד־בֹּאֲכֶם עַד־הַמָּקוֹם הַזֶּה׃ וַאֲשֶׁר
עָשָׂה לְדָתָן וְלַאֲבִירָם בְּנֵי אֱלִיאָב בֶּן־רְאוּבֵן אֲשֶׁר פָּצְתָה הָאָרֶץ אֶת־פִּיהָ
וַתִּבְלָעֵם וְאֶת־בָּתֵּיהֶם וְאֶת־אָהֳלֵיהֶם וְאֵת כָּל־הַיְקוּם אֲשֶׁר בְּרַגְלֵיהֶם בְּקֶרֶב
ז כָּל־יִשְׂרָאֵל׃ כִּי עֵינֵיכֶם הָרֹאֹת אֶת־כָּל־מַעֲשֵׂה יְהוָה הַגָּדֹל אֲשֶׁר עָשָׂה׃
ח וּשְׁמַרְתֶּם אֶת־כָּל־הַמִּצְוָה אֲשֶׁר אָנֹכִי מְצַוְּךָ הַיּוֹם לְמַעַן תֶּחֶזְקוּ וּבָאתֶם

וִירִשְׁתֶּם אֶת־הָאָרֶץ אֲשֶׁר אַתֶּם עֹבְרִים שָׁמָּה לְרִשְׁתָּהּ: וּלְמַעַן תַּאֲרִיכוּ יָמִים ט
עַל־הָאֲדָמָה אֲשֶׁר נִשְׁבַּע יְהוָה לַאֲבֹתֵיכֶם לָתֵת לָהֶם וּלְזַרְעָם אֶרֶץ זָבַת
ששי י חָלָב וּדְבָשׁ: כִּי הָאָרֶץ אֲשֶׁר אַתָּה בָא־שָׁמָּה לְרִשְׁתָּהּ לֹא כְאֶרֶץ י
מִצְרַיִם הִוא אֲשֶׁר יְצָאתֶם מִשָּׁם אֲשֶׁר תִּזְרַע אֶת־זַרְעֲךָ וְהִשְׁקִיתָ בְרַגְלְךָ כְּגַן
הַיָּרָק: וְהָאָרֶץ אֲשֶׁר אַתֶּם עֹבְרִים שָׁמָּה לְרִשְׁתָּהּ אֶרֶץ הָרִים וּבְקָעֹת לִמְטַר יא
הַשָּׁמַיִם תִּשְׁתֶּה־מָּיִם: אֶרֶץ אֲשֶׁר־יְהוָה אֱלֹהֶיךָ דֹּרֵשׁ אֹתָהּ תָּמִיד עֵינֵי יְהוָה יב
אֱלֹהֶיךָ בָּהּ מֵרֵשִׁית הַשָּׁנָה וְעַד אַחֲרִית שָׁנָה: וְהָיָה אִם־שָׁמֹעַ יג
תִּשְׁמְעוּ אֶל־מִצְוֹתַי אֲשֶׁר אָנֹכִי מְצַוֶּה אֶתְכֶם הַיּוֹם לְאַהֲבָה אֶת־יְהוָה אֱלֹהֵיכֶם
וּלְעָבְדוֹ בְּכָל־לְבַבְכֶם וּבְכָל־נַפְשְׁכֶם: וְנָתַתִּי מְטַר־אַרְצְכֶם בְּעִתּוֹ יוֹרֶה יד
וּמַלְקוֹשׁ וְאָסַפְתָּ דְגָנֶךָ וְתִירֹשְׁךָ וְיִצְהָרֶךָ: וְנָתַתִּי עֵשֶׂב בְּשָׂדְךָ לִבְהֶמְתֶּךָ טו
וְאָכַלְתָּ וְשָׂבָעְתָּ: הִשָּׁמְרוּ לָכֶם פֶּן־יִפְתֶּה לְבַבְכֶם וְסַרְתֶּם וַעֲבַדְתֶּם אֱלֹהִים טז
אֲחֵרִים וְהִשְׁתַּחֲוִיתֶם לָהֶם: וְחָרָה אַף־יְהוָה בָּכֶם וְעָצַר אֶת־הַשָּׁמַיִם וְלֹא־ יז
יִהְיֶה מָטָר וְהָאֲדָמָה לֹא תִתֵּן אֶת־יְבוּלָהּ וַאֲבַדְתֶּם מְהֵרָה מֵעַל הָאָרֶץ הַטֹּבָה
אֲשֶׁר יְהוָה נֹתֵן לָכֶם: וְשַׂמְתֶּם אֶת־דְּבָרַי אֵלֶּה עַל־לְבַבְכֶם וְעַל־נַפְשְׁכֶם יח
וּקְשַׁרְתֶּם אֹתָם לְאוֹת עַל־יֶדְכֶם וְהָיוּ לְטוֹטָפֹת בֵּין עֵינֵיכֶם: וְלִמַּדְתֶּם אֹתָם יט
אֶת־בְּנֵיכֶם לְדַבֵּר בָּם בְּשִׁבְתְּךָ בְּבֵיתֶךָ וּבְלֶכְתְּךָ בַדֶּרֶךְ וּבְשָׁכְבְּךָ וּבְקוּמֶךָ:
וּכְתַבְתָּם עַל־מְזוּזוֹת בֵּיתֶךָ וּבִשְׁעָרֶיךָ: לְמַעַן יִרְבּוּ יְמֵיכֶם וִימֵי בְנֵיכֶם כ כא
עַל הָאֲדָמָה אֲשֶׁר נִשְׁבַּע יְהוָה לַאֲבֹתֵיכֶם לָתֵת לָהֶם כִּימֵי הַשָּׁמַיִם עַל־
שביעי מפטיר הָאָרֶץ: כִּי אִם־שָׁמֹר תִּשְׁמְרוּן אֶת־כָּל־הַמִּצְוָה הַזֹּאת אֲשֶׁר אָנֹכִי כב
מְצַוֶּה אֶתְכֶם לַעֲשֹׂתָהּ לְאַהֲבָה אֶת־יְהוָה אֱלֹהֵיכֶם לָלֶכֶת בְּכָל־דְּרָכָיו
וּלְדָבְקָה־בוֹ: וְהוֹרִישׁ יְהוָה אֶת־כָּל־הַגּוֹיִם הָאֵלֶּה מִלִּפְנֵיכֶם וִירִשְׁתֶּם גּוֹיִם כג
גְּדֹלִים וַעֲצֻמִים מִכֶּם: כָּל־הַמָּקוֹם אֲשֶׁר תִּדְרֹךְ כַּף־רַגְלְכֶם בּוֹ לָכֶם יִהְיֶה מִן־ כד
הַמִּדְבָּר וְהַלְּבָנוֹן מִן־הַנָּהָר נְהַר־פְּרָת וְעַד הַיָּם הָאַחֲרוֹן יִהְיֶה גְּבֻלְכֶם: לֹא־ כה
יִתְיַצֵּב אִישׁ בִּפְנֵיכֶם פַּחְדְּכֶם וּמוֹרַאֲכֶם יִתֵּן ׀ יְהוָה אֱלֹהֵיכֶם עַל־פְּנֵי כָל־הָאָרֶץ
ראה אֲשֶׁר תִּדְרְכוּ־בָהּ כַּאֲשֶׁר דִּבֶּר לָכֶם: רְאֵה אָנֹכִי נֹתֵן לִפְנֵיכֶם הַיּוֹם כו
בְּרָכָה וּקְלָלָה: אֶת־הַבְּרָכָה אֲשֶׁר תִּשְׁמְעוּ אֶל־מִצְוֹת יְהוָה אֱלֹהֵיכֶם אֲשֶׁר כז
אָנֹכִי מְצַוֶּה אֶתְכֶם הַיּוֹם: וְהַקְּלָלָה אִם־לֹא תִשְׁמְעוּ אֶל־מִצְוֹת יְהוָה אֱלֹהֵיכֶם כח
וְסַרְתֶּם מִן־הַדֶּרֶךְ אֲשֶׁר אָנֹכִי מְצַוֶּה אֶתְכֶם הַיּוֹם לָלֶכֶת אַחֲרֵי אֱלֹהִים אֲחֵרִים
אֲשֶׁר לֹא־יְדַעְתֶּם: וְהָיָה כִּי יְבִיאֲךָ יְהוָה אֱלֹהֶיךָ אֶל־הָאָרֶץ אֲשֶׁר־ כט

אתה בא־שמה לרשתה ונתתה את־הברכה על־הר גרזים ואת־הקללה
ל על־הר עיבל: הלא־המה בעבר הירדן אחרי דרך מבוא השמש בארץ
לא הכנעני הישב בערבה מול הגלגל אצל אלוני מרה: כי אתם עברים את־
הירדן לבא לרשת את־הארץ אשר־יהוה אלהיכם נתן לכם וירשתם אתה
לב וישבתם־בה: *ושמרתם לעשות את כל־החקים ואת־המשפטים אשר לוי
יב א אנכי נתן לפניכם היום: אלה החקים והמשפטים אשר תשמרון לעשות
בארץ אשר נתן יהוה אלהי אבתיך לך לרשתה כל־הימים אשר־אתם
ב חיים על־האדמה: אבד תאבדון את־כל־המקמות אשר עבדו־שם הגוים
אשר אתם ירשים אתם את־אלהיהם על־ההרים הרמים ועל־הגבעות
ג ותחת כל־עץ רענן: ונתצתם את־מזבחתם ושברתם את־מצבתם ואשריהם
תשרפון באש ופסילי אלהיהם תגדעון ואבדתם את־שמם מן־המקום
ד ה ההוא: לא־תעשון כן ליהוה אלהיכם: כי אם־אל־המקום אשר־יבחר
יהוה אלהיכם מכל־שבטיכם לשום את־שמו שם לשכנו תדרשו ובאת
ו שמה: *והבאתם שמה עלתיכם וזבחיכם ואת מעשרתיכם ואת תרומת ישראל
ז ידכם ונדריכם ונדבתיכם ובכרת בקרכם וצאנכם: ואכלתם־שם לפני
יהוה אלהיכם ושמחתם בכל משלח ידכם אתם ובתיכם אשר ברכך יהוה
ח אלהיך: לא תעשון ככל אשר אנחנו עשים פה היום איש כל־הישר בעיניו:
ט כי לא־באתם עד־עתה אל־המנוחה ואל־הנחלה אשר־יהוה אלהיך נתן
י לך: ועברתם את־הירדן וישבתם בארץ אשר־יהוה אלהיכם מנחיל אתכם
יא והניח לכם מכל־איביכם מסביב וישבתם־בטח:** והיה המקום אשר־ שני
יבחר יהוה אלהיכם בו לשכן שמו שם שמה תביאו את כל־אשר אנכי
מצוה אתכם עולתיכם וזבחיכם מעשרתיכם ותרמת ידכם וכל מבחר
יב נדריכם אשר תדרו ליהוה: ושמחתם לפני יהוה אלהיכם אתם ובניכם
ובנתיכם ועבדיכם ואמהתיכם והלוי אשר בשעריכם כי אין לו חלק ונחלה
יג יד אתכם: השמר לך פן־תעלה עלתיך בכל־מקום אשר תראה: כי אם־במקום
אשר־יבחר יהוה באחד שבטיך שם תעלה עלתיך ושם תעשה כל אשר
טו אנכי מצוך: רק בכל־אות נפשך תזבח | ואכלת בשר כברכת יהוה אלהיך
טז אשר נתן־לך בכל־שעריך הטמא והטהור יאכלנו כצבי וכאיל: רק הדם
יז לא תאכלו על־הארץ תשפכנו כמים: לא־תוכל לאכל בשעריך מעשר

דְּגָנְךָ וְתִירֹשְׁךָ וְיִצְהָרֶךָ וּבְכֹרֹת בְּקָרְךָ וְצֹאנֶךָ וְכָל־נְדָרֶיךָ אֲשֶׁר תִּדֹּר וְנִדְבֹתֶיךָ
וּתְרוּמַת יָדֶךָ׃ כִּי אִם־לִפְנֵי יְהוָה אֱלֹהֶיךָ תֹּאכְלֶנּוּ בַּמָּקוֹם אֲשֶׁר יִבְחַר יְהוָה יח
אֱלֹהֶיךָ בּוֹ אַתָּה וּבִנְךָ וּבִתֶּךָ וְעַבְדְּךָ וַאֲמָתֶךָ וְהַלֵּוִי אֲשֶׁר בִּשְׁעָרֶיךָ וְשָׂמַחְתָּ
לִפְנֵי יְהוָה אֱלֹהֶיךָ בְּכֹל מִשְׁלַח יָדֶךָ׃ הִשָּׁמֶר לְךָ פֶּן־תַּעֲזֹב אֶת־הַלֵּוִי כָּל־יָמֶיךָ יט
יא עַל־אַדְמָתֶךָ׃ כִּי־יַרְחִיב יְהוָה אֱלֹהֶיךָ אֶת־גְּבֻלְךָ כַּאֲשֶׁר דִּבֶּר־לָךְ כ
וְאָמַרְתָּ אֹכְלָה בָשָׂר כִּי־תְאַוֶּה נַפְשְׁךָ לֶאֱכֹל בָּשָׂר בְּכָל־אַוַּת נַפְשְׁךָ תֹּאכַל
בָּשָׂר׃ כִּי־יִרְחַק מִמְּךָ הַמָּקוֹם אֲשֶׁר יִבְחַר יְהוָה אֱלֹהֶיךָ לָשׂוּם שְׁמוֹ שָׁם כא
וְזָבַחְתָּ מִבְּקָרְךָ וּמִצֹּאנְךָ אֲשֶׁר נָתַן יְהוָה לְךָ כַּאֲשֶׁר צִוִּיתִךָ וְאָכַלְתָּ בִּשְׁעָרֶיךָ
בְּכֹל אַוַּת נַפְשֶׁךָ׃ אַךְ כַּאֲשֶׁר יֵאָכֵל אֶת־הַצְּבִי וְאֶת־הָאַיָּל כֵּן תֹּאכְלֶנּוּ הַטָּמֵא כב
וְהַטָּהוֹר יַחְדָּו יֹאכְלֶנּוּ׃ רַק חֲזַק לְבִלְתִּי אֲכֹל הַדָּם כִּי הַדָּם הוּא הַנָּפֶשׁ וְלֹא־ כג
תֹאכַל הַנֶּפֶשׁ עִם־הַבָּשָׂר׃ לֹא תֹּאכְלֶנּוּ עַל־הָאָרֶץ תִּשְׁפְּכֶנּוּ כַּמָּיִם׃ לֹא כד כה
תֹּאכְלֶנּוּ לְמַעַן יִיטַב לְךָ וּלְבָנֶיךָ אַחֲרֶיךָ כִּי־תַעֲשֶׂה הַיָּשָׁר בְּעֵינֵי יְהוָה׃ רַק כו
קָדָשֶׁיךָ אֲשֶׁר־יִהְיוּ לְךָ וּנְדָרֶיךָ תִּשָּׂא וּבָאתָ אֶל־הַמָּקוֹם אֲשֶׁר־יִבְחַר יְהוָה׃
וְעָשִׂיתָ עֹלֹתֶיךָ הַבָּשָׂר וְהַדָּם עַל־מִזְבַּח יְהוָה אֱלֹהֶיךָ וְדַם־זְבָחֶיךָ יִשָּׁפֵךְ כז
עַל־מִזְבַּח יְהוָה אֱלֹהֶיךָ וְהַבָּשָׂר תֹּאכֵל׃ שְׁמֹר וְשָׁמַעְתָּ אֵת כָּל־הַדְּבָרִים כח
הָאֵלֶּה אֲשֶׁר אָנֹכִי מְצַוֶּךָּ לְמַעַן יִיטַב לְךָ וּלְבָנֶיךָ אַחֲרֶיךָ עַד־עוֹלָם כִּי תַעֲשֶׂה
שלישי הַטּוֹב וְהַיָּשָׁר בְּעֵינֵי יְהוָה אֱלֹהֶיךָ׃ כִּי־יַכְרִית יְהוָה אֱלֹהֶיךָ אֶת־ כט
הַגּוֹיִם אֲשֶׁר אַתָּה בָא־שָׁמָּה לָרֶשֶׁת אוֹתָם מִפָּנֶיךָ וְיָרַשְׁתָּ אֹתָם וְיָשַׁבְתָּ
בְּאַרְצָם׃ הִשָּׁמֶר לְךָ פֶּן־תִּנָּקֵשׁ אַחֲרֵיהֶם אַחֲרֵי הִשָּׁמְדָם מִפָּנֶיךָ וּפֶן־תִּדְרֹשׁ ל
לֵאלֹהֵיהֶם לֵאמֹר אֵיכָה יַעַבְדוּ הַגּוֹיִם הָאֵלֶּה אֶת־אֱלֹהֵיהֶם וְאֶעֱשֶׂה־כֵּן גַּם־
אָנִי׃ לֹא־תַעֲשֶׂה כֵן לַיהוָה אֱלֹהֶיךָ כִּי כָל־תּוֹעֲבַת יְהוָה אֲשֶׁר שָׂנֵא עָשׂוּ לא
לֵאלֹהֵיהֶם כִּי גַם אֶת־בְּנֵיהֶם וְאֶת־בְּנֹתֵיהֶם יִשְׂרְפוּ בָאֵשׁ לֵאלֹהֵיהֶם׃ אֵת יג א
כָּל־הַדָּבָר אֲשֶׁר אָנֹכִי מְצַוֶּה אֶתְכֶם אֹתוֹ תִשְׁמְרוּ לַעֲשׂוֹת לֹא־תֹסֵף עָלָיו וְלֹא
תִגְרַע מִמֶּנּוּ׃
כִּי־יָקוּם בְּקִרְבְּךָ נָבִיא אוֹ חֹלֵם חֲלוֹם וְנָתַן אֵלֶיךָ אוֹת אוֹ מוֹפֵת׃ וּבָא הָאוֹת ב ג
וְהַמּוֹפֵת אֲשֶׁר־דִּבֶּר אֵלֶיךָ לֵאמֹר נֵלְכָה אַחֲרֵי אֱלֹהִים אֲחֵרִים אֲשֶׁר לֹא־
יְדַעְתָּם וְנָעָבְדֵם׃ לֹא תִשְׁמַע אֶל־דִּבְרֵי הַנָּבִיא הַהוּא אוֹ אֶל־חוֹלֵם הַחֲלוֹם ד
הַהוּא כִּי מְנַסֶּה יְהוָה אֱלֹהֵיכֶם אֶתְכֶם לָדַעַת הֲיִשְׁכֶם אֹהֲבִים אֶת־יְהוָה
אֱלֹהֵיכֶם בְּכָל־לְבַבְכֶם וּבְכָל־נַפְשְׁכֶם׃ אַחֲרֵי יְהוָה אֱלֹהֵיכֶם תֵּלֵכוּ וְאֹתוֹ ה

תִּירָאוּ וְאֶת־מִצְוֺתָיו תִּשְׁמֹרוּ וּבְקֹלוֹ תִשְׁמָעוּ וְאֹתוֹ תַעֲבֹדוּ וּבוֹ תִדְבָּקוּן׃
ו וְהַנָּבִיא הַהוּא אוֹ חֹלֵם הַחֲלוֹם הַהוּא יוּמָת כִּי דִבֶּר־סָרָה עַל־יְהוָה אֱלֹהֵיכֶם
הַמּוֹצִיא אֶתְכֶם ׀ מֵאֶרֶץ מִצְרַיִם וְהַפֹּדְךָ מִבֵּית עֲבָדִים לְהַדִּיחֲךָ מִן־הַדֶּרֶךְ
ז אֲשֶׁר צִוְּךָ יְהוָה אֱלֹהֶיךָ לָלֶכֶת בָּהּ וּבִעַרְתָּ הָרָע מִקִּרְבֶּךָ׃ כִּי יְסִיתְךָ
אָחִיךָ בֶן־אִמֶּךָ אוֹ־בִנְךָ אוֹ־בִתְּךָ אוֹ ׀ אֵשֶׁת חֵיקֶךָ אוֹ רֵעֲךָ אֲשֶׁר כְּנַפְשְׁךָ
בַּסֵּתֶר לֵאמֹר נֵלְכָה וְנַעַבְדָה אֱלֹהִים אֲחֵרִים אֲשֶׁר לֹא יָדַעְתָּ אַתָּה וַאֲבֹתֶיךָ׃
ח מֵאֱלֹהֵי הָעַמִּים אֲשֶׁר סְבִיבֹתֵיכֶם הַקְּרֹבִים אֵלֶיךָ אוֹ הָרְחֹקִים מִמֶּךָּ מִקְצֵה
ט הָאָרֶץ וְעַד־קְצֵה הָאָרֶץ׃ לֹא־תֹאבֶה לוֹ וְלֹא תִשְׁמַע אֵלָיו וְלֹא־תָחוֹס עֵינְךָ
י עָלָיו וְלֹא־תַחְמֹל וְלֹא־תְכַסֶּה עָלָיו׃ כִּי הָרֹג תַּהַרְגֶנּוּ יָדְךָ תִּהְיֶה־בּוֹ בָרִאשׁוֹנָה
יא לַהֲמִיתוֹ וְיַד כָּל־הָעָם בָּאַחֲרֹנָה׃ וּסְקַלְתּוֹ בָאֲבָנִים וָמֵת כִּי בִקֵּשׁ לְהַדִּיחֲךָ
יב מֵעַל יְהוָה אֱלֹהֶיךָ הַמּוֹצִיאֲךָ מֵאֶרֶץ מִצְרַיִם מִבֵּית עֲבָדִים׃ וְכָל־יִשְׂרָאֵל
יג יִשְׁמְעוּ וְיִרָאוּן וְלֹא־יוֹסִפוּ לַעֲשׂוֹת כַּדָּבָר הָרָע הַזֶּה בְּקִרְבֶּךָ׃ כִּי־
יד תִשְׁמַע בְּאַחַת עָרֶיךָ אֲשֶׁר יְהוָה אֱלֹהֶיךָ נֹתֵן לְךָ לָשֶׁבֶת שָׁם לֵאמֹר׃ יָצְאוּ
אֲנָשִׁים בְּנֵי־בְלִיַּעַל מִקִּרְבֶּךָ וַיַּדִּיחוּ אֶת־יֹשְׁבֵי עִירָם לֵאמֹר נֵלְכָה וְנַעַבְדָה
טו אֱלֹהִים אֲחֵרִים אֲשֶׁר לֹא־יְדַעְתֶּם׃ וְדָרַשְׁתָּ וְחָקַרְתָּ וְשָׁאַלְתָּ הֵיטֵב וְהִנֵּה
טז אֱמֶת נָכוֹן הַדָּבָר נֶעֶשְׂתָה הַתּוֹעֵבָה הַזֹּאת בְּקִרְבֶּךָ׃ הַכֵּה תַכֶּה אֶת־יֹשְׁבֵי
הָעִיר הַהִוא לְפִי־חָרֶב הַחֲרֵם אֹתָהּ וְאֶת־כָּל־אֲשֶׁר־בָּהּ וְאֶת־בְּהֶמְתָּהּ לְפִי־
יז חָרֶב׃ וְאֶת־כָּל־שְׁלָלָהּ תִּקְבֹּץ אֶל־תּוֹךְ רְחֹבָהּ וְשָׂרַפְתָּ בָאֵשׁ אֶת־הָעִיר
וְאֶת־כָּל־שְׁלָלָהּ כָּלִיל לַיהוָה אֱלֹהֶיךָ וְהָיְתָה תֵּל עוֹלָם לֹא תִבָּנֶה עוֹד׃
יח וְלֹא־יִדְבַּק בְּיָדְךָ מְאוּמָה מִן־הַחֵרֶם לְמַעַן יָשׁוּב יְהוָה מֵחֲרוֹן אַפּוֹ וְנָתַן־לְךָ
יט רַחֲמִים וְרִחַמְךָ וְהִרְבֶּךָ כַּאֲשֶׁר נִשְׁבַּע לַאֲבֹתֶיךָ׃ כִּי תִשְׁמַע בְּקוֹל יְהוָה אֱלֹהֶיךָ
לִשְׁמֹר אֶת־כָּל־מִצְוֺתָיו אֲשֶׁר אָנֹכִי מְצַוְּךָ הַיּוֹם לַעֲשׂוֹת הַיָּשָׁר בְּעֵינֵי יְהוָה
א אֱלֹהֶיךָ׃ בָּנִים אַתֶּם לַיהוָה אֱלֹהֵיכֶם לֹא תִתְגֹּדְדוּ וְלֹא־תָשִׂימוּ יב רביעי
ב קָרְחָה בֵּין עֵינֵיכֶם לָמֵת׃ כִּי עַם קָדוֹשׁ אַתָּה לַיהוָה אֱלֹהֶיךָ וּבְךָ בָּחַר יְהוָה
ג לִהְיוֹת לוֹ לְעַם סְגֻלָּה מִכֹּל הָעַמִּים אֲשֶׁר עַל־פְּנֵי הָאֲדָמָה׃ לֹא
ד תֹאכַל כָּל־תּוֹעֵבָה׃ זֹאת הַבְּהֵמָה אֲשֶׁר תֹּאכֵלוּ שׁוֹר שֵׂה כְשָׂבִים וְשֵׂה
ה ו עִזִּים׃ אַיָּל וּצְבִי וְיַחְמוּר וְאַקּוֹ וְדִישֹׁן וּתְאוֹ וָזָמֶר׃ וְכָל־בְּהֵמָה מַפְרֶסֶת פַּרְסָה
ז וְשֹׁסַעַת שֶׁסַע שְׁתֵּי פְרָסוֹת מַעֲלַת גֵּרָה בַּבְּהֵמָה אֹתָהּ תֹּאכֵלוּ׃ אַךְ אֶת־זֶה
לֹא תֹאכְלוּ מִמַּעֲלֵי הַגֵּרָה וּמִמַּפְרִיסֵי הַפַּרְסָה הַשְּׁסוּעָה אֶת־הַגָּמָל וְאֶת־

הָאַרְנֶבֶת וְאֶת־הַשָּׁפָן כִּי־מַעֲלֵה גֵרָה הֵמָּה וּפַרְסָה לֹא הִפְרִיסוּ טְמֵאִים הֵם
לָכֶם׃ וְאֶת־הַחֲזִיר כִּי־מַפְרִיס פַּרְסָה הוּא וְלֹא גֵרָה טָמֵא הוּא לָכֶם מִבְּשָׂרָם ח
לֹא תֹאכֵלוּ וּבְנִבְלָתָם לֹא תִגָּעוּ׃ אֶת־זֶה תֹּאכְלוּ מִכֹּל אֲשֶׁר בַּמָּיִם ט
כֹּל אֲשֶׁר־לוֹ סְנַפִּיר וְקַשְׂקֶשֶׂת תֹּאכֵלוּ׃ וְכֹל אֲשֶׁר אֵין־לוֹ סְנַפִּיר וְקַשְׂקֶשֶׂת י
לֹא תֹאכֵלוּ טָמֵא הוּא לָכֶם׃ כָּל־צִפּוֹר טְהֹרָה תֹּאכֵלוּ׃ וְזֶה אֲשֶׁר יא יב
לֹא־תֹאכְלוּ מֵהֶם הַנֶּשֶׁר וְהַפֶּרֶס וְהָעָזְנִיָּה׃ וְהָרָאָה וְאֶת־הָאַיָּה וְהַדַּיָּה לְמִינָהּ׃ יג
וְאֵת כָּל־עֹרֵב לְמִינוֹ׃ וְאֵת בַּת הַיַּעֲנָה וְאֶת־הַתַּחְמָס וְאֶת־הַשָּׁחַף וְאֶת־הַנֵּץ יד טו
לְמִינֵהוּ׃ אֶת־הַכּוֹס וְאֶת־הַיַּנְשׁוּף וְהַתִּנְשָׁמֶת׃ וְהַקָּאָת וְאֶת־הָרָחָמָה וְאֶת־ טז יז
הַשָּׁלָךְ׃ וְהַחֲסִידָה וְהָאֲנָפָה לְמִינָהּ וְהַדּוּכִיפַת וְהָעֲטַלֵּף׃ וְכֹל שֶׁרֶץ הָעוֹף יח יט
טָמֵא הוּא לָכֶם לֹא יֵאָכֵלוּ׃ כָּל־עוֹף טָהוֹר תֹּאכֵלוּ׃ לֹא־תֹאכְלוּ כָל־נְבֵלָה כ כא
לַגֵּר אֲשֶׁר־בִּשְׁעָרֶיךָ תִּתְּנֶנָּה וַאֲכָלָהּ אוֹ מָכֹר לְנָכְרִי כִּי עַם קָדוֹשׁ אַתָּה לַיהוָה
אֱלֹהֶיךָ לֹא־תְבַשֵּׁל גְּדִי בַּחֲלֵב אִמּוֹ׃
חמישי *עַשֵּׂר תְּעַשֵּׂר אֵת כָּל־תְּבוּאַת זַרְעֶךָ הַיֹּצֵא הַשָּׂדֶה שָׁנָה שָׁנָה׃ וְאָכַלְתָּ כב כג
לִפְנֵי ׀ יְהוָה אֱלֹהֶיךָ בַּמָּקוֹם אֲשֶׁר־יִבְחַר לְשַׁכֵּן שְׁמוֹ שָׁם מַעְשַׂר דְּגָנְךָ תִּירֹשְׁךָ
וְיִצְהָרֶךָ וּבְכֹרֹת בְּקָרְךָ וְצֹאנֶךָ לְמַעַן תִּלְמַד לְיִרְאָה אֶת־יְהוָה אֱלֹהֶיךָ כָּל־
הַיָּמִים׃ וְכִי־יִרְבֶּה מִמְּךָ הַדֶּרֶךְ כִּי לֹא תוּכַל שְׂאֵתוֹ כִּי־יִרְחַק מִמְּךָ הַמָּקוֹם כד
אֲשֶׁר יִבְחַר יְהוָה אֱלֹהֶיךָ לָשׂוּם שְׁמוֹ שָׁם כִּי יְבָרֶכְךָ יְהוָה אֱלֹהֶיךָ׃ וְנָתַתָּה כה
בַּכָּסֶף וְצַרְתָּ הַכֶּסֶף בְּיָדְךָ וְהָלַכְתָּ אֶל־הַמָּקוֹם אֲשֶׁר יִבְחַר יְהוָה אֱלֹהֶיךָ בּוֹ׃
וְנָתַתָּה הַכֶּסֶף בְּכֹל אֲשֶׁר־תְּאַוֶּה נַפְשְׁךָ בַּבָּקָר וּבַצֹּאן וּבַיַּיִן וּבַשֵּׁכָר וּבְכֹל אֲשֶׁר כו
תִּשְׁאָלְךָ נַפְשֶׁךָ וְאָכַלְתָּ שָּׁם לִפְנֵי יְהוָה אֱלֹהֶיךָ וְשָׂמַחְתָּ אַתָּה וּבֵיתֶךָ׃ וְהַלֵּוִי כז
אֲשֶׁר־בִּשְׁעָרֶיךָ לֹא תַעַזְבֶנּוּ כִּי אֵין לוֹ חֵלֶק וְנַחֲלָה עִמָּךְ׃ מִקְצֵה ׀ כח
שָׁלֹשׁ שָׁנִים תּוֹצִיא אֶת־כָּל־מַעְשַׂר תְּבוּאָתְךָ בַּשָּׁנָה הַהִוא וְהִנַּחְתָּ בִּשְׁעָרֶיךָ׃
וּבָא הַלֵּוִי כִּי אֵין־לוֹ חֵלֶק וְנַחֲלָה עִמָּךְ וְהַגֵּר וְהַיָּתוֹם וְהָאַלְמָנָה אֲשֶׁר כט
בִּשְׁעָרֶיךָ וְאָכְלוּ וְשָׂבֵעוּ לְמַעַן יְבָרֶכְךָ יְהוָה אֱלֹהֶיךָ בְּכָל־מַעֲשֵׂה יָדְךָ אֲשֶׁר
ששי תַּעֲשֶׂה׃ *מִקֵּץ שֶׁבַע־שָׁנִים תַּעֲשֶׂה שְׁמִטָּה׃ וְזֶה דְּבַר הַשְּׁמִטָּה א ב
שָׁמוֹט כָּל־בַּעַל מַשֵּׁה יָדוֹ אֲשֶׁר יַשֶּׁה בְּרֵעֵהוּ לֹא־יִגֹּשׂ אֶת־רֵעֵהוּ וְאֶת־אָחִיו
כִּי־קָרָא שְׁמִטָּה לַיהוָה׃ אֶת־הַנָּכְרִי תִּגֹּשׂ וַאֲשֶׁר יִהְיֶה לְךָ אֶת־אָחִיךָ תַּשְׁמֵט ג
יָדֶךָ׃ אֶפֶס כִּי לֹא יִהְיֶה־בְּךָ אֶבְיוֹן כִּי־בָרֵךְ יְבָרֶכְךָ יְהוָה בָּאָרֶץ אֲשֶׁר יְהוָה ד
אֱלֹהֶיךָ נֹתֵן־לְךָ נַחֲלָה לְרִשְׁתָּהּ׃ רַק אִם־שָׁמוֹעַ תִּשְׁמַע בְּקוֹל יְהוָה אֱלֹהֶיךָ ה

ו לִשְׁמֹר לַעֲשׂוֹת אֶת־כָּל־הַמִּצְוָה הַזֹּאת אֲשֶׁר אָנֹכִי מְצַוְּךָ הַיּוֹם: כִּי־יְהוָה
אֱלֹהֶיךָ בֵּרַכְךָ כַּאֲשֶׁר דִּבֶּר־לָךְ וְהַעֲבַטְתָּ גּוֹיִם רַבִּים וְאַתָּה לֹא תַעֲבֹט וּמָשַׁלְתָּ
ז בְּגוֹיִם רַבִּים וּבְךָ לֹא יִמְשֹׁלוּ: כִּי־יִהְיֶה בְךָ אֶבְיוֹן מֵאַחַד אַחֶיךָ יג
בְּאַחַד שְׁעָרֶיךָ בְּאַרְצְךָ אֲשֶׁר־יְהוָה אֱלֹהֶיךָ נֹתֵן לָךְ לֹא תְאַמֵּץ אֶת־לְבָבְךָ
ח וְלֹא תִקְפֹּץ אֶת־יָדְךָ מֵאָחִיךָ הָאֶבְיוֹן: כִּי־פָתֹחַ תִּפְתַּח אֶת־יָדְךָ לוֹ וְהַעֲבֵט
ט תַּעֲבִיטֶנּוּ דֵּי מַחְסֹרוֹ אֲשֶׁר יֶחְסַר לוֹ: הִשָּׁמֶר לְךָ פֶּן־יִהְיֶה דָבָר עִם־לְבָבְךָ
בְלִיַּעַל לֵאמֹר קָרְבָה שְׁנַת־הַשֶּׁבַע שְׁנַת הַשְּׁמִטָּה וְרָעָה עֵינְךָ בְּאָחִיךָ הָאֶבְיוֹן
י וְלֹא תִתֵּן לוֹ וְקָרָא עָלֶיךָ אֶל־יְהוָה וְהָיָה בְךָ חֵטְא: נָתוֹן תִּתֵּן לוֹ וְלֹא־יֵרַע
לְבָבְךָ בְּתִתְּךָ לוֹ כִּי בִּגְלַל ׀ הַדָּבָר הַזֶּה יְבָרֶכְךָ יְהוָה אֱלֹהֶיךָ בְּכָל־מַעֲשֶׂךָ
יא וּבְכֹל מִשְׁלַח יָדֶךָ: כִּי לֹא־יֶחְדַּל אֶבְיוֹן מִקֶּרֶב הָאָרֶץ עַל־כֵּן אָנֹכִי מְצַוְּךָ
יב לֵאמֹר פָּתֹחַ תִּפְתַּח אֶת־יָדְךָ לְאָחִיךָ לַעֲנִיֶּךָ וּלְאֶבְיֹנְךָ בְּאַרְצֶךָ: כִּי־
יִמָּכֵר לְךָ אָחִיךָ הָעִבְרִי אוֹ הָעִבְרִיָּה וַעֲבָדְךָ שֵׁשׁ שָׁנִים וּבַשָּׁנָה הַשְּׁבִיעִת
יג תְּשַׁלְּחֶנּוּ חָפְשִׁי מֵעִמָּךְ: וְכִי־תְשַׁלְּחֶנּוּ חָפְשִׁי מֵעִמָּךְ לֹא תְשַׁלְּחֶנּוּ רֵיקָם:
יד הַעֲנֵיק תַּעֲנִיק לוֹ מִצֹּאנְךָ וּמִגָּרְנְךָ וּמִיִּקְבֶךָ אֲשֶׁר בֵּרַכְךָ יְהוָה אֱלֹהֶיךָ תִּתֶּן־
טו לוֹ: וְזָכַרְתָּ כִּי עֶבֶד הָיִיתָ בְּאֶרֶץ מִצְרַיִם וַיִּפְדְּךָ יְהוָה אֱלֹהֶיךָ עַל־כֵּן אָנֹכִי
טז מְצַוְּךָ אֶת־הַדָּבָר הַזֶּה הַיּוֹם: וְהָיָה כִּי־יֹאמַר אֵלֶיךָ לֹא אֵצֵא מֵעִמָּךְ כִּי אֲהֵבְךָ
יז וְאֶת־בֵּיתֶךָ כִּי־טוֹב לוֹ עִמָּךְ: וְלָקַחְתָּ אֶת־הַמַּרְצֵעַ וְנָתַתָּה בְאָזְנוֹ וּבַדֶּלֶת
יח וְהָיָה לְךָ עֶבֶד עוֹלָם וְאַף לַאֲמָתְךָ תַּעֲשֶׂה־כֵּן: לֹא־יִקְשֶׁה בְעֵינֶךָ בְּשַׁלֵּחֲךָ
אֹתוֹ חָפְשִׁי מֵעִמָּךְ כִּי מִשְׁנֶה שְׂכַר שָׂכִיר עֲבָדְךָ שֵׁשׁ שָׁנִים וּבֵרַכְךָ יְהוָה
אֱלֹהֶיךָ בְּכֹל אֲשֶׁר תַּעֲשֶׂה:
יט כָּל־הַבְּכוֹר אֲשֶׁר יִוָּלֵד בִּבְקָרְךָ וּבְצֹאנְךָ הַזָּכָר תַּקְדִּישׁ לַיהוָה אֱלֹהֶיךָ לֹא שביעי
כ תַעֲבֹד בִּבְכֹר שׁוֹרֶךָ וְלֹא תָגֹז בְּכוֹר צֹאנֶךָ: לִפְנֵי יְהוָה אֱלֹהֶיךָ תֹאכְלֶנּוּ
כא שָׁנָה בְשָׁנָה בַּמָּקוֹם אֲשֶׁר־יִבְחַר יְהוָה אַתָּה וּבֵיתֶךָ: וְכִי־יִהְיֶה בוֹ מוּם
כב פִּסֵּחַ אוֹ עִוֵּר כֹּל מוּם רָע לֹא תִזְבָּחֶנּוּ לַיהוָה אֱלֹהֶיךָ: בִּשְׁעָרֶיךָ תֹּאכְלֶנּוּ
כג הַטָּמֵא וְהַטָּהוֹר יַחְדָּו כַּצְּבִי וְכָאַיָּל: רַק אֶת־דָּמוֹ לֹא תֹאכֵל עַל־הָאָרֶץ
תִּשְׁפְּכֶנּוּ כַּמָּיִם:
א שָׁמוֹר אֶת־חֹדֶשׁ הָאָבִיב וְעָשִׂיתָ פֶּסַח לַיהוָה אֱלֹהֶיךָ כִּי בְּחֹדֶשׁ הָאָבִיב טז
ב הוֹצִיאֲךָ יְהוָה אֱלֹהֶיךָ מִמִּצְרַיִם לָיְלָה: וְזָבַחְתָּ פֶּסַח לַיהוָה אֱלֹהֶיךָ צֹאן וּבָקָר
ג בַּמָּקוֹם אֲשֶׁר יִבְחַר יְהוָה לְשַׁכֵּן שְׁמוֹ שָׁם: לֹא־תֹאכַל עָלָיו חָמֵץ שִׁבְעַת

יָמִים תֹּאכַל־עָלָיו מַצּוֹת לֶחֶם עֹנִי כִּי בְחִפָּזוֹן יָצָאתָ מֵאֶרֶץ מִצְרַיִם לְמַעַן
תִּזְכֹּר אֶת־יוֹם צֵאתְךָ מֵאֶרֶץ מִצְרַיִם כֹּל יְמֵי חַיֶּיךָ: וְלֹא־יֵרָאֶה לְךָ שְׂאֹר בְּכָל־ ד
גְּבֻלְךָ שִׁבְעַת יָמִים וְלֹא־יָלִין מִן־הַבָּשָׂר אֲשֶׁר תִּזְבַּח בָּעֶרֶב בַּיּוֹם הָרִאשׁוֹן
לַבֹּקֶר: לֹא תוּכַל לִזְבֹּחַ אֶת־הַפָּסַח בְּאַחַד שְׁעָרֶיךָ אֲשֶׁר־יְהוָה אֱלֹהֶיךָ נֹתֵן ה
לָךְ: כִּי אִם־אֶל־הַמָּקוֹם אֲשֶׁר־יִבְחַר יְהוָה אֱלֹהֶיךָ לְשַׁכֵּן שְׁמוֹ שָׁם תִּזְבַּח ו
אֶת־הַפֶּסַח בָּעָרֶב כְּבוֹא הַשֶּׁמֶשׁ מוֹעֵד צֵאתְךָ מִמִּצְרָיִם: וּבִשַּׁלְתָּ וְאָכַלְתָּ ז
בַּמָּקוֹם אֲשֶׁר יִבְחַר יְהוָה אֱלֹהֶיךָ בּוֹ וּפָנִיתָ בַבֹּקֶר וְהָלַכְתָּ לְאֹהָלֶיךָ: שֵׁשֶׁת ח
יָמִים תֹּאכַל מַצּוֹת וּבַיּוֹם הַשְּׁבִיעִי עֲצֶרֶת לַיהוָה אֱלֹהֶיךָ לֹא תַעֲשֶׂה
מְלָאכָה: שִׁבְעָה שָׁבֻעֹת תִּסְפָּר־לָךְ מֵהָחֵל חֶרְמֵשׁ בַּקָּמָה תָּחֵל ט
לִסְפֹּר שִׁבְעָה שָׁבֻעוֹת: וְעָשִׂיתָ חַג שָׁבֻעוֹת לַיהוָה אֱלֹהֶיךָ מִסַּת נִדְבַת יָדְךָ י
אֲשֶׁר תִּתֵּן כַּאֲשֶׁר יְבָרֶכְךָ יְהוָה אֱלֹהֶיךָ: וְשָׂמַחְתָּ לִפְנֵי ׀ יְהוָה אֱלֹהֶיךָ אַתָּה יא
וּבִנְךָ וּבִתֶּךָ וְעַבְדְּךָ וַאֲמָתֶךָ וְהַלֵּוִי אֲשֶׁר בִּשְׁעָרֶיךָ וְהַגֵּר וְהַיָּתוֹם וְהָאַלְמָנָה
אֲשֶׁר בְּקִרְבֶּךָ בַּמָּקוֹם אֲשֶׁר יִבְחַר יְהוָה אֱלֹהֶיךָ לְשַׁכֵּן שְׁמוֹ שָׁם: וְזָכַרְתָּ כִּי־ יב
עֶבֶד הָיִיתָ בְּמִצְרָיִם וְשָׁמַרְתָּ וְעָשִׂיתָ אֶת־הַחֻקִּים הָאֵלֶּה:

מפטיר חַג הַסֻּכֹּת תַּעֲשֶׂה לְךָ שִׁבְעַת יָמִים בְּאָסְפְּךָ מִגָּרְנְךָ וּמִיִּקְבֶךָ: וְשָׂמַחְתָּ בְּחַגֶּךָ יג יד
אַתָּה וּבִנְךָ וּבִתֶּךָ וְעַבְדְּךָ וַאֲמָתֶךָ וְהַלֵּוִי וְהַגֵּר וְהַיָּתוֹם וְהָאַלְמָנָה אֲשֶׁר
בִּשְׁעָרֶיךָ: שִׁבְעַת יָמִים תָּחֹג לַיהוָה אֱלֹהֶיךָ בַּמָּקוֹם אֲשֶׁר־יִבְחַר יְהוָה כִּי טו
יְבָרֶכְךָ יְהוָה אֱלֹהֶיךָ בְּכֹל תְּבוּאָתְךָ וּבְכֹל מַעֲשֵׂה יָדֶיךָ וְהָיִיתָ אַךְ שָׂמֵחַ: שָׁלוֹשׁ טז
פְּעָמִים ׀ בַּשָּׁנָה יֵרָאֶה כָל־זְכוּרְךָ אֶת־פְּנֵי ׀ יְהוָה אֱלֹהֶיךָ בַּמָּקוֹם אֲשֶׁר יִבְחָר
בְּחַג הַמַּצּוֹת וּבְחַג הַשָּׁבֻעוֹת וּבְחַג הַסֻּכּוֹת וְלֹא יֵרָאֶה אֶת־פְּנֵי יְהוָה רֵיקָם:

The Maftir for Shabbat Rosh Ḥodesh, page 1030

שופטים יד אִישׁ כְּמַתְּנַת יָדוֹ כְּבִרְכַּת יְהוָה אֱלֹהֶיךָ אֲשֶׁר נָתַן־לָךְ: שֹׁפְטִים יז יח
וְשֹׁטְרִים תִּתֶּן־לְךָ בְּכָל־שְׁעָרֶיךָ אֲשֶׁר יְהוָה אֱלֹהֶיךָ נֹתֵן לְךָ לִשְׁבָטֶיךָ וְשָׁפְטוּ
אֶת־הָעָם מִשְׁפַּט־צֶדֶק: לֹא־תַטֶּה מִשְׁפָּט לֹא תַכִּיר פָּנִים וְלֹא־תִקַּח שֹׁחַד יט
כִּי הַשֹּׁחַד יְעַוֵּר עֵינֵי חֲכָמִים וִיסַלֵּף דִּבְרֵי צַדִּיקִם: צֶדֶק צֶדֶק תִּרְדֹּף לְמַעַן כ
לוי תִּחְיֶה וְיָרַשְׁתָּ אֶת־הָאָרֶץ אֲשֶׁר־יְהוָה אֱלֹהֶיךָ נֹתֵן לָךְ: *לֹא־ כא
תִטַּע לְךָ אֲשֵׁרָה כָּל־עֵץ אֵצֶל מִזְבַּח יְהוָה אֱלֹהֶיךָ אֲשֶׁר תַּעֲשֶׂה־לָּךְ: וְלֹא־ כב
תָקִים לְךָ מַצֵּבָה אֲשֶׁר שָׂנֵא יְהוָה אֱלֹהֶיךָ: לֹא־תִזְבַּח לַיהוָה א יז
אֱלֹהֶיךָ שׁוֹר וָשֶׂה אֲשֶׁר יִהְיֶה בוֹ מוּם כֹּל דָּבָר רָע כִּי תוֹעֲבַת יְהוָה אֱלֹהֶיךָ
הוּא: כִּי־יִמָּצֵא בְקִרְבְּךָ בְּאַחַד שְׁעָרֶיךָ אֲשֶׁר־יְהוָה אֱלֹהֶיךָ נֹתֵן ב

לָךְ אִישׁ אוֹ־אִשָּׁה אֲשֶׁר יַעֲשֶׂה אֶת־הָרַע בְּעֵינֵי יְהוָה־אֱלֹהֶיךָ לַעֲבֹר בְּרִיתוֹ:
ג וַיֵּלֶךְ וַיַּעֲבֹד אֱלֹהִים אֲחֵרִים וַיִּשְׁתַּחוּ לָהֶם וְלַשֶּׁמֶשׁ ׀ אוֹ לַיָּרֵחַ אוֹ לְכָל־צְבָא
ד הַשָּׁמַיִם אֲשֶׁר לֹא־צִוִּיתִי: וְהֻגַּד־לְךָ וְשָׁמָעְתָּ וְדָרַשְׁתָּ הֵיטֵב וְהִנֵּה אֱמֶת נָכוֹן
ה הַדָּבָר נֶעֶשְׂתָה הַתּוֹעֵבָה הַזֹּאת בְּיִשְׂרָאֵל: וְהוֹצֵאתָ אֶת־הָאִישׁ הַהוּא אוֹ
אֶת־הָאִשָּׁה הַהִוא אֲשֶׁר עָשׂוּ אֶת־הַדָּבָר הָרָע הַזֶּה אֶל־שְׁעָרֶיךָ אֶת־הָאִישׁ
ו אוֹ אֶת־הָאִשָּׁה וּסְקַלְתָּם בָּאֲבָנִים וָמֵתוּ: עַל־פִּי ׀ שְׁנַיִם עֵדִים אוֹ שְׁלֹשָׁה
ז עֵדִים יוּמַת הַמֵּת לֹא יוּמַת עַל־פִּי עֵד אֶחָד: יַד הָעֵדִים תִּהְיֶה־בּוֹ בָרִאשֹׁנָה
לַהֲמִיתוֹ וְיַד כָּל־הָעָם בָּאַחֲרֹנָה וּבִעַרְתָּ הָרָע מִקִּרְבֶּךָ:
ח כִּי יִפָּלֵא מִמְּךָ דָבָר לַמִּשְׁפָּט בֵּין־דָּם ׀ לְדָם בֵּין־דִּין לְדִין וּבֵין נֶגַע לָנֶגַע
דִּבְרֵי רִיבֹת בִּשְׁעָרֶיךָ וְקַמְתָּ וְעָלִיתָ אֶל־הַמָּקוֹם אֲשֶׁר יִבְחַר יְהוָה אֱלֹהֶיךָ
ט בּוֹ: וּבָאתָ אֶל־הַכֹּהֲנִים הַלְוִיִּם וְאֶל־הַשֹּׁפֵט אֲשֶׁר יִהְיֶה בַּיָּמִים הָהֵם וְדָרַשְׁתָּ
י וְהִגִּידוּ לְךָ אֵת דְּבַר הַמִּשְׁפָּט: וְעָשִׂיתָ עַל־פִּי הַדָּבָר אֲשֶׁר יַגִּידוּ לְךָ מִן־
יא הַמָּקוֹם הַהוּא אֲשֶׁר יִבְחַר יְהוָה וְשָׁמַרְתָּ לַעֲשׂוֹת כְּכֹל אֲשֶׁר יוֹרוּךָ: *עַל־ ישראל
פִּי הַתּוֹרָה אֲשֶׁר יוֹרוּךָ וְעַל־הַמִּשְׁפָּט אֲשֶׁר־יֹאמְרוּ לְךָ תַּעֲשֶׂה לֹא תָסוּר
יב מִן־הַדָּבָר אֲשֶׁר־יַגִּידוּ לְךָ יָמִין וּשְׂמֹאל: וְהָאִישׁ אֲשֶׁר־יַעֲשֶׂה בְזָדוֹן לְבִלְתִּי
שְׁמֹעַ אֶל־הַכֹּהֵן הָעֹמֵד לְשָׁרֶת שָׁם אֶת־יְהוָה אֱלֹהֶיךָ אוֹ אֶל־הַשֹּׁפֵט וּמֵת
יג הָאִישׁ הַהוּא וּבִעַרְתָּ הָרָע מִיִּשְׂרָאֵל: וְכָל־הָעָם יִשְׁמְעוּ וְיִרָאוּ וְלֹא יְזִידוּן
יד עוֹד:** כִּי־תָבֹא אֶל־הָאָרֶץ אֲשֶׁר יְהוָה אֱלֹהֶיךָ נֹתֵן לָךְ וִירִשְׁתָּהּ טו שני
טו וְיָשַׁבְתָּה בָּהּ וְאָמַרְתָּ אָשִׂימָה עָלַי מֶלֶךְ כְּכָל־הַגּוֹיִם אֲשֶׁר סְבִיבֹתָי: שׂוֹם תָּשִׂים
עָלֶיךָ מֶלֶךְ אֲשֶׁר יִבְחַר יְהוָה אֱלֹהֶיךָ בּוֹ מִקֶּרֶב אַחֶיךָ תָּשִׂים עָלֶיךָ מֶלֶךְ לֹא
טז תוּכַל לָתֵת עָלֶיךָ אִישׁ נָכְרִי אֲשֶׁר לֹא־אָחִיךָ הוּא: רַק לֹא־יַרְבֶּה־לּוֹ סוּסִים
וְלֹא־יָשִׁיב אֶת־הָעָם מִצְרַיְמָה לְמַעַן הַרְבּוֹת סוּס וַיהוָה אָמַר לָכֶם לֹא תֹסִפוּן
יז לָשׁוּב בַּדֶּרֶךְ הַזֶּה עוֹד: וְלֹא יַרְבֶּה־לּוֹ נָשִׁים וְלֹא יָסוּר לְבָבוֹ וְכֶסֶף וְזָהָב לֹא
יח יַרְבֶּה־לּוֹ מְאֹד: וְהָיָה כְשִׁבְתּוֹ עַל כִּסֵּא מַמְלַכְתּוֹ וְכָתַב לוֹ אֶת־מִשְׁנֵה הַתּוֹרָה
יט הַזֹּאת עַל־סֵפֶר מִלִּפְנֵי הַכֹּהֲנִים הַלְוִיִּם: וְהָיְתָה עִמּוֹ וְקָרָא בוֹ כָּל־יְמֵי חַיָּיו
לְמַעַן יִלְמַד לְיִרְאָה אֶת־יְהוָה אֱלֹהָיו לִשְׁמֹר אֶת־כָּל־דִּבְרֵי הַתּוֹרָה הַזֹּאת
כ וְאֶת־הַחֻקִּים הָאֵלֶּה לַעֲשֹׂתָם: לְבִלְתִּי רוּם־לְבָבוֹ מֵאֶחָיו וּלְבִלְתִּי סוּר מִן־
הַמִּצְוָה יָמִין וּשְׂמֹאול לְמַעַן יַאֲרִיךְ יָמִים עַל־מַמְלַכְתּוֹ הוּא וּבָנָיו בְּקֶרֶב
יח א יִשְׂרָאֵל: לֹא־יִהְיֶה לַכֹּהֲנִים הַלְוִיִּם כָּל־שֵׁבֶט לֵוִי חֵלֶק וְנַחֲלָה שלישי

עַם־יִשְׂרָאֵל אִשֵּׁי יְהוָה וְנַחֲלָתוֹ יֹאכֵלוּן׃ וְנַחֲלָה לֹא־יִהְיֶה־לּוֹ בְּקֶרֶב אֶחָיו ב
יְהוָה הוּא נַחֲלָתוֹ כַּאֲשֶׁר דִּבֶּר־לוֹ׃ וְזֶה יִהְיֶה מִשְׁפַּט הַכֹּהֲנִים ג
מֵאֵת הָעָם מֵאֵת זֹבְחֵי הַזֶּבַח אִם־שׁוֹר אִם־שֶׂה וְנָתַן לַכֹּהֵן הַזְּרֹעַ וְהַלְּחָיַיִם
וְהַקֵּבָה׃ רֵאשִׁית דְּגָנְךָ תִּירֹשְׁךָ וְיִצְהָרֶךָ וְרֵאשִׁית גֵּז צֹאנְךָ תִּתֶּן־לּוֹ׃ כִּי בוֹ ד ה
בָּחַר יְהוָה אֱלֹהֶיךָ מִכָּל־שְׁבָטֶיךָ לַעֲמֹד לְשָׁרֵת בְּשֵׁם־יְהוָה הוּא וּבָנָיו כָּל־
הַיָּמִים׃ וְכִי־יָבֹא הַלֵּוִי מֵאַחַד שְׁעָרֶיךָ מִכָּל־יִשְׂרָאֵל אֲשֶׁר־הוּא ו רביעי
גָּר שָׁם וּבָא בְּכָל־אַוַּת נַפְשׁוֹ אֶל־הַמָּקוֹם אֲשֶׁר־יִבְחַר יְהוָה׃ וְשֵׁרֵת בְּשֵׁם ז
יְהוָה אֱלֹהָיו כְּכָל־אֶחָיו הַלְוִיִּם הָעֹמְדִים שָׁם לִפְנֵי יְהוָה׃ חֵלֶק כְּחֵלֶק יֹאכֵלוּ ח
לְבַד מִמְכָּרָיו עַל־הָאָבוֹת׃ כִּי אַתָּה בָּא אֶל־הָאָרֶץ אֲשֶׁר־יְהוָה ט
אֱלֹהֶיךָ נֹתֵן לָךְ לֹא־תִלְמַד לַעֲשׂוֹת כְּתוֹעֲבֹת הַגּוֹיִם הָהֵם׃ לֹא־יִמָּצֵא בְךָ י
מַעֲבִיר בְּנוֹ־וּבִתּוֹ בָּאֵשׁ קֹסֵם קְסָמִים מְעוֹנֵן וּמְנַחֵשׁ וּמְכַשֵּׁף׃ וְחֹבֵר חָבֶר יא
וְשֹׁאֵל אוֹב וְיִדְּעֹנִי וְדֹרֵשׁ אֶל־הַמֵּתִים׃ כִּי־תוֹעֲבַת יְהוָה כָּל־עֹשֵׂה אֵלֶּה וּבִגְלַל יב
הַתּוֹעֵבֹת הָאֵלֶּה יְהוָה אֱלֹהֶיךָ מוֹרִישׁ אוֹתָם מִפָּנֶיךָ׃ תָּמִים תִּהְיֶה עִם יְהוָה יג
אֱלֹהֶיךָ׃ כִּי ׀ הַגּוֹיִם הָאֵלֶּה אֲשֶׁר אַתָּה יוֹרֵשׁ אוֹתָם אֶל־מְעֹנְנִים וְאֶל־קֹסְמִים יד חמישי
יִשְׁמָעוּ וְאַתָּה לֹא כֵן נָתַן לְךָ יְהוָה אֱלֹהֶיךָ׃ נָבִיא מִקִּרְבְּךָ מֵאַחֶיךָ כָּמֹנִי יָקִים טו
לְךָ יְהוָה אֱלֹהֶיךָ אֵלָיו תִּשְׁמָעוּן׃ כְּכֹל אֲשֶׁר־שָׁאַלְתָּ מֵעִם יְהוָה אֱלֹהֶיךָ טז
בְּחֹרֵב בְּיוֹם הַקָּהָל לֵאמֹר לֹא אֹסֵף לִשְׁמֹעַ אֶת־קוֹל יְהוָה אֱלֹהָי וְאֶת־הָאֵשׁ
הַגְּדֹלָה הַזֹּאת לֹא־אֶרְאֶה עוֹד וְלֹא אָמוּת׃ וַיֹּאמֶר יְהוָה אֵלָי הֵיטִיבוּ אֲשֶׁר יז
דִּבֵּרוּ׃ נָבִיא אָקִים לָהֶם מִקֶּרֶב אֲחֵיהֶם כָּמוֹךָ וְנָתַתִּי דְבָרַי בְּפִיו וְדִבֶּר אֲלֵיהֶם יח
אֵת כָּל־אֲשֶׁר אֲצַוֶּנּוּ׃ וְהָיָה הָאִישׁ אֲשֶׁר לֹא־יִשְׁמַע אֶל־דְּבָרַי אֲשֶׁר יְדַבֵּר יט
בִּשְׁמִי אָנֹכִי אֶדְרֹשׁ מֵעִמּוֹ׃ אַךְ הַנָּבִיא אֲשֶׁר יָזִיד לְדַבֵּר דָּבָר בִּשְׁמִי אֵת אֲשֶׁר כ
לֹא־צִוִּיתִיו לְדַבֵּר וַאֲשֶׁר יְדַבֵּר בְּשֵׁם אֱלֹהִים אֲחֵרִים וּמֵת הַנָּבִיא הַהוּא׃ וְכִי כא
תֹאמַר בִּלְבָבֶךָ אֵיכָה נֵדַע אֶת־הַדָּבָר אֲשֶׁר לֹא־דִבְּרוֹ יְהוָה׃ אֲשֶׁר יְדַבֵּר כב
הַנָּבִיא בְּשֵׁם יְהוָה וְלֹא־יִהְיֶה הַדָּבָר וְלֹא יָבֹא הוּא הַדָּבָר אֲשֶׁר לֹא־דִבְּרוֹ
יְהוָה בְּזָדוֹן דִּבְּרוֹ הַנָּבִיא לֹא תָגוּר מִמֶּנּוּ׃ כִּי־יַכְרִית יְהוָה אֱלֹהֶיךָ א יט
אֶת־הַגּוֹיִם אֲשֶׁר יְהוָה אֱלֹהֶיךָ נֹתֵן לְךָ אֶת־אַרְצָם וִירִשְׁתָּם וְיָשַׁבְתָּ בְעָרֵיהֶם
וּבְבָתֵּיהֶם׃ שָׁלוֹשׁ עָרִים תַּבְדִּיל לָךְ בְּתוֹךְ אַרְצְךָ אֲשֶׁר יְהוָה אֱלֹהֶיךָ נֹתֵן ב
לְךָ לְרִשְׁתָּהּ׃ תָּכִין לְךָ הַדֶּרֶךְ וְשִׁלַּשְׁתָּ אֶת־גְּבוּל אַרְצְךָ אֲשֶׁר יַנְחִילְךָ יְהוָה ג
אֱלֹהֶיךָ וְהָיָה לָנוּס שָׁמָּה כָּל־רֹצֵחַ׃ וְזֶה דְּבַר הָרֹצֵחַ אֲשֶׁר־יָנוּס שָׁמָּה וָחָי ד

ה אֲשֶׁר יַכֶּה אֶת־רֵעֵהוּ בִּבְלִי־דַעַת וְהוּא לֹא־שֹׂנֵא לוֹ מִתְּמֹל שִׁלְשֹׁם׃ וַאֲשֶׁר
יָבֹא אֶת־רֵעֵהוּ בַיַּעַר לַחְטֹב עֵצִים וְנִדְּחָה יָדוֹ בַגַּרְזֶן לִכְרֹת הָעֵץ וְנָשַׁל הַבַּרְזֶל
ו מִן־הָעֵץ וּמָצָא אֶת־רֵעֵהוּ וָמֵת הוּא יָנוּס אֶל־אַחַת הֶעָרִים־הָאֵלֶּה וָחָי׃ פֶּן־
יִרְדֹּף גֹּאֵל הַדָּם אַחֲרֵי הָרֹצֵחַ כִּי יֵחַם לְבָבוֹ וְהִשִּׂיגוֹ כִּי־יִרְבֶּה הַדֶּרֶךְ וְהִכָּהוּ
ז נָפֶשׁ וְלוֹ אֵין מִשְׁפַּט־מָוֶת כִּי לֹא־שֹׂנֵא הוּא לוֹ מִתְּמוֹל שִׁלְשׁוֹם׃ עַל־כֵּן אָנֹכִי
ח מְצַוְּךָ לֵאמֹר שָׁלֹשׁ עָרִים תַּבְדִּיל לָךְ׃ וְאִם־יַרְחִיב יְהוָה אֱלֹהֶיךָ אֶת־גְּבֻלְךָ
כַּאֲשֶׁר נִשְׁבַּע לַאֲבֹתֶיךָ וְנָתַן לְךָ אֶת־כָּל־הָאָרֶץ אֲשֶׁר דִּבֶּר לָתֵת לַאֲבֹתֶיךָ׃
ט כִּי־תִשְׁמֹר אֶת־כָּל־הַמִּצְוָה הַזֹּאת לַעֲשֹׂתָהּ אֲשֶׁר אָנֹכִי מְצַוְּךָ הַיּוֹם לְאַהֲבָה
אֶת־יְהוָה אֱלֹהֶיךָ וְלָלֶכֶת בִּדְרָכָיו כָּל־הַיָּמִים וְיָסַפְתָּ לְךָ עוֹד שָׁלֹשׁ עָרִים
י עַל הַשָּׁלֹשׁ הָאֵלֶּה׃ וְלֹא יִשָּׁפֵךְ דָּם נָקִי בְּקֶרֶב אַרְצְךָ אֲשֶׁר יְהוָה אֱלֹהֶיךָ נֹתֵן
לְךָ נַחֲלָה וְהָיָה עָלֶיךָ דָּמִים׃
יא וְכִי־יִהְיֶה אִישׁ שֹׂנֵא לְרֵעֵהוּ וְאָרַב לוֹ וְקָם עָלָיו וְהִכָּהוּ נֶפֶשׁ וָמֵת וְנָס אֶל־
יב אַחַת הֶעָרִים הָאֵל׃ וְשָׁלְחוּ זִקְנֵי עִירוֹ וְלָקְחוּ אֹתוֹ מִשָּׁם וְנָתְנוּ אֹתוֹ בְּיַד
יג גֹּאֵל הַדָּם וָמֵת׃ לֹא־תָחוֹס עֵינְךָ עָלָיו וּבִעַרְתָּ דַם־הַנָּקִי מִיִּשְׂרָאֵל וְטוֹב
יד לָךְ׃ לֹא תַסִּיג גְּבוּל רֵעֲךָ אֲשֶׁר גָּבְלוּ רִאשֹׁנִים בְּנַחֲלָתְךָ אֲשֶׁר ששי
טו תִּנְחַל בָּאָרֶץ אֲשֶׁר יְהוָה אֱלֹהֶיךָ נֹתֵן לְךָ לְרִשְׁתָּהּ׃ לֹא־יָקוּם עֵד
אֶחָד בְּאִישׁ לְכָל־עָוֺן וּלְכָל־חַטָּאת בְּכָל־חֵטְא אֲשֶׁר יֶחֱטָא עַל־פִּי ׀ שְׁנֵי
טז עֵדִים אוֹ עַל־פִּי שְׁלֹשָׁה־עֵדִים יָקוּם דָּבָר׃ כִּי־יָקוּם עֵד־חָמָס בְּאִישׁ לַעֲנוֹת
יז בּוֹ סָרָה׃ וְעָמְדוּ שְׁנֵי־הָאֲנָשִׁים אֲשֶׁר־לָהֶם הָרִיב לִפְנֵי יְהוָה לִפְנֵי הַכֹּהֲנִים
יח וְהַשֹּׁפְטִים אֲשֶׁר יִהְיוּ בַּיָּמִים הָהֵם׃ וְדָרְשׁוּ הַשֹּׁפְטִים הֵיטֵב וְהִנֵּה עֵד־שֶׁקֶר
יט הָעֵד שֶׁקֶר עָנָה בְאָחִיו׃ וַעֲשִׂיתֶם לוֹ כַּאֲשֶׁר זָמַם לַעֲשׂוֹת לְאָחִיו וּבִעַרְתָּ
כ הָרָע מִקִּרְבֶּךָ׃ וְהַנִּשְׁאָרִים יִשְׁמְעוּ וְיִרָאוּ וְלֹא־יֹסִפוּ לַעֲשׂוֹת עוֹד כַּדָּבָר הָרָע
כא הַזֶּה בְּקִרְבֶּךָ׃ וְלֹא תָחוֹס עֵינֶךָ נֶפֶשׁ בְּנֶפֶשׁ עַיִן בְּעַיִן שֵׁן בְּשֵׁן יָד בְּיָד רֶגֶל
כ א בְּרָגֶל׃ כִּי־תֵצֵא לַמִּלְחָמָה עַל־אֹיְבֶךָ וְרָאִיתָ סוּס וָרֶכֶב עַם רַב
ב מִמְּךָ לֹא תִירָא מֵהֶם כִּי־יְהוָה אֱלֹהֶיךָ עִמָּךְ הַמַּעַלְךָ מֵאֶרֶץ מִצְרָיִם׃ וְהָיָה
ג כְּקָרָבְכֶם אֶל־הַמִּלְחָמָה וְנִגַּשׁ הַכֹּהֵן וְדִבֶּר אֶל־הָעָם׃ וְאָמַר אֲלֵהֶם שְׁמַע
יִשְׂרָאֵל אַתֶּם קְרֵבִים הַיּוֹם לַמִּלְחָמָה עַל־אֹיְבֵיכֶם אַל־יֵרַךְ לְבַבְכֶם אַל־
ד תִּירְאוּ וְאַל־תַּחְפְּזוּ וְאַל־תַּעַרְצוּ מִפְּנֵיהֶם׃ כִּי יְהוָה אֱלֹהֵיכֶם הַהֹלֵךְ עִמָּכֶם
ה לְהִלָּחֵם לָכֶם עִם־אֹיְבֵיכֶם לְהוֹשִׁיעַ אֶתְכֶם׃ וְדִבְּרוּ הַשֹּׁטְרִים אֶל־הָעָם

לֵאמֹר מִי־הָאִישׁ אֲשֶׁר בָּנָה בַיִת־חָדָשׁ וְלֹא חֲנָכוֹ יֵלֵךְ וְיָשֹׁב לְבֵיתוֹ פֶּן־יָמוּת
בַּמִּלְחָמָה וְאִישׁ אַחֵר יַחְנְכֶנּוּ: וּמִי־הָאִישׁ אֲשֶׁר נָטַע כֶּרֶם וְלֹא חִלְּלוֹ יֵלֵךְ ו
וְיָשֹׁב לְבֵיתוֹ פֶּן־יָמוּת בַּמִּלְחָמָה וְאִישׁ אַחֵר יְחַלְּלֶנּוּ: וּמִי־הָאִישׁ אֲשֶׁר אֵרַשׂ ז
אִשָּׁה וְלֹא לְקָחָהּ יֵלֵךְ וְיָשֹׁב לְבֵיתוֹ פֶּן־יָמוּת בַּמִּלְחָמָה וְאִישׁ אַחֵר יִקָּחֶנָּה:
וְיָסְפוּ הַשֹּׁטְרִים לְדַבֵּר אֶל־הָעָם וְאָמְרוּ מִי־הָאִישׁ הַיָּרֵא וְרַךְ הַלֵּבָב יֵלֵךְ ח
וְיָשֹׁב לְבֵיתוֹ וְלֹא יִמַּס אֶת־לְבַב אֶחָיו כִּלְבָבוֹ: וְהָיָה כְּכַלֹּת הַשֹּׁטְרִים לְדַבֵּר ט
שביעי טז אֶל־הָעָם וּפָקְדוּ שָׂרֵי צְבָאוֹת בְּרֹאשׁ הָעָם: כִּי־תִקְרַב אֶל־עִיר י
לְהִלָּחֵם עָלֶיהָ וְקָרָאתָ אֵלֶיהָ לְשָׁלוֹם: וְהָיָה אִם־שָׁלוֹם תַּעַנְךָ וּפָתְחָה לָךְ יא
וְהָיָה כָּל־הָעָם הַנִּמְצָא־בָהּ יִהְיוּ לְךָ לָמַס וַעֲבָדוּךָ: וְאִם־לֹא תַשְׁלִים עִמָּךְ יב
וְעָשְׂתָה עִמְּךָ מִלְחָמָה וְצַרְתָּ עָלֶיהָ: וּנְתָנָהּ יהוה אֱלֹהֶיךָ בְּיָדֶךָ וְהִכִּיתָ אֶת־ יג
כָּל־זְכוּרָהּ לְפִי־חָרֶב: רַק הַנָּשִׁים וְהַטַּף וְהַבְּהֵמָה וְכֹל אֲשֶׁר יִהְיֶה בָעִיר כָּל־ יד
שְׁלָלָהּ תָּבֹז לָךְ וְאָכַלְתָּ אֶת־שְׁלַל אֹיְבֶיךָ אֲשֶׁר נָתַן יהוה אֱלֹהֶיךָ לָךְ: כֵּן תַּעֲשֶׂה טו
לְכָל־הֶעָרִים הָרְחֹקֹת מִמְּךָ מְאֹד אֲשֶׁר לֹא־מֵעָרֵי הַגּוֹיִם־הָאֵלֶּה הֵנָּה: רַק טז
מֵעָרֵי הָעַמִּים הָאֵלֶּה אֲשֶׁר יהוה אֱלֹהֶיךָ נֹתֵן לְךָ נַחֲלָה לֹא תְחַיֶּה כָּל־נְשָׁמָה:
כִּי־הַחֲרֵם תַּחֲרִימֵם הַחִתִּי וְהָאֱמֹרִי הַכְּנַעֲנִי וְהַפְּרִזִּי הַחִוִּי וְהַיְבוּסִי כַּאֲשֶׁר צִוְּךָ יז
יהוה אֱלֹהֶיךָ: לְמַעַן אֲשֶׁר לֹא־יְלַמְּדוּ אֶתְכֶם לַעֲשׂוֹת כְּכֹל תּוֹעֲבֹתָם אֲשֶׁר יח
עָשׂוּ לֵאלֹהֵיהֶם וַחֲטָאתֶם לַיהוה אֱלֹהֵיכֶם: כִּי־תָצוּר אֶל־עִיר יט
יָמִים רַבִּים לְהִלָּחֵם עָלֶיהָ לְתָפְשָׂהּ לֹא־תַשְׁחִית אֶת־עֵצָהּ לִנְדֹּחַ עָלָיו גַּרְזֶן
כִּי מִמֶּנּוּ תֹאכֵל וְאֹתוֹ לֹא תִכְרֹת כִּי הָאָדָם עֵץ הַשָּׂדֶה לָבֹא מִפָּנֶיךָ בַּמָּצוֹר:
רַק עֵץ אֲשֶׁר־תֵּדַע כִּי לֹא־עֵץ מַאֲכָל הוּא אֹתוֹ תַשְׁחִית וְכָרָתָּ וּבָנִיתָ מָצוֹר כ
עַל־הָעִיר אֲשֶׁר־הִוא עֹשָׂה עִמְּךָ מִלְחָמָה עַד רִדְתָּהּ:
כִּי־יִמָּצֵא חָלָל בָּאֲדָמָה אֲשֶׁר יהוה אֱלֹהֶיךָ נֹתֵן לְךָ לְרִשְׁתָּהּ נֹפֵל בַּשָּׂדֶה א כא
לֹא נוֹדַע מִי הִכָּהוּ: וְיָצְאוּ זְקֵנֶיךָ וְשֹׁפְטֶיךָ וּמָדְדוּ אֶל־הֶעָרִים אֲשֶׁר סְבִיבֹת ב
הֶחָלָל: וְהָיָה הָעִיר הַקְּרֹבָה אֶל־הֶחָלָל וְלָקְחוּ זִקְנֵי הָעִיר הַהִוא עֶגְלַת ג
בָּקָר אֲשֶׁר לֹא־עֻבַּד בָּהּ אֲשֶׁר לֹא־מָשְׁכָה בְּעֹל: וְהוֹרִדוּ זִקְנֵי הָעִיר הַהִוא ד
אֶת־הָעֶגְלָה אֶל־נַחַל אֵיתָן אֲשֶׁר לֹא־יֵעָבֵד בּוֹ וְלֹא יִזָּרֵעַ וְעָרְפוּ־שָׁם אֶת־
הָעֶגְלָה בַּנָּחַל: וְנִגְּשׁוּ הַכֹּהֲנִים בְּנֵי לֵוִי כִּי בָם בָּחַר יהוה אֱלֹהֶיךָ לְשָׁרְתוֹ ה
וּלְבָרֵךְ בְּשֵׁם יהוה וְעַל־פִּיהֶם יִהְיֶה כָּל־רִיב וְכָל־נָגַע: וְכֹל זִקְנֵי הָעִיר הַהִוא ו
מפטיר הַקְּרֹבִים אֶל־הֶחָלָל יִרְחֲצוּ אֶת־יְדֵיהֶם עַל־הָעֶגְלָה הָעֲרוּפָה בַנָּחַל: וְעָנוּ ז

ח וְאָמְרוּ יָדֵינוּ לֹא שפכה אֶת־הַדָּם הַזֶּה וְעֵינֵינוּ לֹא רָאוּ: כַּפֵּר לְעַמְּךָ יִשְׂרָאֵל שָׁפְכוּ
אֲשֶׁר־פָּדִיתָ יהוה וְאַל־תִּתֵּן דָּם נָקִי בְּקֶרֶב עַמְּךָ יִשְׂרָאֵל וְנִכַּפֵּר לָהֶם הַדָּם:
ט י וְאַתָּה תְּבַעֵר הַדָּם הַנָּקִי מִקִּרְבֶּךָ כִּי־תַעֲשֶׂה הַיָּשָׁר בְּעֵינֵי יהוה: כִּי־ כי תצא
יא תֵצֵא לַמִּלְחָמָה עַל־אֹיְבֶיךָ וּנְתָנוֹ יהוה אֱלֹהֶיךָ בְּיָדֶךָ וְשָׁבִיתָ שִׁבְיוֹ: וְרָאִיתָ
יב בַּשִּׁבְיָה אֵשֶׁת יְפַת־תֹּאַר וְחָשַׁקְתָּ בָהּ וְלָקַחְתָּ לְךָ לְאִשָּׁה: וַהֲבֵאתָהּ אֶל־
יג תּוֹךְ בֵּיתֶךָ וְגִלְּחָה אֶת־רֹאשָׁהּ וְעָשְׂתָה אֶת־צִפָּרְנֶיהָ: וְהֵסִירָה אֶת־שִׂמְלַת
שִׁבְיָהּ מֵעָלֶיהָ וְיָשְׁבָה בְּבֵיתֶךָ וּבָכְתָה אֶת־אָבִיהָ וְאֶת־אִמָּהּ יֶרַח יָמִים וְאַחַר
יד כֵּן תָּבוֹא אֵלֶיהָ וּבְעַלְתָּהּ וְהָיְתָה לְךָ לְאִשָּׁה: וְהָיָה אִם־לֹא חָפַצְתָּ בָּהּ
וְשִׁלַּחְתָּהּ לְנַפְשָׁהּ וּמָכֹר לֹא־תִמְכְּרֶנָּה בַּכָּסֶף לֹא־תִתְעַמֵּר בָּהּ תַּחַת אֲשֶׁר
טו עִנִּיתָהּ: *כִּי־תִהְיֶיןָ לְאִישׁ שְׁתֵּי נָשִׁים הָאַחַת אֲהוּבָה וְהָאַחַת לוי
טז שְׂנוּאָה וְיָלְדוּ־לוֹ בָנִים הָאֲהוּבָה וְהַשְּׂנוּאָה וְהָיָה הַבֵּן הַבְּכֹר לַשְּׂנִיאָה: וְהָיָה
בְּיוֹם הַנְחִילוֹ אֶת־בָּנָיו אֵת אֲשֶׁר־יִהְיֶה לוֹ לֹא יוּכַל לְבַכֵּר אֶת־בֶּן־הָאֲהוּבָה
יז עַל־פְּנֵי בֶן־הַשְּׂנוּאָה הַבְּכֹר: כִּי אֶת־הַבְּכֹר בֶּן־הַשְּׂנוּאָה יַכִּיר לָתֶת לוֹ פִּי שְׁנַיִם
יח בְּכֹל אֲשֶׁר־יִמָּצֵא לוֹ כִּי־הוּא רֵאשִׁית אֹנוֹ לוֹ מִשְׁפַּט הַבְּכֹרָה: *כִּי־ ישראל
יִהְיֶה לְאִישׁ בֵּן סוֹרֵר וּמוֹרֶה אֵינֶנּוּ שֹׁמֵעַ בְּקוֹל אָבִיו וּבְקוֹל אִמּוֹ וְיִסְּרוּ אֹתוֹ
יט וְלֹא יִשְׁמַע אֲלֵיהֶם: וְתָפְשׂוּ בוֹ אָבִיו וְאִמּוֹ וְהוֹצִיאוּ אֹתוֹ אֶל־זִקְנֵי עִירוֹ וְאֶל־
כ שַׁעַר מְקֹמוֹ: וְאָמְרוּ אֶל־זִקְנֵי עִירוֹ בְּנֵנוּ זֶה סוֹרֵר וּמֹרֶה אֵינֶנּוּ שֹׁמֵעַ בְּקֹלֵנוּ
כא זוֹלֵל וְסֹבֵא: וּרְגָמֻהוּ כָּל־אַנְשֵׁי עִירוֹ בָאֲבָנִים וָמֵת וּבִעַרְתָּ הָרָע מִקִּרְבֶּךָ
כב וְכָל־יִשְׂרָאֵל יִשְׁמְעוּ וְיִרָאוּ: ** וְכִי־יִהְיֶה בְאִישׁ חֵטְא מִשְׁפַּט־מָוֶת שני
כג וְהוּמָת וְתָלִיתָ אֹתוֹ עַל־עֵץ: לֹא־תָלִין נִבְלָתוֹ עַל־הָעֵץ כִּי־קָבוֹר תִּקְבְּרֶנּוּ
בַּיּוֹם הַהוּא כִּי־קִלְלַת אֱלֹהִים תָּלוּי וְלֹא תְטַמֵּא אֶת־אַדְמָתְךָ אֲשֶׁר יהוה
כב א אֱלֹהֶיךָ נֹתֵן לְךָ נַחֲלָה: לֹא־תִרְאֶה אֶת־שׁוֹר אָחִיךָ אוֹ אֶת־
ב שֵׂיוֹ נִדָּחִים וְהִתְעַלַּמְתָּ מֵהֶם הָשֵׁב תְּשִׁיבֵם לְאָחִיךָ: וְאִם־לֹא קָרוֹב אָחִיךָ
אֵלֶיךָ וְלֹא יְדַעְתּוֹ וַאֲסַפְתּוֹ אֶל־תּוֹךְ בֵּיתֶךָ וְהָיָה עִמְּךָ עַד דְּרֹשׁ אָחִיךָ אֹתוֹ
ג וַהֲשֵׁבֹתוֹ לוֹ: וְכֵן תַּעֲשֶׂה לַחֲמֹרוֹ וְכֵן תַּעֲשֶׂה לְשִׂמְלָתוֹ וְכֵן תַּעֲשֶׂה לְכָל־אֲבֵדַת
ד אָחִיךָ אֲשֶׁר־תֹּאבַד מִמֶּנּוּ וּמְצָאתָהּ לֹא תוּכַל לְהִתְעַלֵּם: לֹא־
תִרְאֶה אֶת־חֲמוֹר אָחִיךָ אוֹ שׁוֹרוֹ נֹפְלִים בַּדֶּרֶךְ וְהִתְעַלַּמְתָּ מֵהֶם הָקֵם תָּקִים
ה עִמּוֹ: לֹא־יִהְיֶה כְלִי־גֶבֶר עַל־אִשָּׁה וְלֹא־יִלְבַּשׁ גֶּבֶר שִׂמְלַת אִשָּׁה
כִּי תוֹעֲבַת יהוה אֱלֹהֶיךָ כָּל־עֹשֵׂה אֵלֶּה:

יז כִּי יִקָּרֵא קַן־צִפּוֹר ׀ לְפָנֶיךָ בַּדֶּרֶךְ בְּכָל־עֵץ ׀ אוֹ עַל־הָאָרֶץ אֶפְרֹחִים אוֹ בֵיצִים ו
וְהָאֵם רֹבֶצֶת עַל־הָאֶפְרֹחִים אוֹ עַל־הַבֵּיצִים לֹא־תִקַּח הָאֵם עַל־הַבָּנִים:
שַׁלֵּחַ תְּשַׁלַּח אֶת־הָאֵם וְאֶת־הַבָּנִים תִּקַּח־לָךְ לְמַעַן יִיטַב לָךְ וְהַאֲרַכְתָּ ז
שלישי יָמִים: כִּי תִבְנֶה בַּיִת חָדָשׁ וְעָשִׂיתָ מַעֲקֶה לְגַגֶּךָ וְלֹא־תָשִׂים דָּמִים ח
בְּבֵיתֶךָ כִּי־יִפֹּל הַנֹּפֵל מִמֶּנּוּ: לֹא־תִזְרַע כַּרְמְךָ כִּלְאָיִם פֶּן־תִּקְדַּשׁ הַמְלֵאָה ט
הַזֶּרַע אֲשֶׁר תִּזְרָע וּתְבוּאַת הַכָּרֶם: לֹא־תַחֲרֹשׁ בְּשׁוֹר־וּבַחֲמֹר י
יַחְדָּו: לֹא תִלְבַּשׁ שַׁעַטְנֵז צֶמֶר וּפִשְׁתִּים יַחְדָּו: גְּדִלִים תַּעֲשֶׂה־לָּךְ יא יב
עַל־אַרְבַּע כַּנְפוֹת כְּסוּתְךָ אֲשֶׁר תְּכַסֶּה־בָּהּ: כִּי־יִקַּח אִישׁ אִשָּׁה יג
וּבָא אֵלֶיהָ וּשְׂנֵאָהּ: וְשָׂם לָהּ עֲלִילֹת דְּבָרִים וְהוֹצִא עָלֶיהָ שֵׁם רָע וְאָמַר יד
אֶת־הָאִשָּׁה הַזֹּאת לָקַחְתִּי וָאֶקְרַב אֵלֶיהָ וְלֹא־מָצָאתִי לָהּ בְּתוּלִים: וְלָקַח טו
אֲבִי הַנַּעֲרָ וְאִמָּהּ וְהוֹצִיאוּ אֶת־בְּתוּלֵי הַנַּעֲרָ אֶל־זִקְנֵי הָעִיר הַשָּׁעְרָה: וְאָמַר טז
אֲבִי הַנַּעֲרָ אֶל־הַזְּקֵנִים אֶת־בִּתִּי נָתַתִּי לָאִישׁ הַזֶּה לְאִשָּׁה וַיִּשְׂנָאֶהָ: וְהִנֵּה־ יז
הוּא שָׂם עֲלִילֹת דְּבָרִים לֵאמֹר לֹא־מָצָאתִי לְבִתְּךָ בְּתוּלִים וְאֵלֶּה בְּתוּלֵי בִתִּי
וּפָרְשׂוּ הַשִּׂמְלָה לִפְנֵי זִקְנֵי הָעִיר: וְלָקְחוּ זִקְנֵי הָעִיר־הַהִוא אֶת־הָאִישׁ וְיִסְּרוּ יח
אֹתוֹ: וְעָנְשׁוּ אֹתוֹ מֵאָה כֶסֶף וְנָתְנוּ לַאֲבִי הַנַּעֲרָה כִּי הוֹצִיא שֵׁם רָע עַל בְּתוּלַת יט
יִשְׂרָאֵל וְלוֹ־תִהְיֶה לְאִשָּׁה לֹא־יוּכַל לְשַׁלְּחָהּ כָּל־יָמָיו: וְאִם־אֱמֶת כ
הָיָה הַדָּבָר הַזֶּה לֹא־נִמְצְאוּ בְתוּלִים לַנַּעֲרָ: וְהוֹצִיאוּ אֶת־הַנַּעֲרָ אֶל־פֶּתַח כא
בֵּית־אָבִיהָ וּסְקָלוּהָ אַנְשֵׁי עִירָהּ בָּאֲבָנִים וָמֵתָה כִּי־עָשְׂתָה נְבָלָה בְּיִשְׂרָאֵל
לִזְנוֹת בֵּית אָבִיהָ וּבִעַרְתָּ הָרָע מִקִּרְבֶּךָ: כִּי־יִמָּצֵא אִישׁ שֹׁכֵב ׀ כב
עִם־אִשָּׁה בְעֻלַת־בַּעַל וּמֵתוּ גַּם־שְׁנֵיהֶם הָאִישׁ הַשֹּׁכֵב עִם־הָאִשָּׁה וְהָאִשָּׁה
וּבִעַרְתָּ הָרָע מִיִּשְׂרָאֵל: כִּי יִהְיֶה נַעֲרָ בְתוּלָה מְאֹרָשָׂה לְאִישׁ כג
וּמְצָאָהּ אִישׁ בָּעִיר וְשָׁכַב עִמָּהּ: וְהוֹצֵאתֶם אֶת־שְׁנֵיהֶם אֶל־שַׁעַר ׀ הָעִיר כד
הַהִוא וּסְקַלְתֶּם אֹתָם בָּאֲבָנִים וָמֵתוּ אֶת־הַנַּעֲרָ עַל־דְּבַר אֲשֶׁר לֹא־צָעֲקָה
בָעִיר וְאֶת־הָאִישׁ עַל־דְּבַר אֲשֶׁר־עִנָּה אֶת־אֵשֶׁת רֵעֵהוּ וּבִעַרְתָּ הָרָע
מִקִּרְבֶּךָ: וְאִם־בַּשָּׂדֶה יִמְצָא הָאִישׁ אֶת־הַנַּעֲרָ הַמְאֹרָשָׂה וְהֶחֱזִיק־ כה
בָּהּ הָאִישׁ וְשָׁכַב עִמָּהּ וּמֵת הָאִישׁ אֲשֶׁר־שָׁכַב עִמָּהּ לְבַדּוֹ: וְלַנַּעֲרָ לֹא־תַעֲשֶׂה כו
דָבָר אֵין לַנַּעֲרָ חֵטְא מָוֶת כִּי כַּאֲשֶׁר יָקוּם אִישׁ עַל־רֵעֵהוּ וּרְצָחוֹ נֶפֶשׁ כֵּן
הַדָּבָר הַזֶּה: כִּי בַשָּׂדֶה מְצָאָהּ צָעֲקָה הַנַּעֲרָ הַמְאֹרָשָׂה וְאֵין מוֹשִׁיעַ כז
לָהּ: כִּי־יִמְצָא אִישׁ נַעֲרָ בְתוּלָה אֲשֶׁר לֹא־אֹרָשָׂה וּתְפָשָׂהּ וְשָׁכַב כח

כט עִמָּהּ וְנִמְצָאוּ׃ וְנָתַן הָאִישׁ הַשֹּׁכֵב עִמָּהּ לַאֲבִי הַנַּעֲרָ חֲמִשִּׁים כָּסֶף וְלוֹ־תִהְיֶה
כג א לְאִשָּׁה תַּחַת אֲשֶׁר עִנָּהּ לֹא־יוּכַל שַׁלְּחָהּ כָּל־יָמָיו׃ לֹא־יִקַּח אִישׁ
ב אֶת־אֵשֶׁת אָבִיו וְלֹא יְגַלֶּה כְּנַף אָבִיו׃ לֹא־יָבֹא פְצוּעַ־דַּכָּא וּכְרוּת
ג שָׁפְכָה בִּקְהַל יְהוָה׃ לֹא־יָבֹא מַמְזֵר בִּקְהַל יְהוָה גַּם דּוֹר עֲשִׂירִי
ד לֹא־יָבֹא לוֹ בִּקְהַל יְהוָה׃ לֹא־יָבֹא עַמּוֹנִי וּמוֹאָבִי בִּקְהַל יְהוָה גַּם
ה דּוֹר עֲשִׂירִי לֹא־יָבֹא לָהֶם בִּקְהַל יְהוָה עַד־עוֹלָם׃ עַל־דְּבַר אֲשֶׁר לֹא־קִדְּמוּ
אֶתְכֶם בַּלֶּחֶם וּבַמַּיִם בַּדֶּרֶךְ בְּצֵאתְכֶם מִמִּצְרָיִם וַאֲשֶׁר שָׂכַר עָלֶיךָ אֶת־בִּלְעָם
ו בֶּן־בְּעוֹר מִפְּתוֹר אֲרַם נַהֲרַיִם לְקַלְלֶךָּ׃ וְלֹא־אָבָה יְהוָה אֱלֹהֶיךָ לִשְׁמֹעַ אֶל־
בִּלְעָם וַיַּהֲפֹךְ יְהוָה אֱלֹהֶיךָ לְּךָ אֶת־הַקְּלָלָה לִבְרָכָה כִּי אֲהֵבְךָ יְהוָה אֱלֹהֶיךָ׃
ז ח לֹא־תִדְרֹשׁ שְׁלֹמָם וְטֹבָתָם כָּל־יָמֶיךָ לְעוֹלָם׃ *לֹא־תְתַעֵב אֲדֹמִי רביעי
ט כִּי אָחִיךָ הוּא לֹא־תְתַעֵב מִצְרִי כִּי־גֵר הָיִיתָ בְאַרְצוֹ׃ בָּנִים אֲשֶׁר־יִוָּלְדוּ לָהֶם
י דּוֹר שְׁלִישִׁי יָבֹא לָהֶם בִּקְהַל יְהוָה׃ כִּי־תֵצֵא מַחֲנֶה עַל־אֹיְבֶיךָ יח
יא וְנִשְׁמַרְתָּ מִכֹּל דָּבָר רָע׃ כִּי־יִהְיֶה בְךָ אִישׁ אֲשֶׁר לֹא־יִהְיֶה טָהוֹר מִקְּרֵה־לָיְלָה
יב וְיָצָא אֶל־מִחוּץ לַמַּחֲנֶה לֹא יָבֹא אֶל־תּוֹךְ הַמַּחֲנֶה׃ וְהָיָה לִפְנוֹת־עֶרֶב יִרְחַץ
יג בַּמָּיִם וּכְבֹא הַשֶּׁמֶשׁ יָבֹא אֶל־תּוֹךְ הַמַּחֲנֶה׃ וְיָד תִּהְיֶה לְךָ מִחוּץ לַמַּחֲנֶה
יד וְיָצָאתָ שָׁמָּה חוּץ׃ וְיָתֵד תִּהְיֶה לְךָ עַל־אֲזֵנֶךָ וְהָיָה בְּשִׁבְתְּךָ חוּץ וְחָפַרְתָּה
טו בָהּ וְשַׁבְתָּ וְכִסִּיתָ אֶת־צֵאָתֶךָ׃ כִּי יְהוָה אֱלֹהֶיךָ מִתְהַלֵּךְ ׀ בְּקֶרֶב מַחֲנֶךָ
לְהַצִּילְךָ וְלָתֵת אֹיְבֶיךָ לְפָנֶיךָ וְהָיָה מַחֲנֶיךָ קָדוֹשׁ וְלֹא־יִרְאֶה בְךָ עֶרְוַת דָּבָר
טז וְשָׁב מֵאַחֲרֶיךָ׃ לֹא־תַסְגִּיר עֶבֶד אֶל־אֲדֹנָיו אֲשֶׁר־יִנָּצֵל אֵלֶיךָ מֵעִם
יז אֲדֹנָיו׃ עִמְּךָ יֵשֵׁב בְּקִרְבְּךָ בַּמָּקוֹם אֲשֶׁר־יִבְחַר בְּאַחַד שְׁעָרֶיךָ בַּטּוֹב לוֹ לֹא
יח תּוֹנֶנּוּ׃ לֹא־תִהְיֶה קְדֵשָׁה מִבְּנוֹת יִשְׂרָאֵל וְלֹא־יִהְיֶה קָדֵשׁ מִבְּנֵי
יט יִשְׂרָאֵל׃ לֹא־תָבִיא אֶתְנַן זוֹנָה וּמְחִיר כֶּלֶב בֵּית יְהוָה אֱלֹהֶיךָ לְכָל־נֶדֶר כִּי
כ תוֹעֲבַת יְהוָה אֱלֹהֶיךָ גַּם־שְׁנֵיהֶם׃ לֹא־תַשִּׁיךְ לְאָחִיךָ נֶשֶׁךְ כֶּסֶף
כא נֶשֶׁךְ אֹכֶל נֶשֶׁךְ כָּל־דָּבָר אֲשֶׁר יִשָּׁךְ׃ לַנָּכְרִי תַשִּׁיךְ וּלְאָחִיךָ לֹא תַשִּׁיךְ לְמַעַן
יְבָרֶכְךָ יְהוָה אֱלֹהֶיךָ בְּכֹל מִשְׁלַח יָדֶךָ עַל־הָאָרֶץ אֲשֶׁר־אַתָּה בָא־שָׁמָּה
כב לְרִשְׁתָּהּ׃ כִּי־תִדֹּר נֶדֶר לַיהוָה אֱלֹהֶיךָ לֹא תְאַחֵר לְשַׁלְּמוֹ כִּי־דָרֹשׁ יט
כג יִדְרְשֶׁנּוּ יְהוָה אֱלֹהֶיךָ מֵעִמָּךְ וְהָיָה בְךָ חֵטְא׃ וְכִי תֶחְדַּל לִנְדֹּר לֹא־יִהְיֶה
כד בְךָ חֵטְא׃ מוֹצָא שְׂפָתֶיךָ תִּשְׁמֹר וְעָשִׂיתָ כַּאֲשֶׁר נָדַרְתָּ לַיהוָה אֱלֹהֶיךָ נְדָבָה
כה אֲשֶׁר דִּבַּרְתָּ בְּפִיךָ׃ כִּי תָבֹא בְּכֶרֶם רֵעֶךָ וְאָכַלְתָּ עֲנָבִים כְּנַפְשְׁךָ חמישי

כו שָׂבְעֶךָ וְאֶל־כֶּלְיְךָ לֹא תִתֵּן׃ כִּי תָבֹא בְּקָמַת רֵעֶךָ וְקָטַפְתָּ מְלִילֹת
כד א בְּיָדֶךָ וְחֶרְמֵשׁ לֹא תָנִיף עַל קָמַת רֵעֶךָ׃ כִּי־יִקַּח אִישׁ אִשָּׁה וּבְעָלָהּ
וְהָיָה אִם־לֹא תִמְצָא־חֵן בְּעֵינָיו כִּי־מָצָא בָהּ עֶרְוַת דָּבָר וְכָתַב לָהּ סֵפֶר
ב כְּרִיתֻת וְנָתַן בְּיָדָהּ וְשִׁלְּחָהּ מִבֵּיתוֹ׃ וְיָצְאָה מִבֵּיתוֹ וְהָלְכָה וְהָיְתָה לְאִישׁ־
ג אַחֵר׃ וּשְׂנֵאָהּ הָאִישׁ הָאַחֲרוֹן וְכָתַב לָהּ סֵפֶר כְּרִיתֻת וְנָתַן בְּיָדָהּ וְשִׁלְּחָהּ
ד מִבֵּיתוֹ אוֹ כִי יָמוּת הָאִישׁ הָאַחֲרוֹן אֲשֶׁר־לְקָחָהּ לוֹ לְאִשָּׁה׃ לֹא־יוּכַל בַּעְלָהּ
הָרִאשׁוֹן אֲשֶׁר־שִׁלְּחָהּ לָשׁוּב לְקַחְתָּהּ לִהְיוֹת לוֹ לְאִשָּׁה אַחֲרֵי אֲשֶׁר הֻטַּמָּאָה
כִּי־תוֹעֵבָה הִוא לִפְנֵי יְהוָה וְלֹא תַחֲטִיא אֶת־הָאָרֶץ אֲשֶׁר יְהוָה אֱלֹהֶיךָ נֹתֵן
ה לְךָ נַחֲלָה׃ כִּי־יִקַּח אִישׁ אִשָּׁה חֲדָשָׁה לֹא יֵצֵא בַּצָּבָא וְלֹא־יַעֲבֹר ששי
עָלָיו לְכָל־דָּבָר נָקִי יִהְיֶה לְבֵיתוֹ שָׁנָה אֶחָת וְשִׂמַּח אֶת־אִשְׁתּוֹ אֲשֶׁר־לָקָח׃
ו ז לֹא־יַחֲבֹל רֵחַיִם וָרָכֶב כִּי־נֶפֶשׁ הוּא חֹבֵל׃ כִּי־יִמָּצֵא אִישׁ גֹּנֵב נֶפֶשׁ
מֵאֶחָיו מִבְּנֵי יִשְׂרָאֵל וְהִתְעַמֶּר־בּוֹ וּמְכָרוֹ וּמֵת הַגַּנָּב הַהוּא וּבִעַרְתָּ הָרָע
ח מִקִּרְבֶּךָ׃ הִשָּׁמֶר בְּנֶגַע־הַצָּרַעַת לִשְׁמֹר מְאֹד וְלַעֲשׂוֹת כְּכֹל אֲשֶׁר־
ט יוֹרוּ אֶתְכֶם הַכֹּהֲנִים הַלְוִיִּם כַּאֲשֶׁר צִוִּיתִם תִּשְׁמְרוּ לַעֲשׂוֹת׃ זָכוֹר אֵת אֲשֶׁר־
י עָשָׂה יְהוָה אֱלֹהֶיךָ לְמִרְיָם בַּדָּרֶךְ בְּצֵאתְכֶם מִמִּצְרָיִם׃ כִּי־תַשֶּׁה
יא בְרֵעֲךָ מַשַּׁאת מְאוּמָה לֹא־תָבֹא אֶל־בֵּיתוֹ לַעֲבֹט עֲבֹטוֹ׃ בַּחוּץ תַּעֲמֹד
יב וְהָאִישׁ אֲשֶׁר אַתָּה נֹשֶׁה בוֹ יוֹצִיא אֵלֶיךָ אֶת־הַעֲבוֹט הַחוּצָה׃ וְאִם־אִישׁ עָנִי
יג הוּא לֹא תִשְׁכַּב בַּעֲבֹטוֹ׃ הָשֵׁב תָּשִׁיב לוֹ אֶת־הַעֲבוֹט כְּבוֹא הַשֶּׁמֶשׁ וְשָׁכַב
יד בְּשַׂלְמָתוֹ וּבֵרְכֶךָּ וּלְךָ תִּהְיֶה צְדָקָה לִפְנֵי יְהוָה אֱלֹהֶיךָ׃ לֹא־ שביעי
טו תַעֲשֹׁק שָׂכִיר עָנִי וְאֶבְיוֹן מֵאַחֶיךָ אוֹ מִגֵּרְךָ אֲשֶׁר בְּאַרְצְךָ בִּשְׁעָרֶיךָ׃ בְּיוֹמוֹ
תִתֵּן שְׂכָרוֹ וְלֹא־תָבוֹא עָלָיו הַשֶּׁמֶשׁ כִּי עָנִי הוּא וְאֵלָיו הוּא נֹשֵׂא אֶת־נַפְשׁוֹ
טז וְלֹא־יִקְרָא עָלֶיךָ אֶל־יְהוָה וְהָיָה בְךָ חֵטְא׃ לֹא־יוּמְתוּ אָבוֹת
יז עַל־בָּנִים וּבָנִים לֹא־יוּמְתוּ עַל־אָבוֹת אִישׁ בְּחֶטְאוֹ יוּמָתוּ׃ לֹא
יח תַטֶּה מִשְׁפַּט גֵּר יָתוֹם וְלֹא תַחֲבֹל בֶּגֶד אַלְמָנָה׃ וְזָכַרְתָּ כִּי עֶבֶד הָיִיתָ
בְּמִצְרַיִם וַיִּפְדְּךָ יְהוָה אֱלֹהֶיךָ מִשָּׁם עַל־כֵּן אָנֹכִי מְצַוְּךָ לַעֲשׂוֹת אֶת־הַדָּבָר
יט הַזֶּה׃ כִּי תִקְצֹר קְצִירְךָ בְשָׂדֶךָ וְשָׁכַחְתָּ עֹמֶר בַּשָּׂדֶה לֹא תָשׁוּב כ
לְקַחְתּוֹ לַגֵּר לַיָּתוֹם וְלָאַלְמָנָה יִהְיֶה לְמַעַן יְבָרֶכְךָ יְהוָה אֱלֹהֶיךָ בְּכֹל מַעֲשֵׂה
כ יָדֶיךָ׃ כִּי תַחְבֹּט זֵיתְךָ לֹא תְפַאֵר אַחֲרֶיךָ לַגֵּר לַיָּתוֹם וְלָאַלְמָנָה
כא יִהְיֶה׃ כִּי תִבְצֹר כַּרְמְךָ לֹא תְעוֹלֵל אַחֲרֶיךָ לַגֵּר לַיָּתוֹם וְלָאַלְמָנָה יִהְיֶה׃

כב וזכרת כי־עבד היית בארץ מצרים על־כן אנכי מצוך לעשות את־הדבר
ה א הזה: כי־יהיה ריב בין אנשים ונגשו אל־המשפט ושפטום
ב והצדיקו את־הצדיק והרשיעו את־הרשע: והיה אם־בן הכות הרשע
ג והפילו השפט והכהו לפניו כדי רשעתו במספר: ארבעים יכנו לא יסיף
ד פן־יסיף להכתו על־אלה מכה רבה ונקלה אחיך לעיניך: לא־תחסם שור
ה בדישו: כי־ישבו אחים יחדו ומת אחד מהם ובן אין־לו לא־
תהיה אשת־המת החוצה לאיש זר יבמה יבא עליה ולקחה לו לאשה
ו ויבמה: והיה הבכור אשר תלד יקום על־שם אחיו המת ולא־ימחה שמו
ז מישראל: ואם־לא יחפץ האיש לקחת את־יבמתו ועלתה יבמתו השערה
אל־הזקנים ואמרה מאן יבמי להקים לאחיו שם בישראל לא אבה יבמי:
ח ט וקראו־לו זקני־עירו ודברו אליו ועמד ואמר לא חפצתי לקחתה: ונגשה
יבמתו אליו לעיני הזקנים וחלצה נעלו מעל רגלו וירקה בפניו וענתה
י ואמרה ככה יעשה לאיש אשר לא־יבנה את־בית אחיו: ונקרא שמו
יא בישראל בית חלוץ הנעל: כי־ינצו אנשים יחדו איש ואחיו
וקרבה אשת האחד להציל את־אישה מיד מכהו ושלחה ידה והחזיקה
יב יג במבשיו: וקצתה את־כפה לא תחוס עינך: לא־יהיה לך בכיסך
יד אבן ואבן גדולה וקטנה: לא־יהיה לך בביתך איפה ואיפה גדולה וקטנה:
טו אבן שלמה וצדק יהיה־לך איפה שלמה וצדק יהיה־לך למען יאריכו ימיך
טז על האדמה אשר־יהוה אלהיך נתן לך: כי תועבת יהוה אלהיך כל־עשה
אלה כל עשה עול:
יז יח *זכור את אשר־עשה לך עמלק בדרך בצאתכם ממצרים: אשר קרך מפטיר
בדרך ויזנב בך כל־הנחשלים אחריך ואתה עיף ויגע ולא ירא אלהים:
יט והיה בהניח יהוה אלהיך ׀ לך מכל־איביך מסביב בארץ אשר־יהוה
אלהיך נתן לך נחלה לרשתה תמחה את־זכר עמלק מתחת השמים
לא תשכח:

כי תבוא כא

כו א והיה כי־תבוא אל־הארץ אשר יהוה אלהיך נתן לך נחלה וירשתה וישבת
ב בה: ולקחת מראשית ׀ כל־פרי האדמה אשר תביא מארצך אשר יהוה
אלהיך נתן לך ושמת בטנא והלכת אל־המקום אשר יבחר יהוה אלהיך
ג לשכן שמו שם: ובאת אל־הכהן אשר יהיה בימים ההם ואמרת אליו

הִגַּדְתִּי הַיּוֹם לַיהוָה אֱלֹהֶיךָ כִּי־בָאתִי אֶל־הָאָרֶץ אֲשֶׁר נִשְׁבַּע יְהוָה לַאֲבֹתֵינוּ
ד לָתֶת לָנוּ: *וְלָקַח הַכֹּהֵן הַטֶּנֶא מִיָּדֶךָ וְהִנִּיחוֹ לִפְנֵי מִזְבַּח יְהוָה אֱלֹהֶיךָ: לוי
ה וְעָנִיתָ וְאָמַרְתָּ לִפְנֵי ׀ יְהוָה אֱלֹהֶיךָ אֲרַמִּי אֹבֵד אָבִי וַיֵּרֶד מִצְרַיְמָה וַיָּגָר שָׁם
ו בִּמְתֵי מְעָט וַיְהִי־שָׁם לְגוֹי גָּדוֹל עָצוּם וָרָב: וַיָּרֵעוּ אֹתָנוּ הַמִּצְרִים וַיְעַנּוּנוּ
ז וַיִּתְּנוּ עָלֵינוּ עֲבֹדָה קָשָׁה: וַנִּצְעַק אֶל־יְהוָה אֱלֹהֵי אֲבֹתֵינוּ וַיִּשְׁמַע יְהוָה אֶת־
ח קֹלֵנוּ וַיַּרְא אֶת־עָנְיֵנוּ וְאֶת־עֲמָלֵנוּ וְאֶת־לַחֲצֵנוּ: וַיּוֹצִאֵנוּ יְהוָה מִמִּצְרַיִם בְּיָד
ט חֲזָקָה וּבִזְרֹעַ נְטוּיָה וּבְמֹרָא גָּדֹל וּבְאֹתוֹת וּבְמֹפְתִים: וַיְבִאֵנוּ אֶל־הַמָּקוֹם
י הַזֶּה וַיִּתֶּן־לָנוּ אֶת־הָאָרֶץ הַזֹּאת אֶרֶץ זָבַת חָלָב וּדְבָשׁ: וְעַתָּה הִנֵּה הֵבֵאתִי
אֶת־רֵאשִׁית פְּרִי הָאֲדָמָה אֲשֶׁר־נָתַתָּה לִּי יְהוָה וְהִנַּחְתּוֹ לִפְנֵי יְהוָה אֱלֹהֶיךָ
יא וְהִשְׁתַּחֲוִיתָ לִפְנֵי יְהוָה אֱלֹהֶיךָ: וְשָׂמַחְתָּ בְכָל־הַטּוֹב אֲשֶׁר נָתַן־לְךָ יְהוָה
יב אֱלֹהֶיךָ וּלְבֵיתֶךָ אַתָּה וְהַלֵּוִי וְהַגֵּר אֲשֶׁר בְּקִרְבֶּךָ: *כִּי תְכַלֶּה שני (ישראל)
לַעְשֵׂר אֶת־כָּל־מַעְשַׂר תְּבוּאָתְךָ בַּשָּׁנָה הַשְּׁלִישִׁת שְׁנַת הַמַּעֲשֵׂר וְנָתַתָּה
יג לַלֵּוִי לַגֵּר לַיָּתוֹם וְלָאַלְמָנָה וְאָכְלוּ בִשְׁעָרֶיךָ וְשָׂבֵעוּ: וְאָמַרְתָּ לִפְנֵי יְהוָה
אֱלֹהֶיךָ בִּעַרְתִּי הַקֹּדֶשׁ מִן־הַבַּיִת וְגַם נְתַתִּיו לַלֵּוִי וְלַגֵּר לַיָּתוֹם וְלָאַלְמָנָה
יד כְּכָל־מִצְוָתְךָ אֲשֶׁר צִוִּיתָנִי לֹא־עָבַרְתִּי מִמִּצְוֹתֶיךָ וְלֹא שָׁכָחְתִּי: לֹא־אָכַלְתִּי
בְאֹנִי מִמֶּנּוּ וְלֹא־בִעַרְתִּי מִמֶּנּוּ בְּטָמֵא וְלֹא־נָתַתִּי מִמֶּנּוּ לְמֵת שָׁמַעְתִּי בְּקוֹל
טו יְהוָה אֱלֹהָי עָשִׂיתִי כְּכֹל אֲשֶׁר צִוִּיתָנִי: הַשְׁקִיפָה מִמְּעוֹן קָדְשְׁךָ מִן־הַשָּׁמַיִם
וּבָרֵךְ אֶת־עַמְּךָ אֶת־יִשְׂרָאֵל וְאֵת הָאֲדָמָה אֲשֶׁר נָתַתָּה לָנוּ כַּאֲשֶׁר נִשְׁבַּעְתָּ
טז לַאֲבֹתֵינוּ אֶרֶץ זָבַת חָלָב וּדְבָשׁ: ** הַיּוֹם הַזֶּה יְהוָה אֱלֹהֶיךָ מְצַוְּךָ שלישי
לַעֲשׂוֹת אֶת־הַחֻקִּים הָאֵלֶּה וְאֶת־הַמִּשְׁפָּטִים וְשָׁמַרְתָּ וְעָשִׂיתָ אוֹתָם בְּכָל־
יז לְבָבְךָ וּבְכָל־נַפְשֶׁךָ: אֶת־יְהוָה הֶאֱמַרְתָּ הַיּוֹם לִהְיוֹת לְךָ לֵאלֹהִים וְלָלֶכֶת
יח בִּדְרָכָיו וְלִשְׁמֹר חֻקָּיו וּמִצְוֹתָיו וּמִשְׁפָּטָיו וְלִשְׁמֹעַ בְּקֹלוֹ: וַיהוָה הֶאֱמִירְךָ
יט הַיּוֹם לִהְיוֹת לוֹ לְעַם סְגֻלָּה כַּאֲשֶׁר דִּבֶּר־לָךְ וְלִשְׁמֹר כָּל־מִצְוֹתָיו: וּלְתִתְּךָ
עֶלְיוֹן עַל כָּל־הַגּוֹיִם אֲשֶׁר עָשָׂה לִתְהִלָּה וּלְשֵׁם וּלְתִפְאָרֶת וְלִהְיֹתְךָ עַם־קָדֹשׁ
לַיהוָה אֱלֹהֶיךָ כַּאֲשֶׁר דִּבֵּר:
כז א וַיְצַו מֹשֶׁה וְזִקְנֵי יִשְׂרָאֵל אֶת־הָעָם לֵאמֹר שָׁמֹר אֶת־כָּל־הַמִּצְוָה אֲשֶׁר אָנֹכִי רביעי
ב מְצַוֶּה אֶתְכֶם הַיּוֹם: וְהָיָה בַּיּוֹם אֲשֶׁר תַּעַבְרוּ אֶת־הַיַּרְדֵּן אֶל־הָאָרֶץ אֲשֶׁר־
ג יְהוָה אֱלֹהֶיךָ נֹתֵן לָךְ וַהֲקֵמֹתָ לְךָ אֲבָנִים גְּדֹלוֹת וְשַׂדְתָּ אֹתָם בַּשִּׂיד: וְכָתַבְתָּ
עֲלֵיהֶן אֶת־כָּל־דִּבְרֵי הַתּוֹרָה הַזֹּאת בְּעָבְרֶךָ לְמַעַן אֲשֶׁר תָּבֹא אֶל־הָאָרֶץ

אֲשֶׁר־יהוָה אֱלֹהֶיךָ | נֹתֵן לְךָ אֶרֶץ זָבַת חָלָב וּדְבַשׁ כַּאֲשֶׁר דִּבֶּר יהוָה אֱלֹהֵי־
ד אֲבֹתֶיךָ לָךְ: וְהָיָה בְּעָבְרְכֶם אֶת־הַיַּרְדֵּן תָּקִימוּ אֶת־הָאֲבָנִים הָאֵלֶּה אֲשֶׁר
ה אָנֹכִי מְצַוֶּה אֶתְכֶם הַיּוֹם בְּהַר עֵיבָל וְשַׂדְתָּ אוֹתָם בַּשִּׂיד: וּבָנִיתָ שָּׁם מִזְבֵּחַ
ו לַיהוָה אֱלֹהֶיךָ מִזְבַּח אֲבָנִים לֹא־תָנִיף עֲלֵיהֶם בַּרְזֶל: אֲבָנִים שְׁלֵמוֹת תִּבְנֶה
ז אֶת־מִזְבַּח יהוָה אֱלֹהֶיךָ וְהַעֲלִיתָ עָלָיו עוֹלֹת לַיהוָה אֱלֹהֶיךָ: וְזָבַחְתָּ שְׁלָמִים
ח וְאָכַלְתָּ שָּׁם וְשָׂמַחְתָּ לִפְנֵי יהוָה אֱלֹהֶיךָ: וְכָתַבְתָּ עַל־הָאֲבָנִים אֶת־כָּל־דִּבְרֵי
ט הַתּוֹרָה הַזֹּאת בַּאֵר הֵיטֵב: וַיְדַבֵּר מֹשֶׁה וְהַכֹּהֲנִים הַלְוִיִּם אֶל־כָּל־
יִשְׂרָאֵל לֵאמֹר הַסְכֵּת | וּשְׁמַע יִשְׂרָאֵל הַיּוֹם הַזֶּה נִהְיֵיתָ לְעָם לַיהוָה אֱלֹהֶיךָ:
י וְשָׁמַעְתָּ בְּקוֹל יהוָה אֱלֹהֶיךָ וְעָשִׂיתָ אֶת־מִצְוֹתָו וְאֶת־חֻקָּיו אֲשֶׁר אָנֹכִי מְצַוְּךָ
יא יב הַיּוֹם: *וַיְצַו מֹשֶׁה אֶת־הָעָם בַּיּוֹם הַהוּא לֵאמֹר: אֵלֶּה יַעַמְדוּ לְבָרֵךְ חמישי
אֶת־הָעָם עַל־הַר גְּרִזִּים בְּעָבְרְכֶם אֶת־הַיַּרְדֵּן שִׁמְעוֹן וְלֵוִי וִיהוּדָה וְיִשָּׂשכָר
יג וְיוֹסֵף וּבִנְיָמִן: וְאֵלֶּה יַעַמְדוּ עַל־הַקְּלָלָה בְּהַר עֵיבָל רְאוּבֵן גָּד וְאָשֵׁר וּזְבוּלֻן
יד טו דָּן וְנַפְתָּלִי: וְעָנוּ הַלְוִיִּם וְאָמְרוּ אֶל־כָּל־אִישׁ יִשְׂרָאֵל קוֹל רָם: אָרוּר
הָאִישׁ אֲשֶׁר יַעֲשֶׂה פֶסֶל וּמַסֵּכָה תּוֹעֲבַת יהוָה מַעֲשֵׂה יְדֵי חָרָשׁ וְשָׂם בַּסָּתֶר
טז וְעָנוּ כָל־הָעָם וְאָמְרוּ אָמֵן: אָרוּר מַקְלֶה אָבִיו וְאִמּוֹ וְאָמַר כָּל־הָעָם
יז יח אָמֵן: אָרוּר מַסִּיג גְּבוּל רֵעֵהוּ וְאָמַר כָּל־הָעָם אָמֵן: אָרוּר
יט מַשְׁגֶּה עִוֵּר בַּדָּרֶךְ וְאָמַר כָּל־הָעָם אָמֵן: אָרוּר מַטֶּה מִשְׁפַּט גֵּר־יָתוֹם
כ וְאַלְמָנָה וְאָמַר כָּל־הָעָם אָמֵן: אָרוּר שֹׁכֵב עִם־אֵשֶׁת אָבִיו כִּי גִלָּה כְּנַף אָבִיו
כא וְאָמַר כָּל־הָעָם אָמֵן: אָרוּר שֹׁכֵב עִם־כָּל־בְּהֵמָה וְאָמַר כָּל־הָעָם
כב אָמֵן: אָרוּר שֹׁכֵב עִם־אֲחֹתוֹ בַּת־אָבִיו אוֹ בַת־אִמּוֹ וְאָמַר כָּל־הָעָם
כג כד אָמֵן: אָרוּר שֹׁכֵב עִם־חֹתַנְתּוֹ וְאָמַר כָּל־הָעָם אָמֵן: אָרוּר
כה מַכֵּה רֵעֵהוּ בַּסָּתֶר וְאָמַר כָּל־הָעָם אָמֵן: אָרוּר לֹקֵחַ שֹׁחַד לְהַכּוֹת
כו נֶפֶשׁ דַּם נָקִי וְאָמַר כָּל־הָעָם אָמֵן: אָרוּר אֲשֶׁר לֹא־יָקִים אֶת־דִּבְרֵי
הַתּוֹרָה־הַזֹּאת לַעֲשׂוֹת אוֹתָם וְאָמַר כָּל־הָעָם אָמֵן:
כח א וְהָיָה אִם־שָׁמוֹעַ תִּשְׁמַע בְּקוֹל יהוָה אֱלֹהֶיךָ לִשְׁמֹר לַעֲשׂוֹת אֶת־כָּל־מִצְוֹתָיו כב
ב אֲשֶׁר אָנֹכִי מְצַוְּךָ הַיּוֹם וּנְתָנְךָ יהוָה אֱלֹהֶיךָ עֶלְיוֹן עַל כָּל־גּוֹיֵי הָאָרֶץ: וּבָאוּ
ג עָלֶיךָ כָּל־הַבְּרָכוֹת הָאֵלֶּה וְהִשִּׂיגֻךָ כִּי תִשְׁמַע בְּקוֹל יהוָה אֱלֹהֶיךָ: בָּרוּךְ
ד אַתָּה בָּעִיר וּבָרוּךְ אַתָּה בַּשָּׂדֶה: בָּרוּךְ פְּרִי־בִטְנְךָ וּפְרִי אַדְמָתְךָ וּפְרִי בְהֶמְתֶּךָ
ה ו שְׁגַר אֲלָפֶיךָ וְעַשְׁתְּרוֹת צֹאנֶךָ: בָּרוּךְ טַנְאֲךָ וּמִשְׁאַרְתֶּךָ: בָּרוּךְ אַתָּה בְּבֹאֶךָ

ששי וברוך אתה בצאתך: יתן יהוה את־איביך הקמים עליך נגפים לפניך בדרך ז
אחד יצאו אליך ובשבעה דרכים ינוסו לפניך: יצו יהוה אתך את־הברכה ח
באסמיך ובכל משלח ידך וברכך בארץ אשר־יהוה אלהיך נתן לך: יקימך ט
יהוה לו לעם קדוש כאשר נשבע־לך כי תשמר את־מצות יהוה אלהיך
והלכת בדרכיו: וראו כל־עמי הארץ כי שם יהוה נקרא עליך ויראו ממך: י
והותרך יהוה לטובה בפרי בטנך ובפרי בהמתך ובפרי אדמתך על האדמה יא
אשר נשבע יהוה לאבתיך לתת לך: יפתח יהוה | לך את־אוצרו הטוב יב
את־השמים לתת מטר־ארצך בעתו ולברך את כל־מעשה ידך והלוית
גוים רבים ואתה לא תלוה: ונתנך יהוה לראש ולא לזנב והיית רק למעלה יג
ולא תהיה למטה כי־תשמע אל־מצות | יהוה אלהיך אשר אנכי מצוך
היום לשמר ולעשות: ולא תסור מכל־הדברים אשר אנכי מצוה אתכם יד
היום ימין ושמאול ללכת אחרי אלהים אחרים לעבדם:
והיה אם־לא תשמע בקול יהוה אלהיך לשמר לעשות את־כל־מצותיו טו
וחקתיו אשר אנכי מצוך היום ובאו עליך כל־הקללות האלה והשיגוך: טז יז יח
ארור אתה בעיר וארור אתה בשדה: ארור טנאך ומשארתך: ארור פרי־ יט
בטנך ופרי אדמתך שגר אלפיך ועשתרת צאנך: ארור אתה בבאך וארור כ
אתה בצאתך: ישלח יהוה | בך את־המארה את־המהומה ואת־המגערת
בכל־משלח ידך אשר תעשה עד השמדך ועד־אבדך מהר מפני רע מעלליך כא
אשר עזבתני: ידבק יהוה בך את־הדבר עד כלתו אתך מעל האדמה כב
אשר־אתה בא־שמה לרשתה: יככה יהוה בשחפת ובקדחת ובדלקת כג
ובחרחר ובחרב ובשדפון ובירקון ורדפוך עד אבדך: והיו שמיך אשר כד
על־ראשך נחשת והארץ אשר־תחתיך ברזל: יתן יהוה את־מטר ארצך כה
אבק ועפר מן־השמים ירד עליך עד השמדך: יתנך יהוה | נגף לפני איביך
בדרך אחד תצא אליו ובשבעה דרכים תנוס לפניו והיית לזעוה לכל כו
ממלכות הארץ: והיתה נבלתך למאכל לכל־עוף השמים ולבהמת הארץ כז
ובטחורים ואין מחריד: יככה יהוה בשחין מצרים ובעפלים ובגרב ובחרס אשר לא־ כח כט
תוכל להרפא: יככה יהוה בשגעון ובעורון ובתמהון לבב: והיית ממשש
בצהרים כאשר ימשש העור באפלה ולא תצליח את־דרכיך והיית אך ל
ישכבנה עשוק וגזול כל־הימים ואין מושיע: אשה תארש ואיש אחר ישגלנה בית לא
תבנה ולא־תשב בו כרם תטע ולא תחללנו: שורך טבוח לעיניך ולא תאכל

מִמֶּנּוּ חֲמֹרְךָ גָּזוּל מִלְּפָנֶיךָ וְלֹא יָשׁוּב לָךְ צֹאנְךָ נְתֻנוֹת לְאֹיְבֶיךָ וְאֵין לְךָ מוֹשִׁיעַ׃
לב בָּנֶיךָ וּבְנֹתֶיךָ נְתֻנִים לְעַם אַחֵר וְעֵינֶיךָ רֹאוֹת וְכָלוֹת אֲלֵיהֶם כָּל־הַיּוֹם וְאֵין
לג לְאֵל יָדֶךָ׃ פְּרִי אַדְמָתְךָ וְכָל־יְגִיעֲךָ יֹאכַל עַם אֲשֶׁר לֹא־יָדָעְתָּ וְהָיִיתָ רַק עָשׁוּק
לד לה וְרָצוּץ כָּל־הַיָּמִים׃ וְהָיִיתָ מְשֻׁגָּע מִמַּרְאֵה עֵינֶיךָ אֲשֶׁר תִּרְאֶה׃ יַכְּכָה יְהוָה
בִּשְׁחִין רָע עַל־הַבִּרְכַּיִם וְעַל־הַשֹּׁקַיִם אֲשֶׁר לֹא־תוּכַל לְהֵרָפֵא מִכַּף רַגְלְךָ
לו וְעַד קָדְקֳדֶךָ׃ יוֹלֵךְ יְהוָה אֹתְךָ וְאֶת־מַלְכְּךָ אֲשֶׁר תָּקִים עָלֶיךָ אֶל־גּוֹי אֲשֶׁר
לז לֹא־יָדַעְתָּ אַתָּה וַאֲבֹתֶיךָ וְעָבַדְתָּ שָּׁם אֱלֹהִים אֲחֵרִים עֵץ וָאָבֶן׃ וְהָיִיתָ לְשַׁמָּה
לח לְמָשָׁל וְלִשְׁנִינָה בְּכֹל הָעַמִּים אֲשֶׁר־יְנַהֶגְךָ יְהוָה שָׁמָּה׃ זֶרַע רַב תּוֹצִיא הַשָּׂדֶה
לט וּמְעַט תֶּאֱסֹף כִּי יַחְסְלֶנּוּ הָאַרְבֶּה׃ כְּרָמִים תִּטַּע וְעָבָדְתָּ וְיַיִן לֹא־תִשְׁתֶּה וְלֹא
מ תֶאֱגֹר כִּי תֹאכְלֶנּוּ הַתֹּלָעַת׃ זֵיתִים יִהְיוּ לְךָ בְּכָל־גְּבוּלֶךָ וְשֶׁמֶן לֹא תָסוּךְ כִּי
מא מב יִשַּׁל זֵיתֶךָ׃ בָּנִים וּבָנוֹת תּוֹלִיד וְלֹא־יִהְיוּ לָךְ כִּי יֵלְכוּ בַּשֶּׁבִי׃ כָּל־עֵצְךָ וּפְרִי
מג אַדְמָתֶךָ יְיָרֵשׁ הַצְּלָצַל׃ הַגֵּר אֲשֶׁר בְּקִרְבְּךָ יַעֲלֶה עָלֶיךָ מַעְלָה מָּעְלָה וְאַתָּה
מד תֵרֵד מַטָּה מָּטָּה׃ הוּא יַלְוְךָ וְאַתָּה לֹא תַלְוֶנּוּ הוּא יִהְיֶה לְרֹאשׁ וְאַתָּה תִּהְיֶה
מה לְזָנָב׃ וּבָאוּ עָלֶיךָ כָּל־הַקְּלָלוֹת הָאֵלֶּה וּרְדָפוּךָ וְהִשִּׂיגוּךָ עַד הִשָּׁמְדָךְ כִּי־
מו לֹא שָׁמַעְתָּ בְּקוֹל יְהוָה אֱלֹהֶיךָ לִשְׁמֹר מִצְוֹתָיו וְחֻקֹּתָיו אֲשֶׁר צִוָּךְ׃ וְהָיוּ בְךָ
מז לְאוֹת וּלְמוֹפֵת וּבְזַרְעֲךָ עַד־עוֹלָם׃ תַּחַת אֲשֶׁר לֹא־עָבַדְתָּ אֶת־יְהוָה אֱלֹהֶיךָ
מח בְּשִׂמְחָה וּבְטוּב לֵבָב מֵרֹב כֹּל׃ וְעָבַדְתָּ אֶת־אֹיְבֶיךָ אֲשֶׁר יְשַׁלְּחֶנּוּ יְהוָה בָּךְ
בְּרָעָב וּבְצָמָא וּבְעֵירֹם וּבְחֹסֶר כֹּל וְנָתַן עֹל בַּרְזֶל עַל־צַוָּארֶךָ עַד הִשְׁמִידוֹ
מט אֹתָךְ׃ יִשָּׂא יְהוָה עָלֶיךָ גּוֹי מֵרָחֹק מִקְצֵה הָאָרֶץ כַּאֲשֶׁר יִדְאֶה הַנָּשֶׁר גּוֹי אֲשֶׁר
נ נא לֹא־תִשְׁמַע לְשֹׁנוֹ׃ גּוֹי עַז פָּנִים אֲשֶׁר לֹא־יִשָּׂא פָנִים לְזָקֵן וְנַעַר לֹא יָחֹן׃ וְאָכַל
פְּרִי בְהֶמְתְּךָ וּפְרִי־אַדְמָתְךָ עַד הִשָּׁמְדָךְ אֲשֶׁר לֹא־יַשְׁאִיר לְךָ דָּגָן תִּירוֹשׁ
נב וְיִצְהָר שְׁגַר אֲלָפֶיךָ וְעַשְׁתְּרֹת צֹאנֶךָ עַד הַאֲבִידוֹ אֹתָךְ׃ וְהֵצַר לְךָ בְּכָל־שְׁעָרֶיךָ
עַד רֶדֶת חֹמֹתֶיךָ הַגְּבֹהֹת וְהַבְּצֻרוֹת אֲשֶׁר אַתָּה בֹּטֵחַ בָּהֵן בְּכָל־אַרְצֶךָ וְהֵצַר
נג לְךָ בְּכָל־שְׁעָרֶיךָ בְּכָל־אַרְצְךָ אֲשֶׁר נָתַן יְהוָה אֱלֹהֶיךָ לָךְ׃ וְאָכַלְתָּ פְרִי־בִטְנְךָ
בְּשַׂר בָּנֶיךָ וּבְנֹתֶיךָ אֲשֶׁר נָתַן־לְךָ יְהוָה אֱלֹהֶיךָ בְּמָצוֹר וּבְמָצוֹק אֲשֶׁר־יָצִיק
נד לְךָ אֹיְבֶךָ׃ הָאִישׁ הָרַךְ בְּךָ וְהֶעָנֹג מְאֹד תֵּרַע עֵינוֹ בְאָחִיו וּבְאֵשֶׁת חֵיקוֹ וּבְיֶתֶר
נה בָּנָיו אֲשֶׁר יוֹתִיר׃ מִתֵּת ׀ לְאַחַד מֵהֶם מִבְּשַׂר בָּנָיו אֲשֶׁר יֹאכֵל מִבְּלִי הִשְׁאִיר־
נו לוֹ כֹּל בְּמָצוֹר וּבְמָצוֹק אֲשֶׁר יָצִיק לְךָ אֹיִבְךָ בְּכָל־שְׁעָרֶיךָ׃ הָרַכָּה בְךָ וְהָעֲנֻגָּה
אֲשֶׁר לֹא־נִסְּתָה כַף־רַגְלָהּ הַצֵּג עַל־הָאָרֶץ מֵהִתְעַנֵּג וּמֵרֹךְ תֵּרַע עֵינָהּ בְּאִישׁ
נז חֵיקָהּ וּבִבְנָהּ וּבְבִתָּהּ׃ וּבְשִׁלְיָתָהּ הַיּוֹצֵת ׀ מִבֵּין רַגְלֶיהָ וּבְבָנֶיהָ אֲשֶׁר תֵּלֵד

כִּי־תֹאכְלֵם בְּחֹסֶר־כֹּל בַּסָּתֶר בְּמָצוֹר וּבְמָצוֹק אֲשֶׁר יָצִיק לְךָ אֹיִבְךָ בִּשְׁעָרֶיךָ׃
נח אִם־לֹא תִשְׁמֹר לַעֲשׂוֹת אֶת־כָּל־דִּבְרֵי הַתּוֹרָה הַזֹּאת הַכְּתֻבִים בַּסֵּפֶר הַזֶּה
נט לְיִרְאָה אֶת־הַשֵּׁם הַנִּכְבָּד וְהַנּוֹרָא הַזֶּה אֵת יהוה אֱלֹהֶיךָ׃ וְהִפְלָא יהוה אֶת־
מַכֹּתְךָ וְאֵת מַכּוֹת זַרְעֶךָ מַכּוֹת גְּדֹלֹת וְנֶאֱמָנוֹת וָחֳלָיִם רָעִים וְנֶאֱמָנִים׃
ס סא וְהֵשִׁיב בְּךָ אֵת כָּל־מַדְוֵה מִצְרַיִם אֲשֶׁר יָגֹרְתָּ מִפְּנֵיהֶם וְדָבְקוּ בָּךְ׃ גַּם כָּל־חֳלִי
וְכָל־מַכָּה אֲשֶׁר לֹא כָתוּב בְּסֵפֶר הַתּוֹרָה הַזֹּאת יַעְלֵם יהוה עָלֶיךָ עַד הִשָּׁמְדָךְ׃
סב וְנִשְׁאַרְתֶּם בִּמְתֵי מְעָט תַּחַת אֲשֶׁר הֱיִיתֶם כְּכוֹכְבֵי הַשָּׁמַיִם לָרֹב כִּי־לֹא
סג שָׁמַעְתָּ בְּקוֹל יהוה אֱלֹהֶיךָ׃ וְהָיָה כַּאֲשֶׁר־שָׂשׂ יהוה עֲלֵיכֶם לְהֵיטִיב אֶתְכֶם
וּלְהַרְבּוֹת אֶתְכֶם כֵּן יָשִׂישׂ יהוה עֲלֵיכֶם לְהַאֲבִיד אֶתְכֶם וּלְהַשְׁמִיד אֶתְכֶם
סד וְנִסַּחְתֶּם מֵעַל הָאֲדָמָה אֲשֶׁר־אַתָּה בָא־שָׁמָּה לְרִשְׁתָּהּ׃ וֶהֱפִיצְךָ יהוה בְּכָל־
הָעַמִּים מִקְצֵה הָאָרֶץ וְעַד־קְצֵה הָאָרֶץ וְעָבַדְתָּ שָּׁם אֱלֹהִים אֲחֵרִים אֲשֶׁר
סה לֹא־יָדַעְתָּ אַתָּה וַאֲבֹתֶיךָ עֵץ וָאָבֶן׃ וּבַגּוֹיִם הָהֵם לֹא תַרְגִּיעַ וְלֹא־יִהְיֶה מָנוֹחַ
סו לְכַף־רַגְלֶךָ וְנָתַן יהוה לְךָ שָׁם לֵב רַגָּז וְכִלְיוֹן עֵינַיִם וְדַאֲבוֹן נָפֶשׁ׃ וְהָיוּ חַיֶּיךָ
סז תְּלֻאִים לְךָ מִנֶּגֶד וּפָחַדְתָּ לַיְלָה וְיוֹמָם וְלֹא תַאֲמִין בְּחַיֶּיךָ׃ בַּבֹּקֶר תֹּאמַר
מִי־יִתֵּן עֶרֶב וּבָעֶרֶב תֹּאמַר מִי־יִתֵּן בֹּקֶר מִפַּחַד לְבָבְךָ אֲשֶׁר תִּפְחָד וּמִמַּרְאֵה
סח עֵינֶיךָ אֲשֶׁר תִּרְאֶה׃ וֶהֱשִׁיבְךָ יהוה ׀ מִצְרַיִם בָּאֳנִיּוֹת בַּדֶּרֶךְ אֲשֶׁר אָמַרְתִּי לְךָ
לֹא־תֹסִיף עוֹד לִרְאֹתָהּ וְהִתְמַכַּרְתֶּם שָׁם לְאֹיְבֶיךָ לַעֲבָדִים וְלִשְׁפָחוֹת וְאֵין
סט קֹנֶה׃ אֵלֶּה דִבְרֵי הַבְּרִית אֲשֶׁר־צִוָּה יהוה אֶת־מֹשֶׁה לִכְרֹת אֶת־
בְּנֵי יִשְׂרָאֵל בְּאֶרֶץ מוֹאָב מִלְּבַד הַבְּרִית אֲשֶׁר־כָּרַת אִתָּם בְּחֹרֵב׃
כט א וַיִּקְרָא מֹשֶׁה אֶל־כָּל־יִשְׂרָאֵל וַיֹּאמֶר אֲלֵהֶם אַתֶּם רְאִיתֶם אֵת כָּל־אֲשֶׁר עָשָׂה שביעי
ב יהוה לְעֵינֵיכֶם בְּאֶרֶץ מִצְרַיִם לְפַרְעֹה וּלְכָל־עֲבָדָיו וּלְכָל־אַרְצוֹ׃ הַמַּסּוֹת
ג הַגְּדֹלֹת אֲשֶׁר רָאוּ עֵינֶיךָ הָאֹתֹת וְהַמֹּפְתִים הַגְּדֹלִים הָהֵם׃ וְלֹא־נָתַן יהוה
ד לָכֶם לֵב לָדַעַת וְעֵינַיִם לִרְאוֹת וְאָזְנַיִם לִשְׁמֹעַ עַד הַיּוֹם הַזֶּה׃ וָאוֹלֵךְ אֶתְכֶם
אַרְבָּעִים שָׁנָה בַּמִּדְבָּר לֹא־בָלוּ שַׂלְמֹתֵיכֶם מֵעֲלֵיכֶם וְנַעַלְךָ לֹא־בָלְתָה מֵעַל
ה רַגְלֶךָ׃ לֶחֶם לֹא אֲכַלְתֶּם וְיַיִן וְשֵׁכָר לֹא שְׁתִיתֶם לְמַעַן תֵּדְעוּ כִּי אֲנִי יהוה
ו אֱלֹהֵיכֶם׃ וַתָּבֹאוּ אֶל־הַמָּקוֹם הַזֶּה וַיֵּצֵא סִיחֹן מֶלֶךְ־חֶשְׁבּוֹן וְעוֹג מֶלֶךְ־הַבָּשָׁן מפטיר
ז לִקְרָאתֵנוּ לַמִּלְחָמָה וַנַּכֵּם׃ וַנִּקַּח אֶת־אַרְצָם וַנִּתְּנָהּ לְנַחֲלָה לָראוּבֵנִי וְלַגָּדִי
ח וְלַחֲצִי שֵׁבֶט הַמְנַשִּׁי׃ וּשְׁמַרְתֶּם אֶת־דִּבְרֵי הַבְּרִית הַזֹּאת וַעֲשִׂיתֶם אֹתָם
לְמַעַן תַּשְׂכִּילוּ אֵת כָּל־אֲשֶׁר תַּעֲשׂוּן׃

עשרת הדברות שבפרשת ואתחנן

THE TEN COMANDMENTS IN PARASHAT VA'ETHANAN

בטעם העליון

אָנֹכִי יהוה אֱלֹהֶיךָ
אֲשֶׁר הוֹצֵאתִיךָ מֵאֶרֶץ מִצְרַיִם מִבֵּית עֲבָדִים לֹא־יִהְיֶה לְךָ אֱלֹהִים אֲחֵרִים
עַל־פָּנַי לֹא תַעֲשֶׂה־לְךָ פֶסֶל ׀ כָּל־תְּמוּנָה אֲשֶׁר בַּשָּׁמַיִם ׀ מִמַּעַל וַאֲשֶׁר בָּאָרֶץ
מִתַּחַת וַאֲשֶׁר בַּמַּיִם ׀ מִתַּחַת לָאָרֶץ לֹא־תִשְׁתַּחֲוֶה לָהֶם וְלֹא תָעָבְדֵם כִּי
אָנֹכִי יהוה אֱלֹהֶיךָ אֵל קַנָּא פֹּקֵד עֲוֺן אָבוֹת עַל־בָּנִים וְעַל־שִׁלֵּשִׁים וְעַל־
רִבֵּעִים לְשֹׂנְאָי וְעֹשֶׂה חֶסֶד לַאֲלָפִים לְאֹהֲבַי וּלְשֹׁמְרֵי מצותו: לֹא מִצְוֹתָי
תִשָּׂא אֶת־שֵׁם־יהוה אֱלֹהֶיךָ לַשָּׁוְא כִּי לֹא יְנַקֶּה יהוה אֵת אֲשֶׁר־יִשָּׂא אֶת־
שְׁמוֹ לַשָּׁוְא: שָׁמוֹר אֶת־יוֹם הַשַּׁבָּת לְקַדְּשׁוֹ כַּאֲשֶׁר צִוְּךָ ׀ יהוה
אֱלֹהֶיךָ שֵׁשֶׁת יָמִים תַּעֲבֹד וְעָשִׂיתָ כָּל־מְלַאכְתֶּךָ וְיוֹם הַשְּׁבִיעִי שַׁבָּת ׀
לַיהוה אֱלֹהֶיךָ לֹא־תַעֲשֶׂה כָל־מְלָאכָה אַתָּה וּבִנְךָ־וּבִתֶּךָ וְעַבְדְּךָ־וַאֲמָתֶךָ
וְשׁוֹרְךָ וַחֲמֹרְךָ וְכָל־בְּהֶמְתֶּךָ וְגֵרְךָ אֲשֶׁר בִּשְׁעָרֶיךָ לְמַעַן יָנוּחַ עַבְדְּךָ
וַאֲמָתְךָ כָּמוֹךָ וְזָכַרְתָּ כִּי־עֶבֶד הָיִיתָ ׀ בְּאֶרֶץ מִצְרַיִם וַיֹּצִאֲךָ יהוה אֱלֹהֶיךָ
מִשָּׁם בְּיָד חֲזָקָה וּבִזְרֹעַ נְטוּיָה עַל־כֵּן צִוְּךָ יהוה אֱלֹהֶיךָ לַעֲשׂוֹת אֶת־יוֹם
הַשַּׁבָּת: כַּבֵּד אֶת־אָבִיךָ וְאֶת־אִמֶּךָ כַּאֲשֶׁר צִוְּךָ יהוה אֱלֹהֶיךָ
לְמַעַן ׀ יַאֲרִיכֻן יָמֶיךָ וּלְמַעַן יִיטַב לָךְ עַל הָאֲדָמָה אֲשֶׁר־יהוה אֱלֹהֶיךָ נֹתֵן
לָךְ: לֹא תִרְצָח: וְלֹא
תִנְאָף: וְלֹא תִגְנֹב: וְלֹא־
תַעֲנֶה בְרֵעֲךָ עֵד שָׁוְא: וְלֹא
תַחְמֹד אֵשֶׁת רֵעֶךָ וְלֹא
תִתְאַוֶּה בֵּית רֵעֶךָ שָׂדֵהוּ וְעַבְדּוֹ וַאֲמָתוֹ שׁוֹרוֹ וַחֲמֹרוֹ וְכֹל אֲשֶׁר לְרֵעֶךָ:

According to the Gr"a and Heidenheim, the first commandment until מִבֵּית עֲבָדִים *should be read with the regular trop.*

הפטרות
HAFTAROT

הפטרת בהעלותך
HAFTARAT BEHA'ALOTEKHA

ZEKHARYA

ב יד רני ושמחי בת־ציון כי הנני־בא ושכנתי בתוכך נאם־יהוה: טו ונלוו גוים רבים
אל־יהוה ביום ההוא והיו לי לעם ושכנתי בתוכך וידעת כי־יהוה צבאות
שלחני אליך: טז ונחל יהוה את־יהודה חלקו על אדמת הקדש ובחר עוד
בירושלם: יז הס כל־בשר מפני יהוה כי נעור ממעון קדשו: ג א ויראני
את־יהושע הכהן הגדול עמד לפני מלאך יהוה והשטן עמד על־ימינו
לשטנו: ב ויאמר יהוה אל־השטן יגער יהוה בך השטן ויגער יהוה בך הבחר
בירושלם הלוא זה אוד מצל מאש: ג ויהושע היה לבש בגדים צואים ועמד
לפני המלאך: ד ויען ויאמר אל־העמדים לפניו לאמר הסירו הבגדים הצאים
מעליו ויאמר אליו ראה העברתי מעליך עונך והלבש אתך מחלצות:
ה ואמר ישימו צניף טהור על־ראשו וישימו הצניף הטהור על־ראשו וילבשהו
בגדים ומלאך יהוה עמד: ו ויעד מלאך יהוה ביהושע לאמר: ז כה־אמר
יהוה צבאות אם־בדרכי תלך ואם את־משמרתי תשמר וגם־אתה תדין
את־ביתי וגם תשמר את־חצרי ונתתי לך מהלכים בין העמדים האלה:
ח שמע־נא יהושע | הכהן הגדול אתה ורעיך הישבים לפניך כי־אנשי מופת
המה כי־הנני מביא את־עבדי צמח: ט כי | הנה האבן אשר נתתי לפני יהושע
על־אבן אחת שבעה עינים הנני מפתח פתחה נאם יהוה צבאות ומשתי
את־עון הארץ־ההיא ביום אחד: י ביום ההוא נאם יהוה צבאות תקראו איש
לרעהו אל־תחת גפן ואל־תחת תאנה: ד א וישב המלאך הדבר בי
ויעירני כאיש אשר־יעור משנתו: ב ויאמר אלי מה אתה ראה ויאמר ראיתי (ואמר)
והנה מנורת זהב כלה וגלה על־ראשה ושבעה נרתיה עליה שבעה ושבעה
מוצקות לנרות אשר על־ראשה: ג ושנים זיתים עליה אחד מימין הגלה ואחד
על־שמאלה: ד ואען ואמר אל־המלאך הדבר בי לאמר מה־אלה אדני: ה ויען
המלאך הדבר בי ויאמר אלי הלוא ידעת מה־המה אלה ואמר לא אדני:
ו ויען ויאמר אלי לאמר זה דבר־יהוה אל־זרבבל לאמר לא בחיל ולא בכח
כי אם־ברוחי אמר יהוה צבאות: ז מי־אתה הר־הגדול לפני זרבבל למישר
והוציא את־האבן הראשה תשאות חן | חן לה:

HAFTARAT SHELAH
הפטרת שלח

ב א וַיִּשְׁלַח יְהוֹשֻׁעַ בִּן־נוּן מִן־הַשִּׁטִּים שְׁנַיִם אֲנָשִׁים מְרַגְּלִים חֶרֶשׁ לֵאמֹר לְכוּ YEHOSHUA
רְאוּ אֶת־הָאָרֶץ וְאֶת־יְרִיחוֹ וַיֵּלְכוּ וַיָּבֹאוּ בֵּית אִשָּׁה זוֹנָה וּשְׁמָהּ רָחָב וַיִּשְׁכְּבוּ־
ב שָׁמָּה: וַיֵּאָמַר לְמֶלֶךְ יְרִיחוֹ לֵאמֹר הִנֵּה אֲנָשִׁים בָּאוּ הֵנָּה הַלַּיְלָה מִבְּנֵי יִשְׂרָאֵל
ג לַחְפֹּר אֶת־הָאָרֶץ: וַיִּשְׁלַח מֶלֶךְ יְרִיחוֹ אֶל־רָחָב לֵאמֹר הוֹצִיאִי הָאֲנָשִׁים
ד הַבָּאִים אֵלַיִךְ אֲשֶׁר־בָּאוּ לְבֵיתֵךְ כִּי לַחְפֹּר אֶת־כָּל־הָאָרֶץ בָּאוּ: וַתִּקַּח
הָאִשָּׁה אֶת־שְׁנֵי הָאֲנָשִׁים וַתִּצְפְּנוֹ וַתֹּאמֶר כֵּן בָּאוּ אֵלַי הָאֲנָשִׁים וְלֹא יָדַעְתִּי
ה מֵאַיִן הֵמָּה: וַיְהִי הַשַּׁעַר לִסְגּוֹר בַּחֹשֶׁךְ וְהָאֲנָשִׁים יָצָאוּ לֹא יָדַעְתִּי אָנָה הָלְכוּ
ו הָאֲנָשִׁים רִדְפוּ מַהֵר אַחֲרֵיהֶם כִּי תַשִּׂיגוּם: וְהִיא הֶעֱלָתַם הַגָּגָה וַתִּטְמְנֵם
ז בְּפִשְׁתֵּי הָעֵץ הָעֲרֻכוֹת לָהּ עַל־הַגָּג: וְהָאֲנָשִׁים רָדְפוּ אַחֲרֵיהֶם דֶּרֶךְ הַיַּרְדֵּן
ח עַל הַמַּעְבְּרוֹת וְהַשַּׁעַר סָגָרוּ אַחֲרֵי כַּאֲשֶׁר יָצְאוּ הָרֹדְפִים אַחֲרֵיהֶם: וְהֵמָּה
ט טֶרֶם יִשְׁכָּבוּן וְהִיא עָלְתָה עֲלֵיהֶם עַל־הַגָּג: וַתֹּאמֶר אֶל־הָאֲנָשִׁים יָדַעְתִּי
כִּי־נָתַן יְהוָה לָכֶם אֶת־הָאָרֶץ וְכִי־נָפְלָה אֵימַתְכֶם עָלֵינוּ וְכִי נָמֹגוּ כָּל־יֹשְׁבֵי
י הָאָרֶץ מִפְּנֵיכֶם: כִּי שָׁמַעְנוּ אֵת אֲשֶׁר־הוֹבִישׁ יְהוָה אֶת־מֵי יַם־סוּף מִפְּנֵיכֶם
בְּצֵאתְכֶם מִמִּצְרָיִם וַאֲשֶׁר עֲשִׂיתֶם לִשְׁנֵי מַלְכֵי הָאֱמֹרִי אֲשֶׁר בְּעֵבֶר הַיַּרְדֵּן
יא לְסִיחֹן וּלְעוֹג אֲשֶׁר הַחֲרַמְתֶּם אוֹתָם: וַנִּשְׁמַע וַיִּמַּס לְבָבֵנוּ וְלֹא־קָמָה עוֹד רוּחַ
בְּאִישׁ מִפְּנֵיכֶם כִּי יְהוָה אֱלֹהֵיכֶם הוּא אֱלֹהִים בַּשָּׁמַיִם מִמַּעַל וְעַל־הָאָרֶץ
יב מִתָּחַת: וְעַתָּה הִשָּׁבְעוּ־נָא לִי בַּיהוָה כִּי־עָשִׂיתִי עִמָּכֶם חָסֶד וַעֲשִׂיתֶם גַּם־
יג אַתֶּם עִם־בֵּית אָבִי חֶסֶד וּנְתַתֶּם לִי אוֹת אֱמֶת: וְהַחֲיִתֶם אֶת־אָבִי וְאֶת־אִמִּי
וְאֶת־אַחַי וְאֶת־אחותי וְאֵת כָּל־אֲשֶׁר לָהֶם וְהִצַּלְתֶּם אֶת־נַפְשֹׁתֵינוּ מִמָּוֶת: אַחְיוֹתַי
יד וַיֹּאמְרוּ לָהּ הָאֲנָשִׁים נַפְשֵׁנוּ תַחְתֵּיכֶם לָמוּת אִם לֹא תַגִּידוּ אֶת־דְּבָרֵנוּ זֶה
טו וְהָיָה בְּתֵת־יְהוָה לָנוּ אֶת־הָאָרֶץ וְעָשִׂינוּ עִמָּךְ חֶסֶד וֶאֱמֶת: וַתּוֹרִדֵם בַּחֶבֶל
טז בְּעַד הַחַלּוֹן כִּי בֵיתָהּ בְּקִיר הַחוֹמָה וּבַחוֹמָה הִיא יוֹשָׁבֶת: וַתֹּאמֶר לָהֶם
הָהָרָה לֵּכוּ פֶּן־יִפְגְּעוּ בָכֶם הָרֹדְפִים וְנַחְבֵּתֶם שָׁמָּה שְׁלֹשֶׁת יָמִים עַד שׁוֹב
יז הָרֹדְפִים וְאַחַר תֵּלְכוּ לְדַרְכְּכֶם: וַיֹּאמְרוּ אֵלֶיהָ הָאֲנָשִׁים נְקִיִּם אֲנַחְנוּ מִשְּׁבֻעָתֵךְ
יח הַזֶּה אֲשֶׁר הִשְׁבַּעְתָּנוּ: הִנֵּה אֲנַחְנוּ בָאִים בָּאָרֶץ אֶת־תִּקְוַת חוּט הַשָּׁנִי הַזֶּה
תִּקְשְׁרִי בַּחַלּוֹן אֲשֶׁר הוֹרַדְתֵּנוּ בוֹ וְאֶת־אָבִיךְ וְאֶת־אִמֵּךְ וְאֶת־אַחַיִךְ וְאֵת
יט כָּל־בֵּית אָבִיךְ תַּאַסְפִי אֵלַיִךְ הַבָּיְתָה: וְהָיָה כֹּל אֲשֶׁר־יֵצֵא מִדַּלְתֵי בֵיתֵךְ ׀
הַחוּצָה דָּמוֹ בְרֹאשׁוֹ וַאֲנַחְנוּ נְקִיִּם וְכֹל אֲשֶׁר יִהְיֶה אִתָּךְ בַּבַּיִת דָּמוֹ בְרֹאשֵׁנוּ
כ אִם־יָד תִּהְיֶה־בּוֹ: וְאִם־תַּגִּידִי אֶת־דְּבָרֵנוּ זֶה וְהָיִינוּ נְקִיִּם מִשְּׁבֻעָתֵךְ אֲשֶׁר

הִשְׁבַּעְתָּנוּ׃ וַתֹּאמֶר כְּדִבְרֵיכֶם כֶּן־הוּא וַתְּשַׁלְּחֵם וַיֵּלֵכוּ וַתִּקְשֹׁר אֶת־תִּקְוַת כא
הַשָּׁנִי בַּחַלּוֹן׃ וַיֵּלְכוּ וַיָּבֹאוּ הָהָרָה וַיֵּשְׁבוּ שָׁם שְׁלֹשֶׁת יָמִים עַד־שָׁבוּ הָרֹדְפִים כב
וַיְבַקְשׁוּ הָרֹדְפִים בְּכָל־הַדֶּרֶךְ וְלֹא מָצָאוּ׃ וַיָּשֻׁבוּ שְׁנֵי הָאֲנָשִׁים וַיֵּרְדוּ מֵהָהָר כג
וַיַּעַבְרוּ וַיָּבֹאוּ אֶל־יְהוֹשֻׁעַ בִּן־נוּן וַיְסַפְּרוּ־לוֹ אֵת כָּל־הַמֹּצְאוֹת אוֹתָם׃ וַיֹּאמְרוּ כד
אֶל־יְהוֹשֻׁעַ כִּי־נָתַן יהוה בְּיָדֵנוּ אֶת־כָּל־הָאָרֶץ וְגַם־נָמֹגוּ כָּל־יֹשְׁבֵי הָאָרֶץ
מִפָּנֵינוּ׃

HAFTARAT KORAḤ — הפטרת קורח

On Rosh Ḥodesh Tammuz read the Haftara on page 1092.

I SHMUEL

וַיֹּאמֶר שְׁמוּאֵל אֶל־הָעָם לְכוּ וְנֵלְכָה הַגִּלְגָּל וּנְחַדֵּשׁ שָׁם הַמְּלוּכָה׃ וַיֵּלְכוּ יא יד טו
כָל־הָעָם הַגִּלְגָּל וַיַּמְלִכוּ שָׁם אֶת־שָׁאוּל לִפְנֵי יהוה בַּגִּלְגָּל וַיִּזְבְּחוּ־שָׁם
זְבָחִים שְׁלָמִים לִפְנֵי יהוה וַיִּשְׂמַח שָׁם שָׁאוּל וְכָל־אַנְשֵׁי יִשְׂרָאֵל עַד־
מְאֹד׃ וַיֹּאמֶר שְׁמוּאֵל אֶל־כָּל־יִשְׂרָאֵל הִנֵּה שָׁמַעְתִּי בְקֹלְכֶם לְכֹל יב א
אֲשֶׁר־אֲמַרְתֶּם לִי וָאַמְלִיךְ עֲלֵיכֶם מֶלֶךְ׃ וְעַתָּה הִנֵּה הַמֶּלֶךְ ׀ מִתְהַלֵּךְ לִפְנֵיכֶם ב
וַאֲנִי זָקַנְתִּי וָשַׂבְתִּי וּבָנַי הִנָּם אִתְּכֶם וַאֲנִי הִתְהַלַּכְתִּי לִפְנֵיכֶם מִנְּעֻרַי עַד־הַיּוֹם
הַזֶּה׃ הִנְנִי עֲנוּ בִי נֶגֶד יהוה וְנֶגֶד מְשִׁיחוֹ אֶת־שׁוֹר ׀ מִי לָקַחְתִּי וַחֲמוֹר מִי ג
לָקַחְתִּי וְאֶת־מִי עָשַׁקְתִּי אֶת־מִי רַצּוֹתִי וּמִיַּד־מִי לָקַחְתִּי כֹפֶר וְאַעְלִים עֵינַי
בּוֹ וְאָשִׁיב לָכֶם׃ וַיֹּאמְרוּ לֹא עֲשַׁקְתָּנוּ וְלֹא רַצּוֹתָנוּ וְלֹא־לָקַחְתָּ מִיַּד־אִישׁ ד
מְאוּמָה׃ וַיֹּאמֶר אֲלֵיהֶם עֵד יהוה בָּכֶם וְעֵד מְשִׁיחוֹ הַיּוֹם הַזֶּה כִּי לֹא מְצָאתֶם ה
בְּיָדִי מְאוּמָה וַיֹּאמֶר עֵד׃ וַיֹּאמֶר שְׁמוּאֵל אֶל־הָעָם יהוה אֲשֶׁר ו
עָשָׂה אֶת־מֹשֶׁה וְאֶת־אַהֲרֹן וַאֲשֶׁר הֶעֱלָה אֶת־אֲבוֹתֵיכֶם מֵאֶרֶץ מִצְרָיִם׃
וְעַתָּה הִתְיַצְּבוּ וְאִשָּׁפְטָה אִתְּכֶם לִפְנֵי יהוה אֵת כָּל־צִדְקוֹת יהוה אֲשֶׁר־עָשָׂה ז
אִתְּכֶם וְאֶת־אֲבוֹתֵיכֶם׃ כַּאֲשֶׁר־בָּא יַעֲקֹב מִצְרָיִם וַיִּזְעֲקוּ אֲבֹתֵיכֶם אֶל־יהוה ח
וַיִּשְׁלַח יהוה אֶת־מֹשֶׁה וְאֶת־אַהֲרֹן וַיּוֹצִיאוּ אֶת־אֲבוֹתֵיכֶם מִמִּצְרַיִם וַיֹּשִׁבוּם
בַּמָּקוֹם הַזֶּה׃ וַיִּשְׁכְּחוּ אֶת־יהוה אֱלֹהֵיהֶם וַיִּמְכֹּר אֹתָם בְּיַד סִיסְרָא שַׂר־צְבָא ט
חָצוֹר וּבְיַד־פְּלִשְׁתִּים וּבְיַד מֶלֶךְ מוֹאָב וַיִּלָּחֲמוּ בָּם׃ וַיִּזְעֲקוּ אֶל־יהוה וַיֹּאמְרֻ י
חָטָאנוּ כִּי עָזַבְנוּ אֶת־יהוה וַנַּעֲבֹד אֶת־הַבְּעָלִים וְאֶת־הָעַשְׁתָּרוֹת וְעַתָּה
הַצִּילֵנוּ מִיַּד אֹיְבֵינוּ וְנַעַבְדֶךָּ׃ וַיִּשְׁלַח יהוה אֶת־יְרֻבַּעַל וְאֶת־בְּדָן וְאֶת־יִפְתָּח יא
וְאֶת־שְׁמוּאֵל וַיַּצֵּל אֶתְכֶם מִיַּד אֹיְבֵיכֶם מִסָּבִיב וַתֵּשְׁבוּ בֶּטַח׃ וַתִּרְאוּ כִּי יב

נָחָשׁ מֶלֶךְ בְּנֵי־עַמּוֹן בָּא עֲלֵיכֶם וַתֹּאמְרוּ לִי לֹא כִּי־מֶלֶךְ יִמְלֹךְ עָלֵינוּ וַיהוָה
יג אֱלֹהֵיכֶם מַלְכְּכֶם: וְעַתָּה הִנֵּה הַמֶּלֶךְ אֲשֶׁר בְּחַרְתֶּם אֲשֶׁר שְׁאֶלְתֶּם וְהִנֵּה נָתַן
יד יהוה עֲלֵיכֶם מֶלֶךְ: אִם־תִּירְאוּ אֶת־יהוה וַעֲבַדְתֶּם אֹתוֹ וּשְׁמַעְתֶּם בְּקוֹלוֹ
וְלֹא תַמְרוּ אֶת־פִּי יהוה וִהְיִתֶם גַּם־אַתֶּם וְגַם־הַמֶּלֶךְ אֲשֶׁר מָלַךְ עֲלֵיכֶם אַחַר
טו יהוה אֱלֹהֵיכֶם: וְאִם־לֹא תִשְׁמְעוּ בְּקוֹל יהוה וּמְרִיתֶם אֶת־פִּי יהוה וְהָיְתָה
טז יַד־יהוה בָּכֶם וּבַאֲבֹתֵיכֶם: גַּם־עַתָּה הִתְיַצְּבוּ וּרְאוּ אֶת־הַדָּבָר הַגָּדוֹל הַזֶּה
יז אֲשֶׁר יהוה עֹשֶׂה לְעֵינֵיכֶם: הֲלוֹא קְצִיר־חִטִּים הַיּוֹם אֶקְרָא אֶל־יהוה וְיִתֵּן
קֹלוֹת וּמָטָר וּדְעוּ וּרְאוּ כִּי־רָעַתְכֶם רַבָּה אֲשֶׁר עֲשִׂיתֶם בְּעֵינֵי יהוה לִשְׁאוֹל
יח לָכֶם מֶלֶךְ: וַיִּקְרָא שְׁמוּאֵל אֶל־יהוה וַיִּתֵּן יהוה קֹלֹת וּמָטָר בַּיּוֹם
יט הַהוּא וַיִּירָא כָל־הָעָם מְאֹד אֶת־יהוה וְאֶת־שְׁמוּאֵל: וַיֹּאמְרוּ כָל־הָעָם אֶל־
שְׁמוּאֵל הִתְפַּלֵּל בְּעַד־עֲבָדֶיךָ אֶל־יהוה אֱלֹהֶיךָ וְאַל־נָמוּת כִּי־יָסַפְנוּ עַל־
כ כָּל־חַטֹּאתֵינוּ רָעָה לִשְׁאֹל לָנוּ מֶלֶךְ: וַיֹּאמֶר שְׁמוּאֵל אֶל־הָעָם
אַל־תִּירָאוּ אַתֶּם עֲשִׂיתֶם אֵת כָּל־הָרָעָה הַזֹּאת אַךְ אַל־תָּסוּרוּ מֵאַחֲרֵי
כא יהוה וַעֲבַדְתֶּם אֶת־יהוה בְּכָל־לְבַבְכֶם: וְלֹא תָּסוּרוּ כִּי | אַחֲרֵי הַתֹּהוּ אֲשֶׁר
כב לֹא־יוֹעִילוּ וְלֹא יַצִּילוּ כִּי־תֹהוּ הֵמָּה: כִּי לֹא־יִטֹּשׁ יהוה אֶת־עַמּוֹ בַּעֲבוּר שְׁמוֹ
הַגָּדוֹל כִּי הוֹאִיל יהוה לַעֲשׂוֹת אֶתְכֶם לוֹ לְעָם:

HAFTARAT ḤUKAT / הפטרת חוקת

When Ḥukat and Balak are read together read the Haftara on page 1081.
On Rosh Ḥodesh Tammuz read the Haftara on page 1092.

SHOFETIM יא א וְיִפְתָּח הַגִּלְעָדִי הָיָה גִּבּוֹר חַיִל וְהוּא בֶּן־אִשָּׁה זוֹנָה וַיּוֹלֶד גִּלְעָד אֶת־
ב יִפְתָּח: וַתֵּלֶד אֵשֶׁת־גִּלְעָד לוֹ בָּנִים וַיִּגְדְּלוּ בְנֵי־הָאִשָּׁה וַיְגָרְשׁוּ אֶת־יִפְתָּח
ג וַיֹּאמְרוּ לוֹ לֹא־תִנְחַל בְּבֵית־אָבִינוּ כִּי בֶּן־אִשָּׁה אַחֶרֶת אָתָּה: וַיִּבְרַח יִפְתָּח
מִפְּנֵי אֶחָיו וַיֵּשֶׁב בְּאֶרֶץ טוֹב וַיִּתְלַקְּטוּ אֶל־יִפְתָּח אֲנָשִׁים רֵיקִים וַיֵּצְאוּ
ד ה עִמּוֹ: וַיְהִי מִיָּמִים וַיִּלָּחֲמוּ בְנֵי־עַמּוֹן עִם־יִשְׂרָאֵל: וַיְהִי כַּאֲשֶׁר־
נִלְחֲמוּ בְנֵי־עַמּוֹן עִם־יִשְׂרָאֵל וַיֵּלְכוּ זִקְנֵי גִלְעָד לָקַחַת אֶת־יִפְתָּח מֵאֶרֶץ
ו ז טוֹב: וַיֹּאמְרוּ לְיִפְתָּח לְכָה וְהָיִיתָה לָּנוּ לְקָצִין וְנִלָּחֲמָה בִּבְנֵי עַמּוֹן: וַיֹּאמֶר
יִפְתָּח לְזִקְנֵי גִלְעָד הֲלֹא אַתֶּם שְׂנֵאתֶם אוֹתִי וַתְּגָרְשׁוּנִי מִבֵּית אָבִי וּמַדּוּעַ
ח בָּאתֶם אֵלַי עַתָּה כַּאֲשֶׁר צַר לָכֶם: וַיֹּאמְרוּ זִקְנֵי גִלְעָד אֶל־יִפְתָּח לָכֵן עַתָּה

שַׁבְנוּ אֵלֶיךָ וְהָלַכְתָּ עִמָּנוּ וְנִלְחַמְתָּ בִּבְנֵי עַמּוֹן וְהָיִיתָ לָּנוּ לְרֹאשׁ לְכֹל יֹשְׁבֵי
גִלְעָד׃ וַיֹּאמֶר יִפְתָּח אֶל־זִקְנֵי גִלְעָד אִם־מְשִׁיבִים אַתֶּם אוֹתִי לְהִלָּחֵם בִּבְנֵי ט
עַמּוֹן וְנָתַן יהוה אוֹתָם לְפָנָי אָנֹכִי אֶהְיֶה לָכֶם לְרֹאשׁ׃ וַיֹּאמְרוּ זִקְנֵי־גִלְעָד י
אֶל־יִפְתָּח יהוה יִהְיֶה שֹׁמֵעַ בֵּינוֹתֵינוּ אִם־לֹא כִדְבָרְךָ כֵּן נַעֲשֶׂה׃ וַיֵּלֶךְ יִפְתָּח יא
עִם־זִקְנֵי גִלְעָד וַיָּשִׂימוּ הָעָם אוֹתוֹ עֲלֵיהֶם לְרֹאשׁ וּלְקָצִין וַיְדַבֵּר יִפְתָּח אֶת־
כָּל־דְּבָרָיו לִפְנֵי יהוה בַּמִּצְפָּה׃ וַיִּשְׁלַח יִפְתָּח מַלְאָכִים אֶל־מֶלֶךְ יב
בְּנֵי־עַמּוֹן לֵאמֹר מַה־לִּי וָלָךְ כִּי־בָאתָ אֵלַי לְהִלָּחֵם בְּאַרְצִי׃ וַיֹּאמֶר מֶלֶךְ יג
בְּנֵי־עַמּוֹן אֶל־מַלְאֲכֵי יִפְתָּח כִּי־לָקַח יִשְׂרָאֵל אֶת־אַרְצִי בַּעֲלוֹתוֹ מִמִּצְרַיִם
מֵאַרְנוֹן וְעַד־הַיַּבֹּק וְעַד־הַיַּרְדֵּן וְעַתָּה הָשִׁיבָה אֶתְהֶן בְּשָׁלוֹם׃ וַיּוֹסֶף עוֹד יד
יִפְתָּח וַיִּשְׁלַח מַלְאָכִים אֶל־מֶלֶךְ בְּנֵי עַמּוֹן׃ וַיֹּאמֶר לוֹ כֹּה אָמַר יִפְתָּח לֹא־ טו
לָקַח יִשְׂרָאֵל אֶת־אֶרֶץ מוֹאָב וְאֶת־אֶרֶץ בְּנֵי עַמּוֹן׃ כִּי בַּעֲלוֹתָם מִמִּצְרָיִם טז
וַיֵּלֶךְ יִשְׂרָאֵל בַּמִּדְבָּר עַד־יַם־סוּף וַיָּבֹא קָדֵשָׁה׃ וַיִּשְׁלַח יִשְׂרָאֵל מַלְאָכִים ׀ יז
אֶל־מֶלֶךְ אֱדוֹם לֵאמֹר אֶעְבְּרָה־נָּא בְאַרְצֶךָ וְלֹא שָׁמַע מֶלֶךְ אֱדוֹם וְגַם
אֶל־מֶלֶךְ מוֹאָב שָׁלַח וְלֹא אָבָה וַיֵּשֶׁב יִשְׂרָאֵל בְּקָדֵשׁ׃ וַיֵּלֶךְ בַּמִּדְבָּר וַיָּסָב יח
אֶת־אֶרֶץ אֱדוֹם וְאֶת־אֶרֶץ מוֹאָב וַיָּבֹא מִמִּזְרַח־שֶׁמֶשׁ לְאֶרֶץ מוֹאָב וַיַּחֲנוּן
בְּעֵבֶר אַרְנוֹן וְלֹא־בָאוּ בִּגְבוּל מוֹאָב כִּי אַרְנוֹן גְּבוּל מוֹאָב׃ וַיִּשְׁלַח יִשְׂרָאֵל יט
מַלְאָכִים אֶל־סִיחוֹן מֶלֶךְ־הָאֱמֹרִי מֶלֶךְ חֶשְׁבּוֹן וַיֹּאמֶר לוֹ יִשְׂרָאֵל נַעְבְּרָה־נָּא
בְאַרְצְךָ עַד־מְקוֹמִי׃ וְלֹא־הֶאֱמִין סִיחוֹן אֶת־יִשְׂרָאֵל עֲבֹר בִּגְבֻלוֹ וַיֶּאֱסֹף סִיחוֹן כ
אֶת־כָּל־עַמּוֹ וַיַּחֲנוּ בְּיָהְצָה וַיִּלָּחֶם עִם־יִשְׂרָאֵל׃ וַיִּתֵּן יהוה אֱלֹהֵי־יִשְׂרָאֵל כא
אֶת־סִיחוֹן וְאֶת־כָּל־עַמּוֹ בְּיַד יִשְׂרָאֵל וַיַּכּוּם וַיִּירַשׁ יִשְׂרָאֵל אֵת כָּל־אֶרֶץ
הָאֱמֹרִי יוֹשֵׁב הָאָרֶץ הַהִיא׃ וַיִּירְשׁוּ אֵת כָּל־גְּבוּל הָאֱמֹרִי מֵאַרְנוֹן וְעַד־הַיַּבֹּק כב
וּמִן־הַמִּדְבָּר וְעַד־הַיַּרְדֵּן׃ וְעַתָּה יהוה ׀ אֱלֹהֵי יִשְׂרָאֵל הוֹרִישׁ אֶת־הָאֱמֹרִי כג
מִפְּנֵי עַמּוֹ יִשְׂרָאֵל וְאַתָּה תִּירָשֶׁנּוּ׃ הֲלֹא אֵת אֲשֶׁר יוֹרִישְׁךָ כְּמוֹשׁ אֱלֹהֶיךָ כד
אוֹתוֹ תִירָשׁ וְאֵת כָּל־אֲשֶׁר הוֹרִישׁ יהוה אֱלֹהֵינוּ מִפָּנֵינוּ אוֹתוֹ נִירָשׁ׃ וְעַתָּה כה
הֲטוֹב טוֹב אַתָּה מִבָּלָק בֶּן־צִפּוֹר מֶלֶךְ מוֹאָב הֲרוֹב רָב עִם־יִשְׂרָאֵל אִם־
נִלְחֹם נִלְחַם בָּם׃ בְּשֶׁבֶת יִשְׂרָאֵל בְּחֶשְׁבּוֹן וּבִבְנוֹתֶיהָ וּבְעַרְעוֹר וּבִבְנוֹתֶיהָ כו
וּבְכָל־הֶעָרִים אֲשֶׁר עַל־יְדֵי אַרְנוֹן שְׁלֹשׁ מֵאוֹת שָׁנָה וּמַדּוּעַ לֹא־הִצַּלְתֶּם
בָּעֵת הַהִיא׃ וְאָנֹכִי לֹא־חָטָאתִי לָךְ וְאַתָּה עֹשֶׂה אִתִּי רָעָה לְהִלָּחֶם בִּי יִשְׁפֹּט כז
יהוה הַשֹּׁפֵט הַיּוֹם בֵּין בְּנֵי יִשְׂרָאֵל וּבֵין בְּנֵי עַמּוֹן׃ וְלֹא שָׁמַע מֶלֶךְ בְּנֵי עַמּוֹן כח

כט אֶל־דִּבְרֵי יִפְתָּח אֲשֶׁר שָׁלַח אֵלָיו: וַתְּהִי עַל־יִפְתָּח רוּחַ יהוה
וַיַּעֲבֹר אֶת־הַגִּלְעָד וְאֶת־מְנַשֶּׁה וַיַּעֲבֹר אֶת־מִצְפֵּה גִלְעָד וּמִמִּצְפֵּה גִלְעָד
ל עָבַר בְּנֵי עַמּוֹן: וַיִּדַּר יִפְתָּח נֶדֶר לַיהוה וַיֹּאמַר אִם־נָתוֹן תִּתֵּן אֶת־בְּנֵי עַמּוֹן
לא בְּיָדִי: וְהָיָה הַיּוֹצֵא אֲשֶׁר יֵצֵא מִדַּלְתֵי בֵיתִי לִקְרָאתִי בְּשׁוּבִי בְשָׁלוֹם מִבְּנֵי
עַמּוֹן וְהָיָה לַיהוה וְהַעֲלִיתִהוּ עוֹלָה:
לב לג וַיַּעֲבֹר יִפְתָּח אֶל־בְּנֵי עַמּוֹן לְהִלָּחֶם בָּם וַיִּתְּנֵם יהוה בְּיָדוֹ: וַיַּכֵּם מֵעֲרוֹעֵר
וְעַד־בּוֹאֲךָ מִנִּית עֶשְׂרִים עִיר וְעַד אָבֵל כְּרָמִים מַכָּה גְּדוֹלָה מְאֹד וַיִּכָּנְעוּ בְּנֵי
עַמּוֹן מִפְּנֵי בְּנֵי יִשְׂרָאֵל:

הפטרת בלק
HAFTARAT BALAK

When Ḥukat and Balak are read together read this Haftara.

MIKHA

ה ו וְהָיָה ׀ שְׁאֵרִית יַעֲקֹב בְּקֶרֶב עַמִּים רַבִּים כְּטַל מֵאֵת יהוה כִּרְבִיבִים עֲלֵי־עֵשֶׂב
ז אֲשֶׁר לֹא־יְקַוֶּה לְאִישׁ וְלֹא יְיַחֵל לִבְנֵי אָדָם: וְהָיָה שְׁאֵרִית יַעֲקֹב בַּגּוֹיִם בְּקֶרֶב
עַמִּים רַבִּים כְּאַרְיֵה בְּבַהֲמוֹת יַעַר כִּכְפִיר בְּעֶדְרֵי־צֹאן אֲשֶׁר אִם עָבַר וְרָמַס
ח ט וְטָרַף וְאֵין מַצִּיל: תָּרֹם יָדְךָ עַל־צָרֶיךָ וְכָל־אֹיְבֶיךָ יִכָּרֵתוּ: וְהָיָה
י בַיּוֹם־הַהוּא נְאֻם־יהוה וְהִכְרַתִּי סוּסֶיךָ מִקִּרְבֶּךָ וְהַאֲבַדְתִּי מַרְכְּבֹתֶיךָ: וְהִכְרַתִּי
יא עָרֵי אַרְצֶךָ וְהָרַסְתִּי כָּל־מִבְצָרֶיךָ: וְהִכְרַתִּי כְשָׁפִים מִיָּדֶךָ וּמְעוֹנְנִים לֹא יִהְיוּ־
יב לָךְ: וְהִכְרַתִּי פְסִילֶיךָ וּמַצֵּבוֹתֶיךָ מִקִּרְבֶּךָ וְלֹא־תִשְׁתַּחֲוֶה עוֹד לְמַעֲשֵׂה יָדֶיךָ:
יג יד וְנָתַשְׁתִּי אֲשֵׁירֶיךָ מִקִּרְבֶּךָ וְהִשְׁמַדְתִּי עָרֶיךָ: וְעָשִׂיתִי בְּאַף וּבְחֵמָה נָקָם אֶת־
ו א הַגּוֹיִם אֲשֶׁר לֹא שָׁמֵעוּ: שִׁמְעוּ־נָא אֵת אֲשֶׁר־יהוה אֹמֵר קוּם רִיב
ב אֶת־הֶהָרִים וְתִשְׁמַעְנָה הַגְּבָעוֹת קוֹלֶךָ: שִׁמְעוּ הָרִים אֶת־רִיב יהוה וְהָאֵתָנִים
ג מֹסְדֵי אָרֶץ כִּי רִיב לַיהוה עִם־עַמּוֹ וְעִם־יִשְׂרָאֵל יִתְוַכָּח: עַמִּי מֶה־עָשִׂיתִי לְךָ
ד וּמָה הֶלְאֵתִיךָ עֲנֵה בִי: כִּי הֶעֱלִתִיךָ מֵאֶרֶץ מִצְרַיִם וּמִבֵּית עֲבָדִים פְּדִיתִיךָ
ה וָאֶשְׁלַח לְפָנֶיךָ אֶת־מֹשֶׁה אַהֲרֹן וּמִרְיָם: עַמִּי זְכָר־נָא מַה־יָּעַץ בָּלָק מֶלֶךְ מוֹאָב
וּמֶה־עָנָה אֹתוֹ בִּלְעָם בֶּן־בְּעוֹר מִן־הַשִּׁטִּים עַד־הַגִּלְגָּל לְמַעַן דַּעַת צִדְקוֹת
ו יהוה: בַּמָּה אֲקַדֵּם יהוה אִכַּף לֵאלֹהֵי מָרוֹם הַאֲקַדְּמֶנּוּ בְעוֹלוֹת בַּעֲגָלִים בְּנֵי
ז שָׁנָה: הֲיִרְצֶה יהוה בְּאַלְפֵי אֵילִים בְּרִבְבוֹת נַחֲלֵי־שָׁמֶן הַאֶתֵּן בְּכוֹרִי פִּשְׁעִי
ח פְּרִי בִטְנִי חַטַּאת נַפְשִׁי: הִגִּיד לְךָ אָדָם מַה־טּוֹב וּמָה־יהוה דּוֹרֵשׁ מִמְּךָ כִּי
אִם־עֲשׂוֹת מִשְׁפָּט וְאַהֲבַת חֶסֶד וְהַצְנֵעַ לֶכֶת עִם־אֱלֹהֶיךָ:

HAFTARAT PINEḤAS הפטרת פינחס

If this Parasha falls before the 17th of Tammuz, read this Haftara.
If it falls afterwards, read the Haftara on the next page.

I MELAKHIM

מו יח וְיַד־יהוה הָיְתָה אֶל־אֵלִיָּהוּ וַיְשַׁנֵּס מָתְנָיו וַיָּרָץ לִפְנֵי אַחְאָב עַד־בֹּאֲכָה
א יט יִזְרְעֶאלָה: וַיַּגֵּד אַחְאָב לְאִיזֶבֶל אֵת כָּל־אֲשֶׁר עָשָׂה אֵלִיָּהוּ וְאֵת כָּל־אֲשֶׁר
ב הָרַג אֶת־כָּל־הַנְּבִיאִים בֶּחָרֶב: וַתִּשְׁלַח אִיזֶבֶל מַלְאָךְ אֶל־אֵלִיָּהוּ לֵאמֹר
כֹּה־יַעֲשׂוּן אֱלֹהִים וְכֹה יוֹסִפוּן כִּי־כָעֵת מָחָר אָשִׂים אֶת־נַפְשְׁךָ כְּנֶפֶשׁ אַחַד
ג מֵהֶם: וַיַּרְא וַיָּקָם וַיֵּלֶךְ אֶל־נַפְשׁוֹ וַיָּבֹא בְּאֵר שֶׁבַע אֲשֶׁר לִיהוּדָה וַיַּנַּח אֶת־
ד נַעֲרוֹ שָׁם: וְהוּא־הָלַךְ בַּמִּדְבָּר דֶּרֶךְ יוֹם וַיָּבֹא וַיֵּשֶׁב תַּחַת רֹתֶם אחת וַיִּשְׁאַל אֶחָד
אֶת־נַפְשׁוֹ לָמוּת וַיֹּאמֶר ׀ רַב עַתָּה יהוה קַח נַפְשִׁי כִּי־לֹא־טוֹב אָנֹכִי מֵאֲבֹתָי:
ה וַיִּשְׁכַּב וַיִּישַׁן תַּחַת רֹתֶם אֶחָד וְהִנֵּה־זֶה מַלְאָךְ נֹגֵעַ בּוֹ וַיֹּאמֶר לוֹ קוּם אֱכוֹל:
ו וַיַּבֵּט וְהִנֵּה מְרַאֲשֹׁתָיו עֻגַת רְצָפִים וְצַפַּחַת מָיִם וַיֹּאכַל וַיֵּשְׁתְּ וַיָּשָׁב וַיִּשְׁכָּב:
ז ח וַיָּשָׁב מַלְאַךְ יהוה ׀ שֵׁנִית וַיִּגַּע־בּוֹ וַיֹּאמֶר קוּם אֱכֹל כִּי רַב מִמְּךָ הַדָּרֶךְ: וַיָּקָם
וַיֹּאכַל וַיִּשְׁתֶּה וַיֵּלֶךְ בְּכֹחַ ׀ הָאֲכִילָה הַהִיא אַרְבָּעִים יוֹם וְאַרְבָּעִים לַיְלָה עַד
ט הַר הָאֱלֹהִים חֹרֵב: וַיָּבֹא־שָׁם אֶל־הַמְּעָרָה וַיָּלֶן שָׁם וְהִנֵּה דְבַר־יהוה אֵלָיו
י וַיֹּאמֶר לוֹ מַה־לְּךָ פֹה אֵלִיָּהוּ: וַיֹּאמֶר קַנֹּא קִנֵּאתִי לַיהוה ׀ אֱלֹהֵי צְבָאוֹת
כִּי־עָזְבוּ בְרִיתְךָ בְּנֵי יִשְׂרָאֵל אֶת־מִזְבְּחֹתֶיךָ הָרָסוּ וְאֶת־נְבִיאֶיךָ הָרְגוּ בֶחָרֶב
יא וָאִוָּתֵר אֲנִי לְבַדִּי וַיְבַקְשׁוּ אֶת־נַפְשִׁי לְקַחְתָּהּ: וַיֹּאמֶר צֵא וְעָמַדְתָּ בָהָר לִפְנֵי
יהוה וְהִנֵּה יהוה עֹבֵר וְרוּחַ גְּדוֹלָה וְחָזָק מְפָרֵק הָרִים וּמְשַׁבֵּר סְלָעִים לִפְנֵי
יב יהוה לֹא בָרוּחַ יהוה וְאַחַר הָרוּחַ רַעַשׁ לֹא בָרַעַשׁ יהוה: וְאַחַר הָרַעַשׁ אֵשׁ
יג לֹא בָאֵשׁ יהוה וְאַחַר הָאֵשׁ קוֹל דְּמָמָה דַקָּה: וַיְהִי ׀ כִּשְׁמֹעַ אֵלִיָּהוּ וַיָּלֶט
פָּנָיו בְּאַדַּרְתּוֹ וַיֵּצֵא וַיַּעֲמֹד פֶּתַח הַמְּעָרָה וְהִנֵּה אֵלָיו קוֹל וַיֹּאמֶר מַה־לְּךָ פֹה
יד אֵלִיָּהוּ: וַיֹּאמֶר קַנֹּא קִנֵּאתִי לַיהוה ׀ אֱלֹהֵי צְבָאוֹת כִּי־עָזְבוּ בְרִיתְךָ בְּנֵי יִשְׂרָאֵל
אֶת־מִזְבְּחֹתֶיךָ הָרָסוּ וְאֶת־נְבִיאֶיךָ הָרְגוּ בֶחָרֶב וָאִוָּתֵר אֲנִי לְבַדִּי וַיְבַקְשׁוּ אֶת־
טו נַפְשִׁי לְקַחְתָּהּ: וַיֹּאמֶר יהוה אֵלָיו לֵךְ שׁוּב לְדַרְכְּךָ מִדְבַּרָה דַמָּשֶׂק
טז וּבָאתָ וּמָשַׁחְתָּ אֶת־חֲזָאֵל לְמֶלֶךְ עַל־אֲרָם: וְאֵת יֵהוּא בֶן־נִמְשִׁי תִּמְשַׁח לְמֶלֶךְ
עַל־יִשְׂרָאֵל וְאֶת־אֱלִישָׁע בֶּן־שָׁפָט מֵאָבֵל מְחוֹלָה תִּמְשַׁח לְנָבִיא תַּחְתֶּיךָ:
יז וְהָיָה הַנִּמְלָט מֵחֶרֶב חֲזָאֵל יָמִית יֵהוּא וְהַנִּמְלָט מֵחֶרֶב יֵהוּא יָמִית אֱלִישָׁע:
יח וְהִשְׁאַרְתִּי בְיִשְׂרָאֵל שִׁבְעַת אֲלָפִים כָּל־הַבִּרְכַּיִם אֲשֶׁר לֹא־כָרְעוּ לַבַּעַל וְכָל־

יט הכה אשר לא־נשק לו: וילך משם וימצא את־אלישע בן־שפט והוא חרש
שנים־עשר צמדים לפניו והוא בשנים העשר ויעבר אליהו אליו וישלך
כ אדרתו אליו: ויעזב את־הבקר וירץ אחרי אליהו ויאמר אשקה־נא לאבי
כא ולאמי ואלכה אחריך ויאמר לו לך שוב כי מה־עשיתי לך: וישב מאחריו
ויקח את־צמד הבקר ויזבחהו ובכלי הבקר בשלם הבשר ויתן לעם ויאכלו
ויקם וילך אחרי אליהו וישרתהו:

HAFTARAT PINEḤAS OR MATTOT הפטרת פינחס או מטות

Read this Haftara on the first Shabbat that falls after the 17th of Tammuz.

YIRMEYAHU

א א ב דברי ירמיהו בן־חלקיהו מן־הכהנים אשר בענתות בארץ בנימן: אשר
היה דבר־יהוה אליו בימי יאשיהו בן־אמון מלך יהודה בשלש־עשרה
ג שנה למלכו: ויהי בימי יהויקים בן־יאשיהו מלך יהודה עד־תם עשתי־
עשרה שנה לצדקיהו בן־יאשיהו מלך יהודה עד־גלות ירושלם בחדש
ד ה החמישי: ויהי דבר־יהוה אלי לאמר: בטרם אצורך בבטן ידעתיך אצרך
ו ובטרם תצא מרחם הקדשתיך נביא לגוים נתתיך: ואמר אהה אדני יהוה
ז הנה לא־ידעתי דבר כי־נער אנכי: ויאמר יהוה אלי אל־תאמר נער אנכי כי
ח על־כל־אשר אשלחך תלך ואת כל־אשר אצוך תדבר: אל־תירא מפניהם
ט כי־אתך אני להצלך נאם־יהוה: וישלח יהוה את־ידו ויגע על־פי ויאמר יהוה
י אלי הנה נתתי דברי בפיך: ראה הפקדתיך | היום הזה על־הגוים ועל־
יא הממלכות לנתוש ולנתוץ ולהאביד ולהרוס לבנות ולנטוע: ויהי
דבר־יהוה אלי לאמר מה־אתה ראה ירמיהו ואמר מקל שקד אני ראה:
יב יג ויאמר יהוה אלי היטבת לראות כי־שקד אני על־דברי לעשתו: ויהי
דבר־יהוה | אלי שנית לאמר מה אתה ראה ואמר סיר נפוח אני ראה ופניו
יד טו מפני צפונה: ויאמר יהוה אלי מצפון תפתח הרעה על כל־ישבי הארץ: כי |
הנני קרא לכל־משפחות ממלכות צפונה נאם־יהוה ובאו ונתנו איש כסאו
טז פתח | שערי ירושלם ועל כל־חומתיה סביב ועל כל־ערי יהודה: ודברתי
משפטי אותם על כל־רעתם אשר עזבוני ויקטרו לאלהים אחרים וישתחוו
יז למעשי ידיהם: ואתה תאזר מתניך וקמת ודברת אליהם את כל־אשר אנכי
יח אצוך אל־תחת מפניהם פן־אחתך לפניהם: ואני הנה נתתיך היום לעיר

מבצר ולעמוד ברזל ולחמות נחשת על־כל־הארץ למלכי יהודה לשריה
לכהניה ולעם הארץ: ונלחמו אליך ולא־יוכלו לך כי־אתך אני נאם־יהוה יט
להצילך: ויהי דבר־יהוה אלי לאמר: הלך וקראת באזני ירושלם ב א ב
לאמר כה אמר יהוה זכרתי לך חסד נעוריך אהבת כלולתיך לכתך אחרי
במדבר בארץ לא זרועה: קדש ישראל ליהוה ראשית תבואתה כל־אכליו ג
יאשמו רעה תבא אליהם נאם־יהוה:

HAFTARAT MAS'E — הפטרת מסעי

Read the Haftara even when it is Rosh Ḥodesh Av.

YIRMEYAHU

שמעו דבר־יהוה בית יעקב וכל־משפחות בית ישראל: כה | אמר יהוה ב ד ה
מה־מצאו אבותיכם בי עול כי רחקו מעלי וילכו אחרי ההבל ויהבלו:
ולא אמרו איה יהוה המעלה אתנו מארץ מצרים המוליך אתנו במדבר ו
בארץ ערבה ושוחה בארץ ציה וצלמות בארץ לא־עבר בה איש ולא־
ישב אדם שם: ואביא אתכם אל־ארץ הכרמל לאכל פריה וטובה ותבאו ז
ותטמאו את־ארצי ונחלתי שמתם לתועבה: הכהנים לא אמרו איה יהוה ח
ותפשי התורה לא ידעוני והרעים פשעו בי והנביאים נבאו בבעל ואחרי
לא־יועלו הלכו: לכן עד אריב אתכם נאם־יהוה ואת־בני בניכם אריב: כי ט י
עברו איי כתיים וראו וקדר שלחו והתבוננו מאד וראו הן היתה כזאת:
ההימיר גוי אלהים והמה לא אלהים ועמי המיר כבודו בלוא יועיל: שמו יא יב
שמים על־זאת ושערו חרבו מאד נאם־יהוה: כי־שתים רעות עשה עמי יג
אתי עזבו מקור | מים חיים לחצב להם בארות בארת נשברים אשר לא־
יכלו המים: העבד ישראל אם־יליד בית הוא מדוע היה לבז: עליו ישאגו יד טו
כפרים נתנו קולם וישיתו ארצו לשמה עריו נצתה מבלי ישב: גם־בני־נף טז (נִצְּתוּ)
ותחפנס ירעוך קדקד: הלוא־זאת תעשה־לך עזבך את־יהוה אלהיך בעת יז (וְתַחְפַּנְחֵס)
מוליכך בדרך: ועתה מה־לך לדרך מצרים לשתות מי שחור ומה־לך לדרך יח
אשור לשתות מי נהר: תיסרך רעתך ומשבותיך תוכחך ודעי וראי כי־רע יט
ומר עזבך את־יהוה אלהיך ולא פחדתי אליך נאם־אדני יהוה צבאות:
כי מעולם שברתי עלך נתקתי מוסרותיך ותאמרי לא אעבוד כי על־כל־ כ (אֶעֱבוֹר)
גבעה גבהה ותחת כל־עץ רענן את צעה זנה: ואנכי נטעתיך שורק כלה כא

כב זֶרַע אֱמֶת וְאֵיךְ נֶהְפַּכְתְּ לִי סוּרֵי הַגֶּפֶן נָכְרִיָּה׃ כִּי אִם־תְּכַבְּסִי בַּנֶּתֶר וְתַרְבִּי־לָךְ
כג בֹּרִית נִכְתָּם עֲוֺנֵךְ לְפָנַי נְאֻם אֲדֹנָי יֱהֹוִה׃ אֵיךְ תֹּאמְרִי לֹא נִטְמֵאתִי אַחֲרֵי
הַבְּעָלִים לֹא הָלַכְתִּי רְאִי דַרְכֵּךְ בַּגַּיְא דְּעִי מֶה עָשִׂית בִּכְרָה קַלָּה מְשָׂרֶכֶת
כד דְּרָכֶיהָ׃ פֶּרֶה ׀ לִמֻּד מִדְבָּר בְּאַוַּת נפשו שָׁאֲפָה רוּחַ תַּאֲנָתָהּ מִי יְשִׁיבֶנָּה כָּל־ נַפְשָׁהּ
כה מְבַקְשֶׁיהָ לֹא יִיעָפוּ בְּחָדְשָׁהּ יִמְצָאוּנְהָ׃ מִנְעִי רַגְלֵךְ מִיָּחֵף וגורנך מִצִּמְאָה וּגְרוֹנֵךְ
כו וַתֹּאמְרִי נוֹאָשׁ לוֹא כִּי־אָהַבְתִּי זָרִים וְאַחֲרֵיהֶם אֵלֵךְ׃ כְּבֹשֶׁת גַּנָּב כִּי יִמָּצֵא
כז כֵּן הֹבִישׁוּ בֵּית יִשְׂרָאֵל הֵמָּה מַלְכֵיהֶם שָׂרֵיהֶם וְכֹהֲנֵיהֶם וּנְבִיאֵיהֶם׃ אֹמְרִים
לָעֵץ אָבִי אַתָּה וְלָאֶבֶן אַתְּ ילדתני כִּי־פָנוּ אֵלַי עֹרֶף וְלֹא פָנִים וּבְעֵת רָעָתָם יְלִדְתָּנוּ
כח יֹאמְרוּ קוּמָה וְהוֹשִׁיעֵנוּ׃ וְאַיֵּה אֱלֹהֶיךָ אֲשֶׁר עָשִׂיתָ לָּךְ יָקוּמוּ אִם־יוֹשִׁיעוּךָ
בְּעֵת רָעָתֶךָ כִּי מִסְפַּר עָרֶיךָ הָיוּ אֱלֹהֶיךָ יְהוּדָה׃

Ashkenazim add:

ג ד הֲלוֹא מֵעַתָּה קראתי לִי אָבִי אַלּוּף נְעֻרַי אָתָּה׃ קָרָאת

Sepharadim add:

ד א אִם־תָּשׁוּב יִשְׂרָאֵל ׀ נְאֻם־יְהוָה אֵלַי תָּשׁוּב וְאִם־תָּסִיר שִׁקּוּצֶיךָ מִפָּנַי
ב וְלֹא תָנוּד׃ וְנִשְׁבַּעְתָּ חַי־יְהוָה בֶּאֱמֶת בְּמִשְׁפָּט וּבִצְדָקָה וְהִתְבָּרְכוּ בוֹ גּוֹיִם
וּבוֹ יִתְהַלָּלוּ׃

HAFTARAT DEVARIM — הפטרת דברים

YESHA'YAHU

א א חֲזוֹן יְשַׁעְיָהוּ בֶן־אָמוֹץ אֲשֶׁר חָזָה עַל־יְהוּדָה וִירוּשָׁלָםִ בִּימֵי עֻזִּיָּהוּ יוֹתָם
ב אָחָז יְחִזְקִיָּהוּ מַלְכֵי יְהוּדָה׃ שִׁמְעוּ שָׁמַיִם וְהַאֲזִינִי אֶרֶץ כִּי יְהוָה דִּבֵּר בָּנִים
ג גִּדַּלְתִּי וְרוֹמַמְתִּי וְהֵם פָּשְׁעוּ בִי׃ יָדַע שׁוֹר קֹנֵהוּ וַחֲמוֹר אֵבוּס בְּעָלָיו יִשְׂרָאֵל
ד לֹא יָדַע עַמִּי לֹא הִתְבּוֹנָן׃ הוֹי ׀ גּוֹי חֹטֵא עַם כֶּבֶד עָוֺן זֶרַע מְרֵעִים בָּנִים
ה מַשְׁחִיתִים עָזְבוּ אֶת־יְהוָה נִאֲצוּ אֶת־קְדוֹשׁ יִשְׂרָאֵל נָזֹרוּ אָחוֹר׃ עַל מֶה תֻכּוּ
ו עוֹד תּוֹסִיפוּ סָרָה כָּל־רֹאשׁ לָחֳלִי וְכָל־לֵבָב דַּוָּי׃ מִכַּף־רֶגֶל וְעַד־רֹאשׁ אֵין־
בּוֹ מְתֹם פֶּצַע וְחַבּוּרָה וּמַכָּה טְרִיָּה לֹא־זֹרוּ וְלֹא חֻבָּשׁוּ וְלֹא רֻכְּכָה בַּשָּׁמֶן׃
ז אַרְצְכֶם שְׁמָמָה עָרֵיכֶם שְׂרֻפוֹת אֵשׁ אַדְמַתְכֶם לְנֶגְדְּכֶם זָרִים אֹכְלִים אֹתָהּ
ח וּשְׁמָמָה כְּמַהְפֵּכַת זָרִים׃ וְנוֹתְרָה בַת־צִיּוֹן כְּסֻכָּה בְכָרֶם כִּמְלוּנָה בְמִקְשָׁה
ט כְּעִיר נְצוּרָה׃ לוּלֵי יְהוָה צְבָאוֹת הוֹתִיר לָנוּ שָׂרִיד כִּמְעָט כִּסְדֹם הָיִינוּ לַעֲמֹרָה

דמינו: שמעו דבר־יהוה קציני סדם האזינו תורת אלהינו עם י
עמרה: למה לי רב־זבחיכם יאמר יהוה שבעתי עלות אילים וחלב מריאים יא
ודם פרים וכבשים ועתודים לא חפצתי: כי תבאו לראות פני מי־בקש זאת יב
מידכם רמס חצרי: לא תוסיפו הביא מנחת־שוא קטרת תועבה היא לי יג
חדש ושבת קרא מקרא לא־אוכל און ועצרה: חדשיכם ומועדיכם שנאה יד
נפשי היו עלי לטרח נלאיתי נשא: ובפרשכם כפיכם אעלים עיני מכם טו
גם כי־תרבו תפלה אינני שמע ידיכם דמים מלאו: רחצו הזכו הסירו רע טז
מעלליכם מנגד עיני חדלו הרע: למדו היטב דרשו משפט אשרו חמוץ יז
שפטו יתום ריבו אלמנה: לכו־נא ונוכחה יאמר יהוה אם־יהיו יח
חטאיכם כשנים כשלג ילבינו אם־יאדימו כתולע כצמר יהיו: אם־תאבו יט
ושמעתם טוב הארץ תאכלו: ואם־תמאנו ומריתם חרב תאכלו כי פי יהוה כ
דבר: איכה היתה לזונה קריה נאמנה מלאתי משפט צדק ילין כא
בה ועתה מרצחים: כספך היה לסיגים סבאך מהול במים: שריך סוררים כב כג
וחברי גנבים כלו אהב שחד ורדף שלמנים יתום לא ישפטו וריב אלמנה
לא־יבוא אליהם: לכן נאם האדון יהוה צבאות אביר ישראל כד
הוי אנחם מצרי ואנקמה מאויבי: ואשיבה ידי עליך ואצרף כבר סיגיך כה
ואסירה כל־בדיליך: ואשיבה שפטיך כבראשנה ויעציך כבתחלה אחרי־כן כו
יקרא לך עיר הצדק קריה נאמנה: ציון במשפט תפדה ושביה בצדקה: כז

HAFTARAT VA'ET-ḤANAN הפטרת ואתחנן

YESHA'YAHU

נחמו נחמו עמי יאמר אלהיכם: דברו על־לב ירושלם וקראו אליה מ א ב
כי מלאה צבאה כי נרצה עונה כי לקחה מיד יהוה כפלים בכל־
חטאתיה: קול קורא במדבר פנו דרך יהוה ישרו בערבה ג
מסלה לאלהינו: כל־גיא ינשא וכל־הר וגבעה ישפלו והיה העקב ד
למישור והרכסים לבקעה: ונגלה כבוד יהוה וראו כל־בשר יחדו כי פי ה
יהוה דבר: קול אמר קרא ואמר מה אקרא כל־הבשר חציר ו
וכל־חסדו כציץ השדה: יבש חציר נבל ציץ כי רוח יהוה נשבה בו אכן ז
חציר העם: יבש חציר נבל ציץ ודבר אלהינו יקום לעולם: על ח ט
הר־גבה עלי־לך מבשרת ציון הרימי בכח קולך מבשרת ירושלם הרימי

י אַל־תִּירָאִי אִמְרִי לְעָרֵי יְהוּדָה הִנֵּה אֱלֹהֵיכֶם׃ הִנֵּה אֲדֹנָי יֱהֹוִה בְּחָזָק יָבוֹא
יא וּזְרֹעוֹ מֹשְׁלָה לוֹ הִנֵּה שְׂכָרוֹ אִתּוֹ וּפְעֻלָּתוֹ לְפָנָיו׃ כְּרֹעֶה עֶדְרוֹ יִרְעֶה בִּזְרֹעוֹ
יב יְקַבֵּץ טְלָאִים וּבְחֵיקוֹ יִשָּׂא עָלוֹת יְנַהֵל׃ מִי־מָדַד בְּשָׁעֳלוֹ מַיִם
וְשָׁמַיִם בַּזֶּרֶת תִּכֵּן וְכָל בַּשָּׁלִשׁ עֲפַר הָאָרֶץ וְשָׁקַל בַּפֶּלֶס הָרִים וּגְבָעוֹת
יג יד בְּמֹאזְנָיִם׃ מִי־תִכֵּן אֶת־רוּחַ יְהֹוָה וְאִישׁ עֲצָתוֹ יוֹדִיעֶנּוּ׃ אֶת־מִי נוֹעָץ וַיְבִינֵהוּ
טו וַיְלַמְּדֵהוּ בְּאֹרַח מִשְׁפָּט וַיְלַמְּדֵהוּ דַעַת וְדֶרֶךְ תְּבוּנוֹת יוֹדִיעֶנּוּ׃ הֵן גּוֹיִם כְּמַר
טז מִדְּלִי וּכְשַׁחַק מֹאזְנַיִם נֶחְשָׁבוּ הֵן אִיִּים כַּדַּק יִטּוֹל׃ וּלְבָנוֹן אֵין דֵּי בָּעֵר וְחַיָּתוֹ
יז יח אֵין דֵּי עוֹלָה׃ כָּל־הַגּוֹיִם כְּאַיִן נֶגְדּוֹ מֵאֶפֶס וָתֹהוּ נֶחְשְׁבוּ־לוֹ׃ וְאֶל־
יט מִי תְּדַמְּיוּן אֵל וּמַה־דְּמוּת תַּעַרְכוּ־לוֹ׃ הַפֶּסֶל נָסַךְ חָרָשׁ וְצֹרֵף בַּזָּהָב יְרַקְּעֶנּוּ
כ וּרְתֻקוֹת כֶּסֶף צוֹרֵף׃ הַמְסֻכָּן תְּרוּמָה עֵץ לֹא־יִרְקַב יִבְחָר חָרָשׁ חָכָם יְבַקֶּשׁ־לוֹ
כא לְהָכִין פֶּסֶל לֹא יִמּוֹט׃ הֲלוֹא תֵדְעוּ הֲלוֹא תִשְׁמָעוּ הֲלוֹא הֻגַּד מֵרֹאשׁ לָכֶם
כב הֲלוֹא הֲבִינֹתֶם מוֹסְדוֹת הָאָרֶץ׃ הַיֹּשֵׁב עַל־חוּג הָאָרֶץ וְיֹשְׁבֶיהָ כַּחֲגָבִים
כג הַנּוֹטֶה כַדֹּק שָׁמַיִם וַיִּמְתָּחֵם כָּאֹהֶל לָשָׁבֶת׃ הַנּוֹתֵן רוֹזְנִים לְאָיִן שֹׁפְטֵי אֶרֶץ
כד כַּתֹּהוּ עָשָׂה׃ אַף בַּל־נִטָּעוּ אַף בַּל־זֹרָעוּ אַף בַּל־שֹׁרֵשׁ בָּאָרֶץ גִּזְעָם וְגַם נָשַׁף
כה בָּהֶם וַיִּבָשׁוּ וּסְעָרָה כַּקַּשׁ תִּשָּׂאֵם׃ וְאֶל־מִי תְדַמְּיוּנִי וְאֶשְׁוֶה יֹאמַר
כו קָדוֹשׁ׃ שְׂאוּ־מָרוֹם עֵינֵיכֶם וּרְאוּ מִי־בָרָא אֵלֶּה הַמּוֹצִיא בְמִסְפָּר צְבָאָם לְכֻלָּם
בְּשֵׁם יִקְרָא מֵרֹב אוֹנִים וְאַמִּיץ כֹּחַ אִישׁ לֹא נֶעְדָּר׃

הפטרת עקב — HAFTARAT EKEV

YESHA'YAHU

מט יד טו וַתֹּאמֶר צִיּוֹן עֲזָבַנִי יְהֹוָה וַאדֹנָי שְׁכֵחָנִי׃ הֲתִשְׁכַּח אִשָּׁה עוּלָהּ מֵרַחֵם בֶּן־בִּטְנָהּ
טז גַּם־אֵלֶּה תִשְׁכַּחְנָה וְאָנֹכִי לֹא אֶשְׁכָּחֵךְ׃ הֵן עַל־כַּפַּיִם חַקֹּתִיךְ חוֹמֹתַיִךְ נֶגְדִּי
יז יח תָּמִיד׃ מִהֲרוּ בָּנָיִךְ מְהָרְסַיִךְ וּמַחֲרִבַיִךְ מִמֵּךְ יֵצֵאוּ׃ שְׂאִי־סָבִיב עֵינַיִךְ וּרְאִי
כֻּלָּם נִקְבְּצוּ בָאוּ־לָךְ חַי־אָנִי נְאֻם־יְהֹוָה כִּי כֻלָּם כַּעֲדִי תִלְבָּשִׁי וּתְקַשְּׁרִים
יט כַּכַּלָּה׃ כִּי חָרְבֹתַיִךְ וְשֹׁמְמֹתַיִךְ וְאֶרֶץ הֲרִסֻתֵךְ כִּי עַתָּה תֵּצְרִי מִיּוֹשֵׁב וְרָחֲקוּ
כ מְבַלְּעָיִךְ׃ עוֹד יֹאמְרוּ בְאָזְנַיִךְ בְּנֵי שִׁכֻּלָיִךְ צַר־לִי הַמָּקוֹם גְּשָׁה־לִּי וְאֵשֵׁבָה׃
כא וְאָמַרְתְּ בִּלְבָבֵךְ מִי יָלַד־לִי אֶת־אֵלֶּה וַאֲנִי שְׁכוּלָה וְגַלְמוּדָה גֹּלָה ׀ וְסוּרָה
כב וְאֵלֶּה מִי גִדֵּל הֵן אֲנִי נִשְׁאַרְתִּי לְבַדִּי אֵלֶּה אֵיפֹה הֵם׃ כֹּה־
אָמַר אֲדֹנָי יֱהֹוִה הִנֵּה אֶשָּׂא אֶל־גּוֹיִם יָדִי וְאֶל־עַמִּים אָרִים נִסִּי וְהֵבִיאוּ
כג בָנַיִךְ בְּחֹצֶן וּבְנֹתַיִךְ עַל־כָּתֵף תִּנָּשֶׂאנָה׃ וְהָיוּ מְלָכִים אֹמְנַיִךְ וְשָׂרוֹתֵיהֶם

מיניקתיך אפים ארץ ישתחוו־לך ועפר רגליך ילחכו וידעת כי־אני יהוה
כד אשר לא־יבשו קוי: היקח מגבור מלקוח ואם־שבי צדיק
כה ימלט: כי־כה ׀ אמר יהוה גם־שבי גבור יקח ומלקוח עריץ ימלט ואת־
כו יריבך אנכי אריב ואת־בניך אנכי אושיע: והאכלתי את־מוניך את־בשרם
וכעסיס דמם ישכרון וידעו כל־בשר כי אני יהוה מושיעך וגאלך אביר
נ א יעקב: כה ׀ אמר יהוה אי זה ספר כריתות אמכם אשר שלחתיה
או מי מנושי אשר־מכרתי אתכם לו הן בעונתיכם נמכרתם ובפשעיכם
ב שלחה אמכם: מדוע באתי ואין איש קראתי ואין עונה הקצור קצרה ידי
מפדות ואם־אין־בי כח להציל הן בגערתי אחריב ים אשים נהרות מדבר
ג תבאש דגתם מאין מים ותמת בצמא: אלביש שמים קדרות ושק אשים
ד כסותם: אדני יהוה נתן לי לשון למודים לדעת לעות את־יעף
ה דבר יעיר ׀ בבקר בבקר יעיר לי אזן לשמע כלמודים: אדני יהוה פתח־לי
ו אזן ואנכי לא מריתי אחור לא נסוגתי: גוי נתתי למכים ולחיי למרטים פני
ז לא הסתרתי מכלמות ורק: ואדני יהוה יעזר־לי על־כן לא נכלמתי על־כן
ח שמתי פני כחלמיש ואדע כי־לא אבוש: קרוב מצדיקי מי־יריב אתי נעמדה
ט יחד מי־בעל משפטי יגש אלי: הן אדני יהוה יעזר־לי מי־הוא ירשיעני הן
י כלם כבגד יבלו עש יאכלם: מי בכם ירא יהוה שמע בקול עבדו
יא אשר ׀ הלך חשכים ואין נגה לו יבטח בשם יהוה וישען באלהיו: הן כלכם
קדחי אש מאזרי זיקות לכו ׀ באור אשכם ובזיקות בערתם מידי היתה־
נא א זאת לכם למעצבה תשכבון: שמעו אלי רדפי צדק מבקשי
ב יהוה הביטו אל־צור חצבתם ואל־מקבת בור נקרתם: הביטו אל־אברהם
ג אביכם ואל־שרה תחוללכם כי־אחד קראתיו ואברכהו וארבהו: כי־נחם
יהוה ציון נחם כל־חרבתיה וישם מדברה כעדן וערבתה כגן־יהוה ששון
ושמחה ימצא בה תודה וקול זמרה:

HAFTARAT RE'E — הפטרת ראה

This Haftara is read even on Erev Rosh Ḥodesh Elul. On Rosh Ḥodesh Elul, however Ashkenazim read the Haftara on page 1092, while Sepharadim read this Haftara.

YESHA'YAHU

נד יא עניה סערה לא נחמה הנה אנכי מרביץ בפוך אבניך ויסדתיך בספירים:

יב וְשַׂמְתִּי כַּדְכֹד שִׁמְשֹׁתַיִךְ וּשְׁעָרַיִךְ לְאַבְנֵי אֶקְדָּח וְכָל־גְּבוּלֵךְ לְאַבְנֵי־חֵפֶץ׃
יג יד וְכָל־בָּנַיִךְ לִמּוּדֵי יהוה וְרַב שְׁלוֹם בָּנָיִךְ׃ בִּצְדָקָה תִּכּוֹנָנִי רַחֲקִי מֵעֹשֶׁק כִּי־לֹא
טו תִירָאִי וּמִמְּחִתָּה כִּי לֹא־תִקְרַב אֵלָיִךְ׃ הֵן גּוֹר יָגוּר אֶפֶס מֵאוֹתִי מִי־גָר אִתָּךְ
טז עָלַיִךְ יִפּוֹל׃ הֵן אָנֹכִי בָּרָאתִי חָרָשׁ נֹפֵחַ בְּאֵשׁ פֶּחָם וּמוֹצִיא כְלִי לְמַעֲשֵׂהוּ הִנֵּה
יז וְאָנֹכִי בָּרָאתִי מַשְׁחִית לְחַבֵּל׃ כָּל־כְּלִי יוּצַר עָלַיִךְ לֹא יִצְלָח וְכָל־לָשׁוֹן
תָּקוּם־אִתָּךְ לַמִּשְׁפָּט תַּרְשִׁיעִי זֹאת נַחֲלַת עַבְדֵי יהוה וְצִדְקָתָם מֵאִתִּי נְאֻם־
ה א יהוה׃ הוֹי כָּל־צָמֵא לְכוּ לַמַּיִם וַאֲשֶׁר אֵין־לוֹ כָּסֶף לְכוּ שִׁבְרוּ וֶאֱכֹלוּ
ב וּלְכוּ שִׁבְרוּ בְּלוֹא־כֶסֶף וּבְלוֹא מְחִיר יַיִן וְחָלָב׃ לָמָּה תִשְׁקְלוּ־כֶסֶף בְּלוֹא־
לֶחֶם וִיגִיעֲכֶם בְּלוֹא לְשָׂבְעָה שִׁמְעוּ שָׁמוֹעַ אֵלַי וְאִכְלוּ־טוֹב וְתִתְעַנַּג בַּדֶּשֶׁן
ג נַפְשְׁכֶם׃ הַטּוּ אָזְנְכֶם וּלְכוּ אֵלַי שִׁמְעוּ וּתְחִי נַפְשְׁכֶם וְאֶכְרְתָה לָכֶם בְּרִית
ד ה עוֹלָם חַסְדֵי דָוִד הַנֶּאֱמָנִים׃ הֵן עֵד לְאוּמִּים נְתַתִּיו נָגִיד וּמְצַוֵּה לְאֻמִּים׃ הֵן
גּוֹי לֹא־תֵדַע תִּקְרָא וְגוֹי לֹא־יְדָעוּךָ אֵלֶיךָ יָרוּצוּ לְמַעַן יהוה אֱלֹהֶיךָ וְלִקְדוֹשׁ
יִשְׂרָאֵל כִּי פֵאֲרָךְ׃

הפטרת שופטים
HAFTARAT SHOFETIM

YESHA'YAHU

א יב אָנֹכִי אָנֹכִי הוּא מְנַחֶמְכֶם מִי־אַתְּ וַתִּירְאִי מֵאֱנוֹשׁ יָמוּת וּמִבֶּן־אָדָם חָצִיר
יג יִנָּתֵן׃ וַתִּשְׁכַּח יהוה עֹשֶׂךָ נוֹטֶה שָׁמַיִם וְיֹסֵד אָרֶץ וַתְּפַחֵד תָּמִיד כָּל־הַיּוֹם
יד מִפְּנֵי חֲמַת הַמֵּצִיק כַּאֲשֶׁר כּוֹנֵן לְהַשְׁחִית וְאַיֵּה חֲמַת הַמֵּצִיק׃ מִהַר צֹעֶה
טו לְהִפָּתֵחַ וְלֹא־יָמוּת לַשַּׁחַת וְלֹא יֶחְסַר לַחְמוֹ׃ וְאָנֹכִי יהוה אֱלֹהֶיךָ רֹגַע
טז הַיָּם וַיֶּהֱמוּ גַּלָּיו יהוה צְבָאוֹת שְׁמוֹ׃ וָאָשִׂם דְּבָרַי בְּפִיךָ וּבְצֵל יָדִי כִּסִּיתִיךָ
יז לִנְטֹעַ שָׁמַיִם וְלִיסֹד אָרֶץ וְלֵאמֹר לְצִיּוֹן עַמִּי־אָתָּה׃ הִתְעוֹרְרִי
הִתְעוֹרְרִי קוּמִי יְרוּשָׁלִַם אֲשֶׁר שָׁתִית מִיַּד יהוה אֶת־כּוֹס חֲמָתוֹ אֶת־קֻבַּעַת
יח כּוֹס הַתַּרְעֵלָה שָׁתִית מָצִית׃ אֵין־מְנַהֵל לָהּ מִכָּל־בָּנִים יָלָדָה וְאֵין מַחֲזִיק
יט בְּיָדָהּ מִכָּל־בָּנִים גִּדֵּלָה׃ שְׁתַּיִם הֵנָּה קֹרְאֹתַיִךְ מִי יָנוּד לָךְ הַשֹּׁד וְהַשֶּׁבֶר
כ וְהָרָעָב וְהַחֶרֶב מִי אֲנַחֲמֵךְ׃ בָּנַיִךְ עֻלְּפוּ שָׁכְבוּ בְּרֹאשׁ כָּל־חוּצוֹת כְּתוֹא
כא מִכְמָר הַמְלֵאִים חֲמַת־יהוה גַּעֲרַת אֱלֹהָיִךְ׃ לָכֵן שִׁמְעִי־נָא זֹאת עֲנִיָּה וּשְׁכֻרַת
כב וְלֹא מִיָּיִן׃ כֹּה־אָמַר אֲדֹנַיִךְ יהוה וֵאלֹהַיִךְ יָרִיב עַמּוֹ הִנֵּה לָקַחְתִּי
מִיָּדֵךְ אֶת־כּוֹס הַתַּרְעֵלָה אֶת־קֻבַּעַת כּוֹס חֲמָתִי לֹא־תוֹסִיפִי לִשְׁתּוֹתָהּ עוֹד׃

כג וְשַׂמְתִּיהָ בְּיַד־מוֹגַיִךְ אֲשֶׁר־אָמְרוּ לְנַפְשֵׁךְ שְׁחִי וְנַעֲבֹרָה וַתָּשִׂימִי כָאָרֶץ גֵּוֵךְ
נב א וְכַחוּץ לַעֹבְרִים׃ עוּרִי עוּרִי לִבְשִׁי עֻזֵּךְ צִיּוֹן לִבְשִׁי ׀ בִּגְדֵי תִפְאַרְתֵּךְ
ב יְרוּשָׁלַ͏ִם עִיר הַקֹּדֶשׁ כִּי לֹא יוֹסִיף יָבֹא־בָךְ עוֹד עָרֵל וְטָמֵא׃ הִתְנַעֲרִי מֵעָפָר
ג קוּמִי שְּׁבִי יְרוּשָׁלָ͏ִם התפתחו מוֹסְרֵי צַוָּארֵךְ שְׁבִיָּה בַּת־צִיּוֹן׃ כִּי־כֹה הִתְפַּתְּחִי
ד אָמַר יהוה חִנָּם נִמְכַּרְתֶּם וְלֹא בְכֶסֶף תִּגָּאֵלוּ׃ כִּי כֹה אָמַר אֲדֹנָי
ה יֱהוִֹה מִצְרַיִם יָרַד־עַמִּי בָרִאשֹׁנָה לָגוּר שָׁם וְאַשּׁוּר בְּאֶפֶס עֲשָׁקוֹ׃ וְעַתָּה
מַה־לִּי־פֹה נְאֻם־יהוה כִּי־לֻקַּח עַמִּי חִנָּם מֹשְׁלָו יְהֵילִילוּ נְאֻם־יהוה וְתָמִיד
ו כָּל־הַיּוֹם שְׁמִי מִנֹּאָץ׃ לָכֵן יֵדַע עַמִּי שְׁמִי לָכֵן בַּיּוֹם הַהוּא כִּי־אֲנִי־הוּא הַמְדַבֵּר
ז הִנֵּנִי׃ מַה־נָּאווּ עַל־הֶהָרִים רַגְלֵי מְבַשֵּׂר מַשְׁמִיעַ שָׁלוֹם מְבַשֵּׂר טוֹב
ח מַשְׁמִיעַ יְשׁוּעָה אֹמֵר לְצִיּוֹן מָלַךְ אֱלֹהָיִךְ׃ קוֹל צֹפַיִךְ נָשְׂאוּ קוֹל יַחְדָּו יְרַנֵּנוּ
ט כִּי עַיִן בְּעַיִן יִרְאוּ בְּשׁוּב יהוה צִיּוֹן׃ פִּצְחוּ רַנְּנוּ יַחְדָּו חָרְבוֹת יְרוּשָׁלָ͏ִם כִּי־נִחַם
י יהוה עַמּוֹ גָּאַל יְרוּשָׁלָ͏ִם׃ חָשַׂף יהוה אֶת־זְרוֹעַ קָדְשׁוֹ לְעֵינֵי כָּל־הַגּוֹיִם וְרָאוּ
יא כָּל־אַפְסֵי־אָרֶץ אֵת יְשׁוּעַת אֱלֹהֵינוּ׃ סוּרוּ סוּרוּ צְאוּ מִשָּׁם טָמֵא
יב אַל־תִּגָּעוּ צְאוּ מִתּוֹכָהּ הִבָּרוּ נֹשְׂאֵי כְּלֵי יהוה׃ כִּי לֹא בְחִפָּזוֹן תֵּצֵאוּ וּבִמְנוּסָה
לֹא תֵלֵכוּן כִּי־הֹלֵךְ לִפְנֵיכֶם יהוה וּמְאַסִּפְכֶם אֱלֹהֵי יִשְׂרָאֵל׃

HAFTARAT KI TEẒE — הפטרת כי תצא

If the Haftara of Re'e was not read (because of Rosh Ḥodesh Elul), it is read at the end of this Haftara.

YESHA'YAHU

נד א רָנִּי עֲקָרָה לֹא יָלָדָה פִּצְחִי רִנָּה וְצַהֲלִי לֹא־חָלָה כִּי־רַבִּים בְּנֵי־שׁוֹמֵמָה מִבְּנֵי
ב בְעוּלָה אָמַר יהוה׃ הַרְחִיבִי ׀ מְקוֹם אָהֳלֵךְ וִירִיעוֹת מִשְׁכְּנוֹתַיִךְ יַטּוּ אַל־
ג תַּחְשֹׂכִי הַאֲרִיכִי מֵיתָרַיִךְ וִיתֵדֹתַיִךְ חַזֵּקִי׃ כִּי־יָמִין וּשְׂמֹאול תִּפְרֹצִי וְזַרְעֵךְ
ד גּוֹיִם יִירָשׁ וְעָרִים נְשַׁמּוֹת יוֹשִׁיבוּ׃ אַל־תִּירְאִי כִּי־לֹא תֵבוֹשִׁי וְאַל־תִּכָּלְמִי כִּי
ה לֹא תַחְפִּירִי כִּי בֹשֶׁת עֲלוּמַיִךְ תִּשְׁכָּחִי וְחֶרְפַּת אַלְמְנוּתַיִךְ לֹא תִזְכְּרִי־עוֹד׃ כִּי
בֹעֲלַיִךְ עֹשַׂיִךְ יהוה צְבָאוֹת שְׁמוֹ וְגֹאֲלֵךְ קְדוֹשׁ יִשְׂרָאֵל אֱלֹהֵי כָל־הָאָרֶץ יִקָּרֵא׃
ו כִּי־כְאִשָּׁה עֲזוּבָה וַעֲצוּבַת רוּחַ קְרָאָךְ יהוה וְאֵשֶׁת נְעוּרִים כִּי תִמָּאֵס אָמַר
ז ח אֱלֹהָיִךְ׃ בְּרֶגַע קָטֹן עֲזַבְתִּיךְ וּבְרַחֲמִים גְּדֹלִים אֲקַבְּצֵךְ׃ בְּשֶׁצֶף קֶצֶף הִסְתַּרְתִּי
ט פָנַי רֶגַע מִמֵּךְ וּבְחֶסֶד עוֹלָם רִחַמְתִּיךְ אָמַר גֹּאֲלֵךְ יהוה׃ כִּי־מֵי נֹחַ
זֹאת לִי אֲשֶׁר נִשְׁבַּעְתִּי מֵעֲבֹר מֵי־נֹחַ עוֹד עַל־הָאָרֶץ כֵּן נִשְׁבַּעְתִּי מִקְּצֹף עָלַיִךְ

י וּמְגַעַר־בָּךְ׃ כִּי הֶהָרִים יָמוּשׁוּ וְהַגְּבָעוֹת תְּמוּטֶנָה וְחַסְדִּי מֵאִתֵּךְ לֹא־יָמוּשׁ
וּבְרִית שְׁלוֹמִי לֹא תָמוּט אָמַר מְרַחֲמֵךְ יְהוָה׃

הפטרת כי תבוא
HAFTARAT KI TAVO

ס א ב קוּמִי אוֹרִי כִּי בָא אוֹרֵךְ וּכְבוֹד יְהוָה עָלַיִךְ זָרָח׃ כִּי־הִנֵּה הַחֹשֶׁךְ יְכַסֶּה־אֶרֶץ YESHA'YAHU
ג וַעֲרָפֶל לְאֻמִּים וְעָלַיִךְ יִזְרַח יְהוָה וּכְבוֹדוֹ עָלַיִךְ יֵרָאֶה׃ וְהָלְכוּ גוֹיִם לְאוֹרֵךְ
ד וּמְלָכִים לְנֹגַהּ זַרְחֵךְ׃ שְׂאִי־סָבִיב עֵינַיִךְ וּרְאִי כֻּלָּם נִקְבְּצוּ בָאוּ־לָךְ בָּנַיִךְ
ה מֵרָחוֹק יָבֹאוּ וּבְנֹתַיִךְ עַל־צַד תֵּאָמַנָה׃ אָז תִּרְאִי וְנָהַרְתְּ וּפָחַד וְרָחַב לְבָבֵךְ
ו כִּי־יֵהָפֵךְ עָלַיִךְ הֲמוֹן יָם חֵיל גּוֹיִם יָבֹאוּ לָךְ׃ שִׁפְעַת גְּמַלִּים תְּכַסֵּךְ בִּכְרֵי מִדְיָן
ז וְעֵיפָה כֻּלָּם מִשְּׁבָא יָבֹאוּ זָהָב וּלְבוֹנָה יִשָּׂאוּ וּתְהִלֹּת יְהוָה יְבַשֵּׂרוּ׃ כָּל־צֹאן
קֵדָר יִקָּבְצוּ לָךְ אֵילֵי נְבָיוֹת יְשָׁרְתוּנֶךְ יַעֲלוּ עַל־רָצוֹן מִזְבְּחִי וּבֵית תִּפְאַרְתִּי
ח ט אֲפָאֵר׃ מִי־אֵלֶּה כָּעָב תְּעוּפֶינָה וְכַיּוֹנִים אֶל־אֲרֻבֹּתֵיהֶם׃ כִּי־לִי ׀ אִיִּים יְקַוּוּ
וָאֳנִיּוֹת תַּרְשִׁישׁ בָּרִאשֹׁנָה לְהָבִיא בָנַיִךְ מֵרָחוֹק כַּסְפָּם וּזְהָבָם אִתָּם לְשֵׁם יְהוָה
י אֱלֹהַיִךְ וְלִקְדוֹשׁ יִשְׂרָאֵל כִּי פֵאֲרָךְ׃ וּבָנוּ בְנֵי־נֵכָר חֹמֹתַיִךְ וּמַלְכֵיהֶם יְשָׁרְתוּנֶךְ
יא כִּי בְקִצְפִּי הִכִּיתִיךְ וּבִרְצוֹנִי רִחַמְתִּיךְ׃ וּפִתְּחוּ שְׁעָרַיִךְ תָּמִיד יוֹמָם וָלַיְלָה לֹא
יב יִסָּגֵרוּ לְהָבִיא אֵלַיִךְ חֵיל גּוֹיִם וּמַלְכֵיהֶם נְהוּגִים׃ כִּי־הַגּוֹי וְהַמַּמְלָכָה אֲשֶׁר לֹא־
יג יַעַבְדוּךְ יֹאבֵדוּ וְהַגּוֹיִם חָרֹב יֶחֱרָבוּ׃ כְּבוֹד הַלְּבָנוֹן אֵלַיִךְ יָבוֹא בְּרוֹשׁ תִּדְהָר
יד וּתְאַשּׁוּר יַחְדָּו לְפָאֵר מְקוֹם מִקְדָּשִׁי וּמְקוֹם רַגְלַי אֲכַבֵּד׃ וְהָלְכוּ אֵלַיִךְ שְׁחוֹחַ
בְּנֵי מְעַנַּיִךְ וְהִשְׁתַּחֲווּ עַל־כַּפּוֹת רַגְלַיִךְ כָּל־מְנַאֲצָיִךְ וְקָרְאוּ לָךְ עִיר יְהוָה צִיּוֹן
טו קְדוֹשׁ יִשְׂרָאֵל׃ תַּחַת הֱיוֹתֵךְ עֲזוּבָה וּשְׂנוּאָה וְאֵין עוֹבֵר וְשַׂמְתִּיךְ לִגְאוֹן עוֹלָם
טז מְשׂוֹשׂ דּוֹר וָדוֹר׃ וְיָנַקְתְּ חֲלֵב גּוֹיִם וְשֹׁד מְלָכִים תִּינָקִי וְיָדַעַתְּ כִּי אֲנִי יְהוָה
יז מוֹשִׁיעֵךְ וְגֹאֲלֵךְ אֲבִיר יַעֲקֹב׃ תַּחַת הַנְּחֹשֶׁת אָבִיא זָהָב וְתַחַת הַבַּרְזֶל אָבִיא
כֶסֶף וְתַחַת הָעֵצִים נְחֹשֶׁת וְתַחַת הָאֲבָנִים בַּרְזֶל וְשַׂמְתִּי פְקֻדָּתֵךְ שָׁלוֹם
יח וְנֹגְשַׂיִךְ צְדָקָה׃ לֹא־יִשָּׁמַע עוֹד חָמָס בְּאַרְצֵךְ שֹׁד וָשֶׁבֶר בִּגְבוּלָיִךְ וְקָרָאת
יט יְשׁוּעָה חוֹמֹתַיִךְ וּשְׁעָרַיִךְ תְּהִלָּה׃ לֹא־יִהְיֶה־לָּךְ עוֹד הַשֶּׁמֶשׁ לְאוֹר יוֹמָם וּלְנֹגַהּ
כ הַיָּרֵחַ לֹא־יָאִיר לָךְ וְהָיָה־לָךְ יְהוָה לְאוֹר עוֹלָם וֵאלֹהַיִךְ לְתִפְאַרְתֵּךְ׃ לֹא־יָבוֹא
עוֹד שִׁמְשֵׁךְ וִירֵחֵךְ לֹא יֵאָסֵף כִּי יְהוָה יִהְיֶה־לָּךְ לְאוֹר עוֹלָם וְשָׁלְמוּ יְמֵי אֶבְלֵךְ׃
כא וְעַמֵּךְ כֻּלָּם צַדִּיקִים לְעוֹלָם יִירְשׁוּ אָרֶץ נֵצֶר מטעו מַעֲשֵׂה יָדַי לְהִתְפָּאֵר׃ מַטָּעַי
כב הַקָּטֹן יִהְיֶה לָאֶלֶף וְהַצָּעִיר לְגוֹי עָצוּם אֲנִי יְהוָה בְּעִתָּהּ אֲחִישֶׁנָּה׃

הפטרת שבת ראש חודש

HAFTARAT SHABBAT ROSH ḤODESH

The Maftir for Shabbat Rosh Ḥodesh, Bemidbar 28:9-15, is on page 1030.

YESHA'YAHU

כֹּה אָמַר יהוה הַשָּׁמַיִם כִּסְאִי וְהָאָרֶץ הֲדֹם רַגְלָי אֵי־זֶה בַיִת אֲשֶׁר תִּבְנוּ־לִי א ס
וְאֵי־זֶה מָקוֹם מְנוּחָתִי: וְאֶת־כָּל־אֵלֶּה יָדִי עָשָׂתָה וַיִּהְיוּ כָל־אֵלֶּה נְאֻם־יהוה ב
וְאֶל־זֶה אַבִּיט אֶל־עָנִי וּנְכֵה־רוּחַ וְחָרֵד עַל־דְּבָרִי: שׁוֹחֵט הַשּׁוֹר מַכֵּה־אִישׁ ג
זוֹבֵחַ הַשֶּׂה עֹרֵף כֶּלֶב מַעֲלֵה מִנְחָה דַּם־חֲזִיר מַזְכִּיר לְבֹנָה מְבָרֵךְ אָוֶן גַּם־הֵמָּה
בָּחֲרוּ בְּדַרְכֵיהֶם וּבְשִׁקּוּצֵיהֶם נַפְשָׁם חָפֵצָה: גַּם־אֲנִי אֶבְחַר בְּתַעֲלֻלֵיהֶם ד
וּמְגוּרֹתָם אָבִיא לָהֶם יַעַן קָרָאתִי וְאֵין עוֹנֶה דִּבַּרְתִּי וְלֹא שָׁמֵעוּ וַיַּעֲשׂוּ הָרַע
בְּעֵינַי וּבַאֲשֶׁר לֹא־חָפַצְתִּי בָּחָרוּ: שִׁמְעוּ דְּבַר־יהוה הַחֲרֵדִים ה
אֶל־דְּבָרוֹ אָמְרוּ אֲחֵיכֶם שֹׂנְאֵיכֶם מְנַדֵּיכֶם לְמַעַן שְׁמִי יִכְבַּד יהוה וְנִרְאֶה
בְשִׂמְחַתְכֶם וְהֵם יֵבֹשׁוּ: קוֹל שָׁאוֹן מֵעִיר קוֹל מֵהֵיכָל קוֹל יהוה מְשַׁלֵּם גְּמוּל ו
לְאֹיְבָיו: בְּטֶרֶם תָּחִיל יָלָדָה בְּטֶרֶם יָבוֹא חֵבֶל לָהּ וְהִמְלִיטָה זָכָר: מִי־שָׁמַע ז ח
כָּזֹאת מִי רָאָה כָּאֵלֶּה הֲיוּחַל אֶרֶץ בְּיוֹם אֶחָד אִם־יִוָּלֵד גּוֹי פַּעַם אֶחָת כִּי־
חָלָה גַּם־יָלְדָה צִיּוֹן אֶת־בָּנֶיהָ: הַאֲנִי אַשְׁבִּיר וְלֹא אוֹלִיד יֹאמַר יהוה אִם־אֲנִי ט
הַמּוֹלִיד וְעָצַרְתִּי אָמַר אֱלֹהָיִךְ: שִׂמְחוּ אֶת־יְרוּשָׁלַם וְגִילוּ בָהּ כָּל־ י
אֹהֲבֶיהָ שִׂישׂוּ אִתָּהּ מָשׂוֹשׂ כָּל־הַמִּתְאַבְּלִים עָלֶיהָ: לְמַעַן תִּינְקוּ וּשְׂבַעְתֶּם יא
מִשֹּׁד תַּנְחֻמֶיהָ לְמַעַן תָּמֹצּוּ וְהִתְעַנַּגְתֶּם מִזִּיז כְּבוֹדָהּ: כִּי־כֹה ׀ אָמַר יב
יהוה הִנְנִי נֹטֶה־אֵלֶיהָ כְּנָהָר שָׁלוֹם וּכְנַחַל שׁוֹטֵף כְּבוֹד גּוֹיִם וִינַקְתֶּם עַל־צַד
תִּנָּשֵׂאוּ וְעַל־בִּרְכַּיִם תְּשָׁעֳשָׁעוּ: כְּאִישׁ אֲשֶׁר אִמּוֹ תְּנַחֲמֶנּוּ כֵּן אָנֹכִי אֲנַחֶמְכֶם יג
וּבִירוּשָׁלַם תְּנֻחָמוּ: וּרְאִיתֶם וְשָׂשׂ לִבְּכֶם וְעַצְמוֹתֵיכֶם כַּדֶּשֶׁא תִפְרַחְנָה וְנוֹדְעָה יד
יַד־יהוה אֶת־עֲבָדָיו וְזָעַם אֶת־אֹיְבָיו: כִּי־הִנֵּה יהוה בָּאֵשׁ יָבוֹא וְכַסּוּפָה טו
מַרְכְּבֹתָיו לְהָשִׁיב בְּחֵמָה אַפּוֹ וְגַעֲרָתוֹ בְּלַהֲבֵי־אֵשׁ: כִּי בָאֵשׁ יהוה נִשְׁפָּט טז
וּבְחַרְבּוֹ אֶת־כָּל־בָּשָׂר וְרַבּוּ חַלְלֵי יהוה: הַמִּתְקַדְּשִׁים וְהַמִּטַּהֲרִים אֶל־הַגַּנּוֹת יז
אַחַר אחד בַּתָּוֶךְ אֹכְלֵי בְּשַׂר הַחֲזִיר וְהַשֶּׁקֶץ וְהָעַכְבָּר יַחְדָּו יָסֻפוּ נְאֻם־יהוה: (אַחַת)
וְאָנֹכִי מַעֲשֵׂיהֶם וּמַחְשְׁבֹתֵיהֶם בָּאָה לְקַבֵּץ אֶת־כָּל־הַגּוֹיִם וְהַלְּשֹׁנוֹת וּבָאוּ יח
וְרָאוּ אֶת־כְּבוֹדִי: וְשַׂמְתִּי בָהֶם אוֹת וְשִׁלַּחְתִּי מֵהֶם ׀ פְּלֵיטִים אֶל־הַגּוֹיִם יט
תַּרְשִׁישׁ פּוּל וְלוּד מֹשְׁכֵי קֶשֶׁת תֻּבַל וְיָוָן הָאִיִּים הָרְחֹקִים אֲשֶׁר לֹא־שָׁמְעוּ אֶת־
שִׁמְעִי וְלֹא־רָאוּ אֶת־כְּבוֹדִי וְהִגִּידוּ אֶת־כְּבוֹדִי בַּגּוֹיִם: וְהֵבִיאוּ אֶת־כָּל־אֲחֵיכֶם ׀ כ

מִכָּל־הַגּוֹיִם ׀ מִנְחָה ׀ לַיהוָה בַּסּוּסִים וּבָרֶכֶב וּבַצַּבִּים וּבַפְּרָדִים וּבַכִּרְכָּרוֹת
עַל הַר קָדְשִׁי יְרוּשָׁלִַם אָמַר יְהוָה כַּאֲשֶׁר יָבִיאוּ בְנֵי יִשְׂרָאֵל אֶת־הַמִּנְחָה
כא כב בִּכְלִי טָהוֹר בֵּית יְהוָה׃ וְגַם־מֵהֶם אֶקַּח לַכֹּהֲנִים לַלְוִיִּם אָמַר יְהוָה׃ כִּי כַאֲשֶׁר
הַשָּׁמַיִם הַחֲדָשִׁים וְהָאָרֶץ הַחֲדָשָׁה אֲשֶׁר אֲנִי עֹשֶׂה עֹמְדִים לְפָנַי נְאֻם־יְהוָה
כג כֵּן יַעֲמֹד זַרְעֲכֶם וְשִׁמְכֶם׃ וְהָיָה מִדֵּי־חֹדֶשׁ בְּחָדְשׁוֹ וּמִדֵּי שַׁבָּת בְּשַׁבַּתּוֹ יָבוֹא
כד כָל־בָּשָׂר לְהִשְׁתַּחֲוֺת לְפָנַי אָמַר יְהוָה׃ וְיָצְאוּ וְרָאוּ בְּפִגְרֵי הָאֲנָשִׁים הַפֹּשְׁעִים
בִּי כִּי תוֹלַעְתָּם לֹא תָמוּת וְאִשָּׁם לֹא תִכְבֶּה וְהָיוּ דֵרָאוֹן לְכָל־בָּשָׂר׃
וְהָיָה מִדֵּי־חֹדֶשׁ בְּחָדְשׁוֹ וּמִדֵּי שַׁבָּת בְּשַׁבַּתּוֹ יָבוֹא כָל־בָּשָׂר לְהִשְׁתַּחֲוֺת לְפָנַי
אָמַר יְהוָה׃

הפטרת שבת ערב ראש חודש

HAFTARAT SHABBAT EREV ROSH ḤODESH

כ יח יט וַיֹּאמֶר־לוֹ יְהוֹנָתָן מָחָר חֹדֶשׁ וְנִפְקַדְתָּ כִּי יִפָּקֵד מוֹשָׁבֶךָ׃ וְשִׁלַּשְׁתָּ תֵּרֵד מְאֹד I SHMU'EL
וּבָאתָ אֶל־הַמָּקוֹם אֲשֶׁר־נִסְתַּרְתָּ שָּׁם בְּיוֹם הַמַּעֲשֶׂה וְיָשַׁבְתָּ אֵצֶל הָאֶבֶן
כ כא הָאָזֶל׃ וַאֲנִי שְׁלֹשֶׁת הַחִצִּים צִדָּה אוֹרֶה לְשַׁלַּח־לִי לְמַטָּרָה׃ וְהִנֵּה אֶשְׁלַח
אֶת־הַנַּעַר לֵךְ מְצָא אֶת־הַחִצִּים אִם־אָמֹר אֹמַר לַנַּעַר הִנֵּה הַחִצִּים ׀ מִמְּךָ
כב וָהֵנָּה קָחֶנּוּ וָבֹאָה כִּי־שָׁלוֹם לְךָ וְאֵין דָּבָר חַי־יְהוָה׃ וְאִם־כֹּה אֹמַר לָעֶלֶם
כג הִנֵּה הַחִצִּים מִמְּךָ וָהָלְאָה לֵךְ כִּי שִׁלַּחֲךָ יְהוָה׃ וְהַדָּבָר אֲשֶׁר דִּבַּרְנוּ אֲנִי
כד וָאָתָּה הִנֵּה יְהוָה בֵּינִי וּבֵינְךָ עַד־עוֹלָם׃ וַיִּסָּתֵר דָּוִד בַּשָּׂדֶה וַיְהִי
כה הַחֹדֶשׁ וַיֵּשֶׁב הַמֶּלֶךְ עַל־הַלֶּחֶם לֶאֱכוֹל׃ וַיֵּשֶׁב הַמֶּלֶךְ עַל־מוֹשָׁבוֹ כְּפַעַם ׀ אֶל־
בְּפַעַם אֶל־מוֹשַׁב הַקִּיר וַיָּקָם יְהוֹנָתָן וַיֵּשֶׁב אַבְנֵר מִצַּד שָׁאוּל וַיִּפָּקֵד מְקוֹם
כו דָּוִד׃ וְלֹא־דִבֶּר שָׁאוּל מְאוּמָה בַּיּוֹם הַהוּא כִּי אָמַר מִקְרֶה הוּא בִּלְתִּי טָהוֹר
כז הוּא כִּי־לֹא טָהוֹר׃ וַיְהִי מִמָּחֳרַת הַחֹדֶשׁ הַשֵּׁנִי וַיִּפָּקֵד מְקוֹם דָּוִד
וַיֹּאמֶר שָׁאוּל אֶל־יְהוֹנָתָן בְּנוֹ מַדּוּעַ לֹא־בָא בֶן־יִשַׁי גַּם־תְּמוֹל גַּם־הַיּוֹם
כח אֶל־הַלָּחֶם׃ וַיַּעַן יְהוֹנָתָן אֶת־שָׁאוּל נִשְׁאֹל נִשְׁאַל דָּוִד מֵעִמָּדִי עַד־בֵּית לָחֶם׃
כט וַיֹּאמֶר שַׁלְּחֵנִי נָא כִּי זֶבַח מִשְׁפָּחָה לָנוּ בָּעִיר וְהוּא צִוָּה־לִי אָחִי וְעַתָּה אִם־
מָצָאתִי חֵן בְּעֵינֶיךָ אִמָּלְטָה נָּא וְאֶרְאֶה אֶת־אֶחָי עַל־כֵּן לֹא־בָא אֶל־שֻׁלְחַן
ל הַמֶּלֶךְ׃ וַיִּחַר־אַף שָׁאוּל בִּיהוֹנָתָן וַיֹּאמֶר לוֹ בֶּן־נַעֲוַת הַמַּרְדּוּת
לא הֲלוֹא יָדַעְתִּי כִּי־בֹחֵר אַתָּה לְבֶן־יִשַׁי לְבָשְׁתְּךָ וּלְבֹשֶׁת עֶרְוַת אִמֶּךָ׃ כִּי כָל־

הַיָּמִ֗ים אֲשֶׁ֤ר בֶּן־יִשַׁי֙ חַ֣י עַל־הָֽאֲדָמָ֔ה לֹ֥א תִכּ֖וֹן אַתָּ֣ה וּמַלְכוּתֶ֑ךָ וְעַתָּ֗ה שְׁלַ֨ח
וְקַ֤ח אֹתוֹ֙ אֵלַ֔י כִּ֥י בֶן־מָ֖וֶת הֽוּא׃ וַיַּ֙עַן֙ יְה֣וֹנָתָ֔ן אֶת־שָׁא֖וּל אָבִ֑יו לב
וַיֹּ֧אמֶר אֵלָ֛יו לָ֥מָּה יוּמַ֖ת מֶ֥ה עָשָֽׂה׃ וַיָּ֨טֶל שָׁא֧וּל אֶת־הַחֲנִ֛ית עָלָ֖יו לְהַכֹּת֑וֹ וַיֵּ֙דַע֙ לג
יְה֣וֹנָתָ֔ן כִּֽי־כָ֥לָה הִ֛יא מֵעִ֥ם אָבִ֖יו לְהָמִ֥ית אֶת־דָּוִֽד׃ וַיָּ֧קָם יְהוֹנָתָ֛ן לד
מֵעִ֥ם הַשֻּׁלְחָ֖ן בָּֽחֳרִי־אָ֑ף וְלֹא־אָכַ֞ל בְּיוֹם־הַחֹ֤דֶשׁ הַשֵּׁנִי֙ לֶ֔חֶם כִּ֤י נֶעְצַב֙ אֶל־
דָּוִ֔ד כִּ֥י הִכְלִמ֖וֹ אָבִֽיו׃ וַיְהִ֣י בַבֹּ֔קֶר וַיֵּצֵ֧א יְהוֹנָתָ֛ן הַשָּׂדֶ֖ה לְמוֹעֵ֣ד דָּוִ֑ד לה
וְנַ֥עַר קָטֹ֖ן עִמּֽוֹ׃ וַיֹּ֣אמֶר לְנַעֲר֔וֹ רֻ֗ץ מְצָ֥א נָא֙ אֶת־הַ֣חִצִּ֔ים אֲשֶׁ֥ר אָנֹכִ֖י מוֹרֶ֑ה לו
הַנַּ֣עַר רָ֔ץ וְהֽוּא־יָרָ֥ה הַחֵ֖צִי לְהַעֲבִרֽוֹ׃ וַיָּבֹ֤א הַנַּ֙עַר֙ עַד־מְק֣וֹם הַחֵ֔צִי אֲשֶׁ֥ר יָרָ֖ה לז
יְהוֹנָתָ֑ן וַיִּקְרָ֨א יְהוֹנָתָ֜ן אַחֲרֵ֤י הַנַּ֙עַר֙ וַיֹּ֔אמֶר הֲל֥וֹא הַחֵ֖צִי מִמְּךָ֥ וָהָֽלְאָה׃ וַיִּקְרָ֨א לח
יְהוֹנָתָ֜ן אַחֲרֵ֤י הַנַּ֙עַר֙ מְהֵרָ֥ה ח֖וּשָׁה אַֽל־תַּעֲמֹ֑ד וַיְלַקֵּ֞ט נַ֤עַר יְהוֹנָתָן֙ אֶת־הַ֣חִצִּ֔י הַחִצִּ֔ים
וַיָּבֹ֖א אֶל־אֲדֹנָֽיו׃ וְהַנַּ֖עַר לֹא־יָדַ֣ע מְא֑וּמָה אַ֤ךְ יְהוֹנָתָן֙ וְדָוִ֔ד יָדְע֖וּ אֶת־הַדָּבָֽר׃ לט
וַיִּתֵּ֤ן יְהוֹנָתָן֙ אֶת־כֵּלָ֔יו אֶל־הַנַּ֖עַר אֲשֶׁר־ל֑וֹ וַיֹּ֣אמֶר ל֔וֹ לֵ֖ךְ הָבֵ֥יא הָעִֽיר׃ הַנַּ֘עַר֮ מ מא
בָּא֒ וְדָוִ֗ד קָם֙ מֵאֵ֣צֶל הַנֶּ֔גֶב וַיִּפֹּ֨ל לְאַפָּ֥יו אַ֛רְצָה וַיִּשְׁתַּ֖חוּ שָׁל֣שׁ פְּעָמִ֑ים וַֽיִּשְּׁק֣וּ ׀
אִ֣ישׁ אֶת־רֵעֵ֗הוּ וַיִּבְכּוּ֙ אִ֣ישׁ אֶת־רֵעֵ֔הוּ עַד־דָּוִ֖ד הִגְדִּֽיל׃ וַיֹּ֧אמֶר יְהוֹנָתָ֛ן לְדָוִ֖ד מב
לֵ֣ךְ לְשָׁל֑וֹם אֲשֶׁ֨ר נִשְׁבַּ֜עְנוּ שְׁנֵ֣ינוּ אֲנַ֗חְנוּ בְּשֵׁ֤ם יְהוָה֙ לֵאמֹ֔ר יְהוָ֞ה יִהְיֶ֣ה ׀ בֵּינִ֣י
וּבֵינֶ֗ךָ וּבֵ֥ין זַרְעִ֛י וּבֵ֥ין זַרְעֲךָ֖ עַד־עוֹלָֽם׃

READING FOR FAST DAYS
קריאה לתענית ציבור

The following is read on a fast day (except Tisha B'Av, page 1047) in both Shaharit and Minha. At Minha, the person called up for Shelishi also reads the Haftara.

It is customary for the congregation to say aloud the passages marked by arrows, followed by the Reader.

לב יא וַיְחַל מֹשֶׁה אֶת־פְּנֵי יהוה אֱלֹהָיו וַיֹּאמֶר לָמָה יהוה יֶחֱרֶה אַפְּךָ בְּעַמֶּךָ אֲשֶׁר SHEMOT
יב הוֹצֵאתָ מֵאֶרֶץ מִצְרַיִם בְּכֹחַ גָּדוֹל וּבְיָד חֲזָקָה: לָמָּה יֹאמְרוּ מִצְרַיִם לֵאמֹר
בְּרָעָה הוֹצִיאָם לַהֲרֹג אֹתָם בֶּהָרִים וּלְכַלֹּתָם מֵעַל פְּנֵי הָאֲדָמָה ◄ שׁוּב מֵחֲרוֹן
יג אַפֶּךָ וְהִנָּחֵם עַל־הָרָעָה לְעַמֶּךָ: ◄ זְכֹר לְאַבְרָהָם לְיִצְחָק וּלְיִשְׂרָאֵל עֲבָדֶיךָ
אֲשֶׁר נִשְׁבַּעְתָּ לָהֶם בָּךְ וַתְּדַבֵּר אֲלֵהֶם אַרְבֶּה אֶת־זַרְעֲכֶם כְּכוֹכְבֵי הַשָּׁמָיִם
יד וְכָל־הָאָרֶץ הַזֹּאת אֲשֶׁר אָמַרְתִּי אֶתֵּן לְזַרְעֲכֶם וְנָחֲלוּ לְעֹלָם: וַיִּנָּחֶם יהוה
עַל־הָרָעָה אֲשֶׁר דִּבֶּר לַעֲשׂוֹת לְעַמּוֹ:

לד א וַיֹּאמֶר יהוה אֶל־מֹשֶׁה פְּסָל־לְךָ שְׁנֵי־לֻחֹת אֲבָנִים כָּרִאשֹׁנִים וְכָתַבְתִּי עַל־ לוי
ב הַלֻּחֹת אֶת־הַדְּבָרִים אֲשֶׁר הָיוּ עַל־הַלֻּחֹת הָרִאשֹׁנִים אֲשֶׁר שִׁבַּרְתָּ: וֶהְיֵה
ג נָכוֹן לַבֹּקֶר וְעָלִיתָ בַבֹּקֶר אֶל־הַר סִינַי וְנִצַּבְתָּ לִי שָׁם עַל־רֹאשׁ הָהָר: וְאִישׁ
לֹא־יַעֲלֶה עִמָּךְ וְגַם־אִישׁ אַל־יֵרָא בְּכָל־הָהָר גַּם־הַצֹּאן וְהַבָּקָר אַל־יִרְעוּ
ד אֶל־מוּל הָהָר הַהוּא: *וַיִּפְסֹל שְׁנֵי־לֻחֹת אֲבָנִים כָּרִאשֹׁנִים וַיַּשְׁכֵּם מֹשֶׁה ישראל
בַבֹּקֶר וַיַּעַל אֶל־הַר סִינַי כַּאֲשֶׁר צִוָּה יהוה אֹתוֹ וַיִּקַּח בְּיָדוֹ שְׁנֵי לֻחֹת אֲבָנִים:
ה ו וַיֵּרֶד יהוה בֶּעָנָן וַיִּתְיַצֵּב עִמּוֹ שָׁם וַיִּקְרָא בְשֵׁם יהוה: וַיַּעֲבֹר יהוה ׀ עַל־פָּנָיו
ז וַיִּקְרָא ◄ יהוה ׀ יהוה אֵל רַחוּם וְחַנּוּן אֶרֶךְ אַפַּיִם וְרַב־חֶסֶד וֶאֱמֶת: נֹצֵר חֶסֶד
לָאֲלָפִים נֹשֵׂא עָוֺן וָפֶשַׁע וְחַטָּאָה וְנַקֵּה ◄ לֹא יְנַקֶּה פֹּקֵד ׀ עֲוֺן אָבוֹת עַל־בָּנִים
ח וְעַל־בְּנֵי בָנִים עַל־שִׁלֵּשִׁים וְעַל־רִבֵּעִים: וַיְמַהֵר מֹשֶׁה וַיִּקֹּד אַרְצָה וַיִּשְׁתָּחוּ:
ט וַיֹּאמֶר אִם־נָא מָצָאתִי חֵן בְּעֵינֶיךָ אֲדֹנָי יֵלֶךְ־נָא אֲדֹנָי בְּקִרְבֵּנוּ כִּי עַם־קְשֵׁה־
י עֹרֶף הוּא ◄ וְסָלַחְתָּ לַעֲוֺנֵנוּ וּלְחַטָּאתֵנוּ וּנְחַלְתָּנוּ: ◄ וַיֹּאמֶר הִנֵּה אָנֹכִי כֹּרֵת
בְּרִית נֶגֶד כָּל־עַמְּךָ אֶעֱשֶׂה נִפְלָאֹת אֲשֶׁר לֹא־נִבְרְאוּ בְכָל־הָאָרֶץ וּבְכָל־הַגּוֹיִם
וְרָאָה כָל־הָעָם אֲשֶׁר־אַתָּה בְקִרְבּוֹ אֶת־מַעֲשֵׂה יהוה כִּי־נוֹרָא הוּא אֲשֶׁר אֲנִי
עֹשֶׂה עִמָּךְ:

HAFTARA – FAST DAYS הפטרה לתענית ציבור

At Minḥa of a fast day, the person called up for Shelishi also reads the Haftara

YESHA'YAHU

דִּרְשׁוּ יְהוָה בְּהִמָּצְאוֹ קְרָאֻהוּ בִּהְיוֹתוֹ קָרוֹב: יַעֲזֹב רָשָׁע דַּרְכּוֹ וְאִישׁ אָוֶן ו ז נה
מַחְשְׁבֹתָיו וְיָשֹׁב אֶל־יְהוָה וִירַחֲמֵהוּ וְאֶל־אֱלֹהֵינוּ כִּי־יַרְבֶּה לִסְלוֹחַ: כִּי לֹא ח
מַחְשְׁבוֹתַי מַחְשְׁבוֹתֵיכֶם וְלֹא דַרְכֵיכֶם דְּרָכָי נְאֻם יְהוָה: כִּי־גָבְהוּ שָׁמַיִם ט
מֵאָרֶץ כֵּן גָּבְהוּ דְרָכַי מִדַּרְכֵיכֶם וּמַחְשְׁבֹתַי מִמַּחְשְׁבֹתֵיכֶם: כִּי כַּאֲשֶׁר יֵרֵד י
הַגֶּשֶׁם וְהַשֶּׁלֶג מִן־הַשָּׁמַיִם וְשָׁמָּה לֹא יָשׁוּב כִּי אִם־הִרְוָה אֶת־הָאָרֶץ וְהוֹלִידָהּ
וְהִצְמִיחָהּ וְנָתַן זֶרַע לַזֹּרֵעַ וְלֶחֶם לָאֹכֵל: כֵּן יִהְיֶה דְבָרִי אֲשֶׁר יֵצֵא מִפִּי לֹא־ יא
יָשׁוּב אֵלַי רֵיקָם כִּי אִם־עָשָׂה אֶת־אֲשֶׁר חָפַצְתִּי וְהִצְלִיחַ אֲשֶׁר שְׁלַחְתִּיו:
כִּי־בְשִׂמְחָה תֵצֵאוּ וּבְשָׁלוֹם תּוּבָלוּן הֶהָרִים וְהַגְּבָעוֹת יִפְצְחוּ לִפְנֵיכֶם רִנָּה יב
וְתַחַת וְכָל־עֲצֵי הַשָּׂדֶה יִמְחֲאוּ־כָף: תַּחַת הַנַּעֲצוּץ יַעֲלֶה בְרוֹשׁ תחת הַסִּרְפַּד יַעֲלֶה יג
הֲדַס וְהָיָה לַיהוָה לְשֵׁם לְאוֹת עוֹלָם לֹא יִכָּרֵת: כֹּה אָמַר יְהוָה א נו
שִׁמְרוּ מִשְׁפָּט וַעֲשׂוּ צְדָקָה כִּי־קְרוֹבָה יְשׁוּעָתִי לָבוֹא וְצִדְקָתִי לְהִגָּלוֹת: אַשְׁרֵי ב
אֱנוֹשׁ יַעֲשֶׂה־זֹּאת וּבֶן־אָדָם יַחֲזִיק בָּהּ שֹׁמֵר שַׁבָּת מֵחַלְּלוֹ וְשֹׁמֵר יָדוֹ מֵעֲשׂוֹת
כָּל־רָע: וְאַל־יֹאמַר בֶּן־הַנֵּכָר הַנִּלְוָה אֶל־יְהוָה לֵאמֹר הַבְדֵּל יַבְדִּילַנִי יְהוָה ג
מֵעַל עַמּוֹ וְאַל־יֹאמַר הַסָּרִיס הֵן אֲנִי עֵץ יָבֵשׁ: כִּי־כֹה | אָמַר ד
יְהוָה לַסָּרִיסִים אֲשֶׁר יִשְׁמְרוּ אֶת־שַׁבְּתוֹתַי וּבָחֲרוּ בַּאֲשֶׁר חָפָצְתִּי וּמַחֲזִיקִים
בִּבְרִיתִי: וְנָתַתִּי לָהֶם בְּבֵיתִי וּבְחוֹמֹתַי יָד וָשֵׁם טוֹב מִבָּנִים וּמִבָּנוֹת שֵׁם עוֹלָם ה
אֶתֶּן־לוֹ אֲשֶׁר לֹא יִכָּרֵת: וּבְנֵי הַנֵּכָר הַנִּלְוִים עַל־יְהוָה לְשָׁרְתוֹ ו
וּלְאַהֲבָה אֶת־שֵׁם יְהוָה לִהְיוֹת לוֹ לַעֲבָדִים כָּל־שֹׁמֵר שַׁבָּת מֵחַלְּלוֹ וּמַחֲזִיקִים
בִּבְרִיתִי: וַהֲבִיאוֹתִים אֶל־הַר קָדְשִׁי וְשִׂמַּחְתִּים בְּבֵית תְּפִלָּתִי עוֹלֹתֵיהֶם ז
וְזִבְחֵיהֶם לְרָצוֹן עַל־מִזְבְּחִי כִּי בֵיתִי בֵּית־תְּפִלָּה יִקָּרֵא לְכָל־הָעַמִּים: נְאֻם ח
אֲדֹנָי יֱהוִה מְקַבֵּץ נִדְחֵי יִשְׂרָאֵל עוֹד אֲקַבֵּץ עָלָיו לְנִקְבָּצָיו:

HAFTARA FOR TISHA B'AV הפטרה לתשעה באב

The Torah Portion for Tisha B'Av, Devarim 4:25-40, is on page 1047.

YIRMEYAHU

אָסֹף אֲסִיפֵם נְאֻם־יְהוָה אֵין עֲנָבִים בַּגֶּפֶן וְאֵין תְּאֵנִים בַּתְּאֵנָה וְהֶעָלֶה נָבֵל יג ח
וָאֶתֵּן לָהֶם יַעַבְרוּם: עַל־מָה אֲנַחְנוּ יֹשְׁבִים הֵאָסְפוּ וְנָבוֹא אֶל־עָרֵי הַמִּבְצָר יד
וְנִדְּמָה־שָּׁם כִּי יְהוָה אֱלֹהֵינוּ הֲדִמָּנוּ וַיַּשְׁקֵנוּ מֵי־רֹאשׁ כִּי חָטָאנוּ לַיהוָה: קַוֵּה טו

טז לְשָׁלוֹם וְאֵין טוֹב לְעֵת מַרְפֵּה וְהִנֵּה בְעָתָה: מִדָּן נִשְׁמַע נַחְרַת סוּסָיו מִקּוֹל
מִצְהֲלוֹת אַבִּירָיו רָעֲשָׁה כָּל־הָאָרֶץ וַיָּבוֹאוּ וַיֹּאכְלוּ אֶרֶץ וּמְלוֹאָהּ עִיר וְיֹשְׁבֵי
יז בָהּ: כִּי הִנְנִי מְשַׁלֵּחַ בָּכֶם נְחָשִׁים צִפְעֹנִים אֲשֶׁר אֵין־לָהֶם לָחַשׁ וְנִשְּׁכוּ אֶתְכֶם
יח יט נְאֻם־יְהוָה: מַבְלִיגִיתִי עֲלֵי יָגוֹן עָלַי לִבִּי דַוָּי: הִנֵּה־קוֹל שַׁוְעַת
בַּת־עַמִּי מֵאֶרֶץ מַרְחַקִּים הַיהוָה אֵין בְּצִיּוֹן אִם־מַלְכָּהּ אֵין בָּהּ מַדּוּעַ הִכְעִסוּנִי
כ כא בִּפְסִלֵיהֶם בְּהַבְלֵי נֵכָר: עָבַר קָצִיר כָּלָה קָיִץ וַאֲנַחְנוּ לוֹא נוֹשָׁעְנוּ: עַל־שֶׁבֶר
כב בַּת־עַמִּי הָשְׁבָּרְתִּי קָדַרְתִּי שַׁמָּה הֶחֱזִקָתְנִי: הַצֳרִי אֵין בְּגִלְעָד אִם־רֹפֵא אֵין
כג שָׁם כִּי מַדּוּעַ לֹא עָלְתָה אֲרֻכַת בַּת־עַמִּי: מִי־יִתֵּן רֹאשִׁי מַיִם
ט א וְעֵינִי מְקוֹר דִּמְעָה וְאֶבְכֶּה יוֹמָם וָלַיְלָה אֵת חַלְלֵי בַת־עַמִּי: מִי־יִתְּנֵנִי בַמִּדְבָּר
מְלוֹן אֹרְחִים וְאֶעֶזְבָה אֶת־עַמִּי וְאֵלְכָה מֵאִתָּם כִּי כֻלָּם מְנָאֲפִים עֲצֶרֶת
ב בֹּגְדִים: וַיַּדְרְכוּ אֶת־לְשׁוֹנָם קַשְׁתָּם שֶׁקֶר וְלֹא לֶאֱמוּנָה גָּבְרוּ בָאָרֶץ כִּי מֵרָעָה
ג אֶל־רָעָה ׀ יָצָאוּ וְאֹתִי לֹא־יָדָעוּ נְאֻם־יְהוָה: אִישׁ מֵרֵעֵהוּ הִשָּׁמֵרוּ וְעַל־כָּל־
ד אָח אַל־תִּבְטָחוּ כִּי כָל־אָח עָקוֹב יַעְקֹב וְכָל־רֵעַ רָכִיל יַהֲלֹךְ: וְאִישׁ בְּרֵעֵהוּ
ה יְהָתֵלּוּ וֶאֱמֶת לֹא יְדַבֵּרוּ לִמְּדוּ לְשׁוֹנָם דַּבֶּר־שֶׁקֶר הַעֲוֵה נִלְאוּ: שִׁבְתְּךָ
ו בְּתוֹךְ מִרְמָה בְּמִרְמָה מֵאֲנוּ דַעַת־אוֹתִי נְאֻם־יְהוָה: לָכֵן כֹּה
אָמַר יְהוָה צְבָאוֹת הִנְנִי צוֹרְפָם וּבְחַנְתִּים כִּי־אֵיךְ אֶעֱשֶׂה מִפְּנֵי בַּת־עַמִּי:
ז חֵץ שוחט לְשׁוֹנָם מִרְמָה דִבֵּר בְּפִיו שָׁלוֹם אֶת־רֵעֵהוּ יְדַבֵּר וּבְקִרְבּוֹ יָשִׂים שָׁחוּט
ח אָרְבּוֹ: הַעַל־אֵלֶּה לֹא־אֶפְקָד־בָּם נְאֻם־יְהוָה אִם בְּגוֹי אֲשֶׁר־כָּזֶה לֹא תִתְנַקֵּם
ט נַפְשִׁי: עַל־הֶהָרִים אֶשָּׂא בְכִי וָנֶהִי וְעַל־נְאוֹת מִדְבָּר קִינָה כִּי
נִצְּתוּ מִבְּלִי־אִישׁ עֹבֵר וְלֹא שָׁמְעוּ קוֹל מִקְנֶה מֵעוֹף הַשָּׁמַיִם וְעַד־בְּהֵמָה
י נָדְדוּ הָלָכוּ: וְנָתַתִּי אֶת־יְרוּשָׁלִַם לְגַלִּים מְעוֹן תַּנִּים וְאֶת־עָרֵי יְהוּדָה אֶתֵּן
יא שְׁמָמָה מִבְּלִי יוֹשֵׁב: מִי־הָאִישׁ הֶחָכָם וְיָבֵן אֶת־זֹאת וַאֲשֶׁר
דִּבֶּר פִּי־יְהוָה אֵלָיו וְיַגִּדָהּ עַל־מָה אָבְדָה הָאָרֶץ נִצְּתָה כַמִּדְבָּר מִבְּלִי
יב עֹבֵר: וַיֹּאמֶר יְהוָה עַל־עָזְבָם אֶת־תּוֹרָתִי אֲשֶׁר נָתַתִּי לִפְנֵיהֶם
יג וְלֹא־שָׁמְעוּ בְקוֹלִי וְלֹא־הָלְכוּ בָהּ: וַיֵּלְכוּ אַחֲרֵי שְׁרִרוּת לִבָּם וְאַחֲרֵי הַבְּעָלִים
יד אֲשֶׁר לִמְּדוּם אֲבוֹתָם: לָכֵן כֹּה־אָמַר יְהוָה צְבָאוֹת אֱלֹהֵי יִשְׂרָאֵל
טו הִנְנִי מַאֲכִילָם אֶת־הָעָם הַזֶּה לַעֲנָה וְהִשְׁקִיתִים מֵי־רֹאשׁ: וַהֲפִצוֹתִים בַּגּוֹיִם
אֲשֶׁר לֹא יָדְעוּ הֵמָּה וַאֲבוֹתָם וְשִׁלַּחְתִּי אַחֲרֵיהֶם אֶת־הַחֶרֶב עַד כַּלּוֹתִי
טז אוֹתָם: כֹּה אָמַר יְהוָה צְבָאוֹת הִתְבּוֹנְנוּ וְקִרְאוּ לַמְקוֹנְנוֹת

יז וּתְבוֹאֶינָה וְאֶל־הַחֲכָמוֹת שִׁלְחוּ וְתָבוֹאנָה: וּתְמַהֵרְנָה וְתִשֶּׂנָה עָלֵינוּ נֶהִי
יח וְתֵרַדְנָה עֵינֵינוּ דִּמְעָה וְעַפְעַפֵּינוּ יִזְּלוּ־מָיִם: כִּי קוֹל נְהִי נִשְׁמַע מִצִּיּוֹן אֵיךְ
יט שֻׁדָּדְנוּ בֹּשְׁנוּ מְאֹד כִּי־עָזַבְנוּ אָרֶץ כִּי הִשְׁלִיכוּ מִשְׁכְּנוֹתֵינוּ: כִּי־
שְׁמַעְנָה נָשִׁים דְּבַר־יְהוָה וְתִקַּח אָזְנְכֶם דְּבַר־פִּיו וְלַמֵּדְנָה בְנוֹתֵיכֶם נֶהִי
כ וְאִשָּׁה רְעוּתָהּ קִינָה: כִּי־עָלָה מָוֶת בְּחַלּוֹנֵינוּ בָּא בְּאַרְמְנוֹתֵינוּ לְהַכְרִית עוֹלָל
כא מִחוּץ בַּחוּרִים מֵרְחֹבוֹת: דַּבֵּר כֹּה נְאֻם־יְהוָה וְנָפְלָה נִבְלַת הָאָדָם כְּדֹמֶן
כב עַל־פְּנֵי הַשָּׂדֶה וּכְעָמִיר מֵאַחֲרֵי הַקּוֹצֵר וְאֵין מְאַסֵּף: כֹּה | אָמַר
יְהוָה אַל־יִתְהַלֵּל חָכָם בְּחָכְמָתוֹ וְאַל־יִתְהַלֵּל הַגִּבּוֹר בִּגְבוּרָתוֹ אַל־יִתְהַלֵּל
כג עָשִׁיר בְּעָשְׁרוֹ: כִּי אִם־בְּזֹאת יִתְהַלֵּל הַמִּתְהַלֵּל הַשְׂכֵּל וְיָדֹעַ אוֹתִי כִּי אֲנִי יְהוָה
עֹשֶׂה חֶסֶד מִשְׁפָּט וּצְדָקָה בָּאָרֶץ כִּי־בְאֵלֶּה חָפַצְתִּי נְאֻם־יְהוָה:

הלכות תפילה

GATES TO PRAYER

The text (*nusaḥ*) of the siddur that we use today is based on the siddur of the Geonim, primarily *Seder Rav Amram Gaon* from the ninth century. The *nusaḥ* we call "*Nusaḥ Ashkenaz*" refers to the prayer texts and customs of Ashkenazi Jewry, which included the Jews of Germany and northern France. When Ashkenazi Jews moved eastward, they brought their practices with them to Poland and Russia, as well as Lithuania, Bohemia, Moravia, Austro-Hungary, Romania and the Balkans. Similarly, Ashkenazi Jews moved westward to Switzerland, France, Belgium, Holland, Northern Italy, England and, lastly, to Israel and America.

There is no single, authoritative version of *Nusaḥ Ashkenaz*. Certain differences in *nusaḥ* developed between the Jews of western Germany and eastern Germany (known today as *Minhag Polin*). For the most part, *Minhag Polin* is what Ashkenazi Jews follow today. But not exclusively. In the eighteenth century, Ḥasidic Jews adopted a new *nusaḥ* based on the Ari (R. Isaac Luria, 1534–1572), which strongly resembles the *nusaḥ* of Sephardi Jewry. As a result, many Jews of Ashkenazi descent now follow what is called "*Nusaḥ Sepharad*." Another variation on *Nusaḥ Ashkenaz* was developed by the Vilna Gaon (R. Eliyahu b. Shelomo, 1720–1797) and is called "*Minhag HaGra*." Students of the Vilna Gaon who moved to Israel in the nineteenth century brought *Minhag HaGra* with them, and it is the dominant Ashkenazi practice in Israel today.

In this Siddur we have tried to present *Nusaḥ Ashkenaz* as it is typically practiced in Ashkenazi congregations in the United States and Israel, with the differences noted in the instructions. Some practices referred to as "Israeli" are also followed by select congregations in the United States. In the pages below, we also note certain practices of *Nusaḥ Sepharad* which have become more common in Ashkenazi circles.

Rabbi Eli D. Clark

GUIDE TO THE SUMMER MONTHS

TAMMUZ

Shiva Asar B'Tammuz (17th of Tammuz)

1 According to the Mishna (*Ta'anit* 4:6), the fast of the 17th of Tammuz commemorates five calamities that befell the Jewish people on that date: (1) Moses broke the tablets, (2) the daily *Tamid* sacrifice was interrupted (in Second Temple times), (3) the walls of Jerusalem were breached by Titus, (4) Apostemus burned the Torah, and (5) an idol was introduced to the Temple.

2 The fast begins at dawn [שו״ע או״ח, תקנ: ב]. One is permitted to wake before dawn to eat and drink, but only if one had the intention to do so before going to sleep [שו״ע או״ח, תקסד: א].

3 Eating and drinking are forbidden, but other activities (bathing, wearing leather shoes) are permitted [שו״ע או״ח, תקנ: ב]. Pregnant and nursing women are exempt from fasting [רמ״א, שם: א].

4 If the 17th of Tammuz falls on Shabbat, the fast is postponed to Sunday [שו״ע או״ח תקנ, ג].

5 Shaḥarit: for weekdays. During the Repetition of the Amida, the *Shaliaḥ Tzibbur* says עֲנֵנוּ between the seventh and eighth blessings (page 155) [שו״ע או״ח, תקסו: א]. This is followed by *Seliḥot, Avinu Malkenu* and *Taḥanun* [ערוה״ש או״ח, תקסו: ח].

6 Torah Reading: Page 1095. The Torah is read only if at least six people (according to some: three people) are fasting. Only people who are fasting are called up. It is customary for the congregation to say the following passages aloud: the last seven words of Ex. 32:12: שׁוּב מֵחֲרוֹן אַפֶּךָ, וְהִנָּחֵם עַל־הָרָעָה לְעַמֶּךָ, the "Thirteen

Attributes of Mercy": יהוה יהוה אֵל רַחוּם וְחַנּוּן אֶרֶךְ אַפַּיִם וְרַב־חֶסֶד וֶאֱמֶת: נֹצֵר חֶסֶד לָאֲלָפִים נֹשֵׂא עָוֹן וָפֶשַׁע וְחַטָּאָה וְנַקֵּה, and the last four words of Ex. 34:9: "וְסָלַחְתָּ לַעֲוֹנֵנוּ וּלְחַטָּאתֵנוּ וּנְחַלְתָּנוּ" [משנ״ב, שם (ג)].

7 Minḥa: for weekdays, except that after *Ashrei* and Half Kaddish, the Torah is read. The reading is the same as that of the morning. The third *oleh* reads the Haftara (page 1096) [רמ״א, או״ח, תקסו: א]. After the Torah is returned to the Ark, the *Shaliaḥ Tzibbur* says Half Kaddish, and Minḥa continues as for weekdays.

8 During the silent Amida, those who are fasting say עֲנֵנוּ as part of the sixteenth blessing, שׁוֹמֵעַ תְּפִלָּה (page 277). During the Repetition of the Amida, the *Shaliaḥ Tzibbur* says עֲנֵנוּ between the seventh and eighth blessings, as in the morning (page 271). After the eighteenth blessing (מוֹדִים), the *Shaliaḥ Tzibbur* says the paragraph relating to *Birkat Kohanim* (page 281). For the final blessing of the Amida, שִׂים שָׁלוֹם is said instead of שָׁלוֹם רָב. After the Amida, the congregation says *Avinu Malkenu*. This is followed by *Taḥanun*, Full Kaddish and *Aleinu*.

9 From the 17th of Tammuz until Tisha B'Av (the "Three Weeks"), certain mourning rituals are observed: one does not cut one's hair, shave, listen to music, buy new things, or hold weddings and other parties [שו״ע או״ח תקנא, א]. Some permit shaving during this period.

AV

10 From Rosh Ḥodesh Av through Tisha B'Av (the "Nine Days") additional mourning rituals are observed: one abstains from eating meat or drinking wine, clothes are not laundered or pressed, and one generally minimizes joyful activities [שו״ע ורמ״א או״ח, תקנא].

Shabbat Ḥazon (Shabbat preceding Tisha B'Av)

11 The Shabbat preceding Tisha B'Av is known as *Shabbat Ḥazon*, named for the first word of the Haftara, חֲזוֹן. On Friday night, many congregations sing *Lekha Dodi* to the melody of אֱלִי צִיּוֹן. The special Haftara (Is. 1:1–27) is read to the tune of *Eikha*.

12 On Motza'ei Shabbat, *Kiddush Levana* is not said [רמ״א או״ח, תקנא: ח].

Erev Tisha B'Av (8th of Av)

13 *Taḥanun* is omitted from Minḥa.

14 The *Se'uda Mafseket* (final meal) is eaten after Minḥa. The custom is to eat no more than one cooked item. Three adult males should not eat together, so that no *zimmun* is said. Some have the custom to sit on the floor and eat eggs with ashes [שו״ע ורמ״א או״ח, תקנב].

15 When the final meal is eaten on Shabbat afternoon, these restrictions do not apply; however, the meal must be finished before sunset [שם: י].

Tisha B'Av (9th of Av)

16 According to the Mishna (*Ta'anit* 4:6), the fast of the 9th of Av commemorates five calamities that befell the Jewish people on that date: (1) God decreed that the children of Israel would not be allowed to enter the land of Israel, (2) the First Temple was destroyed, (3) the Second Temple was destroyed, (4) Beitar was captured, and (5) Jerusalem was plowed over.

17 The fast begins at sunset. In addition to eating and drinking, one is prohibited from washing and anointing oneself and from wearing leather shoes. Marital relations are likewise forbidden. One abstains from Torah study, except for topics such as mourning laws, *Eikha*, Job, and the unhappy portions of Jeremiah [שו״ע או״ח, תקנד: א–ב]. One does not greet other people or inquire after their welfare [שם: כ].

18 Ma'ariv: for weekdays. The Amida is followed by Full Kaddish, the reading of *Eikha* and the recitation of *Kinot*. The congregation says וְאַתָּה קָדוֹשׁ (page 345), followed by Full Kaddish (omitting the line beginning תִּתְקַבַּל), *Aleinu* (page 359), and Mourner's Kaddish. When Tisha B'Av falls on Motza'ei Shabbat, וְיִתֶּן־לְךָ is omitted.

19 If the fast falls (or is observed) on Motza'ei Shabbat, וִיהִי נֹעַם is omitted, and Havdala is not said. The blessing בּוֹרֵא מְאוֹרֵי הָאֵשׁ is said on a flame [שו״ע או״ח, תקנו: א].

20 Shaḥarit: Neither tallit nor tefillin is worn in the morning [שו״ע או״ח, תקנה: א]. During the Repetition of the Amida, the *Shaliaḥ Tzibbur* says עֲנֵנוּ between the seventh and eighth blessings (page 155). *Taḥanun* is omitted.

21 Torah Reading: page 1047. Three men are called up. The third *oleh* reads the Haftara: page 1096 [רמ״א או״ח תקנד, ד]. Afterwards, the first three blessings following the Haftara (page 649) are said. After the Torah is returned to the Ark,

Kinot are said. This is followed by *Ashrei*, וּבָא לְצִיּוֹן (omitting the verse וַאֲנִי זֹאת בְּרִיתִי, see page 231), Full Kaddish (omitting the line beginning תִּתְקַבַּל), *Aleinu*, and Mourner's Kaddish.

22 During Minḥa both tallit and tefillin are worn.

23 Minḥa starts with the Daily Psalm (pages 243–251), *Ashrei* and Half Kaddish. The Torah is read: page 1047. Three men are called up; the third reads the Haftara: page 1096. After the Torah is returned to the Ark, the *Shaliaḥ Tzibbur* says Half Kaddish.

24 During the silent recitation of the Amida (page 275), the congregation says נַחֵם as part of the fourteenth blessing (בּוֹנֵה יְרוּשָׁלָיִם), עֲנֵנוּ as part of the sixteenth blessing (שׁוֹמֵעַ תְּפִלָּה) (unless one is not fasting), and שִׂים שָׁלוֹם in place of שָׁלוֹם רָב (page 281). During the Repetition of the Amida, the *Shaliaḥ Tzibbur* says עֲנֵנוּ between the seventh (גּוֹאֵל יִשְׂרָאֵל) and eighth (רוֹפֵא חוֹלֵי עַמּוֹ יִשְׂרָאֵל) blessings, נַחֵם as part of the fourteenth blessing, the paragraph relating to *Birkat Kohanim* [שו״ע ורמ״א או״ח, תקנז: א], and שִׂים שָׁלוֹם. Minḥa ends with Full Kaddish and *Aleinu*.

25 After Ma'ariv, *Kiddush Levana* is said (page 365). When Tisha B'Av begins on Motza'ei Shabbat, Havdala is said on Sunday night, preferably over a cup of wine or grape juice; no blessing is made over spices or a flame.

26 Although the fast is broken after nightfall, it is customary to continue the other mourning customs until midday of the 10th of Av. However, if the 10th of Av falls on Friday, one is permitted to bathe and otherwise prepare for Shabbat prior to midday [רמ״א או״ח, תקנח: א].

Shabbat Naḥamu (Shabbat following Tisha B'Av)

27 Named for the first word of the Haftara, נַחֲמוּ. The first of the seven Shabbatot (שבע דנחמתא) between Tisha B'Av and Rosh HaShana, on which a Haftara is read from Isaiah containing words of consolation.

Tu B'Av (15th of Av)

28 According to the Mishna (*Ta'anit* 4:8), on the 15th of Av, the young women of Jerusalem would put on borrowed white dresses and dance together in the vineyards. Young men would come out to watch them, and the women would urge the men not to be swayed by beauty, but to be drawn to women of good family.

29 *Taḥanun* is omitted during Shaḥarit and Minḥa. If it falls on Shabbat, אַב הָרַחֲמִים is omitted during Shaḥarit, and צִדְקָתְךָ during Minḥa.

ELUL

30 Beginning on the first day of Elul (the second day of Rosh Ḥodesh) and for the entire month of Elul, it is customary to say לְדָוִד, יהוה אוֹרִי (page 255) in the evening at the end of Ma'ariv and in the morning after saying the Psalm of the Day [אשי ישראל, פמ״ה: ג].

31 In addition, four shofar blasts are sounded at the end of weekday morning prayers, prior to (or following) recitation of לְדָוִד, יהוה אוֹרִי [רמ״א או״ח, תקפא: א].

Pre-Rosh HaShana Customs

32 On the Motza'ei Shabbat prior to Rosh HaShana, the congregation gathers at midnight to say *Seliḥot*. This is often preceded by a sermon from the rabbi. If Rosh HaShana falls on Monday or Tuesday, the first recitation of *Seliḥot* is moved back to the preceding Motza'ei Shabbat [רמ״א או״ח, תקפא: א].

33 The congregation says *Seliḥot* each weekday thereafter through Erev Yom Kippur. Although the original custom was to say *Seliḥot* every night after midnight and before dawn, most congregations today say them prior to Shaḥarit; some say them during the preceding evening [ערוה״ש שם, ב–ד].

34 The *Shaliaḥ Tzibbur* chosen to lead the *Seliḥot* should preferably be distinguished in Torah scholarship and personal virtue, over the age of thirty and married [רמ״א או״ח, תקפא: א].

35 One who is praying alone is permitted to say *Seliḥot* without a *minyan*, provided one omits the י״ג מידות ("Thirteen Attributes of Mercy") and the Aramaic passages [תקפא: ד]. However, one who is alone may read the י״ג מידות with *ta'amei hamikra* [שו״ע או״ח תקסה: ה].

Erev Rosh HaShana (29th of Elul)

36 The recitation of *Seliḥot* (the longest of the year) precedes regular Shaḥarit for weekdays. The congregation omits *Taḥanun* and shofar blowing [שו״ע ורמ״א או״ח, תקפא: ג].

37 It is customary to say the formula of התרת נדרים, the Annulment of Vows, in front of three adult males after Shaḥarit [חיי אדם, קלח: ח]. The formula may be said at any time of the day [שו״ע יו״ד, רלד: נו] and may be said any day prior to Yom Kippur.

38 Some have the custom to immerse in the mikveh. Other customs include fasting and visiting the graves of departed relatives [שו״ע או״ח, תקפא: ב; רמ״א, שם: ד].

39 When Rosh HaShana falls on Thursday and Friday, each household must prepare an *Eiruv Tavshilin*; this makes it permissible to prepare food on Friday for the Shabbat meals [שו״ע או״ח, תקכו].

DAILY PRAYER

ON WAKING

40 The custom is to say מוֹדֶה אֲנִי immediately on waking, even before washing hands [משנ״ב או״ח, א:ח].

Laws of Washing Hands; בִּרְכַּת אֲשֶׁר יָצַר; אֱלֹהַי נְשָׁמָה

41 Upon waking, one is obligated to wash hands [שבת, קח:]. Some hold that one should not walk four *amot* (around six feet) prior to washing hands [משנ״ב או״ח, א:ב (בשם הזוהר)].

42 According to some authorities, there is a separate obligation to wash hands prior to prayer [ערוה״ש או״ח, ד:ה]. One who washes and says the blessing of עַל נְטִילַת יָדַיִם after waking, does not repeat the blessing when washing prior to prayer [רמ״א או״ח, ו:ב].

43 Hands should preferably be washed using a cup, but a cup is not required [שו״ע ורמ״א, או״ח: ד, ז]. The custom is to pour water from the cup onto the right hand, then the left, and repeat a total of three times [משנ״ב, שם: י]. Where water is unavailable, one may clean one's hands using any appropriate material; in that case, the blessing is changed to עַל נְקִיּוּת יָדַיִם [שו״ע או״ח, ד:כב].

44 The blessing of עַל נְטִילַת יָדַיִם may be said before drying one's hands or afterward [משנ״ב, ד:ב].

45 A number of reasons have been offered for washing hands upon waking. The Gemara states that, during the night, hands are enveloped by an "evil vapor," רוח רעה, which is removed by washing one's hands [שבת, קח:]. In addition, there is a concern that, while sleeping, one's hands may have touched an unclean part of

the body [רא״ש ברכות, פ״ט: כג]. Finally, it is noted that a person who wakes is like a newborn; therefore, one needs to sanctify oneself by washing [שו״ת רשב״א ח״א, קצא].

46 The blessing of אֲשֶׁר יָצַר should be said each time after relieving oneself. It is recommended that one should go to the bathroom immediately after washing hands, then say the blessings of עַל נְטִילַת יָדָיִם followed by אֲשֶׁר יָצַר. However, even if one does not relieve oneself, one is permitted to say אֲשֶׁר יָצַר after washing hands [רמ״א או״ח, ד: א]. One should not postpone going to the bathroom [שו״ע או״ח, ג: יז].

47 According to the Gemara, the blessing of אֱלֹהַי נְשָׁמָה should be said upon waking [ברכות, ס:]. The contemporary custom is to say אֱלֹהַי נְשָׁמָה immediately after אֲשֶׁר יָצַר [משנ״ב, שם: יב]. However, some rule that one who stays up all night should not say אֱלֹהַי נְשָׁמָה and the blessing הַמַּעֲבִיר שֵׁנָה מֵעֵינַי, and should instead hear them from others [משנ״ב, מו: כד].

48 The custom is to say the *Birkhot HaTorah* after אֲשֶׁר יָצַר, because one should not read or recite Torah verses before making the requisite blessings on Torah study [שו״ע ורמ״א, או״ח: מו, ט].

Laws of Tzitzit

49 Putting on a four-cornered garment with tzitzit attached fulfills an affirmative mitzva from the Torah. The obligation applies only during the daytime [מנחות, מג.]. Since wearing tzitzit is a time-bound mitzva, women are exempt [שו״ע או״ח, יז: ב].

50 The accepted practice is to wear a *tallit katan* all day long and to wear a *tallit gadol* during Shaharit [שו״ע או״ח, כד: א]. The dominant Ashkenazi custom is to begin wearing a *tallit gadol* when one marries [משנ״ב, יז: י], but Jews of German and Sephardi descent begin wearing the *tallit gadol* at an earlier age. Nevertheless, the custom is to wear a *tallit gadol* – even if unmarried – when acting as *Shaliaḥ Tzibbur*, reading from or being called up to the Torah, opening the Ark or performing *hagbaha* or *gelila*.

51 One should put on the *tallit katan* immediately upon dressing. One should first examine the strings of the tzitzit to ensure that they are not torn [שו״ע או״ח, ח: ט]. Then, while standing [שו״ע או״ח, ח: א], one should say the blessing of עַל מִצְוַת צִיצִית and immediately put on the garment [רמ״א או״ח, ח: ו]. One does not say the blessing if (a) one is about to put on a *tallit gadol*, and (b) one will have in mind the *tallit katan* when saying the blessing on the *tallit gadol*. On the other hand, if there is a substantial interruption between the time one puts on the *tallit katan* and one puts on the *tallit gadol*, one should say the separate blessing on the *tallit katan* [שו״ע או״ח, ח: יג].

52 The blessing on tzitzit may be said at daybreak, but not before [רמ״א או״ח, יח: ג].

53 Similarly with the *tallit gadol*, one should first examine the strings, then while standing, say the blessing לְהִתְעַטֵּף בַּצִּיצִית and put on the *tallit gadol*. The word לְהִתְעַטֵּף means to wrap oneself; one should initially wrap the *tallit gadol* around to cover one's head and face for a few moments, after which it is sufficient that it cover the torso [מג״א, ח: ב].

54 If one removes the *tallit gadol* for any reason, one should repeat the blessing when putting the tallit back on [שו״ע או״ח, ח: יד]. The blessing is not repeated if the *tallit gadol* is put back on soon after taking it off, and either (a) one was wearing a *tallit katan* all along, or (b) one's original intention was to put the tallit back on shortly [משנ״ב, שם: לז].

55 If one's head is otherwise covered, there is no requirement to cover one's head with the *tallit gadol* [ט״ז או״ח, ח: ג]. Some authorities nevertheless require married men to cover their heads with the *tallit gadol* throughout Shaḥarit, because it promotes reverence in prayer [ב״ח או״ח, ח: ג (בשם הרדב״ז)]. Others have the custom to cover their heads during the Amida only, or from *Barekhu* through the end of the Amida. Unmarried persons should not wear the *tallit gadol* over their heads [קידושין, כט:].

Laws of Tefillin

56 Putting on tefillin fulfills an affirmative mitzva from the Torah. The obligation applies only on weekdays [שו״ע או״ח, לא]. Since wearing tefillin is a time-bound mitzva, women are exempt [שו״ע או״ח, לח: ג].

57 One puts on tefillin after the tallit, because the former are more sacred, and we follow the principle of "ascending in sanctity" (מעלין בקודש) [שו״ע או״ח, כה: א].

58 The *tefillin shel yad* is worn on the weaker arm, meaning that right-handed people wear it on the left arm, and left-handed people wear it on the right arm [שו״ע או״ח, כז: ו].

59 The *tefillin shel yad* is put on first, by placing the box on the biceps near the elbow joint, angled toward the heart, and saying the blessing לְהָנִיחַ תְּפִלִּין. One then tightens the strap around the muscle and wraps the strap around the forearm seven times. Without speaking or otherwise becoming distracted [שו״ע או״ח, כה: ט–י], one places the *tefillin shel rosh* on the head above the hairline, centered over the nose, and says the blessing עַל מִצְוַת תְּפִלִּין. One then adjusts the straps, so that the knot rests at the base of the skull and the two straps hang down the front of one's chest, and says בָּרוּךְ שֵׁם כְּבוֹד מַלְכוּתוֹ לְעוֹלָם וָעֶד [רמ״א או״ח, כה: ה].

Finally, one wraps the strap of the *tefillin shel yad* around the fingers, while saying וְאֵרַשְׂתִּיךְ (See page 15).

60 The box of the *tefillin shel yad* and the *tefillin shel rosh* must rest directly on the arm and head respectively, without any barrier between them [שו״ע או״ח, כז: ד]. This rule does not apply to the straps of the tefillin [רמ״א, שם].

61 One should regularly touch first the *tefillin shel yad,* then the *tefillin shel rosh,* so as to remain conscious that one is wearing them. In particular, one should touch the appropriate tefillin when saying the relevant verses of the Shema [שו״ע או״ח, כח: א] (see law 79). It is also customary to touch them when saying the verse פּוֹתֵחַ אֶת־יָדֶךָ during *Ashrei.*

62 At a minimum, tefillin should be worn while saying the Shema and the Amida [שו״ע או״ח, כה: ד]. The custom is to keep them on until one has heard the *Kedusha* three times and Kaddish four times [רמ״א, שם: יג], which means that one should not remove the tefillin until after the Mourner's Kaddish following *Aleinu* [משנ״ב, שם: נו]. In theory, one should wear tefillin all day. The custom, however, is to take the tefillin off after praying, because it is difficult to maintain a constant awareness of the tefillin and the requisite purity of mind and body throughout the day [שו״ע או״ח, לז: ב].

63 The order in which one removes tefillin is the reverse of the order in which they were put on. Thus, one first unwinds the strap of the *tefillin shel yad* from one's fingers, then removes the *tefillin shel rosh* and wraps it in its case. One then unwinds the *tefillin shel yad* from the arm, removes the box from the muscle and wraps the tefillin in its case [שו״ע או״ח, כח: ב]. This entire process should be performed standing up [משנ״ב, כח: ו].

SERVICES

Laws of Birkhot HaShaḥar and Pesukei DeZimra

64 According to the Gemara [ברכות, ס:], *Birkhot HaShaḥar* (Morning Blessings) were originally said separately, in conjunction with the performance of the associated activity. Thus, upon dressing one would say the blessing of מַלְבִּישׁ עֲרֻמִּים, and upon standing up one would say the blessing of זוֹקֵף כְּפוּפִים. However, the custom now is to say all of the blessings together in the synagogue [שו״ע או״ח, מו: ב].

65 The insertion of the verse (or verses) of Shema after *Birkhot HaShaḥar* was not meant to satisfy the individual's obligation to say the Shema every morning [רמ״א, שם: ט]. However, as discussed in further detail in law 72, the three paragraphs of Shema must be said within the first half of the morning (measured as ¼ of the time from daybreak to nightfall). Since some congregations hold Shaḥarit services late, especially on Shabbat, and as such the communal recitation of the Shema in Shaḥarit may take place too late to fulfill the halakhic obligation, under such circumstances it is recommended to say all three paragraphs of Shema after *Birkhot HaShaḥar* [משנ״ב, שם: לׂא].

66 One should say the biblical verses describing the קרבן תמיד (page 45), preferably with the congregation [רמ״א או״ח, מח]. Some authorities require one to stand [משנ״ב, שם: ב].

67 The fifth chapter of מסכת זבחים and the ברייתא דרבי ישמעאל were added after the biblical passages regarding sacrifices to institutionalize the daily study of Scripture, Mishna and Gemara [שו״ע או״ח, נ: א].

68 Saying Kaddish, *Barekhu* or *Kedusha* requires the presence of a *minyan* (ten adult males) [שו״ע או״ח, נה: א].

69 One should not utter idle speech from the beginning of the words בָּרוּךְ אַתָּה יהוה in *Barukh SheAmar* until one completes the Amida [שו״ע או״ח, נא: ד]. Certain responses are permitted, as detailed in the chart on pages 1128–1130.

70 If one comes late to the synagogue, one may skip all, or portions, of *Pesukei DeZimra*, as follows:

a If there is sufficient time, say *Barukh SheAmar*, Psalms 145–150, and *Yishtabaḥ*.

b If there is less time, say *Barukh SheAmar*, Psalms 145, 148, 150, and *Yishtabaḥ*.

c If there is less time, say *Barukh SheAmar*, Psalm 145, and *Yishtabaḥ*.

d If there is less time, omit *Pesukei DeZimra* altogether. Complete the rest of the service with the congregation, then say *Pesukei DeZimra* privately, omitting *Barukh SheAmar* and *Yishtabaḥ* [רמ״א ושו״ע או״ח, נב].

Morning Shema – קריאת שמע של שחרית

71 Saying the three paragraphs of the Shema each morning and each night fulfills an affirmative mitzva from the Torah. Since saying the Shema is a time-bound mitzva, women are exempt [שו״ע או״ח, ע: א]. Nevertheless, women are required to say the first verse to express their acceptance of עול מלכות שמים ("the yoke of the kingdom of Heaven") [ב״ח, שם]. Women are permitted to say the Shema and its preceding and following blessings [משנ״ב, שם: ב].

72 There is a set time period every morning during which the Shema may be said. The optimal time is immediately before sunrise, when there is assumed to be sufficient light to recognize an acquaintance from a distance of four *amot* (around 6 feet). If necessary, the Shema may be said from daybreak [שו״ע או״ח, נח: ג]. After sunrise, the earlier the Shema is said, the better [שם: ב]. At the latest, the Shema must be said during the first quarter of the day (in halakhic terminology, three halakhic "hours," where each hour represents 1⁄12 of the day; regarding the measure of a "day." There is a dispute between halakhic authorities whether the day is measured from daybreak to nightfall (Magen Avraham), or from sunrise to sunset (Vilna Gaon). One should follow local communal practice in this regard.) [שם: א]. After that time, one is permitted to say the Shema with the blessings during the fourth halakhic "hour," that is, until the end of the first third of the day. After that, the Shema may be said without the blessings, but this does not fulfill the mitzva [שם: ו].

73 If one says the Shema without its preceding and following blessings, one has still fulfilled the mitzva. However, one should say the blessings afterward, preferably repeating the Shema as well [שו״ע או״ח, ס: ב].

74 The Shema must be said with concentration and awe [שו״ע או״ח, סא: א]. Each word and syllable should be pronounced correctly and carefully, without slurring consonants [שו״ע או״ח, סא: טו–כא].

75 Some authorities ruled that one should say the Shema with *Ta'amei HaMikra*. Today, however, most people do not do so [שו״ע ורמ״א, שם: כד].

76 The custom is to cover the eyes with the right hand while saying the first verse, so as not look at anything that might disturb one's concentration [שו״ע או״ח, סא: ה].

77 It is customary to draw out one's pronunciation of the letters ח and ד in the word אֶחָד to emphasize God's sovereignty over creation [שו״ע או״ח, סא: ו].

78 The sentence בָּרוּךְ שֵׁם כְּבוֹד מַלְכוּתוֹ לְעוֹלָם וָעֶד is said quietly, because it does not appear in the biblical text of the Shema [שו״ע שם: יג; משנ״ב, שם: ל].

79 As discussed in law 61 above, the custom is to touch the *tefillin shel yad* when saying וּקְשַׁרְתָּם לְאוֹת עַל־יָדֶךָ and to touch the *tefillin shel rosh* when saying וְהָיוּ לְטֹטָפֹת בֵּין עֵינֶיךָ [שו״ע או״ח, כח: א].

80 If one enters the synagogue and hears the congregation about to begin saying the Shema, one is required to say the first verse of the Shema together with the congregation [שו״ע או״ח, סה: ב].

Laws of the Shaḥarit Amida

81 There is a set time period every morning during which the Amida may be said.

In general, the Amida should be said at or after sunrise. At the latest, the Amida should be said during the first third of the day, (four halakhic "hours"; regarding the measure of a "day," see law 72). If the Amida was said between daybreak and sunrise, the mitzva has been fulfilled. If necessary, it is permissible to say the Amida after the first third of the day, but before midday [שו״ע או״ח, פט:א].

82 One who must leave for work (or a journey) before sunrise is permitted to say the Amida from daybreak [שו״ע שם סע׳ ח]. If one did not say the Shaḥarit Amida prior to midday, one should say the Minḥa Amida twice [משנ״ב, שם:ס״ק ז].

83 One should not eat or drink before saying the Amida, although drinking water is permitted. Moreover, anyone who needs to eat or drink in order to concentrate on his prayers is permitted to do so [שו״ע או״ח, פט:ג–ד].

84 The Amida is said facing the site of the Temple in Jerusalem. Thus, outside Israel, one faces the land of Israel; inside Israel, one faces Jerusalem; and inside Jerusalem, one faces the Temple Mount [שו״ע או״ח, צד:א]. If one is praying in a synagogue, one should pray facing the Ark [משנ״ב, שם:ס״ק י].

85 The Amida is said standing with feet together in imitation of the angels who, according to tradition, present the appearance of having only one leg [ברכות, י:, רש״י, ד״ה ״ורגליהם״]. One should bow one's head and imagine one is standing in the Temple, like a servant before his master [שו״ע או״ח, צה:א–ב].

86 One who is traveling in a vehicle should, if possible, say the Amida standing; if this is not possible, one is permitted to sit [שו״ע או״ח, צד:ה].

87 When saying the Shaḥarit Amida, one may not allow any interruption or disruption between the conclusion of the blessing גָּאַל יִשְׂרָאֵל and the introductory words to the Amida [שו״ע או״ח, סו:ח; שם, קיא:א]. This includes not responding to Kaddish, *Barekhu*, *Kedusha* or *Modim*, although on Shabbat one may do so [רמ״א, שם]. One may also answer "Amen" if one hears someone else concluding the blessing גָּאַל יִשְׂרָאֵל [רמ״א או״ח, סו:ז].

Laws of Havinenu

88 When circumstances require, one is permitted to substitute a special paragraph (*Havinenu*, page 1007) for the thirteen middle blessings of the Amida. This is only permitted in exceptional cases, such as when one is incapable of concentrating during a full-length Amida or expects interruptions. One says this abbreviated form of the Amida while standing, and one does not need to repeat the full-length Amida afterward. *Havinenu* is not said during the winter months or on Motza'ei Shabbat [שו״ע או״ח, קי:א].

Laws of חזרת הש״ץ

89 During the Repetition of the Amida, the congregation is required to listen attentively to the blessings and respond "Amen" [שו״ע או״ח, קכד:ד].

90 In order to begin the Repetition of the Amida, at least nine men are required to be listening attentively [שם].

91 Some require the congregation to stand during the Repetition of the Amida [רמ״א, שם].

92 Under extenuating circumstances, the *Shaliaḥ Tzibbur* may begin saying the Amida aloud, while the congregation says the Amida quietly along with him. The *Kedusha* is said aloud in the customary fashion and, after the *Shaliaḥ Tzibbur* finishes the blessing הָאֵל הַקָּדוֹשׁ, he and the congregation continue saying the Amida quietly [רמ״א, שם:ב].

93 At the conclusion of the Repetition of the Amida, it is recommended that the *Shaliaḥ Tzibbur* say quietly the verse יִהְיוּ לְרָצוֹן אִמְרֵי־פִי, except when Full Kaddish immediately follows the Repetition of the Amida [משנ״ב קכג:כא]. Some also say this verse during the individual's silent Amida.

Laws of Kedusha

94 There are different customs regarding what the congregation says during the *Kedusha*: (1) The congregation says only the biblical verses (...קָדוֹשׁ; ...בָּרוּךְ; ...יִמְלֹךְ) [שו״ע או״ח, קכה:א]; (2) The congregation says every word of the *Kedusha*, with the *Shaliaḥ Tzibbur* repeating each sentence [בה״ט, שם (בשם האר״י)]; (3) The congregation says נְקַדֵּשׁ and all the biblical verses [ערוה״ש, שם:ב].

Laws of Birkat Kohanim

95 The Kohen has an affirmative obligation from the Torah to bless the congregation, provided there are at least ten males aged 13 or over (including the Kohen himself) [שו״ע או״ח, קכח:א–ב].

96 The Kohen is required to wash his hands (without a blessing) before saying *Birkat Kohanim*. It is customary for a Levi to pour the water [שם, ו]. If there is no water, or if the Kohen did not have enough time to wash, he may say *Birkat Kohanim*, provided that: (a) he washed his hands before Shaḥarit, and (b) since washing for Shaḥarit he has not touched anything unclean, even his own shoes [משנ״ב, שם:כ].

97 Each Kohen removes his shoes before ascending to say *Birkat Kohanim* [שם, ה]. When the *Shaliaḥ Tzibbur* begins רְצֵה, the Kohanim ascend to the Ark and

stand with their backs to the congregation [שם, ח: ו–י]. After the congregation answers "Amen" to the blessing הַטּוֹב שִׁמְךָ וּלְךָ נָאֶה לְהוֹדוֹת, if there is more than one Kohen, the *Shaliaḥ Tzibbur* calls out "Kohanim," and they turn around and say the blessing. If only one Kohen has ascended to the Ark, he starts the blessing without being prompted [שם: י–יא]. The *Shaliaḥ Tzibbur* does not answer "Amen" at the end of the blessing [משנ״ב, שם: עא].

98 The *Shaliaḥ Tzibbur* reads each word of *Birkat Kohanim* and the Kohanim repeat it in unison. At the end of each verse, the congregation answers "Amen" [שו״ע ורמ״א, שם: יג]. The *Shaliaḥ Tzibbur* does not answer "Amen" at the end of each verse [שו״ע, שם: יט].

99 If the *Shaliaḥ Tzibbur* is himself a Kohen, some rule that he should not say the blessing, unless no other Kohanim are in the synagogue [שו״ע, שם: יט]. However, the custom today is for the *Shaliaḥ Tzibbur* to participate in the blessing [משנ״ב, שם: עה].

00 During *Birkat Kohanim,* the congregation should stand silently with eyes lowered and concentrate on the words of the Kohanim. One should not look at the faces or hands of the Kohanim [שו״ע, שם: כג].

01 In most congregations in Israel, *Birkat Kohanim* is said every day in Shaḥarit and, where applicable, in Musaf, as well as in *Ne'ila* on Yom Kippur. It is also said in Minḥa on a fast day [שו״ע או״ח, קכט: א]. *Birkat Kohanim* is not said in Shaḥarit of Tisha B'Av or in a mourner's house [משנ״ב, קכא: ו], although in Jerusalem, the custom is to say *Birkat Kohanim* even in a mourner's house [גשר החיים, כ: ה]. On those occasions and when no Kohen is present, the *Shaliaḥ Tzibbur* says אֱלֹהֵינוּ וֵאלֹהֵי אֲבוֹתֵינוּ (page 181).

02 The custom outside Israel and in certain northern Israeli congregations, is for the *Shaliaḥ Tzibbur* to say אֱלֹהֵינוּ וֵאלֹהֵי אֲבוֹתֵינוּ instead of the Kohanim saying *Birkat Kohanim,* except in Musaf of Yom Tov [רמ״א או״ח, קכח: מד].

Laws of Taḥanun

03 נפילת אפיים ("Lowering the Head," page 203/289) is said immediately after the Shaḥarit Amida on Sundays, Tuesdays, Wednesdays and Fridays, and after the Minḥa Amida on every weekday except for Friday. In Shaḥarit on Mondays and Thursdays, *Taḥanun* begins with וְהוּא רַחוּם (page 203), and יהוה אֱלֹהֵי יִשְׂרָאֵל (page 207) is added.

4 On fast days (except on Tisha B'Av, when neither *Avinu Malkenu* nor *Taḥanun* is said) and during the *Aseret Yemei Teshuva, Avinu Malkenu* (page 189) is said before *Taḥanun.*

105 One should not speak between the Amida and **נפילת אפיים** [שו״ע או״ח, קלא: א].

106 **נפילת אפיים** should be said while sitting [שם: ב], with one's head lowered against one's weaker forearm. If one is wearing tefillin however, one lays one's head against the arm lacking tefillin [שו״ע ורמ״א, שם: א]. The head is lowered only where there is a Sefer Torah [רמ״א, שם: ב], except in Jerusalem, where the custom is to lower the head in any case [שו״ת אגרות משה יו״ד ח״ג, קכט (ב)].

107 For days on which *Taḥanun* is not said, see list on page 195 [שו״ע ורמ״א או״ח, קלא: ד; משנ״ב, שם: כו].

Laws of Torah Reading

108 To ensure that the Torah is read at least once every three days, Moses established the public reading of the Torah on Shabbat, Yom Tov, Ḥol HaMo'ed, Rosh Ḥodesh, and Monday and Thursday mornings. Ezra added the public reading in Shabbat Minḥa [רמב״ם הלכות תפילה פי״ב ה״א].

109 On weekdays and Shabbat Minḥa, three people are called up [שו״ע או״ח, קלה: א]. On Shabbat morning, seven are called up, though additional individuals (*hosafot*) may also be called [שו״ע או״ח, רפב: א]. On Yom Kippur morning, six are called up, five on Yom Tov, and four on Ḥol HaMo'ed and Rosh Ḥodesh.

110 If a Kohen is present, he is called up first. If a Levi is also present, he is called up second; for subsequent *aliyot*, one calls up a Yisrael [שו״ע או״ח, קלה: ג]. If a Kohen is present but a Levi is not, the same Kohen is called up for the first two *aliyot* [שם: ח]. If a Levi is present and a Kohen is not, the Levi need not be called up, but if the Levi is called up, he should be first [שו״ע ורמ״א או״ח, קלה: ו].

111 The custom is to avoid calling up a Kohen after a Yisrael, except for Maftir and, in some communities, for **אחרון**, provided it is a *hosafa* [רמ״א, שם: י].

112 Other individuals who are given priority for an *aliya* include: a bridegroom on his wedding day and the Shabbat preceding and following the wedding; a Bar Mitzva; the father of a newborn baby; one commemorating a parent's *yahrzeit*; and a person obligated to say *Birkat HaGomel* [בה״ל, קלו: ד״ה ״בשבת״].

113 It is considered bad luck to call up two brothers or a father and son one after the other [שו״ע או״ח, קמא: ו]. While the custom is to avoid the practice, if one is called up after one's brother or father, one should accept the *aliya*.

114 One who is called up to the Torah should take the shortest route to the *bima* [שו״ע, שם: ו]. He should open the scroll to locate where the *aliya* begins. Still holding the handle, he should say the blessing, taking care to look away from

the Torah (or close the scroll or his eyes), so as not to appear to be reading the blessing from the scroll itself [שו״ע ורמ״א או״ח, קלט:ד].

115 If, after the blessing is said, the *ba'al koreh* discovers that the blessing was said over the wrong passage of the Torah, the scroll is rolled to the correct location and the *oleh* repeats the blessing. The blessing does not need to be repeated if the correct passage was visible when the blessing was said [שו״ע או״ח, קמ:ג; משנ״ב, שם:ט].

116 The Torah is read standing [שו״ע או״ח, קמא:א]. The *oleh* is also required to stand. The rest of the congregation is not obligated to stand, but it is proper to do so [ערוה״ש, שם:ב].

117 The *oleh* should read the words quietly along with the *ba'al koreh* [שו״ע או״ח, קמא:ב].

118 If the *ba'al koreh* makes an error that affects the meaning of the words, he needs to reread the Torah portion from the location of the error [שו״ע ורמ״א או״ח, קמב:א].

119 If an error is found in the Torah scroll, the reading is stopped, a new scroll is brought out, and the reading is continued from the location of the error [שו״ע או״ח, קמג:ד]. It is not required to call up all of the *aliyot* a second time to read from the new scroll, but if the remainder of the reading can be divided into the appropriate number of *aliyot* for that day, it is preferable to do so [משנ״ב, שם:טז].

120 It is customary to say a prayer for a sick person (מִי שֶׁבֵּרַךְ, page 643) at the conclusion of the Torah reading, or between *aliyot*.

121 On the Shabbat before a *yahrzeit*, it is customary to say a prayer for the deceased relative (אֵל מָלֵא רַחֲמִים, page 645), usually after the Shabbat Minḥa Torah reading.

122 After completing the reading from a Torah scroll, the open scroll is raised and displayed to the entire congregation. The congregation says וְזֹאת הַתּוֹרָה (page 647) [שו״ע ורמ״א או״ח, קלד:ב].

Laws of Birkat HaGomel

123 After being saved from mortal danger, one should say *Birkat HaGomel* [שו״ע או״ח, ריט:א, ו–ט; משנ״ב, שם:לב] (see page 643). The blessing should be said no later than three days after the event [שו״ע, שם:ו]. *Birkat HaGomel* is said only in the presence of a *minyan*; the custom is to say the blessing after the Torah reading [שם:ג]. If one will not be in the presence of *minyan* within three days, one is permitted to say the blessing without a *minyan* [משנ״ב, שם:ח].

124 A husband may say *Birkat HaGomel* for his wife, or a father for his children [משנ״ב, שם:יז]. But, according to most authorities, it is preferable that a woman say *Birkat HaGomel* for herself in the presence of a *minyan*.

Laws of Mourner's Kaddish

125 The Mourner's Kaddish is generally said after specific chapters of Psalms at the beginning and end of a service. It is said by one who is either (a) in mourning for a relative, or (b) commemorating the *yahrzeit* of a relative. When no such person is present, the Mourner's Kaddish is generally omitted, except after *Aleinu* at the end of Shaharit [רמ״א או״ח, קלב: ב], when it is said by one whose parents have died or whose parents do not object to their child saying the Mourner's Kaddish [שם].

126 Historically, the Mourner's Kaddish was said by one individual. A set of rules developed for allocating among different mourners the various opportunities for saying it [ביאור הלכה, שם; קונטרס מאמר קדישין, י]. Today, most congregations allow group recitation of the Mourner's Kaddish. In such cases, they should say the words in unison [סידור יעב״ץ].

Laws of the Minḥa Amida

127 There is a set time period every afternoon during which the Minḥa Amida may be said. At the earliest, one may say the Amida one half of a halakhic "hour" from midday (a halakhic hour is 1/12 of the day measured from daybreak to nightfall). At the latest, the Amida must be said before nightfall. It is preferable to say the Amida at least 3½ halakhic "hours" after midday [שו״ע או״ח, רלג: א].

128 One should wash hands before saying Minḥa, even if they are not dirty; but if no water is available, one need not wash [שו״ע או״ח, רלג: ב]. No blessing is said on the hand-washing.

Laws of the Evening Shema and Ma'ariv

129 There is a set time period every night during which the Shema may be said. At the earliest, one may say the Shema from nightfall [שו״ע או״ח, רלה: א]. It is preferable to say the Shema before midnight (measured from nightfall to daybreak), but one is permitted to say the Shema until daybreak [שם: ג].

130 Some congregations hold Ma'ariv services early, with the result that the communal recitation of the Shema in Ma'ariv may take place too early to fulfill the halakhic obligation. Under such circumstances, one should repeat all three paragraphs of Shema after nightfall [שו״ע, שם: א].

131 If one enters the synagogue and hears the congregation about to begin saying the Amida, one should say the Amida together with the congregation, then afterward say the Shema with its preceding and following blessings [שו״ע או״ח, רלו: ג].

132 After the blessings of the Shema, the congregation says בָּרוּךְ יהוה לְעוֹלָם (page 311),

except in Israel. One who begins Ma'ariv late should omit בָּרוּךְ יהוה לְעוֹלָם in order to say the Amida with the congregation, then say בָּרוּךְ יהוה לְעוֹלָם after Ma'ariv, without the final blessing [משנ״ב, שם: יא].

Laws of Keri'at Shema al HaMita (the Shema Before Sleep at Night)

133 *Keri'at Shema al HaMita* should be said before retiring, when one is feeling sleepy [משנ״ב או״ח, רלט: ג], after which one should not eat, drink or speak [רמ״א, שם: א].

LAWS OF HAND-WASHING, HAMOTZI AND *BIRKAT HAMAZON*

134 Before eating bread, one is required to wash one's hands [שו״ע או״ח, קנח: א]. After washing but before drying the hands, one says the blessing עַל נְטִילַת יָדַיִם; however, if one forgot, one may say the blessing after one's hands are dry [רמ״א, שם: יא]. One should dry one's hands carefully before touching the bread [שו״ע, שם: יב].

135 Hands should be washed using a cup or other container that holds at least a *revi'it* (about 4.4 ounces) of liquid [שו״ע או״ח, קנט: א]. Holding one's hands under flowing water is not valid [שו״ע, שם: ז].

136 One should wash each hand up to the wrist, although the minimum requirement is to wash the fingers up to the knuckle furthest from the nail [שו״ע או״ח, קסא: ד]. Hands should be free of dirt or other material that one normally removes. In addition, rings should be removed before washing [שם: א–ג].

137 If the hands are clean, it is sufficient to pour water once on each hand [שו״ע או״ח, קסב: ב], but twice on each hand is preferable [מ״ב שם, כא].

138 After washing, one should take care not to allow one's wet hands to touch the unwashed hands of another. If they do so, one must dry them and wash them again [שו״ע שם, ד].

139 If one makes the blessing הַמּוֹצִיא לֶחֶם מִן הָאָרֶץ on bread, no blessing need be said on foods that are part of the meal. If one eats foods that are not eaten with bread or are not part of the meal, such as fruit eaten as dessert, they require a separate blessing [שו״ע, קעז: א].

140 If wine is served during the meal, the blessing בּוֹרֵא פְּרִי הַגָּפֶן must be said, as the blessing on bread does not cover wine [שו״ע או״ח, קעד: א]. But if wine is drunk

before the meal (or as part of Kiddush), the blessing need not be repeated when drinking wine during the meal [שם: ד].

141 One should not remove bread from the table until after *Birkat HaMazon* is said [שו״ע או״ח, קפ: א].

142 Prior to saying *Birkat HaMazon*, one should wash the grime off one's fingers with *mayim aḥaronim* [שו״ע או״ח, קפא: א]. Some have the custom not to wash with *mayim aḥaronim*, because the original reasons for the practice no longer apply [שם, י; משנ״ב שם, כב], but a fastidious person who washes after a meal should wash with *mayim aḥaronim* before *Birkat HaMazon* [שו״ע: שם].

143 Women are obligated to say *Birkat HaMazon* [שו״ע או״ח, קפו: א].

144 *Birkat HaMazon* should be said where one ate. If one forgot to say *Birkat HaMazon* and went elsewhere, one should return to the site of the meal to say *Birkat HaMazon*. If one cannot return to the site of the meal, one is permitted to say *Birkat HaMazon* as soon as one remembers to do so [שו״ע ורמ״א או״ח, קפד: א; משנ״ב, שם: ו].

145 If one forgets to say *Birkat HaMazon* at the end of the meal, it must be said afterward, so long as one does not feel hungry [שו״ע או״ח, קפד: ד]. If one wants to eat again, one may wash hands and say הַמּוֹצִיא again; the subsequent *Birkat HaMazon* then covers the first meal as well [רמ״א או״ח, קעח: ב].

146 On Ḥanukka or Purim, one adds עַל הַנִּסִּים to the second blessing. If one forgets עַל הַנִּסִּים, one is not required to repeat *Birkat HaMazon* [שו״ע או״ח, תרפב: א; שו״ע ורמ״א או״ח, תרצה: ג].

147 On Shabbat, one adds רְצֵה (page 985) to the third blessing. On Rosh Ḥodesh, Yom Tov and Ḥol HaMo'ed, one adds יַעֲלֶה וְיָבוֹא (page 985) to the third blessing; if it is also Shabbat, one says רְצֵה, then יַעֲלֶה וְיָבוֹא. If one forgets to say the required addition on Shabbat or Yom Tov, one repeats the entire *Birkat HaMazon*. Alternatively, if one remembers before beginning the fourth blessing, one may say a special blessing in honor of Shabbat or the appropriate Yom Tov [שו״ע או״ח, קפח: ה–ו]. If one forgets the required addition on Rosh Ḥodesh or Ḥol HaMo'ed, one is not required to repeat *Birkat HaMazon* [שם: ז].

148 If one started eating while it was Shabbat, Rosh Ḥodesh or other days on which additions to *Birkat HaMazon* are said, and continued the meal after sunset, one still says the additions to *Birkat HaMazon* [שם: י] (see laws 146–147 above).

149 If three adult males eat a meal together, they are required to preface *Birkat HaMazon* with *zimmun* (page 979). If women are present, they are required to join in the *zimmun* as well. Three adult females may also form a *zimmun*, but are not obligated to do so. If ten or more males are present, the word אֱלֹהֵינוּ is added to the formula [שו"ע או"ח, קצב: א].

50 *Zimmun* is required if all three participants ate bread. If only two participants ate bread, but a third person either eats a *kezayit* (about 1.5 ounces) of any food, or drinks a *revi'it* (about 4.4 ounces) of any beverage (other than water), the three should say *zimmun* [שו"ע או"ח, קצז: ג; משנ"ב, שם: כב].

51 Even if the participants are not sitting together, as long as some of the participants can see each other, they can join together in a *zimmun* [שו"ע או"ח, קצה: א].

52 If one of the three participants said *Birkat HaMazon* by himself, he may still join the other two to make a *zimmun*, but if two of them (or all three) said *Birkat HaMazon* by themselves, then no *zimmun* may be said [שו"ע או"ח, קצד: א].

53 At a *Sheva Berakhot* meal, a special addition is made to the *zimmun* [שו"ע אבה"ע, סב: יג; ערוה"ש, שם: יח], and the *Sheva Berakhot* are said after *Birkat HaMazon* [שו"ע, שם: ו].

54 At the meal after a Brit Mila, a special *zimmun* is said, and a series of prayers is added before the end of *Birkat HaMazon*.

55 At a meal in a house of mourning, a special addition is made to the *zimmun*, and the third and fourth blessings are changed) [ערוה"ש יו"ד, שעט: א–ב].

ROSH ḤODESH PRAYER

56 On Rosh Ḥodesh, יַעֲלֶה וְיָבוֹא is added to the seventeenth blessing of the Amida (רְצֵה) in Ma'ariv, Shaḥarit and Minḥa [שו"ע או"ח, תכב: א], and to the third blessing of *Birkat HaMazon* (page 177) [שם, תכד: א].

57 If one forgets to say יַעֲלֶה וְיָבוֹא in its proper place in the Amida, but realizes before beginning the blessing הַמַּחֲזִיר שְׁכִינָתוֹ לְצִיּוֹן, one should immediately say יַעֲלֶה וְיָבוֹא and continue with the rest of the blessing. If one realizes the omission immediately after completing the blessing הַמַּחֲזִיר שְׁכִינָתוֹ לְצִיּוֹן, one should say יַעֲלֶה וְיָבוֹא and continue with the following blessing. If one realizes the omission after beginning the words מוֹדִים אֲנַחְנוּ לָךְ, one must repeat the Amida from the beginning of the seventeenth blessing (from the word רְצֵה). If one realizes the omission after completing the Amida, one must repeat the Amida from the beginning [שו"ע או"ח, תכב: א].

58 If one forgets to say יַעֲלֶה וְיָבוֹא in Ma'ariv, one does not repeat the Amida [שם].

159 Shaḥarit: as for weekdays, although one adds special verses for Rosh Ḥodesh in the *Korbanot* (page 51) [שו״ע או״ח, תכא: א]. יַעֲלֶה וְיָבוֹא is added to the Amida (see laws 156–157). After the Repetition of the Amida, *Taḥanun* is omitted, and the congregation says Half Hallel [שו״ע או״ח, תכב: ב], followed by Full Kaddish.

160 Torah reading: page 1029. Four men are called up [שו״ע או״ח, תכג: א]. Note that the second *aliya* begins by repeating the last verse of the first *aliya* [שו״ע או״ח, תכג: ג]. Half Kaddish is said before the Torah is returned to the Ark. The service continues with *Ashrei*, וּבָא לְצִיּוֹן and Half Kaddish. The tefillin are then removed [שו״ע או״ח, תכג: ד], and the congregation says Musaf for Rosh Ḥodesh. This is followed by *Aleinu*, Mourner's Kaddish, the Daily Psalm, Psalm 104 (בָּרְכִי נַפְשִׁי), and Mourner's Kaddish.

Laws of Hallel

161 Hallel is said standing [שו״ע או״ח, תכב: ז]. On Rosh Ḥodesh and the last six days of Pesaḥ, the abridged form, Half Hallel, is said [שו״ע או״ח, תכב: ב; תצ, ד], omitting the first halves of Psalm 115 (לֹא לָנוּ) and Psalm 116 (אָהַבְתִּי, כִּי־יִשְׁמַע).

162 At the beginning of Psalm 118 (הודו לַיהוה כִּי־טוֹב, page 849), it is customary for the *Shaliaḥ Tzibbur* to say each of the four verses out loud, and the congregation responds with הודו לַיהוה כִּי־טוֹב, כִּי לְעוֹלָם חַסְדּוֹ [משנ״ב תכב, כ]. Some advise the congregation to quietly say each verse with the *Shaliaḥ Tzibbur*.

SHABBAT PRAYER

EREV SHABBAT

3 Minḥa: as for weekdays. *Taḥanun* is omitted [שו"ע או"ח, רסז: א].

SHABBAT EVE

4 Candle lighting: At least two candles are lit [שו"ע או"ח, רסג: א]. There is a custom to light one candle for each member of the household. After lighting, one says the blessing **לְהַדְלִיק נֵר שֶׁל שַׁבָּת** [שו"ע ורמ"א או"ח, רסג: ה]. It is customary to cover one's eyes when saying the blessing [רמ"א, שם].

5 The custom is to light Shabbat candles 18 minutes prior to sunset. In any case, the candles must be lit before sunset, at which time all labor must cease [שו"ע ורמ"א או"ח, רסא: א]. After lighting the candles, one may not perform any labor, even if one lit prior to sunset, unless one's intention to perform necessary labor before sunset is articulated explicitly prior to lighting [רמ"א או"ח, רסג: י; משנ"ב, שם: מב].

The candles must be lit in a location where one will benefit from the light before the candles burn out [שו"ע, שם: ט].

If one is not eating at home on Friday night, one should still light candles at home [שו"ע, שם: ו]. If one is not sleeping at home on Friday night, one should light where one sleeps or make a nominal payment to one's host, so as to participate in the host's candle lighting. This is not required if a family member is at home and lights candles with one in mind [שו"ע, שם: ו].

168 Kabbalat Shabbat: Many congregations sing *Yedid Nefesh* before Kabbalat Shabbat. Because Kabbalat Shabbat is not considered part of Ma'ariv, it is customary for the *Shaliaḥ Tzibbur* to stand at the *bima*, rather than at the front of the synagogue [אשי ישראל, לו:יד]. For the same reason, it is permissible for a male under the age of 13 to lead Kabbalat Shabbat.

169 When saying the last stanza of *Lekha Dodi*, the custom is to stand facing the door or the rear, which is usually the western side, of the synagogue [משנ״ב או״ח, רסב:י].

170 By custom, mourners who are sitting *shiva* remain outside the synagogue for Kabbalat Shabbat, entering when the congregation finishes *Lekha Dodi*. As they enter, the congregation calls out in unison הַמָּקוֹם יְנַחֵם אֶתְכֶם בְּתוֹךְ שְׁאָר אֲבֵלֵי צִיּוֹן וִירוּשָׁלָיִם (page 425) [ערוה״ש יו״ד, ת:ה].

171 The congregation says the last two psalms of Kabbalat Shabbat, מִזְמוֹר שִׁיר לְיוֹם הַשַּׁבָּת (Ps. 92) and יהוה מָלָךְ (Ps. 93). This is followed by the Mourner's Kaddish and the second chapter of Mishna *Shabbat* (בַּמֶּה מַדְלִיקִין) [שו״ע או״ח, ער:א]. Some congregations outside Israel say בַּמֶּה מַדְלִיקִין after Full Kaddish at the end of Ma'ariv instead [משנ״ב, שם:ב].

172 Ma'ariv for Shabbat and Yom Tov: וְהוּא רַחוּם is omitted [טור או״ח, רסז]. The *Shaliaḥ Tzibbur* moves to the front of the synagogue to say *Barekhu*. It is preferable for Ma'ariv to begin after nightfall. If it does not, the congregation needs to repeat the Shema after nightfall [משנ״ב או״ח, רסז:ג]. The conclusion of הַשְׁכִּיבֵנוּ is different from the weekday formula, and בָּרוּךְ יהוה לְעוֹלָם is omitted [שו״ע שם, ג]. If one erroneously concludes הַשְׁכִּיבֵנוּ with the weekday blessing, one should say the correct blessing, provided one remembers immediately. If not, one does not repeat the blessing [משנ״ב, שם:ט]. It is customary to say וְשָׁמְרוּ (page 457) before the Amida [משנ״ב, שם]. If it is also Yom Tov, one adds the verse relating to the Festival (וַיְדַבֵּר מֹשֶׁה).

173 The Shabbat Ma'ariv Amida is said (page 459). On Rosh Ḥodesh, יַעֲלֶה וְיָבוֹא is added in the fifth blessing (page 467). On Ḥanukka, עַל הַנִּסִּים is added in the sixth blessing.

174 If one begins to say the Amida for weekdays on Shabbat and remembers in the middle of the Amida, one should complete the blessing already started, then begin the fourth blessing for the appropriate Shabbat Amida [שו״ע או״ח, רסח:ב]. If one remembers after completing the Amida, the correct Amida should be said from the beginning [שם:ד].

175 One who says the Amida for the wrong Shabbat service (e.g., saying the Amida for Shaḥarit during Minḥa), does not repeat the Amida. The exception is one who says the wrong Amida during Musaf, or the Musaf Amida during a different

service, in which case the Amida must be repeated [שם: ו]. If, however, one remembers during the Amida, one goes back to the beginning of the fourth blessing of the correct Amida [משנ״ב, שם: טו].

6 After the Amida, the *Shaliaḥ Tzibbur* and congregation say וַיְכֻלּוּ (page 475) [שו״ע או״ח, רסח: ו]. The *Shaliaḥ Tzibbur* says the abbreviated Repetition of the Amida, unless prayers are said in a location where (a) services are not held in a regular fashion, or (b) there is no Torah scroll [משנ״ב, שם: כד]. The *Shaliaḥ Tzibbur* says the Full Kaddish. Some congregations say בַּמֶּה מַדְלִיקִין (page 433) at this point. From Shabbat Ḥol HaMo'ed Pesaḥ until Shavuot, the Omer is counted. The congregation says *Aleinu*, followed by the Mourner's Kaddish. From the 1st of Elul through Shemini Atzeret, Psalm 27 (page 487) is said. It is customary to conclude with the singing of Yigdal or Adon Olam.

7 Some congregations have the custom to say Kiddush in the synagogue prior to *Aleinu*. However, since Kiddush should generally be said where the Shabbat meal is eaten, where possible, the Kiddush wine should be drunk by a child (or children) under the age of bar/bat mitzva. If this is not possible, the person making Kiddush may drink the wine [שו״ע או״ח, רסט: א].

8 Upon returning home, the custom is to say (or sing) a number of traditional songs and prayers. Some have the custom to bless their children. The Kiddush for Shabbat is an affirmative mitzva from the Torah. By custom, one person says Kiddush and the others listen attentively, fulfilling their obligation by proxy (based on the principle of שומע כעונה – "one who hears is as one who says"). Women are obligated in this mitzva, and a woman is permitted to say Kiddush for herself and others [שו״ע או״ח, רעא: ב]. It is customary to punctuate the meal with *Zemirot*. After the meal, one adds רְצֵה to the third blessing of *Birkat HaMazon* (page 985). On Rosh Ḥodesh, יַעֲלֶה וְיָבוֹא (page 985) is added after רְצֵה [שו״ע או״ח, קפח: ה].

SHABBAT DAY

One does not put on tefillin. Prayers begin as on weekdays, although one adds special verses for Shabbat in the section of *Korbanot* (page 51) [שו״ע ורמ״א או״ח, מח: א]. *Pesukei DeZimra*: as for Shabbat and Yom Tov (page 517) [שו״ע או״ח, נא: ט]. After אָז יָשִׁיר, the congregation says *Nishmat*. The *Shaliaḥ Tzibbur* for Shaḥarit begins from the words שׁוֹכֵן עַד.

180 Shaḥarit: as for Shabbat and Yom Tov. After *Barekhu*, the congregation says הַכֹּל יוֹדוּךָ (page 583). The Shabbat Amida is said. On Rosh Ḥodesh, יַעֲלֶה וְיָבוֹא is added in the fifth blessing (page 623). On Ḥanukka, עַל הַנִּסִּים is added in the sixth blessing. After the Repetition of the Amida, on Rosh Ḥodesh, the congregation says Half Hallel [שו״ע או״ח, תכב: ב]. The *Shaliaḥ Tzibbur* then says Full Kaddish. Some congregations follow the Sephardi custom of saying at this point the Daily Psalm (Ps. 92) and, if applicable, Ps. 104 or 27 (see law 183), followed by the Mourner's Kaddish.

181 Torah Reading: see laws 108–122. Seven are called up, though additional individuals may also be called up [שו״ע או״ח, רפב: א]. After completing the final *aliya*, the *Ba'al Koreh* says Half Kaddish. The Maftir is called up, and the appropriate portion is read, followed by the Haftara. After the Haftara and its blessings, the congregation says *Yekum Purkan* and the blessing for the congregation (page 651) [רמ״א או״ח, רפד: ז]. This is followed by the prayers for the government and the State of Israel. On a Shabbat immediately preceding Rosh Ḥodesh, *Birkat HaḤodesh* is said (page 665), except on the Shabbat preceding Tishrei.

182 The congregation says אַב הָרַחֲמִים, except (a) on days when *Taḥanun* is omitted, (b) when *Birkat HaḤodesh* is said (except for the months of Iyar and Sivan), and (c) on *Shabbat Shekalim, Zakhor, Para* and *HaḤodesh* [רמ״א או״ח, רפד: ז]. *Ashrei* is said, the Torah is returned to the Ark, and the *Shaliaḥ Tzibbur* says Half Kaddish.

183 Musaf for Shabbat: On Rosh Ḥodesh, the entire fourth blessing follows a special formula (אַתָּה יָצַרְתָּ, page 687); on Ḥanukka, עַל הַנִּסִּים is added in the sixth blessing. The *Shaliaḥ Tzibbur* repeats the Amida. This is followed by Full Kaddish, *Ein Keloheinu*, the Rabbis' Kaddish, *Aleinu*, Mourner's Kaddish, and the Daily Psalm (Ps. 92). On Rosh Ḥodesh, Psalm 104, *Barekhi Nafshi* (page 251), is added; from the 1st of Elul to Shemini Azeret, Psalm 27 is added (page 723). Mourner's Kaddish, *Anim Zemirot* (page 727), Mourner's Kaddish, and Adon Olam.

184 The time for saying Musaf is immediately after Shaḥarit. Musaf should be said no later than the seventh halakhic "hour" of the day, which is 7/12 of the period from daybreak to nightfall. However, if one said Musaf at any time before sunset, one has fulfilled the obligation [שו״ע או״ח, רפו: א].

185 Shabbat Morning Kiddush should be said where one eats the Shabbat meal [שו״ע או״ח, רפט: א]. If no wine or grape juice is available, one may say Kiddush over a cup of liquor or other beverage, but not over water or bread [שם: ב].

186 Minḥa: After *Ashrei* and וּבָא לְצִיּוֹן, the *Shaliaḥ Tzibbur* says Half Kaddish, the congregation says וַאֲנִי תְפִלָּתִי־לְךָ (page 765), and the Torah is taken from the Ark [שו״ע ורמ״א או״ח, רצב: א]. Three are called up, and the beginning of the following week's

Torah portion is read. Half Kaddish is not said. After the Torah is returned to the Ark, the *Shaliaḥ Tzibbur* says Half Kaddish, and the congregation says the Shabbat Minḥa Amida. On Rosh Ḥodesh, יַעֲלֶה וְיָבוֹא is added in the fifth blessing (page 783). On Ḥanukka, עַל הַנִּסִּים is added in the sixth blessing. After the Repetition of the Amida, the congregation says צִדְקָתְךָ, except on a day when *Taḥanun* is omitted [שם:ב]. This is followed by Full Kaddish, *Aleinu* and Mourner's Kaddish.

87 Some congregations say Psalm 104 (בָּרְכִי נַפְשִׁי) and the fifteen psalms beginning שִׁיר הַמַּעֲלוֹת, Ps. 120–34 after Shabbat Minḥa, from *Shabbat Bereshit* until *Shabbat HaGadol* [רמ"א, שם].

88 It is customary to read a chapter of the Ethics of the Fathers (*Pirkei Avot*, page 799) after Shabbat Minḥa, from the Shabbat after Pesaḥ to the Shabbat before Rosh HaShana [שם].

89 One should have a third meal (*Se'uda Shelishit*) on Shabbat [שו"ע או"ח, רצא:א]. Women are also obligated to eat *Se'uda Shelishit* [שם:ו]. The meal should begin with bread, unless one is too full to eat bread [שם:ה]. After the meal, one adds רְצֵה (page 985) to *Birkat HaMazon*, even if the meal extends past nightfall.

MOTZA'EI SHABBAT

90 In some congregations, Psalms 144 and 67 (page 341) are sung before Ma'ariv.

91 Ma'ariv: as for weekdays (page 299). In the fourth blessing of the Amida, אַתָּה חוֹנַנְתָּנוּ (page 319) is added [שו"ע או"ח, רצד:א]. On Rosh Ḥodesh, יַעֲלֶה וְיָבוֹא (page 327) is added in the seventeenth blessing. If one forgets either of these additions, one does not repeat the Amida [שם]. After the silent Amida, unless Yom Tov falls in the following week, the *Shaliaḥ Tzibbur* says Half Kaddish and the congregation says וִיהִי נֹעַם and וְאַתָּה קָדוֹשׁ (pages 343–345) [רמ"א או"ח, רצה:א]. The *Shaliaḥ Tzibbur* then says Full Kaddish. From the second day of Pesaḥ until Shavuot, the Omer is counted. Some have the custom to say וְיִתֶּן־לְךָ (page 351) [שם]. In most congregations, the *Shaliaḥ Tzibbur* says Havdala [שו"ע, שם]. The congregation says *Aleinu*, followed by Mourner's Kaddish. From the 1st of Elul to Shemini Azeret, Psalm 27 is said (page 363).

92 After nightfall, one may not perform labor until one says Havdala or hears it said. If one says אַתָּה חוֹנַנְתָּנוּ in Ma'ariv (page 319), one may perform labor after nightfall prior to Havdala [רמ"א או"ח, רצט:י].

93 Each month, one says Kiddush Levana (page 365) on seeing the New Moon

at night. Kiddush Levana may be said from the eve of the fourth day of the new month until the middle day of the month. By custom, it is said on the first Motza'ei Shabbat that falls within the time span, preferably outdoors with a *minyan*. [שו״ע ורמ״א או״ח, תכו].

194 Havdala is said at home if (a) one did not say אַתָּה חוֹנַנְתָּנוּ or hear Havdala in the synagogue; (b) one said אַתָּה חוֹנַנְתָּנוּ or heard Havdala, but intended not to fulfill one's obligation; or (c) someone at home did not yet hear Havdala [שו״ע או״ח, רצו: ג; משנ״ב, שם: לב]. Women may say Havdala for themselves [משנ״ב, שם: לה–לו]. If one forgets to say Havdala on Motza'ei Shabbat, one may say it as late as Tuesday night.

195 After Shabbat, one should eat a meal, the *Melaveh Malka*, as a way of marking the end of Shabbat [שו״ע או״ח, ש: א].

TABLE OF PERMITTED RESPONSES

	Pesukei DeZimra (from Barukh SheAmar to Yishtabaḥ)	*Within a paragraph of the Shema or the preceding blessings*[1]	*Between the paragraphs of the Shema or the preceding blessings*	*Between concluding the blessing* גָּאַל יִשְׂרָאֵל *and beginning the Amida*[2]
אָמֵן יְהֵא שְׁמֵהּ רַבָּא; אָמֵן following דַּאֲמִירָן בְּעָלְמָא[3]	Permissible	Permissible	Permissible	Forbidden [שו״ע או״ח סו, ט; משנ״ב נא, ח]
אָמֵן following any blessing	Permissible	Forbidden	Permissible	Forbidden[4]
בָּרוּךְ הוּא וּבָרוּךְ שְׁמוֹ; בְּרִיךְ הוּא	Forbidden[5]	Forbidden	Forbidden	Forbidden
Tallit	Put on the tallit, but say the blessing between paragraphs [משנ״ב נג, ה]	Put on the tallit, but say the blessing after the Amida [שו״ע ורמ״א או״ח סו, ב]	Put on the tallit, but say the blessing after the Amida	Forbidden [שו״ע או״ח סו, ח]
Tefillin	Put on the tefillin, but say the blessings between sections [משנ״ב נג, ה]	Before the Shema: forbidden; within the Shema, put on the tefillin and say the blessing [משנ״ב סו, טו]	Permissible	Put on the tefillin, but say the blessings after the Amida [שו״ע או״ח סו, ח]

1. The paragraphs are as follows: from the blessing יוֹצֵר אוֹר to יוֹצֵר הַמְּאוֹרוֹת; from אַהֲבָה רַבָּה or אַהֲבַת עוֹלָם to Shema; from Shema to וּבִשְׁעָרֶיךָ; from וְהָיָה אִם שָׁמֹעַ to עַל־הָאָרֶץ; from וַיֹּאמֶר to גָּאַל יִשְׂרָאֵל [שו״ע או״ח סו, ה]. Responses permitted within a paragraph are also permissible within a verse, though it is preferable to respond only at the end of a thought.
2. Some rule that on Shabbat one may respond to Kaddish, *Barekhu*, *Kedusha* or *Modim* [רמ״א או״ח קיא, א]. See law 87.
3. Only these are required responses; the other responses of אָמֵן in Kaddish are only a custom [משנ״ב סו, יז].
4. One may answer אָמֵן if one hears another concluding the blessing גָּאַל יִשְׂרָאֵל [רמ״א או״ח סו, ז].
5. These responses are only a custom, as they are not mentioned in the Gemara [משנ״ב נא, ח].

	Pesukei DeZimra (from Barukh SheAmar to Yishtabaḥ)	*Within a paragraph of the Shema or the preceding blessings*[1]	*Between the paragraphs of the Shema or the preceding blessings*	*Between concluding the blessing* גָּאַל יִשְׂרָאֵל *and beginning the Amida*[2]
Barekhu[6]	Permissible	Permissible	Permissible	Forbidden
Shema	Say the first verse with the congregation [משנ״ב סה, יא]	Forbidden, except to close one's eyes and sing the melody of the Shema	Forbidden, except to close one's eyes and sing the melody of the Shema[7] [שו״ע או״ח סה, ב]	Forbidden
Kedusha	Permissible[8] [משנ״ב נא, ח]	Say only the verses beginning קָדוֹשׁ and בָּרוּךְ	Say only the verses beginning קָדוֹשׁ and בָּרוּךְ	Forbidden [משנ״ב סו, יז]
אָמֵן after הָאֵל הַקָּדוֹשׁ and שׁוֹמֵעַ תְּפִלָּה	Permissible	Permissible	Permissible	Forbidden [רמ״א או״ח סו, ג]
Modim DeRabanan	Permissible	Say only the words מוֹדִים אֲנַחְנוּ לָךְ	Say only the words מוֹדִים אֲנַחְנוּ לָךְ	Forbidden [משנ״ב סו, כ]
Being called up to the Torah[9]	Permissible	Permissible – but not in the middle of the first verse of the Shema or בָּרוּךְ שֵׁם כְּבוֹד מַלְכוּתוֹ לְעוֹלָם וָעֶד	Permissible	Forbidden [משנ״ב סו, כו]

6. Whether before the blessings of the Shema or before the Reading of the Torah. The blessings said by the עוֹלֶה are like any other blessing [משנ״ב סו, יח].
7. If the congregation is saying *Aleinu*, one should stand and bow with them [ערוה״ש או״ח סה, ו].
8. Say only the biblical verses [אשי ישראל פט״ז, לא; see law 94].
9. The Gabba'im should not call up to the Torah one who is in the middle of prayer; however, if only one Kohen is present, he may be called up. Likewise, if only one person knows how to read the Torah, he may interrupt his prayers in order to be the *ba'al koreh* [משנ״ב סו, כו].

	Pesukei DeZimra (from Barukh SheAmar to Yishtabaḥ)	*Within a paragraph of the Shema or the preceding blessings*[1]	*Between the paragraphs of the Shema or the preceding blessings*	*Between concluding the blessing* גָּאַל יִשְׂרָאֵל *and beginning the Amida*[2]
אֲשֶׁר יָצַר	Say the blessing between paragraphs [בה״ל, נא ד״ה צריך]	Wash one's hands, but say the blessing after the Amida	Wash one's hands, but say the blessing after the Amida	Wash one's hands, but say the blessing after the Amida [משנ״ב סו, כג]
Blessing on thunder or lightning	Permissible	Forbidden	Permissible, if the opportunity may not recur	Forbidden [משנ״ב סו, יט]

GENERAL RULES

MA'ARIV

The rules regarding responses are identical to those of Shaḥarit. After the blessing שׁוֹמֵר עַמּוֹ יִשְׂרָאֵל לָעַד until Half Kaddish, is considered to be between paragraphs, even in the middle of בָּרוּךְ יהוה לְעוֹלָם אָמֵן וְאָמֵן [ביאור הלכה סו ד״ה ואלו].

HALLEL

The laws regarding responses during Hallel are identical to those of the Shema [שו״ע או״ח תפח, א]. If a Lulav is brought in the middle of Hallel, one should say the blessing between paragraphs of Hallel [משנ״ב תרמד, ז].

REMOVING A CRYING CHILD

One should remove a crying child from the synagogue even while saying the Amida, in order to avoid disturbing others who are praying [אשי ישראל פל״ב, יג (בשם החזון איש)].

KADDISH DURING PESUKEI DEZIMRA

A mourner is permitted to say Kaddish during *Pesukei DeZimra*, if he will be unable to say it afterwards [אשי ישראל פט״ז הערה קט].

SOME FREQUENTLY ASKED QUESTIONS ABOUT TEFILLA

Why pray?

- I pray because I want a connection with God. If you consider the gap that exists between an all-knowing, all-powerful God and a limited finite human being, it would be absurd to imagine that any connection is even possible. Yet God revealed to us that through prayer contact is possible. The difference is that when God initiated contact with man, He did so through prophecy; when man initiates the contact it is through prayer.
- I believe that I am made up of a body and a soul. I'm not really sure what the soul is. I do know that it is something that makes up who I am, the inner essence of me, the part of me that others cannot see. It longs to be nourished. I therefore pray for the sake of nourishing my soul, no less than I eat in order to nourish my body. The body needs to be fed else it will wither; the soul needs to be fed else it, too, will wither. Prayer is the vitamin for the soul.
- The Rabbis tell us that each person is unique; there are no two people in the world who are the same, either in body or soul. As much as I celebrate my uniqueness, there is also a part of me that is sometimes lonely, when my inner essence makes me feel like I am so different from anyone else that there is no one else who truly understands me, no one else who knows my innermost thoughts, feelings, fears. The only One who truly can is God, since my uniqueness comes from Him. Prayer enables me to connect and overcome my loneliness.

◂ I pray

- I pray because it is a mitzva to do so.
- There have been times when I was so happy that I could burst. Something great happened to me or I saw something so amazing or so beautiful that I just needed to express myself besides saying "Wow!" Prayer enables me to express my feelings of wonder, awe, amazement, gratitude, appreciation or humility. Similarly, there have been times when I have been very sad or when I am so overcome by the distress or sadness around me that I just want to scream. Prayer provides me with the opportunity and the language with which to express myself when words fail, when I want to express my anger, my sorrow, my pain. It also enables me to encounter Hashem at those moments for He is the source for the goodness, and often the source of the sadness that I am experiencing.
- There are things that I need. Whether it's a better grade, a material possession, help with an activity, a job or a relationship. In prayer, I turn to Hashem to ask for the things that I need.
- There are things that I am afraid of. In prayer I can ask for help with my fears and insecurities, my anxieties and my worries. Sometimes, when I can just share those feelings with Someone who understands, it provides relief.
- One opinion says that the Hebrew word for prayer *lehitpalel* comes from the root *pilel* which means to judge. The reflexive form, *hitpalel*, therefore means to judge oneself. *Tefilla* is about holding up a mirror to oneself a few times a day. It's about reminding oneself of what's important and what one's values are, and how one can use the hours ahead most productively.
- Similarly, when I assess my own needs, I become conscious of the needs of others. When I ask God for something or become conscious of the ethics which guide His behavior as indicated by the prayers, then I grow more sensitive to the ethics that I should live by, the responsibilities I have toward others. Prayer makes me a better person.
- When I pray, I connect myself with the Jewish people of the past. I use the same words they did, I refer to experiences they had, I recall the beliefs that we all share, in the same language that has been used for thousands of years. In prayer, I become a part of the chain of tradition.

- When I pray, I connect myself to my fellow Jews in the present wherever they may be. Prayers are almost always in the plural, reminding me that I am concerned not only with myself but with my extended family, just as they are concerned with me in their prayers. I join with the people around me to form a cohesive group and am thus provided with a constant source of community, even if the people around me are strangers.
- Prayer heightens awareness. When I recite a blessing regarding a particular event, it raises the event to something more transcendent.
- The very act of prayer, mandated as it is by halakha to specific times, forces me to take time out of my day to be conscious of all of the above, even if it doesn't always succeed in doing so. Prayer provides me with self-discipline.
- I pray because I cannot not pray.

Why do I need to use a Siddur?

- EXPRESSING YOUR FEELINGS CAN BE DIFFICULT. WE ALL NEED HELP

  One practical reason is that we're not so good at coming up with ways to express our feelings. Consider the fact that when you go to the store to buy a birthday card for someone, you usually have two choices: one card is blank, while the other has a pre-printed message. The vast majority of us choose the card with the message. Filling a blank card can be too difficult, especially if you do it every day.

- YOUR PRAYERS SHOULD BE JEWISH

  One of the things that distinguish our prayers from those of other faiths or spiritual practices, is that our prayers are Jewish. They are based upon things in our belief system and in our history. These are uniquely Jewish beliefs and Jewish history. Were we to only use our own prayers, it is likely that our prayers would not have this dimension.

- JEWISH PRAYER HAS A PARTICULAR STRUCTURE

  The most famous example is the structure of שבח, בקשה, הודאה – *praise, request ,thanks*. Were we to only use our own prayers, we probably would not think to use that structure. Yet we are told that praying this way can be particularly meaningful and powerful.

- JEWISH PRAYER CONSISTS OF PARTICULAR CONTENTS

The prospect of finite man being able to communicate with an infinite God would be an absurd impossibility if not for the fact that the Torah says that such a thing is possible. From the Tanakh we learn the way that God can be approached, the kinds of things that can be said and the way that they can be said. These are incorporated in the Siddur. Were we only to use our own prayers, we would probably not speak to God in these uniquely Jewish terms.

- JEWISH PRAYER CONSISTS OF VARIOUS FORMS OF COMMUNICATION

There are verses from the Torah and teachings of the Talmud; there are texts based upon deep philosophical thoughts and mysterious kabbalistic insights; there is complex poetry and lyrical prose. Were we only to use our own prayers, we would most likely use but one form, and lose the rich opportunities provided by the Siddur.

- JEWISH PRAYER IS RECITED IN HEBREW

While this is not an absolute requirement (*Shulḥan Arukh* 60:2, 101:4 and *Mishna Berura* there), praying in Hebrew can be much more enriching and meaningful than in English. This is both because of the nuanced meaning of Hebrew and because it is לשון קודש, the mystical holy language that Jews have used to communicate with God for millennia. Were we to only use our own prayers, we would probably just use English rather than our uniquely Jewish language. Consider, for example, the famous expression אדון עולם, used in the song that is sung at the conclusion of services or said early in the morning. Most often it is translated as Master of the Universe. But the word עולם can also mean "world" and so the expression can also mean "Master of the Planet." Alternatively, the word עולם is related to the word נעלם meaning "hidden," thus rendering the expression to mean that God is hidden or mysterious. One could have one of these meanings or any combination of them in mind when you say this expression,

◂ depending

depending on your mood or what you want to convey. English limits you to only one possibility.

- JEWISH PRAYER IS USUALLY IN THE PLURAL

In Judaism, you seldom are praying for yourself alone. We see ourselves as part of a quorum, a community, a people. Being a part of these groups is a critical part of Jewish prayer. Were we to only use our own prayers, we probably would only use the self-centered and often selfish singular. If there are things which I need but am not thinking about for myself, there's a pretty good chance that someone else in the *minyan* will have them in mind. I get included in his prayers simply because he's saying it in the plural and we join our prayers to one another.

- JEWISH PRAYER ATTACHES YOU TO JEWISH HISTORY

Jewish prayer is the composite work of thousands of years of Jewish history. The Siddur contains whole sections from the Torah and Nevi'im and Ketuvim. Other prayers and blessings were composed during Mishnaic and Talmudic times. פיוטים (liturgical poems) were composed and included in the liturgy of the Middle Ages in all countries of Europe and North Africa and the Middle East. In our own era, contemporary concerns and sensitivities have been added, such as the prayers for the welfare of Israeli soldiers, American soldiers, and the State of Israel. When we use the Siddur, we thus join ourselves to thousands of years of Jewish history and the Jewish people, we utter words that have been used for millenia and words that join us to Jews around the world. Were we to only use our own prayers, we probably would think most of the time only about ourselves and our own time.

- JEWISH PRAYER JOINS YOU TO OTHER JEWS

When I was in the ninth grade I went to Belarus with my school to visit the Jewish community there. Although we could barely communicate with the people there, the words of the *Shema* and *Tefilla* connected us. Two completely different people with completely different languages and histories came together as one. (Ethan Stein)

◂ *So how do I make prayer*

So how do I make prayer more personal?

- BRING YOUR OWN FEELINGS TO THE WORDS ON THE PAGE
  Always remember that one of the most important (if not *the* most important) things about *tefilla* is *kavana,* the intent that you bring to the task. The words in the Siddur serve multiple purposes as we described above. While the literal meaning of the words is important, there is nothing wrong with bringing your own meaning to them. In other words (excuse the pun), the words can be understood metaphorically as well.
  For example, in the *Shemoneh Esreh,* we say the prayer for the revival of the dead. This is considered the supreme example of Hashem's mastery over nature, which is the theme of that particular blessing (*Gevurot*) in *Shemoneh Esreh.* Now when we say this blessing, we should certainly try to bear in mind the belief that Hashem can perform the miraculous act of revival of the dead. But if that's not where your head is that day, then consider other possibilities that have been suggested: (1) He supports and cures those who were at death's door whom doctors said could not be cured. Hashem thus revives the dead in this way. (2) Hashem has mercy on the evil, who are called "dead" in their lifetimes. (3) Hashem grants life to those who are downcast or enveloped by sadness, who may feel like they are dead. (4) Hashem sends rain on a regular basis which revives life on earth. (5) Hashem enables us to awake every morning when we are otherwise like dead people.
  Each of these is in keeping with the theme of the blessing of *Gevurot,* His mastery over the world, but they are not limited to the literal meaning alone. Be creative. Acknowledge the literal meaning but let your heart be free.

- ADD YOUR OWN REQUESTS
  Contrary perhaps to popular belief, you are allowed, in fact encouraged, to add your own prayers. If *tefilla* is supposed to be service of the heart, then let your heart do the talking. The *Shulḥan Arukh* (119:1) specifically says that if you have individual requests in *Shemoneh Esreh* then you should add them in the appropriate place. If you want to ask for material things, then ask in the blessing of *Barekh Aleinu;* if you

want to pray on behalf of someone who is ill, then do so in the blessing of *Refa'enu*. Every blessing has a theme; find the theme appropriate for your particular request and add it in before you conclude the blessing. Alternatively, insert your own prayer into the blessing of *Shema Kolenu*, a catch-all blessing where anything goes. Or, insert it toward the end of the blessing of *Elokai Netzor*.

In short, it's a mistake to think that the Siddur is impersonal. It's as personal as you want to make it using the guidelines it provides. The Gemara (*Berakhot 28b*) suggests that one should not make his prayer the same every day. Yet how does one do that if in fact the prayers are the same every day?! The answer: you are different every day and therefore what you bring to the prayer makes it a different prayer. Whether prayer is the same old thing day in and day out or whether it is a way to express new feelings or hopes or needs depends entirely upon you.

What if I'm not in the mood to pray?

- This is one of the biggest misconceptions about *tefilla*. *Ḥazal* absolutely understood that people were not always in the mood to *daven*. Precisely because we can too often take life and the beauty of the world around us for granted, precisely because we can forget to be thankful for what we have or fail to note our dependency on God, precisely because we can so easily get lost in our own fatigue or our own concerns about the day, *Ḥazal* forced us to stop in our tracks three times a day and take note of these things. In other words, the Siddur is not there only for when we are in the mood; rather, the Siddur is there to help put us in the mood.

What if prayer really doesn't do it for me?

- An artist was once asked: "How long did it take to produce this remarkable painting?" He replied: "Ten hours to apply the paints, but forty years to learn how." Prayer is an art, not only a mechanical act. It takes time and patience and persistence. It's the exercise of a muscle, the development of a relationship, the cultivation of love.

◂ *What value*

What value is there to saying something even if you don't mean it?

- The story is told of a small town where the only watchmaker passed away. Over time, the clocks in the town failed to tell the correct time and so the people didn't bother with them any more. Yet one man continued to wind his clock every day, even though it continued to tell the wrong time. Finally, a new watchmaker came to town. When everyone brought their clocks to be fixed he told them that each was too difficult to fix for the mechanisms had rusted and run down. Only the person who had kept winding his clock had a machine that could be easily restored to working order.

  Moreover, there is something to be said for the very act of going to *shul* even if one is not in the mood and even if one's prayers amount to just mumbling the words. The very act of attending *shul* is itself a statement to Hashem that I'm committed and I recognize that You are a part of my life. In addition, it is a statement to myself that I see myself as part of the community and that the community needs my presence.

What value is there to saying something I don't understand?

- Pray in English if you need to. While Hebrew is richer, the most important thing is *kavana,* so say it in whatever language you want. And if at times you don't have a translation available, let the very act of praying serve as a prayer.

  (When you can, try to focus on one blessing in Hebrew. Learn the translation. Think about the meaning. The added beauty and significance of the words will come in time, one blessing at a time.)

Does God really answer prayers?

- In the *Shemoneh Esreh,* we declare that Hashem is a *Shome'a Tefilla*: He *hears* prayer. Sometimes, that's like having a cell phone conversation with someone when the signal isn't so strong; the other person hears you even though you cannot hear them, and so you continue to speak, knowing that their very act of listening is response enough. As Rabbi Sacks once wrote, "Prayer is the place where speaking

◂ meets God's

meets God's listening, and in ways we will never understand, we are transformed."

- Maybe He did answer you. It was just in another form, which was perhaps far more worthwhile than your original intention.
- Maybe He yet will answer. Prayer, as someone said, is not a slot machine where you put in a coin and you get the jackpot. Sometimes, you need to have the patience to wait...and keep trying.
- Maybe what you asked for was not appropriate. You may think it would be good for you or for another person but really it is not. Maybe it would be bad for someone else. Maybe it would be bad for you.
- Maybe you asked in an inappropriate way. Were you just paying lip service to what you said? Were you testing God to see if He really exists? Were you testing prayer to see if it really works? Were you really praying?
- Maybe you need to do something to change yourself before you are deemed suitable for what you want.
- Sometimes the answer is "no." That may not be the answer to our prayers that we wanted, but it still means that our prayer was answered.

  Moreover, as Rav Noaḥ Weinberg once wrote, if a billionaire father handed over unlimited cash on a silver platter, his child would grow up spoiled and irresponsible. So too, if God gave us everything automatically, we may never define for ourselves what we want in life. True, life would be easy. But we would not grow. Since God has our best interests at heart, He wants us to earn it. Because that's what will make us great.

RABBIS' KADDISH

Mourner: Yitgadal ve-yitkadash shemeh raba. (*Cong:* Amen)
Be-alema di vera khir'uteh, ve-yamlikh malkhuteh,
be-ḥayyeikhon, uv-yomeikhon,
uv-ḥayyei de-khol beit Yisrael,
ba-agala uvi-zman kariv,
ve-imru Amen. (*Cong:* Amen)

All: Yeheh shemeh raba mevarakh le'alam ul-alemei alemaya.

Mourner: Yitbarakh ve-yishtabaḥ ve-yitpa'ar ve-yitromam ve-yitnaseh
ve-yit-hadar ve-yit'aleh ve-yit-hallal
shemeh dekudsha, berikh hu. (*Cong:* Berikh hu)
Le-ela min kol birkhata
ve-shirata, tushbeḥata ve-neḥemata, da-amiran be-alema,
ve-imru, Amen. (*Cong:* Amen)

Al Yisrael, ve-al rabanan,
ve-al talmideihon, ve-al kol talmidei talmideihon,
ve-al kol man de-asekin be-oraita
di be-atra (*In Israel:* kadisha) ha-dein ve-di be-khol atar va-atar,
yeheh lehon ul-khon shelama raba,
ḥina ve-ḥisda, ve-raḥamei,
ve-ḥayyei arikhei, um-zonei re-viḥei,
u-furkana min kodam avuhon di vish-maya,
ve-imru Amen. (*Cong:* Amen)

Yeheh shelama raba min shemaya
ve-ḥayyim (tovim) aleinu ve-al kol Yisrael,
ve-imru Amen. (*Cong:* Amen)

Bow, take three steps back, as if taking leave of the Divine Presence, then bow, first left, then right, then center, while saying:
Oseh shalom bim-romav,
hu ya'aseh ve-raḥamav shalom aleinu, ve-al kol Yisrael,
ve-imru Amen. (*Cong:* Amen)

MOURNER'S KADDISH

Mourner: Yitgadal ve-yitkadash shemeh raba. (*Cong:* Amen)
Be-alema di vera khir'uteh, ve-yamlikh malkhuteh,
be-ḥayyeikhon, uv-yomeikhon,
uv-ḥayyei de-khol beit Yisrael,
ba-agala uvi-zman kariv,
ve-imru Amen. (*Cong:* Amen)

All: Yeheh shemeh raba mevarakh le'alam ul-alemei alemaya.

Mourner: Yitbarakh ve-yishtabaḥ ve-yitpa'ar ve-yitromam ve-yitnaseh
ve-yit-hadar ve-yit'aleh ve-yit-hallal
shemeh dekudsha, berikh hu. (*Cong:* Berikh hu)
Le-ela min kol birkhata
ve-shirata, tushbeḥata ve-neḥemata,
da-amiran be-alema,
ve-imru, Amen. (*Cong:* Amen)

Yeheh shelama raba min shemaya
ve-ḥayyim aleinu ve-al kol Yisrael,
ve-imru Amen. (*Cong:* Amen)

Bow, take three steps back, as if taking leave of the Divine Presence, then bow, first left, then right, then center, while saying:

Oseh shalom bim-romav,
hu ya'aseh shalom aleinu, ve-al kol Yisrael,
ve-imru Amen. (*Cong:* Amen)

קורן ירושלים